THE ISLES

NORMAN DAVIES

THE ISLES

A HISTORY

OXFORD
UNIVERSITY PRESS

OXFORD
UNIVERSITY PRESS

Oxford   New York

Athens   Auckland   Bangkok   Bogotá   Buenos Aires   Calcutta
Cape Town   Chennai   Dar es Salaam   Delhi   Florence   Hong Kong   Istanbul
Karachi   Kuala Lumpur   Madrid   Melbourne   Mexico City   Mumbai
Nairobi   Paris   São Paulo   Singapore   Taipei   Tokyo   Toronto   Warsaw

and associated companies in
Berlin   Ibadan

Copyright © 1999 by Norman Davies

Published by Oxford University Press, Inc.
198 Madison Avenue, New York, New York 10016

First published 1999 by Macmillan
an imprint of Macmillan Publishers Ltd
25 Eccleston Place, London SWIW 9NF
Basingstoke and Oxford
Associated companies throughout the world

Oxford is a registered trademark of Oxford University Press

The publishers are grateful to Random House Group Ltd
for permission to quote from *The Queen and I* by Sue Townsend.

Library of Congress Cataloging-in-Publication Data
Davies, Norman.
The Isles: a history / by Norman Davies.
p. cm.
Includes bibliographical references and index.
ISBN 0-19-513442-7
1. Great Britain—History.   2. Great Britain—Civilization—European Influences.
4. Great Britain—Relations—Europe.   5. Europe—Relations—Great Britain.
6. Ireland—Relations—Europe.   7. Europe—Relations—Ireland.   8. Ireland—History.
I. Title.
DA30.D355   1999
94—dc21   99-29052

9 7 5 3   2 4 6 8
Printed in the United States of America
on acid-free paper

To the memory of

RICHARD SAMSON DAVIES

(1863–1939)

English by birth, Welsh by conviction,
Lancastrian by choice, British by chance

Acknowledgents

Acknowledgements

The author plays only a supporting role in the preparation and production of a large book. For institutional assistance, therefore, I wish to register my debt to Wolfson College and to the Wolfson Library, where much of the book was written, and to the Librarian, Adrian Hale. I am also especially indebted to the Division of the Pacific and Asian History, Australian National University, which provided me with a research fellowship, and more importantly with a most friendly environment for writing and first-rate office support. My genial host in Canberra, Professor Hank Nelson, deserves to be mentioned in all despatches. Equally, the Department of History, University of Adelaide, under its Chairman, Professor Ric Zuckerman, gave me the very welcome chance to work for an extendid period on their campus and to make full use of the excellent Barr Smith Library.

Among many individuals, in first place I owe a special debt of gratitude to my wife, Myszka, who, having considerable writing talents herself, fully understands the needs and foibles of a creative writer. I have received sterling assistance beyond the call of duty from my chief Researcher, Roger Moorhouse, and from my PA, Ewa Huggins. Numerous other friends and colleagues have made valuable contributions, among them the incomparable Ian and Margaret Willis, Professor Keith Brown, Professor Henry Loyn, Jude Shanahan, Cathy Brocklehurst, Lewis Mayo, Rhoda Macdonald, Alistair Moffat, Manon Williams, Rieko Karatani, Iain Smith, Athena Syriatou, David Morgan, Deanna Gallagher, Ray Chubb, Kevin Donnelly, Gavin Parsons, Dr Anthony Faulkes, Ceri Wyn-Richard, Pat Maclean, Revd Janet Ridgeway, Jos Paels, Philip Skingley, Graham Caie, The Scots Language Society, and many others.

My publishers, Macmillan, know exactly what it needs to keep an author in good heart and on the right path. I thank them for their efficiency and flexibility, especially my enthusiastic desk editor, Nicholas Blake, the book designer, Wilf Dickie, and my chief editors, Tanya Stobbs and Georgina Morley. In the darkest days of the greatest pressure, Georgina Morley proved to be an unflappable team leader, a wonderful manager, and a skilled psycho-therapist. The typesetters, SetSystems of Saffron Walden, responded to an extraordinarily tight schedule with speed and precision. My agent, David Godwin, has also been a tower of strength.

Every chapter has been submitted for comment to a team of specialist academic readers. Their advice has been absolutely invaluable. My warmest thanks go, therefore, to Professor Barry Cunliffe; Professor John Gillingham, Dr. Halina Hamerow, Dr Edwin Jones, Professor Iain McCalman, Martin Meanaugh, Dr Heather O'Donoghue, Professor Wilfrid Prest, Professor Peter Salway, Dr John Stevenson, and Dr Bjorn Weiler. The extent to which their advice was followed was my sole responsibility. All errors are exclusively my own doing. I would wish to take credit, however, for anything which happens to be accurate.

NORMAN DAVIES
The Day of the Total Eclipse
11 *August 1999*

CONTENTS

List of Illustrations

Section One

Section Two

Section Three

Section Four

List of Maps

List of Tables

List of Appendices

INTRODUCTION

To write a comprehensive history of one's own country is a forbidding task. The subject matter is copious and complex. The emotional overtones emanating from one's own life and family can be intrusive. And one could easily quake at the thought of all the historical giants who have travelled the same road. They and their books fill the shelves at every turn – from Hume to Trevelyan.

Fortunately, I was never sufficiently aware of such considerations to be bothered by them. As chance would have it, I found lodgings for one summer in a house that had once belonged to G. M. Trevelyan. There was a commemorative plaque over the front door; and two or three pictures of the grand old man still hung in the hallway. I particularly remember one which showed a maid serving the tea as he sat in the garden with his books. History-writing must be a good life, I mused. I was a postgraduate enrolled in the Cambridge Intensive Russian Course. Trevelyan, in his time, was 'the most influential and the most widely read historian of his generation.'[1] It never struck me for one moment that I might someday be writing history myself, still less that I might tackle a subject of which Trevelyan was the last great exponent.

Yet in that very same year an idea was planted that is only now bearing fruit more than thirty years later. In 1965, my former Oxford tutor, A. J. P. Taylor, published the fifteenth and final volume of the *Oxford History of England*, on the period 1914–45. In his usual mischievous way, Taylor explained in the preface that, given the 'assignment of English history' his book would not be dealing directly with 'the Welsh, the Scotch [sic], the Irish, or the British overseas'.[2] It was a typical Taylorian shaft. But it led me to reflect. Evidently, none of Taylor's eminent editors had ever clarified some key questions. Exactly which country's history was their series supposed to address? What precisely was the remit of English and of British history? Where did English history stop and British history begin? Or were they the same thing? And how do the Welsh, Scottish, and Irish components fit in? The answers involved far more than a mere play on words. In fact, it now looks as though they could run to more than a thousand pages.

Many years later, having written *Europe: a history*, I was invited to give a lecture at University College, Dublin. After the presentation, someone in the audience asked about my current project. I started to reply that I was thinking of writing a history of 'the British—'. I then realized that in Dublin, of all places, one cannot fairly talk of 'the British Isles'. The Isles ceased to be British precisely fifty years ago when the Republic of Ireland left the Commonwealth, though few people in the British residue have yet cared to notice. Various clumsy alternatives were discussed, such as 'the British and Irish Isles', 'Europe's Offshore Islands', and the 'Anglo-Celtic Archipelago'. In the end, it was decided that the only decent name for the forthcoming book was 'A History of These Islands'. And such was one of several working titles until, after much trial and error, I eventually arrived at *The Isles: A History*.

And today, as I sit with my papers in a gumtree's shade on a friendly Australian campus, the only thing missing is the maid to serve the tea. I will never be able to emulate Trevelyan.

This book necessarily presents a very personal view of history. Indeed, by some academic standards, it may well be judged thoroughly unsound. As I wrote in relation to a previous work, it presents the past 'seen through one pair of eyes, filtered by one brain, and recorded by one pen'. It has been assembled by an author who, though a British citizen and a professional historian, has no special expertise in the British historical field. Although every chapter has been read and commented on by specialist readers, almost all the factual material has been culled from standard accounts and reference works that can be found in any decent library. As always, the 11th Edition of *Encyclopædia Britannica* has been constantly at my elbow, as has *The History Today Companion to British History* and *The Oxford Companion to Irish History*. I was greatly encouraged early on by Hugh Kearney's *The British Isles – A History of Four Nations* (1989), which has acted as a pathfinder for many historians seeking a fresh approach. I have repeatedly consulted Michael Lynch's *Scotland: a new history* (1991), John Davies' *A History of Wales* (1993), and Roy Foster, ed., *The Oxford History of Ireland* (1989). I also acknowledge a special debt to Edwin Jones and his *The English Nation: the great myth* (1998), which I encountered at a very late stage and entirely by accident thanks to the generous open shelves policy of the Barr Smith Library. Even so, one cannot satisfy everybody. One of my most distinguished readers, who took an instant dislike to his designated chapter, advised me to 'jettison the lot'. I suspect that other professionals may exhibit similar allergies.

For, unlike some other recent surveys of the subject, the present work does not aim to summarize the reigning consensus. I definitely share the widespread anxiety about the slough of ultra-specialization, of pedagogical theorizing, and of public disinterest into which History has fallen; and I wish to contribute my pennyworth for the rehabilitation of the subject. Yet I do not see the solution in further recycling the specialist debates and I have totally avoided all post-modern discourses which try to invalidate every discourse except their own. For once, I intend to escape from the professional game, to address the established record of the past more directly, and in particular to re-examine the general framework within which all the more detailed studies are presented.

As a historical writer devoted increasingly to the problems of general synthesis, I have no hesitation in stating my admiration and respect for colleagues who study history at the other end of the spectrum, 'under the microscope'. No historical generalist could begin to function without reliance on the monographs and academic articles of people working at a completely different level of magnification. I would only ask that some of the specialists would show similar understanding for the skills and labours of the popularizers and *simplifacteurs*. It is in no one's interest that the false division between 'popular' and 'academic' history should be perpetuated.

Nonetheless the almost universal assumption amongst professionals seems to be that the broad framework of British history was set in stone by the great scholars of past generations, and that historians nowadays should leave it alone. They should devote all their time and ingenuity to ever shrinking patches of virgin territory. As the torrent of historical data expands exponentially, so, too, does the temptation to fix one's gaze on those tiny areas. For fifty years now the tendency has been to make history less of an art and more of a pseudo-science, and hence for everyone in the profession to know 'more and more about less and less'. As a result, 'Sorry, that is not my field' has become the watchword. Young historians have been led to believe that debating arcane issues among themselves in learned jargon is more important than communicating in plain language with the public. Students are raised on an *à la carte* menu, which never supplies them with a coherent picture of anything; and teachers are left picking 'n' mixing according to their likes and dislikes. The public has switched off.

At least, the public is in danger of switching off. I have deliberately overstated the case. Things are not so bad as the pessimists imply. I am well aware that in recent years a number of courageous historians have dared to buck the trend and have climbed to the top of the best-seller lists with large, ambitious, wide-horizoned history books. None of them, before publication, can have been sure of meeting success with their unlikely winners. Authors such as Simon Schama, Felipe Fernández-Armesto, and Orlando Figes have gained well-deserved acclaim through their originality of approach, their obvious passion for the subject, and their skill as writers.[3] The public, as it turns out, has an unquenched thirst for feisty history written with flair. A major article in the *New York Times* revealed, to the writer's obvious astonishment, that blockbuster history books could reach the best-seller lists.[4]

I am also aware that some of the best historians in the British field have broken clear of the herd, and have been exploring exciting new directions. The old Anglocentric straitjacket is bursting at the seams. The fundamental question of 'British identity' is being subjected to fierce scrutiny. Authors such as David Cannadine and Linda Colley, Hugh Kearney, Patrick O'Brien, and Rees Davies have shown convincingly that the old ways will no longer suffice. I was lucky enough to attend the ground-breaking Anglo-American Conference in London in 1994, which, despite its ill-suited title, demonstrated that the old Anglo-framework of insular history was unsustainable. As a graduate of Magdalen College I was also aware that scholars and influential mentors such as the late Angus McIntyre, himself a Hiberno-Australian Scot, were inspiring a group of disciples interested in Britain's 'multiple identities' and 'composite kingdoms'.[5] Their painstaking work will have its reward.

Even so, it is depressing to see the degree of complacency and bewilderment which often prevails with regard to the simplest historical matters. Everyone has heard those stories about supermarket attendants who see a total of £10.66 on their check-out screen and who remark, 'There we go – the Battle of Waterloo.' Education has much to answer for. Fifty years ago all children still learned the history and development of what they called 'England' – that is of the United Kingdom with its empire and colonies. They learned it in a spirit of pride and patriotism, being regaled with accounts of kings and queens, heroes and heroines, victories, glorious defeats, and national achievements. They understood what it meant, and what its civic and patriotic purposes were. Fifty years on, very little of the old approach was left. It undoubtedly had its faults. But it has never found a worthwhile replacement. Once the Empire collapsed, patriotic history fell out of fashion. Wars and battles had few admirers, especially among teachers. Dates and facts about kings and queens were judged injurious to the health of young minds. Their placed in the classroom was taken by critical discussions on skills and sources, and more frequently by exercises in empathy. Political history lost its traditional link with geography and gave way to social and economic studies. Indeed, with the advent of new subjects such as technology, ecology, and economics, History was in danger of being relegated to a secondary option in the national curriculum for state schools in England and Wales. As reported in the press in March 1999, government plans, if implemented, would further diminish history's already low standing. Primary schools, ordered to devote more time to raising standards in English and mathematics, were set to abandon any attempt to teach an outline of national history. Teachers were to be urged to concentrate still more on inculcating historical skills to pupils who were devoid of systematic historical knowledge. Secondary schools were due to abandon event-based history altogether. Pupils were to 'study how British society was shaped by the movement and settlement of different peoples'. In lessons on the twentieth century, the only compulsory subject would be the Nazi Holocaust – which does not even belong directly to British affairs. In the opinion of the director of the History Curriculum Association, the changes would confirm 'the disappearance of the landmarks of British History'.[6] One could only hope for a change of heart or for confirmation that the reports were exaggerated.

That such a prospect should even be discussed, however, indicated the alarming decline of History in recent decades. If the reports were accurate, the rot was well advanced. A generation had been educated without any basic historical awareness. And a society unaware of its history is like a person suffering from amnesia. It simply cannot function efficiently. One should not be in the least surprised that on every hand one met people who do not care about the difference between 'England' and 'Britain' or between 'Great Britain' and 'the United Kingdom'. Such distinctions, which are rooted in historical change, were simply not noticed.

The true extent of this morass of mix-ups is marvellous to behold. One of the most extraordinary aspects of the current scene lies in the number of citizens of the United Kingdom who do not appear to be familiar with the basic parameters of the state in which they live. They often do not know what it is called; they do not distinguish between the whole and the constituent parts; and they have never grasped the most elementary facts of its development. Confusion reigns on every hand. Nor is it confined to the old bad habit of using 'England' as a shorthand for the United Kingdom as a whole, and hence of travellers who imagine that they carry an 'English' as opposed to a 'British' passport. Such lapses are commonplace. But they form the tip of a far larger iceberg. The scale of the problem only begins to emerge when one observes the inability of prominent authorities to present the history of our Isles in accurate and unambiguous terms.

For a preliminary sounding, one only needs to enter a bookshop and examine the opening passages of the most popular volumes on British history. My own experiment was conducted in a bookshop where, to my query about the best books in circulation, the assistant pointed out three titles: Roy Strong, *The Story of Britain* (1992), *The Oxford History of Britain* (1999), and Antonia Fraser, *The Lives of the Kings and Queens of England* (revised edition, 1997).[7] All three books undoubtedly possess manifold virtues in those aspects of the subject which most concern them. I was not making a general assessment. The point of the experiment was simply to test how they define and introduce the overall subject.

Roy Strong's volume, for instance, was inspired by an admirable and passionate belief in the present generation's need for a straightforward narrative history. Yet it opens with the baffling sentence 'Britain is an island.'[8] One is tempted to mutter, 'Well, yes and no.' On the facing page, Strong offers a physical map showing an unnamed archipelago consisting of two large islands and several smaller ones. Uninitiated readers, say from Mars or Japan, would be forgiven for asking which of the islands was called 'Britain'. And they would not be helped by the answer, 'It all depends on what you mean.'

Initiated readers, of course, would quickly recognize the familiar outline of the 'British Isles'. For their part, they would be justified in wondering whether the book dealt with the history not of one

island but of all of them. Judging by the contents, it would seem
that Strong is using 'Britain' as the accepted shorthand for the
United Kingdom. The trouble there lies in the fact that, in its present
form, the United Kingdom consists of two parts – Great Britain and
Northern Ireland. So it is not 'an island' (singular) in the present
tense. Indeed, it has not been one island since 31 December 1800.

Roy Strong's misconception follows in the steps of numerous
predecessors. One of these was A. L. Rowse, who published a survey
with the same title as Strong's. Rowse's *Story of Britain* (1979, 1993)
opens in almost exactly the same way:

> The story of Britain is that of the island which has influenced
> the outside world more than any other island in history.[9]

There it goes again – the one island fixation, embellished with an
imperial flourish. And it is still there in the final sentence of Rowse's
epilogue:

> It remains to be seen how the people . . . work out their fate;
> and whether in this lucky island it will be worthy of so
> remarkable a history.[10]

At this point, many readers may want to reach for their
dictionary. The latest edition of the ultimate authority, *The Oxford
English Dictionary*, defines 'Britain' as follows:

> The proper name of the whole island containing England,
> Wales, and Scotland, with their dependencies; more fully called
> Great Britain; now also used for the British state or empire as
> a whole.[11]

For the adjective *British*, the *OED* supplies five basic meanings:

1. Of or pertaining to the ancient Britons
2. Of or belonging to Great Britain, or its inhabitants
3. Of, or belonging to, Brittany, Breton. *Obs*(olete)
4. *ellipt.* as *sb. pl.* British people, soldiers etc. [i.e. 'The British']
5. *comb.*, *British-born*, *-built*, *-owned* adjs., *British-man*.[12]

From this, one learns that 'Britain' can refer to any one of three different entities – to the geographical unit of 'Great Britain', to the British state, and/or to the British Empire. Incongruously, however, *British* has somewhat different geographical connotations. It can only refer apparently to Ancient Britain, to Great Britain, and to Brittany. It does not pertain to the United Kingdom, therefore, except in that short period of history when the Kingdom was coterminous with 'Great Britain', i.e. from 1707 to 1800. Surely that cannot be right for a dictionary published in 1994.

If one turns for elucidation to *The Shorter Oxford English Dictionary*, the plot thickens. The meanings of 'British' are essentially the same as in the *OED*, although point 5 is omitted. The main definition of *Britain* is also essentially the same, except for one curious amendment. Where the *OED* reads 'now also used for the British state or empire as a whole', the *SOED* has 'now used for the British empire as a whole'.[13] For some reason, among its definitions of 'Britain', the *SOED* has chosen to drop the 'British state'. If this is correct, then Roy Strong's *Story of Britain* could be a history *either* of the island of Great Britain *or* of the British Empire, but not of the United Kingdom.

The inconsistencies are legion. They centre on the thorny question of what constituted the United Kingdom at any particular time. In their further explanations to their definitions of Britain, both the *OED* and *SOED* use a similar formula. The *OED* states:

> After the O(ld) E(nglish) period, *Britain* was used only as a historical term, until about the time of Henry VIII and Edward VI, when it came again into practical politics in connexion with the efforts made to unite England and Scotland; in 1604 James I was proclaimed 'King of Great Britain'; and this name was adopted for the United Kingdom, at the union in 1707 . . .[14]

The *SOED* uses a condensed version of this information, while the *OED* adds some further details:

After that event [the union of 1707], *South Britain* and *North Britain* are frequent in acts of Parl. for England and Scotland respectively; the latter is in occasional (chiefly postal) use. (So *West Britain*, humorously or polemically for 'Ireland'.) *Greater Britain* is a modern rhetorical device for 'Great Britain and the colonies', 'the British Empire', brought into vogue in 1868.[15]

These comments are instructive, of course, as far as they go. But one cannot help feeling that the Oxford editors have been stranded in a rather distant period of history. Indeed, they appear to have progressed very little beyond 1707. They do not let on that the name and territory of the United Kingdom have changed twice in the last two centuries. *West Britain*, for example could only have applied when Ireland formed part of the United Kingdom between 1801 and 1922. *Britain* as shorthand for both 'Great Britain' and the 'United Kingdom' only remained unambiguous during the lifetime of the united 'Kingdom of Great Britain' between 1707 and 1800. Ever since 1800, as the dictionary definitions indicate, *Britain* has had to assume alternative meanings.

Nor is the matter much clarified by turning to the dictionary for an explanation of the term *England*. The *SOED* seems to offer three definitions:

1. The territory of the Angles. Only in O[ld] E[nglish]
2. The southern part of the island of Great Britain . . . Often: the English (or British) nation or state . . .
3. Short for *The King of England*, also for the English or a portion of them . . .[16]

Looked at closely, this entry reveals that the *SOED* is actually offering seven definitions of *England*. Point 2 alone contains five. These five are:

– The southern part of the island of Great Britain – i.e., a geographical or territorial unit.
– The English nation – i.e., a community of people.
– The English state – i.e., a political entity.

- The British nation.
- The British state.

It is unfortunate that the editors elide all five definitions into a single point. One possibility is that they considered both 'English' and 'British', like 'nation' and 'state', to be synonyms and that all four terms are coterminous with 'the southern part . . . of Great Britain'. If so, they have laid themselves open to some serious queries.

In this light, or twilight, one can turn to *The Oxford History of Britain* (1999). The editor's foreword opens as follows:

> The distinctiveness, even uniqueness, of the British as a people has long been taken for granted . . . Visitors from overseas, from those ubiquitous Venetian ambassadors in the late fifteenth century, through intellectuals like Voltaire or Tocqueville, to American journalists in the twentieth century, have all been convinced of the special quality of British Society.[17]

The key phrases here are 'the British as a people' and 'British society'. They immediately arouse suspicions of anachronism. There can be no doubt that Voltaire in the eighteenth century, de Tocqueville in the nineteenth, and the American journalists in the twentieth were all reporting on a people and a society that could properly be called 'British'. But there has to be a question mark over what exactly was visited by those Venetian ambassadors in the late fifteenth century. More than two hundred years before the formation of the British state, one has to suspect that the Venetian ambassadors had only visited England and that their comments were confined to the special qualities of the English people and of English society. It is surely out of place to suggest that the 'English society' of the fifteenth century was simply an earlier version of the 'British society' of the eighteenth century and later.

Reading on, one's hopes for clarification are dashed when one meets a statement containing a still more convoluted muddle:

> A basic premise of this book is that it deals with the history of

> Great Britain, two partitioned, poly-cultural islands, and not
> merely with England.[18]

The book does not deal 'merely with England'. That is fair enough.
It supposedly deals with the 'history of Great Britain'. Yet *Great
Britain* cannot possibly be equated with 'two partitioned, poly-
cultural islands'. As the *OED* confirms, Great Britain is the full name
of 'the whole island containing England, Wales, and Scotland, with
their dependencies'. It does not include Ireland. Unlike 'Britain', it
can't be made to refer to 'two islands', whether 'partitioned' or
'poly-cultural' or otherwise. So one is faced here not just with an
anachronism or with an ambiguity but with a fundamental error. It
is rather disturbing. It would appear that the mix-ups are being
disseminated by the very works that should be disentangling them.

Investigation of the constituent chapters of *The Oxford History of
Britain* provides little reassurance. Despite the editor's declaration,
the 'basic premise' is largely ignored. The chapter on the sixteenth
century, for example, is entitled 'The Tudor Age'. It begins with a
section on 'Population Changes', which contains no information on
the population of anywhere other than England, and opens with a
statement that:

> The age of the Tudors has left its impact on the Anglo-
> American mind as a watershed in British history.[19]

Surely, the age of the Tudors, who reigned in England, Wales, and
Ireland but not in Scotland, is an important period in the history of
England. But it hardly represents a watershed in British history.

The chapter following, entitled 'The Stuarts, 1603–1688', offers
meagre improvement. Once again, Scotland and Ireland are ignored;
and the chapter opens with a remark about the Stuarts being 'one
of England's least successful dynasties'.[20] Such a judgement on an
ancient Scottish dynasty which reigned only briefly in England is, to
say the least, out of place.

In his foreword, the editor of the *Oxford History* makes a heartfelt
appeal to the patriotism of Britain. 'This rooted patriotism,' he

writes, 'embracing Welsh, Scots and Ulstermen over the centuries – though, significantly, never the southern Irish – endured and remained unchangeable.'[21] One has to suppose that southern Irishmen like the Duke of Wellington do not come into the reckoning. But if Welsh, Scots, or Ulster readers take the trouble to seek out what is, and what isn't, said about their countries, their presumed patriotic feelings are due for a dousing. If British historians are to continue to appeal to the patriotism of the non-English, they will have to address non-English concerns with rather more accuracy and sensitivity.

If one now turns to *The Lives of the Kings and Queens of England*, one finds still more sources of confusion. Lady Antonia begins by saying that 'in one sense . . . the volume . . . needs no introduction.'[22] A glance at the table of contents, however, reveals that on one point at least an introductory explanation is sorely needed. For the contents open with William the Conqueror and close with Elizabeth II. For no apparent reason they exclude the ten pre-Conquest monarchs from Edward the Elder to Harold Godwinson, who were undoubtedly Kings of England, whilst including the eleven representatives of the Houses of Hanover, Sachsen-Coburg und Gotha, and Windsor who have been monarchs not of England but of the United Kingdom. All the Queen's loyal but non-English subjects have good cause to feel aggrieved.

This Sceptred Isle was a book published to accompany the highly successful BBC Radio series in 1995–6.[23] Liberally laced with trenchant extracts from Winston Churchill's *History of the English Speaking Peoples* (1954–6), its fifty-five episodes cover the two thousand years from Julius Caesar to Queen Victoria. Both the book and the radio series revealed the public's appetite for old-fashioned narrative history and for a comprehensive chronological framework to historical knowledge. Yet, as the adoption of Shakespeare's catch-phrase implies, the interpretation (see page 507, below) is Anglocentric to a fault. It accepts without a word of hesitation that England is the only part of the Isles that counts and that British history is a mere continuation of English history.

Finally, one last book needs a mention. Paul Johnson's *Offshore Islanders* (1995) bears a subtitle, *A History of the English People*. It opens on the frontispiece with a quotation from Milton's *Areopagitica*:

> Lords and Commons of England – consider what nation it is whereof you are and of which you are governor . . .[24]

Amen to that.

Nowhere is the reigning confusion better illustrated than in the classification system of major libraries. The seeker for truth in the libraries of Oxford University, for example, has some curious puzzles to solve. On OLIS, the University on-line catalogue, historical subjects are commonly organized by country. French history can be found under <FRANCE -- HISTORY>, Italian history under <ITALY -- HISTORY>, and so on. So, logically, one might expect modern British history to be catalogued under <UNITED KING-DOM -- HISTORY>. But it is not. Indeed, OLIS is not aware of the United Kingdom having a history of its own at all. If one enters <UNITED KINGDOM -- HISTORY> one receives no response whatsoever other than a line of arrows on the screen indicating where the non-existent entry would have been located between <UK HARPISTS' ASSOCIATION> and <UNITED KINGDOM I.T.A. FEDERATION> – I.T.A. standing for Initial Teaching Alphabet. There is not even a cross-reference to any other related headings such as <GREAT BRITAIN -- HISTORY>, or <NORTHERN IRELAND -- HISTORY>. After all, as the well informed will know, the state in which Oxford University and its libraries live and work is called the 'United Kingdom of Great Britain and Northern Ireland'.

Scrolling through the catalogue headings, one comes up to <UNITED ARAB EMIRATES -- HISTORY> and down to <UNITED NATIONS -- HISTORY> and <UNITED STATES -- HISTORY>. Indeed, as far one can ascertain, every single member state of the United Nations from <AFGHANISTAN> to <ZIM-

BABWE> has a main heading together with a sub-heading for its history. But not the United Kingdom.

The next step is to have a guess and to enter <GREAT BRITAIN, HISTORY>. After all, many people equate the 'United Kingdom' with 'Great Britain'. This time, the response is positive. <GREAT BRITAIN –– HISTORY> appears on the screen between <GREAT BRITAIN –– HISTORIOGRAPHY – PERIODICALS> and a very long list of further subdivisions under GREAT BRITAIN, HISTORY by period. At the latest count it was showing a total of 641 entries. These, one presumes, relate to general works on British history. It is rather slipshod; but understandable. If one explores a bit further, however, and keys in <ENGLAND, HISTORY>, one is in for a shock. For <ENGLAND –– HISTORY> not only carries a cross-reference back to <GREAT BRITAIN –– HISTORY> but also shows the same tally of 641 entries. On examination all the entries under <GREAT BRITAIN –– HISTORY> and <ENGLAND –– HISTORY> turn out to be absolutely identical. They both start with 1. Chronicles of St. Bride's; and they both end with 641. Zins, Henryk, Historia Anglii (The History of England), Wrocław, 1979. There can only be one conclusion. Whoever it was that determined the classification of history books in the libraries of the United Kingdom's senior university, a decision was taken to treat <GREAT BRITAIN> and <ENGLAND> as one and the same thing. In this corner of the official mind, 'British History' does not relate to the United Kingdom; and it is indistinguishable from 'English History'.[25]

Oxford librarians are always on guard against troublemakers. They feign surprise. But then, after persistent questioning, one of them lets slip that the Bodleian follows the same policy as the Library of Congress in Washington D.C. even on matters relating to the United Kingdom. Long ago, it seems, long before the age of computers, the astute librarians of the US Congress established a dominant hold on the market by selling compact sets of their subject-headings printed on index cards. So now almost all libraries in the English-speaking world have adopted the American system. It is a brilliant case of informational imperialism. Once the index cards had been transferred onto inter-linked computerized catalogues, the compatibility of subject-headings became still more desirable – with the obvious results.

The Subject Headings of the Library of Congress are published in three grand red-bound volumes; and they are accompanied by a splendid cataloguing manual. The previous experiment can now be repeated. Once again, under <UNITED KINGDOM – HISTORY>, one draws a blank. Indeed, this time the 'United Kingdom' itself does not exist. Between <UNITED FRUIT COMPANY> and <UNITED NATIONS>, there is not so much as a line of arrows. How can the USA have a 'special relationship' with an ally that does not exist?

So one turns to the first of the grand red volumes, and looks up <GREAT BRITAIN>. It is not only there; it has an explanatory note:

> Here are entered works on the United Kingdom of Great Britain and Northern Ireland, which comprises England, Northern Ireland, Scotland and Wales, as well as works on the island of Great Britain ... Works on the non-jurisdictional group comprising the islands of Great Britain, Ireland and smaller adjacent islands, are entered under British Isles.[26]

This is both impressive and encouraging. These Americans seem to know what they are talking about. They give precise definitions both of the 'United Kingdom' and of the 'British Isles'; and they know that Great Britain is just one island.

Turning to the sub-heading <GREAT BRITAIN, *History*>, however, the old bogey raises its head. <GREAT BRITAIN, History> is followed by the instruction <U(se) F(or) ENGLAND, History>: not <U.F. ENGLAND, History> and <U.F. SCOTLAND, History>, but just <U.F. ENGLAND, History>. What a mess! Notwithstanding their superior information, the Americans are every bit as mixed up as the Brits. As in Oxford, the Washington librarians are determined to present British history and English history as one and the same thing. In both cases, there is no awareness either that British history has encompassed Scotland as well as England (and Ireland in the nineteenth century) or that England, like Scotland, possessed its own separate history prior to the Union of 1707.

For librarians wrestling with these arcaneries – two pages of guidance are provided:

> BACKGROUND: The heading **Great Britain** is used in both descriptive and subject cataloguing as the conventional form for the United Kingdom, which comprises England, Northern Ireland, Scotland, and Wales. This instruction sheet describes the usage of **Great Britain**, in contrast to **England**, as a subject heading. It also describes the usage of **Great Britain**, **England**, **Northern Ireland**, **Scotland** and **Wales** in local subdivision.[27]

So far, so good. But then, one meets 'the exception':

> Exception: Do not use the subdivisions **History** or **Politics and Government** under England. For a work on the history, politics, or government of England, assign the heading **Great Britain**, subdivided as required for the work. References in the subject file reflect this practice. Use the subdivision **Foreign relations** under **England** only in the restricted sense described in the scope note under **England – Foreign relations**.[28]

There is no point in reading further. The libraries of Washington do not intend to apply their excellent knowledge to the task in hand. Objectively speaking, there is no good reason why the Library of Congress, and every other library in the world, should not have adopted one heading for 'United Kingdom', another for 'Great Britain', and another for the 'British Isles'. Logically, England requires a separate heading equivalent to those for Scotland, Ireland, Northern Ireland, and Wales. <ENGLAND, History> needs just three main sub-divisions:

> England, History – prior to the Union with Scotland (1707)
> England, History – 1707–1800, within the Kingdom of Great Britain
> England, History – since 1801 within the United Kingdom

Unfortunately, 'the conventional form' dictates otherwise. The chances of unscrambling a convention which is more deeply ingrained than the millennium bug are minimal. One suspects that <UNITED KINGDOM – HISTORY> will never be introduced as a subject-heading until the United Kingdom has passed into history.

This is hardly the place to attempt a comprehensive explanation of the reigning confusion. But two or three observations may not be amiss. One of these would refer to the widespread, unthinking, and unshakeable belief in the unbroken continuity of 'our island history'. The belief is so strong that it crushes any sense of the need to change the names to match the changing reality. England is assumed to be fixed and eternal. Hence many historians do not hesitate to talk of 'England' in those centuries of the first millennium long before the creation either of an English state or nation. And they continue to talk of 'England' as a mistaken synonym for the United Kingdom long after England had been merged into a wider unified state.

In a similar way, English people seem particularly unwilling to recognize that their united Kingdom has undergone two successive transformations since its creation in 1707. After much delay, the public accepted that 'Great Britain' was a more fitting label for the United Kingdom than 'England' had been. But when the kingdom changed its name in 1801 and again in 1922, no further attempt was made to readjust the shortened form. The eighteenth-century designation was set in mental stone, and has proved amazingly persistent ever since. In the early twentieth century, when British motor vehicles were first required to carry an international identification plate, the out-of-date and inappropriate abbreviation of 'GB' was chosen in place of 'UK'. Vehicles from Northern Ireland, which has never been part of Great Britain, run around on GB plates to this day. On the world's money markets, the currency of the United Kingdom, the pound sterling, is abbreviated not to 'UKP' but to 'GBP'. By the same token, when British government departments were allocated electronic domain names in the 1990s, many inadvertently adopted the suffix of <gov.gb>, only changing to the more suitable form of <gov.uk> at the second attempt.

Lastly, one observes a blanket change that was widely instituted in the 1970s and 80s. When historians finally realized that the traditional designation of 'English History' was clearly out of place for the period after 1707, the English label was indiscriminately replaced by the British one. In consequence, a completely new set of anachronisms became entrenched. The wholesale use of 'British' for all periods in the history in the Isles is turning the whole story upside down. The Tudors, who as Kings of England had always been correctly described as an English dynasty (of Welsh origin), have now been turned into a British dynasty, which they patently were not. The ultimate development in this regard was perpetrated in a recent TV advertisement which unceremoniously amended Shakespeare and came up with the ineffable line:

'This blessed plot, this earth, this realm, this *Britain*.'

The advertisers must not be blamed. After all, they are imitating the most distinguished academics.

One would be hard put to find another state or country which is so befuddled about the basic framework of its past. One of the few parallels that does exist can be found in the textbooks of the late and unlamented Soviet Union. Although the Soviet Union was not created until 1923, Soviet historians customarily pretended that Soviet history stretched back to prehistoric times, just as it was destined to stretch up and away into the eternal future. The standard textbook of the Stalinist era, A. M. Pankratova's *A History of the USSR*, appeared in Moscow in three volumes in 1947–8. Only the third volume treated the formation and development of the USSR. The first volume opened with a section on 'The Primitive Community System in Our Country', and closed with 'Important Dates in the History of the USSR since Ancient Times until the end of the Seventeenth Century'. In this period of the 'Soviet past', space was found both for the ancient Greek cities of the Crimea and for

Genghis Khan. The second volume opened with a chapter on 'The Founding of the Russian Empire' and closed with 'Important Dates in the History of the USSR in the Eighteenth and Nineteenth Centuries'. The first date on this last list is '1682–1725 . . . Reign of Peter I'.[29] One may be amused. But to state that the reign of Peter the Great formed part of Soviet history is no less eccentric than stating that the reign of Henry VIII formed part of British history. Soviet historians at least could plead that they were writing to the prescription of ideological commissars. British historians have no such excuse. It is worth pointing out that many people in the West did not realize that 'Russia' and the 'Soviet Union' were not the same thing until the Soviet Union, finally, collapsed, leaving fifteen independent republics in its wake.

So what is to be done? I would say that my present goals are fivefold. The first is to suggest that the conventional framework of the history of the Isles is in urgent need of revision. The second is to pay due respect to all the nations and cultures in the history of the Isles and to the detriment of none. The third is to put the existing body of knowledge on certain key subjects, such as the rise and fall of 'Britishness', into a firm chronological and analytical setting. The fourth is to make a contribution to the contemporary British debate, helping to show how the present state of affairs has been reached. And finally, to assist the above, I aimed to present a clear and simple exposition of the overall historical narrative, concentrating on the formation and transformation of the states within whose fluctuating bounds every layer of our shifting and multiple identities has been formed. Until I started writing, I myself did not realize just how many different states the Isles have supported over the centuries:

- The High Kingship of Ireland, to AD 1169
- The Ancient British tribal principalities, to c. AD 70
- Independent 'Pictland', to the ninth century AD
- Roman Britannia, 43–c. 410 AD

- The independent British/Welsh principalities, from the fifth century to 1283, including Cornwall, Cumbria, and Strathclyde
- The Anglo-Saxon kingdoms, from the fifth to the tenth centuries
- The Kingdom of the Scots, from the ninth century to 1651, and 1660–1707
- The Kingdom of England, from the tenth century to 1536, together with its dependencies including the Channel Islands, the Isle of Man, the Welsh March, and English-occupied Wales and Ireland
- The Kingdom of England and Wales, 1536–1649, 1660–1707
- The Kingdom of Ireland, 1541–1649, 1660–1800
- The Commonwealth and Free State of England, Wales, and Ireland, 1649–1654
- The Commonwealth of Great Britain and Ireland, alias the 'First British Republic', 1654–1660
- The united Kingdom of Great Britain, 1707–1800
- The United Kingdom of Great Britain and Ireland, 1801–1922
- The Irish Free State (later Éire, then the Republic of Ireland), since 1922
- The United Kingdom of Great Britain and Northern Ireland, since 1922

In relating this long and rather complicated story, I preferred to adopt the standpoint of an outsider looking inwards, rather than that of an insider observing the immediate surroundings. One reason for this was to lead my readers into the insular affairs of the earlier periods only after giving them a taste of the wider context. Another reason, by starting the narrative of each chapter at slightly eccentric locations, was to demonstrate the extent to which any historical narrative is dependent on the historian's chosen perspective.

I have also taken care to be as precise as possible about nomenclature. Having questioned the reigning conventions, I must endeavour to be more accurate myself. I have been careful to show what is English and what is not, and only to use the British adjective in relation to the two periods where it is relevant – one ancient and one modern.

To bypass the prevailing anachronisms, I decided to transpose all the names in the first chapter into imaginary but time-neutral forms. In Chapter Four, I have replaced the usual 'Anglo-Saxons' with 'Germanics'. I don't use the word 'British' in its modern sense before the formation of the united Kingdom in 1707. And in the title of the book, I have used the simplest formula of all.

The structure of the book follows a consistent pattern. Each chapter consists of three sections. The opening sections take the form of a 'snapshot', that is, the detailed treatment of some brief episode which puts the main theme of the chapter into its wider context. The middle sections are devoted either to a summary account of the period in hand, or, in Chapters Seven to Ten, to summaries of a series of salient themes from the period. The concluding sections, which vary considerably in length, aim to sketch in outline how each period of history was reflected in the historiography and literature of later times. No such brief survey can hope to be complete. But one hopes that it is sufficiently extensive to reveal the truth that the history of those islands has not been one of smooth, seamless, linear progress. Rather, it has been one of kaleidoscopic change and of repeated, turbulent transformations.

I cannot say exactly what inspired me to undertake the present task. Having spent several decades writing about foreign places, I wished to embark for once on an adventure round my native shores. But I wanted to do it in a particular way. I wanted to return to the path which Trevelyan trod with such distinction, of showing that history is an art as well as a science. Trevelyan understood that history is there to enthuse the millions, not just to provide employment for academics. He once described himself as 'a man of letters disguised as a don.' I find that an attractive model to follow.[30]

Adelaide, S.A.
March 1999

CHAPTER ONE

THE MIDNIGHT ISLES

THE CANYON CAVE MAN. Not long after the last Ice Age, not far from the western sea, a young man was buried in a cave set high in the walls of a limestone canyon. Beside him lay a strange long object made of antler bone, variously described as some sort of sceptre or perhaps a spear-straightener. The shallow grave on the cave floor was surrounded by thousands of flints – the non-perishable parts of Stone Age spears, knives, scrapers, and burins. These in turn were accompanied by heaps of bones from the birds and animals which had supplied the cave dweller's diet: hence wild horse, reindeer, and red deer; blue hare, brown bear, Arctic fox, and willow grouse; pig, ptarmigan, peregrine falcon; and one solitary, and much older, mammoth bone. The cave and its contents remained undisturbed until rediscovered in modern times.

Caves were one of the favourite places of refuge for prehistoric people. They provided shelter in all seasons, an even temperature, and protection from wild animals. Unlike a neighbouring cavern, which had once served as a den for hyenas and which had been used by humanoids in far remoter ages, the 'Canyon Cave' had not been inhabited before the last ice had melted. Its cool, but never freezing, air was ideal for the growth of stalactites and, in our own times, for the fermentation of cheese. When the Anglo-Saxons arrived some seven or eight thousand years after the cave burial, they founded the nearby village, and called it Ceodor – their word for a canyon or ravine. When the Normans came five hundred years after the Anglo-Saxons, they called the ravine a *gorge* – their word both for a throat and for a narrow valley.

Very little is known about the person who was buried in the Canyon Cave. Though he lived and died in a country which would much later be called England, he was certainly not English. We do not know what tribe or people he belonged to. We do not know what language or languages he spoke; or whether the language of his people was comprehensible to others living in the vicinity. We do not know what thoughts he may have had about his world, or whether he had any concept of the era into which he was born. We may suppose that he was a hunter, or at least that he was supported by the hunters and gatherers of his tribe. We may also surmise, since the meat of animals and the fruits of the forest were the staff of his life, that he was inured to constant wandering. He followed the herds over hill and dale in the cool, dry 'boreal' climate of that first post-glacial phase. Since his cave lay barely a day's walk from the open sea, he must often have climbed up the canyon wall to the grassy track on the ridge and strolled along it towards the beach. Even if the coast were further out than it is today, we may reasonably imagine that he had cruised along it in his dugout, that he had crossed the nearby estuary to its northern shore, or even that he had made the more adventurous crossing of the long Inner Bay to a landfall beyond the sunset.

For ninety years after its discovery in 1903 in Gough's Cave, Cheddar Gorge, the skeleton of 'Cheddar Man' was kept in London's Natural History Museum. But in 1996 it was the subject of an extraordinary experiment. It was sent to the Institute of Molecular Medicine in Oxford for DNA testing, and samples of its mitochondrial DNA were compared with a score of similar samples taken from volunteers among the villagers in the present-day Cheddar district. 'To the astonishment of the scientists', as The Times reported, 'a close match was found between Cheddar Man and Mr [Adrian] Targett', a forty-two-year-old history teacher at the Kings of Wessex Community School in Cheddar Village. The experiment had proved beyond reasonable doubt that a man living in late twentieth-century Britain was a direct descendant through the maternal line of a person living in the same locality in the Middle Stone Age.[1]

The implications of the Targett Case are very far-reaching. If the result is not just a mistake or a chance in a billion, it would indicate that a substantial proportion of people in modern Britain form part of local kinship groups which have had a continuous existence for three or four hundred generations. This in its turn means that each of those generations has adapted itself to every successive cultural, linguistic, and political wave that has taken place over the millennia. The old idea that Britain's 'island race' was the sum total of numerous massive invasions, from the mesolithic relations of Cheddar Man, who repopulated the islands after the Ice Age, to the Celts, Romans, Saxons, Vikings, Normans, and Angevins of historic times, who all but obliterated their prehistoric predecessors, has been under attack for many years. It is now virtually untenable. The prehistoric gene pool must undoubtedly have been supplemented and modified by more recent arrivals. But it is still there.

There are other crucial considerations. British people are taught in a way which leads them to assume unthinkingly, that 'Cheddar Man lived on the island of prehistoric Britain'. Yet, if one reflects, every single part of that sentence is inaccurate. For when Mr Targett's ancestor was buried in the cave, the canyon was not yet Cheddar Gorge. So whoever he was, 'the Canyon Cave Man' could not have been Cheddar Man. What is more, neither he nor his relations could possibly have known that they were 'prehistoric'. And their homeland was still many millennia away from being England or Britain. Most surprisingly, since nine thousand years represents a mere moment in the overall timetable of prehistory, their country was not yet an island. The latest carbon dating for the death of the Canyon Cave Man was 8980 $\perp$ 150 radiocarbon years. Adjusted to calendar years, this gives a date inside the eighth millennium BC and precedes by a clear margin the median date at which geologists estimate the formation of Europe's offshore islands (see page 8, below). Even if he had been born exactly where he died, there can be virtually no doubt that 'the Canyon Cave Man' was a Continental.

THE MIDNIGHT ISLES

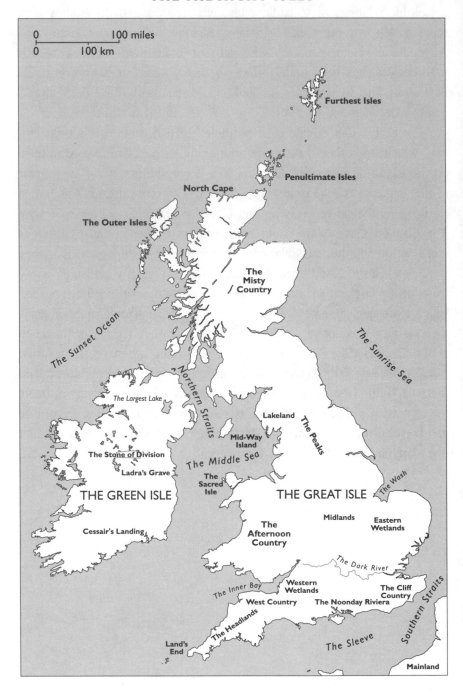

0   100 miles
0   100 km

Furthest Isles

Penultimate Isles

North Cape

The Outer Isles

The Misty / Country

The Sunset Ocean

Northern Straits

The Largest Lake

Lakeland

The Peaks

The Sunrise Sea

Mid-Way Island

The Stone of Division

The Middle Sea

Ladra's Grave

The Sacred Isle

THE GREEN ISLE

THE GREAT ISLE

The Wash

Cessair's Landing

Midlands

Eastern Wetlands

The Afternoon Country

The Dark River

The Inner Bay

Western Wetlands

The Cliff Country

West Country

The Noonday Riviera

Southern Straits

The Headlands

Land's End

The Sleeve

Mainland

THE HISTORY OF MANKIND on the peninsula which we now call 'Europe' has lasted for some seven hundred or eight hundred thousand years. For over 99 per cent of that vast expanse of time, man lived in the Stone Age, using rough stone or flint tools of very slowly increasing sophistication. He supported life through hunting, trapping, fishing, and gathering the wild plants and crustaceans. Though various convenient caves and open sites were occupied, abandoned, and reoccupied over long periods, there was little permanent settlement as the human troops followed the herds across the ever-changing seasons and feeding-grounds. If the passage of time in the Peninsula's human prehistory is counted on a scale of 1 to 100, the emergence of modern man, *Homo sapiens sapiens*, would have occurred at about point 94: the last retreat of the northern Ice Sheet and the onset of the mesolithic somewhere after point 98: the earliest origins of the so-called 'Neolithic Revolution' around point 99. At no stage before the final point were there any major islands off the Peninsula's north-west coast.

For most of prehistory, the lands which are now called the British or the British and Irish Isles formed a broad promontory of the Continental land mass, an oceanside peninsula of the Peninsula. (See map, page 2.) It consisted of two parts, the main north–south trunk and a long arm protruding on the western side. Its sparse population came and went during the Ice Ages, sometimes encouraged by the warmer conditions of the interglacials, sometimes deterred by the icebound or sub-tundra conditions of the glacial advances. At the height of the terminal Ice Age, all human habitation ceased. Resettlement resumed c. 10,000 BC after an interval of perhaps seven or eight millennia. From then on, humans have been

present without a break until the present day. By the time of the
Canyon Cave Man the southern valleys were overgrown by ever
denser post-glacial woodland; the inhabitants increasingly set up
camp on coastal sites or moved into the outer islands, the remoter
uplands and most northerly districts, where in due course hut-circles
would become a standard form of settlement.

The transformation of the oceanside peninsula into a group of
offshore islands took place in the course of the seventh or sixth
millennium BC. In all probability it took place gradually, not as the
result of a dramatic geological catastrophe or a sudden onrush of
the sea. It was partly caused by the tilting of land surfaces rendered
unstable by the retreating ice, and partly by the rising levels of
warmer seas. As the outer coastal range sank, its peaks were left as
a string of stormbound islets. The mountains of the north tipped
upwards. The western arm of the peninsula broke free, creating two
separate islands, the 'Green Isle' and the 'Great Isle'. The ocean
tides surged into the long inner bay not only from the south but
also through the new and turbulent northern straits, turning the top
of the bay into the 'Middle Sea'. Next, to the east, the Continental
coastal flats retreated southwards as the shallow salt water advanced.
This greatly extended the 'Sunrise Sea'. It also reduced the peninsula's Continental landlink to a narrow low-lying southern isthmus
less than a hundred miles wide, between two chalk ridges. Finally,
as the sea continued to rise, the isthmus itself began to shrink. It
first turned to wet, salty marshland and then began to flood. After
that, the currents from the west aided the currents from the east to
wash away the remaining chalk, gravel, and sand. Sometime
between 6000 and 5500 BC the landlink disappeared entirely. 'The
Sleeve' was born, with its pinchpoint at the 'Southern Straits'.[2]

The consequences of the birth of 'the Sleeve' are often misrep-
resented or exaggerated. It is often said that the new-formed islands
were 'isolated' from the Continent or 'cut off'. But this is hardly
correct. Of course, in strictly geographical terms, the islands *were*
isolated, since 'to isolate' means 'to turn into an island'. Where once
there was a strip of land, there now was a stretch of water. This

would have been a serious blow for the migrating herds of animals, who could no longer cross the isthmus. The livestock on the islands, especially the larger beasts, could no longer be replenished by Continental migrants. The great elk, for example, became extinct on the Isles just as the mammoth had done. Yet man, unlike the animals, could readily adapt to the changed circumstances. Indeed, he could turn them to his advantage. There is every indication that communications actually improved. Even with the primitive boats then available, one could paddle or sail from one side of the Sleeve to the other more rapidly than one could previously have tramped across the isthmus or, in the intermediary phase, waded through the marshes. The birth of the Sleeve must have stimulated sailing techniques and marine transport of various kinds. In the period during the emergence of the Isles, the islanders became expert sailors. The islands were *not* cut off. Communication was simply made more dependent on boats.

The exploration and utilization of the western seaways appears to have begun as soon as they were opened up. Little is known about the vessels and the navigational techniques of those mesolithic mariners. But the archaeological evidence is decisive in showing that people and goods were shipped back and forth across all the channels and between all the islands. After all, the distances involved were not great enough to deter fair-weather voyages by hide-bound coracles and kayaks, by dugouts, or even by rafts. Even the 'Great Crossing' between the Mainland and the Great Isle at the most convenient section of the Sleeve did not exceed sixty miles. It could be completed in a day, at most in a day and night. The passage between the two largest islands was forty-eight miles at its widest and only twelve miles at its narrowest. Navigation round the Middle Sea, greatly assisted by stopovers on 'Midway Island', was particularly attractive. One should not assume, therefore, as classical scholars once did, that the arts of sailing and navigation necessarily originated in the Mediterranean. And tentative beginnings in the mesolithic would be greatly expanded in succeeding ages – especially in the fourth millennium, when a further rise in sea level occurred.[3]

As a result, human settlement was increasingly concentrated in areas adjacent to the seaways and maritime trade routes. A western group of mesolithic communities developed round the shores of the Middle Sea. It was an integral part of a cultural region directly linked to the oceanside peninsulas of the Mainland. Archaeologists have given the modern name of Tardenoisian to the material culture of those western seaways. An eastern group of communities developed on all the shores of the Sunrise Sea in a region linking the east coast of the Great Isle with the Mainland's northern and north-eastern coasts. In between, the sparsely populated and landlocked midlands and uplands of the Great Isle were left in relative obscurity.

Eight thousand years ago is too far back for prehistorians to know anything about the Peninsula's languages or place names. Alphabets were not yet invented. No words or voices were recorded. Not surprisingly, therefore, prehistorians have fallen into the habit of calling the most ancient places by the most modern names. For some purposes, this may be unavoidable. But it puts prehistory into a false, totally anachronistic, and frequently nationalistic context. A little historical imagination might reconstruct some more realistic solutions. The somewhat mythological ring of invented names is a small price to pay if one is to avoid the cardinal sin of anachronism.

It is not unreasonable to assume, for example, that prehistoric people would have named the principal features of the landscape after what they saw; and many of their descriptive names, translated into later languages, would have survived into historic times. It is not entirely fanciful, therefore, in those distant days when the Sleeve was forming, to imagine troops of hunters camped generation after generation atop the high cliff which commands the southern shore of the Southern Straits. They would come to breathe the fresher air, perhaps to make signals, above all to get a better view of the herds that wended their way across the shrinking isthmus below. As time passed, they would have watched with growing perplexity as the herds floundered in the marshland and eventually refused to cross. Standing on the cliff top with the midday sun on their backs, or in later times paddling out into the waters of the Sleeve, they would have seen the magnificent line of undulating white cliffs that glinted ahead in the sunlight. In due course, they must have sailed across to the new-formed island shore, and cruising along it have caught sight of the finest group of cliffs of all. And they would have called them the 'Eight Sisters'. (How the Eight became the Seven is a matter of conjecture.) One day, on the way back, they would have seen the shadows lengthening on the north-facing escarpment of their own home cliff, and would have called it the equivalent of 'Grey Nose Head'. These names are less likely to have been invented by people standing on the shore than by sailors out to sea. By extension, it would have been perfectly natural for the whole of the land beyond the chalk cliffs to have become known as 'the Cliff Country'.[4]

Ancient man navigated by sun and stars. 'East' was the direction of the sunrise, and is so called in many languages to this day. The west was 'Sunset', the south 'Midday', the north 'Midnight'. For example, in Latin *oriens*, 'the rising sun', 'the east'; *occidens*, 'evening', 'the west'; *meridies*, 'noon', 'the south'; *septemtrio*, 'the north' – *septemtriones*, the constellation of the Great Bear. Similarly, in modern Polish *wschód*, *zachód*, *południe*, and *północ* mean respectively 'sunrise' and 'east', 'sunset' and 'west', 'midday' and 'south', and 'midnight' and 'north'. What is more, one knows from anthropological studies that illiterate peoples will often take their bearings when facing the sunrise. From this position, the east is seen to be 'in front', the west is 'behind', the north is 'the left hand', and the south, 'the right hand'. We simply do not know what the Peninsula's northern offshore islands were called in prehistoric times, but it is not beyond the realms of reason to suppose that they were called by something equivalent to 'the Left-Hand Isles' or, more poetically, 'the Midnight Isles'.

The introduction of arable and livestock farming during the so-called 'Neolithic Revolution' did more to transform mankind's way of life than anything before or since. It created permanent, settled communities, which may be seen as the kernel of civilization as we now understand it. Its economy was based on the increasingly intensive exploitation of crops and domesticated animals, whose products promised a varied diet, a potential surplus in good years, and greater opportunities for regular trade and commerce. Its social structures saw a marked division between the food producers, who invested immense efforts of physical labour into their primitive agriculture, and the specialized castes of craftsmen, merchants, miners, administrators, and soldiers, who could be supported from the food surplus. Its politics put a premium on the control of land, on the protection of settlements, and hence on the formation of territorial polities – in other words, of nascent states. Its geographic patterns transformed the landscape, which was henceforth divided into the familiar sectors of cultivated countryside, of urban areas, and of the residual primeval wilderness. Its religious ideology saw a waning of the cult of the Great Earth Mother, with its prime emphasis on birth and the reproduction of a tiny, fragile species, and a corresponding move towards a concern for the fertility of the fields – where the sun and rain, the changing seasons, and the gods of river and harvest gained absolute priority. The priestly caste busied itself with astronomy, geodesy, and climatology. Matriarchy gave way to patriarchy.[5]

At one time, prehistorians were apt to assume that mesolithic people would have accepted the 'Neolithic Revolution' with alacrity as part of the march of progress. Now they are not so sure. Well-tried communities of hunter-gatherers may have had neither the interest nor the inclination to submit to the unfamiliar and demanding routines of agricultural life and to the back-breaking initial work of tree-felling, stone-clearing, and ditch-digging. Here guesswork is as good as a thesis. But it may well be that the neolithic innovators gained the upper hand through their one undoubted advantage, namely the concentrated military power to occupy land and hold it.

The 'Neolithic Revolution', however, was an intercontinental movement of great duration. Its origins, c. 8000 BC in the River Valley civilizations of the Near East, pre-dated the mesolithic era. Its terminal phase, c. 2000 BC in the farthermost reaches of the European Peninsula, coincided with the onset of Minoan civilization in

Crete. Even so, there is no consensus about the means of its expansion. One supposition is that bands of neolithic agriculturalists steadily pushed their way across the Peninsula in their insatiable hunger for suitable land. In this case, the newcomers would have simply supplanted the hunter-gatherers, killing or expelling those whom they could not recruit. The picture resembles that of the later conquistadores in Mexico or of American pioneers on the Oregon Trail. And the fate of the hunter-gatherers resembled that of native Americans or Australian Aboriginals. The more recent and fashionable supposition is that, while neolithic farmers did not necessarily migrate themselves, their farming techniques did. In this case, the old population of successive regions was not displaced, but was steadily converted to the new lifestyle by a process of acculturation. The mesolithic hunter-gatherers were not the victims of the neolithic revolutionaries but their ancestors. The third supposition, and the most likely one, is that the 'Neolithic Revolution' spread through a mixture both of migration and of acculturation. The difficulty is to estimate the relative proportions of the two methods. Recent studies of modern European DNA strongly support the hypothesis of acculturation. One research group concluded that 'the major extant lineages throughout Europe predate the Neolithic expansion and . . . the spread of agriculture was a substantially indigenous development'.[6]

Neolithic agriculture reached the Midnight Isles some time towards the end of the fifth or the beginning of the fourth millennium. Common sense demands that the first sack of seedcorn and the first domesticated cattle were landed on the northern shore of the Sleeve from a boat. What is not known is whether they were brought over by a band of Continental migrants or perhaps by an island entrepreneur engaged in a brilliant import venture. At all events, the agriculturalists flourished on the islands. They would have been assisted by the large expanses of uninhabited land, by the rich variety of culturable soils, and by the onset of a milder and moister oceanic climate with stimulating seasonal fluctuations. Their flocks of sheep and cattle could graze on lusher and higher pastures.

Their crops of wheat and barley, based on the infield–outfield system, grew more readily, even in the uplands and the most northerly latitudes. Gradually, inexorably, the way of life of the hunter-gatherers faded from the record.

The period of transition was obviously a long one; and the activities of hunting and gathering never entirely died out. There is evidence that the late mesolithic inhabitants of the central Peaks, for example, had already learned the art of herding domesticated deer. So neolithic cattle-ranching was not a total novelty. Similarly, even when arable crops supplied the staple food, farming families did not cease to supplement their diet in the old ways. Stag-hunting, angling, grouse-shooting, blackberry-picking, and cockle-collecting never stopped. Local delicacies, such as the windblown samphire that grows on the coastal fenland, were prized in neolithic times, as they still are today.[7]

The technological and organizational standards of neolithic settlements have been shown to be rather more sophisticated than originally suspected. The earliest neolithic house to be unearthed in the Isles so far is located on the crown of a hill to the west of the Largest Lake on the Green Isle. Pottery on the site has been carbon-dated to c. 3795 BC. The house, measuring 21 ft 4 in by 19 ft 8 in, had two clay hearths and walls of upright oaken planks. It closely resembles a dwelling type from the central Continental Mainland that is associated with the Linear Pottery Culture. In the Cliff Country, a neolithic settlement perched on Windy Hill near one of the great stone circles gave its name to a widespread archaeological culture lasting in southern parts till the Bronze Age. It may be compared to a contemporary settlement built on an island in a lake in the west of the Green Isle, which was a similar centre of religious and ritual activity. The houses there had wattle-and-daub walls standing on stone foundations.

Yet the best preserved neolithic settlement is undoubtedly the one found hiding behind the coastal dunes on one of the Penulti-mate Isles. There, a late neolithic community of cattle-herders and shellfish-collectors lived in an isolated world where arable agriculture, metalworking, and warfare were all unknown. Their hamlet of six interconnected houses was served by covered alleyways and by a communal sewerage system of slab-lined drains. Each house contained a spacious living room together with one or more side cells as storerooms or privies. In the absence of local timber, peat burned in the central hearth; and all the internal furniture – box beds, benches, cooking stands, shelves, and cupboards – was made of local flagstones. By the time that the hamlet was buried c. 1500 BC in the sandstorm which was to preserve it intact like a mini-Pompeii, the rest of the Isles had entered the Bronze Age.

The net result of the 'Neolithic Revolution' was not just that the population of the Isles multiplied significantly, perhaps to as many as a million scattered through several tens of thousands of settlements. More importantly, the Isles made up the backlog of the Ice Ages and caught up with trends on the Continent.

The consolidation of settlement stimulated both trade in general and the western seaways in particular. The Middle Sea, where sailors could steer by reference to the circle of surrounding summits, was criss-crossed by routes linking all the Isles with each other and with the western peninsulas of the Continent. Two of the earliest commodities were semi-finished flintstones and ready-made axes. The former were produced in quantity on the Green Isle in the vicinity of the 'Northern Straits' and in various locations on the southern coast of the Cliff Country. The latter, which were polished and sharpened for export, originated in factories situated among the outcrops of granite and tuff in western Lakeland. The scale of the operations can be seen at an excavated neolithic flint mine near the Wash, where eight hundred separate shafts were sunk, or at one single axe factory in Lakeland, where the debris of an estimated seventy-five thousand discarded axe-heads has been found.

With time, the emphasis gradually shifted to the trade in precious metals – copper, gold, tin, and eventually iron. By the end of the third millennium, when the neolithic was giving way to the Bronze Age, copper-smiths were well established in the north-western Highland Zone and marine transport was capable of moving seriously heavy freight. The classic illustration of this last capacity can be found in the operation c. 1700 BC which moved eighty-two fifty-ton bluestones over a distance of over two hundred miles from the far south-west of 'the Afternoon Country' to 'the Great Stone Circle'. The operation illustrates another cardinal feature of the era – the obsession with megaliths.

The development of the seaways was matched by the development of overland trackways, especially in the southern Cliff Country. Warm wet winds blew in from the ocean; dense deciduous woodland overgrew the valleys and the lowlands; and the treeless ridges of the chalk hills stood out as a high-level zone of free movement and large-scale construction. In late neolithic times scores of huge earthwork enclosures were built on the upper contours of the southern hills, each surrounded by ditches and each served by springs or dewponds. They also served no doubt as refuges for the local population and their chattels in times of alarm, and possibly as fairgrounds or tribal assembly points. They were frequently linked to each other by grassy ridgeway tracks. Before long, an extensive network of tracks took shape where the enclosures acted as 'stations' on the freeway, and the freeways wound their paths along the lines of all the major watersheds of the chalk country. The principal junction was located in the upper reaches of the Dark Water Valley at a point where the largest artificial earthen mound in the Isles was erected. A traveller could stride for days along the daisy-strewn ridges without ever having to cross a stream or ford a river. From the northernmost hill station of the system in the Midlands one could walk in twenty or thirty easy stages over two hundred miles to the Noonday Riviera. A similar journey would take one from the main western terminus on the Riviera, or from the far eastern terminus near the Sunrise Coast, all the way to the Eight Sisters and the Southern Straits. It would be nice to think that some of the port stations on the Riviera offered a regular link via the Great Crossing to partner ports on the Mainland and to a parallel network of Continental throughways.[8]

Much speculation has been expended on the origins of the

figures cut into the chalk beside many of the ancient trackways. Some of them, such as the famous White Horse in the upper Dark River Valley, have been confirmed as prehistoric. Others, like the nearby White Giant replete with club and phallus, are less certain. Most are relatively modern.

The megaliths or 'Great Stones' are the most impressive physical manifestation of a neolithic culture, or civilization, which flourished in all the western regions of the Peninsula. They were once thought to have had precedents in the cyclopean temples of Gozo in Malta and in the pyramids of Egypt, both of which associated religious concepts and practices with building on a colossal scale. But their particular origins are now judged to lie in the spiritual tensions arising from the confrontation between mesolithic and neolithic peoples. They all apparently share some form of religious or ritual function together with some type of solar, lunar, or stellar align-ment. Despite the mysteries and speculations which surround them, they clearly show that the worldview of their constructors bound the fate of mankind to the changing face of the skies and the seasons. They can be found at all points near the western seaways from the most northerly of the Midnight Isles to the most southerly shores of the Mainland and the Gates of the Ocean. The megalith builders threw themselves into their colossal labours in the fourth millennium at a time when metalworking was already affecting the cultures of the central Mainland and when the Aegean had entered the Bronze Age.

Megaliths are usually classified in one of four types – chambered tombs and passage-graves, cromlechs, alignments and menhirs, and dolmens. Each of them had a distinct function. It is very common, however, for particular locations to display examples of more than one type of megalith as they pass through successive phases of development.

In many ways, the chambered tombs resembled the earthen longbarrows which had provided the standard form of collective burial in the preceding age and which in some areas continued in use. The megalithic fashion was to construct a long passageway lined and roofed with enormous stone slabs and leading to a central inhumation chamber. When complete, the whole structure was covered by a long rounded cairn of boulders. Some of the finest extant examples, which were built in the Valley of Kings on the Green Isle in the late fourth millennium, measured nearly 330ft. They would have demanded tens of thousands of man-hours of hard physical labour to build.

Like the longbarrows, the chambered tombs were not laid down in haphazard fashion. In each region of the Isles, they all faced particular directions. In the far west of the Green Isle most faced the sunset. In the far north-east of the Misty Country most faced the sunrise. Though regional traditions varied, all megalith builders clearly saw a conjunction between the sky and the dead. In some of the larger tombs, more sophisticated refinements can be observed. Over the lintel of the entrance of the most spectacular example, an aperture was carved in the shape of a giant letter box. Experiments have shown that for a few days on either side of the winter solstice, the rays of the rising sun would have gleamed through this opening, and briefly illuminated the resting place of the dead.

For reasons that remain obscure, stones laid out in circular patterns came into fashion around the turn of the fourth and the third millennia. The result was a long series of stone circles, rings, and 'henges'. In the earlier phases, the circles probably served some simple ritual purpose, such as the laying out and blessing of the dead. In later phases, both the structures and their uses became far more complex. 'The Great Circle', for instance, which for more than fifty centuries has been the prime wonder of the Isles, passed through four distinct stages. In the initial stage, c. 3200 BC, it consisted of a simple earthen ring surrounding a solitary wooden centrepost. In the following millennium it was completely renovated with the construction of a double circle of the imported bluestones and of an earthen avenue set in the direction of the nearest river. There is clear evidence of a solar alignment, since the midsummer sun rises directly over the heelstone at an azimuth of 51°. Only two centuries after that, the still unfinished bluestone circles were removed, and were replaced by a ring of sarsen stones surrounding a horseshoe of trilithons. Finally, c. 1600 BC, the bluestones returned from disfavour, and were re-erected. No other megalithic monument in the Peninsula can match the grandeur of the Great Circle. The total number of lesser circles built in all parts of the Midnight Isles runs into thousands. One is easily misled, however, by the chance nature of what survives and what has disappeared. Recent excavations beneath Windy Hill, for example, show that the Great Circle formed only one section of a much larger complex, the largest part of which was built from timber. The existence of the adjacent timber circle, once 765 yards in circumference and 10 yards high, was not suspected until 1989.[9]

An alignment is defined as 'three or more stones deliberately placed in a straight line'. Some of the alignments, like that at 'the Farm by the Cairn' sited on a promontory of the far north-west coast, do take the minimum form, whilst others like the 'Great Circle of the North' on the Outer Isles, or the 'Multiple Rows' laid out near the remote North Cape, are as puzzling as they are complicated. No less than seventy stone rows were laid out on the 'Lower Moor' site alone. The supposition here has to be that the alignments are in some way connected to the movements of the moon as well as to those of the sun. For if solar movements are regular and relatively simple, the lunar cycles of 18.61 years require observations of great precision and duration. The correspondence of many alignments with the solar and lunar extremes can hardly be a coincidence.

Speculation, of course, is essential to the game, and should not in itself be derided, even when its results must be received with caution. One prehistorian, for instance, has suggested that the megalithic year was divided into sixteen equal periods, each marked by a particular astronomical event. The regular occurrence of midsummer, midwinter, and the two equinoxes is a well-proven fact; and it is not so terribly fanciful to see them as the possible basis of a calendar or calendars, which launched seasonal festivals surviving into historic times. The existence of a prehistoric 'Sixteen-Month Calendar' is something which has to be left hovering somewhere between the possible and the probable.[10]

Similar speculation surrounds the significance of the single standing stones, the menhirs, and of the trilithic dolmens. It may be that they were no more than straightforward markers denoting boundaries, routes, or burials. On the other hand, they may be part of far more extensive alignment systems. The most risky speculations maintain that every single standing stone is linked to sun, moon, or stars and that they form the links in countrywide alignments. One extreme theory suggests that all the standing stones in the Isles were triangulation points in a system established by Continental surveyors who linked the insular system with the Continental one through lines joining the insular Land's End with the Continental Land's End.[11]

Not too long ago, a heated controversy erupted over a theory maintaining that all mounds, beacons, and standing stones were markers on a coordinated network of dead-straight lines. Some of the enthusiasts for these 'ley lines' have even implied that they form a kind of National Grid round which mystic forces circulate. Their fantasies exceed proof or disproof. Yet a network of marker posts and signal stations specially erected to assist early travellers does not lie completely beyond the realm of possibility.[12]

Knowing that the general trend in prehistory moved from the harsh conditions and primitive technology of the Stone Age to the far friendlier environment and more advanced technology of the Iron Age, it would be tempting to imagine that improvements followed each other in regular and smooth succession. In reality, 'three steps forward and two steps back' would be a gross oversimplification of far more complex patterns. For example, a general 'standstill' occurred in the middle of the third millennium, c. 2500 BC. Archaeologists' reports from some regions sound more like a setback. Explanations differ. But the megalith builders slowed down. Tombs were blocked up and camps abandoned. On the southwestern moorlands, fields dating from the Bronze Age that had been cross-ploughed for generations with the neolithic ard, or 'crook plough', reverted to waste. Elsewhere, woodland returned to the valleys cleared earlier. Contacts with the Mainland never ceased. But there were marked variations in their variety and intensity. What is more, social conditions changed, not necessarily for the better. As revealed by the content of grave goods, social structures grew more differentiated. Local groupings spawned wealthy and powerful elites. Chiefdoms were established. Local fighting, and with time large-scale tribal warfare, became endemic.

Into this changing and uncertain world stepped the Beaker Folk – at least that is how prehistorians used to put it. The Beaker Folk were the manufacturers and users of a highly characteristic brand of fine, red-coloured, cord-decorated and bell-shaped pottery which reached the Isles at the start of the second millennium. Various types of corded wares – that is, pottery whose decorations had been fashioned through impressions of twisted cords onto the wet clay – were widely used on the Mainland in the early Bronze Age; and they were often associated with other 'ideological' changes, such as the replacement of large collective tombs with small round barrows and individual graves. Yet the bell-beakers are outstanding in quality. And they are located in such a way that prehistorians long thought of the people associated with them as a distinct ethnic group that migrated to the Isles from their original homes on the southern shores of the Sunrise Sea. Once again, however, the invasion theory does not seem to work. The Beaker Folk are now viewed as the product of an advanced material culture, which was able to spread without any major movements of people. They certainly underline the fact that the islanders cannot be viewed as a race apart from the Continentals. They were a martial people. They were archers, using flint-tipped arrows; and in the eastern districts at least their warriors still carried the polished stone battleaxes which had made such a career on the Mainland in the preceeding period. They also admired ornaments. Their clothes were festooned with polished buttons, and round their necks hung double strings of jet beads or even torcs of gold.[13]

With the 'standstill' behind them, the islanders of the second millennium BC reasserted themselves with new vigour. Many of the existing megaliths were renovated or remodelled. In the southern Cliff Country huge new mounds and circles were raised. On the Sacred Island direct copies of older passage-graves from the Green Isle were made. Most importantly, metalworking began – first in copper, then in bronze and gold, and from c. 1500 BC in tin. Metallurgy in its turn revived Continental trade. Imports of Baltic amber, even of objects deriving from the Aegean, reveal the expanding range of commerce. As the millennium closed, contacts with the Low Countries were particularly strong. The islands' earliest example of a sea-going ship, which sank c. 1100 BC, has been found off the coast in the Southern Straits.

The Bronze Age, therefore, which lasted in the Isles from c. 1800 to 600 BC, had more to recommend it than bronze. At first it was the age of renewed megalith-building and also of the Beaker Folk and their exquisite pottery. Later it was the scene of distinctive new cultures which archaeologists once associated unambiguously with conquering Continental colonists but whose conquests may have been somewhat less sanguinary than was once supposed. Two such groups became specially prominent – the 'Flanged-axe Warriors' and the 'Urnfield People'.

The Bronze Age 'Flanged-axe Warriors' are better known to archaeologists by the modern name of the region of the southern Cliff Country where their settlements were first identified.[14] But it seems wrong to give them an insular label when it is abundantly clear not just that their elite elements came from the Mainland c. 1700 BC but also that they brought their Continental lifestyle with them. Their chief advantage lay in an arsenal of much-improved weaponry which included efficient bronze axes with side flanges, long offensive rapier-like daggers, and stone maces. There is little doubt that their equipment, and their Continental experience, would have enabled them to subdue the local population rapidly. However, it is not necessary to imagine their arrival as a pre-run of the Norman Conquest. It is more likely that small groups of raiders established an efficient overlordship, and perpetuated their kind by taking the local women as wives. It is also possible that local leaders simply imitated the weapons and the techniques that they had observed on the other side of the Sleeve. In these ways, the political and cultural scene could change abruptly, whilst the basic population and the gene pool changed only slightly. Cultural innovations included new burial customs based on bell-barrows, cremations, and elaborate grave goods for use in the afterlife. One such burial in a valley of the chalk hills in the vicinity of the Great Circle presents a fully caparisoned warrior in all his glory. 'He possessed an axe and two massive daggers, one of which had a hilt sparkling with a gold inlay and was hooked to his belt from a finely chased gold plate. Two other gold plates enriched his dress, and as a badge of rank he carried a curious sceptre with a stone head and elaborately cut bone mounts. Such sceptres suggest a truly princely pomp.'[15]

Three centuries after the Flanged-axe Warriors, the Urnfield People made their appearance. They have been named from the large incinerators which were made for funerary use. But their most striking characteristic lay in a particular combination of pastoral and arable economy which enabled them to reclaim large stretches of poorer land in a steady, peaceful manner. As a result, having taken over the areas previously dominated by the Beaker Folk, the Urnfield People moved into the uplands, pressed on into the empty spaces of the Misty Country, and crossed over in force to the Green Isle. Two new crops assisted their success. The first was barley, which thrived in the bleaker northern lands. The second was flax, which was spun into fine linen to accompany the warm clothes made from wool and sheepskins. The Urnfielders were master artisans perfecting the flint, copper, gold, and bronze of previous times. When they died, their cremated ashes were placed in the traditional urn, and buried in a deep pit. Where megalithic tombs or stone circles still stood in the vicinity, the urn pits would share the sacred ground of the older monuments. Where this was not possible, they huddled together in dedicated cemeteries. One such site lies on the wild western slopes of the Peaks. Beneath the ground, a central pit lined with stout oaken posts contained the urns of two obviously illustrious people.

Above ground, a causeway led across an open ditch to the stone entrance, and a ring of high posts linked the palisade which surrounded the whole. It was not just a tomb; it was a monument.[16]

The final phase of the Bronze Age, which followed the turn of the first millennium, witnessed new variants on the preceding themes. Several smaller cultures emerged, which may or may not have been backed by migrant colonizers. Agricultural techniques improved. 'The hoe gave way to the plough, and the woman to the ox.' Hardier strains of wheat were grown. Great attention was paid to the delineation of fields, whose boundaries in the southern chalklands were permanently marked with deep white furrows. Textile techniques also advanced. Upright looms held the warp threads taut with cylindrical clay weights, whilst spindles sprouted side whorls to increase the speed and balance of the spin. Religious fervour may have declined. Urnfield cremations were still practised. But the time had passed when the aura of the megaliths inspired elaborate ritual and ceremony.

Three late Bronze Age sites illustrate the variety of settlement, and of human fortune, at that time. The first of them, on an inland plain towards the eastern end of the Noonday Riviera, was a solid farmstead. It was presumably established by a family of Continental migrants, since it bore little likeness to other Urnfield settlements in the same neighbourhood. A cluster of round thatched huts was surrounded by earthen banks and linked by well-worn tracks to the cattle compounds beyond. Four or five small squarish cornfields completed the ensemble. The community used pottery with handles and with incised decorations, much as was used at that time on the opposite shore of the Sleeve.[17]

Three hundred miles to the north, another site of the same vintage was situated beside a stream flowing from the desolate eastern foothills of the central Peaks. It poses a puzzle in that the poverty of its location in a wild dank cave does not match the wealth of its contents. Whoever its inhabitants were, they possessed an astonishing array of equipment. Their weapons included socketed bronze axes, spears, and swords: their tools, an elegant shouldered

bucket or *situla* and a mould and tongs for bronze founding: their
ornaments, a golden armlet and ring. Nor were they short of food.
In a short spell of residence, they managed to eat huge amounts of
beef, mutton, and game, and to smash a great pile of crockery.
There are evident traces of wheeled vehicles, possibly chariots. The
supposition has to be that here was the temporary halt of a man of
rank, perhaps a defeated chieftain followed into exile by his faithful
retinue. Their end came suddenly, perhaps from a spat in the ravine.
The cave was abandoned with all its treasure in the company of
three corpses.[18]

Three hundred miles further north still, a hamlet of ranchers
huddled behind the dunes near the longest promontory of the
Furthest Isles. They herded shorthorn cattle and two breeds of
sheep, whilst cultivating a few small fields, fishing, fowling, and
hunting seals. They lived in sturdy stone-built houses designed to a
unique plan, where an open hearth burned in a central courtyard
from which four or five side-chambers and a cattle stall were set
into the surrounding wall. For many generations, they fashioned
their implements from local materials slate, quartz, and whale-
bone. But the day came when a bronze-smith arrived and set up his
workshop in one of the courtyards. The Bronze Age had reached
the Furthest Isles at the very time that the Iron Age was reaching
the southern shores of the Cliff Country.[19]

The abandonment of the megaliths may indicate a shift in
religious belief in this period. A site on the edge of the Eastern
Wetlands hints at what the shift may have involved. Four million
timber piles were driven into the flooded marsh to support an
avenue leading to an artificial 'holy island'. Votive offerings of
broken swords, jewellery, and sacrificial victims, both animal and
human, were cast into the lake. If the sacred of the neolithic had
been largely perceived in the skies, the sacred of the late Bronze
Age was increasingly associated with the gods of river, lake, and
forest. Natural springs attracted votive offerings right up to Christian
times.

The Iron Age may well have begun on the Isles with the

importation of Continental artefacts, especially swords and daggers, rather than with indigenous manufacture. At least a thousand years separates the very earliest instances of iron-smelting in foreign areas, with which the islanders could have maintained some form of contact, and the establishment on the Isles of societies dependent on iron-based technology. Yet the Isles possessed plentiful sources of iron. It was only a matter of time before the benefits of ferrology were generally adopted. Iron ore was plentiful; copper and tin were scarce. Even so, the transition from Bronze to Iron lasted many centuries. At first the bronze-smiths copied the designs of imported iron tools and weapons without changing the metal in their crucibles. Later they would retain bronze for certain items whilst increasingly turning to iron for swords and sickles. Finally, they abandoned bronze altogether, and became full-time ferrophiles.

A moment from the long transitional phase has been preserved in a hoard of loot dumped on the bed of a lake in the hills of the southern Afternoon Country. According to a distinguished archaeological team, a raiding party of hillsmen must have looted a farmstead on the nearby plain belonging to a warrior with Continental connections. They escaped with a fine haul, but were then forced by the hot pursuit to offload it. They never recovered it from the lake, perhaps because their pursuers caught up and killed them.[20] According to another distinguished archaeologist, this interpretation is – well, a different sort of offload. The deposit in the lake is more probably a votive offering. Nonetheless, whichever interpretation one follows, the important fact is that the items in the hoard are a mixture of bronze and iron. Traditional bronze spears and axes and a bronze razor lay alongside a crude iron sickle fashioned in a bronze-style shape, and a great iron sword in a fine winged scabbard.

Iron, however, was not the only innovation of the Iron Age. Horse-power was equally important. The presence of horses on the Isles, initially for riding, is well attested from 1000 BC at the latest. In the following centuries they were increasingly used as draught animals to pull wheeled wagons, and for military purposes as chariot-teams or cavalry mounts.

The advance of military techniques clearly raised the threshold of fear and insecurity. As a result, one of the prominent features of the Iron Age lay in the rapid multiplication of hill forts. These were not the same as the crude enclosures of the neolithic period. They were usually significantly smaller, but much more thoroughly protected with steep approaches, deep V-shaped ditches, elevated stone-faced multiple ramparts, high wooden palisades, and fortified gateways.[21] Indeed, at several of the best-known sites, an Iron Age fort could huddle in a corner of an ancient enclosure, just as later Roman camps might be located alongside, within, or atop an older hill fort. Over three thousand hill forts and 'cliff castles' were built in the early centuries of the first millennium, especially in the south and western Cliff Country and in the Afternoon Country. Such, indeed, was their proliferation that they had clearly become an essential part of the social and military system of local areas. A detailed study of an area immediately to the south of the upper reaches of the Dark River reveals a dense network of hill forts each averaging 12 acres in size and each controlling a territory of some 120–150 square miles.[22]

Hill forts, of course, came in many shapes and sizes. In the north-east corner of the Afternoon Country, so-called 'vitrified forts' can be found, where the stone-faced ramparts were fused by heat into a solid mass with the underlying rock. In the 'Headlands' so-called 'ring-forts' of circular shape were the fashion from the third century onwards. So, too, were the 'cliff-castles', which exploited the natural coastal defences and which closely resembled counterparts on the other side of the Sleeve. One such surviving example protected a hamlet of eight or nine courtyard houses lined up along a cobbled street. The inhabitants were tin-miners, who extracted the precious metal from long subterranean galleries underneath the fort.[23] By the time the Romans came, several of the larger forts supported communities large enough for the Romans to call them *oppida* – 'towns'.

The presence of tin in the Headlands had many consequences. It revived the western seaways after a long period of slow progress.

It revitalized the intercourse of the Isles with the Mainland to the
point where the Continental tribe of the Venetii built a powerful
fleet to protect their sea trade. Trade grew to the point where barter
was no longer sufficient. According to some authorities, the first
insular currency, used far and wide beyond its original sphere in
the tin trade, was wrought from standardized iron bars. Most
portentously the tin trade attracted merchants from the distant
Mediterranean.

These Mediterranean adventurers brought the Isles into the
realm of literate and recorded history. One of them, Pytheas of
Marseilles, made the perilous voyage in 325 BC, and wrote an account
of it where he calls his destination 'the Tin Islands'. He relates how
the natives brought the tin in carts to a small coastal island, where
they met the foreign traders. His full text has not survived, but key
extracts are known from later authors. One further consequence *is*
certain. The Greeks, who ran the southern stage of the trade, were
familiar with coinage. Before long, the chieftains of the Isles would
be minting coins of their own.

In districts where natural defences did not exist, well-defended
settlements were constructed in the middle of lakes or swamps.
Lake villages had been invented in the central Mainland in the mid-
first millennium. They appeared in the Isles two or three centuries
later. The technique was to build a huge raft of logs, float it away
from dry land, fix it to the lake-bed with stakes, cover it with
a floor of stones mixed with brushwood and clay, and then use the
man-made pontoon as the base for a complete, palisaded village.
Archaeologists have discovered several such pontoons. But the best
known example lies in the Western Wetlands (not far from the
Canyon Cave). Dating from the second century BC, it was still
functioning in the early Roman period. Its palisade enclosed an area
of some 12,000 square yards (2.5 acres) within which sixty spacious
round huts were linked by cobbled alleyways. A fortified causeway,
wide enough for carts, led to cornfields and pastures on the higher
ground. A landing-stage offered mooring for the boats and dugouts
of fowlers and fishermen. Craftsmanship reached particularly high

standards. Blacksmiths forged sickles which could pass muster in any later age. Bronze-smiths concentrated on fine domestic vessels, like bowls and cauldrons. The carpenters had mastered both the construction of heavy work platforms and the delicate lathe-turning of rounded ladles, handles, and spoons. The weavers used an improved loom with bone bobbins. The millers ground flour from a hand-operated rotary quern.[24]

Iron Age artefacts were often as beautiful as they were utilitarian. A school of decorative art flourished that had no parallel in earlier ages. It may well be that a measure of inspiration was drawn from the fine Greek and Roman goods which were now finding their way into all the 'barbarian lands'. But just as Scythian and Sarmatian jewellers and craftsmen on the Pontic steppes took classical models and transformed them into something wonderfully brilliant and original,[25] so Iron Age artists at the western extremities of the Peninsula achieved a similarly unique aesthetic fusion of their own. 'The orderly human spirit of classical taste fled before the free, flamboyant, visionary spirit which now inspired barbarian genius to yield at last one of the most masterly abstract arts which Europe has known'.[26] A drinking cup was not just a container to aid consumption of the newly fashionable and much-appreciated Mediterranean import – wine; it was a slender, elegant, shining object to admire. A sword or a shield was no longer a mere weapon; it provided the occasion for exquisite mouldings, inlays, and edgings in patterns of striking beauty. A horse-harness was not simply a device for controlling the beast; the bits, rings, and dainty snaffles, and even more the elaborate head armour, were a source of pride, and a sign of status, of the horse's owner.

The old debate of conquest or acculturation reappears in Iron Age studies in its acutest form. At least two major tribes of Continental migrants have been identified for certain in the Cliff Country and several more in the Green Isle. But two from thirty or forty such tribes does not add up to a decisive element (see Chapter Two).

Coastal salt pans added one last innovative feature of the Iron

Age landscape. The greatly increased demand for salt probably arose from the new, inestimable capacity to lay down surplus meat as salt beef and salt pork, and hence to allay the immemorial terror of winter starvation. Henceforth, salt became a staple necessity, and the salt trade a major, Continent-wide business. Prehistoric man was edging away from the age-old concerns of life on the very brink of daily subsistence.

Viewed as a whole, the Prehistoric Age in the Midnight Isles displays immense variations in time and space. Historians must necessarily generalize. But in so doing they inevitably select, rationalize, and oversimplify. One standard oversimplification already mentioned is chronological: the tendency to reduce the complex rhythms of change and reaction to fit periods and sub-periods of perceived progress. Another one is geographical. The Isles have never displayed uniformity. Important regional variations were always present: but they cannot be described through the conventional pattern of core and periphery. It is perfectly true, of course, that the south-eastern lowlands of the Cliff Country enjoyed important advantages that carried increasing weight as the density of settlement intensified. They were sheltered from the worst ocean storms, and possessed an attractive variety of light soils and pasture, a wide-ranging network of river valleys and dry trackways, and the readiest access to the Mainland. Yet it is not true to describe these advantages as either determinant or decisive. There were times and spheres where the Green Isle marched ahead of developments in the Cliff Country. And it was only in the terminal Iron Age that the inland areas of the Cliff Country could match the achievements of the older coastal settlements.

Constant discernment is required. There can be little doubt, for instance, that the remote northern and western uplands of the Great Isle were less developed than most parts of the Green Isle. The northern Highlands of the Misty Country were settled late and sparsely. The Outer Isles lay at the very terminus of the long-distance seaways and on the wrong side of the turbulent Northern Strait. Only the long northerly coastlands of the Sunrise Sea, which stretched in the lee of the Highlands as far as the Penultimate and the Furthest Isles, offered a comparable habitat to those further south.[27]

The mountainous parts of the Afternoon Country no doubt experienced similar challenges. Archaeologists once assumed that it was the last stop on a civilizational line running east–west from the Southern Strait to the Middle Sea: in other words, that it was inevitably the most backward of all regions. In reality, the land link with the southern Cliff Country was probably less vital than the sea link with the Green Isle. The coastal settlements on all sides of the Middle Sea formed a natural cultural and commercial community which was not in the least isolated. A famous copper mine on a promontory opened c. 1700 BC must have attracted numerous Bronze Age merchants and prospectors from near and far.[28]

The Green Isle, like the Misty Country, was slow to throw off its post-glacial lethargy. The first mesolithic settlers were few and far between. A well-examined site close to the most northerly coast was inhabited for about five centuries on either side of 7000 BC. This means that those first settlers may possibly have walked across the land bridge before it was severed.[29] In later ages, however, the Green Isle was in no sense retarded. On the contrary, it was doubly linked to the outside world, both by the short sea routes to the Great Isle and by the longer but well-tried route to Iberia. In the neolithic age its farmsteads were as sturdy, and its megaliths and their decorations as numerous and impressive, as anything else-where. In the age of metallurgy, its mineral wealth gave it exceptional prominence in metal manufacture, in the metal trade, and in metal-based art. Estimates which compare the total quantity of ore mined with the total number of artefacts manufactured suggest that less than 1 per cent of prehistoric metal implements have survived to the present day. Even so, the Green Isle excelled in certain categories. The abundance of copper led to specialization in the heaviest, and most expensive, type of bronze axes and of high-quality bronze cauldrons. The presence of gold inspired the production of magnificent hammered sun-discs and crescent-shaped *lanulae* or gorgets which found their way very far abroad. One great hoard of 146 gold objects from the west coast contains a collection of gold collars, bracelets, and dress-fasteners of such massiveness that they may only have been worn on ceremonial occasions. But it also illustrates the unusual quantity of disposable wealth of the Green Isle's Bronze Age society.[30] In the Iron Age, all the usual developments are found, from horse-drawn transport to dazzling decorative art. But the total number of hill forts, not exceeding fifty, was much smaller than in the Cliff Country, and lake villages were unknown.[31]

Several features of the most prominent sites point to the very special nature of the Green Isle's legacy. One such feature lies in its unusual continuity. Whereas many of the enclosures or fortresses of neolithic origin in the Cliff Country were reoccupied and reabandoned in different periods of their history, several sites on the Green Isle reveal continuous utilization from the Stone or Bronze Age right down to the dawn of Christian times. Such sites evidently combined a place of sacred ritual with the seat of princely power. A huge circular shrine in the north was built c. 100 BC on top of nine occupation levels stretching back to the Bronze Age. Forty-seven yards in diameter, it was supported by rings of timber posts and roofed with six or seven overlapping sheaths of thatch. From the single entrance, a long earthen ramp led down to the bottom of a pit at whose centre a massive pole was erected – presumably as some sort of totem. For reasons that are obscure but not unique the whole structure was deliberately burned to the ground shortly after its completion, and covered with a cairn of stones. The ruins contained the bones of a Barbary ape, which can only have come from North Africa and whose existence, probably as a gift, implies the high status of its owner.[32]

The so-called 'Fort of Kings', on the banks of the Royal River, contains a complex of remains of still greater antiquity. At one side stands 'the Mound of Hostages', a megalithic passage-grave dated to c. 2000 BC. Next to the Mound is a rectangular space which was once wrongly dubbed 'the Banqueting Hall' but is now thought to mark the gateway where many ancient tracks from all over the island converged. On the other side, one finds two adjacent double-ditched ringforts. In the middle of the larger one 'The Stone of Destiny' still stands, a manifestly phallic object of ritual importance. 'The Fort of Kings' is one of three or four such 'royal places' on the Green Isle. Its real importance lies in the fact that it continued to be used as the seat of the island's High Kings until c. AD 900. It stands 'in the dim shadows where mythology and history converge'.[33]

At which point, a word must be said about the nature and limitations of archaeology. Archaeology is a wonderful discipline, to which we owe the bulk of our knowledge about the world before historical and literary records. Its methods grow ever more ingenious, its analyses ever more sophisticated. It makes use of a wide range of auxiliary sciences, from epigraphy to numismatics, and it has co-opted a dazzling array of high-tech procedures, including carbon dating, aerial photography, and DNA testing. Yet archaeology will never fully overcome its fundamental reliance on material evidence, and its inevitable focus on material culture. What is more, it has naturally attracted a scientific body among which scholars with a materialist philosophy, including Marxists and *Marxisants*, hold prominent positions. In consequence, it tells us much about past technologies, economies, societies, and even collective cultural practices. But its views on the higher realms of human life, like religion, are limited by the material nature of its evidence. It has little to say about individual human beings – their faces, their personalities, their quirks, their feelings, their ideas, their aspirations.

From this situation, one of the few sources of salvation can be found in mythology; and here again it is the Green Isle which comes to the rescue. Unlike the Cliff Country, which later experienced three or four major subjugations that effectively cut its inhabitants off from knowledge of their prehistoric roots, the Green Isle saw only one significant civilizational shift – the coming of Christianity – between prehistoric and mid-medieval times. The folklore and mythology of 'the Green Isle' are much more in touch with local

prehistoric events than are their counterparts in the neighbouring
isle.

Generally speaking, historians keep their distance from mythology. They demand reliable sources, and much prefer digs and
documents to oral traditions. As a result, they are capable of writing
books on prehistory which lack any sense of the human condition.
They may be missing a trick. For if mythology is unreliable in the
standard informational sense, it certainly isn't irrelevant. It shelters
some of the few tenuous chains of information which link the
historical with the prehistoric past.

No one needs to be reminded too strongly about the dangers of
trying to relate myth to history. Nor can one fail to take account of
Romantic nationalist inventions and of the verbose mumbo-jumbo
of New Age and neo-pagan commentaries. Even so, the fact remains
that among the froth, the forgeries, and the flights of pure imagination, the myths and legends are inhabited by the fleeting echoes of
the prehistoric past. By the time that 'the Green Isle' became literate
its residents were Celtic-speaking Christians. But they were well
aware that they had a pre-Christian, and a pre-Celtic, past.

One of the very first works of literature from the Green Isle, the
'Book of Invasions', sets out to record the sequence of peoples who
made up the island's pedigree. Written by medieval monks who had
been taught that the world was created only four or five thousand
years before their own time, it contains the story of Cessair, Ladra,
Bith, and Fintan – in effect, the Green Islanders' Foundation Myth.
One may make of it what one will. One is wasting one's time to
relate it to any modern system of chronology. Through all the layers
of poetic licence, of charlatanry, of misattribution, and of confused
memory, however, there run the delicate gossamer threads which
convey a strange but intriguing strand of truth.

The first expedition to the Green Isle was reportedly organized
by the goddess Cessair. Before setting out, she told her followers,
'Take an idol . . . and worship it.' And the idol said, 'Make a voyage,
embark upon the sea.' So Cessair gathered her company together –
her father Bith (Cosmos), her brother Ladra (the Aged One), the

helmsman Fintan the White, son of the Ocean, and fifty maidens, one from every nation on earth. And they took ship and set sail. After many adventures, they landed on the southern shore of the Isle, at the confluence of 'The Three Sisters', that is of the three rivers, whose sources lie in the mountains that gave birth to the island-goddess Eriu.

Cessair was drowned by a Great Flood which carried her companions far and wide. Bith was carried to the far north, taking seventeen maidens with him. He died on the mountain named after him, where the maidens buried him under a great cairn on the mountaintop. Ladra was carried up the eastern coast, taking sixteen maidens with him. 'He died of excess of women' (or, as a mischievous monk added in the margin of the earliest text, 'it is the shaft of the oar that penetrated his buttock'). At all events, he was buried on the shore under a great mound that stands there to this day. Ladra was 'the first dead man who went under the soil of Erin'.[34]

As for Fintan, he survived because he had the power to turn himself into fish, falcon, or eagle. During the Flood, he chose the form of a leaping salmon, but lost an eye to a marauding hawk which pounced as he leapt from the water. After that, he made his way to the very centre of the Isle, to the place where the great stone circle would be built on the Hill of Uisnech. There he planted the berry which grew into the sacred Ash, the central tree of all the Isle. It was Fintan, too, who later designated the island's five provinces. Standing on the Stone of Divisions on the Hill of Uisnech, he was asked, 'How has our island been divided?' He replied: 'By Knowledge in the West, Battle in the North, Prosperity in the East, Music in the South, Royalty at the Centre.' Most importantly, Fintan could commune with the birds and the beasts. On one occasion he conversed at length with the Hawk of Achill, the bird that had plucked out his eye, and related his whole life story:

> My life before the black flood
> Was fifteen years of years.

After the Flood God gave me
Five thousand five hundred years.[35]

Known to later generations as Fintan mac Bochra, the sole survivor
of the Green Isle's first immigrant ship lived on in legend until the
coming of Christianity. Summoned then by the High King, he was
the oldest man on the Isle, and could recount the whole of its
history:

> . . .
> I was [already] in Erin
> When Erin was a wilderness
> until Agnoman's son came,
> Nemed, pleasant in his ways.
> . . .
> The Fir Bolg and Fir Galion
> came; it was long [thereafter].
> The Fir Domnann came;
> they settled in Irrus in the West.
>
> Then came the Tuatha Dé
> in clouds of dark mist,
> and I lived among them
> though it was a long life.
> . . .
> After that came the sons of Mil
> out of Spain to the south,
> and I lived among them
> though mighty was their combat.
>
> I had attained to long life,
> I will not hide it,
> when the Faith came to me
> from the King of the cloudy heaven.
>
> I am white Fintan
> Bochra's son, I will not hide it.

Ever since the Deluge here
I am a high and noble sage.

By using similar sources, scholars attempt to retrieve a world of prehistoric culture which sceptics have always thought beyond recall. In contrast, some mythologists are convinced that in the myths and legends of the Green Isle there are fragments not just *about* the prehistoric past but *from* the prehistoric past. 'The Song of Amheirgin', for example, was supposedly composed by the chief bard of the Milesians, who Fintan mac Bochra said came from Iberia. It was passed down by word of mouth for countless generations until finally written down in medieval times. Reconstructed by a modern English poet, its origins are said to begin in 1268 BC:

I am a stag:	*of seven tines,*
I am a flood:	*across a plain,*
I am a wind:	*on a deep lake,*
I am a tear:	*the Sun lets fall,*
I am a hawk:	*above the cliff,*
I am a thorn:	*beneath the nail,*
I am a wonder:	*among the flowers*
I am a wizard:	*who but I*
	sets the cool head aflame
	with smoke?
I am a spear:	*that rears for blood*
I am a salmon:	*in a pool,*
I am a lure:	*from paradise,*
I am a hill:	*where poets walk,*
I am a boar:	*ruthless and red,*
I am a breaker:	*threatening doom,*
I am a tide:	*that drags to death*
I am an infant:	*who but I*
	peeps from the unhewn
	dolmen arch?
I am the womb:	*of every holt*

I am the blaze:　　*on every hill*
I am the queen:　　*of every hive*
I am the shield:　　*for every head*
I am the grave:　　*of every hope.*[36]

MOST EUROPEAN NATIONS are aware that their present territory was once ruled by foreign powers, dominated by different cultures or inhabited by alien peoples. If pressed, the French know full well that France only started its career after the arrival of the Franks, the Italians that the ancient Latins occupied only a small part of their peninsula whilst the rest was occupied by Celts, Etruscans, or Greeks. The Spaniards cannot overlook the fact that Spain only came into being after eight hundred years of Moorish, Muslim rule. The Magyars know that their forefathers crossed the Carpathians in AD 895 to settle in 'Hungaria', the former land of the Huns. Wherever one looks on the map of Europe, except perhaps in Iceland, one sees layer upon layer of settlement, statehood, and occupation.

On the other hand, present-day nations and regimes have a strong inclination to believe that they and their forebears have 'possessed' their present territory since time immemorial. Belief in the unbreakable bond between 'Blood and Soil' was one of the most powerful psychological motors of nineteenth-century nationalism. Europeans were thoroughly indoctrinated with the notion that every inch of ground within their national frontiers was eternally 'theirs' and hence inherently 'French' or 'German' or 'Polish' or whatever. Popular gurus of prehistory attracted their audiences by evoking 'the ancestral heritage', by urging an imaginary leap over vast spans of time, by magnifying the links between 'us' and 'them', by identifying the people and places of a remote past with the people and places of the present. 'I have led [my reader] . . . over mountains and up dales', cooed the author of a pioneering guidebook to 'Prehistoric

Britain', '. . . and have journeyed to and fro over the past hundred thousand years':

> It has been a long way to go in both time and space, but I think we have seen all the finest of our ancestral monuments, all the places where the past stirs the imagination: the places where formerly we were and from which we have come.[37]

Thanks to such evocations, prehistory and archaeology have inevitably developed in an intensely political context. Nationalism has never been far beneath the surface. Immense efforts have been made to discover a past to which modern people could relate, and, where necessary, to exclude those elements of the past that were politically inconvenient. Prussian archaeologists would prove beyond question that the prehistoric monuments of Prussia's eastern borderlands were indisputably Germanic. A few decades later Polish archaeologists working with identical material established that the selfsame monuments were indisputably, and *ab origine*, Slavonic. Neither side paused to ask whether those monuments were not, at least in part, Celtic. Nowadays, the Ancient Celts have few advocates in Central Europe. But similar exercises are still in progress. Since 1992, the creation of FYROM – the Former Yugoslav Republic of Macedonia – has provoked furious quarrels with Greece over the classification and national attributions of the ancient Kingdom of Macedon.

This is a useful starting point from which to ponder the perceptive comment that 'every generation gets the Stonehenge which it deserves – or desires'.[38] What sort of Stonehenge will match the needs of the next millennium?

Early in 1997 a British archaeologist specializing in stone circles produced a hypothesis that promised the new answer. Stonehenge, he argued, displays several characteristics that are alien to other stone circles in these islands; it could not, therefore, have been the work of native builders. His solution postulated that Stonehenge was designed and constructed by the same people who built the great megalithic monuments at Carnac in Brittany. So, with the

United Kingdom an active member of the European Union, the UK's prehistoric showpiece was set to be Europeanized.

Fortunately or unfortunately Dr Burl's hypothesis did not receive universal acclaim. In fact, most of the professionals were distinctly sceptical. But one of the most interesting aspects of the whole affair was the manner in which it was discussed. Under a corny headline SO GALLING − ANCIENT BRETONS MAY HAVE BUILT STONEHENGE, *The Times* reported 'England's greatest monument, Stonehenge, may have been built by the French': 'Dr Aubrey Burl says that the stones were not manhandled into position by burly Britons but by visiting Gallic engineers overseen by French overlords'.[39] Under the headline STONEHENGE IS FRENCH IMPOSTER, the archaeology correspondent of *The Independent* fumed with similar pseudo-indignation: 'Stonehenge − the pre-eminent symbol of Britain's ancient heritage − was not built by the British at all but by the French'.[40] Humour apart, such sentiments are barely distinguishable from those of an irate Greek correspondent reporting on the latest announcement by FYROM's Department of Antiquities. The language of scholarly reactions was hardly more circumspect. A report prepared for the Archaeological Institute of America began, 'A British scholar has claimed that Stonehenge, England's most famous prehistoric monument, was built by the French.'[41]

It is a nice irony that Dr Burl himself has entered the lists on the vexed question of prehistoric nomenclature. He has been at pains to dismiss the 'pseudo-antiquarianism' and 'bogus romanticism' of scholars who allegedly sow confusion by abandoning the conventional names of prehistoric sites and by replacing them with newly invented or obscure, usually Celtic variants. A particular target for his ire was Mr Magnus Magnusson, the well-known broadcaster, who in the preface to a book on the Standing Stones of Callanish in the Outer Isles dared to use the neo-Gaelic form of Calanais.[42] As Dr Burl announced, the oldest recorded form of the site's name was neither the Gaelic Calanais nor the Anglicized Callanish. It was the Old Norse Kalladarnes, meaning 'the promontory from which a ferry can be hailed'. The Vikings, it seems, provided the oldest layer of surviving place names in the Outer Hebrides. Which is no doubt the case. Dr Burl is arguing that to adopt Kalladarnes would sow just as much confusion as to adopt Calanais. Callanish, he implies, has gained the right to acceptance through long usage. 'Names,' he protests, 'should be respected.' Familiarity and practicality are to be the dominant criteria. 'Stonehenge', for instance, is the accepted, conventional form. No one in their right mind would consider dropping it for the older Anglo-Saxon Stan-heng or the still older Latin form of Circea Gigantum, 'The Giants' Ring'.[43] After all, Stonehenge is administered by English Heritage.

Which is all very well. It is reminiscent of the arguments that go on all over the world. Geographers argue whether the highest summit of the Himalayas should be known as Mount Everest, as the Nepalese Sagarmatha, as the Chinese-influenced Chu-mu-lang-ma Feng, or as the native Tibetan Chomolungma. Australians debate whether the most famous natural feature in Australia should be called by the English name of Ayers Rock or by the most common Aboriginal name of Uluru. There is no easy answer. For names carry cultural associations, and in some instances indications of owner-ship. The real point about the prehistoric sites of the Isles is that none of the historical names applied to them possesses the right associations. Conventional names are conventional, and nothing more. All modern names which have been coined in the absence of their unknown prehistoric counterparts are equally inappropriate.

So, to begin at the beginning. When the second stage of Stonehenge was built on Salisbury Plain c. 2700 BC, it could not have been called Stonehenge, which is an English name. The English had not yet arrived. The English language had not been invented. The Plain would have been there; but it could not have been named after Salisbury, since Salisbury itself had not been founded. One may deduce that a year equivalent to 2700 BC once existed; but no such date could have been conceived before the birth of Christ or the concept of a Common Era. There was no country called 'France', and nothing equivalent to it; there was no 'England', and there was no 'Britain', and no 'Brittany'. As yet, there were no Ancient Gauls, no Ancient Britons, and no Ancient Bretons. This holds good even if each of those later communities would owe much to the gene pool of their unidentifiable predecessors. Only two things can be said with absolute certainty about prehistoric life on 'the Midnight Isles' at that period: it was *not* English; and it was *not* British.

CHAPTER TWO

THE PAINTED ISLES

c. 600 BC to AD 43

THE CELTS IN PREHISTORIC EUROPE

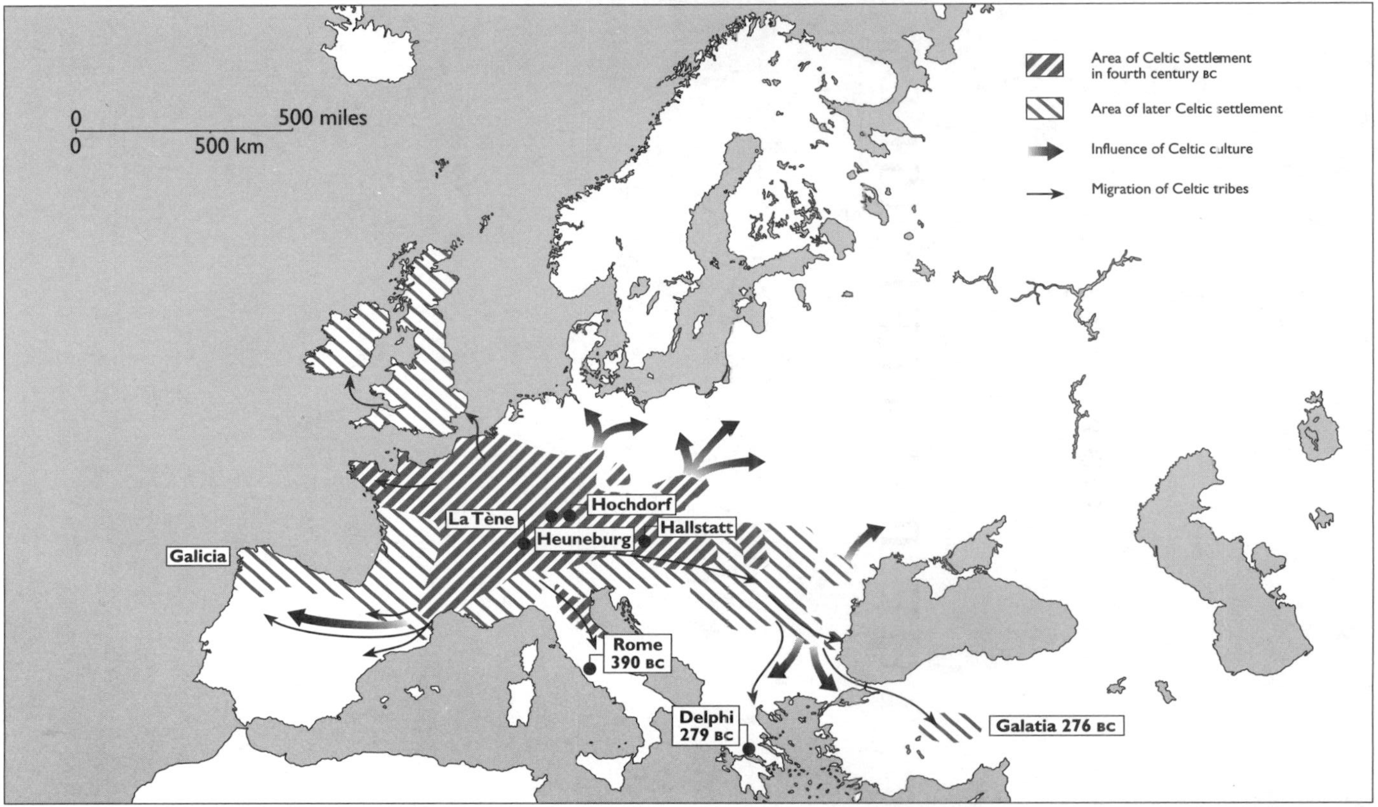

Area of Celtic Settlement in fourth century BC

Area of later Celtic settlement

Influence of Celtic culture

Migration of Celtic tribes

500 miles

500 km

Galicia

La Tène

Hochdorf

Heuneburg

Hallstatt

Rome 390 BC

Delphi 279 BC

Galatia 276 BC

... er bod parodrwydd i gredu yn y posibilrwydd bod Pobl y Diodlestri yn siarad iaith Indo-Ewropeaidd ac i ystyried fod Proto-Geltiaid (ta beth yw'r rheini) ym Mhrydain o gyfnod cynnar iawn. Serch hynny, yr uniongrededd bresennol yw mai grwpiau bychain, heb fod yn ddigon niferus i newid cyfansoddiad hiliol y gymdeithas, ond a oedd yn ddigon grymus a hyderus i fod yn ddiwylliannol arglwyddiaethol, a gyflwynodd yr iaith Geltaidd a hanfodion y diwylliant Celtaidd i Brydain yn y canrifoedd ar ôl 600 CC.[1]

Thus, in a British history book recently published in London by one of the largest British publishers, a leading British historian uses a modern variant of the British language to summarize the origins of the British peoples. In this passage, since the ancient British formed just one branch of a much wider Celtic community, he writes about the arrival of Celtic civilization in the Isles c. 600 BC. Most readers today, including many who may think of themselves as British, will not find such a text so very easy to decipher. They may be able to pick out a few words like *Indo-Ewropeaidd* (Indo-European), or *Celtaidd* (Celtic), or *Brydain* (Britain), but not much more. And they will wonder whether *Celtaidd* and *Geltaidd*, or *Brydain* and *Mhrydain*, are the same words or perhaps misprints. So, for them, the same publishers put out a translation:

... there is some readiness to believe in the possibility that the Beaker Folk spoke an Indo-European language and that there were Proto-Celts (whatever that may be) in Britain from a very early age. Nevertheless, the current orthodox view is that the Celtic language and the essentials of Celtic culture were brought to Britain in the centuries after 600 BC by small groups of migrants who were not large enough to change the basic racial composition of society but who were powerful and confident enough to be culturally dominant . . .[2]

The Celtic British established themselves on the Great Isle, whilst another, non-British branch of the Celts took over the Green Isle. Together, they established a Celtic supremacy — indeed, a virtual Celtic monopoly — which was to last for six or seven centuries until the coming of the Romans.

Another recent history book, using a modern variant of another old Celtic language, covers the whole history of the insular Celts from the earliest times to the end of the Roman Conquest. The first passage quoted below talks about the early Celts in Europe; the second about their love of myths and legends; and the third about Celtic survivals:

> Fadó, fadó sular tháinig an Róimh chun cinn ba iad na Ceiltigh a bhí i gceannas ar chuid mhór den Eoraip — ó Éirinn agus ón mBreatain sa tuaisceart, ó dheas go dtí an Fhrainc agus an Spáinn agus chomh fada soir leis na Balcáin agus leis an Tuirc. Ní raibh siad aontaithe faoi rí amháin. Ba iad a dteanga agus a gcultúr a thug le fios gur aon dream amháin iad. Cé gur fada an lá ó tháinig meath ar a gcumhacht tá tionchar theanga agus chultúr na gCeilteach le brath i gcónaí . . .[3]

Once again, though the book was designed for younger people, most average readers are likely to have difficulties. They may be able to pick out *Róimh* (Rome), or *Eoraip* (Europe) or *chultúr* (culture), but not much more. So, for them, the publishers produced an English edition:

> Long, long ago, before Rome became a power in the ancient world, the people we call Celts dominated much of Europe. Their influence ranged from Britain and Ireland in the north to France and Spain in the south, and east as far as the Balkans and Turkey. They were united not by a common ruler but by a common language and culture. Though it is now many centuries since their power declined, the influence of the Celtic language and culture remains . . .[4]

> . . . Celts loved to tell stories of their tribes, their leaders and their gods. They also liked to invent stories of imaginary heroes and

heroines. These were passed from one generation to the next by word of mouth, and many of them must have been lost or forgotten. In Britain and Ireland, however, some of these stories and legends were written down after the decline of the Druids, and can still be read today . . .

Irish literature gives us the largest number of Celtic legends. Many of them were written down by Christian monks, but even so they tell tales of the old Celtic gods and goddesses, as well as of mortal heroes and heroines. They are one of our best sources for finding out how the Celts looked at life . . .[5]

After the conquest of the Celtic lands by the Romans, many Celts adopted Roman ways. The Druids were suppressed, and people were encouraged to practise other religions, including . . . Christianity. . . .

On mainland Europe, 'Romanisation' was quite thorough. In some of the old Celtic lands . . . Celtic culture disappeared completely . . . Though most British Celts also adopted Roman ways, many of the tribes bitterly opposed Roman rule. Therefore Celtic culture survived more successfully than on the mainland of Europe . . .

Although the Celtic languages died out in most of Europe, they survived in Britain, Ireland and Brittany. Most of them have recently undergone a revival as people have become more aware of the importance of their Celtic inheritance. Erse, Gaelic, Welsh and Breton are still spoken, . . . while Manx, which was spoken on the Isle of Man, and Cornish, have only recently died out.[6]

It is not a bad idea to begin at the elementary level. Few British people have been taught these things at school.

Elsewhere in the Isles, in the Highlands and Islands of the far north-west, a small band of schoolchildren still do their learning in a third Celtic language. All their textbooks are written in Gaelic. Their school atlas, for example, starts with a map which shows them the names and locations of the main places in their own and the neighbouring countries. (See Table 1, overleaf.)

The story of the Celts is rooted in language. For the Celts were, and still are, a conglomeration of peoples speaking a series of related

Table 1. Gaelic place names in the Isles

Alba	Scotland
A' Ghaidhealtachd	The Highlands, literally 'the Home of the Gaels'
A' Ghalltachd	The Lowlands, literally 'the Home of the Strangers'
Innse Gall	The Hebrides
An t-Eilean Sgitheanach	The Isle of Skye
Dùn Eideann	Edinburgh
Glaschu	Glasgow
Eirinn	Ireland
Baile Atha Cliath	Dublin
Eilean Mhanainn	Isle of Man
Sasainn	England
Lunnainn	London[7]

languages. They are a linguistic group, not a national, ethnic, or racial one. What is more, as the most ancient authorities attest, the Celts laid great store on language and on the culture which the language conveyed. Their bards and poets have always been held in great esteem. Their chiefs retained a corps of bards, who underwent a rigorous training of great length and complexity and who enjoyed a status unrivalled except by the Celtic religious caste, the druids. Unfortunately for us – though not necessarily for them – they long upheld a ban on writing, which they saw as a threat to their oral tradition. Even when they came into prolonged and intimate contact with the literate civilizations of Greece and Rome they largely resisted the temptation of literacy, and did not take to letters until Christian times. As a result, the world of the ancient Celts has become one of those many mysterious 'lost civilizations'. Having no recorded voice of their own, the ancient Celts are regarded by sympathetic observers as 'a great people maligned by history', or 'the people who came out of the darkness'.[8]

The Celtic languages form one of the main constituent branches of the Indo-European linguistic family. In this, they are a counterpart to the Germanic, Romance, Baltic, and Slavonic groups. They include both dead and living languages, though they are all descended by one route or another from the long-lost Proto-Celtic, which in turn was an early progeny of Proto-Indo-European (see Appendix 9). So much today is common knowledge. But it was not always so. It was not until comparatively recently that the Scottish scholar George Buchanan and Welshman Edward Lluyd (see page 91, below) showed that all the surviving Celtic languages possessed common roots. It was not until the eighteenth century that the orientalist Sir William Jones (1746–94), the London-born son of a family from Llanfihangel in Anglesey, who served as a judge in Calcutta, established the fact that Sanskrit was closely related to Greek and Latin. And it was not until the nineteenth century that the German philologist Kaspar Zeuss (1806–56) completed the puzzle by showing that the Celtic group formed part of the wider Indo-European family. No popular sense of common Celtic roots could be cultivated until these scholarly discoveries had been made and disseminated. By that time, all but a handful of the Celtic languages were extinct; and the reconstruction of the lost world of the ancient Celts was in large measure left to the archaeologists.

It is perhaps worth noting that for the purists the 'Celtic' label is unacceptable. The modern name for the Celts derives from the classical Greek word *keltoi*, which had the meaning of 'strangers' but which was only used by Greek writers for peoples living in central parts of the Continental interior during the first millennium BC. In its origins, therefore, it did not refer to peoples living further to the north and west, especially in the Isles; and it was not used to describe the Celtic linguistic group as a whole until the era of modern scholarship. As usual, the ancients had a myth to explain the phenomenon. Celtus, the first of the Celts, was born from the liaison of his mother, Celtina, with Hercules. The Romans, in contrast to the Greeks, used the term 'Galli'. In retrospect, modern scholars might have been better advised to adopt 'Gallic' rather than 'Celtic' for the overall label. It is closer to what many of the Celts call themselves, namely 'Gaels'. But by the time the issue arose, 'Gallic' had already been reserved for reference to ancient Gaul, and by extension, to modern France. So 'Celtic' stuck. Only the most pedantic or hostile commentators continue to make an issue of it. Nonetheless, one may take comfort from the fact that the general location of the Greeks' *keltoi* coincided very closely with that of the archaeological sites where modern scholars have established the arrival in Europe of a distinctive Iron Age culture in the same period.

The early Celtic heartland has been fixed in the region of the upper reaches and tributaries of the Rhine, the Rhône, and the Danube. It can be no accident that all these rivers have retained names from the Celtic. Two stunning archaeological discoveries confirmed this geographical setting. The first of them, at modern Hallstatt in the Salzkammergut Mountains, was excavated between 1846 and 1899, and gave its name to the earliest known phase of Celtic culture, starting c. 800–700 BC. The second, at modern La Tène on Lake Neuchâtel, came to light in 1874, and has lent its name to the following phase starting c. 450 BC. A third, at Vix in Burgundy, suggested strong links between northern Europe and northern Italy. Two recent finds made spectacular additions to existing knowledge. One at Heuneburg on the upper Danube showed a fort community carrying on a prosperous trade with the Greeks of Massilia. Another, at Hochdorf in the same vicinity, revealed a sixth-century Celtic chieftain buried with his horses and war-chariot and other sumptuous fittings.[9]

Explorations further afield suggest that the original definitions of the Celtic heartland may have been too narrow. The district of Carniola, now in Slovenia, for example, yielded a mass of exquisite finds, most of which found their way into the Mecklemburg Collection of the Peabody Museum at Harvard. Bohemia, too, has proved a rich Celtic hunting ground, having taken its name from a fierce tribe of classical times whom the Romans called Boii. Even Silesia and southern Poland can now claim to have belonged to that early Celtic heartland long before the arrival of the Slavs. Silesia possesses several religious sites with possible Celtic connections; the Holy Cross Mountains in central Poland possess impressive prehistoric Celtic iron-workings; and the rivers and villages of the district around Kraków abound in Celtic place names. According to some commentators, the earliest legends about the foundation of Kraków itself in the struggle of King Krak and the Dragon contain unmistakably Celtic overtones. Most recently, the discovery of the grave of a Celtic chief buried in the modern district of Kujawy to the west of the Lower Vistula showed that the Celtic presence reached far to the north.[10]

The expansion of the Celtic world took place by two contrasting methods. On the one hand, there are well-documented migrations and invasions, whereby Celtic tribes physically moved out of the old heartland and settled in new territories, especially in the south. One mass of Celts, for example, crossed the Alps and settled in northern Italy, creating what the Romans called Gallia Cisalpina. They sacked Rome in 390 BC. Another group of Celts moved into Greece, sacking Delphi in 279 BC. A third group moved further south-eastwards into Thrace and crossed after some delay into Asia Minor, establishing themselves in the province of Bithynia, thereafter named Galatia, 'the Land of the Celts'. In the second century, the Celtic tribe of Helvetii left their home east of the Alps and settled in the vicinity of Lake Lemanus.

Celtic influences spread not just by the movement of people but also by the export of culture and language. In the last centuries of the first millennium BC the classical world acted as a great stimulus for trade beyond the frontiers of the growing Roman Empire; and the Celts acted as the middlemen between the Mediterranean and the peoples of the north and west. As wine and wine merchants permeated the lands 'beyond the known world', dealing in salt and slaves and swords and fine jewellery, the language of the Celts seems to have become first the *lingua franca* and, with time, the native language of peoples far beyond the earlier heartland.[11]

By the time that Julius Caesar (d. 44 BC) came on to the scene, the Romans had already conquered the Celtic lands of Cisalpine and Transalpine Gaul and of Iberia. Caesar in his *Gallic Wars* was describing the campaigns to absorb the remaining lands of the western Celts. *Omnis Gallia*, he famously declared, *divisa est in partes tres*: 'The whole of Gaul is divided into three regions.' As he smashed his way through their country in three brutal campaigns, he noted that the numerous Gallic tribes spoke different and mutually incomprehensible dialects. He also decided that the defeated Gallic tribes could best be held in submission if he subdued their Celtic kinsmen in the neighbouring Isles. As a result, he mounted two expeditions in successive seasons, in 55 and 54 BC. He came; he saw; he did not conquer: but he took hostages, withdrew, and claimed a triumph. He headed south for the Alps, and fatefully recrossed the frontier of the Roman Republic on the Rubicon – his point of no return.

The classical world had come to know the Isles by a variety of names. Herodotus in the fifth century BC called them the Nêsoi Kassiterides, 'the Tin Islands', though he was more than vague about where they actually lay. For several centuries the Carthaginians seem to have maintained a blockade on shipping beyond the Pillars of Hercules to protect their lucrative metal trade. Nonetheless, at least one Greek sailor, Pytheas of Massilia, sailed through the cordon in the fourth century and left a record of his journey. The names which he noted are clearly Celtic in character – Pretaniké for the Isles as a whole, Ierne for the smaller, western isle, and Nesos Albionon for the larger, eastern isle. This would be decisive except for the fact that the original account by Pytheas was lost and has only survived in fragments of a much later date. There is immense scope for scholars to question the reliability of the sources, and to speculate about the variants, the connotations, and the transformations of the terms involved. Nonetheless, though the details are debatable, the main derivations look pretty solid. The Greek Ierne, which appeared at a later stage as the Latin Hibernia, is clearly the classical transcription of a Celtic name, an ancestor of the modern Irish Éire or Erin. Rufus Avienus writes of it as 'the Sacred Isle' inhabited by the tribe of Hierni. The Greek Albionon, in contrast, became the Latin Albionum. Whether one accepts the Roman or the Celtic etymology (see page 57, below), it seems more than likely that the name of Albion, which has lasted till modern times, was inspired by those magnificent white cliffs, which greet every visitor to the island. As for Pretaniké, which changed in Latin to Britannia, it is clearly cognate with the Welsh Prydain, and at one stage further removed with the modern English Britain. Etymologists link it with a Celtic term for 'painted' or 'coloured'; and this in turn can be associated with the islanders' well-known habit of painting their bodies with woad. In which case, it would not be out of place for English-speaking historians of this period to talk of 'the Painted Isles'.

THE CELTS OF THE ISLES, or 'insular Celts', clearly had much in common; but it would be wrong to think of them as one homogeneous nation. On the contrary, they were divided amongst themselves into fiercely competing tribes. The people of Éire differed in several respects from the people of Albion. And it is far from certain whether the tribes inhabiting the far north of Albion had yet been absorbed into the Celtic orbit. (Remembered today as 'Picts', from the Latin designation of Picti, they kept the attribute of 'painted people' long after the others had lost it. (See page 131, below.))

Above all, though no written records survive, there seems to be every reason to believe that the Celtic language of Albion had already diverged from that of Éire. At some point in prehistory, a fundamental sound-shift had occurred in the mainstream of Celtic linguistic evolution, leaving two separate streams – the older Q-Celtic or Goidelic in Éire, and the younger P-Celtic or Brythonic in Albion and Gaul. This sound-shift has persisted until the present day, and can be easily illustrated in its simplest forms from Irish and Welsh vocabulary:

Table 2. Q-Celtic (Goidelic) and P-Celtic (Brythonic)

Q-Celtic (Irish)	P-Celtic (Welsh)	English equivalent
mac	map	son
clann	plentyn	children
ceann	pen	head
ceathair	pedwar	four
cúig	pump	five

THE CELTIC TRIBES IN THE ISLES

CORNOVII	– Tribal Names
Ulaidh	– Regional Names
Lughdun o	– Place Names

0 ——— 100 miles
0 ——— 100 km

CORNOVII

CALEDONII

PICTII

DAMNONII

VOTADINI

SELGOVAE

NOVANTAE

Ulaidh

Cualinge
Ard Macha o

BRIGANTES

PARISII

Cruchain

Mide

MON

Tara o

GANGANI

DECEANGLI

ORDOVICES

CORITANI

ICENI

Laighin

CATUVELLAUNI

CORNOVII

TRINOVANTES

Camulodunum

Mumha

DEMETAE

DUBUNNI

SILURES

Lughdun

ATREBATES

Tamesis

CANTIACI

BELGAE

DUROTRIGES

Mai Din

DUMNONII

Din Albion

In due course, in the first millennium AD, both the Goidelic and the Brythonic languages were to diverge still further. The Goidelic gave rise to Erse (modern Irish Gaelic), to Gáidhlig (Scots Gaelic), and to Gailck (Manx Gaelic). The Brythonic gave rise to Cumbrian, Cymraeg (Welsh), Kernak (Cornish), and Brezoneg (Breton). (See Chapter Four.) It is necessary to give warning that the Q>P sound change was only one among many, and that some philologists regard the Q-Celtic and P-Celtic labels as unwarrantably simplistic. The latest edition of the *Encyclopædia Britannica* has rejected the traditional classification altogether.[12]

An interesting observation from all this indicates that in discovering the name Pretaniké, Pytheas of Massilia can only have been talking to P-Celts and not to Q-Celts. He obviously took his information from a P-Celt source either in Albion, or perhaps on the Continental shore. (In his search for the tin mines, he visited a small islet called Ictis where merchants brought tin ore and which may well have been St Michael's Mount in Cornwall.) If he had talked instead to a Q-Celt, he would have been told that the Isles were not inhabited by Priteni but rather by something like Quriteni or Qurtani. Transposing this into his native Greek, he would not have come up with Pretaniké but with something more akin to Krutheniké. The Romans would then have turned this not into the Britanni but into the Cruteni. Eventually, we would have ended up not with the 'Brits' but with the 'Cruts'.[13] For some reason, Cruttish does not have the same ring as British; but there are people today who regard the existence of prehistoric Cruthins as fact.

Numerous theories, both ancient and modern, compete to explain the origin and provenance of the insular Celts. Archaeologists once favoured the notion that material cultures coincided with ethnic populations. First the Beaker People and later the Urnfield People were put forward as prospective 'proto-Celts' or ancestors of the Celts. But this is nowadays discounted, not least on chronological grounds. Few respected authorities now suggest that the Celts reached the Isles prior to the early centuries of the first millennium. What is more, Éire has relatively few remains with either Hallstatt

or La Tène connections. This tends to cramp the archaeologists'
generalizations.

The mythologists have rather more to offer, though nothing of
absolute certainty. In Éire, they most frequently point to the
legendary Milesians or 'Sons of Mil', who feature in the 'Book of
Invasions' as the fourth wave of the Green Isle's invaders. (See pages
35–9, above.) In so doing, they imply a long period of pre-Milesian
and non-Celtic settlement. Mil, who is also known as Golamh, as
the Latin Milesius, and by the later epithet of Míle Easpain or
'Soldier of Spain', is widely thought to be the legendary personification of a Celtic migration from Iberia. If correct, this might help
explain the separate language of the Q-Celts in the Green Isle. In
Irish legend, Mil set out to avenge the death of his nephew, who
had been killed by the island's previous masters, the Tuatha Dé
Danann. Mil, however, was also killed, as was his second wife,
Scota, and it was left to their sons – Eber, Eremon, and Amairgen –
to complete the conquest of the island. Of the three brothers
Amairgen was both poet and warrior. It was he whose famous song
is recorded in the 'Book of Invasions', and who decreed that
jurisdiction over the island should be divided between his brothers.
When Eber demurred, he was slain in combat by Eremon, who
then emerged as the sole chief of the Milesians and the first High
King to reign at Tara. Eremon's mother, Scota, is remembered at
Scotia's Glen near Tralee, Co. Kerry.

Much confusion has been generated by the recurrence of two
different mythological ladies both called Scota, and both presented
as daughters of different pharaohs of Egypt. The first Scota, wife of
Mil, is said to have been daughter to an otherwise unknown
pharaoh, Nectanebus. The second Scota, allegedly the daughter of a
known pharaoh, Cingris, married a visitor to Egypt from the Green
Isle. She then returned with her husband and their infant son,
Goidel, to her husband's home. This is a clear illustration of the
frequent way in which the old pagan legends become entwined with
later Christian and Hebrew stories. The young Goidel was said to
have been healed of an ailment by Moses. What is certain is that in

the earliest times the ancient Gaels of Éire preferred to call them-selves Scots, and that one or another of the Scotas, or both, was seen as their ancestral mother. The Romans called them Scotti. For his part, Scota II's son, Goidel, gave his name both to the Gaels in general and, through the ingenuity of modern scholars, to the languages which they speak – the Goidelic or Q-branch of Celtic.

Putting an exact date on the arrival of the Milesians is well nigh impossible. But that does not stop scholars from trying. As recently as 1911, a contributor to the *Encyclopædia Britannica* stated firmly that it occurred in 3500 AM, that is, 3,500 years since the creation of the world, or, by a rough calculation, 504 BC.[14]

In Albion, the mythological record was much further removed from the coming of the Celts than it was in Éire. The medieval chronicler Geoffrey of Monmouth repeats a story whereby Albion appears as a giant son of the island's ruling Sea God. An Irish legend talks of a fugitive Nemedian warrior called Britan who fled across the sea after the battle on Tory Island, and gave his name to the neighbouring Isle. But this looks suspiciously like wisdom long after the event. Ralph Holinshed (died 1580), using many intermediary materials, came up with a story whereby Albion was first populated by the Princess Albina and her band of fifty women, all of whom had killed their husbands. One is at a loss to make something sensible of this, though the band of women is rather reminiscent of Cessair's boat-party (see pages 35–6, above). The obvious lesson seems to be that Éire and Albion did *not* share the same foundation myths.

Similar divergence is suggested by the archaeological record. Hallstatt culture, meagre in Éire, is well evidenced in south-east Albion. La Tène culture equally made its presence felt in the same region somewhat later through typical burial rites and fine metal-working. This would confirm the obvious fact that Albion was in closer material and cultural contact with the Celts of the Continent than Éire was.

The Celts held undisputed sway over the Isles for the best part of a thousand years. Their beginnings go back to the start of the

first millennium BC. The scholarly consensus holds that, after a long
period of penetration, they were fully established by 600 BC. And
they ruled unchallenged until the first century AD. This period is
longer than that enjoyed by any other of the islands' subsequent
masters. Even after the Roman invasion, they controlled the greater
part of the Isles for another thousand years. They are not just a
passing episode or a minor prelude.

Until very recently, prehistorians waxed eloquent over scenes of
the Celtic conquests. Fierce 'Hallstatt warriors' were said to have
landed, swinging their huge iron longswords and driving all before
them. Stages were mapped out – Stage A Invasion followed by Stage
B Settlement and Stage C Assimilation. Then, 'when the first
Hallstatt settlers were arriving in this country their kinsfolk . . . in
southern Germany were building up a new culture which came to
represent the height of early Celtic achievement'. In due course, the
next wave of still fiercer and more sophisticated warriors arrived:

> It seems that about 250 BC numbers of such warriors began . . .
> to cross to Britain, sailing probably from the mouth of the
> Seine, and to introduce for the first time the La Tène Culture
> which was to bear its final and most mature fruits in these
> islands.

Their coming allegedly 'provoked consternation among the British
peasants'.[15]

This picture is now refuted. The Continental Celts did not so
much invade as percolate and permeate. They did not supplant the
existing population. They mingled, merged, and in time gained
cultural ascendancy. Though the phases of cultural transformation
are opaque, the Celtic languages and Celtic customs spread from
one end of the Isles to the other. Pockets of pre-Celtic culture would
have survived in remoter parts, possibly into the Christian era.
There are hints of a revolt by subservient Firbolg tribute-payers in
Éire as late as the first century AD. But no authority contests the
predominantly Celtic character of all the Isles long before Roman
times.

The historical record of those centuries is virtually beyond recall, particularly in Albion. In Éire there is something to be gleaned by trying to sift the historical from the fantastical in the mythological cycles and from the royal genealogies and lists of kings which the bards of later times would recite. It is obvious that the king lists, which were drawn up to eulogize the ancestry of their patrons, contain a large element of pure invention. The great medieval Irish chiefs were keen to show that they were descended from the Celtic gods or from Noah or the pharaohs of Egypt. On the other hand, when the names of heroes and tribes and battles recur in plausible sequences, especially in the less distant centuries, one may reasonably suspect that they are underpinned by some degree of reality. The nearer the genealogies approach to historical times, the more the fictional element recedes and the factual element rises. And date-guessing by the calculation of generations and by comparison of king lists is a much-practised art. Needless to say, the results of the game are as tentative as they are colourful. Historians of the scientific tendency dismiss them out of hand. Nonetheless, they do contain enough credible material to merit attention. According to these bardic sources, Slaigne the Firbolg was the first Ard Rí or High King of Éire. From his accession to AD 1, there were a hundred and seven High Kings – nine Firbolgs, nine Tuatha Dé Danann, and eighty-nine Milesians. Following the rebellion in the early first century AD, the High Kingship was re-established, and an unbroken line of eighty-one more monarchs stretches out until the ill-fated Ruaidhrí Ua Conchubhair (Rory O'Connor) who in 1175 surrendered his overlordship to Henry Plantagenet, King of England. It was a long run.

Of course, there can be little certainty about the historicity of all the names on the lists, still less about the dates which are traditionally attributed to them. It is also important to recognize the anachronism whereby prehistoric chiefs are given the same powerful status which the High Kings enjoyed in those early medieval times when the lists were drawn up. Whatever truth there may be in the establishment of Milesian rule at Tara – which was named after

Eremon's wife, Tea – one must accept the probability that a still more ancient ritual centre was being adapted to a new political function, and that the authority of those early High Kings could not have been enforced beyond the immediate vicinity. According to legend, the Lia Fáil or 'Stone of Destiny' on which the High Kings were crowned had been brought to Éire by the tribe of the Tuatha Dé Danann. It was said to roar with delight whenever it felt the touch of a legitimate king's foot.

As one descends the prehistoric bardic genealogies, it is fascinating to see how the High Kings gradually emerge from a world of gods and spirits into the realms of recognizable reality. Conaire Mór, for example, can hardly be a historical figure. Son of the bird god Nemglan, he attracted the wrath of the gods for breaking a *geis* or 'personal taboo' and was slain in battle. Ollamh Foóla, in contrast, the eighteenth High King, supposedly acceded in 714 BC and is credited with giving the country its first law code. He is said to be buried at Tailltin. And *Ollamh* was the highest of the seven grades of bards. The real significance of this shadowy figure may be that he illustrates the High King's dual role as ruler and chief poet. Tighernmas, 'the Lord of Death', was a High King who supposedly initiated the cult of an idol called Cromm Cruach, 'the Blood Crescent', on 'the Plain of Adoration'. He was killed in a frenzied riot at the Feast of Samhain during the worship of his own idol. Ugaine More, who supposedly reigned during the fifth century BC, married a Gaulish princess. His realm briefly bestrode both Éire and Gaul. But on his death Éire was divided into twenty-five parts between his twenty-five children, and was not reunited for three centuries. Mac Mong Ruadh or 'Macha of the Red Tresses' is listed as the seventy-seventh monarch, acceding in 377 BC. She bore the name of Macha, Goddess of War, sometime consort of Nemed, and is sometimes awarded divine properties. But she also seems to have some very concrete achievements. She built Ard Macha ('Macha's Height'), the future Armagh, and established the nearby Emain Macha or 'Fort of Navan' as capital of Ulster. The hospital which she founded, the Bron-Bherg or 'House of Sorrow', supposedly survived until destroyed by fire in AD 22.[16]

In this semi-legendary setting, historians should probably give more prominence to the better evidenced existence of the five provinces than to the shadowy idea of a nominal unity. Éire had been divided into 'fifths' from pre-Celtic times; and the rivalries of the provincial tribes and heroes furnish the central theme of the island's history. The northern Fifth of Ulaidh (Ulster) was said to have been founded by Rudraidhe, son of Partholón; and its people were first known as the Clan Rudraidhe or Rudricans. Their affairs are particularly well known through the *Epic of the Red Branch*, i.e., the Ulster Cycle; and they played a prominent part in Éire's history right down to the destruction of traditional Ulster society in the seventeenth century. (See Chapter Eight.) The western Fifth of Cruchain (Connaught) was Ulster's chief rival. Ruled by Queen Medb for a record eighty years, it provides the setting for *The Cattle Raid of Cooley* (see below). The south-eastern Fifth of Laighin (Leinster) was earlier known as Galian. It had the closest proximity to, and strongest ties with, Albion. The south-western Fifth of Mumha (Munster) was dominated by its mountains and wild ocean coast. In legend it was often associated with the Otherworld, its lochs and beaches leading to the sunken 'Land of the Dead'. The central Fifth of Mide (Meath) had little more than local significance until the first century AD when as 'Royal Meath' it became the strongest of the provinces. The fact that Meath, where Tara was situated, did not gain prominence until such a late date underlines the likelihood that in the preceding centuries the High Kingship possessed symbolic but not necessarily military or political pre-eminence.

One might imagine that the historical record of Éire would be so much sparser than that of Albion. Éire, after all, was inevitably more insulated than Albion from the winds of change blowing from the Continent. In fact, as Kearney has noted, it is British evidence from Albion that is signally lacking: 'We are in the paradoxical position of knowing more about the "traditional" area of the Celtic world than about its "modernising" sector.'[17] Pessimists might conclude that there are precious few topics to discuss. Historians, who must justify their existence, can always find something.

The Celtic tribes, whose presence in Albion has been well ascertained in the first millennium BC, were the original Ancient Britons. They spoke a P-Celtic or Brythonic variant of the Celtic languages, and, with the possible exception of the far north, they spread all over the island. They were closely related to the Continental Gauls. Sadly, their names are only known in the Latinized forms which were given them by classical authors or by their later conquerors, and which set a false tone to discussions from the start. (See map, page 56.) Attempts have been made to reconstruct the Celtic forms, but most archaeologists and prehistorians do not even bother. A few tribal names have obvious etymologies; but many do not. The 'Hammer-fighters' or 'Hammerers' came out in Latin as the Ordovices; the 'Hill Folk' – from the Celtic *briga* meaning 'hill' – were turned into Brigantes. The Catuvellauni in some way derived their Latin name from *catu* meaning 'battle'; so perhaps they were 'the Warrior Folk' or 'the Victors'. The Belgae may have had some affinity with the old Firbolg of Ireland, 'the Bog Men'. But the exact connotations are beyond recall. 'The Proud Ones' has been suggested. The Dumnonii were 'the People of the Deep', but whether the link was with mining or fishing or with the Otherworld or with something else, one cannot tell. The Belgic Atrebates were 'the Settlers', which, since they had counterparts of the same name in northern Gaul, fits well with the notion of them being a migrant group. The Cornovii were 'the Horned People'. This could mean that their warriors wore horns on their helmets, that they inhabited a horn-shaped territory, or that they worshipped the Horned God, or none of these things. The majority of the more obscure names are usually thought to be linked with long-lost local deities or totems.

At one time, great emphasis was laid on the warlike disposition of the Ancient Britons, on their alleged love of a quarrel, and hence on their internecine, intertribal warfare. The hill forts were explained as a necessary feature of this deeply disturbed society. Of course, the tribes did fight. Warlords rose and fell. Tribal territories waxed and waned. But exploration of some of the key sites has modified the picture. The largest of those forts, Mai Dun or 'the Great Fort', which was the stronghold of the Durotriges in the West Country, was so enormous that it was ill designed for purely defensive purposes. A similar structure, which served as the upland HQ of the Brigantes,[18] enclosed 750 acres and was surrounded by earthen ramparts six miles long. Though both of these places were fortified, and were destined to fall to the Romans in last-ditch stands (the one in AD 44, the other in AD 74), it seems likely that they had also fulfilled some non-military functions – perhaps as popular meeting grounds, as festival sites, or as regional fairs.

One of the most meticulously excavated sites in southern Albion stood some thirty miles from the southern coast in the land of the Atrebates. It was inhabited for some five hundred years until destroyed by fire c. 100 BC. Though defended by fortifications, it was clearly a stronghold designed for permanent residence. It had internal streets laid out on a regular plan, a rectangular shrine in the centre, and circular houses sheltering in the shadow of the ramparts. Most interestingly, the very numerous granary pits provided storage capacity for quantities of grain far beyond the needs of the three hundred to five hundred residents. It served as a commercial centre, therefore, as well as a political and religious one. The granaries may well have held the accumulated tribute in kind of the whole tribe. Its modern English name meaning 'the Fort of the Danes' conceals the fact that it was really 'the Fort of the British'.[19]

Two tribes or tribal confederations are usually listed as migrants who crossed to Albion from the Continent. One of them, the Parisii, seems to have been a sept (clan) of the parent tribe in Gaul which has left its name in the capital city of modern France. They moved to a clearly defined location immediately to the north of the Three Rivers Estuary on the east coast. Archaeologists have recognized traces of their presence in the highly specific burial sites marked by inhumations, vehicular grave goods, and square surrounding trenches.[20] The other group, the Belgae, were mentioned by Caesar as having sailed to Albion to raid, and having stayed to settle. In the last century of the first millennium BC they became a dominant element in the south-east and the valley of the Tamesis. Retaining close contacts with their kinsfolk on the Continent, they participated in the intensification of trade across the Sleeve which resulted in something resembling a socio-economic revolution.

The rapprochement between Albion and Gaul in the first century BC was political, economic, and cultural. Political ties intensified through the presence of related tribes on both sides of the strait. There were instances of chiefs who exercised authority both in Albion and Gaul. More often, disaffected parties in the tribal conflicts took refuge on the other side of the water, and sought assistance. Above all, both Britons and Gauls watched anxiously as the forces of Rome crossed the Alps, created the province of Gallia Narbonensis in 124 BC, and then projected their power far beyond the imperial frontier.

Economic life, too, was affected by the Roman advance. Roman wealth greatly stimulated trade. The Celts acquired a taste for Italian wine, and found that they could fund their thirst by exporting slaves, metals, and agricultural products. Roman merchants, armed with money, ventured far to the north. Trading posts were set up, and trading posts turned into towns.

Cultural rapprochement was based on the common language and common customs. But it was boosted by the attractions of Roman civilization. Caesar mentions the fact that during his Gallic wars British warriors fought both in his own ranks and in the ranks of his opponents. Britons who returned to Albion, either from trading expeditions or from war service on the Continent, had been brought into intimate contact with Roman ways. In the last century of British independence, the sons of high-born British families were already learning Latin.

Nothing better reflects these developments than the growth of a port on Albion's Noonday Riviera. It has been called 'the first truly

urban community in Britain'.[21] Ideally situated on a narrow peninsula on the seaward side of a large protected harbour, and crowned
by a hill forming a natural stronghold, it occupied a site which had
repeatedly attracted human habitation since the Stone Age. It was
reoccupied by Celtic Iron Age people from c. 700 BC, and at some
point thereafter was fortified by a double line of dykes and ramparts
running across the narrowest point of its isthmus. To the north, it
looked across the placid waters of the harbour to two rivers flowing
from the most fertile and most densely cultivated valleys in the
region. To the south, it looked out across the more turbulent
currents of the Sleeve to the mouth of the Sequana in Gaul, some
120 miles distant. Its ancient British name has not survived. It is
known today by a totally inappropriate pseudo-Anglo-Saxon name
invented by Romantic Victorians. So if a new name could be
invented, it would be far more fitting to call it by a Brythonic name.
'Altrose' has been put forward. But the most appropriate thing
would be to call it, after the Sea God's giant son, Din Albion, 'Fort
Albion'.

Modern excavations at Din Albion have revealed a hive of
commercial and manufacturing activity, and a community living in
considerable affluence. One of the first digs brought to light the
largest hoard of Roman and Celtic coins ever found in the Isles. The
Roman coins – in gold, silver, and bronze – ranged from republican
denarii to imperial *aurei* of the Antonine period. The Celtic coins,
from southern Albion and northern Gaul, indicate the existence
both of coastal trade and of long-range commerce linking Armorica
with the Rhine. Manufacturing activities in the Fort included iron-
stone works, glassworks, bead and armlet factories, pottery kilns,
and a wide variety of metal smelting and casting. There is strong
suspicion, though no firm evidence, of a local mint. A profusion of
large Italian amphorae attests to the wholesale wine trade. Though
iron ore was obtainable from local quarries, copper, silver, lead, and
gold had to be imported as ingots or as scrap for later fashioning
and finishing.

'Din Albion' was clearly the leading example of urbanization in its time. But similar developments elsewhere in the south and east had similar effects. Hill forts were abandoned, and communities began to concentrate in locations more suitable for trade and commerce. The enterprising archaeologist whose labours have thrown the greatest light on Din Albion has written enthusiastically of 'a period which saw the end of the old order, and the establishment of a settled urban economy . . ., a time of dramatic change.'[22] This may be no exaggeration for the most favoured districts. But it did not apply in the deep interior. As Caesar observed from his two brief visits, the Britons of the south closely resembled the Gauls, whilst the pastoral tribes of the west and north 'still lived in skins'.

Din Albion escaped the direct impact of the two abortive Roman expeditions of 55 and 54 BC. The legions twice landed in the south-eastern 'Corner Land', i.e., Cantium, having chosen the shortest crossing and directed their operations to territory round the estuary of the Tamesis. Yet after their departure it was the chiefs and tribes which had confronted them, together with their cities of Camulodunum and Lughdun, that came to the fore. This may simply have reflected a shift in political power. It would also have been helped by the fact that the tribes who paid tribute to Rome enjoyed a monopoly in contracts with Roman merchants.

Caswallawn has the distinction of being the first Ancient Briton to be known by name. As such, he has an entry in *The Dictionary of National Biography*, under the Latinized form of his name – Cassivellaunus.[23] Chief of the Catuvellauni, he led the British resistance to Caesar's second invasion of Albion in 54 BC, and features prominently in Caesar's *Gallic War*. He is also noted as one of the first British rulers to have minted gold coins, and hence to have launched a valuable new source of information about the late Iron Age.

Caswallawn's strategy in the campaign of 54 BC against Caesar was apparently to draw the Roman columns deep into the interior, and thereby to expose the landing site of their fleet to a counter-attack. He certainly knew how nervous the Romans were about the vulnerability of their naval supply lines, having seen how storm

damage to the Roman fleet in the previous year swiftly caused
Caesar to retreat. His problem was to persuade fellow chiefs to
follow a common policy. His own base lay some twenty miles to
the north of the estuary of the Tamesis. But he had a running feud
with his immediate eastern neighbours, the Trinovantes, who submitted to Caesar without a fight; and he failed to rally the Cantians
in good time. He could not match the heavy armour of Caesar's
legions in close combat. But his four thousand charioteers wreaked
havoc among the Romans as they struggled to ford the Tamesis,
and his warriors put up a stubborn defence of their tribal hill fort[24]
before fleeing deeper into the Midlands. This was the moment when
a counterattack on the Romans' rear in Cantium would have had
maximum effect. When Caswallawn found that it could not be
organized, he, too, submitted. He gave Caesar hostages, promised
to leave the Trinovantes in peace, and agreed to pay Rome an
annual tribute. He then watched Caesar sail away across the Strait,
and probably resumed his activities exactly as before. His exploits
and his Celtic name survive in Welsh legend.[25]

By the time that Caswallawn's grandson or great-grandson,
Cunobelin, took charge some fifty or sixty years later, the Catuvellauni had already absorbed the territory of the Trinovantes, and
Cunobelin ruled from the former Trinovantian capital at Camulodunum. A prince of the Trinovantes, Dubnovellaun, had taken
refuge in the court of the Emperor Augustus, complaining no doubt
of the broken treaty; and Cunobelin judged it prudent to sign on as
a Roman ally to avoid yet another threatened invasion.

Cunobelin – whose name has been rather dubiously decoded as
'Hound of the God Belin' – is best remembered as the prototype for
Shakespeare's Cymbeline, King of Britain. The historical consensus
holds that Shakespeare's dramatic plot, filtered through centuries of
legend and the poetic licence of Geoffrey of Monmouth and Raphael
Holinshed, bears little resemblance to reality. Holinshed's own
account, gleaned from a variety of sources, is colourful but
unreliable:

> Kymbeline or Cimbeline the sonne of Theomantius was of the
> Britains made king after the deceasse of his father, in the yeare
> of the world 3944, after the building of Rome 728, and before
> the birth of our Sauiour 33. This man (as some write) was
> brought vp at Rome, and there made knight by Augustus
> Caesar, vnder whome he serued in the warres, and was in such
> fauour with him, that he was at libertie to pay his tribute or
> not. . . . The best approoued [writers] affirme, that he reigned
> 35 years and then died, & was buried at London, leauing behind
> him two sonnes, Guiderius and Aruiragus.[26]

This passage reflects the interesting phase when the British chief
was a formal ally of Rome, but it places Cunobelin's regnal years
quite wrongly as 33 BC to AD 2. In any case, Shakespeare had no
cause to follow Holinshed in a slavish manner. He was creating 'a
fantastical drama' not a historical account. Occasional details in the
play, however, ring true. The poet's Cassibelan is clearly Caswallawn, and Tenantius may well be a distortion of Cunobelin's known
father and predecessor, Tasciovan. Apart from that, the prominent
theme of Britain's much resented annual tribute to Rome may not
be completely fanciful:

> There may be many Caesars
> Ere such another Julius. Britain is
> A world by itself, and we will nothing pay
> For wearing our own noses.[27]

One must not forget of course, that lines such as these, composed
in 1609, were probably directed as much to the groundlings' memory
of the Spanish Armada as to their interest in ancient history. When
the Queen responds with stirring words about 'the fam'd Cassibelan
. . . who made Lud's Town with rejoicing fires bright / And Britons
strut with courage!', she, too, was playing to the Tudor gallery.

One other detail deserves consideration. Shakespeare, in line
with the chronicles, calls Cymbeline 'King of Britain'; and this
matches the epithet of the Roman author Suetonius, who calls
Cunobelin *Rex Britannorum*. One is entitled to ask whether Albion,

like Éire, did not possess a tradition of High Kings to whom all the other tribal chiefs owed allegiance. Another hint may be found in the etymology of Caswallawn, which may not have been a personal name but rather a Celtic title meaning 'Ruler of the League'. Tasciovan even issued a coin with the inscription TASCIO RIGON – *Rigon* being a Brythonic term for 'Giant King'. Holinshed, for his part, had no doubts that there had been ancient British kings enjoying supreme authority over the whole island. He even supplies the name of his candidate for 'the first king of Britaine who was crowned with a golden crowne' and who had supposedly acceded to the throne in a year equivalent to 447 BC:

> Mulmucius began his reigne over the whole monarchie of Britain
> in the yeare of the world 3529, after the building of Rome 314
> and after the delivrance of the Israelites out of captivitie 97, and
> about the 26 yeare of Darius Artaxerxes Longimanus, the fifth
> king of the Persians.[28]

The evidence is obviously inconclusive. But if the Celtic tradition of High Kings held good in Éire, as it did at a later date in Scotland, it could conceivably have applied in some form in Celtic Albion.

The numismatic evidence throws no light on that particular problem. But its contribution to the corpus of knowledge about this last, pre-Roman period is invaluable. Coins provide hard information, often about precise dates, specific locations, and particular rulers. Celtic coinage began its career in the fourth century BC with Continental copies of Greek originals. Many of these, together with Greek and Roman coins, found their way to the Isles. British coinage began its career early in the first century with Cantian-cast imitations of bronze coins from the Ambiana tribe in northern Gaul. The earliest known example, which bears no date or inscription, shows the splendid profile of a long-haired charioteer. Horses, in fact, were the favourite emblem. Albion was entering the money economy, or something quite like it. Six southern tribes opened their own mints. During Caesar's Gallic wars, the circulation of coins suddenly increased. Uniface bronze staters of the Ambiani, otherwise classed as Gallo-Belgic E, have been described as 'the sinews of the Belgian war effort'. Great quantities of them reached Albion, presumably in payment for the assistance which, as Caesar complained, the British tribes were giving to their Gallic kinsfolk. The bronze staters degenerated in weight and quality. Silver coins appeared.[29]

After 51 BC the independent Gaulish mints were replaced by Roman ones. The British minters were left to their own devices. For some decades they were content with old designs. But in or about 10 BC Tasciovan, Chief of the Catuvellauni, took the signal step of striking a coin bearing his own name. By AD 10, after an interregnum, the mint at Camulodunum was turning out fine gold coins inscribed in full with CUNOBELINUS. One of its most impressive products took the form of a gold *aureus* bearing the head of the Emperor Augustus and the inscription AUGUSTUS DIVUS, 'the Divine Augustus'. This was a clear sign that the Catuvellauni did indeed accept Roman overlordship at that time. Coins from the early part of Cunobelin's reign carried the head of Augustus or Tiberius on the obverse, and some reference to CUN or CAM on the reverse. Nevertheless, by the end of his reign, Cunobelin had issued coins which, in addition to his own Romanized bust, bore the inscriptions either of CUNOBELLINUS REX or of CUN. and TASCIO F – in other words, 'King Cunobelin, son of Tasciovan'. Here was an indication that the ageing Cunobelin now wished to harness his legitimacy not to a Roman overlord but to his sovereign British pedigree.

British coins of this era carry much information that cannot be found elsewhere. They have been invaluable, for instance, in establishing the line of succession of the various tribal dynasties. Several of the more obscure chiefs of the minor tribes, such as Volisios of the Coritani or Bodvoc of the Dobunni, would never have been heard of except for their coins. Still more important for the study of an illiterate society is the iconography. More than a thousand issues over a century and a half portray a vast array of tribal emblems, mythological figures, and artistic designs. There was the Wild Boar of the Iceni, the Eagle of Cantium, the Dragon of the Atrebates, the Vine Leaf of Verica, and any number of variants on warriors, horsemen, and charioteers. One finds dahlias and sunflowers, starfish and tridents, sphinxes, spirals, and even a human eye. Cunobelin alone was responsible for coins depicting ears of wheat, a sow, a lion, a butting bull, a two-headed Janus, a seated metalworker, and, of course, himself. Each of these vivid images carried religious or political symbolism that would not have been lost on their users. And often they were fashioned with exquisite artistry. Celtic coinage was once dismissed as crude and primitive. But experts now admire both the technical skill and the creative designs. The transformation of an elegant, classical Head of Apollo into an abstract composition of swirling tresses and compressed facial features is worthy of advanced modernism. The step-by-step stylization of a prancing horse from a realistic animal into a dismembered steed or an elongated line drawing would not have disgraced a Picasso. 'Those Celtic designers knew exactly what they were doing.' Every issue helps to define the personality of the people who made them. Even the mundane and the repetitive issues have a message to convey. As a leading numismatist remarked about the specially unremarkable coins of the Coritani:

> A Coritanian coin is unmistakeable; it can be told at a glance from all other Celtic coins. The coinage points to a people . . . lacking the more imaginative Celtic gifts, avoiding any temptations to flirt with Rome, but fully endowed with the technical skills of the time and place and pursuing its self-contained conservative cause.[30]

How much poorer is our knowledge of those tribes, like the Parisii and the Brigantes, who never struck a coin of their own!

Ancient Celtic civilization, like the languages which the Celts spoke, displays great diversity within the overarching framework of common traditions. Like the members of a family, the Celtic peoples were both recognizably similar and yet individually different. The great attractions of their ancient culture are only heightened by the air of mystery surrounding the lack of literary records.

Ancient Celtic religion, for example, was governed by belief in a world filled with the supernatural and inhabited by a vast array of deities, by magical spells and curses and by tribal heroes. It assumed the existence of spiritual forces, both good and evil, and its complex rites and rituals were designed 'to constrain the powers of magic to beneficent ends'. It had no theology in the conventional sense, no ethics beyond the realm of effective propitiation, and certainly no scriptures. It was enshrined in myth and legend. It had more in common with the Indo-European belief system of the ancient Hindus than with that of the contemporary Greeks and Romans.

Indeed, misguided parallels with the classical world seem to be a major source of confusion. When the Romans encountered the Celts, and then conquered them, they assumed that the multiplicity of Celtic Gods was organized in a way similar to their own. Modern scholars with a classical education tend to do the same, or to suggest half-heartedly that the classical model 'can be useful'. It can't. Attempts to equate Lugh with Mercury, Maponos with Apollo, or Brigit with Mercury are wide of the mark. The Celts did recognize a pantheon of a sort, but it had few features in common with its Olympian counterpart. Considerable uncertainty surrounds the existence of a 'Father of the Gods' exercising supreme command. There was no central Celtic Olympos; and there were few specialized functions to which particular gods were allocated. For the Celtic concept of divinity encompassed a high-intensity magic which enabled the divine ones constantly to change the nature of their emanations. Four major features appear to have been at work.

Firstly, through transmogrification or 'shape-shifting' – like Fintan who turned himself into a salmon – all deities had the ability to adopt zoomorphic forms according to the needs of the moment. Secondly, they indulged in triplicity, that is they used the 'magic power of three' to have three names, to present themselves in three different guises, or to be one part of a threefold collective. Thirdly, they gained or lost their position in the divine league in accordance with the shifting success or failure of their adherents. Fourthly, they frequently presented themselves in male and female pairs. The overall picture was one of incessant, kaleidoscopic change and baffling complexity. One historian, referring to the religion of the insular Celts, has called it 'fertile chaos'.[31]

The insular Celts recognized major gods who recurred throughout the Celtic world. Dagda, 'the All-Competent', 'the Lord of Knowledge', was a club-swinging giant of great strength. He is sometimes equated with the Dis-Pater of Gaul mentioned by Caesar, though the same claims are made for Cernunnos, 'the Horned One'. Cernunnos was usually represented in a Buddha-like sitting posture, and he too carried a club. Lugh of the Longarm, 'the Shining One', was God of all arts and crafts. Known as Lugus in Gaul and as Lleu in Wales, he has left his mark in many Roman and modern place names from Lyons (Lugdunum) and Laon to Luguvallium (Carlisle), Léon in Spain, Leiden in Holland, and Legnica in Poland. He was patron of the summer harvest festival – in Irish Lugnasadh and in English Lammas. Epona, 'the Divine Mare', became popular with Roman cavalrymen stationed in Gaul, who took her cult to Rome. She was cognate with various other equine deities. There was also a 'Raven Queen', who wreaked havoc on the field of battle. In Éire, she was the triune Morrigan, who was interchangeable with Macha, Badb, and Nemain. She left one of her names at Ard Macha (Armagh), one of the oldest prehistoric sites on the Isles.

At the same time, there were insular gods with no known Continental equivalent. Such was the magnanimous Lud, otherwise 'Nud of the Silver Hand', who in Albion may have acquired the status of supreme deity. According to later legend, a temple to Lud once occupied the present site of St Paul's Cathedral in London, to which city he may possibly have bequeathed his name (Lud's Fort). The derivation of Ludgate in London is more certain. Lud was later known in Wales as Lludd Llaw Ereint, where with Mordaf and Rhydderch he was a member of a triad, and in Éire as Nuade, where he had led the third invasion, that of the Dé Danann. As Nodens, he was co-opted by Roman soldiers in Britain who built a temple in his honour.[32]

Rites and rituals were designed to keep the bewildering forces of the supernatural in check. The Celtic year was made up of propitious and unpropitious days, and of regular festivals. In Gaul, it is known from the famous Coligny Calendar, and in the Isles from Irish practices that have not entirely died out even today. The Festival of Samhain on 1 November is reflected in Hallowe'en and in the later Christian All Souls' Day. It inspired annual tribal gatherings. It arose from a critical moment in the cycle of pastoral societies, when animals were slaughtered before the winter. At Tara in Éire, the High King took on the role of the Dagda by publicly copulating with a maiden incarnating the river deity, Boann (Goddess of the Boyne), thereby ensuring the survival of the seed until the next season. The early spring festival of Imbok on 1 February was prompted by the lactation of ewes. It is connected with the Sanskrit cult of Brhati, 'the Exalted One', with the Dagda's daughter, Brigid, and of course with St Brigid's Day. The Festival of Beltine on 1 May was marked by fire ceremonies and the fumigation of cattle, and Lugnasadh on 1 August by the onset of the harvest. Commentators note the contrast between Christian harvest festivals, which thank God *after* the event, and the pagan rites of propitiation, which have to be completed *before* it.

Classical visitors entertained mixed feelings about Celtic practices. They were perfectly familiar with sacred groves, with votive offerings cast into holy lakes and wells, with sacrifices, and with the reading of the auguries. All such things could be seen in Rome itself. Yet two practices repeatedly provoked comment – the head cult, and the persistence of human sacrifice.

The Celts believed that the essence of a person resided in the head. As a result, they paid special attention to head forms in their sculpture, and to skulls in their decorative motifs. Their warriors decapitated defeated enemies and slung their heads from their saddles. Further Celtic tradition held that particular gods could only be propitiated by particular forms of ritual murder – by drowning, hanging, or burning. This is attested by numerous and suitably grisly archaeological discoveries of the victims' remains. Yet why it should have been found repellent by the Romans, who wallowed for centuries in public shows of mass killing, is not clear. At all events, the substitution of animal for human sacrifice in the Celtic world was at best partial. Ritual death even awaited the High Kings and tribal chiefs. Just as the young king was initiated by uniting with a nubile young woman, so a sick or ageing king had to face a violent end in the company of an old hag. In this way, the Celts gave expression to their own involvement in Nature's cycles of death and renewal, of barrenness and fecundity.

Over all such events, it was the corps of druids which presided. The druids, both male and female, formed a hierarchical caste, commanding the greatest authority in Celtic society. The etymology of their name is variously derived from 'oak' and 'knowledge'. Guardians of the tribal lore, in which they were systematically trained for decades, they were priests, judges, magicians, shamans and healers, bards, seers, and diplomats – all rolled into one. Their decisions were paramount, and were enforced by spells and curses. They ruled the groves, gave orders to kings and warriors, and left the strongest of all romanticized legacies. The Isles were said by Caesar to be the greatest centre of their learning. And within the Isles, their most sacred groves were to found on the island of Mon. Their most famous representative has come down to us as Myrddin or Merlin. According to legend, before Albion was populated, it had been known as Clas Myrddin – 'Merlin's Grove'.

Ancient Celtic society, as seen through Roman eyes, was a strange hierarchical mixture of nobles (who were not quite the landowning nobles of the Roman style), and ordinary people who were 'almost in the position of slaves'. Clearly, a stratified order of some sort operated. But it could only have functioned by custom as opposed to formal law; and it did not conform to classical structures. The basic groupings were the *túath*, or territorial tribe, and the *fine*, or clan. At the top there stood a powerful caste of specialized warriors, from which the top rank of druids and the kings were chosen. In the middle there was a stratum of free commoners, among them farmers and craftsmen of special importance, such as iron-workers and blacksmiths. At the bottom, it has been suggested that the labour force was organized in a system of age-cohorts who worked their way through a succession of social tasks suitable to their age and strength, rather than in a permanent arrangement of fixed classes. If so, one might speculate that boys started work as shepherds, grooms, and cow-hands, young men hunted and trained in the arts of war, and older men reared horses or toiled in the fields and the mines. Girls and women would begin with child-minding, milking, and kitchen chores, would move into the adult occupations of child-rearing and gardening, and would finish as domestic cooks and matrons. Given the emphasis on tribal identity, it is highly probable that the collective realm dominated over the individual one. At harvest time, all hands were sent out to bring in the crops. In time of war, everyone stood at the disposal of the military leaders.

One social institution of the ancient Celtic world, which attracted the attention of many observers, was the *corps d'élite* of 'knights' or 'free nobles'. As early as the second century BC the ancient historian Polybius described what he wrongly took to be a separate tribe of Gaesetae, literally 'spearmen', who at the Battle of Telamon in 225 BC fought apart from the other Celtic warriors, and who were clearly highly motivated by religion. In all probability, this was the first recorded appearance of similar warrior bands who stayed on the scene until medieval times. They were highly trained, intensely indoctrinated by the druids, separated from the rest of the tribe, and sworn to defend each other and their chief to the death. They supplied the champions, both male and female, who were immortalized in legend. In Gaul, their prowess was noted by Caesar. In Éire they appear as the Fianna or 'Fenians', the High King's bodyguard, reputedly founded c. 300 BC by the High King Fiachadh. Their daring deeds and the exploits of their champion, Fionn MacCumhaill or 'Finn MacCool', gave rise to the oldest of the Irish epic cycles. They were the prototypes of 'King Arthur' and his 'Knights of the Round Table', who rode out to fame many centuries later.

Ancient Celtic art survives mainly in the design and decoration of durable artefacts. Though there was no figurative representation, abstract patterns were preferred, and the shape of all figures became highly stylized in order to harmonize with the overall design. The essential components were drawn from a few basic shapes – spirals, interlacing, fretwork, and swastikas – which were woven together into an intricate curvilinear network. Stunning effects were obtained from the delicacy of line and the endless ingenuity of the variations. The main styles are inimitable, unmistakable. At one time, they were thought to be derivatives of superior classical design, but are now seen to be great art in their own right. The original input came as much from oriental, possibly from Scythian, as from Mediterranean inspiration. Celtic Art, wrote one of its most influential exponents, 'is far from primitiveness and simplicity; is refined in thought and technique; elaborate and clever, full of paradoxes, restless, puzzlingly ambiguous, rational and irrational, dark and uncanny – far from the lovable humanity and transparency of Greek art'. Yet it is a real style, 'the first great contribution of the barbarians to the European arts'. It is, in fact, both the antithesis and the equal of Classical Art – the first stage on the road to the Gothic, the Romantic, and the Modern.[33]

From all that is known, music was no less prominent in Celtic consciousness than art and poetry. 'The sound of song and of the harp filled Tara's Halls.' The Celtic harp, the *telen*, is still extant. But the music was lost on the ancient air.

One must emphasize, of course, that it is wrong to present the ancient Celts as complete illiterates. Numerous inscriptions survive to show that the Celts were familiar with the alphabets of their neighbours. The druids of central Europe knew Greek letters. In Gaul and Iberia they were familiar with Latin letters, in northern Italy with Etruscan. After the Roman conquest of particular districts, bilingual epigraphy on funerary and religious monuments was not uncommon. In two places, however, the Celts developed writing systems of their own. On the confines of Italy and Gaul, one finds examples of the so-called Lepontine script.[34] In Éire, from the end of the first millennium BC, one finds Ogam.[35] For whatever reason, the Celts never put their knowledge of letters to the service of literature.

Ancient Celtic literature is one of the marvels of civilization. By rights it should have been extinct long since, and unknown. But it isn't. Its origins lie deep in pagan prehistory; and in ancient times it was never written down. Like its Homeric contemporary in Ancient Greece, it descended from an immemorial oral tradition where gods and myths and kings and heroes and tales and poetry all merged into one. In Gaul, Caesar's men had listened to the *fili*, or bards, who had to memorize over two hundred epics before winning their full licence. Caesar reckoned that the druids had banned writing to preserve secrecy. In Gaul, Celtic literature died an early death thanks to the thorough Roman occupation, as it would do in Roman Britannia. But it survived in Éire, where the Romans never came and where it was given a final spin by the Christian monks who would finally write it down in the early Middle Ages. And it would survive with greater difficulty in Wales, which as a Roman military zone received only the lightest veneer of Latin culture. Most appropriately, the chief patron of Celtic poetry was Birgit, equally the Goddess of Hearth and Home, and as St Brigid, the leading patroness of Christian Ireland.

By common consent, it is the four great literary cycles from Éire which form at once the largest and the oldest segment of the ancient Celtic corpus. They contain elements with the most archaic, Continental Celtic connections, elements adopted by the Celts from the pre-Celtic peoples of the Isles, and elements generated after the Celts' arrival on the Isles. The so-called Mythological Cycle contains two works, the *Dissenchus* or 'History of Places' and the *Leabhar Gabhála Éireann* or 'Book of Invasions of Éire'. The Ulster Cycle recounts the exploits of the Ulaidh or 'Men of Ulster', otherwise 'the Red Branch Company', under their king, Conchobar mac Nessa, and their champion, Cú Chulainn. The Fenian Cycle, as mentioned earlier, deals with the Fianna, the 'Fenians'. In contrast with the Ulster Cycle, which was recited at royal feasts, it was said to be preferred by the common people. The fourth or Royal Cycle centres on Conn Cétchathach, alias 'Conn of the Hundred Battles', and on Cormac mac Airt, both of whom make journeys to the underworld. The youngest of the four cycles, it deals principally with events of the early Christian era.[36]

Not that any strict chronology can be easily established. Each of the cycles contains episodes from widely separate periods, and each of them evolved over many centuries, if not millennia. Even so, many of the actions described, from tribal warfare to cattle-raiding and horse-stealing, belonged to a way of life that was almost timeless. It is often superfluous to know whether a particular battle or hero has been placed by the experts in the third century BC or the third century AD. The 'Heroic Age' has no clear beginning and no clear end. One could argue that the traditions first embodied in Cú Chulainn continued in unbroken line until the last tragic stand of the clansmen at Culloden in 1746 (see Chapter Nine). They certainly survived in institutional form in Ireland until the suppression of the bardic schools by Cromwell (see Chapter Eight).

It is in this context that the action of the *Táin Bó Cuailgne*, the central story in the Ulster Cycle, unfolds. Claims are made that it is absolutely the oldest fragment of West European literature. Cattle-raiding was endemic among the pastoral tribes of the north. It provided a few days or weeks of excitement amidst months of lonely herding, and the occasion for deeds of courage, honour, and treachery. In this instance, the raid was mounted by the Men of Connaught in the west led by their King Ailill and his ferocious Queen, Medb. Their aim is to capture the fabulous Bull of Cooley – Cooley being a district on the eastern coast of Ulster. It all began when the royal couple of Connaught quarrelled over which of them was wealthier.

It happened once, when Ailill and Medb were in their royal
bedchamber at Cruachan, that they fell into argument.

— 'It is true what they say,' declared Ailill, 'that a rich man's
wife enjoys a life of comfort. I was just thinking how much
better off you are today with me than on the day I married
you . . .'

— 'That's not how it was at all,' retorted Medb. 'My father was
Eochaid, King of Ireland, and of all of his six daughters . . . I
was the best at fighting and the most generous. I had fifteen
hundred soldiers in my pay . . . My father gave me a province
to rule on my own . . . As for suitors, I was wooed by [five
kings] . . . When I chose you, I showered you with gifts . . . I
gave you a splendid chariot with seven serving-maids, and the
width of your face in red gold . . . You are nothing more than
a kept man.'

— 'That's a lie. I, too, am the son of a king, and my two
brothers are kings . . .'

— 'The fact remains,' said Medb, 'that my riches far outweigh
yours.'

— 'Never,' cried Ailill. 'No one has a greater treasure than I.'

— 'Very well,' Medb challenged, 'let us put it to the test!'[37]

When all the cattle and jewels of the king and queen were counted,
they were found to be exactly equal, except for one item. The
Queen's great bull was missing. So, to get even with her husband,
she resolved to steal the Bull of Cooley from the Ulstermen.

Medb is confident of success. She has paralysed the Men of
Ulster with a curse. Surely, they cannot resist. But as she prepares
to leave, she encounters a prophetess who foresees disaster:

The young woman was sitting on the shaft of a chariot, staring
at her. She had golden hair, and a cloak of many colours . . .
Her skin was as pale as the snow of a single night, her eyes
had triple irises, and her voice was like the gentle strumming
of a harp. In her hand, she held a sword of white bronze,
which she turned around as if weaving a web . . .

— 'What is your name, young maiden?'

— 'I am Fedelm, the Prophetess of Connaught.'

— 'And where have you come from?' asked Medb.

— 'From [across the northern water], where I learned to read the signs . . .'

— 'Then look into the future, and tell what you see for my people.'

The girl obeyed and said, 'I see crimson on them. I see red.'

— 'That cannot be,' answered Medb, 'for Conchabar lies stricken at Emain Macha . . . We have nothing to fear from the Ulstermen . . .'

— 'I see crimson on them. I see red,' the girl repeated.

— 'Impossible!' said Medb once again . . . 'Look again, maiden.' . . .

— 'I see crimson on them. I see red,' uttered the girl for the final time.

— 'I see a man, low in stature, performing great feats of arms. I see many wounds on his smooth skin, but victory on his brow. He is young, beautiful, modest to women, and fierce as a dragon. I do not know him . . . but he will redden the men of your army with their own blood. The dead will lie thick on the ground, and he will carry away many heads.'[38]

The beautiful young man is, of course, Cú Chulainn, who holds Medb's army at bay single-handedly until his countrymen recover from the curse. And on it goes, for thousands upon thousands of lines of epic verse. The Irish monk who wrote it all down, perhaps in the ninth century, added his own Latin gloss at the end:

I, who copied this history down, or rather this fantasy, do not believe in all the details. Several things in it are devilish lies. Others are the invention of poets. And others again have been thought up for the entertainment of idiots.[39]

≈

The final act of independent Albion closed in the last year of King Cunobelin (d. AD 42) and the second year of the Roman Emperor Claudius (r. AD 41–54). The rich and powerful tribes of the south-east, like the Catuvellauni, were chafing under their nominal alliance with Rome. At the same time, they had been using their muscle at the expense of their neighbours. Once again, exiled British chiefs had appeared in the imperial court seeking the aid of the legions in Gaul. The Cantians, in particular, harboured a strong sense of grievance; and they controlled the prospective landing beaches. They knew that a serious feud at Camulodunum was dividing the sons of Cunobelin, who was on his deathbed. When he died, he left his kingdom to his two younger sons, Caractacus and Togodamnos. The eldest son, Adminius, fled to Gaul.

Unlike Caesar, Claudius did not see the troubles of Albion as a threat to his security. But he was eager for glory, and he listened to the blandishments of courtiers eager to please. So he gave the fateful order for the legions to sail. The Celts of Éire were not in his sights. They would remain masters of their fate for a thousand years more. But most of the Britons of Albion would never be free again.

EVEN THOUGH THE ANCIENT CELTS were the earliest group of ethnically and culturally identifiable inhabitants of the Isles, few general histories pay them much attention. Most histories of 'England', 'Britain', or 'the British Isles' begin with the coming of the Romans, starting either with Caesar's expeditions in 55 and 54 BC or with the Claudian conquest. The preceding period of the Celtic supremacy, which lasted for the same length of time as that dividing Claudius from Bede or Tony Blair from the Black Prince, is usually glossed over or simply cut. At the most, it is treated as a hurried prelude to the more important things that follow. The prestigious *Oxford History of England* series is a good case in point. The editors have had two attempts to produce the opening volume on Roman Britain, but they have not thought fit to recast their scheme in order to take in the pre-Roman period. They show no real interest in the heritage of the Celts *per se*.[40]

One reason for this neglect lies in the fact that the pre-Roman era is usually judged to belong to prehistory rather than to history. After all, students of Roman Britain can read the works of classical authors, starting with Caesar himself. Students of the ancient Celts, in contrast, are struggling almost exclusively in the realms of archaeology and mythology. The distinction, however, hardly holds up to examination. Archaeology is vital to the study of Roman Britain, as mythology is to the study of early Anglo-Saxon England. No native documentary sources exist from any period prior to the late sixth and early seventh centuries. In which case, if historical sources are to be the criterion, no history of the Isles should start before the second half of the first millennium AD.

Three further factors may have contributed to the exclusion of the Celtic Supremacy from mainstream history. One of these relates to classical prejudices, a second to the predilections of archaeology, a third to the peculiar development of Celtic Studies. Yet the net result can hardly be contested. As the authors of a long-running and well-respected textbook of British history once put it:

> . . . about the time that Alexander the Great was revealing the East to the eager curiosity of the Greeks, Pytheas was introducing Britain to the civilized world. Little did the half-barbaric islanders realise what this meant. Nor could they foresee . . . that there would be a time when educated Englishmen would know far more about Ancient Greece than about Ancient Britain.[41]

So long as classical education and classical prejudices prevailed, educated Englishmen inevitably saw Ancient Britain as an alien land.

Archaeology has advanced very far from the amateurish digs and guesses which still prevailed only a century ago. Yet archaeologists are reluctant to enter those realms of research and speculation in which their well-tried scientific methodology is not relevant. On the Ancient Celts, for example, the leading authority to approach the subject from the archaeological standpoint presents a magnificent illustrated volume where the reader can taste everything except myth and literature. A short passage which briefly mentions the contents of the Ulster Cycle is followed by another dismissing claims about the Cycle's prehistoric pedigree. The opinion of one scholar, who has studied 'the material culture' in the Cycle and takes it to be connected to 'the Dark Ages', is preferred to rival views holding the Cycle to be 'A Window on the Iron Age'.[42] The gulf between the materialists and the culturalists is deep. Indeed, there are scholars who suggest that the ancient Celts are nothing more than a modern invention. 'More and more archaeologists are concluding', said one of them, 'that the Ancient Celts as usually conceived never really existed.'[43]

The important thing to realize here is that the findings of

archaeology, like those of any other scientific subject, can sometimes be used for entirely unscientific purposes. Archaeology does not operate in a neutral, sterile environment. It is subject to pressure from all sorts of political and ethnic interests, eager to find confirmation of the particular results they seek.[44] There are archaeologists working with the Celtophiles, and others working against them, often suspected of dire English nationalism.[45] The idea that archaeology is a neutral science is a mirage.

A rare if not exceptional attempt to bridge the gulf between archaeology and philology was made by Professor Colin Renfrew in a study in which the puzzle of the ancient Celts takes a prominent place. Renfrew supports a very early date for the emergence of the insular Celts, quoting with approval fellow prehistorians whose linguistic arguments seem to underpin his own archaeological conclusions:

> If the earliest Celtic settlements date from the Bronze Age, the question whether the invaders were Goidels or Brythons does not arise. Linguistic innovations that distinguish the Brythons may be much later, some of them innovations (u > i; qu > p) which spread from some centres on the continent and never reached the 'lateral' areas of Ireland and Spain.[46]

It is not unfair to suggest that such interdisciplinary observations are not enough.

Celtic Studies, too, have tended to develop inside their own watertight compartment. For many centuries they were the exclusive concern of local Celtic communities. Irish monks copied and studied the remnants of ancient Irish literature. Welsh monks and Gaelic monks preserved the Welsh and the Scots-Gaelic heritage. Modern Celts virtually monopolize modern Celtic Studies.

Most famous of the historically minded monks who set out to preserve the ancient Celtic heritage for posterity was the Breton Gaufridus (1100–55), better known as Geoffrey of Monmouth. His *Historia Regum Britanniae* ('History of the Kings of Britain'), which was written in Oxford Castle in 1138–9, claims to be based on an ancient manuscript from Brittany. There is little evidence for this. Like its Irish counterparts, the *Historia* is an inimitable mélange of improbable legends, classical accretions, vivid fantasy, and a residue of conceivably historical fact. It traces the story from the first alleged monarch, Brute or Brutus, a survivor of the Trojan War, to the seventh-century Welsh Prince Cadwalladr:

> Britain, best of islands, lieth in the Western Ocean betwixt Gaul and Ireland, and containeth eight hundred miles in length and two hundred in breadth. Whatsoever is fitting for the use of mortal men the island doth afford in unfailing plenty . . .
>
> Brute chose . . . to set sail in quest of the island which the divine monition had prophesied should be his own . . . and after loading his ships with all the treasures and luxuries he had acquired, he re-embarked and with a prosperous wind sought the promised island, where he landed at last in safety at Totnes.
>
> At that time, the name of the island was Albion, and none of it was inhabited save a few giants. Nonetheless, the pleasant aspect of the land . . . did fill Brute and his companions with no small desire that they should dwell therein. Wherefore, . . . after exploring certain districts they drove the giants to take refuge in the caverns of the mountains, and divided the country among them by lot . . . They began to till the fields and to build them houses in such sort that after a brief space ye might have thought it inhabited since time immemorial. Then at last Brute calleth the island Britain, and his companions Britons after his own name . . . Wherefore afterward, the country speech, which aforetime had been called Trojan or crooked Greek, was called British.[47]

Gaufridus produced a similarly implausible explanation for the origins and naming of London:

> After that he had seen his kingdom, Brute was minded to build him a chief city . . . When he came to the river Thames, he walked along the banks till he found the spot very best suited to his purpose. He therefore founded his city there and called it

New Troy . . . By this name it was known for many ages until at last, by corruption of the word, it became Trinovantum . . .

But afterward Lud, the brother of Cassibellaunas, who fought with Julius Caesar . . . surrounded the city with right noble walls . . . commending that it be called Kaerlud, that is 'City of Lud' . . . and after that, by corruption of the name Kaerlondon. In a later day, by the changing of the tongues it was called London, and yet later, after the landing of the foreign folk . . . hath it been called Londres.[48]

The amateur etymology of Gaufridus was no more convincing than his historical fact-checking. His work was soon condemned as inaccurate, notably by William of Newburgh (d. 1198). But its colourful narrative continued to attract readers, and, in the absence of more authoritative accounts, to exercise wide influence. Twice translated into Anglo-Norman, it became a popular historical text for the French-speaking elite of the twelfth and thirteenth centuries and a major source for later chroniclers such as Laʒamon, Higden, and Holinshed. It was Gaufridus who fixed the association between the history of the Ancient Britons and fanciful story-telling. Such, after all, was the Celtic style. Shakespeare inherited the association at several stages removed; and it was perhaps no accident that the greatest of his three 'British' plays, *King Lear*, deals with the theme of madness. The most important achievement of Gaufridus, however, was to establish the general chronology. For all his faults as a historian, Gaufridus taught generations of readers that before the Normans, before the Anglo-Saxons, and before the Romans, the Isles were ruled and inhabited by ancient Celts and Britons. As the influence of the surviving Celts declined, that basic information was invaluable.

In modern times, when antiquaries, scholars, and collectors took a renewed interest, the only people with the necessary linguistic qualifications belonged to families of Celtic descent. In Ireland, the Franciscan friar Michael O'Clerigh (d. 1636) compiled *The Annals of the Four Masters* with the deliberate purpose of combating the hostile stereotypes of the 'Wild Irish' which were circulating in the works of Tudor and Jacobean propagandists.

In England, the great pioneer is generally taken to be Edward Lluyd or Lloyd (1660–1709), an Oswestry man, who became a Fellow of Jesus College, Oxford, and sometime keeper of the Ashmolean Museum. Lluyd travelled widely in Ireland, Wales, the Scottish Highlands, and Brittany, collecting antiquities, manuscripts, folklore, and linguistic information. His *Archæologia Britannica* (1707) is often regarded as the founding survey of Celtic studies. It contains a fundamental chapter classifying Q-Celtic and P-Celtic. Typically, after Lluyd died young and in poverty the University of Oxford sold off his effects to pay his debts. These effects included the sole original manuscripts both of the *Book of Leinster* and the *Yellow Book of Lecan*, now in the library of Trinity College, Dublin. Since most of Lluyd's papers remained unpublished, his work was less well known than that of a far less reliable contemporary, Theophilus Evans, whose gushing epic *Drych y Prif Oesoedd* ('The Mirror of Past Ages', 1716) tried to link historical Wales with the Tower of Babel. 'The Welsh were for generations to view their past through the romantic eyes of . . . Evans rather than through the scholarly eyes of Lluyd.'[49] Another of Lluyd's contemporaries and an acquaintance at Oxford, John Toland (1670–1722), was a native Irish speaker and a philosopher-theologian who invented the concept of 'pantheism'. He may be regarded as the pioneer of the return to religion's pre-Christian, Celtic roots.[50]

In Scotland, apart from the Revd James Macpherson and his scam on Ossian (see page oo, below), pride of place must go to three historians all by the name of Robertson – William Robertson (1721–93), friend of Gibbon and author of *The History of Scotland* (1760), James B. Robertson (1800–77), professor at the Catholic University of Dublin, and Eben W. Robertson (1815–74), a resident of England, and author of *Scotland Under her Early Kings to the Thirteenth Century* (1862). This last work was bitterly attacked by the English historian Freeman for daring to suggest that the early Scots kings enjoyed independent status.

In that same period, both government policies and the new ideas of the Enlightenment combined to provoke a distinct Celtic Revival. The repression of the Jacobite Risings in Scotland, the continuing injustices of English rule in Ireland, and the official neglect of Welsh culture in Wales had created a growing store of resentments. And the assertions of learned men that the humiliation of the non-English peoples was a necessary stage in the march of progress only added insult to injury. Ireland, in particular, was parodied as a savage land of bogs and bards.

One reaction, led by the Revd Dr William Stukeley (1687–1765), Rector of Stamford, was to revive the cult of the druids. Stukeley, who had visited Stonehenge, convinced himself that druidism was the aboriginal religion of the Isles, and he laid out a druidical temple in his garden, replete with an old apple tree overgrown with mistletoe. He was the pioneer of all the pseudo-druidical orders of modern times. His friends called him 'Arch-Druid Chyndonax'. After Culloden, they saw Stukeley's next garden adorned with a memorial gate to the '45 and a statue to Flora MacDonald. Stukeley was an eccentric; and he was clearly in error on many issues, not least on his fatal link between the druids and Stonehenge. But his numerous publications promoted an important trend which held that the Celtic past was worth studying.[51]

Another reaction was to take an interest in Celtic poetry. All over the Isles, the Celtic bardic tradition was singled out as a source of illiterate superstition and sedition until Celtophiles pointed out that the savagery was not quite so one-sided. An ode by Thomas Gray to *The Bard* (1757) struck a defiant note, though it spread the wrong-headed idea that the medieval English conquest of Wales was attended by a massacre of bards. It coincided very closely with the publication of Macpherson's pseudo-Ossianic *Fragments of Ancient Poetry Collected in the Highlands* ... (1759). Both found their admirers; but both were comprehensively panned, notably by Dr

Johnson. Johnson's own *Journey to the Western Islands* (1775), together with Boswell's *Journal* of the same tour, acted as catalysts to the debate.

Protests against the denigration of the bards came thick and strong. Learned Scots writers like Donald McNicol in his *Remarks . . .* (1779) questioned Johnson's good faith. '[Johnson] systematically discredits "the Poems of Ossian – the whole Gallic language – our seminaries of learning", he fumed, "and the veracity of all Scotch and particularly Highland narration. The utter extinction of the two former seems to have been the principal motive of [his] journey.'[52] Welsh writers moved to assist on the other flank. Evan Evans (1731–89), defending Gray's ode, published his *Paraphrase of the 137th Psalm Alluding to the Captivity of the Welsh Bards by King Edward I*, following it with his patriotic defence of Wales, *The Love of Our Country* (1772). The harpist and antiquary Edward Jones (1752–1824) published his collected *Musical and Poetical Relicks of the Welsh Bards* (1784). To cap it all, a Celtic Harpists' Festival was organized in Belfast on Bastille Day 1792 – 'to revive and perpetuate the ancient Music and Poetry of Ireland'. The Ancient Celts were at last finding their modern advocates and admirers. Cromwell's forcible closure of the bardic schools in Ireland had not achieved its goal.

Yet the process went further. The modest Celtic Revival of the late eighteenth century was to have a long-term effect on nascent national feelings in Ireland, Scotland, and Wales. (See Chapter Ten.) But it was also to leave a strong mark on English literature. By contesting the all-powerful rationalism of the Enlightenment, and by cultivating 'the mystical and the sublime', it took a giant step in the direction of Romanticism. By 1789 William Blake had already penned his own song to 'The Voice of the Ancient Bard':

> Youth of delight, come hither,
> And see the opening morn,
> Image of truth new born.
> Doubt is fled, & clouds of reason,

Dark disputes & artful teazing.
Folly is an endless maze,
Tangled roots perplex her ways,
How many have fallen there!
They stumble all night over bones of the dead
And feel they know now what but care
And wish to lead others when they should be led.[53]

Celtic mysticism was finally flowing into the English stream.

The credentials of the Celtic Revival have naturally been called
into question. Not content with the manifest truth that the Celtic
Revival, like all revivalist movements, contained its share of exaggeration and wishful thinking, the Celtophobes are apt to suggest that
its advocates were engaged in the romantic creation of an imaginary
past, not in the rediscovery of a historic past – in short, in the
propagation of a myth. The Ancient Celts, they would argue, belong
to an 'invented tradition'.[54]

Nonetheless, by the nineteenth century Celtic archaeology,
Celtic languages, and Celtic literature had all found their place
in British academic life. They are now underpinned by a proliferation of distinguished academic journals, and by an array of
distinguished university chairs. They were given a major boost by
the rise of cultural nationalism, especially in Ireland and Wales,
by the work of bodies such as the Irish Archaeological and Celtic
Society (1853) and the Cambrian Archaeological Association (1846),
and by the foundation of new universities such as the (Catholic)
University of Dublin (1855) and the University of Wales, Lampeter
(1827). Scottish interest in Scotland's Gaelic heritage was first
frowned on by the British Establishment then adapted in a particularly false and sentimental embrace. (See Chapter Nine.) In
Ireland, interest in the Gaelic past by W. B. Yeats in *The Celtic
Twilight* (1893) was a landmark event. Another landmark in the
subject occurred in 1911 with the publication in the influential
Eleventh Edition of the *Encyclopædia Britannica* of a huge and
erudite entry on 'The Celts'. The author was Edgar Mungo Quiggin,

a rising star from the new Department of Celtic and Anglo-Saxon Studies at Cambridge, who died tragically young.[55] In the twentieth century, Celtic Studies were further boosted by the creation of an Irish Free State (1922), and in the United Kingdom by the belated adoption in the 1960s of official policies protecting the country's Celtic cultures. The Canolfan Uwchefrydiou Cymreig a Cheltaidd, the Centre for Advanced Welsh and Celtic Studies at Aberystwyth, dates from 1985.

The obvious limitation of these considerable achievements lies in the failure to integrate the love and knowledge of Celtic culture into the mainstream of British intellectual life. Celtic Studies have found their niche. By and large, however, the Celts of the Isles are still left delving into their Celtic heritage in isolation, whilst the English majority press on regardless with their own Anglocentric concerns.

A prime example of the gaping hole in English awareness can be found in a personal anecdote recently recorded by a professor of literature who at the time was an official of the British Comparative Literature Association:

> Some years ago, on a visit to the Slovak Academy of Sciences in Bratislava, I was asked by [a] well-known Slovak comparatist . . . to give him the names of colleagues in Britain working on British Comparative Literature. Having been a founder of the BCLA, . . . I felt I had a sound sense of who was working on what, so I duly provided him with a list of names of colleagues in French, German and English Departments and the few specifically designated Comparative Literature programmes. He appeared perplexed by this and repeated his request for names of colleagues working on British Comparative Literature . . . We looked at each other across our cups of coffee in bafflement.
>
> It took several minutes before it dawned on me what he was asking for. He simply wanted to know who was comparing the literatures of the British Isles . . . When I told him that there were no such programmes of research or teaching, that the

BCLA had never even considered this question, my statement was met with disbelief.[56]

Three hundred years after Edward Lluyd had set Celtic Studies on their way, they were still not part of established literary interest.

Another incident illustrates a different aspect of the prevailing lack of awareness. In 1982 Penguin Books published an anthology of *Contemporary British Poetry*. It excluded all poets writing in Celtic languages, even in translation, whilst including several non-British poets writing in English. In a poem entitled 'Open Letter', an Irish poet, and future Nobel Prize winner, was moved to protest at some length at the improper use of the word 'British'.

> You'll understand I draw the line
> At being robbed of what is mine,
> My patria . . .[57]

Seamus Heaney was right. All too often, the English casually subsume the insular Celts, or callously ignore them, as the mood dictates.

In the meantime, a second Celtic Revival is thriving far beyond the narrow realms of academe and high culture. For the last ten or twenty years, 'Celticity' has been increasingly promoted as an anti-dote both to the stresses of contemporary life and to the dominant interests of the United Kingdom's cultural establishment. It combines a romantic attachment to a perceived Celtic heritage with a fascination for the mysticism and animist spirituality that are taken to form its essential adjunct. It is linked to the reinvigorated nationalist movements, to the ecological movement, which shares a similar empathy for the spirits of nature, and also to the rise of 'New Age' neo-paganism. In short, it appeals to all those people who feel the strains of modern civilization, and who seek, however impractic-ally, to recover the benefits of the world before civilization. In the Isles, the world before civilization was the world of the ancient Celts.

In this new climate, a veritable explosion has occurred – a

spontaneous outburst of enthusiasm for everything Celtic in a dozen different fields. Celtic music and dance, for instance, has met unprecedented success. Irish and Scottish folk groups, such as the Clancy Brothers, the Fureys, the Chieftains, the Corries, and Clannad, have gained a worldwide following. Irish singers have won the European Song contest time and again. Hundreds of CDs with titles like *Celtic Moods*, *Celtic Spirit*, *Celtic Magic*, and *Celtic Dreamtime* exploit the same soothing, echoing style, with haunting pipes and ethereal harps; and they sell in millions. Dance troupes such as 'Lords of the Dance', and *Riverdance* with its severe formalized postures, enjoy global acclaim. In the realm of arts and crafts, all manner of specialities from needlework and jewellery to ceramics, glassware, calligraphy, engraving, and knitting patterns exploit traditional Celtic designs. There is a vogue for Celtic folklore, for anthologies of Celtic poetry and legend, for popular histories of the Celtic countries, even for primers of the Celtic languages for self-taught amateurs. Celtic tourism flourishes, especially from abroad. Chains of Celtic stores sell a vast variety of Celtic merchandise. Celtic Studies proliferate, especially as alternative courses in less conventional colleges. To cap it all, the film industry has broken into the act. Mel Gibson's *Braveheart* (1995) won the Oscar for best film. Set amidst glorious Highland scenery, it made an unashamed appeal to undiluted Scottish nationalist sentiment. Michael Caton-Jones' *Rob Roy* (1995) exploited another story from Scottish history and from Walter Scott's historical novel, on the same anti-English and anti-Establishment pitch. *Waking Ned Devine* (1998), filmed entirely on the Isle of Man, adds social subversion to whimsical Irish humour.

An international Celtic League was founded in 1961 to tap some of the energy of these diffuse activities. Run by a General Council consisting of representatives of the six Celtic nations including Brittany and Man, it coordinates the work of the separate national organizations. It aims to foster cooperation between the Celtic peoples and to publicize their struggles and achievements. It looks forward to the time when six independent Celtic republics can join together in a Pan-Celtic Federation. Its ideologists see their task to free the Celts from both cultural and political 'imperialism'.[58]

The huge diaspora of Celts round the world is playing a prominent role in the current revival. Long divided by oceans and continents both from each other and from their ancestral homelands, they are now being reunited by modern transport and communications. The heartbreak of the great migrations (see Chapter Nine) is finally being mended. Australia alone has eight million citizens of Irish extraction from a total population of eighteen million, together with large Scots, Welsh, Cornish, and Manx contingents. The Celtic Council of Australia presides over countless Hibernian and Caledonian societies, the Australian Federation of Cornish Associations, and the Australian Manx Associations. Celtic Conferences and Celtic Festivals form part of the regular agenda. As in the USA, many of these Celtic bodies, fed by nostalgia, are more unswervingly committed 'to the cause' than are their relatives in the Isles.

The growth of the Internet has proved a boon to these scattered communities. The 'Celts of Cyberspace' are among the busiest in the business. Given the command 'Celtic Revival – SEARCH', any of the standard search engines will immediately throw up a minimum of fifty thousand relevant sites. The scale and range of the fare is astonishing. *Celtic Connection* offers a newspaper serving the Celtic communities of Vancouver, Canada; *Celtic Dreams* offers a worldwide delivery service for Irish and Scottish gifts; and *Celtic Artlink* offers an electronic display of the Celtic visual arts . . . The academic offerings are as serious and diverse as the commercial ones. At ⟨**gopher://cheops.anu.edu.au:70/0waisdocid%** . . . **1/cornish-studies**⟩ an electronic debate is in progress on the Cornish national movement. At ⟨**http://www.smo.uhi.ac.uk/saoghal/mionchanain/brezhoneg**⟩ a Breton linguist working at the Gaelic College on the Isle of Skye provides lessons in his native language for one and all.[59]

In the religious sphere, Christian and non-Christian strands overlap in their common love and awe of Nature. Contemporary anthologies abound. Celtic Christianity is famous for its prayers and its blessings. One well-known blessing comes from Iona:

> Deep peace of the running wave to you
> Deep peace of the flowing air to you
> Deep peace of the quiet earth to you
> Deep peace of the shining stars to you
> Deep peace of the Son of Peace to you[60]

Another, originally in Irish Gaelic, has reached English via Welsh:

> May the blessing of light be on us, light without and light within.
> May the blessed sunlight shine upon us and warm our hearts,
>   till they glow like a great peat fire . . .
> And may the light shine out of the eyes of us, like a candle
>   set in the windows of a house, bidding wanderers come in
>   from the storm.
> And may the blessing of the rain be on us – the soft sweet rain . . .
> And may the blessing of the great rains be on us, that they
>   beat upon our spirits and wash them fair and clean . . .
> And may the blessing of the earth be on us – the great round earth;
>   may we ever have a kindly greeting for those we pass on the
>   road . . .
> And now may the Lord bless us, and bless us kindly![61]

Celtic neo-paganism is one of numerous contemporary movements that have rushed into the vacuum left by the decline in Christian practice. It has no fixed form. Some of its adherents endeavour to follow the old 'Druid Way'. They do not seem to mind whether their supposedly druidical doings are spurious or authentic. Some of them, like the British Order of Druids or the Reformed Druids of North America, don garb reminiscent of the Ku Klux Klan and engage in elaborate rituals. Others again are 'creating a lifestyle' based on a distinct brand of 'Celtic sexuality', and Celtic polytheism, or indulging in *wiccan* 'white magic'. Most are engaged in some form of 'earth quest' or 'earth magic'; and all who retain an overtly Celtic link observe the seasonal festivals of Samhain, Imbok, Beltane, and Lugnasadh.[62]

A curious aspect of contemporary 'Celticity' lies in the fact that it often aims to recruit English people as much as anyone else. The English, who might otherwise be considered the butts of the phenomenon, are very definitely included. The assumption seems to be that 'Englishness' is no more than a modern cultural veneer overlying a broad ancestral community that is only just awakening to its lost Celtic roots. Most English families can find Irish, Welsh, Cornish, or Scots branches in their family tree. It only requires a simple switch of attitude to stress the non-English as opposed to the English elements in their make-up. Genealogy, therefore, occupies a central position. The 'Anglo-Celtic' constituency is potentially the largest of all. For them, the important thing is *not* to try to become fluent in Irish or Welsh or Gaelic, which few will be able to do, but simply to learn to respect the Celtic part of their inheritance.

The Celtica Centre at Machynlleth in Powys is an unabashed temple to this contemporary Celtic Revival. Founded in 1992 in a mansion once belonging to a Marquis of Londonderry, it invites its visitors 'to experience the Mysterious and Magical World of the Celts'. Everything is presented in a bilingual Welsh and English setting with the assistance of modern audiovisual and information technology. Visitors pass from the historical Exhibition and Interpretative Centre dedicated to the Celtic past across the centuries, to a series of locations where one participates in reconstructions of ancient Celtdom. The Celts are called 'husbands of the earth' who live in 'openness of spirit and time'. The ancient Celts knew the 'Magical Time'. They lived in a landscape alive with the spirits of nature. The foundry and roundhouse of an ancient Celtic settlement, whose actors recount their own stories, are approached through a Corridor of Time. Then one goes through the Magical Forest to the Otherworld where one peers into the Vortex and tries to see the future by reflecting on the past. One is transported from the murder of the druids to the suppression of the miners' strike in the 1980s. As the Centre's brochure announces, this is 'an imaginative view of history':

> Mae Celtica yn atyniad newydd unigryw sy'n olrhain hanes y Celtaid – pobl y bu eu diwylliant yn dylanwadu ar hanes Ewrop ers 3,000 o flynyddoedd. Cewch ddiwrnod llawn hwyl yn y ganolfan a chyfle i ddysgu rhywbeth newydd. Mae'r ganolfan yn adlewyrchu treftadaeth Geltaidd Cymru, Ile gydag awyrgylch Gymreig, cewch gân, crefft a chyfle i brofi byd hud a lledrith y Celtaidd.
>
> *(Celtica is a unique new attraction telling the story of the Celts – a people whose culture has influenced European history for over 3,000 years. A great place for an enjoyable and informative day out, Celtica reflects Wales's distinct Celtic inheritance; a magical blend of myth and music, landscape and language, reflecting a nation which, in common with the other Celtic lands on the fringes of Western Europe, is as proud of its past as it is of its present and future.)*[63]

The unimaginative, the sceptics, and the entrenched English are unlikely to be impressed. Indeed, some of them could take offence, seeing it as a good example, to use Tennyson's phrase, of 'the blind hysterics of the Celt'. But as one leaves the Celtica Centre it will be a hard heart indeed which remains unmoved by the music, as a passionate Welsh choir belts out a full-blooded rendering of the neo-Celtic anthem, *'Yma o hyd'*, 'We're still here!'. The message is abundantly clear:

YMA O HYD

'Dwyt ti'm yn cofio Macsen
'Does neb yn ei 'nabod o
Mae mil chwe chant o
    flynyddoedd
Yn amser rhy hir i'r co'
Ond daeth Magnus Maximus o
    Gymru

(WE'RE STILL HERE!

You don't remember Macsen;
No one here ever knew him.
One thousand and six hundred
    years
Is too long ago to recall.
But Magnus Maximus left
    Wales

Yn y flwyddyn tri chant wyth
  tri
A'n gadael yn genedl gyfan
A heddiw, deled hi!

Cytgan
R'yn ni yma o hyd
R'yn ni yma o hyd
Er gwaetha pawb a phopeth
Er gwaetha pawb a phopeth
Er gwaetha pawb a phopeth
R'yn ni yma o hyd
R'yn ni yma o hyd

*In the year three hundred and eighty-
  three.*
He left the nation as one.
And today, just look at her!

Chorus
We're still here (We're still standing)
We're still here.
Despite everybody and everything.
Despite everybody and everything.
Despite everybody and everything.
We're still here.
We're still here . . .)*

---

* See Appendix 48.

1. The Isles – separated from the Continental mainland
c. 6000–5500 BC, rejoined by the Channel Tunnel AD 1994.

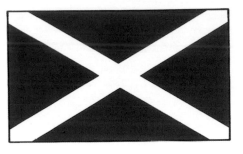

2. St Andrew

3. St George

4. St Patrick

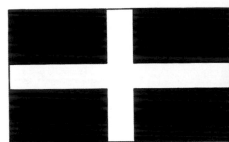

5. St Piran

6. Welsh Dragon

7. Manx *Trinacria*

8. Guernsey

9. Jersey

10. Commonwealth Jack, 1649

11. Protectorate Jack, 1658

12. Union Jack, 1707

13. Union Jack, 1801

14. Northern Ireland

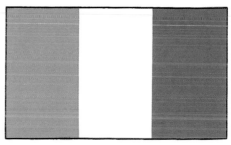

15. Irish Republic

16. Orkney

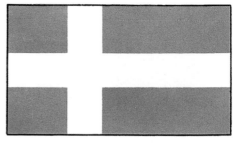

17. Shetland

18. St Edward the Confessor, King of England, 1042–66 (canonized 1161)

19. Two Norman lions passant gardant. The Conqueror and successors, 1066

20. Scottish lion rampant. Guillaume le Lion and successors, c. 1165

21. Three Plantagenet lions. Richard Cœur de Lion and successors, 1198

22. 'France Quartered'. Edouard III and successors, 1340

23. James VI, I, & I, self-proclaimed King of Great Britain, King of Ireland, King of France, 1603

24. Standard of the Lord Protector, Richard Cromwell, 1658

25. 'Dutch Pretence'. William III & II, Stadholder of the United Provinces, 1694–1702

26. 'Scotland Impaled'. Anne, Queen of Great Britain, France, and Ireland, 1707–14

27. 'Hanover Quartered'. George I, II, III, Electors of Hanover, Kings of Great Britain, France, and Ireland, 1714–1801

28. 'Hanover Crowned'. George III to William IV, Kings of the United Kingdom and Hanover, 1816–37

29. Victoria to Elizabeth II, 1837–?

30. Celtic Bard – bearer of the older tradition.

31. Last invasion of the Northmen (1066): Guillaume le Conquérant
examines the body of Harold Godwinson.

32. Defeat of the Spanish Armada (1588): England triumphant and triumphantly Protestant.

33. George IV enters Holyrood (1822) – the first British monarch to visit Scotland.

34. 'King Billy Rides Again' – Loyalist mural, Belfast, 1970.

35. Mrs Susan McCarron with tea guest, Glasgow, 1999.

6. Roman Centurion at Hadrian's Wall (c. AD 122). 'I've served in Britain forty years.'

37. Vortigern, the 'Vawr-Tigherne or Overlord', welcomes Hengest and Horsa, AD 428 or 449.

38. *Left:* 'King Arthur' transformed from early Celtic warlord into the champion of medieval chivalry.

39. *Below:* Sveyn Forkbeard, King of Denmark and England, lands on Humberside, 1003.

40. *Opposite, top:* Magna Carta, signed at Runnymede in 1215, when England was a papal fief.

41. *Opposite, bottom:* 'Constitutional history was for the few, Robin Hood for the many.'

42. c. 7000 BC Cheddar Man –
'almost certainly a Continental'.

43. Bishop Patricius (b. c. AD 372) – Roman-
British churchman, patron saint of Ireland

44. Alfred, King of Wessex (d. 899) –
'the hero of our race'.

45. Macbeth of Moray, King of Scots (r. 104
– 'very pleasant was the handsome you

46. Owain ap Gruffydd Glyn Dŵr
(c. 1359–1416) – the last Prince of Wales.

47. Margaret Tudor, Queen of Scotland,
1503–13 – 'a keystone marriage'

48. Thomas Cromwell, ideologue,
cuted 1540 – inventor of 'The Great Myth'.

49. Hugh O'Neill, Earl of Tyrone
(1540–1616) – the last native chief of Ulster.

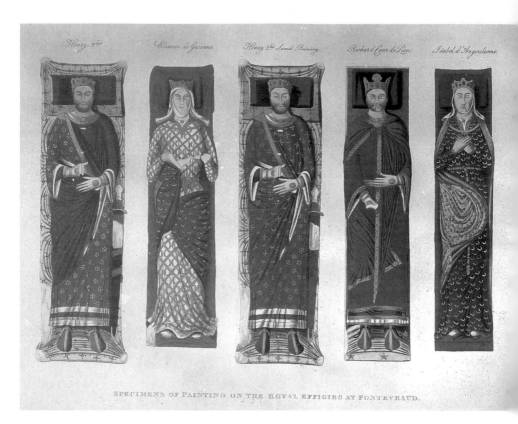

SPECIMENS OF PAINTING ON THE ROYAL EFFIGIES AT FONTEVRAUD.

Henry 2nd.   Eleanor de Guienne   Henry 2nd Second Painting.   Richard Cœur de Lion.   Isabel d'Angoulesme.

Alexander Rex Scotie   lewellin princeps wallie

50. *Above:* The Plantagenê
tombs at Fontevrault –
'French citizens who had
returned home.'

51. *Left:* Edouard I in
Parliament: flanked by
Alexander, King of Scotla[nd]
and Llywelyn, Prince of
Wales.

52. *Opposite, top:* Bravehe[art]
(1305) – 'Scots, wha hae
wi' Wallace bled.'

53. *Opposite, bottom:* Edou[ard]
I Plantagenêt pays homa[ge]
to the King of France (12[?])

54. *Above:* The Battle of Sluys (1340) – 'the fish could have learned French'.

55. *Right:* Henry V at Harfleur (1415) – 'Once more unto the breach, dear friends, once more.'

CHAPTER THREE

THE FRONTIER ISLES

43 to c. 410

*(The Senate and Roman people [dedicated this monument] to
Tiberius Claudius Caesar Augustus Germanicus, son of Drusus,
Pontifex Maximus, during his eleventh tenure of tribunician power,
Consul five times, hailed as Victorious Commander twenty-two times,
Censor, Father of the Fatherland, having caused eleven kings of the
Britons to surrender, having conquered them without loss, and having
first brought the barbarian tribes beyond Ocean under the authority
of the Roman people.)*

According to the Roman historian and satirist Suetonius, it was vanity
which drove Claudius into the campaign from which all the preceding
emperors since Caesar had refrained:

> Expeditionem unam omnino suscepit eamque modicam. Cum decretis
> sibi a senatu ornamentis triumphalibus leuiorem maiestati principali
> titulum arbitraretur uelletque iusti triumphi decus, unde adquireret
> Britannium potissimum elegit neque temptatam ulli post Diuum
> Iulium et tunc tumultuantem ob non redditos transfugas.[3]

> *(He undertook only one campaign, and a minor one at that. The
> Senate had already voted him the ornamental trappings of a triumph.
> But he rated such a [dubious] honour to be lèse-majesté, an insult to
> his imperial dignity, and he wanted the glory of a proper triumph.
> So, as the best place for realizing his wish, he chose Britain, which
> no one since the Divine Julius had tried to invade, and which
> happened to be in turmoil at the time over an issue of unreturned
> fugitives.)*

In other words, a local dispute with the tribes in Albion offered the
Emperor Claudius the chance of an easy conquest. And he took it.

Certainly, there was no compelling reason why in AD 43 Claudius
should have suddenly reversed the cautious policy of his predecessors.
Caesar had established a sort of informal protectorate over the more
important British tribes; tribute had been paid on and off; trade had
flourished. The Britons posed no danger to the Empire. As Cicero had
concluded on receiving a letter from his brother, who had accompanied
Caesar's second expedition, 'De Britannicis rebus,' he wrote, 'cognovi ex

tuis litteris nihil esse nec quod metuamus nec quod gaudeamus.'[4] (Concerning British affairs, I have realized from your letters that there is nothing there over which we should either tremble or rejoice.)

The geographer Strabo had expressed the clear view that invasion would be unwise. 'Local chieftains,' he said, 'have made virtually the whole island a Roman possession.' The costs of occupation would exceed the resultant revenues. So the matter was driven by the politics of Rome, and in particular by considerations of the Emperor's image.

Historians who refuse to accept that the Roman Empire was not following a grand strategic policy find arguments for rationalizing its conduct. The Emperor might be foolish, but the Empire had to be rational. They say, for example, that the growing unification of the British tribes under Cunobelin posed a potential threat to Rome; that the rising economic prosperity of Albion made it a plum ripe for the picking; that the Straits of Ocean was not a satisfactory frontier. These, they say, are 'the real reasons'.[5] But they are not reflected in the sources. What is more, the detailed examination of Roman frontier policy, in various parts of the Empire and at various periods, fails to reveal any consistent conduct. On the contrary, arbitrary moves were more common than calculated ones. The main rationale arose from the requirements of the Roman army, which needed to win land for its veterans, and to recoup the huge costs of its upkeep. The instinct of Roman generals was to march on to glory, and to think later. Most tellingly, they possessed little developed spatial sense and no sophisticated military intelligence. They had linear itineraries and probably some sort of maps of the territory inside the Empire that had been surveyed. But Caesar thought that Albion was triangular in shape, and knew nothing about its overall size. Even after Albion had been conquered, Tacitus thought Hibernia lay 'between Britain and Spain'. Both Caesar and Claudius sent large expeditions across Ocean without knowing in advance where exactly they would land. They must not be endowed with skills and knowledge that were not available at the time. The Roman frontier in the Isles, as elsewhere, was to be established by nothing better than trial and error.[6]

The invasion force of AD 43 was commanded by a 'distinguished senator', Aulus Plautius, at the head of four legions and their usual auxiliaries. In all, his troops must have numbered about fifty thousand men. Of the four legions, three were drafted from the imperial frontier on the Rhine, and one from Pannonia. The II Augusta came from Argentoratum, the XIV Gemina from Mogontiacum, the XX Valeria Victrix from Novaesium, and the IX Hispana from Pannonia. Together they sailed down the Rhine, picked up some auxiliaries in Batavia, and rounded the sea coast to northern Gaul. After crossing the Ocean Straits in three separate flotillas, they regrouped in Cantium not far from their landing ground, and marched north. They went completely unchallenged until they reached a major river crossing:

> The barbarians thought that the Romans would not be able to cross without a bridge, and bivouacked rather carelessly on the opposite bank. But [Plautius] sent over a detachment of Batavians, who were accustomed to swim easily in full armour across the most turbulent streams. These fell unexpectedly on the enemy, and . . . wounded the horses that drew their chariots. In the confusion, not even the enemy's mounted warriors could save themselves.[7]

From there, it was only one or two days' march to Lugh's Town and the Tamesis.

At which point Plautius set up camp, and sent for the Emperor in Rome. Claudius wanted to see the decisive battle in person. He sped in a fast ship from Ostia to Massilia, and thence over the roads of Gaul to Ocean. He stayed in Albion only sixteen days. But it was long enough for him to watch the legions of Plautius as they forced the Tamesis and captured the Britons' capital at Camulodunum. From there, he hurried back to Rome, where he persuaded the Senate to give him his triumph, build his arch, award his wife a front seat at the Circus, and call him 'Britannicus'.

Claudius' triumph was echoed by a large chorus of sycophants. A minor Roman poet dedicated some dubious lines of verse to the event:

> Distant Tiber used to bound your realms, Romulus;
> That was your boundary, religious Numa,
> And your power, Divine One, consecrated in your sky,

Stood on this side of farthest Ocean.
But now Ocean flows between twin worlds:
What once was a limit of the Empire is part of it.[8]

The citizens of Cyzicus, a Greek city in Asia Minor, hoping no doubt for imperial favour, built a copy of the Claudian Arch in their own forum. The Guild of Touring Athletes from Antioch in Syria wrote a letter of congratulations in Greek (now in the British Museum).

From then on, the conquest proceeded year in, year out, for more than forty years. It was ruthlessly pursued by all means available. One military campaign followed another. In the four remaining years of Plautius' governorship, the legions pushed forward to a line joining Isca in the south-west with Lindum Colonia in the north-east. Best known from this period are the exploits of the II Augusta, under the future emperor Vespasian, who captured the Isle of Vectis, stormed twenty Celtic hill forts including Mai Dun, harried the lands of the Dumnonii, and built the fort at Isca. At the same time, care was taken to make allies of those tribes, such as the Atrebati in the south, the Iceni in the east and the Brigantes in the north, who preferred to steer clear of the fighting. On the ideological front, temples were raised to the Olympian gods and the natives were invited to worship. In 60–61 and conclusively in 78–79 determined action was taken to break the power of the druids, by storming their most sacred groves on the island of Mona. Towns were founded, roads were built, country villas established.

British resistance centred on three successive leaders – two male and one female. Caradog (Caractacus), son of Cunobelin, who had faced the Emperor Claudius on the Tamesis in 43 and had seen his brother killed there, moved out westwards to the lands of the Silures. He was finally beaten, tracked down, and taken in chains to Rome in 51. Released by Claudius, he is said to have exclaimed, 'Why do you, who possess so many palaces, covet our poor tents?' Boudicca, or Boadicea, Queen of the Iceni, was the wife of a Roman ally. But after her husband's death she saw his kingdom plundered. She herself was arrested and flogged. Her daughters were raped. A huge temple to the deified Claudius was erected in the provincial forum at Camulodunum. It was, wrote Tacitus, 'a blatant stronghold of alien rule'. Roman tax-collectors were pitiless. The Procurator, Decianus Catus, was notoriously greedy. According to Tacitus, 'it was his rapacity which drove the province to war'. In contrast, Cartimandua, the 'Sleek Pony', Queen of the Brigantes, had handed the fugitive Caradog to the Romans. But her consort, known as Venutius, would have no truck with the invaders. He made his last stand at a great fort in the north in 71.

The abortive rising of the Iceni in the reign of Nero was probably the most crucial event of the whole conquest. It brought the new Roman province to the brink of collapse. It started in 60 or 61 when the tribesmen, provoked beyond endurance, swarmed into the cities of Camulodunum, Verulamium, and Londinium, burning and butchering everything in their path. Tacitus says seventy thousand people were killed indiscriminately, both Roman and British. The IX Legion, which stood in their path, was cut to pieces. In one account, the red-haired Boudicca, addressing her troops, poured contempt on the 'so-called conquerors'. 'They are', she said, '. . . men who bathe in warm water, eat artificial dainties, drink unmixed wine, anoint themselves with myrrh, sleep on soft couches with boys for bedfellows . . . and are slaves to an incompetent lyre-player.'[9]

The rising ended when the Governor, Suetonius Paulinus, rallied the remaining legions, defeated Boudicca's army, and sent his men on a rampage of even greater proportions than the original one. This time, the dead were counted at eighty thousand. Roman apologists write things like 'Suetonius had prevented Britain from falling back into its aboriginal barbarism.'[10] By their reckoning, massacres committed by barbarians are barbaric. Massacres committed by civilized people are part of the civilizing mission.

The most interesting, and best recorded, campaigns of the conquest were those of Julius Agricola, Governor of Britannia from 77/78 to 83/84. Born in Forum Julii in southern Gaul, he had been educated in Massilia, and had twice served as a soldier in Britannia. Vespasian made him Consul and then Governor of Britain. It was quite clear that Agricola intended to subdue all the Isles. In 78 he reduced the Ordovices, the last tribe still holding out in the western military zone. In 79 he moved out of Deva on the first of five campaigns against the Caledonians of the north

He sent ships to round the northern cape and to survey the coasts. And at Mons Graupius, somewhere in the farthest Highlands, he broke Caledonian resistance once and for all. He even wanted to cross to Éire, which he thought he could have subdued with just one legion. But then he was recalled. (We know all about him because Tacitus married his daughter.) The 'Long March' had ended, but at terrible cost. The verdict of Tacitus did not mince words. '*Auferre, trucidare, rapere*', he wrote bitterly, '*falsis nominibus imperium atque ubi solitudinem faciunt pacem apellant.*'[11] (Looting, killing and raping – by twisting their words they call it 'empire'; and wherever they have created a wilderness, they call it 'peace'.) The fate of northern Albion echoed that of Carthage and of many another territory 'liberated from barbarians' in the future. In the inimitable judgement of Edward Gibbon, 'After a war of about forty years, under-taken by the most stupid, maintained by the most dissolute and terminated by the most timid of all emperors, the greater part of the island submitted to the Roman yoke.'[12]

Of course, the yoke could never stay perfectly in place. The Lowland Zone had been effectively secured. But the Upland Zone remained unstable. The tribes of the north were licking their wounds; they had not been eliminated. And Éire remained free – a constant source of potential complications, a place of refuge for troublemakers, a permanent reminder that the old Celtic way of life was still in being. So the work of the legions in Britannia was never done.

In frontier provinces like Britannia, as in Rome itself, the horns of a permanent dilemma were painfully evident. To advance, to extend the Empire was the tradition of several centuries, rooted in the days of Coriolanus and the wars against the Volscians and the Samnites. It promised glory, loot, and revenues for paying more troops to march on to more glory, more loot, and more revenues. Yet it risked what a historian has recently called 'imperial overstretch', both at the local and the central level. To retrench by choice, therefore, to withdraw to more defensible lines and to consolidate previous gains, always carried the opposite attraction. In practice, periods of expansion alternated with periods of entrenchment.

There was also a definite correlation between the Roman army's activities in one sector of the Empire's frontiers and its posture in other sectors. It did not possess the resources to wage battle on all fronts simultaneously. The Claudian invasion of Britannia, for example, could only have taken place once the first phase of establishing the imperial *limes* (boundary) in Germany had been terminated. Similarly, Agricola's campaigns were timed to follow Vespasian's conquest of the Agri Decumates.* It was no accident that the subsequent thirty years' lull in Britannia coincided with the Emperor Trajan's long campaigns on the Middle Danube and the conquest of Dacia.

For historians of Britannia, the story of the Roman *limes* in Germany is particularly instructive. A long line of forts was built along the Lower Rhine at the end of Caesar's Gallic wars in 51 BC. An even longer system of roads and legionary camps followed the left bank of the Middle and Upper Rhine all the way to Brigantium and beyond. Yet Roman ambitions did not stop there. Early in the reign of Augustus, in 12 BC, Drusus Senior crossed the Rhine, and in three years subdued the tribes of Germania Magna all the way to the Elbe. It proved to be a step too far. By AD 9 the tribes had regrouped under a chieftain called Herman (Arminius), who laid an ambush. Falling on the three legions of Quinctilius Varus as they struggled to cross an upland pass in the Teutoburger Forest, Herman annihilated them, thereby achieving the most chilling defeat ever of Roman arms.[13] The Emperor Augustus sobbed incoherently: 'Give me back my legions.' He then sent Germanicus, son of Drusus, to restore order. Germanicus reorganized the defences on the Rhine in the last years of Augustus, and then, in the first three years of Tiberius, 14–17, magnificently emulated his father's march to the Elbe a quarter of a century earlier. Yet his success only aroused the emperor's envy. Tiberius swiftly packed him off to Syria where, allegedly, he was duly poisoned. The territorial gains in Germany were left wide open for more than fifty years. Only under Vespasian (r. 69–79) was the decision taken to secure the Agri Decumates, the wedge of territory configured by the elbow of the Rhine. Only under Vespasian's son, Domitian (r. 81–96)

---

* 'Tithe Lands', where Gauls were settled on terms requiring the payment of one tenth of their produce (a decimal) to the state.

was the main frontier line of the Limes of Upper Germania, established between the Main and Neckar. But even that was not enough. Fifty years after Domitian, Antoninus Pius pushed the German frontier line still further out, as he did in Britain, building yet another great line of forts and palisades stretching all the way from the Rhine to the Danube. It is a complicated tale. But one thing is certain: the *limes* advanced by fits and starts, in piecemeal fashion, just as, in due course, it would retreat.[14] (See map, page 104.)

The case of Dacia, another peripheral province, offers yet another variation. At the very time that Agricola was battling the Caledonians, a Dacian chieftain called Decebalus was causing such havoc on the Danube that the Emperor Domitian was obliged to buy him off and to pay him annual tribute. The Empire's humiliation lasted until Trajan set about ending it. As from 101 Trajan drove the Dacians back through their own lands – where, after five years' campaigning, he set up one of the Empire's fairest provinces (the future Transylvania). Decebalus killed himself. Trajan, having taken the name of Dacicus, awarded himself a triumph in Rome, laid on a festival of games lasting 123 days, and built himself a column. Dacia, one of the last provinces to be formed, would be the first to be abandoned.

The distribution of the Empire's legions gives some indication of the tensions in different sectors of the frontier. The four legions which were sent to Albion in 43 represented about 15 per cent of the Empire's total forces. The fact that they stayed there throughout the first century, guarding a relatively small frontier area, points to the Britannic province's vulnerability and perhaps to the stamina of British resistance. (See Table 3, overleaf.)

The elaborate precautions which the Roman Empire took to guard and define its frontiers reveal a characteristic psychological trait of the ancient world. Quite apart from the practicalities of frontier management, they underline the strong desire of the Romans to separate themselves from 'the barbarians'. The trait had been inherited from the Greeks, who had invented and developed the concept of 'barbarity' and who had passed it on with so much else to their Roman pupils. At one time, the barbarians had been no more than the label suggests, foreigners who spoke an

Table 3. The number of legions stationed in the Empire's European provinces[15]

	AD 24	AD 74	AD 150
Britannia	—	4	3
Iberia	3	1	1
Germania Inferior	4	4	2
Germania Superior	4	4	2
Pannonia	3	2	4
Moesia	2	4	5
Dalmatia	2	1	1
Dacia	—	—	2

unintelligible ba-ba or 'babble'. But in the hands of Greek writers of the Golden Age it had assumed a derogatory air, turning all non-Greeks or non-Romans not just into aliens but into primitive, savage, hostile, and unpleasant aliens. Indeed it tended to turn all foreigners into savages, even when, as with the Persians, they were highly civilized.[16] For the Greeks the key encounter lay in their early meeting with the Scythians on the Pontic steppes. For the Romans it lay in their experiences of the Celts. A perspicacious author has recently spelled out the momentous consequences:

> In this particular encounter [of the Greeks with the Scythians] began
> the idea of 'Europe' with all its arrogance, all its implications of
> superiority, all its assumptions of priority and antiquity, all its
> pretensions to a natural right to dominate.[17]

The Romans possessed that arrogance in full measure. Objectively speaking, the Greeks and the Romans could often be barbarous, just as the barbarians could in some ways be civilized.

The time for general retrenchment arrived at the end of Trajan's reign. For Trajan had not confined his expansions to Dacia. He had also added Armenia, Arabia, and Mesopotamia to the collection. Indeed, he had personally marched all the way to the Persian Gulf, whence he was returning when he died. He was no slouch. Yet while he was far away in the East the tribes in the West began to grow restless. In Britannia sometime in the period 115–20, the northern tribes came out of the hills and assaulted the Roman garrison. At one time, historians thought that the city of Eboracum had been sacked, and the IX Legion wiped out. The turmoil is now seen to have been less drastic. (Eboracum was not yet a city.) But the crisis was serious, and it was matched by similar turbulence on the German *limes* and in Dacia. When Trajan's death was announced, his successor, Hadrian, then at Antioch, must already have known that his task was to consolidate on all fronts.

P. Aelius Hadrianus (76–138), though a veteran of the Dacian wars, was more of a builder than a battler. Three times Consul, he had been Governor both of Pannonia and of Syria, where in August 117 he succeeded to the purple at the age of forty-one. He immediately abandoned Trajan's conquests beyond the Euphrates, turned the newly founded province of Armenia into a tributary kingdom, then set off to quell the uproar on the Danube. Between 120 and 131 he patiently toured every province of the Empire, pacifying, building, and legislating. He made extensive administrative and legal reforms, among other things codifying the Praetor's Edict. His favourite residence was in Athens, which he restored and adorned with many grandiose temples. In Rome, he built the Pantheon, the Temple of Venus, his own Mausoleum (the Castello San Angelo), and the famous villa at Tivoli. Unlike most emperors, who took vanity names to match their military triumphs, he chose to call himself Olympeius, the 'Olympian', in celebration of the Temple of Zeus, which he built in Athens.

Hadrian arrived in Britannia in the spring of 122 and stayed for the best part of a year. It was the second port of call on his 'world tour' after Gaul and the Rhine. He arrived in the company of the VI Vetera Victrix Legion, which he had brought with him to replace the unfortunate IX Hispana. A Roman historian recalled the event:

Adeptus imperium ad priscum se statim morem instituit et tenendae per orbem terrarum paci operan intendit. Nam deficientibus iis nationibus, quas Traianus subegerat, Mauri lacessebant, Sarmatae bellum inferebant, Britanni teneri sub Romana dicione non poterant, Aegyptus seditionibus urgebatur, Libya denique ac Palaestina rebelles animos efferebant . . .[18]

(Having taken over the Empire, [Hadrian] immediately reverted to the earlier policy [of Augustus], setting out to establish a worldwide peace. For of all the peoples whom Trajan had subjugated, the Moors were launching raids, the Sarmatians were waging war, the Britons could not be held under Roman control, Egypt was rocked by seditions, and both Libya and Palestine were rebellious.)

... Ergo conversis regio more militibus Britanniam, in qua multa correxit murumque per octoginta milia passuum primus duxit, qui barbaros Romanosque divideret.[19]

(Hence, having reformed the soldiery in regal manner, he travelled to Britannia. There he put a great many things in order, and was the first to build a wall eighty [Roman] miles long, which would divide the Romans from the barbarians.)

This is the one solitary mention of 'Hadrian's Wall' in ancient literature. It was constructed in the years following 122.

The emperor's visit inspired the minting of three commemorative coins. The first marked his arrival, the second the restoration of the army. The third, a bronze *sestertius*, displayed the seated figure of a personified Britannia and the slogan of BRITANNIA S.C. − 'Britannia, issued by decree of the Senate'.[20] When the Wall was completed, an imposing monument was set into it at a point near the eastern end. Two important fragments of the huge inscription have survived:

[DIVORUM] OMNIUM FIL[IUS]
IMP. CAESAR TRAIANUS] HADR[IANUS]
[AUGUSTUS IMPOSIT]A NECESSITAT[E IMPERII]
[INTRA FINES CONSER]VATI [DIV]INO PR[AECEPTO]
[. . . C]OS II[I . . .]
DIFFVSIS [BARBARIS ET]
PROVINC[IA RECIPERATA]
BRITANNIA AD[DIDIT LIMITEM INTER]
VTRVMQUE O[CEANI LITUS PER MP LXXX]
EXERCITUS PR[OVINCIAE OPUS VALLI FECIT]
SUB CUR[A A PLATORI NEPOTIS LEG AUG PR PR][21]

(Son of all the deified [emperors], HADR [IAN AUGUSTUS]
through the necessity of [keep]ing [the Empire within its limits that
had been laid upon him] by [div]ine co[mmand] ... thrice Consul
... having dispersed [the barbarians] [and] [recovered] the province
of Britannia, ad[ded] a frontier system between both [shores of] the
O[cean for 80 miles]. The army [of the] pr[ovince built the Wall]
under the direction [of Aulus Platorius Nepos, Pro-Praetorian legate
of the Emperor.])

From then on. the province of Britannia was well and truly established.

CALEDONIA, HIBERNIA AND ROMAN BRITANNIA

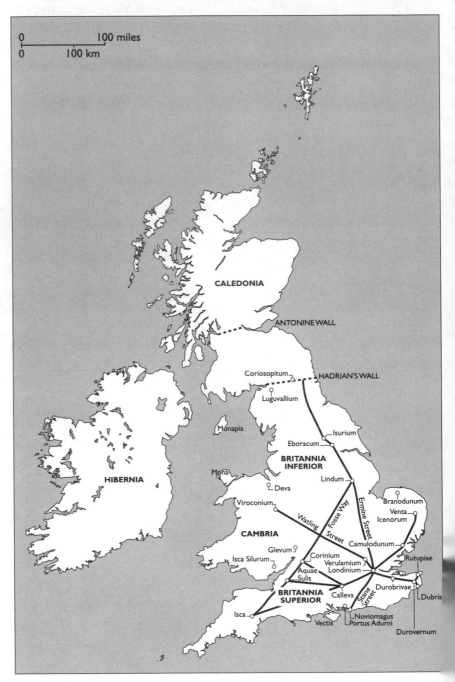

THE ESTABLISHMENT OF ROMAN BRITANNIA divided the Isles into two distinct areas – the occupied Roman one and the unoccupied non-Roman one. Each of these two areas can be divided in turn into various sub-zones. The Roman Province, for instance, consisted in the first place of a large lowland zone in the south and east, and in the second place of the two highland zones in the north and west. The lowland zone, which was gradually subjected to a thoroughgoing civil administration, was to receive the highest degree of Romanization; the highland zones, which largely remained in the hands of a military administration, were to receive a much lower degree. Similarly, the non-Roman parts consisted on the one hand of the free, northern half of Albion, and on the other hand of the island of Éire. The former, though outside the Empire, was seen by the Romans as a sphere of their influence and of occasional military operations. Éire was left inviolate. In short, *Britannia omnis divisa est in partes quattuor.* The Painted Isles were divided into four parts. Each part would develop in different ways; and the differences would strongly affect subsequent developments.

The main civilian part of the Roman Province, therefore, which bore the heaviest impact of imperial rule, accounted for little more than 30 per cent of the total territory of the Isles (c. 40,000 of 120,000 square miles). This should be borne in mind, seeing that 'Roman Britannia' is often presented as the only topic worthy of discussion. A large part of Britain was not Roman; and some important parts of the Isles were not even in Britain.

≈

The history of Celtic Éire is characterized by its remarkable continuity. Whilst Albion was completely reconstructed by the Roman conquest, her sister isle was left undisturbed. The High Kings ruled on at Tara. The druids officiated. The pagan rites were performed without interruption. The tribal wars and cattle-raids raged on unabated.

The High Kings of the late pagan era moved in a world where historical fact is still encrusted with legend and fantasy. Sceptical historians talk of 'pseudo-history', or even of the absence of history. Yet there are too many echoes of verifiable reality for them to be dismissed out of hand. Like King Arthur, their British counterpart of a later age, who is now accepted as a real personage (see page 194, below), the High Kings of Éire are more likely to be historical figures embellished by the bards than names plucked from pure fiction. And the nearer they come to a literate, better recorded age, the more convincing are the accounts of their deeds. In the late first century AD, for instance, there are echoes in the legends of a great popular rising that overturned the High King of the day. The rebels, known as the People of Aithech, have been variously linked with the Attacotti, who appear in Roman records, or as the under-race of Firbolgs, who had finally rebelled against their Milesian overlords. (They could be both.) In the second century, a central position is held by King Tuathal Techtmar 'the Legitimate' (r. c. 130–60). Tuathal either restored the High Kingship to Tara or, in some estimations, founded it. At all events, he established a long-lasting dynasty whose power-base lay in the central plain of Meath, and whose fortresses he successfully defended against all comers. He is also said to have imposed the *bóramha* or 'cattle-tribute' on the neighbouring kingdom of Leinster, which continued to pay it for the next eight hundred years. Tuathal's grandson and successor, Conn Cétchathach (d. 177), 'Conn of the Hundred Battles', is best known for his mythical exploits, though his wars with a great rival – Mog Nuadat, King of Munster – were probably real enough. The wars ended with the permanent division of Éire into two equal parts

– the Leth Cuinn or 'Conn's Half' in the north and the Leth Moga or 'Mog's Half' in the south.

In the third century it is Cormac Mac Airt (r. 254–77) who steals the centre stage. He was said to be the offspring of Art Aenfer 'the Solitary', who had secretly slept with a smith's daughter on the eve of his death in battle; and he was the father of the High King Muredach, who overran Ulster. But his main claim to fame came from being a brilliant patron of art and learning and lord of the Fenians. He was disfigured in a fight with the tribe of the Dési, who were thereby expelled to Dyfed in western Britannia. In the late fourth century one High King – Eochaid Muig Medon (r. 358–66), the 'Horse' – is said to have given his name to the English word 'jockey', whilst another – Níall Noígiallach or 'Níall of the Nine Hostages' (r. 379–405) – sent raiding parties into the faltering province of Roman Britain. This Níall was supposedly the progenitor of the famous clan O'Neill, which played a prominent part in Irish politics until the final 'Flight of the Earls' during the Elizabethan conquest. (See Chapter Seven.)

The Fianna or 'Fenians' were the archetypal company of Celtic knights, the prototype of Arthur and his Round Table. Whether or not they had been founded by King Fiachadh many centuries before is a matter for debate. But it was at the court of Cormac Mac Airt that they, and their fearless champion Finn MacCool, performed their celebrated acts of derring-do.

Finn MacCool – Fionn MacCumhaill – is the most renowned of all Irish heroes. He was the son of a druid's daughter, who had eloped with her lover-knight to escape her father's wrath and who bore the boy-child after the revenge killing of its father. Mother and son, Murna and Demna, were taken in by the kindly druid Finnegas, who educated the boy as his own and changed his name to Fionn. Once grown, Fionn embarked on a devil-may-care career of duelling, fighting, hunting, sorcery, love, and passion. In one episode he saved the life of Cormac Mac Airt, and was made the captain of the royal bodyguard. In another he wooed the Goddess

Sadb, who had been changed into a fawn and who reverted to womanhood for long enough to give birth to their son Oisín or Ossian ('Little Fawn'), the greatest of all the ancient Celtic bards. One version of Fionn's death tells how he is not really dead but sleeping in a mountain cave, awaiting the hour of his recall. This legend is remarkably similar to the much later Germanic legends about Frederick Barbarossa.

One of the best-loved stories brings together the 'three Finns' – Finn MacCool, Finegas, the kindly druid, and Fintan, the oldest inhabitant of Éire:

> Making his way to the River Boyne, Finn now headed for the home of Finnegas or Finn Eces, the druid. Finnegas had lived in this place for seven years, hoping to catch sight of the Salmon of Knowledge. For it had been prophesied that whoever ate the salmon would be blessed with boundless wisdom. This same prophecy also stated that the salmon would be eaten by one called Finn, and Finnegas had supposed that this referred to him. He had no suspicions, therefore, when a lad called Demna asked to be his pupil.
>
> Then, one day, the druid witnessed a sight that brought him great joy. There, by the river's edge, lay the fish he had been waiting for. It was much larger than a normal salmon and, on its shiny skin, all the colours of the rainbow seemed to dance and swirl. Taking it up, Finnegas carried the salmon back to his house and told his pupil to cook it
>
> Finn did as he was told, and soon the smell of cooked salmon wafted through the house. Finnegas sat at the table, and as the fish was brought to him, he asked the lad if he had tasted it. 'No,' Finn replied, but he hesitated . . . 'I have not eaten any part of it,' he continued, 'but as I was cooking the fish, I burnt my thumb on it, and sucked it to ease the pain.' The druid was perplexed. 'You say your name is Demna, yet according to the prophecy it must be Finn . . .'
>
> Then Finn told him about his nickname, and Finnegas understood it all. He bade the lad sit down and eat the salmon.

Finn did as he was told. By this means, he came to possess the power of divination that was in the Salmon of Knowledge.[22]

Oisín MacFinn (pronounced Osheen), or 'Ossian', was a warrior turned poet. He shared many of the adventures of the Fenians, but preferred to indulge his love of poetry and women. He refused to participate, for example, in the Fenians' vengeful pursuit of the eloped lovers Diarmaid and Gráinne, even though Gráinne had been Finn MacCool's betrothed. With his flaxen-haired wife Eobhir he was father to yet another famous warrior, Oscar. With Niamh, daughter of the Sea God, he sired Plur na mBan, 'The Flower of Women'. He lived with Niamh for three hundred years in her father's kingdom, 'The Land of Promise'. This was long enough for him to emerge and greet St Patrick.

The poems of Ossian, if known at all, are known only to the most advanced of advanced Celtic scholars. As the Revd James Macpherson (1736–96) might have said, they can't be reproduced here. For in the hands of Macpherson they were the object of one of history's most extraordinary literary scams, or as some would have it, 'creative transpositions'. In 1760 that obscure Scottish clergyman, posing as the translator of the still more obscure bard of pre-Christian Ireland, succeeded in persuading half the literati of all Europe that Ossian was a literary giant. Without actually producing the manuscripts, he claimed to be in possession of ancient Irish verses preserved in the farthest glens of the Scottish Highlands. Sceptics headed by Dr Johnson quickly shouted 'forgery', 'foul', and 'fabrication', complaining bitterly of 'sentimental cant' and 'old Irish manuscripts sullied with smoke and snuff'. But to no avail. An important cross-section of modern Europeans were ready to believe almost anything in their desire to recover the lost Celtic heritage. As Macpherson confided to the writer of his Preface, a Dr Blair, 'The public may depend on the following fragments as genuine remains of ancient Scottish poetry . . . The versification in the original is simple, and to such as understand the language, very smooth and beautiful . . . The translation is extremely literal':

My love is a son of the hill. He pursues the flying deer.
His gray dogs are panting around him; his bow-string sounds
                                                        in the wild.
Whether by the front of the rock or by the stream of the
                                                mountain thou liest;
Then the rushes are nodding with the wind, and the mist is
                                                flying over thee,
Let me approach my love unperceived, and see him from the
                                                        rock . . .[23]

One has to wonder what exactly these lines contain to have persuaded so many eager readers to judge them both genuine and genial.

Oscar, the 'Deer Lover', was the Fenians' last commander. He possessed a heart 'like a twisted horn sheathed in steel' and headed a battalion called 'The Terrible Broom', because they swept all opponents from the field. Their prowess aroused the wrath of the new High King, Cairbere MacCormac, who determined to curb his overmighty subjects. In the decisive battle, Oscar kills the High King in single combat, but is himself mortally wounded; and the Fenians are destroyed. Both Finn MacCool and Oisín leave the Otherworld to attend Oscar's funeral, where Oisín helps to carry his son's remains to the final consuming pyre.

The legendary elements of the Fenian Cycle are obviously legendary. But the historical setting is largely historical. It is firmly based in the Éire of the third century AD. This also happens to be the era to which the oldest surviving inscriptions in the Ogham alphabet can be dated. Ogham or Ogam may well have originated earlier, but it flourished in the three or four centuries which begin with the age of Cormac Mac Airt. It takes its name from its legendary inventor Ogma, son of the Dagda and God of Eloquence, who was recorded in Gaul as 'Ogmios' and whose tasks included that of conveying souls to the 'Otherworld'. It was used for funerary monuments, for marker stones, and for divination, but very definitely *not* for literary texts. It was most common in Munster,

Table 4. The Ogam alphabet

LETTER	TREE	BIRD	COLOUR	DATES
B	beithe *birch*	besan *pheasant*	White	24 Dec. – 20 Jan.
L	luis *rowan*	lacha *duck*	Light Grey	21 Jan. – 17 Feb.
N	nion *ash*	naoscach *snipe*	Transparent	18 Feb. – 18 Mar.
F	fearn *alder*	faoileán *gull*	Crimson	19 Mar. – 14 Apr.
S	saileach *willow*	seabhac *hawk*	Fire	15 Apr. – 12 May
H	(h)uath *hawthorn*	(h)adaig *night crow*	Earth	13 May – 9 Jun.
D	dair *oak*	dreoilin *wren*	Black	10 Jun. – 7 Jul.
T	tinne *holly*	truit *starling*	Grey	8 Jul. – 4 Aug.
C	coll *hazel*	corr *crane*	Brown	5 Aug. – 1 Sept.
M	muin *vine*	meantán *titmouse*	Motley	2 Sept. – 29 Sept.
G	gort *ivy*	géis *mute swan*	Blue	30 Sept. – 27 Oct.
Ng	(n)getal *broom*	(n)gé *goose*	Green	28 Oct. – 25 Nov.
R	ruis *elder*	rocnat *rook*	Blood-red	26 Nov. – 23 Dec.
A	ailme *pine*	airhircleog *lapwing*	Piebald	Winter Solstice, 1
O	onn *furze*	odoroscrach *cormorant*	Dun	Vernal Equinox
U	úr *heather*	uiseóg *skylark*	Resin	Summer Solstice
E	edad *poplar*	ela *whistling swan*	Red	Autumn Equinox
I	iúr *yew*	illait *eaglet*	White	Winter Solstice, 2

B = Birchday/Sunday; S = Willowday/Monday; T – Hollyday/Tuesday; N – Ashday/Wednesday; D = Oakday/Thursday; Q = Appleday/Friday; F= Allerday/Saturday[24]

especially in Kerry, though examples have also been found in various parts of Albion, notably in Dyfed, whence it was presumably taken by the migrating Dési. It used a system of notches that could be easily cut into wood or stone. It is sometimes known as the Beithe-Luis, after the initial letters. Every letter was associated with a tree, an animal or a bird, and with some sort of divinatory connotation. (See above.)

Relations between Éire and the Roman province of Britannia operated at many levels. The recent discovery of a large Roman fort on Éire's east coast spread panic among Celtic scholars when it briefly raised the prospect, if not of a Roman occupation, then at least of a Roman expedition. But it is now taken to be no more than a large trading post. In the religious sphere, the gradual spread of Christianity throughout the Roman Empire and beyond held momentous consequences for both islands (see below, pages 140–42). In the fourth century turbulence in Ulster, and the raiding parties of the High King Níall, prepared the way for Irish migration to northern Albion. This was the first step in the long process whereby the concept of a 'Land of the Scots' was to be moved wholesale from Éire to a new home across the sea.

The northern reaches of Albion, which Agricola had sought to conquer, were long left as an unstabilized and fluctuating frontier region. Hadrian's adopted son and successor, Antoninus Pius (r. 138–61), renewed the assault on the north, evacuated his father's Wall, and built another fortified line a hundred miles beyond it. This Antonine Wall was abandoned shortly after its founder's death; the legions returned to Hadrian's Wall, rebuilt it in stone, and held it thereafter as the formal limit of the province.

As a result of these fluctuations, three distinct northern frontier districts can be identified. The first, between the fully colonized sector of Britannia and Hadrian's Wall, was largely taken up by the lands of the Brigantes. Once conquered in the first century, it always remained formally a part of the province, sometimes known as Britannia Secunda. The second area, between the two great Walls, was twice overrun, by Agricola and by Antoninus Pius, and twice abandoned. It was the abode of the external tribes with whom the Romans had most frequent contact. The third area, to the north of the Antonine Wall, though the subject of two major Roman incursions, usually lay beyond the Empire's immediate reach (see map, page 118).

The Brigantes or 'Uplanders' of Britannia Secunda formed a tribal federation occupying a great swath of territory from coast to coast. They were watched on one side by the garrison of Hadrian's Wall, and from the south by the legionary camps at Deva and

Eboracum. Their tribal capital was located on the eastern side of the Pennine Hills at Isurium, which from the second century became the centre of a self-governing *civitas*. Some of the constituent tribes are known by their Latinized names – the Setantii, the Lopocares, the Gabrantovices, the Tectoverdi, and the Carvetii. The last one, 'the Deer People', lived in the extreme north-west corner of the province. By the third century they had established a separate *civitas* based at Luguvallium.[25]

Hadrian's Wall, which cut Albion into two almost equal parts, is the subject of many misunderstandings. Although its stone wall, towers, and vallum clearly possessed a defensive function, the primary intention was to lay out an unmistakable marker of the Empire's jurisdiction and to set up a system of transfrontier traffic control. No barbarians could stray into the Province by accident or unnoticed. If they presented themselves at the gates of the Wall, they would have to explain their purposes and to pay their dues. If they chose to swarm over the Wall in a concerted attack or to circumvent it by taking to their boats, they could be hunted down by the legions and annihilated. For this reason, the fortifications of the Wall extended from the very beginning to a long line of coastal towers and mileposts all along the adjacent western shore. And they were always supplemented by cavalry patrols which roamed far beyond the Wall to the north. The Romans were as alert to sea-borne intruders from Hibernia as to foot-slogging intruders from Caledonia.[26]

The *vici*, or urban settlements, which grew up beside the military installations have yielded the richest of archaeological harvests. They not only reflect the composition of the imperial garrison, which was drawn from units of the widest imaginable provenance, but also the interplay of everyday military and civilian life. At Vercovicium, a cliff-top fort on the central sector of the Wall, the luxurious quarters for a cohort of 1,000 men commanded panoramic views across the open landscape. Coriosopitum, a large supply centre set a couple of miles behind the Wall, has yielded many valuable finds to the archaeologists, though its buildings were vandalized in the late seventh century for the construction of St Wilfred's Abbey at nearby Hexham. At Cilurnum an opulent military bathhouse has been preserved. Vindolanda near Vercovicium offered up one of the rarest treasures – a collection of Roman letters written in ink on birchbark tablets.[27]

Nothing is more eloquent, however, than the inscriptions to be found on the Roman altars and tombstones left by those long-lost military garrisons. The career of a third-century fort commander called Silvanus Pantheus, for example, can be traced from the remnants of his tombstone erected by his wife at the fort of Bremenium:

>] COH ✶I✶ VARDVL | [　　　　] COH I AVG | LVSITANOR
> ITEM COH I | BREVCOR SVBCVR VIAE | FLAMINIAE ET ALIMENT |
> SVBCVRA OPERVM PVBL | IVLIA LVCILLA C F MARITO | B M VIXIT
> AN XLVIII | M VI D B XXV[28]

> (*To the Tribune of the First Cohort of Vardulli, sometime Prefect of the First Augustan Cohort of Lusitanians and of the First Cohort of Breuci, and sometime sub-curator both of the Via Flaminia and of Food and Public Works, the senatorial lady Iulia Lucilla [raised this monument] for a well-deserving husband who lived 48 years, 6 months and 25 days.*)

It is a nice thought that a senior military officer who died in Britannia had once served as the civilian administrator of the great road linking Britannia with Rome.

Most tombstones are far more modest. One from Magnis dedicated to the wife of a third-century soldier contains hints that she may have been a Christian:

> D ✶ M | AVR ✶ T F AIAE | D ✶ SALONAS | AVR ✶ MARCVS | 7 ✶
> OBSEQ ✶ CON | IVGI ✶ SANCTIS | SIMAE ✶ QVAE ✶ VI | XIT ✶
> ANNIS XXXIII | SINE VLLA MACULA

> D(IS) M(ANIBUS) AUR(ELIAE) T(ITI) F(ILIAE) AIAE, D(OMO)
> SALONAS, AUR(ELIUS) MARCVS C(ENTURIAE) OBSEQ(UENTIS),

CONIUGI SANCTISSIMAE QUAE VIXIT ANNIS XXXIII SINE ULLA
MACULA (POSUIT)[29]

(By the hands of Fate, Aurelius Marcus, Recorder of the Century, [set up this stone] to Aurelia Tita, daughter of Aia and a native of Salonas, his most holy spouse who lived without any stain for 33 years.)

Yet another stone, this time from Verteris, is inscribed in Greek, the language of the Eastern Empire. It carries the epitaph of a boy from Commagene in Syria, perhaps the son of a trader, and a poetic reference to 'The Land of the Cimmerians':

ΕΚΚΑΙΔΕΚΕΤΗ ΤΙC | ΙΑѠΝ ΤΥΜΒѠ CΚΕΦΘΕΝΤ |
ΥΠΟ ΜΟΙΡΗC * ΕΡΜΗ | ΚΟΜΜΑΓΗΝΟΝ ΕΠΟC |
ΦΡΑCΑΤѠ ΤΟΔ ΟΔΕΙΤΙC | ΧΑΙΡΕ CΥ ΠΑΙ ΠΑΡ
ΕΜΟΥ | ΚΗΝΠΕΡ ΘΝΗΤΟΝ ΒΙΟ | ΕΡΠΗC *
ѠΚΥΤΑΤ ΕΠ | ΤΗC ΓΑΡ ΜΕΡΟΠѠΝ ΕΠΙ |
ΚΙΜΜΕΡΙѠΝ ΓΗ * ΚΟΥ ΨΕΥ | CΕΙ Α [. . .] ΓΑΡ Ο
ΠΑΙC ΕΡΜΗC |

(Should any traveller chance to see sixteen-year-old Hermes of Kommagene, foredoomed by fate to the grave, let him speak as follows: 'My greetings to you, boy, fast though you pass(ed) your mortal life; for you flew to the land of the Cimmerians.' And you won't be wrong, for he was a good, chaste-living boy.)[30]

'The Land of the Cimmerians', described by Homer as 'shrouded in mist and cloud', was the last stop for Odysseus before his visit to the Underworld. But it may well be a suitable place of association for someone who died far from home in northern Britain.

Most typically, the briefest of inscriptions record the briefest of lives. One at Brocavum shows the picture of a standing boy in a cloak, and the Celtic name of his parents:

ANNAMORIS ★ PATER | ET RESSONA ★ MATER | F ★ C[31]

The bereaved family were clearly natives.

The area between the Hadrianic and the Antonine Walls was

sometimes known informally as Britannia Barbarica, a district briefly
included in the Province, but never really wrested from the natives.
It was home to four British tribes recorded both by Ptolemy and by
Tacitus – as the Damnonii on the banks of the Clota, the Novantae
in the west adjacent to Éire, the Selgovae in the centre, and the
Votadini on the east coast. The Selgovae, or 'Hunters', who were to
give their name to the Solway Firth, abandoned their hill-fort capital
after Agricola's campaigns. The Votadini, who also abandoned a
large number of hill forts, were the founders of Celtic Dunedin
(later Edinburgh). They were the precursors of the Brythonic-
speaking Gododdin who were to play a prominent role in early
medieval battles for 'the Borders'. (See Chapter Four.)

The Antonine Wall, only thirty-seven miles in length, occupied
the most effective line of defence, from sea to sea. Its stone base
was topped by a turf rampart, and could have been manned by half
the number of troops required by Hadrian's Wall. But it was in use
for barely twenty years. The Roman governors of the Province
presumably decided that the military advantages gained by a shorter
Wall were outweighed by the increased political burden of holding
down an extra complement of barbarians.[32]

In many ways, the military zone in the west closely resembled
the frontier regions of the north. Although a permanent part of the
province from the early decades, it was never effectively colonized
or Romanized. Known at one time as Britannia Prima, it was
controlled by the legionary bases at Isca Silurum and at Deva, and
by the forts on the island of Mona. Deva, in particular, was
constructed as a city of quasi-capital proportions. The Silures and
Ordovices had led the initial British resistance, and were not granted
the status of *civitates* until well into the second century. After that
the fertile southern vales supported towns and villas. Few roads or
towns were built in the interior, where mining proved to be the
Romans' main attraction. At Dolaucothi, for instance, an elaborate
complex of gold mines was worked by a huge workforce of servile
or local bonded labourers. Two large aqueducts brought millions of
gallons of water per day to the site for driving stone-crushers and

for washing the ore. The underground galleries were kept dry by the baling action of man-powered waterwheels (one of which survives in the National Museum of Wales). It may be no accident that an auxiliary unit stationed nearby came from Asturias in northern Iberia, the home of the Roman Empire's most extensive gold mines.[33] Overall, the British complexion of the population in the west remained intact. Indeed, it was probably changed less by Romanized Latins than by the influx of Q-Celts from Éire.

The land to the north of the Antonine Wall was known to the Romans as 'Caledonia', to the Celts of Éire and their kinsfolk as 'Alba', and to the local inhabitants as some unknown Pictish equivalent of Pictland. The confusions and theories generated by this nomenclature are endless, but largely unnecessary. The name of Caledonia, for example, is easily explained. The Caledonians were the first tribe to be encountered by the Romans when they crossed the River Clota; and the name for that one tribal locality was soon extended to all parts further north. (One sees the same mechanism at work in 'Siberia', which was the name of the first Tatar khanate encountered by the Russians on the far side of the Urals but was soon applied to all the lands between the Urals and the Pacific.) 'Alba' and 'Pict' are best explained by reference to the changes brought about by the creation of the Roman Province. Alba is obviously cognate with Albion. Prior to the Roman conquest it referred to the whole of the Great Isle (the modern Great Britain). After the conquest, when the southern half became Britannia, Alba remained in the usage of the Q-Celts as the name for the unoccupied northern half. It is still the standard term in modern Irish and modern Gaelic for the country which much later the English were due to rename Scotland.

As for the 'Picts', they, too, could derive their various appellations to the time before the conquest. Picti, or 'Painted People', is a nickname which the Romans awarded to all those islanders who were given to wearing tattoos and woad. It is the exact equivalent of the Celtic terms 'Pretani' and 'Quriteni', which those same inhabitants used to describe themselves and from which the name of 'British' derives. After the Romans overran a large slice of the 'Pretanic Isles', however, and after various other names were found for the peoples of Éire, the one remaining group of Picti was the one which lived to the north of the Antonine Wall. It is a matter of conjecture how long they continued to paint and tattoo themselves. At all events, 'Pictland', together with 'Alba' and 'Caledonia', are all appropriate synonyms in the Roman period for the country which was not yet Scotland.

The problem with the Pictish label, of course, is that it says absolutely nothing about the ethnic or linguistic associations of the people concerned. It does not necessarily imply that they were Celts, still less that they were Q-Celts or P-Celts. Modern Celtic scholars tend to argue in favour of the Picts belonging to one or other of the Celtic communities. Others argue against it, holding instead that the Picts were 'non-Celtic', or 'pre-Celtic'. Both arguments could be correct if the northern Picts were the last remnant of a pre-Celtic population which, like the rest of the islands, was gradually being Celtified. Place names starting with Pit-, such as Pitlochry, which are found at all ends of 'Pictland', are thought to be Pictish in origin. But Pit- has no obvious Celtic significance, and does not offer any overall solution.[34]

One recent theory holds that the Picts of Caledonia/Alba were descended from 'the Ancient Kindred' of northern Éire, that is from the pre-Celtic population of the Green Isle who had been driven across the sea from their homeland by the incoming Gaels. In this case, the Picts of Caledonia/Alba were composed of emigrant proto-Ulstermen, who would have moved into Caledonia in the middle of the first millennium BC.[35] Such ideas are non-disprovable. Yet one thing seems probable. In the era of Roman Britannia, Caledonia/Alba was inhabited by three separate, if overlapping, ethnic groups. The first, in the north, most commonly called Picts, were non-Celticized or lightly Celticized pre-Celtic tribes. The second, particularly in the south, were British P-Celts – the kinsfolk of border tribes like the Votadini and of the Romano-British. The third, in the west, were the forerunners of the Q-Celtic Scots from Éire, already drifting across the Celtic Sea into the Highlands and Islands. The picture is not so terribly complicated.

In so far as the Picts can ever be known without access to their undeciphered language, it is only through their material and their pictorial legacy. Here, many scholars have seized on the Pictish 'symbolic stones' as the most accessible key to the puzzle. Some two hundred carved megaliths and cave inscriptions have yielded a pool of remarkable graphic symbols which are usually divided into the categories of animal and abstract. They do not resemble any of the standard forms of Roman, Anglo-Saxon, or Irish art, although some similarity has been noticed with the creatures drawn in early medieval insular manuscripts. Celticists have tried to link the commonest animals such as the bull and the horse with Celtic nature cults, though the correlation is not close. Most of the inscriptions are dated between the fourth and the seventh centuries, though the symbolic forms may be older. Some of the most elaborately carved stones, which include crosses and biblical references such as Daniel and the Lions' Den, are evidently from the later Christian era. In most cases the craftsmanship, whether in shallow-relief or embossed style, is superb; and the artistic effect dramatic. The St Andrews Shrine, for instance, is a candidate for 'the finest Dark Age Sculpture north of the Alps'. The Glamis Manse Stone carries an intricately interlaced cross: a seal head and triple desk symbol: a centaur with axes, and a lion: two axemen in combat: two figures falling into a cauldron: a serpent, a fish, and a mirror symbol. The Aberlemno Slab carries the figures of long-beaked birds (as in the Lindisfarne Gospels), monsters, and a battle scene. Observers can only goggle and guess.[36]

The 'Civil Zone' of the Britannic Province comprised the whole lowland area from Ocean in the south to the confines of the Brigantes in the north. It was bounded in the east by the coast of the Mare Germanicum and the west by the line joining Deva and Isca. In the third century, it was split along the middle by a new administrative division which created two provinces from one – Britannia Superior or 'Upper Britain' governed from Londinium, and Britannia Inferior or 'Lower Britain' governed from Eboracum.

Civil Britannia – if one may adopt a convenient label – closely resembled the older Roman provinces in neighbouring Gaul. Indeed, it has been suggested that both Britannia and Gallia came to belong to a common Romano-Celtic culture that prevailed in all the north-western provinces of the Empire.[37] These were Celtic countries conquered by Rome, and subsequently colonized and Latinized by the conquerors. The resultant blend in the Civil Zone was as much Roman as Celtic, whereas in the military zones the Celtic invariably predominated over the Roman.

Of course, Civil Britannia can have been little more than a pale replica of Gallia. It was smaller, less populous, further from Rome, more exposed to the inroads of barbarians, and ultimately more dispensable. Even so it possessed all the essential attributes of imperial life – a large military garrison, a fine network of roads, several imposing cities and many towns, an orderly rural society dominated by agrarian villa-based estates, and a complex adminis-tration combining central control with wide-ranging local autonomy.

The Roman army's impact was ubiquitous, and by no means weaker in the civil as opposed to the military zones. The presence of four legions in one small province, together with their auxiliaries and logistical support, affected all aspects of provincial life. Military duties apart, it was the army which often built the roads and the cities, and which brought in the main influx of Latinizing elements from all over the Empire. Generally speaking, the policy of *divide et impera* determined that units of the Imperial army did not serve in the provinces where they were raised. As a result, Britannia was largely garrisoned by soldiers from abroad, whilst levies raised in Britannia were most usually sent to serve on the Rhine–Danube frontier. What is more, though the most senior officers might circulate between Rome and a number of provinces, the legions were strongly attached to their local bases. At the end of their service, legionary veterans could expect to receive a grant of land in the province. In this way, since all legionaries were required to read and speak Latin, the army became the major colonizing and Romanizing force.

As for units raised in the province, there is ample evidence of their activities in distant parts. Among the cavalry units, both the *ala Britannica* and the *ala I Brittonum* dated from the first century, and were sent to Pannonia. The former seems to have been raised from citizens of the province, and the latter from various Celtic 'Britons' in twelve known British infantry units who were not citizens. The *cohors I Brittonum Ulpia torquata civium Romanorum* distinguished itself in Trajan's Dacian wars. The *cohors I Cornoviorum* was raised from loyal men of the Cornovii tribe. The fleet of the province, the *Classis Britannica*, was largely manned by Germans and Mediterraneans, though there were some Gauls and Britons among the marines. The *Classis Germanica*, in contrast, contained many men from Britannia. Yet not all Britons served abroad. A second-century tombstone from the Antonine Wall marks the grave of a Brigantian, Nectovelianus son of Vindex, who had been serving in the Second Thracian Cohort.[38]

The Roman roads of the province radiated from the bridge built c. AD 50 over the Tamesis at Londinium. They formed the outline of a communications grid that survives to this day. The main Continental link road (the later Watling Street) came in from Durovernum, which was joined to the two Ocean terminals at Rutupiae and Dubris. It continued north-west out of Londinium to Verulamium and thence for a hundred and fifty miles or so to the legionary fortresses at Viroconium. The main road to the north (the later Ermine Street) headed first to Lindum Colonia and after that to Eboracum and the eastern end of the Wall. Shorter roads left Londinium north-eastwards for Camulodunum and Venta Icenorum and south-westwards (the later Stane Street) to the coast at Noviomagus. The principal western route stretched straight as a die from Londinium to Calleva. From there, three branches diverged – one

to Corinium, one to Abone and Aquae Sulis and one all the way
to Isca. Isca also provided the southern terminus of the main
transversal sal road (the later Fosse Way) which crossed the Midlands to Lindum. In all, more than three thousand miles of paved
carriageway served up to a hundred urban centres.[39]

The cities belonged to one of three grades. The top-ranking
colonia, like Lindum or Glevum, was legally constituted as a corporation of full Roman citizens. The *municipium* was a smaller town
with fewer autonomous powers. The *civitas* was the cantonal capital
of self-governing tribal areas. Small settlements with no independent
legal status were usually classed as *vici*.

Londinium, which only gained the rank of a *colonia* under
Hadrian, was an important commercial and communications centre
long before that. It stretched along the north bank of the Tamesis,
with its Trajanic military fort at one end and its Hadrianic forum at
the other. Its life centred on the riverfront and on the unending
traffic of the bridge. Destroyed by Boudicca in AD 61, it was rebuilt
in the time of Procurator Alpinus Classicianus, whose tombstone is
now in the London Museum. It was completely enclosed by a stone
wall in the third century (see Appendix 7).[40]

By far the finest surviving example of a Roman city, however, is
Calleva, the capital of the Atrebates, which was never reconstructed
in later times. Like all of its counterparts, it displayed local variations
on the standard Roman pattern. A planned grid of straight paved
streets crossing each other at right angles was surrounded by the
city walls in the shape of an irregular polygon. There were five
gates. The central Forum was lined on three sides by a covered
portico. The fourth side was occupied by the municipal meeting
hall, the Basilica. There was a large inn, a temple, and a sumptuous
public bathhouse. The other plots were taken up by small private
buildings, many of them shops and workshops over which the
proprietors lived. All the more substantial houses were built of stone
and possessed their own individual bath suites. The city amphithea-
tre lay outside the walls, close to the Eastgate. Total population did
not exceed five thousand.

The multiplication of cities attested to the proliferation of commerce. Roman Britannia was fully integrated into the imperial trade systems. Eager Roman merchants had always marched on the heels of the legions. Indeed they had clearly set foot in Britannia before Claudius did. A study of amphorae from a pre-Boudiccan site at Camulodunum shows that 60 per cent of the city's bottled imports came from Baetica in southern Iberia. Apart from wine, the prominent items were olive oil, *garum* (fish sauce), and *defrutum* (grape syrup), all essential elements for a Mediterranean palate. Wine came mainly from Campania, but also from Rhodos, Tarraca, and the northern Aegean. Analysis of pottery from a fourth-century site at Glevum reveals an even wider spectrum of provenance. In this case, the two leading suppliers were located in the Samian ware factories in southern Gaul and in Palestine, closely followed by Campania, Rhodos, and Central Gaul. By that time, Britannia was more than self-sufficient in its staple export commodity – wheat. When the Emperor Julian (r. 360–63) was facing a food crisis for the legions on the Rhine, he was able to ship in emergency supplies from Britannia.

The prosperity of Roman society depended to a large degree on the fruitful interplay between the urban centres and the surrounding countryside. All the cities were supplied by a ring of satellite villas. At least thirty have been discovered in the vicinity of Londinium, and many more must once have existed. By far the greatest density, however, was to be found in the south and east, where by the second century an affluent, Romanized, agrarian aristocracy was thriving, as Britannia became a substantial exporter of grain. Nonetheless, the grandest of the villas was built in the first century on the outskirts of Noviomagus on the shore of Ocean. Designed in the Mediterranean Roman courtyard style, this opulent rural palace belonged to an important Roman client-king, Cogidubnus, of the Regnenses and other tribes, who took over the site of a Claudian fort for his personal use. Its sumptuous layout included formal gardens irrigated by ceramic pipes, colonnades, bathhouses, a guest wing, a regal audience chamber, and a private port with access to the sea. By the fourth century, the most spectacular concentration of villas lay in the hills south and east of Glevum.

The Roman administration of Britannia evolved considerably over the four hundred years of its existence. Lessons were no doubt learned after the Boudiccan revolt which had been provoked, among other things, by the grandiose and arrogant transformation of the Trinovantian capital into a full-blown Roman *colonia*. After that, the Roman governors stepped more warily, and far-reaching autonomy was granted to the loyal tribes (*civitates*), each with its elected magistrates and its tribal capital. Within each of the smaller districts, or *pagi*, councils would manage their local affairs. At the end of the third century, the two provinces of Upper and Lower Britannia were increased to four – Britannia Prima, Britannia Secunda, Flavia Caesariensis, and Maxima Caesariensis. This was probably intended to reduce the power of each provincial governor. The Vicarius, or Governor-General, whose seat was in Londinium, reported to the Praetorian Prefect of the Gauls at Augusta Treverorum.

Extensive improvements had to be made to the coastal defences in the south-east. Pirates and sea-raiders had started to infiltrate from the far side of the Mare Germanicum. A line of forts and watch towers was built from Portus Adurni to Branodunum under the command of a Count of the Saxon Shore – the *comes litoris Saxonici per Britanniam*. As part of this defensive strategy, the Roman authorities in Britannia installed several groups of Germanic auxiliaries to strengthen the reserves of troops. These newcomers enjoyed the same status as the Franks who were being settled in that same era along the Rhine. They may be seen as the advance guard of the subsequent 'Anglo-Saxon' invaders.

The face-off between Romans and barbarians was incessant. The barbarians viewed the Empire with a mixture of admiration and resentment. Many of them sought permission to settle or to be hired as auxiliaries. Some of their most determined incursions were fired by the refusal of imperial governors either to meet their demands or to buy them off. Roman governors of frontier provinces saw constant vigilance as the price of civilization. In the two centuries following Hadrian and Antoninus Pius, no less than seven ruling Emperors visited Britannia to repel barbarian attacks. Two of them – Commodus in 185 and Constantine I in 315 – took the title of Britannicus to mark their success. Septimus Severus campaigned in Caledonia for five seasons. He died at Eboracum in 211. His sons, Geta and Caracalla, cut their losses and took the decision to pull back again to Hadrian's Wall. In 306, Constantine's father, Constantius, the western Augustus, also died in Eboracum, having earlier staged a triumph in Londinium. Constantine's son, Constans, came to Britannia in 342–3, the last emperor to do so.

Despite Rome's concern for its distant colony, there can be little doubt that the Roman lifestyle was only adopted by a minority of the total population. Archaeological excavations naturally focus on the towns, villas, and legionary forts, where evidence abounds of their wine-drinking, Latin-speaking, toga-wearing, and hypocaust-heated inhabitants. Yet the statistics argue against the Romanized strata being typical of overall society. Given an estimated population in the Province of two to three million, the urban dwellers living in a hundred or so very small towns would not have exceeded about two hundred thousand, or less than 10 per cent. This would scarcely have been doubled by the addition of the military garrison and their families, perhaps fifty to sixty thousand, and of the Romanized element living among the local labour force on some three thousand villa estates, perhaps another fifty to sixty thousand. In other words, it is hard to see how the Romano-British could have reached more than one-fifth, or at most one quarter of the whole. The proportions are quite different than in the Empire's Continental provinces. The Romans in Britannia were not only heavily outnumbered by the Britons among whom they lived. They must also have felt the presence of the free Celts and Caledonians beyond the Wall and across the Hibernian Sea. As the political stability of the Empire declined, they must have felt distinctly embattled. It is not without significance that the Roman cities in Britannia, unlike their early counterparts in Gaul, were walled.

One is tempted to expand on the fascinating details of life in

Roman Britain. It provides the subject of great scholarly expertise, of intensive research, and of widespread popular interest. On the other hand, one must constantly face the fact that it constitutes a passing phase in the history of the Isles and left precious little behind it. Unlike Roman Gaul, which represents one of the formative experiences in the emergence of modern France, Roman Britain left no lasting legacy of note. In the long run, since its achievements were to be almost completely erased by subsequent barbarians, it has less significance in the evolution of the Isles than what its historians are pleased to call 'the British Background'. The Roman 'foreground' proved a cul-de-sac. In the eyes of its detractors, Latin civilization proved to be a veneer, an implantation that did not take root. As the Professor of Archaeology at Oxford has dared to write: 'For nearly four hundred years, Britain was occupied and governed by an alien power. Yet, remarkably, the impact of that long period of rigid control was comparatively slight.'[41]

Britannia in 400 was a very different country from what it had been before the Claudian conquest. But most of the achievements were subsequently lost. It may not be too much of a *reductio* to state that the legacy of Roman Britain consisted of a few roads, a few ruins, a few genes, and – as the sole substantial item, not itself Roman in origin – Christianity.

From its beginnings in the Roman province of Judaea, the Christian religion spread to all the other provinces of the Empire. It was frowned on by the imperial authorities, and periodically persecuted due to the Christians' refusal to worship the deified emperors and the Romans' fear of secret societies. But it was not halted by persecution. Writing c. 200, one of the Fathers of the Church, Origen the Alexandrian, stated that the Faith had 'even reached Britain'. In 313, by the Edict of Milan, the Emperor Constantine raised it to be one of the tolerated cults, and in 391, Theodosius the Great finally and officially declared it to be the sole religion of the Empire. From being the persecuted, the Christians were tempted to become the persecutors.

Evidence for the Christian presence in Britannia is sparse but indisputable. Several accounts confirm the martyrdom at Verulamium of St Alban, a former Roman soldier who perished for sheltering a fugitive priest either in 209 or in 304. Archaeologists have identified the foundations of a dozen churches, most certainly at Camulodunum, Calleva, and Rutupiae, and a similar number of Christian tombs and cemeteries. Christian iconography such as the Chi-Ro symbol has been found on a variety of building materials, lead tanks, and portable hoard items. One of the largest villas, near Durobrivae in Cantium, possessed a Christian chapel whose walls were painted with Chi-Ro symbols and with figures at prayer.[42]

Everything points to the likelihood that the early Christian Church in Britannia was an outpost of the more senior Church in Gaul. In 314, five Britons attended the Gallic Council of Arles. Later in the fourth century, the veneration of St Martin of Tours appears to have spread widely. Two of the best-known products of Britannic Christianity, Pelagius the theologian (c. 350–425), known to his Continental friends as 'Brito', and Bishop Patricius (c. 372–460), spent decades of study at Gallic monasteries.

Given the catastrophe which would soon assail it at the hands of pagan invaders, the most important step of the Britannic Church was to spread its influence to places beyond the pagans' reach. In this, the lead was taken by St Ninia or Ninian (c. 360–432), the 'apostle of the Picts', who evangelized the district beyond Hadrian's Wall. His best-known foundation, a monastery of St Martin, called the *Candida Casa* or 'White House', lay in the lands of the Novantae. Ninian's successor, Abbot Caranoc, is credited by tradition with first taking the Christian Faith to Éire.

Bishop Patricius, whose baptismal name was Succatus, was the son of a well-established Britannic Christian family. His father, Calpornius, was a deacon, his grandfather, Potitus, a married priest. He lived in a town called Bannavem Taberniae, somewhere on the western coast, possibly to the north of Hadrian's Wall. A formative episode began sometime in the 380s when, as a boy, he was kidnapped by Hibernian pirates and carried off to eight years' slavery in Éire as the swineherd of King Milchu. When he finally escaped by ship back to Britannia, he promised to return and to convert his captors to Christianity. He fulfilled his vow many decades later. In the meantime, he travelled to Gaul, where he was received into the clergy by St Germanius of Auxerre, and studied at the monastery of St Honorat on the Île de Lerins. During his absence, the Roman administration of Britannia started to collapse.

The disorders evident in the second half of the fourth century were the culmination of a long process of political disintegration. The fate of Britannia could not be disentangled from the inexorable enfeeblement of the Western Empire. As barbarian attacks multiplied, the Roman army grew increasingly frustrated and politicized by the authorities' inability to take effective action. Already in the mid-third century, from 259 to 274, a separatist Gaulish Empire had seceded from Roman rule under the self-proclaimed Emperor Posthumus and had taken both Iberia and Britannia with it. Not long after, the commander of the *Classis Britannica*, M. Aurelius Carausius, awarded himself the purple, as did his short-lived assassin, Allectus. By 339, when the Emperor Constantine moved the imperial capital from Rome to Byzantium, he implicitly confirmed the priority that was to be given to the wealthier and less vulnerable provinces of the East. In 350, Magnentius, who usurped the throne of the Emperor Constans, led the Western Empire into war against Constantinople. His three-year rule ended in defeat and in the persecution of his supporters, especially in Britannia.

By then, the Empire's overstretched resources could no longer guarantee more than intermittent security. The troubles in Britannia coincided increasingly with barbarian incursions and military revolts. In 367, Picts, Scots, and Saxons all descended on Britannia in concert from north, west, and east. Count Theodosius restored order but then had to hurry off to deal with the crisis on the Rhine. In 378, the Ostrogoths and their allies gained a signal victory over the imperial legions at Adrianopolis, thereby launching the thirty-year Gothic rampage which, after the sack of Athens, eventually peaked with the sack of Rome itself. In 383–8 an army commander from Spain, Magnus Maximus, who had made his reputation fighting the Picts, exploited the reigning distractions to set himself up as Emperor, and for five years ruled the West from Augusta Treverorum. Magnus had married a British chieftain's daughter, Elen Lwddog, and appears in later Welsh lore as Macsen Wledig. According to the historian Ammianus Marcellinus, he took the Roman garrison troops from Britannia, and marched with a battle standard bearing a dragon on a purple field. Once again, however, the Empire was saved, and Magnus was put to death. But less than a decade later, in 396, Britannia was overrun by the barbarians in such numbers that a rescue expedition had to be mounted by Rome's own great semi-barbarian general, Flavius Stilicho. No sooner had Stilicho pacified the diocese, however, when he rushed off to fight the Visigoths in Italy, taking the garrison of Britannia with him. That was in 402. For the first time in 360 years, the province was virtually defenceless.

Four years later, the dam burst. In December 406 a vast horde of Vandals, Suevi, and Alans poured over the frozen Rhine into Gaul in an unstoppable flood, effectively cutting Britannia off from imperial assistance. A second Germanic horde of Burgundians was heading from the middle Rhine for the vicinity of Lugdunum, where they would create the first of the barbarian kingdoms within the Western Empire. In Britannia, no less than three imperial usurpers – Marcus, Gratian, and 'Constantine III' – appeared and disappeared in swift succession, thoroughly discrediting the administration that they sought to salvage. In 409, with the Saxons redoubling their raids, the Roman administrators appointed by Constantine III were expelled. In 410, the year when Rome was sacked by Alaric, the local Romano-British leaders were said to have appealed to the beleaguered Emperor Honorius. According to one source, an imperial rescript told them that they must look to their own defences. Even if the rescript was never sent, as some historians maintain, the situation was not changed. The Emperor Honorius had no intention of withdrawing the Empire's authority from Britannia. But equally he had no means of restoring it. For all practical purposes, imperial rule had come to an end. The Romano-British were on their own.

In retrospect, one can see that the Roman Empire had played as ephemeral a role in the history of the Isles as the Isles had played in the history of the Empire. After 410, the Roman Empire was to survive for 1,043 years more. The Isles had no further part in it.

MODERN ATTITUDES TO the era of 'the Frontier Isles' have never been uniform. But there has been a heavy preponderance of interest in Roman Britain as opposed to the non-Roman part of the story. Of course, the surviving Celts of the Isles have preserved a strong and special attachment to their own heritage. The Irish, in particular, are fiercely proud of the fact that Éire's youthful virginity was never embraced by a Roman occupation. Ever since the early Christian monks of the Celtic Church set themselves the task of recording and adapting the achievements of Celtic paganism, a long line of Celtic antiquaries and scholars have devoted themselves to the same task right to the present day. Yet to admire the ancient Celts and their ways could not fail to carry an element of protest against the reigning English and Christian Establishment; and there have always been signs of sneaking admiration for the British rebels like Boudicca and Caractacus. In the late twentieth century, Celtomania has become an essential part of New Age neo-paganism. But its strongest manifestations were felt in the era of Romanticism. No one gave more eloquent voice to them than the popular Irish poet, Thomas Moore (1779–1852):

> The harp that once through Tara's halls,
> The soul of music shed.
> Now hangs as mute on Tara's walls
> As if that soul were fled.
> So sleeps the pride of former days,
> So glory's thrill is o'er,
> And hearts that once beat high for praise
> Now feel that pulse no more!

No more to chiefs and ladies bright
The harp of Tara swells.
The chord, alone, that breaks at night
Its tale of ruin tells.
Thus Freedom now so seldom wakes,
The only throb she gives,
Is when some heart indignant breaks
To show that she still lives.[43]

In the two centuries since Moore wrote those lines, in a mood of near despair, the rising tides of indignation have risen ever higher; and the cause of Celtic Freedom has not died.

Such thoughts, however, are completely alien to most British people, and especially to the majority of the English majority. For the English have been taught for centuries that their civilization is superior to that of the Celts. As a result, the weight of popular admiration, and indeed a strong sense of identification has been attached to the Roman occupiers of Britain rather than to the native British. The reasons for this have been partly territorial, partly cultural, but mainly political.

For fundamental reasons of geography, the area of active Roman occupation was confined to the lowland territory which would later become England. The Roman presence is missing from Irish history, and is marginal to the history of Scotland and Wales. But it is evident on all sides in the towns and the countryside of England. Roman remains can be seen every day not only in the major centres such as London, York, or Canterbury but also in curious backwaters like Ribchester on the Ribble or Blackstone Edge. Old Roman pipes still bring water to the Roman Baths at Bath. All English children are schooled in the knowledge that they live in a land where once the Romans lived. So Roman Britain has been attached, quite inappropriately, to 'the English Heritage'. Many English people believe, quite falsely, that Hadrian's Wall has always marked the frontier between England and Scotland. (It doesn't today, and it never did in the past.) But that's beside the point. The English have decided that Hadrian's Wall is 'theirs'. Only a spoilsport would care to remind them that in Hadrian's time the ancestors of the English were still in Germany, or that the 'Scots' were still in Ireland, and that neither England nor Scotland yet existed.

Still more important is the realization that all those generations of British people (largely men), who were educated in the classics, were being taught to understand and to sympathize with the Greeks and the Romans. When thinking of the long confrontation between Celts and Romans, therefore they instinctively sided with the Romans. They would all have read Tacitus's warning: 'Remember, they are barbarians . . .' For the Romans were seen as the bearers of civilization and the ancient Britons as the uncivilized. The fact that the English of that era still lingered in the backwoods of Germany, in conditions considerably more barbaric than those prevailing among the Britons, was not allowed to spoil the equation.

All manner of pressure was brought to bear to ensure that British schoolboys empathized with Rome. From the sixteenth century to the mid-twentieth, every educated person was required to learn Latin. Caesar and Tacitus were among the very first authors which all those pupils were obliged to read. Yet no one taught them anything about the Celts, let alone a Celtic language. Even today, when the teaching of classics in the United Kingdom has sharply declined and Celtic studies receive a measure of official support, for every British schoolchild that learns even a little about the native Celtic heritage, there are a hundred that still learn about the heritage of Rome.

A whole literary genre was devoted to strengthening the bond of identity between modern Britons and Ancient Romans. Any number of books and poems have been written to invite the reader to stand in Roman shoes, to put oneself shoulder to shoulder with the legions in the eternal struggle of civilization against barbarity. The premier poet of the British Empire, for example, imagined the lot of the Roman centurion stationed on British soil:

Legate, I had the news last night – my cohort ordered home
By ship to Portus Itius and thence by road to Rome.
I've marched the companies aboard, the arms are stowed below:
Now let another take my sword. Command me not to go!

I've served in Britain forty years, from Vectis to the Wall.
I have none other home than this, nor any life at all.
Last night I did not understand, but, now the hour draws near
That calls me to my native land, I feel that land is here.

Here where men say my name was made, here where my work
                                                    was done;
Here where my dearest dead are laid – my wife – my wife and son;
Here where time, custom, grief and toil, age, memory, service, love.
Have rooted me in British soil. Ah, how can I remove?

. . .

Let me work here for Britain's sake – at any task you will –
A marsh to drain, a road to make or native troops to drill.
Some Western camp (I know the Pict) or granite Border keep,
Mid seas of heather derelict, where our old messmates sleep.

Legate, I come to you in tears – My cohort ordered home!
I've served in Britain forty years. What should I do in Rome?
Here is my heart, my soul, my mind – the only life I know.
I cannot leave it all behind. Command me not to go![44]

Historical novels were written to serve exactly the same purpose. One of the most exciting books of many a boyhood was called *With the Eagles*. It recounts the adventures of Mandorix, a plucky Gallic orphan, who starts as a servant boy in one of Caesar's legions and who ends as a centurion of the Praetorian Guard. It is a great read. But just in case the young reader misses it, the message is spelled out at the very beginning, as Mandorix recounts his family history:

My father was a Gaul by birth, of the great tribe of the Aedui, but seeing, as did some four-fifths of his people, that the future greatness of our nation lay not in resisting the Roman conquerors but in accepting their rule and learning from them the arts of war and peace, he early declared his loyalty to Rome.[45]

To side with Rome was wise and prudent. To side with the enemies and victims of Roman power was foolish.

It may be surprising that the British of a later age sympathized more with the pagan Roman Empire than with the Roman Christianity that the late Western Empire introduced. After all, the modern British were predominantly Christian until very recent times, and may have been expected to look back to the Romano-British Church as the foundation of their tradition. The fact is, they did not and they do not. There are probably very good reasons for this, not least the aversion of English Protestants to anything smacking of 'Roman' religion. But St Alban did not inspire a cult in his native Britain. Modern Celts pay due respect to the Romano-British Church as the springboard of Celtic Christianity. But the modern English have treated it with cool detachment. They acknowledge its existence, and are prepared to remember its martyrs and heroes as figures of minor, local significance. But they do not empathize with it in the way that many of them have empathized with Roman Britannia's pagan rulers and its emperor-worshipping soldiers.

At its root, therefore, this empathy for Rome was driven by the imperial imperative. The leading imperialists of the modern world saw common cause with the leading imperialists of the ancient world. The British in general, and the English in particular, saw themselves as an imperial race. They had an empire to run, and an imperial establishment to sustain. Educating young men in the traditions of the greatest Empire that had ever reached our shores was an excellent means to an end. British educators of the Victorian vintage made no bones about the values to be instilled. Active participation in the civilizing mission of a multinational empire was good. Resisting that mission was at best wildly romantic, and if truth were told, positively harmful. The Fellow of Magdalen College who was joined by Rudyard Kipling in producing that very popular *History of England* (1911) which included 'The Song of the Centurion' harboured no doubts. 'This book is written for all boys and girls', he stated in the Preface, 'who are interested in the story of Great Britain and its Empire.' And, then, in his reflections on the beneficial effects of Roman Britain, he concluded with a statement of regret:

> It was, however, a misfortune for Britain that Rome never conquered the whole island [sic]. The great warrior Agricola did penetrate far into Scotland but he could leave no trace of civilisation behind him, and Ireland he never touched at all. So Ireland never went to school, and has been a spoilt child ever since.[46]

And as for the British tribes whom the Romans conquered he had no time whatsoever. 'I will not even tell you,' he growled, 'the Latinized forms of their barbarous names.'[47] In other words, please remember the Romans and please forget the natives.

CHAPTER FOUR

THE GERMANICO-CELTIC ISLES

c. 410 to 800

THE MARE GERMANICUM OF HENGEST AND HORSA

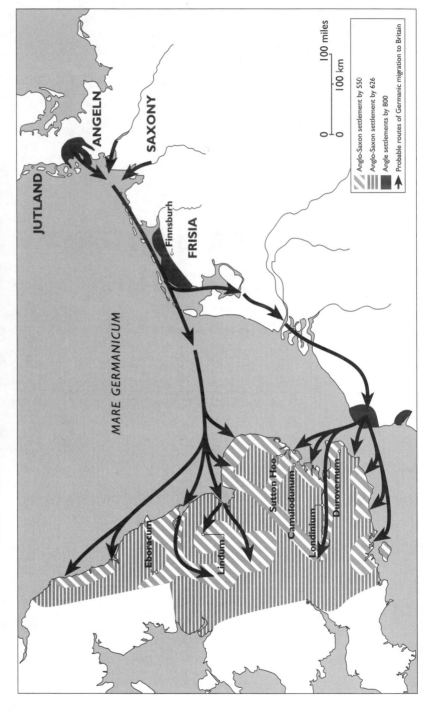

JUTLAND

ANGELN

SAXONY

Finnsburh

FRISIA

MARE GERMANICUM

Eboracum

Lindum

Sutton Hoo

Camulodunum

Londinium

Durovernum

Anglo-Saxon settlement by 550

Anglo-Saxon settlement by 626

Angle settlements by 800

Probable routes of Germanic migration to Britain

0   100 km

0   100 miles

FINNSBURH, FRISIA. Sometime in the second quarter of the fifth century, a fight took place in the royal hall of Finn, King of the Frisians. Finn was married to a Danish princess, Hildeburgh of the Scyldings; and Hildeburgh's brother, Hnæf, was staying with them together with his retinue of sixty warriors. Finn's guard, partly Frisians and partly Jutes, picked a quarrel with their 'half-Danish' guests, and one night they treacherously attacked them in the dark. Warned by the clink of armour, Hnæf quickly posted men by the doors of the hall, and managed to hold off the initial onslaught. The battle reportedly raged for five days. As the poet told it:

> Ne gefrægn ic næfre wurþlicor   æt were hilde
> sixtig sigebeorna   sēl gebæran,
> ne nēfre swānas hwītne medo   sēl forgyldan,
> ðonne Hnæfe guldan   his hægstcaldas.

> *(Never have sixty sword men in a set fight*
> *borne themselves more bravely; or better I have not heard of.*
> *Never was the bright mead better earned*
> *than that which Hnæf gave his guard of youth.)*[1]

But then the spears began to draw blood. Hnæf fell dead, as did the son of Finn and Hildeburgh. Both sides were so sorely depleted that none could continue the fight. At last, a truce was agreed between Finn and the Half-Danes' second-in command, Hengest.

The pact which ended the fight gave the Half-Danes equal standing with the Frisians' other guests. Finn swore on oath to honour the battle-survivors, and to give them accommodation alongside the Jutes. But he also insisted that if any complaint were voiced against the pact, the sword would again be unsheathed. Only then could they burn the dead on a common pyre:

> Āð wæs geæfned,   ond incgegold
> āhæfen of horde.   Here-Scyldinga
> betst beadorinca   wæs on bǣl gearu;
> æt þǣm āde wæs   ēþgesȳne
> swātfāh syrce,   swȳn ealgylden,
> eofer īrenheard,   æþeling manig
> wundum āwyrded   – sume on wæle crungon.
> Hēt ðā Hildeburh   æt Hnæfes āde
> hire selfre sunu   sweoloðe befæstan,
> bānfatu bærnan,   ond on bæl dōn
> ēame on eaxle.   Ides gnornode,
> geōmrode giddum;   gūðrinc āstāh;
> wand tō wolcnum   wælfȳra mǣst,
> hlynode for hlāwe.   Hafelan multon,
> bengeato burston   ðonne blōd ætspranc,
> lāðbite līces.   Līg ealle forswealg,
> gǣsta gīfrost,   þāra ðe þǣr gūð fornam
> bēga folces;   wæs hira blǣd scacen.

> (The pyre was erected, the ruddy gold
> brought from the hoard, and the best warrior
> of Scylding race was ready for the burning.
> Displayed on his pyre, plain to see,
> were the bloody mail-shirt, the boars on the helmets,
> iron-hard, gold-clad; and gallant men about him
> all marred by their wounds; mighty men had fallen there.
> Hildeburgh then ordered her own son
> to be given to the funeral pyre of Hnæf
> for the burning of his bones; bade him be laid
> at his uncle's side. She sang the dirges,
> bewailed her grief. The warrior soared:
> the greatest of corpse fires coiled to the sky,
> roared before the mounds. There were melting heads
> and bursting wounds, as the blood sprang out

from weapon-bitten bodies. Blazing fire,
most insatiable of spirits, swallowed the remains
of both nations. Their valour was no more.) [2]

Hengest, however, was sick at heart. By taking service with Finn, he was breaking the warrior's code of honour. It was improper to serve the slayer of one's own prince. After they had safely wintered at Finnsburh, therefore, one of his men pointedly laid a sword across his knees. He knew what had to be done. Hengest's followers fell on Finn, just as Finn's followers had fallen on Hnæf. Finn was killed with all his troop. His widow was captured, and carried off. His hall was ransacked, all its treasures and furnishings looted. The revenge of the Scyldings was complete:

> Hīe on sǣlāde
> drihtlice wīf   tō Denum feredon
> lǣddon tō lēodum.

> *(Journeying back, they returned to the Danes their*
> *true-born lady, and restored her to her people.)* [3]

For all who held the memory of Hengest in high regard, this was a rousing tale. Honour had been saved from the jaws of defeat.

There is every likelihood that the *Freswael*, the 'Fight at Finnsburh', actually took place. It is described in convincingly similar detail in two separate texts. One of them is no more than the copied fragment from a long-lost epic. The other forms a saga within a saga, a discrete episode within the much longer (and much later) epic poem of *Beowulf*. There, it is presented as an ancient tale told in the hall at Heorot on the island of Sjaelling about the heroes of the past:

> Songs were sung in Hrothgar's presence to the accompaniment of music. The harp was struck, and many ballads recited. Then, by way of entertainment, Hrothgar's poet sang in the hall of how Hnæf, the leader of a small Danish clan, fell by the hands of Finn's men in a Frisian quarrel . . . [4]

The peoples who composed these epics were Angles and they were recalling their long-lost homeland on the Continent. The 'Fight at

Finnsburh' has been called the 'Origin Myth of the Angles'. The reason why that particular adventure was remembered rather than countless others of the same sort was probably due to the presence of Hengest. For Hengest would be back. His decisive act of revenge had given him an international reputation.

In the early fifth century, Frisia or 'Friesland' stood at the crossroads of one of the busiest regions to be affected by the migrations of the Germanic peoples. Lying immediately to the east of the Rhine delta, on the very edge of the Roman Empire, it occupied the long windswept Continental coastland of the Mare Germanicum. Its outer coastline had been breached by the sea, and had been turned into a string of over twenty islands stretching all the way to the Cimbrian Peninsula. Its mainland shore was also subject to frequent flooding, being penetrated by several deep channels like the Middlemeer or the IJssel which one day would expand into the Zuider Zee. Its inhabitants, who had first arrived at the end of the Bronze Age, fought an endless war with the sea. They built their villages on low, artificial mounds called *terpen* standing six to ten feet above the flood-plain. They said, 'God created the sea, but we created the shore.' Like their neighbours on the Rhine, the Franks, the Saxons on the Elbe, and the Jutes and Angles on Jutland, they spoke one of a group of West Germanic dialects which had probably been mutually intelligible in early times and which together formed the most important corporate ancestor of Old English.

Finn's Fort was built on a typical mound beside the Middlemeer, at a site close to the modern town of Ljouvert (Leeuwarden). It would have been well supplied from the rich seaside pastures, and from local fishing in both salt and fresh water. But above all, it was a convenient stopping-place on the great maritime freeway, where boats could sail in relatively protected sea lanes between the islands and the mainland. It would be two or three centuries before the northern sea-rovers would develop the technique and the confidence to row and sail nonstop across the larger stretches of open sea. But the Frisian freeway provided the ideal route for every barbarian pirate and warrior-band who sought their fortunes in ever increasing numbers along the coasts of the crumbling Empire.

Those sea-rovers were drawn from all the peoples of the North. Finn's own guard was made up from Frisians and Jutes. Hnæf and Hengest were Danes in command of Half-Danes, obviously another mixed company. The Angles came from a district north of the River Eider, Angeln, which still bears their name, the Jutes from the area beyond them on the southern shores of the Skagerrak. The Danes in this period were concentrated in the more easterly islands of their present homeland, off the Baltic side of Jutland. Beowulf's people – the Geats – occupied the southern region of modern Sweden. The Swedes lived higher up still, looking across the eastern sea to the lands of the Finns and the Balts. The Saxons, who had easy access to the sea from the north German rivers, were perhaps the most numerous. Yet there must also have been sizeable contingents of fugitive slaves from Gaul and of former prisoners from all over the Empire. Frisia was both the meeting-place for all of them and the jumping off ground. It was in Frisia that the pirate captains filled their 'keels', sheltered from the winter storms, took on supplies, and laid their plans for the raiding season. From Frisia, they lay only a day or two's sail from the rich cities of northern Gaul or from the Saxon shore of Britannia.

The popular migrations which were triggered by the collapse of the Western Empire constituted one of the grandest spectacles and one of the key movements in the formation of Europe as we know it.[5] German historians once coined the term *Völkerwanderung*, the 'wandering of peoples'. This is a fine phrase so long as the wanderings were not confined to the Germanic tribes alone. For the Germanic tribes were being pushed from behind the scenes by nomadic Huns and Avars, as was the largest of all the European families, the Slavs. At the time when the *Freswael* was fought, the Visigoths, Vandals, Burgundians, and Franks were carving up Gaul. But the prime sensation arose from the long-feared arrival of the Huns. A passing reference in a later Anglo-Saxon poem, *Widsith*, 'Far Traveller', suggests that the Huns may have stirred up the Slavs in Eastern Europe much as they disturbed the neighbouring Germanic tribes.[6]

At all events, the Eastern Roman Empire was to face the *Völkerwanderung* of the Slavs in the sixth century, much as the Western Empire suffered from the Germanics in the fifth. The Western Slavs marched along the northern plain as far as the River Elbe and the Weser; and they appropriated the old Celtic country of Bohemia. In due course, the southern Slavs would cross the Danube, take over the greater part of the Balkan peninsula and wash against the very walls of Constantinople. Entirely new countries such as 'Bulgaria', 'Serbia', and 'Croatia' were created in this period by much the same sort of events that would also produce 'France' and 'England'.

Of course, the impact of these various invasions varied enormously. In southern Gaul, for example, the Visigoths left virtually no trace of their presence whatsoever. When they moved over the Pyrenees into Iberia, they soon became the dominant political force but were readily assimilated into the culture of the Latinized Celto-Iberians. Their experience was mirrored by that of the Franks, who replaced them in Gaul, and by the Ostrogoths and Lombards in northern Italy. Despite the Germanic conquests, the Spaniards, the French, and the Italians all emerged with their original Latinate languages and cultures essentially intact. Elsewhere, existing cultures were submerged. In Poland and Bohemia, the Slav migrants obliterated all traces of their predecessors. In the Roman provinces south of the Danube, too, whether Greek- or Latin-speaking, the Slavs established a dominant position, if not a monopoly. In the former Moesia, the Turkic-speaking Bulgars subdued the preceding wave of Slavonic migrants, only to be Slavicized in their turn. In Greece, the Slavs overran the whole of the Peloponnese, only to find themselves being Hellenized by the reassertion of Greek culture under Byzantine auspices. The ethnic, linguistic, and cultural mix, and the eventual products, were different in every case. All of which gives food for thought over the fate of Britannia.

The invasion of the Huns was exactly contemporary with the *Freswael*. Indeed, it is almost certain that the Huns and the Frisians would have come into contact. The Hunnic Chieftain, Attila, 'the Scourge of God', ruled the Hunnic horde from 434 to 453; and it was in those same two decades that he left a trail of destruction right across Western Europe.

For years, the Huns were content to raid the Empire, to sell themselves as mercenaries to all and sundry, and to extract large sums in protection money. But exactly in 450 – one of the key dates in the Hengest story – the Romans decided to fight Attila instead of paying him. One year later, the last great general of the Western Empire, Aetius, caught up with him on the Catalaunian Fields of north-eastern Gaul, and, overcoming conditions that favoured the Hunnic cavalry, repulsed their assault. Attila was still to devastate Italy, and to storm Rome – but soon he was dead, and his empire died with him. His base on the plains of the former Pannonia, which he had been turning into 'Hungary', was broken up by resentful Germanic tribes, who then used it as their own springboard into the south. 'Hungary' remained a disputed land until it was finally settled by yet another wave of migrant nomads, the Magyars, at the end of the ninth century.

The Legend of St Ursula provides one of the few echoes of the passage of the Huns in the age and the vicinity of the *Freswael*. Ursula was a Christian woman martyred with her companions in the city of Colonia (Cologne). The date of her martyrdom is unknown, but local tradition holds that it occurred at the hands of the Huns, who captured Cologne on their way to fight Aetius. The same tradition maintains that she and her eleven companions who grew in time to be her 'Eleven Thousand Virgins' – were exiles from Britannia. It is not impossible.[7]

Though the Huns dispersed, their assault left the Western Empire in its death throes. Aetius was soon assassinated by the jealous emperor whose realm he had just salvaged. After him, there was no Roman general to take command, and no emperors worth the name to give the orders. In 455 Rome was sacked once again by Vandals coming from North Africa; the rest of Italy was controlled by the sometime allies of Aetius, the Ostrogoths. For a time, the Ostrogothic chiefs observed the niceties of appointing titular emperors. The last time they did so, in 476, they chose a non-entity with the ironic name of Romulus Augustulus. Thereafter, they did not even bother to mask the fact that the Western Empire was dead. The only Roman emperor whom they recognized was the one in Constantinople.

Such was the setting for the further adventures of Hengest and for the ultimate fate of Britannia.

Once the Roman legions leave Britannia, historians have to rely on a new set of sources. Archaeological evidence apart, the description closest to the events of the fifth century is found in the writings of the British cleric Gildas (c. 475–550), especially in his *De Excidio Britanniae Liber Querulus*, 'A Polemical Book Concerning the Ruin of Britain'. Gildas's account, which serves as a historical preface to a tirade against the rulers of his own day, has often been discounted. His Celtic admirers gave him the epithet of *Sapiens*, 'The Wise Man'. But English commentators have often dismissed him as 'a prejudiced authority, as all national writers are'[8] (English writers by definition are not 'national'). After Gildas, there is an important *Kentish Chronicle*, which deals with events between 425 and 460, and the work of a chronographer who strove to sort out the confused dating of fifth-century events. Both of these texts originated in a period close to that of Gildas although they only survived in the middle of a much later compilation, heaped together by the Welshman Nennius as the so-called *Historia Brittonum*. There are the *Annales Cambriae*; and lastly, there is the 'Venerable Bede', whose *History of the English Church and People* (731) has often been given the stamp of superior reliability. In reality, however, Bede's comments on the fifth century are transcribed almost word for word from Gildas, and on the sixth century are virtually non-existent. Bede only comes into his own after the first event which really interests him, namely the landing of St Augustine of Canterbury in 597. 'Before 597, Bede is a secondary writer.'[9] In addition, there is a significant scatter of Continental and Irish records, and a body of royal genealogies which can be used to check the outline of events in disintegrating Britannia.

Precise dates from the fifth century are specially hard to come by. Gildas hardly bothered with them; Bede made several verifiable mistakes; and the editors of *The Anglo-Saxon Chronicle* working four hundred years after the events only added to the confusion. Modern archaeologists, taking Bede and *The Anglo-Saxon Chronicle* as gospel, established a dating scheme that stayed unquestioned for too long. The independent work of German colleagues using Continental comparisons has helped rectify matters. The traditional dates found in modern English textbooks have sometimes erred on the early side, sometimes on the late side. In practice, there is very little hard evidence for Germanic settlement prior to the second half of the century.

Nonetheless, if definitive dating is impossible, the main sequence of events can be established with some confidence. The scholar who did most to revise the traditional scheme identified three periods in the history of fifth-century Britannia. The first period, starting in 410, saw native rulers struggling, like their Roman predecessors, to stem the tide of barbarian attacks. The second period, starting about 442, saw twenty years of intense conflict between the British authorities and a group of barbarian mercenaries, who succeeded in turning themselves into permanent colonists. The third period, from the 460s to the 490s, saw a new generation of British leaders waging a long, stubborn and effective campaign of containment against the newcomers.[10]

The decades following the withdrawal of the legions from Britannia are called by some 'sub-Roman', by others 'the period of Celtic revival'. The former label stresses the elements of continuity in the life of Roman institutions and the Latin-speaking elite, the latter the reassertion of British Celtic culture and of non-Roman, tribal forces. Both labels can be justified. Indeed, it was probably the diverging interests of the various post-Roman interest groups which generated the fateful civil war.

Opinions vary with regard to economic conditions. Some historians follow the statement of Gildas, who reported that the prosperity of late Roman Britannia was not interrupted.[11] Certainly, there was no sudden end to the commercial activity of the main cities such as Augusta, which now reverted to its previous name of Londinium. On the other hand, the numismatic and archaeological evidence suggests radical deterioration. No new coins were minted after 410, and the decreasing circulation of only low-value bronze *sesterces* indicates a dwindling money economy. The abandonment of high-quality ceramic manufacture, one of the staples of

Roman trade, points in the same direction. A failing monetary system would inevitably have crippled centralized taxation, and with it the chances of raising and maintaining an effective defence force.

Fractures were also apparent in the religious sphere. The Roman state religion, Christianity, had been left with no state to enforce its orthodoxy and its legal monopoly. As shown by a near-contemporary *Vita*, St Germanus of Auxerre paid two visits to Britannia after 429, principally to combat the spread of the Pelagian heresy. He reported on the helplessness of the Britons in face of the raiding by Scots and Picts; and he may well have observed the revival of Celtic paganism.[12]

The course of political life in the headless province is exceedingly obscure, although several contending groups can be identified. Firstly, there were the *cives*, 'the citizens', the Romano-British elite living in their scattered and vulnerable cities and villas, especially in the south-east. Rural landowners, who either served as city magistrates or controlled them, would have predominated. Having relied for centuries on the legions, the undefended citizens must have been in desperate need of leadership and protection. Secondly, there were the Celtic *civitates* or self-governing districts and tribes of the north and west, many of whom would have retained much higher degrees of self-sufficiency, administrative autonomy, and military training. Thirdly, there were the remnants of the Army of the North, who would have been left behind under their traditional *dux* or 'commander' at Eboracum when the main legionary body marched off. Later genealogies suggest that the last Roman commander was a soldier whom the Welsh call Coel Hen and who has survived in the English nursery-rhyme as 'Old King Cole'. Such commanders, bereft of higher orders, would have quickly turned themselves into kinglets who founded some of the shadowy local dynasties of the later fifth and sixth centuries. By all appearances they held the line of the Wall intact, since it shows no signs of being stormed or suddenly evacuated. This means that the marauding Picts, of whom everyone complained, must have taken to their boats like the Saxons and penetrated the province along stretches of unprotected coastline. Lastly, there were the Germanic settlers of the Saxon Shore, whose shadowy presence is not well attested but may be reasonably surmised. Having formed round the nuclei of Roman-trained auxiliary units, their settlements would probably have been the best armed and the least involved in the initial power struggle.

Nothing certain can be gleaned about particular developments, but the reigning confusion can be well imagined. At first, the *cives* would have assumed responsibility for maintaining law and order. Yet except for the magistrates in quieter localities they can have had no effective means of enforcing their writ. Before long, therefore, they would have been seeking the protection of more powerful parties. Gildas says that they eventually appealed for help to Flavius Aetius in Gaul much as a previous generation had appealed to Stilicho. But Aetius was steeling himself to face the Huns, and could do nothing. (He may have had a hand in the second mission of Bishop St Germanus.) So the *cives* had to fall back for protection on their Celtic neighbours. The Celtic tribes and *civitates*, however, can hardly have been prepared for taking overall control. Rivalries and conflicts must have proliferated. Nennius writes of a war fought in the 430s between two warlords, one called Ambrosius Aurelianus 'whose ancestors wore the purple' and the other called Vitalinus. Memories of Ambrosius survived in Welsh lore under the name of Emrys. Vitalinus has been identified with the figure who came to dominate the scene for three or four decades and who appears repeatedly in a wider fan of sources as the Vawr-Tigherne, the Gwrthcyrn, the Vortigern, the 'Supreme Leader', the 'Overlord'.

Assessments of the Vortigern are far from unanimous. He probably hailed from the western colonia of Glevum. Gildas calls him a *tyrannus*, which probably means no more than absolute ruler, though he seems to have ruled in conjunction with some sort of provincial Council. Medieval Welsh genealogies mention him with pride as the progenitor of the dynasty of Powys. Modern detractors claim that he had reverted to paganism and practised polygamy. Modern Celtomanes can't decide. On one side, he is judged to have re-established the ancient Celtic practice of a High Kingship, putting Britannia on a par with Éire. On the other, he is regarded as the 'arch-traitor' and personification of folly.[13] For it was the Vortigern who called in Hengest.

The problem lay less in the civil war as such as in the combination of civil war with the uncontrollable Irish, Pictish, and Saxon raids which the war encouraged. The Vortigern could never cement his overlordship

while he was struggling to protect Britannia from the marauding bands.
As the *cives* put it in their appeal to Aetius, 'The barbarians drive us
into the sea, and the sea drives us back into the barbarians.' The Vortigern's solution was the oldest one in the Roman repertoire – to tame the
barbarians with the help of other barbarians.

It isn't known how the Vortigern's messengers contacted Hengest, nor
what Hengest had been doing in the years since the *Freswael*. One or two
hints suggest that his activities on the Continent had made him so
unwelcome that he was more than ready for an assignment in the Isles.
He was clearly an early form of contract-killer, a warrior whose sword
was up for sale. The Vortigern was hiring a small but highly professional
band of hardened mercenaries. Most sources agree that Hengest and his
brother Horsa landed from three 'keels' or warships on Thanet, the 'Bright
Island'. Bede calculated that they landed in 449, and almost everyone has
followed suit. In this particular, he was almost certainly wrong. The
chronographer in Nennius goes for 428, 'the fourth year of the Vortigern's
reign'. Nonetheless, the event itself can hardly be in doubt. *The Kentish
Chronicle* states:

> Then came three 'keels', driven into exile from Germany. In them
> were the brothers Horsa and Hengest . . . Vortigern welcomed them
> . . . and handed over to them the island that in their language is
> called Thanet, in ours Ruoihm.[14]

Gildas waxes more eloquent, boiling with indignation:

> All the members of the council, and the proud tyrant were struck
> blind . . . To hold back the northern peoples, they introduced into the
> island the vile unspeakable Saxons, hated of God and man alike . . .
> What raw hopeless stupidity! Of their own free will, they invited in
> under the same roof the enemy they feared worse than death . . .
>
> So the brood of cubs burst from the lair of the barbarian lioness
> in three 'keels', as they call warships in that language . . . Their
> dam, learning of the success of the first contingent, sent over a larger
> draft of satellite dogs . . . [They] were introduced in the guise of
> soldiers running great risk for their kind 'hosts' . . . They demanded

'supplies' which were granted, and which for a long time 'shut the dog's mouth'.[15]

Despite his angry rhetoric, Gildas used the correct late Roman vocabulary for hiring auxiliaries, where *hospites*, 'hosts', were required to offer *annona*, 'supplies'. Bede tried to place the event in a wider context:

> In the year of our Lord 449, Martian became emperor with Valentinian, the forty-sixth successor to Augustus, ruling for seven years. In his time, the Angles or Saxons came to Britain at the invitation of King Vortigern in three longships, and were granted lands in the eastern part of the island on condition that they protected the country; nevertheless, their real intention was to attack it.[16]

The Anglo-Saxon Chronicle expands on the mercenaries' origins:

> 449. In this year Mauricius and Valentinian obtained the kingdom and reigned seven years. In their days, Hengest and Horsa, invited by Vortigern, King of the Britons, came to Britain at a place which is called Ypwines fleot [Ebbsfleet] at first to help the Britons, but later they fought against them. They then sent to Angeln, ordered [them] to send more aid and to be told of the worthlessness of the Britons and of the excellence of the land. They then sent them more aid. These men came from three nations of Germany: from the Old Saxons, from the Angles, [and] from the Jutes.[17]

Analogies can be found to show that the Vortigern's deployment of mercenaries was not quite so stupid or outrageous as Gildas thought. One leading historian has argued, for instance, that Cunedda, a chief of the Votadini and the traditional protoplast of a dynasty that was to rule Gwynedd for eight centuries, was actually brought south by the Vortigern in order to deal with undesirable settlers from Éire who had been putting down roots in western Britannia. The Votadini were known in the Celtic form as the Gododdin. Their lands to the north of the Wall were being ravaged by the Picts; and it would have been quite consistent for their chiefs to seek better fortunes in the Vortigern's service. A document in Nennius provides the outline, although the date, once again, is dubious:

Cunedag, ancestor of Mailcunus [Maelgwn] came with his eight sons
from the north, from the district called Manan Guotodin, CXLVI
years before Mailcunus reigned, and expelled the Irish ... with
enormous slaughter, so that they never came back to live there
again.[18]

There are parallels between the story of Cunedda in Wales and that of
Mil and his eight sons in Ireland. It is conceivable that they are no more
than related myths. On the other hand, if Cunedda is accepted as a
historic personage, it is clear that the people of Hengest and Horsa held
no monopoly in mercenary service, migration, and massacre.

The figure of Hengest is beset with problems concerning his name,
his identity, and his ethnic origins. Hengest means 'Stallion', just as
'Horsa' means 'Horse'. These were not usual personal names. They may
just be nicknames, or emblems from the standards under which they
fought. They have a suitable piratical flavour. But equally, one must also
face the possibility that the two equine pirates and their famous 'three
keels' were figments of some ancient imagination. Horsa, in particular,
has come under the strong suspicion of being a purely mythical figure,
whilst the 'three keels' recur so often in Anglo-Saxon lore that they may
well be no more than a formulaic convention.[19]

Furthermore, there is no absolute proof that the Hengest who fought
at Finnsburh is the same Hengest who later sailed into Ebbsfleet. J. R. R.
Tolkien – beside whose bust these lines have been written – wrote the
authoritative paper on the subject, and admits that it would not have been
impossible to have two different warriors with the same exotic nickname
roaming the same seas at the same time. But the supposition is unlikely,
and has nothing to support it.[20]

Much ink has been wasted in attempts to connect Hengest and his
followers to one exclusive ethnic group. Bede started the goose chase
when he called them Jutes. Yet that attribution is unlikely, unless the first
fight of the *Freswael* was fought between Jute and Jute. If he was a
kinsman of Hnæf, he would have been a Dane – which he could well
have been. So one historian comes up with 'a Jutlander of the Danish
allegiance'.[21] But Frank Stenton thinks he was a Frank.[22] Yet he was first

observed in Frisia. So other historians argue that the Jutes most probably migrated via Frisia. Then why did he send for reinforcements to Angeln? And might he not have been a 'half-Saxon'? The answer has to be that all of these things are possible; but they don't really matter. One has no more reason to put an ethnic tab on Hengest's band of pirate-mercenaries than to imagine everyone in the Foreign Legion to be French. They were a band of sea-rovers from the Mare Germanicum, which in the fifth century facilitated links between Jutland, Frisia, and Francia and was awash with all sorts of Germanics. And that's enough.

The task assigned to Hengest's band in the former Britannia was to curb the Pictish raids. One might wonder how such a small force could have had much effect. But by all accounts, they performed well. The point about the Picts is that they, like the 'Scots', were what Gildas called *transmarini*. They were coming down the east coast in small boats and coracles, and evading the frontier defences. It may well have been Picts, and not Saxons, who demolished some of the isolated watchtowers on the Saxon Shore. And the point about Hengest's men is that they were not just professional warriors. They were seasoned sailors in seagoing warships. Their mission must surely have been to sweep the Pictish raiders from the sea, and then to destroy their bases, and to harry the interior of Pictland. If this were so, there are signs from gravesites that some of Hengest's men stayed on in the north. The city of Dumfries — 'Fort of the Frisians' — is thought to derive from that episode.[23]

Once the Pictish mission was completed, relations between the 'Stallion' and the 'Overlord' deteriorated. Hengest was bringing in reinforcements from the Continent who were not wanted and who couldn't be paid. The Council of Britannia thought that the mercenaries should withdraw. The mercenaries felt that more was to be gained by staying. The account in *The Kentish Chronicle* rings true:

> The King undertook to supply the Saxons with food and clothing without fail . . . But the barbarians multiplied their numbers, and the British could not feed them. When they demanded the promised food and clothing, the British said, 'We cannot feed and clothe you, for your numbers are grown. Go away, for we do not need your help.'[24]

The result was a long stand-off. It has been suggested that the Vortigern now drew much closer to Hengest, using the mercenaries to combat internal enemies. He may even have taken Hengest's daughter as one of his many wives, and have agreed to the import of still more reinforcements. In which case, this would also have been the best moment for Cantium to have been ceded to Hengest by treaty.

Yet the basic problem remained. The Vortigern's ability to pay was shrinking as fast as his political power. The moment came when Hengest decided to seize by force what he was no longer being freely given. His decision provoked a general barbarian rebellion, a great exodus, and after that a protracted war, which in a sense has never been properly concluded.

The barbarian rebellion, now thought to have started in the 440s rather than the 450s, has been traditionally portrayed as a vast overwhelming conflagration, as a result of which 'Britain passed into the power of the Saxons'. The chief culprit here is undoubtedly Gildas, whose purple passages teeter on the brink of distortion. Many of his reports of murder and mayhem, and of the flames of disorder 'blazing from sea to sea' can be justified by reference to isolated incidents. But as generalizations they were greatly exaggerated. They only hold good in those eastern localities, such as Caister-by-Norwich where the barbarian onslaught was particularly ruthless and effective:

> Swords flashed and flames crackled. Horrible it was to see the foundation towers and high walls thrown down bottom upward in the squares, mixing with holy altars and fragments of human bodies, as covered with a purple crust of clotted blood in some fantastic wine-press. There was no burial save in the ruins of the houses or in the bellies of the beasts and birds.[25]

Archaeological evidence paints a less drastic picture. It is simply not true that 'all the greater towns fell' or that 'all their inhabitants . . . were mown down together'. Londinium did not fall. Nor did Noviomagus. Major cities in the west, like Viconium, were untouched. Eboracum and Lindum, in the main line of attack, may possibly have been evacuated. If so, they were quickly reoccupied. At Verulamium, the citizens built a large grain-drying store — a sign that the surrounding countryside was no longer secure. Most surprisingly, Hengest's men do not seem to have broken out of their base on Thanet.

Several conclusions may be drawn. The main strength of the barbarians at this stage lay not with the mercenaries but with the Germanic colonists in their shoreline redoubts. The rebels may have been able to dominate the countryside and to raid far to the western sea. But they did not have the capacity for a general takeover. The damage which they inflicted destroyed the economy and the political order, but not the mass of the population. Even so, one act of treachery must have had shattering consequences. When the Vortigern invited Hengest to attend a conference with three hundred members of the British Council, Hengest told his men to conceal daggers in their shoes and then to murder the unarmed elders wholesale. The Vortigern alone was saved, a broken man. Henceforward, he fades from the record.

There were also reports of widespread flooding due to climatic deterioration and rising sea levels. The reports coincide with environmental evidence on the Continent. If the floods did indeed coincide with the rebellion or its aftermath, they would certainly have assisted the sea-rovers and the boatloads of Germanic colonists, who were penetrating the river valleys deep into the interior.

The 'Great Exodus', which followed the rebellion, is known from the well-recorded influx of British exiles into a northern Gaul still held by ex-Roman forces. It was significant for the sort of people who left. They would have been the surviving leaders and families of the Britannic elite. Twelve thousand exiles have been mentioned. They were settled in the districts on either side of the lower Seine where there are still clusters of villages all called Bretteville.

The campaign to punish Hengest was waged by the Vortigern's son, Vortimer. In the decade following the rebellion, both Celtic and Germanic sources mention three battles on the borders of Londinium and Cantium. Sites and sequences are disputed; but in one of the battles, at a ford called Riobogael, or 'Horseford', Hengest's brother was killed. At another, Vortimer himself fell, on the verge of victory. Overall, however, Hengest made good his claims. He was never driven out. On the contrary, he and his son Oisc or Æsc stayed on as the protoplasts of the Germanic dynasty which was to rule the land of 'Kent' throughout the sixth and seventh centuries.

The transformation of Christian Cantium into pagan Kent could not have taken place overnight. For several decades, the remnants of the Cantii lived alongside the ever-swelling communities of settlers, traditionally identified as Jutes. Within one or two generations the Celtic speech of the natives was drowned in the rising tide of Germanic dialects. The chief city, Durovernum ('the Fort by the Swamp'), became Cantwaraburg, 'the Fort of the Kentishmen'. The ports of Ripuarium and Dubris became Richborough and Dover. The population exchanged the name of Cantii for that of Kentings. The last of the Cantian kings gave way to the rule of the Oiscingas. The Church of St Martin in Canterbury was abandoned. The Roman arch at Richborough was left to collapse. Grass grew between the stones on the road to Ocean.

The last mention of Hengest is found in the entry in *The Anglo-Saxon Chronicle* for 473, when the old warrior was still seen battling it out with the natives. 'Here Hengest and Æsc fought against the Welsh and seized countless war-loot, and the Welsh fled from the English like fire.'[26] He probably lived on until the succession of Oisc ten years afterwards. The exact date of his death cannot be definitely calculated. But given that he had been fighting as a young man at Finnsburh in the 420s, it would probably have occurred well before the turn of the century. By that time, the Huns had come and gone; the Western Empire had disappeared; Rome was run by the Ostrogoths; Gaul was being turned into 'Francia' by the Franks; and Britannia had been shattered into many fragments. The Germanic bridgehead in Kent, together with its Anglian counterpart to the north of the Tamisa, would soon be joined by a Saxon bridgehead on the south coast, where the company of Ælle and his three sons, like Hengest and Horsa before them, would allegedly come ashore 'in three keels'.[27]

The fore-fathers of these assorted Germanic wanderers had been Continentals. Their descendants, like the British enemy among whom they had come to live, would be islanders. And in due course they would learn to call themselves Englisc, 'English'. The Celtic peoples of the Isles, both in Éire and in Britain, called all the newcomers without distinction Saxons. Modern commentators, too, do not usually bother to differentiate, calling

them either Anglo-Saxons or, more simply but anachronistically, English
— as if the English landed pre-mixed, pre-cooked, and pre-packaged. That
was not how it happened. So it is safer to call the newcomers by the only
label which fits them all — Germanics. In which case, through the long
centuries when those Germanics disputed the Isles with the native Celts,
it is not unreasonable to talk of 'the Germanico-Celtic Isles'.

THE GERMANICO–CELTIC ISLES

RHEGED – Celtic Kingdoms
ELMET – Germanic Kingdoms
Lincoln – Towns
Catterick – Battles

0 _____ 100 miles
0 _____ 100 km

PICTLAND

Nechtansmere
AD 685 ×
Dunkeld o

Iona o

DALRIADA

GODODDIN
BERNICIA
Degsastan ×
AD 603
STRATHCLYDE
NORTHUMBRIA

DÁL RÍATA
ULSTER
Bangor o
RHEGED

Catterick × DEIRA
AD 613

CONNAUGHT
ELMET

Tara o
MEATH
Clanmacnoise o
Kildare o
Chester Lincoln o
AD 615

LEINSTER
GWYNEDD
EAST
ANGLIA

Cashel o
MERCIA
Sutton Hoo o

MUNSTER
POWYS
Essex

Cork o
DYFED
Abingdon
GLYWYSING
London o

Dyrham
× AD 577
WESSEX
KENT
SUSSEX

Tintagel o
o Cadbury
Hill

DUMNONIA

IMPERIAL RULE REACHES its term in different places in different ways; and in this the Roman Empire was no exception. In Dacia, the Romans staged an orderly withdrawal: having held the province for only a hundred and sixty-nine years, they pulled out in 275, not only with the legions but also with that part of the civilian population which wanted to leave. They then created on the southern bank of the Danube the new province of Dacia Ripuarensis. In North Africa, they awaited the arrival of the Vandal horde which in 429 would take the province by force of arms. In Aquitaine, they bowed to the terms of an imperial treaty which in 425 opened the province to the rule and settlement of the Visigoths. In Britannia, none of these things happened. Britannia was neither evacuated, nor stormed, nor ceded by treaty. It was left to its own devices for a temporary period which, in the event, turned out to be permanent.

The era which begins with the Roman retreat was once called the Dark Ages. This term is no longer accepted by most historians because they dislike the derogatory overtones once applied to everything 'non-Roman', 'sub-Roman', or 'post-Roman'. They also reject the old idea that no valid historical sources exist and hence that the events of the period are lost in impenetrable obscurity. Even so, the scarcity of reliable information is undeniable. There is no period which contains more formative events in the history of the Isles but which is also the object both of wild speculation and of nationalistic theorizing.

The political void which was opened by the disorderly nature of the Roman retreat from Britannia was not filled for centuries. What is more, it seriously affected the relations between the former Britannia and all other parts of the Isles. In the short term, it set in motion a long chain of migrations and resettlements, not only by the likes of Hengest and Horsa but also by a rich assortment of other Germanic- and Celtic-speakers. In the long term it facilitated the complex mixing of peoples from which, towards the end of the millennium, there would emerge the basic fourfold division of the Isles into England, Ireland, Scotland, and Wales.

One of the commonest oversimplifications is to reduce the complex interplay of peoples to a straightforward confrontation between 'Celts and Saxons'. This pseudo-racial stereotype simply does not fit the facts, beloved though it may be both by the Celtophiles of recent times and by the older advocates of Anglo Saxon superiority. The fact is that Celts fought Celts over power and territory just as Germanics fought Germanics. In the shifting kaleidoscope of alliances, Celtic warlords could call in their Saxon counterparts for assistance as readily as, on other occasions, they engaged them in battle. Angles battled Saxons; and Saxons battled Saxons no less frequently than at a later stage they all waged war against the Danes. The idea that Celtic society was somehow noble and peace-loving whilst Germanic society was mean and murderous leads to nonsensical assertions about Celtic warriors being 'enthusiastic' and Saxon raiders 'genocidal'. Once the shield of Roman legions was withdrawn from Britannia, all parts of the Isles reverted to the state of incessant warfare which had often prevailed beyond the Empire and which would remain the normal order of things for centuries.

It is equally important to refrain from anachronistic nomenclature that ruins all attempts to reconstruct an accurate historical picture of the age. It is not just a linguistic point to insist that the English names from later times do not match an era when the earliest form of the English language was only just emerging. The countries of England, Scotland, and Wales did not exist in the fifth century. Their emergence provides the main theme of this period, and cannot be assumed to be the inevitable outcome. Even Ireland, which takes pride in having much longer traditions than other parts of the Isles, did not really match the insular concept which was to become its later trademark. For in the first half of the fifth century, 'the lands of the Irish' were well established on both sides of the 'Celtic Sea'. Indeed, it is quite possible to imagine a future in which the 'Irish' would have been the dominant element in both of the main islands. That this did not happen has less to do with the rise of the Germanic settlements in the east as with the unforeseeable concentration of British Celts in western Britannia and with the appearance of a completely new and separate kingdom of the Scots in the north. The latter, of course, was founded by people of Irish origin.

There is a special problem with the Germanic settlements in the former Britannia. Despite widespread agreement about the long process of state- and nation-building which starts with the landing of Hengest and Horsa, the prevailing nomenclature continues to talk about 'the coming of the English' and 'the English settlements'. Celtophile commentators similarly use the blanket term of Saxons, using an analogy with more modern terms of Saesnaeg and Sassenach, thereby giving another false impression of Germanic homogeneity. Surely, the whole point of the story is that a sense of Englishness, and at one stage further removed a kingdom of England, were the end-products of the process, not its motor or springboard. Neither Hengest nor any of his contemporaries were English, and no one ever uttered the name of England until at least three hundred years after Hengest's death. Throughout that very long span of time, other names and concepts were in use, and they are the ones which historians of the period should promote. Otherwise they will undermine the credibility of any lesser facts and figures which they unearth within the wider framework. For example, when Hengest's fellow pirate Ælle briefly claimed over-lordship over the other rulers of his day, he took the title of Bretwalda, that is 'Lord of Britain'. All Germanic rulers with the same pretensions used the same title for centuries. In other words, if anyone had asked them what exactly they were claiming to be overlords of, they would all have replied 'the former Roman province of Britannia'. For they were *not* lords of 'England', *not* lords of the whole island later called 'Great Britain', and *not* lords of all the Isles.

The Christianization of Éire neither started nor ended with St Patrick. It began in the fourth century, when contacts with Britannia had intensified, and it continued to the seventh century, when in the formal sense at least, it was completed. The first 'Bishop for the Irish', Palladius, was sent out in 431 by Pope Celestine, whom a contemporary chronicle reported 'to be labouring to keep the Roman island Catholic whilst also making the barbarian island Christian'. The names of a dozen other pre-Patrician saints and bishops are known. Their achievements, principally in the southern half of the island, were largely effaced by the all-embracing cult of St Patrick, which in medieval times would brook no rival.

Patricius, or St Patrick as he became, returned to Éire in inauspicious circumstances. Earlier missionaries had made little progress, and the Britannic Church was in no position to support him. The pagan order in Éire had not been seriously challenged. But Patrick believed in frontal assault. After setting up his first church in a barn in Ulster, and after converting Milchu's realm, where he had once lived, he made straight for Tara. Lighting the Paschal fire on the Hill of Slane in full view of Tara, where the Council of the High King Laoghaire was meeting, he dared the pagans to do their worst. The confrontation ended with King Laoghaire's baptism. After that the gates were opened. Seven years evangelizing in Connaught were followed by seven years in Munster. The supreme See of Armagh was founded in 445. According to legend, Patrick lived on in his barn-church at Saul on Strangford Loch until he died in 493 at the age of one hundred and twenty!

Legends are an unavoidable part of the story. One of them tell how Patrick cleared the island of snakes and demons. Another explains how his crozier was the Staff of Jesus, given to him as holy relic at Lerins. A third shows him expounding the doctrine of the Trinity to King Laoghaire with the aid of a three-leafed clover, the shamrock. Two of the writings attributed to St Patrick, however, are definitely judged historical. His *Confession* includes a long polemic with the Britannic Church. His *Epistle to Coroticus* berates a Christian tyrant for the sort of lawlessness which the pagans were wont to practise. Once thought to be the lord of Dumbarton, Coroticus was more likely a Roman Briton who had taken to piracy in Éire. His gang would seem to have attacked a group of Patrick's followers immediately after their baptism, to have killed the men and to have sold the women into slavery with the Picts:

> I Patrick, a sinner, very badly educated, declare myself to be a bishop in Ireland. I am quite certain that I have received from God that which I am. Consequently, I live among barbarian tribes as an exile and refugee for the love of God ...
>
> I have written and set down with my own hand these words to be solemnly given, carried and sent to the soldiers of Coroticus. I do not say 'To my fellow citizens' ... but 'To the fellow citizens of the devils', because of their wicked behaviour ...
>
> The day after the newly baptized, still bearing the chrism, still in their white dress ... had been ruthlessly massacred and slaughtered, I sent a letter by a holy presbyter ... along with clergy ... They laughed at them.
>
> I am the object of resentment ... I am greatly despised. Here were your sheep savaged ... by gangsters at the behest of Coroticus. One who betrays Christians into the hands of Scots and Picts is far from the love of God. Voracious wolves have swallowed up the flock of the Lord in Ireland which was increasing nicely through hard work ...
>
> It is the custom of the Roman Gauls who are Christians to send to the Franks ... and to ransom baptized people who are captured. You, on the contrary, murder them, and sell them to an outlandish people who know not God. You are virtually handing the members of Christ to a brothel ...

So I mourn for you, my dearest . . . But again I rejoice, for
those baptized believers have departed this world for Paradise
. . . The good will feast in confidence with Christ. They shall
judge nations and rule over wicked kings for ever and ever.
Amen.[28]

Given a fragmented tribal society, with numerous rival power
centres and few towns, the standard diocesan organization of the
Roman Church was slow to take root. Monasticism, in contrast,
took hold at an early date and in a form stressing the autonomy,
both spiritual and organizational, of individual houses. Abbots operating through *paruchiae* or 'monastic networks' have traditionally
been seen as wielding greater power than bishops in the early
centuries, though this view has been subject to recent questioning.
The greatest houses, founded at Kildare, Cork, Clonmacnoise, and
Iona, were major ecclesiastical centres, though numerous remote
hermitages came into being as well.[29]

It is also clear that Irish Christianity triumphed after making
numerous compromises, borrowings, and mergers with previous
religious practices. Some would say that Celtic paganism survived
hale and hearty underneath its Christian cloak. Numerous pagan
shrines were adapted for new purposes, and at all levels, from the
primatial see of Armagh to the ubiquitous local holy wells. The
widespread veneration of Brigid, the saint of Kildare, can only be
interpreted as the continuation under Christian sponsorship of the
cult of a well-known prehistoric goddess. The Celtic Cross, where
the symbol of Christianity is superimposed on the sunburst, is a
prime example of ideological fusion.

The most important side-product of Christianization was the rise
of a formidable literate elite and of the educational institutions to
support it. Christianity freed Éire from the age-old Celtic ban on
letters, releasing energies that bore fruit in every branch of secular
and religious life. The great monasteries promoted schools, libraries,
and book-factories. Their pupils, trained in both Irish and Latin,
made signal contributions not just to biblical studies and patristics

but also to Church and social law, to poetry, history, and literature of all sorts. They engineered an extraordinary fusion of late classical and traditional Celtic cultures. Their law codes, for instance, drew on both biblical and customary practices. Their retelling of ancient myths and legends interwove Christian and non-Christian themes. Most importantly perhaps, having taken in and preserved a huge draught of classical and Christian sources, they were able at a later stage to re-export their acquisitions to countries, like Britannia and Gaul, which had been overrun by the barbarians. The claim in a recent book – *How the Irish saved Civilisation* – is only a mild exaggeration of the truth.[30]

The early phases of Christianization in the fifth and sixth centuries are only known in the barest outline. But the productive phase, which began in the mid-seventh century, has left a wealth of texts of great variety. The text known as *De mirabilibus sacrae scripturae*, for instance, 'On the Wonders of Holy Scripture', which is dated to 655, shows that its compilers were fully familiar with all the Fathers and Doctors of the Church. The works of Adomnán (d. 704), ninth Abbot of Iona, reveal a churchman wielding great influence on either side of the Celtic Sea. In that same era, a group of ecclesiastical publicists at Armagh produced a stream of works establishing the primacy of St Patrick. In the legal sphere, the treatise named *Collectio canonum hibernensis* (early eighth century), which systematized many branches of Church and social law, was disseminated all over Western Europe. In the Gaelic literary sphere, few documents survive beyond the interlinear inscriptions of Latin texts; but it is clear that many of the components of the great mythical and literary cycles, not systematized until the eleventh century, were already being collected.

No name in this tradition is more revered than that of Colum Cille (Dove of the Church), otherwise St Columba (c. 521–97). Reputedly a descendant of the pagan High King Níall of the Nine Hostages, and certainly a member of the prominent clan Uí Néill (O'Neill), he was one of the many high-born ordinands who dominated the Irish Church. He had already founded two monasteries, at Derry and at

Durrow, before taking disciples with him into exile on the island of Iona. From Iona, he ministered to the kingdom of eastern Dál Riata and prepared the way for the conversion of Pictland.

Columba's contemporary, St Columbanus (c. 540–615), ventured further afield. A monk from Bangor in Ulster, he was already in middle age when he set off for the Continent with a band of companions, including St Gall. He established a string of monasteries centred on Luxeuil in the Vosges, where he issued a rigorous monastic rule, that for a time was a rival for that of St Benedict. Living in the age of Pope Gregory the Great, with whom he corresponded, and of Merovingian Gaul, the papacy's most loyal servant, he was one of the first to conceive of Europe as a civilizational unit centred on Rome. He died at his last foundation, the monastery at Bobbio in Lombardy – the greatest of the Irish *peregrini*.

Like everything else, the ancient institution of High Kingship was strongly affected by new Christian principles. Churchmen married old Celtic practices to the demands of the new religion. Adomnán writes of an early dynast and ancestor as 'ruler of the whole of Ireland ordained by God'. In practice, historians now argue, it is unlikely that any of the kings claiming overlordship were ever able to reduce all of their rivals to submission. Even the powerful Uí Néills, whose ancestral base lay in the north-east and who took the title of Kings of Tara, were incapable of making their claims stick. The real concentrations of power lay in the great regional kingships of Ulster, Munster, Leinster, and Connaught, whose dynasts had long been turning smaller local kinglets into a subservient nobility. Their internecine rivalries revolved round the control both of territory and of the rich Church foundations. In this regard, in addition to the Uí Néill, one would have to mention the Laigín and their descendants, the Uí Dúnlainge and the Uí Chennselaig of Leinster, the Uí Fiachrach and Uí Briúin (O'Brien) of Connaught, and the Eóganacht of Munster. Pan-Irish unity, like many of the details of the royal genealogies, was fictitious.[31]

Analysis of the law codes shows that early Irish society was rigidly hierarchical. Important legal distinctions divided the laity and the clergy, the lord and the commoner, the bond and the free. Christianity seems to have made little difference to the prevalence of slavery, polygamy, concubinage, and divorce. Contemporary knowledge of early Irish law is based on a sizeable body of surviving legal tracts from the seventh and eighth centuries. The tracts, sometimes written in prose sometimes in poetry, summarize laws regarding a great variety of topics, from the status of clergy, marriage, and kinship to hostages, hunting, dogs, and bee-keeping. The laws, often known as Brehon law from the Gaelic *breitheamh*, or 'judge', reflect an original fusion of common Celtic and Christian elements.[32]

In St Patrick's day, thanks to the open seas, the Irish world included several well-established outposts on the western shores of Britannia – in Dál Riata (Dalriada), in Man, in Dyfed and the Lleyn Peninsula, and even in the far south-west. Of those settlements, Dál Riata alone was destined to survive, though its Irish connection would eventually be severed. (See page 183, below.)

The Isle of Man is sometimes said to take its name from the Irish mythical hero Manannán mac Lir. That is less certain than the fact that the Irish came in sufficient numbers in the early Christian era not only to convert the inhabitants but also to dominate their language. The modern Manx language is one of the three branches of Q-Celtic Gaelic. Man in the seventh century features as the destination for expeditions of both Ulstermen and Northumbrians, although the extent of their political control over the island is unclear. The monastery of Maughold and numerous primitive hermitages date from that same period.

As a result of the numerous movements of peoples, the geographical configuration of 'Irishdom' was slow to take its final shape. The *Glossary* of Cormac of Cashel (d. 908) paints a vivid picture of its formal extent:

The power of the Irish over the Britons was great, and they had divided Britain between them into estates . . . and the Irish

lived as much east of the sea as they did [to the west], and
their dwellings and royal fortresses were made there. Hence is
Dirid Tradui . . . that is, the triple rampart of Crimthann, King
of Ireland and Britain as far as the . . . Channel. From this
division originated the fort of the sons of Liathan in the lands
of the Britons of Cornwall . . . And they were in that control
for a long time, even after the coming of St Patrick . . .[33]

These outposts were successively surrendered in the early Christian
era. In Dyfed, though the Irish dynasty of the Dési is thought to
have lasted until the tenth century, bilingualism seems to have died
out much earlier and the population thoroughly absorbed into the
emergent Welsh identity of the region. The name of Lleyn derives
from the Laigin of Leinster; that of Porth Dinllaen indicates 'the
harbour of the fort of the Leinstermen'. As Nennius records, they
came under attack from Cunedda, one of the earliest princes of
North Wales. In the south-west of Britain their fate is still less
certain, though there are many Irish echoes in the historical background to the legends of Tristan. Needless to say, it is only when
the Irish settlements in Britannia cease to function that one can start
to employ the modern insular concept of 'Ireland'.

The evolution of Caledonia/Alba, that is, the land to the north of
Hadrian's Wall, proceeded through the interaction of four distinct
peoples – the Picts, the British, the Irish, and the Angles. Contrary
to popular impressions, it is not a simple bipolar story of Picts and
Scots. The Picts, beyond the Clota, were one of the most mysterious
peoples in the Isles (see above). The British, converts of Ninian,
were alone to have embraced Christianity. The Irish were present
in the highlands and islands of the west, into which their kingdom
of Dál Riata had expanded. The Germanic Angles, the latest intruders, had penetrated the north-eastern segment of the former Britannia and were filtering up the east coast. In the early fifth century,
when Roman Britannia collapsed, these four peoples had nothing in

common. Four hundred years later, they were experiencing the first
stages of integration and were forging a unified kingdom with a
completely new identity. In order to trace the twists and turns, it is
necessary to keep an eye on the two most dynamic groups – the
Irish of Dalriada and the Angles of Northumbria.

To modern readers, the process whereby the kingdom of Dál
Riata appeared to migrate from north-east Éire to western Caledonia
may seem a little confusing. But it is perfectly comprehensible once
one accepts the sea to be a unifier and then observes the successive
steps taking place over a very long time. The original territorial base
of the kingdom lay in what later became County Antrim, in a district
where the Giant's Causeway points a path across the sea and where
on a fine evening the setting sun lights up the hills over the water.
In the first half of the first millennium Irish migrants crossed the
Northern Strait into lands previously inhabited by Picts; and they set
up a colony consisting of three settlements, on Islay, Lorn, and
Kintyre. They called it Ar-gael, or Argyll, literally 'the Eastern Irish'
For a period the two parts of the kingdom were ruled as one. But in
the late sixth century the Picts briefly recovered Argyll; and it was
from a Pictish king that St Columba received the island of Iona.
Shortly afterwards, the appearance of a vigorous King of Dál Riata,
Aidan mac Gabhráin (r. 574–608), upset not only the Picts, whose
possessions he ravaged as far afield as Orkney and Man, but also the
High King of Éire, whose overlordship he was flouting. At the
Convention of Drumccat (575), which St Columba attended, Aidan
agreed to pay the High King military tribute whilst reserving maritime tribute for himself. This appears to have been a wise choice,
since Dalriada's naval prowess enabled its kings to survive a series of
devastating defeats on land. In 603 Aidan's army was cut to pieces
by the Angles at the unidentified battlefield of Degsastan. Bede,
writing a century later, boasted that 'no Irish kin in Britain had dared
to wage war on the English since'. Then in 637, at the battle of Mag
Rath, the Uí Néill destroyed the forces of Aidan's grandson, Domnall
Brecc, effectively bringing his control of the Dalriadan homeland to
an end. After that, the Dalriadans had little choice but to fall back

on Argyll and to carve out a new power-base for themselves in
Caledonia. Such was their task in the seventh and eighth centuries.
Cultural and dynastic links were long maintained between western
Dál Riata and eastern Dalriada. But the former had been drawn
definitively into the Irish sphere, whilst the latter was becoming a
crucial force in the Caledonian/Alban sphere. The links were finally
cut by the naval power of the Vikings, who conquered the coastland
of Éire and sank the name of Dalriada for good.

A remarkable seventh-century document provides a unique
insight into the workings of the Dalriadan kingdom. The *Senchus fer
n'Alba*, 'Tradition of the Men of Alba', which survives in a tenth-
century copy, is a Gaelic forerunner of the English 'Domesday
Book', listing local land holdings and assessing their state tribute.
Though less elaborate than 'Domesday Book', it confirms that the
upkeep and manning of a naval force constituted the principal
obligation of Dalriada's subjects.

In order to follow subsequent developments, however, accurate
historical nomenclature, as always, is vital. The difference between
Dál Riata and Dalriada is merely one of Irish and non-Irish spelling.
It is more important to know that, whilst the Dalriadans at home
had called themselves Gaels, in Caledonia they were given the old
Roman label for all transmaritime Irish migrants, i.e., Scotti, or
Scots. This label stuck with them, and with all the lands they came
to govern or dominate. It is still in use today, more than a thousand
years after all current usage of Dalriada has stopped.

The Angles, who flooded into Britannia in the fifth century,
organized themselves in two main areas on either side 'of the River
Humber'. Their more northerly colony, Northumbria, was to play a
pivotal role not only in the affairs of the former Britannia but also
in the affairs of Caledonia. In the early centuries, Northumbrian
politics were dominated in turn by two rival dynasties – one based
in the more northerly kingdom of Bernicia with its capital of
Bamburgh, and the other in the kingdom of Deira with its capital at
Eboracum. Their rivalries continued without a break until the last
quarter of the seventh century, when the Deiran dynasty died out

in the male line and the Bernicians took over all the land from the Humber to the Forth.

The expansion of Northumbria largely took place at the expense of British tribes. It is well documented, partly because Bede, a Northumbrian, was an unashamed apologist. Like their kinsman of Deira, the Bernician kings claimed descent from Woden. Their first historical king was Ida the Flamebearer (r. 547–60), the builder of Bamburgh. Bernicia's principal opponents, the Novantiae and the Votadini, had both created tribal kingdoms, known respectively as Rheged and Gododdin. They have been saved from total obscurity by their Celtic bards. Taliesin of Rheged (sixth century) sang the deeds of the still earlier King Urien. Parts of his *Book of Taliesin* contain the first surviving fragments of Welsh literature:

> Uryen yr echwyd. haelaf dyn bedyd.
> lliaws a rodyd y dynyon eluyd.
> Mal y kynnullyd yt wesceryd.
> llawen beird bedyd tra vo dy uuchyd.
> ys mwy llewenyd gan clotuan clotryd.
> ys mwy gogonyant vot vryen ae plant.
> Ac ef yn arbennic yn oruchel wledic.
> yn dinas pellennic. yn keimyat kynteic.
> lloegrwys ac gwydant pan ymadrodant.

> (*Urien of Echwyd, most liberal of Christianmen*
> *Much do you give to men in this world*
> *As you gather, so you dispense*
> *Happy the Christian bards so long as you live. . . .*
> *Sovereign supreme ruler all highest*
> *The strangers' refuge strong champion in battle.*
> *This the English know when they tell tales.*
> *Death was theirs rage and grief are theirs*
> *Burnt are their homes bare are their bodies.*)[34]

Feeble English translations do not convey the declamatory power of the original, which has been described as 'the oldest living European literature'.[35]

Aneirin (turn of the seventh century) wrote an epic poem, *Y Gododdin*, about a catastrophic expedition against the Bernicians in which he had personally participated. He describes the attack on Catraeth (Catterick):

Gwŷr a aeth Gatraeth, oedd ffraeth eu llu,
Glasfedd eu hancwyn a gwenwyn fu,
Trychant trwy beiriant yn catáu,
A gwedi elwch tawelwch fu.
Cyd elwynt lannau i benydu,
Dadl ddiau angau i eu treiddu.

(Warriors went to Catraeth, their host was swift,
Fresh mead was their feast and it was bitter,
Three hundred fighting under command,
And after the cry of jubilation there was silence.
Though they went to churches to do penance,
The certain meeting with death came to them.)

Gwŷr a aeth Gatraeth, feddfaeth feddwn,
Ffyrf, ffrwythlon, oedd cam nas cymhwyllwn.
I am lafnawr coch, gorfawr gwrmwn,
Dwys, dengyn, ydd ymleddyn aergwn.

(Warriors went to Catraeth, a mead-nourished host,
Sturdy and vigorous, it would be wrong if I did not praise them.
Along with blood-red blades in great dark-blue sockets,
In close ranks, grimly, the war-hounds fought.)

Ar deulu Brynaich, baich barnaswn,
Eiliw dyn yn fyw nis adawswn.
Cyfaill a gollais, difflais oeddwn,
Rhugl yn ymwrthryn, rhyn ryadwn.
Ni mynnws gwrol gwaddol chwegrwn,
Maban i Gian o Faen Gwyngwn.

(Of the host of Bernicia – I should have considered it a burden –
No one in the shape of a man would I have spared.
A friend have I lost – I was faithful –

Swift in combat, it was hard for me to leave him.
The hero desired no father-in-law's dowry,
The young son of Cian from Maen Gwyngwn.)

Gwŷr a aeth Gatraeth gan wawr
Trafodynt eu hedd eu hofnawr,
Milcant a thrychant a ymdaflawdd.
Gwyarllyd gwynoddyd waywawr,
Ef gorsaf wriaf yng ngwriawr,
Rhag gosgordd Mynyddog Mwynfawr.

(Warriors went to Catraeth with the dawn,
Their fears departed from their dwelling-place,
A hundred thousand and three hundred charged against each other.
He stains spears with blood,
The most valiant resister in battle,
Before the retinue of Mynyddog Mwynfawr.) [36]

The battle occurred c. 600. Thereafter, the road to the north
from Northumbria lay open. In the 630s Edwin, King of Northumbria, occupied the capital of the Gododdin, Dunedin, which, as
Edinburgh, is often wrongly thought to have been named after its
Anglian conqueror. In that same century, both Rheged and the
Gododdin disappear from the record. The remnants of the Gododdin
are said to have migrated south to the Celtic bastion of western
Britain, leaving the south-eastern lowlands of Caledonia, later to be
known as 'the Borders', as an unchallenged bastion of Germanic
settlement.

In this region, a new Germanic language began to germinate. It
was related to, but distinct from, the other Germanic idioms further
south. To begin with, in an age when all those idioms were in a
state of competitive flux, the most northerly variant enjoyed no
special status. But just as one of the southern variants was destined
to be raised above the others through its association with a powerful
political community, so too, in time, was its northern counterpart.
Many centuries into the future it would become the language of
courts and kings. Its earliest known form has survived in the runic

inscriptions on an old seventh-century church cross near Dumfries, that quote fragments of a poem on *The Dream of the Rood*:

> ongeredae hinae god almehtig
> tha he walde on galgu gistiga
> medig fore alle menn
> ahof ic ricnae kyninge
> haefunes hlafard haelda ic ni dorstae

> *(Girded him then God Almighty*
> *before he stepped on the scaffold,*
> *made for all men.*
> *I held aloft the King of Heaven,*
> *Nor dared to bend.)*[37]

One effect of the Northumbrian advance was to split British territory in Caledonia into two. By the eighth century at the latest, the southern chunk that was soon to be called Cumbria, i.e., a second Cymru, was completely separated by Bernician territory from the British kingdom of Strathclyde, with its capital at Dumbarton. Another effect was to blur the ancient dividing line between Caledonia and Britannia. Five more centuries would pass before a new permanent border was established between Caledonia's successor and Britannia's successor.

Strathclyde's doughty monarchs, from St Patrick's correspondent, Ceredig, to Owain the Bald (d. 1018), had to defend their birthright against all comers. For long they held their own, scoring signal victories over the Dalriadans at Strathcarron in 642, and over the Picts at Mugdock near Glasgow in 750. But as from the late eighth century they were forced to submit successively to Northumbrian and to Pictish overlordship, and then to see their country increasingly invaded by Germanic, Anglian migrants. A major invasion of Germanic settlers took place after a joint Picto-Northumbrian campaign of 756. The P-Celtic (Welsh) language of Strathclyde came under threat from the spread both of the Gaelic and of Anglian Germanic. In the last period of its existence, therefore,

Strathclyde displayed rich cultural diversity, not least when Viking Norse was added to the mix.

The critical element in the eventual outcome, however, was always going to lie with the Picts – the people who controlled the largest expanse of land together with the unassailable mountain fastnesses beyond the reach of their enemies. Pictland stretched from the Outer Isles in the far north to the River Forth. It was defended by a formidable navy as well as by an army drawn from the bands of the numerous warlords, whose far-flung territories constituted the basis of their confederation. Its rulers, whose names are known from surviving king-lists, were not elevated by hereditary succession but by election from a pool of candidates including foreigners. Despite continuous wars with Dalriada, Strathclyde, and Northumbria, its southern frontier did not change significantly from the fifth to the ninth centuries. Indeed, the Picts were not really in danger from open battle. They twice overran Dalriada, and must have come close to extinguishing it. They eventually extended their hegemony over Strathclyde. Most importantly, at the Battle of the Dunnichen (Nechtansmere) on Tayside on 20 May 685, they so crushed the Northumbrians that Anglian expansion beyond the Forth was halted for good. As Bede did *not* say, 'No Anglian king in Britain has dared to wage war on the Picts since.' That battle had fundamental consequences. In effect, it ensured that the division between the Highlands and the Lowlands of Caledonia would coincide with ethnic and cultural divisions, thereby establishing one of the permanent features of the political landscape of the Isles.

The history of Pictland can only be pieced together from occasional glimpses. Bede observed that in his day the northern Picts were separated from the southern Picts. The first historical king, Bridei mac Maelcon (mid-sixth century), had a father with a British name and a stronghold in the Great Glen. At some point, however, a central royal establishment appeared in a region called Fortriu or Fortrenn. The royal hall at Forteviot was located on the banks of the River Earn. In the seventh century, part of southern Pictland was occupied by the Northumbrians until recovered by Brude mac

Bili (r. 672–93), the victor of Nechtansmere. This may explain Bede's observation. In the eighth century, one king, Necton mac Derelei (r. 706–39), overran Dalriada but failed to conquer Strathclyde. Collectively, the rulcs were known as the Kings of Fortrenn.[38]

In the event, therefore, the fate of Pictland was decided less by invading armies than by the spread of culture, and especially by the particular circumstances of Christianization. The adoption of the Christian religion in its Irish form went hand in hand with the adoption of the Gaelic language and of Gaelic customs. The resultant symbiosis of Pict and Scot in the north and west of Caledonia prepared the ground for the exchange of kings and for the painless unification of the two kingdoms.

Not that the religious story was uncomplicated. Though the role of St Columba was important, it was so inflated by his later cult that it is sometimes wrongly presented as a monopoly operation. Columba's ordination of Aidan Mac Gabhráin and his conversion of Dalriada obviously provided a stepping stone for subsequent developments. The *paruchia* of Iona, that is, the network of sister monasteries and ecclesiastical centres spawned by the Iona mission, proliferated to all points round the Celtic Sea. It provided a long-lasting bridge between the Churches in Éire and in Caledonia. On the other hand, despite his visit to Bridei mac Maelcon, there is no evidence that Columba ever attempted the conversion of the Picts. That task was first undertaken by the rival *paruchia* of another Irishman, St Donnán, who was martyred before the altar of his church on the island of Eigg in 617, but who left religious communities scattered all through the western Isles and all round the northern shores of Pictland. SS Congall of Bangor, Moluag of Lismore, Maelrubha of Applecross, and Brendan the Voyager were also active participants in the export of the Celtic Church to Caledonia. Nor can one overlook the continuing presence of St Ninian's mission among the Caledonian British. An invitation to revitalize that mission which was issued by the ruler of Strathclyde to St Kentigern (d. 617) created a further focus of activity. Kentigern, otherwise known as Mungo, is variously described as a native of Lothian, a Welshman and a Northumbrian once exiled to Wales. He was the founder of the church in Glasgow.

Seen overall, therefore, the evangelization of Caledonia was multi-positional not mono-directional. Given Aidan's mission to Northumbria (see below, page 201), Iona's share in the Caledonian process was arguably no greater than in the Anglian sphere. Indeed, a duality emerged in Pictland similar to that in Northumbria. One major religious centre, at Dunkeld, which was founded by missionaries from Iona, was an outpost of the Celtic Church. Another, at Kilrymont (St Andrews), refounded on the orders of King Oengus to accommodate a relic of St Andrew, was an outpost of the Roman Church. The full amalgamation of the Celtic, British, and Roman Churches in Caledonia was the work of long centuries.

By the early ninth century, the relationship of Dalriada to Pictland was characterized by an odd combination of political subservience and cultural ascendancy. The independence of Dalriada had been lost; but the expansion of Celtic Christianity, of the Gaelic language and of Irish settlement was gathering pace. The name of the district of Athfotla, or Atholl, literally 'New Ireland', which first appeared in the Pictish heartland in 739, may be taken as a sign either of migrating Scots or of expanding Gaelic or of both. What is more, the ruling house of Dalriada, though fragmented into competing septs and constrained by Pictish overlords, continued to involve itself in high Pictish politics. No less than three Dalriadan underkings, helped by the Pictish custom of marrying their daughters to prominent foreigners, found their way to supreme power in Pictland. The third of them, Cenedd or Kenneth Mac Alpin (r. 840–57), lord of Kintyre, not only succeeded in seizing control of Pictland but also in introducing a hereditary monarchy that would rule Picts and Scots in unison for the duration. To emphasize the permanence of his intentions, he is said to have brought the 'Stone of Destiny' from his western homeland and to have installed it for his inauguration in the church at Scone. A Gael of Irish origin with a British given name, he himself did not use the Scottish title officially. But henceforth the joint kingdom, forged by his dynasty, started to call itself Scotia, that is, 'Scotland'.

Further south, in the former Britannia, a similar patchwork of peoples and settlements came into being. In this case, the external migrants were coming exclusively from the East and were all, in one ilk or another, Germanic. The residents, with whom they came into contact, were all Celts of the British variety. Once the initial coastal settlements had been established – by Hengest in Kent, by the 'South Saxons' on the Channel coast, and by the Angles in three main groups on the east coast – the interior could be penetrated either by marching overland or by sailing up the rivers. The 'South Saxons', who had few major rivers at their disposal, went in for military conquest. The 'West Saxons', who had set up an early settlement at Abingdon, like the 'East Saxons' further downstream, had obviously reached their future homelands by sailing up the Thames. The Mercians, or 'marcher folk', found their way into the Midlands along the tributaries of the Humber and the Trent. The Northumbrian Angles, in addition to moving north, crossed the island from east to west by advancing up the Tyne valley.

One of the most persistent notions in the story, propagated by Bede and widely repeated thereafter, concerns the neat threefold division of the newcomers into 'Angles, Saxons, and Jutes'. The picture thus created suggests that each of these three groups – one from Angelus or Angeln, one from Saxony, and one from Jutland – settled down in Britannia in ready-made ethnic communities. Yet the picture does not fit the facts. For one thing, the number of known groups among the newcomers is nearer to six or seven than to three. For another, comparative archaeological study of the relevant Continental and insular homelands has not produced the right correlations. Fifth-century gravesites in supposedly 'Jutish' Kent do not match fifth-century graves in Jutland. So who were the Jutes? The best guess would seem to be that the communal labels known later on to Bede were adopted by groups of mixed origin *after* their arrival in Britannia, not before it. In which case, the labels would reflect sixth-century post-invasion identities not fifth-century pre-invasion identities.

The peculiar layout of the island played an important part in the way in which it would eventually be divided up. The scale of distances was such that no inland location lay further than one or at the most two days' march from the coast or from the leading riverheads. This gave a marked advantage to maritime invaders. Equally, the lie of the estuaries – notably of the Solway, the Dee, the Severn, the Thames, and the Humber – meant that each of the principal mountain fastnesses – in Cumbria, in the western peninsula, and in the south-west – could be safely blocked off and isolated by the invaders. It was no accident that at the end of the migratory period the residue of undefeated Celts should have been concentrated in these three mountainous localities. From the geopolitical point of view, the key to their fate would lie with the capture or loss of the cities and fortresses commanding these estuaries. Up to that point, the Celtic kingdoms such as Rheged in the north or Elmet in the east were not in serious danger.

The transformation of the chaotic patchwork of statelets into a map containing fewer but much larger and more integrated political and cultural units was the work of half a millennium. It was not a foregone conclusion. Through a thousand military conflicts, marriages, mergers, and mishaps, the teeming territories of the fifth century amalgamated in the course of two hundred years to form a dozen rival kingdoms. After two hundred years more, the kingdoms of the seventh century had been still further reduced, leaving two distinct zones – one predominantly Celtic, the other exclusively Germanic.

There are several ways of viewing this process. Most commonly, it is viewed from the Germanic perspective that was established by medieval chroniclers such as Henry of Huntingdon. According to this scheme, where only 'Anglo-Saxon' principalities count, the first stage sees the creation of a Heptarchy, i.e., seven major states, and the second stage sees the Heptarchy reduced to one. In Celtic eyes, in contrast, a shrinking Britannia sees its constituent parts chewed up and consumed by the voracious 'Saxon cancer' until only three heroic remnants survive – in Cumbria, Cymru, and Kerno. Needless to say, both these schemes are teleological and, as such, essentially unhistorical.

The concept of 'British Resistance' assumes that the Germanic advance was recognized at the time as an island-wide menace and that the British rulers were capable of a concerted response. Neither assumption is certain. There are many indications, of course, that the British did not submit without prolonged rearguard actions. The fifth- and sixth-century refortifications of West Country hill forts such as Cadbury Hill or Tintagel tell an unambiguous story. But it takes a quantitative leap of the imagination to say that the forts were the headquarters of a national Celtic campaign and of its champion, the shadowy 'King Arthur'. Historians mostly now agree that an Arthur-like British warlord really did exist and that Gildas's account of a famous British victory at 'Mons Badonicus' is basically trustworthy. What they can't say with any confidence is who Arthur was, where his political base was located, or in what circumstances the battle near the unidentified Mount Badon was fought. The traditional date for the battle is 500, at the start of a long period of respite for the contending parties. But whether Arthur was there, whether he was as Welsh tradition holds a local prince of Morgannwg or as medieval legend maintained an all-conquering overlord, are matters for speculation. Arthur's role in history is less important than his role in creative fiction. To call the entire post-Roman era 'The Age of Arthur' seems to be an unjustified conceit.[39]

Most modern accounts are spoiled by the fact that everyone knows what the final outcome will be. Little attention is paid to the climate of the extremely long period when the outcome hung in the balance. One hundred years after Hengest's landing, the Germanics had still reached neither the Severn nor the Dee nor the Solway. Turning points came in 577 after the Battle of Dyrham, when the men of Wessex captured Aquae Sulis and Glevum: in 600, after Catraeth, when the Gododdin were devastated: in 616 after the Battle of Chester, when the Britons of the west were cut off from their compatriots in the north, and in 682, when Cadwaladr, King of Gwynedd, was killed in distant Northumbria. Until then, an ultimate British victory was entirely possible. In the 580s, Urien of Rheged raided deep into the Midlands; Cadwaladr's father, Cadwallon, reached Lindisfarne in Northumbria, just as the Northumbrians had reached Angelsey. In the 630s, a Celto-Germanic alliance between Cadwallon and Penda, King of Mercia, looked set to create the dominant force. It was not to be. A medieval scribe, adding a gloss in the margin of the *Annales Cambriae* under 682, wrote 'And from that time onwards the Britons lost the crown of the kingdom and the Saxons won it.'[40] No such crown existed. But it's clear what he meant.

Nonetheless, even if teleology is out of order, the end result of the struggles is not without interest. For the net product in the former Britannia was very different from that, for instance, in the former Gaul. In Gaul, the political triumph of the invading Germanics did not save them from assimilation into the language and culture of the native Gallo-Romans. The language which emerged, first called *Romain* and later *Français*, i.e., Frankish, was in effect the Frankish variant of neo-Latin. In the former Britannia, in contrast, the invading Germanics avoided cultural assimilation; and the language which eventually emerged was not a fusion of Latin, Celtic, and Germanic, but a new, original idiom of an almost purely Germanic character. How was it, one is entitled to ask, that the British Celtic majority did not absorb the scattered and disunited communities of Angles, Saxons, Jutes, Frisians, and others? How was it that the culture of the Gallo-Romans triumphed whereas the culture of the Romano-British went under?

The simplest answer is extermination. Celtophiles love to relate how the murderous Saxons massacred the defenceless Britons and supposedly wiped them out. The word genocide is used. It is completely out of place. Though atrocious massacres *did* occur, both of civilians and of churchmen, as at Anderida in Sussex in 491 or on the eve of the Battle of Chester in 616, there is plentiful evidence that the bulk of the British population continued to live on under Germanic rule, and to speak their own language. The law code of Ine, King of Wessex, from the late seventh century, for instance, makes special provision for the British still living in his domain.

A second answer invokes numbers. The native Celts were supposedly swamped by the overwhelming tide of Germanics. This too, is unlikely. Though fifth-century boat convoys might bring in enough migrants to fill the initial colonies, it is unthinkable that they could have repopulated the entire country. Apart from that, there is every indication that repopulation did *not* take place. Modern genetic research is showing quite convincingly that the Germanic invasions, like the Celtic invasions before them, were insufficient to transform the existing gene pool to any major degree.[41]

A third answer concerns the prevailing linguistic patterns in late Roman Britannia. The Germanics were moving into the most heavily Romanized regions of the south-east where Latin, not Brythonic, was the main language. Celtic survivals there would naturally be less marked than in other regions where Brythonic had not been so seriously undermined. This makes sense.

Two further factors may have had some impact. The bubonic plague which devastated Western Europe in the mid-sixth century is thought by some commentators to have hit the Celts harder than the Germanics. And physical displacement had its effect. The advance of the Germanics from the east undoubtedly drove some of the British Celts westwards from the former civilian zone whilst forcing others to flee to the Continent.

In the end, one is perhaps best advised to examine the various mechanisms which served in the first phase to insulate the Germanic minority and then, in the later phases, to submerge the Celtic majority in a particularly thorough-going fashion. There are two sorts of arguments – one spatio-economic, and the other cultural.

On the economic front, the agrarian character of Germanic colonization has to be taken into consideration. Ever-expanding areas of solid Germanic rural colonization, created and fed by the plantation of strings of nuclear villages on the heaviest soils, resulted in a settlement pattern where the Germanics came to live alongside the British, not to intermingle with them. Existing British settlements and cities were not so much destroyed as steadily surrounded and slowly strangled.

On the cultural front, the clue, one suspects, lies with the unusually slow pace of Christianization and with the peculiar links between religious and vernacular culture. In the former Britannia, the conversion of the Germanic settlers did not commence until 597, a hundred and fifty years after their arrival. It was not even formally complete until eighty or ninety years after that. This compares with the fifteen years which elapsed between the passing of the last ruler of Roman Gaul and the once-and-for-all conversion of the conquering Franks by Clovis. It meant that in Britannia the Celtic Christians and the Germanic pagans had seven or eight generations in which to reinforce and to ritualize their cultural differences. From all accounts, the Celts were as loath to share their religion with pagans as the pagans were to accept it. What is more, when the Germanics eventually accepted Christianity, they did so from Irish or Roman missionaries, not from their British neighbours. And they did so with the full weight of political and social power behind them. The result was a peculiarly pedantic and oppressive approach to religious matters, where the enforcement of ecclesiastical norms was linked to the promotion of the language and lifestyle of the now dominant Germanic elites. The outward manifestation of this approach was a long wrangling campaign over clerical tonsures and the methods of calculating Easter. The accompanying (but unwritten) message said that no forms of cultural pluralism would be tolerated. It was in that hostile social climate of the seventh and eighth centuries, therefore, not in the hurly-burly of the invasions, that the dwindling Celtic element finally faded away. The British Celts and the Germanics of

Britannia had so schooled themselves in their separateness that in the end they could neither live together nor significantly influence each other's language and culture.

It is an extraordinary fact that the emerging common language of Britannia's Germanic settlers, which had passed its formative centuries in a predominantly Celtic environment, contained barely a handful of Celtic words. This is seized on by the exterminationists to argue that there were no Celtic mothers around to teach the Celtic vocabulary to the children of mixed families. But there may be other explanations. It is hard to believe that the dialects of the illiterate migrants did not make any borrowings from the languages of the partly literate country to which they had come. On the other hand, it is all too easy to believe that at a much later stage those same Germanic educators who were following the norms of Roman Christianity so slavishly would also have favoured linguistic purism and would have purged all Celtic traits from their speech. The early mongrel dialects would never have been recorded. Only the late, purged, and purified language was current when the Germanics finally became literate.

There can be little doubt that a critical point was reached in the former Britannia when the Roman Church dispatched a mission to recapture the paganized country. St Augustine of Canterbury (d. 605), who landed in 597 at the head of forty missionaries, was successful in winning over the King of Kent, and in founding episcopal sees at Rochester and, for the East Saxons, at London. After his death, his missionary team pressed on, despite reversals and apostasies. Within sixty years all the kingdoms of the so-called Heptarchy – Kent, Essex, Wessex (634), Mercia (655), Northumbria (680), Sussex (709,) and East Anglia (c. 700) – had been subordinated to Augustine's see at Canterbury.

The ethos of the Roman mission, however, contrasted sharply with that of the older Celtic Church. Augustine's Germanic converts were apt to adopt the new religion thinking that it would bring them political and material benefits. Bede relates the action of a pagan high priest, Coifi, who desecrated his own shrine because it had failed to bring his people victory in war. Augustine's arrival, in fact, provided the Germanic kingdoms with an ideological cause that was previously lacking. As the evidence of post-Roman cemeteries suggests, pagan cremation rites had been reasserting themselves among the Celts. Old British Christianity was declining. Religious-based antagonism was probably diminishing fast, until St Augustine restoked it. Bede reports this, and approved. For it was no pagan king but St Augustine himself who set the wheels of violent conflict in motion. In 603, Augustine summoned the leaders of the British Church to a conference at a place on the borders of Wessex which in Bede's time was still called 'Augustine's Oak'. There he invited them to accept his brand of Christianity – or else. For its part, the British delegation, which contained a large contingent from the monastery at Bancornaburg (Bangor), had consulted a wise hermit on the way to the conference. 'If Augustine is meek and lowly of heart,' they were advised, 'it shows that he bears the yoke of Christ and offers it to you. But if he is haughty and unbending, then he is not of God, and you should not listen to him.' When Augustine did not even bother to rise and greet them, they had their answer. The conference ended with Augustine issuing threats:

> If they refused to unite with their fellow-Christians, they would
> be attacked by their enemies . . .; and if they refused to preach
> the Faith of Christ to them, they would eventually be punished
> by meeting death at their hands. And, as though by divine
> judgement, all these things happened as Augustine foretold.[42]

Immediately afterwards, Æthelfrith, King of Northumbria, fresh from his victory at Degsastan, 'made a great slaughter of the faithless Britons'. Bede wanted to compare him to Saul, King of Israel, 'except that he was ignorant of true religion'. Æthelfrith had recently captured Deva, and renamed it Legacestir, 'the City of the Legions'. He raised an army there to do battle with the local British. Before the battle, he noticed that a body of 1,200 monks from Bangor-in-Coed were praying for the other side. So he had them butchered. Bede's comment on this pagan warrior, who furthered the interests of the Roman mission, was to quote Isaac's blessing for Benjamin. 'Benjamin shall ravage like a wolf: in the morning he shall devour the prey, and at night he shall divide the spoils.' In this alliance of neophyte fervour and political power, there was no room for Christian charity. The critical phase of the Germanic conquest was pursued in close correlation with Roman evangelization.

The methods of evangelization were relevant to the final success. For if St Augustine was less than charitable towards the British Christians, he proceeded with considerable care and restraint in relation to the Germanic pagans. And he did so on the explicit orders of Pope Gregory, who painstakingly answered all of his queries:

> Augustine's Eighth Question. May an expectant mother be baptized? How soon after childbirth may she enter church? And how soon after birth may a child be baptized if in danger of death? How soon after childbirth may a husband have relations with his wife? And may a woman enter church at certain periods? And may she receive communion at these times? And may a man enter church after relations with his wife before he has washed? Or receive the sacred mystery of communion? These uncouth English people require guidance on all these matters.

Gregory was especially solicitous to adapt heathen practices to Christian usage:

> We have come to the conclusion that the temples of idols . . . should on no account be destroyed. He [Augustine] is to destroy the idols, but the temples themselves are to be aspersed with holy water, altars set up, and relics enclosed in them . . . In this way, we hope that the people may abandon idolatry . . . and resort to these places as before . . . And since they have a

custom of sacrificing many oxen to devils, let some other solemnity be substituted in its place . . . They are no longer to sacrifice beasts to the Devil, but they may kill them for food to the praise of God . . . If the people are allowed some worldly pleasures . . . they will come more readily to desire the joys of the spirit. For it is impossible to eradicate all errors from obstinate minds at a stroke; and whoever wishes to climb to a mountaintop climbs step by step . . .[43]

Not surprisingly, therefore, the progress of Christianization was inextricably tied to the affairs of the strongest Germanic kingdom of the era – Northumbria. Northumbria, which had risen to prominence through the merger of Bernicia and Deira, had first been introduced to Christianity through the activities of an Irish monk from Iona, St Aidan (d. 651), founder of the monastery of Lindisfarne on Holy Island. Aidan won over the long-lived Northumbrian king, Oswy (r. 641–70). Thanks to the crushing defeat in 655 of his pagan Mercian rivals, who were thereby obliged to convert, Oswy gained a commanding position and took the lead in reconciling the traditions of the British and Roman Churches. For Oswy had a delicate problem. Thanks to the discrepancy of the Roman and the Celtic calendars, he was celebrating Easter when his Kentish queen was still celebrating Palm Sunday. The Synod of Whitby (664), which was called to find solutions, made a momentous decision to accept Roman practices; and the decision was then extended to all the Germanic kingdoms. At Whitby, St Wilfred of York (634–710), whose aim in life was 'to extirpate the rank weeds sown by the Irish', had abused his Celtic adversary, Aidan's successor Cólman. And he succeeded in pressing the case not only for the Roman calendar but also for a centralized Roman diocesan structure. But he did not get his way in everything. The Archbishop of Canterbury, Theodore of Tarsus, a Greek (d. 687), disciplined Wilfrid and imposed some compromises. The Mercian see at Lichfield went to an Irish disciple of Aidan, St Chad (d. 672): and the Northumbrian Church, inspired by Lindisfarne, was allowed to flourish in a style which produced a wonderful synthesis of the Germanic and Celtic forms. In the eyes of his admirers, Theodore's moderation shaped his Church 'for all time'.[44] Certainly the see of Canterbury, which he graced, and which governed the bishops now attached to each of the Germanic kingdoms within its frontiers, began to sow the seeds of a common identity.

The formal triumph of Christianity, however, was slow to bring results of a more deep-seated nature. Rædwald of East Anglia (d. 625) is remembered as the king who hedged his bets by building both a Christian altar and a pagan shrine under one roof. He is also regarded by archaeologists to be the most likely person to have been buried in the magnificent ship-tomb at Sutton Hoo, where the presence of Christian objects cannot disguise the essentially pagan character of the site.[45] The same ambiguity must have characterized many of his Germanic kinsfolk, perhaps for generations.

The advent of Christianity did nothing to curb the incessant bloodthirsty warfare of both British and Germanic kingdoms. In the eighth century, King Æthelbald of Mercia (r. 716–57), who murdered his way to the throne and was eventually murdered by his own war-band, established a 'Mercian hegemony' over British neighbours and Germanic rivals alike. His successor, Offa (r. 757–96), organized a Christian coronation in the manner of Charlemagne: minted the earliest common coinage on the island;[46] and built the famous earthworks to mark his western frontier. Offa's Dyke, from the Dee to the Severn, is 'the most spectacular piece of evidence for the existence of prolonged and continuous hostility between Britons and Saxons'.[47] There had been no general ethnic blending. Instead, there was deep and permanent division.

Late eighth-century society under the Mercian hegemony has often been described as colonial. It was certainly colonial with respect to the relations between Germanics and Celts. As several *wergild* tariffs show, the 'blood-money' required for the killing of a British freeman was much lower than that for the killing of a Germanic freeman. But colonialism is not too wide of the mark for the methods of systematic domination practised by the Mercians

over their various subjects. Whither this might have led if the
hegemony had lasted is anyone's guess. All one can say is that it
was due to be rudely interrupted. As an entry in *The Anglo-Saxon
Chronicle* records:

> 787. Her nam Breohtric cining Offan dohter Eadburge. ꞁ on his
> dagum comon | ærest ·iii· scipu Norðmanna of Hereða lande.
> ꞁ þa se ge refa þær to rad. ꞁ he wolde drifan to ðes cininges
> tune þy he nyste hwæt hi wæron. ꞁ hine man of sloh þa.

> (787. *In this year, King Beorhtric [of Wessex] took to wife Eadburh,
> daughter of King Offa. And in his days came first three ships of
> Norsemen from Hörthaland: and the reeve rode thither and tried to
> compel them to go to the royal manor, for he did not know what they
> were: and they slew him.*)[48]

The reeve's name was Beaduheard; and he had ridden over from
the royal manor at Dorchester, believing the newcomers to be
merchants. The law of Wessex required all foreign traders to register
with him and to declare how many persons were in their party. It
was recorded that Beaduheard spoke to the Norsemen haughtily.
His demeanour, which cost him his life, probably arose from the
shock on realizing that the visitors were not traders but raiders.

Later historians have often been obsessed with the question of
unity. Yet unity was the rarest of commodities. It is perfectly clear
that there was no love between rival sets of Celts and Germanics,
and very little sense of an ultimate destiny. If people ever thought
where they lived, they continued to think of Britannia. True enough,
Bede did express his longings for a future unity. Yet these longings
were religious and ecclesiastical, not national. In the closing sentences of his *History*, it is still Britannia that concerns him:

> Hic est impraesentiarum universae status Brittaniae, anno
> adventus Anglorum in Brittaniam circiter ducentesimo octoge-
> simo quinto, Dominicae autem incarnationis anno septingentes-
> imo tricesimo primo: in cuius regno perpetuo exultet terra, et

congratulante in fide eius Brittania laetentur insulae multae,
et confiteantur memoriae sanctitatis eius.

*(This, then is the present state of all-Britain about two hundred and
eighty-five years since the coming of the English to Britain, and seven
hundred and thirty-one years since our Lord's incarnation. May the
world rejoice under his eternal rule, and Britannia glory in his Faith.
Let the countless isles be glad, and sing praises to the honour of his
holiness!)*[49]

The same sentiment is implicit in that title of Bretwalda (Power-
Wielder of Britain) which various princes adopted to express their
claim to overlordship over lesser rulers. According to Bede, seven
kings had the title Ælle of Sussex (d. 491), Ceawlin of Wessex
(d. 593), Æthelberht of Kent (c. 552–616), Rædwald of East Anglia,
and Edwin (d. 633), Oswald (d. 642), and Oswy (d. 670) of Northumbria. The list almost certainly should also contain the three
all-powerful kings of Mercia – Æthelbald (r. 716–57), Offa, and
Coenwulf (r. 796–821) – to whom Northumbrians like Bede would
not have given undesirable publicity. The title might equally have
fitted some of the British kings such as Cadwallon or Cadfan whose
Latin epitaph at Llangadwaladr in Anglesey reads '*Catamanus Rex
sapientissimis opiniatissimus omnium regum*' (King Cadfan, the wisest
and most renowned of all kings).[50] It was still being used by *The
Anglo-Saxon Chronicle* for rulers in the ninth century. The point is:
nearly five hundred years after the departure of the Romans, the
only higher political entity to which they all felt they belonged was
Britannia. Whether any of the bretwaldas ever exercised effective
overlordship is another matter.

On the Germanic side of the cultural divide, one of the few
significant advances towards greater coherence was made in the
realm of language. The motley collection of Germanic settlers of the
fifth century had spoken a number of languages with varying degrees
of mutual intelligibility. Three hundred years later, it was still very
unlikely that an uneducated Northumbrian could have freely com-
municated with an uneducated West Saxon or East Anglian. Yet

Christianity brought literacy with it: and literacy brought the practice of writing and reading both in Latin and in the vernacular languages. A common script encouraged a common literary idiom and a common readership. King Ine's law code (c. 690) was written in this new language, as was a growing body of literature in the following century. Interestingly enough, for a long time there was no name either for the emerging language or for the people who spoke it. The Celts had already decided that the common denominator among the Germanics was to be labelled the equivalent of 'Saxon'. But the Germanics adopted a name reflecting the origins of the dominant power at the time of the new linguistic community's emergence. Bede (d. 735) used the ultra-modern formula of *gens anglorum*. Offa (d. 796) was the very first ruler in the former Britannia to call himself *Rex Anglorum*, 'King of the English'.

The western districts of the former Britannia, the least Romanized and the furthest removed from the Germanic colonies, were the natural candidates for re-Celtification. As the area of Germanic control expanded, the western districts offered the most accessible places of refuge for displaced Celts. Hence, as the Germanic character of the eastern regions intensified so, too, did the Celtic character of the west. The west was not simply an eternal P-Celtic homeland, whose inhabitants had nothing to do but survive. Both east and west were drawn into the same processes of filtration, of a new crystallization and of apartheid.

One must also point out that in the post-Roman era the western seaways thrived. With Roman coastal defences abandoned, and turmoil on the landward side, the Celtic Sea returned to its earlier function as the great open conveyer of goods, people, and culture. The western districts of Britannia were in the closest possible touch with Éire, and continued to be so until the appearance of the next maritime inhibitor – the Vikings.

The Celtic Church was one of the chief beneficiaries of the open seaways. British churchmen worked and studied in Éire, as did Irish

men in western Britannia. Regular contact was maintained with
Dumnonia, and from there with the Continent. As a result, while
British Christianity faded in the central and eastern parts of post-
Roman Britannia, especially under pagan Germanic rule, it saw a
marked resurgence in the West. The central figure was St Illtud,
who flourished in the early sixth century – 'renowned teacher of the
Britons, learned in the teachings of the Church, in Latin culture and
in the teachings of his own people'. Monasteries of the Irish type
were founded at the saint's birthplace, Llanilltud Fawr (Llantust), at
Llandeilo, and at Bangor-in-Coed, all of which became major centres
of learning, evangelization, and education. In its day, Llanilltud was
probably the largest and most influential monastery in the Isles.
Among its pupils were St Samson of Dol, the father of monasticism
in Brittany, Paul Aurelian, a central figure in Dumnonia, and the
historian Gildas.

In the next generation, a more ascetic form of monasticism
made its appearance. Anchorites living in remote locations may have
been motivated in part by the mid-sixth-century plague. Their
greatest leader, Abbot Dewi (c. 530–89), inspired more than a
thousand churches in his name. He had many followers in Éire and
his admirers permit themselves to opine that 'Irish monasticism was
the child of [his] monasticism'.

Until the end of the sixth century, all the main communities of
Celtic Britannia were linked by swaths of continguous territory. Still
very conscious of their Roman heritage, they called themselves
Cumbrogi, 'co-citizens' or 'compatriots', whilst they were called by
the Germanics Welsch – a word meaning 'stranger' that is cognate
with the Vlachs, the Roman survivals in the Balkans. But from the
seventh century onwards successive Germanic advances gradually
severed the links, drastically curtailing contact between the isolated
Celtic enclaves. Mercian expansion into southern Rheged, coupled
with the Northumbrian drive to the Solway, cut off the 'Men of the
North' both from the western peninsula and from the British
Kingdom of Strathclyde. West Saxon expansion to the Severn and
along the south coast cut off the 'South-Western Men' from all

except seaborne support. The building of Offa's Dyke by the Mercians was the last act in coralling the 'Western Men' into their mountainous peninsula.

The 'Men of the North' – Cymry as Aneirin called them – were subdued politically but not culturally. Despite their conquest by the Northumbrians, they were destined to rise again and to enjoy a second period of independence. They stayed in contact with their kinsfolk in the western peninsula, mainly no doubt by sea, long after the land link was broken. For the common community to which they and the 'Men of the West' still belonged Aneirin never used any other term but Brythonaid, 'Britons'.

The 'Men of the South-West' were descendants of the Dumnonii. They maintained their separate existence into the eighth century. The kingdom of Dumnonia was still functioning under its last known ruler in 708–9, when King Geraint was accused by his Saxon neighbours of observing the Celtic Easter. The critical moment occurred shortly afterwards when a joint attack of the South and the West Saxons captured Isca After that, the kingdom fragmented. The district on the Severn estuary lost its local British dynasty and became Somerset. The part to the east of the Tamar retained its original name but in Germanic form, Defensascir, i.e., 'Saxon Dumnonia', and became Devon. Only the land to the west of the Tamar remained in British hands. To the Saxons, it was known as Kern-wealhas, i.e., Cornwall. To the natives, it was, and still is, Kerno.[51]

Kerno formed the central pier of the double sea-bridge joining Éire with the Gallic remnants in Armorica. In late Roman times, therefore, it was subject to Irish settlement and possibly to Irish rule. It has been argued with some plausibility that Irish, not Saxon, pressure provoked the initial fifth-century British exodus to Armorica, causing the appearance of 'Lesser Britannia' across the water. There is ample evidence of Celtic churchmen operating on both sides of the sea at a time when as yet there were no Saxons in sight. It is true that the Roman part of Kerno's heritage held steady for a considerable period before the Celtic British part could assume dominance. All the circumstances in the historical background to the love-legend of 'Tristan and Isolt' point to the Latinate character of the court of Marcus Quonimorus. King Mark's kinsman, Tristan, is prince of the lost land of Lyonesse, but Isolt is an Irish princess. A sixth-century memorial stone, which still stands by the roadside at Menabilly, records the real person behind the legend: *'Drustans hic iacet Cunomori filius'* (Here lies Tristan son of Quonimorus).[52]

Despite many uncertainties of detail, there is no doubt that Continental Brittany came into being through pre-medieval British migration. Arguments proliferate over the chronology and over the extent of the British and the Gallo-Roman elements in the final mix. There seem to have been two main migratory waves. Only the later one was provoked by the Saxon advance into Dumnonia. The Breton language, Brezoneg, clearly derives from Brythonic, but developed along different lines from either Cornish or Welsh. Its history is as distinct and as remote from French as the P-Celtic languages of Britain are from English. Britannia Minor or 'New Britain' across the sea became a permanent feature of the map, a natural partner for the Celtic rim in the Isles. Many, many centuries later, the term 'Great Britain' had to be coined to distinguish the old Britannia from the new Brittany. (See Chapter Eight.)

The 'Men of the West', living on the peninsula defined by Severn and Dee, had no discernibly separate identity at the end of the Roman period. On the contrary, it was among them that Romano-British customs and culture persisted longest, reinforced no doubt by the influx of refugees from beyond the Severn. The earliest churchman of the region known by name, Dubricius (St Dyfryg, c. 425–509), was a diocesan bishop of the Roman type officiating, it has been suggested, from Arconium. A memorial stone at Penmarchon refers to a Justinus, appointed consul in 540. The local territorial units of later, medieval times, the *carefi* are thought to be a direct continuation of the Roman *pagi*. And almost all the dynasties which figure in the seventh-century 'Welsh Heptarchy' – in Gwynedd, Powys, Ceredigion, Dyfed, Brycheiniog Glywysing, and Caer-went (Gwent) – claimed descent from late

Roman dignitaries, most frequently from Magnus Maximus. The formation of larger kingdoms through the merging of lesser ones mirrored the process at work among the Germanics to the east. The kingdom of Gwynedd was assembled in the mid-sixth century by Maglocunus (Maelgwyn Fawr), a descendant of Cunedda. The powerful kingdom of Morgannwg (Glamorgan) was put together by the dynasty of Meurig ap Tewdrig, who merged Glywysing, Ercing, and Gwent.

The first strategic priority of the new territorial kingdoms was to tame the Irish settlements of the west coast. The ruling dynasties of both Dyfed and Brycheiniog were of Irish origin: and Irish colonies planted in late Roman times would have been encouraged by the open seaways to strengthen their ties with the homeland. A memorial stone at Castelldioyran inscribed both in Latin and in Ogham records the name of Voteporix (Gwrthefyr), the *tyrannus Demetarum* in Dyfed, and one of the post-Romano-British rulers whom Gildas excoriates for his sins. His lands, and those of his counterparts further up the coast, were overrun in the sixth century. After that, according to divergent interpretations, they were either 'de-Romanized', 'Brittonicized', or 're-Brittonicized'.

No sooner had the Irish problem been resolved than the Germanic advance assumed a menacing aspect. The fall of Glevum (575) and of Deva (614) severely constricted British access to the Midlands. In the early seventh century, the wars of Gwynedd and Northumbria, which had raged all the way from Ynys Glannauc to Ynys Medgawdd, ended with the victory of a third party, namely Mercia. In the south, the repulse c. 630 of the West Saxons by the 'Men of Gwent' led to a permanent frontier at the gorge of the River Wye. In the centre, a prolonged struggle was joined by Celtic Powys and Germanic Mercia over the rich valley of the Upper Severn. The struggle began in the early seventh century. There is a note from the life of St Beuno, who in 610 was so shocked on hearing 'Saxon' spoken on the opposite bank of the Severn that he fled the scene. The struggle was regulated in the eighth century by the building of Wat's Dyke by Æthelbert of Mercia and by the demarcation of a continuous boundary during the reign of Offa. Contrary to popular impressions, however, Offa's Dyke did not appropriate all the best land for the Mercians, leaving the British to languish in their mountain retreats. At several points, it makes careful detours to the east in order to preserve specific strongpoints or fertile fields for the British. Care taken for the interests of Powys and Gwent helped Mercia to make the line permanent.

The creation of a firm, fixed frontier, however, could not fail to have far-reaching consequences. It was probably intended to give the Mercians respite from the British and to assist Offa's bid for hegemony over the other Germanic kingdoms. Instead, it had a greater impact on the British. It ensured that the 'Men of the West' would never escape from the isolation of their peninsula, that their language and culture would develop in directions not shared by other insular Celts, and that far into the future they would assume a separate national identity.

In 400, the language of the western peninsula was Brythonic – a highly inflected P-Celtic tongue with grammar as complicated as Latin. Two hundred years later, in the seventh century, it was losing its inflections and, like the closely related northern language of Taliesin and Aneirin, was giving rise to a new literary form. Although it had not yet assumed a new name, it had taken the decisive linguistic turn that would propel it into its own distinct orbit. And it left a few monuments. An inscription on the Cadfan Stone in the church at Tywyn, Gwynedd, dating from c. 700 is thought to contain its earliest surviving traces. The transcription of the Cadfan Stone, let alone its interpretation, has been the subject of lengthy erudite debate, and no definite decipherment has so far proved possible. Even so, among the hotly contested readings of the memorial texts, there are unmistakable words of a late Brythonic or an early Welsh character:

> Cengrui cimalted gu (reic)
> adgan
> ant erunc du but marciau

cun ben celen: tricet nitanam

(Ceinrwy wife of Aiddian [lies here] close to Bud [and] Meirchiaw)

(Cun, wife of Celyn: grief and loss remain)[53]

More than a century later, a cell full of manuscripts is said to have been seen at Dinbych-y-Pysgod (Tenby) in the ninth century, but they are lost. So scholars have been left reconstructing the earliest form of the language from the marginalia of Latin texts. The vernacular literature of the period, including the *Pedair Cainc y Mabinogi* (*The Four Branches of the Mabinogi*), is only known from later medieval copies.

Throughout these centuries, the 'Men of the West' would have continued to call themselves Brythonaid, Britons, making no known distinction from their compatriots elsewhere. They also used the term Cumbrogi, though again with no regional differentiation. The chronicler Nennius, who was active in the early ninth century, was still calling himself *cives*. The Saxons were already thinking of a discrete territory, the 'Land of the Welsh', or Wales. Yet, as it has been pointed out, this idea only existed in Saxon heads. Only once, in a praise poem to Cadwallon dated to 633, does a new British word occur in reference to the land of the western Cumbrogi. That word was Cymru.

Everything said above only serves to underline how reluctant historians must be to jump the historical gun, how careful not to use later names for earlier things. For names reflect consciousness. They are only applied when people became aware of phenomena which they previously did not recognize. One can be reasonably sure if the sources show no regular trace of a particular name that the phenomenon did not yet exist. Talking of the centuries after 400, one of the most respected historians in these matters has dared to write, 'This was the era when . . . the nations of the Welsh, the English and the Scots crystallised.'[54] The judgement is a bold, not to say a rash one. It would be more realistic to conclude that by 800 the conditions had been created where England, Ireland, Scotland, and Wales could begin the initial and most tentative phase of their crystallization.

PERHAPS THE OUTSTANDING FEATURE of the centuries following the Roman collapse lies in the fact that the Germanic and the Celtic peoples did not mix. What is more, the political and cultural divide which came into being at that time was going to be reinforced by the emergence of the four nations. The Celtic nations showed no great solidarity among themselves, except in their common dislike of the English. For their part, the English cultivated a variety of attitudes to their Celtic neighbours stretching from lofty detachment to scathing disdain. Their notorious ignorance about Celtic matters was most usually attended by relaxed complacency and occasionally by fierce pride. All these attitudes and feelings have found full expression in the perpetual debates about the period of history when the chasm first opened up.

Nowadays, it seems not only legitimate but entirely natural for Irish, Welsh, and Scots to look to the origins of their nationhood and to do so without a chorus of derision. Such things are often considered a basic human right. The Irish, for example, look back at the very least to St Patrick as the founder of a Christian nation, and more often to the pagan Irish civilization which Patrick Christianized. The Welsh look at least to St David, who was young when Patrick was old. And at any Welsh *eisteddfod* one is told that the rules of such bardic competitions were drawn up at a festival held at Carmarthen in 693. The Scots cannot claim quite such venerable antiquity unless they appeal to such events as the founding of Dalriada or of Dunedin. But every modern genealogy of the Kings of Scots starts with Kenneth Mac Alpin and his coronation at Scone. No one expresses surprise if all these narratives contain an element of legend and myth. After all, every nation on earth, including the

English, takes pride in its legends and its foundation myths as well as in the better verified histories of more recent times.

Matters, however, were not ever thus. In the formative period of the British Union, the English were so jealous of their own history, and of their own exclusive right to a history, that all non-English histories in the Isles were either ignored or ridiculed. The great figures of the Enlightenment were particularly scathing. Here, for instance, is Edward Gibbon playing to the gallery as he writes about the ancient Caledonians on the far side of Hadrian's Wall:

> The native Caledonians preserved their wild independence for which they were not less indebted to their poverty than their valour. Their incursions were frequently repelled and chastised, but they were never subdued. The masters of the fairest and most wealthy climates of the globe, turned with contempt from gloomy hills assailed by the winter tempest, from lakes concealed in a blue mist, and from cold and lonely heaths, over which the deer of the forest were chased by naked barbarians.[55]

Gibbon's contemporary and acquaintance David Hume, a Scot, adopted the same line and tone. Having failed, as he thought, to make his mark as a philosopher, Hume wrote an enormous eight-volume *History of England* (1754–62), in which any sympathy for the Scots' perspective was totally lacking. It is curious in itself that a staunchly pro-Unionist should choose not to write an all-British work but to prefer the narrow Anglocentric approach. It is even more remarkable that in the few passages which he devotes to his native country he treats it with ill-disguised disdain. Although he starts with a ringing paragraph on 'the curiosity of all civilised nations' about 'the exploits of their ancestors', he clearly takes the Germanics to be the only set of ancestors worth discussing. On the settlement of Scotland, for instance, his one and only comment refers to the advance of the Northumbrians:

> How far [the Northumbrian] dominions extended into the country now called Scotland is uncertain; but it cannot be

doubted that all the Lowlands . . . were peopled in great measure from Germany: though the expeditions by the several Saxon
adventurers have escaped the records of history. The language
spoken in those countries, which is purely Saxon, is a stronger
proof of this event than can be opposed by the imperfect, or
rather the fabulous annals which are obtruded by the Scottish
historians.[56]

He has nothing whatsoever to say of the British of Strathclyde, the
Picts of the north, or the Gaels of Dalriada, all of whom appear to
be subsumed by 'the other inhabitants of the island'. And as for the
disputes over ancient settlement between 'Scotch and Irish antiquaries', he notes: 'We shall not enter into any detail on so uninteresting
a subject'.[57] He is no kinder to the Welsh. Having devoted considerable space to Hengest and Horsa and to Bede's line on the Angles,
Saxons, and Jutes, he objects strongly to other conflicting evidence.
'These stories', he comments, 'seem to have been invented by the
Welsh authors in order to palliate the weak resistance made . . . by
their countrymen'.[58] More dismissive one cannot get. In certain
regards, therefore, one might not object too strongly to J. S. Mill's
assessment of Hume as 'the profoundest negative thinker on
record'.[59]

 Ninety years later, when Charles Dickens came to write his
Child's History of England, he was consciously pitching his narrative
for the youngest readers, and was deliberately confining himself to
his own country. Even so, the book is full of bold judgements and
original observations:

> The Romans had scarcely gone away from Britain when the
> Britons began to wish they had never left it. For . . . the
> Picts and Scots came pouring in over the broken and unguarded
> Wall . . . in swarms. They plundered the richest towns, and
> killed the people, and came back so often for more booty and
> more slaughter that the unfortunate Britons lived a life of
> terror . . .
> At last, the Britons . . . resolved . . . to invite the Saxons to

come to their country and helped them keep out the Picts and Scots.

It was a British Prince called VORTIGERN who took this resolution and who made a treaty of friendship with HENGIST and HORSA, two Saxon chiefs. Both these names, in the Old Saxon language, signify Horse; for the Saxons, like many other nations in a rough state, were fond of giving men the names of animals, as Horse, Wolf, Bear, Hound. The Indians of North America—a very inferior people to the Saxons though—do the same to this day.[60]

In Victorian times, the idea of 'superior' and 'inferior' peoples was never far away.

The principal exponent of 'historical Darwinism', however, was John Richard Green (1837–83), whose *Short History of the English People* (1874) enjoyed great popular success for twenty or thirty years. Green's book opens with the statement that, since the Anglo-Saxons were not native to the Isles, 'For the fatherland of the English race, we must look far away from England itself.' Later, in a passage on the landing of Hengest and Horsa at Ebbsfleet, he remarked: 'No spot in Britain can be so sacred to Englishmen as that which first felt the tread of English feet.' Such views fitted well enough with the pro-Germanic sentiments of mid-Victorian times. They faded fast in the years of Anglo-German rivalry after 1895; and they were killed stone dead by two World Wars.[61]

When it comes to modern scholarship, academics still tend to be far more lenient to the Germanic than to the Celtic side of the story. It is not that the various accounts of English origins are treated uncritically, nor that the Celtic sources are dismissed out of hand. But the Bedean school has been revered so long, and the tradition of Gildas so thoroughly derided, that analysis of the two schools is rarely undertaken in the same temper or in the same language. A work on the *Lebar Gabála*, for instance, and 'The Irish National Origin-legend', concludes that the medieval monks who assembled it were engaged in 'synthetic pseudo-history':

[The *Lebar Gabála*] and other texts were written to address a specifically Irish need; they sought to develop a vision of history which would accommodate and reconcile . . . the rich corpus of native legendary lore and the Latin learning introduced into Ireland by the Church. In this they were outstandingly successful . . .[62]

Such a conclusion is unobjectionable. The real question, however, is whether, if 'English need' were substituted for 'Irish need' and 'England' for 'Ireland', exactly the same comments could not be fairly directed at Bede; and in particular at Bede's early chapters. The scholars who have called Bede a 'synthetic pseudo-historian' are few and far between.

One is not revealing the prejudices of hugely distant generations. One has only to look at recent syllabuses from England's senior university. For most of the century since its foundation in 1851, undergraduate students at Oxford's Faculty of Modern (sic) History spent two of their seven teaching terms preparing for one exam in 'Anglo-Saxon England' and another on the Latin text of Bede's *Historia*. The examination decrees were reformed in the 1990s. It was not Bede plus Gildas or Bede plus Nennius, but Bede, just Bede. Students in Oxford's Faculty of English meanwhile were gearing themselves up for a degree in which the Old English text of *Beowulf* constituted the only compulsory item of study. This state of affairs was not seriously challenged until 1998, when 'modernist' Oxford dons finally made a move 'to slay Beowulf'. As one student put it, 'most people coming to do English literature don't expect to be learning a foreign language'.[63] Traditionalist dons would argue that studying *Beowulf*, like studying Bede, is absolutely essential because it involves the study of 'English roots'. And they are the likeliest source of information for statements in major reference works that say that *Beowulf* is 'the earliest European epic'.[64]

Nonetheless, two of the Oxford dons who were deeply devoted to the traditional study of Old English made a remarkably popular impact far beyond the groves of academe. J. R. R. Tolkien

(1892–1973), who was Professor of Anglo-Saxon and later of English at Oxford, developed an immensely appealing sideline in writing for children. *The Hobbit* (1937) and *The Lord of the Rings* (1954–5) revolve round an imaginary 'Middle Earth' which has its own myths, its own monsters, its own half-imaginary language, and its own magic spells:

> One Ring to rule them all, One Ring to find them,
> One Ring to bring them all and in the darkness bind them.[65]

Tolkien's colleague at Oxford, C. S. Lewis (1898–1963), possessed multifaceted talents that led him, among other things, into religious and ethical issues, beginning with *The Lion, the Witch and the Wardrobe* (1950). His 'Chronicles of Narnia' revolve around another fabulous land of myths and marvels. Both Tolkien and Lewis had serious achievements to their name in the arcane fields of Old and Middle English philology and literature. But they both knew that the most priceless legacy of the period, whether from the anonymous author of *Beowulf* or from the Celtic bards, lay in the age-old art of storytelling.

It could be argued, of course, that English literature stole the most valuable treasure of the Celtic tradition by appropriating the Arthurian romances, and that the impenetrable wall between Germanic and Celtic was thereby breached. That in a sense is true. 'King Arthur' and Sir Galahad and the Knights of the Round Table have indeed been incorporated into the English sphere, and have made their contribution to a shared sense of common modern 'Britishness'. On the other hand, it is important to realize that the Arthurian romances followed a tortuous route through medieval Brittany and France before finding their way with great delay to England. They were not borrowed from the British Celts directly. By the time that Sir Thomas Malory composed *Le Morte D'Arthur* in the fifteenth century, he and Chrétien de Troyes were paying homage not to the post-Roman Celts of Britain but to the heroes of medieval French chivalry:

yet som men say in many p[art]ys of Inglonde that Kynge Arthur
ys nat dede, but h[ad] by the wyll of oure Lorde Jesu into
another place; and men say that he shall come agayne, and he
shall wynne the Holy Crosse. Yet I woll nat saye that his shall
be so, but rather I wolde say: here in thys worlde he chaunged
his lyff. And many men say that there is wrytten upon the
tumbe thys:

HIC IACET ARTHURUS REX QUONDAM REXQUE FUTURUS[66]

For some reason, the gulf between the Germanic and the Celtic
traditions only grew wider with time. By the late nineteenth century,
respectable Victorian scholars were trying to explain it in crude
racial terms. Nothing illustrates this development better than an
experiment conducted in London with the blessing of the Royal
Historical Society in 1884. A researcher seeking to assess the relative
value of the Germanic and the Celtic elements to the British 'race'
was invited to measure the skulls of the Society's Fellows. He
concluded, since the 'brain-pans' of the Fellows with Anglo-Saxon
names were larger on average than those with Celtic names, that the
former were of superior stock. ('There is no hope for the Davieses.)
Fourteen hundred years after it happened, 'the Saxon invasion' was
proved a racial success.[67]

Another curious problem refers to the reasons why England's
collective memory of early Christianity by-passed the first two phases
– of the Romano-British and of the Celtic Churches – and concentrated instead on the somewhat unattractive figure of St Augustine
of Canterbury. The answer must surely lie in part in the millennium
and more when the see of Canterbury has headed the English
Church, and has urged its loyal communicants to give precedence
to the see's initiator. Yet one equally suspects, as with the cult of
Bede and *Beowulf*, that St Augustine has attracted a following
because his mission was linked with England's narrow ethnic roots.
SS Alban, Aidan, Patrick, and David were all fine Christian gentlemen no doubt, and they all laboured in the vineyard of the future
England, but they were not English; and that, in the eyes of some,

was a grave disability. Nor when Reformation England broke with the Roman Church and adopted a very anti-Roman stance did anyone think of cultivating the country's Celtic heritage as a counterweight to St Augustine. The non-hierarchical and evangelical character of the Celtic Church might possibly be thought closer to Protestantism than St Augustine's Papism was. But it attracted little attention among the English before the Romantic period, when the lonely grandeur of its long-abandoned island sites probably proved as great a pull as the nature of its organization or its theology. If the early Protestant historians were interested in anything relating to the origins of Christianity in the Isles, it was in the legends which hinted that the Gospel might have been imported direct from the Holy Land. The Legend of Joseph of Arimathea coming to Glastonbury is a case in point. For Protestant polemicists, the idea that Rome was completely irrelevant, even in the sixth century, was very attractive.[68]

The physical remains of the early Celtic and English Churches are few and far between. Most of the earliest buildings, as at St David's or at Canterbury, have been replaced by, or incorporated into, much later ecclesiastical piles of medieval vintage. Yet most of the sites are known, and can be visited; and they well repay the pilgrim's toils. One should start at Whithorn Priory in Galloway, where c. 397 Ninian built the first known stone church in Britain. It is a place which few English people have heard about, let alone seen. Yet it bears witness to Romano-British Christianity; and it belongs to the world in which St Patrick lived before he went to Ireland. Ninian's Cave is still marked on the map. Ninian's Chapel on the nearby Isle of Whithorn was rebuilt in the twelfth century. But it is very close to nature, and it exudes the spirit of its founder who said that 'the fruit of study was to perceive the eternal world of God reflected in every plant and insect, every bird and animal, and every man and woman'.[69]

The next stop, if one does not follow St Patrick's wake across the sea, should be the island of Iona. Columba's church was destroyed by Vikings. Its replacement is a thirteenth-century Benedictine monastery, and a twentieth-century community. But the mission of 'the Columcille' still sits at the centrepoint of the post-Roman Celtic Church. Iona is the stepping stone between Patrick's Ireland and Aidan's Northumbria. When Columba was dying, and collapsed by the wayside, legend tells how an old horse came and laid its head in the saintly lap. Columba forbade his attendant to drive the beast away. 'This dumb creature possesses no reason,' he said, 'but it has been told by the Creator himself that I am about to leave.'[70]

On the way from Iona to Lindisfarne one stops off to see the tomb of St Kentigern in Glasgow Cathedral. Kentigern is said to have exchanged pastoral staffs with Columba. He is the patron of Strathclyde, a reminder that in his day the heart of what today is Scotland was the most northerly outpost of British 'Wales'.

Holy Island is to the east coast what Iona is to the west. Lindisfarne, like Iona, was destroyed by Vikings. The Priory, whose ruins still stand, dates from Norman times. Yet the site is for ever associated with St Aidan and with his disciples Cuthbert, Chad, and Cedd. These are the Christian pioneers who created the wonderful fusion between the Celtic Church and the Germanic Angles, of whose legacy the Lindisfarne Gospels, now in the British Museum, are the supreme exemplar. Most appropriately the tomb of St Cuthbert, Abbot of Lindisfarne, lies close to the tomb of the Venerable Bede, historian of the English, both in Durham Cathedral. Cuthbert lies behind the high altar, Bede in the Galilee Chapel. Durham became the religious centre of Northumbria, when Lindisfarne was no more.[71]

Northumbria, which cedes no precedence to Canterbury in England's Christian tradition, is the correct starting point for sites further south. The first stop has to be at St Hilda's Abbey on the cliffs overlooking the bay at Whitby. The buildings which hosted the Synod of 664 are long gone; but the ruins of a medieval church keep watch over its memory. From there, the pilgrim has many choices. But preference must surely be given to the very few sites that preserve the simple, modest air of the infant Christian community. One of them is the church of St Cedd at Bradwell-on-Sea in Essex, which was built c. 654 from the stones of a nearby Roman fort. Another is the Abbey of Dorchester-on-Thames, built c. 635 by St Birinus, a Roman missionary and the first bishop of the West Saxons. And thence, as Chaucer said, 'to Caunterbury'. Pope Gregory had intended to make London the seat of his chief representative in England; and Canterbury's splendour belongs to another time.

Cornwall's 'Age of the Saints' took place in the period before the Germanic inroads into western Dumnonia.[72] It was the meeting-ground of colourful Irish churchmen like St Feock, who rode across the sea on a granite boulder, and of Welshmen like St Pol de Leon or St Samson of Dol, who, having bought a chariot in Rome, used it to transport his holy books. Many of them moved freely between Cornwall and Brittany. The result is a profusion of magnificent Celtic crosses, even in remote locations like Bodmin Moor, and a wealth of parishes dedicated to obscure Celtic Christians, of whom little is known beyond their names: hence St Austell, St Blazey, St Kew, St Levan, St Mabyn, St Nest, St Wenn, St Winnow ... Cornwall's answer to St Patrick and St David was St Perrin or Piran, a sixth-century abbot.

Nothing in Great Britain, however, compares to the wealth of Ireland's legacy from the early centuries of Christianity. The physical scale of beehive hermitages and Celtic high crosses may sometimes be modest; but their significance for the survival of civilization in the Isles was vast. The tiny, windowless Gallarus Oratory on the Dingle Peninsula, Co. Kerry, is said to be the best-preserved original Celtic building in the Isles; the Celtic monastery on Skellig Michael, eight miles off the Kerry Coast, is definitely the most remote; and St Kevin's Refuge at Glendalough in the Wicklow Mountains is one of the most idyllic. Of St Kevin, they say that a blackbird laid its eggs in his hands when he was wrapped in prayer. Rather than disturb the bird, he stayed on his knees till the eggs were hatched.

The most venerated sites in Ireland, of course, are connected with St Patrick. The centre of the cult nowadays is the mountain of Croagh Patrick in Co. Mayo, where the patron once fasted in the wilderness for forty days and forty nights. Nowadays, pilgrims piously climb the mountain, singing a modern version of St Patrick's hymn, 'The Breastplate':

> At Tara today in this fateful hour
> I place all heaven with its power,
> And the sun with its brightness,
> And the snow with its whiteness,
> And the fire with all the strength it has,
> And the lightning with its rapid wrath,
> And the winds with their swiftness,
>   Along their path,
> And the sea with its deepness,
> And the rocks with their steepness,
> And the earth with its starkness;
>   All these I place,
> By God's Almighty help and grace,
> Between myself and the powers of darkness.[73]

The important historical fact about St Patrick is that he was British. He is the obvious candidate to be the Patron of Christian Unity in the Isles.

Fortunately, there have always been a select band of stalwarts who aim to unite rather than to divide. The Germanic and the Celtic traditions can indeed be bridged, and sometimes are. Two academic Cambridge households were once a good case in point. Hector Munro Chadwick (1870–1947) was Professor of Anglo-Saxon at Cambridge – Tolkien's opposite number on the Cam – whilst his wife Nora Chadwick, née Kershaw was a rising author with a special interest in the early Celtic Church. Chadwick's student Alison Hingston, a numismatist and archaeologist, married Chadwick's colleague Dr E. B. Quiggin, the university's precocious lecturer both in Celtic Studies and in German. Quiggin, a Manxman, reputedly had a command of Polish, Russian, Yiddish, Swedish, Finnish, Hungarian, and Turkish in addition to Old Irish and Old Welsh and other common languages. He had obtained a Ph.D. from the University of Greifswald in Prussia with a thesis on *The Cattle Raid of Cooley*. Apart from his famous article on 'The Celts' in the *Encyclopædia Britannica*, he had published a monograph on the Gaelic dialect of Donegal. He died tragically young. But out of this milieu, under Chadwick's leadership, there emerged Cambridge's unique Department of Anglo-Saxon, Norse, and Celtic. In the late 1990s, this department sheltered scholars working on a huge range of topics from St Patrick and *Beowulf* to medieval Welsh poetry, Old Norse sagas, and insular Latin. Their motto might well be a saying of Quiggin's uttered almost a century ago: 'today . . . we struggle against the anaesthetic of anglocentricity'.[74]

But those struggling academics are not alone. Their holistic views of the period are sometimes echoed further afield. In 1996, for example, the novelist and broadcaster Melvyn Bragg (b. 1939) published an off-beat fictional work called *Credo*, set in his native Cumbria in the seventh century. One of the aims was to reconstruct the encounters of an age when Irish saints still lived on the shores of Lakeland, and the local Welsh mingled with the advancing Angles. In particular, Bragg seeks to reanimate the life of St Bega, a figure who 'hovers between the historic and the mythic'. Bega, an Irish woman, who left her name at St Bees, spent many years in a lonely hermitage on the western bank of a mountain-girt lake which the Vikings would later call Bassenthwaite. She lived in the age of SS Aidan, Hilda, Cuthbert, and Wilfrid; and her mission operated in the southern section of the British kingdom of Rheged in the decades separating the Council of Whitby from the Battle of Dunnichen. There were descendants of the Romano-British in the nearby city of Caerel; there were pagans in the hills; there were Picts on the prowl across the border, and powerful Northumbrian overlords from the other end of the Wall; and, in the crucial phase of general Christianization, there were fears on every hand:

> In Bega's chapel, the nuns were fearful that night . . . For it was the hour of the ghosts for them, too. Even the most pious of the nuns saw ghosts as they hurried from the tiny chapel to their sleeping quarters. Every day most of those who lived by the lake or by a stream or waterfall would make an offering to the gods of water, those powerful gods of the Celts who would never die. All over this valley, the adjoining valleys, all over Rheged . . . as darkness put its grip on the world, the nightly battles began between life and death, between survival and extinction, between dreams and truth, and, for the Christians, between good and evil.[75]

Did Wordsworth, or any other of the Lakeland poets, ever harbour similar thoughts? For in the cultural sphere at least, this mingling of the Germanic and the Celtic has to be the principal touchstone of true 'Britishness'.

CHAPTER FIVE

THE ISLES IN THE WEST

795 to 1154

THE SCANDINAVIAN WORLD OF THE VIKINGS

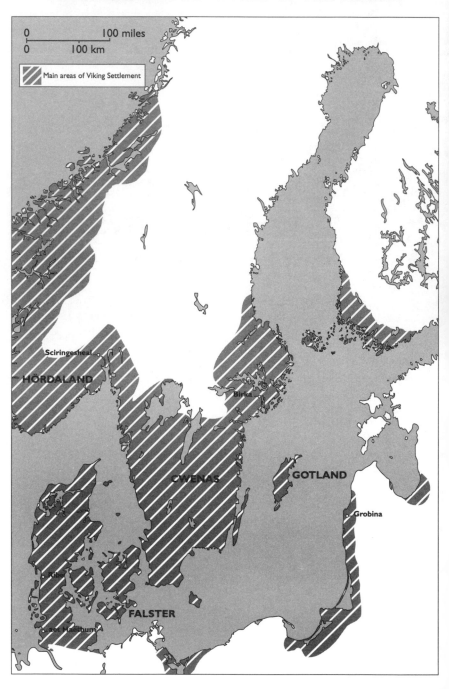

0 — 100 miles
0 — 100 km

Main areas of Viking Settlement

Sciringesheal

HORDALAND

Birka

CWENAS

GOTLAND

Grobina

Ribe

FALSTER

Haithum

SOMETIME IN THE LATE NINTH CENTURY, a Norse merchant living in England visited King Alfred and presented him with a detailed account of his homeland. The merchant's name was Ottar, though his West Saxon hosts called him Ohthere. His account, as copied down in Old English by the royal scribes, has survived as part of a geographical introduction to King Alfred's edition of Orosius's *Historia adversum paganos*:

> Ohthere told his lord, King Alfred, that the farm he lived on lay further north than [that of] any Norseman ... on the coast of the ocean. Yet, he said, the country stretched a very long way farther north, uninhabited except that here and there Lapps had their encampments ...
>
> He was a very rich man in the sort of thing their wealth is counted in, that is to say, wild beasts. When he visited the king, he still owned six hundred tame beasts not yet sold – the sort of beasts they call 'reindeer'. Six of them were decoy deer, which are especially valuable because the Lapps use them to catch wild reindeer. He was among the most important men of that country, but for all that he possessed no more than twenty cattle and twenty pigs, and what little he ploughed he ploughed with horses.
>
> Their wealth comes mostly from the tax the Lapps pay them [consisting of] animal pelts, bird's down, whale-bone and ships' cables made from the skins of whale and seal. Each pays according to his rank ...
>
> He said that Norway was very long and narrow. All the land fit for grazing lies along the sea-coast [which] is very rocky in places. To the east and higher up, wild fells lie alongside the worked land [which] in the south may be sixty miles across. In the middle, [the arable is] thirty or more [miles across]; and, in the north, he said,

where it is narrowest, it may be [only] three miles to the fell. And
then the fell is in some parts as broad as can be crossed in two
weeks . . .

Alongside the southern part of this land, beyond the fells, is
Sweden . . . And alongside the northern part is the territory of the
Cwenas. Sometimes the *Cwenas* attack the Norwegians, and sometimes the Norwegians attack them. Scattered over the fells are very
large fresh-water lakes, and the *Cwenas* carry their boats overland
to the lakes, and from there attack the Norwegians . . .

Ohthere called the district he lived in Halogaland. He said that
nobody lived north of him. But there was a certain market-town in
the south of the land called *Sciringesheal* [Kaupang]. He said that it
took at least a month to get there under sail if you laid up at night
and had a favourable wind every day. All the time you must sail
along the coast. To starboard, there is, first, Ireland; and then the
islands that lie between Ireland and England . . . And to port,
Norway all the time.

South of this place a great sea opens out into the land, broader
than anyone could see across . . . From *Sciringesheal* he said he
sailed in five days to the trading town called *aet Haethum* (Hedeby).
This is set between the lands of the Wends, the Angles and the
Saxons; and it owes allegiance centrally to the Danes. When he
sailed there from *Sciringesheal* he had Denmark to port and open
sea to starboard for three days; then, two days before arriving at *aet
Haethum*, he had to starboard Jutland and Sillende and a lot of
islands – these are the lands the Angles lived in before they came to
England – and for two days there were to port the islands that are
part of Denmark.[1]

Sciringesheal (Kaupang) stood on the northern shore of the Skagerrak
near the entrance to Norway's most important fjord. Aet Haethum stood
on the eastern shore of Jutland.

Ottar belonged to a group of peoples who were beginning to have a
huge impact on European history. They are now called 'Scandinavians',
though historically they were called 'Northmen'. They are most frequently
remembered in the Isles as *Vikings*, that is, by the Old English word for

'pirates'. As Ottar's story shows, this hardly does them justice, since piracy was only one aspect of their rich and complex history. It is not without significance that King Alfred, at the height of his Viking wars, had offered his protection to a Viking merchant. (That is why Alfred is addressed as Ottar's lord.) Since most Scandinavians of that era were pagan illiterates, however, history has generally been written without their point of view. Indeed, it has often been assumed that as mere rapists and pillagers they had nothing to offer by way of historical reflections. In fact, a considerable body of literary material exists, especially in the medieval Icelandic sagas, which record events from all ends of the Viking world, and in Old Norse skaldic poetry. A Viking *skald*, or 'bard', for example, who visited Northumbria, recorded the start of his voyage:

> Vestr fórk of ver,
> en ek Viðris ber
> munstrandar mar,
> svá's mitt of far;
> drók eik á flot
> við isa brot,
> hlóðk mærðar hlut
> míns knarrar skut.
>
> (*West over sea I came*
> *With me I carried*
> *The Sea of Odin's breast.*
> *Such is my profession.*
> *At breaking of the ice-floes*
> *I dragged my oak-ship to sea.*
> *I loaded my vessel's hold*
> *With its cargo of praise.)*[2]

Skaldic poetry gained its effect through short, pithy four- or six-syllable lines of regular metre, through rhymes and alliterations, and through the characteristic device of kennings. A kenning was a cryptic puzzle-phrase, whose meaning the listener had to guess or otherwise decipher in order to make sense of the passage. In the verse above, 'the sea of Odin's breast' refers to the mystic mead which Odin once stole and which endows the gift of poetry. The last sentence of the verse reveals that we are being introduced to a 'praise-poem' eulogizing the feats of the Viking leader whose court the poet is setting out to visit.

Of course, the sagas can only be used as a historical source by exercising the greatest caution. They were not written down until centuries after the Viking Age, and present a fictionalized, romanticized view of the past. Skaldic poetry, too, is concerned with other things than historical accuracy. Even so, it is the memories of the Viking past which often provide the inspiration. Descriptions of the dangers and excitement of the sea voyage form a favourite topic:

> Þél høggr stórt fyr stáli
> stafnkvígs á veg jafnan
> út með éla meitli
> andærr jǫtunn vandar,
> en svalbúinn selju
> sverfr eirar vanr þeiri
> Gestils ǫlpt með gustum
> gandr of stál fyr brandi.

> *(Before the stem of the prow-beast*
> *The hostile monster of the mast*
> *With his strength hews out a file*
> *On ocean's even path.*
> *With it the chill wolf of the willow*
> *With its gusts files away,*
> *Showing no mercy to Gestil's swan,*
> *Over the stem, before the prow.)*[3]

'The prow-beast' is a kenning for the ship. So, too, is the swan of Gestil (a sea god). The wind, that is, 'the monster of the mast' or the 'wolf of the willow', turns the sea into sharp waves or teeth which file away without mercy at the hull.

When a Viking ship of the pirate sort landed, as in Portland, a verbal confrontation with the natives could often ensue. The Viking spokesman would demand tribute to avoid bloodshed. The natives, if they could summon up the courage, would hurl back defiance. An Old English poem recalls the moment exactly;

> On the beach there stood, calling out harshly
> A Viking envoy; he spoke these words.
> With threats he presented the sea-rovers' demands
> To the earl, standing there on the shore.
> 'This tough crew of seamen sent me to you.
> They've instructed me to tell you to send at once
> Arm-rings in return for security. It is better for you
> To buy off this surge of war with blackmail
> Than for us, rough fighters as we are, to engage in battle . . .
> With your money we will return to our ships,
> Put to sea and leave you in peace.'
> Byrhtnoth spoke, he raised his shield,
> Brandished his slim spear-shaft, spoke these words,
> Angry, determined, spoke these words.
> 'Sea-rover, can you hear what these people say? . . .
> Spokesman of the seamen, report my reply . . .
> That here stands a nobleman, dauntless among his retinue
> Who intends to defend his native land,
> Æthelred's realm, my lord's
> People and country. It is the heathen fighters
> Who will fall in battle. Too great a shame, it seems to me,
> That you should go to your ships with our property
> Without a fight, seeing you have come so far
> Here into our country.
> Wealth will not come to you so easily.
> Spear-point and sword's edge will decide between us,
> Fierce sport of warfare, before we give tribute.'[4]

The epic monologues capture the ritual taunting which might precede a fight. The arm-rings that the Viking demanded were made of gold, and were worn both as ornaments and as a sign of personal wealth. They were the first target of muggings. Though the scene employs a measure of poetic licence, it is likely that the Viking speaking in Norse and the earl speaking in Old English could make themselves understood.

As often as not, battle ensued. And gory battle scenes were part of
the standard poetic fare.

Svá beit þá sverð
ór siklings hendi
váðir Váfaðar
sem í vatn brygði.
Brǫkuðu broddar.
Brotnuðu skildir.
Glumruðu gylfringar
í gotna hausum.

Trǫddusk tǫrgur
fyr Týs ok bauga
hjalta harðfótum
hausa Norðmanna.
Róma varð í eyju,
Ruðu konungar
skírar skjaldborgir
í skatna blóði.

. . .

Brunnu beneldar
i blóðgum undum.
Lutu langbarðar
at lýða fjǫrvi.
Svarraði sárgymir
á sverða nesi.
Fell flóð fleina
í fjǫru Storðar.

Blendusk við roðnar
und randar himni.
Skǫglar veðr léku
við skýs of bauga.
Umðu oddláar
i Óðins veðri.

Hné mart manna
fyr mækis straumi.[5]

(Then the sword in the prince's hand
Bit through Odin's clothing as if thrust into water.
Spear-shafts rattled, shield shattered,
Swords crashed down into the skulls of men.

Shields, skulls were trampled down by the hilts' harsh feet
Of the ring-God of the Northmen.
The island rang with the clash of battle. The king stained
The bright wall of shields with the blood of heroes.

Wound-fires flamed in bloody gashes.
Lombard blades sought out men's lives.
Battle-sea surged against swords' headland.
The spears' torrent swept down to Stord shore.

Beneath the rim's heaven the red blood mingled.
Skogul's storm-winds played against the bossed sky.
In Odin's storm the spear-seas thundered.
A host of men cowered before the sword's current.)

In the poet's eye, seas and storms provide one great metaphor for warfare.
The kennings are inimitable. 'Odin's clothing' is armour. Swords are 'wound-
fires'; blood is 'battle-sea' and 'spears' torrent'; a shield is 'the swords'
headland'.

Many of the early raiders were simply out for glory and loot. But
as time went on, growing numbers of Vikings were searching for
somewhere to live. If they did not manage to settle in one place,
they moved on to the next. The peregrinations of one such would-be
colonist called Aud, who eventually settled in Iceland, have been closely
recorded:

There was a king of a band of fighting-men called Oleif the Fair, son
of King Ingiald Helgason ... Oleif the Fair went on many a Viking
raid in the west, took over Dublin and the region dependent on it,

and became king there. He married Aud the Deeply Wealthy, daughter of Ketil Flatnef. Their son was called Thorstein the Red. Oleif fell in battle in Ireland. Thereupon Aud and Thorstein went to the Hebrides. There Thorstein married Thurid, daughter of Eyvind the Norwegian and sister of Helgi the Skinny. They had a large family . . .

Thorstein [like his father Oleif] became king of a band of fighting-men. He joined up with Earl Sigurd the Mighty [of the Orkneys], son of Eystein Glumra. They took over Caithness and Sutherland, Ross and Moray, and half of Scotland. There Thorstein became king until the Scots failed him and he fell in battle.

Aud was in Caithness when she heard of Thorstein's death. She had a ship built secretly in the forest; and when it was complete she set out for the Orkneys. There she married off Thorstein the Red's daughter Groa [who] became mother to Grelod whom Thorfinn the Skull-splitter wed. After that, Aud made for Iceland . . . with twenty freemen.

Aud came first to the Faroes where she married off Alof [another of Thorstein's daughters]. Then she sailed to Iceland, reaching Vikraskeid [where] she was cast ashore. So she went on to Kialarnes to her brother's . . . He invited her to stay with half her crew. She thought that a mean offer, and said he would always be a small-minded man . . .

Next spring Aud and her company went looking for land along Breidafiord . . . They landed at a headland where Aud lost her comb. This she called Kambsnes [Comb-Head]. And took all the dale-land at the inner end of the fjord between the rivers . . . She lived at the place called Audartoptir . . . and gave land both to her crew and to her freed slaves.

Aud was a woman of great dignity. When old age wearied her, she invited her relatives in and made ready a splendid feast. When it had gone on for three days, she picked out gifts for her friends and wished them well . . . Next night, she died. She was buried as she had stipulated on the foreshore between high and low water marks. As a baptised Christian she did not want to be interred in unhallowed ground. After that, her family's faith declined.[6]

By Aud's time, in the second half of the ninth century, there were Viking footholds at many points along the western seaways. She spent her life moving from one to another, as the fortunes of her menfolk waxed and waned. As a matriarch among warriors her first duty was to see that her family's progeny were sufficient to outbreed their numerous losses. As a Christian among pagans, she attracted the attention of the later chroniclers who preserved her memory. She died with impressive composure, sitting upright in bed.

As often as not, a Viking's story ended under a pile of stones on a distant shore. The poet imagined a dead warrior being buried in the company of a slave:

> Einn byggvik stǫ́ steina,
> stafnrúm Atals hrafni,
> esat of þegn á þiljum
> þrǫng, býk á mar ranga.
> Rúm es bǫðvitrum betra,
> brimdýri knák stýra,
> lifa mun þat með lofðum
> lengr, en illt of gengi.[7]

> (*Alone in this berth of stones I lie*
> *In the sea-king's raven's hold.*
> *No press of men on the decking.*
> *On the waves' steed I live.*
> *Better for the battle-skilled fighter*
> *Is space than this low companion.*
> *The sea-beast is my command.*
> *Long will that stand in man's memory.*)

The greatest achievement was to have earned a lasting reputation. The Vikings did not always win a good name among their enemies. Yet every one of them would have wished to be remembered well:

> Deyr fé,
> deyja frændr,
> deyr sjálfr it sama;

ek veit einn
at aldri deyr:
dómr um dauðan hvern.[8]

(Cattle die, kin die.
The man dies too.
One thing I know that never dies,
The good name of the dead.)

Sometimes, especially if the rover came home, his grave would be marked with a stone and a runic inscription:

Hann vaʀ manna
mestr oniðingʀ.
Eʀ a Ænglandi
aldri tynði

This stone was raised by one Gaut in memory of his son Ketil.
He was most admirable of men
Who lost his life in England.[9]

Runes were the only form of writing known to pagan Scandinavia. Runes began at a very early date as a collection of magic symbols used in divination:

In time, they developed into an alphabet that could be used to transcribe the Old Norse language. Like their Celtic counterpart, Ogam, they were designed to be easily incised in wood or stone. In their most advanced form, they were known as Futhark, from the order of their first six letters:

They were never applied to literary texts, and have mainly survived on memorial stones.[10]

The ancient Scandinavian world had functioned smoothly for centuries on the northern rim of late Iron Age Europe. It was largely self-sufficient. The fjords offered rich fishing. The deep valleys provided good ground for mixed farming. The forests contained an endless supply of wood and timber for fuel and building. The environment was harsh, but stimulating. The 'northerners' were well enough known to the rest of Europe. But apart from the merchants who travelled to the Baltic and northern Germany, they had kept largely to themselves.

Scandinavian life centred on the routines of isolated peasant communities living on the edge of the outer wilderness. In Denmark and Sweden the peasants tended to live in compact villages. In Norway they lived in huge, scattered farmsteads or 'long houses'. The long, dark, and snow-bound winters kept people indoors for weeks at a time. The short, bright summers demanded periods of intense labour with the crops and the animals. But the critical moment came in the sudden spring, when ice floes broke up on the lakes and fjords, the sun shone and boats were launched. The 'Spring Expedition', when the young men sailed off on a long journey or a fishing trip, became an established event. In the times when sea-roving was rife, the warrior bands would usually sail off twice a year – once in the spring and again in the autumn. The important thing was to be home for harvest.

The craft skills of these Scandinavian villages were exceptionally high. Everything had to be made at home. Food was preserved by drying, salting, or freezing. Milk was kept underground in winter, in vats lined with ice blocks. Clothes were fashioned from home-spun wool and linen. Every locality had its forge, where iron was smelted by charcoal. Every farm had its chest of high-grade tools. Metalwork of every kind was practised. So, too, was bone carving and jewellery. But the greatest pride of the Norsemen was their carpentry. House-building and ship-building techniques were well in advance of their time. As naval architecture evolved and improved, the tub-like *knörr*, which was used for trade, was joined by the long, elegant *dreki* or 'dragon ship', the warship of the fjords. With masts of pine and planks of oak, equipped both with oars and with sail, with keel and side-rudder, the *dreki* knew no rival on the northern seas.

Scandinavian society consisted of three distinct estates – nobles, freemen, and slaves. The nobility provided the professional warriors and the elite crews of the dragon ships and dominated politics. The freemen provided the backbone of the agricultural system. The slaves were drawn either from the underclass born into servitude or from prisoners-of-war. As in many slave-holding societies, the free classes were eager democrats. All Scandinavian localities had their *thing* or 'popular assembly', which settled disputes and elected magistrates and other officials. Representatives from several such assemblies would meet together in a regional or country-wide *Althing*. The existence of these ancient assemblies inevitably delayed the growth of centralized kingship. Local 'kings' and chieftains proliferated. In Norway, for instance, the foundations of a unified monarchy were not laid until the days of Harald Hárfagri, 'Fine-Hair', in the late ninth century.

Women were not thought equal to men. But they were trained in self-reliance. Polygamy was prevalent; and, together with a high birth rate, it compensated for high mortality among young martial men. The first, legitimate wife had often to manage the farm or the estate during her husband's long absences. She habitually carried the keys of all the farm-buildings on a ring at her waist; and she was the mother of all her husband's legal heirs. All subsequent 'wives' enjoyed the lower but fully accepted status of concubines.

Scandinavia was the last bastion of Germanic paganism, with its rich panoply of gods, myths, heroes, and spirits. The Norsemen believed in a three-tiered cosmos, where the gods resided in an upper realm called Asgard. Human kind lived in the middle realm supported by a vast evergreen ash-tree called Yggdrasill. After death, if they deserved it, they passed into Valhalla, the glorious hall of eternal heroes. Four main deities ruled over Asgard. Odin – the nearest counterpart to classical Zeus – was the cosmic grand strategist, master of knowledge and victory. He rode round the sky on his eight-legged stallion, Sleipnir, escorted by the two black ravens Hugin (Thought) and Munin (Memory). Thor, 'the Thunderer', son of Odin, was stronger than all men. He travelled in a chariot pulled by two billy-goats. Wielding his enormous hammer, Mjöllnir, he was the breaker of giants, the dispeller of evil spirits, and hence the most popular protector of ordinary folk. Freyr was the good and generous god of fertility. His sister Freyja, goddess of beauty, was general of the female army of Valkyries, or 'Choosers of the Slain', who hovered over every battlefield. It was they who decided who to take with them to Valhalla, and who to leave behind.

Like the Celts before them, the Norsemen also believed in a vast array of sprites, elves, fairies, and spirits of river and forest. Unlike the Celts, however, they did not recognize a priestly caste. Every father was the religious leader of his family, holding simple open-air ceremonies for the propitiation of evil forces. Every chieftain and king was the chief priest of his band or tribe. Religious attitudes and social mores overlapped in the widespread cult of heroes. Patronized by kings, *skalds* recited stylized poetry in the warriors' halls whilst others spun the *sagas* or 'epic stories' of the past. Like their Celtic equivalents, the old Norse sagas were not written down until Christian times. But by then the gallery of legendary heroes and idealized historical figures were part of the established lore recorded in poetic form. Apart from entertainment on long winter nights, one of the main purposes of the sagas was to keep the memories and traditions of the old times alive. The so-called 'kings' sagas' were compendiums of fictional general history, whilst the 'family histories' recounted the valorous deeds which legitimized claims to particular lands or settlements.

Despite their apparent belief in an afterlife, the Northmen customarily cremated their dead, though burial was also practised. The greatest honour was to end one's earthly sojourn in a vessel, either cremated amidships or buried with all the trappings of a long voyage. Most spectacularly, a dragonship would sometimes be readied with the dead chief aboard, and then, with the sail fully trimmed for a lonely trip into the sunset, would be set alight and cast adrift. One of the few surviving accounts of the preparations for the cremation of a Viking chief was made by a foreign merchant who observed every detail and wrote them down. He described how the corpse was lovingly washed and laid out in the finest underwear and regalia, and how one of the chief's slave-girls was ritually killed in order to accompany him. Assured that she would stay by her master's side in Valhalla, the girl apparently volunteered. She took several strong potions to drink, offered herself in sexual intercourse to each of the leading warriors in turn, cut off the head of a live chicken, then entered the tent where she was to be stabbed and strangled by a presiding hag. A cacophony of shrieks was raised to mask her last cries.

The central puzzle of early Scandinavia is to know why, after an age of passive isolation, the Norse communities suddenly exploded, sending wave after wave of fleets, warriors, and colonists into every corner of Northern Europe. In many ways it resembles the puzzle of the nomads who from time to time expanded explosively from the steppes of Central Asia. The answer obviously has something to do with a serious ecological imbalance between demographic levels and the available resources for human life support. Historians refer to changes in climate; and it may well be that a favourable phase in the climatic cycle had encouraged unsustainable increases in population density. At all events, the point was reached when finite areas of arable land could no longer support the rising numbers of people trying to exploit it. In the first instance overpopulation encouraged the growth of a violent and divided society, where bands of pirates and land-grabbers habitually preyed on their neighbours and disturbed the peace. In the second instance, it pushed these same pirates to seek their fortunes overseas: and in the last instance it provoked mass emigration.[11]

Yet another technical factor must also have been at work. In the previous era of the Anglo-Saxon invasions, there were no ocean-going ships. Hengest and Horsa could not have sailed to Iceland and Greenland, let alone to America. But in the intervening period, improvements in ship design and navigation had given the 'Northmen' much greater confidence and potential. At 130 feet plus, the dragonships were significantly longer and stronger than anything afloat. The combination of a narrow beam and heavy side-rudder gave them the ability to ride out the tallest waves and the wildest storms. The combination of thirty oars and a huge sail helped them to keep up speed in most weathers, and the oars and double-ended construction gave them forward and reverse man-oeuvrability in narrow rivers. Methods had even been devised to move overland on rollers during portages. Professional shipyards, like the one discovered on the Danish island of Falster, facilitated larger-scale, continuous production of the biggest and most sophisticated vessels. When the Northmen felt the urge to set sail, they were not confined to creeping round the coasts. They must have felt that there was nowhere in the world they could not reach – swiftly and directly.[12]

Once overseas expansion began, the Northmen from Sweden concentrated on the Baltic seaways, and in particular on the Baltic–Black Sea route along the Dnieper. The Northmen from Denmark tended to move south, against Germany and later against eastern England. Those from Norway sailed west. The Western route proved to be the most rewarding of all. It was helped by a chain of landfalls that acted as stepping-stones across the ocean. The Shetlands lie two hundred miles or two days' good sailing from the Norwegian coast. The Faroes lie conveniently another two hundred miles beyond Shetland. From Shetland, one has a choice between a further ocean cruise towards Iceland and Greenland or a delightful exercise in island-hopping along the old western seaways of the Isles. The main stops on the line included Orkney, the Outer and Inner Hebrides, Ulster, Man, Anglesey, South Wales, Lundy, and Cornwall. In the Channel, one could expect to meet other Vikings who had sailed down the east coast of the Isles or across the 'German Sea'. (See map, page 228.)

Looking at a modern atlas, one sees that the Isles lie to the south and southwest of Scandinavia. The islanders called the Scandinavian invaders 'Northmen' because they came from the north. And one might have expected that the Northmen would have called the islanders 'Southerners'. Yet the Northmen saw it differently. To reach the Isles, they always thought of 'sailing west'. To their way of thinking, they were not heading so much for 'the Southern Isles' as for 'the isles in the West'.

THE VIKINGS IN THE ISLES IN THE LATE NINTH AND EARLY TENTH CENTURIES

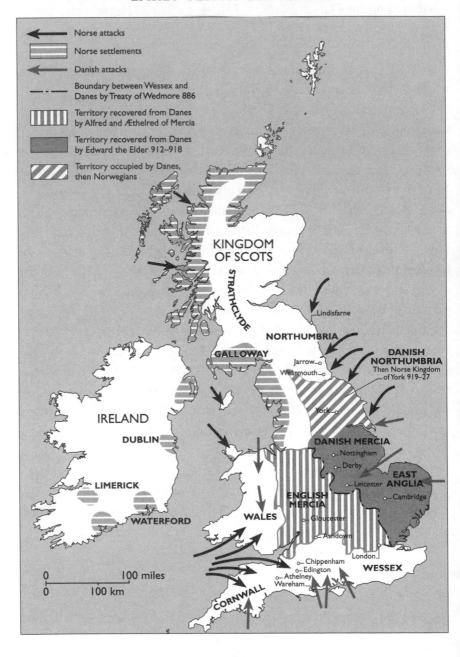

Norse attacks

Norse settlements

Danish attacks

Boundary between Wessex and Danes by Treaty of Wedmore 886

Territory recovered from Danes by Alfred and Æthelred of Mercia

Territory recovered from Danes by Edward the Elder 912–918

Territory occupied by Danes, then Norwegians

KINGDOM OF SCOTS

STRATHCLYDE

GALLOWAY

NORTHUMBRIA

Lindisfarne

DANISH NORTHUMBRIA
Then Norse Kingdom of York 919–27

Jarrow
Wearmouth

York

IRELAND

DUBLIN

DANISH MERCIA

Nottingham
Derby
Leicester

EAST ANGLIA

Cambridge

LIMERICK

ENGLISH MERCIA

WATERFORD

WALES

Gloucester

Ashdown

London

Chippenham
Edington
Athelney
Wareham

WESSEX

CORNWALL

0   100 miles
0   100 km

THE MEN WHO KILLED THE KING'S REEVE on the beach at Portland in 789 came from Hordaland, the district round Hardanger Fjord in what is now south-western Norway. Different versions of *The Anglo-Saxon Chronicle* called them 'Northmen' or 'Danes' interchangeably. In terms of their general lifestyle and activities, however, they belonged like Hengest's men centuries before to the category of sea-rovers. They were the rowmen of the longships which set sail from the fjords and specialized in seasonal expeditions and lightning raids. They were the forerunners of the more extensive Scandinavian forces which were to descend on the Isles with large-scale armies and with a view to permanent settlement. For reasons of convenience, modern scholarship calls both sorts of Scandinavians 'Vikings', thereby blurring the distinction. Furthermore, there is another mistaken tendency to identify the 'Northmen' or 'Norsemen' with modern Norway, and the 'Danes' with modern Denmark. This is not appropriate for the simple reason that in the period in question the separate Scandinavian nations of Norwegians, Danes, and Swedes had not yet come into existence.

The Viking appellation, therefore, needs to be glossed. It refers to an activity, not to an ethnic group. It probably derives from the Old Norse word *Viken*, which was used in the region of the modern Oslo with the sense of 'men of the fjords'. But it was soon picked up by Old English to designate any sort of 'Scandinavian pirate' irrespective of their particular place of origin. Yet it was only one of numerous names that were used at the time to refer to the various types of Scandinavians who landed in the Isles between the late eighth and mid-eleventh centuries. Churchmen like Asser were apt to call them all simply 'pagans'. This was particularly appropriate in that all contemporary commentators explained the Viking invasions by regarding them as God's punishment for people's sins.

Similarly, in its origins, the name of 'Dane' was not a national or an ethnic one. It is akin to the Old English *thegn*, and in the sense of 'warrior' was applied to the Northmen who took to fighting in consolidated bands, especially on the northern marches of the Carolingian Empire. In due course, when these battling Northmen established themselves in a permanent homeland, they called it Danmark or 'Denmark'. When they invaded England in force, they were usually dubbed *Daniscmen*; and the territory which their armies controlled was called the Danelagh or 'Danelaw'.

There is no point in disguising Viking violence. Viking raiders practised murder and pillage routinely, deliberately sowing terror among the settled and isolated communities whom they attacked. Some modern historians have reacted against the conventionally negative image. Yet the idea that Vikings were 'little more than long-haired tourists who occasionally roughed up the natives', is surely eccentric.[13] It is no less misplaced than the conviction of previous generations that gratuitous violence was the be-all and end-all of pagan Scandinavian culture.

Care must also be taken with the particular community of Scandinavians which settled in the early tenth century round the estuary of the Seine and which founded the modern province of 'Normandy'. These 'Normans', who intermarried with the local population and rapidly adopted the Christian religion and the Old French language of their hosts, are usually consigned to the French category. Yet one should not be too eager to jump the historical gun. The 'Northmen' of Normandy did not become homogenized Frenchmen overnight. Like their counterparts who settled in the Danelaw of eastern England at a slightly earlier date, they long retained a strong sense of their separate origins and culture. Even when they followed the 'Danish' example by conquering England, their poets and chroniclers continued to sing their praises as a distinct and providential people.[14] In the history of the Isles, there is no less reason to regard them as 'the last wave of the Northmen' than as 'the first wave of the French'.

Nonetheless, it is easy to spread confusion unless a consistent system of names is adopted. In the following pages, 'Northmen' is used as the general term. The pertinent adjective is 'Norse'; and the language which the Northmen spoke is 'Old Norse'. The Viking term is confined to the Norse pirates/sea-raiders/sea-rovers: the label of Dane to the soldiers and dependants of the great Norse armies. Normans will be Normans. To sum it up, all 'Vikings', 'Danes', and 'Normans' were 'Northmen' to one degree or another. But not every Northman was a Viking, a Dane, or a Norman.

If one thinks about it, Portland in Dorset was the unlikeliest place to have witnessed the Northmen's first landfall in the Isles. Portland is just about as far as one could sail from Hordaland without landing on the Continent. So it is reasonable to ask what those Northmen were doing when the King's Reeve apprehended them. One doesn't know from which direction they arrived, nor in which direction they left. But since there are no other reports of Viking raids either that year or for the next five years, it seems unlikely that the first shipload of Northmen to be sighted were actively engaged in an aggressive mission. It is rather more probable that they were reconnoitring, possibly that they were circumnavigating the Isles to work out their bearings and distances. For once they had made contact, their operations followed a steadily escalating pattern. In the first phase, they mounted regular raids for loot and plunder. In the second phase, they established fortified bases and winter outposts, sometimes known as *longhports*, from which the raiding could be better organized. And in the third phase, they brought in settlers to establish permanent colonies.

The first of the raids took place on 8 June 793, when Holy Island was attacked. As the Peterborough MS of *The Anglo-Saxon Chronicle* records:

793. Here terrible portents came about over the land of Northumbria, and miserably frightened the people: there were
immense flashes of lightning, and fiery dragons were seen
flying in the air. A great famine immediately followed these
signs; and a little after that . . . the raiding of heathen men
miserably devastated God's church in Lindisfarne by looting
and slaughter. And Sicga passed away on 22 February.[15]

Writing from the Carolingian court, the great Northumbrian scholar,
Alcuin, commiserated with his countrymen. In a letter to Bishop
Higebald, he sought to explain the disaster:

What can we say except weep with you in our hearts before
the altar of Christ and say 'Spare thy people, O Lord' . . . lest
the heavens should ask 'Where is the God of the Christians?'
. . . This indeed has not happened by chance; it is a sign that
someone has well deserved it . . .[16]

After Lindisfarne, it was the turn of Jarrow (794), Monkwearmouth,
Rechru, and Iona (795). A second assault on Iona in 806 led to the
dispersion of the Columban community, one group moving to Kells
in Éire, the other to Dunkeld. These sudden forays, which their
perpetrators called *strandhögg* or 'beach raids', resulted in much
pillage, arson, and wanton killing. The raiders departed as swiftly as
they came, carrying off treasure, cattle, women, and prisoners to be
sold into slavery. Henceforth, churches all over Europe would repeat
the prayer, 'Deliver us, O Lord, from the fury of the Norsemen . . .'
   One of the first of the Northmen's staging-posts was established
in the late eighth century in the island group of Hjaltland (Shetland),
the most northerly territory of the Picts. It is almost exactly two
hundred miles from the headland of Lamba Ness on Uist to the
coast of Hordaland and a similar distance to the Faroes. Hjaltland,
therefore, soon became a vital port of call both for ships heading
westwards across 'The Glacial Sea' to Iceland and Greenland and for
those heading south to the Isles and to western Europe. From
Shetland, one can proceed by a series of easy stages to Fridarey (Fair

Isle), to the Orkneyjar or 'Orkneys', to the mainland coast of Caithness and Sutherland, to the Hebrides, to Ireland, to Man and western Britannia, and thence along the old western seaways to Brittany, Biscay, and the Basque country. All of these destinations were visited by the dragonships in the early ninth century; and all the stops along the western sea-route through the Isles received forts and staging-posts of their own. In time, all the staging-posts in the Isles grew into compact Norse colonies with a Norse-speaking population. Such was the work of the ninth century.

Early Norse adventures in Hjaltland and the Orkneyjar (Orkneys) can be well charted thanks to the famous *Orkneyinga Saga*, or 'History of the Earls of Orkney'. Written by an unknown Icelander in a mixture of prose and poetry, the saga covers the period from the days of the legendary sea-kings to the late twelfth century. The historical part of the chronicle begins c. 891 when King Harald Fine-Hair mounted an expedition to crush the rebellious Vikings of the islands. Harald Fine-Hair was the first of the Norwegian rulers to bring a measure of unity and order to the twenty-seven sub-kingdoms and far-flung settlements of his realm. He was specially incensed that the Norsemen of Shetland had taken to regular plundering in Norway itself. Accompanied by his faithful retainer Ragnvald of More and Ragnvald's brother, Sigurd the Powerful, 'the forecastleman' of the royal flagship, he imposed his rule on all the Vikings from Shetland to Man. At the end of the expedition, he offered the islands to Ragnvald; but Ragnvald passed them on to Sigurd, who thereby became the very first Earl of Orkney. In the next generation, the islands were contested by Ragnvald's illegitimate son, Einarr, and King Harald's disobedient son, Halfdan Long-Leg. Einarr killed Halfdan, and, having built a burial mound, he composed a verse:

> Rekit telk Rǫgnvalds dauða,
> rétt skiptu því nornir,
> nú 's folkstuðill fallinn,
> at fjórðungi mínum.

Verpið, snarpir sveinar,
þvít sigri vér róðum,
skatt velk hónum harðan,
at Háfœtu grjóti.

(The folk-lord is fallen
the fee paid for Rognvald;
sweetly the Norns shaped
for me my quarter-share.
Cast the stone, keen
lads, on Long-leg's cairn
as we celebrate here
the settling of the Scot.)[17]

Einarr was remembered for his foresight in introducing the art of peat-burning. He was the progenitor of a line of earls who ruled Orkney and Shetland under Norwegian suzerainty until 1472.

The counties of Caithness and Sutherland were conquered from the Picts and settled by Norse colonists from the neighbouring earldom. Their place names remain predominantly Norse to the present day. Caithness was Kaitness. From the viewpoint of Vikings coming from the earldom, Sudrland (Sutherland) – the most northerly district of Great Britain – was the 'Southernland'. Thórsá (Thurso) was 'Thor's River'; Höfn (Ham) was 'the Harbour' for crossing to Orkney; Skarabólstadr (Scrabster) was 'the homestead on the edge'; Vik (Wick) was 'the bay'. In the Norse sagas, Skotland, 'the land of the Irish', did not include these northern parts, but lay far to the south beyond the Breida Fjord (the Moray Firth).

In the Sudreyjar, or Hebrides, the arrival of the Northmen interrupted a long-running contest between Picts and Dalriadans. They were first sighted there in 794. Through persistent attacks they established a dominant presence. In the mid-ninth century, when solid colonization began, a Danish expedition became embroiled in fighting among the Norse settlers already there. An early chieftain, Ketil Flatnose (d. c. 860), failed to establish a dynasty. But place-name evidence suggests that Scandinavians came to form the majority of the population.

Norse control of Man (the Isle of Man) flowed from their control over the Hebrides. Harald Fine-Hair is said to have laid it waste. The Northmen left traces in the Manx language which diverged henceforth both from Irish and from Scots Gaelic. But they left a permanent legacy in the island's assembly or *Tynwald*, which continues to meet to the present day as a living embodiment of Viking democracy. From their bases on Man, they were equidistant from the coasts of Éire and of north-western Britannia.

Viking raids on Ireland were an annual event from the 790s onwards. From the 830s much larger fleets sailed regularly into the Liffey, the Boyne, and the Shannon. In 839–41 there were sixty longships on the Liffey where a Viking captain called Thorgisl conquered Ulster, marched south, and built a *longhport*. He called it Dublin after the Irish Dubh linn, or 'Black Pool', and declared himself king. Ten years later, the Danish expedition which had reached the Hebrides joined in the fray, making common cause with the local Irish. From then on, the Irish allegedly distinguished between the *Finngaill*, 'the fair foreigners' (the Norse) and the *Dubhgaill*, the 'dark foreigners' (the Danes). The Norsemen held the upper hand, however; and under the two brothers Olaf the White and Ivar the Boneless (d. 873) they turned Dublin into a major slaving centre and a base for attacking Britannia. For many years a Viking fleet was based on the inland waters of Lough Neagh. In Ireland they called themselves *Ostmen*, 'Men of the East', to distinguish themselves from the Irish whom they called *Vestmenn*, or 'West Men'. As such they established a number of coastal bases at Wexford, Waterford, and Limerick. They were inevitably drawn into Ireland's wars, having arrived at a time when the dominant Uí Néill in the northern Conn's Half were being seriously challenged by Kings of Cashel from the southern Mug's Half. The fearsome King-Bishop of Cashel, Feidlimid mac Crimhthainn (d. 847), had the reputation of razing far more churches than the Norsemen ever did. The feud

which he started was not ended until the reign of Flann Sinna, King
of Tara, who utterly destroyed the southerners and their Norse
allies at the Battle of Belagh Mugna in 908. The fluidity of arrangements at this juncture is well illustrated both by the story of Aud
the Deeply Wealthy (see above, page 235) and by the fate of Dublin.
Though apparently well established, Dublin was abandoned by the
Ostmen in 902 in the face of Flann Sinna's advance. The Ostmen
moved for a decade or two to Man and to Britannia. They came
back in force in 917.

Norse settlement in north-west Britannia, which dated from the
mid-ninth century, flowed naturally from movement along the
island sea-routes. It was an integral part of the realm of Dublin,
Man, and the Hebrides. The original base was set up on the Wirral,
where the Mersey estuary provided the classic setting for a Viking
harbour. From these, expeditions were mounted with varying success in all directions. The greatest success was found in Northumbria, however, where, after a signal victory at Corbridge in 915, two
adventurous *Ostmen*, Ragnvald and Sygtrygg the Squint-Eyed, seized
control of the Danish Kingdom of Jorvik.

In the tenth century, Viking fortunes began to approach their
limits. They were absolute masters of the sea. But they did not
possess either the manpower or the military forces to match
the overall impact of the Danes. In mainland Britannia, their
colonies were confined to two or three localities – one in Dalriadan
territory in Argyll, one in the former Rheged between Mersey
and Ribble, and another, possibly, on Mona (which they called
Anglesey). Almost all of the offshore islands in those parts from
Bardsey to Lundy were given Norse names, thereby indicating
a measure of Norse settlement. Their hold on the Kingdom of
Jorvik was precarious; their settlements in Ireland were constantly
under threat. Limerick was sacked in 965 by the King of a renascent
Cashel:

[The Irish] carried off their jewels and their best property, their
beautiful foreign saddles, their gold and silver, and their fine

woven cloth of all colours and all kinds. Afterwards they
reduced the good town to a cloud of smoke and red fire. All
the captives were collected on the hills of Saingel. Every one of
them fit for war was killed; every one who was fit for a slave,
was enslaved.[18]

Dublin was sacked in 981 by the King of Tara, and again in 999 by
the triumphant King of Cashel, Brian Boru, who thereupon pronounced himself 'emperor of the Irish'.

The final act of Ireland's Viking wars came at Clontarf in 1014,
the site of Brian Boru's culminating victory and death. Thanks to
the subsequent eulogies of the O'Briens, the significance of the
battle has clearly been exaggerated. Irish were fighting Irish, with
Norse allies on both sides. The Norse King of Dublin did not take
part. Even so, the battle certainly marked the term of Norse
ambitions to play a major role in Ireland. And it was important
enough to be remembered in Icelandic poetry:

> Var ek þar, er bragnar bǫrðusk;
> brandr gall á Írlandi;
> margr, þar er mœttusk tǫrgur,
> málmr gnast í dyn hjálma;
> sókn þeira frá ek snarpa,
> Sigurðr fell í dyn vigra;
> áðr téði ben blœða;
> Bríann fell ok helt velli.

> *(I was there when warriors fought*
> *Swordblades rang on Ireland's coast*
> *Metal yelled as shield it sought*
> *Spearpoints in the well-armed host.*
> *I heard swordblows many more*
> *Sigurd fell in battle's blast*
> *From his wounds there sprang hot gore*
> *Brian fell, but won at last.)*[19]

Other Norse ambitions, in Britannia, were dashed at an earlier date, and in two separate episodes.

For a brief period in the early tenth century, the prospect had loomed that a strategic Norse hegemony could be formed by the junction of the Dublin Norse and their kinsmen in the Kingdom of Jorvik. There was no love lost between the Dublin Norse and the Northmen of the Danelaw; and Jorvik had only passed into Norse hands through Danish preoccupations with the resurgent power of Wessex. What is more, there were several sturdy allies to hand – in Man, in Scotland, and in Strathclyde. The issue came to a head in the 930s. On gaining control of Jorvik Sygtrygg the Squint-eyed had relinquished his kingship at Dublin to his brother Guthfrith. He had also tried to bolster his position by marrying a sister of the great Athelstan, King of Wessex, and by accepting Christianity. Within a year, however, he had been forced by his heathen subjects to renounce both bride and faith. Athelstan thereupon seized York, killed Sygtrygg, defeated Guthfrith, and rapidly gained a position to dominate the whole of the north. A coalition rapidly formed against him. By 937, Olaf Guthfrithson, the new King of Dublin, had sealed an alliance with Constantine II, King of Scots, with Owain Mac-Domhnuil, King of Strathclyde, probably with Aralt, King of Man and the Isles, and possibly with other Celtic chieftains. His army sailed to meet his allies in Britannia, and Athelstan marched to meet them at Brunanburh.

Some historians insist that the site of Brunanburh has not been identified. But nothing fits it so well as Bromborough on the Mersey shore of the Wirral. The Wirral, after all, was the regular place for Norse fleets from Dublin to land, and an obvious target for the Saxons to attack. At all events the battle was one of the bloodiest, and most definitive in the history of the Isles. Five (unnamed) kings, seven Norse earls, and two of Athelstan's own cousins were slain. Both the Icelandic *Saga of Egil Skallagrimsson* (who had fought for Athelstan) and *The Anglo-Saxon Chronicle*, which broke into purple verse for the occasion, agreed that 'greater carnage had not been in this island ever':

> . . . the field streamed with warriors' blood
> When rose at morning tide the glorious star
> The sun, God's shining candle, until sank
> The noble creature to its setting.
> As fled the Scots, weary and sick of war
> Forth followed the West Saxons, in war bands
> Tracking the hostile folk the livelong day.
>   . . . There lay five kings
> Whom on the battlefield swords put to sleep,
> And they were young, and seven of Olaf's earls
> With Scots and mariners, an untold host . . .[20]

Celtic tradition sees Brunanburh in rather different light. Less concerned with the fate of the Northmen, Celtic commentators grieve over the last occasion when the Celts of the Isles might conceivably have united to expel the Saxons once and for all. Speculation about the identity of the five dead kings opens up fascinating vistas of Athelstan being confronted not just by Norse, Scots, and northern British but by Irish, western British, and Cornish as well. Unfortunately, there is no shred of evidence for the presence at Brunanburh of Hywel Dda, paramount King of western Britain, despite the proximity of his lands to the battle (see below). All there is is a stirring poem – Armes Prydein Vawr, 'the Prophecy of Great Britain' – written in Dyfed in Hywel's reign and calling on the British to join the Norse and, under the banner of Dewi Sant, to drive the Saxons into the sea.[21]

Twenty years later, as an epilogue to the disaster of Brunanburh, the Northmen of Jorvik shook off their Saxon overlord and welcomed as their king the most notorious Norse adventurer of the age. Eirik Blóðox, or Eric Bloodaxe (d. 954), son of Harald Fine-Hair, had succeeded his father in 933 only to provoke a civil war with his brothers and, after a brief and violent reign, to be driven into exile. He came to Jorvik at the end of two decades of brawling the length and breadth of the Viking world. As the sometime King of all-Norway, he enjoyed unusual prestige; and the irony of his position at Jorvik, where he had expelled Athelstan's brother, Eadred, was increased by the fact that Norway had been taken over by his own half-brother Hákon Haraldsson, Athelstan's foster son. Eric set up a grand pagan court in the land of St Aidan which had been predominantly Christian for three hundred years. It didn't last long. In 954, Eadred re-established Saxon rule in York by force of arms. The 'Blood-axe' was last reported treacherously murdered on the wastes of Stainmoor by one Maccus Olafson – in all probability the son of the defeated Norse leader at Brunanburh.

By that time, of course, the Vikings were losing their drive. Though Norway itself remained pagan, many of the Norse colonies in the Isles were adopting the Christianity of their neighbours. The pagan marauders were being tamed. The raids of the longships had ceased. Much of the surplus population of the fjords had sailed to Iceland, and from Iceland were sailing to Greenland and to America.

Yet the Vikings' impact on the Isles must not be minimized. By conquering much of Pictland, and by cutting off Dalriada from Éire, they created the preconditions for the consolidation of the 'Kingdom of the Scots' (see page 263, below). Their presence in the islands was long-lasting. There were people still speaking Norse in Orkney and Shetland in the eighteenth century. In Éire, by founding numerous commercial ports, they greatly stimulated the country's maritime trade. And, by introducing compact warrior colonies, they acted as a catalyst for the wars which eventually, under Brian Boru, provoked a measure of unity. Indeed, they constituted a permanent element in the make-up of the country which they were the first to call 'Ireland'.

For some reason, the Vikings largely left their runes behind when they sailed to the Isles. Though a number of runic inscriptions are known from various locations along the western seaways, the Isle of Man was the only place to receive a substantial collection. This gap only adds to the mystery with which the Vikings continue to be surrounded.

≈

In the former Britannia, the Vikings made less impact perhaps than elsewhere. Their Britannic exploits were less formidable than those of the Danish armies. But their example, of sturdy sea-rovers and fearless sons of Thor, must have aroused more than fear. Indeed, in the hearts of everyone in Britannia who thought themselves to be the heirs of Hengest and Horsa it must have inspired considerable admiration.

As soon as the initial raiding phase was over, the Northmen moved quickly into full-scale campaigns of invasion. Unlike the Vikings, whose small squadrons sailed directly across the North Sea and down the western sea-routes, the Danes came in much larger numbers and with far greater fleets. They edged along the Continental coasts, and approached the Isles from the south. From their initial campaigning grounds south of the Danevirke in Schleswig, they had razed Hamburg before being repulsed by Charlemagne. They then established one major base area near the mouth of the Rhine, and another near the mouth of the Seine. From there, it was only one short step to the coast of Kent or of the South Saxons. For much of the ninth century, in fact, the Saxon chronicles did not call them Danes, but just 'heathen men' or 'the local host'.

In the 830s, Egbert, King of Wessex (r. c. 815–39) had already assumed the dominant position previously held by Offa of Mercia. For some years, he had served as a captain in Charlemagne's guard, and on his return from the Continent dealt some crushing blows to the ambitions of Mercia. His victory at Ellendown (825) gave Wessex the upper hand among his rivals, and briefly gave him the title of Bretwalda. This was a fortunate circumstance from the point of view of the West Saxons, because they were based in the swathe of territory furthest removed from the areas most attractive for Danish colonization. It would be a factor in their ability to ride the coming invasion and in the eventual outcome. Whilst Egbert was still alive, *The Winchester Chronicle* recorded: '832. Her heathene men ofer hergodon Sceap ege.' (Here [in fact in 835] heathen men raided across Sheppey.)[22]

Lying off Kent, the Isle of Sheppey was an ideal site, like Thanet for Hengest, to gain the initial toehold. Next year, King Egbert fought against 'thirty-five shiploads' *aet carrum* 'on the rocks', that is, at a site called Cernemude in the West Country. There was great slaughter, but the Danes held their ground. In 838, a great ship-army of Danes joined the 'Kerno Welsh'; and Egbert only held his own by calling out the whole fyrd of Wessex. The crucial battle was fought at Hengestdune. In 839, King Egbert passed away, after a reign of thirty-two years and seven months. It was the same year that Thorgisl was founding Dublin.

From the mid-830s the scale of operations multiplied enormously. Every two or three years fleets of several hundred ships sailed from Denmark carrying thousands of fighting men to the various fronts. Hamburg was again ransacked. But for forty years it was Paris that provided the prime target. Rouen, Chartres, Tours all fell. Charlemagne's grandson, Charles the Bald (r. 843–77), built successive defence lines; fought endless battles; paid huge sums in tribute, the Danegeld; and repeatedly recruited one Danish chieftain to fight another. Finally, in 886, thirty-five thousand Danes besieged a Paris defended by only two hundred knights. Fire, heroic sallies by Count Odo, plague, floods all failed to force a resolution. The eventual way out was for the Frankish king, Charles the Fat (r. 882–7), to pay the Danes to move off and attack his neighbours in Burgundy.

During these lengthy operations on the Continent, parts of the Danish ship-army regularly peeled off to attack the poorly defended coasts across the Channel, and the greater part of the former Britannia was effectively conquered. The Danish conquest made deeper and more rapid inroads into the island than that of the 'Angles and Saxons' four centuries before. Yet it is little known, partly because the illiterate Vikings left virtually no records of their own and partly because West Saxons' accounts are more concerned to publicize their later triumphs than their earlier near-disasters. One factor, however, is beyond doubt. The defenders of the Isles possessed neither the ships nor the skill to confront the Scandinavians' mastery of the seas. The islanders, one historian wrote, 'had forgotten their sea-faring heritage'. From time to time they notched up a local victory on land. But they had no means of intercepting or interdicting the massive fleets of ships which landed huge numbers of disciplined warriors on all their shores.

From the first major incursions of the 'Heathen Army' in 840 to the treaty which fixed the boundaries of their jurisdiction, only forty-six years passed. The onslaught came in two great waves. Initially, in 840, the southern coast of Wessex was targeted – first in the Solent with its port of Ham and then on the open beach at Cernemude. But no prominent beachhead was set up. In 841, two massive assaults materialized – one in the Thames estuary, another in the Wash. The former, with five hundred ships, overwhelmed everything in the region except the city of London itself. The latter opened the way for the penetration of the Midland rivers. In 844 Northumbria was invaded, and its king, Redwulf, killed. During the ensuing lull, when the fleets sailed off to Hamburg and Aquitaine, it would not have been hard to conclude that the east was far more vulnerable than the south. In 851, though, the West Saxons inflicted a crushing defeat at Aclea. London was captured. Fearing perhaps a British coalition with the Vikings, Æthelwulf of Wessex even found time for a foray into western Britannia. But the respite was brief, as from 854 several heathen formations joined forces to create a 'Great Host' which harried far and wide without mercy. Northumbria was overrun, its last two kings killed. After York was stormed, the southern section, the old kingdom of Deira, re-emerged as the Scandinavian 'Kingdom of Jorvik'. In 870, East Anglia was annihilated and its king, Edmund, martyred. After East Anglia, it was the turn of Mercia, whose king, Burgred, was forced to flee. The eastern half was put under the direct rule of the 'Five Boroughs' and their five jarls of Derby, Nottingham, Lincoln, Leicester, and Stamford. The western half was left in the hands of a renegade Mercian earl, Ceolwulf.

By the 870s, the Great Host controlled the whole of the former Britannia between Scotland and the Thames. Of the old Germanic kingdoms, Wessex alone was holding out. So the decisive attack developed against Wessex – first under two doughty chieftains, and then under the new Danish lord of East Anglia, Guthrum. The strategy was simple. A huge impregnable military base was built at Reading on the middle Thames, to challenge the defending Wessex forces. A grand fleet would then round Kent, and land the decisive strike force on the south coast. The Reading base proved impregnable. The forces of Wessex were effectively tied down. In 871, six battles were fought with no clear outcome, except that the attackers could ride out and pillage at will. In the spring of 878, the new young King of Wessex, Alfred, was reduced to taking refuge in the Somerset marshes at Athelney. People were fleeing abroad. Final victory for the Danes seemed imminent. It was prevented by three developments. In 876, a great storm destroyed over a hundred longships and their crews off the coast at Swanage. Then, by a mixture of guile and guts, Alfred was able to revive the flagging defenders. And lastly, Guthrum was gradually convinced that a negotiated settlement might offer him more than a fight to the finish. Fighting continued with intervals till 896. Before then, the line of demarcation between Wessex and the Danelaw or 'Danish Jurisdiction' was defined by treaty. The critical point on the line, at the confluence of the rivers Thames and Lea, put the city of London in Wessex and control of London's sea trade in the hands of the Danes. (Curiously enough, that point lies on the bank of the Thames exactly opposite the site where a Millennium Dome would be built over eleven hundred years later.)

Alfred (r. 871–99), later called 'the Great', gained his enormous reputation partly through his astonishing powers of survival, and partly, in his later years, through the unusually wide range of his interests. He was victorious warrior, law-giver, sage administrator, strategic planner, cultural patron, and, through the support of his hagiographical biographer Asser, creator of his own legend. (Asser's integrity has been questioned more than once.) Alfred's reign was built on the remarkable arrangement reached in 878 with Guthrum. Emerging from the marshes of Athelney, Alfred improvised an army that somehow inflicted an important reverse at Edington Down; he then took Guthrum in as his guest, and persuaded him to accept Christian baptism, and, by the Treaty of Wedmore, to withdraw. From that stage onwards, the Wessex Chronicle drops the epithet of the *heathen men* and starts to talk of the *Deningoais*, 'the Danes'. Alfred thereby won the respite to lay the foundations not just of a restored state but also of a new united nation.

Of Alfred's many achievements, three deserve particular mention. Firstly, as a literate man, he assembled the scholarly and educational infrastructure for maintaining a permanent royal-sponsored cultural elite. Secondly, he built up a comprehensive defence system. On land, he constructed a network of over thirty fortified *burhs*. At sea, he constructed a standing fleet of sixty-oar longships which were superior to those in use by the Danes. Thirdly, he engineered a complex amalgamation of West Saxon institutions with those of the overrun kingdom of Mercia. Law codes were integrated, territorial shires introduced. He married one of his daughters to Ceolwulf's successor, and returned London to Mercian rule. By these and other acts of enlightened generosity, he turned Mercia into a West Saxon dependency, thereby creating the basis for the enlarged kingdom of the future.[23]

The establishment of the Danelaw, and the protracted struggle between the Danes and West Saxons, had important consequences for the Celts of western Britannia. Effectively hedged in since the late eighth century by Offa's Dyke, they might have expected a contest to the death with the rising power of Mercia. Instead, with Mercia subdued by the Danes, they experienced a long period of isolation during which they could develop their own institutions, promote their own language, and consolidate their separate identity. No united Celtic realm emerged. But intermarriage between the ruling houses, the rise and fall of dominant leaders, and life under common laws and customs nourished the rise of a distinct national community.

Between 800 and 1100, no less than four Welsh princes succeeded

in expanding their local power-bases into realms covering most of
the territory west of the dyke. What this indicated was not a
national polity, but a cohesive cultural area within which enterprising princes could seek their fortunes. Rhodri ap Merfyn (r. 844–77),
for instance, started as Prince of Gwynedd in the north. He took
over Powys in the centre from his mother's relatives and Seisyllwg
in the south from his wife's relatives. He died as Rhodri Mawr,
'Rhodri the Great', ruling a realm from Anglesey to Gower. Rhodri's
grandson, Hywel Dda, 'Hywell the Good' (r. 900–50), started from
a southern base in Seisyllwg and Dyfed and ended by taking over
Gwynedd. He was a regular visitor to the courts of Alfred's heirs,
by whom he was heavily taxed, and is known to have visited Rome.
Maredudd ap Owain (r. 986–99), Prince of Deheubarth (the principality created by Hywel's linkage of Seisyllwg and Dyfed), also
ruled, like Hywel, in Gwynedd.

Hywel's epithet of 'the Good' probably derived from his reputation as a law-giver. The Law of Hywel, combining justice with
mercy, codified the Celtic folk law of centuries past, providing a
body of rules and customs that continued to evolve throughout the
Middle Ages. It addressed an exclusively rural society, where the
bonheddwyr, the 'well born', lorded it over various gradations of
freemen and slaves. It is known from a total of forty-two variant
texts, copied from earlier versions in the thirteenth century mainly
in Welsh but partly in Latin. It offered a strong secular counterweight to the canon law of the Church.

No Welsh prince, however, was quite so successful as the brutal
Grufudd ap Llewellyn (r. 1039–63). In a thirty-year rampage of
violence against all his neighbours, he murdered and marauded his
way to a fitting end. Starting in Gwynedd, he took over every
corner of Wales, including Gwent and Glamorgan, before attacking
Mercia and driving out the English settlers from the Border beyond
the dyke. Married to a high-born Mercian lady – Ealdgyth, granddaughter of Lady Godiva – and allied to Mercians opposed to the
West Saxon hegemony, he was finally driven back to his lair in 1063
by Harold Godwinson, the future King of England. Grufudd was

killed in Snowdonia by the son of one of his Welsh victims. His widow was taken in marriage by Harold. Thus, briefly, 'Wales was one, under one ruler, a feat with neither precedent nor successor'; and Ealdgyth 'was in turn Queen of Wales and Queen of England'.[24]

Not that violence was Wales's sole heritage from those turbulent times. Celtic literature and history flourished among the fighting. The tenth century saw the composition both of *Armes Prydein* (see above) and of the *Annales Cambriae*, the 'Annals of Wales'. The eleventh century saw a burst of hagiography, including the *Latin Life of St David* and c. 1060, at the height of Grufudd ap Llewellyn's depredations, the masterpiece of legend, the *Pedair Cainc y Mabinogi*, 'The Four Branches of the Mabinogi'.[25]

The establishment of the Danelaw, and particularly of the Northmen in Jorvik, had similar consequences for the nascent Kingdom of Scotland. The period from 800 to 1050 is usually seen as the period of the consolidation of the Mac Alpin dynasty, and hence of the Gaelic supremacy. No less than fourteen male descendants of Kenneth Mac Alpin ruled in succession from his death in 858 to the death of Malcolm II in 1034. By one means or another, they managed to obliterate the culture and community of the Picts whose previous rulers they displaced.

Yet this simple picture demands a number of refinements. Kenneth Mac Alpin is described in the genealogies as King of 'Pictavia'; and it is his grandson, Donald II (r. 889–900), who first uses the Gaelic form *rí Alban*, or 'King of Alba'. (The Latin form of 'Albania' also occurs.) So the progress of the Gaelic supremacy occurred gradually, not as the result of some imaginary 'black dinner' at which all the Pictish leaders were eliminated. What is more, one has to remember that the Scotia or 'Scotland' which emerged through the fusion of the Hiberno-Celtic Gaels and the fading Picts, and which was ruled from Scone on the Tay, covered no more than the central parts of ancient Caledonia. It did not include the Western Isles, Orkney and Shetland, or Caithness and

Sutherland, all of which were firmly in Norse hands. It may not have included Moray, whose rulers were called *jarls* in Norwegian sources, *ri* or kings in Irish sources, and *mormaer* in later Scottish sources. It certainly did not include the land of Lothian south of the Forth round Edinburgh, which was now inhabited by Angles and which in the Latin chronicles of the Gaels was called 'Saxonia'. And it did not include the surviving British kingdom of Strathclyde, which had spread into Cumbria.

In this patchwork of changing ethnic communities and fluctuating hegemony, the Mac Alpin kings operated through a complicated system of temporary alliances and shifting clientage. They could have harboured no hope of setting themselves up as sole kings of Pan-Caledonia. Whilst building up the substance of their central Gaelic power base, they gradually established a fragile overlordship over the other ruling houses. At a later stage, their propagandists would try to contrast the true Christian kingship of Scotia with the mere kinglets and underlords of neighbouring lands. The important thing for them was that they were shielded from turbulence to the south in the former Britannia by the extensive intermediate buffer zone of Strathclyde–Cumbria, Lothian, Jorvik, and the bridgeheads in Britain of the Kingdom of Dublin.

In the middle of the eleventh century the Mac Alpin dynasty ran into trouble. Automatic primogeniture had never been practised. But Malcolm II (r. 1005–34) and the various candidates for the throne – Duncan I (r. 1034–40), Malcolm II's grandson, Macbeth of Moray (r. 1040–57), Malcolm II's nephew, and Lulach of Moray (r. 1057–8), Macbeth's stepson – all became embroiled in an elaborate feud. This was nothing unusual in medieval dynasties, but the sensational treatment of the episode by William Shakespeare has turned it into an archetype of bloodthirsty treachery and usurpation, replete with witches and sexual jealousy:

> I am in blood
> Stepp'd in so far that, should I wade no more,
> Returning were as tedious as go o'er.[26]

Shakespeare did not hint to his English audience that similar
tragedies had occurred nearer home; and he dragged the whole of
Scottish history into that same sea of gore and nihilism:

> Out, out brief candle!
> Life's but a walking shadow, a poor player
> That struts and frets his hour upon the stage
> And then is heard no more: it is a tale
> Told by an idiot, full of sound and fury,
> Signifying nothing.[27]

These may be lines of unsurpassed magnificence. Yet they hardly
match the historical record. Macbeth was sufficiently sure of his
throne to be the only King of Scots to visit Rome, where 'he
scattered money like seed to the poor'. He held on to the sceptre
despite the defeat at Dunsinnan (1054), and he was finally killed by
Duncan's son, Malcolm Canmore. As part of his military strategy,
he imported the first contingent of Norman knights to Scotland.
This event signalled a trend which in the next generation would
transform the cultural and ethnic landscape of the Lowlands.[28]

Far to the south, whilst the Danes worked to colonize and to
assimilate the vast lands under their jurisdiction in the former
Britannia, the House of Wessex sought to recover its once dominant
position. Over the years both sides succeeded in these aims; and it
is from the resultant fusion of the Danish and of the Wessex-led
Anglo-Saxon elements that the first 'Kingdom of England' was born.
Such, of course, is not the traditional picture. English nationalist
historians have always tried to discount the Viking–Danish invasions
as a mere interlude, and to put the emergence of an English national
community much further back. In reality, it is doubtful whether
any sense of an all-English identity could have emerged without
the Viking impulse. It took the Vikings and the Danes to break the
particularisms of the previous period, especially in Mercia and
Northumbria, and to present the one remaining local dynasty, the

House of Wessex, with a consolidated objective. To suggest that the political entity of England emerged thanks to a pre-existing and long-standing cultural and linguistic unity is to put the wagon before the ox.

The Danish impact, therefore, was considerable. The 'Great Army' brought in colonists and settlers in such numbers that place names with the typical Danish endings *-by*, *-thorpe*, and *-dale* became a standard feature of the north-east, the east, and the Midlands. From Grimesthorpe to Grimsby, from Ashby to Hornby to Whitby, Danish names came to predominate in many parts. An early form of Old Norse was introduced as the official language of the Danelaw, and its presence helped the long process of changing Anglo-Saxon Old English into medieval Middle English (see below). What is more, as Frank Stenton showed in an early work, Viking social customs exerted a liberating effect on the nascent traditions of early English society. Basing his research on his homeland in the heart of the Danelaw, Stenton found that the Danish villages possessed better farming methods, more freemen, and greater commercial contacts than their Anglo-Saxon counterparts.[29] The Danelaw was the most populous and most prosperous region of the country. Once the pagan barrier was lifted, it was well fitted to play an active part in the cultural and political unification which the West Saxons were trying to promote.

Since the Norse-speaking population was so large, it may seem surprising that it left so few traces. Written evidence of Norse is particularly rare. One has to presume that the art of writing went hand in hand with conversion to Christianity, but that the incoming Anglo-Saxon or Anglo-Saxon trained clergy would only have taught the converts to write either in Latin or in Old English. Norse would have slowly declined as a neglected, rural, unwritten vernacular. Yet a handful of Norse inscriptions *have* survived, most typically on village sundials. These may possibly have some connection with the undeclared remnants of pagan practices within Christianized communities. One of them, from Aldborough (E. Yorkshire), bears these words round the edge of the stone dial:

VLF[HE]T AROERAN CYRICE FOR HA[A]NVM ꟁ FOR
GYN[WARA] SAVLA

*(Ulf ordered the church (to be built) for himself & for
Gunwara's soul)*

The revival of Wessex under Alfred's successors is the stuff of
conventional English history. It is often presented as if it was bound
to happen. Edward the Elder (r. 899–924) conquered the whole of
the Danelaw south of the Humber. Athelstan (r. 924–39) harboured
still greater ambitions. Having taken the Welsh princes under his
wing, and in 934 having raided deep into Scotland, he took the title
not just of Bretwalda but of Basileus, 'Emperor'. At Brunanburh
(see page 254, above), he cut short the prospect of a Celto-Norse
coalition against the growing hegemony of Wessex; and he initiated
the recovery of Northumbria that was eventually completed by
the overthrow of Eric Bloodaxe. He even lent a fleet to Louis
d'Outremer, exiled King of the West Franks. The culminating act
occurred in 973 when King Edgar (r. 959–75) was rowed down the
River Dee by 'eight British Kings' as a sign of their submission. As
revealed at his coronation, Edgar's regal style, like that of Athelstan,
had distinctly imperial connotations.

Caution needs to be applied, however, to these passing moments
of symbolic success. Later English historians tend to seize on them
as proof of permanent English suzerainty. The reality was more
prosaic. In an age when precise legal and territorial definitions were
lacking, all monarchs had to vaunt their pretensions and to exagger-
ate their standing vis-à-vis their neighbours. Historians cannot take
all these pretensions at face value. Athelstan, for example, tested the
mettle of Harald Fine-Hair, and Fine-Hair tested Athelstan:

At this time, a young king called Athelstan the Good ruled
England ... He sent messengers to King Harald in Norway
with this errand. The envoy came into the King's presence, and
presented him with a sword, its scabbard all splendid with gold
and silver and set with gems.

The envoy said, 'My lord King, here is a sword that Athelstan, king of England sends you as a gift.' When the King took hold of the hilt, the envoy said at once, 'You accepted it as our king expected you to. Now you must be his man after this "sword-taking".' . . .

Now King Harald had no intention of being Athelstan's man, nor indeed the man of anybody else in the world. Yet he concluded that it was not kingly behaviour to kill the envoys of another king if they carried their lord's message unadorned. Rather guile should be met with guile . . .

Next summer King Harald sent a ship west to England, and put it in charge of his best friend Hauk Habrok. He also put under his care a lad called Hakon, whom Thora Morstrong, his servant-girl, had given birth to . . .

So Hauk met up with King Athelstan in London. When the tables were cleared, the King bade him welcome. Then Hauk said, 'Lord, King Harald of Norway has sent you his kind regards. Further he has sent you a white bird, well trained, and asks you to train it even better in the future.' He pulled the lad out of the lap of his cloak, and put him on the King's knee . . .

Then Athelstan said, 'Whose child is this?' Hauk answered, 'The mother is a servant girl. She says King Harald is the father. Now that you have taken the lad on your own knee, you must treat him as if he were your own son.' . . . So Athelstan had Hakon brought up at his court, and ever since he has been known as *Aðalsteinsfóstri*, 'Athelstan's foster-son'.[30]

As the saga concludes, 'each of the kings wanted to be recognized as higher than the other'. In reality, neither of them exercised any formal overlordship.

The standard (English) story of this period tells how the native Anglo-Saxons won back England from the Danish intruders. It is called a 'reconquest' because the assumption is that England had existed much earlier. 'The Making of England' is usually placed in the centuries preceding Alfred, not in the century following Alfred.[31] Nonetheless it might be more precise to say that one section of the

Old Germanics, that is, the West Saxon elite, created England in the course of the tenth century by subduing the New Germanics (the Danes) together with the rest of the Old Germanics who had passed under Danish rule. For it does not follow that the warriors of Wessex were less heavy-handed or more welcome than the Danes. On the contrary, they formed the vanguard of an imperial war machine whose ethos was anything but peaceful and gentle. The nearest parallel in European history may be that of the *conquistadors* of Castile whose long career of global conquest grew out of the centuries-long *Reconquista* in Spain. It took a Welshman, of course, to see the comparison:

> England was united under very remarkable circumstances: all her kingdoms other than Wessex were conquered by the Danes, and it was a crusade under the leadership of the House of Cerdic which brought all the English under the rule of one king. The kingdom of England was created by *conquistadores* campaigning to restore their country to their race and their faith, an experience which fostered an imperial spirit among them, as it did in not wholly dissimilar circumstances among the men of Castile centuries later.[32]

What is more, having finally turned the dubious claims of the old Bretwaldas into reality, the victors ensured that their achievement would be permanently enshrined in political consciousness. They gave their unified kingdom a famous name – the name of *Engla land*, 'England'. As a tenth-century chronicler put it, 'Britain is now called England, thereby assuming the name of the victors.'[33] The exact moment or authorship of this stroke of 'consummate mastery' has not been recorded. But its effects were to last. It gave the new kingdom a clear identity, a brand name which none of the other countries in the Isles yet possessed; and it served to bind the various peoples of the kingdom more closely together. Naturally, it could not create a homogeneous 'nation' of the modern sort. One of King Edgar's law codes talked of 'all the nation, whether Englishmen, Danes, or Britons'. This indicates that each of the communities within the kingdom – what the Latin chroniclers called *gentes* – were still regarded as separate entities. But over them all, there now existed the over-arching concept of a unified realm. The subjects of this realm were to remain convinced of its permanence even when foreign invaders reappeared, even when the House of Wessex was overthrown, even when the victors were themselves vanquished. 'English-consciousness', wrote a recent analyst, was 'strong enough to survive the extinction of the class that had created it . . .'[34] Here, not earlier, in the long phase when Wessex held the initiative in the Viking wars, was the time when England was made.

For the Viking wars were far from over. After a long pause in the mid-tenth century, Viking raiders and Danish invaders reappeared in what some historians have called the Second Viking Age. Coastal raiding again became the order of the day, 'sometimes with a savage intensity'. Some of the raiders penetrated deep inland. In 980, for instance, not just the city but the whole shire of Chester were devastated. Viking armies, some of them every bit as powerful as those of the ninth century, landed in 1003, 1014, 1066, and 1098.

Nor was the Kingdom of England at ease with itself once the House of Wessex had completed its conquest. On the contrary, the long reign of Æthelred the 'Unready' (r. 978–1016) saw many of the old problems revive. It began with the murder of the king's brother and moved rapidly into conflict with foreign Vikings and local Danes. Æthelred was humiliated when forced once again to pay the Danegeld. Tension arose between the royal court at Winchester and the inhabitants of the former Danelaw who looked increasingly to a resurgent Denmark for aid and consolation. Seeing his grip loosening, Æthelred turned for support to the Duke of Normandy, Richard, whose daughter he had married. He was playing the oldest card in the pack, courting one band of barbarians to hold off the rest. Finally, in 1002, he gave the ultimate order of desperation. He ordered the massacre of all Danes living in England. Far from ending the disputes, the attempted massacre caused a general Danish rising. The next year, Sveyn Forkbeard, King of Denmark, landed in the Humber at the head of another 'Great

Army'. Within a decade, he and his allies had put the Army of England to flight, driven Æthelred into exile, and taken control of the entire country. Sveyn I had created an Anglo-Danish, or rather a Dano-English, Empire. After two hundred years of conflict, the contest between the Anglo-Saxons and the Northmen was reaching the point of almost total Norse supremacy.

A curious literary episode emphasizes the integration of the Isles into the pan-Viking world at this juncture. The *Jómsvíkingasaga* tells of the founding of a Viking settlement in the Baltic, the training of the crews and the attitudes to death and suffering. But it contains a persistent storyline linking Jómsborg with 'Bretland'. The chief hero, Pálna Tóki, is a historical figure and foster-father to Sveyn Fork-beard. In the saga, he marries Alof, the wise and beautiful daughter of a Viking earl in Bretland; and his chief companion is one Bjorn hinn brezki, 'Bjorn the Briton'. For the historian, everything turns on the identification of 'Bretland', where most of the adventures take place. Bretland could possibly be a literary device like Shake-speare's 'coast of Bohemia'. But it is more likely to be Wales or Cumbria or Strathclyde. The medieval saga-writer assumed that Bretland, wherever in the Isles it was, was a natural place to go.[35]

The short-lived Danish Empire of the early eleventh century was one of those brief historical dawns which never broke into day. Based on the strongest naval forces of the age, with the capacity to project political power across considerable distances, it had huge potential as a maritime, military, and commercial complex. It might well have opened up the whole North Sea–Scandinavia–Baltic region, as the Hansa did in a later age. All it needed was the period of consolidation – which it never got. There was certainly a large fleet in existence; and there was a network of active entrepôts stretching from London and Bristol in the Isles, Kaupang on the Skagerrak, Bremen in north Germany and Hedeby in Schleswig, to Birka in Sweden and to a long line of bases on the southern Baltic shore – Strzasłowo (Stralsund), Wolin, Truso. Sveyn I's queen, Knútr's mother, Świętosława, was a Polish princess. Novgorod the Great was already flourishing at the head of the transit route from the Baltic to the Black Sea. Viking adventurers had opened up permanent communication lines all the way from their northern homelands to Byzantium, the Caucasus, and the Caspian. Hoards of Arab *dirhams* or 'silver deniers' from Mesopotamia and Central Asia are a common archaeological find throughout the Viking north. Finally, as well demonstrated in the foundation both of Kievan Rus and of Normandy, there was a well-established tradition of adopting Norse rule to local customs and conditions.

One should also mention the curious question of Anglo-Saxon mercenaries serving at this time in the famous Varangian Guard of the Byzantine Empire. The fact is attested by well-respected author-ities.[36] Yet it contains a problem. The Varangians were eastern Vikings, most probably from Sweden, who among other feats had founded the state of Kievan Rus. From orthodox Kiev to orthodox Byzantium was just one step. Yet who were the recruits from pre-Conquest England? They could have been exiled Anglo-Saxon warriors, or Norse professionals from the Danelaw, or neither. The interesting aspect of the matter lies in the apparent readiness of an elite Viking force to treat men from England as their own.

When Sveyn Forkbeard died in 1014, his empire was divided between his sons, Harald and Knútr. Knútr (r. 1014–35), however, quickly reassembled it. Known in Old English as Cnut and in modern form as Canute, he defeated Æthelred's son, Edmund Ironside, in battle at Assandun (1016), married Æthelred's widow, Emma (1017), and, having accepted the Christian faith, was crowned at London. On Harald Sveynsson's death he succeeded to his brother's senior position in Denmark. From then to his own demise, he worked to weld the disparate parts into a new whole. He divided England into four earldoms – Northumbria, East Anglia, Mercia, and Wessex – thereby recognizing their separate histories and reversing the centralizing drive of the West Saxon monarchs. As shown by the legend of him sitting on his throne on the beach and commanding the tide to stop, he wanted to demonstrate the limitations of kingship, and relied on the skills of his earls. Among these, the key figure was Godwin, Earl of Wessex, the man appointed to supplant the influence of the previous ruling house.[37]

One can find many reasons for the collapse of Knútr's Dano-English Empire. The most obvious cause was dynastic failure, in that neither of Knútr's sons – Harald I (r. 1035–40), and Harthacnut (r. 1040–2) – produced viable heirs. It is also fair to point out that pagan Denmark and Christian England were not readily compatible, and that the Danish court was too involved in its own quarrels to pay much attention to England. But one can already see the disruptive effects of the Norman factor, which had been at work since Æthelred's early years and which enabled the House of Wessex to return. For Æthelred's queen, Emma, was daughter of a Norman duke; Edmund Ironside was half-Norman; and Edmund's son, Edward the Confessor (r. 1042–66), had been raised and educated in Normandy. The leaderless Anglo-Danish nobility accepted Edward's return from exile, but they soon resented the Normans who crowded his entourage. From their point of view – and of some historians – Edward the Confessor may have been presented as King Alfred's heir. But in practice, he was not so much a standard-bearer of the Old English interest, or shield against the Danes, as a Trojan horse for the rising power of the third Scandinavian force – Normandy.

Ragnvald, Earl of More, companion to Harald Fine-Hair, King of Norway, and brother of Sigurd the Powerful, first Earl of Orkney, married Ragnhild, daughter of a certain Hrolf Nose. Ragnvald and Ragnhild produced a son whom they called Hrolf after his maternal grandfather. This boy grew into a warrior of such enormous stature that he was dubbed Hrolf Göngu or Göngu Hrolf, 'Hrolf Walker'. He was so big that no horse could carry him; so he had to walk.

Göngu Hrolf must have been born in the 860s, sometime after his father's return to Norway. He would have reached the age of adventuring and have sailed from the fjords on his first expedition in the 880s. He may well have been among the Northmen who joined the siege of Paris in 885. He was certainly among the Vikings who stayed on in the lower valley of the Seine after the failure of the siege and made it their permanent home. The sagas have no doubt that it was Hrolf the Viking who was to make history, though the issue is somewhat confused by the presence of someone known as 'Rolf the Dane' – possibly the same man, possibly someone else.

Just at the time that Hrolf, or Rolf, was settling into his new residence, the Carolingian Empire was finally breaking up. After the threefold division of Charlemagne's possessions in 842, the three constituent parts gradually pulled apart. The western kingdom, Neustria, centred on Paris, looked back to its Gallo-Roman roots and spoke Frankish Latin. The eastern kingdom, Austrasia, part Frankish and part Saxon, possessed a strongly Germanic character. The central kingdom, Lotharingia, became an eternal bone of contention between its western and eastern neighbours. Northern Italy, too, pulled away. The idea that the imperial crown could pass to any of Charlemagne's descendants caused such dissension that it was abandoned. The tenth and last crowned emperor of the Carolingian series, Louis King of Provence, died in 905. Neustria was ruled for thirty-one years, from 893 to 928 by one of Charlemagne's great-great-grandsons, Charles III the Simple, who followed his father's fashion and called himself King of France. But his powers were limited. In the decades since Charlemagne's death each of the old Carolingian counties of Neustria – Toulouse, Flanders, Anjou, Gascony, Poitou, Burgundy, and Auvergne – had sprouted semi-independent hereditary dynasties of their own.

For this was the era when the military-territorial system which historians call feudalism was being regularized. Especially in France, the havoc wreaked by several generations of Norse invasions acted as a major stimulus. Princes of weakened states, unable to raise taxes or armies, began to delegate their authority over a given tract of land in return for a sworn contract promising political loyalty and military service. The lord swore to protect his vassal; the vassal swore to serve his feudal lord. A king's principal vassals, the tenants-in-chief, very often the hereditary counts that had grown up in the

Carolingian period, were encouraged to make similar arrangements with lesser vassals or 'sub-tenants', they ceded jurisdiction over portions of their own feudal lands in return for specified obligations of loyalty and service, usually calculated in terms of the supply of knights and of castle-builders. For behind the new feudalism lay a fundamental problem – how to guarantee the vast outlay of men and money required to support the latest military techniques of stone castles and heavy cavalry.

Such was the context in which Charles III the Simple, King of France, wondered what to do with his Scandinavian squatters on the Seine. Their depredations continued unchecked. There was no force at hand to tame them. There were no more funds to pay Danegeld. So the best way out was to recruit them. In or about 911, therefore, King Charles met Göngu Hrolf at the monastery of St Clair-sur-Epte. In the resultant treaty, the king agreed to give Hrolf the high title of Duke and to award him in fief all the land in the valley of the Seine between the rivers Epte and Bresle. In return, Hrolf agreed to become the king's vassal and – in order to validate the vassal's oath of homage – to accept Christian baptism. Henceforth, Hrolf's adventurers were formally integrated into the French feudal order. The Latin scribes, who recorded the deed, gave Hrolf's name the Latinate form of Rollo; and they gave his new dukedom the name of Normandia – literally 'the land of the Norsemen'. (His French neighbours called him Rollon le Piéton.) The deal was to be far more solid and successful than the one which King Alfred had reached a generation earlier when setting up the Danelaw.

The assimilation of Rollo's men into French society proceeded with great rapidity. All of them who did not return to their families in Scandinavia received a *mannshlutr* or 'man's share' of land. An estimated five thousand warriors received Christian baptism, took Frankish wives, and became a ruling class. Viking laws and institutions, such as the *Althing*, were abandoned in favour of hierarchical feudal jurisdictions. Pagan rituals and the Norse language died out quickly, though polygamy apparently persisted. The ducal castle was built at Rouen, and a religious centre at the Abbey of Bayeux.

Hrolf–Rollo, having married Popa, daughter of Count Béranger of Bretagne, founded a dynasty that was to rule the dukedom for 250 years.[38]

As neophytes, the Normans zealously pursued their commitment to France, feudalism, and Christianity. They regarded themselves as the most loyal of servants, both to their king and to the Roman Pope. When the king's demesne was attacked by Burgundy they raced to his defence, receiving a large extension to their duchy in payment. When ecclesiastical and monastic reforms were introduced by William of Volpiano (962–1031), they were quick to adopt them. When the last of the French Carolingians died in 987 they took a leading part in establishing the new dynasty founded by Hugh Capet. By the end of the tenth century, after only three or four generations, they were by all appearances completely Frenchified. The key question was: were they still Vikings at heart, ready to sail away on impulse on every new adventure? The answer would seem to be positive. In 1059–60, for instance, Count Roger d'Hauteville and his brothers sailed away to conquer Sicily in the name of the Pope. They never came home. The military-feudal kingdom which they set up in 'the two Sicilies' was a precursor to the similar state which their cousins were to set up in England.

The Normans' interest in England was as old as the day when the first of them looked across the Channel. Bands of warriors had often left the *Here* of the Seine to join in the wars of the Danelaw. But the House of Rollo must have felt a certain affinity with the House of Wessex. Both were military imperialists, both making a career by bringing order to the prevailing chaos. The marriage of Emma to Æthelred in 991 was a two-way deal. Æthelred was looking for Norman support against the Danes in England. But the Normans were looking for West Saxon support in their problems on the Continent, notably with their troublesome neighbours in the counties of Maine and Anjou.

In 1035, the death of Knútr the Great, King of Denmark and England, coincided with the death in Normandy of Duke Robert le Magnifique, and the accession of Robert's son, Guillaume le Bâtard

(William the Bastard). Guillaume knew all about succession crises. His own father had seized the Norman throne by murdering his uncle; his grandfather's sister, Emma, had twice been married to successive Kings of England; and four of her sons had sat on the English throne. Emma's son, Edward the Confessor, Guillaume's cousin, had lived in Normandy for many years, and may well have recognized Guillaume's claim to be his natural successor. Guillaume may also have extracted an oath of recognition from Harold Godwinson after the latter was shipwrecked on the Norman coast. At all events, it was obvious throughout Guillaume's early reign that the failure of the House of Wessex to produce a direct heir after Edward would provoke a storm in which he would be very personally involved. So Guillaume prepared his campaign thoroughly. He possessed the most modern of armies; and he obtained the backing of the Pope. His half-brother, the Comte de Mortain, offered a hundred and twenty dragonships: the Comte d'Avranches sixty.

Edward the Confessor's reign (1042–66) has been called England's 'Norman Prelude'. This label was hardly appropriate for the country as a whole, though it fitted the state of affairs in the royal court. Edward surrounded himself with Norman advisers. He imported Norman clerics to run the English church, and built his new royal abbey at Westminster in Norman style. Court politics were reduced to a confrontation between the Anglo-Norman party of the king's favourites and the Anglo-Danish party led by Harold Godwinson. When the king died childless in January 1066, the expected storm broke. Harold Godwinson took the throne as Harold II.

But Harold immediately faced three powerful challengers. Apart from Guillaume le Bâtard, there was Sveyn II, Knútr's successor in Denmark, and Harald Hardráði, King of Norway. Every single one of them was a Viking, or a client of Vikings, or a descendant of Vikings. This fact puts rather a different spin on the story than that which tells how 1066 saw a famous battle between the English and the French. In effect, 1066 saw a complicated scramble for the final Viking spoils in England. (See Appendix 16.) Nor was the contest decided by one single clash of arms.

Of the contestants, Harald Sigurdarson Hardráði was far and
away the most colourful. Brother of the sainted Olaf, he had spent
much of his career in the Varangian Guard of the Byzantine Empire.
(He was dubbed Hardráði, 'Ruthless', from his penchant for drastic
decisions.) He had fought in Africa and Sicily, had visited Jerusalem,
and had married a Kievan princess. One legend tells how he was
cast into a lion's den for flirting with a Byzantine lady, only to tear
the lion apart with his bare hands. Another tells how he blinded the
Byzantine Emperor in revenge for wrongful accusations of stealing
gold:

> Náði gorr enn glóðum,
> Gríklands, jǫfurr handa,
> stólþengill gekk strǫngu
> steinblindr aðalmeini.
>
> *(The prince took even more*
> *Glowing embers of the arm.*
> *The emperor of the Greeks became*
> *Stone-blind with savage injury . . .)*[39]

Some historians have called Hardráði 'the last of the Vikings'. He
set sail as soon as he heard of the Confessor's demise, landed in
Northumbria, gathered an army in the land of Eric Bloodaxe, and
marched south. He was met at Stamford Bridge in Yorkshire on 26
September 1066 by Harold Godwinson at the head of his huscarls.
The Vikings were cut to pieces. Hardráði took an arrow full in the
chest. As the battle raged, Guillaume le Bâtard was waiting with his
fleet in the port of St Valéry hoping for a fair wind. Two days later,
he sailed.

The march of Harold Godwinson's men from Stamford Bridge
to Hastings is one of the grandest epics of English history. They
covered two hundred and fifty miles in twelve days. They found
that the Normans had moved along the coast from their landing-
ground at Pevensey and had set up a strong beachhead. On the
morning of 14 October, St Calixtus's Day, they drew up their ranks

on the crest of Senlac Hill, and awaited the Norman assault. Wave upon wave of knights were broken on the line of their shields and battle-axes. The feudal cavalry made little impression, until they feigned retreat and were pursued, drawing the defenders out of position. In the late afternoon, Harold was killed by an arrow. His huscarls stood their ground and fought to the death of the last man.

Guillaume, now le Conquérant, 'the Conqueror', took two months to get himself crowned in Westminster Abbey on Christmas Day, and three years to impose his rule on the greater part of England. His method was to build impregnable stone castles like the Tower of London and then to terrorize the inhabitants of the surrounding countryside into submission. In 1067 the West Country was ravaged, in 1068 Wales was invaded. In 1069, the Normans marched against their Norse rivals in Jorvik. Sveyn of Denmark was cruising the coast, ready to pounce. The Conqueror could not conquer Northumbria. But he stopped the Northumbrians from conquering him.

The model feudal state of 'Angleterre' which the Conqueror established was a highly successful implant. Having created Normandy by submerging themselves into the French order, the descendants of Rollo now expected to repeat the experiment by giving absolute priority to the political, social, and linguistic culture of their earlier adoption. It is sometimes argued that the Conqueror originally intended to leave the Old English system intact. If so, he was soon persuaded against such a policy by the outbreak of numerous revolts. In any case, the horde of Norman, Breton, and Flemish knights who took part in the Conquest were straining to be rewarded. Within twenty years, they had divided up virtually all the land in the kingdom between them. Tens of thousands of manors, large and small, passed into French hands. All but two of the king's tenants-in-chief were from France. Under Lanfranc (1010–89), some-time Prior of Bec and now Archbishop of Canterbury, the Church was similarly purged. The entire ruling class of Church and state spoke French. Pre-Conquest England, with its Anglo-Saxon and Danish connections, was completely submerged. The long-standing link with the Scandinavian world was severed. And the new order was kept in place by an administration of unusual energy. In 1085, the Conqueror told his Council that he wanted to know exactly what had happened to every single piece of land in the kingdom. So in 1086 his agents scoured every corner of England, conducting a survey of unparalleled precision. They extracted details from forty-five thousand landholdings in fourteen thousand named locations, recording each one's pre-Conquest assessment for Danegeld, its valuation 'when the Confessor died' (i.e. in 1066), and its valuation 'now'. Their findings were preserved in two huge volumes in the royal treasury at Winchester. They contained statistical, social, and economic information that had no parallel in Europe for centuries to come. Together, they soon became known as Domesday Book.

Dissensions in the ruling family were greatly increased by the fact that Normandy continued to be regarded as both a senior and a separate possession. Just as Sveyn Forkbeard had designated his elder son for Denmark and his younger son for England, so the Norman Conqueror designated his elder son, Robert, for Normandy, and his younger son, Guillaume le Roux, or 'Rufus', for England. Indeed, Robert grew so disaffected awaiting his inheritance that he sought support from the King of France to seize Normandy by force. The Conqueror met his death in 1087, fighting against his French liege and his appointed heir in the disputed district of the Vexin. The years from 1087 to 1096, when Robert held Normandy and Rufus held England, were filled with rebellions on both sides of the Channel. So, too, were the years 1100 to 1106, when Rufus's successor, Henri Beauclerc (r. 1100–35), was challenged for the control of Normandy by Robert's heir, Guillaume Cliton. The notion that England, as the larger possession, was necessarily the more important was not shared by the House of Rollo. For Normandy was not a dependency of the English kings. It was a feudal duchy of France. And despite its monarchical status the Normans' Kingdom of England was an off-shoot of Normandy.

Special provisions had also to be made for the lands which from the earliest stages of the Norman Conquest had been carved out as private principalities in the marches of Wales. The Conqueror needed to erect a barrier between himself and the Welsh, and some of the largest land-grants and earldoms were made in the Marches to his closest kinsmen and followers – William Fitzosbern at Hereford, Roger Montgomery at Shrewsbury, Hugh d'Avranches at Chester. But as an aftermath of the intervention into Wales by Harold Godwinson the Welsh were still fighting among themselves, and fell an easy prey to the armoured newcomers. Fitzosbern, for instance, extinguished the seven hundred-year-history of the Kingdom of Gwent at one blow. Some five hundred temporary castles were erected; and huge stone fortresses began to rise at Chepstow, Monmouth, Montgomery, and Rhuddlan. In the wake of these first Norman earls came a phalanx of lesser, but no less aggressive marchers – Ralph Mortimer of Wigmore, Roger de Lacy of Weobley, Ralph de Toeni of Clifford, Osbern Fitzrichard, Bernard de Neufmarché, Robert Fitzhammo, Balliol, and de Breos. In 1081 the Conqueror made a pilgrimage to St David's, perhaps as a sign of respect to the Welsh, perhaps to give notice of his presence, perhaps to reconnoitre. Domesday Book shows him taking tribute from Welsh princes and Norman marchers alike – £40 from Rhys ap Tewdwr in Deheubarth, and £40 from a cousin of the Earl of Chester for lands to the west of the River Clwyd.

Under Rufus, the marchers made a second rush into Wales. Fitzhammo brought a force from his lands near Gloucester, overran Glamorgan, and set himself up as lord of Cardiff. Bernard de Neufmarché captured Brycheiniog, building a fortress at Aberhonddu (Brecon) before attacking Deheubarth. Rhys ap Tewdwr was killed in that campaign (1093). The most spectacular breakthrough, however, was achieved by the army of the Montgomery Earl of Shrewsbury. Marching hard through the mountains of Powys, they reached the sea in the Bay of Ceredigion, turned south, built a fortress at Aberteifi (Cardigan), then pressed on into Dyfed. Having seized the ocean-bound cantref of Penfro as his base, Arnulf de Montgomery founded the castle of Pembroke, the most powerful of the Norman strongholds in Wales.

Despite their great liberties, it is important to remember that the marcher lords were locked into a network of holdings and loyalties that tied them both to England and, for several generations, to the Duchy of Normandy. The Montgomeries, for instance, having set themselves up in the March, did not relinquish their ancestral home at Montgoméry, near Lisieux. What is more, open rebellion against the king spelled instant forfeiture. In 1102 Henri I abolished the Montgomeries' Earldom of Shrewsbury and seized their castle at Pembroke. Pembroke was given to the loyalist family of de Clare, whose principal post-Conquest 'honour' lay in Suffolk. Gilbert de Clare, first Earl of Pembroke (d. c. 1148), father of Richard Strongbow, rose to become one of the greatest of the marchers.

The cultural impact of the March was enormous. The Normans imported administrators, churchmen, monks, city dwellers, and colonists, all of whom helped to change the cultural landscape. Gerald of Windsor, for instance, royal castellan of Pembroke, married Nest, the widow of Rhys ap Tewdwr. Their grandson was Giraldus Cambrensis (c. 1146–1223), 'Gerald of Wales', the famous chronicler. Norman clerics attacked the aberrations of the Welsh church. Bernard, Bishop of St David's from 1115, abolished the old *clas* or Celtic monastery, whilst propagating the cult of St David throughout the March. Benedictine, Cistercian, and Augustinian monasteries proliferated, notably at Valle Crucis, Strata Florida, and Tintern. Towns with municipal privileges sprang up round the military strongholds, notably at Cardiff, Carmarthen, and Haverfordwest. English peasant settlers moved into the Vale of Glamorgan. A large contingent of Flemish colonists was brought into Pembroke, obliterating the native Welsh and launching the county's reputation as 'Little England beyond Wales'. Geoffrey of Monmouth, a Breton (d. 1155) and second Bishop of St Asaph's, wrote a fantastic and highly influential *Historia Regum Britanniae*, 'History of the Kings of Britain'. Whilst launching the Arthurian myth onto a wider stage, and greatly boosting Celtic self-awareness, Geoffrey was unambiguous in his advocacy of the political hegemony of England.

By the first decade of the twelfth century, the March was settling into the form which would last for four hundred years. It was 'the lawless Frontier' where the king's writ did not run and where robber barons held sway through force, fear, and treachery. It did not form part of the Kingdom of England, yet lay beyond the call of the Welsh princes. The marcher lords were regarded as feudal subjects of the English king. They paid him fees and homage in return for a greater measure of freedom than any of the English barons. They administered the law of the March, i.e. 'Welsh law as seen through Norman eyes', as they saw fit, often with great cruelty. They were free to build castles and to wage war, but in the knowledge that the king had no obligation to help them. As Domesday Book said of Osbern Fitzrichard, 'He has what he can take – no more.' Time would prove that he and his like could not take very much. The Welsh counterattacked, especially during the great 'Anarchy' after 1135; and the border stabilized. Owain ap Gruffudd (r. 1137–70), grandson of Rhys ap Tewdwr and Prince of Gwynedd, exercised a wide hegemony over the Welsh heartlands. He recovered Ceredigion, much of Dyfed, and parts of Powys, and extended his realm in the north to the walls of Chester. The overall effect of the Norman onslaught, therefore, was not to subdue Wales, but to partition it. Henceforth, the distinction between Marchia Walliae, 'the March of Wales' and Wallia Pura, 'Wales Proper', was permanently established.[40]

The definition of a permanent border between Scotland and England proved more indecisive than the creation of the Welsh March. For the Anglo-Normans, the Scottish border was the 'postern gate' which could never be properly shut. For the Scots, it was the high road to fame and fortune – much as France was for England. When Macbeth died, Cumbria was still in Scottish hands; Northumbria was in uproar; and it took the best part of a century before a new line of demarcation was fully recognized. Malcolm II had briefly submitted to Knútr in 1031. But Malcolm III Canmore, 'Bighead' (r. 1058–93), was able to avoid such concessions. His first marriage was to the widow of Thorfinn, Earl of Orkney: his second, in 1069, to Margaret, sister to the exiled English pretender, Edgar the Ætheling. He led no less than five invasions of England – in 1061, 1070, 1079, 1091, and 1093. On each occasion, he provoked fierce English counter-invasions. In 1072 the Conqueror rode as far as the Tay, and at Abernethy forced Malcolm 'to be his man'. This is often seen as the first step in 'Scotland's descent into a client state'. Yet the Scots had not been brought to their knees. The balance of power was affected more permanently by the building of two Norman strongholds – one by Robert Courteheuse at the New Castle on Tyne (1080), another by Rufus at Carlisle (1091). Rufus turned Cumbria into a Norman military colony poised to strike against the northern invaders. Yet this did not prevent Malcolm III, on his final incursion in 1093, from laying the foundation stone at Durham Cathedral.

Anglo-Norman grappling with Scotland undoubtedly provided the background to the last great Norse invasion of the Isles. Magnus Barfot or 'Barefoot', King of Norway (r. 1093–1103), felt the need to reassert his claims to the Earldom of Orkney, to the Western Isles, and to Man. So in 1098 his fleet sailed along the old western route, bringing all the Norse territories into line. But it did not stop there. Magnus saw fit to give the Normans a taste of their own medicine. He landed on Anglesey, and struck out for England. He was met by a force under two of the marcher lords, Hugh de Montgomery, second Earl of Shrewsbury and Robert of Rhuddlan. 'And the French fell from their horses like fruit from the branches.'[41] Before retiring Magnus slew Earl Hugh in personal combat. In Scotland, he persuaded the Scots court to reconfirm his lordship of the Isles.

Malcolm III's death in an English ambush near Alnwick precipitated a long phase of dynastic confusion in which the Gaelic establishment of Scotland was steadily undermined. Malcolm III's brother, Donald III Bane (r. 1093–4, 1094–7) was elevated by the Scots magnates in order to drive out Queen Margaret's English courtiers. Malcolm III's eldest son, Duncan II (r. 1094), a Celt trained as a Norman knight, briefly took the throne 'on condition that he never introduce English or French into the land'. Yet he only replaced his uncle thanks to an Anglo-Norman army provided by Rufus. Malcolm III's next son, Edgar (r. 1097–1107), was also installed as king 'in fealty to King William'. After that the marriage of Alexander (r. 1107–24) to an illegitimate daughter of Henri I, and Henri I's marriage to Edith-Maltilda, daughter of Malcolm III and Margaret, and sister to four Scottish kings, tied the dynastic, political, and cultural strands of the knot for several generations. David I (r. 1124–53), youngest son of Malcolm and Margaret, was brought up at the English court as David fitzMalcolm, Earl of Huntingdon and Northampton. At Henri's insistence, he obtained widespread jurisdictions in southern Scotland during Alexander's reign, acting like a marcher lord and Henri's virtual viceroy. He was backed by a group of Anglo-Norman adventurers based in Northumbria and by the strong military garrison of French knights stationed in Cumbria. The first act of his reign in 1124 was to grant the vast border estate of Annandale to the Norman family of De Brus. It was the first of many. Like his counterparts in the March of Wales, he was an energetic founder of royal burghs – like Berwick, Perth, and Aberdeen – and an eager patron of monasteries. He introduced a territorial administration on the Anglo-Norman model of sheriffdoms; and he minted Scotland's earliest native coins. He authored 'the Davidian Revolution'. None of which prepared the English for David's searing expedition into northern England in 1138 at the head of 'an incredible army of semi-barbarians'.

The linguistic arrangements of the Anglo-Norman state held serious consequences for the future. Although some documents, like *The Anglo-Saxon Chronicle*, continued to be written in Old English, England's new masters spoke French and wrote in Latin. The Norman court and administration were entirely French. The Norman church, which exercised a virtual monopoly on education, was strongly ultramontane; and the importance of Latin increased. The speech of the common people reverted to a series of unwritten vernaculars that were evolving in different directions in different parts of the kingdom.[42]

The affairs of England, however, could not be disentangled from the broader scene of Continental politics. As Dukes of Normandy, the Conqueror's successors continued to be feudal vassals of the Kings of France; and their standing in France rapidly came under pressure from several quarters. The alliance with Flanders, which had facilitated the Conqueror's invasion of England, soon broke down. Thereafter, Flanders and Normandy became rivals and competitors. Similarly, the Conqueror had benefited in his early years from the internal dissensions in neighbouring Anjou. This period of relief ended as soon as Anjou was whipped into shape by the aggressive Count Fulk le Réchin (see below). Most seriously, the Capetian Kings of France grew ever more resentful about the overseas success of their Norman vassals. The Conqueror had died fighting Philip I. Rufus inherited the Conqueror's feud with Duke Robert. And Henri I (r. 1100–35), who only gained control of Normandy in the seventh year of his English reign, spent the best part of two decades fighting an anti-Norman coalition of Flemings, Angevins, and Capetians. Indeed, his initial strategy was to make himself independent of France through political marriages. His daughter Matilda was married to the Holy Roman Emperor, Henry V, and eight of her bastard sisters were distributed round the ruling houses to secure their father's realm. Yet in 1120, when Henri's only son and heir was drowned in the disaster of 'the White Ship', the strategy changed tack. Matilda was brought back from Germany and married to the heir of Anjou, Geoffroi Plantagenêt. This ensured conflict, and England's permanent embroilment in French affairs. From the political point of view, England, which a century earlier had been a dependency of Denmark, was now becoming little more than an extension of France.

In that early twelfth century, the Viking impulse had waned. If Harald Hardráði was not absolutely the last Viking, the conditions which had produced him were fast disappearing. Scandinavia's surplus population had largely been offloaded. The iron plough had arrived. Agrarian production was increasing. Trade routes were well established. The Scandinavians had largely adopted Christianity; and their Christian kings had formally taken their places in Christendom – Denmark in 960, Norway in 995, Sweden in 1008. Many of the traditional destinations had been closed off to adventurers. The Baltic–Black Sea route was controlled by Kievan Rus. The coastlands of the North Sea were policed by the Kings of England, the Dukes of Normandy, and the Holy Roman Emperors. The dragonships were no longer setting sail.

In the Isles, the Viking heritage was soon forgotten. History was written by monks, whose negative views on pagan pirates were fixed, and were not contradicted by any more positive sources. The Old Norse sagas, for example, were written down far away, mainly in Iceland, and were not known to the outside world till modern times. The Viking age was seen as a nasty storm that had blown itself out and need not be remembered. The moments when there had been a real prospect of the Isles passing permanently into the Scandinavian sphere left no trace in collective memory.

In Ireland, the Celtic supremacy established by Brian Boru was left unchallenged. The Norman Kings of England made no attempt to cross the Celtic Sea. The Norse settlements were steadily integrated, leaving a host of place names, a few words in Gaelic, and a far more developed system of maritime communication. The hundred and fifty years following the Battle of Clontarf are generally seen as a last 'Golden Age' of Irish independence. The Irish church was energetically modernized by figures such as Mael Ísa, consecrated Bishop of Waterford by St Anselm, Gilla Espaic, Bishop of Limerick, and Máel Máedoc (St Malachy, 1096–1148), who died at Clairvaux in St Bernard's arms. The new Cistercian order was introduced with houses at Mellifont (Louth) and Boyle (Roscommon). A national synod came into being, together with thirty-six diocesan bishoprics. St Malachy, who as legate re-established Ireland's close links with the papacy, oversaw the creation of four bishoprics at Armagh, Cashel, Dublin, and Tuam. A new generation of diocesan schools shone in their Irish and Latin learning. An

analytical grammar of the Irish language was completed, the second
of the genre in western Europe, after its Norse equivalent. The
college of Armagh, under the guidance of St Laurence O'Toole
(1128–80), resembled a university. In politics, in the wake of Brian
Boru's clean sweep, the supreme status of the high-kingship was
restored. The significance of scores of sub-kings declined sharply.
Given the example of a powerful feudal state in England across the
water, it looked as if the dynasty of Toirdelbach Ua Conchubair
(O'Connor) from Connaught might be on the verge of launching
a hereditary monarchy on the English model. The accession of
Toirdelbach's son Ruaidhrí (Roderick or Rory O'Connor) in 1166,
and the convening of an assembly of clergy and chieftains in the
following year, seemed specially promising. But it was not to be. As
the Irish textbooks say, 'it was the last gleam of sunlight'. For the
great traitor, Diarmaid MacMurchada (Dermot Macmurrough, or
'Diarmaid of the Foreigners'), was already on his way to the English
court.

In Wales, the Viking impact was once assessed as no more than
the 'backwash' of events elsewhere.[43] It left virtually no trace either
in the Welsh language or on Welsh place names, though it largely
determined the form which English-language place names would
take in Wales along the north and southern coasts. It exercised its
greatest influence in the later phase when the regular route of
Dublin–Anglesey–Chester was established, and when Bristol developed as a major Viking slave port. It is known from *The Anglo-Saxon
Chronicle*, for example, that islands in the Severn Estuary bore the
Old English names of Bradan Reolice and Steapan Reolice before
they were given their permanent names of Flatholme and Steep-
holme by the Norsemen. Overall, by dominating the coastlands of
Wales, the Norsemen served to emphasize the importance of the
mountainous Welsh heartland. Indirectly, they served to encourage
a long period when the Welsh and the English, instead of fighting
each other, preferred a state of coexistence.

In Scotland, the effect of the second Viking age was very
different from that of the first. Following the consolidation of Scots

power and of the Gaelic language under the Mac Alpin dynasty, the eleventh century saw the rapid Anglicization of the Lowlands at the expense of the Strathclyde British, whilst the twelfth century saw the influx of numerous powerful Norman families. If Malcolm III (r. 1058–93), under the influence of his English queen, was decidedly Anglophile, David I (r. 1124–53) was decidedly Normanophile. It was under his patronage that Norman families such as the Frasers, the Bruces, the Haigs, and the Stewarts received their estates. The effect was a marked shift of political gravity away from the Gaeltacht and towards an entente with England.

These trends clearly underline the differences between the 'Making of Scotland' and the 'Making of England'. In the former Caledonia, it was taking longer to weld together a rich mix of ethnic groups – Gaels, Picts, Norse, British, Angles, Normans. On the other hand, within the arena provided by the expanding kingdom of Scotland, a modus vivendi was being forged between Celt and non-Celt. In the former Britannia, a certain communal sense of Englishness was observed prior to the developments provoked by the Danish invasions and prior to the construction of a united kingdom of England. Yet both the Kingdom and its Englishness were only achieved by the permanent separation of the English from the Celts. 'Scottishness' was slower to crystallize, but was more inclusive. Caledonia was witnessing the halting rise of one modern nation – the Scots. Britannia witnessed two: the English and the Welsh.

In England itself, few people associated the Norman Conquest with the previous Viking and Danish invasions. After all, the Normans justified their operations in Normandy and in England by the order which they brought to the preceding Viking-bred chaos. And yet there was a strong Norse element in the make-up both of the conquerors and the conquered. For the Normans were not just ordinary Frenchmen. And the English were not just 'Anglo-Saxons'. The common denominator between the knights of Guillaume of Normandy and the subjects of Harold Godwinson lay in the important strand of their Viking descent. It was a proper conclusion to 'The Age of the Vikings'.

ALTHOUGH THE VIKING AGE lasted for three centuries, and Scandinavians were present in the Isles as conquerors, colonists, and kings, it is remarkable that in the popular imagination they are remembered almost exclusively in their initial role as pirates. Paintings such as W. Bell Scott's *Descent of the Danes at Tynemouth* (1856) say it all. A group of fierce warriors in horned helmets emerge from the morning mist on the beach. The priory church burns. The terrified local population flee their homes and take to the hills.[44]

In recent times, the pirate image of the Vikings has inspired a distinct genre of fictional and juvenile literature. It provides an excellent pretext for adventure stories which combine stirring action with exotic historical settings. The dangerous lives of wandering sea-rovers obviously have a special attraction for today's cosseted suburban youth. Favourite themes include voyages of exploration, especially to Iceland and Vínland:[45] the feats of young Viking warriors, who have to prove their manhood:[46] and most frequently, tales of Anglo-Saxon children sold into slavery by their Viking captors either in the Muslim world or in Byzantium.[47] One observes that almost all the authors view the Vikings as a foreign, external phenomenon, which only impinged on the outer edges of insular life. The place for Vikings is on the open sea, on exposed coasts and islands, and in distant foreign countries. They are rarely presented as an integral part of English (or Scottish or Irish) life. Both geographically and culturally they remain aliens and outsiders. Young British readers are invited to identify with the native victims of Viking piracy, and sometimes with Viking warriors, but not with the Scandinavian migrants attempting to build a new life in the Isles or with Scandinavian rulers confronting their Anglo-

Saxon opponents. To all intents and purposes the Vikings were considered to be pagan brutes, and as such unworthy of further attention.[48]

By and large, the conceptual opposition of brutish Viking and civilized native has held good ever since. One of the few voices raised against the conventional picture was that surprisingly of Charles Dickens. In his *Child's History of England* he reminded his readers that the Christian Anglo-Saxons could be every bit as barbaric as the pagan Northmen. He supported his opinion with the example of the Massacre of St Brice's Day in 1002:

> And now, a terrible deed was done in England, the like of which was never done on English ground before or since. On the thirteenth of November, in pursuance of secret instructions sent by the king over the whole country, the inhabitants of every town and city armed, and murdered all the Danes who were their neighbours. Young and old, babies and soldiers, men and women, every Dane was killed.[49]

English interest in the Anglo-Saxon period was very slow to develop. Indeed it hardly existed at all for six or seven hundred years. Medieval legal experts developed a certain taste for pre-Conquest law and government which came to be seen as a lost golden era of liberty preceding the post-Conquest tyrannies. This theme was present all the way through from Henry of Huntingdon in the twelfth century to parliamentary ideologues like Edward Coke in the seventeenth (see below, page 576), and it would remain an essential ingredient of the ultimate mix. Yet most other aspects of pre-Conquest life were completely forgotten. The Old English language was totally lost until the work of George Hickes (d. 1715). The *Anglo-Saxon Chronicle* was not translated until 1819. The manuscript of *Beowulf* was not published until 1815.

When popular English interest did eventually occur, the central hero was bound to be King Alfred. For Alfred was a lawgiver and a patron of learning as well as a doughty warrior; and he could be used to demonstrate the superior civilizational qualities of his people. What is more, by staving off the Danes at their most expansive moment, he could be presented not just as the progenitor but as the saviour of 'Englishness', the man without whom the English would have had no future. Though consigned to virtual oblivion for the best part of a millennium, he rapidly became the symbol of that most valuable English historical commodity – continuity. He went ahead; and we came later.

Oddly enough, the English cult of Alfred was first inspired by the installation of the House of Hanover. Obsequious subjects of the Hanoverians thought it fitting to advertise the idea that the new dynasty from Germano-Saxony had illustrious Anglo-Saxon forebears. In 1723, Sir Richard Blackmore dedicated his *Alfred: an epick poem* to George I, declaring Alfred to be 'a prince sprung from the ancient Saxon race of your native land'. Before long, a trickle of such eulogies was becoming a flood. In 1740, both Thomson and Mallett and Dr Arne produced masques on the theme of *Alfred*; in 1773, Garrick produced another masque; and in 1778 a dramatic tragedy appeared. The War of American Independence provided an occasion to elaborate on the theme of Alfred as the fount of all English liberties (such as those the Americans were fighting for). A biography in 1777 of *The Great King of the Anglo-Saxons* by Alexander Bichnell described a lost Golden Age; and in his pro-American polemic *Take Your Choice* (1777), the ebullient Major Cartwright gave Alfred the line that 'the English should be as free as their thoughts'. 1801 saw Henry Pye's epic poem on *Alfred* in six books. 1831 saw J. S. Knowles presenting William IV with yet another biography of *The Patriot King*.[50]

The advent of Victoria, and her marriage to a genuine Saxon prince, could only boost the Alfredian cult. Albert was proclaimed to be Alfred incarnate. In William Theed's statue in Windsor Chapel he is portrayed as an Anglo-Saxon warrior, the embodiment of Teutonic manhood. In 1856 a prize was awarded in Oxford to one William Powell James for a poem entitled *King Alfred Surveying Oxford University at the Present Time*. It was a masterly piece of flattery. James imagined the spirit of the ancient monarch coming back to see how 'the Saxon's sons' were getting on and expressing his royal satisfaction:

> O England, I have mark'd with pride and joy
>   Thy goodly corn-lands ripe on many a plain,
> Thy rich towns safe from Northman's fierce annoy,
>   Or sword of fair-hair'd Dane:
>
> How wide the realms, from India's burning strand
>   To the vast West, thy children hold in fee;
> How proud thy fleets that pass from land to land,
>   From sea to subject sea.[51]

Yet the deftest piece of flattery, from Alfred's own lips, was directed at donnish vanity:

> But dearest flower in all thy wreath of fame,
>   Rise these proud halls where truth and knowledge dwell,
> Where the glad mind drinks largely, none to blame,
>   Of learning's sacred well.[52]

No wonder the would-be poet won the prize.

Forty years later, near the end of Victoria's reign, a poet laureate with similarly forgettable talents recalled the Queen's coronation in 1837:

> With grave utterance and majestic mien
> She with her eighteen summers filled the throne
> Where Alfred sate: a girl, withal a Queen,
> Aloft, alone.[53]

The apogee of the cult was reached shortly after Queen Victoria's death during the 'King Alfred Millenary' of 1901. The City of Winchester funded an eighteen-foot statue. A memorial volume was prepared, prefaced by a poem on *The Spotless King* by the same poet laureate:

> Through the distance of a thousand years
> Alfred's radiance falls on us at last.[54]

The Prime Minister, Lord Salisbury, was present at the statue's unveiling. And a speech of superlative municipal immodesty was delivered by the mayor:

> Since it is acknowledged that the English-speaking people . . . still derive great and incalculable benefits from Alfred's indefatigable works . . ., it was felt that the memorial to 'the hero of our race' should be worthy not only of the city and neighbouring counties but also of the Anglo-Saxon race.[55]

The tone was set by the Bishop of London, who had assured his listeners that 'the blood of Alfred still ran in the veins of her Most Gracious Majesty, Queen Victoria'.[56] He didn't risk a percentage.

The racial aspect in these matters had surfaced some fifty years earlier, especially in the early work of Edward Augustus Freeman (1823–92). Freeman, like many of his Victorian contemporaries, held a roseate view of pre-Conquest England and of its supposed predilection for constitutional liberties. But he was driven by a visceral hatred of everything French, and by a historical vision in which the Normans were the ultimate villains. In Freeman's eyes, the whole of medieval and modern English history had been a painstaking struggle to reverse the verdict of 1066. His verdict was unashamedly triumphalist:

> We have conquered, we have conquered,
>   Though not on tented plain,
> And the laws and tongue of Alfred
>   We have won them back again.
> The boasted might of Normandy
>   For aye is laid to rest,
> But the name of Saxon freedom
>   Still warms each faithful breast.[57]

It was Freeman who, as a historian, insisted on the modern term 'English' being substituted for the older 'Anglo-Saxon', thereby creating the impression that the subjects of Alfred had been just an earlier version of the subjects of Victoria. When he came to write his colossal six-volume *History of the Norman Conquest: its causes and its results* (1875–9), he combined a panegyric for the Old English state with a sustained polemic against 'the Norman Yoke'. To his way of thinking, the Battle of Hastings was the ultimate trauma:

> It is from the memorable day of Saint Calixtus that we may fairly date the overthrow . . . of our ancient and free Teutonic England. In the eyes of men of the next generations that day was the fatal day of England, the day of the overthrow of our dear country, the day of her handing over to foreign lords . . . till it was a shame to be called an Englishman, and the men of England were no more a people.[58]

The inconsistencies in this diatribe hardly need to be underlined. But the deep-seated Francophobia, to which Freeman gave expression, helps explain why the French aspects of Norman civilization were being emphasized at the expense of its Viking connections.

No Anglo-Saxon monarch has ever matched the Victorian popularity of King Alfred. But the tragic fate of Harold Godwinson has attracted its share of modern sentiment. The Victorian writer Edward Bulmer-Lytton (1803–73) wrote a historical romance called *Harold: the last of the Saxons* (1848); and Lord Tennyson composed a poetic drama on the same subject. Bulmer-Lytton's conclusion anticipated Freeman's:

> Eight centuries have rolled away, and where is the Norman now? . . . In many a noiseless field, your relics, O Saxon heroes, have won back the victory from the bones of the Norman saints . . . Smile, O soul of our Saxon Harold, smile, appeased on the Saxon's land.[59]

A far more sensitive tribute to King Harold and to his stricken kingdom was paid by the poet and novelist Charles Kingsley (1819–75). In his poem *The Swan-Neck* (1851), Kingsley imagined the scene after the battle at Hastings, where Harold's lady-love was searching for his body among the corpses of the fallen. And he did so in a quasi-Old English style that admirably fits the content:

> Rousing erne and sallow glede,
> Rousing gray wold off his feed,
> Over franklin, earl, and thane,
> Heaps of mother-naked slain,
> Round the red field tracing slow,
> Stooped that Swan-neck white as snow;
> Never blushed nor turned away,
> Till she found him where he lay;
> Clipt him in her armés fair,
> Wrapt him in her yellow hair,
> Bore him from the battle-stead,
> Saw him laid in pall of lead,
> Took her to a minster high,
> For Earl Harold's soul to cry.
>
> Thus fell Harold, bracelet-giver;
> Jesu rest his soul for ever;
> Angles all from thrall deliver;
> Miserere Domine.[60]

Kingsley was also responsible for one of the few literary works which views the last period of pre-Conquest England from an Anglo-Danish as distinct from the Anglo-Saxon perspective. Kingsley's historical novel *Hereward the Wake* (1866) carries the subtitle of *The Last of the English*. But it is made abundantly clear at the outset that the hero is not the conventional sort of Anglo-Saxon. 'Hereward the Wake, Lord of Bourne' is an inhabitant of the former Danelaw and the descendant of Danish settlers:

> When the men of Wessex, the once conquering, and even to the last the most civilised race of Britain, fell at Hastings once and for all . . . the men of the Danelagh disdained to yield to the Norman invader. For seven long years they held their own, not knowing like true Englishmen when they were beaten . . .

They were a changed folk since first they settled in that Danelagh ... [They] had long ceased to burn farms, sack convents, torture monks for gold, and slay every human being they met in mere Berserker lust for blood ... Gradually they had settled down on the land, intermarried with the Angles and Saxons, and colonised all of England north and east of Watling Street ... as far as the Tees. Gradually, they had deserted Thor and Odin for 'the White Christ' ... The convents which the fathers had destroyed, the sons, or at least the grandsons, rebuilt ...[61]

Despite his own admission of the far-reaching assimilation of the Danes, Kingsley chooses to stress the contrast between them and the previous population:

The Anglo-Saxon race was wearing out. The men of Wessex, priest-ridden and enslaved by their own aristocracy, quailed before the free Norsemen, among whom was not a single serf. The God-descended line of Cerdic and Alfred was exhausted. Vain, incapable, profligate kings ... were no match for such heroes as Thorkill the Tall ... or Swend Forkbeard. The Danes had seized not only their own Danelagh and Northumbria but great parts of Wessex ...[62]

Hence Hereward was the only man left to stand and fight for Old England's ancient virtues. When he is finally trapped and killed, after seven years and forty-one chapters of non-stop heroics, he takes a dozen Normans with him:

> Then died far off within the boundless mist
> And left the Frenchman master of the land.[63]

The country was covered with Norman castles; and the victorious 'French' cast the down-trodden English into unspeakable bondage:

They took those they suspected of having some goods, both men and women, and put them in prison for their gold and silver, and tortured them ... They hung some by the feet and smoked

> them with foul smoke: some by the thumbs or by the head . . .
> They put them in dungeons wherein were adders and snakes
> and toads . . . Some they put into a crucet-house . . .[64]

All was lost save 'The Spirit of Freedom, which can never die'.[65]

Once this Victorian enthusiasm wore out, historians took over from the poets and novelists, and more balanced views of pre-Conquest England prevailed. In the years before the First World War, three new and major studies of the subject were circulating – by Ramsay, Hodgkin, and Oman;[66] and in 1908 a young scholar called Frank Stenton wrote a piece that strongly echoed the opinions of Kingsley. Thirty-five years later, the mature Stenton published the work that has set the benchmark for Anglo-Saxon history ever since.[67] As a fellow son of the Danelaw, he still repeated some Herewardian touches, such as his low judgement on 'the national degeneracy' of the late Anglo-Saxon monarchy and his soft spot for Cnut, 'the first Viking to be admitted into the civilised community of Christian Kings'. But he had grown altogether more positive about the Anglo-Saxon world as a whole. Like most English patriots, he was convinced of the self-evident destiny of unification, that supposedly came about step by step from Bede's time on. Alfred was 'the most effective ruler in western Europe since Charlemagne'; and Athelstan and Offa were 'statesmen of the first rank'. The Anglo-Saxon church, after the monastic reforms, was a fortress of learning and civilization. Most significantly perhaps, he demonstrated that the contrast between pre-Conquest and post-Conquest England was not quite as stark as previously supposed. In the social sphere, for example, 'the general drift from freedom to servitude' among the pre-Conquest peasantry did not amount to a feudal system; but to some degree it anticipated what the Normans introduced. In the last resort, however, Stenton clearly admired the Anglo-Saxons whilst disliking the Normans:

> The Normans who entered into the English inheritance were a
> harsh and violent race. They were the closest . . . to the
> barbarian strain in the continental order. They had produced

little in art or learning, and nothing in literature, that could be set beside the work of Englishmen. But politically they were masters of their world.[68]

Stenton's volume appeared in 1943, in the middle of the Second World War. It is incongruous to see him still writing about 'race' in the Victorian manner. At the same time his reference to the Normans being close to 'the barbarian strain' carried the germ of a valid but unusual idea. It implied that the Normans belonged no less to the world before 1066 than to the world after it. In other words, that 1066 was *not* a total and absolute break.

1066 is engraved on modern English consciousness like no other event in history. In the immortal words of Sellers and Yeatman, 'In 1066, there occurred the other memorable date in English History'[69] (the first memorable date remaining unidentified). Never a truer word was spoken in jest. People who cannot say who fought the Battle of Hastings, still less who won, will nonetheless confirm that 1066 was supremely important. It is a quasi-magic figure that has been seized on by the English because it confirms their deep but dubious belief that their island has been inviolate ever since. The fact is confirmed in *Alice in Wonderland*. When the Mouse is asked to repeat 'the driest thing he knows', he comes up with a brief résumé of 1066. 'William the Conqueror, whose cause was favoured by the Pope, was soon submitted to by the English, who wanted leaders . . .'[70] 'The favour of the Pope' is an important detail. One recurrent source of modern English animus against the Normans derived from the strange conviction that they were Papists – as if Alfred and Harold Godwinson were Protestants.

Another element may also have been at work. Most people in later times may have disliked the Normans; but not a few admired them. In particular they have admired the 'vigour' of the administrative machine which the Normans imposed; and they contrast it with the supposedly fractious characteristics of the late Anglo-Saxon regime which the Normans overthrew. This opinion is not well viewed among current specialists. But it has its advocates, who, in the most forthright instances, have been ready to credit Norman feudalism with the origins of the modern state.[71] It certainly lends academic credence to the popular view that the Norman Conquest represented a complete, and a necessary, new beginning.

As always, the blank spot in this particular array of English attitudes lies in the absence of any sort of recognition of events beyond England's borders. It is as if Anglo-Saxon England were bordered by an ocean to the north and the west as well as by a channel to the south. The mental planet that is peopled by Alfred and the Danes and Harold and the Conqueror has no place whatsoever for Hywel Dda, for Brian Boru, for Kenneth Mac Alpin or Macbeth. The Celtic peoples no doubt inhabit historical planets of their own. But all such non-English bodies revolve in their own orbits, out of sight and beneath the horizon. They do not even belong to the same galaxy.

Of course, one could well argue that Welsh, the Scots, and the Irish suffer from the same form of the tunnel-vision that afflicts the English. This may well be true in many instances. In the Victorian era, for example, when Irish nationalists were trawling their early history in search of Irish heroes, they found Brian Boru and set him up in parallel to the English cult of Alfred. What they needed, just as the English nationalists did, was a grand figure from before the Great Catastrophe. And they needed him to prove that despite appearances all had not been lost. They were not interested in the real Brian Boru, still less in the complex interaction in Irish society of Gael and Norse. They wanted a symbol of Gaelic valour and survival, a symbol to prove that in Ireland as in England there was 'a spirit of freedom which can never die'.[72]

Nonetheless, a very special fate overtook the memory of the Gaelic Kings of the Scots, and particularly of Macbeth. Unlike its neighbours, early Scotland did not experience a 'Great Catastrophe' comparable to the Norman conquest of England or the Plantagenet invasion of Ireland. The Gaelic monarchy of Scotland was not overthrown by violent external attack. It was undermined by the internal policies of later kings from the House of Canmore who destroyed the Gaelic supremacy from within. By the thirteenth century at the latest (see Chapter Six), Scotland's centre of political gravity had shifted decisively away from the Gaeltacht and into the Lowlands. Power moved into the hands of a Lowland aristocracy, which had strong Norman connections, which spoke Scots not Gaelic, and which viewed the Highland Gaels as troublesome aliens. When the new Scottish elite began to trace their roots, therefore, they found that they had nothing in common with illustrious predecessors like Macbeth. Macbeth, in fact, was an embarrassment. He had been overthrown by Malcolm Canmore, an ancestor of the Stewarts. In reality Macbeth was no assassin; but his reputation had to be assassinated. Step by step, the stains were spread. Already by the fourteenth century the Scots chronicler John of Fordon, who invented the figure of Banquo, was calling Macbeth a usurper. And early in the fifteenth century, Andrew of Wyntoun was putting the tag of murder onto Duncan's death. Yet it was the sixteenth-century scholar Hector Boece who did the decisive damage. Boece turned the historical Queen Gruoch into the hideous Lady Macbeth and introduced the theme of conspiracy. As one of Boece's many Scots imitators put it:

> [Macbeth's] wife, impatient of lang tarry (as all women ar) specially quhar they are desirus of any purpos, gaif him gret artation to pusew the weird that sche might be ane queene, callend him off tymis febye cowart and nocht desirus of honouris, sen he durst not assailze the thing with manheid and curage quilk is offerit to hym be the benivolence of fortoun . . .[73]

Boece wrote in Latin. But his spin was picked up by the two leading historical writers of the next generation – George Buchanan in Scotland and Raphael Holinshed in England. Hence, when William Shakespeare was looking for a story for an intended Scottish play, he found it ready made. All he had to do was to add the words. And he gave the world a Macbeth of whom 'the devil himself could not pronounce a title more hateful to mine ear'.

A historical source that is much closer in time to the historical Macbeth provides the following portrait:

> The strong one was fair, yellow-haired, and tall.
> Very pleasant was the handsome youth to me.
> Brimful of food was Scotland, east and west,
> During the reign of the ruddy, brave king.[74]

One may be forgiven for suspecting that myths are more powerful than history.

CHAPTER SIX

THE ISLES OF
OUTREMER

1154 to 1326

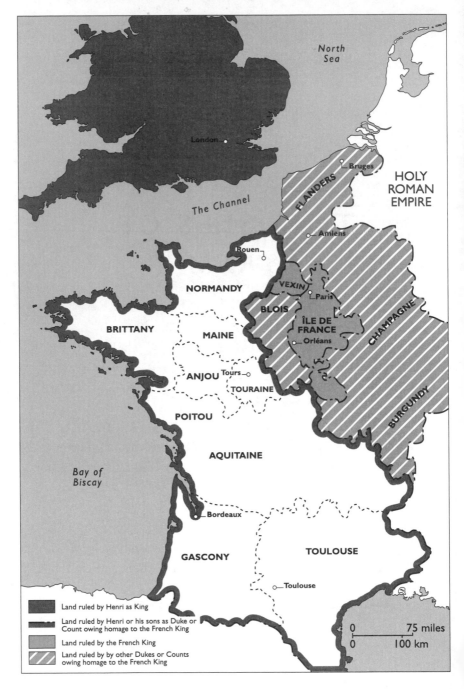

CAPETIAN AND ANGEVIN FRANCE, c. 1174

North
Sea

London

HOLY
ROMAN
EMPIRE

The Channel

Bruges

FLANDERS

Amiens

Rouen

NORMANDY

VEXIN

Paris

BLOIS

ÎLE DE
FRANCE

CHAMPAGNE

BRITTANY

MAINE

Orléans

ANJOU Tours

TOURAINE

BURGUNDY

POITOU

AQUITAINE

Bay of
Biscay

Bordeaux

GASCONY

TOULOUSE

Toulouse

Land ruled by Henri as King

Land ruled by Henri or his sons as Duke or
Count owing homage to the French King

Land ruled by the French King

Land ruled by by other Dukes or Counts
owing homage to the French King

| 0 | 75 miles |
| 0 | 100 km |

24 June 1148, Acre, Palestine. Having paid their respects at the Holy Sepulchre, the leaders of the Second Crusade came down to the main port of the Kingdom of Jerusalem for a grand assembly with the dignitaries of Outremer. Fifty years exactly after the First Crusade had created the Latin states of the Holy Land, Louis VII, King of France, and Conrad III von Hohenstaufen, King of the Romans, had 'taken the cross' to defend the Christian colonies against the encroachments of the surrounding Muslim princes. Louis VII, the sixth monarch of the Capetian dynasty, was accompanied by the Counts of Perche, Champagne, and Flanders and by the English Earls of Worcester and Warenne. Conrad, the first of the Hohenstaufen, was accompanied, among others, by Heinrich Jasimirgott, Duke of Austria, by Friedrich Barbarossa, the future Holy Roman Emperor, by Welf or 'Guelph' of Bavaria and by one of the Polish princes. They were received by Baudouin III, the fifth Latin King of Jerusalem, by his widowed mother, Queen Mélisende de Bouillon, by the Patriarch Fulcher, and by the Grand Masters of both the Templars and the Hospitallers. The Papal Legate, Bishop Theotwin of Porto, and the Bishops of Metz and Toul, were welcomed by a strong cohort of local clerics headed by the Archbishops of Caesarea and Nazareth, and the Bishops of Acre, Sidon, Beirut, Banyas, and Bethlehem. Together, they represented the highest echelons of secular and ecclesiastical power in Latin Christendom — a tightly knit community of warrior princes and princely prelates united by a common ethos and close family ties.

This latest band of crusaders had survived a series of disasters on the long overland road from Western Europe. And now, having decided to attack the great city of Damascus, they were embarking on the final folly of an enterprise which the finest historian of the crusades labelled with the simple word, 'Fiasco'.[1] The English chronicler Henry of Huntingdon summed it up as a well-deserved judgement of the Divine will:

1148 Eodem anno exercitus imperatoris Alemannie et regis Francorum, qui summis ducibus illustrati cum summa incedebant superbia, ad nichilum deuenerunt, quia 'Deus spreuit eos'. Ascendit enim in conspectu Dei incontinentia eorum, quam exercebant in fornicationibus non occultis. In adulteriis etiam quod Deo ualde displacuit. Postremo in rapinis et omnium genere scelerum. Prius ita namque prosternati proditione imperatoris Constantinopolitani, postea ferro hostili, emarcuerunt. Rex autem Francie et imperator Alemannie, cum paucissimus prius Antiocham, postea Ierosolimam, ignominiose aufugerunt. Tunc uero rex Francie, quasi aliquid acturus ad detrimentum fame refocillandum, auxilio militaru templi quod est in Ierussalem, et uiribus undique congestis, possedit Damascum, sed gratia Dei carens et ideo nichil proficiens rediit in Galliam.[2]

(1148. In this year, the armies of the Emperor of Germany and the King of France were annihilated, though . . . they had commenced their march under the greatest leaders and in the proudest confidence. But God despised them . . . for they abandoned themselves to open fornication . . . to robbery and every sort of wickedness. First they were starved by famine, through the false conduct of the Emperor of Constantinople, and afterwards were destroyed by the enemy's sword. King Louis and the emperor took refuge, at Antioch, and afterwards in Jerusalem with the remnant of their followers. And the French king, wishing to do something to restore his reputation, laid siege to Damascus with the aid of the Knights Templars of Jerusalem, and a force drawn from all quarters. But lacking the favour of God, and therefore having no success, he returned to France.)

There was considerable interest in England in the fortunes of the Second Crusade; and there was considerable knowledge among the crusaders about the affairs of England. That interest and knowledge did not only derive from the fact that many of the individual crusaders had strong connections in England. England as a whole in that era formed an integral part of the feudal world to which all those crusaders belonged. As that most patriotic English historian G. M. Trevelyan once wrote, England was 'a mere extension of Franco-Latin Europe'.[3]

What is more, when the leaders of the Second Crusade had marched off overland in the previous year, a strong English contingent had sailed for the Holy Land by sea. Despite the ravages of a civil war in England (see below), the English had answered the call of the Pope, the Blessed Eugenius III, to protect Jerusalem from the advancing Muslims; and they had intended to reach Palestine in stages, first crossing the Bay of Biscay and then entering the Mediterranean through the Straits of Gibraltar. However, when they landed at the mouth of the Douro in Portugal, they found a Holy War against the Muslims in progress there; and they decided to participate. Alfonso Henriques, Count of Portugal (r. 1128–85) was one of the warrior heroes of the *Reconquista*. Known as 'Ibn Errik' by the Moors, he was also one of the legendary figures of medieval romance. He had just broken free of Castilian suzerainty, and had placed his county under the direct protection of the Papacy. He had recently stormed the fortress of Santarèm and was advancing to the siege of Lisbon. It was an opportunity which the English crusaders could not resist. They joined in the siege, entering Lisbon in the company of the conquering Count on 24 October 1147. They helped him to establish the boundary of his nascent kingdom on the River Tagus, and were offered territorial fiefs in return. Many of them stayed. One of their number, Gilbert of Hastings, became the first Bishop of Lisbon. They laid the foundations of England's oldest alliance. All plans for proceeding to Palestine were dropped.

Henry of Huntingdon devoted only a few sentences to the Lisbon crusade, though he compared its success to the failure at Damascus:

> Interea quidam exercitus naualis uivorum non potentum, nec alicui magno duci innixi . . . quia humiliter profecti sunt, optime profecerunt . . . Meanwhile, a naval force made up of poor rather than powerful men, and with no great leader, fared much better, because they set out in humility. Though few in number, but with God's help, they captured a city in Spain called Ulixis Bona (Lisbon) and another called Almeriá, together with the adjacent territories. Truly, 'God

resists the proud and gives favour to the humble.' For the armies of the French king and the Emperor were greater and more splendid than that which had formerly conquered Jerusalem ... Yet no multitude could withstand the force of poor men, which I just mentioned. The greater part of them had come from England.[4]

A much fuller account was written by an anonymous English participant. Nothing is known about the author of the late twelfth century *De expugnatione Lyxbonensi* ('The Conquest of Lisbon') except that his name began with 'R' and he served in the retinue of Hervey de Granvill, a knight from East Anglia. He may well have been a chaplain. He describes how a fleet of 164 ships sailed from Dartmouth on 23 May 1147, taking large numbers of Rhinelanders and Flemings as well as English. They were recruited in Portugal by the Bishop of Oporto and reached Lisbon by sea. They played an active role in the seventeen-week siege, building the ninety-foot siege tower which eventually brought the city to surrender. When the end came, the defenders were granted their lives, though all their houses and property were forfeit.

'R''s main interest, however, lay in the religious sphere. He carefully noted the slurs and blasphemies with which the Christian besiegers were assailed. The details are better left, in the best Gibbonian tradition, in the decent obscurity of the Latin:

Hec et hiis similia adversum nos calumpniantes obtrectabant. Crucis insuper signum cum magna irrisione ostentare nostris; atque in illam expuentes, feditatis sue posteriora extergebant ex illa, sicque demum micturientes in illam quasi obprobrium quoddam, crucem nostram nobis proiciunt. Videbatur vero iterum Christus actualiter ab incredulis blasphemari.[5]

The conclusion was that of a true Christian. 'Once again, it was truly observed', he wrote, 'how Christ was actually insulted by the unbelievers.'

Yet after the capitulation of the Moors, 'R' was magnanimous. He was at great pains to insist that the victorious crusaders should examine their own consciences:

Videntes ergo sed non intelligentes divine adimadversionis iudicium hostibus inculcatum, conscientie nostre immunditiam atque impuritatem consideremus ... Observing therefore but not understanding the judgement of divine chastisement imposed on the enemy, let us consider the impurity of our own consciences, and with fear and trembling let us say unto God 'Spare, now Lord, spare the work of Thy hands' ... But rather if it be possible let their sorrow be turned into joy, 'in order that they may know Thee, the only living and true God, and Jesus Christ whom Thou hast sent, even Thy Son, who liveth and reigneth for ever and ever.' Amen.[6]

Here, at least, was one crusader who knew what Christian charity meant.

Louis VII had travelled to the Holy Land in the company of his Queen, Aliénor d'Aquitaine, a woman whose destiny would be closely linked to England. His decision to attack Damascus, 'the city of blood', was born of sheer desperation. The Emir of Damascus was the only friendly Muslim leader in the region and had signed a treaty of alliance with the King of Jerusalem. For he, like the four Latin states, was directly threatened by the rising power of Nur ed-Din, Sultan of Mosul. After all, it was Nur ed-Din's seizure of the inland Latin principality of Edessa in 1144 which had raised the initial alarm, and had inspired the Pope to announce the crusade. Yet bitter rivalries and dissensions among the crusaders ruled out all the more sensible destinations. Nur ed-Din's city of Aleppo, for example, had been the preferred target of the circle of knights connected with Aliénor d'Aquitaine, and with her uncle, Raimond de Poitiers, Prince of Antioch. But the visit of France's royal pair to Antioch, on their way to Jerusalem, had caused such a furious domestic storm that Aliénor had threatened to divorce Louis, and Prince Raimond had left the crusade in disgust. Still more acute animosities flared in Antioch's fellow principality of Tripoli. Tripoli was ruled by another Prince Raimond, bastard son of Raimond IV de Toulouse, Marquis de Provence, leader of the First Crusade. Prince Raimond's half-brother, Alphonse-Jourdain, Raimond IV's legitimate heir and the current Count of Toulouse, had arrived in the

Holy Land in the French king's retinue, only to die of suspected poisoning soon after landing. So the fingers of suspicion were pointed both at his half-brother and at Queen Mélisende; and the Prince of Tripoli, like the Prince of Antioch, withdrew to his tent. After that, despite the grandiose display of solidarity at Acre, the resources of the crusaders were strained to breaking point. Much of the infantry had been lost on the road through Asia Minor and a short campaign against a nearby city was all that could be contemplated. It was Damascus or nothing. So the column moved off in mid-July on the eighty-mile march to the Syrian city. The King of Jerusalem, boasting local knowledge, led the van. The French king held the centre: the German king brought up the rear. They laid siege on 24 July, camping in the lush orchards below the city's southern walls. They called their Muslim opponents 'the Infidels', 'the unbelievers'. The Infidels called the crusaders the 'Franj', the 'Franks'.

Once he recovered from his surprise, the Emir of Damascus, Mu'in al-Din Unar, urged his subjects to sally forth and resist the Franj. Amongst the defenders streaming out of the city, he noticed a renowned Moroccan theologian called Al-Findalawi.

> Upon seeing him walking ahead, [the Emir] greeted him and said, 'Venerable old man, your advanced age exempts you.' He asked him to turn back. But Al-Findalawi refused saying 'I have sold myself and God has bought me.' Thus did he refer to the words of the Almighty 'God has bought the persons and property of the faithful and will grant them paradise in return.' Al-Findalawi marched forward, and fought the Franj until he fell under the blows.[7]

At that juncture, the tide of battle was flowing in the crusaders' favour. The principal historian of the Kingdom of Jerusalem, Guillaume de Tyre, who was alive at the time, recorded the scene:

> During this engagement, the emperor* . . . is said to have slain a Turkish knight in a most remarkable way . . . With one blow of his

---

* Conrad III, King of the Romans, never formally received the Imperial crown; but as the ruler of Germany and successor to the German Emperors, he was popularly known as 'emperor'.

sword, he severed from the body of his enemy the head and the neck, the left shoulder with the arm attached and part of the side . . . This feat caused such terror . . . even to those who merely heard of it, that they lost all hope of resisting.[8]

Yet resistance stiffened. Emir Unar called on his rival, Nur ed-Din, for assistance. Turkish and Arab cavalry poured into the city's northern gate. Well-placed bribes seduced part of the besieging force, whilst the leaders fell again to squabbling. The Count of Flanders demanded that Damascus should be ceded to him. The knights of Jerusalem demanded that it be made a fief of the kingdom under Guy de Brisebarre, Lord of Beirut. On the third day, a counterattack drove the besiegers from the cover of the orchards, and pushed them into arid terrain on the city's eastern side. There, for lack of water and lack of common purpose, the crusaders' resolve crumbled. On the fifth day, they retreated. Muslim commentators could not contain their surprise:

> The Franj were not what they used to be. Negligence and disunity among military commanders, it seemed, were no longer the unhappy prerogative of the Arabs. The Damascenes found this amazing. Was it possible that this powerful Frankish expedition, which had caused the entire Orient to tremble, was disintegrating after only four days of battle? *It was thought that they were preparing some trick*, Ibn al-Qalanisi says. But no. The new Frankish invasion was really finished. *The German Franj*, Ibn al-Athar says, *returned to their country which lies over yonder, beyond Constantinople, and God rid the faithful of this calamity.*[9]

Indeed, Conrad III departed without delay. Louis VII was stranded, with a disaffected wife and no active allies. Guillaume de Tyre quoted Job, 'My harp is turned to mourning, and my organ into the voice of those who weep.'[10]

Louis of France, who had been the first to take the cross, was the last to leave. Two years before, at Vézelay, he had listened to the passionate Easter sermon of St Bernard calling for the crusade. It was said that Queen Aliénor and her ladies had dressed as Amazons on that occasion to urge the King's courtiers to follow his example. But now he felt abandoned by all. He felt betrayed by the Byzantine emperor, whose troops had attacked his crusaders: betrayed by Conrad III, who had gone off to Constantinople to join up with the Byzantines: betrayed by the Latins of Outremer: betrayed by his quarrelling vassals: and betrayed by his own Queen, whose dalliances were spawning gossip. His Chancellor, Abbot Suger, was begging him to return home in haste; but he lingered in the Holy Land until the Easter celebrations of 1149. He then sailed for Sicily, hoping in vain to mount another crusading expedition and leaving his wife to follow him. To crown his misfortunes, his squadron was intercepted and interned by hostile Byzantine ships, and he landed in Calabria as a destitute castaway. Aliénor reached Palermo in a different ship.

Meanwhile, in the Holy Land, the last sordid acts were played out. Bertrand de Toulouse, son of the dead Alphonse-Jourdain, stayed behind to take revenge on Raimond, Prince of Tripoli. The Prince defended himself by calling in the Emir Unar, and Bertrand landed in a Muslim jail. 'It was a fitting end to the Second Crusade that the last crusader should be held captive by the Moslem allies of the fellow-Christian prince whom he tried to despoil.'[11]

The chief beneficiary, however, was Nur ed-Din, the Muslim ruler whose ambitions the crusaders were supposed to check. In 1149, having seized Antioch, he despatched a silver casket containing the head of its Latin prince, Aliénor's uncle, to the Caliph in Baghdad. He had set his sights on Damascus.

England, though geographically distant from the Latin states of Outremer, was in no sense distant from its political, social, and cultural affairs. For the Anglo-Norman ruling class, which had annexed England after 1066 and which was now advancing rapidly into the other kingdoms of the Isles, was an offshoot of that wider French-dominated feudal community of which Outremer was the furthest limb. England's French elite not only shared that inimitable concoction of feudalism and militant Catholicism which constituted the ethos of the 'Age of Crusade'. They were also intimately related to the leading personalities among the crusaders. They were the kith and kin of Outremer's own elite. Raimond, Prince of

Antioch, for example, uncle to Queen Aliénor of France, had been resident
at the English court of his relative, Henri I, before he sailed away in 1135
to marry the Norman heiress of Antioch. The matchmaker for that
marriage was none other than Fulk V d'Anjou, King of Jerusalem, who
had himself sailed out to the Holy Land to marry Mélisende, heiress of
Baudouin II, a few years previously. King Fulk's younger son, Baudouin
III, was the youth who welcomed the Second Crusade. Fulk's elder son,
Geoffroi le Bel, 'Plantagenêt', who had taken over as Count of Anjou,
was married to Mathilde (Matilda), heiress of Henri I. Matilda in turn
had previously been married for eleven years to the Emperor Henry V,
Conrad III's predecessor in the Empire. Henri I had never taken the cross.
On the contrary, he had stayed home and had seized the Kingdom of
England in 1100, when his elder brother, Robert Courteheuse (Curthose),
was absent on the First Crusade. As a result, he had been forced to fight
for his realms on Robert's return. After his victory at Tinchebrai (1106),
he confirmed his hold on both Normandy and England, but only at the
cost of holding Robert as a lifelong prisoner in Cardiff Castle, for twenty-
eight years. Modern readers have to reach for their genealogical tables to
work all this out. But the feudal nobles, whose lifeblood ran through this
maze of kinship, would have known it all by heart. (See Appendix 19.)

At the time of the Second Crusade, in 1147–8, England found itself in
a state of unparalleled confusion. The conflict between the two rivals for
the throne, Étienne de Blois, Comte de Boulogne, and Henri's heiress,
Matilda, had opened the country both to internal wars and to external
invasion. Whilst the factions of the contenders fought a series of battles
and sieges in the Midlands and the South, the Welsh overran the Marches;
Ranulph, Earl of Chester carved out an independent principality for
himself; and Geoffroi de Mandeville, Earl of Essex, ravaged much of the
eastern counties. Most ominously, Scottish armies seized the whole of
England to the north of the Ribble and the Tyne. Despite a serious reverse
at the Battle of the Standard (1138), David I, King of Scotland, a
supporter of Matilda, set up his capital in Carlisle.

Étienne de Blois (better known in English textbooks as King Stephen)
had seized the English throne much as Matilda's father, Henri I, had
seized it from Robert Curthose thirty-five years earlier. He was descended

on the paternal side from the standard-bearer of Robert Curthose on the First Crusade, and on the maternal side was a grandson of the Conqueror. His brother was the powerful Bishop of Winchester; and he quickly gained the backing of the Church and of all those Norman barons who resented Matilda's marriage into the rival House of Anjou. In 1141, during Matilda's chief campaign in England, he was captured and deposed. Recovering, he had to be recrowned in Westminster Abbey. But he could not defend Normandy from the ravages of the Plantagenêt who by 1144 had taken a complete grip on the duchy. Étienne's heir, Eustace, had made a splendid match to Constance, sister to Louis VII, who, in his fear of the Angevins, variously supported both Étienne and the earlier English pretender, Guillaume Cliton (William Clito), son of Curthose. Clito (1101–28), sometime Count of Flanders, was wed to Sybilla, daughter of Fulk V d'Anjou and Geoffroi Plantagenêt's sister, who later married Thierry de Flandres, the would-be claimant to Damascus. In middle age, Sybilla left her husband, took religious vows, and fled to the protection of her father in Jerusalem. During the Second Crusade, though half-sister to King Baudouin III, she was a nun in the Abbey of St Lazarus in Bethlehem. She had clearly tired of the infernal complications of feudal politics – as many readers of this paragraph will also do. But it would be surprising if she never spared a thought for the outcome of the struggles in England, where, in other circumstances, she would have been queen.

Henry of Huntingdon (d. 1156), who was an accomplished Latin poet as well as a chronicler, has left a vivid and sometimes gruesome account of England's troubles as he saw them. The last book of his *History*, 'De Hoc Presenti', is entirely devoted to contemporary affairs:

> Successu uero temporis atrocissimi quod postea per Normanorum rabiosas prodiciones exarsit, quicquid Henricus fecerat, uel tirannice uel regie, comparatione deteriorum uisum est peroptimum . . . But in the dreadful time that followed [Henry I's death] which was set on fire by the mad treacheries of the Normans, whatever Henry had done, whether in royal or tyrannical manner, looked by comparison to be the height of excellence. For without delay came Stephen, the younger brother of Count Theobold of Blois, a man of great vigour

and effrontery ... [who] challenged God by seizing the crown of the Kingdom. William, Archbishop of Canterbury, who had been the first to take the oath — prohdolor, alas! — blessed him as king.[12]

The chronicler believed in divine portents. He described how the new reign had begun in very bad odour:

Rex namque Henricus prima die Decembris obierat. Cuius corpus allatum est Rotomagum ... King Henry had died on the first day of December [1135]. His body was brought to Rouen, and there his entrails, brain and eyes were buried together. The remainder of the corpse was cut all over with knives, sprinkled with a great deal of salt and wrapped in ox hides to stop the strong pervasive stench which was already causing the deaths of those who watched over it. It even killed the man who had been hired for a great fee to cut off the head with an axe and extract the stinking brain ... so he was badly rewarded for his fee. He was the last of many whom King Henry put to death ... See then, how the body of a most mighty king, whose crowned head had sparkled with gold and the finest jewels, ... was so miserably cast down ... Learn to hold such things in contempt ... At last, the royal remains were brought to England ... and [to] the Abbey of Reading ... King Stephen came there from the court which he had held in London at Christmas ... together with the Archbishop of Canterbury ... and they buried King Henry with the respect due to so great a man.[13]

Henry of Huntingdon had not welcomed the reign of Étienne de Blois. But he felt obliged to support a crowned monarch. And he particularly appreciated the King's energetic action against the invading Scots:

Stephanus rex impiger, tercio anno ... The energetic King Stephen, in the third year of his entry into England, rushed out to Bedford, which he besieged on Christmas Eve [1137] ... many considered this displeasing to God, since he was treating the most solemn of festivals as being of little importance. Bedford surrendered to him, and he advanced his army into Scotland. For the King of Scots, under cover of piety, having sworn an oath to King Henry's daughter, commanded his men in barbarous deeds. For they ripped open pregnant women and tore out the unborn foetuses. They tossed children on the points of their lances. They dismembered priests on their altars. They put the heads cut off crucifixes onto the bodies of the slain, and, changing them round, put the heads of the dead onto crucifixes ... So King Stephen invaded, burned and laid waste the southern areas of King David's kingdom.[14]

When the Empress Matilda entered the field in 1141 and her rival was captured in battle by one of her knights, Guillaume de Cahagnes, the chronicler accepted it as an act of divine judgement. The King's subsequent release could only be explained as a miracle:

Dei igitur iudicio circa regem peracto ... God's judgement on the king having been carried out, he was ... put into Bristol castle as a prisoner. The empress was received as *domina*, 'their lady', by all the English nation except for the men of Kent, where the queen and William of Ypres opposed her with all their might ... But she was lifted up to an insufferable arrogance ... and alienated the hearts of almost everyone. So either at the instigation of crafty men or by God's will ... she was driven out of London. Provoked by this into a womanly rage, she ordered the king, the Lord's anointed, to be put in irons ... Eventually, the London army came, and with augmented numbers they fought against the empress and forced her to flee. In the rout, many were captured. One of the captives was Robert [of Gloucester,] the empress's brother, by whose capture alone the king could escape ... So the King ... was miraculously freed by God's mercy, and was received by the English nobility with great rejoicing.[15]

Yet the misdeeds of the contending parties continued unchecked. The despairing chronicler was moved to verse:

> Quis michi det fontem ... lacrimarum
> Vt lacrimer patrie gesta nefanda mee?
> Aduenit caligo Stigis dimissa profundo,
> Que regni faciem conglomerata tegit.

Ecce furor, fremitus, incendia, furta, rapine,
 Cedes, nulla fides, consociata ruunt.[16]

(Who will give me a fountain of tears,
 That I may weep for my country's infamous deeds?
 Stygian gloom has arrived, released from the depths,
 And it veils the face of the Kingdom,
See how fury, uproar, robbery, pillage, murder
 And faithlessness, rush headlong to ruin . . .)

Fountains, pure or polluted, supplied the favourite metaphor:

De pressura Anglie

Garrula puri   uenula fontis
Sorde repleta   reddere priscas
Gurgite presso   abnuit undas.
Prodita iacti   germina grani
Grandine strata,   flore subacto
Spem dominorum   arbore querna
Diruta ponunt . . .
Si quoque seuis   Anglia merens
Pressa tyranis,   sorde repleta
Diruta fraude,   dulcia seuis
Mella uenenis   anxia mutat[17]

(The babbling trickle from a pure fountain is now filled with dirt,
 obstructed, it fails to release its flow
laid low by hail, the fruits of the harvest are destroyed,
the flower subdued; betrayed, their owners are left to put their hope in the
 oak alone . . .
So, too, grieving England, oppressed by harsh tyrants,
 filled with dirt, overthrown by deceit,
in troubled mood exchanges sweet honey for savage poisons.)

By the time of the Second Crusade, a dozen years since the death of Henri
Beauclerc, no end to the anarchy was in sight.

≈

Louis VII of France (r. 1137–80) was the central pivot in this political web of personal and territorial relationships. As the sixth monarch of the Capetian dynasty, his political influence was much greater than the size of the royal domain in the Île de France might have suggested. Successor, as he claimed, to Charlemagne, he would have ceded precedence to none, not even to the kings and emperors of Germany, whose formal status, enhanced by papal investiture, was technically superior. Although he often lacked the means to hold his numerous vassals to their oaths of loyalty and obedience, he had personally received the homage of all the great dukes and counts of his kingdom. Among the crusaders of 1148 he was the direct feudal superior of the Counts of Perche, Champagne, Flanders, and Provence, as also of the families from which all the princes and kings of Outremer were descended. In the unfolding drama of England, he was the active feudal lord of all the interested parties – the Dukes of Normandy, the Counts of Anjou, the Count of Boulogne, and, as would soon emerge, the Dukes of Aquitaine. Modern English historians often ignore this point. They rightly insist that the Kingdom of England as created by its West Saxon rulers was a sovereign realm, legally independent of all neighbouring jurisdictions. Yet they underplay the other important fact that every claimant to the medieval English throne from 1066 onwards possessed honours, titles, estates, and family connections which subordinated them to the French monarchs. In the feudal order, no King of England ever stood so high as the Kings of France. England's independence was a technical abstraction. The people who ran England were not fully independent.

What is more, Louis VII, like his predecessors and successor, was constantly forced to defend the northern borders of the royal domain against the shameless depradations of his Norman and Angevin subjects. And he was inevitably concerned by the extra strength and resources which those subjects received from their cross-Channel possessions. As a result, like all French kings, he was deeply involved in the English succession. The French lost no love on Henri I Beauclerc; and they supported in turn each of the candidates who challenged the hold of Beauclerc's circle on England and Normandy – i.e., William Clito to 1128, Étienne de Blois, and from 1152 his brother-in-law Eustace de Boulogne.

Louis, however, had married outside the incestuous circles of northern France. In July 1137, still in his father's lifetime, he had travelled to Bordeaux to marry Aliénor de Poitiers, who was already Duchess of Aquitaine in her own right. Five days after the marriage, he learned that his royal father was dead. He hastened back to Paris, alone, to launch a reign that would last for forty-three years.

Not surprisingly, therefore, immense consequences hung on the outcome of the domestic rift between Louis VII and his queen, Aliénor d'Aquitaine, that had become public during the Second Crusade. After the quarrel at Antioch, where she had shunned her husband's company for that of her dashing uncle, Aliénor had been physically dragged to the royal ship for all to see. And she had reportedly shouted that she was married 'not to a king, but to a monk'. The King's pious disposition was not to her liking; and her frivolity was not reciprocated. Most damningly, after eleven years of marriage, the Queen had still not borne an heir. At Tusculum, near Rome, on the way back from the crusade, Pope Eugenius had greeted the royal pair and had personally ordered them to sleep in one bed. Aliénor conceived, only to give birth to the second of two daughters. Louis was displeased. He was already consulting his ecclesiastical advisers about the feasibility of annulling his marriage on the grounds of consanguinity. Like many such couples, Louis and Aliénor had common relatives within the forbidden degrees. But then the tale took another twist. In the summer of 1151, Geoffroi 'Plantagenêt', Count of Anjou and Duke of Normandy, brought his young son, 'Henry Fitz-Empress', to St Denis to have him invested in the duchy. Aliénor, it was rumoured, took more than a usual liking to both father and son. Both Anjou and Normandy were key pieces in the English puzzle.

Anjou was one of the great fiefs of France.[18] Like its neighbours, Normandy and Poitou, it had emerged during Carolingian times, though its fortunes were largely made during the long reign of its ferocious count, Fulk III Nerra (r. 987–1040). Two generations later, Fulk IV le Réchin was remembered for letting the fief decay and for letting his wife become the mistress of the King. But Fulk V le Jeune (r. 1109–31) restored the family fortunes. Threatened by the rise of Normandy, he made every possible effort to hitch his children to the Norman star. One daughter was married off to William the Aetheling, heir to Henri Beauclerc. When the Aetheling died, the next daughter Sibylla was married (as mentioned above) to William Clito, heir to Robert Curthose. When Clito died, Fulk's son and heir Geoffroi le Bel — the first of the clan to wear a sprig of broom (i.e., *plantagenêt*) in his helmet — was married to Beauclerc's heiress, the Empress Matilda. As a widower, Fulk then felt free to sail for the Holy Land, to marry *secondo voto* Queen Mélisende and to rule in Jerusalem for fifteen years. Fulk had died in 1143, the year before Geoffroi completed the conquest of Normandy. Geoffroi died in 1151, the same year he and his son, Henry FitzEmpress, had made the acquaintance of their Queen, Aliénor of Aquitaine.

In the mid-twelfth century Aquitaine was the largest of the French duchies. At the time, it was the only French fief to approach the Mediterranean coast and the only one to be dominated by the southern culture of the *langue d'oc*. Its origins went all the way back to the Romans. In the fifth century AD one of its early bishops, Fortunatus of Poitiers, wrote the famous Christian hymn *Vexilla regis prodeunt*, 'The Royal Banners Forward Go', which later became the favourite marching song of the crusaders. In medieval times it crystallized round the lands held by one of Charlemagne's companions, St Guillaume de Gellone (c. 735–812). The first Dukes of Aquitaine exercised power from their home county of Auvergne; the later ones from the county of Poitou. Guillaume VIII (r. 1058–86) created a Greater Aquitaine, '*la Joyeuse*', including Poitou, Saintonge, Gascogne, and Auvergne, much as his contemporary, Fulk Nerra, created a Greater Anjou. His son, the ninth duke, was Guillaume le Troubador (r. 1086–1127), who was not just a patron but a practitioner of Occitan minstrelsy:

> Farai chansoneta nueva
> ans que vent ni gel ni plueva;
> ma dona m'assai'e'm prueva,
> quossi de qual guiza l'am;
> e ja per plag que m'en mueva,
> no'm solvera de son liam.
>
> . . .

Que plus ez blanca qu'evori,
per qu'ieu autra non azori.
Si'm breu non ai ajutori
cum ma bona dompna m'am,
morrai, pel cap sanh Gregori
si no'm bayz'en cambr'o sotz ram.

. . .

Qual pro y auretz, dompna conja,
si vostr'amors mi deslonja?
Par queus vulatz metre monja.
E sapchatz, quar tan vos am,
tem que la dolors me ponja,
si no'm faitz dreg dels tortz qu'ie 'us clam.

. . .

Per acquesta fri e tremble,
quar d
e tan bon'amor l'am;
qu'anc no cug qu'en nasques semble
en semblan del gran linh n'Adam.[19]

(MODERN FRENCH)
Je ferai un chant nouveau
avant qu'il ne vente, gèle et pleuve,
Ma dame ma tente et m'éprouve
et veut voir de quelle façon je l'aime.
Malgré ses querelles, jamais
je ne me délierai d'elle.

. . .

Elle, plus blanche qu'ivoire
elle plus que toute autre adorée.
Si elle ne m'assiste vite
de son amour, ma dame fine,
j'en mourrai par saint Grégoire;
si elle ne me baise en chambre ou sous la ramée.

. . .

Que gagnerez-vous, dame fine,
à m'éloigner de votre amour?
Vous voulez vous faire nonne?
Sachez-le, mon amour est tel
que je crains de mourir de douleur
si vous ne changez d'idée en écoutant ma plainte.

. . .

Pour elle, je frisonne et tremble
car je l'aime d'un tel amour.
Je ne crois par qu'il en nacquît jamais de pareille
de tout ce grand lignage depuis messire Adam.

(MODERN ENGLISH)
I shall make a new song
Before it blows, freezes and rains.
My lady tests and tries me
Wishing to see in what manner I love her.
Despite her complaints, never
Will I untie myself from her.
. . .
She, whiter than ivory,
Is adored above all other.
If she does not swiftly come to my side
With her love, my good lady,
By St Gregory, I shall die;
Or if she does not kiss me, in the chamber or behind the screen.
. . .
My fine lady, what will you gain
If you distance me from your love?
Do you really wish to be a nun?
Make no mistake, such is my love,
That I fear to die from pain
If, hearing my plea, you do not change your mind.
. . .
For that woman, I shake and tremble
For I do love her with such passion.

I do not believe that an equal love might be born
From all of Adam's great lineage.

It was in the Troubadour's court at Poitiers, and under his influence, that the young Aliénor had passed her earliest years. His poetry is often seen as the starting point of Occitan literature. The style was dictated by the conventions of 'courtly love' – the earliest wave of Europe-wide secular culture. It was a world away from the austere clerical circle which determined the climate at St Denis. The Troubadour's one signal act of piety was to organize the foundation, on the northern border of Poitou and Anjou, of the great Benedictine Abbey of Fontevrault.

Aliénor's immediate family was marked by a wayward streak. Her father, Guillaume X (r. 1127–36), the last Count of Poitiers, had curried disfavour in France by taking the side of the anti-Popes in the long-running Investiture Conflict which at one point had simultaneously produced two popes and three emperors. He had died in mysterious circumstances on pilgrimage at Santiago di Compostella, leaving Aliénor as the sole heiress of all his lands and recommending her as a match for the heir of France. His wife and countess was already dead. His brother, the above-mentioned Raimond de Poitiers, Prince of Antioch, who had gone off as a young man to England and thence to the Holy Land, was passed over, despite being the sole surviving male; his younger daughter, Aélithe, known as Petronilla, Aliénor's only sibling, was every bit as impetuous as her sister.

Petronilla caused enormous trouble. In fact, it could be said that she caused the Second Crusade. Unmarried, Petronilla followed Aliénor to the French court where she, as the King's sister-in-law, started an open but illicit liaison with one of the royal courtiers, Raoul de Vermandois. As it happened, her lover was Seneschal of France, and her lover's wife was sister to the powerful Count of Champagne, who was mightily offended by the affair. In fact, when Louis VII failed to intervene against the Seneschal's repudiation of his wife in favour of Petronilla, the Count of Champagne declared war on his suzerain and invaded the royal domain. That was in 1142. Three years later the war was turning nasty. The royal troops, commanded by the Seneschal, were caught in a pincer with the

Champagnards pushing in from the east and the Normans (of Geoffroi Plantagenêt) pressing down from the north. Desperate and infuriated by the hostility of the local population in the little town of Vitry-en-Perthois, they herded more than a thousand men, women, and children into the church and burned them to death. Louis VII saw the atrocity, but did not stop it. Afterwards, wracked by remorse, he offered to do penance. And his penance, announced at Christmas 1145, was to launch a crusade for the relief of Edessa. In this way, Petronilla's peccadilloes had provoked the royal pair's departure for Palestine.

As for Fontevrault, the Troubadour's foundation, it was to offer a secure refuge for all the women oppressed by these uncontrolled political storms.[20]

In the spring of 1152, the King of France's advisers urged that a final resolution to his marital problems must be instigated. Accordingly, an ecclesiastical court was convened at Beaugency on the Loire, and on 21 March the assembled lawyers and clerics declared the royal marriage to be null and void on the grounds of consanguinity. Aliénor, who was present, did not contest it. She was to hand over her two daughters to the King, but she was to receive restitution of all her hereditary lands including Poitou, Saintonge, Marche, Angoumois, Périgord, Auvergne, Limousin, the Bordelais, the Agenois, and Gascogne. Louis VII, who had assumed the title of Duke of Aquitaine, was to restore the title to her. Reportedly, the one formal condition of the annulment was that she could not remarry without the King's explicit permission. Yet she defied the legal terms and remarried, shockingly, within two months of leaving Beaugency. Her second spouse, seventeen years younger than herself, was to be, equally shockingly, Henri FitzEmpress Plantagenêt.

Given the speed of Aliénor's remarriage, many people assumed that the whole operation was secretly prepared long in advance. There is little evidence one way or the other. Not that Henri would have needed much prompting. Dozens of eligible bachelors were preening their feathers. On the way back to Poitiers from Beaugency, Aliénor survived two attempted kidnaps. She escaped from one would-be suitor by fleeing from her host's castle at dead of night. She evaded the other – none other than Henri's younger brother – by switching her itinerary. In the world of feudalism, the choicest bride in Christendom was not just a hot property; she was, in all senses of the phrase, fair game.

Henri FitzEmpress was at Lisieux in Normandy when news of the royal annulment arrived. He was discussing the affairs of England with his barons. By 1152, years of conflict had failed to cement the position of Étienne de Blois and the Angevins could still revive their claim. Whether or not Aliénor sent Henri a missive announcing her freedom, as some accounts affirm, is a matter for speculation. At all events, he rode south without delay. Since his father's recent death, he was already Count of Anjou, comprising Anjou, Maine, and Touraine; and for two years past he had been installed as Duke of Normandy. As sole heir to the Empress Matilda, he could also expect to assume the latent claim to England. But Aquitaine was not a lesser prize than England. So England would have to wait. Henri rode into Poitiers with a purpose. The preliminaries were brief. Henri and Aliénor were married by an English bishop in the cathedral of St Fortunatus on 18 May, 'without fitting pomp and ceremony'. For pomp can hardly have been foremost in their minds. As peers of France and royal tenants-in-chief, both bride and groom were wilfully breaking the spirit if not the letter both of their feudal bonds, and of Aliénor's annulment. The King, their suzerain and her ex-husband, was sure to respond violently. It was no time for ceremonies.

There are few traces of that famous day in the cathedral at Poitiers. The old Romanesque nave was remodelled in Gothic style shortly afterwards, and the bright polychrome decorations, which would have provided a colourful set for the wedding, have long since disappeared. The east window, which Henri and Aliénor presented to the cathedral as part of the general renovation initiated in remembrance of their marriage, is all that survives. The window, in stained glass, reminiscent of St Denis, shows the crucifixions both of Christ and of (the inverted) St Peter. The kneeling figures of Henri and Aliénor appear at the base.[21]

The expected war was swiftly abandoned. Louis VII cobbled together a coalition of malcontents whose only common interest was their resentment of Henri Plantagenêt's success. Among them were the King's brother, Robert de Dreux, his son-in-law, Eustace de Boulogne, pretender to the English crown, and Henri's own brother, Geoffroi d'Anjou. A Capetian army marched into Poitou, whilst another besieged and captured the Norman fortress of Neufmarché. But that was the limit of their exertions. The Plantagenêt already commanded far more resources than the King did, and an ailing Louis VII had no stomach for an extended wrangle. He eventually resigned his claim to Aquitaine in return for a payment. Apart from anything, he needed to adjust to the news from Germany, where the imperial electors had just elevated the energetic Friedrich I Barbarossa to the throne. Oddly enough, Barbarossa had just put aside his own wife on the grounds of consanguinity.

So Henri FitzEmpress could turn at last to England, a country which he had visited only twice in his twenty years. As a boy of seven or eight, he had accompanied his mother, the Empress Matilda, in her vain attempt to drive out Étienne de Blois in 1141–2; and he had stayed on among Matilda's supporters in the West Country, receiving an extended period of tuition in Bristol. He had returned for the campaigning season of 1149 under the protection of his maternal uncle, David I, King of Scotland, who formally initiated the sixteen-year-old into knighthood. The Scots army had camped all summer at Carlisle, facing down a royal English army at York. But the threatened battle did not materialize, and the novice knight returned home to Le Mans unblooded. He had spent the next two years with his father, sorting out the transfer of Normandy and Anjou. Following the elder Plantagenêt's sudden death in September 1151, through a chill caught swimming in the River Cher, Henri had returned to his mother. They might have planned his marriage with Aliénor. They must definitely have discussed the deteriorating condition of England.

Notwithstanding nearly two decades of civil war, Étienne de Blois had repeatedly failed to stamp his authority on England. Many of the magnates who had obeyed Henri I in swearing allegiance to Matilda had only broken their oaths and accepted Étienne in the hope of a quiet life. Now that Étienne was patently incapable of providing a quiet life, they were turning against him. And Étienne seemed to have no answer except to punish the waverers and to lay waste their estates. Worst of all, he was losing the confidence of the Church. When both bishops and barons resolutely refused to recognize the claim to succession of Étienne's son, Eustace de Boulogne, his cause was manifestly on the wane.

In the winter of 1152–3 Henri FitzEmpress undoubtedly knew that his fortunes in England would soon be put to the test. In the event, he was forced to test his chances rather sooner than expected. Having fulfilled the prime duty of a would-be dynast by impregnating Aliénor with the first of their five sons, he took ship in one of the Norman ports with a view to sailing to another place further along the coast. Providence decreed, however, that a sudden storm blew his ships out to sea. Henri was driven helplessly across the Channel and onto a beach of his would-be kingdom, probably in Dorset:

> When the glorious duke was blown by a tempest onto the shores of England the land rustled with rumours like a reed-bed ... The news spread quickly, as usual, bringing joy and happiness to some, fear and sorrow to others ... Some thought that crossing the stormy sea in the middle of winter was brave, others found it rash. But the brave duke gathered his supporters together ... and hating delay above all laid siege to Malmesbury Castle.[22]

A lesser man might have beaten the retreat. But word of the Plantagenêt's arrival was rallying men to the cause. Any sign of weakness would have sown confusion. So Henry took the field – unprepared, unannounced, and almost unaccompanied. He had landed as a lonely pretender; he would not leave until he was the undisputed heir to the throne.

The remarkable reversal of fortunes which occurred in that year of 1153 shows that the existing regime had slipped much further than surface events betrayed. The King, Étienne de Blois, set out manfully to meet the challenge. At Malmesbury, a hard-fought battle was avoided by the intervention of the English weather:

> The day after [the King's] arrival, he drew up his army containing a great number of excellent and distinguished knights ... and many

barons, their banners glittering with gold, beautiful and terrible indeed. But God, in whom alone is safety, was not with them. For the floodgates of heaven opened, and such bitter gusts of wind and pouring rain were driven into their faces, that God himself seemed to be fighting for the duke . . . He and his men had the gale at their backs; the King's men had it in their faces, so that they could barely hold their weapons or their dripping lances . . . Since neither side would cross the rain, the King, no longer able to withstand such floods of rain, retraced his steps to London, his discomfiture complete.[23]

At Wallingford on the Thames, a strategic stronghold, another grand battle seemed imminent. But again it did not materialize:

When the royal army saw the unexpected sight of their enemies drawn up before them, they were struck by sudden panic . . . But the King was not afraid and ordered his men to march out from camp in battle array. But the barons, those betrayers of England, . . . were unwilling to fight, as they did not wish either side to win. . . . The King and the duke had a conference alone together, across a small stream, about making a lasting peace . . . and each complained about the treachery of his nobles.[24]

But in August Providence delivered the decisive blow. Eustace de Boulogne, the King's heir, died at the height of his powers. The King had nothing more to strive for. He could fight to a futile finish, or he could do a deal. He chose wisely. If the Plantagenêt camp would let him reign for his lifetime, he would forget the feud with Matilda and would make Matilda's son his official heir. Suddenly, the King turned generous. He went out to meet the young duke and personally escorted him to a series of rousing welcomes:

What inestimable joy! O blessed day! when the King himself received the young prince at Winchester with a magnificent procession of bishops and nobles through the cheering crowds.

The King received him as his adoptive son, and recognised him as his heir. From Winchester the king took the duke to London, where he was received with no less joy by enormous crowds and splendid processions ... Thus, by God's mercy, peace dawned on the ruined realm of England, putting an end to its troubled night.[25]

At the Treaty of Winchester the contract was signed and sealed. Étienne de Blois could reign till he died. His one surviving son, Guillaume de Warenne, could keep his lands and title. And the Plantagenêt was to be heir to the throne. One last event awaited before he left. At Oxford in January, Henri was invited to meet an assembly of barons and churchmen, to drink and carouse with his future tenants-in-chief, to receive their fealty, and to reconfirm the Treaty in good cheer. Barring accidents, which in medieval times were frequent, he was all set to add yet another title to his collection. Henri Plantagenêt, 'Henry FitzEmpress', Henri du Mans, Henri Courtmanteau, Comte de Maine et de Tours, Duc d'Anjou, de Normandie, et d'Aquitaine, was due to become Henri II, Roi de l'Angleterre.

As it happened, he did not have long to wait. Étienne de Blois, exhausted, expired on 25 October 1154. Henri II left his French home, took his wife and child, and sailed to collect his throne. He was crowned at Westminster on 19 December. The 'Plantagenet Era' had begun. In Normandy and Anjou it would last for fifty years more, in Poitou for seventy-one years, in Aquitaine for two hundred and ninety-nine years: in England it would last for three hundred and thirty-one. The people of England heaved a huge sigh of relief. Henry of Huntingdon broke into heroic hexameters:

> Anglia letali iamdudum frigore terpens,
> Nunc solis feruore noui rediuiua calescens,
> Erigis impressum terre caput, et uacuatis
> Mesticie lacrimis, pre leticia lacrimaris.
> Cum lacrimis hec verba tuo profundis alumpno:
> 'Spiritus es, caro sum, te nunc intrante reuixi.'[26]

(England, long numbed by mortal chill, you now grow warm, revived by the heat of a new sun. You lift the country's bowed head, and wiping away the tears of sorrow, you weep for joy. With tears, you utter these words to your foster child: 'You are spirit, I am flesh: now as you enter I am restored to life.')

Not far from Huntingdon, another English monk at Peterborough Abbey had been keeping up the annals of *The Anglo-Saxon Chronicle*. He was to make the very last entry within a month of Henry's coronation:

> 1154. In this year King Stephen died and was buried where his wife and son were buried at Faversham, the minster they had made ... The earl was beyond the sea, but no man dared do other than good through great awe of him. Then when he came to England, he was received with great honour and was consecrated as king in London on the Sunday before mid-winter day, and there held a great court.
>
> Then the very day that Martin, abbot of Peterborough, should have gone [to that court in London] he fell sick and died on 2 January. Within the day, the monks chose another from themselves who is called William de Vatteville, a good clerk and a good man well loved by the king and by all good men. [They] buried the abbot in the morning, and immediately the abbot-elect and the monks with him travelled to the King at Oxford [where] the King gave him the abbacy. And he made his way immediately to Lincoln and was there blessed as abbot before he came home, and was afterwards received at Peterborough with a great procession ... and is now abbot and has made a fine beginning. Christ grant that he may end thus![27]

The English undercurrent was waning. The French supremacy in England was set to last. The idea that English history can be separated from French history in this period is an illusion.

In the Age of the Crusades, England was more comprehensively involved in Continental affairs than at any time before or since. As Frenchmen, and as dependants of the Kingdom of France for an important part of their holdings, the Norman and Plantagenet Kings of England never completely distanced themselves from their French roots. By maintaining the French connection, they anchored all their subjects in the French orbit. Indeed, with time, they would come up with a claim to be the rightful occupants of the French throne. What is more they turned their relations with the Irish, the Scots, and the Welsh, over whom they exercised increasing control, into a function of their French fixation. Although the Isles escaped direct Continental rule, the shadow of France lay across them for the best part of four hundred years. The Plantagenets only served to strengthen the French link which the Normans had forged.

One must also recognize the expansive nature of the France with which the Isles were so closely associated. Like England, both the Kingdom of the Two Sicilies and the Crusader States in the Holy Land were outposts of the same French feudal order. They were not exactly colonies on the modern model. Yet they were not far from it. They all saw the influx of a considerable body of French settlers and the imposition not just of French dynasties but of a French ruling class, which treated the culture of their non-French subjects with imperial disdain. For as long as that ruling class maintained its separation from the people at large – and it did so longest in England – there was little chance that the countries concerned could begin to build a strong sense of their own separate identity. England, Sicily, and Jerusalem all formed part of what some historians have seen as the first experiment in the overseas export of European civilization. When Henri Plantagenêt claimed the English throne, like the Conqueror before him, or Robert Guiscard in Sicily or Baudouin de Bouillon in Jerusalem, he was doing what they all did. He sailed overseas. Like them, his contemporaries would have numbered him as one of the numerous French princes ruling in 'France overseas' – à l'Outremer.[28]

THE ISLES IN THE LATE TWELFTH CENTURY

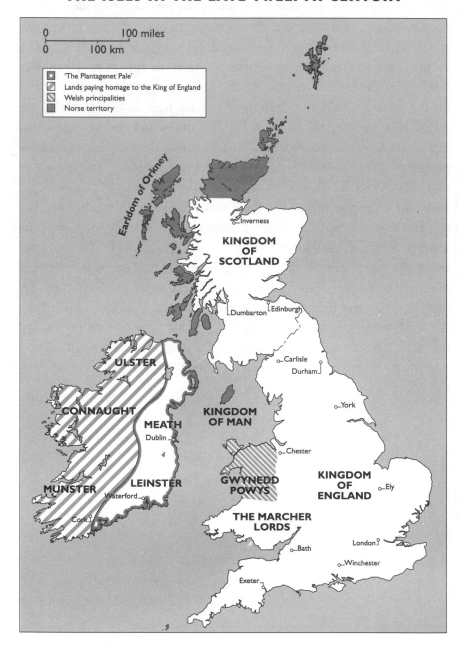

0   100 miles

0   100 km

- 'The Plantagenet Pale'
- Lands paying homage to the King of England
- Welsh principalities
- Norse territory

Earldom of Orkney

Inverness

KINGDOM
OF
SCOTLAND

Dumbarton   Edinburgh

ULSTER

Carlisle
Durham

CONNAUGHT

KINGDOM
OF MAN

York

MEATH
Dublin

MUNSTER   LEINSTER
Waterford

Chester

GWYNEDD
POWYS

KINGDOM
OF
ENGLAND

Ely

Cork

THE MARCHER
LORDS

London

Bath

Winchester

Exeter

HISTORIANS HAVE COINED THE TERM 'the Plantagenet Empire'. It is not historically correct. But it is a convenient way of describing the huge agglomeration of lands which fell into the lap of Henri Plantagenêt in those few years in the mid-twelfth century. That agglomeration did not really constitute an empire. There was no capital city, no central focus, no clear domination of one part over the others, no common ideology, no unified administration except for the tireless figure of the Duke/Count/King, who rode constantly back and forth across his domains for thirty-five years. Not surprisingly, the 'empire' proved no more durable than its guardians. When the Plantagenets took to scrapping among themselves, their united inheritance was doomed. By a strange turn of fate, the only one of Henri Plantagenêt's five sons to pass on even a part of the family's holdings was the youngest, Jean Sans Terre (1167–1216), 'John Lackland', who had received nothing in his father's initial carve-up. It was also far from predictable that of all the major pieces in the Plantagenet collection the only two territories to retain a close link with each other were not the Conqueror's lands in Normandy and England, nor the first Plantagenet's lands in Normandy and Anjou, but Matilda's Kingdom of England and Aliénor's Duchy of Aquitaine. This fact was to have immeasurable consequences for the development both of France and of the Isles. (See opposite.)

The central strategic problem for the Plantagenet Empire was posed by the continuing hostility of the Capetian Kings. Though Louis VII had been obliged to accept the defiant marriage of Henri and Aliénor, it is clear that his successors could not indefinitely accept that Paris be always surrounded on three sides by Plantagenet territory. It must also have been clear that the French counterattack would be concentrated on the lands adjacent to the Île de France in Normandy, Anjou, and Poitou rather than on the more distant positions in England or Aquitaine. By the same token, it is not difficult to work out that the best way for the Plantagenets to bolster their resources and thereby to resist the Capetian counter-attack would be to expand into more remote territories which they could absorb without fear of the expected Capetian intervention. What this meant in practical terms was that Henri Plantagenêt must have had his eyes from an early stage on the one remaining independent territory in western France, the Duchy of Brittany, and the one remaining fully independent kingdom in the Isles, namely Ireland. It is well known, for example, that in 1155 Henri persuaded the English Pope, Adrian IV, to issue the Bull of *Laudabiliter* and to authorize the conquest of Ireland. He made this move many years before there was any chance of putting the Pope's authorization into effect. The first step in the direction of Brittany was taken in 1156 when Henri's brother, Geoffroi d'Anjou, was installed at Nantes as Count of Lower Brittany. Everything was interconnected. Even the event for which Henri's reign is best remembered in England – the murder of Thomas à Becket, Archbishop of Canterbury – must be seen in the context of strains between Church and state not just in England but right across Western Europe.

Much has been written about 'Angevin Kingship' in England as if it developed in isolation from the rest of the Plantagenet realms. Yet Henri's concerns must have been for the whole of the 'empire'. His English policies were tailored to the interests of the whole. One cannot escape from the fundamental fact that in the fifty years after 1154 the Plantagenet monarchs spent only a third of their time in England. Henri's prime aims in England, therefore, were firstly to restore the law and order that had collapsed during the previous disputed reign, and secondly to create a self-sustaining adminis-tration that could function during his long absences. The emphasis was necessarily on laying the foundations of a permanent system of justice with regular courts, professional judges, established procedures, and written records. Hence the reign of Henri II (1154–89) saw the appearance both of the office of Justiciar or viceroy, which was long held by Richard de Lucy (d. 1179), an erstwhile supporter of King Stephen, and of the Pipe Rolls of the Exchequer. But nothing was more characteristic of the age than the King's itinerary and the institution which derived from it, the General *Iter* or 'Eyre'. Henri II was constantly on the move, plodding methodically round every corner of his realms, on horseback, dispensing justice, collecting taxes, bringing the barons into line, supervising the sheriffs, and taking the entire court in his train. In any one year, he could find himself in dozens of locations hundreds of miles apart.

In 1170, for example, the year of Becket's murder, Henri II spent fourteen weeks in England as opposed to thirty-eight in various parts of France. A detailed list of his stop-overs reveals his remarkable energy:

1170		Location	Business	Approximate mileage
January		Nantes	spends Christmas and New Year with Prince Geoffroi in Lower Brittany	
February	2	Sécs	corresponds with Becket from Normandy	200
	20	Caen		
March	3	Portsmouth	lands in England for the first time in four years	100
		Shaftesbury (Wilts) Feckenham (Worcs)		120
April	5	Windsor	celebrates Easter: creates a Commission of Enquiry into the governance of England	100
	10	London	Great Council: most English sheriffs dismissed	25
May		Woodstock (Oxon.)		60
		Silverstone (Northants)		30

June	10	London	Council – to receive reports of Commission of Enquiry	60
	14	Westminster	Prince Henry crowned by the Archbishop of York	5
	15		King William of Scotland and his brother pay homage	60
	24	Portsmouth	sails to Barfleur (Normandy)	80
	30	Falaise		100
July		Argentan to La Ferté Bernard		50
	20	Vendôme	meets King Louis VII of France	50
	22	Fréte val	meets Becket and is apparently reconciled	10
August	10	Mote-de-Ger	falls seriously ill, and makes his will	100
September	29	(Quercy)	makes a pilgrimage to Rocamadour after his recovery	250
October	12	Amboise	further meeting with Becket at Chinon	200
November	26	Loches, Mont Luçon, Bourges (Berry)	arranges truce with Louis VII over the dispute in Berry	200
December			[Becket lands at Sandwich on his way to Canterbury]	
		Normandy	Bayeux: Henry II spends Christmas at Bar-le-Roi [Becket murdered in Canterbury Cathedral]	200
1171				
January	1	Argentan	Henry II receives news of Becket's death	50

Total miles on land 2050[29]

Even though Henri did not visit the extremities of his dominions in northern England, Wales, or Gascony, and even though he stayed still for several weeks in Brittany, in London, and, during his illness, in Normandy, he still managed to cover over two thousand miles within the year.

Since the King could not be everywhere at once, however, he

restored and expanded Henri I's Commission of the General Eyre which regularly sent royal officials and judges round the country on similarly unending circuits. The system brought a much higher degree of coherence and of central control to English government. But it opened the gate to new forms of royal power, which in due course would be regarded as intolerable forms of abuse. By declarations *ira et malevolentia*, i.e. 'the King's displeasure', or by arbitrary actions classed as *vis et voluntas*, i.e. 'the King's enforceable will', Henri II and his sons would regularly extract gifts and concessions from their tenants-in-chief on pain of fines, distraint, or arrest. They were preparing the ground for the showdown between King and barons which in 1215 would give rise to the Magna Carta.

As dynasts, Henri Plantagenêt and Aliénor d'Aquitaine knew their duty. Despite the Queen being in her thirties at marriage, they produced five sons and three daughters in sixteen years of cohabitation. Aliénor returned alone to Aquitaine in 1168, where she re-established her troubadour court. She was to spend fifteen years, 1174–89, under close arrest, after openly supporting the rebellion of her sons. But she would live on to the age of eighty-four, when she died in peace at Fontevrault. Henri, meantime, fathered a dozen bastards, including four by Alice de France, daughter of Louis VII and, at the time, fiancée of his son Richard. His most famous love, however, was Rosamund Clifford, Abbess of Godstow Priory near Oxford, renowned in the ballads.

> Yea Rosamonde, fair Rosamonde,
> Her name was called so,
> To whom our queene, dame Ellinor
> Was known a deadly foe . . .[30]

No wonder that Aliénor signed herself 'by the wrath of God, Queen of England'.

Henri II's tussle with Becket was fuelled by their rivalry over control of the Church in England. But it was a local emanation of a much wider and much longer conflict. The secular and the ecclesiastical authorities in Latin Christendom had been at odds ever since the start of the so-called Investiture Contest a hundred years earlier. In 1159, and again in 1165, the Papacy was rent by schism and by the quarrels of popes and anti-popes and their various sponsors. Henri's frustration with Becket was compounded by the serious complications engendered in his relations with both France and the Empire. He was by no means the only medieval king to have ordered the killing of a prelate. Once he had performed the necessary acts of public penance at Becket's shrine, his position was not significantly weakened.

Henri Plantagenêt's domestic turmoil was reflected in his wars. He never managed to tame either the ambition of his sons or the anger of the Capetians. In 1169, the three eldest surviving sons – Henri le Jeune, Richard Cœur de Lion, and Geoffroi – paid homage to Louis VII and were then invested respectively with Normandy and Anjou, Aquitaine, and Brittany. In 1170 and again in 1172, the eldest son, Henri, was twice crowned King of England, at Westminster and Winchester, in his father's lifetime. But his intrigues with Louis VII, with his brothers, with his mother Aliénor and with the King of Scotland, Guillaume le Lion, led to a grand coalition which in 1173 promised to overwhelm the empire. In the event it was crushed by the Old King's military brilliance. For six or seven years, the Plantagenet Empire at its zenith held steady. But the accession of Phillipe-Auguste to the French throne in 1180, the death of England's 'Young King' in 1183, the death of Geoffroi in 1186, and the calling of the Third Crusade in 1187 spelt an end to peace. After three decades of ceaseless struggle, Henri Plantagenêt's plans were in total tatters. He spent his last years fighting desultory campaigns either with Richard against Philippe-Auguste or against Richard and Philippe-Auguste together. At the end, having been driven from his native Anjou, he was forced by the humiliating Treaty of Azay-le-Rideau to accept Richard as his sole heir, to let him marry Alice, and to pay a huge indemnity of 20,000 marks. Two days later he was dead. Richard was free to leave on crusade. The youngest son, Jean, whom to Richard's annoyance he had favoured, had been granted the lordship of Ireland. The Plantagenets were not noted for their generosity. One can well understand the image on the wall of the Painted Chamber at Winchester, where four eaglets are shown pecking out the eyes of the dying Eagle.

The extent to which the lives of these Plantagenets were tied to France is well illustrated by their deaths. The 'Young King' died at Château Martel in Turenne, and was buried first in the cathedral at Le Mans, later alongside the Conqueror at Rouen. Like his brother Richard, he was married to a daughter of Louis VII. Geoffroi, the fourth son, who had established his position in Brittany by marrying the Duke's daughter, was killed in an accident during a tournament in Paris, and was buried in Notre-Dame. Henri (the Old King), having died at Chinon, was buried at Fontevrault, where Aliénor would later join him. Richard, the third son, was to die at Chalus in the Limousin. He, too, would be buried at Fontevrault, as would Isabelle d'Angoulême, the widow of his younger brother and successor, Jean sans Terre. The idea that these people were English is a later fiction. There is no evidence that any of them could speak a word of the English language. Eight centuries after their deaths, Queen Victoria was to make a formal request that the two kings and two queens of England buried at Fontevrault (which in her day was a state penitentiary) 'be returned'. The Prefect of Maine-et-Loire, to whom the request was referred, declined. According to his peculiar view of history, the Plantagenets were French citizens who had long since returned home.

Of course, whilst conceding the total French character of the monarchy at this time, it is perfectly possible to stress the distinction between the ruling class and the country at large and to argue that many of the most important innovations in Plantagenet England, like Magna Carta, continued in force long after the Plantagenets themselves had disappeared. This is a valid point. England and the Plantagenet monarchy were two different things. On the other hand, it is not difficult to underestimate the huge span of time when the two of them were intimately related. The effect of each upon the other was obviously substantial, even in those spheres where the 'Englishness' of the country eventually predominated over the 'Frenchness' of the monarchy. In this regard, one of many questions which historians have to address is why a French ruling class did *not* completely Frenchify England, whilst a ruling class from England did in large measure Anglicize Ireland.

The conquest of Ireland, which began in 1169, and the subsequent wave of foreign settlement, is generally recognized as a landmark in Irish history. 'No event except the preaching of the gospel by St Patrick', writes one of the standard authorities, 'has so changed the destinies of Ireland.' It is traditionally called 'the English Conquest'. This term is doubly dubious. For one thing, the people who launched it were not English and were not even acting on behalf of England. (Punctilious historians call them 'Cambro-Normans'.) For another, the operation ended in what may at best be rated a half-conquest. This, too, would have its consequences.

In the decades before 1169, the ancient isolation of Ireland was gradually dissolving. One reason for this was trade. The Viking seaways, no longer dominated by predators, were opening up again to commerce. Dublin was closely bound both to Chester and in particular to Bristol. Church affairs, too, were bringing the two islands together. The Irish ecclesiastical reforms of the early twelfth century had reforged the link with Rome. But they had also provoked resistance from people who sought assistance in England. In 1121, for example, the burghers of Dublin had appealed to the Archbishop of Canterbury. In 1152 it was the inauguration of an independent metropolitan of Ireland in Dublin which provoked the Archbishop of Canterbury's protest to the Pope and by extension the Bull of *Laudabiliter*. The first incumbent of the Irish metropolitan see, and the last of Irish descent, Abbot Lorcan ua Tuathail (St Laurence O'Toole, 1128–80) had been taken as a child by the MacMurroughs as a hostage, and was the dastardly Dermot's brother-in-law.

By this time, Dublin had reached pre-eminence above all Irish cities. It still contained a substantial Norse population, and its local 'king' was an Irish Norseman, Askulf MacTurkill, who had relatives in the Orkneys and Hebrides. But the city's status was also recognized by the other Irish kings. After his long struggle with Murtoch MacLochlainn and Dermot MacMurrough in 1166, it was in Christ Church Cathedral, Dublin, that Rory O'Connor, the last Ard Rí, was crowned.

In its origins, the Conquest began with a small private expedition. It resulted from a fruitful partnership of an exiled Irish chief and a dispossessed Norman baron from Wales. The exile was Dermot MacMurrough, sometime tyrant of Leinster. The baron was Richard fitzGilbert de Clare, Earl of Pembroke, commonly known in later accounts as 'Strongbow'. He was a widower recently stripped of his lands by royal decree. MacMurrough had sought out Henri Plantagenêt in Aquitaine, and had asked him to restore his kingdom. All he got was a sheaf of letters-patent calling on all of Henri's liegemen, English, Norman, Welsh, and Scots, to note that 'Dermot, Prince of Leinster, has been received into the bosom of our grace and benevolence' and that any assistance to the said Dermot would not be viewed with disfavour. Thus armed, Dermot made for Bristol, whence he was put in touch with Strongbow's circle at Pembroke. The deal was simple. If the knights of Pembroke would help MacMurrough to recover the Kingdom of Leinster, Strongbow would be given the hand of MacMurrough's daughter in marriage and the reversion of her father's kingdom. If the burghers of Bristol would supply the ships, they would be given control of the city of Dublin.

The 'Pembroke Circle' is worth examining, if only because it generated so many of the famous names of future Irish history. Apart from Strongbow, whose forfeited earldom of Pembroke had been granted to his father in 1138, the central figures were all related to the fair and infamous Nesta, Princess of Deheubarth, sometime mistress of Henri I, wife *primo voto* of Gerald de Windsor, Castellan of Pembroke, *secondo voto* of Étienne, Constable of Cardigan, and 'queen-bee of the Cambro-Norman swarm'. Central to the operation were two of Nesta's many sons, the half-brothers Maurice fitzGerald

(d. 1176) and Robert fitzStephen (d. 1183). The former was the progenitor of the ubiquitous 'Geraldines', Earls of Kildare and Dukes of Leinster and of the related Earls of Desmond; the latter, sometime lord of Cardigan, had been captured by the Welsh and joined the Irish expedition as a means of effecting his release. In addition, there were four of Nesta's grandsons: Raymond fitzGerald le Gros (d. 1182), Strongbow's chief companion; Maurice fitzGerald's second son, Thomas fitzMaurice: Robert de Barry, son of Nesta's daughter Angharad; and Meiler fitzHenry, grandson of Nesta and King Henri I. To cap it all, another of Nesta's grandsons, Gerald de Barry, alias the historian Giraldus Cambrensis, was to visit Ireland in person and was to be the author of the *De Expugnatione Hibernica* (1189), the principal but by no means unbiased account of the Conquest.

The invasion took place in several stages. Dermot sailed for Ireland late in 1167, taking a small force of Norman mercenaries with him. He was soon hollering for help. In May 1169, Robert de Barry landed at Bannow Bay in the far south-east of Ireland accompanied by Robert fitzStephen, Hervey de Montmorency, and Maurice de Prendergast, with mounted knights, men-at-arms, and archers. Joined by Dermot, they stormed the Norse town of Wexford. Next year, in May 1170, the advance guard of Strongbow's own army arrived. Led by Raymond Carew 'le Gros', one of the Fitzgeralds, they occupied the rocky headland of Baginbun near Waterford and fortified it. They weathered an Irish attack by driving a herd of cattle into the advancing warriors:

> At the creek of Baginbun
> Ireland was lost and won.[31]

Then, on 23 August 1170, Strongbow landed at nearby Passage, joined up with le Gros to storm Waterford with great cruelty, and summoned Dermot to fulfil his bargain. As (wrongly) portrayed in a fresco in the Palace of Westminster, Strongbow married Dermot's daughter Aífe on the battlefield. Finally Strongbow and Dermot marched on Dublin. Outflanking the Irish defence lines by climbing the Wicklow Hills, they appeared before the city walls and called on the Norse garrison to surrender. On 21 September 1170 Raymond le Gros and others broke into the city. Askulf fled to his ships. The Normans held Dublin. Furious counterattacks by Norse and Irish failed. In 1171 Dermot died. Strongbow was proclaimed King of Leinster.

Nearly thirty years passed before Strongbow's conquests were directly linked to the Kingdom of England. In the first twist to the story, Henri Plantagenêt took fright at Strongbow's success. In fact, he had tried to send orders to stop Strongbow from sailing. He could hardly allow Strongbow to carve out a private kingdom across the sea, whence he might be tempted to return and re-conquer his forfeited lands in Wales. So Henri sailed to Ireland in person. He landed at Waterford with a huge army in October 1171 and spent six months in Ireland. Strongbow went to meet him. No fighting was necessary. All the lesser Irish kings and all the bishops submitted voluntarily. Strongbow was granted Leinster in fief. Dublin and its hinterland was reserved as royal demesne. The King's viceroy, Guillaume fitzAudelin (d. 1198), was left behind to administer it. One of fitzAudelin's knights, Hugh de Lucy, was granted the Kingdom of Meath. He married Rory O'Connor's daughter. Another of them, Jean de Courcy, set off without permission to capture the Kingdom of Ulster. In 1175, by the Treaty of Windsor, Henri agreed to recognize Rory O'Connor's high-kingship over all the non-occupied lands, and to receive in return a tenth of all the island's cattle as tribute. The treaty proved a dead letter. O'Connor was not capable of keeping his side of the bargain.

One of the few surviving eye-witness accounts of this initial phase of the Conquest was written by King Dermot's official interpreter, Maurice Regan. It took the form of an epic poem of 3,459 lines, covering the years 1169 to 1175 in rhyming French couplets. It is called *Le Chansun de Dermot e li quens Richard Fitz-Gilbert*. Regan is not objective. His admiration for French chivalry is unbounded. His contempt for King Dermot's 'traitorous' opponents is unwavering. The style is rambling. But the details are vivid:

A la Banue ariverent
Od tant de gent cum erent;
Quant il furent arivez
E erent tuz issuz de nefs,
Lur gent firent herberger
Sur la rive de la mer.[32]

(They arrived at Bannow;
They came with so many men-at-arms
When they had landed,
And all had left the ships,
They ordered their men to set up camp
On the shore of the sea.)

Interestingly, though all the knights were French-speakers and most of them from Wales, Regan calls them 'les Engleis'. And it's clear that in the fighting with the Irish, heads were still collected in the old Celtic fashion – *unze vint testes le jour!* ('On that day, 220 heads!').[33] And the battle-cry of the invaders was 'Saint David':

Le fiz Henri, le ber Meiller,
En haut se prit a hucher
Devant ala escriant:
'Passez, chevalers! Que alez targant'?
En l'ewe ço mist icil errent;
Ultre l'aport le cheval blanc.
Quant passé esteit le chevaler,
'Sein Davi' escriad haut e cler,
Kar il esteit [sun] seignur
Suz dampnedeu le creatur,
E li chevaler par grant duçor
Sein Davi reclama nuit e jur.[34]

(Henry's son, Baron Meiller,
started to shout aloud,
Going in front crying

'Knights, pass along! Why so slow?'
Then he plunged into the water,
And his white horse carried him across
When the knight had crossed [the river]
He cried 'Saint David' loud and clear
For [David] was his lord
Under Almighty God, the Creator;
And the knight with great sweetness
Would appeal to the saint both night and day.)

Meiler fitzHenry (1155–83) was the natural son of Henri II.

In the next twist of the tale, the King decided to award 'the lordship of Ireland' to his youngest and landless son, Jean. The decision was implemented by the Council of Oxford in May 1177, when the fiefs of the leading barons in Ireland were also confirmed. The plan, which was part of the King's vain attempts to effect an equitable division of his realms among his fractious sons, envisaged Ireland as a separate kingdom. Owing to papal opposition, however, this could not be put into effect, even though Henri had already ordered an Irish crown from Rome. As it was, Prince Jean briefly visited Dublin in 1185, and made a thoroughly bad impression both on the Irish kings and the Norman barons. He was left ruling Ireland through his personal household. And so it would have remained, quite distinct from the government of England, if any of Jean's older brothers had lived or had produced surviving male issue.

So the last twist occurred on 27 May 1199 when, against all earlier expectations, Prince Jean succeeded to the English throne. On the day he was crowned at Westminster, the lordship of Ireland was fused with the Kingdom of England. The fusion stayed unaltered until Henry VIII revived Henri II's plan, and formally declared Ireland to be a kingdom in 1541.

Seen in the wider perspective, the invasion of Ireland formed part of the expansion of France Outremer in ways that had already reached England, Wales, and Scotland at various junctures during the previous hundred years. England had received it with the Norman Conquest: Wales with the establishment of the March: Scotland with the 'Davidian Revolution'.

Scotland in the reigns of Malcolm IV (r. 1153–65) and of Guillaume le Lion (r. 1165–1214) consolidated the influx of English influence and of Anglo-Norman culture that had occurred earlier. Norman settlement took permanent root, spreading into new districts like Moray. Sixteen royal burghs began to flourish. The network of church parishes spread nationwide, as did the secular system of sheriffdoms. The religious orders grew from fragile newcomers into rich and powerful fixtures. Melrose Abbey, refounded by David I as the first Cistercian house in Scotland, gradually rose to its full splendour. Sweetheart Abbey in Galloway dates from the same period. So, too, did the Augustinian Canonry at Holyrood Abbey in Edinburgh, whose western front was 'one of the grandest things of its kind'.

Malcolm IV 'the Maiden', grandson of David I, is sometimes cited as the first beneficiary of primogeniture in the Scottish monarchy. Crowned at Scone, he died young – but not before paying homage to Henri Plantagenêt and relinquishing Scotland's hold on Cumbria. This last act had been waiting to happen for years. David I's campaign into northern England had ended disastrously at the Battle of the Standard (1138). But for the chaos of Stephen's reign, Cumbria, undefended by the Scots, would probably have been taken back much earlier. Henceforth, the English–Scottish border would be permanently fixed on the Solway and the Tweed.

Guillaume le Lion, the 'most Anglo-Norman of the MacMalcolm kings', 'gloried in the aura of French knightly culture'.[35] His reign in Scotland ran parallel to the reigns in England of Henri II, Richard I, and Jean; and no King of Scots was more thoroughly dovetailed into the English interest. The brother of Malcolm IV, he was the second son of David I's second son, Henry, Earl of Huntingdon and Northumberland. He married Ermengarde de Beaumont-le-Maine, a granddaughter of Henri Beauclerc at Woodstock. Henri Plantagenêt had every reason to regard him as his vassal many times over. Indeed, after his coronation at Scone, Guillaume tarried long at the English court. In the family wars between the Plantagenêt and his sons, Guillaume took the part of the 'Young Kings'. In 1168, he signed the first formal treaty between Scotland and France, the starting-point of 'the Auld Alliance'. So when he was captured at Alnwick by Leinstermen in Plantagenet service, he could expect a rough ride. He was paraded through the streets of Northampton in his English earldom, with his feet tied beneath his horse, then taken in captivity to Falaise in Normandy. There, in December 1174, he was forced to accept the treaty which, by English reckoning, placed Scotland permanently under English suzerainty. The King of Scots, together with all his nobles, both clerical and lay, paid homage both to Henri Plantagenêt senior and to Henri Plantagenêt junior.

The implications of the Treaty of Falaise have exercised historians as much as they exercised contemporaries. The Treaty was the culmination of a century-long creeping process which had started at Abernethy in 1072, when Malcolm III had 'promised to be the Conqueror's man' but which now saw a King of Scots paying homage 'for Scotland and all his other lands'. (The Scots would still be reminded of it in the English pamphlets which preceded the Act of Union of 1707!) No objective analyst, however, could sustain the more extreme English claims. For one thing, as an act of feudal homage, the Treaty of Falaise did not rate as a permanent constitutional union between the two countries. It was a lifelong, personal arrangement between one ruler and another. For another, it was not renewed by Henri Plantagenêt's successors. In 1189 Richard I chose to commute his expected dues for a quit-claim of 10,000 marks; and in 1200, Guillaume was able to qualify his homage to Jean with a far-reaching clause 'saving only his own rights'. One cannot deny that the Kings of England exercised a certain shifting suzerainty over the Scottish monarchs in this period. But it was similar in nature and scope to the suzerainty which the Kings of France wielded over the Kings of England. The real significance of the Treaty of Falaise, therefore, was the fact that Guillaume le Lion was being woven into an international web of feudal dependencies centred not in England but in France.

Similar developments were afoot in Wallia Pura, which remained quite distinct from the Welsh March. The Welsh Princes could hold their own without serious difficulty against the Cambro-Norman colonists, but they lacked the resources and the common purpose to oppose the English crown directly. For his part, Henri Plantagenêt had too many distractions elsewhere to consider a sustained campaign of conquest. The modus vivendi, therefore, took the form of shifting feudal arrangements which the King used to minimize the waywardness of the Welsh princes and which the princes accepted in order to maintain a large measure of freedom. When Henri made his first incursion into Wales in 1157 he was assisted by the Prince of Powys; and the episode ended with all the main princes proffering oaths of allegiance. In 1165, in contrast, when Henri's advancing army came to grief in the Berwyn Mountains, the two leading princes of the time, Owain Gwynedd of Gwynedd and Rhys ap Grufydd of Deheubarth, both took full advantage. Owain Gwynedd destroyed the royal castle at Rhuddlan, and in 1168 took a leaf out of the Scots' book by making soundings in Paris about an alliance with France. Rhys ap Grufydd, who took Robert fitzStephen prisoner, made such inroads into the Cambro-Norman colony of the south-west that his ascendancy gave distinct encouragement to the Conquest of Ireland. Henri's third visit, in 1177, was attended by great feudal pomp and ceremony. On that occasion, Rhys ap Grufydd was elevated to the office of royal Justiciar in South Wales, whilst Owain's son, Dafydd of Gwynedd, was given the King's half-sister Emma in marriage. The Welsh princes, like the Scots barons, were being systematically locked in to the feudal network.

An interesting compromise was also reached by Welsh and Normans in ecclesiastical affairs. The entry into Wales of the Cistercian Order, which began with the foundation of Whitland in Pembrokeshire in 1140, could easily be seen as a marked advance of

Norman influence. In practice, since the Cistercians were a supra-national order based in Burgundy, they were not natural Plantagenet agents, whilst their affinity for remote mountain areas and particularly for sheep-farming brought them close to the spirit and interests of the native Welsh. Between Strata Florida (1164) and Valle Crucis (1202), every single Welsh prince of standing founded a Cistercian abbey on his territory. And it was in these houses that the campaign for studying, copying, and preserving ancient Welsh literature was largely undertaken. The one campaign which did not succeed was that so doughtily championed by Giraldus Cambrensis, namely to elevate the bishopric of St David's to the rank of a metropolitan see equal to Canterbury.

No Welsh prince of the age, however, matched the stature of Llewellyn ap Iorwerth, Prince of Gwynedd from 1194 to 1240. 'Llewellyn the Great' made common cause with the Plantagenets, swearing allegiance to Jean sans Terre, and marrying the King's illegitimate daughter. He then used his position to infeudate most of the lesser Welsh princes to himself and to build up a centralized Welsh government on the English model. When the English barons rebelled, he joined them, and like Owain Gwynedd before him explored the possibility of a French alliance. In May 1215, on the eve of Magna Carta, he would be holding Shrewsbury. This would enable him to insist on the most crucial of the Charter's Welsh Clauses (No. 56) – that English law should hold in England, Marcher law in the March, and Welsh law in Wallia Pura.

Laws and customs, no less than language, were motors of medieval identity; and it was the fierce Welsh attachment to their law as well as to their language which helped them hold English power at bay. Giraldus Cambrensis, once described as 'the first non-Welsh speaking Welshman', also noted the strong Welsh proclivity for breaking the law which they so much valued. For a man who felt himself a Norman among Welshmen and a Welshman among Normans, this was a sign of Wales's doom. His patriotism was at best ambiguous. Yet it was Giraldus who recorded those most patriotic of words when an old man of Pencader addressed Henri

Plantagenêt in person. 'This Welsh people will never be destroyed except by the anger of God alone,' the old man declared. 'For on the Day of Judgement, no people or nation other than that of Wales will answer before the Supreme Judge for this little corner of the world.'[36] It would seem that the King concurred. 'The Welsh', he wrote in a letter to the Byzantine Emperor, 'are a people, who cannot be tamed.'[37]

Comments such as this indicate a marked shift of attitudes that had occurred since the Norman Conquest. In pre-Conquest times, Anglo-Saxons tended to view themselves in distinction to a pagan 'other'. Paganism had been the test whether a foreigner belonged to 'us' or to 'them'. Yet after the Conquest, since everyone in the Isles was by now a Christian, the English adopted a new secular test of otherness. English commentators began to denounce all non-English as 'barbarians' as if the English alone were civilized. Their growing xenophobia was not linguistic in origin. All the nations of the Isles were living in a multilingual environment. The source of the sentiments lay partly in contempt for divergent legal systems, partly in disdain for the pastoral economies of the north and west, and partly in the apparent horror at lax sexual mores. Given the gross sexual licence of both Norman and Angevin Kings of England, it seems hard to understand why the English chroniclers could take offence at Irish kings who kept concubines or Welsh families which thrived in polygamy. But xenophobia is not rational. The anonymous 'R' of the 'Conquest of Lisbon', for instance, who was a highly charitable man, had a distinct propensity for foreign stereotypes. *Quis enim Scottos barbaros esse neget?* he asked once, provoking marginal comments from Scottish students to this day. 'Who [on earth] would deny that the Scots are barbarians?' Henry of Huntingdon was no better. Scottish barbarianism is innate; English barbarianism is just punishment. The historian who has most closely analysed such attitudes has called them 'the beginnings of English imperialism'.[38]

≈

On Henri II's death, the Plantagenet Empire passed to his third and eldest surviving son, Richard, Duke of Aquitaine. Richard was promptly invested as Duke of Normandy and crowned as King of England at Westminster. Since Richard was intent on joining the Third Crusade, however, the lands in Aquitaine were put in the charge of his mother, Aliénor, newly released from arrest; Ireland was left under the sole control of Jean Sans Terre; England was entrusted to two royal Justiciars, whose authority 'Prince Jean' was eager to challenge. Contrary to earlier prospects, the youngest son was now moving on to the highest rungs of the dynastic ladder. In the meantime, Richard sailed off to the Holy Land where his bravery and brutalities earned him the sobriquet of 'Cœur de Lion' (Lionheart). He looked on his duchies and his kingdom as a credit bank for his expeditions. Having been captured by the Duke of Austria on his return journey from Palestine, he was subjected to the vast ransom of 150,000 silver marks. So his subjects had to pay. Officeholders had to pay to keep their offices. All knights were charged 20 shillings. The entire wool-crop of the Cistercians was requisitioned. In London, a special *Scaccarium Redemptionis* or 'Ransom Chest' was set up in St Paul's Cathedral. But then, when Richard was freed, he spent his entire time waging war against his erstwhile royal crusading partner, Philippe-Auguste. He was killed by a chance arrow at the siege of Chalus in April 1199. Before he died, he ordered the offending archer to be spared – but his companions skinned the wretched captive alive. He had been King of England for ten years, but had spent less than six months in his kingdom.

Absentee monarchs are not generally well regarded. But the absence of a wastrel monarch can be a blessing in disguise. Despite conflicts between the Justiciars in the early 1190s, the administration of England established by Henri Plantagenêt withstood the test. The attempted rebellion of Prince Jean, who had briefly assumed the illegal title of *Summus Rector totius regni*, was frustrated. And reforms introduced by the new Chief Justiciar, Hubert Walter, including the appointments of justices of the peace, helped to hold the leaderless kingdom together.

The career in Church and state of Hubert Walter (d. 1205), Archbishop of Canterbury from 1193, well illustrates where the strands of strength and continuity lay. A Baron of the Exchequer and the right-hand man of Ranulf de Glanville, Henri II's Justiciar, he had served under Richard as Chaplain-General to the Third Crusade. He was loved by the ordinary crusaders for his care and compassion. Yet he was no weakling. As Archbishop, he did not hesitate to order the firing of the church of St Mary-le-Bow in London in order to flush out a rebel. He was King Richard's natural choice as England's virtual viceroy. (His elder brother, Theobald Walter, known as 'Le Botiller', who had accompanied Prince Jean to Ireland, was the ancestor of the Irish Butlers, Earls of Ormonde.) He crowned 'Le Roi Jean', after delivering a speech on the electoral basis of English kingship. When the Archbishop died, the monarch declared, 'Only now am I truly King of England.'

King Jean's reputation as Satan incarnate may well be as undeserved as Richard's reputation as a fine and famous king. He was devious, suspicious, and arbitrary; but one can argue that his oppressions were no greater than those of his predecessors. He was libelled in a systematic way by ecclesiastical chroniclers, starting in his own lifetime with Roger of Wendover.[39] It is also probable that he was on the receiving end of animosities that had been accumulating throughout the Angevin period. Yet one thing cannot be contested. Jean had a genius for making enemies. He angered his liege-lord, the King of France; he offended the Church beyond forgiveness. And he drove his tenants-in-chief to the archetypal baronial revolt of English history.

English historians have obviously paid the greatest attention to the baronial revolt and to the resultant Magna Carta, which was signed 'in the meadow called Ranimed between Windlesora and Stanes' on 15 June in the seventeenth year of the reign. For people looking back in later ages for the roots of English liberties, Magna Carta provided a document of prime interest. Its sixty-three articles covered every conceivable aspect of feudal dues and rights down to those of widows, hostages, and dispossessed Welshmen. Some of them, such as the ban on trials without witnesses (No. 38) or the condemnation of the arrest of freemen 'save by the judgement of their peers', were to be fundamental to the subsequent growth of the rule of law. Indeed, the basic idea underlying the charter, that good government depends on agreed rules of conduct observed by all, is the cornerstone of constitutionalism.

At the same time, it would be idle to suppose that Plantagenet England had any serious capacity for constitutional government. It is perfectly possible to argue that for the general framework within which the Isles were to develop, the Great Charter was less important than some of the other crises of the reign.

Jean's succession itself had been problematical. Four years of strife were spent in settling it. In 1199, Jean had seized the Plantagenet treasure at Chinon; but Aquitaine wished to remain under the elderly Aliénor, while the lords of Brittany, Anjou, Maine, and Touraine, supported by the King of France, opted for Jean's twelve-year-old nephew, Arthur de Bretagne. For a brief period, the prospect loomed that England and Normandy alone would stay together as in the Conqueror's time. The other Plantagenet lands, for which young Arthur had paid formal homage to Philippe-Auguste, would effectively pass under French control. Jean restored his fortunes by a lightning raid on the castle of Mirabeau in Poitou where he took two hundred knights and most of his political opponents captive, including Arthur. Jean allegedly murdered Arthur in a drunken rage at Rouen, and threw his body into the Seine.

Jean's conflict with the Church started with a disputed election to the late Archbishop Walter's see at Canterbury. When the Pope imposed Cardinal Stephen Langton, and personally invested him in Rome without the King's knowledge, the King forcibly expelled the clergy of Canterbury and seized their property. In consequence, England in 1208 was placed under interdict. In theory, all places of worship were closed, all the sacraments suspended, and all people who died were denied salvation. In 1209, Jean was excommunicated; and in 1212, the King of France was commissioned to implement the bull of excommunication. Jean did not submit until 1213, when a

French invasion fleet gathered at Damme, near Bruges, then Arch-bishop Langton was welcomed to England; and all expelled clergy were promised restitution. Most surprisingly, the Kingdom of Eng-land and the Lordship of Ireland were formally turned into papal fiefs, with an annual tribute of 700 and 300 marks respectively. This episode demonstrated Jean's vacillatory nature. It also demonstrated the more important fact that the Kingdom of England was not a modern sovereign nation state, but an integral part of that great inchoate feudal commonwealth of Latin Christendom, of which, in theory at least, the Pope was head.

In the long run, however, the 'Loss of Normandy' was arguably the most momentous event of the early Plantagenet age. It did not sever England's connections with France, as some English commen tators have suggested. But it severed England's direct connection with the French province which was both contiguous to England and which for a hundred and fifty years had been the ancestral home of a large section of England's ruling class. At a stroke, its loss broke the central link in the cross-Channel Plantagenet empire; and it represented a crucial step in the consolidation of the Kingdom of France. Anglo-French relations would never be the same again.

The casual way in which the Plantagenet possessions in northern France and Normandy seemed to be abandoned between 1204 and 1214 was one of many factors which maximized the mistrust between Jean and his subjects. Intermittent warfare on the frontier between the Plantagenets and the Capetians had been in progress for genera-tions. Castles were won and lost. Small districts like the Vexin changed hands several times. But neither side seemed capable of forcing a clear resolution. So when Philippe-Auguste was allowed to overrun the whole of Normandy in 1204 without serious resistance, the English and Norman barons were seriously dismayed. And when France's Court of Peers declared Jean as a recalcitrant Duke of Normandy to have forfeited all his French lands, they must have realized that the prospects were uncommonly grave. Jean's response, apparently, was to say that he could win it all back in a single day as he had recovered from the previous threat posed by Arthur of

Brittany. This time, no swift recovery was possible. Instead, John sought to claw back his position by patiently building a coalition between all of Philippe-Auguste's discontented neighbours, feudaries, and enemies. By 1214 the Coalition was in place, and it was a powerful combination, containing among others the Emperor Otto IV, the Count of Flanders, the Count of Boulogne, and the Count of Toulouse. Jean's plan was to draw off the French forces to the south-west by leading an offensive out of his Queen's home territory of Angoulême, thereby facilitating a decisive attack on Paris from the north by his Imperial allies. Philippe-Auguste saw the danger. He tied Jean up in a siege and advanced to meet the Imperialists. The giant clash of arms involving almost a hundred thousand men took place on 27 July 1214 on the plain of Bouvines near Lille. After a day of fickle fortunes, when the French king was unhorsed, the Emperor forced to flee, and the men of Reginald, Comte de Boulogne covered themselves in desperate glory, the French won the field. The Earl of Salisbury, commander of the English contingent, was captured by the battling Bishop of Beauvais. The Imperial army withdrew. All hope for the recovery of the Plantagenet lands was lost. English textbooks tend to treat Bouvines as an obscure Continental skirmish. French textbooks call it *notre première victoire nationale*, 'our first national victory'.

Nor are English readers well served by the continuing habit of English historians to stick with that most misleading of labels, 'the Loss of Normandy'. The effects of the Battle of Bouvines were far more serious than the label implies. For the Plantagenets did not lose Normandy alone. They also lost their own home-base in the provinces of Anjou, Maine, and Touraine. What was more, thanks to Jean's murder of the young Duke Arthur, they had lost their promising stake in Brittany as well. On the eve of Bouvines, Duke Arthur's sister Alix was married to Pierre, Comte de Dreux; and it was from that match that an independent dynasty would develop in Brittany until the end of the fifteenth century. Taken together, the provinces of Normandy, Anjou, Maine, Touraine, and Brittany constituted a swath of well-populated territory that was almost

three-quarters the size of England itself. Their loss was no mere
setback. It was a catastrophe of unparalleled proportions. French
gains after the Battle of Bouvines were of the same order of
magnitude as Norman gains after the Battle of Hastings.

Historians can separate out the various strands which contributed to the complex crisis of Jean's final years. But the most
interesting aspect is to see how the different strands affected each
other. Archbishop Langton, whose appointment by Pope Innocent
III had provoked the Interdict, was a leading organizer of the
baronial revolt. Jean's surprising submission to the Pope in 1213 was
an essential precondition to the completion of the anti-French
Coalition. The defeat at Bouvines goes a long way to explain Jean's
conciliatory stance at Runnymede.

It is not always realized how far Jean went in winning back lost
ground in England. The Pope, Jean's feudal superior, excommunicated all the barons who had forced him to sign the Great Charter.
Magna Carta, according to the highest law of the day, was invalidated. When the King was struck down by a sudden fever in
October 1216, he was conducting a merciless campaign of retribution
against the length and breadth of England. He was buried before
the altar at Worcester Cathedral, the first English king since Harold
Godwinson to be born and to die in England.

For much of the thirteenth century, the configuration of power in
the Isles remained little different from the position that had evolved
by King Jean's death. The loss of northern France markedly
increased the relative importance of England within the Plantagenet
Empire, whilst the resultant separation of the Isles from distant
Aquitaine inhibited all thoughts of consolidation. The empire had
been effectively split into two. England's beachhead in Ireland was
greatly strengthened, whilst her reassertion of hegemony over Wales
and Scotland would eventually lead to open conflict. For several
decades, however, a weakened English monarchy struggled to stand
its ground against the centrifugal might of the barons, against a

Church at the height of its prestige, and against the influence of new social classes.

Between the death of Jean in 1216, and the accession of his great-grandson ninety-one years later, only two men sat at the heart of Plantagenet affairs – Henri III (r. 1216–72) and Edouard I (r. 1272–1307). Henri III, one of the few Englishmen to feature in Dante's *Divina Commedia*, was consigned, perhaps unjustly, to the 'Ring of the Indolent'. Edouard I was a man of action.

As always, relations with the Kingdom of France were crucial. These can hardly be classed as 'foreign relations'. The Plantagenets, still French-speaking and still both vassals and close relatives of the French kings, were not foreigners in Paris. And England with its dependencies was still an integral part of the French-run feudal network. The French victory at Bouvines had not given rise to a formal peace treaty but only to a temporary, but many times extended, truce. The Plantagenets and the Capetians, therefore, remained technically at war. Desultory fighting flared along a border which was steadily pushed southwards as the French overran Poitou. Peace came at the Treaty of Paris in 1259. Only then did the King of England finally agree to rejoin France's House of Peers, to do homage for Aquitaine (Bordeaux, Bayonne, and Gascony) and for his many interests in the dioceses of Limoges, Perigueux, and Cahors, and to resign for ever the family claims to Normandy, Anjou, Maine, Touraine, and Poitou. This treaty laid the foundation for the long period of cross-Channel stability which gave the Plantagenets the chance to extend their hegemony in the Isles. England's relations with Ireland, Wales, and Scotland remained, in large measure, a function of her relations with France.

Having lost out to the Capetians in northern France, the Plantagenets broadened their international involvement. Henri III's younger brother, Richard, Earl of Cornwall, pursued a glittering career which in 1257 saw him elected King of the Romans and prospective German Emperor. One of their sisters, Isabelle, had earlier married Frederick II, the *stupor mundi*, and had been crowned Empress. Another sister, Joan, had been wedded to Alexander II, to seal the hold on Scotland, whilst the youngest, Eleanor, married the Norman adventurer, Simon de Montfort, whose turbulent career in England all but unhinged the dynasty (see page 361, below). Henri's widowed mother, Isabelle d'Angoulême, took the daring step of marrying Hugues de Lusignan, whose complaint to the French court against her earlier marriage to King Jean had been the catalyst of the loss of the Plantagenet family lands. After much delay, Henri III himself married Eleanor de Provence, a daughter of the ubiquitous Bérenger clan. One of the English queen's sisters was Marguérite de Provence, Queen of France: another, Béatrice de Provence, was Duchesse d'Anjou: and a third, Sanchia de Provence, became Richard of Cornwall's second wife. Of Henri III's sons, Edmund was crowned King of Sicily, whilst Edouard married a daughter of the King of Castile. The tentacles of the family stretched from the Orkneys to the Mediterranean (see Appendix 20).

The Plantagenets ruled in an age when the authority of the Roman Church was still accepted as supreme in international affairs. The Vatican stood at the height of its influence in the decades between the Lateran Decrees (1215), where Pope Innocent III (r. 1198–1216) re-invigorated ecclesiastical life, and the Jubilee Year of 1300, when thousands of pilgrims walked to Rome. Henri Plantagenêt had stored up great trouble by misunderstanding Becket and his backers; whilst Jean had demonstrated that the papacy could be both a formidable foe and an effective ally. In the thirteenth century, the international influence of the Church was strengthened by the founding of the Friars – the mendicant orders who were independent of the episcopal hierarchy – and by the spread of the universities whose clerical graduates formed an international fraternity of educated scholars. In England, Oxford, which claimed origins in the previous century as an offshoot of Paris, and Cambridge, which was launched in 1229, established themselves as centres of academic excellence long unchallenged in the Isles. The famous Dominican Roger Bacon (1214–94), who is often considered an early pioneer of scientific thought, is just the best-known scholarly name among many. Ecclesiastical courts jealously defended their particular sphere of competence within the systems of justice, and learned clerics wielded very special influence within the royal bureaucracy and in a largely illiterate society. Canon law provided an international framework for all discussions on jurisprudence. The lords spiritual, bishops and abbots, maintained a status on a par with that of their greatest temporal counterparts. Prelates, such as Robert Grosseteste (d. 1253), Bishop of Lincoln, were among the greatest figures in the land. Scholar, author, philosopher, sometime rector of the Franciscans at Oxford, Grosseteste did not shrink from excommunicating recalcitrant opponents nor from fighting his corner against the demands of both Pope and King. He won Bacon's accolade '*Solus unnus scivit scientias ut Lincolniensis episcopus*'.

The thirteenth century could also be described as the heyday of the feudal barons. The forceful monarchy of the Normans and early Plantagenets was faltering, whilst municipal and representative institutions were in their infancy. To some extent, the rise of the great barons could be seen as a centrifugal development. Already in Jean's reign, 'the Northerners' were showing signs, like the 'Welsh Marchers', of being a law unto themselves. And the mid-century Barons' War was an episode of maximum disruption. Yet circumstances contrived to forge an English baronial community that had not previously existed. After the loss of northern France, the Plantagenets required their English tenants-in-chief to abandon their former lands and allegiances on the Continent, wherever such holdings might cause a conflict of loyalties. Many of the great Norman and Angevin families were forced to choose. Though the Plantagenets themselves continued to do homage to the French king, they made it difficult for their barons to do the same. As a result, the English baronage steadily assumed a separate identity, and came to resent the Continental interlopers whom the Plantagenets from time to time preferred. (It is a wonderful irony that the most successful of those interlopers, Simon de Montfort Jnr, was to be seen as the champion of Englishmen against the King's foreign counsellors.) It is also important that some of the most prominent barons, like the sometime Regent, Guillaume le Maréchal (d. 1231), or Hubert de

Burgh (d. 1243), the Justiciar, married into the ruling house, thereby adding some local leaven into the Plantagenets' predominantly Continental connections.

None of the barons, however, matched the extraordinary cosmopolitan figure of Richard of Cornwall (1207–72). Apart from his earldom, Richard held lands, honours, and castles all over England, from Knaresborough to Tintagel, making him the largest landowner after the King. He was also one of the greatest bankers of the age, closely involved with English Jewry, lending money to monarchs, courts, and legates. He financed the great recoinage of 1247–8 from capital which he recouped many times over. In the 1230s he dallied with the baronial opposition. He and Simon de Montfort were joint godfathers of the Lord Edward. But then in 1240–2 he went off to the Holy Land on crusade; and from 1257 to his death he was preoccupied by his attempts to rule Germany. His son and heir, Henri d'Almayne, was murdered at Viterbo by the sons of Simon de Montfort. He died at his castle of Berkhamstead, and was buried with his second wife at their foundation at Hayles in Gloucestershire.[40]

Social changes were of no little importance. The mass of the population remained serfs or villeins, and as such played no part in political life. Some leading historians hardly mention them, especially as the 'submerged English' had no role to play as yet in England's cultural history. Yet the bonds of servile tenure were loosening, and were preparing the ground for dramatic developments after the Black Death (see below). What is more, important shifts were afoot both in town and countryside in the middle reaches of society. The knights, the sub-tenants of the barons, were gaining a margin of manoeuvre, whilst the growth of towns and trade strengthened the urban elements of merchants, lawyers, and town politicians. It can be no accident that in the two great political crises of the century, when 'Parliaments' first arose in England, one sees the debut both of knights of the shire and of municipal burgesses.

Simon V de Montfort (1208–65) was an unlikely champion of English liberties. His home, like that of generations of his forefathers bearing the same name, was at Montfort l'Amaury in Touraine not far from Chartres. His father, Simon IV, had chosen the Capetian as opposed to the Plantagenet allegiance, and rose to be commander of France's royal army in the Albigensian Crusade. Simon V, a younger son, had other ideas. He set out as a penniless youth for the Plantagenet court in England, taking with him his grandmother's moribund claim to the defunct earldom of Leicester. In the 1230s, when Henri III was relying heavily on Poitevin, Gascon, and Provençal counsellors to counterbalance the obstreperous English barons, de Montfort appeared to be just another of the detested foreign courtiers. He was inevitably suspected of pro-French and pro-Papal sympathies. Yet astute political manoeuvring between the court and the discontented earls brought him the highest possible rewards – first the coveted earldom of Leicester, and then, in 1238, the hand of the King's widowed sister. In the 1240s, already a man of substance, he was emerging as a natural arbiter in England's running political strife, though his friendship with the King steadily deteriorated. In 1248 he was handed the unenviable task of governing Gascony. When he returned in 1252 to face charges of maladministration, the King's ingratitude pushed him firmly into the dissident, reforming camp. Within a few years, his search for justice would inspire comparisons with Thomas à Becket:

> Thomas martir nuncupatur,
> Sicut Christus, sicut datur
> Symon pro iusticia.[41]

Matthew Paris, a monk of St Albans and the leading chronicler of the period, said that Henri III 'feared the Earl of Leicester more than thunder and lightning'.[42]

The baronial reform movement can be traced back to Magna Carta and beyond. On the one side stood the King and the royal court, hard pressed by the constant demands to defend Aquitaine, by the need for mercenary troops, and by the shortage of ready cash. On the other side stood the English magnates, who refused to let the King use their knights in 'foreign service', who increasingly resented the King's arbitrary exploitation of feudal dues, and who increasingly sought to regulate his insatiable demands for money by various forms of legal and institutional restraint. One of the devices which they came to prefer was the calling of 'Parliaments'. In its origins, the English Parliament, like the French *Parlement*, was a purely judicial assembly designed to facilitate the regular presentation and recording of petitions. Unlike its French counterpart, however, it evolved in the thirteenth century by assuming non-judicial functions and by providing a forum for the incipient stirrings of representative government. Constitutional historians have seen the critical moment of its evolution either in the assembly which was summoned by Simon de Montfort in the middle of the Barons' War, or in the Parliament of Edouard I (1298).

Prior to the general crisis of 1258–65, the reign of Henri III saw several abortive overseas expeditions and numerous baronial revolts. The crisis came to a head at the time when the absent King, having failed in a hopeless scheme to intervene in the Sicilian succession,[43] was trying to negotiate a comprehensive settlement with the King of France: when the absent Lord Edouard had recently plunged into the affairs of Castile: when the King's absent brother, Richard of Cornwall, had just been elected as King of the Romans in Germany, when one of the King's Lusignan relatives, Bishop Aymer of Winchester, was proving particularly obnoxious, and when the magnates had already refused the King a grant in aid. The conduct of the 'foreigners', and the demands of foreign embroilments, seemed to be running out of control. From the point of view of the English barons, it was difficult to say which was the more dangerous – a feckless king or his overambitious relatives. By the Provisions of Oxford (1258), a committee of barons and courtiers agreed a raft of measures to keep the King in his place, among them plans for regular *parlamenz*, for a permanent council, and for the accountability of ministers. Amidst the accelerating conflict, Simon de Montfort was charged with treason, absolved by his peers, and forced into exile. The King obtained papal absolution from his oath supporting the Provisions, whilst the Papal Legate was busy trying to reinstate Aymer de Lusignan.

Early in 1264, three of the English barons appealed to Louis IX to act as arbiter in the dispute. But in his arbitration, the so-called 'Mise d'Amiens', the French king took the part of his royal brother, annulled the Provisions, and rejected the central demand 'that the realm of England be [only] ruled by native-born men'. This was the breaking point. In the first round of the Barons' War, which culminated at the Battle of Lewes (14 May 1264), Simon de Montfort triumphed, capturing both the King and the Lord Edouard. His cause was celebrated in song, in the *Carmen de bello Lewensi*:

> Iam respirat anglia sperans libertatem
> Cui des gracie det prosperitatem . . .[44]
>
> (*Now may England breathe freely in the hope of liberty
> which by God's Grace will bring prosperity*).

Holding the King hostage, de Montfort proceeded to summon a Parliament attended by a hundred and twenty churchmen, twenty-three barons, two knights for every shire, and two burgesses for every borough. In the second round, the royalists had their bitter revenge. The Lord Edouard, having escaped from captivity, led a force which trapped Earl Simon returning from his allies in the Welsh marches. At the Battle of Evesham (4 August 1265) Earl Simon was killed. His corpse was decapitated. His head was carried off as a trophy, with his testicles strung round the ears.

Simon de Montfort was revered by contemporaries and by later constitutionalists alike. He was seen as a person of principle, and in some quarters as a saint:

> Symon, Symon modo dormis!
> Quam mors tua sit enormis
> Clamat vox ad sidera.[45]
>
> (*Simon, Simon, you are but sleeping!
> Our voice exclaims to the stars
> the enormity of your death.*)

His many English admirers have rarely stressed his Frenchness.

Simon de Montfort's career has always given historians food for considerable thought. At one time, it would be invoked by stalwarts of the English School to show that England had always been 'more free' than 'the Continent'. Nowadays, in contrast, it stands at the centre of a debate that is asking just how different England really was. The baronial reformers of de Montfort's day may well have been following French ideas. Concern for the protection of non-nobles, which is found both in Magna Carta and in de Montfort's camp, is mirrored in French and German charters of the same vintage. Matthew Paris shared the opinion of Geraldus Cambrensis that England was less free than France. 'A comparison of good and harmonious government between England under Henry III and France under Louis XI', writes a recent specialist, 'would have all been in favour of France'.[46]

England's baronial brawls gave a long period of respite to the rest of the Isles. Though there was plenty of local turbulence, especially in Ireland, no major English interventions were possible.

Thirteenth-century Ireland experienced two important developments. One of these was the creation of a centralized government for the main area of Norman settlement on the east coast; the other was an unending series of military campaigns and castle-building by the Norman barons in the supposedly native areas. Dublin Castle was built by King Jean. Sheriffs were appointed. Coinage was struck. The jury system was introduced. By 1260, seven English-style counties were in operation at Louth, Waterford, Cork, Tipperary, Limerick, Kerry, and Connaught. By 1297, an Irish Parliament had been summoned from these counties in parallel to the Parliament in England. Meanwhile, step by step, fortress after fortress, the great Norman families spread their tentacles throughout the land. In Ulaidh (Ulster) it was the de Courcys: in Meath the de Lacys. The McCarthy 'Kingdom of Cork' was annexed by the fitzStephens, the

O'Brien's 'Kingdom of Limerick' by de Braose. Most active were the Geraldines, especially Maurice III fitzGerald, Justiciar 1232–45, who used crown forces to extend the family's private estates in Sligo, Mayo, and Galway. The native chieftains were pushed back into the hills and the peripheries. One of them, Brian O'Neill of Tír Eoghain (Tyrone) in the north, was the last ever to claim to be 'King of the Kings of Ireland'. His head was sent back to London to amuse Henri III. Little effective resistance was offered until the battles of Callan (1261) and Áth in Chip (1270). The former kept the Normans out of southern Kerry. The latter stopped them in their tracks in Roscommon. In many places, the Norman lords brought in English colonists. But elsewhere they did not. 'Munster, under Norman influence, became one of the most French of countries outside France.'[47]

In Wales, the problem of fitting Wallia Pura into the overall scheme of government was repeatedly posed. Henri III plundered the lands of Gwynedd so mercilessly that Llewellyn the Great's successor, Prince Dafydd, vainly appealed to the Pope to take him on as a papal vassal. By the Treaty of Woodstock (1247), the King obliged Dafydd's successor, Llewellyn II ap Gruffydd (r. 1246–82), to accept the standard status of an English baron. Matthew Paris wrote 'Wales has been reduced to nothing.'

But then the wind changed. In the late 1250s, the men of Gwynedd swept through Wallia Pura and much of the March, forcing the local chiefs and magnates to recognize their overlordship. By 1264–5 Llewellyn II was strong enough to ally with Simon de Montfort, to marry his daughter, and, through the Pipton Agreement (June 1265) – one of Simon's last acts – to hold the whole Principality of Wales as a fief of the (captive) King. The substance of the agreement was confirmed by the liberated King at the Treaty of Montgomery (1267). Wales was established as a discrete entity within the Plantagenet realms, but not as a province of England. 'Llewellyn II', wrote the leading English historian of the period, 'was the keystone in an arch of kings.' The Welsh population was growing rapidly: towns were sprouting, the educated class expanding. Welsh historians, not necessarily of the romantic persuasion, have talked of a determination 'to resolve upon nationhood' and of 'an embryonic state'.[48]

The status of thirteenth-century Scotland was considerably less problematical. Both Alexander II (r. 1214–49) and Alexander III (r. 1249–86) were married to sisters of the English king, and Scotland, though a separate kingdom, was considered by most interested parties as an extension of the Plantagenet realms. This was confirmed by the restoration of the confiscated earldom of Huntingdon on the day in 1221 when Alexander II became simultaneously Henri III's brother-in-law and vassal. Internal Scottish politics were dominated by the rise of powerful regional magnates, notably of the Stewarts in the West, the Comyns in the North, and the Anglo-Scottish Baliols.

Yet the key event of the century undoubtedly lay in the annexation of the Western Isles.[49] The Stewarts had been snapping at the Lordship of the Isles for decades, but it was only in 1244 that the Scottish crown joined them in a diplomatic and military offensive against Norwegian rule. Alexander II died on the Isle of Kerra with his offensive incomplete. He is portrayed in *Hakon's Saga* as an evil king who died from the sacrilege of attacking St Columba's patrimony. The Scottish advance resumed after the minority of Alexander III. In 1262 the Earl of Ross laid waste to the Isle of Skye. The Battle of Largs (1263), when a Norwegian counterattack was repulsed, stands close in Scots tradition to Stirling Bridge and Bannockburn. And the subsequent death of the King brought the warring parties to the negotiating table. By the Treaty of Perth (1266), Scotland assumed the Lordship of the Isles for the down payment of 4,000 marks plus a smaller annuity. Scotland's western border was now as well defined as its southern one. What is more, the centre of gravity of the kingdom had shifted both geographically and culturally. The Gaelic and the Norse connections were both revived to offset the predominantly Anglo-Norman orientation of preceding reigns. The Gaelic traditions of the Hebrides were added to the pool of national consciousness, and at Alexander III's coronation the King's genealogy going back to the legendary Scota was recited in Gaelic. At his death in 1286, when he fell from his horse at night, it was fully expected that the throne would pass to his sole Scandinavian grandchild, Margaret 'Maid of Norway'. Alexander III had never paid homage to the English king. The Plantagenet connection appeared to be fading fast.

The dilapidation of the Plantagenet hegemony must have been manifest to all close observers several years before the Lord Edouard succeeded his father. Baronial grievances in England had been stifled but not addressed. Ireland, like Aquitaine, had largely been left to its own devices. The Welsh, by the Treaty of Montgomery, and the Scots, by the Treaty of Perth, had both built platforms from which they might escape from strict control. In 1272, the Lord Edouard was absent on crusade. But from the moment he returned home, his task was clear. It was to halt the prevailing drift.

Edouard I (r. 1272–1307), like the Cœur de Lion before him, was a warrior of huge physical strength, a crusader, an *animus magnificus* beloved of the Gascon troubadours. His knights called him 'Longshanks'. But he was also a great churchman, the associate of popes and cardinals, and a monarch unusually dedicated to the details of administration.

Contrary to a once fashionable notion, he was not a visionary modernizer. By the standards of his time, he was conventional, conservative, even conformist, but vigorously adept at exploiting the feudal conventions to his own great advantage. 'He was playing with Feudalism, not against it.'[50] The sobriquets most usually applied to him in England are 'the English Justinian' and 'the Hammer of the Scots'. Neither does him full justice. As legislator he did much more than simply codify existing practices. And it was not just the

Scots whom he hammered. His energy was felt in all parts of the
Isles – so much so that he has been said to initiate a 'British
Century'.

Modern, insular perceptions of this most forceful of the Plantagenets, however, can be misleading. It is very instructive to examine
how he reacted to his accession to the English throne. He had left
on crusade in 1270, making his way to North Africa from Bordeaux,
hoping to join St Louis at Tunis. But he arrived there after St Louis's
death. So he pressed on to the Holy Land, where, among other
things, he distinguished himself by slaughtering the entire population
of Nazareth. In the Holy Land he was once heard speaking a few
sentences of English, which was sufficiently unusual to catch a
chronicler's attention, though, as an official biographer has noted,
'he can scarcely be looked on as an Englishman'.[51] He learned of his
father's death when in Sicily. But it took him nearly two years to
find his way to England. His first priority was to ride to Paris and
to do homage to the King of France. His next step was to make for
Gascony, and to spend many months suppressing the rebellion of
Gaston de Bèarn. Only then did he think of heading for England
and for his coronation at Westminster Abbey.

More than thirty years of incessant royal legislation, litigation,
and writ-mongering can hardly be summarized in one page. The
sheer quantity of the material is overwhelming; and the intricate
feudal terminology in which it is couched, from *seisin* and *mortmain*
to *replevin*, *escheat*, and *trailbaston* demands pre-requisite courses in
advanced Middle French and in medieval property law. Between the
statute *Districciones Scacarii* of 3 Ed. I and *De Conjunctione Feoffatio* of
34 Ed. I, there flowed a score of major acts, a constant stream of
commissions, inquiries, and trials, and an unending series of institutional innovations. At the risk of naive oversimplification, one may
say that Edouard I engaged in three sorts of operation. The first was
to establish what the precise state of existing laws, customs, rights,
and privileges actually was. In the famous statue of *Quo Warranto*
(1290), for example, he required all the magnates to produce all the
warrants and ancient charters on which their holdings were based.

Secondly, he used the information received to punish wrongdoers, to correct irregularities, to enforce discipline, to insist on the 'Confirmation of the Charters', and, by no means incidentally, to fill the royal coffers. Thirdly, by calling regular Parliaments with an extended franchise, he sought to gain a measure of public support, thereby insulating the crown against resentments over ministers and feudatories.

Some historians have seen him as a tyrant and manipulator; others as a successor to Simon de Montfort. 'The victor of Evesham was the true heir of the vanquished.' At all events, he reconciled the great earls to the crown, and built a governmental machine that worked. 'By 1300', a medievalist has recently concluded, '"a body politic of England" was already visible in a parliament . . . with the king at its head.'[52] An effective body politic was the essential basis for the King's other passion – warfare.

The immediate causes of Edouard I's Welsh wars do not seem commensurate with the ruthlessness displayed by the King and his Marcher allies. Llewellyn II was judged to have breached the terms of the Treaty of Montgomery, and in particular to have retained his hold on Powys and Glamorgan. But the English response was cataclysmic, not to say exterminatory. In the campaign of 1277, which took English soldiers into the heart of Snowdonia, the King mobilized not just the feudal host of England, but a mercenary army paid by loans from the bankers of Lucca, a corps of archers and crossbowmen, a fleet of ships from both the Cinque Ports and Bayonne, and a vast logistical force of masons, miners, woodmen, and reapers. Whilst the soldiers kept the natives at bay, the infrastructure of Welsh life was systematically destroyed. Military roads and castles were built, forests cleared, food supplies requisitioned. A fragile peace, which saw the beginnings of imposed English justice and a continuing offensive against 'Welsh robbers', collapsed. The winter campaign of 1282–3 took the form of a fight to the finish. Anglesey was captured by an amphibious force. The Menai Straits were bridged. A threefold offensive edged forward along the north and west coasts and through the centre. From his HQ at Rhuddlan the King raised additional huge loans, and extracted subsidies from the English cities and 'extraordinary gifts' from the clergy. The 'Double Parliament' of January 1283, held in two separate assemblies at York and Northampton, voted a specially large property tax of a thirtieth. The impregnable walls of Harlech, Conway, Caernarvon, Criccieth, and Bere rose above the Welsh countryside, whilst the 'rebels' were hunted down in the hills. The despatch which told the King of the death of Llewellyn at Builth, allegedly by treachery, has survived:

> Sachez, sire, ke vos bones gens . . . se combatirent av Leweln le finz Griffin en le paes de Buelt le vendredy pchain apres la feste seint Nhoilas, issi ke Leweln . . . est mort . . . et tote la flour de se gent morz.[53]

> (Know, sire, that your faithful men fought with Llewellyn son of Griffin (Gruffydd) in the country of Builth on the Friday following the Feast of St. Nicholas, also that Llewellyn was killed, and all the flower of his people dead also.)

Then came a Gascon Army, and 5,000 more infantry and 400 knights and 800 more woodsmen. By June, Edouard I was combing Cadair Idris for Llewellyn's brother Dafydd, hunting down the Welsh remnants.

One of the chroniclers recorded two completely contradictory epitaphs to the late Llewellyn. One was written by a Welsh monk, the other by an Englishman:

> Here lies the scourge of England
> Snowdonia's guardian sure,
> Llewellyn Prince of Wales,
> In character most pure.
> Of modern kings the jewel
> Of kings long past the flower,
> For kings to come a pattern,
> Radiant in Lawful power.
>
> . . .

Here lies the prince of errors,
    A traitor and a thief
A flaring, flaming firebrand,
    The malefactors' chief.
The wild Welsh evil genius,
    Who sought the good to kill.
Dregs of the faithless Trojans
    And source of every ill.

It is curious to note that the English monk thought that his compatriots were heirs to the ancient Greeks.

The Statute of Rhuddlan (1284) was a dictated peace par excellence. Justiciars or viceroys were appointed for North and South Wales. Five new counties were created, in Anglesey, Caernarvon, Merioneth, Cardigan, and Carmarthen. The fortress towns were declared free boroughs. The Marchers took back their own and more. In Glamorgan, Gilbert de Clare emerged as a virtual 'fellow sovereign'.

The Conquest of Wales was one of the most decisive events in the history of the Isles. Unlike the attack on Ireland, which had been less than half a conquest, and unlike the abortive Edwardian conquest of Scotland, it was, both in military and political terms, a complete success. 'The Welsh polity, which Llewellyn and his ancestors had fostered, was uprooted.' In the words of a Welsh historian, that polity 'as yet has had no successor'.[54] The separation of the March from Wallia Pura was perpetuated. Indeed the contempt of the Marchers for the 'free Welsh', like the contempt of the Scots Lowlanders for the Gaelic Highlanders in a later age, was used as an instrument of official policy. Welshness was a quality that could only take refuge in some of the hearts, and in part of the population, of Wales. Those magnificent Edwardian castles have remained ever since, 'the magnificent badges of our subjection'.

In 1284, during Edouard I's triumphant progress through Wales, his Queen gave birth at Caernarvon to their son and heir. In reality, that son, 'Edouard de Caernarvon', was created 'Prince de Galles' seventeen years later at Lincoln. But in legend he was lifted aloft on his father's shield at Caernarvon as an infant; and the populace asked jokingly whether their new Prince spoke English or Welsh. They were told that he spoke neither, since he could not speak at all. Later legend had forgotten that the royal family of England only spoke French.

Shortly after the Welsh War Edouard I expelled the Jews from England, thereby terminating a Jewish presence that had existed since the Conqueror. Plantagenet England shared all the prejudices of crusading Europe, and the incidence of attacks on Jews had been rising. The blood-libel, which consisted of false accusations against Jews of killing Christian boys in mockery of Christ's crucifixion, had first been recorded in the case of William of Norwich (d. 1144). It culminated in the shocking case of St Hugh of Lincoln (d. 1255), who was canonized for miracles attributed to him, and was buried alongside Bishop Grosseteste. A 'pogrom' was perpetrated in London on the night of Richard I's coronation in 1190; and from 1218 Jews were required to wear yellow badges. Simon de Montfort removed all Jews from his earldom of Leicester. The statute *De Judaismo* (1275) was presented as a move to regulate usury. But since it forbade Jews to engage in finance, it was for all practical purposes a prelude to the expulsion which soon followed in 1290. There was to be no Jewish presence in England for three hundred and sixty-five years.

The Anglo-Scottish Wars, which erupted in 1296, stemmed in the first instance from the failure of the MacMalcolm dynasty and from the resultant succession crisis. But they had deeper undercurrents. They represent a milestone in the hardening of both English and Scots identities. For a time, by involving both Ireland and Wales, they 'raised the spectre of a Pan-Celtic international'.[55]

The crisis began in 1286, when a regency council of Scotland's 'Guardians of the Realm' was convened for the minority of 'the Maid of Norway'. It rapidly deepened when the Maid drowned at sea. She had no heir. In 1290 Edouard I asserted a claim of over-lordship, insisting that he act as arbiter of a commission convened to appoint a successor. After two years of solemn legal pleading, 'the Great Cause' concluded with a decision in favour of Jean II de Baliol, Lord of Galloway (1249–1315).

The Baliols were an archetypal example of the Francogenae clans, who still dominated all parts of the Isles in this period. Descendants of Guido de Bailleul, a companion of the Conqueror, they held lands in Normandy, in England, and in Scotland. Their main base in England was at Barnard Castle in County Durham. Jean I de Baliol (d. 1271), Guido's great-great-great-grandson, a close adherent of Henri III, had already endowed the Oxford college which still bears his misspelled name, before being captured with the King at Lewes. His marriage to the heiress of Galloway made him a leading baron on both sides of the border. Their son, Jean II de Baliol (1249–1315), who had married a Warenne, was a natural client of Edouard I. After his unhappy foray into kingship, he would retreat to his ancestral lands, dying at Chateau-Gaillard.

The miserable reign of Jean de Baliol (King John I, r. 1292–96) – known in Scots tradition as Toom Tabard or 'Empty Jacket' – was beset by every manner of machinations. Baliol had only become a contestant for the Scottish throne by signing up in advance to the English king's questionable claim to superior overlordship. He was obliged to swear fealty to Edouard prior to his coronation at Scone, and to pay homage after it. He was comprehensively trapped. No sooner crowned, he was summoned to appear in court at Westminster and to act as witness in a case where the King of England sought to prove a right to hear all Scottish appeals. His failure to appear led to a judgement of contumacy and the forfeiture of his English lands. In 1294 he did attend an English Parliament in London, but withdrew when he saw that he was expected to support England's coming war with France. His Scots subjects were incensed. A Scots Parliament at Scone angrily rejected the English demand for knight service in France. The forfeiture of all English barons holding lands in Scotland was announced. In 1295 Baliol signed an alliance with Philip IV of France, each undertaking to aid the other against English aggression. From then on, there was no way out. In 1296 the English attacked the French from Gascony. The Scots attacked the English in Cumbria. And Edouard I invaded Scotland. Having taken Berwick, he was handed Baliol's formal renunciation of fealty. 'Has the foolish fellow done such folly?' he shouted in French. 'If he won't come to us, we shall go to him!' A huge English army, including 11,000 Welshmen, captured Edinburgh and pressed on to Elgin. Baliol had no stomach for the fight. At Montrose, he surrendered, and was ritually humiliated. His tabard, hood, and girdle were stripped from him in the ceremony reserved for treasonable knights. The English king's words were (in translation), 'A man does good business when he rids himself of a turd.' The Great Seal of Scotland was smashed. The Stone of Destiny, the Scottish regalia, and St Margaret's holy relic of the Black Rood were carried off to London. So, too, was Baliol, to languish in the Tower. The King of England presided over a Scots Parliament at Berwick. 'Scotland had become a virtual colony.'[56]

Such, however, was only the start. Edouard I had broken the fundamental assumption of all feudal contracts – that subjects paid service, and lords provided protection. In Scots eyes, he was a tyrant, not a protector. He was going to lose 'the business' he had begun. Both by the standards of the feudal age, as by modern standards of decent behaviour, he deserved to lose. Indeed, he was seen by no less than Dante as a prime case of pride:

> Lì si vedra la superbia ch'asseta
> che fa lo Scotto e l'Inghilese folle,
> sí che non può soffrir dentro a sua meta.[57]

Unfortunately, he did not live to see the Scots' revenge. He had left his son, Edouard II (r. 1307–27), an untenable legacy.

England's hold on Scotland, seized with haste, crumbled at leisure. Huge armies of occupation, annually renewed, piled up the King's debts and the disillusionment of the barons. Alternating policies of reconciliation and reprisal sidelined would-be Scots collaborators. Guerrilla warfare against scattered English garrisons, open conflict between competing Scots magnates, and relentless Scottish raids into northern England gradually rendered the English position untenable. First into the field was William Wallace (c. 1272–1305), a Baliol supporter and legendary patriot, whose murder of an English sheriff at Lanark in 1297 sparked off a general revolt. His victory at Stirling Bridge (1298) propelled him into the office of 'Guardian of the Realm'. His savage treatment after capture, grue-somely recreated in the film *Braveheart*, turned him into a national martyr.[58] The English victory at Falkirk (1298), gained by the skill of Welsh and Gascon mercenaries, deterred the Scots' eagerness for open confrontation. For several years, the Guardianship was held jointly by two bitter rivals, Robert de Bruce of Annandale, and Jean Comyn de Badenoch, Baliol's nephew. The best part of a decade would elapse before 'the Bruce' emerged as the focus of Scots resistance.

About this time, at the turn of the fourteenth century, one of the earliest surviving Scots poems mourns the 'perplexity' of Scot-land in the dozen years 'since King Alexander died'.

> Sen Alexander our king wes deid
> That Scotland left in luve and lee
> Away wes sonse of aill and breid,
> Of wine and wax, of gamin and glee.
> The gold wes changit all in leid,
> The frute failyeit on everilk tree.
> Christ succour Scotland and remeid
> That stad is perplexitie.[59]

As for William Wallace, his achievement would come to be praised lavishly by a prominent English historian with strong connections in Northumberland, whose sympathies might be expected to have lain elsewhere:

All seemed finished. All in fact was about to begin. Deserted by her nobles, Scotland discovered herself. The governors whom Edward I left behind him were incapable and cruel, and the foreign soldiery made the Scots feel their subjection. . . . [A] guerrilla chief of genius, a tall man of iron strength, who suddenly appears on the page of history as if from nowhere, defeated at Stirling Bridge an English army under its blundering feudal chief the Earl of Warenne, of *quo Warranto* fame. Thence William Wallace broke ravaging into Northumberland and Cumberland.

This unknown knight, with little but his great name to identify him in history, had lit a fire which nothing since has ever put out. Here, in Scotland, contemporaneously with the very similar doings in Switzerland, a new ideal and tradition of wonderful potency was brought into the world; it had no name then, but now we should call it democratic patriotism. It was not the outcome of theory. The unconscious qualities of a people had given it reality in a sudden fit of rage.

Theories of nation-hood and theories of democracy would follow afterwards to justify or explain it. Meanwhile, it stood up, a fact.[60]

Robert VIII de Bruce (1274–1329) was the latest of eight generations of French barons bearing the same name. Robert I, Sire de Bréaux (d. 1094), a companion of the Conqueror, had established the senior English seat of the family at Skelton in Cleveland. Robert II (d. 1141), a companion of David I at the English court, moved to Scotland when granted the lands of Annandale in Dumfriesshire. Robert VI (d. 1295), known as 'the Competitor', a companion of Henri III at the Battle of Lewes, had competed in the Great Cause against Jean de Baliol. Robert VII (d. 1304), 'le Veil', had accompanied the 'Lord Edouard' on crusade in 1269–74, and in 1296 had asked for Baliol's crown. He received the ironic reply from the King of England: '*Ne avons ren autres chos a fere/ Que a vous reamgs ganere*' (We really have nothing much better to do/ than to hand out realms to people like you!). Robert VIII, Earl of Carrick, known as 'Le Jovenne', therefore, was born into the heart of the Francogenic Anglo-Scottish aristocracy. Together with his father, he paid homage to Edouard in 1296 for his Scottish lands.

'The Bruce' long held to an ambivalent position in the Anglo-

Scottish Wars. He briefly helped Wallace in 1297, but in the campaign of 1303–4 he was an open advocate of the English invaders. His loyalty seems to have flipped in the autumn of 1305 when he travelled to London to attend a joint Anglo-Scottish Parliament. He saw the head of Wallace still hanging from London Bridge, and like many Scottish lords would have been dismayed by the Parliament's proceedings. The resultant Ordinance for Scotland, which resembled the earlier Statute of Rhuddlan for Wales, sought to introduce English law and government, whilst banning all Scots and Gaelic customs. Immediately after his return home, the Bruce murdered his Comyn rival before the high altar at Dumfries, and seized his chance to be crowned at Scone.

From 1306 to 1314, the Bruce took the patriotic cause in Scotland from near extinction to total triumph. Driven into exile on Rachlin Island in Ulster, he learned of his three brothers' executions. According to legend, he learned from watching a spider on the wall 'to try, and try, and try again'. But he also learned of Edouard I's death in Northumbria, and the accession of his weakling son. After that, inspired by Wallace's memory, he was able to reduce all the English garrisons in Scotland one by one. He even led an expedition to the Isle of Man. By 1313, Stirling alone remained in English hands; and in the following year, a huge invasion force of 100,000 men moved off from Berwick to relieve it. Bruce met the incoming English on the Bannock Burn near Stirling. On the eve of the battle, he rode up to the English lines on his Highland pony, picked out an English earl on a warhorse, and, standing high in his stirrups, cleft the earl with a single blow of his axe. Here in single combat was an enactment in miniature of the next day's general clash. A well-chosen site, cool command, and patriotic determination achieved one of the most decisive victories in the history of the Isles. Thirty thousand English dead lay piled high on the field. The flower of English chivalry perished. On 24 June 1314, the Battle of Bannockburn 'decided the independence of Scotland'. England's plans were confounded. The Bruce, at a stroke, put an end to the notion that the English could reduce 'the whole island to a centralised empire under one head, untrammelled by the bonds of constitutional monarchy'.[61]

The question of Scotland's independence had hung in the balance for a generation. Edouard I had formally recognized it at the Treaty of Brigham in 1290, when he was negotiating for the hand of Alexander III's daughter, Margaret. But he regarded the treaty as null and void since Margaret had died before he could marry her. In 1300, Pope Boniface VII had attempted to act as arbiter, by staking a claim to be 'lord paramount' over both England and Scotland. This caused an English Parliament at Lincoln in 1301 to reject the competence of the Pope 'in the temporal affairs of England' and to declare Scotland 'dependent'. In their depositions sent to the Pope, the English argued (following Geoffrey of Monmouth) that their forebear, Locrine, held prior claim over Brutus's younger son, Albanacht. The Scots for their part argued that 'Albany' referred to the whole of the island and that all its sons were equal. Bannockburn terminated all such wrangling. The war of words gave way to the war of swords. But it took many years or the counter-claims of the Scots to be formally confirmed. On 6 April 1320, by the Declaration of Arbroath, a Scottish Parliament was still calling on the Pope to give his blessing to the country's independence:

> . . . While there exist a hundred of us we will never submit to England. We fight not for glory, wealth or honour, but for that liberty without which no virtuous man will survive. Wherefore we most earnestly request your Holiness, as His viceregent who gives equal measure . . . to all persons and nations, that you would admonish [the King of England] to content himself with his own dominions . . . and allow us Scotsmen, who dwell in a poor and remote quarter and who seek for naught but our own, to dwell in peace.[62]

The Scots had long been thwarted by English agents who held the ear of the Pope. So the Declaration ended with a pretty pointed warning about the consequences of its rejection:

But if your Holiness puts too much faith in the tales the English tell and will not give sincere belief to all this, nor refrain from favouring them to our prejudice, then the slaughter of bodies, the perdition of souls, and all the other misfortunes that will follow, inflicted by them on us and by us on them, will, we believe, be surely laid by the Most High to your charge.[63]

The substance of the Declaration was granted by the Papacy in 1323, and recognized by the King of France in 1326. It was finally conceded by an English Parliament convened at York to consider the preliminaries for a peace treaty. Despite many later recriminations, it was never reversed. The key article to the preliminaries signed on 8 February 1328 stated that 'Scotland according to its ancient bounds in the days of Alexander III should remain to Robert King of Scots, his heirs and successors, free and divided from the kingdom of England, without any subjection, right or service or claim or demand, and that all writs executed at any time to the contrary should be held void.'[64] Within a year, Robert the Bruce was dead of leprosy.

The Bruce's success had caused major repercussions in Ireland. In 1315, at the invitation of Donal O'Neill, grandson of the last nominal High King, Edouard de Bruce, Robert's brother, landed in Ulster, and was declared 'King of Ireland'. He joined O'Neill in sending the Pope a Remonstrance, similar to and earlier than the Declaration of Arbroath, recounting Ireland's long independent history and her maltreatment by the English. They were opposed by Roger Mortimer, the royal Justiciar, who possessed land both in Meath and in the Welsh Marches. For three years, the colony was plunged into turmoil, especially in 1317 when Robert de Bruce joined his brother in a far-ranging campaign from Ulster to Waterford. Ireland was pulled from the English into the Scottish sphere. But then, at the Battle of Faughart (1318), Edouard de Bruce was killed, and his enterprise collapsed. Once again, Ireland reverted to a state of neglect. Central government lost all purpose beyond the salvaging of its ever-shrinking finances. Honours owned by absentees proliferated. Magnate fought with magnate, chief with chief, baron and chief against baron and chief. Mortimer rewarded the Geraldines with the new earldoms of Kildare, Ormonde, and Desmond. The Geraldines feuded with the de Burghs in Ulster and Connaught. One of the de Burghs, fully Gaelicized, took the name of Éamonn Albanach MacWilliam Burke, and ran Connaught as a totally independent realm. Everywhere the native chiefs were breaking free from the close feudal or royal control to which they had been subjected. Their courts fostered the rise of *Danté gradha*, a form of Gaelic poetry derived from the courtly poems of the French troubadours. A Parliament met in Dublin, but only to complain of dwindling income, unrepaired fortresses, empty lands, and rampant Hibernization. In the Statutes of Kilkenny (1366), which codified fifty years of legislation and fixed the frontier of a much reduced Pale, the colonists can be seen to be using Welsh Marcher custom or Brehon law, to be wearing Irish costume and speaking Gaelic, and to undermine attempts at maintaining law and order. Englishmen from England were specifically forbidden from calling these beleaguered *Francogenae* as 'Irish dogs'.

The Anglo-Scottish wars undoubtedly stimulated the growth of national identity both in England and in Scotland. Yet the 'Englishness' and 'Scottishness' that emerged had little to do with language and much to do with the conscious formation of 'a community of the realm'. The ground had been well prepared by historians and jurists over the previous century. But open conflict sharpened the existing trends. In England, Henri de Bracton (d. 1268), a royal judge, figured strongly in a tradition which traced the country's legal system, and hence its ultimate authority, to the native laws of Edward the Confessor. Bracton's treatise *On the Laws and Customs of England* is nowadays attributed to an earlier colleague. But it became the bible of English common lawyers. In Scotland, an entirely separate legal tradition was launched.

A sequence of English chroniclers from Henry of Huntingdon to Roger of Wendover and Matthew Paris promoted the Anglocentric tradition which diminished or ignored all the non-English events in the Isles. The educated classes in England were still thinking in French, but more and more were thinking of themselves as English. The attempt by Edouard I to create one unified Plantagenet community of the Isles had failed. Instead, the community of the English realm was mentally turning in on itself. Its long-standing tendency to xenophobia would be further emphasized by the coming struggle with France.

By the fourteenth century, therefore, there could be no doubt that the Isles were inhabited by four historic peoples. Two of the four – the English and the Scots – enjoyed an identity which coincided with a state polity. The other two – the Welsh and the Irish – possessed a strong identity but no statehood.[65]

English apologists are quick to plead that the Scots had exploited a time of peculiar English weakness. This is perfectly correct. (All political contests, like all boxing matches, are decided by the relative strengths and weaknesses of the contestants 'on the day'.) Yet the reign of Edouard II de Caernarvon presented a sorry spectacle indeed. All the old troubles resurfaced. The young King cleaved to foreign favourites, notably to yet another Gascon, Pierre Gaveston. His household tried to assert a hold over royal government; his debts mounted; and his barons rebelled. By the Ordinances of 1311 he found the royal prerogative constrained, and in the view of a famous medievalist, constitutional government was established 'by historical accident'.[66] In the course of a baronial revolt he was overthrown by the intrigues of his mother, Queen Isabelle, and her lover, Roger Mortimer. He was deposed by the illegal decree of the pseudo-Parliament of Kenilworth (1326), incarcerated in Berkeley Castle, and foully murdered in secret. Before he died, Edouard II of England composed the saddest of poems:

> En temps de iver me survynt damage,
> Fortune trop m'ad traversé:
> Eure m'est faili tut mon age.
> Bien sovent l[e]ay esprové:

Pener me funt cruelement –
E duint qe bien l'ai deservi.
Lour fausse fai en parlement
De haut en bas mc descendi.[67]

To PUT EVEN A SIMPLE question about the Middle Ages to ordinary men and women today is to invite a blank stare. Mention of 'the early Plantagenets' is a surefire conversation stopper. If confronted with the word 'medieval', most people would struggle to conjure up anything beyond the popular TV parodies such as Monty Python's *Holy Grail* (which is vaguely twelfth century in setting) or Rowan Atkinson's *Blackadder* (which is vaguely fourteenth or fifteenth century). This is not simply because medieval history is rarely taught in schools. The contemporary world with its emphasis on materialism and secular culture is profoundly out of sympathy with an age when the Christian religion was paramount and the universal Church was the most important of all institutions. The 'jokey tendency' in historical consciousness is encouraged because few people feel any serious connotations. Matters were not ever thus.

The English may have special problems of their own. For centuries after the Reformation, they were taught to look askance at an era when England was a minor kingdom in Catholic Europe and when the sun of national greatness had not yet risen. They were profoundly unimpressed by the French-run world to which England had been joined by the Conquest of 1066. Even prominent historians would make little distinction between the Norman period, when England was tied to the neighbouring Duchy of Normandy, and the Plantagenet period, when she formed part of a far more extensive and more complex realm. Present-day attitudes may conceivably change through membership of the European Union. But until now English attitudes, if they exist at all, have been markedly parochial. The Irish and the Welsh can both be expected to know something

about the era when their national misfortunes began. The Scots
have been well fed on a diet of Wallace and Robert the Bruce and
the assertion of Scottish independence. But the English have little
cause to remember. English memories focus on three issues – on
Magna Carta, and hence on the perceived growth of English liberties; on Robin Hood and the struggle of the common people against
alien oppression; and, as a bad third, on the crusades. Each of these
topics has inspired a substantial body of interest both in historiography and in literature.

Magna Carta is famous because it is the centrepiece of a very
particular historical myth that for many years gained a virtual
monopoly over English perceptions of the past. To use an organic
metaphor well suited to the myth, it was the acorn 'from which the
mighty oak did grow'. The oak, of course, was the English constitution as described by generations of legal and administrative historians; and the English constitution was seen as the repository of
popular liberty against the tyranny of (foreign) kings. The tree has
two branches. One branch is 'the law' enshrined in a vast stream of
documents as interpreted by a long line of constitutionalists. The
other is the institutional framework, centred on Parliament, through
which the unwritten constitution mysteriously dispenses its blessings. Together, legalists and parliamentarians assembled such a
magnificent construct that by the early twentieth century British
history was widely thought to be 'basically the history of the English
State'.[68]

It is worth noting that when Shakespeare wrote his historical
play *King John* (1596), he did not mention Magna Carta once. He
picked up the patriotic theme, which had circulated since the
fourteenth-century *Brut* chronicle, but he steered clear of the constitutional issues. Later Tudor and early Stuart England was familiar
enough both with 'the struggle for the restoration of the good old
lawes' and with the rise of Parliament. Both had found a place in
Polydore Vergil's *Anglicae Historia* (1534). But opinion was uncertain; and a court dramatist would probably not care to stir sensitive
issues in preference to topics of stirring national pride:

Come the three corners of the world in arms,
And we shall shock them. Naught shall make us rue
If England to itself do rest but true.[69]

For Shakespeare was still active in 1616 when King James dismissed the lawyer Sir Edward Coke, who played the most prominent part in launching the English constitutional myth on its long career. Coke was an advocate for the interests of the landed aristocracy, and he used his researches on medieval documents as a weapon in his attack on the royal prerogative. He formulated the ultraconservative, and quite unsustainable theory that England possessed a body of immemorial law of Anglo-Saxon vintage which had been regularly 'reaffirmed', most prominently by Magna Carta. He assumed that any innovations made by the King were improper. Quoting Bracton completely out of context, he concluded *Quod rex non debet esse sub homine sed sub Deo et lege* ('The King should be subject not to man but to God and the law'). In Bracton's day, the law had included the canon law of the universal Church. In Coke's day, it meant the common law and parliamentary statutes as interpreted by Coke and his friends. Yet Coke's ideology was adopted by the victorious parliamentary cause, and it became the basis of a lasting national tradition.

Throughout the seventeenth century, several legal and medieval scholars challenged Coke's partisan position. In his *Ius feudale* (1603), Coke's contemporary Sir Thomas Craig (1538–1608), a French-educated Scot, demonstrated that feudal law was not fixed but evolving. The antiquary and jurist Sir Henry Spelman (1564–1641) studied legal records of the Anglo-Saxon and Norman periods and argued that medieval kingship was not the subordinate institution suggested by Coke. In his studies of the medieval Church and baronage, the great student of rolls and charters Sir William Dugdale (1605–86) collected the material for a more balanced view of medieval institutions. Yet it was Robert Brady (1627–1700), who in the closing years of Charles II's reign made one last effort to restrain those who were using their appeals to immemorial laws 'to bomb and batter the governments'. Brady's *Introduction to the Old English History* (1684) was written in answer to one William Petyt, who, among other things, had maintained that knights and burgesses had 'always' sat in Parliament. By 'always', Brady asked, 'did he mean eternity, or Adam, or [just] since the Britons, Romans and Saxons?'[70]

Brady also took an interest in Simon de Montfort and in that 'Nick of Time' between 1258 and 1265 which was vital to the germination of Parliament. But he himself was writing at a juncture that was not conducive to fair-minded scholarship. Once the Whigs had triumphed in that 'Glorious Revolution' of 1688–9, their view of history triumphed with them. Everything that happened prior to 1688 was to be viewed teleologically as tending towards that glorious goal. All history post-1688 was building on the glorious achievement. This 'Whig Interpretation' did not come under serious attack for two hundred and fifty years. In the eighteenth century, things medieval fell out of fashion. David Hume's monumental *History of England* (sic) saw feudalism as a modest advance on the preceding chaos. But Hume treated the Church as an enemy to civilization. And his treatment of English policy to the Welsh and the Scots betrayed an 'almost total neglect of truth and justice'.[71]

Nineteenth-century historians approached the Middle Ages with enthusiasm. But, with one or two exceptions, their enthusiasm was misdirected by Whig bias, by Protestant prejudice, and by narrow English nationalism. It was born of the general Romantic urge of the century, and boosted by the proud realization that the *ancien régime* in the United Kingdom, unlike France, had remained intact. The great names and works were those of the Whig politician Henry Hallam (1777–1859), whose *Europe during the Middle Ages* (1818) and *Constitutional History of England* (1827) pioneered their subjects, of Bishop William Stubbs (1825–1901), Regius Professor of History at Oxford, whose *Constitutional History of England* (1873–8) was long the standard work on the period; and F. W. Maitland (1824–97), Downing Professor of Law at Cambridge, whose *History of English Law* (1895) took the narrative up to the critical reign of Henri III. Despite their immense erudition, and their enormous services to the subject, all these scholars positively crowed with nationalistic self-satisfaction. None of them gained a reputation outside the English-speaking world. Referring to Magna Carta, Hallam praised 'England's first national event' which 'brought all free men together in an almost sacramental communion'. In his inaugural lecture in Oxford in 1867, Bishop Stubbs expounded his view that English constitutional history embodied 'the spirit of liberty' and 'the principle of freedom'. As for Maitland, the legalist par excellence, he saw an unbreakable bond between the Common Law and 'our land and race'; and he eulogized the judges of Henri III's reign – Pateshull, Raleigh, and Bracton:

> It was for the good of the whole world that one race stood apart from its neighbours and turned away its eyes at an early time from the fascinating pages of the *Corpus Iuris* [Roman law] . . . These few men [Pateshull, Raleigh, and Bracton] were penning writs that would run in the name of kingless commonwealths on the other shore of the Atlantic Ocean; they were making right and wrong for our children.[72]

History in the hands of lawyers will always turn lawyers into heroes.

Maitland's reference to 'kingless commonwealths' across the ocean underlines the important fact that the legal system of the USA traces its roots to the English common law and to the same Whiggish 'spirit of liberty'. American lawyers are still trained in the insular spirit which once characterized their English colleagues. It is entirely appropriate that the site of Magna Carta at Runnymede is graced by a memorial to an American president.

Interest in legal and constitutional matters led naturally to curiosity about the workings of government and administration. Professor T. F. Tout (1855–1929) of Manchester University created a field which explained medieval politics in terms of the competing departments of court and state. His *Chapters in the Administrative History of Mediaeval England* (1920–23) was a fitting partner for the earlier work of Stubbs and Maitland.[73]

The grand historical construct of the English medieval state knows few equals. It was assembled by formidable scholars with a strong sense of mission. Yet its very size and prestige left little space for the competition. Indeed, by establishing such a dominant vision over what is supposedly important, it positively deterred enquiry into less developed fields of study. By concentrating on one of several medieval state machines in the Isles, it ignored all others that were functioning at the time; and by stressing its own continuities, it implied that most other things in England's past were continuous. Above all, by assuming that England was unique, it denied the value of comparative history. England in the period when its Continental connections were most intense was effectively (and damagingly) divorced from the essential Continental context.

One of the few major English historians to dissent from the dominant school was John Lingard (1771–1851), a specialist in the Anglo-Saxon and medieval periods. Educated abroad in the English college at Douai, he was free from the usual nationalist bias of his contemporaries; and as a Catholic priest, he did not share the prevailing Protestant antipathy to the medieval Church. His eight-volume *History of England* (1819–30) ran into six editions, and was translated into several European languages. His manifestly sympathetic approach to the medieval world influenced receptive readers such as the Pre-Raphaelites and William Morris. The emphasis which he gave to the early Plantagenet period was entirely at odds with that of Hallam, Stubbs, or Maitland. It says much for the limited horizons of English historiography that Lingard never found his way into the company of recognized 'greats'.[74]

Professional medievalists did not mount a concerted attack on the Stubbsian school for more than a century. In 1963, H. G. Richardson and G. O. Sayles published *The Governance of Mediaeval England* which exposed the essentially teleological character of conventional views.[75] They contested the idea that the Parliament of Edouard I could be a 'model of every other succeeding assembly bearing the name', and ridiculed the practice of using the English constitution as a blueprint for all the ex-colonial countries of the late twentieth century. In other works, they located the origins of the English Parliament in the judicial as distinct from the legislative sphere. Whatever evolutions may subsequently have occurred, the implication is that the early English Parliament was analogous to the French *Parlement*.[76] Needless to say, any such suggestion would have been anathema to the older generation.

Constitutional history was for the few. Robin Hood was for the many. Tales of the brave outlaw and his band of merry men, who lived in the greenwood off the King's venison and who robbed the rich to pay the poor, have fed one of the largest and most variegated stocks of popular lore and entertainment. Versified ballads about Robin Hood were circulating widely in the fifteenth century, although they clearly drew on material from earlier times. Street plays about Robin Hood from the late medieval period grew into regular theatrical comedies in the early modern period: Shakespeare's contemporary Michael Drayton wrote in 1596:

> In this our spacious isle I think there is not one
> But 'he of Robin Hood hath heard' and Little John.
> And to the end of time the tales shall ne'er be done
> Of Scarlet, George-a-Green, and Much the Miller's son,
> Of Tuck, the merry Friar, who many a sermon made
> In praise of Robin Hood, his outlaws and their trade.[77]

In the nineteenth century, Robin Hood was one of the stock figures of Victorian melodrama and vaudeville. In the twentieth, he became one of the mainstays of the film industry. Douglas Fairbanks (1922), Errol Flynn (1939), Richard Greene (1953), and Michael Praed (1984) are just the best-known names to have featured in the role.

The favourite setting for the tales is Sherwood Forest near Nottingham in the 1190s. Robin is a nobleman wrongfully banished from his lands. His chief oppressors are the Sheriff of Nottingham and the Sheriff's master, Prince John, who has taken to cruel exploitation of the people during King Richard's absence on crusade.

Apart from Will Scarlet and Much the Miller's son, leading members of the band include Robin's giant deputy, Little John, the fugitive Franciscan, Friar Tuck, and the dashing minstrel, Allan-a-Dale. Their most frequent victim, and involuntary guest at their forest banquets, is the well-fed Bishop of Hereford. A happy ending is conventionally provided by the return of King Richard in disguise, the restoration of Robin to his lands, and his long-awaited marriage to his greenwood sweetheart, Maid Marion. A different effect can be provided by the variant ending where a stricken Robin fires an arrow through the window of his abbey sickroom, and asks to be buried under the oak where the arrow falls:

> Here underneath this little stone
> Lies Robert, Earl of Huntingdon;
> Never archer as he so good,
> And people called him Robin Hood.
> Such outlaws as he and his men
> Will England never see again.[78]

This is all very attractive. The problem for historians is that virtually none of these details are reflected in contemporary sources.

The earliest documentary references to Robin Hood date from the thirteenth century. One Robin Hood, a servant of the Abbot of Cirencester, is recorded as committing a murder sometime before 1216 during the Barons' War against King Jean. This event is usually dismissed as a coincidence. But in 1228–32, there are reports of an outlaw or *fugitivus* named Robert Hood operating in Yorkshire. His nickname seems to have been 'Hobbehod'. Thirty years later, another *fugitivus* called William Robehod was recorded in Berkshire. This man can be identified as the outlawed son of Robert le Fevere from Enborne on the Hampshire border. But nothing else about him fits the actions and locations popularized in the later ballads. Adam de la Halle's *Jeu de Robin et Marion*, a French-language drama, is dated to c. 1280. By that time, the legend was clearly beginning to circulate widely. But no certain sighting of a historical Robin Hood had been

made. Several medieval Scottish sources place the stories firmly in
the thirteenth century. One of them gives both a precise date, 1283,
and precise places:

> Litil Iohun and Robert Hude
> Waythmen war commendit gud;
> In Inglewood and Bernnysdaile
> Thai oyssit at this tyme thar trawale.[79]

Unfortunately, there are two Barnsdales, one in south Yorkshire
contiguous to Sherwood, the other eighty miles away in Rutland.
The more southerly Barnsdale Forest, which lies between Oakham
and Stamford, is less favoured than its Yorkshire counterpart. Yet it
is particularly rich in local mementoes – a 'Robin Hood's Cave', a
'Robin Hood's Cross', a 'Robin Hood's Stone', several 'Robin Hood's
Fields', and a 'Robin-a-tiptoe Hill'. In 1354, a man called Robin
Hood was awaiting trial for offences in the nearby royal forest of
Rockingham.

Similar searches can be conducted in the medieval undergrowth
for various maids Marion and for each of the merry men. References
to Little John are particularly strong in Derbyshire, where his grave
at Glossop is extant. A specially curious item derives from Lindfield
in Sussex in 1417, where a former chaplain called Robert Stafford
took to banditry and adopted the name of 'Friar Tuck'. Yet there is
no way of telling whether this cleric turned robber was the original
'jovial friar' or just an impersonator. In such circumstances, negative
judgements are more trustworthy than optimistic ones. The famous
scene where Friar Tuck is boxed about the ears by the disguised
King Richard, for example, is historically impossible. Richard I died
twenty years before the mendicant orders were founded.

The academic industry of Hoodology, therefore, has had rich
veins to mine. It began with the Stamford antiquarian, William
Stukeley (see page 92, above) whose *Palæographia Britannica* (1746)
contains 'The Pedigree of Robin Hood, Earl of Huntingdon'. Stukeley identified Robin Hood with Robert Fitzooth, 'pretended earl of
Huntingdon', who died in 1274 and who was supposedly descended

from an Anglo-Saxon nobleman. This was accepted by Joseph Ritson
in the introduction to his influential anthology of the Robin Hood
ballads which appeared in 1832;[80] but it is now generally accepted as
an illustration of the gentrification of the legend that occurred in
the seventeenth and eighteenth centuries. Since then, hundreds if
not thousands of titles have appeared. If anything, the chances of a
positive identification are receding with every speculative attempt.
For the task of harmonizing the evidence of a burgeoning late
medieval oral tradition with the contradictory fragments of documentary evidence from the early Plantagenet era is all but impossible. Proliferating romanticization of the legends can be more surely
demonstrated than a single historical beginning.

As in many other fields, Victorian and Edwardian commentators
chose to highlight the perceived 'racial' angle to the Robin Hood
stories. After a dismissive Protestant comment about the medieval
Church, the fashion was to place the stories into the context of
'Saxon versus Norman':

> This was the day, not only of oppression by Church and State
> but also of the struggle between the Saxon land-holders and
> their Norman conquerors. Robin Hood was, first of all, a Saxon
> who stood out for the rights of the people, waging war against
> knights, sheriffs, abbots and money-lenders, whose sway was so
> heavy. But he was fair in war, a protector of women and
> children: courteous . . . kind . . . generous . . . a respecter of
> honest labouring men and tradesfolk . . . brave to rashness,
> proud and adventurous . . . skilled and adroit and resourceful;
> finally a man of frank open countenance, singing among the
> lights and shadows of the good greenwood, and jesting in the
> face of death itself.
>   . . . Is there any wonder that the common people loved
> him?[81]

The mention of 'money-lenders' is gratuitous; and linking the 'common people' with the 'Saxons' two or three hundred years after the
Conquest is both simplistic and anachronistic. But the generations

who were taught that Alfred was their royal champion were more
than willing to see Robin Hood as the champion of their proletarian
forebears.

Some of the responsibility both for popularizing the scenario of
worthy Saxon versus nasty Norman and for choosing a setting in the
reign of Richard I must fall on Sir Walter Scott. The doyen of
historical novelists set most of his works in Scotland and in later
times. But *Ivanhoe* (1820) was set firmly in the England of the 1190s.
And *Ivanhoe* was a best-seller among the best-selling Waverley
novels. It tells the story of the disinherited son of a Saxon nobleman,
Wilfrid of Ivanhoe, who sets out to beat the Normans at their own
favourite game, fighting in the lists at chivalric tournaments. It takes
place in 'the pleasant district of merry England watered by the River
Don between Sheffield and Doncaster'; but its most outstanding
characteristic is the state of virtual apartheid prevailing 'betwixt the
descendants of the victor Normans and the vanquished Saxons':

> Four generations had not sufficed to blend the hostile blood of
> the Norman and Anglo-Saxon, or to unite . . . two hostile races,
> one of which still felt the elation of triumph, while the other
> groaned under all the consequences of defeat. The power had
> been completely placed in the hands of the Norman nobility,
> and it had been used . . . with no moderate hand . . . All the
> monarchs of the Norman race had shown the most marked
> predilection for their Norman subjects: the laws of the chase,
> and many others, unknown to the milder and more free spirit
> of the Saxon constitution, had been fixed upon the necks of the
> subjugated inhabitants, to add weight, as it were, to the feudal
> chains with which they were loaded. At court, and in the castles
> of the great nobles . . . Norman French was the only language
> employed . . . while the far more manly and expressive Anglo-
> Saxon was abandoned to the use of rustics and hinds, who knew
> no other . . . [82]

Scott showed considerable interest in the language issue. In the
famous opening scene of *Ivanhoe*, two Saxon serfs, Gurth and

Wamba, are sitting in 'the rich grassy glades' of the forest. Gurth, a swineherd, wears a serf-collar bearing the inscription 'Gurth the son of Beowulf is the bornthrall of Cedric of Rotherwood'. He is explaining to 'Wamba, the son of Witless' how the English *swine*, which he herds, become French *pork* on the castle table. In due course, when Prince Jean appears in villainous form, it turns out that he can't understand a word of English. The good King Richard, in contrast, speaks enough to share the English toast of *Waes hael*, *drinc hael* – a rather dubious proposition in itself.

The principal storyline concerns Ivanhoe's feud with a Templar, the Knight of the Black Raven, Brian de Bois-Guilbert. From their first meeting at the tourney of Ashby-de-la-Zouche, which Ivanhoe enters incognito, to the final clash where the Black Raven dies, the contest is presented in stark terms of patriotic underdog challenging proud oppressor. Ivanhoe's shocking toast is raised 'To all true English hearts, and to the confusion of foreign tyrants!' and when choosing the Lady Rowena as queen of the tourney, he dares to proclaim, 'Long live the race of the immortal Alfred.'

In the final scene, Scott orchestrates Ivanhoe's reconciliation with his father in the presence of both King Richard and Robin Hood. The occasion is played out at one of the outlaws' 'sylvan repasts'. Ivanhoe receives his father's forgiveness and the promise of Lady Rowena's hand in marriage. And the King throws off his disguise:

> 'As yet you have known me but as the Black Knight of the Fetterlock – Know me now as Richard Plantagenet!'
>
> 'Richard of Anjou!' exclaimed Cedric, stepping backward with the utmost astonishment.
>
> 'No, noble Cedric – Richard of England, whose dearest interest, whose deepest wish it is to see her sons united with each other – And, how now, worthy Thane! hast thou no knee for thy prince?'[83]

The idea that Cœur de Lion held England in such high regard is straining the historical record to breaking point. Richard I reigned in an age when democracy was unknown, and in a century when Parliament had never met. What he did to persuade Victorian parliamentarians to acquire a grand statue cast in his memory for the Great Exhibition of 1857 and to re-erect it in the precinct of the Palace of Westminster remains a mystery. Nothing is more incongruous than the sight of a monarch who was not even Anglo-Norman, let alone English, being turned into a totem of English national pride.[84]

British interest in the crusades, however, has been strictly limited. The crusades are frequently featured in school textbooks, where they have customarily appeared as a colourful episode of long ago or as an excuse to recount the adventures of Cœur de Lion. But they are not presented as an episode for young people to identify with, and have not inspired much creative literature. The reasons for the neglect are obvious. In the eyes of Protestant commentators from John Foxe onwards, the crusaders were fatally contaminated by Catholicism. In the opinion of the Enlightenment, they were fanatics. David Hume's condemnation was absolute. The crusades, he said, were 'the most signal and durable monument to human folly that has yet appeared in any age or nation'.[85] Modern historians are no more forgiving. 'The Holy War itself', concluded Steven Runciman, 'was nothing more than a long act of intolerance in the name of God, which is the sin against the Holy Ghost.'[86] Here is the crux of the matter. To wage war on behalf of the Gospel of Love is contrary to basic Christian teaching. For this reason, nine hundred years after the First Crusade was preached, Christian pilgrims in the 1990s are now travelling to the Holy Land to ask humbly for forgiveness.

In other circumstances, Cœur de Lion might easily have become the hated symbol of foreign domination. King Jean, who did England the inestimable service of losing 'Normandy', might well have been remembered as the genial monarch who put England back onto the road to regaining her inheritance. Yet that is not what happened.

English nationalist history has always been dominated first by a reluctance to look beyond the Isles and secondly by the need to demonstrate a permanent attachment to the growth of 'Liberty'. So Magna Carta is big; and King Jean has to be bad. What is more, the people who cultivated the theme of disinheritance in England did not often apply it to the other countries of the Isles. The Irish certainly thought that Ireland had been disinherited by the Plantagenet Conquest. The Welsh thought that Wales had been disinherited by Edouard I. But in later years the English rarely reflected on the fact that England's policy of expansion involved the disinheritance of others. Edouard I, after all, was a fine, far-sighted king who was only trying to accelerate the formation of the United Kingdom.

For much of modern history, British perceptions of the Middle Ages suffered from a large blind-spot. The centrality of the Church to medieval life could not be overlooked. But the fact that the ecclesiastical provinces in England, Ireland, Scotland, and Wales formed part of a grand international universal Catholic community was seriously underplayed. The cathedrals of England were presented as national achievements, as if Canterbury, Wells, or York did not belong in the same company as Cologne, Chartres, or Milan. England's greatest churchmen have often been dressed up in English garb, whilst in reality they were executives of a multinational spiritual firm. If one examines the Archbishops of Canterbury from the time of the Conqueror to that of Edouard II, for example, one finds that they were predominantly either foreigners or English-born clerics with substantial foreign experience. Prelates like Thomas à Becket or Walter Reynolds, whose life and careers were limited to England, were rarely the most effective.

By the same token, the international character of the religious orders, which played such a vital role in the social, educational, and economic life of the Middle Ages, was not always recognized. The standard survey of the subject was not published until after the Second World War. In his Epilogue, Professor Dom David Knowles

compared the Dissolution of the Monasteries during the Reformation in England to the Revolution in France and talked of 'a spectre
that defied exorcism':

> In a still more powerful way, the ghost of medieval monasticism
> remained and remains to haunt this island. The grey walls and
> broken cloisters, the . . . bare ruin'd choirs, where late the sweet
> birds sang, speak more eloquently for the past than any his-
> torian would dare, and pose for every beholder questions that
> words cannot answer.[87]

The European dimension to England's internal affairs was one of
many things that the Reformation destroyed.

Had later history followed a different course, Nicholas Breakspear might conceivably have become the most famous medieval
Englishman of all. Possibly born in St Albans, where his widowed
father entered the Benedictine monastery, probably in the reign
of William Rufus, Breakspear left England as a lad, and went to
study at Arles. Rising through the ranks of the ecclesiastical hierarchy, he was made Abbot of the Canonry of St Rufus at Valence,
and in 1146 Cardinal-Archbishop of Albano. Sent as legate to the
infant churches in Scandinavia, he gained the reputation of 'the
Apostle of the North'. He ascended the throne of St Peter in the
same year as Henri Plantagenêt ascended the throne of England. As
things stand, this is not considered a particularly memorable
achievement.

For the tradition in England until well into the twentieth century
was to minimize if not to deny completely the country's long
association with the Papacy. From Thomas Cromwell's preambles
(see page 456, below) to Bishop Stubbs' Charters and beyond,
English Protestant historians worked to project post-Reformation
assumptions onto their descriptions of pre-Reformation England. In
particular, they sought to inflate both the supposed independence of
the English monarchy and the supposedly national character of the
English medieval Church. To this end, their contentious interpretations of Becket's death in the twelfth century and of the various

Statutes of Praemunire, regarding control of clerical finance, in the fourteenth, served a preconceived purpose. These episodes could not be properly treated, writes a recent analyst of the historiography, 'Until the whole context had been set right, until medieval England was seen, at last, as a self-conscious part of a greater whole – the Christian community of Europe.'[88]

The essentially Catholic and theocratic parameters of the medieval world-view are best preserved in literature. The monk and the nun from Chaucer's *Prologue*, for example, were timeless figures, who could have been observed in the Isles at any time between the sixth and the sixteenth centuries:

> Ther was also a Nonne, a Prioresse,
> That of hir smylyng was ful symple and coy;
> Hir gretteste ooth was but by Seinte Loy;
> And she was cleped madame Eglentyne.
> Ful weel she soong the service dyvyne,
> Entuned in hir nose ful semely;
> And Frenssh she spak ful faire and fetisly,
> After the scole of Stratford atte Bowe,
> For Frenssh of Parys was to hire unknowe.
> At mete wel ytaught was she with alle;
> She leet no morsel from hir lippes falle,
> Ne wette hir fyngres in hir sauce depe;
> Wel koudeshe carie a morsel and wel kepe
> That no drope ne fille upon hire brest.
> In curteisie was set ful muchel hir lest.
> Hir over-lippe wyped she so clene
> That in hir coppe ther was no ferthyng sene
> Of grecem whan she dronken hadde hir draughte.
> Ful semely after hir mete she raughte.
> And sikerly she was of greet desport,
> And ful plesaunt, and amyable of port,
> And peyned hire to countrefete cheere
> Of court, and to been estatlich of manere,
> And to ben holden digne of reverence.

> But for to speken of hire conscience,
> She was so charitable and so pitous
> She wolde wepe, if that she sagh a mous
> Kaught in a trappe, if it were deed or bledde.
> Of smale houndes hadde she that she fedde
> With rasted flessh, or milk and wastel-breed.
> But soore wepte she if oon of hem were deed,
> Or if men smoot it with a yerde smerte;
> And al was conscience and tendre herte.
> Ful semyly hir wympul pynched was,
> Hir nose tretys, hir eyen greye as glas,
> Hir mouth ful smal, and therto softe and reed.
> But sikerly she hadde a fair forheed;
> It was almoost a spanne brood, I trowe;
> For, hardily, she was nat undergrowe.
> Ful fetys was hir cloke, as I was war.
> Of smal coral aboute hire arm she bar
> A peire of bedes, gauded al with grene,
> And thereon heng a brooch of gold ful sheene,
> On which ther was first write a crowned A,
> And after *Amor vincit omnia*.[89]

Chaucer's pilgrims, of course, were making for the shrine of Thomas à Becket at Canterbury. Becket's shrine had been growing, since the late twelfth century, into England's premier place of popular pilgrimage. During the Reformation, it was demolished without trace. Nothing says more about the gulf separating modern from medieval thinking.

Scotland alone escaped conquest by the early Plantagenets. So the first three decades of the fourteenth century became the classic era of Scottish independence, celebrated by Scots at the time and ever since. Robert the Bruce, the victor of Bannockburn, was set on a pedestal as Scotland's national hero. The panegyrics began shortly after his death:

> A! Fredome is a noble thing!
> Fredome mays man to haiff liking;
> Fredome all solace to man giffis;
> He levys at es that frely levys!
> A noble hart may haiff nane es,
> Na ellys nocht that may him ples,
> Gyff fredome failyhe: for fre liking
> Is yharnyt our all othir thing . . .[90]

Four hundred years after John Barbour, the Scots national bard, Robbie Burns was praising the national heroes in similar vein:

> Scots, wha hae wi' Wallace bled,
> Scots, wham Bruce has aften led,
> Welcome to your gory bed
> 　　　Or to victorie!
> Now's the day, and now's the hour:
> See the front o' battle lour,
> See approach proud Edward's power –
> 　　　Chains and slaverie!
>
> . . .
>
> Lay the proud usurpers low!
> Tyrants fall in every foe!
> Liberty's in every blow!
> 　　　Let us do, or die![91]

Burns, who detested the Union with England, was writing on an ebbing tide of Scots national feeling. During the long heyday of the British Empire, memories of Scotland's medieval triumphs were held in check. But two hundred years after Burns, when Scots patriotism revived, there was only one period of history which could provide the focus for Scots pride:

> O flower of Scotland
> When will we see
> Your like again,
> That fought and died for

Your wee bit hill and glen
>> And stood against him
>> Proud Edward's army
>> And sent him homeward
>> Tae think again.[92]

CHAPTER SEVEN

THE ENGLISHED ISLES

1326 to 1603

THE HUNDRED YEARS WAR, 1337–1453

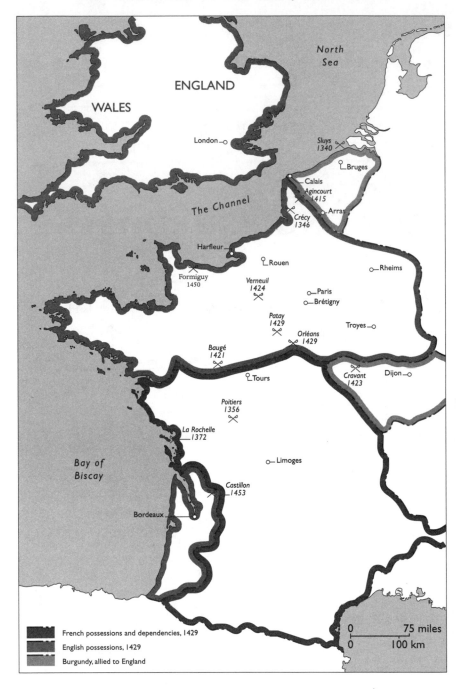

North
Sea

ENGLAND

WALES

London—o

Sluys
1340

Bruges

Calais
Agincourt
1415

The Channel

Crécy
1346

Arras

Harfleur—

Rouen

Rheims

Formiguy
1450

Verneuil
1424

Paris
Brétigny

Patay
1429

Troyes—o

Baugé
1421

Orléans
1429

Tours

Cravant
1423

Dijon—o

Poitiers
1356

La Rochelle
—1372

Limoges

Bay of
Biscay

Castillon
—1453

Bordeaux—

French possessions and dependencies, 1429

English possessions, 1429

Burgundy, allied to England

| 0 | 75 miles |
| 0 | 100 km |

AMIENS (PICARDIE), 6 JUNE 1329. In the choir of the cathedral, Edouard III, Plantagenêt, King of England, paid homage to the newly crowned King of France, Philippe VI de Valois. At the time, 'Edouard de Windsor' was barely sixteen years old. Philippe, a close relative, was thirty-five. The ceremony took place before the high altar, under the splendid Gothic vault constructed in the previous century, and beside the reliquary of St John the Baptist's head, which had been brought to Amiens from Constantinople in 1206. It was preceded by the customary ritual protestations. The Seigneur Milo de Noyers protested that his master, the King of France, had no mind to cede any of the rights held by his predecessors. The Bishop of Lincoln protested that *his* master, the King of England, would not renounce any of the rights that were due to him. The Chamberlain of France then proposed that the act of *hommage simple* should go ahead, subject only to those (undefined) reservations. Kneeling, head bared, the King of England said, '*Vraiement*,' 'Truly.' 'The hands of the King of England were placed between the hands of the King of France, and the latter kissed the King of England on the mouth.' Finally, Edouard, speaking in his native French, pronounced the oath of homage in line with an agreed formula:

> I become your man for the Duchy of Guyenne and its appurtenances
> . . . as Duke of Guyenne and Peer of France, according to the form
> of peace made between your predecessors and ours, [and] according
> to the services which we and our ancestors, Kings of England and
> Dukes of Guyenne, have done for the Duchy to your predecessors,
> Kings of France.[1]

To the participants, the ceremony must have seemed almost routine. It was something which every King of England had performed, whether for

Aquitaine, for Anjou, or for Normandy, since the days of Conqueror. Indeed, Edouard III had already performed a similar act of homage in 1325 with the previous French king, Charles IV.

The ritual protestations formed an essential part of the proceedings. They would enable both parties to argue that the act of homage had been invalid if at some future date insuperable differences arose. Yet the ceremony was an important event in itself. It gave public expression to the relative standing of the two monarchs within the feudal order. Every English king paid homage to the King of France.

The homage of Amiens took place at the insistence of the French. Knowing that Edouard III had challenged his assumption of the throne, Philippe VI had wanted to secure his English cousin's loyalty as soon as possible. Yet the act of simple homage was only the first stage in the feudal process. It was usually followed by an act of 'liege hommage' which bound the parties together not merely as 'lord and man' but as partners in a detailed contract of rights and obligations, including military service. In the following year, therefore, Philippe VI called on Edouard to return to France and to commit himself to the stricter terms of liege homage. Edouard baulked; he temporized; he prevaricated. On 31 March 1331 he wrote a letter containing the following words:

> We recognize that the homage which we did at Amiens to the King of France was, is, and ought to be accounted liege homage; and we promise him faith and loyalty, as Duke of Guyenne, Peer of France and Count of Ponthieu and Montreuie.[2]

This was a clever legal gambit, but not enough to give the French full satisfaction. Though proposed as a makeshift solution, it marked the passing of an era. It turned out to be the last occasion in history when an English king was willing to accept the status of a feudal inferior to the King of France. A major change was in the making in the history both of England and of the Isles.

Having squared his feudal superior, however, the young King had next to square his relations with the Church. He had come to the throne during 'the Babylonian Captivity' of the popes in Avignon. To some degree, the weakness of the Papacy enhanced his own position; but it caused endless complications that were best avoided. The Church, after all, was a force to be reckoned with. The English bishops played a central role in baronial politics; and the English monasteries were at the height of their number, wealth, and influence.

As it happened, the see of Canterbury fell vacant shortly after the young King was crowned. Archbishop Walter Reynolds, a former royal clerk and treasurer, who had presided at the coronation, had been notoriously corrupt; and his death was no great loss. But the choice of a successor posed problems. The Regents wanted to appoint the subservient Bishop of Lincoln. They wanted even more to prevent the appointment of the able Bishop of Winchester, John Stratford. In the end, by way of a compromise, they agreed to accept a seriously undistinguished canon of Chichester, Simon de Meopham. The Canterbury chapter was persuaded to support de Meopham's elevation; and he was then packed off to Avignon to obtain the belated approval of Pope John XXII.

De Meopham's five-year tenure as England's primate left little trace in the history books; but it provides a brief illustration of the international ecclesiastical web in which the medieval kingdom of England was so thoroughly enmeshed. Like both of his successors at Canterbury, Stratford 1333–48, and the learned *doctor profundus*, Thomas Bradwardine in 1349, Archbishop de Meopham had been a student at Merton College, Oxford. But he was no scholar, and he was no shining administrator. So while Bishop Stratford launched himself into a career as royal chancellor, the new Archbishop tried to put some order into his see. His task was thankless. When he convened a convocation of the clergy from the province, he found that the expected grant for the King was refused. When he tried to execute his duty as visitor to the diocese of Exeter, he found Exeter's gates barred against him. And when he rashly picked a quarrel with the powerful Prior of St Augustine's in Canterbury, he found himself summoned to the court of the papal commissioner. When he refused to attend, he was fined £700, and was then judged contumacious. He died excommunicate, and the monks of St Augustine's opposed his Christian burial. The English church, like the English king, had a long way to go before enjoying complete freedom of manoeuvre.

In the meantime, Edouard III came of age. During the baronial wars of his father's reign he had become the helpless instrument of his mother, Queen Isabella, and of her paramour, Roger Mortimer. Isabella and Mortimer had arranged his marriage to Philippa d'Hainault, like that of his infant sister Joanne to the infant King of Scotland, David II. They had dictated the rapprochement with France and the acceptance of Scotland's independence; and they had had his father killed. But now he was ready to stand on his own two feet. 1330 saw the birth of his son and heir, Edouard de Woodstock (d. 1376), known to later history as the Black Prince, and the fall of Mortimer. The young King captured Mortimer in person, having broken into Nottingham Castle through a secret underground tunnel, then took him to London to be hanged at Tyburn as a traitor. Isabella was gracefully asked to retire.

Edouard III inherited the towering physique and personality of his royal grandfather. A knight's knight, and a lady's man, he possessed all the chivalrous virtues and vices which his wretched bisexual father had lacked. A champion jouster and enthusiastic warrior, he soon established himself as the natural leader of the barons. His amorous depredations, which in a later age might have given him the label of 'rapist', came as welcome relief to a court scandalized in the previous reign by the King's gay dalliances and by the suppression of the Templars on false charges of heresy, wizardry, and pederasty. His love of pomp and pageantry provided the country with a sense of purpose and unity. Yet after 1331 the differences between England and France multiplied fast. They arose from a further round of civil wars in Scotland, the close friendship of England and Flanders, and the long-running question of the French succession.

Scotland's civil wars flared anew thanks to the old rivalry of Bruce and Baliol. The accession of the infant David II de Bruce (r. 1329–71) was challenged by the son of 'Toom Tabard', Edward Baliol. The former, who benefited from papal recognition of Scotland's independence, was the first Scottish monarch to be both crowned *and* anointed, his agents in Rome having overcome traditional English opposition to a Scottish ceremony of unction. Before that, he had earned the unkind epithet of 'David Drip-on-altar'. The nickname derived from an incident which occurred at a meeting of the Scots and English barons at Berwick, where they had publicly burned Edouard I's charter granting Scotland to John de

Baliol as a perpetual English fief. The child-King was then formally betrothed to Edouard III's sister Joanna: 'On being dedicated at the altar, the child, who was suffering from diarrhoea, dirtied himself. At this, the Scotsman James Douglas said to his friends: "I fear he will besmirch the whole kingdom of Scotland." '[3]

It was a poor augury. As for Edward Baliol, he enjoyed the support of all the lords and magnates exiled during the previous reign, and entered Scotland at the head of an invasion force. Edouard III calculated that England could not lose if he supported both contenders. So he gave assistance first to his brother-in-law David de Bruce and then to Edward Baliol, who in 1332–3 had his moments of glory first at a coronation in Scone and then, at Halidon Hill, a major victory. In due course, in 1334, Baliol paid formal homage to Edouard III at Newcastle. The price for English assistance, however, was pitched too high. At Newcastle, Edouard III insisted not only that the five southern counties of Scotland be ceded to England, but also that he be restored to Edouard I's old title of 'Lord Paramount'. This united all the Scots against him. Both Baliol and de Bruce took refuge abroad. In desperation, David II paid homage to Philippe VI. The Scottish Douglases and the Northumbrian Percys waged battle over the borders. Peace was gradually restored by the feats of David II's half-brother, Walter, sixth hereditary High Steward of Scotland. The Stewards or 'Stewarts' were only one step away from the supreme prize.

England's friendship with Flanders had been strengthened by the dynastic link between the Plantagenet King and the House of Hainault. But it was based on older and harder economic interest, especially on the growing importance of the wool trade. Wool cloth was fast becoming not only the chief manufacture of England but also a leading item in the King's revenue, 'the flower and strength . . . and blood of England'. Fine English wool was in great demand in the great Flemish textile cities of Bruges, Ghent, and Ypres, where it competed with the previously dominant supply of merino wool from Spain. Edouard III made efforts to stimulate both home production and the export trade. He and his courtiers wore only English cloth. With the help of his Queen, he brought in Flemish weavers, who were settled in Norwich and in London; and he

Table 5. The costs of a typical wool sample, 1337

	(per sack, approximate)	
Cost of 205 sacks of wool bought in parts in Lindsey	£40 10d	3s 10d
Cartage, packing, storage, drying, re-packing, wrapping materials, porterage, hoistage, lighterage, freightage, shipping, pilotage, armed guard and port dues:		34s 4½d
Value of wool lost from damaged sacks		2s 4¾d
For the expenses of [William de la Pole's] 5 merchants: Richard Sletholme, John Bole, Henry of Manfield, William Keyser, and Nicholas Hustweyt: from 12 September to 5 May, [regnal years] 9–10	£17 6d	1s 8½d
Paid to the collectors of royal custom at Hull.		26s 8d
Total		£3 11s 11¼d[4]

imposed strict controls on wool exports, reintroducing the Ordinance of the Staple (1313), which Isabella and Mortimer had abandoned. The policy of creating home and foreign 'staples', or trading centres enjoying royal monopoly, was still in flux and would not be stabilized until the Statute of the Staple (1354), which fixed the main wool staple at Calais. In the meantime, a number of different outlets were used. Judging by the costs and difficulties which the transport of goods involved in medieval times, the profits must have been considerable.

The accounts of one sample consignment, which was sent in September 1337 from Hull to Dordrecht by William de la Pole, a merchant financier and Baron of the Exchequer, shows something of what was involved. Calculations are necessarily rather tentative. But the journey by land and sea of 205 sacks of Lincolnshire wool from Lindsey via Barton-on-Humber lasted no less than 235 days; and transport costs (less customs) totalled a staggering 38s 5¾d per sack, a figure more than ten times the original purchase price. (See above.)

The enormous customs payment of 26s 8d per sack raised the total outlay on the consignment including the purchase price to £737 15s 8¾d. This meant that to make even the most marginal profit, William de la Pole's merchants would have had to sell their wool at a figure not less than eighteen times what they paid for it. Clearly there were wool traders in Dordrecht who were willing to pay it.

Edouard III's claim to the throne of France was not capricious. It was based on his position as grandson of Philippe IV, and might well have been judged superior to that of Philippe de Valois, who was Philippe IV's nephew. But it was extremely inconvenient politically, and would have required the French barons to accept the final triumph of the Plantagenets after nearly two centuries of rivalry. It had been put to the Parlement of Paris in 1328 and rejected. Initially, Edouard had no choice, under his mother's tutelage, other than to recognize the Valois. Yet the limitations placed on England's freedom of action, particularly in Scotland and Flanders, led to a gradual rethink. At first, no overt declarations were made. As late as 1336, Edouard seems to have 'crossed secretly in France' to try and settle matters privately. No reference was made to the King's claim in the manifesto of grievances which Edouard issued early in 1337.[5] But when the Bishop of Lincoln was told to travel to Paris and to call Philippe VI to his face *le soi-disant Roi de France*, the 'Self-proclaimed King of France', the offence was deliberate.

The conflict between France and England came to a head in the summer of 1337. The French would not grant the English a free hand in Scotland. Indeed, by taking David II under their protection they were openly obstructing English hopes of reversing the gains of Robert the Bruce. For their part, the English could not bring themselves to abandon their partners in Flanders, let alone to do their duty and serve their sovereign's liege lord. So Edouard III was declared in Paris to be in contempt. War was the only resort. Philippe VI opened the lists by invading Gascony.

Edouard III threw himself into the conflict with gusto.

At that same juncture, in 1337, Edouard de Woodstock, Prince of Wales, was raised to the lands and dignity of 'Duke of Cornwall'. It was the first dukedom in English history, initiating a new, top layer of the peerage that was equivalent to the 'princes of the fleur-de-lis' in France. Here was yet another sign that the English monarchy was beginning to see itself as equal to its French counterpart. Henceforth, the leading princes of the blood royal would normally be given their dukedoms; and would become the most frequent contenders for the throne. In 1362, Edouard III's second and third surviving sons, Lionel d'Anvers (1338–68) and Jean de Gand (John of Ghent or 'Gaunt', 1340–99), would be created respectively Duke of Clarence and Duke of Lancaster. The latter was the direct ancestor of the House of Lancaster that was to dominate the monarchy in the next century. The rival House of York was to trace its origins to Edouard III's fourth surviving son, Edmund de Langley (1341–1402), who would not be created Duke of York until after his father's death.

It is essential to stress that France in the mid-fourteenth century was a very different creature from the kingdom faced by Henri II a hundred and fifty years before. The France which had taken the field at Bouvines was a small northern kingdom, whose Capetian kings controlled only a fraction of its nominal territory. It exercised direct control over an area of some 115,000 km^2, which was similar to that of England but considerably inferior to that of the Plantagenet Empire as a whole. Even after Bouvines, where it recovered most of the provinces north of the Loire, it still possessed very few lands within the Mediterranean watershed. Yet the thirteenth and early fourteenth centuries had seen a dramatic series of expansions. Louis IX planted the French flag on the Mediterranean shore. In 1271, the French took control of all Languedoc west of the Rhône, in 1311 of the metropolis of Lyons, and in 1348 of Dauphiné as far the ridge of the southern Alps. At some 300,000 km^2, therefore, the realms of Edouard III's rival, Philippe VI, were twice the size of England, and significantly exceeded the much reduced holdings of the Plantagenets. The balance of power had shifted. Thanks to the Channel, and to a lack of naval transport, it was unclear whether the Valois would be able to bring his military advantage to bear on the Isles. At the same time, the Plantagenets could never really hope to conquer France, still less to hold it down permanently. They were condemned from the outset to a strategy of aggressive disruption, weakening France by constant raids and expeditions, sowing dissension among the French magnates, and forming endless coalitions with France's other neighbours. England was hard to defeat. But she was incapable of delivering the knock-out blow. So long as the English were not given a taste of their own medicine, they could prolong the indecisive war indefinitely.

Edouard's first response to the outbreak of war was to contact his in-

laws in Hainault and to organize an anti-French coalition. And from 1337,
English envoys resided in Valenciennes, the capital of Hainault, distribut-
ing largesse and courting the princes of the Low Countries. Everyone took
the English King's money. £60,000 bought the good intentions of the
Emperor Louis IV of Bavaria and the title of Imperial Vicar-General of the
Holy Roman Empire. In theory, 129,000 'helmed men' were to be made
available. But there were few signs of solid military assistance. In 1338, a
small English force was driven back from Brabant, and further largesse
had to be distributed in order to encourage the allies. The Flemings, in
particular, were slow to respond. Threatened with a papal interdict if they
openly rebelled against the King of France, they argued that Edouard III
would have to claim the French throne formally to facilitate their decision.
So in 1340 Edouard III took the fateful step. He accepted the lordship of
Flanders and declared himself to be the lawful King of France. He changed
his coat-of-arms accordingly, quartering the fleur-de-lys of France with
the three lions passant gardant of the Plantagenets. He had launched a
claim that would not be rescinded until 1801. All English monarchs up to
Queen Anne, and all British monarchs up to George III, were to bear the
French title among their honours.

The assumption of France's royal title was contained in a proclamation
dated 8 February 1340 which Edouard III issued at Ghent and which was
intended to be affixed to all the church doors in France:

Eduardus, Dei Gratiae Rex Franciae et Angliae, Dominus Hiberniae
. . . Since, therefore, the kingdom of France has by divine disposition
devolved upon us by the clearest right owing to the death of Charles
of noted memory, brother german to our lady mother, and [since]
the Lord Philip of Valois, son of the king's uncle and thus further
removed from the royal blood . . . has intruded himself by force into
the kingdom while we were of tender years, and holds that kingdom
against God and Justice, . . . we have recognized our right to the
kingdom . . . resolving . . . to do justice to all men, . . . to revive the
good laws and customs which were in force in the time of Louis, our
predecessor, . . . and to cast out the usurper when the opportunity
shall seem most propitious.[6]

This proclamation had to be accompanied by an English statute providing an express guarantee 'that our realm of England and the people of the same, of whatsoever estate or condition they be, shall not in any time to come be put in subjection to us, nor to our heirs and successors as kings of France'.[7]

Naval supremacy is a very different concept in the Middle Ages. Neither England nor France possessed sufficient ships of sufficient power to maintain a year-round, all-weather patrol on the Channel. The French alone possessed a small professional navy, consisting by 1336 of thirteen war-galleys built in the Clos des Gallées at Rouen and at La Rochelle, supplemented by twelve transferred from the Mediterranean, and in 1338 twenty hired from Genoa and seventeen from Monaco.[8] In time of war the English could only rely on converted merchant cogs impressed for service from the Cinque Ports, London, and Southampton. Even so, it was inevitable that each side would endeavour to gain the upper hand on the seas. Under the pretext of preparing a crusade, Philippe VI had steadily assembled a fleet in the estuary of the Zwin at Sluys (Écluse) in Flanders: after a series of successful English raids, especially that of January 1340 which destroyed eighteen galleys in Boulogne, he retained four French and two Genoese galleys, and twenty-two barges, with two hundred and two ships.[9] In June 1340, when the English believed that a cross-Channel invasion was being prepared, they attacked with fury. In the morning of the 24th, they bore down on the French ships, which were chained together for safety 'like a line of castles'. Archers firing with the sun behind them inflicted the initial damage; whilst hand-to-hand fighting continued through the hours of darkness, illuminated by the glare of burning vessels. In all 190 ships were captured (the galleys, which had not moored, escaped). Over 16,000 men were killed. So many men drowned, it was said that the fish could have learned French. In strategic terms, the Battle of Sluys (1340) arguably held a more significant place in the unfolding sequence of events than all the better known and much publicized land battles at Crécy (1346), Poitiers (1356), or Agincourt (1415). Sluys did not stop the French from raiding England's south coast and burning English ports, which they did regularly. It did not prevent French or indeed Castilian warships from sailing up and down the Channel. But it killed all ideas in France for a major cross-Channel expedition. It largely determined that the Hundred Years War would be fought on French territory and not in the Isles.

By the end of 1340, however, Edouard III was bankrupt. He had debts to the tune of £300,000 – a sum equal to perhaps ten times his annual income. He could not return from the Continent until he had sold part of the crown jewels to pay the troops. Yet this early financial crisis had long-term benefits. It forced him to match his ambitions to his means; and it encouraged the ever closer partnership of King and Parliament that was to become the hallmark of English governance. The King would never escape from the clutches of his Italian bankers; and parliamentary taxation would often place intolerable burdens on the backs of the peasantry. But the prosecution of the war against France created a long-running national enterprise which demanded the support of all classes. Once the immediate crisis was eased, England was to prove capable of sustaining the military effort almost indefinitely. As early as 1338, in the Walton Ordinances, provision had been made to make regular financial estimates, 'to enquire into the extent of the King's debts and liabilities and to estimate the revenue necessary to meet them' – in other words to prepare a budget. One of the few such rudimentary financial exercises to leave documentary evidence dates from a slightly later decade when the system would already have been in operation for over twenty years. (See Table 6, overleaf.)

The prominence of the wool trade is self-evident. The sources of income in the estimates did not mention parliamentary taxation, or other means such as loans and ransoms whereby the deficit might be covered. But it shows that the concept of financial control was operating.

The state of war, the growth of trade, and the efforts to bring order to the King's finances all increased the urgency of reforming the coinage. By 1343, there was a serious shortage of the silver pennies which had been circulating since the last major reforms under Edouard I. The old silver groat, worth 4d, had been abandoned; and the smaller units, the halfpenny and farthing, were virtually unobtainable. So in January 1344, the seven royal mints launched England's first gold coinage. A gold

Table 6. Royal revenues and expenses of Edward III (1362–3)

Les reuenues et despens notre seignour le roi en lan xxxvij^me

Viscountez, fermes et aultres reuenuez Dengleterre [*shrievalties, farms and other English revenues*]	3,984 marȝ. 8s. 4d.
Item les custumez et subsides de leynes en touz les portz Dengleterre [*Customs from wool*]	46,910. marȝ.
Le hanaper en la chauncellerie amonte par an [*in the hamper*]	<u>2,400. marȝ.</u>
La somme totale qe remeynt	54,294. marȝ. 10s. 5d.
Les despensez del an passe amountent [*The expenses of the past year amount to*]	136,190. marȝ. 12s. 2d.
Et issint amounte la summe des paiementz outre la summe receu [*Hence total payments exceed receipts by*]	<u>82,896. marȝ. 1s. 9d.</u>[10]

'Florin', designed by two Florentine goldsmiths, was issued at a value of 72d. But it was withdrawn almost immediately in favour of the fine 'Ship Noble' worth 80d. The latter coin depicted the King with drawn sword in a two-castled ship. It presumably commemorated the victory at Sluys. It was accompanied by half-nobles and quarter nobles, and in the next decade by long-running silver groats and half-groats. After several years of severe fluctuation, the gold–silver ratio settled down at 12–1, and the currency remained undisturbed until well into the next century.

The victory at Sluys gave a period of respite. But in the mid-1340s the English court was preparing itself again for a general military confrontation with France. Failure to act would inevitably lead to the permanent loss of Gascony. What is more, Philippe VI was meddling in Brittany and, by mending his fences with the Emperor, was threatening England's allies in the Low Countries. In 1342–3, a small English force was sent to Brittany to support the de Montfort duke against his Valois rival. But the preparations were not solely military. Many obstacles had to be overcome before the ground was cleared for a full-scale Continental expedition. In Parliament, for example, the King had become embroiled in a dispute over his dismissal of all the country's sheriffs. In 1343, he had to accept the nullification of earlier acts on this subject, and he had to work with a Parliament now formally divided into two separate 'houses' of Lords and Commons. Given the perilous state of the King's private finances, harmony in Parliament was a precondition for a warlike posture.

In the royal court, Edouard III sought to strengthen the collective will of the barons by cultivating their chivalrous instincts. In 1344, after a tournament at Windsor, he staged a re-enactment of King Arthur's Round Table, starring in the role of Arthur. (In this, he was repeating a similar event which his grandfather had laid on at Nefyn in 1284 following the conquest of Wales.) But he pressed on with plans to found a permanent Order of Chivalry dedicated to St George. Windsor Castle was refurbished and the foundations laid for the home for the Order's ceremonies at St George's Chapel. In due course, twenty-six knights were inducted as founder members, the Order took the curious name of 'the Garter', and the still more curious motto of HONI SOIT QUI MAL Y PENSE (shamed be he who evil thinks). The name and the motto were said to derive from an incident and a quip when the King's mistress, the Countess of Salisbury, lost her garter during a dance, and the King, picking it up, uttered the medieval French equivalent of 'No nasty insinuations, please.' It became an in-joke for the insiders of the royal circle.

Finally, in the summer of 1346, Edouard III was ready to mount the long-awaited invasion of France. He sailed from the Solent in early July with a thousand ships and a huge retinue of knights attended by 15,000 men-at-arms and archers. He officially set off for Gascony but landed at La Hogue in Normandy. This indicates either a deception plan worthy of the D-Day landings or an opportunism that would follow the wind in any direction so long as the French were attacked as soon as possible. A month's progress through the French countryside saw the English force trailed by an army many times its own size; and the march had to turn north in an attempt to regain one of the Channel ports. On 26 August Edouard III drew up his lines near the village of Crécy-en-Ponthieu in the district which had once formed his mother's dowry. Fifteen or sixteen overeager charges by the French cavalry failed to disturb the English position, whilst deadly showers of English arrows wreaked havoc among the mailed knights. French casualties were probably as high as at Sluys. One could say, with a little bravado, that the worms learned French. For the English had adopted the unchivalrous tactic of killing rather than capturing their foes. (No matter that a similar slaughter of English knights would have given the worms yet another French lesson.) Edouard's army was able to withdraw intact. Beyond that, the results of the battle were rather meagre. Crécy marks an important point in the evolution of military technology and in the decline of the feudal host. But it didn't significantly alter the imbalance in the potential strength of the two sides; it didn't remove the French from Gascony; and it didn't even force a truce. Only an Englishman would think of listing it among 'the decisive battles of world history'.[11]

The principal consequence of Crécy was to facilitate the capture of nearby Calais, and thereby to give lasting effect to the earlier naval victory at Sluys. And that was no trifling matter. The fortified port with its double walls of towers and ditches withstood a merciless siege and blockade for eleven months. Starvation forced it to submit on 1 August 1347. The French governor and six of the leading burghers, barefoot and haltered, were made to carry the city's keys to Edouard in person, and to beg forgiveness. Disinclined to mercy, the English King is said to have relented only at the tearful imprecations of his pregnant queen. The citizens were then expelled, to be replaced by English settlers and soldiers. Calais become 'a little piece of England', the first English colony. In conjunction with the port of Dover, it permitted English ships to command the straits whichever way the wind was blowing; and it provided a near-impregnable base for further expeditions into France. It was to remain in English hands until 1558.

With the English king embroiled in France, the French called on their Scots allies to attack England. So David II, only recently restored to his throne, marched south. On 17 October 1346, at Neville's Cross near Durham, his troops were assaulted by the same deadly display of Welsh-style archery that had won the day at Crécy. David II was captured, and held prisoner for eleven years while he raised a crushing ransom. In his absence, Walter le Steward's son, Robert, served as Guardian of the Realm. 'England's Back Door' was well and truly shut.

By 1346, a still more deadly danger was advancing. The Black Death had already reached Europe from the East. A Genoese galley carried its cargo of infected rats from Crimea to Sicily. Thence the bubonic plague spread with devastating rapidity. Within four years, perhaps a third of all Europeans were dead. It was an unprecedented catastrophe. It reached Paris in the summer of 1348, England and Wales in the winter of that year, Scotland and Ireland in 1349. It even forced the warring French and English to call a truce. Its causes were not understood. It could only be explained as God's retribution for human sin. Its consequences included deep psychological trauma, crowds of penitent flagellants, widespread pogroms, especially in Germany, and irreversible social changes, especially in England. One of the bravest attempts to describe it was made by a Welsh poet:

> We see death coming into our midst like black smoke, a plague which cuts off the young, a rootless phenomenon which has no mercy for fair countenance ... Woe is me of the shilling of the armpit ... It is of the form of an apple, like the head of an onion, a small boil that spares no one. Great is the seething, like a burning cinder, a grievous thing of ashy colour ... They are similar to the seeds of black peas, broken fragments of brittle sea-coal ... cinders of the peelings of the cockle weed, a mixed multitude, a black plague like half pence, like berries.'[12]

It is hard to imagine the level of shock experienced by countries which had lost a third of their people. Historians most usually concentrate on the socio-economic turmoil: the sudden rise in prices, the shortage of labour, and the Statute of Labourers (1351) whereby the English Parliament endeavoured to control wage inflation. No European monarch, however, perished in the plague; and the immediate political impact on the Isles was slight. Some of the most interesting and long-lasting changes took place in the realm of language and culture.

Culture, however, must be understood in the widest sense. The combination of the Black Death and the French Wars affected English social culture, for example, in some curious ways. Some time after the Black Death, Edouard III noticed that the supply of his battle-winning archers was drying up. Men had taken to playing worthless games. So, with some considerable delay, he wrote to all his sheriffs:

The King to the Sheriff of Kent. Whereas the people of our realm,
. . . usually practised in their games the art of archery, whereby . . .
we gained not a little help in our wars, by God's favour: and now
. . . the people amuse themselves with throwing stones . . . or playing
handball or football or 'stick ball' [*pila cacularis*] or hockey or cock-
fighting . . . so that the kingdom becomes destitute of archers. We
. . . order you, that in all places in your shire . . . everyone in the
shire on festival days . . . shall learn and exercise himself in the art
of archery, and use for his games bows and arrows, or crossbows
and bolts, . . . forbidding all and single to meddle or toy in any way
with [those other] games . . . which are worthless, under pain of
imprisonment. By the King himself.[13]

Henceforth, the requirement for all the menfolk of England to meet on the
village green on their holidays and to practise their archery cannot have
failed to affect their collective outlook. The prime topic of conversation
during archery practice can only have been the state of the French wars,
and the likelihood of the men being called to military service. This, in
turn, can only have helped to foster patriotic attitudes. But for the Valois
King, and his ridiculous claim to the French throne, everyone could have
stayed at home to play *pila cacularis* (which has tentatively been identified
as cricket). Such considerations must surely have crossed the minds of the
gossips on the green when the French War restarted over the unresolved
problems of Aquitaine.

Ever since 1259, the old Duchy of Aquitaine which the Plantagenets
had acquired from Queen Aliénor (see Chapter Six) had been much
reduced. Although it still stretched from the Charente to the Pyrenees,
and still subsumed Gascony, it had lost important districts both to the
north in Poitou and in the south-west. Known to the French as Guyenne
– a medieval form of the Latin Aquitania – and to the English just as
Gascony, its territory swelled and shrank in line with fortunes of its
governors at Bordeaux. Its economic prosperity was closely linked to the
Bordeaux wine trade with England. Every year, the royal court of Edouard
III would import and consume up to 1,000 tons of 'Gascon wine'. In the
1350s the duchy was rocked by the rebellion of the Count of Armagnac,

who had declared his loyalty to the new King of France, Jean II le Bon (r. 1350–64). On 1 October 1355 the 'Black Prince', the newly created Prince of Aquitaine as well as Prince of Wales and Duke of Cornwall, sailed eagerly from Plymouth to sort him out.

Edouard de Woodstock, Prince of Wales, never set foot in Wales. He rarely visited his ducal castle of Restormel in Cornwall. He spent most of his active adult life as Lord Lieutenant of Gascony at Bordeaux. French sources called him 'un bon capiteine et un féroce pillard' (a good commander and ferocious plunderer). Edouard's son, Richard de Bordeaux (1367–1400), was to inherit the English throne. Edouard's brother, Jean de Gand, Duke of Lancaster, joined him in the wars of Gascony which in the 1360s would spill over the Pyrenees. Gand, who fathered thirteen children from three marriages, was deeply involved in Iberia. He became titular King of Castile and succeeded his brother as 'Prince of Aquitaine'. His descendants filled the fifteenth century, not only in the House of Lancaster, but equally in Portugal and Castile.

In the short term, the Black Prince's wars brought fame and glory. In 1355, he laid waste the County of Armagnac, burning first Carcassonne – a city larger than London – and then Narbonne. In 1356, he advanced northwards to the Loire, punishing all the people and places who had remained loyal to the Valois. On 19 September, at Nouailles near Poitiers, he won a famous victory in which the French king, Jean II, was taken into English captivity. Once again, the tactics of Crécy paid off hand-somely. In the long term, however, the English position proved unsustain-able. To pay for his wars, the Black Prince oppressed his subjects in Guyenne with merciless taxation and reprisals. He unwittingly prepared the ground for the French reconquest, much of which he would live to see in his embittered middle age.

Whenever the English tried to capitalize on their victories, they met repeated disillusionment. They seemed to enjoy every possible advantage. They had settled with the Scots, and in 1358 they saw France further weakened by the far-flung atrocities of the fearsome Jacquerie or 'peasant rising' and by Étienne Marcel's rebellion in Paris itself. They fixed Jean II's ransom at the astronomic figure of four million golden crowns (c. £700,000): and in 1359 they demanded the return of the Plantagenet homelands in Maine, Touraine, Normandy, and Anjou. Enforcing their demands was a different matter. Late in 1359 Edouard III and his sons set off from Calais, hoping to force their way into Reims for a coronation. But Reims was well defended, and a siege in a winter of heavy rains proved impractical. Followed by a baggage train of 12,000 carts, each pulled by three horses, and accompanied by teams of falconers and packs of hounds, so that they could live off the land, they ravaged the French countryside without mercy. They then marched on Paris only to find that the city had been pacified by the Dauphin. What is more, their armies were demoralized by a series of violent storms. So they were forced to negotiate. In a treaty signed at Brétigny near Chartres in May 1360, the English king agreed to lower the ransom demand to three million crowns. The French agreed to recognize Edouard III as the sovereign ruler of Guyenne. The treaty was solemnly blessed at a joint mass in Paris at Notre-Dame. But it, too, was to prove unenforceable.

In that same year, 1360, Master John Wyclif (c. 1329–84) was appointed Master of Balliol College, Oxford. This 'morning star of the Reformation' would soon be organizing the translation of the Bible into English. Also, £16 was paid from the royal exchequer for the release of a young English prisoner who had been captured by the French near Reims. The prisoner was one Geoffrey Chaucer (c. 1340–1400). He would make his poetical debut within the decade with *The Book of the Duchesse*, a long poem dedicated to Gaunt's late wife, Blanche de Lancastre, who had died from a recurrence of the bubonic plague:

> I have gret wonder, be this lyghte,
> How that I lyve, for day ne nyghte
> I may nat slepe wel nygh nought;
> . . .
> So when I saw I might not slepe
> Til now late, this other night,
> Upon my bedde I sat upright
> And bad oon reche me a book,

A romance, and he it me tok
To rede and drive the night away.[14]

Elsewhere in England, an obscure priest called William Langland (c. 1330–86) was about to complete his *Vision of Piers Plowman*, whose earliest known text is dated to 1362. Langland's Vision, or rather visions, were apparently conceived whilst wandering on the Malvern Hills. They reveal a deeply religious disposition disturbed by the social upheavals of the day. They plead for human charity, and foresee disaster, if each of the social estates does not keep to its divinely ordained function:

> In a somer sesoun, whanne softe was the sonne,
> I shop me in-to a shroud, as I a shep were;
> In abite as an ermyte, unholy of werkis,
> I wente wyde in this world, wondrs to here.
> But on a May morwenyng on Malverne hilles
> Me befel a ferly, of fairie me thoughte . . .[15]

> (*In a summer season, when soft was the sunlight,*
> *I shook on some shreds of shepherd clothing,*
> *And habited like a hermit, but not a holy one,*
> *Went wide in this world, watching for wonders.*
> *But on a May morning on a Malvern hill-top,*
> *A marvel befel me, as might a fairy-tale. . . .*)

Langland's poem is a fitting partner for the mystical religious writings such as the anonymous *Cloud of Unknowing* which probably dates from the same decade. Literary historians regard it as the centrepiece of the Alliterative Revival.

This arcane Revival refers to the re-emergence of a particular poetical style which had not been seen in England since late Anglo-Saxon times. Its real significance, however, lies less in the literary technique than in the extraordinary fact that works like *Piers Plowman* were written in a virtually new language. Although the Middle English of Langland, Chaucer, and Wyclif was clearly a derivative of the Old English used for literary purposes two or three centuries earlier, it differed greatly from its pre-Conquest ancestor. It was at least as far from the language of Alfred or Ælfric as modern English is from modern Dutch or German.

The re-emergence of English in a completely new form poses a wonderful puzzle for the philologists. Scholars hold varying views on the causes and timing and on the degree of continuity. But almost all agree that the very specific political and social conditions of the mid-fourteenth century were crucial. A new political climate had been formed by the prolonged wars with France and by a growing feeling that England's established French culture was no longer entirely appropriate for the ruling class. The growing assertiveness of the English-speaking lower classes was encouraged by the Black Death.

English historians of English culture tend to enthuse patriotically over these developments. 'For anyone who speaks English,' writes one, 'the most exciting thing about the period is not the drums and tramplings of the futile war with France, or the sorry strife of the peasants, or the divisions of religious sectaries, but the redemption of our language.'[16] Redemption is an emotive word. It suggests that English had been saved from slavery.

Contemporaries appear to have paid rather less attention to the linguistic revolution. Apart from a handful of literary texts read by a small sector of the tiny educated class, there were few visible signs of change. The royal court continued to speak French until the end of the century and beyond. The oldest surviving legal document in English was not drawn up until 1376. The oldest parliamentary document in English, a Petition for the Mercers' Company (1386), the oldest English will (1387), and the oldest English guild returns, from London and Norwich (1389), all date from after the Peasants' Revolt (1381). Richard II was said to have addressed Jack Cade's rebels in their native tongue. This does not change the fact, as observed by the French Ambassador, that the same 'Richard de Bordeaux' was himself a native French speaker.

Language is not something that can be learned overnight. It is obvious that a considerable time lag must ensue between changing intentions and changed effects. In 1363, for example, the Lord Chancellor was said to have opened a parliamentary session for the first time in English. That same session passed the so-called Statue of Pleadings: 'The King has ordained . . . that all pleas which shall be pleaded in any court whatsoever . . . shall be pleaded, shown, defended, answered, debated and judged in the English tongue, and that they shall be entered and enrolled in Latin.'[17] How soon the ordinance came into full effect is impossible to tell. One assumes that there could not have been any sudden transformation. Even so, the complexity of the overall linguistic picture is fascinating. After centuries of conducting their business in French, the moment had to come when all the courts of England – including, one presumes, the High Court of Parliament – were told to conduct the greater part of their public business in English. The majority of the public at large could not easily follow anything else. Yet English was not given a monopoly. The rolls and records were still to be kept in Latin. And French would be retained as the professional language of the lawyers until 1600. Bilingual English government was becoming trilingual.

The chronology of the shift has to be reconstructed from a number of scattered sources. In or around 1300, the chronicler Robert of Gloucester noted (in French) the strange subjection of English: '. . . unless a man knows French, he is thought little of. But humble men keep to English and their own speech still. I reckon there are no countries in the whole world that do not keep to their own speech, except England only.'[18] About the same time, the author of a long didactic poem, the *Cursor Mundi* or 'World Courier', explained why he had translated his mainly Latin sources:

> Efter haly kirces state
> Þis ilke bok it es translate,
> Into Inglis tong to rede,
> For þe love of Inglis lede,
> Inglis lede of Ingeland,
> For þe commun at understand.[19]
>
> (*After the manner of the Holy Church,*
> *This same book has been translated*
> *to be read in the English tongue,*

> *For the love of English people,*
> *The English people of England,*
> *For the common folk to understand.)*

William of Nassington, author of the *Speculum Vitae* (1325), openly expressed irritation at a state of affairs where a language that was familiar by then to everyone in England was still neglected:

> No Latyn will I speke no waste,
> But English þat men vse mast,
> Þat can eche man vnderstande
> Þat is born in Ingelande.[20]

The fact is that educated English society in the fourteenth century was multilingual, and would long remain so. Monks, chroniclers, poets, and administrators chose to use a particular language in particular conditions for particular purposes. They all needed Latin to follow international trends, to address a universal audience, or to participate in Church affairs. They still needed French to communicate with the nobility, the court, and administration. They needed English to communicate with the uneducated masses and sometimes to perpetuate thoughts in their native idiom. The overall situation had not radically altered since the early part of the previous century, when a monk of Reading Abbey had noted down perhaps the earliest of known Middle English lyrics in his commonplace book, but had then added Latin instructions on how to sing it:

> Sumer is icumen in, Lhude sing cuccu.[21]

Even so, the balance between England's languages was on the move. One indicator of this can be found in the popular Mystery Plays. The earliest examples, such as *Le Jeu d'Adam* or the *Ludus Coventriae*, were composed in French or in Latin. But as from 1311, when the Church turned the Feast of Corpus Christi into an official Holy Day, the plays were increasingly written and performed in English. Another indicator lies in the increasing frequency of translation. Translation was nothing new. Laȝamon's Chronicle, the English *Brut* (c. 1200), for example, drew heavily on Wace's French *Roman de Brut*, which in turn purported to be based on 'an ancient book in the British tongue', presumably in Welsh. Yet as time passed a greater need was felt 'to english' a greater number of works. Such was the case with the huge Latin *Polychronicon* (1352) written by Ranulph Higden, a monk of St Werburg's in Chester, which was translated into English thirty-five years after its first appearance.

Higden, who took the history of the world down to 1327, wrote a famous passage on the state of the English language. After noting that all English schoolchildren were educated in French, he went on to give one of the principal reasons why this was so:

> Also, though Englishmen always had three forms of speech from the start – Southern, Northern and Middle – being descended from three different sorts of people from Germany, nonetheless, through mixing and melling with Danes and Normans, the language has been greatly impaired: and some of them [speak with] a strange stammering, chattering, snarling and guttural tooth-biting.[22]

Higden clearly didn't like regional accents or dialects. But between the lines he was also saying that English was in no fit state to be adopted as the universal vehicle of instruction. Indeed, it may well be that Lallans or Lowland Scots was in a much fitter state for such purposes than any of the variants of English in England.

In that era prior to the Black Death, it is notable that more attention was paid to the decline of French than to the rise of English. According to Froissart, the English Parliament of 1332 urged the nobility to keep teaching their children French. The foundation statutes of two Oxford colleges – Oriel (1326) and Queen's (1340) – both underline the necessity for all students to be proficient in French as well as Latin.

Elsewhere in Europe, of course, the virtues of the vernacular were preoccupying some of the greatest minds of the age. Dante Alighieri had written *De vulgari eloquentia* before the end of the previous century. The Italian works of Dante (d. 1321), Petrarch (d. 1374), and Boccaccio (d. 1375) were all known to Chaucer. The seed of an idea had been planted that education need not necessarily be confined either to the language of the Church or to the language of the ruling class. It was already possible to conceive of a time when the language which people spoke at home and the language which they learned at school would be one and the same.

Higden's translator, John of Trevisa, came from Cornwall. He must have started work on the translation in the 1370s, if not in the 1360s. Much had changed since Higden's day. So when he reached the passage quoted above on education and the state of the English language, he added an insertion of his own. He knew from his own observations that practices were no longer the same:

> Þys manere was moche y-vsed tofore þe furste moreyn, and ys seþ the somdel ychaunged . . . so þat now, þe ȝer of oure Lord a þousond þre hondred foure score and fyue, of þe secunde Kyng Richard after þe Conquest nyne, in al þe gramerscoles of Engelond children leueþ Frensch and construeþ and lurneþ an Englysch . . . Also gentil men habbeþ now moche yleft for to teche here childern Frensch.[23]

> *(This practice [of teaching all children French] was much used before the first plague, but since then is somewhat changed . . . so that now, in the year of Our Lord one thousand three hundred and eighty-five, the ninth year of the second King Richard since the Conquest, children in all the grammar schools of England are leaving French, and are construing and learning in English. Similarly, noble men have now largely abandoned teaching their children French.)*

Trevisa was one of the very few observers to record what was happening. He says that the key language change in education had taken place after the *furste moreyn*, 'the first plague', i.e. the outbreak of the Black Death in 1348–50. (Elsewhere, he claims less convincingly that the change had been initiated by a schoolmaster in Cornwall.) But by the time in the 1380s when he was vicar of Berkeley in Gloucestershire and working on Higden's text, he says that all the grammar schools were using English as the language of instruction. Indeed they no longer appear to have seen the need to teach French even as a second language. If Trevisa was right, that last generation of fourteenth-century schoolchildren was the first both to speak and to learn in some form of English.

Nonetheless, it is significant that Trevisa saw no reason to add a gloss to Higden's earlier account of the mutually unintelligible English dialects:

> Al þe longage of þe Norþhumbres, and specialych at ʒork, ys so scharp, slyttying, and frotyng, and vnschape, þat we Souþeron men may þat longage vnneþe vndurstonde. Y trowe þat þat ys because þ at a buþ nyʒ to strange men and aliens, þat spekeþ strangelych, and also bycause þat þe kynges of Engelond woneþ alwey fer fram þat contray.[24]

> (All the language of the Northumbrians, and especially at York, is so sharp, piercing, rasping and unformed that we Southerners can rarely understand it. I believe that the reason for this is because they are near to foreigners and aliens who speak in strange ways, and also because the Kings of England have always lived far away from that country.)

The North–South divide was still so strong that England did not yet possess a single common vernacular.

The decline of French, therefore, was no more than a starting point — the first link in a long chain of shifts – which would gradually lead first to the rise of standard English and later to the propagation of standard English throughout the Isles. England's growing political and cultural power would march hand in hand with her growing isolation from the Continent. The process would never be absolutely complete, and it would proceed as much by the force of circumstance as by conscious policy. So many other things were happening to the subjects of Edouard III and his successors. Most of them would never have noticed that, like Higden's chronicle, they, too, were being Englished.

THE THREE STUART KINGDOMS

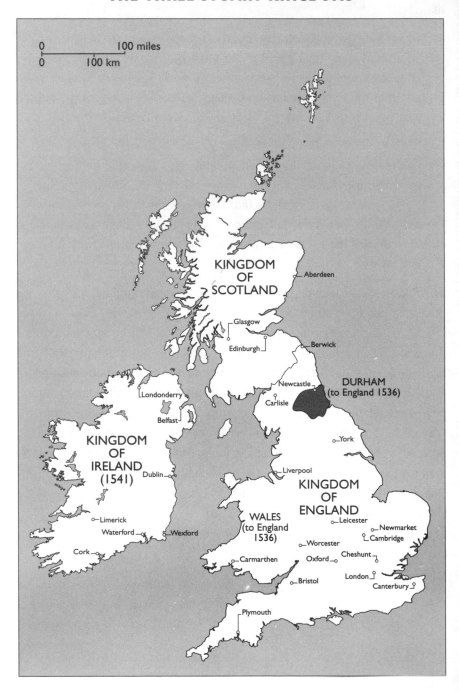

0 | 100 miles

0 | 100 km

KINGDOM
OF
SCOTLAND

Aberdeen

Glasgow

Edinburgh

Berwick

Newcastle

DURHAM
(to England 1536)

Londonderry

Carlisle

Belfast

KINGDOM
OF
IRELAND
(1541)

Dublin

York

Liverpool

KINGDOM
OF
ENGLAND

WALES
(to England
1536)

Leicester

Newmarket

Cambridge

Limerick

Worcester

Waterford

Wexford

Carmarthen

Oxford

Cheshunt

Cork

London

Bristol

Canterbury

Plymouth

(1) A Salutary Failure: the Hundred Years War

Once Edouard III had been persuaded to adopt the title of King of France, and to add the fleur-de-lys to his royal standard, he was condemning his subjects both in England and in Gascony to the prospect of perpetual war. With hindsight, one can see that he had set himself a trap from which neither he nor any of his Plantagenet successors could ever escape. He seems to have sensed the danger when, at the Treaty of Brétigny, he surrendered his royal French title in return for full sovereignty over Gascony. But he was soon forced to backtrack nine years later by France's repudiation of the Treaty. After that, there was no possibility of easy withdrawal. In the age of chivalry, the English claim to the French throne could not just be abandoned when it proved impractical. Honour demanded that all the King's loyal subjects press his claim, and fight to enforce it. At the same time, the peculiar logistics of England's insular and France's Continental position rendered any decisive military result unlikely. England could attack France repeatedly, but could never deliver the terminal blow. France could recover repeatedly from English victories, but could not project her power across the Channel. The result was twelve decades of exhausting, bloody, almost ritualistic Anglo-French conflict. Campaign followed campaign, and truce followed truce for 118 years. When later historians came to analyse this complex pattern of events at their leisure, they called it, somewhat imprecisely, the 'Hundred Years War'.[25]

The Hundred Years War provides the framework for the period when England finally emerged as a country that was recognizably English in the modern sense. Under the early Plantagenets, the 'community of the realm' in England had certainly acquired a distinct identity from its neighbours; but it had essentially remained an outpost of the French world from which its dominant class originated. Now, under the later Plantagenets (from Edouard [Edward] III (r. 1327–77) to Edward IV (r. 1461–83)), who failed in the high stakes of claiming the French throne for themselves, it was set to become predominantly English by culture as well as by allegiance.

England's obsession with its prolonged French war also set the framework for the development of the other countries in the Isles. Generally speaking, when English fortunes in France rode high, the English had time and energy to assert themselves against their insular neighbours. When English fortunes in France faltered, the Scots, Irish, and Welsh gained space for manoeuvre. Throughout the War, Scotland systematized 'the Auld Alliance' with France that had already operated earlier. Ireland was largely left to its own devices. Wales, still divided between the March and the conquered land of Wallia Pura, was able to do little except in England's most disadvantageous moments.

The nature of the fighting, however, rarely took the form of regular military campaigns. Major set battles were few and far between. Only one English king – Henry V – was to follow the example of Edouard III and the Black Prince in mounting full-scale expeditions. Already during the truce of the 1360s bands of English or English-led marauders made their appearance. Captains such as Sir John Hawkwood, who had served as a *condottiere* in the wars of the Italian cities, saw new pastures for the picking. And it was their parasitic practices which usually predominated. Large parts of France were turned for decades into lawless and defenceless fields for loot and plunder on a scale that had not occurred since the age of the Vikings.

If the first three phases of the war had seen England on the offensive (see Appendix 25), the next phase, in 1369–96, saw a remarkable French recovery. Piecemeal attacks on strategic towns and castles quickly limited the extent of English-held territory. The greatest general of the age, Bertrand du Guesclin, conceived a sustained programme of reducing English strongholds in the south-west which left the residue of Aquitaine dangerously exposed. By the time that the ageing Edouard III died, only Bordeaux in the south and Calais in the north stood firm.

The Anglo-French truce signed in 1396 was intended to last for thirty years. It held for only nineteen. But it well expressed the military stalemate that had been reached. The time was filled by dynastic and political turmoil in each of the combatant camps. In England, Henri de Bolingbroke, Duke of Lancaster, usurped the throne of Richard de Bordeaux, emerging in 1399 as 'Henry IV'. It was the start of the feud within the Plantagenet dynasty between the rival houses of Lancaster and York. In France, a parallel feud developed between the houses of Burgundy and Armagnac, which broke into open domestic warfare in 1407. It was fuelled by the insanity of Charles VI (r. 1380–1422) and by disputes regarding control of the royal court, army, and regency.

In the first decade of the fifteenth century the Welsh staged the last and greatest of their attempts to shake off English domination. England had been plunged into confusion by the overthrow of Richard II, and the House of Lancaster was facing a grand array of enemies in Ireland, Scotland, and Northumbria as well as in France. A group of wishful-thinking Welshmen seized the moment to raise the standard of revolt. On 16 September 1400, Owain ap Grufydd Glyn Dŵr of Glydyfrdwy (c. 1359–c. 1416), known in English as 'Owen Glendower', was proclaimed Prince of Wales at his manor-house near Bala. His followers set off to recover their country's long-lost independence. They attacked a number of English settlements, starting with Ruthin, then began to look for allies. In a letter written in French to the King of Scotland, Glyn Dŵr outlined the basis of his claims:

Brutus, your most noble ancestor and mine, was the first crowned king who dwelt in this realm of England which was formally called Great Britain [*Brataygna graunt*]. Brutus begat three sons, namely Albanactus, Locrinus and Kamber. You are

descended in the direct line from Albanactus. The descendants
of Kamber reigned as kings until Cadwaladr, who was the last
crowned king of my people [*de ma nacioun*]. I, dear cousin, am
descended directly from Cadwaladr.[26]

It was a very long shot. Cadwaladr had lived more than seven
hundred years before. But it gave Glyn Dŵr a step up towards
legitimacy. In short order, his forces had won recognition from all
parts of Wales.

Glyn Dŵr's plans can only be described as grandiose. In a
document known as the Tripartite Indenture, which summarized
the terms of alliance with Henry Percy, Earl of Northumberland
and the marcher lord, Edmond Mortimer, he planned to carve up
the whole of England into three parts. Wales was to be extended to
the Mersey and Trent; two Welsh universities were to be founded;
and the Bishopric of St Asaph's was to become an archbishopric.
Allegiance was to be transferred from the Pope at Avignon to the
'anti-Pope' in Rome. Although Wales had no native parliamentary
tradition, a Welsh Parliament was to be summoned.

For a dozen years, Glyn Dŵr reigned and ruled as a sovereign
prince. In 1404–5 a Welsh Parliament met at Machynlleth. The
independence of Wales was recognized by the King of France. But
the military situation was less promising. Several English castles in
Wales never surrendered. Many others were retaken by royal forces.
A few, like Harlech, protected the rebels. But ships, men, and
gunpowder poured in from Bristol and Chester, until on 10 March
1414 an English earl received the formal submission of Glyn Dŵr's
men at Bala. But Glyn Dŵr himself was never captured. He
disappeared into the mists of the mountains, his fate unknown:

> Owain Glyn Dwr was a truly national figure twice over. For
> those ... who wanted an image of a blustering hot-blooded
> Welshman (as Shakespeare did), he fitted the bill admirably; for
> Welsh intellectuals who pined for a national leader ... he was
> equally well suited, be it as 'the sole head of Wales' (*un pen ar*

Gymru) . . . But he was also a hero at the popular and local level over the centuries . . . a truly national hero.[27]

In August 1415 the youthful Henry V (r. 1413–22), son of Bolingbroke, landed at Harfleur in Normandy. He came with a full-scale army of the kind that had not been seen for fifty years. Moreover he was allied to the Duke of Burgundy, another great vassal of France who had recently declared his independence. At the great battle of Azincourt (Agincourt) in the Pas-de-Calais, fought on St Crispin's Day, 25 October 1415, it appeared that he had succeeded in realizing his wildest dreams. The French had learned nothing in terms of military tactics, and, as at Crécy, a combination of superior generalship and the fearful English longbow wreaked unmitigated slaughter. With the cream of French knighthood destroyed, and the Burgundians pressing from the east, the defenceless heart of France awaited its fate. After much manoeuvring, the French court found a solution by offering Henry V the hand of Catherine de Valois, the French king's daughter, and by recognizing the English king as the official heir to the French throne. These terms were formally incorporated into the Treaty of Troyes (1420), and were duly celebrated in grand style at the queen's coronation staged at West-minster. When Henry's new queen gave birth in 1421 to a son, another Henry, heir after his father to both England and France, it looked as if the victory was complete.

English historians have naturally taken great pride in Agincourt and in the political settlement that it engendered. But it is well worth pausing for a moment to reflect on the prospects to which it gave rise. One cannot know for certain what might have happened. But sober analysis suggests that Henry V may well have been handed a chalice full of poison. It is true that he stood on the very brink of attaining his great-grandfather's goal, and of establishing an Anglo-French monarchy. If he had lived only a few months longer, he would probably have commanded a dual state of still greater proportions than that of his Plantagenet forebears. On the other hand, it is doubtful whether he possessed the means to defend such an empire. France had been laid low by the double misery of domestic strife and foreign invasion. But she was not totally subdued. On the contrary, the greater part of French territory lay beyond English control; and Henry V's brother-in-law, the disinherited Dauphin Charles, survived as the focus of resistance. What is more, it is unlikely that Henry's Burgundian allies would have stood idly by as the Lancastrian threat to their independence outgrew the existing threat from the Valois. Everything one knows about the incurable fractiousness of feudal politics suggests that Henry V would never have been left to enjoy his inheritance in peace. In all probability, he would have been cast into a morass of further unwinnable conflicts and unforgivable treacheries. He would have been leading both his own family and his English homeland into a high-risk lottery. In which case, instead of bemoaning his untimely death, English patriots should rest content that he died when he did.

The fact that Henry V was struck down by dysentery in 1422, and that he was unexpectedly outlived by Charles VI, threw the entire settlement of Troyes into confusion. Having suffered decades of an unstable regency under an insane king, the French nobility were not inclined to accept another regency under an infant foreigner. So a struggle for the French succession was opened up once more. The Dauphin stayed on the defensive. The English occupied Paris, and most of northern France up to the line of the Loire. By 1429, heavily besieged, the city of Orléans on the north bank of the Loire was the sole French strongpoint in the region to be holding out.

At which point, a young girl of seventeen literally rode to France's rescue. Jeanne d'Arc, 'La Pucelle', was a native of distant Domrémy in Lorraine, which had been harried not by the English but by the Burgundians. But she had seen visions, which urged her to don a knight's armour, to gain the blessing of the Dauphin, and to rekindle French resistance. On 4 May 1429, she charged across the bridge at Orléans at the head of a company of French knights and raised the English siege. Assisted by another French victory at Patay, near Orléans, she then accompanied the Dauphin to Reims where he was crowned as Charles VII (r. 1429–61). Shortly afterwards, she was captured by the Burgundians in a skirmish and sold to the English, who had her burned in the market place of Rouen on charges of heresy. Not surprisingly, the martyred Maid of Orléans became the symbol of French resurgence long before she was canonized and France's unofficial patron saint.

Apart from the exploits of La Pucelle, the crucial move in this phase of the war lay on the diplomatic front. By the Treaty of Arras (1435), France was reconciled to Burgundy. The English lost their main ally. Henry VI of England, though crowned as Henry II of France, could not exploit his advantage. Paris was recaptured. By the Truce of Tours (1444), the French gained five years' grace in which to prepare the decisive assault.

In the final phase of fighting, 1449–53, the French confidently launched a powerful two-pronged attack on the English positions in Normandy and Gascony. In 1450, at Formigny near Bayeux, they annihilated the English army with results that were far more durable than those of Crécy or Agincourt. Except for Calais, English rule in northern France was eliminated for ever. Then in 1451, the reconquest of Gascony was launched in earnest. The sparse English garrisons, starved of external support, were unable to resist. In 1453, at Castillon, they made their final, faltering stand. A triumphant French army recaptured Bordeaux after three hundred years of English rule. The Hundred Years War was over. France had survived its baptism by fire. Calais alone remained in English hands.

Though no definitive treaty would be signed for years, England was unable to reassert her claims to France. England was sinking into the same sort of domestic quagmire from which France had just emerged. The reign of the saintly but insouciant Henry VI was proving as disastrous in England as it had once threatened to be in France. 1453 was the first year in which Henry VI fell into an extended state of insanity, forcing his courtiers to compete over the appointment of a Regent. From 1455 to 1485, the Wars of the Roses between the rival proponents of Lancaster and York reduced England to chaos and removed any chance of re-engaging in a Continental war.

France, in contrast, was going from strength to strength. The reign of Louis XI, 'the Universal Spider' (r. 1461–83), saw the wiles of diplomacy flourish whilst the sinews of war were trained and tautened. In 1477 Burgundy was returned to the French fold, though many of its possessions in the Netherlands were absorbed by the rising House of Habsburg. France basked in the sunlight of the early Renaissance. Well could François Villon sing:

> . . .
>
> Et Jehanne la bonne Lorraine
> Qu'Englois brulerent à Rouan;
> Ou sont ilz, ou, Vierge souvraine?
> Mais ou sont les neiges d'antan?[28]
>
> (And Joan, that good woman from Lorraine,
> Whom the English burned at Rouen:
> O sovereign Virgin, where are they all?
> Where are the snows of yesteryear?)

French historians, therefore, have little difficulty in spelling out the consequences of the Hundred Years War. They rightly see them in a most favourable light. The emergence of a fire-hardened French monarchy ruling over a unified territory containing some of the fairest and most populous provinces of Europe set the scene for France's modern greatness.

English historians are more reticent. They tend to see the Hundred Years War as an episode of sporadic glories and of missed opportunities, but not of any great significance. In this, they may be mistaken. They should give more attention to the scenario from which England was saved by defeat. The later Plantagenets had spent much of England's substance in their vain bid to press their French claims. Had they succeeded, they would have inevitably embroiled England in open-ended Continental concerns, and would have been tempted to put England's resources at the disposal of the more important French part of their trans-Channel empire. That they were prevented from doing so might be considered as an occasion for English rejoicing. Defeat in the Hundred Years War gave England the chance to be herself for the first time in four centuries.

The psychological consequences of the long-drawn-out Anglo-French struggle must also be taken into consideration. The English had found themselves in the enviable position of being able to attack a major European power without serious fear of retaliation. Five or six generations of Englishmen had learned to treat the French with contempt, to regard France as a traditional playground for rape, plunder, and derring-do, and to glory in their own impunity. The arrogance born of that impunity was not limited to England's Continental connections. It encouraged similar attitudes towards England's neighbours in the Isles. Just as the English knew that the French were unlikely to cross the Channel in force, they also knew that the Irish were unlikely to cross the Celtic Sea, that the Welsh and Scots did not possess the independent strength to penetrate far beyond the borders. As a result, the heart of England became one of the safest locations in the world. An unusual degree of security in the home base created the grounds for unusual confidence and expansiveness. Once England's foreign dynasty had been replaced by a strong native monarchy, and once England's strength-sapping obsession with France had been terminated, the country possessed enormous potential for political and economic enterprises of all sorts. In this light, and from the narrow English perspective, England's failure to achieve her misplaced goals in the Hundred Years War must be seen as entirely salutary.

(2) NATIVE DYNASTIES: STEWARTS AND TUDWRS

In a feudal age, the character and connections of ruling dynasties played an important role in the formation of popular identity.

People understood that they belonged to a family, to a locality, to a feudal lord, to the Mother Church of Christendom, and possibly to a province or country. Even if they never travelled beyond the bounds of their home village, as many of them didn't, they would meet and know persons, from the reeve to the parish priest, who represented each of the more important groupings. But over and above those local factors they could have little concept of a national community, except as subjects of the ruling prince to whom they and their immediate feudal lord owed allegiance. In late Plantagenet England the mass of the population would not have regarded themselves as English in the modern national sense even though many of them used some form of Middle English speech. They were English because they were subjects of the King of England. In this, they shared a common bond with Welsh, Irish, Gascons, Bordelais, and citizens of Calais, but not with the foreign subjects of the King of Scots. Changes of rulers caused changes in popular identity. In the fifteenth century, three dynasties came into the reckoning in the Isles – the self-destructing Plantagenets, the rising House of Tudwr, and the well-established Scottish House of Stewart.

The Stewarts, whose origins lay with the hereditary stewards of the royal court of the previous period, had taken control of Scotland in the course of the troubled succession to Robert the Bruce. Robert II Stewart (r. 1371–84), who was a grandson of the Bruce on the maternal side, had acted as Guardian of the Realm during the long captivity of David II (see page 408, above) and had then acceded to the throne on David's death. Wearied by the congenital in-fighting of baronial politics, he withdrew in favour of his son, Robert III Stewart (r. 1384–1406). But, dying in 1390, he lived long enough to see his family firmly entrenched. Indeed, whilst the English succession was constantly wracked by childlessness and usurpation, the Scottish succession proceeded in unbroken line through nine generations. James VI Stewart (r. 1567–1625), who was to play a very special role in the history of the Isles, was the great-great-great-great-great-great-great-grandson in direct line of Robert II. (See Appendix 30.)

Not that the Stewarts were lacking in troubles. James I (r. 1406–37) was murdered after spending eighteen years in captivity as a hostage in England. Three of the Stewarts died on the battlefield – James II in 1460 at Roxburgh Castle during the Wars of the Roses, James III in 1488 when he was challenged by his fifteen-year-old son, and James IV in 1513 at the great disaster of Flodden. Of the eight Stewart kings, two married Scots noblewomen, two married English brides, and four married Continental princesses. Of the latter, two were from Denmark – Margaret, queen of James III, who brought the Orkneys and Shetlands in her dowry, and Anne, queen of James VI, who would join her husband on the throne of England. Most fateful of all the Scottish matrimonial connections, however, were those of James V Stewart (r. 1513–42), who in accordance with the 'Auld Alliance' twice married high-born French women. In 1537, at Notre-Dame, he married Madeleine de France, daughter of Francis I. In 1538, he married the widowed Marie de Bourbon, Duchess de Guise-Lorraine. Here lay the root of the French dimension in the tragedy of their daughter. Mary Stewart, Queen of Scots (r. 1542–67) was one of the grandly tragic figures of European history.

Unlike the Stewarts, the Tudwrs could boast only modest beginnings. Owain ap Maredudd ap Tudwr ap Goronwy (c. 1400–61) was a Welshman, who joined Henry V's army in France and later served in the household of Henry V's queen, Catherine de Valois. His forebears came from Abergele in the Four Cantreds of Denbighshire, and had served the princes of Gwynedd for generations. An early ancestor, Cynfrig ap Iorwerth, was the right-hand man of Llewllyn the Great. Another, Goronwy ap Tudwr, was Constable of Beaumaris under Richard II. The family met hard times in the 1400s, having thrown in their lot with the Rising of their kinsman Owain Glyn Dŵr, and having suffered from the subsequent repressions. This, no doubt, was the reason why the young Owain ap Maredudd went off to soldier in the French war.[29]

Once in the English court, however, Owain had trouble with his name. Like all Welshmen, he did not possess a surname in the English fashion, just a string of patronymics standing for 'son of Maredudd (Meredith), son of Tudor, son of Goronwy'. He could easily have added some more to trace his ancestry to the family protoplast – ap Tudur Hen, ap Goronwy, ap Ednyfed, ap Cynfrig. For the simple-minded English these flourishes were unintelligible. So they called him Owen fitz Maredudd, and at a later stage, Owen Tudor. Since 'Tudwr' or 'Theodore' was his grandfather's Christian name, they were making a serious mistake. But the English pay scant regard to other people's conventions. Tudor, in its Anglicized form, became the customary surname of Owain's descendants.

Owain's fortune was made c. 1432 by his romance with and secret marriage to his employer, the widowed queen dowager, Catherine de Valois. The liaison caused consternation at court and an official inquiry. But it was soon accepted. In due course Owain's two sons, Edmund, Earl of Richmond, and Jasper, Earl of Pembroke, half-brothers to Henry VI, emerged as the King's closest kinsmen. Jasper Tudor, in particular, master of the de Clares' old fortress at Pembroke, emerged as one of the doughtiest standard-bearers of the Lancastrian cause during the Wars of the Roses. He became the natural protector of his brother Edmund's posthumous son, Henry Tudor (b. 1457).

The extraordinary twists and turns of the Lancastrian–Yorkist feud is sure to try the patience of the modern reader. But the tensions reached a critical state at two points. In 1461 Henry VI was overthrown by the chief Yorkist pretender, Edward Plantagenet, Earl of March, who was recognized by Parliament and assumed the style of Edward IV. (He had re-adopted the old, disused surname of Plantagenet, in order to stress his claim to superior royal lineage.) In 1470, Edward IV was dethroned in turn by the resurgent followers of Henry VI, only to be reinstated in turn a few months later following the Yorkist victory on the bloody battlefield of Tewkesbury. Henry VI's sole son and heir, Edward, Prince of Wales, was killed at Tewkesbury. The grieving Henry VI was then murdered mysteriously.

At this juncture, Jasper, Earl of Pembroke took his young ward Henry Tudor into exile. They lived in style in Brittany, held by the duke under house arrest at the magnificent Château de Suscinio on the coast of Morbihan, and later at the Château de Largoët near Vannes. They attracted a retinue of Lancastrian refugees, but had no special significance until 1483, when Edward IV died. Here the Yorkists' death-wish took over. Edward IV's two young sons, one of whom briefly reigned as Edward V, were murdered in the Tower of London and usurped by their uncle and Lord Protector, Richard III (r. 1483–5). The murder of the 'Princes in the Tower' left the Yorkist camp without an immediate successor. Henry Tudor, aged twenty, learned in Brittany that he was now the premier pretender to the English throne. Recognized as such by the King of France, he moved to Normandy to prepare the expedition that would determine his fate. His fleet, under Uncle Jasper's command, sailed from Honfleur on 1 August 1485. He had already declared that if successful in removing Richard III he would take a Yorkist bride and thereby 're-unite the roses'.

The Tudors landed at Milford Haven near Pembroke in Jasper's home territory after a voyage of six days. They were accompanied by some four hundred Lancastrian exiles, by a French force under the Savoyard Philippe de Chandeé, and by a company of Scots under Bernard Stewart, Lord of Aubigny. Their march up the Welsh coast to Aberystwyth, then across the Welsh mountains to Shrewsbury, flying the banner of the Red Dragon and collecting reinforcements as they marched, provides one of the great romantic tales of English, and Welsh, history. The decisive clash took place on 22 August at Bosworth Field near Leicester, where Richard III had awaited them. The day was decided by the last-minute intervention of Sir William Stanley, a Lancastrian from Lancashire. Richard III ended a dishonourable life with an honourable death, unhorsed and sword in hand. The rumour that his crown was found on a thornbush started to circulate immediately. Henry Tudor was crowned as 'Henry VII' in Westminster Abbey in October, and married Elizabeth of York, Edward IV's daughter, at the same location in January. The roses were reunited. The domestic wars had finished.

The one threat to the peace of the realm was posed by Yorkist pretenders. Two such impostors appeared in quick succession. Lambert Simnel (c. 1477–1534) was a handsome lad from Oxford who fell into the hands of a scheming priest. He was put forward as the Earl of Warwick, nephew of Edward IV, and recognized as such by the late King's sister, Margaret of Burgundy. Sent to Dublin to be crowned by Yorkist adherents, he landed in Lancashire with a force of Irish and German mercenaries. His bid for power came to an abrupt end after his defeat at the Battle of Stoke (1487). He lived out his life first as a scullion in the royal kitchens, and later as a royal falconer.

Perkin de Werbecque or Warbeck (c. 1474–99) was a still more exotic customer than Simnel. A Fleming born in Antwerp, he had worked as a servant boy in Portugal and Brittany before finding his way into the service of the pro-Yorkist Earl of Kildare. Though not an English speaker, he was proclaimed to be one of the 'Princes in the Tower'. Supported by Margaret of Burgundy, he was paraded round the courts of Europe as the lawful King of England. He was then received by James IV of Scotland, who provided him with an aristocratic wife. But none of his various forays into England bore fruit. He appeared once in Kent, a second time in Northumberland, and a third time in Cornwall. (See page 477, below.) Captured and forced to confess, he was ultimately hanged after trying to escape from the Tower of London.

Unlike the Stewarts, however, the Tudors did not possess the prime dynastic virtues – fertility and longevity. This may well have been due in the second generation to the contraction of syphilis, a disease recently imported from America and raging throughout Europe in its most virulent form. At all events, Henry VII's eldest surviving son, Henry VIII (r. 1509–47), produced only three childless children from six marriages and only one recognized bastard from numerous concubines. The reigns of Edward VI (r. 1547–53), Mary I

(r. 1553–58), and Elizabeth I (r. 1558–1603) were full of stirring pageant; but in dynastic terms they were an empty cul-de-sac. Edward VI, in desperation, set aside his sisters' rights on his deathbed, leaving his throne to Lady Jane Grey, who reigned for only nine days prior to her execution. Elizabeth I, in similar straits, left her inheritance to her cousin, James VI Stewart. (See page 534, below.)

None of these disasters, of course, could have been known to Henry VII. The first of the Tudor monarchs reigned in confident and prudent manner for twenty-four years, despite his inauspicious qualifications. Brought up in Wales and in Brittany, speaking French better than he spoke English, he was thrown into kingship 'feet first'. Yet he coped far better than all his recent predecessors and most of his successors. His reign laid the foundations of England's prowess in 'the Tudor age'. He tamed the barons, calmed the Church, fought off all pretenders, established an efficient legal and financial system, conducted an energetic policy in France and Spain, provided for his children, and died in his bed.

An interesting aspect of Henry's reign can be found in his dynastic propaganda. He was very conscious both of the need to heal past divisions, and of the power of symbols among a largely illiterate public. Although he was only a quarter Welsh (as opposed to half English through his mother, Elizabeth Beaufort), he chose to emphasize his Welshness as an instrument of unification. Courtiers and poets regaled their audiences with tales of his descent from ancient British kings, thereby reclaiming a legacy which set aside the French character of the Normans and Plantagenets and appealed to a far more distant, native past. He called his eldest son Arthur; and if Arthur had lived to succeed him, there is little doubt that England would have been subjected to a still stronger dose of 'Britishness'. As it was, Henry Tudor contented himself with a rich fare of heraldic imagery which addressed his most catholic connections. The bronze gates of his supermagnificent funeral chapel in Westminster Abbey, designed in 1503 soon after Prince Arthur's death, say it all. The panels of the gates combine the Welsh dragon, the Beaufort portcullis, the red and white roses entwined, the crown on thornbush, the Plantagenet leopards, and the lilies of France.

In that same year, 1503, Henry Tudor married his eldest daughter, Margaret, to James IV of Scotland. This step may well have had 'British' overtones, although the Plantagenets had never been slow to tie in their Scottish neighbours through marriage. But its long-term effect made a signal contribution to the gradual construction of a British kingdom. All subsequent holders of the English, Scottish, and British thrones were either closely related to or descended from the partners of that keystone Stewart–Tudor marriage. What is more, the fact that Margaret Tudor's husband, James IV Stewart, was seduced by the 'Auld Alliance' to betray his new-found English relations greatly undermined the position of an independent Scottish monarchy. After the crushing defeat at Flodden, when James IV was killed together with a horrifyingly huge contingent of his leading nobles, Scotland's position vis-à-vis England was irreparably weakened.

Henceforth, the Stewarts headed an enfeebled country which could ill resist the attacks, or blandishments, of an invigorated England. Throughout the sixteenth century they hung onto their one remaining trump card – their heirs and heiresses. The card was first played in 1543 at the Treaty of Greenwich, when Margaret Tudor's infant granddaughter, Mary Stewart, was offered to the infant Tudor prince, Edward. Henry VIII clearly saw the point of the match. In his 'Rough Wooing' of 1544–5, he twice invaded Scotland in his desperate attempts to put the Treaty into effect. By then, however, the religious factor was raising its head; and the Scots held off.

For several decades, the poor and passionate Mary Stewart was the key pawn in this Anglo-Scottish game of dynastic chess. From the age of six days, she was Queen of Scots in her own right; and from the age of eleven, the closest claimant to the Tudor succession. Unfortunately, once Edward VI was dead, the Tudors had no more eligible males to offer in marriage. So Mary was left to make a series of three ill-starred and blood-soaked marriages elsewhere. Her first husband, with whom she lived for only two years, was François II, Dauphin then King of France. He died of an inglorious ear infection. (See page 539, below.) Her second husband, with whom she produced her only child, was a cousin, Henry Stewart, Lord Darnley. He killed her secretary, David Riccio, in the presence of his unborn son, before being killed himself. Her third husband, the Earl of Bothwell, was probably Darnley's unidentified assassin. At the end of all this, abdicating in favour of her infant son, she fled to England, and threw herself on Elizabeth's mercy. She survived under arrest for eighteen years, before involving herself in a Catholic plot. Like so many others in the shadow of the Tudor throne, she died on the scaffold, dressed in crimson robes. Her remains were transferred to Westminster Abbey in 1612 by the son who had done nothing much to save her.

Mary Stewart, daughter of a French queen and the ex-queen of a French king, adopted the custom of signing her name in its French spelling – 'MARIE STUART'. Her son James, even when resident in London, habitually signed himself 'Jacques'. For this reason, when their descendants became Kings both of England and Scotland, they became known not as 'the Stewarts' but as 'the Stuarts'. It is one of those odd ironies of history. The Plantagenets, who were almost completely French until the final Yorkist phase, are widely assumed to have been English. The Tudor-Stewarts, who were similarly un-English in origin, are usually remembered in a form which hints at their French connections. The most important thing about the Tudor–Stewarts, however, is the fact that they were insular natives. They had no home-base beyond the Isles. This can only have emphasized the drift away from Continental affairs in the direction of a separate destiny.

(3) KINGS AND PARLIAMENTS

By the fourteenth century, there were three separate parliamentary systems functioning in the Isles, in England, in Scotland, and in Ireland. There were also – or had been – a number of important local assemblies, in the City of London, in Cornwall, in Wales, in the Isle of Man, and in the Channel Islands. The overall picture was not a simple one.

Yet no subject has suffered more from 'Whiggism' and from 'Anglocentrism' than parliamentary history. Historians of the Victorian era were so immensely proud of the pre-eminent position in the world which Westminster then embodied that they explained everything as an inexorable march towards the desirable end of their own times. They ignored anything which could not be fitted into the Westminster Story; and they tended to assume that parliamentarism was a uniquely English invention.

In reality, parliaments and diets and 'assemblies of the estates' were thick on the ground in late medieval and early modern Europe. England was no exception. It was only in later times that Absolutism came to the fore in Continental polities. The Holy Roman Empire, nominally the senior state of Western Christendom, functioned through an electoral system which took final form in the Golden Bull of 1364 and through an Imperial Diet working in conjunction with the Emperor. The Jagiellonian realms of Poland and Lithuania, which in 1572 would join together into an elective Commonwealth, covered for a time the largest territory in Europe. They had developed a precocious legal and parliamentary tradition, which in several respects – such as the principles of habeas corpus or of 'No Taxation without Representation' – foreshadowed later developments in England. The estates of Aragon, whose statutes governed a large part of the western Mediterranean, were famed for the rumbustious defence of their rights against those of the king. Almost all the great Italian cities, which enjoyed unrivalled cultural splendour and commercial prosperity in late medieval times, possessed constitutional histories of great vigour and variety. They may be divided into those, like Florence, whose parliamentary traditions were suppressed or manipulated by despotic princes, and those, like the Republic of Venice, whose parliamentary oligarchy survived intact.

The Irish Parliament, initiated by King John, was an institution whose competence was strictly limited to the Pale. It did not embrace the larger part of Ireland, which continued to be governed by local customs and by native chiefs. Even so, within its sphere of competence, it achieved a higher degree of representation than its English mentor. As from 1300 both gentry of the shires and burgesses of the towns gained the right of regular attendance, which was also extended – exceptionally in the Isles – to the 'proctors' or representatives of the lower diocesan clergy. In the fifteenth century, when England was distracted by foreign and domestic wars, the Irish Parliament largely ran its own affairs. Under the patronage of the barons, notably of Gerald Fitzgerald (c. 1456–1513), the eighth Earl of Kildare, it had been edging its way to a position of near independence until Henry VII reasserted English authority. Kildare had been involved with the Yorkist plotters who had Lambert Simnel crowned in Dublin in 1487 as 'Edward VI', and who in 1491 set the next pretender, Perkin Warbeck, on his road to annihilation. As a result, in 1495 Henry VII's commissioner, Sir Edward Poynings, obliged the Dublin Parliament to pass a notorious and long-lasting statute which invalidated all Irish legislation not previously approved in England. After several years' arrest in the Tower of London, 'the Great Earl' returned to his post as Lord Deputy. But his relatives were to be the source of constant discontent in the subsequent decades. Poynings' Law remained on the statute book for nearly three hundred years. It was to prove a double-edged weapon, since Irish interests in Westminster learned to use it to take their revenge and to foul up English Government plans.

The Parliament of Scotland possessed a very different character. In origin, it was a baronial council that had adopted the name of *parliamentum*, and it never escaped from the grip of baronial interests. Unlike its English counterpart, it never produced a second chamber; and, unlike its Irish counterpart, it never put the representatives of shires, towns, and clergy on an equal footing with the nobility. For more than a century, the burgesses were only allowed to attend sessions devoted to financial matters; and an act of 1428, which was intended to find a role for 'shire commissioners' (i.e., county delegates), was not implemented. When James II first created the class of 'lords' or peers in 1445, he encouraged a differentiation between greater and lesser baronage. But the step had the unintentional effect of strengthening the grip of the most powerful barons over the country's unicameral assembly. As time passed, the predominance of aristocratic Lowlanders weighed ever more heavily; and it was their sectional interests which eventually led to the merger of the Edinburgh and Westminster parliaments in 1707. Scotland's 'Commons' were all but excluded from political life until the creation of a Presbyterian Kirk in the 1560s, and the rise of the Kirk's General Assembly as a sort of unofficial substitute for a lower chamber. Similarly, no effective place was found in the constitution for the Gaelic-speaking Highland clans who had once dominated the country but who were now sliding into a long period of neglect and subordination.

In England, the remarkable feature of the late medieval Parliament lay in the rise of the House of Commons to a position of near parity with the House of Lords. In this, the influence of the Hundred Years War and of the King's financial problems were paramount. The Commons won the right to a separate chamber in Westminster Hall in 1346, and from 1376 elected their own Speaker. In 1407 the Commons were granted precedence over the Lords in offering funds to the monarch; and in 1414, on the eve of Agincourt, Henry V accepted the principle that he could approve or reject, but not amend, the draft of a Commons bill. It was the very first whisper of a limited monarchy. From 1429, 'forty shilling freeholders' were regarded as the minimum constituency for electing knights of the shire; and from that date until 1832 the pattern of two knights per shire and two burgesses per borough was established as the basis for popular representation. The number of seats in the Commons gradually rose from 296 to 462 by the end of the Tudor period through the creation of new boroughs.

Equally surprising, the Commons began to play a part in high politics. In 1387, a group of dissident barons, known as the 'Lords Appelant' which included the future Henry IV, brought a formal charge of treason to Parliament against the leading courtiers of Richard II. After success on the battlefield, they were able to take over the reins of government; and in the Merciless Parliament of 1388 they pressed their charges to the point of several executions and banishments. The Lancastrians were learning to use support in the Commons against their rivals in the Lords. In 1399 they claimed to have removed Richard II in conjunction with Parliament. In actual fact, being unsure of parliamentary approval, they had carried out the dethronement with the express approval of only a small selection of their own supporters among the bishops, peers, and commoners. Even so, by publicly appealing to parliamentary support, they inevitably strengthened the belief that both Houses of Parliament were an essential element of legitimate government. By the early fifteenth century, under Lancastrian rule, virtually all statutes were issued under the standard formula, 'by advice and assent of the lords spiritual and temporal at the instance of the Commons'. Parliaments continued to meet throughout the Wars of the Roses, and Henry VII made full use of Parliament in securing the final settlement. In later years, however, Henry VII was determined 'to live off his own' and, by avoiding war, to avoid undue dependence on the Commons.

It would be wrong to maintain, therefore, that the House of Lords had been overshadowed. This was not the case. Throughout the Tudor and Stuart periods, the Lords continued to contain the greatest men in the land who not only guarded their right to counsel the King but who also possessed the wealth and means of effective opposition. The hereditary secular peerage, which first came into being through the creation of baronies by royal Letters Patent in 1387, provided a powerful strand of continuity in English politics right until modern times. It was strengthened by a decision of 1516 to exclude the spiritual peers when convenient, and by the abolition in 1540 of the abbots. The Commons, in contrast, were far more exposed to the ire of forceful monarchs, and, as individuals, enjoyed a much lower level of continuous representation. In between parliamentary sessions, the Commons, unlike the Lords, had no voice. What emerged, therefore, was a strong, multifaceted institution which constitutionalists are wont to call 'King-in-Parliament'. No element in this organic product of history was entirely free of the others. Each had clearly defined spheres of competence.

Yet monarchs continued to rule in a regal, not to say a brutally assertive manner. The Tudor monarchs cut down their almighty subjects to size, as they pleased. The Lords continued to lord it over the lesser estates. And the Commons remained commoners, whose influence was dependent on their knowing their place. At no point before the end of the sixteenth century did anyone in Parliament enjoy legal immunity from the royal ire. One spoke one's mind in Parliament at the risk of losing one's head.

Nonetheless, this was the constitutional engine which drove through the 'Tudor Revolution'. Whereas Parliament had met on average only once in every three years between 1485 and 1529, it was summoned almost every single year in the following three decades. Henry VIII used it to execute the Anglican Reformation, the Break with Rome, and the Dissolution of the Monasteries. Elizabeth I used it to execute her ecclesiastical settlement, which brought the turbulence of the English Reformation under control. All the epoch-making decisions of those years, from the Act of Restraint (1529) and the Act of Supremacy (1534) to the incorporation of Wales (1536), the 'kinging' of Ireland (1541), and the Act of Uniformity (1558), were enshrined in parliamentary instruments. It is important to recognize that the underlying ideology of the process was one not of parliamentary but of royal supremacy. The guiding figure of Thomas Cromwell (c. 1485–1540), who masterminded the strategy in the 1530s, was that of a royal, not a parliamentary servant. The essence of the Tudor regime was monarchical. The Parliament was but one wheel in the machine which gave effect to a ruthless, efficient, and centralizing government.[30]

The consequences of Tudor power were visible on every hand. The contrast in political climate with that of the late Plantagenets was self-evident. One cannot claim that England under the Tudors was more stable or less conflictual than in the preceding period. On the contrary, it was riven with conflicts, and soaked in blood, cruelty, and repression. Yet the purposeful conduct of its monarchs and their parliaments generated a confidence in the governmental machine that was lacking both before and after. No small part in the Tudor's success in dominating both their subjects and their neighbours must be ascribed to their unprecedented claim to have no superior on earth under God.

(4) REFORMATION: DIVISIONS AND BARRIERS

By the sixteenth century, it had been true for a thousand years that almost everyone in the Isles was a Catholic Christian. Belonging to the great community of 'Christendom', and acknowledging the supreme spiritual authority of the Pope, virtually every man and woman had been baptized, married, and buried in the Roman faith. Ever since Edouard I had packed his Jews into boats in 1290 and driven them out, no recognized non-Catholic religious community had existed. Organized heresy was marginal: open defiance rare. Hidden deviations lay more in the realm of individual eccentrics or of secret pagan survivals than of real Christian dissidence. Prior to Henry VIII's time no one had ever discussed the prospect of breaking with the Universal Church.

Church reform, in contrast, had been on the agenda for more than a century. The Conciliar Movement had been trying to relaunch a comprehensive review of doctrine, liturgy, and ecclesiastical organization ever since the Council of Constance in 1415. When its advocates within the Church hierarchy finally had their way, and convened the twenty-year Council of Trent (1545–63), they conducted a far-reaching reformation such as the Church had never seen. Unfortunately, their rivals within the ranks of the would-be reformers had not been able to wait. By taking matters into their own hands, they provoked a schism that has never been healed. They came to call their own efforts 'the Protestant Reformation'; and their apologists downgraded the Church's own programme of reform to the status of a 'Counter-Reformation'. The Isles was one of several regions of Europe in which the Protestant Reformers made the running.

One of the earliest precursors of Reform had surfaced in England. John Wyclif, the Oxford theologian and philosopher, (see page ooo, above) denounced the absolute power of the papacy, the luxury of the clergy, and, most ominously, the key doctrine of transubstantiation. When challenged by Pope Gregory XI, he wrote one treatise *On the Truth of Holy Writ* and another *On the Eucharist*. He had the Bible translated into English, and started a movement that was never completely suppressed. His followers, known as 'Lollards', turned a label of derision into a badge of pride. At first they attracted support in high quarters. But when Henry IV's statute *De Heretico Comburendo* (1401) set out to punish heresy with burning, and when the rebellion of Sir John Oldcastle (1414) linked Lollardy with treason, they went underground. They seem to have maintained a small network of secret parishes in England and southern Scotland right into the sixteenth century. They strongly influenced the Bohemian Jan Hus. Hussitism in Bohemia, which survived all assaults on it, strongly influenced the climate of ferment in Central Europe that in 1517 eventually produced the open defiance of the indomitable Martin Luther. Luther was the bull which smashed the china shop.

Once unleashed, Protestantism came in many forms. Luther in Saxony from 1521, Zwingli in Zurich from 1522, the Anabaptists of Münster from 1535, and Calvin in Geneva from 1540, all propagated their views across Europe in an unstoppable flood. For practical purposes, the main division lay between the so-called 'Magisterial Protestants', like Luther and Calvin, who sought to replace the state-backed monopoly of the Catholic Church with similar monopolies of their own, and the so-called 'Radical Protestants', such as the anabaptists and anti-trinitarians, who professed every sort of extreme idea from pacifism to democratic congregationalism and, most dangerously, religious tolerance. Toleration formed no part of the Magisterial Protestant repertoire any more than it did in the world-view of the Spanish Inquisition. Luther, an extreme social conservative, once declared that he preferred 'princes doing wrong to the common people doing wrong'. Calvin was still more narrow-minded. His capture of the radical dissenter Michael Servetus by treachery, and the cruel judicial murder that followed, should cure anyone of the illusion that the Protestants were more tolerant than the Catholics. It is the greatest scandal both of the Reformation and of the Counter-Reformation that all sense of the primacy of Christian charity was lost.

Henry VIII of England was a Catholic prince who hated Martin Luther with a passion. Married to a daughter of Ferdinand and Isabella, the chief patrons of the Holy Inquisition, he had no intention of letting the fulminations of a vulgar ex-monk pass in silence. In 1521, he put his name to a fiercely anti-Lutheran Tract, the *Assertio Septem Sacramentorum*, thereby winning the title of 'Defender of the Faith' from a grateful Pope. Earlier, he had not hesitated to declare war on France because France was waging war on the Pope. Not surprisingly, Henry's papist passions paled quickly when he and his wife failed to produce a son and heir, and the Pope failed to grant him the expected divorce or nullification. In retrospect, one can see that the root cause of the whole problem was to be found in the deficiencies of Henry's own reproductive system, *not* in the shortcomings of his six unfortunate wives, *not* in the weakness of the unreformed English Church and *not* in the tortuous politics of the Vatican chancery. But Henry was not a man to admit to deficiencies. Rather than admit them, he was prepared to put all his subjects in all his realms through years of revolutionary turmoil, and to kill every person who stood in his way.

The plan, as devised by Thomas Cromwell, was terrifyingly

simple. In all matters of faith save one, England was to be held within the strictest bounds of traditional Catholicism. The Pope was to be removed as Head of the Church, to facilitate a divorce. At the same time the wealth of the Church was to be despoiled and divided among Henry's sycophants, to offset political reaction. All the acts of the Reformation Parliament, 1529–36, were designed to these ends. The Act of Restraint on Appeals (1533) cut off the English clergy from Rome and from canon law. The Act for Ecclesiastical Appointments (1534) gave the Crown complete control over the Church hierarchy; the Act concerning Peter's Pence (1534) stopped all financial contributions to Rome; and finally, the Act of Supremacy (1534) created an independent and formally separatist Church of England with the monarch as its head. The Act for the Dissolution of the Monasteries (1536) abolished a few nests of corruption together with the greatest network of social and educational welfare that England had ever known.

Yet the King's matrimonial troubles continued. Having set Catherine of Aragon aside, together with their daughter Mary, Henry was able to marry a series of wives, and to discard them as necessary. A second daughter, Elizabeth, was born in 1533, only to be promptly declared illegitimate. A weakly son, Edward, was born in 1537, though the birth killed his mother, Jane Seymour. Henry finally had his son and heir. Among the casualties were Sir Thomas More, a former chancellor and a leading humanist, executed in 1535 for denying the Act of Supremacy; Elizabeth's mother, Queen Anne Boleyn, executed in 1536 for producing a girl child; Queen Catherine Howard, executed in 1542 for alleged adultery; and Thomas Cromwell himself, executed in 1540 for persuading Henry to marry a plain-looking German woman, Anne of Cleves, 'the Flanders Mare'.

Until recently, little attention was paid to the thoroughgoing ideological system which Thomas Cromwell invented in order to lubricate his legislative programme. Since few doctrinal novelties were introduced at this stage, it was long assumed that little had changed in the realm of ideas. Yet close examination of the Reformation statutes shows that each was prefaced by a preamble containing radical theological and historical postulates. Cromwell was not content to create a new legal framework for Church and state. He took great care to present theoretical arguments to justify the changes. In particular, he set out to demonstrate two things: firstly, that the old order which he was destroying had been illegitimate: and secondly, that England was returning to an older, purer state of affairs, which had been steadily corrupted in the intervening period by the false teaching and corrupt practices of the Papacy. His arguments centred on the themes of England as a 'sovereign empire' of the self-sufficiency of English law: and of historical precedent.

Hence the preamble to the Act in Restraint of Appeals opened with a reference to sundry (but unnamed) 'old authentic histories and chronicles':

> Where ... it is manifestly declared and expressed that this realm of England is an empire, and hath been accepted in the world, governed by one supreme head and king having the dignity and royal estate of imperial crown of the same, unto whom a body politic, compact of all sorts and degrees of people, divided in terms and by names of spirituality and temporality, be bounden and ought to bear, next to God, a natural and humble obedience.[31]

Cromwell was claiming to uphold a historic right whereby England had supposedly always been completely independent of all extraneous authority. He was denying the validity of the status which everyone in England had accepted for more than a thousand years.

The Act for Ecclesiastical Appointments adopted a parallel fiction by claiming that the King's sole right to appoint bishops and archbishops was a practice 'as of old time has been accustomed'. Yet the Act of Supremacy went furthest of all:

> Albeit the King's majesty justly and rightfully is and ought to be the supreme head of the Church of England, and so is

recognized ... yet nevertheless for corroboration and confirmation thereof, and for increase of virtue in Christ's religion
within this realm of England, and to repress and extirp all
errors, heresies and other enormities and abuses ... be it
enacted ... that the King, or our Sovereign Lord, his heirs and
successors ... shall be taken, accepted, and reputed the only
Supreme Head on earth of the Church of England, called
Anglicana Ecclesia.[32]

If one adds the claim to a legal *imperium* or 'absolute sovereignty'
to the claim regarding Supreme Headship of the Church and the
claim regarding historical continuity, one sees the full extent of
Henry VIII's ambitions as formulated by Cromwell. The scholar
who has brought these matters to light asserts that they made Henry
'the most absolute monarch in Europe'. He might have said 'the
most absolute monarch in Latin Christendom'. For the powers that
Cromwell was inventing were most similar to those of the 'Caesaro-
papism' of the Byzantine tradition in the Orthodox Church. Henry
VIII was the Ivan the Terrible of the West. Cromwell's ideological
inventions resemble those in Russia concerning the 'Third Rome'. It
may be no accident that whilst Anglicans have never been able to
reconcile themselves with Roman Catholics, they have had no
difficulty entering into full communion with the Russian Orthodox.

The rewriting of history is evident at many points in the
Reformation statutes: but nowhere more forcibly than in the Act of
Appeals:

the King, his most noble progenitors, and the nobility and
commons of this said realm, at divers and sundry parliaments
as well in the time of King Edward I [1272–1307], Edward III
[1327–77], Richard II [1377–99], Henry IV [1399–1413], and other
noble kings of this realm made sundry ordinances, laws, statutes
and provisions for the entire and sure conservation of the
prerogatives, liberties and pre-eminences of the said imperial
crown of this realm, and of the Jurisdiction spiritual and
temporal of the same, to keep it from the annoyance as well of

the see of Rome as from the authority of other foreign potentates, attempting the diminution or violation thereof, as often, and from time to time, as any such annoyance or attempt to be known or espied.[33]

In order to show that Henry VIII was doing nothing new, Cromwell was prepared to revise the whole long story of Anglo-Papal relations.

The hostility to 'foreign powers' and 'foreign authorities' is manifest in the language used. All non-English jurisdictions are described as 'usurpations', 'depradations', and 'annoyances'. English authority is the emanation of liberty. All foreign authority is despicable 'tyranny', 'subjection', and 'bondage'. Hence, the Erastian propositions of the English Reformation were advanced in a spirit of precocious nationalism. A charge of systematic xenophobia would not be amiss.

What is more, the propositions were supported by a new and terrifying definition of treason. Since the monarch was now to be seen as head of both the temporal and the spiritual sphere any deviation in religious practice or belief could be interpreted as an offence against the crown. Sacrilege was deliberately confused with politics: anyone who did 'slanderously and maliciously publish and pronounce . . . that the king our sovereign lord should be heretic [or] schismatic . . . shall be adjudged traitors' and 'the offenders therein and their aiders, consenters, counsellors and abettors . . . shall have and suffer such pains of death and other penalties, as limited and accustomed in cases of high treason.'[34] Religious noncon-formity, understood in the widest possible context, was punishable by death. The Spanish Inquisitors could not have hoped for more.

To publicize the new ideology, Cromwell assembled a strong team of propagandists. Stephen Gardiner, author of *De Vera Obedien-tia* (1534), was one of the pioneers. So, too, was Thomas Starkey, whose pamphlet 'An Exhortation to Unity and Obedience' (1534) popularized the arguments. But none was so zealous as John Bale (1495–1563), a former Carmelite friar who had turned against his former faith with vengeance. Bale was a historian and an archivist, who collected the records of the dissolved monasteries in order to use them against the Catholic Church. He played an important role in the revision of early Church history; but he should perhaps be best remembered as the sometime room-mate and chief mentor of John Foxe, the most effective of all the Protestant propagandists. (See page 468, below.) Through the powers of censorship, Cromwell's servants and their successors ensured that no voice could be raised against them. Their version of English history, and their justifications, became the official line for centuries.

Opposition to the King's scheme was slow to develop. It broke out in the 'Pilgrimage of Grace' of 1536–7, when social and economic grievances in the northern counties combined with disgust at the fate of the monasteries. The chief organizer was a Yorkshire gentleman, Robert Aske. The pilgrims were mercilessly crushed. Aske was executed in 1537, having accepted Henry's safe conduct.

Resistance was strongest in Henry's lordship of Ireland. The changes ordained by the Reformation Parliament in England were re-enacted by the Parliament in Dublin. But they were largely observed in the breach; and did not apply beyond the Pale. In Gaelic Ulster, as early as 1539, the friars and parish priests were widely preaching:

> that each man ought, for the salvation of his soul, fight and make war against our sovereign lord the king's majesty, and if any of them die in the quarrel his soul . . . shall go to Heaven, as the souls of SS Peter, Paul and others, who suffered death and martyrdom for God's sake.[35]

Ireland, for the time being, was beyond England's reach.

Henry VIII's death in 1547 brought a huge sigh of national relief, and a huge wave of genuine pent-up Protestantism. Henry's Archbishop of Canterbury, Thomas Cranmer (1489–1556), whilst publicly promoting the King's scheme, had secretly married a German Lutheran, and had privately prepared the groundwork for more thoroughgoing Protestant reforms. In Edward VI's reign (1547–53) he was the chief architect of a truly Protestant Church of England. He produced two versions of his magnificent *Book of Common Prayer* (1549, 1553), the Anglican *Ordinal* (1550), which provided a standard form of church service, and the Forty-two Articles of Religion (1553), which supplied the theological principles of his programme. The unauthorized and incomplete translation of the Bible produced in Germany by the English exile, William Tyndale (1494–1536), was now permitted to circulate.

Edward VI's death in 1553 provoked a violent Catholic reaction. Queen Mary, the Catholic daughter of a Catholic queen, who had been officially declared a bastard, had risked death by sticking in private to the Catholic liturgy. She was determined to restore not only the Catholic form of religion but also the papal supremacy. To this end, she married Philip of Spain. She ordered all recalcitrant Protestants to be burned as heretics: she drove tens of thousands into exile, many of them to distant Lithuania; and then she died suddenly, childless, of stomach cancer. Cranmer, who was burned in the city ditch at Oxford where the bishops of London and Worcester also suffered, prevaricated for a while then faced the flames with courage. Prior to his final stand, he had signed a humiliating recantation. 'This was the hand that wrote it,' he said when thrusting it into the fire, 'therefore it shall suffer the first punishment.'[36] One should not forget that the same hand had written the magnificent *Book of Common Prayer*. (See below, page 497.)

Mary's death in 1558 propelled her ill-prepared half-sister, Elizabeth, to the throne. But Elizabeth coped magnificently. The Elizabethan Settlement of Religion, which was introduced a year later, initiated a masterly compromise which has left Anglicans claiming to this day that they are both Catholic and Protestant. The Thirty-nine Articles reinstated most of Cranmer's Forty-two. Elizabeth was made Supreme Governor of the Church, thereby stopping short of absolute doctrinal Headship. The Act of Uniformity (1559) insisted that all the Queen's subjects attend church regularly, and refrain from religious dissent on pain of severe punishment. Contrary to appearances, Elizabeth was no crypto-Catholic, though she had to drop hints in that direction in order to secure the cooperation of the House of Lords. She had little sympathy for the Calvinists, however, who were now making their presence felt in the Commons. She was determined to hold firmly to the middle course. She subscribed to active persecution but only when religious dissent was flaunted in public. Catholic recusants, who lay low and paid their fines, were not harassed further. Nonetheless, a well-balanced crop of radical Puritan and conservative Catholic martyrs was put to death. Among the former, one may count the Puritan separatists like Henry Barrow or John Greenwood, who were executed following the rash of anti-Anglican 'Marprelate' pamphlets denying the Queen's right to rule. Among the latter may be numbered the saintly Edmund Campion SJ (1540–81), son of a London bookseller and historian of Ireland, and the far less saintly Anthony Babington (1561–86), who had tried to recruit Mary, Queen of Scots to his intrigues. Elizabeth found her most able defender in the Revd Richard Hooker (c. 1554–1600), whose *Laws of Ecclesiastical Polity* (1594) trounced the Presbyterian opposition and laid the foundations of systematic Anglican theology.

The Reformation in Scotland followed a very different course. For thirty years after Henry VIII's initial onslaught in England, Scotland remained staunchly Catholic. In 1528, on orders of the Scottish Parliament, an Edinburgh bookseller, Patrick Hamilton, was burned alive for importing the works of Luther. The Anglo-Scottish Wars of the 'Rough Wooing' saw Scottish Catholics fighting English Protestants. The opportunity for the reformers came in 1560, when the Catholic Queen was absent in France and when anti-French and anti-Catholic sentiments combined to inspire the first of several ecclesiastical transformations. John Knox (1513–72) was a Scots Calvinist who had been active in England. He was the author of the splendidly titled *First Blast of the Trumpet Against the Monstrous Regiment of Women* (1558), which had been directed against the two

Marys, but equally offended Elizabeth. In Edinburgh, Knox persuaded Church leaders to break with Rome as Henry VIII had done,
to rule the Church through a General Assembly, in the Queen's
absence, and to introduce an Anglo-Genevan liturgy. This achieved
little for more than a decade except to divide the Scottish nobility
into warring pro-Catholic and pro-Protestant factions. Queen Mary's
fervent Catholicism would normally have given her supporters the
edge on her return from France. But her personal indiscretions
proved sufficiently blatant for her Protestant opponents to gain
ground and eventually to overthrow her. It was only in 1567, when
Mary was driven into exile in England, that the reforms of seven
years earlier were secured. Mary's infant son, James VI, was allowed
to succeed under the close guardianship of the Protestant nobles.

The coronation of the infant James VI on 29 July 1567 reflected
the deep divisions of the day. It took place in the parish church at
Stirling, not at Scone, and was presided over by an odd mixture of
clergy. A sermon from the Book of Kings was preached by John
Knox, whilst the crowning was performed by Robert Stewart, until
recently the Catholic Bishop of Orkney. The rite of anointment was
ignored, as was the child's baptismal name, 'Charles'. The King
would remain a virtual prisoner for eighteen years, whilst the
religious and political disputes swirled around him.

Unlike the Church of England, the Church of Scotland did not
reach a precise definition of its relations to the State. Its *First Book of
Discipline* (1560), which was drafted by Knox and which would have
introduced a thoroughgoing Presbyterian structure on the Geneva
model, could not be fully enforced. It had much less influence in
the evolving structure of the Church than in the realms of liturgy
and education:

> Seeing that God hath determined that his Church here in earth
> shall be taught not by angels but by men ... of necessity it is
> that your Honours be most careful for the virtuous education
> and godly upbringing of the youth of this Realm ... Of
> necessity therefore we judge it that every several church have

a schoolroom appointed, such a one as able, at least, to teach
Grammar, and the Latin tongue, if the town be of any
reputation.[37]

Secular and religious schooling were to go hand in hand.

The Settlement of Leith in 1572 provided an interim ecclesiastical
compromise in which bishops were to be nominated by the crown
but were to answer in spiritual matters to the General Assembly of
the Kirk.

The bitterest religious disputes, however, were only just beginning. They were fuelled by the return to Scotland of Andrew
Melville (1545–1622), a Scots divine who had learned his religion in
Huguenot France and in Geneva. Melville, who served as Principal
first of Glasgow University and then of St Andrews, quickly formed
a party of militant ministers, intent on pushing through radical
Presbyterian reforms. He was the chief spokesman of the Presbyterian Party for thirty years until an exasperated King eventually sent
him back to France. But he enjoyed greater success than Knox in
converting the Scottish populace to Calvinism.

The heart of 'Melvillianism' lay in the theory of 'Two Kingdoms'
and in the resultant demands for the separation of Church and state.
It was once summarized in stark form by Melville in one of his
many direct clashes with the King:

> Thair is twa Kings and twa Kingdoms in Scotland. Thair is
> Christ Jesus the King, and his Kingdom, the Kirk, whase subject
> King James the Saxt is, and whase kingdom nocht a king, nor a
> lord, nor a heid, but a member![38]

A more nuanced version found its way into *The Second Book of
Discipline*, adopted in 1578:

> 1.2. The kirk . . . hes a certane power grantit be God, according
> to the quhilk it uses a proper jurisdiction and governement,
> exerciseit to the confort of the haill kirk. . . .
> 1.3. The policie of the kirk flowing from this power . . . is gevin

immediately to the office-beararis, be whom it is exercisit to the weil of the haill bodie . . .

1.4 This power and policie ecclesiasticall is different and distinct in the awin nature from that power and policie quhilk is callit the civil power, and appertenis to the civill government of the commonwelth; albeit they be both of God . . .

1.5 For this power ecclesiastical flowes immediatlie from God, and the Mediator Jesus Christ, and is spirituall, not having a temporal heid on earth, bot onlie Christ, the onlie spirituall King and Governour of his kirk.

1.7 Therefore this power and policie of the kirk sould lean upon the Word immediatlie, as the onlie ground thereof, and sould be tane from the pure fountaines of the Scriptures, . . .

1.8 It is proper to kings, princes and magistrates, to be callit lordis, and dominators over subjectis, whom they govern civilly; bot it is proper to Christ onlie to be callit Lord and Master in the spirituall government of the kirk: . . .

1.9 Notwithstanding, as the ministeris and uthers of the ecclesiasticall estait ar subject to the magistrat civill, so aught the person of the magistrat be subject to the kirk spiritually . . . The civill power is callit the Power of the Sword, and the uther the Power of the Keys.

1.10 The civill power sould command the spiritual to exercise and doe their office according to the Word of God: the spiritual rewlaris sould requyre the Christian magistrate to minister justice and punish vyce, . . .

1.15. Finally, as ministeris are subject to the judgement and punishment of the magistrat in externall things, if they offend; so aucht the magistratis to sumbit themselfis to the discipline of the kirk gif they transgresse in matteris of conscience and religioun . . .

. . .

III.5 In the order of election it is to be eschewit that na person be intrusit in ony of the offices of the kirk contrar to the will of the congregation to whom they are appointed . . .

. . .

VII.2 Assemblies ar of four sortis. For aither ar they of particular kirks and congregations, ane or ma, or of a province, or of ane haill nation, or of all and divers nations professing one Jesus Christ.

. . .

VII.25 There is . . . an uther mair generall kynde of assemblie, quhilk is of all nations and estaits of persons within the kirk, representing the universall kirk of Christ; quhilk may be callit properlie the Generall Assemblie or Generall Councell of the haill Kirk of God.[39]

Such a treatise, on the power of the Sword and the Power of the Keys, is worthy of a medieval tract from the time of the Investiture Contest. It bore no relation to the theories which Cromwell had imposed on England.

Needless to say, Melville's theory proved less than welcome to the Regents, and to a king who showed an early predilection for his own 'divine right'. In consequence, the pendulum swung back and forth between Kirk and crown, and no stable solution was found. In 1584, a Scots Parliament heavily influenced by the court party passed a series of so-called 'Black Acts' subjecting the clergy to the crown. In 1592, another Parliament passed the so-called 'Golden Act' confirming the privileges of the Kirk, but without repealing the previous legislation. So the outcome was messy ambiguity. The General Assembly of the Kirk remained a power in the land, a counterweight to crown and Parliament, but with no precise constitutional rights. The King kept his bishops: but he looked with envy at his sister monarch in England, who ruled her Church with no such difficulties. The struggle between episcopalians and anti-episcopalians in Scotland was to drag on for more than a hundred years. In the next reign, it was to inspire rebellion.

The expansion of education in Scotland inevitably provided a sparring-ground for Kirk and crown. In Edinburgh, the city council weighed into the struggle to control the staff and curriculum of the 'tounis college' and in 1583 to raise it to the ranks of the country's fourth university. There, the Kirk was rebuffed. Ten years later, Marischal's College was founded in Aberdeen.

From any objective standpoint, the results of the Reformation in the Isles were very divisive. They caused huge internal divisions, and a large measure of international isolation. They divided Ireland, which stayed largely Catholic, from England and Scotland, which had accepted Protestantism. Yet they divided England, which became Anglican, from Scotland, which did not. They divided Protestant Cornwall from Catholic Brittany which until then had maintained close ties of exchange and intermarriage. In the Channel Isles, which turned Huguenot, they erected a steep cultural barrier which cut off the islanders both from Anglican England and Catholic Normandy. In each of the countries, beneath a veneer of settlement, they pitted Puritans against Papists, and would-be peacemakers against Puritans and Papists alike. These religious differences would form the main basis for future political alignments.

Most seriously, the Reformation cut off the Isles from much of the Continent and from that main body of Christendom which had been its spiritual home for the previous millennium. This spiritual isolation was arguably more profound than anything that resulted from all the political invasions and geographical changes since the Ice Age. All the great shifts of previous times, whether the establishment of the Celts, the rule of the Romans, the arrival of the Anglo-Saxons, or the conquests of Normans and Angevins, had usually fostered a rapprochement between the experience of the islanders and that of the Continentals. But the Reformation set them apart. It drove a wedge down the Channel that was higher than any cliffs. It erected a barrier that was as durable as it was forbidding. It left Catholic Ireland stranded on the far side of the Isles, separated from her natural friends and allies. It left Scotland with no congenial neighbours and no 'Auld Alliance': and with Highlands separated from Lowlands. It put England into a position of unprecedented isolation surrounded on all sides by sullen Irish subjects, by reluctant

Scottish allies, and by powerful Catholic powers in France and in
the Spanish Netherlands. Prior to the definitive establishment of an
independent Protestant regime in the United Provinces in 1648, the
nearest friendly ports for Protestant ships from London were in
Bremen, Hamburg, Esbjerg, and Oslo. For the Catholic English, as
for the Catholic Irish, their loneliness represented an unmitigated
disaster. As for the majority of English Protestants, they had no
choice but to regard it as a challenge, and, when they survived it, as
a sign of their God-given destiny.

No person better epitomized the spirit of defiant English Protestantism than John Foxe (1516–87), a sometime Oxford don and
Marian exile. During his time in Geneva, Foxe had picked up the
idea of collecting the history of anti-papal martyrs. His *Acts and
Monuments . . .*, first published in Latin in 1554 and in English in 1563,
quickly became the all-time best-seller of the century. Popularly
known as 'Foxe's Book of Martyrs', it recounted all the grisly details
of the deaths of almost all the men and women killed in England at
the hands of Catholics. And it made their deaths all the more
sensational by the use of lurid illustrations. It never said a word, of
course, about the martyrdom of English Catholics at the hands of
Protestants. By modern standards, its catalogue of burnings, behead-
ings, disembowellings, and mutilations represents an obscene display
of violence in the service of bigotry. But it was long thought to be
a fine display of principled patriotism. What is more, it deliberately
included a list of Scottish Protestant martyrs. In this way, Foxe
unmistakably implied that England and Scotland stood as one in the
great anti-papal cause.

(5) THE SPANISH BOGEY

As luck would have it, the Reformation hit the Isles exactly at the
juncture when their southern neighbour, Spain, was rising to the
status of world power. For centuries Spain had been a peripheral
country, divided against itself and largely ruled by Muslim Moors.

Yet several events transformed it in the space of a few decades. Castile was united with Aragon. The *Reconquista* of Moorish territory was completed. Explorers in Spanish pay, like Christopher Columbus, opened up the Americas. The wealth of the Indies poured in to finance Europe's finest army. Finally, as part of the division of the Habsburg lands on the death of Charles V, Spain received Europe's most prosperous commercial region, the Netherlands. For Protestant England this was the ultimate foreign nightmare.

Tudor England, still suspicious of a resurgent France, had initially set great store by its alliance with Spain. The marriages of Catherine of Aragon, first to Prince Arthur, and then to Prince Henry, were the most obvious expression of the two countries' closeness. Yet within a couple of decades the configurations had been reversed. France was hopelessly embroiled in the Italian Wars and then in the internal Wars of Religion, and was no longer a serious threat. Spain, in contrast, was growing stronger with every day. What is more, when putting aside his wife and breaking with Rome, Henry VIII was perpetrating a double insult on his Spanish relations. It was inconceivable that the Spaniards would not respond.

As it was, Spain bided her time. The masterstroke was Philip II's marriage to Queen Mary. But the masterstroke misfired. Mary was barren. Philip took no part in England's internal politics. All he did was to drag England into a war with France, whose one tangible result was the loss of Calais. Mary died saying, 'You will find Calais engraved on my heart.'

Philip was patient with Elizabeth. He even tried to marry her, though with no great enthusiasm. But with time his patience snapped. In the 1580s English pirates like Francis Drake were plundering Spanish property on both sides of the Atlantic, and with the Queen's full approval. In 1584 the Spanish Ambassador was expelled from London for complicity in a plot by Francis Throckmorton to replace Elizabeth with Mary Stewart. English intervention in the Revolt of the Netherlands and Mary's execution provided the last straws. After that, it was war – undeclared but unmistakably war.

Spain launched three great fleets or *armadas* against England –
in 1588, 1596, and 1597. They are the stuff of English legend. Their
purpose was to escort a still larger fleet of troop transports that had
been assembled in the ports of the Netherlands. As on later
occasions, notably in 1940, England had no serious forces to contest
a major landing force. But the landing was not to be. The first
armada was dispersed by a daring fireship attack off Gravelines, by
fierce storms in the North Sea, and by the rocks of the Scottish and
Irish coasts. The second armada, faced by similar storms, was
ordered back to harbour. The third armada was 'repelled by bad
weather'. Losing her grip on the Netherlands, Spain finally abandoned all thoughts of an English expedition.[40]

England had survived against the odds. Just as the long war
against France had crystallized English identity in the previous
century, so the long contest with Spain gave it an extra dimension.
The English now saw themselves not just as Protestant and triumphant, but as triumphantly Protestant. It was bad news for the
Catholics, and for international reconciliation.

(6) The High Seas: a Slow Start

Medieval seafaring had barely improved on the standards of the
Viking Age. But in the fifteenth century, new sailing techniques and
new navigational instruments gave sailors the confidence to take to
the open sea and to find their way back to port in all weathers. The
pioneer of ocean sailing is generally taken to be Prince Henry 'the
Navigator' of Portugal, a descendant of John of Gaunt. His ships
discovered Madeira, rounded Cape Bojador, and explored the long
west coast of Africa. In sailing terms, the exploits of Vasco da Gama,
who opened the route to India via the Cape of Good Hope were
hardly less impressive than those of Columbus or Amerigo Vespucci.

In the wake of the Portuguese came the Spaniards, who settled
the Canaries in 1496, the Basques, and the Bretons. It was a Breton
ship under Jacques Cartier which first reached Canada in 1534. The

English were not serious competitors at this stage. But Bristol and Plymouth and other western ports were ideally located for transoceanic ventures; and a ship sent out of Bristol in 1497 under the Venetian Giovanni Cabot (c. 1450 – c. 1499) discovered exciting possibilities. Cabot sailed down the east coast of North America from Newfoundland to the confines of Florida, returning a year later to chart the coasts of Nova Scotia. The main interest of his employers at that time lay in the rich cod grounds off eastern Canada, which English fishermen had already visited and which were to provide a prosperous living for West Country skippers.

The steady improvement of maritime communications acted as a lifesaver for England. After the traditional links with Gascony and northern France were cut, and relations with Spain deteriorated, England's ocean-going ships came to her rescue. As the Isles were ever more tightly encircled by hostile powers, their lifeline to the outside world was provided by foreign trade, by transoceanic exploration, and eventually by colonies.

The Scots had similar concerns to the English. The ports of Leith and Aberdeen were developed in the reign of James IV, who founded a permanent royal fleet at a time when England had none. The Scots, however, were drawn more to the North Sea and less to the Atlantic. Their natural maritime links drew them to Scandinavia and to the Baltic. Helped no doubt by Scotland's religious troubles, an important Scots community took root in Danzig (Gdańsk) in Poland, for example, where the district of Szkoty survives to the present day. The great-grandfather of Immanuel Kant in Königsberg was reputedly a Scot from Fife.

For many decades, England's overseas trade was dominated by the Merchant Adventurers Company of London. Reinforced by royal charters from the ever-watchful Henry VII, notably in 1486 and 1505, the MAC operated the principal Continental staples at Calais to 1558, at Antwerp from 1446 to 1564, and at Hamburg from 1567 to 1579. It dealt primarily in wool, and increasingly in fine English woollen cloth. Nonetheless, the Company's mounting difficulties were bound to reflect England's strategic squeeze. The staple

at Calais was lost through Mary's ill-judged French War. It moved
to Bruges, only to find that the Spanish authorities there would not
let it prosper. The staple at Antwerp was lost through the Dutch–
Spanish War and the closing of the Scheldt. The staple at Hamburg
was displaced by Germany's religious troubles. In theory, the MAC
should then have turned to the Baltic. But the Baltic trade was well
and truly sewn up by England's Dutch competitors. The MAC
slipped into irreversible decline.

Yet many new English companies were vying to take its place.
In 1553–4 two English adventurers, Hugh Willoughby and Richard
Chancellor, set out to find the north-eastern passage to China. They
rounded the North Cape of Norway, and entered the White Sea,
where Willoughby froze to death. Chancellor pressed on, and
finding his way to the court of Ivan the Terrible in Moscow,
returned home to found the Muscovy Company (1555). Thanks to
the decline of the Hanseatic League, the Baltic opened up for the
Eastland Company (1577), whilst the defeat of the Ottomans at
Lepanto removed obstacles to the foundation of the Spanish Company (1577), the Turkey Company (1581), the Venice Company (1583),
the Barbary Company (1585), and the Africa Company (1588). The
Levant Company (1592) arose from the merger of several of its
predecessors. The famous East India Company was founded in 1600
in imitation of the successful Dutch corporation of the same name.

In this era, economic practice was governed by the theory of
mercantilism. Mercantilists believed that world trade was a finite
and fixed entity. Hence they argued that every nation's share of
trade would decrease if one nation's trading activities were allowed
to increase. They judged it essential that governments should always
ensure a foreign trade surplus and that the state's stock of bullion
and coin should be protected at all costs. These ideas, which were
commonplace in the sixteenth century, were eventually formulated
with great clarity by Thomas Mun, a director of the East India
Company, in his *A Discourse of Trade, from England unto the East
Indies* (1621) and his *England's Treasure by Forraign Trade, or, the
ballance of our forraign trade is the rule of our treasure* (written c. 1630

but published posthumously in 1664).They inspired much of the commercial and maritime legislation of the subsequent period.

Sixteenth-century trade was hugely affected by inflating prices in the so-called Price Revolution, and by the resultant monetary problems. In this sphere, no one was more knowledgeable than Sir Thomas Gresham (1519–70), founder of London's Royal Exchange (1566). As Elizabeth's Ambassador to the Netherlands, Gresham saw how commercial affairs were distorted by politics. As a financier, he saw how people's attempts to defend their holdings against a debased coinage only leads to more debasement. Gresham's Law states that 'bad money drives out good'. Both England and Scotland suffered severely from monetary crises. Henry VIII deliberately debased the English coinage in 1544, trying to beat the clippers at their own game. He unleashed confusion that raged until the introduction of Elizabeth's reformed coinage of 1562. The Scots were more canny. The Scottish *festoon* or 'shilling piece' of 1553 was the first coin to deter clipping by having machine-made milled edges.

An important but sombre shift in England's trading patterns was signalled by the transatlantic ventures of the Plymouth merchant Sir John Hawkins (1532–95). In 1562–3 Hawkins tried to muscle in on the closed Spanish slave trade. On three voyages, he sailed to West Africa, as the Portuguese had done a hundred years before, carried a cargo of African slaves to the Spanish colonies of central America, and returned with a fortune in doubloons. On the third occasion, he was attacked and nearly captured. As one of Elizabeth's leading naval administrators, he was one of the earliest voices calling for England to find colonies of her own. He was the uncle of Francis Drake. In Spanish eyes, he was a common smuggler.

Francis Drake is best known for his flamboyant exploits on the Spanish Main, whither he first sailed with his uncle Hawkins. He came from a fiercely Protestant family, and his spectacular depredations of Spanish shipping, like the wrecking of the fleet at Cadiz in 1587, were motivated as much by religious prejudice as by patriotism and greed. Yet his finest achievement must surely lie with the voyage of 1577–81, when he rounded Cape Horn, watered in

California (where Drake's Bay can be found to the north of San Francisco), crossed the Pacific, and circumnavigated the globe. Drake's *Golden Hind* was the first English ship ever to enter the Pacific. Drake was only the second navigator in history, after Magellan's captain Juan Sebastian de Elcano, to sail round the earth. He showed beyond doubt that England's sailors were entering the world class. He died in the company of Hawkins on an abortive expedition to the Caribbean in 1596.

Drake's contemporary, Humphrey Gilbert (1539–83), another Devonian, was consumed by his belief in the North-west Passage. It was a puzzle that navigators were still trying to solve three hundred years later. He was also dedicated to colonization, in which his family's experience in Ireland inspired a number of unfulfilled schemes for North America. He formally laid claim to Newfoundland, but drowned with all hands on the return leg.

For English seafaring prowess to enter public consciousness, some skilled publicity was required. Richard Hakluyt (1552–1616) undoubtedly possessed both the skill and the motivation, having inherited the passion of his cognominous uncle. His extraordinary work on *The principall Navigations, Voiages and Discoveries of the English nation* (1589) ran into several ever-expanding editions. He created a taste for exotic lands across the sea which in time would become more familiar to English people than the heart of Europe. Seafaring was becoming entangled both with patriotism and with new cultural horizons.

By the middle of Elizabeth's reign, almost everyone agreed that foreign colonies constituted the natural goal of all exploration and voyaging. Countries with colonies were securing a permanent place in the front rank of commercial powers. The English, however, had a slow start. They were long frustrated in their attempts to emulate the colonial successes of the Spaniards, the Portuguese, the Dutch, and the French. By the centenary of Columbus's 'discovery' of 'the New World', no single English colonial venture had taken root.

Soon after Gilbert's ill-starred trip to Newfoundland, yet another Devonian, Walter Raleigh (1554–1618), made the first of several vain attempts to plant a colony of six hundred English settlers on Roanoke Island. Raleigh was a courtier and close to the Queen; but his repeated forays into colonization were constantly interrupted by soldiering in Ireland, by ungentlemanly scrapes, and by political intrigue. He was condemned to death for his part in the Main Plot of 1603; but execution was stayed. In the meantime, the survivors of would-be Roanoke were rescued by Drake; and in 1587 a second group of settlers were taken to the coast of Virginia. Three years later, the crew of a supply ship found nothing more than a cryptic 'Gone Away' message. The mystery of the Virginians' fate has never been solved. Finally, in 1595, Raleigh sought to recover his fortunes by an expedition to Guiana, the famed 'El Dorado'. He returned with no gold, but with a strange plant for smoking and a rip-roaring travel tale for publishing. The 'Virgin Queen' was to die with no thriving colony to her name. Despite their mastery of sail and tiller, the English of the Tudor Age met with far greater success from their attempts to subdue their neighbours on the Isles than to garner the fruits of the high seas.

(7) Dominium: the Emergence of an English Empire

If one examines the events of the sixteenth century through spatial, or geographical, criteria, as opposed to the more usual thematic or chronological approach, one discovers a remarkable phenomenon. Power and resources were moving inexorably to a main hub in England's south-east. Under the Plantagenets, the crown had been preoccupied with its French interests, and had not prevented the feudal magnates from constructing their states within the state. The further they were from the King, the larger their landholdings and the more powerful their private standing. The Wars of the Roses were fought by feudal barons whose strength, whether for Lancaster or York, lay in their control of large tracts of the North and of Wales. Scotland was completely independent. Ireland was largely autonomous. Wales, after the defeat of Owen Glendower, was dominated by marcher lords enjoying the last golden summer of their existence. In the sixteenth century the pattern was reversed. The Tudors masterminded a massive campaign of centralization and of concentration of power. Every part of the Isles was affected.

The south-east of England had always enjoyed important advantages of climate, location, and fertility. These were now exploited with a will. Boosted by the cloth trade, by its crafts and manufactures, and by its market for agricultural products, London grew to be ten times larger than any other city in the Isles. Under the Tudors, now firmly ensconced on the Westminster–Hampton Court axis, it was a mecca for commerce, for politics, for culture and money. It was surrounded by rich farming districts growing richer through the rapid advance of enclosures: by sturdy country towns from Guildford to Chelmsford, each with its thriving market and its new grammar school: and by a population, dense for the times, which ensured dominant representation in Parliament. It was in close touch with Oxford and Cambridge, whose academics played a special role in the Reformation, and, through the port of London, with all points of the globe. When Queen Elizabeth went down from Greenwich to Deptford, to greet the *Golden Hind* and to knight Francis Drake, she was moving between country-wide and world-wide centres of communication. When Henry VIII or Thomas Cromwell needed vast sums of money to finance their projects, the bankers of the City were the only possible source of assistance in the country.

Cornwall, in contrast, was out on the longest limb. Its affairs had long been divided by two separate interests – the estates of the Duchy of Cornwall, which were assigned for the upkeep of the King's eldest son, and the autonomous Stannaries Parliament, which met in Truro and which administered parts of both Cornwall and Devon. Its wide-ranging exemptions from central taxation derived from the exceptional importance of the tin industry, requiring all relevant English legislation to observe the distinction of either *pro Anglia* or *pro Anglia et Cornubia*. The persistence of the Cornish

language strengthened the belief that Cornwall was not just a county
of England but a country in its own right.

Cornwall, however, offended the Tudors on several occasions.
In 1497 two separate Cornish rebellions erupted. The first was
provoked by Henry VII's heavy taxation for his Scottish wars. It
was fomented by one Michael Joseph *An Gof*, 'The Smith', of St
Keveme near the Lizard and by a lawyer, Thomas Flamank, who
proclaimed that the King's war was 'but a pretence to poll and pill
the people'. Collecting a ragged army of some two thousand men,
and a noble commander in the person of Lord Audley, Joseph and
Flamank marched all the way through Devon and Somerset to
London. On 16 June they faced a force of royal guards at Blackheath
and were decimated. The leaders were executed for treason; the
rank-and-file survivors were pardoned.

Three months later, on 7 September 1497, the Yorkist Pretender
Perkin Warbeck landed at Whitesand Bay, near Land's End, having
sailed from Ireland. In Bodmin he declared himself to be Richard
IV, and quickly attracted a following of some six thousand men.
Marching on Exeter and then on Taunton, the rebels made little
headway against the royal forces, and the Pretender threw himself
on the King's mercy. Once again, Henry VII contented himself with
the execution of a few ringleaders. Perkin Warbeck and most of his
Cornish 'subjects' received pardons.

In 1548–50 Cornwall was again shaken, by two separate out-
breaks. Resentments in the county had been mounting over the
previous decade, partly through the attainder and execution of the
local magnate – Henry Courtenay, first Marquis of Exeter (1498–1539)
– and partly through the dissolution of the monasteries. The King's
Council of the West was supported by an army of occupation, and
was run by a man – John Russell, first Earl of Bedford (1485–1555) –
who had made a fortune from ex-monastic properties. In April 1548,
agitated by the prospect of the Protestant reforms of Edward VI, a
mob attacked the house in Helston of one of Thomas Cromwell's
former agents, William Body, and killed him. The instigators, who

came from Michael Joseph's old parish at St Keveme, were soon rounded up; and the rest dispersed. But more was to come. The Proclamation of the English Prayer Book in January 1549 provoked a year-long revolt of much greater proportions. (See page 494, below.) Even so, it was clear that the periphery could no longer assert itself against the evermore powerful centre.

The events surrounding the Western Rising, which coincided with a similar but smaller explosion in Norfolk, betray several features that would recur in other parts of the Isles. One of these was the elimination of leading feudal magnates and the transfer of their wealth and power to dependants of the crown. Another was the establishment of a regional Council, modelled on the Star Chamber of Henry VII, which through fierce judicial and military powers could physically destroy all opposition. A third, in the final stage of 'normalization', was the replacement of local institutions by all the manifold instruments of Tudor government – hence the crown patronage of landholding, the uniformity of religion, the supremacy of English common law and the central judicial system, the standardization of territorial counties, together with all the officialdom, bureaucracy, and central control attached to them.

Wales, therefore, followed a parallel path to that of the West Country. Ever since Glendower's defeat in the age of Agincourt, Wales had been largely left to itself. The old division between the autonomous lordships of the March and Wallia Pura had survived. The former, 'the last bastion of the Norman realm', still rested mainly in the hands of the old marcher families – the Mortimers, the Clares, and the Herberts. A few new marcher fortunes had appeared, notably those of the Tudors at Pembroke and the Staffords at Newport. Henry Stafford, second Duke of Buckingham (1454–83) received vast grants of land in the marches from Richard III only to lead the abortive rebellion which paved the way for Henry Tudor's takeover. Wallia Pura, in contrast, was a defeated country. Fierce penal laws reminiscent of the Statutes of Kilkenny in Ireland forbade Welshmen to live in boroughs, to acquire land, or to engage in trade. The Welsh were formally excluded from the rights of English citizenship. (A special exception had to be made in court for Owen Tudor when he married the English queen dowager.) Counties on the English model had been introduced in Carmarthen, Merioneth, and Caernarvon. But with little energy or interest emanating from the centre, practical accommodations between the Welsh and the English in Wales had become the order of the day. Welsh inroads into the central March of Worcester and Hereford during Glendower's Rising were never reversed. In these districts, it was the 'Englishries' which were pushed onto the defensive against the steady revival of Welsh fortunes.

The Tudor assault on Wales began in 1521 with the attainder and execution of Edward Stafford, third Duke of Buckingham. The pro-Welsh propaganda of early Tudor times was wearing thin; Henry VIII was paranoically suspicious of Stafford's reconstruction of his family's vast holdings in the March; so he cut him down on nebulous charges of treason. In 1531 Rhys ap Griffith, grandson of an ardent supporter of Henry Tudor from Carmarthenshire, suffered the same fate. In 1536, Thomas Cromwell introduced the Act for the Union of England and Wales which propelled the principality into a new era. The privileges of the marcher lordships were abolished. New counties were established at Denbigh, Radnor, Montgomery, Brecon, and Monmouth. Powys was shared between the old county of Merioneth and the new county of Montgomery. The county of Flint was split into Welsh and English districts. New and old counties alike were given full representation in the English Parliament. The old council was transferred into a new Council for the Marches in Wales under the loyalist presidency of Sir Henry Sidney (1526–86). The border between England and Wales was clearly defined for the first time, even though the Principality's special characteristics disappeared. The Kingdom of England, duly extended, was renamed 'the Kingdom of England and Wales'. After further legislation in 1543, English common law replaced customary Welsh or marcher law throughout the thirteen counties; and English was declared the sole language of administration. Welsh speakers had either to learn English, use an interpreter, or live beyond the law. Crown-appointed sheriffs and JPs took over from marcher officials. After the Dissolution of the Monasteries, large tracts of Church land were redistributed. The English principle of primogeniture was made universal in place of the Welsh practice of partible inheritance. Church tithes were collected by wealthy loyalist laymen. A legion of Tudor clients took the pickings of the best estates: the Wynns of Gwydir, the Vaughans of Trawsgoed, the Mansels of Margam, the Herberts, now Earls of Pembroke. The Wiltshire family of Seymours, who rose to prominence through Queen Jane Seymour and the Protectorate of Edward Seymour, first Duke of Somerset (1500–52), took the lands both of Raglan and of Tintern. 'Wales . . . was now the first province within an English empire.'[41]

The North of England remained a land apart. Indeed, Northerners have always felt more at ease with their Celtic neighbours and with the Scots than with the conformist circles of the south-east. In the sixteenth century, they were markedly more attached to Roman Catholicism and to the old communities of 'good-lordship' than they were to the new Anglican Establishment and to the bureaucratic, southern-based Tudor crown. After the defeat of the Pilgrimage of Grace of 1536, however, the North was fenced in by the aggressive activities of the Council of the North, and in the second round of defiance in 1569–70 the Rising of the Northern Earls had little resonance beyond the region.

The Rising centred on the disaffection of two northern magnates, Charles Neville, sixth Earl of Westmorland (1542–1601), and Thomas Percy, seventh Earl of Northumberland (1528–72). Both were Catholics, and both had been implicated in the flight to England of Mary, Queen of Scots (see above). When Westmorland's Catholic brother-in-law, Henry Howard, Duke of Norfolk was executed in 1569 for alleged treason, they took to arms. Northumberland seized Durham Cathedral, where he ordered Mass to be celebrated. Westmorland roused the men of Cumbria, but was defeated in battle at Naworth by Sir Thomas Radcliffe, third Earl of Sussex (1525–83), Lord President of the Council of the North. The leaders fled to Scotland. Radcliffe pursued them. Their supporters were left to face the merciless consequences.

It is not without significance that Radcliffe, who headed the Council of the North, like Sidney, who had headed the Council of Wales, had recently returned from Ireland. Indeed, Radcliffe and Sidney, who were brothers-in-law, both served as successive lords deputy of Ireland. It was no accident that the Tudors' Irish policy owed a great deal to their policy in Wales and the North.

The breaking of the Fitzgeralds served notice that overmighty subjects were no safer in Ireland than elsewhere. But Henry VIII's Irish policy had been inordinately expensive. And it left a gaping vacuum in Irish government that had somehow to be filled. It had been justified by the rebellion of Lord Kildare, the heir to the Fitzgerald fortune, who could not stomach the Act of Supremacy, and by generalized fears of the legislation which Cromwell was known to be preparing. However, the rise and fall in 1535–40 of the English Lord Deputy of Ireland, Leonard Grey, who was recalled and executed with Cromwell, gave proof of the bedevilment of Irish affairs by intrigues at the English court. These intrigues were a constant, enfeebling factor in the execution of central policies which were often in themselves ambiguous or half-hearted.

The next Lord Deputy after Grey, Sir Anthony St Leger (1496–1559), who held office with only temporary breaks until the middle of Mary's reign, implemented two keystone schemes – the creation of the Kingdom of Ireland, and the land policy of 'surrender and re-grant'. In 1541, the Irish Parliament passed an act which raised Ireland to the status of a sovereign kingdom, with Henry VIII as its hereditary monarch. Some such step was essential, since the earlier English Act of Supremacy (1534) had undermined Ireland's previous status as a lordship conferred by papal title. (See page 334, above.) In effect, it created a personal union of crowns, parallel to that which would link England and Scotland after 1603. It conspicuously avoided the integrationist approach that was applied to Wales. The third, clerical chamber of the Irish Parliament, which had denounced the

Royal Supremacy, was abolished. Yet no Tudor monarch ever took the trouble to visit, let alone to be crowned in, their second kingdom. (One hundred and forty-eight years were to pass before a 'King of Ireland' would actually see his Irish kingdom in person.)

The scheme for 'surrender and re-grant' was greatly assisted by the land fund created by the dissolution of the lesser monastic houses. The idea was to end the independence of the great landowners, whether Gaelic chiefs or Anglo-Irish barons, and to weld them into a uniform system of English-style landowning based on aristocratic titles, primogeniture, and regular taxation. One signal success occurred in 1542 when the chief of the O'Neills accepted the title of Earl of Tyrone and, in theory, everything that went with it. But there were many failures. The chiefs and barons retained their private armies, fought each other with impunity, reacted violently to financial impositions, and generally defied all the crown's attempts at 'inexpensive pacification'. Lord Deputy Radcliffe (1556–65) tried to tame the wayward clans by appointing officially approved 'Captains' over the clan armies. But it spoke worlds that Radcliffe's long-term opponent, Shane O'Neill, was brought low not by the crown but by the O'Donnells.

Queen Mary briefly returned both England and Ireland to Catholic orthodoxy. But in 1560 Elizabeth's Irish Act of Uniformity introduced Anglican-style practices together with the Anglican Prayer Book in English and Latin versions. Gaelic Ireland either ignored the legislation or pretended to obey it. Open Catholic recusancy was strongest among the 'Old English' of the Pale, who viewed religious impositions as an adjunct to the obnoxious influence of the 'New English' now proliferating in the crown bureaucracy and in the new plantations. The most sanguinary episode of the four-year Desmond Rebellion (1579–83) was terminated by the wholesale slaughter, by the young Walter Raleigh among others, of the Baltinglass rebels. The establishment of a Protestant academy at Trinity College, Dublin, for teaching Anglican-style clergy, was delayed until 1592.

The policy of 'plantation', that is, the systematic uprooting of the native population in favour of incoming English colonists, was relaunched in 1557, when the districts of Leix and Offaly were officially renamed 'King's County' and 'Queen's County' in honour of Philip and Mary. Lord Deputy Radcliffe was personally involved in these campaigns, supervising the recruitment of these mainly Catholic colonists in England and their transport to Ireland. Under Elizabeth, expressly Protestant plantations were attempted in Ulster, one by Thomas Smith at Ards (1571–2), the other (1572–3) by Walter Devereux, first Earl of Essex. Neither thrived. Early plantations of Presbyterian Scots in Antrim were alternately encouraged and discouraged by the crown. The Gaelic and the Catholic interests in Ireland were directly threatened and insulted by these measures, which caused resentment out of all proportion to their real importance.

The 'Court of Castle Chamber' – Ireland's equivalent of the Council in Wales and the Council of the North – was created under Lord Deputy William Fitzwilliam in 1572 and located in Dublin Castle. Henceforth, Dublin Castle became the prime symbol of English misrule in Ireland. 'Castle Catholic' became the standard Irish term for a collaborator.

For fifty years, the various Irish interest groups — the 'Old English' Palesmen, the 'New English' settlers, the 'Anglo-Irish' barons, and the Gaelic-Irish clans – all jockeyed for power and influence. Each, in its relations with the crown, had grounds both for aspiration and for discontent. For fifty years, a vacillating English regime sought to satisfy the competing demands and to bring Ireland to order without committing adequate resources to the task. As time passed, however, the English military establishment in Ireland grew, together with the temptation to use it. Even before the major rebellions, 75 per cent of Irish taxation was earmarked for military purposes, whilst 90 per cent of all crown expenditure in Ireland was covered by grants from the English treasury. By the 1580s, when Irish politics became entangled with Catholic plots, court intrigues, and Spanish strategy, patience on both sides reached breaking point. Edmund Spenser, the poet, who served as secretary to Lord Deputy

Grey de Wilton, published *A View of the Present State of Ireland* (1596), which called for a ruthless campaign of military might. Hugh O'Neill, second Earl of Tyrone (1540–1616), the royal commissioner in Ulster, to whom the Irish Gaels looked for leadership against the crown, and crown agents for assistance against dissident Gaels, simmered.

O'Neill finally raised the flag of revolt in 1595, when he seized an English fort on the Blackwater near Armagh. He was declared a traitor, and faced the royal wrath. He placed his trust in Spanish assistance, thereby missing his chance to capitalize on local sympathies. His victory at the Yellow Ford (1598) coincided with the death of Philip II, which precipitated three crucial years of indecision on all sides. In 1599, he faced out the Earl of Essex, the Queen's former favourite, with whom he arranged a truce. But time was working against him. The Deputy whom Essex left behind – Charles Blount, eighth Baron Mountjoy, later first Earl of Devonshire (1563–1606) – was made of sterner stuff than any of his predecessors. A half-hearted Spanish landing at Kinsale in 1601 gave too little support too late. Mountjoy was able to crush the Spaniards, before turning on O'Neill in a pitched battle which the Irish would have been well advised to avoid. In 1602 and 1603 he was harrying the Irish countryside without mercy, burning crops, hanging rebels, razing villages, and praising God for his protection. By the time the old Queen died in distant Greenwich O'Neill was in detention; and a prostrate Ireland awaited her fate.

Tudor policy to Scotland was governed by two bald facts – by the defeat of Flodden (1513), which left the enfeebled Scots vulnerable to English manipulations, and, later, by the ever-growing likelihood that James VI would become Elizabeth's heir. The Reformation did not bring a close rapprochement between the Anglican Establishment of England and the Presbyterian Establishment of Scotland. But, while waiting for an outcome to the French Wars of Religion, it shunned 'the Auld Alliance' for decades; and it opened the way for common purposes based on anti-Catholic and anti-Spanish prejudice. Scotland's interventions in Ireland were tempered by the knowledge that links between the Irish Gaels and Highland Gaels were potentially as dangerous for Edinburgh as for London. In July 1586, therefore, when James VI had grown to maturity, Queen Elizabeth's chief minister, William Cecil, Lord Burghley (1520–98), personally negotiated the terms of an Anglo-Scottish treaty, signed at Berwick. Nothing was overtly agreed about the English succession. But James was to be paid an English pension. And the two countries were to embark on an expanding programme of mutual cooperation. Neither the execution in 1587 of Mary, ex-Queen of Scots, nor the turmoil in Ireland, could persuade the signatories to change their chosen course.

Such were the fruits of Burghley's 'British policy'. He lived long enough to see all parts of the Isles subordinated in one degree or another to the dominant English crown. England and Wales had been one kingdom since 1536. England and Ireland had lived in union under the Tudors since 1541. Cornwall's divergent tendencies had been silenced since 1549: those of the North since 1570. England and Scotland, since 1586, were converging towards a path of common destiny. Queen Elizabeth's death and the submission of the Earl of Tyrone occurred in March 1603 within a few days of each other. *De facto*, if not yet evenly *de jure*, all the Isles lay within the English obedience. In the words of one of the very first historians to view the history of the Isles as a whole, 'a new period of history' had begun: 'It was characterised by the emergence of an "English empire", or, more precisely, an empire based on the wealth, population and resources of southern England over the rest of the British Isles.'[42] And he added, 'and in due course, over the east coast of North America and the West Indies'.

Some historians have objected to the time-frame of this statement. Some insist that the process was far from complete. Others point out, quite correctly, that the process had begun many centuries earlier and was not just the product of the Tudor Age.[43] So one must pick one's words carefully. By 1603, it is fair to say, the

construction of England's 'Inner Empire' had moved from the latent
stage to a point where the impetus for its completion was all but
irreversible.

(8) DEARLY BELOVED: THE SPREAD OF ENGLISH

Granted that John of Trevisa had observed a crucial moment in the
late fourteenth century, when he recorded that English had started
to be used as the language of school instruction (see page oo, above),
English could not possibly have risen to a position of pre-eminence
for many generations. Firstly, only a tiny proportion of the population went to school. Almost all women, and the majority of men,
were untouched by formal education. Secondly, the French-speaking
court and its dependent elite had no urgent reason to change its
habits. And thirdly, Latin remained as the universal lingua franca.
Henry V was the first English king to insist that official documents
were published in English. Yet Henry VI, raised by a French mother,
was considerably less English than his father.

In the early fifteenth century, the English language simply did
not possess the necessary attributes of an all-purpose, universal
language. It was not enough that insular French was in decline, or
that Latin lacked a popular base. English itself had to mature, to
expand, and to evolve. It did so in the fifteenth and sixteenth
centuries through the processes of standardization, expansion, legiti-
mization, and state patronage.

Standardization is just one way of describing the evolution of a
single form of literary English that could then be taught to all pupils
and in all parts of the realm. In John of Trevisa's time there were
numerous forms of English in the Isles. There was no common
orthography, no common pronunciation, no common grammar, no
common vocabulary, no common textbooks. If late-fourteenth-
century schoolboys were indeed being taught in English, each school
can only have been using the particular branch of English that was
current in its locality.

Not surprisingly, since there were two sovereign kingdoms in the Isles, two separate branches of standard English developed. The first to establish itself was Scots English, the language of the leading circles in Lowland Scotland after they had thrown off the attempted embrace of the Plantagenets. The key literary texts, which served to create the essential constituency of literate readers and speakers, were taken from the writings of patriots, such as John Barbour (1325–95), who celebrated the struggle for Scotland's independence, and from the more polished productions of the following century. James I, the third of Scotland's Stewart kings, was writing poetry in Scots English at a point when the Plantagenets were still operating in French. A strong group of Scots poets of the early fifteenth century were patronizingly dubbed by English critics as the 'Scottish Chaucerians'. This is surely a misnomer. The 'aureate' poetry of William Dunbar (b. c. 1460, d. before 1530), for instance, carries strong formalist, Latin tones, not least in his 'Ballat to Our Lady':

> Hale, sterne superne! Hale, in eterne,
> In Godis sicht to schyne!
> Lucerne in derne for to discerne
> Be glory and grace devyne;
> Hodiern, modern, sempitern,
> Angelicall regyne!
> Our tern inferne for to dispern
> Helpe, rialest rosyne.
> *Ave Maria, gracia plena!*
> Haile, fresche floure femynyne!
> yerne us, guberne, virgin matern,
> Of reuth baith rute and ryne![44]

Scots English has had, and is still having, a long career. It held a dominant position in Scotland as long as Scotland was a sovereign country. It would decline rapidly during the first decades of the Union, but not before Robbie Burns had won the laurels of a national bard. (See Chapter Nine.) It was to survive alongside Scots Gaelic in local and unofficial circles until, as an essential element of

Scots identity, it would revive again on the wave of contemporary Scottish nationalism. (See Chapter Ten.)

The standard English of England crystallized somewhat later, at the turn of the fifteenth century. It was based on the dialect of the South-east as spoken in London and as enshrined in the works of Geoffrey Chaucer. The great popularity of *The Canterbury Tales* in the age of Agincourt ensured a critical mass of readers and speakers who could use and propagate that particular form of the language:

> Whan that Aprille with his shoures soote
> The droghte of March hath perced to the roote,
> And bathed every veyne in swich licour
> Of which vertu engendered is the flour –
> . . . .
> Thanne longen folk to goon on pilgrimages,
> And palmeres for to seken straunge strondes,
> To ferne halwes, kowthe in sondry londes;
> And specially from every shires ende
> Of Engelond to Caounterbury they wende,
> The hooly blisful martir for to seke,
> That hem hath helpen whan that they were seeke.[45]

Once established, standard Scots and standard English would evolve through many transformations. Language is never static. It is a dynamic phenomenon which reflects the changing needs and interests of the community that uses it. Chaucer's English differs from contemporary English even more than it did from other forms of regional English in his own day.

The community using standard English expanded along two quite distinct tracks. One of these was geographical, and depended on the rising level of political and commercial contacts between the two capitals, Edinburgh and London, and their respective provinces. The other was social, and largely depended on the patterns of education. In this respect, it was important not only that the universities were growing, but also that new, influential schools were being founded to feed the universities. Between 1400 and 1610,

Scotland's universities rose from one to four, whilst the number of colleges at Oxford and Cambridge more than doubled. Royal patronage increased in response to the growing demand for well-educated, English-speaking, and preferably non-clerical administrators. Bishop William of Wykeham (1324–1404), Chancellor under Edouard III and Richard II, founded both New College, Oxford (1379) and its feeder school, Winchester College (1382). Henry VI founded both King's College, Cambridge (1441) and, in the immediate vicinity of Windsor Castle, Eton College (1440–41). His aim was to create an educational system dependent on the crown rather than the Church. William of Wykeham's motto was 'Manners makyth man'. There can be no doubt that in the course of the decades after his death good manners came to include a good knowledge of standard English.

The graduates of the leading schools and universities became parish priests and schoolmasters all over the country. They took metropolitan English culture with them. But nothing accelerated the spread of standard English more effectively than the innovation of printing. William Caxton (1420–91), who set up his first printing press at Westminster in 1476, was twenty years behind the printing pioneers on the Continent. But his publication of a hundred titles in little more than a decade was an astonishing achievement. In Scotland, Walter Chapman and Andrew Myllar received a printers' licence in Edinburgh in 1507. School books and English language devotional works were high on the list of the printers' productions. Literacy among males rose rapidly to an estimated 30 per cent by 1550. Women, though rarely trained in writing, were frequently able to read. And they, too, would increasingly modify their speech to match what they read.

Underlying all these developments lay the rise of a vernacular ethos. For centuries, reading and writing had been the near-magical preserve of the priestly caste; and the secret language of the caste was Latin. The clergy did not surrender their privileges lightly or swiftly. Conservative attitudes long held that secular literature written in the vernacular language of the common people was a dubious, not to say a subversive activity. A long campaign was waged before the prevailing climate of opinion could fully accept the propriety of vernacular literature and secular education. Two great civilizational movements assisted that campaign: the Renaissance and the Reformation.

The Renaissance did not immediately affect the Isles in some of its more visible aspects such as painting or architecture. But through the prevailing Humanism it profoundly influenced cultural attitudes, especially towards education and literature. The repeated visits of Erasmus to England between 1499 and 1514, and his extensive correspondence thereafter with English admirers, such as William Blount, John Colet, Dean of St Paul's, and Hector Boece of Aberdeen, were landmark events. Colet's foundation of St Paul's School (1519), whose statutes expressly excluded clerical control, was a sign of things to come. The Humanists did not follow any single programme. They were opposed to prevailing Church policies, not to Catholicism as such. But their enthusiasm for classical literature brought a whole new dimension to the learning of Latin; their interest in Greek and Hebrew, for the purpose of preparing critical editions of biblical and patristic works, led them into conflict with the Church authorities; and their resultant anticlerical stance gave weight to the rising chorus of protest against ecclesiastical inflexibility. In the general field of literature, their support for the pre-Christian pantheon of classical authors, and for the secular themes and genres of the classics, inevitably boosted the legitimacy of the growing corpus of non-religious, vernacular literature. In England, this helped the rising interest in English authors such as Thomas Malory, whose *Morte d'Arthur* (1471) was printed by Caxton, or Thomas More, whose *Utopia* (1516) has passed into the canon of world literature. Erasmus's own *Adagia* (1508), or 'Proverbs', published first in Latin and then in English, became the very first printed best-seller.

The Protestant Reformation exercised a still greater influence on Englishness. Access to God through the medium of one's own native language was one of its cardinal principles. Whilst the Counter-Reformation reconfirmed the inviolability of the Latin

Mass, all the leading reformers introduced vernacular liturgies. Bible-reading became the prime duty of every conscientious Protestant. This meant that every new Protestant community sponsored a new translation of the Bible, that Protestant officialdom set special store on education and literacy, and that the general level of literacy in Protestant countries soon surpassed the level in Catholic countries.

The expressed desire of the Scottish reformers to open a school in every parish took many decades to realize, not least for financial reasons. (See below.) But the link between kirk and school in Scotland was a strong one. Children were grilled on Monday morning about the content of the Sunday sermon. In England, secular education received a spectacular boost through the special effects of the Dissolution of the Monasteries. The rash of municipal grammar schools, which were founded during the reign of Edward VI in towns all over the kingdom, was the direct result of the sudden closure of monastic schools. They remained one of the sturdiest pillars of English education until their own precipitate dissolution in the 1960s and '70s. Ex-monks provided a plentiful supply of new schoolmasters. In Scotland, the old Church schools were rarely dissolved, merely reconstituted. In that case, the break with the past was far less traumatic.

As for Bible reading, it proved a huge boom both for translators and for booksellers. Every educated Protestant family aimed to possess its own Bible, even though the early Anglican authorities originally intended to limit circulation to nobles. Unfortunately for them, the number of biblical translations ran completely out of control. By the end of Elizabeth's reign, there were eight main English Bibles circulating in England. In addition to Wyclif and Tyndale, there was Coverdale's revision of Tyndale (1535), the officially authorized Matthew Bible (1537), the Great Bible (1539) sponsored by Cromwell, the Geneva or 'Breeches' Bible (1557–60) preferred by Calvinists, the anti-Genevan Bishop's Bible (1566–72), and the Douai Bible (1582), which was produced by English Jesuits abroad for the use of English-speaking Catholics. In this situation, it is entirely understandable that one of the first acts of the next reign would call for a final, authoritative, authorized version. (See page 549, below.)

In that same period, the everyday use of standard English spread into many parts of the Isles that had previously been relatively immune. Regional dialects and Celtic languages pulled back. The culture of England, now thoroughly Englished, commanded more presses, more publications, more people, and more prestige. It dominated all the major centres of higher learning. It was exported into the deepest recesses of the realm by traders, by officials, by settlers. It was imported by locals who had travelled to London, or had studied at Oxford, or who had attended English schools or served the crown.

Yet the interaction of Reformation trends with the spread of English led to some unexpected results. Despite modern impressions, the English authorities did not always impose the English language at all costs. On the contrary, linguistic policy saw l twists and turns; and with some delay a serious attempt was launched to make the reformed religion accessible to the Celtic peoples in Celtic languages. For the time being at least, the propagation of Protestantism commanded no less a priority than the propagation of standard English.

In Wales, for example, the initial programme of Henrician reform included a clear policy of replacing the Welsh language with English. The wording of the Act of Union with Wales (1536) was as tendentious as it was plain:

Albeit the Dominion, Principality and Country of Wales, justly and righteously is, and ever hath been incorporated, annexed, united and subject to and under the imperial crown of this realm as a very member and joint of the same ... yet notwithstanding, because that in [Wales] ... divers usages, laws, and customs be far discrepant from the laws and customs of this realm, and also because of that the people ... have and do daily use a speech nothing like nor consonant to the natural

mother tongue used to within this realm, some rude and
ignorant people have made distinction . . .

His Highness therefore, of a singular zeal, love and favour
that he beareth his subjects of . . . Wales minding and intending
to reduce them to the perfect order, notice and knowledge of
his laws . . . and utterly to extirp all the singular sinister uses
and customs differing from the same . . . established that this
said country . . . of Wales shall be . . . incorporated, united and
annexed to and with this realm of England . . .

Also be enacted . . . that all justices . . . and other officers
. . . shall proclaim and keep the . . . courts in the English tongue
. . . and also that from henceforth no person or persons that
use Welsh speech or language shall have or enjoy any manner
of office or fees . . . upon pain of forfeiting the same office or
fees, unless he or they use and exercise the speech or language
of English.[46]

Once could not hope for a better example of colonial cultural
policy. Yet the Anglicization of office-holders in Wales did little to
change the religious practices of the mass of the population. So
in the next generation the Elizabethan regime took a different
tack. In 1563, the English Parliament ordered a Welsh translation
of the Anglican Prayer Book. This gave rise four years later to
publications in Welsh both of the Prayer Book and of the New
Testament. The translator was William Salesbury (1520–84), who
had earlier produced a Welsh dictionary. The full translation of the
Welsh Bible by William Morgan, Bishop of St Asaph's, followed in
1588.

Similarly, in Scotland, John Carwell's Gaelic translation of the
Genevan *Book of Common Order* was intended to facilitate the
evangelization of the Catholic clans. Even in Ireland, Protestant
literature and liturgies were translated into Irish Gaelic, though no
full Irish Bible was available until 1690.

The effects of these linguistic policies were far from even. Their
success was entirely dependent on the religious disposition of the
recipient population. The contrast between Wales and Ireland, for

example, could not have been greater. In Wales, where the Protestant religion took deep root, the Welsh language prospered as never before. Modern standard Welsh was created from the religious literature of the Reformation period. The churches, and even more the Nonconformist chapels of the later era, became the fortresses of Welsh culture. Welsh-speaking clergymen, like Richard Davies, Bishop of St David's (1501–81), acted as the patrons of a vibrant Welsh secular culture in which poetry and song took pride of place. In Ireland, exactly the opposite happened. Whilst the English-speaking inhabitants of the former Pale largely adopted the reformed religion, the Mass of the Irish Gaels did not. The Irish Catholic clergy continued to say the Mass in Latin, and to regard Protestant-backed Gaelic literature and Protestant-backed Gaelic schools with abhorrence. As a result, Irish Gaelic never received the injection of cultural fuel that Welsh did. In the long term, it was to prove considerably less resistant than Welsh to the onward march of English. Generally speaking, the Irish Gaels were destined to keep their religion and to lose their language. The Welsh lost their links with Catholicism; but they kept their language.

In the Scottish Highlands, the Protestant offensive brought a meagre harvest. With the exception of the Campbell lands in Argyll and of several islands, where Protestant lairds converted their subjects, the great majority of the clans stuck both to the Gaelic tongue and to the Old Religion.

The most puzzling case was encountered in Cornwall. In the mid-sixteenth century, the majority of Cornwall's population still spoke Cornish. Yet their reaction to the imposition of the English Prayer Book was markedly more violent and sustained than that in Wales. Protests began in June 1549 under the leadership of two members of the gentry, Humphrey Arundell and John Winslade. 'Articles of Supplication' were sent to the King's Protector, Lord Somerset, demanding the retention of iconic images and the continued use of Latin in most church services. Not grasping that the demand for Latin in church was a device for protecting Cornish in the home, Somerset refused. And he added a sarcastic comment, saying that the English-speakers in Cornwall surely outnumbered the Latin-speakers. Whereat, parties of rebels congregated in several camps round Bodmin, before marching on Exeter. Their revised articles, which were now sent to Archbishop Cranmer, contained the famous sentence: 'And so we Cornishmen (whereof certain of us understand no English) utterly refuse this new English.' Cranmer's reply was unbending: 'O ignorant men of Devon and Cornwall,' he wrote, 'you ask you wot not what.' It was the signal for a military assault. Russell moved against the rebels with a professional army and a team of hanging judges. Arundell withstood a month's siege; then he retreated and was chased:

> The hangings and the spoils of the rebel's goods . . . began. There was no danger of Russell being too lenient, and when he went back to Exeter . . . he left [the provost-Marshal] to carry on the good works of hanging . . . We have no account of what happened in those grim tragic days . . . We can only sense the confusion . . . of that the 'Commotion Time' as [the Cornish] called it, the tragedy that came home to them and broke their lives.[47]

The 'Prayer Book Revolt' was lost, and with it the chance of bolstering the Cornish language with official policy. But the Cornish loss may have been a Welsh gain. Elizabeth did not make the same mistake in Wales that Somerset had made in Cornwall.

In the Elizabethan age, all the indications are that English culture, based on a sparklingly fresh and vigorous English language, had finally reached maturity. In the realm of high literature, a huge range of genres had opened up. The long task of translating the corpus of classical authors into English was virtually complete. Chapman's translation of the *Iliad* (1596) was a keystone. Vast collections of sermons were published. In J. Lyly's *Euphues* (1578) the English novel was launched. With Raphael Holinshed's *Chronicles* (1577) and William Camden's *Britannia* (1586), a huge fund of historical, antiquarian, mythological, and genealogical material was presented to the public. In poetry, Thomas Wyatt and others reproduced the Italian sonnet form. Lyric poetry burst into flower in the hands of Philip Sydney, Michael Drayton, Edmund Spenser, Christopher Marlowe. Spenser's *Faerie Queene* (1596), which was a deliberate piece of Tudor artistic propaganda, provided a suitable epitaph to Elizabeth's reign:

> See where she sits upon the grassie green,
>> (O seemely sight!)
> Yclad in Scarlot, like a mayden Queene,
>> And ermines white:
> Upon her head a Cremosin coronet
> With Damaske roses and Daffadillies set:
>> Bay leaves betweene
>> And primroses greene
> Embelish the sweete Violet.[48]

Above all, in drama, English culture scaled heights that have never been surpassed. Theatre moved from the shadowy backwaters of inn-yards into the throbbing heart of London life. The Rose, the Globe, and the Curtain were all purpose-built. Working under the watchful eye of a Tudor censorship which regularly clamped down on 'Matters of Divinitie and State not to be suffered', dramatists such as Marlowe, Ben Jonson, and, from 1588, the young Shakespeare, addressed every conceivable theme of the human condition. They were able to do so because the slowly matured English language could respond to their demands. One of the star writers of the day, Robert Green (1558–92), who had written plays, poetry, and a novel called *Pandosto* (1588), complained about the popularity of Shakespeare – 'an upstart crow dressed in our feathers'. Some crow.

For the common people of England, however, history books, sonnets and dramas, were far, far away. Their experience of the new English language was largely confined to Sunday worship in the parish church. Elizabeth's Act of Uniformity commanded that every man, woman, and child in the kingdom should attend church.

So week after week, year after year, millions would assemble to hear the sonorous cadences of Cranmer's Prayer Book:

AN ORDRE

FOR MATTYNS DAYLY THROUGH THE YERE

The Priest beeyng in the quier, shall begynne with a loude voyce the Lordes prayer, called the Pater Noster.

OURE father whiche arte in heauen, hallowed be thy name. Thy kyngdom come. Thy wyll be done in earth as it is in heauen. Geue vs this daye oure dayly bread. And forgeue us oure trespasses, as we forgeue them that trespasse agaynst vs. And lead vs not into temptacion. But deliuer vs from euell. Amen.

Then lykewyse he shall saye,

O Lorde, open thou my lyppes.
Aunswere   And my mouthe shall shewe forth thy prayse.
Priest   O God, make spede to saue me.
Aunswere   O Lord, make haste to helpe me.
Priest   Glory be to the father, and to the sonne, and to the
    holye ghost. As it was in the begynnyng, is now, and euer
    shalbe world without ende. Amen.
    Prayse ye the Lorde.[49]

There has never been a language school like it; and none equipped with more beautiful or more inspiring texts.

In 1552, numerous minor changes were made to the Prayer Book. In the Order for Matins, for example, the recital of the Lord's Prayer was to be prefaced by the reading of one of five alternate passages, most usually the General Confession. Henceforth, until very recent times, these are the words which the great majority of English people would hear every time, as they took their place on the wooden pews:

Almighty and most mercyfull father, we have erred and strayed from thy wayes, like lost shepe. We have folowed too much

the devises and desyres of our owne hearts. We have offended
against thy holy lawes . . .[50]

Similarly precise, poetic and profound pronouncements awaited
them at all their rites of passage:

PUBLIQUE BAPTISME
Dearely beloued, for asmuche as all men bee conceyued and
borne in synne, and that our Sauiour Christ saith, none can
entre into the kingdom of God (except he be regenerate and
borne a newe of water and the holy Ghost); I beseche you to
call upon God the father through our Lord Jesus Christ, that of
his bounteous mercie, he will graunt to these children, that
thing which by nature they cannot have . . .[51]

Or when they started out on married life:

OF MATRIMONY
Dearely beloued frendes, we are gathered together here in the
syght of God, and in the face of his congregacion, to ioyne
together thys man and this woman in holy matrimonie, which
is an honourable estate, instituted of God in Paradise, in the
time of Man's innocency, signifying unto us the misticall union
that is betwixte Chryste and hys Churche: . . .[52]

Or, when they were laid in their graves:

BURIALL OF THE DEAD
I am the resurreccion and the lyfe (sayeth the Lorde): he that
beleueth in me, yea thoughe he were dead, yet shall he lyue.
And whosoeuer lyueth and beleueth in me, shall not dye for
euer.
     I knowe that my redemer liueth, and that I shall ryse
out of the earth in the last day, and shalbe couered agayne
with my skinn, and shall see God in my fleshe: yea, and I my
self shall beholde hym, not with other but wyth these same
eyes.
     We brought nothing into this world, neither may we cary

anything out of this worlde. The Lord geueth, and the Lord taketh awaye. Euen as it hath pleased the Lord so cometh thynges to pass: blessed be the name of the Lorde . . .[53]

Nothing, in their state of isolation from the rest of Christendom, could have given the English people more comfort.

DESPITE THE MANY RESERVATIONS of historians, the year of 1492 is probably still perceived in the popular mind as the single most important date in history. Rightly or wrongly, the year when Columbus 'sailed the ocean' has traditionally been seen as the dividing line between Europe's medieval and modern history, or, if one prefers finer tuning, between the late medieval and the early modern. In the USA, it is known to most Americans of European origin as the moment when their own particular story began. In the English-speaking world as a whole, it seems all the more convincing because it very nearly coincides with one of the traditional divisions of English history, in which the arrival of the Tudor dynasty plays a key role. The Tudors, who climbed onto the English throne in 1485, supposedly created the framework within which England freed herself from civil war, from misplaced Continental ambitions, from domination by the Roman Catholic Church, from backward medieval thought, and from her lowly ranking among European powers.

The arguments against this approach revolve round the undoubted fact that the great changes of the era were the product of long-drawn-out 'processes', not of sudden 'turning-points'. The Age of Discovery, for example, started long before Columbus, with Henry the Navigator or even with Marco Polo, and continued long, long after his death. The Reformation, too, involved the slow gradual transformation of ecclesiastical authority and theological doctrines. It can never be compressed into the one day in 1517 when Luther nailed his theses to the church door in Wittenberg. Even in England, it can be argued, the Reformation process began with Wyclif in the late fourteenth century and was not complete before the Revolution of 1689. Socio-economic changes connected with 'the

Rise of Capitalism' are similarly considered to belong to the category of the *longue durée*, the 'long term'.

One of the characteristics of long historical processes, however, is that their consequences can only take hold after decades or centuries of gestation. Events such as the initial 'encounter' between Columbus and the Americas or Copernicus comprehending the movement of the planets may well have signalled the transformation of world history. But they did little to transform the lives of people at the time. Indeed, Columbus died without ever realizing what he had achieved; and the theory of Copernicus, published in 1543, lay dormant for the rest of the sixteenth century. England planted its first successful American colony 114 years after the voyage of Columbus. The Royal Society for the study of science in England was founded 121 years after Copernicus launched 'the Scientific Revolution'.

In this light, one has to wonder whether the arrival of the Tudors really did provoke such a fundamental break as is usually supposed. Does the early modern really stand in such stark contrast to the late medieval? If one asks the questions 'What did *not* change?', or 'What was only beginning to change?', as opposed to the more usual 'What changed?', one arrives at a fresh set of answers. In the history of the Isles, in particular, the prominence traditionally given to the Tudors would have to be significantly reduced. In the sphere of ideas, for example, the Protestant Reformation may have turned the Church and its doctrines upside down. But it didn't shake the essential medieval conviction that pluralism of religious thought was abominable and that religious uniformity was an issue to die and to kill for. The key works in the history of scientific thought, Bacon's *Advancement of Learning* (1605) and *Novum Organum* (1620), were not published until the reign of James VI and I. In the sphere of socio-economics, too, the effects of the 'Price Revolution' and of changes in the pattern of landholding did not begin to make themselves felt until the turn of the century. The very first event in the chronicle of England's rise to the status of a world commercial power – the foundation of the East India Company – took place in

1600, not in 1500. In the important sphere of government and politics, the 'Tudor Revolution' may well have transformed the workings of England's internal administration. But it made few serious alterations to the basic state framework within which political life operated. The incorporation of Wales into the Kingdom of England in 1536, and the declaration of a separate Kingdom of Ireland in 1541 were not simply cosmetic reforms. But they gave new constitutional shape to the old fact of English domination that dated to Plantagenet times. Despite the increase of England's relative power and prestige under the Tudors, the essential separation of England and Scotland as independent sovereign states remained intact. For all these reasons, '1603' can be upheld as a more crucial turning point in the history of the Isles as a whole than 1485 could ever be.

In which case, historians have to ask how it was the Tudor age came to be given such extraordinary prominence. One answer obviously lies in the brilliant personalities of the two long-reigning Tudor monarchs who started the story of Protestant England. Though they occupy opposite ends of the charm scale, both Henry VIII and Elizabeth I were 'larger than life'. For sheer human interest, the serial wife-slayer and the Virgin Queen outshine all their predecessors among the Plantagenets and all their successors among the Stuarts.

Yet another reason undoubtedly lies with the systematic state propaganda, which launched an enduring 'English myth' about the causes and effects of those allegedly unparalleled Tudor achievements. The myth was set running by Thomas Cromwell (see above), clothed in golden words by William Shakespeare, reinforced by the Protestant Establishment of the seventeenth and eighteenth centuries, and set in stone by the dominant 'Whig Interpretation' of history. As with all major myths, the ramifications are endless. But for the purposes of a brief exposé, three themes deserve emphasis. One is the denigration of the late medieval period, and particularly of the late medieval Church. The second is the deification of the English monarchy as a focus for the founding of English Protestantism and of modern English patriotism. The third involves the exclusion of all non-English elements in descriptions of the roots of later British greatness. These themes recur throughout a wide variety of literary and historical works devoted to the period.

Protestantism had a fundamental interest in highlighting the supposed 'break with the past' that was seen to have taken place at the Reformation. The most devout Protestants inevitably saw the Reformation as 'an age of God's light' and the preceding period as 'an age of Papist servitude'. Yet Protestant opinion was by no means uniform. At different times and different circles, a great variety of views were expressed; and they were not always mutually compatible. Within the Church of England, for example, an unbridgeable gulf usually separated the puritanical position of the Low Church apologists from that of the High Churchmen. And Puritan often disagreed with Puritan, Episcopalian with Episcopalian.

Nonetheless, despite the kaleidoscope of conflicting opinions during the mid seventeenth century, William Prynne (1602–69) can reasonably be taken as an exemplar of the puritan outlook. Active before, during, and after the civil wars, he changed the focus of his work at several stages in his long career. In the 1630s he was imprisoned and mutilated for insulting the King and Queen in an elaborate attack on the theatre, his *Histrio-Mastix* (1632). In the 1640s and '50s, he turned to politics and argued passionately for a balanced constitution. His influential *Brevia Parliamentaria Reviva* (1662) was no less acceptable to moderate royalists than to moderate parliamentarians. In the 1660s, he set out to show that England's Restoration monarchy was rooted in the country's most ancient traditions. Throughout everything, however, he stuck to three basic principles. These were the Erastian propositions concerning the necessary unity of Church and state: the nationalist proposition concerning the uniqueness of English institutions: and the anti-Papal proposition, which regarded the pre-Reformation English Church as the victim of papal 'depradations' and usurpations.

The titles of his many works speak for themselves – *Lord Bishops: or a Short Discourse wherein is proved that Prelaticall Jurisdiction is not of Divine Institution* (1640); *The Treachery and Disloyalty of Papists* (1643); *The Grand Conspiracy of the Pope and his Jesuited Instruments* (1643); *An Exact Chronological Vindication and Historical Demonstration of our British, Roman, Saxon, Norman, English King's Supreme Ecclesiastical Jurisdiction* (1655–8); *A Seasonable Vindication of the Supreme authority and Jurisdiction of Christian Kings, Lords and Parliaments . . .* (1660–8), and posthumously, *An Exact History of the Pope's Intolerable Usurpation on the Liberties of the King's subjects of England and Ireland* (1670).

After the Restoration, Prynne obtained the official post of Keeper of the Records. This enabled him to lard his later works with a large dose of state documents. But it did not give him much independence of mind. It simply helped him to consolidate the framework of English history that was by then becoming conventional. It 'produced an account of the past that was no whit less insular than its counterparts of the sixteenth century'.[54]

Gilbert Burnet, Bishop of Salisbury (1643–1715), spent over forty years preparing and publishing his massive three-volume *History of the Reformation* (1679, 1681, 1714). An Episcopalian Scot, a fervent Whig, and a member of the Royal Society, he lost his chaplaincy in 1685 and won his see through loyalty to William of Orange. Riding on the coat-tails of the Popish Plot, he constructed the historical ideology of the Whig Revolution, in which a common thread was found in the Protestant struggle for 'Liberty'. His reputation as a prime authority on Reformation history lasted well into the nineteenth century.

Burnet's name for the Middle Ages was 'the Darkness', in which 'this Nation did . . . maintain its Liberty the best it could'. In fact, he made no bones of his views that the medieval period was not even worthy of serious study: 'Indeed, I am not out of countenance to own that I have not much studied those Authors of the medieval period . . . If any one has more Patience that I, [he] can think it worth while to search into that *Rubbish* . . .'[55] Burnet's justification for the English Reformation could have been written by Thomas Cromwell. As he wrote in the dedication of his first volume to Charles II: 'The first step that was made in the Reformation of this Church, was the restoration to Your Royal Ancestors the rights of the Crown, and an entire Dominion over all their Subjects: of which they had been disseised by the craft and violence of an unjust Pretender.'[56] The 'unjust Pretender', was, of course, the Bishop of Rome.

For Protestant episcopalians, the chief obstacle to their historical world-view lay in the problem of the apostolic succession. They were happy to discount the political and financial malversations of the medieval papacy. But they had to find a means of explaining how the special prerogatives of the bishops continued unbroken in the true line of descent from Christ's apostles. Fortunately for them, they could point to the none too edifying figure of Thomas Cranmer, whose appointment as Archbishop of Canterbury had been confirmed prior to the Act of Supremacy, and whose subsequent laying on of hands could be judged to legitimize all his post-Reformation appointments.

Burnet's scholarly reputation eventually collapsed through his manifold errors both great and small. But the unmasking did not happen for nearly two hundred years. Indeed, he seems to have protected himself very skilfully by openly admitting to a long list of minor errors in order to divert attention from the major ones. (His modern editor lists a core of 'ten thousand downright mistakes'.) Among the major errors were examples of falsification and forgery. One of these, discovered by the scholarly nonjuror George Hickes (see below), related to an original manuscript by Luther in possession of Corpus Christi College, Cambridge. Burnet 'deliberately perverted' its meaning in order to present Luther as a subscriber to Burnet's favourite concept of 'comprehension' – that is, to the misguided notion that all Protestants, despite disputes over trivialities, were in full agreement on the essentials.[57] In reality, the only principle on which all the Protestants of the Isles were agreed was 'anti-Popery'. And it was Burnet's colourful anti-Popery that gave his *History* its lasting appeal.

≈

Much to historians' chagrin, Shakespeare's influence on perceptions of the later medieval centuries is much greater than their own. A distinguished Oxford medievalist once made the best of it as follows:

> I have lately begun to realize that the great majority, even of those who claim to be educated, are very hazy ... about everything that happened before [1485]. To the brighter schoolboy, the reign of Richard II suggests (with luck) the Peasants Revolt, while his more sophisticated senior, if he recalls anything, will recall either 'My Kingdom fo. a horse' (Wrong) or 'Not all the water in the rough rude sea . . .' (Right). It is one of the penalties we pay ... that our memory of [Shakespeare's] history plays, however imperfect, will outlast the most lucid account of the history books.[58]

Nonetheless, he continued, many of Shakespeare's scenes so touch the essence of historical situations that they can hardly be bettered. Richard II, for instance, 'made the first attempt of an English King to rule as an autocrat on principle', thereby provoking the clash with Henri Bolingbroke. Hence, 'if all we remember of *Richard II* is the Divine Right speech there is at least this consolation, that it is the heart of the matter':

> Not all the water in the rough rude sea
> Can wash the balm from an anointed king;
> The breath of wordly men cannot depose
> The deputy elected by the Lord.
> For every man that Bolingbroke hath pressed
> To lift shrewd steel against our golden crown,
> God for his Richard hath in heavenly pay
> A glorious angel. Then, if angels fight,
> Weak men must fall; for heaven still guards the right.[59]

Historians discuss whether Richard was mad. Yet his views on kingship were not too far removed from those of the Tudors and Stuarts.

The chronological span of Shakespeare's ten historical dramas runs from *King John* to *Henry VIII*. But it is concentrated in the century separating Richard II's personal rule from the death of Richard III, that is, from 1389 to 1485. They are all set in the era of the Hundred Years War and the Wars of the Roses. The main subject is the monarchy; the chief protagonists are England and France; and the central drama within the cycle of dramas is that of *Henry V* and the campaign of 1415:

> Can this cockpit hold
> The vasty fields of France? or may we cram
> Within this wooden O the very casques
> That did affright the air at Agincourt?[60]

Several of the set speeches from the history plays 'This Royal throne of Kings', 'Once more unto the breach, dear friends', or 'Now is the winter of our discontent' – stand on a par with the great soliloquies of *Hamlet* or *King Lear*. They and the sentiments that go with them are part of the intellectual furniture of every educated English speaker.

Shakespeare, however, had higher things in mind than mere historical accuracy. As a court dramatist in late Elizabethan and early Jacobean times, he avoided contentious political and religious issues; and he served up a diet of 'cabbages and kings' which he knew to be popular both with the censorious Lord Chamberlain and with the groundlings. In between the lines, he was telling how Tudor England, having turned its back on medieval blood and strife, had entered an era of harmony and prosperity. The message, in the era of the Reformation, the Spanish Armada, and the 'Price Revolution' was fairly dubious. But it is what the audience wanted to believe. And it was conveyed amidst the most magnificent language and with every possible rhetorical device.

The most apparently patriotic of all the speeches is put into the improbable mouth of the dying Jean de Gand (John of Gaunt), 'time-honour'd Lancaster', a Plantagenet who had spent much of his life in Aquitaine. The scene is set at Ely House in London in 1399:

> This royal throne of kings, this sceptr'd isle,
> This earth of majesty, this seat of Mars,
> This other Eden, demi-paradise,
> This fortress built by Nature for herself
> Against infection and the hand of war,
> This happy breed of men, this little world,
> This precious stone set in the silver sea,
> Which serves it in the office of a wall,
> Or as a moat defensive to a house
> Against the envy of less happier lands;
> This blessed plot, this earth, this realm, this England . . .[61]

Taken in isolation these lines read like the idyllic fantasy of an uncritical patriot. In the play, however, their dramatic purpose is to supply a contrasting prelude to the descriptions of dire civil strife which follow:

> [England] . . . is now bound in with shame,
> With inky blots and rotten parchment bonds;
> That England that was wont to conquer others
> Hath made a shameful conquest of itself.[62]

Gaunt moves from ecstasy to despair in less than twenty lines. As the action moves on, there is no time to reflect on the hyperbole. No matter that the real John of Gaunt would not have spoken English well enough to recite those glamorous words. No matter that England was not, and never has been, an island. No matter that in the 1390s as in the 1590s 'the sceptr'd isle' was subject to the Scottish as well as to the English sceptre. The point is: the first half of Gaunt's speech matched English prejudices perfectly. In the cold light of analysis, its lavish metaphors and mythical geography have to be taken as a piece of poetic licence, not as statements of fact.

Similar dramatic devices underpin Shakespeare's presentation of the English army at Harfleur in 1415. On the one hand he presents the down-to-earth banter of the rank-and-file – Bardolph, Pistol, and the Welsh wind-bag Fluellen. On the other hand, as befits a royal hero, he lets Henry V speak with pathos and overblown eloquence:

Once more unto the breach, dear friends, once more
Or close the wall up with our English dead.
In peace, there's nothing so becomes a man
As modest stillness and humility;
But when the blast of war blows in our ears
Then imitate the action of a tiger:
Stiffen the sinews, conjure up the blood,
Disguise fair nature with hard favour'd rage.
. . . On, on, you noblest English
Whose blood is fet from fathers of war proof . . .
Dishonour not your mothers; now attest
That those whom you call'd fathers did beget you.
. . . And you, good yeomen,
Whose limbs were made in England, now show us here
The mettle of your pasture . . .
I see you stand like greyhounds in the slips,
Straining upon the start. The game's afoot:
Follow your spirit: and upon this charge
Cry 'God for Harry, England and Saint George!'[63]

The groundlings swell with pride, and no doubt raise a cheer. But then they are brought down flat:

BARDOLPH: On, on, on, on, on! to the breach, to the breach!
FLUELLEN: Up to the breach, you dogs! Avaunt, you cullions![64]

Shakespeare takes his audience through all the emotions, except, of course, sympathy for the French. The fact that his view of the Hundred Years War is one-sided to the point of travesty is of no consequence – if only people would remember that he was writing plays, and not writing history.

Nonetheless, it would be wrong to suppose that the Shakespearean texts are completely worthless as history simply because they are factually inaccurate. The bard may have been careless about event-based narrative; but he was very interested in other ways by which the past is remembered – in myths, legends, ideas, and popular misconceptions. These things, no less than events, form part of the historians' brief; and they should not be dismissed out of hand. John of Gaunt's idyll about 'this sceptr'd isle', for instance, was not designed as an exact description. It was the centrepiece of the dying duke's deluded belief in a lost 'Golden Age' which he had supposedly known as a youth. As soon as readers realize that those magnificent lines refer to historical myth, not to historical realism, they will be standing on much firmer ground.[65]

Shakespeare's heroics mask England's failure in the Hundred Years War. Historians' verdicts, as usual, are mixed. Some English historians bemoan the defeat. Others celebrate England's liberation from misguided policies. The greatest teacher in the English medieval field contrived to do both. 'It is the tragedy of Henry V's reign', he wrote, 'that . . . he led his people in pursuit of the chimera of foreign conquest, an adventure from which they recoiled, exhausted and embittered, after more than thirty years of useless sacrifice.'[66]

The one subject into which Shakespeare did not dare to venture was religion. There has been speculation whether he may have been a secret Catholic. It is quite possible. His father was a known recusant; and it now appears that the young Will's 'missing years' may well have been spent among Catholic recusants at Houghton Towers in Lancashire. But the playwright's private beliefs may be largely irrelevant. For under the rigours of the prevailing censorship, anyone who questioned the religious settlement in the slightest faced the severest penalties. The nearest Shakespeare came to making pertinent religious comment was in his very last play, *Henry VIII* (1612/13). The dramatic action stops prudently short of the Act of Supremacy. It reaches its climax in a splendid pageant of the coronation of Anne Boleyn; and it ends with the birth of Elizabeth:

> This royal infant – Heaven still move about her! –
> Though in her cradle, yet now promises
> Upon this land a thousand, thousand blessings
> Which time shall bring to ripeness.[67]

It is a good example of Tudor sycophancy, spoken by a less than resolute Cranmer. Earlier on, however, a stricken Cardinal Wolsey is made to turn to his colleague, Thomas Cromwell, and to state the central dilemma of the English Reformation:

> O Cromwell, Cromwell!
> Had I but serv'd my God with half the zeal
> I serv'd my King, he would not in mine age
> Have left me naked to mine enemies.[68]

Here was the dilemma which would cost Wolsey's successor, Thomas More, his life. More refused to subscribe to the Act of Supremacy. He was executed because he chose to serve his God rather than to serve his King. In a country where the monarchy had raised itself to the headship of the Church, such truth was treasonable. It could not be openly expounded in England for centuries. In the eyes of admirers, More was one of the greatest of Englishmen. Colet called him a genius; Erasmus was enchanted. Yet he was also a contradictory figure. As Lord Chancellor he did not practise the tolerance which he advocated in *Utopia*. And he approved the burning of heretics. No one demands more careful assessment. But apart from the simple chronicle of his life by his faithful son-in-law, William Roper, no serious study of his literary works and no serious biography was published before the nineteenth or twentieth century. St Thomas More was canonized by the Roman Catholic Church in 1935. Robert Bolt's play about him, *A Man For All Seasons*, appeared in 1960 and was turned into a fine film.[69] An anonymous late-sixteenth-century play about him was never staged until 1964, at the Nottingham Playhouse with Ian McKellen in the starring role.[70]

Nor did More's challenge die with him. Time and again, it was repeated by all the opponents of England's established Church, whether Catholic or Puritan. Forty and fifty years after More's death, the Anglican Church still 'appeared less concerned with seeking the Kingdom of God than with supporting the Kingdom of England'.[71] The language of the Puritans, once they surfaced, was particularly aggressive. Queen Elizabeth was 'a new Pope'; the Prayer Book 'an unperfect book culled . . . from the popish dunghill'.

The destruction of England's most distinguished Catholic

Humanist underlined a cardinal fact that is often overlooked. The 'Break with Rome' had damaging consequences far beyond the political and religious spheres. It cut England off from the cultural and intellectual community to which she had belonged for nearly a thousand years; and it forced her to develop along isolated, eccentric lines. The English have had little chance but to take pride in their isolation and eccentricity. Indeed, they have recruited it as a virtue. Their habit of harping on the story of their survival without any foreign invasion since 1066 is an essential part of the exercise. It conceals the inconvenient fact that England's cultural isolation dates not from 1066 but from 1534. In the late medieval period, England's links with the Continent had been growing steadily. In the era of More and Erasmus, they reached their peak. They were severed by a self-inflicted injury.

Thanks to the cultural monopoly established by England's Protestant Establishment, no substantial alternative account of the causes and effects of the Reformation could be published until the start of religious toleration. Throughout the centuries of discrimination prior to 1829, English Catholic exiles maintained a running commentary of opposition from abroad. But their views did not circulate much at home; and they were easily dismissed as unpatriotic by a public that had never been allowed to read them. As a result, the first Catholic histories of the Reformation in England were written by foreigners; and the first major Catholic-inspired *History of England* did not appear in its eight-volume edition until 1819. Its author was Father John Lingard (1771–1851), the son of a recusant family from Winchester, who had been sent abroad to study at the English Jesuit College at Douai. Lingard was a mild-tempered scholar, who spent much time examining original documents in Continental libraries, and whose professional competence was not challenged. After his return to England, he passed most of his career working quietly in a remote Catholic community in Durham. Yet his history contained its share of dynamite. Indeed, if the style had matched the content, it may have had more success in crossing the sectarian divide. As it was, despite running into six editions by 1855, it was studiously ignored by a British Establishment, which effectively excluded Lingard from the historical roll of honour. Its main achievement, in abridged form, was to provide the standard history textbook for English Catholic schools in the late nineteenth and early twentieth centuries.[72] No catalogue of English historiography would be complete without it. Yet he merits no entry in *Encyclopædia Britannica* (1999).

Lingard's narrative ran from Roman times to 1688. (The abridgements carried continuations beyond that date.) But apart from the Anglo-Saxon period, in which Lingard possessed specialist expertise, the core of the work is concentrated on the Tudor age. In this respect Lingard's opinions are extremely interesting, and not just because they deviate from the established view. They often rely on telling and well-substantiated details, which open up new vistas of interpretation. Furthermore, being grounded in a solid knowledge of Catholic doctrine, they were not afraid to address some of the fundamental religious issues, which his Protestant opponents had been all too willing either to avoid or to bury in obscure theological treatises.

Lingard's description of the Hundred Years War faithfully follows each of the political and military twists of the conflict. But the tone omits the nationalist rhetoric that had been standard since Shakespeare's day; and the narrative does not hesitate to criticize English conduct. The burning of Joan of Arc by the English, for example, is called 'a cruel and unjustifiable tragedy'. The fate of the Duke of Suffolk, who was held responsible for the final loss of English-occupied territory in France, underlines an aspect of the English national character – if such a thing exists – that is more commonly found in Continental histories:

[The Duke] sailed from Ipswich with two small vessels, and sent a pinnace before him to enquire whether he might be permitted to land at Calais. But the pinnace was captured by a squadron of men-of-war ... He was ordered on board and received on deck by the captain with the ominous salutation, 'Welcome, traitor!' On the second morning, a small boat came alongside, in which were a block, a rusty sword, and an execcutioner; the Duke was lowered into it and beheaded.[73]

Blood-stained ruthlessness is not an attribute which the English would always observe in themselves. They think of themselves as a kindly folk.

Lingard's account of the episode in 1521 when Pope Clement endowed Henry VIII with the title of Defender of the Faith quotes the text of the original award. After Luther escaped from the Imperial authorities, the King of England wrote to Charles V to denounce the passivity of the princes and the dangers of doctrinal innovation:

Henry himself was anxious to enter the lists against the German; nor did Wolsey discourage the attempt ... That the treatise in defence of the seven sacraments, which the king published was his own composition, is forcibly asserted by himself; that it was planned, revised, and improved by the superior judgment of the cardinal and the bishop of Rochester, was the opinion of the public. The dean of Windsor carried the royal production to Rome, and in a full consistory submitted it to the inspection and approbation of the pontiff. Clement accepted the present with many expressions of admiration and gratitude, and conferred on the English monarch the title of 'Defender of the Faith'. It may here be observed that in neither of the bulls granting or confirming this title, is there any mention of inheritance. The title belonged to the king personally, not to his successors. (*Tibi perpetuum et proprium*.) But Henry retained it after his separation from the communion of Rome; and in 1543, it was annexed to the crown by act of parliament. Thus it became hereditable by his successors; it was retained even by Philip and Mary, though the statute itself had been repealed. Luther wrote an answer to Henry, but the intemperance of his declamation scandalised his friends, while it gave joy to his enemies. To the king, he allotted no other praise than that of writing in an elegant language; in all other respects, he was 'a fool and an ass, a blasphemer and a liar.'[74]

No one can take heart from the level of this theological debate. And few will miss the absurdity of the consequences. Almost five hundred years later, the initials of F(idei) D(efensor), 'Defender of the Faith', are still carried on all British coins; and Queen Elizabeth II, who is still bound by the laws of the Protestant succession, still sports a papal title that was awarded for doughty opposition to the founder of Protestantism.

Lingard's account of Queen Mary's reign condemns the persecution of Protestants without reservation. He called it 'the foulest blot'. ('Foulest' was changed to 'worst' by the editors of the second abridgement.) At the same time, without overstating the case, he was at pains to show that the return to Catholic orthodoxy was not devoid of public support. A description of Mary's marriage to Philip of Spain makes the point without the need for further comment:

In the beginning of March, 1554, the Spanish ambassador arrived in London, and espoused Mary in the name of the prince of Spain. Both houses [of Parliament] unanimously concurred in an act confirming the treaty of marriage, declaring that the queen . . . should continue to enjoy and exercise the sovereignty as sole queen . . . Philip soon arrived at Southampton, escorted by the combined fleets of England, the Netherlands, and Spain. The moment he set his foot on the beach he was invested with the insignia of the order of the Garter. On the festival of St. James, the patron saint of Spain, July 25th, the marriage was celebrated in the cathedral church at Winchester, before crowds of noblemen collected from every part of Christendom, and with a magnificence which has seldom surpassed. From Winchester the royal pair proceeded, by slow journeys, to Windsor and the metropolis.[75]

Religious persecution was an almost universal phenomenon in sixteenth-century Europe. Catholics persecuted Protestants; Protestants persecuted Catholics; Lutherans persecuted Calvinists. Calvinists persecuted non-conformists like everyone else. Everyone persecuted women suspected of witchcraft. In this context, the English collective memory, which likes to imagine that England largely escaped from wars of religion, is wide of the mark. If anything is remembered, it is 'Bloody Mary', whose excesses were supposedly avoided by her statesmanlike half-sister. (This wrong-headed myth was still being perpetuated in a glamorous film on general release in the 1990s.)[76] Lingard, in contrast, was eager to show an even hand. He first stated the general principle:

> That the teachers of erroneous doctrine ought to be reformed by the authority of the civil magistrate, was a maxim which at that period had been consecrated by the assent and practice of ages. Hence religious intolerance had become part of the public law of Christendom; the principle was maintained and acted upon by the reformers themselves; and whatever might be the predominant doctrine, the dissenter from it invariably found himself subject to civil restrictions, perhaps to imprisonment and death.[77]

He then showed that England was no exception to the rule, neither under Mary nor under Elizabeth:

> Elizabeth continued to persecute all her subjects who did not practise that religious worship which she practised herself. Every other form of service, whether it be that of Geneva or the mass, was strictly forbidden: and both the Catholic and the puritan were made liable to the severest penalties if they presumed to worship God according to the dictates of their consciences . . .[78]

He only betrayed his partisanship when he added: 'Some puritans died martyrs to their religious principles; but their sufferings bore no comparison with those of the Catholics.'[79]

In assessing the Tudor monarchs, therefore, Lingard faced a delicate task. On the one hand, as a patriotic Englishman, he wished to praise their achievements. On the other hand, as a good Catholic, he could not excuse the inexcusable. In the case of Henry VIII, he solved the problem by contrasting the 'Young Henry' with the 'Old Henry': 'When [Henry VIII] ascended the throne, there still existed a spirit of freedom. But in the lapse of a few years that spirit had fled . . . and the King of England had grown into a despot, the people had shrunk into a nation of slaves.'[80]

With regard to Elizabeth, the task was more delicate. The Elizabethan age has frequently been identified as the moment when England rose to greatness; and 'the Virgin Queen' had always attracted more admirers than her repulsive father. Lingard found a way out by confining his worst criticisms to the personality of Elizabeth, who, he judged, was 'irresolute', 'overbearing', 'vain', scandalously 'unchaste', 'irritable', and 'bloodthirsty'. At the same time, he recognized the triumphs of the reign, not least in the national war against Spain; and he bemoaned the absence of nineteenth-century liberalism:

> Elizabeth has been numbered among the greatest and the most fortunate of our sovereigns. The tranquillity which, during a reign of nearly half a century, she maintained within her dominions, while the neighbouring nations were convulsed with intestine dissensions, was taken as a proof of the wisdom of the vigour of her government; and her successful resistance against the Spanish monarch . . . and the spirit displayed by her fleets and armies . . . and even the East Indies, served to give the world an exalted notion of her military and naval power. When she came to the throne, England ranked only among the secondary kingdoms; before her death [England] had risen to a level with the first nations in Europe.[81]

However:

> It is evident that neither Elizabeth nor her ministers understood the benefits of civil and religious liberty. The prerogatives which

she so highly prized have long since withered away; the blood-stained code which she enacted against the rights of conscience has ceased to disfigure the pages of the statute-book; and the result has proved that the abolition of despotism and intolerance adds no less to the stability of the throne than to the happiness of the people.[82]

A paragraph from the first abridgement, but omitted from the second, illustrates some of the subterranean tensions:

The historians who celebrate the golden days of Elizabeth, have described with a glowing pencil the happiness of the people under her sway. To them might be opposed the dismal picture of national misery drawn by the Catholic writers of the same period. But both have taken too contracted a view of the subject. Religious dissensions had divided the nation into opposite parties, of almost equal numbers, the oppressors and the oppressed. Under the operation of the penal statutes, many ancient and opulent families have been ground to the dust; new families had sprung up in their place; and these, as they shared the plunder, naturally eulogized the system to which they owed their wealth and their ascendancy. But their prosperity was not the prosperity of the nation; it was that of one half obtained at the expense of the other.[83]

Even in Lingard's day, criticism of the founders of Anglicanism was unusual among English Protestants. One of the few to share Lingard's low opinion was Charles Dickens. 'Henry VIII', Dickens wrote in his *Child's History of England*, 'was a detestable villain'.[84] The famously outspoken William Cobbett was another. The English Reformation, he declared, was 'engendered in lust and brought forth in hypocrisy and perfidy'.[85]

Lingard exercised restraint regarding the fate of the Catholic martyrs. Subsequent Catholic writers did not. They were incensed by the English public's refusal to judge Catholic and Protestant suffering by the same standards, and by the persistent idea that saintly men like Edmund Campion had been executed for their saintly men like Edmund Campion had been executed for their politics. Campion had answered the charge precisely on the scaffold: 'If you esteem my religion treason, then I am guilty. As for other treason, I never committed any . . . Elizabeth, your Queen and my Queen, unto whom I wish a long quiet reign with all prosperity.'[86] The Catholic Truth Society reckoned that 318 men and women were put to death for the Faith in England between the reigns of Henry VIII and Charles II. And their deaths were every bit as horrible as anything described by John Foxe:

> After being hanged up, they were cut down, ripped up, and their bowels were burned in their faces.[87]

By any objective measure, Lingard's achievement was colossal. There are not many historians who have succeeded in writing a ten- or twelve-volume survey of the whole of English History and have seen their work run into several editions. There are still fewer who have based their conclusions on archival research in many countries, or who have produced an independent, unconventional interpretation. There are almost none who have not been accused by their rivals of serious errors. Yet Lingard passes all these tests. Lord Acton, who was no complacent judge, wrote, 'Lingard never gets anything wrong.'[88] One is left, therefore, with a curious academic mystery. How could Lingard be so consistently overlooked? All those students who pass through the History Departments of Britain's great universities and who never find him on their reading lists should really be wondering why.

Once English Catholics were free to propagate their historical opinions, however, there was no shortage of Protestant champions to refute them. The leading Protestant warhorse was James Anthony Froude (1818–94), a historian who had been an admirer both of Newman and Carlyle. His voluminous *History of England from the Fall of Wolsey to the defeat of Spanish Armada* (1856–70), written in dramatic style, became the standard work on the subject. Froude's motto was 'no theorising', though he patently pursued a dubious contention about the Reformation being 'the root and source of the expansive force which has spread the Anglo-Saxon race over the globe'. Reduced to the barest of bones, Froude's theory held that the British Empire of his own day had grown from the policies of Henry VIII. So Henry VIII had to be rehabilitated, and the whole English myth composed by Thomas Cromwell revamped and relaunched. His lack of academic rigour attracted some academic carping; but his magisterial style carried the field. Warmly received in the USA, elected to the rectorship of St Andrews, he was finally rewarded with the Regius Professorship at Oxford. His achievement was not dented but it was his successors in the Tudor field, A. F. Pollard (1869–1948)[89] and Pollard's pupil, J. E. Neal, with whom the glorification of Elizabeth reached its peak. Another popular militant was C. R. L. Fletcher (1857–1934), Fellow of Magdalen College, Oxford and co-author with Rudyard Kipling of an influential turn-of-the-century history. Fletcher and Kipling on the Reformation and the Tudor age left their readers in no doubt.

Fletcher's text constitutes a prime example of history in what one could call the 'vulgar Protestant mode'. In its chapter on the later Middle Ages, it talks of 'a dreary period' which has no importance except for 'the Seeds of Reformation'. Writing in the era of Entente Cordiale, Fletcher could take no pleasure from the Hundred Years War. Of Henry V's attack on France, he writes: 'This really was wicked'. Of Joan of Arc, he wrote of 'a saint and heroine' who 'lives in the hearts of all good Frenchmen (and Englishmen) . . . until this day.' But in the chapter on 'The Tudors and the Awakening of England' one reaches 'a very different part of history', full of achievement and excitement. Henry VIII, it turns out, was not all bad:

A monster of cruelty and selfishness? Yes . . . But [Henry] was . . . much more. He was a great patriot, a great Englishman. He taught Englishmen to rely on themselves and their ships; and

he taught future English kings to rely on their people. He
shivered in pieces the foreign yoke that had bound the Church
of England since St. Augustine . . .[90]

Mary 'cared little for her countrymen' and was deceived by her
Spanish counsellors. She put to death many Protestant martyrs,
whose fate was not matched (in Fletcher's text) by any Puritan or
Catholic martyrs. But Elizabeth was virtually beyond criticism,
especially after the victory over the Armada: 'Our country, and with
her the great cause of freedom and Protestantism, were saved. Spain
was now known to be mainly a bugbear to children, and England
and Elizabeth ruled the waves.'[91]

When Kipling was invited to supply some poetical embellish-
ments to Fletcher's text on the sixteenth century, he submitted two
poems – one about 'Drake in the Tropics' and another called
'Together':

> When Crew and Captain understand each other to the core,
> It takes a gale and more than a gale to put their ships ashore;
> For the one will do what the other commands, although they are
> > chilled to the bone,
> > And both together can live through weather that neither
> > > could face alone.
>
> . . . .
>
> This wisdom had Elizabeth, and all her subjects too,
> For she was theirs, and they were hers, as well the Spaniard knew:
> For when his grim Armada came to conquer the Nation and
> > Throne,
> > Why, back to back, they met an attack, that neither could
> > > face alone![92]

Another of the Protestant warriors was George Gordon Coulton
(1858–1947), Professor of Medieval History at Cambridge. Baptized
no doubt in honour of the leader of the Protestant riot of 1780,
Coulton did not confine his zeal to academic activities. He stomped
around the country with lectures denouncing the evils of Papal

Infallibility, the English Catholic hierarchy and Catholic doctrine in general; and he polemicized with the leading Catholic writers of the day, first and foremost with Belloc and Chesterton. In his influential *Medieval Studies* (1915), he collected all the possible scandalous tales he could find about the Pre-Reformation Church – immoral monks, failed friars, oppressive priests, and pimping popes – leaving his indignant readers convinced that Protestantism had offered the only possible way out.[93] He was one of the godfathers of the opinion that could still be viewed on a placard in the Anglican cathedral at Guildford in 1998, to the effect that the late medieval Church needed reform 'like footballers after a match need a bath'.

Perhaps because the religious debate about the sixteenth century had been so extensively and so inconclusively aired, more recent historiography has understandably sought pastures new. The field of writing is rich and varied; and it might be invidious to stress a single name. Yet by general acclaim, Geoffrey Rudolph Elton (1921–94) made an outstanding contribution; and at the outset he was a very unlikely candidate to have done so. A Central European Jew, born in Tübingen under the name of Gottfried Ehrenberg, Elton reached the United Kingdom in 1939; and by sheer energy and ability rose through the academic ranks to become a Cambridge professor. Like his fellow immigrant, Lewis (Bernstein) Namier, he homed in on the holiest of holies of native historiography, namely the development of English Government. Namier tackled the late eighteenth century, Elton the early sixteenth. Elton's *Tudor Revolution in Government* (1953) stirred up lasting controversy. His thesis, which centres on the reforms of Thomas Cromwell, contested the idea that the Tudors' 'New Monarchy' had been introduced by Henry VII. Nonetheless, though it moved 'the Tudor Revolution' forward from the last decades of the fifteenth century to the 1530s, it insisted that such a revolution had taken place, causing a decisive break with medieval forms of government. Henry VII had governed a kingdom of the old type. Elizabeth inherited a country administered on modern lines. Elton's critics had much to chew on. They immediately argued that many of Cromwell's reforms were reversed after his fall from grace, that his methods resembled those of Henry VII's ministers, that Henry VIII never relinquished the reins, that Cromwell was not the inventor of the Elizabethan Exchequer . . .[94]

One aspect of Elton's work, however, was strangely at odds with the demands of the day. It was deeply Anglocentric. At the very time when Britain was re-engaging with Europe after four centuries of semi-detachment, one of the leading historians in the country was diverting people's historical gaze away from the European context. The workings of the Tudor government machine no doubt provide the pure historian with as valid a subject of study as anything else. But in the wider intellectual debate of the post-war years, they did little to illuminate the roots of contemporary problems. Above all, on the eve of the realization that 'British History and 'English History' were two separate subjects, they could only help to postpone the long-overdue examination of Britishness.

To be fair, Elton was a much grander figure than such caveats might convey. He brought a very broad range of knowledge to bear on his special interest in Tudor government; and he intervened most energetically in the general historical debates of his generation. A conservative by temperament, he waged incessant war against the motley crew of 'theory mongers' and 'gurus' whom he thought to be poisoning his subject. Marxists, psycho-historians, feminists, economic modellers, 'pseudo-scientists', and other 'charlatans and amateurs' all felt the sharp end of his pen. He took a specially hostile stance against the structuralism and postmodernism of Foucault and Derrida which he likened to a 'virus'. The central object of his concern was 'the historian's craft', whose hard-earned skills the new-fangled theorists neither possessed nor valued. His aim was to pass on 'the essentials' to the next generation of historical practitioners. The essentials may be summed up in the field of historical research by his war-cry of *Ad Fontes* – the need to be familiar with original sources – and in the writing of history by order, clarity, and integrity. No historian deserves to make a mark without some method for 'reducing the mess we call life to some sort of order'. No historian could dispense with a clear style that avoids pomposity and professional jargon, and without a strong sense of moral purpose. And no historian should aspire to finding all the answers overnight. The most one could hope for, after a lifetime's dedication to history, was 'new footholds in the territory of truth'.[95]

Elton's passionate defence of history, as he knew it, led him into a series of personal assaults on the more theoretically minded colleagues who crossed his path, notably on R. H. Tawney, Christopher Hill, and Michel Foucault. But through it all he retained an appealing ability to make fun of himself. In his inaugural lecture in 1968, *The Future of the Past*, he tried to explain why he had chosen to give his new chair the title of 'English Constitutional History'. Both 'English' and 'Constitutional', he suspected, were out of fashion. 'I chose the title myself, and damned myself twice over': 'In the present climate of opinion . . . "Chinese Constitutional History" would have been all right. Perhaps "English Social History" would have been wonderful . . .'[96] But Elton never bowed to fashion.

It is also interesting that Elton, though an outsider who had embraced Englishness wholeheartedly, held very astringent views about the English and their attitudes to their history:

> Now one of the most curious things about the English, I think . . . is that they suppose themselves to be conscious of history and to be enveloped in History. They are not. They are both indifferent and ignorant as far as history is concerned. If you want a really historically conscious country you have to go either to Central Europe, where they have too much history . . . or to the United States, where they have so little of it. I think that England could do with knowing more about the past, but that's always been so.[97]

One could not hope for a better authority on such a theme, even though his views mellowed a bit in his later years.[98]

Even more Anglocentric than Elton was an outsider of a different sort. Born in Cornwall in humble circumstances, A. L. Rowse

(1903–97) somehow penetrated the inner sanctum of the British academic establishment; and, as a long-time Fellow of All Souls, acquired all the superior affectations of a caste to which he didn't belong. Rowse's specialities included the history of Cornwall and Elizabethan England. Writing profusely with verve and wit, he did much to popularize the period. But he unashamedly admired his own opinions and he did little to further the cause either of Cornwall or of non-English perspectives. Rowse's somewhat patronizing approach to Cornwall presented a little land of strange names, exotic saints, and curious antiquities which should thank God for being overrun by the English.[99]

Unlike Wales and Ireland, Scotland remained a fully independent country throughout the sixteenth century. As yet, she had not entangled herself with England, even in the limited union of crowns that was to occur after Elizabeth's death. She experienced her own Reformation, which had followed a very different path from England's and which produced a national Church that survives to the present day. She possessed her own legal system, which also survives: she had her own Parliament, and her own Estate of Nobles, who ran the Parliament. She had her own monarchy, and a ruling dynasty that had held their throne for twice as long as the Tudors. She had venerable political, social, and cultural traditions that were every bit as ancient as those of her English neighbour. Yet none of these topics were destined to find their way into the mainstream of British historiography. When they weren't forgotten entirely, they would be parked in a closed reservation, only to be visited by Scottish antiquarians, by Presbyterian divines, and by the odd eccentric patriot. The extent of mainstream neglect may be gauged by the fact that the sixteenth-century chapter of the recently updated edition of *The Oxford History of Britain* (1999) does not bother to mention the internal affairs of Scotland once.[100]

Exactly why Scotland's vibrant history should have all but disappeared in later times is a conundrum that today's historians have only recently begun to address. One reason may be that Scottish history, once enveloped by the United Kingdom, could not compete with its stronger, self-centred English counterpart. Another may be that it lost its political usefulness. In the era of the Union and of the British Empire, it seemed irrelevant to the problems of the day. Most importantly, in the eighteenth and nineteenth centuries, it ceased to interest Scotland's own intellectual elite. The great historians of the Scottish Enlightenment were far more interested in England's history than in their own. They were busy creating what has been called an 'Anglo-British identity' for which Scotland's past was an embarrassment. To do this, they 'hi-jacked the English Whig tradition and recast it in their own terms'.[101] (See Chapter Nine.) Even Sir Walter Scott, who certainly tried to promote a view on Scottish history, was less valued in Scotland than elsewhere. He was one of the great prophets of romantic national history-writing. Yet, like Lord Byron, he seems to have been a prophet relatively unheeded in his own country. The results were startling. Very few Scottish writers of the Romantic Era cared to write about Scotland's highly romantic past. The chief literary works devoted to Maria Stuart were written not by a Scot but by an Italian, a German, two Frenchmen, and a Pole. The Italian Count Alflieri, who had married the Countess of Albany, widow of the last Stuart, produced the drama *Maria Stuart* (1799) which preceded Schiller's more famous version. Schiller's play, *Maria Stuart* (1800), also sentimentalizes the Scots queen as a Catholic martyr, contrasting her with the heartless tyrant that is Elizabeth. The climax arrives when the two queens meet at Fotheringay, and the captive loses her temper with the captor:

> England is
> Ruled by a bastard, and a noble people
> Corrupted by a cunning trickster!
> If there were justice, it is she
> Who'd kneel to me . . .![102]

The most famous line, in Mary's own mouth, runs, '*Maria Stuart hat noch kein Glücklicher beschützt.*' (No lucky person has ever managed to save Mary Stuart.) The drama was not given a performance in England till the Old Vic production of 1958. *Marie Stuart* (1820), by Pierre Lebrun, popularized the story in France. *Maria Stuart* (1832) by Juliusz Słowacki did not figure among the Polish master's best-known masterpieces. It opens with an unlikely scene in Holyrood Palace where a page announces a street pageant outside featuring Robin Hood and his Merry Men:

> Ujrzałem piękne maski, orszak Robinhoda,
> Tłum tancerzy z dzwonkami, Tuck z czarnym kapturem,
> Mały Janek i strzelce i Marianna młoda . . .[103]

Mary, Queen of Scots was a central figure of Romanticism in almost every country but Scotland. The only English writer of stature to take up the theme was Algernon Swinburne, who comprised a dramatic trilogy *Chastlard* (1865), *Bothwell* (1874), and *Mary Stuart* (1881), inspired by his obsession with femmes fatales.

In the meantime, so long as Scotland's independence lasted, Scots literature, including history-writing, continued to flourish. George Buchanan (1506–82) had studied and taught at the University of Paris before returning home, to become the Master of St Andrews and, at the end of his life, tutor to the infant King. In his youth, he wrote many verses in Latin and Greek, and it was entirely natural that his history of Scotland, the *Rerum scoticarum historia* (1582) was written entirely in elegant Latin. This work, in twenty books, covers the whole span from prehistoric times to the mid-sixteenth century. It adopts the 'Fergusian Theory', which holds that the Scots monarchy began with King Fergus Mac in 330 BC; and it works its way through more than a hundred reigns (85 to 1057) until the author reaches his own day. Its academic value is not highly rated by modern scholars, through its literary merit is beyond question. It was translated into all the main European languages, and was constantly reissued. The final, nineteenth edition of the English version appeared, significantly, in 1762. Buchanan's main claim to fame is that he supplied the only text whereby foreigners could gain access to Scottish history for nearly two hundred years.

In the reign of James VI, Scots poetry was patronized by a king who practised the art himself (see page oo, above). Intimate lyrical poems mingled with the philosophical and the political. Captain Alexander Montgomerie (1545–97), a native of Ayrshire and some-time *equus montanus* or 'Highland Trooper', gained the office of Master of the King's Poetry in 1583. Like Donne and Marvell, he wrote a sonnet 'To His Maistres':

> So swete a kis yistrene fra thee I reft,
> In bowing down thy body on the bed,
> That evin my lyfe within thy lippis I left;
> Sensyne from thee my spirits wald never shed;
> To folow thee it from my body fled,
> And left my corps als cold as ony kie.
> Bot when the danger of my death I dred,
> To seik my spreit I sent my harte to thee;
> Bot it wes so inamored with thyn ee,
> With thee it myndit likwyse to remane:
> So thou hes keepit captive all the thrie,
> More glaid to byde then to returne agane.
> Except thy breath thare places had suppleit,
> Even in thyn armes, thair doutles had I deit.[104]

James VI's father, Lord Darnley, was also a poet. In the short interval between his marriage and his murder, he managed to set his husbandly advice to verse;

To the Queen

Be governour baith guid and gratious;
Be leill and luifand to thy liegis all;
Be large of fredome and no thing desyrous;
Be just to pure for ony thing may fall;
Be ferme of faith and constant as ane wall;
Be reddye evir to stanche evill and discord;
Be cheretabill, and sickerlye thou sall
Be bowsum ay to knaw thy God and Lord.

. . . .

Be traist and conquese thy awin heretage
Be ennemyes of auld now occupyit;
Be strenth and force thou sobir thai man swage
Be law of God – thair may no man deny it;
Be nocht as lantern in mirknes unspyit;
Be thou in rycht thi landis suld be restored,
Be wirschop so thy name beis magnefeit;
Be bowsum ay to knaw they God and Lord.

Be to rebellis strong as lyoun eik;
Be ferce to follow thame quhairevir thai found;
Be to thy liegemen bayth soft and meik;
Be thair succour and help thame haill and sound;
Be knaw thy cure and caus quhy thow was cround;
Be besye evir that justice be nocht smord;
Be blyith in hart; thir wordis oft expound;
Be bowsum ay to knaw thy God and Lord.[105]

Mary, Queen of Scots, hardly had time to act on her husband's advice. But *conquese thy awin heretage* would not be a bad motto for Scotland's condition.

CHAPTER EIGHT

TWO ISLES:
THREE KINGDOMS

1603 to 1707

RELIGIOUS CONFLICTS IN EUROPE IN THE SIXTEENTH AND SEVENTEENTH CENTURIES

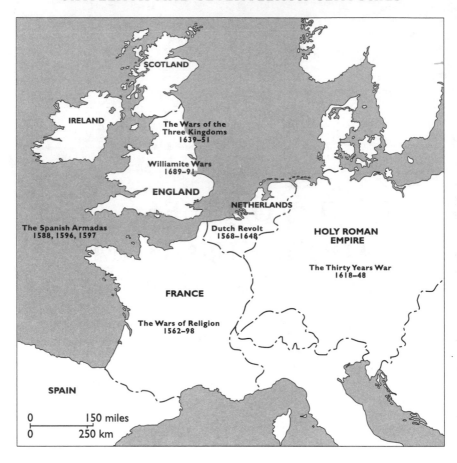

SCOTLAND

IRELAND

The Wars of the
Three Kingdoms
1639–51

Williamite Wars
1689–91

ENGLAND

NETHERLANDS

The Spanish Armadas
1588, 1596, 1597

Dutch Revolt
1568–1648

HOLY ROMAN
EMPIRE

The Thirty Years War
1618–48

FRANCE

The Wars of Religion
1562–98

SPAIN

0   150 miles

0   250 km

EDINBURGH, THURSDAY 31 MARCH 1602/3. After weeks of anxiety and days of considerable commotion, the citizens of Scotland's capital finally received confirmation of the news. Trumpets sounded at Edinburgh Cross; songs were sung; and the official proclamation was read aloud:

> Forsamekle as it hes pleisit the maist heich God to call to his maircie out of this transitorie lyff his Majesteis dearest suster Elisabeth, leat Quene of England, France and Irland, of worthie memorie, for the quhilk as we have just caus of sorrow sua aucht we to rejoyse in that it not only pleissit hir befoir hir depairtar, according to the princilie dispositioun of hir hart towardis his Majestie in all the course of hir lyfe, to declair his Majestie only air maill and lawfull successour in the imperiall crounes of England, France and Irland, bot lykwayis, conforme to hir said will and his Majesteis undoubtit richt, the Lordis spirituall and temporall of England, being assemblet at Londone the xxiiii day of March instant, assistit with his Majesteis lait dearest susteris Previe Counsall, and with greit nowmeris of utheris principall gentlemen of qualitie of that kingdome, the maior, aldermen and citicenis of his Majesteis citie of Londone, and a multitude of utheris guid subjectis and commonis of that realme, be oppin proclamatioun proclaimit his Majestie thair only richteous leige Lord and undoubtit Soverane, . . .[1]

As was the fashion, the text of the Proclamation rolled on and on. The opening sentence alone contained 298 words.

It is doubtful whether the Scots in the crowd would have caught everything. It is certain that little of it could have been understood by the shoals of Englishmen who had already arrived in Edinburgh. But everyone would have grasped the essence. James VI, King of Scots for the past thirty-six years, was also being proclaimed to be James I of England and of Ireland, and for good measure titular King of France.

The long, slow process of the late Queen's passing, and of the new King's succeeding, had lasted throughout the month of March; and it was still incomplete. Elizabeth had been in excellent spirits at Christmas, which she spent at Whitehall. She had still been in spritely form on 6 February, when she had received a Venetian envoy at Richmond and had scolded him roundly. But on hearing of the death of her lifelong companion, the Countess of Nottingham, she had lapsed into a state of inconsolable melancholy. Visited in early March by Sir Robert Carey, she had uttered forty or fifty sighs, and had insisted, uncharacteristically, 'No, Robert, I am not well.'

After that, she had declined rapidly, refusing all food and all medical attention: the Virgin Queen had reached a state where she wanted to die:

> Having performed her last royal duty by nominating James as her successor, she concentrated her mind on Heavenly things, rejoicing in the ministrations of her spiritual physician, her 'black husband', Archbishop Whitgift.
>
> And then she turned her face to the wall, sank into a stupor, and between the hours of two and three in the morning of March 24 1603 passed quietly away, 'as the most resplendent sun setteth at last in a western cloud.'[2]

Most other sources doubt that she had really nominated a successor. In England, 24 March was the last day of the year. It was equally the last day of 'the Age of Gloriana'.

King James had been preparing for this moment all his life, though he was uncertain to the very end that it would actually materialize. Like his mother, Mary, Queen of Scots, he possessed an impeccable claim to the English throne, superior in some respects to that of Elizabeth herself. He was the sole legitimate male heir of both the Tudors and the Stewarts. Yet, having watched from afar as his mother was judicially murdered on Elizabeth's orders, he was familiar enough with the violence and arbitrary twists of English politics. Having conducted a secret and coded correspondence with Elizabeth's leading councillors, notably with Robert Cecil, he knew that they were well disposed towards him; but he could not know if anyone in England would offer resistance. He had inside knowledge via Sir Robert Carey of the Queen's last illness. But he could not tell when her end would come. A letter from Carey had reached him in Edinburgh on 19 March, saying that horses were posted to bring the news north and that Her Majesty had not three days to live. But then nothing happened for the rest of the week. Sometime on 24 March, when unbeknown to him the Queen was already dead, he penned a letter to Henry Percy, Earl of Northumberland, assuring him both of his desire to make no 'alteration in state or government as far as possible' and of his moderation on the all-important question of religion: 'As for the Catholics, I will neither persecute any that will be quiet and will give but an outward obedience to the law, neither will I spare to advance any of them that will by good service worthily deserve it'.[3]

In London, the transfer went very smoothly. Cecil had prepared a draft proclamation, a copy of which was already in James's possession; and at 10 a.m. on the 24th the text was read out by order of the Privy Council at Whitehall Gate. A printed version was distributed on the streets. The Privy Council deliberated all day, and in the evening a 'Missive of Allegiance' to King James was drawn up in conjunction with the Lord Mayor of London. Two official envoys were then entrusted with the Missive and a copy of the morning's Proclamation, and were ordered to deliver it in person to James at Holyrood Palace. When the envoys left, they were twelve hours at least behind Robert Carey, who had defied the Council's explicit orders when he left post haste at 9 a.m.

Carey (1560–1639) had been one of Elizabeth's most influential and colourful courtiers. His father, Henry Carey, first Baron Hunsdon, was the son of Anne Boleyn's sister, Mary, and as such was Queen Elizabeth's closest living kinsman. His elder brother, John, had inherited their father's position as Governor of Berwick and Warden-General of the Scottish Marches. His elder sister Catherine was the Countess of Nottingham whose recent death had triggered the late Queen's decline. Robert Carey himself, soldier, tilter, and diplomat, held the minor office under his brother of Warden of the Middle March. From several embassies to Edinburgh, he knew King James personally. He was now determined to break the news himself come what may.

No one knew the Great North Road better than Carey did. In 1589, he had won an enormous bet of £2,000 by walking on foot from London to Berwick in the record time of twelve days. He now reckoned that he could cover the four hundred miles to Edinburgh in three days flat. One of the curiosities of his ride was that he was leaving London in 1602 and would arrive in Edinburgh in 1603. (Unlike England, Scotland had put New Year's Day back to 1 January three years earlier.)

King James and his family had not left Holyrood Palace for weeks. His Queen, Anne of Denmark, was pregnant. Their younger children, Elizabeth and Charles, were with them. The only one missing was their elder son and heir, Prince Henry, who was being raised apart by order of the Scottish Council under the guardianship of the Earl of Mar at Stirling:

> The Queen was very ill. Holyrood was in a state of expectation. James refused to go anywhere, waiting, always and only, for the final news. The final news lingered yet for days as it had lingered for years. He had been comforted, on the one hand, by a draft of the proposed proclamation which Cecil sent him; on the other, he had been seized by torturing thought. Suppose the Queen lived for years in this state of semi-imbecility, what then could be done? He was on fire to be gone; thirty years of vigil burned in him towards the dawn, and what now if the dawn still delayed?
>
> The Friday night, the Saturday, passed. Holyrood heard no more certain news. As Saturday closed the King retired; he was already in bed when he heard that yet one more rider had halted there, a man known to him, Sir Robert Carey, the English Warden of the Middle March. There was no delay now, and little need for orders. Carey was hurried to the bedchamber. He came in, exhausted by riding, bruised by a fall, his head bloody with a hurt from his horse's hoof. By the bed he kneeled stiffly down; his voice saluted the King of England, Scotland, France, and Ireland. To the sound of that full title James stretched out his hand; Carey touched it with his lips, the

first kiss of the completed royalty. Godmother and mother had unwillingly released their proper crowns. The King of England lay quiet and composed, asking a few questions about the Queen's illness, about her death, whether Sir Robert brought letters from the Council. Sir Robert had not; he had indeed narrowly escaped detention. But he knew that everything in London had been quiet and he was not without a token. He drew out a blue ring, a ring taken immediately and secretly by his sister from the dead Queen's finger, a ring once given her by James. The King looked at it, recognized it, said that Carey was a true messenger, and dismissed him with promises of favour. Indeed, he needed them, for his present office was done – the Marches existed no more. He went out, leaving the first King of England and Scotland to taste the knowledge. For three days it was kept more or less secret; on the third an official embassy arrived, and the homage of England was laid publicly at James's feet.[4]

King James VI and I was 'an original', quite unlike any other monarch in the history of the Isles. Though he was no great physical specimen, he was not the knock-kneed, goggle-eyed twit suggested by Sir Walter Scott in *The Fortunes of Nigel*; and though he had his faults and made his mistakes, he was not the vain, arrogant blunderer which English Whig historians have needed to conjure up to discount an alien monarch at odds with their Parliament. Though he was unusually well educated, he often put his learning to good use; and he did not fully merit the brilliant gibe from a fellow monarch by which he is most usually remembered. It may be true that he was 'one of the most complicated neurotics ever to sit . . . on the throne'.[5] But he overcame his neuroses to bring his kingdoms a large measure of peace and concord. And it was not his fault that the most ambitious political scheme of the century, which he initiated, did not reach fruition. James's neuroses were born before he was. He was present in his mother's womb when her secretary Riccio was dragged from her presence to be killed. He never knew either of his parents. He was taken from his mother before his first birthday, and was brought up to believe that his mother had murdered his father. Three of the four regents who controlled his childhood were violently killed. Even in his teens, when his personal reign began in 1582, he had to suffer the humiliation of being kidnapped by the 'Raiders of Ruthven'. One of the few uplifting anecdotes of his early life, which he must have heard, referred to the day of his birth:

> He was born in Edinburgh Castle, in the little room that is shown there, between nine and ten on the morning of Wednesday, 19th June 1566. About two in the afternoon Darnley came to see his child. Like everybody else in Edinburgh, he had known of the event for hours, since a few minutes after the birth heavy guns, almost at Mary's bedside and without a word of protest from the courageous woman, had roared out their signal to the capital. The nurse put the child into Darnley's arms. 'My Lord', said Mary simply and solemnly, 'God has given you and me a son'. Then she turned to Sir William Stanley: 'This is the son who I hope shall first unite the two kingdoms of Scotland and England.'[6]

The baby's godmother was Queen Elizabeth of England.

James's French connections were strong and intimate. His mother had been Queen of France; and the Scottish court was still under the spell of the 'Auld Alliance'. James spoke French fluently, as many of his courtiers did; and he read the poetry of the Pléiade. In fact, he was so steeped in French that he habitually put an acute accent over the article 'a' when writing in English. Ronsard himself had visited Edinburgh. James's closest companion from the 1580s was the Franco-Scot Esmé Stuart, Seigneur d'Aubigny, whom James raised to be the Duke of Lennox. James's mother had been raised to the French throne after her first father-in-law, Henri II, had been fatally injured in a jousting accident prophesied by Nostradamus. This, indeed, was the prophecy that made Nostradamus's reputation:

> *Le lion jeune le vieux surmontera*
> (The young lion will overcome the older one).
> *En champ bellique par singulier duelle.*
> (In a field of combat, in single fight)
> *Dans caige d'or les yeux lui crevera*
> (He will pierce his eyes in their golden cage)

Deux classes une, puis mourir, mort cruelle.
(Two wounds in one, then he dies a cruel death.)[7]

The words proved spookily accurate. Within three years of their composition, the King of France had died from the splintered lance of his opponent which split the visor of his gilded helmet and pierced both eye and throat. The King's opponent in the tourney was Montgomery, Captain of the Scottish Guard.

Some months later, another prophecy appeared to have been directed at Mary Stewart still more directly:

> Premier fil, veuve, malheurreux mariage
> *(The first son, a widow, an unhappy marriage)*
> Sans nul enfant; deux isles en discorde.
> *(Without children; two islands in discord.)*
> Avant dixhuit incompetante age
> *(Before eighteen years of age, a minor)*
> De l'autre près plus bas sera l'accord.
> *(Still younger than the other will be betrothed.)*[8]

This time, Mary's husband, François II, died at the age of seventeen years, ten months and fifteen days. His younger brother and successor, Charles IX, aged eleven, had just been betrothed to an Austrian princess. If Mary was indeed the childless widow, then 'the two islands in discord', to which she had a claim, were not too hard to identify.

With such a background, James was keenly aware both of the fragility of royal thrones and of the tragic Wars of Religion that rent France asunder throughout his formative years. Mary, Queen of Scots had returned from France a widow, backed by the Catholic Guises and head of the Catholic party in Scotland. Her stormy career was destroyed by the feuds of Catholics and Protestants; and she ultimately lost her life as an English prisoner through the plots of English Catholics against her Protestant cousin. James, who was raised by his guardians as a Presbyterian, wanted nothing of such feuds. Unlike his queen, Anne of Denmark, who was a secret Catholic convert, he never wavered from the Protestant path. But he always talked respectfully of Roman

Catholicism, which he touchingly called 'The Mother Church of our religion'. Above all, he cannot have failed to be impressed by the example of Henry de Navarre, the Protestant king of a small southern kingdom, who fought his way through the bloodbath of the Wars of Religion to win the throne of France and, in a terminal act of reconciliation, to accept the Catholic faith. Henry IV (r. 1589–1610) is known for two bons mots. One was that 'Paris bien vaut une messe' (Paris is well worth a Mass). The other, unfortunately, was the crack about James being 'the wisest fool in Christendom'.

King James was a formidable linguist and no mean author. He once complained that 'They gar me speik Latin ar I could speik Scottis'; but the achievements were beyond dispute. The English Ambassador observed that at the age of eight James could instantly turn Latin texts into French and the French into English. James's native tongue, like that of the Scottish Court, was Lallans, that is, Lowland Scots. But when required he could also use standard southern English, though he never lost a strong Scottish accent. His correspondence is full of rambling Latinate sentences but also of pithy phrases and occasional refreshing vulgarities. He was the only King of England with any claim to literary stature, and he patronized some of the most eminent works of English literature. He first entered print in 1584 with a work on 'The Divine Art of Poetry'. It contained some of his own verses:

SONNETT DECIFRING THE PERFYTE POETE
Ane rype ingyne, ane quick and walkned witt,
With sommair reasons, suddenlie applyit,
For euery purpose vsing reasons fitt,
With skilfulnes, where learning may be spyit,
With pithie wordis, for to expres yow by it
His full intention in his proper leid,
The puritie quhairof weill hes he tryit,
With memorie to keip quhat he dois reid,
With skilfulnes and figuris, quhilks proceid
From *Rhetorique*, with euerlasting fame,
With vthers woundring, preassing with all speid

> For to atteine to merite sic a name:
> All thir into the perfyte Poëte be.
> Goddis, grant I may obteine the Laurell trie.[9]

King James's other publications ranged from religious meditations and political commentaries to his celebrated works on demonology and on the evils of tobacco. His *Basilikon Doron* (1598) was written as a guide to his son in the arts of kingship:

> God gives not Kings the style of Gods in vain,
> For on his throne his Septre do they sway:
> And as their subjects ought them to obey,
> So Kings should fear and serve thier God again.[10]

His *Trewe Law of Free Monarchies* (1598) was written in the period immediately preceding his accession to the English throne. It, too, stresses both the travails of kingship and the divine right of kings.

Despite the quaint language, his *Counterblast to Tobacco* (1604) contains some surprisingly modern sentiments. 'Herein is not only a great vanity,' he fumed, 'but a great contempt of God's good gifts, that the sweetness of man's breath ... should be wilfully corrupted by this stinking smoke.' Contrary to his later reputation, the man had much humanity. He could address a secretary of state as 'my little beagle' and 'in warning his son about the perils of choosing a wife' he urged him 'to think as well upon the business of Christendom as upon the codpiece point'.[11]

James's views on religion revealed a balanced approach and sound good sense. Just like Queen Elizabeth, he disliked the puritan spirit intensely. He never forgave the ministers at Holyrood Abbey who publicly reproved him for marrying on a Sunday. Yet he had to steer a middle course between the Puritans and the politically minded Papists. His very last coded letter to Cecil in March 1603 was intent on making this point:

> My dear 10,
>   The fear I have to be mistaken by you ... enforceth me ... to
> pen ... an answer and clear resolution of my intention. I did ever
> hate alike both extremities in any case, only allowing the middes for

virtue, as my book now lately published doth plainly appear ... I
will never allow in my conscience that the blood of any man be shed
for diversity of opinions in religion, but I would be sorry that
Catholics should so multiply as they might be able to practise their
old principles upon us ...

    Your most loving friend,
      30.[12]

Scotland had plenty of religious fanatics. One of them, Andrew Melville,
had called James 'God's sillie vassal' to his face. But he did not respond
in kind.

In the last decades of Elizabeth's reign Anglo-Scottish relations had
gradually moved away from earlier tensions. James has been blamed for
not protesting more vigorously against his mother's execution. But the
fact is, he was still the prisoner of a Protestant party controlled from
England; he had no means of influencing the outcome, and he left Elizabeth
in no doubt about his feelings. 'We marvel not a little', he had written, 'of
the strange procedure against the Queen, our dearest mother'.[13] The
Treaty of Berwick (1586), which set England and Scotland on the same
anti-Spanish course, paid him a pension of £4,000 p.a. and gave him his
first small measure of financial independence. There were dangerous
moments at the turn of the century when James flirted with the Earl of
Essex on the eve of his rebellion, and when he once opened up a
correspondence with the Vatican. But he was only trying to keep his
options open. And Cecil himself realized that James was an indispensable
player in England's future. It was Cecil who made the first tentative but
secret overtures, without the Queen's knowledge, which in other circumstances could have been judged treasonable.

James's critics, of course, found several weaknesses to exploit. They
said, for example, that he was inordinately fond of hunting and that he
neglected his papers. James responded that regular hunting served to
strengthen his fragile constitution and that in any case he could read as
many state papers in an hour as other monarchs read in a week. The
detractors also said that James was a coward. The charge was hardly
fair. It is true that James had no stomach for physical violence. Having

watched more than one murder, he tended to faint or cower at the sight of cold steel. On the other hand, he could show courage of other sorts. In 1589, for example, when his Danish bride was stranded by storms in Norway, he made a daring winter voyage to Scandinavia to bring her home in person. More serious was James's fondness for 'favourites'. There can be little doubt that he was bisexual by inclination. That in itself did not offend the mores of the day, at least in court circles. But when it drew the King into the habit of giving political preference to otherwise undistinguished individuals, like George Villiers, first Duke of Buckingham, it had far-reaching consequences. Yet the problem can be exaggerated. Certainly in the period when he acceded to the English throne, James was a caring husband and father. The letter which he wrote to his elder son, Henry, before departing for England, reveals genuine paternal affection:

> My son,
>   That I see you not before my parting, impute it to this great occasion, wherein time was so precious . . . Let not this news make you proud, or insolent, for a king's son and heir was ye before, and no more are ye yet. The augmentation that is hereby like to fall unto you is but in cares and heavy burthens. Be therefore merry but not insolent: keep a greatness, but *sine fastu*: be resolute but not wilful . . . Look upon all Englishmen that shall come to visit you as your loving subjects, not with that ceremony as with strangers . . . I send you herewith my book, lately printed; study and profit in it as ye would deserve my blessing . . . Be diligent and earnest in your studies . . . Be obedient to your master . . .: for in reverencing him ye obey me and honour yourself. Farewell.
>   Your loving father,
>   James R.[14]

Generally speaking, therefore, James's greatest failing lay in his lack of charisma. He did not look or behave in the way that was expected of monarchs. He had few of the theatrical talents of his mother or Elizabeth, and none of the fearsome 'presence' of Henry VIII. Though deeply convinced of his divine right, he was not a born leader; and he tended to lecture people instead of laying down the law. Not surprisingly, some of his subjects felt free to discount him.

James's historic journey to England started with tears and ended in a triumphant progress. He left Holyrood on Tuesday 4 April, only five days after the Proclamation. He addressed a weeping crowd of Edinburgh's citizens, and promised them rashly that he would return one year in every three. At Musselburgh, just outside the city, he ran into the funeral cortege of Lord Seton, one of his mother's most fervent supporters. He sat on a wall, and let it pass in silence. Next day at Berwick, as he crossed into his second kingdom, the castle's guns roared their salute. At York, he was presented with the keys of the city. There is no doubt that he entered England with enthusiasm. In an earlier letter to Cecil, he had opined optimistically that 'St George's steed' was easier to ride than 'the unruly colt' of Scotland. 'Saint George surelie rides upon a towardlie rydding horse,' were his exact words, 'quhaire I ame daylie burstin in daunting a wylde unreulie colte.'[15]

In successive English mansions, he was lavishly entertained, not least in the house of a Sir Oliver Cromwell, in Buckinghamshire. At Newmarket, he was waylaid by a delegation of English Puritans, who presented him with the so-called Millenary Petition demanding reform of ecclesiastical abuses. Finally, after nearly a month on the road, he reached Cecil's grand home at Theobalds in Hertfordshire:

Riding slowly, the King came up the great walk; before him the trumpets sounded, and the sheriff of Essex rode with his men. About him were the nobility of England and Scotland, bareheaded, observing no special order, now one, now another, coming up to the King's side and falling back again, according to his Highness's pleasure. At the entrance to the first court the whole glorious company dismounted, all but the King. Four nobles stepped to his horse, two before, two behind, and ceremonially laying their hands upon it, brought him forward into the second court. There he himself dismounted; a young man knelt to present a petition, which the King graciously received. He went forward; he came into the court. He saw before him a gathering of the great ones who had invited him: the Chancellor Egerton, the Treasurer Buckhurst, Henry Howard the Privy Seal. At their head, smaller and greater than any, deformed and decorous, stood the Secretary Robert Cecil, the lord of that house and, under the King, of England. The storm of shouting and cheering went on; the great folk genuflected; on the soft pawing hand of Majesty rested the soft-spoken lips of Cecil. The King raised him; together they passed into the house . . . At that point rather than in the later ceremonial entry into London the accession of James was accomplished.[16]

James was crowned King of England, Ireland, and France at Westminster Abbey on 25 July, St James's Day

As James rode though the Anglo-Scottish borders, it is not possible that he failed to reflect on their blood-soaked history and on the opportunity now presented of ending the ancient hostility. The possibility of a personal union had lived with him since birth. But his mind was now occupied with the idea of introducing something less fragile. He had strong motives for giving it serious attention.

As a Scot, he knew that the smaller partner in a dual state might suffer unless the terms of the union were well regulated. As a dynast, he wanted to bequeath his heirs and successors with a consolidated legacy. The son of Mary, Queen of Scots, who must once have thought that she had joined Scotland with France, was well aware how fickle the fortunes of a personal union could be. If James had been conceived from his mother's first marriage instead of her second, he would now have been reigning in Paris as King of Scotland and France.

One must also give James the credit of understanding the difference between general ideas, which could be expressed in rhetorical formulas, and detailed plans which could only be implemented through the long hard grind of political action. He had stated his long-term goal as early as 13 April 1603, before he had even reached London. 'His wish above all things', he declared, 'was at his death to leave one worship to God: one kingdom, intirely governed: one uniformity of laws.'[17] This was ambition on the grand scale. If his words are to be taken at face value, he was thinking of merging both the kingdoms and the state Churches of England and Scotland and of eliminating all discrepancies in legislation. This degree of unification has never been achieved to the present day. For the time being, however, he was content to press for modest preparatory steps. When he outlined his plans to the English Parliament in the following year, he would combine the rhetoric of his grand vision with practical preliminary proposals. He had also given thought to the issue of nomenclature. The name of 'Great Britain' had been used in a purely geographical sense on several occasions since the late Middle Ages. But it had made its first appearance in the context of a political union between England and Scotland in a tract of 1547, at the time of the 'Rough Wooing'. It was now to be used by James and his supporters as the catchword both for the personal union and for the extended constitutional union which he hoped to introduce.

In the meantime, King James's Scottish subjects had to be kept abreast of developments. On 12 January 1604 the King wrote to the lords of his Privy Council in Edinburgh explaining that the opening session of the English Parliament had been postponed through an outbreak of the plague, and that they should not think of convening the Scottish Parliament before April at the earliest. His thoughts on extending the union were put to them in a fine Scots flourish:

And, for that oure equall ryght to boith the Crownes mon neidis affect us with as equall cair to boith their weillis, and that, being now joyned togidder under ane head, as thay haif bene of lang tyme past in ane religioun, ane language, and ane commoun habitatioun in ane Ile disjonit fra the great Continent of the world, oure princelie cair mon be extendit to sie thame joyne and coalesce togidder in a sinceir and perfyte unioun, and, as two twynis bred in ane bellie, love ane another as no moir twa bot ane estate, we haif to this effect affixt a Parliament within this realme to convene about the twentie day of Marche nixt.[18]

England and Scotland were likened to 'twins bred in one belly'.

The peers and commons of England crowded into the House of Lords to hear the Speech from the Throne on 19 March. They were to be treated to a torrent of further similes and metaphors. The King began by thanking 'the people of all sorts' who, on his entry into England, had 'rid and ran, nay rather flew' to greet their new sovereign. He then praised the benefits of peace. But within five minutes he was launching himself into the grand theme of greater union. He appealed to the precedent of England's union with Wales, though not in the most tactful manner: 'And hath not the union of Wales to England added a greater strength thereto? Which though it was a great Principalitie, was nothing comparable in greatnesse and power to the ancient and famous Kingdome of Scotland.'[19] He appealed to physical geography which made the two kingdoms 'like a little Worlde within it selfe, being intrenched and fortified round about with a naturall and yet admirable strong pond or ditch, whereby all the former feares of this Nation are now cut off'. And he even appealed to Anglo-Saxon history:

> And yet can *Wiltshire* or *Deuonshire*, which were of the *West Saxons*, although their Kingdome was of longest durance, and did by Conquest ouercome diuers of the rest of the little Kingdomes, make claime to Prioritie of Place or Honour before *Sussex*, *Essex*, or other Shires which were conquered by them?[20]

Yet he reserved his strongest words for a sacramental image:

> What God hath conioyned then, let no man separate. I am the Husband, and all the whole Isle is my lawfull Wife; I am the Head, and it is my Body; I am the Shepherd, and it is my flocke: I hope therefore no man will be so vnreasonable as to thinke that I that am a Christian King vnder the Gospel, should be a Polygamist and husband to two wiues; that I being the Head, should haue a diuided and monstrous Body; or that being the Shepherd to so faire a Flocke (whose fold hath no wall to hedge it but the foure Seas) should haue my Flocke parted in two.[21]

In the end, however, when all the florid language was discounted, the speech could be reduced to three simple and practical proposals. The King wanted his English Parliament to embark on the scheme of greater union, firstly by abrogating mutually hostile laws, secondly by introducing free trade, and thirdly by naturalizing as English subjects all Scots residents born before his English accession.

The English Parliament's reaction to the King's proposal, however, was lukewarm. The House of Lords seemed willing on the whole to side with the King. But the majority in the Commons remained unimpressed. The proposed name of 'Great Britain' in particular offended English sensitivities. In June 1604, therefore, Parliament created a Joint Commission to 'perfect' the proposals. Forty-four Englishmen (thirty MPs and fourteen peers) and thirty-one Scots were commissioned to take soundings of public opinion and then to submit an Instrument of Union for further consideration. Their work was to take them two years.

In the meantime, frustrated by the delay, King James took a number of unilateral measures. Firstly, he declared that henceforth the Anglo-Scottish Borders should be known as 'the Middle Shires'. Secondly, on 20 October 1604, he issued a decree pronouncing himself to be 'King of Great-Britain, France, and Ireland'. Thirdly, on 16 November, he signed a decree creating a common Anglo-Scottish currency, including a twenty-shilling piece called a 'Unite'. Pending the commissioners' report, he could do no more.

London in 1604 looked to the future with relish. Though mourning the late Queen, and suffering the ever-watchful restrictions of its strong Puritan contingent, the city thrived with commerce, culture, and confidence. And King James basked in the glow. On the commercial front, London had just witnessed the foundation of the East India Company, a venture which would bring it into intimate contact with the material and the spiritual treasures of the East for generations to come. On the cultural front, royal patronage gave a start to two landmark enterprises. One of these, the commissioning of an Authorised Version of the Holy Bible, would bear fruit seven years later. The other, the granting of a licence for a new theatre, the Globe in Southwark, was intended to unite London's rival troupes of court-sponsored actors. It represented a triumph for the anti-Puritan lobby; and it would literally provide a stage for the greatest of all English talents. William Shakespeare, then aged thirty-seven, had already emerged from the shadow of his late rival Christopher Marlowe; and the stream of dramatic masterpieces was in full flow. By the end of 1604, he had written and produced twenty-six of his thirty-seven plays. He had just written *Measure for Measure* and *Othello*. There were eleven more plays to come.

Apart from the proposed union, the politics of that initial honeymoon phase of King James's reign were dominated by three interconnected issues – religion, foreign war, and Ireland. Like his predecessor, the King wished to set a middle course between the Puritan and the Papist malcontents. The year started with the Hampton Court Conference in January, when the King presided over discussions of issues raised in the Millenary Petition. But the King was in no mood for concessions. As supreme Governor of the Church of England, he did not have to suffer the lectures to which he was treated by the leaders of the Kirk in Scotland; and, as a patron of the theatre, he was not going to diminish Anglican ceremonial. He felt that by giving the Puritans an inch they would take a league. So he told the Puritans that they could either conform or be 'harried out of the land'. What is more, as a gesture of even-handedness, he ordered all unlicensed Catholic priests to leave England forthwith. It was to the Hampton Court Conference, too, that the new translation of the Bible owed its origins. At one point, the King remarked that he had never seen a well-translated Bible, recalling his failure some years previously to persuade the Scottish Kirk to undertake a translation. The remark was taken up, and a committee of the Privy Council convened to supervise the work. When it appeared in 1611, the Authorised Version turned out to be a beloved masterwork that would influence English culture as nothing before or since. It was dedicated by the translators to its 'Prime Mover':

> Great and manifold were the blessing, Dread Sovereign, which Almighty God, the father of all mercies, bestowed upon us, the

people of England, when first he set your Majesty's person to rule and reign over us.[22]

Later that year England made peace with Spain. After two decades of war and hatred, the treaty was a major accomplishment. But it offended all those, whether extreme Protestants or extreme Catholics, for whom the war had been a holy cause. Among the most aggrieved were the Catholic Irish, who had been looking to Spain to protect them from the consequences of defeat, and the militant core of English Catholics who had long dreamed that Spanish arms would mend their fortunes. The latter group, desperate and friendless, determined to act on their own. Some of their numbers, headed by Robert Catesby, laid plans to kill a King who in their eyes had betrayed both his mother and his mother's faith. Their target date was the opening of parliament in November of the following year.

In Ireland, the recent war had been terminated. The rebel leader, Hugh O'Neill, was at liberty. But English officials in Dublin had been deeply worried by his successes, and were pressing for harsh treatment. Much depended on the cautious inclinations of the new King, and on his general policy towards the Catholic Church.

1605 dawned with as much promise as 1604. It saw the publication of Francis Bacon's *Advancement of Learning*, a treatise often seen as the starting point of scientific, critical thought. 'If a man will begin with certainties', Bacon wrote, 'he shall end in doubts. But if he will be content to start with doubts, he shall end in certainties.' In that same season, Shakespeare's *King Lear* was staged. But everything was overshadowed by the discovery on 4 November of the terrible 'Powder Treason'.

Despite endless researches, the full truth of the Gunpowder Plot has never been unearthed. That there was a conspiracy, headed by Catesby, is beyond doubt. That the conspirators managed to stow enough barrels of gunpowder in the cellars of the House of Lords to blow King and Parliament to pieces is equally certain. So, too, is the fact that one of the plotters, Guy Fawkes (1570–1606), was caught in the cellars red-handed by the Yeomen of the Guard. That the conspiracy had been penetrated by Cecil's agents is more than likely. But how and when Cecil knew about it, and how long he let it run, it is impossible to tell. Catesby was killed resisting arrest. Guy Fawkes, though horribly tortured, probably knew little of the ramifications and be betrayed nothing. The public had to be content with the official version. The conspirators had been indiscreet. One had sent a warning of inpending action to the Catholic peer Lord Mounteagle, and his lordship had reported it to Sir Robert Cecil. Cecil, in the nick of time, had ordered the Yeomen to search the cellars. As he himself reported to Parliament four days later: 'And so to have blown up all at a Clapp, if God . . . had not destined it to be discovered, though very miraculously.' For the surviving conspirators, it meant death and mutilation. For Ireland, it greatly reduced the chances of a magnanimous settlement. For the King, it erected a permanent barrier to his repeated efforts for reaching a modus vivendi with the Roman Church and with the Catholic powers. For the English Catholics themselves, it spelt disaster – in effect, over two hundred years of discrimination and disrepute, that most of them had never deserved. 'It was a heavy and doleful tragedy,' writes Lady Antonia Fraser, 'that men of such caliber were driven by continued religious persecution to Gunpowder, Treason and Plot.'[23]

By 1606, therefore, the political wind had turned about. When the Parliamentary Commissioners prepared to present their modified Instrument of Union, they found that English opinion was hardening against it. In part the shift can be explained by the general climate of anxiety fostered by the Gunpowder Plot, which made people less receptive to risk and change. In part, it also signalled a reaction to the influx of hungry, fortune-hunting Scots who had flooded into London and who were particularly noticeable among the King's favourites at court. London was throwing one of its periodic fits of anti-Scottish prejudice; and no one was more aware of it than the King's leading playwright.

The story of Macbeth was common currency in late Elizabethan and Jacobean London. Holinshed's version, circulating since 1580, had inspired various plays and poems. A *Ballad of Macdobeth* was registered for copyright with the Stationers' Company in 1596. Two years later, an unidentified comedy featuring a King of Scotland had so upset the English

Ambassador in Edinburgh that he complained to Lord Burleigh: 'It is regretted that the comedians of London should scorn the King and people of the Land in this play, and it is wished that the matter be speedily amended lest the King and country be striven to answer.'[24] The story of Banquo, with its strange prophecies of the future was also circulating, but independently. Dr Matthew Gwinn, an Oxford don, used it for his play *The Three Sybils* (1605).

Shakespeare, therefore, could have taken up the theme at any time during his earlier career in London. The fact that he only chose to adopt it in 1606 can hardly be accidental. A theme of royal assassination in a setting of Scottish savagery was ideally suited to the moment. Shakespeare would have been composing *Macbeth* at a time when the fate of the Gunpowder Plotters was on everyone's mind; and he must surely have been aware of the King's expertise in witchcraft and demonology. So he was on safe as well as topical ground so long as the evil nature of Macbeth's deed was made abundantly clear. The murdered Duncan could only be a 'most sacred king'. Macbeth and Lady Macbeth could only be presented as 'This dead butcher and his fiend-like queen.' The play was staged in King James's presence in the summer of 1606 either during the revels for the visit of the King of Denmark in July or at Hampton Court in August.

Earlier that year, the King had sought to force the pace on the question of Union. On 12 April 1606, by royal decree, he ordered all the ships of England and Scotland to fly a common flag whose design he had recently approved:

> Henceforth all our subjects of this Isle and Kingdom of Greater Britain and their members thereof shall bear in their main-top the red cross commonly called St George's cross, and the white cross commonly called St Andrew's cross, joined together according to a form made by our heralds, and sent by us to our admiral to be published to our said subjects; and in their fore-top our subjects of south Britain shall wear the red cross only, as they were wont, and our subjects of north Britain in their fore-top the white cross only, as they were accustomed.[25]

The flag was officially named the 'Great Union'. Unofficially it was soon dubbed the 'Union Jack', allegedly since the King's signature on the decree had appeared in the form of 'Jacques'. Ignoring parliamentary debate, which was still to come, the King acted as if a 'Kingdom of Greater Britain' was already in existence. In the decree, he carefully avoided all mention of 'England' and 'Scotland', coining instead the previously unknown terms of 'South Britain' and 'North Britain'.

The Parliamentary session of 1606–7 opened as usual in November. When presented, the Instrument of Union made no mention of a unified 'Kingdom of Greater Britain'. On the contrary, it confined itself to four minimalist measures – the repeal of hostile laws in both kingdoms; the mutual naturalization of the King's English and Scottish subjects; the establishment of free trade; and an Anglo-Scottish extradition treaty. Yet for the English parliamentarians even minimalist measures were unacceptable. Representatives of the London merchants objected to the consequences of free trade. The lawyers, egged on by Sir Edwin Sandys, argued that the adoption of the name of 'Great Britain' would invalidate the whole of English law, and that the proposals for legal harmonization would require a costly and chaotic reorganization of England's entire legal system.[26] These arguments verged on the hysterical, and Sir Francis Bacon was one of the members who tried to call for a more pragmatic discussion. But it was no use. Delay followed delay. Finally, in February 1607, Nicholas Fuller MP rose to give voice to the unspoken prejudices which were blocking progress. He likened England to a fertile field and Scotland to a barren one. It would be madness, he implied, to let the cattle rush back and forth between the two fields at will:

> One man is owner of two pastures, with one hedge to divide them: the one pasture bare, the other fertile and good. A wise owner will not pull down the hedge quite, but make gates and let them in and out . . . if he do, the cattle rush in multitudes and much against their will return . . .[27]

The Scottish Parliament showed no more enthusiasm than the English one. Contrary to the English notion that the Scots would leap at the chance of joining England, the Scots parliamentarians saw plenty of obstacles from the start. Already in 1604 they had expressed fears of James turning into an absentee monarch; and they were unsettled by the prospect that union with England would permanently rule out the possibility of reviving the 'Auld Alliance' with France. In 1606–7 they made it abundantly clear that they would never approve the union unless the English Parliament was willing to address Scottish concerns and to 'meet them half-way'.[28]

In the circumstances, the King felt that he must confront English prejudices head on. On 31 March 1607 he summoned both Houses of Parliament to the Great Chamber of Whitehall Palace, and treated them to a peroration that must have gone on for the best part of two hours. Peppering his text with Latin tags and biblical references, he set out to dispel objections to the proposed union by reasoned argument. The tone was conciliatory. After the customary florid prelude, he admitted his own miscalculation:

> When I first propounded the Vnion, I then thought there could be no more question of it, then of your declaration and acknowledgement of my right vnto this Crowne, and that as two Twinnes, they would have grown vp together. The errur was my mistaking; I knew mine owne ende, but not others feares . . .[29]

And he urged his audience to recognize his moderation:

> I am euer for the *Medium* in every thing. Betweene foolish rashnesse and extreame length, there is a middle way. Search all that is reasonable, but omit that which is idle, curious and unnecessary; otherwise there can neuer be a resolution . . .[30]

For the sake of clarity, he repeated in no uncertain terms what he had told them three years before:

> I desire a perfect Vnion of Lawes and persons, and such a Naturalizing as may make one body of both Kingdomes vnder mee your King. That I and my posteritie (if it so please God) may rule ouer you to the worlds ende; Such an Vnion as was of the Scots and Pictes in Scotland, and of the Heptarchie here in England . . .[31]

And he mentioned, though not in one phrase, the three key terms *unus Rex, unus Grex* and *una Lex*: One King, one Flock, one Law.[32]

From then on, he laboured point by point to refute the prevailing misconceptions: that the Union was being rushed through without preparation, that England would be 'overwhelmed by swarming Scots', that all the benefits would go to Scotland and none to England, and that all English laws and liberties would be lost. He praised the common law of England as 'the best of any Law in the world'. But he spent a good half-hour explaining the special features of Scottish law. He concluded:

> What is now desired, hath oft before bene sought when it could not bee obteined. To refuse it now then, were double iniquitie. Strengthen your own felicitie, *London* must bee the Seate of your King, and Scotland ioined to this kingdome by a Golden conquest, but cymented with love ... What I sweare I will signe, and what I signe, I shall with GODS grace euer performe.[33]

This was the King's last attempt to be reasonable.

Five weeks later, after Parliament continued to prevaricate, the Lords and Commons were called back to Whitehall for a right royal ribbing. King James, in despair, roundly scolded the opponents of union, who:

> spit and blaspheme in this face by preferring war to peace, trouble to quietness, hatred to love, weakness to strength and division to union, to sow the seeds of discord to all our posterities, to dishonour your king, and to make you and me a proverb of reproach in the mouths of all enemies of this nation.[34]

The King's anger was a measure of his failure. He could not force the English Parliament to proceed with the Instrument of Union against their will. An act for the repeal of mutually hostile legislation would be the sole clause of the Instrument to reach the English statute book. It was 2 May 1607.

Added to the King's unilateral actions, the collapse of the scheme for union left a number of serious anomalies in its wake. This was the first step towards a common currency, but no free trade area for it to operate in. There was a Union Flag to be flown by all merchant ships. But it could only be flown in conjunction with one or other of the two national flags which continued to indicate that the ships of England and the ships of Scotland were not the same. Worst of all, King James had declared himself to be monarch of a kingdom which had not come into existence. He had been crowned King of Scots in 1567, and King of 'England, Ireland and France' in 1603; but he had never been crowned 'King of Great Britain' as his self-proclaimed title implied. The royal title could be used in royal documents and could be recognized by foreign monarchs; but it was not recognized by the law-makers of England or Scotland. From the constitutional point of view, England and Scotland remained separate kingdoms. They were separate both from each other and from the Third Kingdom of the Isles – Ireland.

1607 was a year in which a comet appeared over England. At the time, no astronomer knew much about it, except that it was a rare occurrence. Almost a hundred years had to pass before Edmund Halley would make the calculations showing that the comet of 1607 was the same as the comet of 1531 and the comet of 1682. (It was, in fact, the same comet which had appeared in 1066 and which was recorded on the Bayeux Tapestry.) The opportunity to create a 'United Kingdom' was a similar rare occurrence. It did not recur again until the time when Halley was publishing his *Synopsis of the Astronomy of Comets* (1705). By a strange coincidence, the title of 'United Kingdom of Great Britain', which King James had hoped so fervently to construct, eventually came into force exactly one century to the day after King James had vented his wrath on the English peers and commons on 2 May 1607. But that was for the future. For the time being, the best chance there ever was to unite the two kingdoms on an equal basis, and to submerge their separate identities into one British identity, had been missed.[35]

Throughout the seventeenth century, therefore, the Isles remained divided. Since Ireland stayed a dependency of England, they were still, from the political point of view, the 'Anglo-Scottish Isles'. To some degree their subjection to a common dynasty, that was to persist in using its British title, generated the first tentative stirrings of 'Britishness'. It also encouraged the entry into general usage of the purely geographical expression – the British Isles. Yet King James's vision of 'One King, One Flock, One Law' would never come within reach. Two hundred years more would have to pass before all the Isles would be included in a single British state. For the time being, there would be two Isles and three Kingdoms.

THE WARS OF THREE KINGDOMS

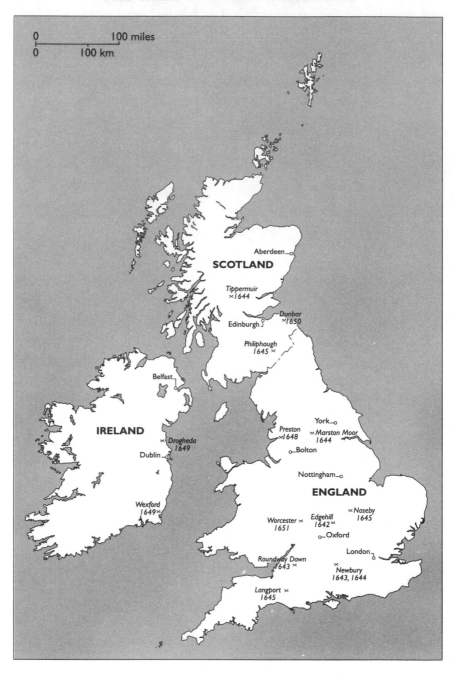

James VI, I, and I was king of three kingdoms – England and Wales, Scotland, and Ireland. By the early seventeenth century, each of the kingdoms had reached its own religious settlement; each was struggling to keep the domestic peace and to maintain a balance between the contending factions. In England, the ecclesiastical establishment brought into being by the Elizabethan Settlement sought to defend the concept of a 'Broad Church', to offset the advocates of a 'High Church' sympathetic in various degrees to Catholicism against those of a 'Low Church' more sympathetic to Calvinism. (The 'Anglican' term did not actually come into general use until after 1660.) In Ireland, the English-linked Church establishment held a much weaker position. It faced on the one hand a Catholic community which was numerically predominant, and on the other an embattled Presbyterian minority in Ulster whose militancy could cause disproportionate trouble. In Scotland, the Presbyterian establishment was beset both by the rivalry of the pro-Anglican (Episcopalian) and anti-Episcopalian wings within the Church of Scotland and by the Roman Catholic elements outside it, especially in the Highlands.

These complex divisions were a recipe for trouble in themselves. Yet nowhere was the religious situation static. In each of the three countries it was in constant motion, responding both to the internal dynamic of competing factions and to external pressures. There is no subject where the historian needs to be more aware of the ceaseless interaction of events and attitudes in all parts of the Isles.

In England, the Gunpowder Plot of 1605 left a baleful legacy of hatred and suspicion. The Elizabethan decision to treat Catholic recusants as political traitors had become a self-fulfilling prophecy. After a small group of desperate Catholics had been caught red-handed in a treasonable conspiracy that came within a whisker of sensational success, the Protestant majority in England tended to regard all Catholics as dangerously unpatriotic. Throughout the seventeenth century and beyond, England was fertile ground for exaggerated tales of Catholic conspiracies. The ultimate nightmare scenario envisaged a vast army of Irish Catholics in the pay of foreign powers invading Great Britain and overturning the Reformation with savage cruelty. The nightmare never happened. But several generations of English people were taught to believe that it could.

The anti-Catholic climate inevitably encouraged radical factions at the opposite end of the spectrum. Indeed, it was during James I's reign that the 'Puritan' label came to be widely applied by the Establishment to denigrate the religious radicals. The Puritans may have lost a battle at the Hampton Court Conference, but they never stopped pressing for their favourite causes – for sober clerical vestments, for an emphasis on sermons over ceremony, for a literal interpretation of the strict observance of the Sabbath, and for a staunchly Protestant foreign policy. They gradually obtained a stronger voice in the House of Commons, notably in the petitions of 1610, when calls for a mixture of religious reform and parliamentary privilege first raised the spectre of Church and King under attack from a militant puritan Parliament. Petitions for the rigorous enactment of the penal laws against Catholics were renewed in 1621 and 1624. In this same period, there was a significant influx of illegal religious tracts from the Continent, much of it with an Anabaptist or Anti-Trinitarian flavour. The extreme Racovian Catechism, for example, published in Poland by the acolytes of the exiled founders of Unitarianism, Lelio and Fausto Sozzini, found its way into England in dozens of different English or Latin editions.[36] For the time being, such literature could only be read in private; but the constant underground stream of stimulating ideas goes a long way to explain the radical ferment in religion which would burst into the open in the next generation. Yet even under James I, various Puritan groups, known to their contemporaries as 'separatists', found life in England intolerable. Some of them were willing to risk their lives by emigrating to the wilderness of North America. The 'Pilgrim Fathers', who set sail in the *Mayflower* from Southampton in August 1620, were intending to join the English colony already established in Virginia. Instead, they landed further north, near Cape Cod, and founded a new colony in Massachusetts where Congregationalist concepts of religion took charge.

During the reign of James I's son, Charles I, the ecclesiastical pendulum swung once again. For most of the two decades under Archbishop George Abbot (1562–1633) moderation prevailed. But under William Laud (1573–1645), Archbishop of Canterbury from 1633, the Church of England took a markedly anti-Calvinist and hence anti-Puritan turn. Laud's circle, which had formed under the patronage of James's favourite, the Duke of Buckingham, were dubbed 'Arminian' because they made a hero of the persecuted Dutch theologian Arminius. In reality they were less interested in Arminian theology and the doctrinal war against Calvinist concepts of predestination than in liturgical reform and the maintenance of uniformity. Laud favoured the revival of Catholic-style ceremonial, and he was prepared to enforce his decrees by the most drastic measures. Thanks to royal support, he was able to use the Star Chamber for the punishment of his critics. William Prynne (1602–69), who had conducted a campaign against the 'decadent' religious practices of the Royal Court, was condemned in 1634 and 1637 to the successive amputation of his ears. Henry Burton (1578–1648), a dismissed cleric who was judged to have slandered the bishops, joined Prynne in the dock in the second trial and, judged guilty of sedition, was condemned to lose both his ears and, in perpetuity, his freedom. These mutilations, reminiscent of the most savage Islamic practice, brought the English Church into popular disrepute.

In Ireland, existing religious divisions were permanently deepened by the consequences of the conflict in Ulster. Although the 'flight of the Earls' deprived the Gaelic Irish of political leadership, the appearance of the Presbyterian colony in their midst rallied them to the Catholic cause (see page 566, below). Nothing ever did more to cement the Catholic identity of the Gaels, whose religious attachments had previously looked fairly indifferent. Henceforth, the Counter-Reformation moved into Ireland in force. The links with Rome were strengthened. Systematic arrangements were made to train Irish clergy on the Continent and, through the swelling stream of new recruits, to reinvigorate Irish Catholicism. Rome's 'Irish Mission' sustained twenty colleges abroad. Catholic bishops were appointed to long-vacant sees. The religious orders, especially the Franciscans, expanded their activities and opened many new houses to replace those that had been lost during the Henrician Dissolution. Thanks to England's military power, the assertively Protestant 'New English' regime in Ireland had won the political contest. But it was losing the religious contest.

Together with the Presbyterian plantation in Ulster, the resurgence of Catholicism among the Gaels left the 'Old English' interest in Ireland seriously exposed. And much politicking surrounded their difficulties. Loyal to the crown but predominantly Catholic, they had lost control of the government of Ireland whilst retaining ownership of a third of the land. In 1613, they were still strong enough to block demands in the Irish Parliament for the general persecution of all Catholics. Yet they still felt increasingly insecure; and they made repeated demands via their friends in England that their special status be guaranteed. In 1628 their prayers seemed to be answered when, in the so-called episode of 'the Graces', Charles I granted them the desired guarantees in return for a large sum of money. As soon as the King's financial straits were eased by the signature of peace with Spain, however, the Graces were repudiated.

Such was the background to the extraordinary career in Ireland of Sir Thomas Wentworth, first Earl of Strafford (1593–1641), Lord Deputy from 1633. Strafford, a blunt Yorkshireman and sometime president of the Council of the North, was determined to make Ireland self-sufficient; and he was prepared to offend all the established interests without fear or favour. In six short years he created an efficient administration that was financially solvent and possessed of considerable military potential. On the road to his goal, he alienated the 'New English' by supporting both Laud's liturgical reforms and the toleration of Catholic recusancy. He then alienated the 'Old English' by supporting the scheme for a new plantation in Connaught; and he alienated the Protestant colonists of Ulster beyond repair by fining them for ignoring the conditions of their land grants and by seizing control of Londonderry from a recalcitrant corporation. In 1634–5 he summoned an Irish Parliament (at a time when no Parliament could meet in England), then proceeded to alienate its members by banning all non-governmental business. By the time that he was recalled, he had offended every single important group in Ireland except the Catholic Gaels. As a result, he returned to England with the reputation not only of a dangerously effective royal administrator but also of a Hibernophile.

In Scotland, religious and political controversy long centred on the King's campaign to remodel the Kirk on Anglican lines. James VI was adamant in his preference for an episcopalian hierarchy; and his attempts to impose the bishops' authority on churches more accustomed to community control created many enemies. Indeed, it was the religious struggles of this reign that persuaded many principled Scots Presbyterians to emigrate to Ulster. Ulster was Scotland's Massachusetts. Yet James's policy was at best only partially successful. The Five Articles of Perth (1618), which insisted among other things on kneeling at communion, on the compulsory observation of Christmas and Easter, and on the confirmation of all clergy by a bishop, were not universally applied. They were only passed in a reluctant Parliament by 86 votes to 59. More seriously, numerous congregations simply withdrew from active participation in the Kirk's affairs. By the time James died, the Scottish Kirk was facing the widespread revolt of underground conventicles. No General Assembly was called for twenty years after 1618. Thanks to the monarchs absence in London, Scotland's religious crisis was allowed to drift.

The accession of Charles I in 1625 ensured that the religious drift proceeded in a climate of heightening tension. The King's first act was to revoke the rights of ownership of all beneficiaries from grants of Church land. The resultant Commission for Surrenders and Teinds echoed the policy of 'surrender and re-grant' by which the Tudors had broken the old aristocracy of Wales and Ireland; and it turned the Scottish nobility into anti-royalists overnight. Then Charles addressed taxation. Edinburgh paid more tax in 1625–6 than in all the years since James's departure for England. In 1633, Charles summoned his Scottish Parliament to raise still more money. He sat on a dais in the centre of chamber, ostentatiously taking notes on who said what. When a respected nobleman dared to pen a petition of protest about the handling of the Parliament, he was put on trial. Lord Balmerino was Scotland's William Prynne. In 1634, Archbishop Spottiswoode, the Kirk's chief hierarch, was appointed chancellor. Finally, in 1636, the King issued a fresh set of Church canons, not by agreement with the Kirk but 'by our prerogative royall . . . in matters ecclesiasticall'. Religious affairs were returning to the top of the agenda in a most unpalatable form.

The most provocative event occurred, however, when the King decided to impose a new Scottish Prayer Book and liturgy prepared by Archbishop Laud. As Primate of the Church of England, Laud held no formal authority in Scotland. But Charles was careless of such niceties. On 23 July 1637 the Dean of the High Kirk of St Giles in Edinburgh opened the first service according to the new Prayer Book in the presence of the two Scottish archbishops, eight Scottish bishops, and members of the Scottish Privy Council. A riot ensued. The congregation staged a walk-out. Abuse was shouted. A stool was hurled. The Bishop of Edinburgh retreated in his carriage through a shower of stones. Protest meetings were held that soon turned political. Demonstrators broke up similar services across the country. By October, Scotland was in a state of revolution. The outcome was the signing of the Scottish National Covenant, and after that, the inevitable war with England.

The Covenant signed at Greyfriars' Church in Edinburgh on 1 March 1638 was a wordy document recounting the whole religious history of Scotland since the Reformation. Yet it contained two explosive passages. One concerned 'the manyfold ordoures' and 'wicked hierarchie' of Popery. The other denounced 'the subversion of our liberties, lawes and estates'. The former sealed the fate of episcopacy; the latter spelled the end of the King's arbitrary habits. The conclusion contained a 'national oath and subscription inviolable', pledging dual allegiance both to the Protestant religion and to the King. The leading Covenanters were grouped round the greatest lords of the land, who no doubt eyed the prospect of office under a changed government. But they obtained the backing of forty thousand signatories from all classes and from all parts of Scotland, thereby creating a truly national movement. They were sworn to defend their principles to the death. Their slogan was 'For Christ's Crown and Covenant'. Their achievement culminated in the long-awaited General Assembly of the Kirk, which met behind locked doors in Glasgow Cathedral for the four weeks prior to Christmas 1638. Ministers of the Kirk and the elders of all Scotland's presbyteries mingled with lairds and their retinues and the representatives of forty seven boroughs. Ignoring the protests of the King's Commissioner, they solemnly abolished the Five Articles, the Canons, the new Prayer Book, and the Bench of Bishops. They ended by declaring the bishops to be deposed and excommunicate. They had launched a manifesto and a cause that would dominate Scottish politics until the restoration of the monarchy more than twelve years later.

King Charles received the news at York. Despite inadequate preparations, he ordered his English army to march. He was launching what the textbooks record as 'the First Bishops' War'. More realistically, he was launching the first act of 'the Wars of the Three Kingdoms'.

Volumes have been written on the causes of the chain of conflict which flowed from the outbreak of the Anglo-Scottish War in 1639. No simple summary of those causes can be attempted. But three points stand out. Firstly, it was matters of religion which acted as the prime source of discontent in that deeply believing age. Secondly, it was religious divisions which underlay the principal political groupings that were to emerge. Thirdly, it was Archbishop Laud's ill-considered programme of religious reform which sowed the seeds of irreconcilable conflict. Laud may well have harboured ambitions to unite all the Churches of this master's three kingdoms. His appointees had taken complete control of the Church of England. His friends in the Scottish episcopate had been running both Church and state. His colleagues in Ireland held the official ecclesiastical ring against Presbyterians and Catholics alike. Some historians say that he and his royal patron were consciously moving in the direction of a pan-British Church. As it was, Laud, like Strafford, had only two years to wait before falling from grace.[37]

(2) The Plantation of Ulster: a 'Fatal Harvest'

At the start of the seventeenth century Ulaidh, or Ulster, was still the most Irish, Gaelic, Catholic, and traditional province in Ireland. Its historical connections were incomparable. It centred on the ancient city of Armagh, the legendary seat of Queen Macha and the see of St Patrick. It had served as the launch pad of Gaelic Scotland (see above, page 183). It was the home base of the O'Neills, the strongest of its clans and the kin of Brian Boru. Moreover, it had largely escaped from the modernizing trends of the Elizabethan era. Apart from Derry and Armagh there were few towns, few English officials, and few English-speakers. Life was dominated by the Gaelic clans and their ancient pastoral economy. A war against the English was in progress, and the clans were feuding among themselves. But that was absolutely normal. Even when Hugh O'Neill surrendered to Lord Mountjoy in March 1603, there could have been few signs that Gaelic Ulster was entering its terminal phase.

Hugh O'Neill, after all, had fought a stalwart fight. His initial tactics of ambush and siege had paid off. His well-equipped army had proved more than a match for the Crown forces in Ulster. It had not eliminated all the English garrisons, especially when, as at Derry in 1600, the English supplied their beleaguered outposts by sea. But it had only been defeated in the far South, at Kinsale, after losing touch with its base and being teased into an unfamiliar battlefield setting. At the Treaty of Mellifont (1603), which ended the Nine Years War, O'Neill was treated leniently, and allowed to return to his estates.

Ireland, however, was to pay the price of O'Neill's impressive performance. Crown officials vowed it must never happen again. They were appalled by the alliance that O'Neill had made with some of the 'Old English', by the opportunity presented for the intervention of England's Spanish enemies, by rumours that O'Neill was due to be appointed 'Papal Viceroy', and by the widespread attacks on 'New English' property. During O'Neill's march to the south, most of the English settlers in the plantations of Leix, Offaly, and Munster had been driven from their lands. Though Mountjoy's campaign of frightfulness effected a quick enough recovery, he and his subordinates believed that the recovery might only be temporary, unless the nest of Gaelic vipers in Ulster was expunged once and for all. At first, the new King in London kept his counsel. But after the Gunpowder Plot his Irish policy was overtaken, like everything else, by the tide of anti-Catholic hostility. Henceforth, Ulster was to be the scene of a particularly ruthless form of colonization. All former 'rebels' were to be expropriated. Their lands were to be redistributed to new settlers specially selected for their devotion to Protestantism and their military competence. The native Irish would be eliminated or marginalized. When the policy moved from proposal to implementation, Hugh O'Neill took flight, fearing arrest. On 3 September 1607 he took ship at Rathmullan in Lough

Swilly, and sailed into voluntary exile on the Continent. Hugh
O'Donnell of Tyrconnell went with him, and ninety other Gaelic
chiefs from Ulster. They left their homeland defenceless and
leaderless.

Up to that point, the English plantations in Ireland had not
received full government backing. Like the early attempts to colonize North America (see page 470, above), the early Irish ventures
had been put in the hands of private entrepreneurs, and the pioneers
had been left to sink or swim. This time the crown would organize
extensive financial support from the City of London, and would
supervise the conditions under which the scheme developed. The
Ulster Plantation was planned at exactly the same time as the third
attempt to plant a colony in Virginia. Derry, renamed Londonderry,
was to be the Irish Jamestown. The native Irish were to play the
same part as the native Americans. Despite initial setbacks, both
Ulster and Virginia were destined to thrive mightily. (See page 570,
below.)

The Flight of the Earls greatly facilitated English planning. In
each of the six counties affected – Armagh, Cavan, Coleraine,
Donegal, Fermanagh, and Tyrone – the native Irish were segregated
and crowded into reservations on the worst land. The rest, and the
best, of the land was then assigned to a network of entirely new
communities. In these areas, lots of 1,000–2,000 acres were offered
at easy rents, but on condition that the leaseholder construct military
defences in the shape of castle and bawn (strong courtyard) and that
the incoming tenants, at ten families per lot, be exclusively Protestant. The ruined city of Derry was assigned for redevelopment to
a City of London Company, which also received special privileges
throughout Tyrone between the River Foyle and the River Bann –
the new county of Londonderry. Another new town was laid out
on the east coast of the Province on Lough Carrickfergus. It was
assigned to Sir Arthur Chichester (1563–1625), the Lord Deputy, and
was to become Belfast.

From the outset, therefore, the new settlers of Ulster operated a
system of social and cultural apartheid. The principal leaseholders

were usually English servitors, that is, former soldiers or crown servants, but the mass of tenants were preponderantly Scots. They built neat new towns and villages of timber-framed or stone cottages, which they fortified like frontier posts and adorned with English names. They renamed Dún Lethglaise as Downpatrick, Ballynalurgan as Castleblayney, Corcreeghagh as Cookstown. They built their own churches, which had no connection either with the official Church or with the old Catholic parishes, and which were usually independent conventicles of the free Presbyterian type. They cleared the land, cut down the forests, and applied themselves to arable farming on a scale never seen before; and they rapidly organized a prosperous trade in timber, cattle, and flax. They had no contact with the native Irish, except those who worked for them as labourers or servants. They had no great love for the crown, nor for the New or Old English, with whom they had little in common. In the Plantation itself, the new breed of Ulstermen represented an absolute majority: in Ireland as a whole an embattled minority. Their self-reliance and truculence were legendary: their devotion to the Protestant cause, unshakeable. Their military prowess was formidable. Their accent, and the new brand of English which they spoke, was inimitable.

Elsewhere in Ireland, the crown encouraged smaller settlements and individual migrants to take up offers of available land. One quarter of Catholic land in Connaught was confiscated for this purpose. The derelict plantations in Munster and in King's and Queen's Counties were restored to health. Altogether, in the first four decades of the seventeenth century, Ireland accommodated an estimated hundred thousand settlers.

In the changed political climate, an important sector of the native Irish took to English ways. Irish landowners, in particular, saw the need to ingratiate themselves with officialdom by adopting English speech, by dressing in the English fashion, by imitating English farming techniques, and by supporting the introduction of English law into their districts. At the landowner level, Anglo-Irish society fused into one. Bit by bit, large tracts of countryside dotted with tasteful residences among enclosed fields began to look more and more like southern England.

Yet the bulk of the native Irish – Gaelic speaking, Catholic, and hugely resentful – had not been reconciled. Especially in Ulster, which had borne the brunt of the innovations, they were merely biding their time. In 1639 they watched the King go to war with the Scots. In 1640 they watched him plunged into unresolved trouble with his English Parliament. So in 1641 they hatched a plot. Headed by Sir Phelim O'Neill, they planned a series of local risings in Ulster itself coupled with an attack on Dublin Castle. The insurrectionaries did not consider themselves rebels. They said they were royalists. They claimed to be defending the King's interests against the militant English Parliament; and all their members were obliged to swear a loyal oath. It could not save them from being treated as traitors. 22 October 1641 was the appointed day. Their plans in Dublin were betrayed, and aborted. But the rash of local actions in Ulster took place, and some two thousand Protestant settlers were killed. Before the year was out, the Ulster Irish were marching south to join up with 'Old English' contingents and to form a 'Catholic Army'. Protestant England's ultimate nightmare seemed to be on the brink of realization.

In these circumstances, it is difficult to make an even-handed assessment of the Ulster Plantation. In Protestant eyes, it had been a grand success: in Catholic eyes, the incarnation of failure. To anyone of an objective disposition, it was clearly the tragic source of endless, irresolvable conflict. As an English Victorian observer put it:

> In its material results, the plantation of Ulster was undoubtedly a brilliant success . . . the foundations of the economic prosperity which has raised Ulster high above the rest of Ireland in wealth and intelligence were laid . . . in the confiscation of 1610 . . . The evicted natives withdrew sullenly to the lands which had been left them by the spoiler; but all faith in English justice had been torn from the minds of the Irishry, and the seed had

been sown of that fatal harvest of distrust and disaffection, which was to be reaped through tyranny and massacre in the age to come.[38]

When James VI, I, and I signed the Act of Confiscation for Ulster, he undoubtedly imagined that his splendid Plantation would help weld his three kingdoms into one. Protestant Ulster, run by the English, manned by Scots, and planted on the Irish, was, in effect, the first British colony; and it benefited from lessons learned from the mistakes of England's previous colonial experiments. Yet Ulster was to remain a state within the state. Its affairs would stay a bone of contention on all sides. Added to the open conflict between England and Scotland, the Ulster Rising of 1641 was to fan the flames of a general conflagration. Nearly four hundred years later, 'the fatal harvest' is still being reaped.[39]

(3) ENGLAND'S KING VERSUS ENGLAND'S PARLIAMENT

English constitutional history was once the flagship subject of historical studies. It attracted many grand figures and in the days when 'documents' were revered above all else, it demanded a precise, legalistic mind to master them. Its chief practitioners commanded great respect and prestige, not least because the standing of Parliament was extremely high in their own day. Constitutionalists were thought to have their finger on the pulse of English greatness. And constitutionalists studying the seventeenth-century crisis were thought to be expounding the well-springs of that greatness. Their one great weakness, of course, lay in their deeply blinkered Englishness. Writing in the era of the United Kingdom, when all the Isles were united under the centralized rule of Whitehall and Westminster, they failed to notice that the early modern state was a very different animal from their own. They paid very little attention to the fundamental fact that seventeenth-century England formed just one part of a 'multiple polity' or 'composite monarchy', where politics depended on the interplay of the three Stuart kingdoms, not just on the English realm alone.[40]

Even so, it cannot be denied that England's position within the multiple polity was especially important, if only because of her relative size and strength. What is more, English constitutional law operated within its own separate compartment; and the failure of English constitutionalists to grasp the wider context of their country's affairs was every bit as evident in the seventeenth century as in later times. As one of the leading advocates of the new 'British History' has put it, the English Parliament pretended that Scotland did not exist. 'If the King [of England] cared to be King of Scots in his spare time, that was nothing to do with them.'[41] It is only in very recent years that some historians and other commentators have begun to move the spotlight away from England and to insist on a comprehensive view of all three kingdoms.

All talk of 'constitutions', inevitably associated with a later, limited monarchy, obscures the far-reaching extent of royal autocracy in Tudor and early Stuart times. For the 156 years between its creation in 1485 and its abolition in 1641, the Court of Star Chamber was arguably more central to the overall functioning of government than Parliament was. From 1540 the Star Chamber encompassed both the Privy Council and the Chief Justices, that is, both the executive and the judiciary, thereby creating a block of influence in permanent session which could dominate the more circumscribed and intermittent sphere of Parliament. Indeed, one can fairly contend that Parliament could never develop its potential until the Star Chamber, together with the underlying political philosophy, were removed. In early seventeenth-century England, the King ruled more commonly by decree than by statute; he could declare martial law at will, thereby suspending all legal constraints; and he could summon or dissolve Parliament as he wished. As yet, there was no Habeas Corpus act, and hence no freedom from arrest and no security for political action. There was no independence for judges, no immunity for jurors, no free press, and no freedom of speech, even for Members of Parliament. There were many crucial areas of royal policy where MPs were not permitted to express an opinion or even to petition the King, let alone influence decisions. As yet, MPs were by no means the equals of peers. Indeed, prior to signature of the Great Contract in 1610 abolishing feudal tenures, the great majority of parliamentarians were still entrapped in a web of feudal dues and loyalties, which rendered all hopes of an independent political career impossible. Though members of the House of Lords enjoyed freedom from arrest and the right to trial by their peers, members of the House of Commons did not. The custom was for the Speaker of the Commons, at the opening of each session, to beg the monarch to grant the Commons the gracious liberty of speaking their mind, but only for the duration of the session. The late Elizabethan era was filled with legal cases involving MPs who had been thrown into jail and who then sought to use their parliamentary status to achieve release.

The one area where the English Parliament in general, and the Commons in particular, wielded traditional competence was in finance. Here was the chink, and as the King's financial problems increased, that could be exploited to the full. By general consent, the key phase in which the House of Commons 'won the initiative' in its dealings with the crown occurred in the middle of the reign of James I. Before that time, the Commons had preserved their customary deference. In 1604, for instance, having obstructed the King's legislative programme, they felt compelled to justify their conduct by an elaborate apology. As it happened, they never had to present the King with their apology, since the King backed off in the meantime. But the episode shows how sensitive an issue had been raised when the Commons did not simply do what the crown had requested. Ten years later, during the Addled Parliament of 1614, they realized what enormous power lay in their grasp. A fierce argument between Lords and Commons over parliamentary privileges forced the King to dissolve Parliament before any subsidies had been granted. As a result, the crown did not get a penny, and was forced to govern for the next few years on a reduced budget. Henceforth, every time Parliament was summoned, the Commons would want to be courted before agreeing to grant any subsidies, whilst the crown understood (with horror) that raising taxation through Parliament involved making political concessions. The conflict of wills between King and Parliament had been launched.

If a new political game emerged during James I's reign, therefore, no one knew the rules. This is where 'the Constitution', and constitutional history, come into their own. For constitutions are nothing other than the body of rules which define how the political game should be played. In early Stuart England, the great unknown centred on the limits of the royal prerogative. This central issue could only be addressed over several decades by trial and error, by the rise of new ideologies, and, when all else failed, by the resort to arms.

The greatest of English constitutional lawyers, Sir William Blackstone (1723–80), defined the royal prerogative as 'that special pre-eminence the King hath over and above all persons and out of the common law in right of his regal dignity; it is singular and eccentric . . .' Yet Blackstone was writing more than a century after the matter had been resolved; and in any case, as any lawyer would agree, the devil lay in the detail. King James loved to give lectures on the subject. Talking to his judges in 1616, he made a generous distinction between his prerogative as a private person, which was no greater than anyone else's, and 'the absolute prerogative of the Crown'. Yet he stated unequivocally that 'the mystery of the King's power is not to be disputed' and 'it is high presumption in a subject to dispute what a king can do'. Such unbending views proved worse than useless in detailed financial issues, such as the granting of royal monopolies, which had been under negotiation with parliamentary representatives since Queen Elizabeth's time. In the absence of any flexibility, they led almost inevitably to the Monopolies Act (1624), which in a signal parliamentary victory declared all existing monopolies void. Even in the realm of foreign policy, where the royal prerogative was not questioned, they did not prove very helpful. In 1621, for example, James called Parliament in an attempt to secure £500,000 to pursue his foreign policy: his son-in-law Frederick,

Elector Palatine, had been made King of Bohemia by the Bohemians in defiance of the Emperor, but removed from his throne by Austrian Habsburg troops under Tilly at the Battle of the White Mountain (1620), and James wanted to restore him. Parliament preferred a naval war with Spain and disliked the proposed marriage of James's son Charles to the Spanish princess Donna Maria; when it presented him with a petition to that effect, it received a stiff rebuff. 'Do not meddle with the royal prerogative or high matters of state,' they were told. 'We mean to punish any man's misdemeanours in parliament.' This was sheer bluster, and everyone concerned knew it. The Commons risked a formal 'Protestation'. The King dissolved Parliament, called the Protestation 'intolerable', then gave an assurance that Parliament would be recalled. He could keep his foreign policy, and fight his war with France. But as he now knew very well, without parliamentary taxes his war could not be won.

In the early years of Charles I, friction over the royal prerogative increased. In 1625, suspicious of the King's motives, Parliament granted the crown the right to receive the import and export duties of tunnage and poundage for one year only. The King, claiming prerogative, ordered them to be levied indefinitely. In 1627, again claiming prerogative, he ordered subscriptions to be made to a forced loan. In a *cause célèbre*, the 'Five Knights' Case' (1627), a group of men who declined to subscribe to the loan were peremptorily imprisoned. Having appealed unsuccessfully to be released on a writ of habeas corpus, they were eventually released under public pressure, but not before forcing the crown to justify its actions in the courts. In 1628, the King was faced by a formal Petition of Right, a document whereby Parliament sought to define and to limit the royal prerogative. He grudgingly accepted it, then ignored it. In 1629 he fined and imprisoned a Cornish MP, Sir John Eliot (1592–1632), who had been campaigning against tonnage and poundage, against Arminianism in religion, and against the King's attitude to the Petition of Right. The ensuing rumpus convinced Charles I that the English Parliament was more trouble than it was worth. So for ten years he simply refrained from summoning a parliament in England.

But he still needed money. His solution was to revive an old levy on port towns in lieu of the supply of ships, and then to extend it to all towns and cities across the country. This 'Ship Money' was a genuine attempt to finance naval construction; and the King's right to raise it was upheld by the judges. But it was a novel, not to say a devious device in times of peace. And it did not pass without surviving yet another legal challenge from yet another doughty parliamentary protester; this time, since Eliot had died in prison, from John Hampden MP (1594–1643).

The incidence of cases involving the royal prerogative brought the King into confrontation with a powerful group of professionals who were well represented in parliamentary circles. English lawyers, who worked the common law, were naturally suspicious of a tendency that threatened to short-circuit legal process altogether. They were appalled when one of their number, Lord Chief Justice Crewe, was dismissed for refusing to rule on the King's forced loan; and they watched with growing apprehension as cowed colleagues successively upheld each of the King's cases. They found a champion in Sir Edward Coke (1552–1634), former MP for Norfolk, former Speaker of the Commons, former Chief Justice of the Common Pleas and Attorney-General. Coke had been a professional rival of Francis Bacon, a noted defender of the royal prerogative. Taking an independent view, he had been dismissed from office in 1616 and in 1622 had spent a period under arrest in the Tower. He drafted the Petition of Right; and was specially critical about the eleven prerogative courts which still functioned in his time.* In a lifetime of writing he moulded the ideology which viewed the historic growth of English common law since Anglo-Saxon times as the heart of the English tradition. He saw the law as the hedge of England's ancient liberties, and legal innovators like Charles I as the chief threat to

---

* Court of Chancery, Court of Requests, Court of the Privy Council, Court of Star Chamber, Council of the North, Council in Wales, Council of the West, Court of Castle Chamber, Court of the Duchy of Lancaster, Court of the County Palatine of Chester, the Court of Stannaries.

established freedom. He was no republican. But his monumental *Institutes of the Laws of England* (1628) was to become a bible for both sides during the Civil Wars.

Since the Parliamentary cause was destined to triumph in its military confrontation with the monarchy, historians were once inclined to see Coke's legal ideology as the way of the future. In terms of the early seventeenth century, however, the Absolutism of the King with its appeal to the divine right of kings must be seen as the progressive, rationalizing, anti-feudal force, whilst Parliament's ideology and the cult of Magna Carta was the force of intense conservatism.

Nonetheless, parliamentary ideology equally encompassed an important radical streak born of long-standing puritan attitudes. Unlike the Catholics, who suffered similar religious disabilities, the Puritans were deeply interested in new forms of non-hierarchical Church organization; and their views on ecclesiastical structures inevitably influenced their views on the state. Hating episcopacy with a passion, they saw all the branches of secular government in which the power of the bishops was exercised, from the House of Lords and the Privy Council to the Court of High Commission, as 'Popish abuses'. Despite their extreme intolerance and colourful language, they practised a form of guided democracy among themselves; and they looked forward to a time when they could introduce a God-ruled democracy in the kingdom at large. For them, there was little to be expected from the existing monarchical and episcopal establishment. But there was much to be aspired to in Parliament and especially in a House of Commons where Puritan voices were increasingly heard. From 1572 onwards, when the Puritans had addressed their First Admonition not to the monarch but to Parliament, they placed their hopes in their own variant of parliamentary democracy. In their view, such a democracy would only work when shorn of the bishops, shorn of the House of Lords, shorn of all ungodly men, and 'if the king were found to be ungodly' shorn of the King himself. The Puritan paradise was no recipe for a general consensus. But it would have its chance.

Such was the state of play when early in 1640 twelve peers of the realm joined Laud and Strafford in advising the King to summon the English Parliament. They warned of numerous current dangers including the threat of Popery from Ireland and the ruinous consequences of the war with Scotland. The King could not refuse. He could only hope to extract the maximum subsidies for the minimum concessions. As for the disgruntled parliamentarians, they were determined to grant the King nothing until their grievances were heard.

The Short Parliament, which convened in April 1640 and broke up at the beginning of May, was short because the King refused to accept the torrent of criticism which he heard. But by sending the members away, he deprived himself of his one and only financial lifeline. So before the year was out a second Parliament was called. This was to be the longest Parliament in English history.

The Long Parliament, though many times re-modelled, was to stay in being through all the troubles until 1660. It opened with a puritanical attack on the Church and state and a barrage of bills to defend the parliamentary interest. In December 1640, a so-called 'Root and Branch Petition' from the City of London ominously made the conjunction between religious and constitutional discontent. It called for the total abolition of episcopacy in the Church of England. 'The Archbishops and Lord Bishops', it began, 'have claimed their calling immediately from the Lord Jesus Christ, which is against the laws of this kingdom, and derogatory to His Majesty.' It could not possibly have named the laws which episcopacy supposedly contravened, and its proposals did not command general support. But it listed a catalogue of twenty-eight grievances, from the proliferation of 'lewd clergy' and 'lascivious books' to increases in 'Popery', 'Sunday Sports' and 'whoredom'. It set the truculent tone on which more purely constitutional measures would thereafter thrive. The Triennial Act (1641), which held that Parliament should automatically reassemble after three years if not summoned by the King, was followed by an act against dissolving Parliament without its consent.

Having overturned the King's right to terminate parliamentary proceedings, the Commons unleashed a furious political offensive. In May they called for the impeachment of the King's ministers. They saw Strafford as the embodiment of secular 'tyranny' and Laud as the incarnation of abominable religious 'innovation'. Both of them were to be sacrificed. But the appetite only grew with the eating. Since the Lords could not be persuaded to expel the bishops, an act was passed to abolish the Court of High Commission, the chief instrument of religious uniformity. Another act abolished Ship Money. On 1 December 1641 the King was presented with a 'Grand Remonstrance on the State of the Kingdom' drafted, among others, by John Pym MP (1584–1643). This was another monster petition in the same spirit as its 'root-and-branch' predecessor, but containing 204 as opposed to 28 articles. Conceived in a climate of Protestant panic fuelled by the news from Ireland (see page 00, above) it ascribed all the present misfortunes to 'the oppressions of the Popish party', which was nowhere defined except by phrases such as 'Jesuits, bishops and courtiers' or 'Papists, Arminians and libertines'. Its more significant practical demands called for the dismissal of the bishops from Parliament and the King's Council, for the selection of ministers from parliamentary leaders, and for the preservation of crown lands in Ireland.

Throughout this barrage, the King kept his cool. With a heavy heart, he sacrificed Strafford and Laud, the former being executed on impeachment, the latter being held under arrest. With reluctance, he gave his assent to the acts diminishing his prerogative. And with great restraint, two days before Christmas, he issued a conciliatory reply to the Grand Remonstrance. He did not understand the talk about 'a Popish Party', he said; and the presence of the bishops in Parliament was perfectly proper. He would defend his right to choose his own councillors and would not entertain any 'naughty general accusations'. But he would take notice of 'particular proofs', as in the case of Strafford. No decisions about Ireland were possible until the outcome of the war was known.

Yet behind the façade of restraint the patience of the King's advisers was wearing thin. They were fighting a couple of wars, in Scotland and in Ireland, but had not received a penny to fight them. They had made concession after concession, but had found no one in Parliament to staunch the torrent of demands. The point had arrived where further unilateral concessions made no sense. So a plot was hatched. On 4 January 1641/2, when the Commons resumed its session after the Christmas recess, the King strode into Westminster Hall to arrest the five most contumacious members in person. He carried charges of treason against Pym, Hampden, Holles, Haselrig, and Strode. As he entered the Commons chamber, surrounded by officers with drawn swords, he realized his mistake. The Five Members had been tipped off. 'I see that the birds have flown,' he stammered. It was an unbearable humiliation. He fled London promptly, and never met his Parliament again.

Throughout those months of protest, everyone in Parliament had claimed to be acting in the King's name. Indeed, they would continue to do so, even when fighting against the King's armies. But henceforth, they were following a political fiction sustained by the argument that Charles Stewart had been illegally seduced or constrained by evil counsellors.

In practice, both King and Parliament were calling their supporters to arms. Both wanted to raise troops to crush the Irish Rebellion. The King had travelled north, appealing to his loyal subjects to join him. In March, the Commons issued the fateful Militia Ordinance. Initially directed to Berkshire, Bedfordshire, and the City of London, it provided an authority 'to raise, lead and employ such persons as necessary, as directed by Parliament'. When the King issued a proclamation forbidding all his subjects to join the parliamentary militia, the Commons responded with an argued defence. The arguments put forward included 'the King cannot withhold Parliament once he has called it', 'the powers of Parliament are more eminent than the King's', and 'the King's justice is not administered by his person but in his courts'. Supreme among all the royal courts stood 'the High Court of Parliament'. To this argument there was no easy answer, even though Parliament was claiming to know the King's business better than the King himself. In all, Charles I formulated three replies to three sets of parliamentary propositions, but with no great hope of reconciliation. By July, when Parliament voted to raise a professional army in addition to the militia 'for the defence of the King's person, Parliament, of true religion, laws, liberty and peace', it was clear that the army was not to be used against the rebels in Ireland but against the royalists in England. From the royalist point of view, there was nothing to be gained from further parleys. The King raised his standard at Nottingham on 22 August 1642. The wars of 'the Great Rebellion' in England was to be added to the wars already underway in Scotland and Ireland.[42]

(4) The Wars of the Three Kingdoms, 1639–51

'The English Civil War' must be one of the worst misnomers in the whole historical repertoire. Not much used at the time, the label ill suits the complex chain of conflicts which were fought out between Scotland, Ireland, and England after 1639, and has misled generations of students and scholars. Royalists called it 'the Great Rebellion', Parliamentarians 'the Cause'. Historians have been looking for a replacement for some time. Some of them fell for the Marxist slogan 'the English Revolution' – which completely misses the point. Others have adopted 'the British Civil Wars', which borders on the anachronistic. Perhaps the best solution is that preferred by many Scots – 'the Wars of the Three Kingdoms'.

English historians always used to pretend that their Civil War was inspired by noble ideals and was fought by gentlemanly combatants showing admirable restraint. They would contrast the honourable conflict in England with the dastardly wars of religion on the Continent, where bigotry, venality, and gratuitous violence were the norm. A favourite quotation came from the correspondence of a Parliamentary general to his friend and colleague in the Royalist camp talking about 'unchangeable affection' and 'this war without an enemy'.

> My affections to you are so unchangeable that hostility itself cannot violate my friendship to your person, but I must be true to the cause I serve. The great God, who is a searcher of my heart, knows . . . with what perfect hatred I look upon this war without an enemy. We are both upon the stage and we must act the parts assigned to us in this tragedy. Let us do it in a way of honour and without personal animosities.[43]

In reality, the wars in the Isles possessed both edifying and disgusting episodes. The religious element was ever present and sometimes led to fanaticism. High ideals were often marred by savagery. It is not in order to draw too strong a distinction between the character of the conflict in the Isles and that of the Wars of Religion in France or of the Thirty Years War in Germany.

The fighting began in Scotland in February 1639, when a force of Covenanters seized the city of Aberdeen. It was the prelude to a series of skirmishes between Covenanters and Royalists in various parts of the country. In the Highlands, the Campbells of Argyll, who supported the Covenant, attacked the Catholic Macdonalds, thereby initiating the clan warfare that was to persist throughout the century. But a full-scale confrontation between King and Covenanters never took place. Charles I, at Berwick, planned a three-pronged offensive into his northern kingdom. Faced in June by a superior Scots army at Duns Law, he preferred to negotiate. The Treaty of Berwick maintained a fragile peace throughout the winter.

The Second Bishops' War, or 'Second War of the Covenant', broke out in August 1640. A formidable Army of Covenanters crossed the Tweed, dispersed the opposing English force at Newburn, and marched into the undefended city of Newcastle-upon-Tyne. Once again, Charles I had failed to act decisively. The Treaty of Ripon (26 October 1640) left Newcastle in Scots hands whilst paying them exorbitant tribute. England could not stand by indefinitely.

The two Bishops' Wars ended in triumph for the Covenanters. They heralded a political revolution in Scotland which anticipated many of the steps taken in England a year or two later. In 1639 the Scottish Parliament's ruling Committee of Estates excluded royal ministers, and declined to receive the King's order for prorogation. In 1640 it claimed the right to vet all executive appointments to both the Privy Council and to the bench of judges; and it passed a Triennial Act eight months before the Long Parliament in England thought of doing the same. Charles I was admitted to Edinburgh in August 1641 on condition that he ratified the changes.

Seen from the Scottish perspective, however, there were many reasons for anxiety. The Covenanters' Revolution was far from secure. The religious settlement, and the abolition of episcopacy, would not last if a strong royalist army were to cross the Borders from England. So it was essential for the Covenanters to find allies in England, and with them to prevent the resurgence of the Royalist cause. It was essential for the Protestant Campbells to stay in control of the Highlands and the Lordship of the Isles. Above all, it was crucial that no pro-Catholic force be allowed to intervene from Ireland. This last danger became a real possibility with the outbreak of the Irish Rebellion.

The Irish Rebellion of 1641 – or the Irish Rising – was fuelled by the conjunction of interests between the Ulster Catholics and the Old English. The former were seeking to overturn the effects of the Protestant Plantation (see page 566, above). The latter had been infuriated by the policies of Strafford. Indeed, they eagerly sent information to Westminster to assist in Strafford's impeachment. Yet when the two groups joined together to form a Catholic Confederation, they were throwing down a challenge which no English government could ignore. Their victory over a small crown detachment at Julianstown Bridge near Drogheda in December 1641 fed exaggerated rumours in London and Edinburgh that the Catholic Irish were about to invade. At the time, neither the English Royalists nor the English Parliament had any troops at their disposal. But the victorious Scots Covenanters did. So in January 1642 a Protestant Scots army sent by the Covenanters landed in Ulster to defend the embattled Protestant planters.

For seven long years, from 1642 to 1649, no resolution to the conflict in Ireland was possible. The Scots never ventured beyond Ulster. The forces loyal to the crown under James Butler, twelfth Earl of Ormonde looked in vain for support from a divided England. They sent an effective force to Scotland in 1644 (see below), but they could not gain mastery at home. The Catholic Confederation could not decide on a consistent policy. The 'Old English' would have preferred an accommodation with King Charles. But the King was in no position to negotiate. Urged on by the Papal Nuncio, Rinuccini, and strengthened by returning exiles, the more extreme Catholic party increasingly dreamed about restoring Ireland to the Faith. They did not possess the means to realize their aims. They enjoyed a few minor victories in local encounters, such as that in 1646 on the Blackwater in Ulster where Colonel Owen Roe O'Neill rebuffed the Scots. In the end, they filled all Protestant hearts with dread without ever gaining a definite advantage. In particular, they so frightened the Parliamentary party in England, which fell increasingly into militant Puritan anti-Catholic hands, that the English Parliamentarians began to prepare for a showdown in Ireland long before it became a realistic proposition. The English Parliament raised loans in the City of London on the security of Irish Catholic lands that were still to be conquered. Hence the final outcome in Ireland was tied to the final outcome in England.

The conflict between King and Parliament in England passed through two distinct phases – the First Civil War of 1642–6, and the Second Civil War of 1648–9. The King, who had wide support in the counties, especially in the North, in the West Country and in Wales, set up his HQ at the college of Christ Church in Oxford. His Royalist party were soon dubbed 'the Cavaliers', from the Spanish word *caballero* meaning 'knight', or 'horseman'. The hostile implication was that all Royalists were feudal gentry who supported

Spanish-style Absolutism and quasi-Catholic religious practices. The Parliamentary party, in contrast, who had a solid base in the City of London and a loyal social constituency in the urban middle classes, were soon dubbed 'Roundheads', supposedly from a close-cropped style of haircut preferred by pre-war Puritans. The hostile implication of this was that all Parliamentarians were either Puritans themselves or dominated by militant Puritans. In actual fact, neither of the stereotypes fitted. All the regions and all social classes in England and Wales were split by rival allegiances to King or Parliament. What is true, beyond the divided centre ground, is that very few Catholics were parliamentarians and very few Puritans were Royalists. It is also true that the Puritan element within the Parliamentary party steadily gained ground until they became the ruling group. The Puritan surge can partly be explained by the career of Oliver Cromwell, partly by the rising influence of the army, in which many Puritans served, and partly by the English Parliament's alliance with the Scots Covenanters.

Oliver Cromwell (1599–1658), one of the great figures of English history, seems to have been converted to Puritanism in the 1630s following some sort of nervous breakdown. Thereafter he displayed extraordinary strength of will and unbending purpose. Elected to the Long Parliament as MP for Huntingdon, he started as a client of Puritan aristocrats and was active in the Eastern Association, a regional body for mobilizing parliamentary support in East Anglia. He made his mark as a military officer in the first major battle of the war, at Edgehill (23 October 1643), where he rallied Parliamentary troops disconcerted by the Royalist cavalry charge. From then on, his star never ceased to rise. In religious affairs, he leaned more to the Puritan independents (or Congregationalists) than to the Presbyterians. In military matters, he was highly critical of the Parliamentary command led by the Earls of Essex and Manchester. He and his circle were instrumental in the formation of Parliament's victorious New Model Army. Above all, he was a man totally convinced of Divine Providence. His comment on the decisive clash at Marston Moor would be: 'It had all the evidences of an absolute

victory obtained by the Lord's blessing upon the godly party . . .
God made them as stubble to our swords.'[44]

Military politics fostered a growing rift in Parliamentary ranks
between the politicians and the professional soldiers. 1643 was a bad
year in Parliament's fortunes. A Royalist attack had come perilously
close to London's western suburbs, and Royalist generals came out
on top in several counties. Matters came to a head after further
reverses in 1644, when Cromwell forced through the Self-Denying
Ordinance, which forbade anyone from being simultaneously both
an MP and a military commander. The effect of the Ordinance in
the first instance was to turn the Parliamentary generals into a
separate political force, and then to facilitate the creation of the
purely professional New Model Army, 'the Ironsides'. Within a few
months of their appearance, the 'Ironsides' became the focus of the
most radical Puritan demands, among them the execution of former
Archbishop Laud. At the same time, they revived Parliament's
fortunes on the battlefield.

Parliament's alliance with the Scots Covenanters flowed naturally from their common fear of a Royalist victory. Yet it took
more than a year to bring it to fruition; and the Scots drove a hard
bargain. They insisted on their demand that the Church of England
adopt Presbyterianism and that all the bishops be dismissed. The
Solemn League and Covenant (September 1643) greatly enhanced
Parliament's military potential. But its doctrinaire approach to
religion invited protests both from centrist Anglicans and from
Puritan Independents. Added to the debut of the New Model Army,
the arrival of the main Scots army under Alexander Leslie greatly
facilitated Cromwell's crushing victory over Prince Rupert at Marston Moor (2 July 1644).

Marston Moor, ten miles west of York, secured the North of
England for Parliament. Cromwell then turned on the South. At
Naseby (14 June 1645), in a contest of great savagery, the New Model
Army under Fairfax defeated Prince Rupert for a second time. A
month later, at Langport in Somerset, they put an end to the King's
Western Army. By May 1646 all remaining Royalist resistance had

been terminated. Charles I chose to put himself in the custody of the Scots.

No description of the major developments of the First Civil War can do justice to the full complexity. Every district, every county, every region had its own civil war. In Lancashire, just to take one example, the people of the county were evenly divided. The gentry of the western districts, many of them Catholic recusants, joined the Earl of Derby and turned their lands into a bastion of Royalism. The townfolk of the towns in the south and east of the county, like Bolton, Blackburn, Oldham, and Rochdale, counted themselves among the staunchest supporters of Parliament. At the height of their fortunes, they conducted a notable siege of the Earl of Derby's home at Knowsley House. But when Prince Rupert appeared on the scene in 1644, on his way to Marston Moor, his troops conducted a general massacre of Bolton's entire population. Two thousand civilians were slaughtered. As a result, at the end of the war, the Earl of Derby was executed in Bolton marketplace, walking out bravely to his death after a last drink in the Man and Scythe Inn.

In Wales, in contrast, indifference largely prevailed. Neither King nor Parliament bothered to publish their propaganda in Welsh. The majority of people aimed simply to avoid trouble. At the same time, the routes to the ports of North and South Wales formed a vital strategic link between the King's HQ in Oxford and his loyal support in Ireland; and there were activists enough to fight over them. What is more, the great landowners like the Earl of Worcester at Raglan Castle had no scruples in conscripting their tenants. Through them Wales became known as 'the nursery of the King's infantry'. Parliamentarians like Thomas Myddleton in the northern counties and Rowland Laugharne in the South successfully cut the royal road to Ireland. Royalists such as the Earl of Carbery or Charles Gerard, assisted by Irish reinforcements, repeatedly opened them up. In 1643, John Williams, Archbishop of York, took pains to re-fortify his native Conway for the King. In 1645 the squires of Glamorgan formed a Peace Army to preserve their county from partisan strife. Charles I briefly visited Raglan following his defeat at Naseby, the first ruling monarch to set foot in the principality since Richard II. But Raglan fell to Parliamentary forces in August 1646. Harlech held out until March 1647.[45]

Meanwhile in Scotland, the Covenanters had been losing their grip. They had fielded one army in Ulster, one of twenty thousand men in England, and several lesser military groups facing pockets of Royalism in various corners of their own country. Nothing could have prepared them for the wave of devastating defeats which ensued from the landing of a small Irish Catholic force in June 1644 at Ardnamurchan on the west coast. The Irishmen were led by Alasdair MacColla, a scion of the Clan Donald, who promptly joined up with James Graham, first Marquess of Montrose, an ex-Covenanter wronged by the Campbells, who had changed sides. On 1 September, at Tippermuir near Perth, they met and defeated an army of Covenanters carrying a banner 'Jesus and no quarter'. Two weeks later, they sacked Aberdeen amidst scenes reminiscent of Bolton. From there, they marched through the snow into the heart of Campbell country. They fought four battles, and won four clear-cut victories. Their 'Highland Charge' was unstoppable, until halted in its tracks on 13 September 1645 by Leslie's main Army of the Covenant at Philiphaugh in the Borders. Montrose's exploits were celebrated by Highland bards. The irony was, Montrose was a Presbyterian. His standard bore the slogan 'For the maintenance and defence of the trew Protestant religion'.

Attempts by the various interested parties to reach an agreement with the captive King proved fruitless. Charles I offended everyone who tried to approach him. He had exasperated the main body of his English subjects by adhering to the Solemn League and by abandoning traditional Anglicanism. He had only been trying to placate his Scots jailers; but he exasperated them as well by encouraging a series of futile Royalist plots. Handed over by the Scots to the English Parliament, he exasperated his new captors by his constant vacillations and by the heavy burden of taxation required to keep the army on a war footing. In the summer of 1648 the army command had to order its troops back into the field in the

'Second Civil War', to suppress a rash of Royalist revolts, principally at Colchester. The country was hit by the worst harvest of the century. Bread was scarce; prices were rocketing: the army was unpaid.

When the Second Civil War was over Cromwell decided that enough was enough. In the previous year he had watched the solidarity of the New Model Army fragment, as radical agitators such as John Lilburne (1614–57) harangued the troops in their camp at Putney. He was forced to take drastic action; and in due course the 'Levellers' were repressed. In 1648, he watched the unity of Parliament crumble, as Presbyterians argued with Independents over the fate of the King. Once again, he was obliged to end the arguments by force, sending Colonel Thomas Pride to Westminster to purge the dissident MPs. So it is not too surprising that he also lost patience with the man who was seen to be the root cause of everyone's misery. 'Charles Stuart, that Man of Blood' was summoned from his prison at Carisbrooke Castle on the Isle of Wight, and put on trial for treason in Westminster Hall. The death verdict was a foregone conclusion. On 30 January 1649 the condemned King stepped through the middle window of the Banqueting House in Whitehall onto a scaffold in the street. Wearing a plain white shirt, he conducted himself with great dignity. In Andrew Marvell's marvellous words, 'he nothing common did or mean'. He prayed, and in a short speech said that he had desired the liberty and freedom of the people as much as any, but also that 'a subject and sovereign are clean different things'.[46] As Parliament's axe fell, he became an instant martyr.

Cromwell was finally free to deal with the long stalemate in Ireland. Landing at Ringsend near Dublin in September, he found that the Lord Lieutenant, the Earl of Ormonde, had recently formed a wide coalition embracing virtually all the Irish factions in the name of the King and in support of universal toleration in religion. As a result, the English invasion force had no one to work with, and everyone to subdue. Cromwell was on a God-given mission to punish the Catholic rebels of 1641 and to end toleration. He needed no allies. He had the finest army in Europe, and an artillery train without equal. There was nobody in Ireland to match it. He marched to nearby Drogheda, fired two hundred cannonballs at the defence lines in one day, overwhelmed the garrison, and put all male combatants to the sword. He justified his action in chilling words. 'This was a righteous judgement of God upon these barbarous wretches . . .' he declared: 'it will prevent the effusion of blood for the future.' He did the same in Wexford, where a crowd of civilian refugees also perished. The Irish were bombarded, battered, and bullied into submission. When Cromwell departed at the end of 1649, Ireland lay bleeding, prostrate, and paralysed. He left his deputies with the task of confiscating all Catholic land, converting the Irish to the Protestant faith and deporting all rebels to the colonies. Recent research suggests that Cromwell's conduct was no better and no worse than the standards of the day.[47] He had launched an operation that would make the Plantation of Ulster look like a mere preliminary.

Which only left Scotland. After Pride's Purge, which removed the Covenanters' English Presbyterian partners, and the execution of the King, which had proceeded without Scottish approval, the Scots parted company with the English Parliament. Regicide had never been on their agenda. Republicanism was a recipe for discord. So when the advisers of the adolescent Charles II told him in his Dutch exile to accept the Covenant, as his father had done, he was invited to Edinburgh in 1650, and promptly crowned. With Scots help, the Royalists aimed to recover both the English and Irish crowns. Cromwell marched north. On 3 September, he annihilated the Army of the Covenant at Dunbar. Exactly a year later, at Worcester, he destroyed another army of assorted Scots and Royalists. Charles II was forced to flee, taking refuge in the 'royal oak' at Boscobel, Shropshire, on the way. The Royalist cause had lost its last active defenders.

The military triumph of the English Parliament was complete throughout the Isles. For the first time in history, England, Ireland, Scotland, and Wales were all obliged to bend the neck directly to

Westminster. The Great Oliver had run out of enemies to fight. But he was faced with political tasks that would baffle even him.

(5) The English Commonwealth (1649–54) and 'the British Republic' (1654–60)

It is sometimes said that that the execution of Charles I ended the threefold Personal Union of Crowns. The regicides would certainly have liked to think so. They had cut off the head on which the three crowns had rested; and they were now searching for something to put in its place. In fact, the matter was not so simple. It could only be determined by reference to theories and interpretations which divided contemporaries as much as they divide historians today. According to the theory of the Divine Right of Kings, in which in all probability the majority of people continued to believe, the death of a monarch can in no way be equated with the death of monarchy. The royal succession is decided by God and not by man. Hence, whatever legislation the regicides passed, Charles I's son and heir automatically succeeded to his father's three kingdoms the instant that his father's head was held aloft. 'The King is dead. Long live the King!' The new King as a minor and an exile was unable to rule; but his inability to rule did not alter the fact that he was already reigning.

Everyone agreed, of course, that serious problems had arisen. England and Wales was ruled by a regime which claimed and believed that it had abolished the monarchy for ever. For all practical purposes, it had become a parliamentary republic. For the time being Scotland was not. Ireland's exact status was debatable, though clearly an English dependency. The Church of England had been officially Presbyterian since 1643. It tolerated Protestant Independents, but not Catholics. The Church of Scotland permitted no deviations. Ireland alone was committed to religious pluralism.

One problem has attracted little comment, though it is vital to a full understanding of the situation. Charles I had followed in his father's footsteps by declaring himself 'King of Great Britain'. His British title was anomalous and did not coincide with the titles proclaimed at his two coronations in London (1625) and Edinburgh (1633). It derived from a claim which was personal in nature and which had also found expression in the Union flags flown by all the ships of the Royal Navy. The claim was personal, and came to an end with the person who made it. Such at least was Cromwell's reasoning. In 1649, he ordered that all Union flags be withdrawn, together with the royal standard. English warships were to sail under a new flag based on the cross of St George. Scottish warships reverted to the flag of St Andrew.

Several months elapsed before the English regicides could devise a constitutional structure for the new order. What they produced in May 1649 was a legislature consisting of a single chamber and an appointed executive, the Council of State. The body politic as a whole was to be called 'The Commonwealth and Free State'. Its writ ran exclusively in England and Wales. (Ireland and Scotland were still separate entities.) The new arrangements were proposed by the Army Council and passed at Westminster by the residue of the old purged Parliament, known derisively as the 'Rump'.

Behind the parliamentary façade, however, all residual power was held by the Army and in particular by the Army Council headed by Cromwell's son-in-law, the Commissary-General of the Horse, Henry Ireton (1611–51). The Army Council was an extraordinary outfit. It was highly political and given to intense debates; it was highly democratic in respect to its own internal procedures, and yet it was highly despotic in its stance to other institutions and to the nation at large. In 1648, it had prepared to make its own private deal with Charles I, its *Heads of Proposals* being considerably more generous than anything proposed by Parliament. It had prevaricated for months over the King's fate, until a surge of protests and peti-tions from junior officers indicated that military opinion favoured execution. (It was not averse to junior officers arguing against and outvoting colonels and generals.) Early in 1649 it came up with a new plan for the regulation of political and religious matters, the so-called *Agreement of the People*. The plan called for parliamentary elections along lines originally proposed in the *Heads*, for a ban on Parliament assuming emergency powers, and for a voluntary approach to church attendance and the payment of tithes. There was to be toleration for all except Roman Catholics and users of the old Prayer Book. The Rump Parliament ignored it. Indeed, the Rump was not prepared to pass a motion unequivocally approving the Regicide. After much cajoling from Cromwell, it refused to do more than to promise loyalty to existing arrangements. As its ranks were swelled by members not purged in 1648 but not present during the King's trial, its complexion was changing. In retrospect, it is easy to see that its days were numbered.

For the time being, however, the army's discontent was contained. The soldiers received a handsome pay award, and were sent off to fight the terminal rounds of the wars in Ireland and Scotland. They would not return to politics for a couple of years.

Apart from the tension between the army and the Rump, the years of the Commonwealth saw three signal developments. Firstly, the conquests of Ireland and Scotland put the English army in control of new territories and new populations where the English Parliament had no previous competence. If the Rump in 1649 was run by a tiny residual clique, unrepresentative of England, by the end of 1651 its standing vis-à-vis Ireland and Scotland was totally illegitimate. Secondly, the political solutions imposed by the army on the conquered countries could only cause controversy. And thirdly, Oliver Cromwell rose to the top of the army command. In 1649, Cromwell had been the army's No. 3. But in 1650 the Commander-in-Chief, Lord Fairfax, who had not attended the King's trial and execution, resigned rather than lead the invasion of Scotland; and in 1651, the No. 2, Henry Ireton, died from overwork whilst serving as Lord Deputy in Ireland. This meant, when he returned to London as the hero-victor of Dunbar and Worcester, that Cromwell was more than just the largest personality in the land. He was the new Commander-in-Chief of the only force that counted. On 10 December 1651 the army officers held an inconclusive discussion about the possible restoration of the monarchy. According to the only recorded witness of the meeting, Cromwell seemed well disposed to the monarchical principle but strongly opposed to the return of the Stuarts.

The Commonwealth's treatment of Ireland was infinitely more 'thorough' than anything that Strafford might have dreamed of. It cemented the Protestant Ascendancy that was to last until the twentieth century. In the eyes of Irish writers 'the Curse of Cromwell' sealed 'the war that finished Ireland'. In some respects these judgements are unfair. The campaign of 1649 came at the end of a decade when plague and famine had killed far more people than Cromwell ever did; and popular views of the Cromwellian massacres are much exaggerated. Like the massacres of Protestants in 1641, which loom large in the Ulster tradition, the disaster of Drogheda has passed into a Catholic folk tradition that recognizes no nuances. Its immediate effects were less horrific than those of the storming of Sligo in 1645 by Sir Charles Coote or the atrocity of Cashel, which had been laid waste by the Gaelic chief Muireadhach O'Brien, in 1647. But its psychological effects are still with us. That is because it quickly became the symbol of the cumulative calamity of which it was the focal point. The statistics speak for themselves. Forty per cent of Ireland's population had died since 1641. Eighty per cent of the land found its way into Protestant ownership compared to half that proportion ten years earlier. Hundreds were executed. Thirty-four thousand Irish soldiers were sent abroad as foreign mercenaries, twelve thousand transported to penal servitude in the West Indies. Thousands of years of the Gaelic heritage were threatened by the closure of bardic schools. Ireland was declared part of the Commonwealth. There was no act of union, though the flag was adapted to the changed circumstances (see illustration). 'This whole episode illustrates the abiding truth that all that any English government ever intended for Ireland was to keep it from being significant.'[48]

Scotland, too, paid a heavy price. The Covenanters had raised a dozen armies, and all had come to grief. One of the last acts of the Cromwellian conquests was the murderous sacking of Dundee by the troops of General George Monck (1608–70). All the other Scottish boroughs paid vast ransoms for fear of the same fate. All parts of the country beyond the untameable Highlands were occupied by hostile English garrisons. All Scots suffered from heavy war losses, material deprivation, punitive taxation, and political chaos. Everything and anything that could be looted was carried off to England. The plunder included all of Scotland's public records and all members of the last Scottish government. Taxes increased tenfold. Vast military works were begun, notably at the fortress of Inverness. After 1649 the Scottish Parliament had fallen into the hands of extreme religious radicals in a 'Rule of Saints'. But now it lost all authority. Six days after the Battle of Worcester, a committee of 'the Rump' in London prepared a bill asserting 'the right of England to Scotland'. The Scottish monarchy and the Scottish Parliament were stated to be redundant. The royal arms were ritually hanged on the gallows in Edinburgh.

At this juncture, John Milton was moved to write a sonnet 'To the Lord General Cromwell'. Milton was serving as Latin secretary to the government of the Commonwealth, and knew its problems from the inside. He hoped and prayed that the Great Oliver would face the challenges of peace with the same success that he had met on the battlefield:

> Cromwell, our cheif of men, who through a cloud
>   Not of warr onely, but detractions rude,
>   Guided by faith and matchless Fortitude
> To peace and truth thy glorious way hast plough'd,
> And on the neck of crowned Fortune proud
>   Hast reard Gods Trophies and his work pursu'd,
>   While *Darwen* stream with blood of Scotts imbru'd
>   And *Dunbarr* feild resounds thy praises loud,
> And *Worsters* laureat wreath; yet much remaines
>   To conquer still; peace hath her victories
>   No less renownd then warr, new foes arise
> Threatning to bind our soules with secular chains:

Help us to save free Conscience from the paw
Of hireling wolves whose Gospell is their maw.[49]

In discussion on the future of the Church of England, Milton had always pressed for toleration of the Protestant radicals. He had licensed the anti-Trinitarian, Racovian Catechism, which was subsequently banned and burned. And he was still fearful that 'Free Conscience' was in danger.

Six years passed before new arrangements for 'a Commonwealth of England, Scotland and Ireland' were properly constituted. A second bill for a 'Tender of Union' became stuck in the legislative logjam caused by Cromwell's dismissal of the Rump in 1653. In April 1654 the Council of State issued an Ordinance of Union, which was eventually given statutory standing in 1657. Scotland received the benefits of free trade; Ireland did not. Scotland sent some fifty members to an enlarged Westminster assembly. As from 1654, a new Union flag was devised. It had four quarters. Quarters 1 and 4 carried the cross of St George, Quarter 2 the lion of Scotland, and Quarter 3 the Irish harp. A British Republic had been created in all but name.

Cromwell's political conundrums multiplied as his power was magnified. In foreign affairs, he was as sure-footed as ever. He fought the First Dutch War, 1652–4, over the Rump Parliament's mercantilist Navigation Acts (1650, 1651), which gave English merchants a monopoly over imports; he took on the 'Barbary Pirates' (1655); and readmitted the Jews to England in 1655 after an interval of 365 years.[50] In this last step, he was following the example of the United Provinces, which had just established their formal independence from a Spain often regarded in that era as the Jews' Chief persecutor. He successfully matched the might of Spain, the New Model Army showing its mettle in its one and only foreign assignment in the Battle of the Dunes near Dunkirk (1658).

But he found no lasting solutions to internal matters. For several years, he had been placing his close friends and relatives, including his sons Richard and Henry, into high positions, thereby creating a form of private oligarchy. On 23 April 1653, for no clear reason, he flew into a rage, and dissolved the 'Rump'. The Council of State was shadowed, then replaced by a Council of Officers which promptly issued an Instrument of Government declaring Cromwell to be the Lord Protector. Later that year, an appointed assembly was convened, commonly called the 'Barebones Parliament' after one of its more colourful members, the Independent Praise-God Barebone (1596–1679). It has been wishfully described as 'the first British Parliament'. In reality, nearly all the delegates were English, including English officers serving in Ireland and Scotland; and, as an unelected body, it was no real parliament. But it fell into dissension, and was dismissed. Another, genuine Parliament was elected, but Cromwell dismissed that one as well. In 1655, a major conflagration in the Scottish Highlands was joined by a very minor Royalist rising in Wiltshire, led by a John Penruddock. This was the pretext for Cromwell to devise a system of military rule. Under the 'Major-Generals' of 1655–8, one senior officer administered each of ten, later eleven, regions. The experiment worked, not least in the realm of financial revenue. But it was only a temporary expedient. In 1657, Cromwell tried yet again and convened the second Parliament of the Protectorate, which worked on a further constitutional scheme called the *Humble Petition and Advice*. But he lost patience with that: and he lost patience with the army, cashiering a group of officers from his old regiment without a court martial. He was turning into a dictator. The Parliamentary cause had reached its term, having no Parliament to direct it.

What's more, the dictator was sick. Early in 1658, he fell into a decline. His handwriting disintegrated before his physical health did. On 3 September, England was rocked by a great storm. In the middle of it, Oliver Cromwell passed away.

(6) Restoration, Re-constituted Kingdoms, and Renewed Religious Bigotry

The return of the Stuarts, and the restoration of the monarchy, might well be seen as a victory for the centralizing, standardizing form of government to which Charles I had been tending before the wars. The Divine Right of Kings, Episcopacy, and Absolutism were all parts of the same philosophical package. Yet, if the Parliamentary cause was spent by the time of Cromwell's death, the Royalist cause had still fewer means of putting its original dreams into effect. All the leading figures in the Restoration drama were acting from positions of political weakness; and everyone concerned, from the King down, realized that painful compromises were necessary. Major concessions would have to be made on all sides.

Yet perhaps the most important concession made by both Parliamentarians and Royalists alike was one that is least discussed. The Parliamentarians had to concede that a restored Parliament in Westminster would have to relinquish the centralized powers over Scotland and Ireland that Cromwell had amassed. The Royalists had to concede that Charles II would not be able to realize his father's and grandfather's claim to be 'King of Great Britain', but would have to be satisfied with recovering his three separate crowns. The British Republic would not be converted into a British Kingdom. If the principle of King in Parliament were to be restored, it would only be restored in the three separate Parliaments of Westminster, Edinburgh, and Dublin. The 'Commonwealth of England, Scotland, and Ireland' would not be replaced by one united triune monarchy, but by one monarch reigning separately over each of his three kingdoms. Under Cromwell's guidance the Interregnum had seen a great centralizing surge. The Restoration would see a great centrifugal reflex.

After Cromwell's death, a political vacuum opened up that could not be filled by existing institutions. The Lord Protector's son, Richard Cromwell (1626–1712), was appointed to succeed him by the ruling oligarchy. But he had little more to him than his surname. The army grew restless. The Protectorate's Parliament, reconvened in January 1659, dallied on the question of the army's arrears; and the Council of Officers demanded its dissolution. The exhausted Protector then moved to dismiss the Council, but faced by mutiny turned tail and dismissed the Parliament as the officers had originally wished. No plans had been laid about the future directions. In April 1659 the Protector retired to his estates. The Council of Officers now recalled the residue of the 'Rump' in a desperate search for a solution before the rising Royalist tide overwhelmed them. Amazingly, forty-two members appeared. But they wanted to control the army, whilst the army intended to control them. So nothing of substance was agreed. Once again, as ten years before, a bad harvest and rising prices exacerbated the political tension. Public finances approached the point of collapse. A Royalist rising in Cheshire was easily suppressed. But religious radicals, Quakers, Levellers, and Independents, were stirring up trouble. On 12 October the army leaders removed the 'Rump'. The country still had no government, and the army still had no pay. In November, Henry Cromwell left his post as Lord-Lieutenant in Dublin, opening the way for a breakaway Protestant regime. In December the Portsmouth garrison mutinied; the Navy blockaded the Thames; Londoners rioted.

The one man who could stop the rot was General George Monck, Cromwell's comrade, and commander of the English army in Scotland. A renegade Royalist turned republican, he had no intention at first of calling in the King. Indeed, he warned publicly against the dangers of a restoration. But he was a loyal Anglican; and he was fearful that the reappearance of religious radicals in 1659 was tending to an attack on the very existence of the Church of England. Moreover he was sick and tired of the incessant bickering. In November, he denounced the dissolution of the 'Rump', and set about forcing a settlement. Unlike his fellow officers in England, he held a substantial treasure chest raised from exorbitant Cromwellian taxation in Scotland. Leaving his Scots troops on one side, he used the treasure to raise new regiments of elite 'Coldstreamers' from the English Borders. In December, he faced down a force sent out to oppose him, then in January marched south unopposed. He was welcomed in London with open arms amidst cries for 'a free Parliament'.

Monck's solution was to demonstrate the supremacy of Parliamentary government over the army not only by re-convening the Commons of the Long Parliament – that is, by recalling both the 'Rump' and the surviving victims of Pride's Purge – but also to proclaim the restoration of a full two-chamber Parliament after fresh elections. When the Long Parliament met for the last time, in March to April 1660, therefore, it knew that its days were numbered. It confirmed Monck as Commander-in-Chief: voted through the heavy taxation needed to pay off the army's arrears: passed a bill to take the local militias away from the radicals: and then dissolved itself.

By then the Royalist tide was already rising fast. What the King's supporters could not achieve on the battlefield, they amply achieved at the elections. In a Convention Parliament, a strongly monarchist Commons was joined by a still more monarchist Lords. It was evident that they would call for the King's return. General Monck acquiesced. In the Declaration of Breda (1 May 1660), Charles II removed the immediate obstacles, proclaiming a general pardon and amnesty for all offences committed during the Interregnum, urging his subjects to love their former enemies, promising to follow the advice of a free Parliament, and (somewhat vaguely) accepting the principle of religious toleration. The Convention responded with a declaration stating that the Government of England was constituted 'by King, Lords, and Commons'. The British Republic had been voted down. The King packed his bags, gathered up his court, landed at Dover, and progressed in triumph to his English capital. Eleven years after his coronation in Scotland, he was crowned in Westminster Abbey on 23 April 1661 as King of England, Ireland and France. All Parliamentary statutes in England since 1641 and in Scotland since 1651 were declared void. The King's regnal years were antedated to 30 January 1649.

Charles II, who loved playing the King, dancing at court, and curing the scrofulous with 'the King's Touch', left the general constitutional settlement to the Convention Parliament at Westminster as confirmed by the Parliaments in Dublin and Edinburgh. It granted him a pension for life, passed the Act of Indemnity and Oblivion for crimes during the Interregnum, and the Act for Judicial Proceedings, which confirmed the validity of all voluntary land sales. Confiscated Church and crown lands were repossessed. The surviving regicides were hunted down and executed. The bodies of the dead regicides, including that of Cromwell, were disinterred and ritually mutilated.

In England, the twenty-five years of 'the Restoration' are best remembered for the collective sigh of relief emanating from a nation weary of strife and fanaticism. A lascivious King and a permissive court set the social tone where 'Restoration comedy' swept the boards of the London theatres. For high society at least, the wit, sexual intrigue, and foppish manners of later comedies such as Etherege's *Man of Mode* (1676) or Vanbrugh's *Provok'd Wife* (1697) mirrored the spirit of the age.

Yet for many English people, Charles II's reign was not so relaxed. Religious matters, in particular, were not settled in the generous spirit originally indicated. Despite the devotion of Roman Catholics to the Royalist cause, there could still be no question of Catholic toleration. And the restoration of the bishops of an Anglican Church of England was accompanied by disabilities placed on all dissenting Protestants. This was the period when English Nonconformity parted company decisively with Anglicanism. In his Worcester House Declaration (1661) Charles II held out hopes to the Presbyterians, to whom he was not at all sympathetic. He once said that 'Presbyterianism is no religion for a gentleman'; and he would have approved Milton's famous quip that 'New Presbyter is but old priest writ large'. There was a spontaneous wave of popular anger against radical religious 'fanaticks', many of whom landed behind bars. The so-called Cavalier Parliament, which sat from 1661 to 1679, was markedly less tolerant than its predecessor; and the four acts of the so-called Clarendon Code (1661–5) severely restricted the lives of all dissenters. A new Act of Uniformity (1662) reinstated the Book of Common Prayer and the Thirty-nine Articles, and required all clergy to renounce the Solemn League and Covenant and to be ordained by a bishop. The Corporation Act (1661) required all office-holders to swear the threefold oaths of allegiance, supremacy, and non-resistance. The Conventicle Act (1664) and the Five Mile Act (1665) were designed to obstruct the worship and residence of dissenting clergy. Persecution, however, only strengthened the dissenters' resolve. The Society of Friends or 'Quakers', founded by George Fox (1624–91), took permanent root at this time. John Milton used the years of his political eclipse to compose *Paradise Lost* (1667) and *Paradise Regained* (1671). John Bunyan (1628–88), an independent or 'Congregationalist' of the Cromwellian flavour, and a fierce critic of the Quakers, spent twelve years in Bedford Gaol for organizing an illegal conventicle. In jail, he wrote one of the great religious classics, *Pilgrim's Progress* (1678).

In Scotland, the King did not need restoring so much as reinstating. He was recrowned at Scone in 1661 for good measure. The Scottish Privy Council was filled with ministers of various hues. The bishops returned to their empty sees, the judges to their benches. And the Scottish Parliament made up for a decade of involuntary inactivity by passing four thousand acts in its first year.

As in England, however, religion proved the most contentious of issues. The Scottish Presbyterians, who had dominated the country for a generation and who had once persuaded Charles II to sign the Covenant, were hoping to preserve their supremacy. But it was not to be. Whether through the machinations of the King's chief minister, Lord Clarendon, or simply through imitation of the 'Cavalier mood' in Westminster, the Scots Parliament opted for a thoroughgoing Anglican-style settlement. Episcopacy was to have a monopoly. No independent conventicles, and no unordained pres-byters, were to be permitted. Whereas the English Act of Uniformity caused the Church of England to lose about a tenth of its clergy, its

Scottish equivalent caused the Church of Scotland to lose up to a third. Once again, illegal conventicles multiplied. Two armed Presbyterian risings, in Kirkcudbrightshire in 1666 and the Cameronian Rising of 1679–80, gave notice of future trouble. Yet Charles II, who had little love for his northern kingdom, left its affairs in the hands of ministers, principally of John Maitland, first Duke of Lauderdale (1616–82), and the unofficial viceroy of the Highlands, Archibald Campbell, ninth Earl of Argyll.

In Ireland, the Restoration Settlement was incapable of righting the disasters of the Cromwellian conquest. Charles II gave promises both to Irish Protestants and to his loyal Irish Catholic supporters. Yet it was impossible both to let the ex-Cromwellians keep their land and to restore all former holdings to the disinherited. As the Earl, now Duke, of Ormonde remarked, 'there must be new discoveries of a new Ireland, for the old Ireland will not serve to satisfy these engagements'.[51] When the all-Protestant Parliament resumed business after an interval of a dozen years, it passed an Act of Settlement (1662) whose land provisions could not be implemented. 'Innocents' and active Royalists were supposed to obtain restitution, and the ex-Cromwellians compensation. In the end, only five hundred 'Innocents' received a fraction of their former property, the Gaelic Irish virtually nothing. Dean Swift (1667–1745), who grew up in Restoration Dublin as the son of a Protestant lawyer, put it this way: 'The Catholics of Ireland . . . lost their estates for fighting in defence of their King. Those who cut off the father's head, [and] forced the son to fly for his life . . . gained by their rebellion what the Catholics lost by their loyalty.'[52]

In matters of religion, the Duke of Ormonde was eager to re-extend toleration to the majority Catholic community, as he had done in 1649. But Catholic attitudes had hardened. The illegal Roman hierarchy rejected the proffered Remonstrance, which contained a clause denying the Pope's right to depose kings, and no agreement was reached. Even so, Ireland's material condition improved. Despite English trade restrictions, Irish commerce grew. Ireland's population headed for two million. And at sixty thousand, Dublin rose to be the second city of the Isles.

No aspect of politics in this era could be free of the religious dimension. England's Second Dutch War (1665–7) was driven by commercial rivalry but it also coincided with the anti-Presbyterian turn of the Restoration Settlement. In a standard royal manoeuvre to secure his financial independence from his Parliaments and to keep a free hand for his prerogative area of foreign policy, Charles II then signed the secret Treaty of Dover (1670) with Louis XIV in return for a French subsidy. The catch was that he should announce his conversion to Catholicism at a suitable time. (He did so on his deathbed after fifteen years' delay.) Nonetheless, he duly entered the Third Dutch War (1672–4) to please the French, combining the move with a well-meant Declaration of Indulgence (1672) that suspended the penal laws against Catholic recusants and Protestant Noncon-formists. The English Parliament was so outraged by this step in favour of toleration that it refused to vote subsidies for the Dutch War until the Declaration was rescinded and replaced by the first of two ferocious Test Acts, institutionalizing religious intolerance. The first Test Act (1673) insisted that all civil and military officers of the crown take the oaths of supremacy, allegiance, and non-resistance and formally renounce the Catholic doctrine of transubstantiation. It brought down the King's brother and prospective heir, James Duke of York (1633–1701), who was a professed Catholic and had been serving as Lord High Admiral. Its provisions were later extended by the second Test Act (1678) to all members of both houses of Parliament. In this way, both domestic and foreign policy became infected by bigotry. The Dutch War had to be abandoned when the United Provinces gained several Protestant allies, against whom the English Parliament refused to fight. The Treaty of Westminster (1674), like its predecessor the Treaty of Breda (1667), is only remem-bered today because it confirmed England's possession of New

Amsterdam – a colony which had been duly renamed, after the admiral of the day, New York.

Watching the early stages of all this from his rural exile in Chalfont St Giles, John Milton was dismayed. He was offended not only by the vices of a dissolute court but also by the coercive attitude of many religious people. He held Cromwell's view that religious bigotry was equal to 'spiritual drunkenness'. So he set down his thoughts in the form of an allegorical *History of Britain* (1670). The book covers the period from the earliest times to the Norman Conquest in wonderful sonorous prose; but its main interest lies in the constant parallels drawn between ancient events and Milton's own day. The 'confused anarchy' which followed the departure of the Roman legions is likened to 'the late civil broils' of the 'Interreign', whilst the supposed decadence of the late Anglo-Saxons made the Norman Conquest a walkover. 'They gave to *William* their Conquerour so easy a conquest.' 'The gaining or loosing of libertie', he wrote, 'is the greatest change to better or worse that may befall a nation'. And hard-won English liberty was again at risk. He feared 'from like Vices without amendment the Revolution of like Calamities'. In Restoration England, the one possible calamity similar to a new Norman Conquest could only have come from Louis XIV's France.[53]

No piece of bigotry, however, could match the furore attending the so called Popish Plot of 1678–9. An English fanatic, Titus Oates (1649–1705), posing as a convert, had gained admission to Jesuit seminaries in Valladolid and St Omer. On return to England he laid a sworn deposition in a magistrate's court, stating that English Catholics were planning to kill the King, to stage a massacre of Protestants, and to install a Catholic ministry. Instead of being treated with the contempt it deserved, this totally false scam was widely believed, not least in Parliament. After the Commons resolved that 'the damnable and hellish plot' was a reality, the enemies of the Duke of York began calling for his exclusion from the throne. Catholics were arrested and tried on trumped-up charges, and several executed. The most prominent victims were

William Howard, first Viscount Stafford (1614–80), the Catholic Archbishop of Dublin, Peter Talbot, who died in prison, and the Catholic Archbishop of Armagh, St Oliver Plunkett (1629–81), who died on the scaffold at Tyburn. Three successive English Parliaments were peremptorily dissolved in close order by the King to prevent them passing an exclusion bill.

Unexpectedly, the Duke of York found much greater favour in Scotland. The Presbyterian risings of 1679–80, which had been sparked by the murder of Archbishop Sharp of St Andrews, attracted support in several localities and were only suppressed with difficulty. The key action took place at Bothwell Bridge near Hamilton on 22 July 1679, when troops under the Duke of Monmouth stormed the insurgents' camp. But it had been preceded by a month-long open-air seminar, reminiscent of the Putney Debates of the English Levellers in 1647, in which various groups of religious radicals discussed their utopias. And it left a long legacy of underground conventicles and smouldering resistance. The inevitable reaction in Edinburgh gave the Duke of York his opening. He travelled north in 1681, and persuaded the Scottish Parliament to pass a body of 'extraordinary legislation' including a loyalty oath on all office-holders in Church and state. It saw off the previous ministers of the crown, and encouraged the rise of a group sympathetic to James. The two Drummond brothers – James, fourth Earl of Perth and John, first Earl of Melfort – were appointed respectively Chancellor and Secretary of State. Both were Catholic converts. The flight of the Duke of Argyll opened the way for a Commission of Highland Justiciary that tackled the endemic problem of clan warfare. 'James was master of Scotland long before Charles II died.'[54]

In this poisoned atmosphere, with England out of step with Ireland and Scotland, the King's life was the sole thread holding back his kingdoms from the brink of chaos. He had several sons, but no legitimate heir beyond his Catholic brother, whom he stoutly refused to renounce. The Protestant mob in London was baying for action. English politicians split for the first time into two opposed camps – one derisively called 'Tories' after an old Irish name for

Catholic rebels, and the other derisively dubbed 'Whigs' or 'Whig-gamores' after an old Scottish name for the Covenanters. The Tories, who saw themselves as heirs of the Cavaliers, wanted to prevent Parliament from dictating the royal succession. The Whigs, led by a group of Protestant aristocrats, wanted to give pride of place to Parliament and above all to exclude James. Their favoured candidate was the King's eldest surviving bastard, James Crofts alias James Scott (1649–85), first Duke of Monmouth. In 1683, during the Rye House Plot, they engaged in a treasonable scheme that sought to kill both the King and his brother as they drove to London from the Newmarket races. Two of their leaders, Algernon Sidney (1622–83), who had once served on the Commonwealth's Council of State, and William, Lord Russell (1639–83), who as a member of 'the Country Opposition' had long warned against the Catholicizing influence of the court, were executed. The Whigs had their martyrs before they got their Parliament. When the King lay on his deathbed in Whitehall Palace in February 1685, he apologized for being 'an unconscionable time a-dying'. The last breath of a tolerant monarch was the last hope for a tolerant future in his three kingdoms.

(7) THE REVOLUTIONARY REIGN OF JAMES VII, II, & II (R. 1685–1701)

It is often said that history is written by the victors. This is not strictly correct. Both winners and losers write history. But it is the winners' version of events which is far more likely to establish itself as the standard account. For historical narrative is a formidable political weapon. The victors are strongly tempted to use it to justify their own actions, to denigrate the motives of the defeated, and to legitimize the resultant settlement. To achieve these goals they need not necessarily suppress the opposing version. They can equally rely on the power of publicity which a victorious regime always possesses, on the selective interpretational spin of servile voices, on the impact of tendentious or well-chosen slogans, and above all on the psychological climate of victory. People are easily induced to accept the historical account of the victors as a natural adjunct to accepting all the other consequences of a military or political struggle.

The period of history which begins in 1685 with the accession of James, Duke of York is a prime case in point. It centred on the conflict between a Catholic King and a Protestant party in Parliament who ultimately prevailed. In almost all the standard accounts, it is presented either under the Whig slogan of 'the Glorious Revolution' or under the manifestly inaccurate slogan of 'the Bloodless Revolution'. It is often dressed up as the culminating phase of England's century-long constitutional crisis, not as a religious war involving all the peoples of the Isles. In many instances, as at the time, it is reduced to a simple struggle between 'liberty' and 'tyranny'. Little prominence is given to the fact that the key issue at every stage of the proceedings was not one of constitutional principle, but the religious coloration of the royal succession. Equally, there is very little discussion of the fundamental truth that, in the absence of liberty for all, one man's freedom was the next man's servitude.

James Stuart, Duke of York and Earl of Ulster, born in 1633 at St James's Palace London, was the second son of Charles I and of Henrietta Maria of France. After escaping from Parliamentary detention in 1648, he spent his formative years abroad in France and the Netherlands. He served as an officer in both the French and the Spanish armies, and received the proud title of Duke of Normandy from Louis XIV. He was frequently at odds with his elder brother, Charles, and long resisted his most Catholic mother's requests for him to convert to Rome. He was notoriously promiscuous, and married Anne Hyde, daughter of the Earl of Clarendon, Charles' chief minister, under the shadow of the shotgun. That first marriage produced eight children of whom only two survived. The girls, Mary and Anne, were consigned to Protestant guardians when each of their parents separately accepted Catholicism. Mary was married in due course to William, Prince of Orange, Count of Nassau-

Dillenburg, Stadholder of the United Provinces, the chief foe of Louis XIV and the leading champion of Protestant Europe. Anne was married somewhat later to Georg von Oldenburg, Prince of Denmark. After Anne Hyde's early death, the widowed James had married in 1673 Maria d'Este, the Catholic daughter of the Duke of Modena, thereby causing an uproar in Parliament. By 1685, this second marriage had produced ten more children, all of whom were dead. James was a stranger neither to family tragedy nor to the contortions demanded of prominent Catholics living within a suspicious Protestant Establishment.

When his royal brother finally expired on 6 February 1685, the Duke of York succeeded to the thrones as James VII of Scotland, James II of England, and James II of Ireland. In Scotland, he was supported by a loyal and largely Catholic government ruling clique over a restless, recently repressed, and predominantly Presbyterian nation. In England, he headed a Protestant Establishment that was dominated by Anglican Tories but challenged by a powerful Whig opposition. In the nation at large, a small group of enthusiastic Catholic subjects were greatly outnumbered by the two Protestant communities, Anglican and Nonconformist, both still humming from the excitements of the Popish Plot. In Ireland, James's accession raised the hopes of the downtrodden Catholic majority, whilst disturbing the ease of the ascendant Protestant minority. The fate of the King and of all his subjects would be decided by the labyrinthine interactions of this complex political tableau. Much would depend on his own good sense.

James sought to be a full-blown Catholic in private, whilst observing the established customs and practices of his three kingdoms in public. Hence on 23 April 1685, when he presented himself at Westminster Abbey for coronation as King of England and Wales according to the Anglican rites, he had already been crowned in private at Whitehall Palace according to the Catholic rite. He was attended on both occasions by his Queen, who unlike his mother fifty-nine years earlier, did not refuse to participate in an Anglican sacrament. In Scotland, where he was publicly crowned by the Presbyterian Kirk, he fitted out the private chapel at Holyrood as a Catholic shrine.

The start of the reign was marked by two armed rebellions, one in England and the other in Scotland. Both proved to be fiascos. On 11 June, James's half-brother, the Duke of Monmouth, landed at Lyme Regis and proclaimed himself King of England. His small band of followers marched into Somerset and captured Taunton before being cut to pieces by a royal force at Sedgemoor (see page 647, below). The West Country was treated to an unparalleled display of hangings and deportations in the so-called 'Bloody Assizes' presided over by the Lord Chief Justice, Judge Jeffries. Almost simultaneously, the Earl of Argyll, Monmouth's partner and a fellow conspirator in the Rye House Plot, landed at Campbelltown in Kintyre, and proclaimed Monmouth king. He attracted no significant following. Both he and Monmouth were summarily executed.

Assured, therefore, of his strong position, and strengthened by a generous financial award granted by Parliament, James set about the main business of his reign as he saw it, which was to sweep away, or at least to diminish, the institutional basis for religious discrimination. Using his power of dispensation under the royal prerogative, the King overrode the Test Act by personal fiat in several key appointments, thereby sending out a signal that recusants and dissenters were at last free to compete for office. In a very short time, half the judges, one fifth of the country's JPs, and a solid block of military and naval officers had been replaced by men previously barred, many of them Catholics. In 1686, the test case of Godden v. Hales was brought before the Court of King's Bench. Hales was a Roman Catholic convert who had received a colonel's commission from the King, and Godden was claiming that the appointment was illegal. Eleven out of twelve judges, quoting precedents going back to Henry VII, decided in favour of Hales and of the King's right of dispensation.[55] Suitably encouraged, James moved on in 1687 to reissue his brother's Declaration of Indulgence in amended form. In addition to the provision for Protestant dissenters to worship in licensed buildings, the declaration permitted Catholics to worship in public, not just in private. Unlike its predecessor of 1673, it failed to guarantee the Church of England as an institution, limiting itself instead to assurances that the rights of worship and the possessions (i.e., the church building), of Anglicans would be protected. As Supreme Governor of the Church of England, the King commanded that the Declaration be read out from the pulpit in all Anglican churches. The Commission of Ecclesiastical Causes was already enforcing discipline in the Church: and a Board of Regulators was at work to free up municipal corporations.

In conventional Protestant accounts, James II has always been dismissed as 'a bigot'.[56] But by all disinterested standards of objectivity, his Declaration of Indulgence was a balanced and reasonable document. It aimed to introduce a desirable measure of even-handed religious toleration. There is nothing in it which gave a clear advantage to one denomination over the others. In any fair-minded society, it would not have caused much stir at all. But Protestant England was in no way fair-minded in such matters. The English had been taught for five or six generations past that Popery was the work of the Devil, and that religious pluralism was a recipe for sinful strife. They assumed, possibly correctly, that Catholics would become the instruments of foreign powers who were just as intolerant as anyone else. In the Restoration era, they demonstrated their deep-seated prejudice not only by falling for the lies of Titus Oates, but also by indulging in a renewed outbreak of witch-burning. In the prevailing climate of prejudice and superstition, therefore, the Declaration of Indulgence was never going to be judged on its objective merits. And King James should have known it. What is more, he should have realized that his motives, however honourable, were bound to be misinterpreted. Whatever his ultimate intentions were – and that is a matter for debate – he should have been in no doubt that a move for tolerating Catholicism would be viewed as a step towards Catholic domination. The Declaration was issued at the very time that thousands of French Huguenot refugees were flooding into England following the revocation of the Edict of

Nantes. The most telling accusations against the King did not concern devious motives but poor preparation and bad timing.

Similar aims were pursued elsewhere in the Isles. In Ireland, King James relied increasingly on the advice of his one-time companion in the Spanish army, Richard Talbot, Earl of Tyrconnell (1630–91), Lord Deputy from 1687. Having disbanded the Protestant militia, they opened the gates of the army and the administration to Catholics, and were preparing for a Parliament that was to revise the abortive Restoration land settlement. Given the preponderance of Catholics in Ireland, their policies were inevitably heading to a regime that would have undermined the Protestant Ascendancy. In Scotland, the Parliament refused point-blank to sanction universal toleration. But indulgences issued via the Privy Council opened a path to office for various Catholics, Quakers, and Nonconformists. Two or three Privy Councillors declined to sign the orders, and a couple of bishops were dismissed. But there were no signs whatsoever of nationwide discontent.

In England, in contrast, the political temperature rose rapidly. The Archbishop of Canterbury, William Sancroft (1617–93), was a dogged customer, but no extremist. He had once lost his fellowship at Cambridge for refusing an oath of loyalty to the Commonwealth, and he would lose his archbishopric for refusing an oath to William and Mary. So when he and six other bishops signed a petition arguing that the Declaration of Indulgence had no legal basis and should not be imposed on the Church of England by royal command, they were only expressing the consensus of their colleagues. The King reacted angrily, and rashly put them on trial for their lives on charges of seditious libel. The Seven Bishops were acquitted. But their trial caused uproar. It was a God-sent gift to the simmering Whigs.

One of the Seven Bishops was the Cornishman Sir Jonathan Trelawny, Bt. (1650–1721), then Bishop of Bristol. His incarceration in the Tower sent shivers through Cornwall. Rumours arose that an army of the West would march on London to free him. (See below.)

Into this political cauldron, in June 1688, there dropped an explosive item of astonishing news. After five stillbirths and five unviable babies, the Queen had been delivered of a healthy son and heir, James Francis Edward. Overnight, the provision that James would be succeeded by his Protestant daughter Mary was invalidated; and the prospect loomed of the King's pro-Catholic regime being prolonged indefinitely. A cabal of Whig and Tory conspirators sounded out Mary's husband, Willem van Oranje (William of Orange), and invited him to invade. The 'Immortal Seven', as they were afterwards styled, included Thomas Osborne, first Earl of Danby, sometime minister to Charles II; Charles Talbot, twelfth Earl of Shrewsbury, an ex-Catholic; Edward Russell; Richard Lumley, first Baron Lumley; Henry Sidney; and Henry Compton, the Bishop of London.

The invitation to William of Orange was one of those technicalities which seek to lend respectability to an act of force already decided on. The Stadholder could have had no illusions that he was embarking on a blatant usurpation, which no form of words could conceal. But his ambition to secure the resources of the three kingdoms for his lifelong struggle against Louis XIV overrode all other considerations; and in the event, the invasion was swiftly accomplished. William landed at Brixham on 11 November from a Dutch fleet armed with Dutch troops and supplied with Dutch money. Though Danby secured the North of England, William had no need to rely on English assistance. He advanced on London and unceremoniously dispersed the garrison of the capital. By all accounts, King James uncharacteristically panicked. He prepared to fight, then withdrew. He fled with his family for the coast, but was stopped. Finally, after communicating with William, he was allowed to leave for France. The Whig version stresses the invitation to William 'from the English people'. In fact, William invited himself. This was a bloodless conquest, but a conquest all the same; and it was to cause the spilling of much blood. No English Parliament had summoned William to England; it was William who summoned the Parliament before he had any legal pretence for doing so.

The Convention Parliament assembled in January 1689 to the sound of rejoicing by Protestant enthusiasts but in the shadow of a fait accompli. Having declared that King James had abdicated – which was simply untrue – it was obliged to offer the crown to William and Mary jointly, since neither of them would agree to Mary acceding alone. In a famous Declaration of Rights, later enshrined in a slightly modified Bill of Rights, it set out the Whig programme of strengthening Parliament and diminishing crown prerogative. Having overruled much of the legislation passed since 1660, it asserted the right of free elections, the right to regular Parliaments, the right of free debate in Parliament, the right of Parliament to control taxation, the suspension of statutes, and a standing army. The one right which it did not mention, and which was the burning issue of the age, was the right of all Christians to worship their God in peace. The Test Acts and the (limited) Toleration Act stayed in place. The succession to the throne was confined to Protestants. No trouble was taken to see whether the arrangements made for England were in any way suited to the wishes of the deposed King's subjects in his two other kingdoms.

In Scotland, opinion was divided between an acquiescent majority and an irreconcilable minority. A Scottish Convention Parliament assembled promptly at Edinburgh and approved the main provisions of its English counterpart. But resistance crystallized around the defiant figure of John Graham of Claverhouse, first Viscount Dundee (1649–89). 'Bonnie Dundee' was a disciple of his late relative, the Marquess of Montrose, and he likewise rallied the Highland clans to the old cause. He was the first 'Jacobite' to take the field. As a soldier, who had once served under William of Orange, he knew the enemy well; and at Killiecrankie (17 July 1689) he engineered a brilliant victory over King William's troops. His death in the hour of triumph, however, caused his following to disintegrate and the clans to relapse into their traditional fraternal fighting. King William adopted the policy of forcing the clan chiefs to swear a public oath of allegiance on pain of retribution. The ultimate consequence of the policy was the notorious Massacre of Glencoe in February 1692, when a party of loyalist Campbells surprised a community of Macdonalds in their beds, and cut their throats.

In Ireland, support for King James was considerably more solid, and not only among Catholics. There was a strong sense that once again the English had unilaterally deposed a legitimate king; there were fears about the implications of a militantly Protestant, and militarily powerful, Parliamentary regime in London; and there was a well-established tradition, first manifest in Ormonde's time, that religious toleration for all was eminently desirable. Tyrconnell somewhat muddied the waters by fixing municipal charters in ways that favoured prospective Catholic candidates for Parliament. When it met in May 1689, 223 out of 230 seats in the 'Patriot Parliament' in Dublin were to be held by Catholics, mainly of the Old English persuasion. Yet the animosity of the day was not directed at Protestants as a whole, but only against those who backed 'the Dutch usurper'.

Soon after his joint coronation with Mary at Westminster in April, Willem van Oranje slipped back to Holland to attend to his duties as Stadholder and to pursue yet another round of his eternal war against France. He had not invaded England because he was worried about James's Catholicism – he was personally quite tolerant – but only from fears that James's troubles would turn England into a French satellite. By the same token, he knew perfectly that his own successful coup in England would provoke French retaliation. So he made another pre-emptive strike, and declared war on France without waiting for a French attack.

'King William's War' (1689–97) saw England and the United Provinces form a Grand Coalition with the Holy Roman Empire, Spain, and Savoy to confront the overwhelming might of Louis XIV at his peak. Since Louis made the deposition of King James a *casus belli*, it might well have been called the 'War of the English Succession'. A clear French victory would undoubtedly have resulted

in King James being restored to his lost thrones. As it was, the
fighting dragged on by land and by sea on several fronts for eight
long years. It was inordinately expensive, not least for England
where it necessitated the formation first of the Commissioners for
Public Accounts (i.e. from 1690) and then, to facilitate large-scale
borrowing, of the Bank of England (1694). In general, by keeping
King William abroad and preoccupied for long spells of time, it
greatly reinforced Parliament's hold on domestic policy. In the end,
the combatants came to terms at the Treaty of Ryswick (1697). Each
side kept what it valued most. Louis XIV kept Strasbourg. Willem
van Oranje kept his barrier fortresses on the frontier of the Spanish
Netherlands; and he kept his title of 'King of England, by the Grace
of God'.

So long as the war lasted, the French constantly threatened to
disrupt the English and the Dutch by landing troops in the outer
reaches of the Isles and by raising the standard for King James. They
had failed to assist Dundee at Killiecrankie. But they put King James
ashore at Kinsale in March 1689, and started the campaign which
would make him or break him.

By the time that King James landed, Williamites and Jacobites
had already fallen to blows in many Irish localities. In Derry, the
long siege had begun the previous December when the Protestant
'Apprentice Boys' slammed the city gates shut in defiance of a
Catholic force led by Lord Antrim. Most of the country was held by
Tyrconnell's Catholic army and its associates, who accompanied
James on his way to Dublin and the 'Patriot Parliament'. As the
Derry Boys bawled 'No Surrender' from the walls, in a cry that was
to become the watchword of Ulster Protestantism, James watched
as the Parliament passed bill after bill depriving Williamites of their
land, compensating the victims of Cromwellian confiscations, and
forbidding Westminster to legislate for Ireland. James refused either
to cancel Poynings' Law or to sanction the transfer of property from
the state Church to the Catholics. In July 1689 the Siege of Derry
came to an end after 105 days, with the defenders triumphant. They
had not surrendered. The Patriot Parliament broke up with the

patriots disgruntled with a King whom they considered half-hearted. Everything waited on the concentrated clash of arms, for which both sides were preparing. The remainder of 1689 passed inconclusively. The Protestant army of Enniskillen, under a leader calling himself 'the Little Cromwell', conducted a trail of slaughter in the south. But a major Dutch force under the Duke of Bromberg sat tight in its camp near Belfast. Willem van Oranje, angry at the lack of progress, delayed his arrival until June 1690.

The Battle of the Boyne (1 July (OS)/11 July (NS) 1690) was contested by the Williamite army advancing southwards from Belfast and the Jacobite army defending the approaches to Dublin. It was a battle of manoeuvre and counter-manoeuvre, and did not inflict major loss of life. Willem van Oranje headed a professional army of Dutchmen, Danes, Huguenots, and English. He was opposed by the Comte de Lauzan and a conglomeration of French regulars, German and Walloon mercenaries, and Catholic Irish. The outcome was determined by an upstream crossing of the river by a detachment of Williamite cavalry. It was far less bloody than the terminal battle of the campaign, at Aughrim a year later, which preceded the Treaty of Limerick (1691). 'King Billy' stood firm in the centre, whilst King James fled the field in despair. His fate was sealed. His cause was lost.

In his terminal years of exile, King James took to ascetic religious exercises. He waited in vain at St Germain-en-Laye for an opportunity for him and his growing son to return home. He outlived his daughter Mary, who died childless in 1694. He saw his other daughter, Anne, defer her claims so that Willem van Oranje could continue as sole monarch. He would have known that Louis XIV's apparent recognition of King William at Ryswick had been done in a form of words that could always be renounced. He knew for certain that William's sister-in-law and heiress, Anne, had borne eighteen pregnancies by 1700, and none successfully. When he died on 16 September 1701, France, England, the United Provinces, and others were embroiled yet again in another war, the War of the Spanish Succession. But the succession to England, Scotland, and

Ireland was still undecided. As he was carried to his last resting place in the chapel of the English Benedictines on the Rue St Jacques in Paris, his thirteen-year-old son was recognized by Louis XIV as James VIII and III.

(8) Union

Seen from the standpoint of the English ruling Establishment – and that was not the only way of looking at it (see below) – the logic for a constitutional union between England and Scotland was growing ever more urgent by the turn of the century. The issue became ever more acute with every day that passed. It was driven by two unresolved questions, the future of the monarchy, and the need to secure the Protestant supremacy. Ever since the abortive republican experiment under Cromwell fifty years earlier, almost everyone in England agreed that the monarchy was essential. But to be effective the monarchy had to be stable; and stability could no longer be provided by the Stuarts. The legitimate line of the Stuarts was Catholic, and a potential source of religious dissension. The ruling line was heirless, and a potential source of political chaos. In the middle of the War of the Spanish Succession, which had been sparked by Louis XIV's intervention in the affairs of the heirless Spanish Bourbons, no one needed reminding of the fatal consequences of a disputed succession. So something needed to be done, and done fast. William III had served England well. He was a Stuart in the maternal line; he was a Protestant, a Dutch Calvinist, but not an officious one; and, as a semi-absent foreigner, he had left Parliament and the Whig oligarchy well alone. But in 1700 he was an ageing widower with no heir other than his worn-out, childless sister-in-law, Anne. The ideal solution for the English Establishment, therefore, was to look around Europe and find a candidate with the same personal profile as King William but without the fatal flaw of infertility.

The catch in the puzzle, of course, was Scotland. Unlike Ireland, which was locked into England by Poynings' Law, Scotland was independent; and a Scots Parliament could make up its own mind about any candidate for the throne. Scotland had the right to choose a different monarch from England, and thereby end the personal union of crowns that had functioned since 1603. What is more, as demonstrated by Montrose and more recently by Dundee, Scotland was more attached to the Scots dynasty of Stuart than England was; and Scotland had a long tradition of the 'Auld Alliance' with France. Lastly, and by no means leastly, Scotland was financially broke. She was a sitting duck for French bribery. If the English could not force, cajole, or buy the Scots to accept the English candidate for the throne, the French might seduce or bully the Scots to accept a French candidate. Seen from London, it was as simple as that. The minute that Louis XIV showed his hand and publicly gave his blessing to Charles III, 'the Old Pretender', the English Government was obliged to find an immediate solution. Every major event of the next fifteen years was subordinated to the resultant plan.

England's Act of Settlement (1701) was passed by Parliament whilst William III was still alive. It was designed to end anxieties over the royal succession once and for all. In the end, it proved so effective that it was never superseded, and is still in being at the time of writing nearly three hundred years later. By overruling the hereditary rights of the House of Stuart, and by overriding the legitimate rights of fifty-seven living claimants (see Appendix 36), it confirmed the fact, implicit in the events of 1688–9, that in the last resort the monarchy was subservient to Parliament. It set the precedent whereby all parts of the constitutional monarchy were to be built on the same legal, man-made foundations. In practice, though not completely in theory, for it did not abolish the sacramental act of coronation, it consigned the Divine Right of Kings to the museum. It transferred the rights of the House of Stuart to the House of Hanover.

The Hanoverians admirably matched the list of credentials which William of Orange's career had shown to be desirable. They had a small proportion of Stuart blood in their veins – not a lot, but enough to help the spin-doctors of the day to publicize the legitimate thread of Stuart descent. (The principal candidate, Sophia, Princess of Bohemia and Dowager Duchess of Hanover and Braunschweig-Lüneburg (1630–1714), had one quarter 'Stuart blood', six grown sons, a propensity for twins, and numerous grandsons.) They were well-established Protestants of the Lutheran variety, who would have few qualms about converting to Anglicanism. And they were total foreigners, who did not speak a word of English and who would be entirely dependent in England on their English advisers. Importantly, too, though they were to establish family links with the rising House of Brandenburg-Prussia, they only belonged to the minor princes of Germany, and did not in themselves possess any strong or independent power-base. Barring accidents, one or other of the Hanoverians was due to be offered the Crown of England and Wales from the day that King William gave his royal assent to the Act of Settlement. Meanwhile, England continued to be racked by the stresses of war and of religious controversy. Both problems were intimately entwined with the omnipresent complications of the royal succession.

During the War of the Spanish Succession (1700–13), a Grand Alliance similar to that of 1690–7 again struggled to contain the expansive designs of France. England – though not Scotland – served as the primary allied naval power, a prominent paymaster and diplomatic coordinator, and a secondary military power. On the domestic front, the war gradually undermined confidence in Godolphin's ruling Whig Junta, who were replaced after 1710 by Harley's first ever Tory ministry. On the foreign front, it set the scene for the sensational career of John Churchill, Duke of Marlborough (1650–1722), whose unblemished record as a battlefield commander made him a fitting partner for Cromwell in England's hall of military fame. It ended for England with the Treaty of Utrecht (1713), which gave international recognition to the Act of Settlement and handed the newly formed United Kingdom a whole new collection of colonies from Newfoundland to Gibraltar.

This time, religious controversy centred on two influential

groups, one of High Anglicans and the other of Nonconformists. The former, known as 'nonjurors', had refused to take the oath of allegiance to William and Mary. They included Archbishop Sancroft, and five of the 'Seven Bishops' from 1688 (though not Trelawny). They felt that the Church of England had become a political football whose spiritual life was being blighted by its link with the state. They refused to sign the Abjuration Act (1702), which precipitated a second round of dismissals. Indeed they were strong enough to maintain their own illegal hierarchy until the early nineteenth century, cultivating close links both with Scots Episcopalians and with French Gallicans. They amply illustrated the national and international ramifications of religious disputes in this period.

The Nonconformists who got into trouble were people who took communion in an Anglican church from time to time in order to satisfy the Test Acts and gain office, but who attended their own chapels and meeting-houses for the rest of the year. Known as 'Occasional Conformists', they aroused the ire of the Tories who were eventually able to stop the practice for a time by the Occasional Conformity Act (1711). Their existence showed that the Toleration Act, which excluded toleration for Catholics, gave considerable leeway to Protestant dissenters.

William III's death in March 1702, and the smooth accession of Queen Anne in England and Scotland, brought the problems surrounding the Succession into their final phase. After Anne, there were no more Protestant Stuarts left. To raise anxieties still higher, the Queen was in poor health; the war dragged on despite Marlborough's victories; and Scotland was still an unknown quantity. William III had tried to interest the English Parliament in union with Scotland, and had been rebuffed. But when the Scottish Parliament in Edinburgh passed its own Act of Security (or Settlement) in 1704, emphasizing Scotland's independent right to choose her own monarchs, the parliamentarians in Westminster were finally stirred into action. In the first place, they produced an Aliens Act (1705), which threatened to expel all non-naturalized Scots residents from England, and then a Bill of Union.

The English Bill of Union (1706) was prepared unilaterally as a document which the Scots could either take or leave. It was presented at a moment when the bargaining power of the Scots was weak; and it was accompanied by the promise of a very large sum of money. It did not have to state in print what everyone suspected in private, namely that a rejection by the Scots of a voluntary union might be followed by the imposition of a union by force on much less generous terms. Even so, the Scots argued the pros and cons fiercely both inside and outside their parliament. But in the end, a delegation travelled to London to say yes. The Scots Parliament voted itself out of existence. The Scottish Government would cease to exist except as a regional department of a central administration in London. Scotland was to enjoy the benefit of free trade with England and to be treated as 'home territory' within the meaning of the Navigation Acts. Scotland was to receive the so-called 'Equivalent', that is the enormous sum of £398,085 calculated as the capitalized value of Scotland's future share of the National Debt. Scottish law, Scottish municipal corporations, the Scottish currency, and the Church of Scotland were not to be touched. But the age-old Scottish monarchy, founded by Kenneth Mac Alpin in the mists of the ninth century and tied since 1371 to the House of Stuart, was to end with the life of Queen Anne. In return, by admitting a contingent of forty-five Scottish MPs, the English Parliament was to be transformed into the sovereign legislature of the new dual state. The state, of which England was only one part, and which did not include England's dependency, Ireland, was to be called as James I would have wished, the 'Kingdom of Great Britain'. The state flag was to be the Union flag that James I had invented more than a century before. The official adjective pertaining to the new state was 'British'. Henceforth, there would be a British state, a British monarchy, a British Parliament, a British Government, a British Empire, a British army, and a community of British subjects.

As it happened, Providence decided that the royal succession did not work out exactly as foreseen. Queen Anne had given birth to one last stillborn child, her nineteenth, after the Act of Settlement; and she lived for seven more years after the Act of Union. Seeing that the heir presumptive, the Dowager Sophia, was advancing in years, it was decided to strengthen the links with her son Georg Ludwig von Braunschweig-Lüneburg, Duke and Elector of Hanover, and his family. The Elector was a less attractive prospect than his mother. He was notoriously irascible; he had divorced his duchess, and shut her up in a castle for life; and he was no longer on speaking terms with his son, Georg Augustus (b. 1683). But such things did not affect his suitability for the appointed role, for which a deaf-mute would not have been entirely amiss. In 1705 the Elector received naturalization as an English subject, and in 1706 his son was made a Knight of the Garter and created Duke of Cambridge. A Regency Act (1706) was introduced to ensure that the Privy Council proclaimed the accession as soon as the old Queen died. It was a time of waiting not dissimilar to that which had preceded the death of the ageing Queen Elizabeth a century earlier. When Queen Anne was approaching her end in the late spring of 1714, the Dowager Sophia was still alive, aged eighty-three. But Sophia died in June, and Anne lingered on until 1 August. On that day, with great dispatch, in the name of the Privy Council in London, the Elector of Hanover was proclaimed 'George I, King of Great Britain, France, and Ireland'. When he heard the news at Osnabrück soon after, he decided for good measure to proclaim himself 'King of Hanover', even though the title would not be recognized internationally for a hundred years.

It is important for historians to put this rather tricky sequence of events into good order. For it provides the context within which the united Kingdom was born. Different accounts give prominence to different points in the sequence. Some highlight the passage of the Bill of Union through the English Parliament in 1706; others stress the day in January 1707 when the Scots delegation delivered its consent, yet others the accession or coronation of George I. They are all slightly off track. The key scene, not often quoted in general histories, unfolded on the afternoon of 6 March 1707.

By ancient custom, no act of parliament can be deemed valid until it has been passed by both Houses and has been given the royal assent. In earlier times, the monarch would give assent to a bill by signing it in person, or by appending the royal seal. But it was another subtle sign of the monarchy's growing subservience that by the beginning of the eighteenth century the granting of the royal assent was often delegated to Parliamentary commissioners. The commissioners usually consisted of the Lord Chancellor and two other lords assisted by the Clerk of Parliament. The Act of Union, however, was too momentous to be left in the hands of commissioners. It would change the character both of the Parliament and of the monarchy. So Queen Anne was present in person. Then, as now, the ceremony began in the House of Lords:

> Her Majesty being seated on Her Royal Throne adorned with her Crown and Regal Ornaments attended with her Officers of the State (the Peers being in their Robes) commanded the Deputy Gentleman Usher of the Black Rod to signify to the House of Commons, 'that it is Her Majesty's Pleasure, they attend Her, presently in the House of Peers'.[57]

On this occasion, the honour fell to a Mr Aston. Dressed in wig and court attire and carrying both sword and staff, he made his way to the door of the Commons' chamber. There, in time-honoured fashion, the door was slammed shut as he approached. Knocking three times with his staff on the closed door, he waited for it to open before walking down the central aisle to stand before the chair of the Speaker, Mr John Smith MP. Bowing to left and right, he repeated the unvarying formula: 'Mr Speaker, Her Majesty commands the presence of this honourable House in the House of Peers.'

Black Rod retired. The Sergeant-at-Arms lifted the mace, and took up position to lead. The Speaker rose from his chair, followed by the Clerk of the House. The members lined up two by two behind them, and then moved off in procession. Earlier, a number of MPs headed by 'Sir William Strickland and others' had complained to the Lords that it would be 'inconvenient' to respond to Her Majesty's command because the passages to their Lordships' Lobby were so crowded. But a message had been sent to the Commons 'To acquaint them that the Lobby and passages leading to the House are cleared as desired.'[58] So the procession arrived without delay. Standing at the entrance to the House of Lords, the Commons would have strained to catch a glimpse of the Queen enthroned at the far end. The Lord Chancellor was seated on the woolsack in front of her. All the other peers in their crimson robes were crammed into their benches on three sides of the chamber. The business would be conducted by three solemn officials. The Reading Clerk would rise to read the royal commission. The Clerk of the Crown would read out the title of the bills. And finally, the Clerk of Parliaments would 'pre-announce' the Royal Assent in the words of a medieval formula – *La Reyne le veult*, 'The Queen wills it.'[59]

Parliament's business proceeded without a break. The Act of Union was only one of eight bills to gain the Royal Assent that day:

1. An Act of Union of the two kingdoms of England and Scotland.
2. 'An Act for better preventing Escapes out of the Queen's Bench and Fleet Prisons.'
3. An act for repairing the Highway between Hockliffe and Woodborne, in the County of Bedford.
4. An Act ... 'repairing the Highways in the County of Hereford'.[60]

To each of these, the Clerk intoned, '*La Reyne le veult*.' Then came four private bills:

5. An Act for enlarging the Passage to the New Palace Yard, the Gate House, Westminster.
6. An Act for the releasing of Sir John Mead of the Kingdom of Ireland, Knight and Baronet.
7. An Act of naturalising Philip van den Enden, Merchant.
8. An Act of making the ship *Supply* a free Ship.[61]

To these, the Clerk recited, *'Soit fait comme il est desiré,'* 'May it be done as desired.' There is something exquisitely inappropriate in the fact that the act embodying the fundamental constitutional treaty between England and Scotland was given the same weight on the agenda as an act for trying to stop the escapes of convicts, and another for mending the road between the villages of Hockliffe and Woodborne.

The Queen then addressed both Lords and Commons from the throne. 'My Lords and Gentlemen,' she said:

> I consider this Union as a matter of the greatest importance to the wealth, strength and safety of the whole island and at the same time a work of so much difficulty and nicety in its own nature that till now all attempts . . . towards it in the course of above a hundred years have proved ineffectual. And therefore, I make no doubt but it will be remembered and spoke of hereafter to the honor of those who have been instrumental in bringing it to such a happy conclusion. I desire and expect from all my subjects of both nations, that from henceforth they act with all possible respect and kindness to one another, that so it may appear to all the world they have hearts disposed to become one people. This will be a great pleasure to me.[62]

In the Queen's estimation, there was still an English and a Scottish nation. But she had expressed the hope that the two nations would grow into one British people.

After returning to the Commons, the Speaker formally announced that the Act of Union was complete. As the *Journal* of the Commons records:

Mr Speaker reported that Her Majesty had been pleased to give the Royal Assent to the Bill intituled An Act for the Union of the Two Kingdoms of England and Scotland: and to the several public and private bills following . . .[63]

Meanwhile, in the Lords, the Clerk of Parliaments had taken down the long vellum scroll on which the text of the Act of Union was written. At the very top of the document, at the left-hand side, he added the words, 'Most Gracious Sovereign, la Reyne le veult'.[64]

After the Easter recess, Queen Anne moved to initiate the next parliamentary session. She was no longer 'Queen of England' and 'Queen of Scotland', but 'Queen of Great Britain' in both substance and style. The Parliament was no longer the Parliament of England. On 29 April 1707, the Queen issued a proclamation requesting Parliament to reassemble in its new form and under its new title:

> . . . by virtue of the Acts of Union. . . . . the Lords of Parliament
> of England and the Sixteen Peers of Scotland and the Members
> of the House of Commons of the said Parliament of England
> and the Forty Representatives of Scotland . . . should assemble
> and meet . . . in the respective Houses of Parliament of Great
> Britain . . . and should be the two Houses of the first Parliament
> of Great Britain.[65]

Two days later, on 1 May 1707, the new Parliament assembled. That was the day on which the British State, the united Kingdom of Great Britain, started to function. It was the day when modern British history began.

(9) FROM UNION TO UNION, 1707–1801

The creation of the united Kingdom of Great Britain left Ireland in a highly unusual position. The Kingdom of Ireland remained intact as a separate entity, though its legislation was still tied via Poynings' Law to the ultimate sanction of Westminster. Yet Westminster no longer housed an English Parliament but the British one; and the English monarchy which had reigned in Ireland since 1541 had merged into the British monarchy. From 1714 British Kings were automatically declared Kings of Ireland; and their assent was required to put the statutes of the Irish Parliament in Dublin into effect. The distinction between British statutes passed at Westminster for application in Ireland and Irish statutes passed in Dublin after approval in London might have been clear enough to constitutional lawyers. But it must have seemed to most ordinary people, as the English would say, 'rather Irish'. Ninety-four years were to pass before these complications were removed, and not in happy circumstances.

At first sight, Ireland in the eighteenth century might be seen as a country of no change. Certainly, no significant reforms were introduced to relieve the two major and related sources of discontent inherited from the previous century – discrimination against Catholics and the land question. Ireland largely missed out on the industrial changes which were beginning to transform several regions of Great Britain, an exception being the growth of linen manufacture in Belfast. Nonetheless, nothing remained static: Ireland in 1800 would not be the same place that it was in 1700.

After the war of 1689–91, the Protestant Establishment tightened its grip. The Banishment Act (1697) formally prohibited the Catholic hierarchy from operating in Ireland. Licences to open churches and chapels were only given to Protestants. The Test Acts excluding Catholics from all office high or low were backed up by the administration of oaths that no Catholic could swear:

> I do solemnly and sincerely, in the presence of God, profess, testify, and declare that I do believe that in the sacrament of the Lord's Supper there is not any transubstantiation of the elements of bread and wine into the body of Christ and that the invocation or adoration of the virgin Mary or any other saint as now used in the church of Rome are superstitious and idolatrous.[66]

In many places, and for several decades, the Catholic population could only worship at so-called 'hedge masses' in the open fields. In Hanoverian times, however, many of the penal laws were observed in the breach. The Catholic hierarchy returned illegally, but was not expelled. Catholic churches were built without licences, but were not demolished. Catholic pilgrimages, such as that to Lough Derg, though forbidden, flourished. Generally speaking, Catholics were allowed to get on with their lives so long as they did not turn to political agitation, did not seek office, and did not try to buy land.

Protestant fears of the Catholic majority were heightened by the presence of large numbers of Irish Catholic soldiers serving abroad, especially in France and Spain. The tradition of these 'Wild Geese' was greatly boosted in 1691, when some twenty thousand Jacobite troops were sent into French service by the Treaty of Limerick. France's 'Irish Brigade' was a large professional formation which supplied trained troops for each of the Jacobite invasions of Great Britain in 1715 and again in 1745. At any one time, a thousand recruits per year were leaving Ireland, and some five hundred Irish officers would be serving in various Continental countries.

In a predominantly peasant society, the divorce of Catholics from land ownership was a catastrophic disability. Confiscations by the Williamites after 1691 more than offset preceding improvements. The Resumption Act (1702), which helped Protestants to recover confiscated land, derived from the English, not the Irish, Parliament. Further acts of 1704 and 1709 forbade Catholics to purchase freehold land and limited Catholic leases to thirty-one years. As could have been foreseen, an important sector of the old Catholic landowners joined the Protestant Church in order to safeguard their property. The proportion of Irish land in Catholic hands fell from 22 per cent in 1688 to 14 per cent in 1700 and to only 5 per cent in 1778. The condition of the landless peasants beggared description. The English agricultural writer Arthur Young (1741–1820), who toured Ireland in the 1770s before touring France, was thoroughly shocked:

The cottages of Irish, called cabins, are the most miserable looking hovels. The furniture in very many [consists] only of a pot for boiling their potatoes, a bit of a table, and one or two broken stools; beds are not found universally, the family lying on straw.[67]

In that same era, the appearance of the 'Whiteboys' in the Irish countryside initiated the long tradition of rural terrorism and of secret societies. From 1765 onwards the ferocious legislation directed against the 'Whiteboys' introduced the death penalty for numerous minor offences, perpetuating and institutionalizing social repression. Ireland had entered a terrible impasse, which well-meaning people on both sides of the religious divide were powerless to alter. Catholic feared Protestant; Protestant feared Catholic; and the British-run government in Dublin Castle, independent of both, ruled with colonial disdain. Pointless protests proliferated. Gaelic bards plied their laments; and Protestant clergymen with a social conscience took to satire. Jonathan Swift, Dean of St Patrick's, marooned at Holyhead on his way home to Dublin, composed a microcosm in doggerel of the prevailing marasmus of impotence:

> Lo here I sit at Holyhead
> I see the ship at anchor ride
> With muddy ale and mouldy bread
> All Christian victuals stink of fish
> I'm where my enemies would wish
> I'm fastened both by wind and tide
> I never was in haste before
> To reach that slavish hateful shore
> I'd go in freedom to my grave
> Than rule yon isle and be a slave.[68]

Gaelic poetry tends more to the melancholic; but it is not without its humour. 'The Lament of Father O'Donnell', for instance, which recalls a priest from Fermanagh who turned Protestant, was turned into a popular song:

Crádh ort, a Dhoiminic Uí Dhomhnaill,
Nach mairg ariamh a chonnaic thu;
Bhí tú 'do shagart Dia Dómhnaigh,
'S ar maidin Dia Luain do mhinistir.
Pill, pill, a rúin ó,
Pill a rúin ó, is ná h-imthigh uaim;
Pill ort, a chuid den tsaol mhór,
No chan fheiceann tu 'n ghlóir mur' bpille tú.[69]

(Woe to you, Dominick O'Donnell,
And woe to all who ever saw you!
On the Day of the Lord you were still a priest,
And on Monday morn a minister.
Come back, come back, my love.
Come back and never leave me.
My share of the world, come back to me,
Or miss eternal glory.)

The one activity the Irish could engage in without hindrance was reproduction. Though population growth was restricted in the early eighteenth century by emigration to the American colonies, especially from Ulster, and by the catastrophic famine of 1741, it accelerated thereafter with unprecedented speed. From 2 million in 1700, Irish numbers had risen by 1791 to 4.4 million, and by the turn of the century at about 5 million to half the combined population of England and Scotland. For the first and last time in its history, the size of Ireland's population closely matched the size of her territory – that is, one third of the Isles as a whole.

The outbreak of the War of American Independence in 1776 caused many people, both in Ireland and in Britain, to see parallels between America and Ireland. The upshot in 1782, after years of intense politicking, was the granting of free trade and a brief period of Irish legislative independence. The central figure in the two subsequent decades of virtual self-government was Henry Grattan (1746–1820), a 'patriot' Protestant lawyer, who after some hesitation supported the rising demands for Catholic emancipation.

News of the French Revolution, however, pushed the trend for moderate constitutional reform into ever more radical channels; and the outbreak of the French Revolutionary Wars revived the spectre of foreign military intervention. The radical society of United Irishmen drew its active membership from Presbyterians in Belfast and from a mixed group of Anglicans and Catholics in Dublin. Its leader, Theobald Wolfe Tone (1763–98), a Protestant Dubliner, was dedicated to the goal of ending British domination through the united efforts of all Irish people of all religious persuasions. He worked with the Catholic Convention of 1792, which was demanding an end to the penal laws. But having failed to obtain concessions from the British government, he travelled to Paris. His mission resulted in the large-scale naval expedition of General Hoche, mounted by the French Directory, and wrecked by a storm on the rocks of Bantry Bay in December 1796. A much smaller French expedition commanded by General Humbert landed at Killala Bay, Co. Mayo, in August 1798, but was defeated by government forces. The general insurrection that it came to reinforce never happened, though the last of several local risings in Co. Wexford had fought a pitched battle at Vinegar Hill (21 June 1798) before being suppressed. Wolfe Tone, captured in a French uniform, killed himself whilst awaiting execution.

The efforts of the United Irishmen persuaded the British Government to end Irish autonomy once and for all. The failure of separatism in the middle of an international war provoked forcible incorporation. Two identical Acts of Union (1800) passed simultaneously in Dublin and London prepared the merger of the British and the Irish Parliaments. Twenty-eight Irish peers joined the British House of Lords, and a block of a hundred Irish MPs entered the House of Commons. Ireland's share of the national debt was assessed at two-seventeenths (11.8 per cent). The Lord Lieutenant and his Chief Secretary were to remain in Dublin Castle at the head of a separate Irish branch of the British administration. Nonetheless, as from 1 January 1801, Ireland became an integral part of the British state. The design of the Union flag was modified to incorporate the spurious cross of St Patrick. And the name of the state was changed to 'the United Kingdom of Great Britain and Ireland'.[70] For the very first time in their history, the whole of the Isles had been placed directly under one united British rule.

SEVENTEENTH-CENTURY LITERATURE is one of the glories of the English heritage. It represents the bedrock of the classical literary canon. Starting in the Jacobean age, with Bacon, the King James Bible, and the later plays and sonnets of Shakespeare, it moves on to the profundities of the Metaphysicals, the sublimities of Milton, the passionate spirituality of Bunyan, the frivolities of Restoration Comedy, and the courtly elegance of Dryden. Seventeenth-century writers concerned to preserve a record of their own times were also writers of quality. The Earl of Clarendon's *History of the Great Rebellion* was superior to anything of the sort produced previously. Samuel Pepys (1633–1703) and John Evelyn (1620–1706) must be rated in the front rank of diarists.

In contrast, literary works inspired by the seventeenth century have been relatively meagre. Writers of the Enlightenment consciously turned away from the conflicts and the religiosity of the preceding age, whilst the Romantics preferred to explore more distant, medieval times and more exotic foreign locations. With one great exception, the seventeenth century did not produce any towering figures who could be the focus of later national pride or moral debate.

The towering exception, of course, is Oliver Cromwell. Any moderately comprehensive library catalogue will list 100 or 150 biographies. They start with the contemporary republican panegyrics, such as Henry Fletcher's *The Perfect Politician* (1660), and the Royalist obloquies, such as James Heath's *Flagellum* . . . (1669), and they continue to the present day. Sometimes for and sometimes against, the best respected positions include Burton (1698), Kimber (1724), Banks (1739), Carlyle (1845), Guizot (1854), Southey (1861),

Gardiner (1899), Morley (1900), Firth (1924), Ashley (1937), C. V. Wedgwood (1939), Paul (1955), Hill (1970) and, most recently, Antonia Fraser (1973). Carlyle, who erected the principles of 'The Hero in History', made some extravagant comments about 'The Great Oliver'. 'God-sent to save England', he called him, grappling 'like a giant, face to face, heart to heart, with the naked truth of things'.[71]

Few historians would contest the Cromwellian archetype of the English 'strong man', though many have wondered whether his strength was necessarily attended by virtue. Clarendon called him 'a brave, bad man'. His principal vice, in the eyes of his detractors, was his Protestant bigotry: his ultimate crime – regicide. Most observers of his character would attest to his honesty. Yet, throughout the four hundred years since his birth, opinions about the paradoxical Lord Protector remain passionately divided. In 1899, on the tercentenary of his birth, the British Parliament sought to erect a monument to a Parliamentarian who had abolished Parliament. The project was agreed, cancelled through the protests of Irish members, then reinstated through pressure, among others, from Jewish members. Lord Salisbury, the Prime Minister, who in the same year had unveiled the statue of King Alfred in Winchester (see page 293, above), unveiled the statue which stands in the House of Commons precinct. His eulogy praised Cromwell as 'a raiser and maintainer of the power of the Empire of England'. In 1911, Winston Churchill, then First Lord of the Admiralty, sought to baptize a battleship after Cromwell. King George V objected: and the ship was launched as the *King George V*. As late as 3 September 1969, the obituary columns of *The Times* carried two rival notices on Cromwell's death-day. One quoted the war-cry of Dunbar: 'Let God arise, let his enemies be scattered.' The other read: 'CROMWELL – to the eternal condemnation of Oliver. Seditionist, traitor, regicide, racialist, proto-fascist and blasphemous bigot. God save England from his like.'[72] In her final word, Antonia Fraser cites the words of Cromwell's own servant: 'A larger soul hath seldom dwelt in a house of clay.'[73]

Cromwell's opponent and chief victim, Charles I, likewise attracts both condemnation and sympathy. His sympathizers can do no better than to repeat Clarendon's verdict:

> And after all this, . . . it is most certain that in that very hour when he was thus wickedly murdered in the sight of the sun, he had as great a share in the hearts and affections of his subjects in general, was as much beloved, esteemed, and longed for by the people in general of the three nations, as any of his predecessors had ever been. To conclude: he was the worthiest gentleman, the best master, the best friend, the best husband, the best father, and the best Christian, that the age in which he lived had produced. And if he was not the best King, if he was without some parts and qualities which have made some kings great and happy, no other prince was ever unhappy who was possessed of half his virtues and endowments, and so much without any kind of vice.[74]

The religious passions of the seventeenth century, which had underlain so many of the political conflicts, rumbled on for two hundred years at least. In some cases, they became institutionalized. The Gunpowder Plot of 1605, for instance, became the occasion for one of England's few annual festivals. On every fifth of November, the Anglican Church has said prayers for 'the deliverance' of the monarch; bonfires blaze, and 'the Guy' is ritually burned in effigy. The festivities were still causing grave offence in mid-Victorian times. Reacting to a letter-writing campaign in *The Times*, which had opposed the restoration of the Roman Catholic hierarchy, a Catholic apologist complained about Bonfire Night being 'a demonstration of insult and ruffianism which, to the disgrace of the country and certainly in violation of the law, has so frequently threatened the peace of various localities'.[75] An unending stream of books and pamphlets, both pro- and anti-Catholic, has endeavoured to explain what 'really' happened. The most recent twist in the historiography is threatening to put the Jacobean hunt for treasonable Jesuits on a par with the paralleled hunt for witches.[76] One thing is certain. No account of the plotting of Catesby and Co. in 1605 can aspire to impartiality without setting the undoubted treason of that small group into the context both of the long-standing and violent persecution of the Catholic community in the preceding generation and of the disproportionate reprisals inflicted on the generations that followed. The most recent historian to take this line does not hesitate to call the plotters 'terrorists'.[77] But their conspiracy was not the one described by their prosecutors; and the English government, too, was engaged in its own kind of terror. Catesby and Co. were driven by noble, idealistic motives. Nearly four hundred years after Fawkes was caught, small English children who know nothing about history or religion, still stop passers-by on the fifth of November and demand 'A penny for the Guy'.

The contest between Cromwell and Charles I also remains controversial because it embodies the continuing discourse between radicals of the Right and radicals of the Left. After the Whig victory of 1689, however, pro-Parliamentary opinions gained an unassailable hold, and became one of the cornerstones of British Liberalism. In the nineteenth century, the 'Whig Interpretation of History' was propagated by Britain's Protestant Establishment; and it was not seriously challenged before the onslaught of Herbert Butterfield in 1931. Butterfield (1900–79), who was a lifelong Methodist, had written eloquently both on the historical novel and on Napoleon, before turning to historiography. What he so devastatingly condemned was 'the study of the past with direct and perpetual reference to the present'.[78] In a sense, his subject was badly labelled since his main target was not so much the Whigs, and the advocates of Whiggish constitutionalism, as the historians of the Reformation and of English Protestantism whose work underpinned Whig ideology. But that is a small quibble. Ever since Butterfield, every student knows what is meant by 'writing History backwards'. Butterfield's censure applies to everyone who imagines the past to be a simple tale of progress. It is particularly relevant to the sins both of the Enlightenment and of modern Marxism. 'It [is] all too easy for any historian, whatever his bias, to go to the past with the present in

mind and to produce an oversimplified abridgement primarily geared
to the demands of his own age.'[79]

As the constitutional obsession faded, contemporary historians
of the seventeenth century have moved ever deeper into economic,
social, and cultural issues. A powerful stimulus in this direction was
supplied by R. H. Tawney, whose *Religion and the Rise of Capitalism*
(1924) proffered a novel thesis concerning the links between religious
faith and economic interest. On the social front, feverish dispute
among professional historians was generated by two opposing and
incompatible analyses of the causes of the Civil War. Tawney and
his associates had recourse to 'the Rise of the Gentry', a phenomenon which took place at the expense of the aristocracy and supposedly explains the conduct of the Parliamentary party. Hugh
Trevor-Roper, in sharp contrast, favoured a view linking the Puritan
radicals not to a rising but to an impoverished squirearchy. They
can't both be right.[80]

Another highly influential figure was Christopher Hill, who
studied at the Stalinist University of Moscow in the late 1940s and
came back with the doubly unfortunate concept of an 'English
Revolution'. Nowadays the notion that the Civil War might properly
be described as either 'English' or as truly 'revolutionary' looks
outdated. Hence Hill's most formidable contributions were probably
in the field of culture and especially religion, where he shed
innumerable shafts of new insight onto the central concerns of the
period in question. In the twenty years after his return from Moscow, Hill enfiladed the historical world with his heavy-calibre intellectual crossfire. A stream of scintillating studies took each of the
main religious and intellectual phenomena of the early seventeenth
century, and subjected them to novel reinterpretations that were
resolutely non-theological. First the Anglican Church of Whitgift
and Laud, then the Puritan movement, then the secular thought of
Bacon, Raleigh, and Coke, and finally the religious radicals of the
1640s – the Levellers, Ranters, Seekers, and Quakers – were all
placed under his learned microscope and subjected to a relentless
materialist analysis. One does not have to share the ideology or the

conclusions to admire Hill's achievement. The odd thing is that he himself is left at the end of his labours praising not the socio-economic motivation of his subjects but their unshakeable Christian faith. He concludes with the words of an English Quaker facing renewed persecution after the Restoration. 'If you should destroy these vessels,' Edward Burroughs told the all-powerful restoration government, 'yet our principles you can never extinguish, but they will live forever, and enter into other bodies to live and speak and act.'[81] That is the finest justification for the study of the history of ideas that one could hope to meet.

The one shortcoming which many of these socio-economists share is the failure to clarify which economy and which society they are using as the basis of their arguments. In the seventeenth century there was no one British state; hence there was no discrete British economy and no British society. But to present English phenomena as if they were the product of clear-cut social and economic structures like those of a later age with a different framework is yet another of those teleological anachronisms which were supposedly long gone.

The academic wrangles, the ultra-specialized topics, and the pseudo-scientific arguments of contemporary scholarship sometimes make one wonder about the progress or regress of the subject. It is certainly refreshing to turn to the older narrative histories for relief and entertainment. In this category, none within the time frame of the seventeenth century surpasses the justly famous *History of England* (1848–55) of Thomas Babington Macaulay (1800–59). Macaulay was everything that the modern scientific scholar would deplore. He was brilliant; he was biased; he was a gripping storyteller – unbothered by philosophy or theorizing. Yet he combined factual accuracy with the most vivid style, thereby bringing the past to life as none of the modern scholars can do. And he was unbelievably industrious. As his colleague Thackeray once observed, 'He reads twenty books to write a sentence; he travels a hundred miles to make a line description.'[82] He took a short span of time – the fifteen years following the accession of James II – and subjected it to the most wide-ranging panoramic treatment. What is more, despite the conventional title of his work, he was not particularly Anglocentric. True enough, his celebrated Third Chapter on 'England in 1685' does not stray beyond the bounds of England. But at many points in his narrative he takes delight in presenting detailed exposés of Scottish and Irish affairs. Here, for example, is Macaulay waxing eloquent on the subject of a city which he had specially visited:

> Eighty years before, during the struggle of the houses of O'Neill and O'Donnell against James the First, . . . the ancient city of Derry had been surprised by one of the native chiefs: the inhabitants had been slaughtered, and the houses reduced to ashes. The insurgents were speedily put down and punished: the government resolved to restore the ruined town: the Lord Mayor, Aldermen, and Common Council of London were invited to assist in the work; and King James the First made over to them in their corporate capacity the ground covered by the ruins of the old Derry, and about six thousand English acres in the neighbourhood.
>
> This country, then uncultivated and uninhabited, is now enriched by industry, embellished by taste, and pleasing even to eyes accustomed to the well tilled fields and stately manor houses of England. A new city soon arose which, on account of its connection with the capital of the empire, was called Londonderry. The buildings covered the summit and slope of a hill which overlooked the broad stream of the Foyle, then whitened by vast flocks of wild swans. On the highest ground stood the Cathedral, a church which, though erected when the secret of Gothic architecture was lost, . . . is not without grace and dignity. Near the Cathedral rose the palace of the Bishop, whose see was one of the most valuable in Ireland. The city was in form nearly an ellipse; and the principal streets formed a cross, the arms of which met in a square called the Diamond. The original houses . . . were in general two stories in height; and some of them had stone staircases on the outside. The dwellings were encompassed by a wall of which the whole

circumference was little less than a mile. On the bastions were planted culverins and sakers presented by the wealthy guilds of London to the colony. On some of these ancient guns, which have done memorable service to a great cause, the devices of the Fishmongers' Company, of the Vintners' Company, and of the Merchant Tailors' Company are still discernible.

The inhabitants were Protestants of Anglosaxon blood. They were indeed not all of one country or of one church, but Englishmen and Scotchmen, Episcopalians and Presbyterians, seem to have generally lived together in friendship, a friendship which is sufficiently explained by their common antipathy to the Irish race and to the Popish religion. During the rebellion of 1641, Londonderry had resolutely held out against the native chieftains, and had been repeatedly besieged in vain. Since the Restoration the city had prospered. The Foyle, when the tide was high, brought up ships of large burden to the quay. The fisheries throve greatly ... The quantity of salmon caught annually was estimated at eleven hundred thousand pounds' weight.[83]

Macaulay was setting the stage for his account of James II's Irish Wars and the Battle of the Boyne. There can be no better introduction to 'the troubles' and the Orange Marches which go on in Derry/Londonderry to the present day.

Generally speaking, English historical fiction has steered clear of the seventeenth century. Despite the turbulence of the times, which lend themselves to tales of adventure and romance, English literature does not possess anything to match the subject matter of an Alexandre Dumas (1802–70) or a Henryk Sienkiewicz (1846–1916).[84] The number of historical novels which take the Civil Wars as their setting, for example, can be counted on the fingers of one hand.

Since the seventeenth century was an age of rampant superstition, witchcraft has been a topic of interest and concern not just for historians but for writers in general. It had a special appeal for the 'Gothick Imagination' of the Romantic period. Here, the central position is W. Harrison Ainsworth's *The Lancashire Witches* (1849), which examines the episode that ended with the execution of the Pendle witches at Lancaster Castle in 1612. Ainsworth's cumbersome novel was hugely popular with the mid-Victorians, but it did not preserve its appeal. More attractive to modern readers is Robert Neill's *Mist over Pendle* (1951), which combines a fine knowledge of local history with a convincing picture of pre-industrial Lancashire.[85]

Sir Walter Scott started his literary career not as a novelist but as an aspiring poet. And the setting for one of his long and aspiring poems, *Rokeby* (1813), was the Battle of Marston Moor:

> XII
>
> Would'st hear the tale? – On Marston heath
> Met, front to front, the ranks of death:
> Flourish'd the trumpets fierce, and now
> Fired was each eye, and flush'd each brow.
> On either side loud clamours ring,
> 'God and the Cause!' – 'God and the King!'
> Right English all, they rush'd to blows,
> With naught to win, and all to lose.
> I could have laugh'd – but lack'd the time –
> To see in phrenesy sublime,
> How the fierce zealots fought and bled,
> For king or state, as humour led;
> Some for a dream of public good,
> Some for church-tippet, gown and hood,
> Draining their veins, in death to claim
> A patriot's or a martyr's name.[86]

Scott admits that he could have laughed. By his time, religious warfare was seen to be ridiculous. In any case, he felt more at ease as a novelist and in his native country.

A Legend of Montrose (1819), like *Rokeby*, was set in 1644, but in the Western Highlands. It evokes the enterprising campaign of the Royalist Earl of Montrose against Scotland's Government of Covenanters, and the resultant warfare of clan against clan. As usual, the principal obstacle to the aspirations of the Gaelic chiefs lay in the pro-government stance of the Campbells of Argyll. One of the most colourful (and historically disputed) elements in the novel revolves round the feud of the Campbells with a force drawn from the outlawed Clan MacGregor, 'the Children of the Mist'. The fictional hero of the novel, Captain Dugald Dalgetty, has pursued a career that is soundly based on those of numerous Scottish soldiers of fortune who served in the Thirty Years War. (In his introduction, Scott quotes the authentic memoirs of the model for his hero, a certain Mungo Gray, who had served between 1626 and 1637 in MacKeye's Regiment, first under the King of Denmark and then under Gustavus Adolphus.) One of Dalgetty's chief adversaries is a historical character, James Stewart of Ardvoirlich, a murderer who was pardoned by the Scottish Parliament in 1644 and became a major in Argyle's Regiment. Scott opens the novel with a summary of the historical background:

> It was during the period of that great and bloody Civil War which agitated Britain during the seventeenth century, that our tale has its commencement. Scotland had as yet remained free from the ravages of intestine war, although its inhabitants were much divided in political opinions; and many of them ... disapproving of the bold measure adopted by sending into England a large army to the assistance of the Parliament, were determined on their part to embrace the earliest opportunity of declaring for the King, and making such a diversion as should at least compel the recall of General Leslie's army out of England ... This plan was chiefly adopted by the northern nobility, who had resisted with great obstinacy the adoption of the Solemn League and Covenant, and by many of the chiefs of the Highland clans, who conceived their interest and authority to be connected with royalty, who had, besides, a decided aversion to the Presbyterian form of religion, and who, finally, were in that half savage state of society, in which war is always more welcome than peace.
>
> Great commotions were generally expected to arise from

these concurrent causes; and the trade of incursion and depre-
dation, which the Scotch Highlanders at all times exercised
upon the Lowlands, began to assume a more steady, anowed,
and systematic form, as part of a general military system.

Those at the head of affairs were not insensible to the peril
of the moment . . . however. They considered, with satisfaction,
that no leader or name of consequence had as yet appeared to
assemble an army of Royalists. It was generally hoped that the
quartering of a sufficient number of troops in the Lowlands
adjacent to the Highland line, would have the effect of restrain-
ing the mountain chieftains . . .

In the West Highlands, [the government] numbered many
enemies; . . . yet . . . as the Campbells had already severely
humbled several of the neighbouring tribes, it was supposed
these would not readily again provoke an encounter with a body
so powerful.

Thus . . . the Scottish Convention of Estates saw no danger
sufficient to induce them to alter the line of policy . . .[87]

The culminating action of the novel, in which Dalgetty is knighted
by Montrose for his services, occurs on the first part of Montrose's
victorious march. It takes place in the Battle of Inverlochy under the
shadow of Ben Nevis:

> *As meets a rock a thousand waves, so Inisfail meets Lochlin.*
>   (Ossian)
> The trumphets and bagpipes, those clamourous harbingers of
> blood and death, at once united in the signal for onset, which
> was replied to by the cry of more than two thousand warriors,
> and the echoes of the mountain glens behind them. Divided
> into three bodies, or columns, the Highland followers of Mon-
> trose poured from the defiles which had hitherto concealed
> them from their enemies, and rushed with the utmost deter-
> mination upon the Campbells, who waited their charge with
> the greatest firmness. Behind these charging columns marched
> in line the Irish, under Colkitto, intended to form the reserve.
> With them was the royal standard, and Montrose himself; and

on the flanks were about fifty horse, under Dalgetty, which by wonderful exertions had been kept in some sort fit for service.

The right column of Royalists was led by Glengarry, the left by Lochiel, and the centre by the Earl of Menteith, who preferred fighting on foot in a Highland dress to remaining with the cavalry.

The Highlanders poured on with the proverbial fury of their country, firing their guns, and discharging their arrows, at a little distance from the enemy, who received the assault with the most determined gallantry. Better provided with musketry than their enemies, stationary also, and therefore taking the more decisive aim, the fire of Argyle's followers was more destructive than that which they sustained. The royal clans, perceiving this, rushed to close quarters, and succeeded on two points in throwing their enemies into disorder. With regular troops this must have achieved a victory; but here Highlanders were opposed to Highlanders, and the nature of the weapons, as well as the agility of those who wielded them, was equal on both sides.

Their strife was accordingly desperate; and the clash of the swords and axes, as they encountered each other, or rung upon the targets, was mingled with the short, wild, animating shrieks with which Highlanders accompany the battle, the dance, or indeed violent exertion of any kind. . . . A steam, like that which arises from a seething cauldron, rose into the thin, cold, frosty air, and hovered above the combatants. . . .

The Marquis of Montrose, in the meanwhile, availing himself of some scattered birch trees, as well as of the smoke produced by the close fire of the Irish musketry, . . . called upon Dalgetty to follow him with the horse, and wheeling round, . . . he commanded his six trumpets to sound the charge. The clang of the cavalry trumpets, and the noise of the galloping of the horse, produced an effect upon Argyle's right wing which no other sounds could have impressed them with. The mountaineers of that period had a superstitious dread of the war-horse, like that entertained by the Peruvians, and had many strange ideas respecting the manner in which that animal was trained to combat. When, therefore, they found, . . . that the objects of their greatest terror were suddenly in the midst of them, the panic, in spite of Sir Duncan's attempts to stop it, became universal. Indeed, the figure of Major Dalgetty alone, sheathed in impenetrable armour, and making his horse caracole and bound, so as to give weight to every blow which he struck, would have been a novelty in itself sufficient to terrify those who had never seen anything more nearly resembling such a cavalier, than a *shelty* waddling under a Highlander far bigger than itself. The repulsed Royalists returned to the charge; the Irish, keeping their ranks, maintained a fire equally close and destructive. There was no sustaining the fight longer. Argyle's followers began to break and fly, most towards the lake, the remainder in different directions.

The Knight of Ardenvohr, with two or three hundred men, all gentlemen of descent and distinguished gallantry, – for the Campbells are supposed to have had more gentlemen in their ranks than any of the Highland clans, – endeavoured, with unavailing heroism, to cover the tumultuary retreat of the common file. . . .

'Good quarter, Sir Duncan,' called out Major Dalgetty . . . Sir Duncan's reply was the discharge of a reserved pistol, which took effect not on the person of the rider, but on that of his gallant horse, . . . Ranald MacEagh, who was one of those who had been pressing Sir Duncan hard, took the opportunity to cut him down with his broadsword . . .

Allan M'Aulay came up at this moment. They were, excepting Ranald, followers of his brother who were engaged on that part of the field. 'Villains!' he said, 'which of you has dared to do this, when it was my positive order that the Knight of Ardenvohr should be taken alive?'

Half-a-dozen of busy hands, which were emulously employed in plundering the fallen knight, whose arms and accoutrements were of a magnificence befitting his quality,

instantly forbore the occupation, . . . laying the blame on the
Skyeman, as they called Ranald MacEagh.

'Dog of an Islander!' said Allan, . . . 'follow the chase, and
harm him no farther, unless you mean to die by my hand.' . . .
The moment was tempting to MacEagh's vengeful spirit – 'That
I should die by your hand, red as it is with the blood of my
kindred,' said he, answering the threat of Allan in a tone as
menacing as his own, 'is not more likely than that you should
fall by mine.' With that, he struck at M'Aulay with such
unexpected readiness, that he had scarce time to intercept the
blow with his target.

'Villain!' said Allan, in astonishment, 'what means this?'

'I am Ranald of the Mist!' answered the Islesman, repeating
the blow; and with that word, they engaged in close and furious
conflict . . .[88]

R. D. Blackmore's ever popular novel *Lorna Doone* (1869) deals
with a different decade and with another romantic location at the
other end of Great Britain. The setting is in Exmoor in Somerset in
the 1680s, in the time of Monmouth's Rebellion. In this epic
romance of seventy-five chapters, Blackmore relates the trials and
tribulations of a worthy farmer's son, John Ridd, and of his love for
the beautiful Lorna, an orphan girl kidnapped by outlaws. Viewed
through the eyes of John Ridd, the narrator, the story is richly
coloured by descriptions of the wild landscape, by the tangy Somerset dialect, in which many of the characters speak, and by the
political and religious complications surrounding the death of
Charles II. The action starts on Exmoor, where the violent and
lawless clan of the Doones live in a remote and secret valley; but it
moves at various points to the Court of Chancery in London, whither
Ridd has to travel as a witness in court, and to the battles, skirmishes, and reprisals of Monmouth's brief campaign. Judge Jeffries,
Major John Churchill, and King James II are all among the historical
figures whom Ridd encounters. 'I am a freeholder,' he answers in
confusion (when confronted by the King), 'ever since the time of
King Alfred. A Ridd was with him in the isle of Athelney, and we

hold our farm by gift of him, or so people say.' Lorna, it turns out, is a disinherited heiress, Lady Dugal, whose identity when duly proven in court opens the way to her marriage to her newly ennobled suitor.

Fiction aside, Blackmore paints some memorable historical moments. One of these, in a chapter called 'Slaughter in the Marshes', sees the narrator on the fringe of the Battle of Sedgemoor:

> Therefore I was guided mainly by the sound of guns and trumpets, in riding out of the narrow ways, and into the open marshes. And thus I might have found my road, in spite of all the spread of water, and the glaze of moonshine; but that, as I followed sound, fog (like a chestnut tree in blossom, touched with moonlight) met me. . . .
>
> It was an awful thing, I say (and to this day I remember it), to hear the sounds of raging fight, and the yells of raving slayers, and the howls of poor men stricken hard and shattered from wrath to wailing; then suddenly the dead low hush, as of a soul departing, and spirits kneeling over it.
>
> At last, when I almost despaired of escaping from this tangle of spongy banks, and of hazy creeks, and reed-fringe, my horse heard the neigh of a fellow-horse, and was only too glad to answer it; upon which the other, having lost his rider, came up, and pricked his ears at us, and gazed through the fog very steadfastly. . . . Therefore, as he might know the way, we followed him very carefully; and he led us to a little hamlet, called (as I found afterwards) West Zuland, or Zealand, so named perhaps from its situation amid this inland sea.
>
> Here the King's troops had been quite lately, and their fires were still burning; but the men themselves had been summoned away by the night attack of the rebels. Hence I procured for my guide a young man who knew the district thoroughly, and who led me by many intricate ways to the rear of the rebel army. We came upon a broad open moor, striped with sullen watercourses, shagged with sedge, and yellow iris, and in the drier

part with bilberries. For by this time it was four o'clock, and the summer sun, arising wanly, showed us all the ghastly scene.

Would that I had never been there! Often in the lonely hours, even now it haunts me: would, far more, that the piteous thing had never been done in England! Flying men, flung back from dreams of victory and honour, only glad to have the luck of life and limbs to fly with, mud-bedraggled, foul with slime, reeking both with sweat and blood, which they could not stop to wipe, cursing, with their pumped-out lungs, every stick that hindered them, or gory puddle that slipped the step, scarcely able to leap over the corses that had dragged to die . . .

'Arl oop wi Moonmo',' shouted one big fellow, a miner of the Mendip Hills, whose weapon was a pick-axe: 'na oose to vaight na moor . . .'

. . .

Then the cavalry of the King, with their horses at full speed, dashed from either side upon the helpless mob of countrymen. A few pikes feebly levelled met them; but they shot the pikemen, drew swords, and helter-skelter leaped into the shattered and scattering mass. Right and left, they hacked and hewed; I could hear the snapping of scythes beneath them . . . How it must end was plain . . .[89]

Another stirring moment, in an earlier chapter called 'The King Must Not be Prayed For', arrives when the parish of Oare first hears of the death of Charles II:

We heard of it first in church, on Sunday, the eighth day of February, 1684–5, from a cousin of John Fry, who had ridden over on purpose from Porlock. He came in just before the anthem, splashed and heated from his ride, so that every one turned and looked at him. . . . He let the anthem go by very quietly . . . and then just as Parson Bowden, with a look of pride at his minstrels, was kneeling down to begin the prayer for the King's Most Excellent Majesty (for he never read the Litany, except upon Easter Sunday), up jumps young Sam Fry, and shouts, –

'I forbid that there prai-er.'

'What!' cried the parson, rising slowly, and looking for some one to shut the door: 'have we a rebel in the congregation?' . . .

'No,' replied Sam, . . . 'no rebel, parson; but a man who mislaiketh popery and murder. That there pri-er be a prai-er for the dead.'

'Nay,' cried the parson, now recognising and knowing him . . . 'you do not mean to say, Sam, that His Gracious Majesty is dead.'

'Dead as a sto-un: poisoned by they Papishers.' And Sam rubbed his hands with enjoyment . . .

'Remember where you are, Sam,' said Parson Bowden, solemnly; 'when did this most sad thing happen? The King is head of the Church, Sam Fry; when did His Majesty leave her?'

'Day afore yesterday. Twelve o'clock. Warn't us quick to hear of 'un?'

'Can't be,' said the minister: 'the tidings can never have come so soon. Anyhow, he will want it all the more. Let us pray for His Gracious Majesty.'

And with that he proceeded as usual; but nobody cried 'Amen,' for fear of being entangled with popery.[90]

Blackmore's description rings true. Ridd is a loyal 'kingist', as he calls himself, unmoved by religious disputes. But the Doones are Catholic recusants; and the universal, irrational fear of 'Popery' is an essential element to the heightened emotions of the tale.

The events of 1688–9 inspired literary works from all ends of the Isles. In England, remembering the last of the great Cornish rebellions, R. S. Hawker (1803–75), vicar of Morwenstowe in north Cornwall, composed his 'Song of the Western Men'. Married to a Polish exile, Hawker was a High Anglican who followed Newman into Roman Catholicism and who described his Cornish parishioners as 'a mixed multitude of smugglers, wreckers and dissenters'. But he retained a soft spot for the defiance of the Seven Bishops and for Bishop Trelawny in particular:

> A good sword and a trusty hand!
> A merry heart and true!
> King James's men shall understand
> What Cornish lads can do.
>
> And have they fixed the where and when?
> And shall Trelawny die?
> Here's twenty thousand Cornishmen
> Will know the reason why!
>
> Out spoke their captain brave and bold
> A merry wight was he:
> If London Tower were Michael's hold,
> We'll set Trelawny free:
>
> We'll cross the Tamar, land to land,
> The Severn is no stay,
> With 'one and all' and hand in hand,
> And who shall bid us nay?
>
> . . .
>
> Trelawny he's in keep and hold,
> Trelawny he may die:
> But here's twenty thousand Cornish bold
> Will know the reason why![91]

For his part, Sir Walter Scott was similarly moved by the fate of Claverhouse, the Earl of Dundee, the victor and the principal casualty of Killiecrankie:

> To the Lords of Convention 'twas Claver'se who spoke
> 'Ere the King's crown shall fall, there are crowns to be broke
> So let each Cavalier who loves honour and me,
> Come follow the bonnet of Bonny Dundee.
> Come fill up my cup, come fill up my can,

Come saddle your horses, and call up your men;
Come open the West Port, and let me gang free,
And it's room for the bonnets of Bonny Dundee!'

. . .

He waved his proud hand, and the trumpets were blown,
The kettle-drums clashed, and the horsemen rode on.
Till on Ravelston's cliffs and on Clermiston's lee
Died away the wild war-notes of Bonnie Dundee![92]

Somewhat surprisingly, James II was not forgotten either. Though clearly a loser in the historical stakes, and leader of the lost Jacobite cause, who died, much maligned, in exile, his place in English history has been kept alive to the present day. His statue by the studio of Grinling Gibbons, in the guise of a Roman emperor, stands in front of the National Gallery on Trafalgar Square:

JACOBVS SECVNDUS

DEI GRATIA

ANGLIÆ SCOTIÆ

FRANCIÆ ET

HIBERNIÆ

REX

FIDEI DEFENSOR

ANNO M.D.C.LXXXVI

Few people expect descriptions of the seventeenth century to end exactly with the year 1700. All historical periods are given suitable endings according to the criteria of the periodizer: but few such endings coincide with the arbitrary divisions of the calendar. 'Long centuries' and 'short centuries' form part of the established historical vocabulary. Histories dominated by English constitutional themes tend to conclude with the 'Glorious Revolution' of 1689. Histories which follow the patterns of ruling dynasties tend to conclude in 1714 with the replacement of the Stuarts by the Hanoverians. Pepys's Diary comes to an end shortly before his death in 1703. Evelyn made his last entry on 3 February 1706. Lord Macaulay, who never reached the intended (but unstated) term of his masterwork, lived to revise his final volume up to his account of 1700 and the death of James II at Versailles. But he left a moving, but unrevised, section dealing with the final hours of his hero, King William:

On the twentieth of February [1702] William was ambling on a favourite horse, named Sorrel, through the park of Hampton Court. He urged his horse to strike into a gallop just at the spot where a mole had been at work. Sorrel stumbled on the mole-hill, and went down on his knees. The King fell off, and broke his collar bone. The bone was set; and he returned to Kensington in his coach. . . . But the frame of William was not in a condition to bear even the slightest shock. He felt that his time was short, and grieved, . . . that he must leave his work but half finished. . . .

He had long known that the relation in which England and Scotland stood to each other was at best precarious, and often unfriendly . . . Recent events had proved that, without doubt, the two kingdoms could not possibly continue for another year to be on the terms on which they had been during the preceding century, and that there must be between them either absolute union or deadly enmity . . . Their union would be the best security for the prosperity of both, for the internal tranquillity of the island, for the just balance of power among European states, and for the immunities of all Protestant countries. On the twenty-eighth of February the Commons listened with uncovered heads to the last message that bore William's sign manual. An unhappy accident, he told them, had forced him to make to them in writing a communication which he would gladly have made from the throne. He had, in the first year of his reign, expressed his desire to see an union accomplished between England and Scotland. He was convinced that nothing could more conduce to the safety and happiness of both. He should think it his peculiar felicity if, before the close of his reign, some happy expedient could be devised for making the two kingdoms one; . . . It was resolved that the message should be taken into consideration on Saturday, the seventh of March.

But on the first of March humours of menacing appearance showed themselves in the King's knee. On the fourth of March he was attacked by fever; on the fifth his strength failed greatly; and on the sixth he was scarcely kept alive by cordials . . . On the seventh of March the Lord Keeper and the clerks of the parliament . . . were detained some hours in the ante-chamber while he was in one of the paroxysms of his malady. Meanwhile the Houses were sitting. It was the day on which the Commons had resolved to take into consideration the question of the union with Scotland. But that subject was not mentioned . . . The following day was Sunday. But there was little chance that William would live through the night. It was of the highest importance that, within the shortest possible time after his decease, the successor designated by the Bill of Rights and the Act of Succession should . . . be publicly proclaimed in the Council.

The King meanwhile was sinking fast . . . His intellect was not for a moment clouded. His fortitude was the more admirable because he was not willing to die . . . From the words which escaped him he seemed to be frequently engaged in mental prayer. Bishop Burnet and [Archbishop] Tenison remained many hours in the sick room. He professed to them his firm belief in the truth of the Christian religion, and received the sacrament from their hands with great seriousness. The antechambers were crowded all night with lords and privy councillors . . . He strained his feeble voice to thank Auverquerque for the affectionate and loyal services of thirty years. To Albermarle he gave the keys of his closet, and of his private drawers. 'You know,' he said, 'what to do with them.' By this time he could scarcely respire. 'Can this,' he said to the physicians, 'last long?' He was told that the end was approaching He swallowed a cordial, and asked for Bentinck. Those were his last articulate words. Bentinck instantly came to the bedside, bent down, and placed his ear close to the King's mouth. The lips of the dying man moved; but nothing could be heard. The King took the hand of his earliest friend, and pressed it tenderly to his heart . . . He closed his eyes, and gasped for breath. The bishops knelt down and read the commendatory prayer. When it ended William was no more.

When his remains were laid out, it was found that he wore next to his skin a small piece of black silk riband. The lords in waiting ordered it to be taken off. It contained a gold ring and a lock of the hair of Mary.[93]

The Union, which King William had so fervently desired, came into being five years and two months after his death. One might imagine that it was an excellent point at which to end any account of seventeenth-century affairs. Yet it is notable that no important work written by an English historian has ever been brought to a close with the Act of Union. Almost all histories of Scotland see 1707 as a key turning point. Almost all histories of England avoid it. The Scots are well aware that in 1707 their forebears entered a new state, the united Kingdom of Great Britain, and that as from 1 May 1707 their representatives were sent to participate in a new British Parliament. Yet the English simply don't see it. Though most of their history books make some mention of the Act which created the United Kingdom and the British Empire, they are not convinced that much had changed. Their complacency is fuelled by many misunderstandings. For one thing, they have been repeatedly told that in 1707 Scotland simply 'merged' into England or that Scottish members were generously 'given the right' of sitting in the English Parliament. The fact escapes them that a treaty was signed by two independent parties to make a fresh start in a new dual partnership. For another, since the English blithely assume that to be merged into England is the height of felicity, they have been taught to believe in the seamless progress of their past. As the Victorian historian J. R. Green put it: 'All that passed away [in 1707] was the jealousy which had parted, since the days of Edward I, two peoples whom a common blood and common speech proclaimed to be one.'[94]

As a result, no English poet ever wrote an ode to celebrate the Act of Union. It was left to Scotland's national bard to denounce it, and to say in no uncertain terms what he thought of 'the rogues' who had succumbed to 'English gold':

> Fareweel to a' our Scottish fame,
>   Fareweel our ancient glory!
> Fareweel ev'n to the Scottish name,
>   Sae famed in martial story!
> Now Sark rins over Solway sands,
>   An Tweed rins to the ocean,
> To mark where England's province stands –
>   Such a parcel of rogues in a nation!
>
> What force or guile could not subdue
>   Thro' many warlike ages
> Is wrought now by a coward few
>   For hireling traitor's wages.
> The English steel we could disdain,
>   Secure in valour's station;
> But English gold has been our bane –
>   Such a parcel of rogues in a nation!
>
> O, would, or I had seen the day
>   That Treason thus could sell us,
> My auld grey head had lien in clay,
>   Wi' Bruce and loyal Wallace!
> But pith and power, till my last hour,
>   I'll mak this declaration:–
> 'We're bought and sold for English gold' –
>   Such a parcel of rogues in a nation![95]

Not everyone would want to leave the last word to the Scots' national bard. Wider reading is required, and a visit to the library The English view of the union must surely be examined. But there one runs head-on once again into the extraordinary way that historical knowledge is classified. In the subject headings of the leading library catalogues (see page xxxii, above), there is no such thing as ⟨ENGLAND – HISTORY – The Union with Scotland⟩. There is ⟨SCOTLAND – HISTORY – The Union, 1707⟩; and there is ⟨IRELAND – HISTORY – The Union, 1800⟩. But even under ⟨GREAT BRITAIN (UF England) – HISTORY⟩, there are no sub-headings for The Unions either of 1707 or of 1800. The signal is crystal clear. Scotland may have united with England in 1707; and Ireland may have united with England and Scotland in 1800. But England has never united with anyone.[96]

CHAPTER NINE

THE BRITISH IMPERIAL ISLES

c. 1700 to 1918

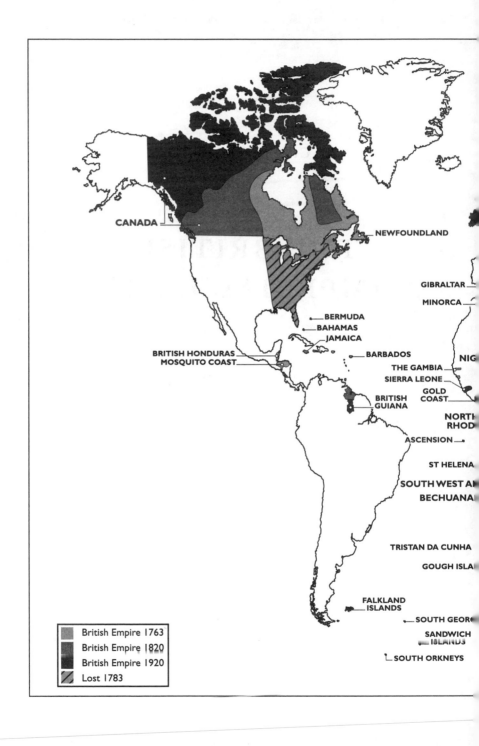

CANADA

NEWFOUNDLAND

GIBRALTAR

MINORCA

BERMUDA
BAHAMAS
JAMAICA

BARBADOS

NIG

THE GAMBIA

SIERRA LEONE

GOLD
COAST

BRITISH HONDURAS
MOSQUITO COAST

BRITISH
GUIANA

NORTH
RHOD

ASCENSION

ST HELENA

SOUTH WEST A

BECHUANA

TRISTAN DA CUNHA

GOUGH ISLA

FALKLAND
ISLANDS

SOUTH GEOR

SANDWICH
ISLANDS

SOUTH ORKNEYS

	British Empire 1763
	British Empire 1820
	British Empire 1920
	Lost 1783

THE GROWTH OF THE BRITISH EMPIRE, 1763–1920

IGOLAND

IONIAN
ISLANDS

CYPRUS
PALESTINE

WEI HAI WEI

IRAQ

INDIA

BENGAL

TRANS-JORDAN

BURMA

ADEN

HONG KONG

Bombay

SOMALILAND

Madras

MALAYA

LOCCADIVES

CEYLON

BORNEO

GILBERT
ISLANDS

NDA

KENYA

SINGAPORE

BRITISH
NEW GUINEA

MALDIVES

Fort York

NAURU

TANGANYIKA

SEYCHELLES

ELLICE
ISLAND

SOUTHERN
RHODESIA

FIJI

MAURITIUS

UNION OF
SOUTH AFRICA

AUSTRALIA

CAPE COLONY

TASMANIA

NEW ZEALAND

CROZET ISLAND

PRINCE EDWARD ISLAND

OCTOBER 1698, THE ISTHMUS OF PANAMA. After an arduous four-teen-week voyage across the Atlantic Ocean, five Scottish ships approached the coast of Central America. They were preparing to lay claim to a piece of territory at the eastern end of the Isthmus and to declare it a sovereign Scottish colony. The ships – the *Caledonia*, the *St Andrew*, the *Unicorn*, the *Dolphin*, and the *Endeavour* – had sailed from Leith, the port of Edinburgh, on 17 July. They were carrying 1,200 would-be colonists, and, as was thought, provisions for nine months. Having rounded the Orkneys and Cape Wrath, they had first made for Madeira where they took on water and fresh supplies. From Madeira, they had headed out to the Caribbean. Yet for reasons of secrecy, no one at home, and none of the ordinary passengers, had been told exactly where their destination lay. All they knew was that they were destined for a land of promise that was to be called 'New Caledonia'. They also knew that their task was to secure a preliminary landing-place. They would soon be supported by a second expedition that was fitting out before they left. As far as they were concerned, they were bound for 'El Dorado', 'the realms of gold'.

In reality, they were bound for a place whose name had already played a key role in the European exploration of America and would remain a synonym for the glorious exultation of discovery. The Spaniards who landed there in 1510 had called it Darién. Santa María del Antigua del Darién claimed to be the earliest European city in the whole of the New World. Before it was abandoned, it served as the base both for the pioneers who pressed on to found Panama City and for the party of explorers who, climbing to the mountainous ridge of the Isthmus, made the very first European sighting of the Pacific:

> Then felt I like some watcher of the skies
>   When a new planet swims into his ken:
> Or like stout Cortez when with eagle eyes
>   He stared at the Pacific – and all his men
> Look'd at each other with a wild surmise –
>   Silent, upon a peak in Darien.[1]

No matter that the poet had confused Vasco Nuñez de Balboa with Hernán Cortéz.

The voyage of 1698 represented Scotland's third or fourth attempt to emulate England's well-established colonial enterprises. Ulster apart, it had been preceded by a group of Scots settlers, who had been sent to the English colony of New Jersey in 1682, and by the abortive settlement of Stuart's Town, South Carolina, which had been wiped out in 1684 by hostile Spaniards. The Scots were well aware of the risks. They would have known that the model English colony of Virginia had only taken root at the third attempt. Like the English pioneers before them, they were well prepared for hardship, but were hoping through perseverance to reap the manifest benefits of overseas empire.

What is more, the expedition of 1698 was backed, organized, and accompanied by one of the most successful entrepreneurs of the age. William Paterson (1658–1719), known as 'the Great Projector', was a lowly farmer's son from Dumfriesshire who had made a startling career in London. Only four years earlier he had founded the greatest financial institution of the century, namely the Bank of England. So when Paterson had presented a scheme for a 'Company of Scotland', it was taken up with alacrity. The expedition to Central America was the Company's opening venture. Paterson was convinced that New Caledonia would become a thriving haven not only of international trade but also of religious toleration.

Paterson's role in the origins of the Bank of England makes an extraordinary story. He only brought his business to London after the Revolution of 1688–9, and he had no high social connections. How exactly he had made his way from rags to riches was a mystery. In later years, there would be rumours of him walking across the Border carrying a pedlar's pack, and equally of him making a fortune as a buccaneer in the West Indies. It was more likely that he had been raised by relatives in Bristol, and that he had sailed as a lad for the Americas. He had spent long enough in Boston (Massachusetts) to marry the widow of a Presbyterian minister there; and he passed enough time in Central America to possess a detailed knowledge of the region. In the 1680s he built up business contacts in several cities of northern Europe, especially in Hamburg and in Amsterdam, where he witnessed the workings of a state bank at first hand. Yet he was remembered in the early 1690s as 'the lonely Scot' forever plying his ingenious schemes in the coffee houses of Lombard Street, one of which was owned by his second wife. He had been a registered member of the Merchant Taylor's Company since the age of twenty-three; but he had made no special mark of distinction. He first came to the attention of the Government in 1692 when, amidst the rising demands of King William's War, the English Parliament formed a committee to find new methods of funding, and he was called in as a witness.

No one denies that Paterson was the originator of the project which grew into the Bank of England. The basic idea was to form a corporation of private subscribers who would create a permanent fund of capital from which the government could borrow on favourable conditions. The subscribers would earn interest on their deposits: the corporation would make a profit by charging a higher rate on its loans to the government; and the government would be assured in perpetuity of a steady source of finance. The days were numbered when kings would be forced to borrow ad hoc from London merchants, or when the City goldsmiths could be ripped off by involuntary loans to a wayward monarch – as had happened under Charles II. Yet Paterson's scheme went through several evolutions before it was found acceptable. The first version, in 1691, was snubbed as 'too Dutch'. The second version, which was considered by the Parliamentary committee, also fell on stony ground. But the third version of 1693–4 rapidly gained the most powerful patronage. The timing was perfect. Charles Montague, William and Mary's ingenious Chancellor of the Exchequer, was facing a shortfall of £1 million in government income, having pinned his hopes on a peculiar form of lottery financed from the salt tax. Montague introduced Paterson to other ministers; and Parliament proved receptive to a request for a special grant to prime the Bank's initial operations. The solution was to divert the revenue from various existing taxes and duties, in particular from the so-called 'tunnage' tax on shipping. As a result, the corporation which would soon emerge as the Bank of England was first known as 'The Tunnage Bank'; and the parliamentary bill which set it on its way had a somewhat misleading title:

> An Act for Granting to their Majesties several rates and duties upon Tunnage of ships and vessels and upon Beer, Ale, and other Liquors ... for securing certain Recompenses and Advantages ... to such persons who shall Voluntarily Advance the sum of Fifteen hundred thousand Pounds towards carrying on the War against France.[2]

The Act received the royal assent on 25 April 1694, and the subscription list was opened in the Mercers' Hall, Cheapside, at 8 a.m. on 21 June.

As Paterson had predicted, the response was phenomenal. No less than £300,000 was subscribed on day one alone. Within ten days, £1.2 million had been raised in shares ranging from the minimum of £25 to the £10,000 maximum put up by Queen Mary herself. By 27 July, 'the Governor and Company of the Bank of England' had received its royal charter. The 1,520 subscribers, who had been required to advance 25 per cent of their share in cash, were now to receive 4 per cent p.a. on their investment. The government was to pay 8 per cent p.a. on its loans plus £4,000 p.a. to cover management costs. Sir John Houblon was appointed the Bank's first governor. Twenty-four directors, who the Charter insisted must all be English subjects, were elected by the subscribers. William Paterson was one of them, which means that he must by then have become a naturalized English subject. Centuries later, when the Bank of England was judged 'the most powerful and firmly entrenched of world institutions',[3] the achievement of 'the Projector' was not forgotten. 'Few of those whose names are blazoned on the scroll of Fame', wrote one of the Bank's many historians, 'have rendered the state such solid and valuable services as this obscure adventurer.'[4]

Paterson did not tarry long in London, however. He remained as director of the Bank for only a few months before cashing in his shares and resigning his directorship. Some commentators have looked for a quarrel with his colleagues. The fact is, he had other things on his mind. His success with the Bank of England gave him the chance to press for a scheme still nearer his heart – the colony in Central America. What is more, Paterson in London had met up with another famous Scotsman of his generation, Andrew Fletcher, Laird of Saltoun (1655–1716). Fletcher happened to be the neighbour of Lord Tweeddale, Scotland's first minister. So in the spring of 1695, Paterson and Fletcher travelled to Scotland together, to seek support in the highest quarters.

Fletcher, who was to gain the sobriquet of 'the Patriot', was, like Paterson, a cosmopolitan figure. Tutored in his youth by Gilbert Burnet, who called him 'a violent republican', he spent the years of his youth adventuring on the Continent – a prisoner in Spain, a mercenary in Hungary, an exile in Brussels and Amsterdam. He joined the expeditions to England both of the Duke of Monmouth in 1685 and of William of Orange in 1688. Sentenced to death by James VII as a traitor, he was later restored to his estates and became the most vociferous Scottish parliamentarian of his day. Lord Macaulay was to describe how the 'monomanias' of Fletcher and Paterson were perfectly matched:

> Fletcher's whole soul was possessed by a sore, jealous, punctilious patriotism. His heart was ulcerated by the thought of the poverty, the feebleness, the political insignificance of Scotland, and of the indignities which she had suffered at the hands of her more powerful and opulent neighbour ... Paterson, on the other hand, firmly believed himself to have discovered the means of making any state which would follow his counsel great and prosperous.[5]

One does not have to share Macaulay's bilious view of Scottish patriots to agree that this fine pair of obsessives were well met.

Scotland in 1695, unlike England, was not at war. But she was experiencing extreme hardship. Her export trade with the Continent was being ruined by the English blockade. Her people were facing starvation in many parts due to the failed harvests of 'the seven ill years'; and, in the aftermath of the Revolutionary Settlement, they stood on the verge of renewed violence. The Highlands were still restless. Scotland's chief minister, the Lord High Commissioner Lord Tweeddale, was under intense pressure to take action against the perpetrators of the Massacre of Glencoe. On the eve of a meeting of the Scottish Parliament, he was looking for a miracle. Paterson's colonial scheme was just what he needed. In the opening session of that year's Parliament, he announced that a bill for promoting a Scottish colony would be introduced forthwith.

Paterson's obsession with the colonial potential of Central America went back more than a decade. He had expended much energy in the 1680s searching in vain for Continental sponsorship. In the 1690s, in London, he had shelved his plans, but not abandoned them. Indeed, when the Scottish Parliament in 1693 had passed an Act to Encourage Foreign Trade, promising government support for colonial ventures, he would probably have jumped at the opportunity but for his preoccupations with the Bank of England. As soon as the Bank was launched, therefore it was natural that he reverted to his earlier concerns. His choice of Panama was based on the calculation that a short porterage of goods across the Isthmus would link the Atlantic trade with the Pacific, thereby reopening the dream of Columbus for a direct western route to the Orient:

> For this purpose it was necessary to occupy in America some spot which might be a resting place between Scotland and India. It was true that almost every habitable part of America had already been seized by some European power. Paterson, however, imagined that one province had been overlooked ... The isthmus which joined the two great continents of the New World remained, according to him, unappropriated. Great Spanish viceroyalties, he said, lay on the east and on the west; but the mountains and forests of Darien were abandoned to rude tribes which followed their own usages and obeyed their own princes.
>
> The havens, he averred, were capacious and secure: the sea swarmed with turtle: the country was so mountainous that, within nine degrees of the equator, the climate was temperate; and yet the inequalities of the ground offered no impediment to the conveyance of goods. Nothing would be easier than to construct roads along which a string of mules or a wheeled carriage might in the course of a single day pass from sea to sea. The soil was, to the depth of

several feet, a rich black mould, on which a profusion of valuable
herbs and fruits grew spontaneously, and yet the exuberant fertilities
of the earth had not tainted the purity of the air. Considered merely
as a place of residence, the isthmus was a paradise. But agriculture
was a secondary object in the colonization of Darien. Let but that
precious neck of land be occupied by an intelligent, an enterprising,
a thrifty race; and, in a few years, the whole trade between India
and Europe must be drawn to that point. The tedious and perilous
passage round Africa would soon be abandoned. The merchant
would no longer expose his cargoes to the mountainous billows and
capricious gales of the Antarctic seas. The greater part of the voyage
from Europe to Darien, and the whole voyage from Darien to the
richest kingdoms of Asia, would be a rapid yet easy gliding before
the trade winds over blue and sparkling waters. The voyage back
across the Pacific would, in the latitude of Japan, be almost equally
speedy and pleasant. Time, labour, money, would be saved. The
returns would come in more quickly. Fewer hands would be required
to navigate the ships. The loss of a vessel would be a rare event.
The trade would increase fast. In a short time it would double; and
it would all pass through Darien. Whoever possessed that door of
the sea, that key of the universe, — such were the bold figures which
Paterson loved to employ, — would give law to both hemispheres;
and would, by peaceful arts, without shedding one drop of blood,
establish an empire as splendid as that of Cyrus or Alexander.

Of the kingdoms of Europe, Scotland was, as yet, the poorest
and the least considered. If she would but occupy Darien, if she
would but become one great free port, one great warehouse, she
would at once take her place in the first rank among nations. No
rival would be able to contend with her either in the West Indian or
in the East Indian trade. The beggarly country, as it had been
insolently called, would be the great mart for all the choicest luxuries.
From Scotland would come all the finest jewels and brocade worn by
duchesses at the balls of St. James's and Versailles. From Scotland
would come all the saltpetre which would furnish the means of war
to the fleets and armies of contending potentates. There would be a
prosperity of which every Scotchman, from the peer to the cadie,

would partake. Edinburgh would vie with London and Paris; and the baillie of Glasgow or Dundee would have as stately and well furnished a mansion and as fine a gallery of pictures, as any burgomaster of Amsterdam.[6]

Once again, one need not share Macaulay's satirical inclinations to recognize the heady mixture of rationality and delusion which drove Paterson forward.

The session of 1695 proved one of the most productive in the history of the Scottish Parliament. Three remarkable acts were passed in a matter of weeks. One of them created the Bank of Scotland, an institution that has long outlasted the government which it was originally designed to serve. Another, the Act for the Settling of Schools, was similarly ahead of its time. It ordained that every parish in the land should build a schoolhouse and pay for the upkeep of a schoolteacher. By general consent, it ensured that within a generation the population of Scotland was among the best educated in Europe. Most famously, a third act created the 'Company of Scotland Tradeing with Affrice and the Indies'. Yet before deciding that the Scots were passing through a phase of untrammelled enlightenment, it is perhaps worth remembering that Edinburgh in 1695 also saw the burning of sixty-three alleged witches and the hanging of a penitent youth for blasphemy. Scotland was desperate. And desperation underlay the various remedies, whether wise or woeful, which were put forward in rapid succession.

The 'Company of Scotland' was not launched simply as the vehicle for Paterson's scheme. It was clearly intended to prepare the legal groundwork for a worldwide Scottish empire – in other words to give Scotland the same imperial capacity that England already possessed. The Act of 26 June 1695,[7] which brought the Company into existence, awarded it the most lavish, global powers. In addition to a thirty-one-year monopoly on Scotland's foreign trade outside Europe, a twenty-one-year exemption from taxes and import duties, and a ten-year licence to build and fit out ships, the Company was given the right to take possession of any 'uninhabited territories'.

The small print of these clauses merited careful examination. Despite the Company's misleading title, the trade monopoly was explicitly directed to 'the Americas' as well as to Africa and Asia. The licence for building ships specifically mentioned warships as well as merchantmen. And 'uninhabited territory' was manifestly not the same as 'unclaimed', 'ungoverned', or 'lordless' territory. As would soon be pointed out in London, there were districts in the Scottish Highlands which were uninhabited but where foreign colonists were unlikely to be welcome. For the time being, of course, all the clauses were hypothetical. But they gave some indication of the planners' intentions. The company's capital was to be raised by public subscription. The Act did not supply details or limitations to this operation, except that any capital raised was to be 'free from arrest'. Yet the fact that a subscription book was first opened in London shows that hopes were primarily directed at the English rather than at the Scottish money market. No lawyer could have failed to notice that any London-based operation would be subject to English law, not to a Scottish statute.

When the Company of Scotland opened its subscription book in London on 13 November 1695, two things happened. First, a flood of investors came forward and quickly took up the whole capital issue of £300,000. Secondly, a howl of protest arose from the English commercial interest. The East India Company, in particular, objected that its rights and interests were being infringed. The House of Lords debated the issue, and all the Company's London-based directors were summoned to appear before it under threat of impeachment. In December, a joint delegation of the English Lords and Commons travelled to the Netherlands to lodge a complaint with King William. They persuaded him to issue a statement declaring himself 'ill-served in Scotland'. As a result, all the English investors in the 'Company of Scotland' were forced to withdraw; and the London end of the Company's business collapsed.

In Scots eyes, the reaction in London to the attempted float constituted yet another case of English bullying. This may well be true. Yet the Company's directors had been injudicious in several regards. In a mercantile age, when every nation's wealth was thought to be finite, they can hardly have been surprised by the anxieties raised about plans that seemed to be using English capital for Scottish purposes. Many English people sincerely believed that 'their money' was being used to undermine their own prosperity. At the same time, the Scots were extremely unwise to have gone ahead without the express approval of King William. Although the Act of 1695 had been touched by the royal sceptre (in the Scottish equivalent to the English ritual of royal assent), and was therefore perfectly legal, it had not been presented to King William in detail. If it had, it would undoubtedly have been amended, especially on those points which loaded the crown with open-ended commitments. It was all very well for the Act to state that the crown would make reparation to the Company for losses inflicted by foreign powers. King William, as King of an impoverished Scotland, could only have made such reparations from his English or his Dutch resources. And in the middle of his French War, he had no intention of doing either. What is more, for the Scottish Parliament to have underwritten the company at the crown's expense, and then to have offered the King in return one hogshead of tobacco per annum, was to add insult to injury. From the King's point of view, it was a very bad deal.

Nonetheless, when the Company's subscription book was reopened in Edinburgh on 26 February 1696, the response was electric. Hundreds flocked to hand over their savings with no questions asked. Hundreds of others were won over by a hard-headed advertising campaign:

> This Company . . . is calculat for the general interest of Our Nation . . . Our Nobility and Gentry who are Landed Men will get their rents better paid and raised . . . The Poor will hereby find Work and Food.[8]

The dominant slogan declared, 'Trade begets trade, and money begets money.' Within a couple of weeks, the total issue of £400,000 had been taken up. 'Perhaps a quarter of [Scotland's] liquid assets were sunk into the enterprise.' The list of subscribers reads like a roll-call of Scottish high society. Maximum shares of £3,000 each were bought by Lord Belhaven, Lord Basil Hamilton, Anne, Duchess of Hamilton, the Duke of Queensberry, the Royal Burrows, the 'Town of Glasgow', the 'Good Town of Edinburgh' . . . Lesser shares, from £2,000 to £100, were bought by everyone from 'William Arbuckle, merchant of Glasgow', to 'Rachel Zeamen, relict of

Mr. George Forster of Knap'.[9] After the end of July, no further subscriptions were accepted. Despite London's cold shoulder, the Company of Scotland had reached its objective. In its moment of supreme confidence, it even approved an issue of paper banknotes.

William Paterson's experiences in that year were not so euphoric. After handing the Company all his papers relating to Darién, he sailed for Hamburg, confident of finding the German and Dutch financial support that had eluded him earlier. He also handed a very large sum of the Company's money to an acquaintance, James Smith, whom he commissioned to make the first purchases for the expedition. When he set up his office in Hamburg, he found that all the local merchants and money-men were deterred by the hostile propaganda of the English resident in the city, Sir Paul Ryant. When he returned to Edinburgh, he learned that James Smith had embezzled the Company's money and disappeared to London. A committee of inquiry acquitted Paterson of any wrongdoing. But it stripped him of office in the Company, thereby leaving plans for the expedition at the mercy of people with rather different priorities. In particular, it opened the way for the infiltration of the expedition by Presbyterian zealots who put missionary zeal above the commercial spirit or brotherly love. These changes could only have bolstered the Company's subsequent decision to postpone all other projects and to pour all its resources into the one expedition to Darién.

The first half of 1698 was spent recruiting personnel and loading the five ships with supplies. For some reason, the meagre provisions were swelled by a large store of bedroom slippers, woollen plaids, and fashionable periwigs. The management of the expedition was entrusted to a Council of Seven. The naval officers were headed by Commodore Robert Pennecuik, a quarrelsome man, who had served in the English Royal Navy. He was destined to quarrel with all his fellow officers, especially with Captain Robert Jolly and with Captain Robert Drummond, commander of the *Caledonia*. The military officers were dominated by Campbells from the regiment of the Duke of Argyll. Among them was Captain Drummond's brother, Thomas, who had taken part in the Massacre of Glencoe. The religious ministers were all drawn from the Presbyterian Kirk of Scotland. Among them was the Revd Francis

Borland, who sailed with the second expedition – one of the few to survive. They insisted on loading a huge cargo of English-language Bibles, which would prove of little use either to the illiterate natives of Darién or to the large contingent of Gaelic-speaking Catholics. The ordinary colonists were drawn from every section of Scottish society. They included many penniless sons of aristocratic families seeking their fortune, and many ex-soldiers. Among them was William Paterson, his new English wife, and their infant son. They all sailed in the greatest fervour of expectation.

Only when the fleet left Madeira were the captains empowered to open the second set of secret orders and to learn of their true destination in Darién. Until then, the majority view that they were headed for the Americas had been offset by a persistent rumour that they would sail south from Madeira to the Cape of Good Hope and thence across the Indian Ocean to one of the uninhabited Spice Islands. As it was, the initial landfall proved an exercise in comedy:

> From Madeira the adventurers ran across the Atlantic, landed on an uninhabited islet lying between Porto Rico and St. Thomas, took possession of this desolate spot in the name of the Company, set up a tent, and hoisted the white cross of St. Andrew. Soon, however, they were warned off by an officer who was sent from St. Thomas to inform them that they were trespassing on the territory of the King of Denmark.[10]

Fortunately, the mishap had been observed by the pirate ship of one William Alliston, who was known to Paterson from earlier days and who had been shadowing the fleet with interest. Only two years before, a force of buccaneers had seized and burned the port of Cartagena. Alliston agreed to act as pilot. Hence it was under the guidance of a buccaneer that the worthy Scots finally dropped anchor in the Gulf of Darién on 2 November 1698.

The first weeks of the colony were tolerable enough. Commander Pennecuik surveyed the shoreline and discovered a harbour 'fit for a thousand sail'. The natives were friendly, and understood the Spanish of the expedition's interpreter. Their chief, Andreas, seemed pleased that the 'new buccaneers' were not Spaniards; and he seemed to agree to the proffered 'treaty'. A long promontory of some thirty acres was selected for the main settlement, and a line of palm-leaf huts was laid out on the leeward side as the centre of the future New Edinburgh. A defensive point called Fort St Andrew was built on a rock at the end of the promontory, and a deep fortified trench was dug to protect it from land attack. The Council of the colony announced that the colonists were freemen and could elect deputies to a Parliament. In due course, a tiny assembly of eight members enacted the colony's thirty-four Rules and Ordinances. Under the influence of the Presbyterian ministers, it was declared that the colony would be ruled by the precepts of Holy Scripture. Hard labour awaited anyone found guilty of profanity, blasphemy, or disrespect to superiors. Death awaited murderers, rapists, robbers, duellers, brawlers, and anyone who corresponded with the colony's enemies. Under Paterson's influence, the colonists' civil liberties were also defined. Everyone was to enjoy the right of trial by jury, and freedom from arbitrary arrest or restraint of property for unproven debt.

Such high-minded considerations, however, were soon overtaken by dire necessity. New Caledonia was assailed by every form of adversity — sickness, disease, tropical storms, starvation, siege, isolation, and internal quarrels. Paterson's clerk, Thomas Fenner, died on the very first night in Darién. Paterson's wife and child followed him to the grave soon afterwards. Dysentery was taking hold. Incessant rain rendered regular work, let alone Scottish-style agriculture, impossible. Worst of all, an early audit revealed that the ships were carrying barely a third of the planned provisions, and that much of the existing food stores were rotten. Half-fed people submitted rapidly to disease. The first executive decision of the Parliament was to demand a search of the ships' holds. The search found that Commodore Pennecuik and Captain Drummond had been hoarding food for their own use. So the colonists fell out with their officers. And Pennecuik quarrelled violently with the Drummonds. An expected relief ship, the *Dispatch*, did not arrive. Unbeknown to the colonists, it had been wrecked on the coast of Islay before leaving Scottish waters. Similarly, the *Dolphin*, when sent for supplies to Cartagena, disappeared without trace. It had been captured by the Spaniards; and its captain and crew were languishing in jail. In February and March, the colony was besieged by a small Spanish force sent out from Panama. The colonists drove the besiegers off. But they now knew for certain that their 'uninhabited' paradise was not unclaimed. After six months, the dispirited population was dwindling fast. New Edinburgh's cemetery contained over three hundred graves.

Early in May, delirious from fever, Paterson penned an appeal to be taken by a relief sloop that was leaving for Jamaica:

> I hope ere this comes to head that Scotland will be sufficiently concerned and busy to support us who are now at the head of the best and greatest undertaking that was ever to the Indies. I assure you that if they do supply us powerfully and speedily we shall in a few months be able to re-imburse them all and make the Company the best fund of any in Europe. But if . . . this little thing should be neglected, then what we have sown others will reap the fruit of . . .[11]

The sloop did not return. No fresh supplies were landed. Two weeks later, a small two-masted boat, a *piragua*, was sent out from New Caledonia. Within a few days it was back with the most bone-chilling news. It had met an English ship whose master gave him a copy of a proclamation recently issued by the English Governor of Jamaica:

> IN HIS MAJESTY'S NAME and by command, strictly to command His Majesty's subjects, . . . that they do not presume, on any pretence whatsoever, to hold any correspondence with the said Scots, nor to give them any assistance of arms, ammunition, provisions, or any other necessaries . . . either by themselves or any other for them, or by any of their vessels, or of the English nation, as they will answer the contempt of His Majesty's command, at their utmost peril.[12]

The proclamation would not have been read over too many times before the realization dawned of what was happening. Far from assisting the Scots colonists, the English government had adopted a deliberate policy of driving them out. The Governor of Jamaica was not acting in isolation. He was following orders issued by the Secretary of State, James

Vernon. All the governors of all the English colonies from Massachusetts southwards would be taking the same line. They would not assist New Caledonia, and they would not prevent the Spaniards from taking armed action against it. The Council of the colony decided on abandonment. Most of the surviving colonists were aboard their four remaining ships when a French ship put into the bay with still more depressing news. A Spanish assault force was about to leave Cartagena. Further delay was pointless. Captain Drummond gave the fateful order to weigh anchor. At the last moment, still delirious, William Paterson was carried aboard, protesting to the last.

Meanwhile, oblivious of the events in Central America, the Company was taking steps to send belated reinforcements. Two small relief ships reached New Caledonia in August with supplies and 300 extra colonists. The *Olive Branch* caught fire within sight of the deserted settlement. The *Hopeful Binning* retreated to the mercy of the English in Jamaica. The long-delayed second expedition, consisting of four ships and 1,300 colonists, reached New Caledonia in November. The *Rising Sun*, the *Duke of Hamilton*, the *Hope of Bo'ness*, and the *Hope* had made excellent time in a nine-week crossing, having sailed directly from the Clyde without waiting for confirmation of the ominous rumours. They were met by Thomas Drummond, who had made it to New York with the *Caledonia* and returned with two sloops. Later, they were joined by Colonel Alexander Campbell, who gave them the will to fight. Together they rebuilt Fort St Andrew, and awaited the expected Spanish attack. The chances of holding out were slim. Five hundred surplus men and women were packed off to Jamaica, and in 1700 Colonel Campbell briefly took the initiative by successfully attacking the Spanish positions at Toubacanti. But in March 1700 two fresh Spanish forces landed, and after a month of siege, intermittent fighting, and recurrent truces, the Articles of Capitulation were agreed. The Spanish commander, Don Juan Pimienta, was generous. The Scots were allowed to sail off with their ships, their guns, their men, and their remaining stores. The name of New Caledonia was to be completely forgotten until reinvented by Captain Cook seventy-four years later when naming a Polynesian island on the other side of the world.

The worst horrors of the Darién disaster, however, were only just beginning. On leaving New Caledonia, the Scots fugitives from Darién faced a terrible dilemma. They could steer for the nearest port, Cartagena, where they would probably be cast into a Spanish dungeon. They could run for Jamaica, where they would face the callous ban of the English authorities. Or they could risk the long Atlantic voyage. Apart from the *Caledonia*, which recrossed the ocean to Scotland via New York, none of the Company's unrepaired ships was fully seaworthy. Their dirty, over-congested holds bred dysentery still more efficiently than the rain-soaked huts of New Edinburgh. One of the ships from the first expedition's fleet, the leaking *Endeavour*, sank slowly to the bottom of the Caribbean. The *Saint Andrew* limped pathetically into Jamaica after seven weeks on the crossing. A hundred and fifty men, and all her naval officers, including Commander Pennecuik, had died. Her replacement commander, Captain Colin Campbell, went ashore, and rode for help to Port Royal (now Kingston):

> In a fine white house above the fort [the Governor], Sir William Beeston received him cordially. A glass of wine, a pipe of tobacco, and an exchange of courtesies, however, were all he was prepared to give the Scot. 'He could by no means suffer me to dispose of any goods for supplying my men, although they should starve.'[13]

Admiral Benbow, riding at anchor in Port Royal harbour, similarly refused assistance. The Royal Navy was unsympathetic because the Spaniards were exacting reprisals on Jamaican shipping 'in the outrageous belief that there was no difference between an Englishman and a Scot'.[14] So Campbell's ship was abandoned. Her remaining crew melted away. Many of the sick were carried ashore to die in the garden of a compassionate English lady. Some sold themselves into slavery on the plantations, or joined the pirates. Others signed on with Admiral Benbow.

The *Unicorn*, in contrast, had sailed north. Dismasted off Cuba, driven out of Matanzas Bay by Spanish musketry, and repeatedly grounded on the coast of Virginia, she miraculously made it to New York only ten days after the *Caledonia*. Over half her complement was dead. She was abandoned as a wreck. But she had fared better than the ships of the second expedition. The *Hope of Bo'ness* was seized by the Spaniards at Cartagena. The *Rising Sun* and the *Duke of Hamilton* were both lost during a hurricane in Charleston harbour. The *Hope* was wrecked with all hands off Cuba. In all, by the end of 1700 only one ship from the Company's two fleets was still afloat. Only a handful of the 3,000 Scots who had set out to make a new life in the colony were still alive.

Morally, still harsher news awaited. When the one surviving ship, the *Caledonia*, docked in at Clydeside on 21 November 1699 there was no rejoicing and no gratitude. The captain, Robert Drummond, had brought his ship home, but only through imposing the most horrendously brutal regime, reminiscent of a slave ship. On the voyage to New York, he had lost 116 men. On the Atlantic crossing, he ordered the sick and dying to be laid out on the open deck on part rations:

> When they complein, to console or comfort them – sweet Christian-like consolation! – 'Dogs! It's too good for you!' Their visits from officers and surgeons were, in the morning, questioning, how many are to be thrown abroad? Answer 4, or perhaps 5. 'Why,' reply they, 'what no more?'[15]

Even the relatives of the survivors were unforgiving. They were told that New Caledonia had failed through the work of cowards, swindlers, traitors, and deserters. In some cases, having lost all their savings, they refused to take in their returning kinsfolk. Paterson, who had reached New York in the *Unicorn* and the Clyde in the *Caledonia*, was barely breathing. He rested in an inn, then crawled for fourteen days from Glasgow to Edinburgh to make his report.

The political fallout of the Darién disaster adversely affected several different spheres. It soured King William's later years. It complicated international affairs at a sensitive moment. And it brought Anglo-Scottish relations to their lowest point since Cromwell's invasion of Scotland in the 1650s.

William III and II was caught in the trap which ultimately derived from the legislative independence of his English and Scottish Parliaments. Frequently abroad on Continental campaigns, or in his Dutch homeland, he had to rely on royal commissioners to keep him informed and his interests safeguarded; but he had no means to guarantee that England and Scotland would always pursue compatible policies. The Darién Scheme revealed this weakness in the most painful manner; and it locked him into commitments that could not be honoured. In October 1699, he received loyal addresses both from the Scottish Parliament and from the Company of Scotland begging him to grant New Caledonia his protection. But the Scots of New Caledonia needed protection not only from Spain but also from his own English government. So he had to refuse. In December he issued a stern warning of his displeasure if he were to be pressured by any further addresses of that sort. He was left with the conviction that a constitutional union between his two disaffected kingdoms was imperative. Twice in the final years of his reign, he was to launch unheeded proposals for an Anglo-Scottish Union.

At the time when the Company of Scotland was formed, England and the Netherlands were at war with France and at peace with Spain. The last thing they wanted was an incident which might rally Spain to the side of Louis XIV. The English government reduced this danger by indulging Spanish interests in the Caribbean at the expense of Scots. The Treaty of Ryswick (1697) supplied a breathing space. But the Darién Scheme was still in being when the next bone of contention arose over the ramifications of the unsettled Spanish Succession. King William had joined in an international consortium to divide up the Spanish empire. Darién had certainly added to the general tension when the Spanish Ambassador at Whitehall, the Marquess of Canales, delivered a vehement protest about English meddling in Spain's most sovereign affairs. The English Ambassador was recalled from Madrid, and Canales was expelled. At that juncture, in the summer of 1700, King William's poor standing in Scotland was matched by his much reduced popularity in England. The House of Commons demanded the removal of his Dutch Guard from Whitehall. On the eve of yet another European war, the complex network of animosity between the King and his two kingdoms was extremely disadvantageous for all concerned.

Bad luck, bad judgement, and sheer bad management had all undoubtedly played their part in the Darién disaster. But in the years when the facts became more widely known, Scottish opinion became ever more convinced that the critical factor lay in England's bad faith. It was disappointing enough that the English Parliament had ruined the original attempt to launch the Company of Scotland as an Anglo-Scottish joint venture. It was appalling that the King's English ministers had abandoned hundreds of his Scottish subjects to their death by denying them vital assistance. But the deepest pit of treachery was felt when suspicions emerged that England had been planning all the time to take Darién for herself. These suspicions could not yet be substantiated. But they were well founded. In his orders of 1699 to the English colonial governors, Vernon had publicly justified his policy of non-assistance on the grounds that the Scots in New Caledonia had violated the territorial rights of His Most Catholic Majesty, the King of Spain. In reality, neither he nor his fellow English ministers were genuinely persuaded of that view. On the contrary, they were all well aware that just two years earlier, in September 1697, the English Commissioners for Trade had advised the King that Darién was *not* possessed by Spain. What is more, the Commissioners had advised that Darién should be occupied by England with all possible speed – 'lest the Scotch be there before us, which is of the utmost importance to the trade of England'.[16] In other words, if England had not been preoccupied by the French War, the Scots fleet might well have been greeted in the Gulf of Darién by English gunfire. With friends like that, Scotland needed no enemies.

The full story would only come out much later, of course. For the time being, Scotland was bathed in tears, anger, and bewilderment. People felt much, but understood little. The Revd Frances Borland returned from New Caledonia with Paterson. As a member of the Calvinist predestined, he took the disaster to be God's judgement on other people's sins. He wrote the longest of eyewitness accounts, couched quite literally in the language of the Old Testament. He richly deserved Macaulay's parody:

> On his first arrival, he tells us, he found New Edinburgh a Ziklag.
> He had subsequently been compelled to dwell in the tents of Kedar.
> Once, indeed, during his sojourn, he had fallen in with a Beer-lahai-roi, and had set up his Ebenezer: but in general Darien was to him
> a Magor Missabib, a Kibroth-hattaavah. The sad story is introduced

with the words in which a great man of old, delivered over to the malice of the Evil Power, was informed of the death of his children and of the ruin of his fortunes: 'I alone am escaped to tell thee.'[17]

This was no preparation for the most critical phase of Scotland's modern history.

England's Act of Succession (1701) was passed on the assumption that Scotland would simply fall into line. Though the English Parliamentarians had treated King William's overtures about union with studied neglect, they took it for granted that the views of the Scots did not really matter. Theirs was a serious misreading not only of the Scottish mood but also of the legal position. The Scots did *not* have a record of simply falling into line. Indeed, on the last three occasions when the royal succession had been questioned, Scotland had followed its own distinct policy. In 1651, the Scottish Parliament had recognized Charles II nine years in advance of its English counterpart. In 1689, the Scottish Convention Parliament did not imitate the English fiction concerning King James's alleged abdication. Instead, it made a ringing declaration about the *deposition* of King James, thereby postulating the claim that a monarch only reigned in Scotland by permission of Parliament. It did not agree to install William and Mary until a two-year wrangle over the religious and financial terms was settled. In 1694, when William succeeded in his own right after Mary's death, the Scots Parliament gave notice yet again that the future of the monarchy in Scotland was subject to Scottish legislation. Hence by taking unilateral action on the succession, the English politicians were casting hostages to fortune. By nominating the Hanoverians as heirs to the throne of England, but without waiting for clarification of Scottish views, they risked a serious rift. Indeed, they soon discovered that Scotland would not follow suit automatically. They fired a debate in Scotland which would last for six years. It was a debate in which William Paterson would be firmly in favour of constitutional union and his old partner, Fletcher of Saltoun, would be passionately against.

It is hard to imagine the deep contempt in which Scotland was held by most English people of the period. Very few English travellers ventured beyond the Border, and those who did were warned in advance that 'Scotland was the most barbarous country in the world'. In the pre-Romantic Age, the English felt no love for Scotland's scenery. They despised both the Jacobites and the Presbyterians who made up most of Scotland's population. And they tended to believe that Scots were to blame for their poverty. 'The people are proud, arrogant, vainglorious, boasters, bloody barbarous and inhuman butchers,' wrote one English visitor. 'Couzenance and theft is perfection among them. Their Church services are "blasphemy as I blush to mention".'[18]

In 1702 the stakes were immediately raised when England, under Queen Anne, joined in the War of the Spanish Succession. The war stood no less to determine the English succession, in that defeat would probably have resulted in the deposition of Queen Anne and the reinstatement of James III, 'the Old Pretender', whom Louis XIV had recognized. Once again, from the English standpoint, Scotland was a loose cannon on the deck. Scotland was more likely than England to welcome the senior and legitimate Stuart line; and she could conceivably offer a landing-ground to an anti-English expedition from the Continent. This time, the Scottish Privy Council swiftly followed the English lead by declaring war on France. But once again the Scottish Parliament had not been consulted. And the Scottish Parliament could always cause trouble by demanding a separate peace.

Not surprisingly, the Scots wished to address their own concerns. On 28 May 1703, Fletcher of Saltoun rose in the Scottish Parliament to speak at length on the negative effects of Scotland's links with England. His principal fears centred on the subservience of Scottish ministers to an absentee court resident in London:

> *My Lord Chancellor*
> When our Kings succeeded to the crown of England, the ministers of that nation took a short way to ruin us; . . . and the great places and pensions, conferred upon Scotsmen by that court, made them willing instruments in the work . . . And as our laws, before the union of the crowns, are full of acts to secure our liberty, those laws that

have been made since that time are directed chiefly to extend the prerogative . . .

All our affairs since the union of the crowns have been managed by the advice of English ministers, and the principal offices of the kingdom [of Scotland] filled with such men, as the court of England knew would be subservient to their designs: by which means . . . we have from that time appeared to the rest of the world more like a conquered province than a free independent people.

The account is very short: whilst our princes are not absolute in England, they must be influenced by that nation; our ministers must follow the directions of the prince, or lose their places . . . So that there is no way to free this country from a ruinous dependence upon the English court, unless by placing the power of conferring [Scottish] offices and [Scottish] pensions in the parliament, so long as we shall have the same king with England.[19]

In the conclusion to his speech, Fletcher proposed that Scotland should either choose a different monarch from England, or, if the joint monarchy were to continue, that the monarchy should be legally subordinated to the will of the Scottish Parliament. Either way, the arbitrary prerogative powers of the crown should be curbed. Of Fletcher's 'Twelve Limitations', the most radical clauses concerned foreign policy, defence, and justice:

6. THAT the king without consent of parliament shall not have the power of making peace and war; or that of concluding any treaty with any other state or potentate.

7. THAT all places and offices, both civil and military, and all pensions formerly conferred by our kings shall ever after be given by parliament.

8. THAT no regiment or company of horse, foot, or dragoons be kept on foot in peace or war, but by consent of parliament.

9. THAT all the fencible men of the nation, betwixt sixty and sixteen, be with all diligence possible armed with bayonets, and firelocks all of a calibre, and continue always provided in such arms with ammunition suitable.

10. THAT no general indemnity, nor pardon for any transgression against the publick, shall be valid without consent of parliament.

. . .

> 12. THAT if any king break in upon any of these conditions of government, he shall by the estates be declared to have forfeited the crown.[20]

Three months later, the Scottish Parliament passed the Act of Security (1703). It was a thoroughgoing confirmation of Scotland's independence. It would have moved the status of the Scottish ruler closer to that of a Dutch *stadholder* than that of an English constitutional monarch:

> And further upon the said death of her Majestie without heirs of her body or a successor lawfully designed and appointed as above . . . the foresaid Estates of Parliament Conveened or Meeting are hereby Authorized and Impowered to Nominat and Declare the Successor to the Imperial crown of this Realm and to settle the succession thereof upon the heirs of the said successor's body; The said successor and heirs of the successor's body being allwayes of the Royal line of Scotland and of the true protestant Religion: Provideing allwayes that the same be not successor to the Crown of England unless that . . . there be such conditions of Government settled and enacted as may secure the honour and sovereignty of this Crown and Kingdom, the freedom frequency and power of Parliaments, the religion liberty and trade of the Nation from English or any foreigne influence . . .[21]

During the passage of the act, the Lord Advocate, Lord Stuart of Goodtrees, successfully inserted a clause making free trade throughout the English empire a condition for any continuation of the joint monarchy:

> It is hereby specially statuted, enacted and declared, That it shall not be in the Power of the said meeting of the Estates, to name the Successor of the Crown of England, to be Successor to the Imperial Crown of this Realm; nor shall the same Person be capable in any event to be King or Queen of both Realms, unless a free Communication of Trade, the Freedom of Navigation, and the Liberty of the Plantations be fully agreed to, and established by the Parliament and Kingdom of England, to the Kingdom and Subjects of Scotland, at the sight, and to the satisfaction of this, or any ensuing Parliament of Scotland . . .[22]

Queen Anne baulked; but she approved the act at the second attempt in 1703, though only after Stuart's clause had been excised. Essentially, the Scots were putting themselves into a position from which they could negotiate with the English on an equal footing. Daniel Defoe, who was working in Scotland as an English spy, saw the development clearly. 'The measures taken in Scotland seemed to be well grounded,' he wrote; they 'effectually Settl'd and Declar'd the independency of Scotland and put her in a posture fit to be treated with either by England or by any other Nation.'[23]

Of course, the practical limitations on Scotland's independence were self-evident. Fletcher of Saltoun had voiced some bitter truths. The Scottish Government was appointed by a monarch dominated by English ministers. The Scottish army of 3,000 men was insufficient to control the Highlands let alone to resist an English assault. The Scottish navy consisted of two frigates, one patrolling the west coast, the other the east coast. There were no Scottish embassies abroad. The Scottish treasury was empty. Scotland's strongest card lay in the fact that England was at war.

In 1704, however, Anglo-Scottish relations deteriorated alarmingly. Patriotic opinion in both countries rose to boiling point, and all the animosities surrounding the Darién disaster revived. It was the year when the Royal Navy captured Gibraltar and when the English army under Marlborough enjoyed the great victory of Blenheim. The Company of Scotland was still trading; and the English were offended that ships flying the Scottish colours were defying their blockade. So, at the instigation of the East India Company, the Royal Navy seized a Scottish merchantman, the *Annandale*, in the Channel and interned it. In retaliation, an English ship, the *Worcester*, which had innocently entered the port of Leith, was seized by the Scots. Yet worse was to come. On investigation, Scottish magistrates found that the *Worcester*'s master, Captain Thomas Green, had recently returned from India. They calculated that he must have been in the vicinity off the Malabar Coast, when another Scottish ship, the *Speedy Return*, had been boarded by pirates and scuttled. Four years before, the *Speedy Return* had been one of the three relief ships sent out in vain to save the second expedition to New Caledonia; and she had since been taken over by none other than Captain Robert Drummond, the former master of the *Caledonia*. So her fate was seen to be a last tragic appendix to the Darién disaster. And Captain Green was going to pay the price. On no firm evidence whatsoever, a Scottish court charged Green with piracy, together with his chief mate and his gunner, then sentenced them all to hang. The sentence was carried out on Leith Sands on 11 April 1705. An eyewitness account reported the fury of the mob and the stoicism of the three victims. The convicted men were

> huzza'd, in triumph as it were, and insulted with the sharpest and most bitter invectives. Being come to the place of execution, good God what a moving sight was it to see those men stand upon the very verge of life, just launching into eternity, and at the same time see the whole multitude transported with joy. Some with pleasure asking: 'Why their countrymen did not come and save them?' Others, loading them with Scotch prayers, told 'em their old master would have 'em immediately. All of which they bore with invincible patience, like innocent men, English men and Christians, and made no other returns than by forgiving them, and desiring their charity.[24]

An English historian with strong Scottish sympathies described the background:

> Too much was bitterly remembered. Ten years before, the nation had created a noble mercantile company, and three years later a colony on Darien that could have been the trading hub of the world. Nine fine ships, built or bought for this enterprise, had been sunk, burnt, or abandoned. Nearly half a million pounds sterling had been freely offered from Scotland's meagre purse, and that which had been taken was now without hope of return. Over two thousand men, women and children had left the Forth and Clyde for Darien, and never returned. They were buried on Panama, drowned in the Caribbean, rotting in Spanish prisons, or lost for ever as indentured servants in English colonies. There was scarcely a family in Scotland below the Highland Line that had not lost a son, or a father, a cousin, nephew or friend in this disaster. This was why Scotland hanged Thomas Green, Madder and Simpson, and this was why there could be no forgiveness.[25]

For weeks afterwards, Scots balladeers extracted cruel delight in the revenge taken on the English. One ballad was called 'A Pill for the Pork Eaters, or a Scots Lancet for an English swelling':

> Then England for its treachery should mourn,
> Be forced to fawn, and truckle in its turn:
> Scots Pedlars you no longer durst upbraid
> And DARIEN should with interest be repaid.
> 'Money begets money, and trade begets trade.'[26]

Such was the prelude to the culminating scenes of the union debate.

The mood in England was growing equally truculent. In February 1705, the English Parliament, stung by the Scottish Security Act, had passed its own Aliens Act. The new measure called on the one hand for commissioners to be appointed to negotiate with Scotland. On the other hand it threatened to treat all non-domiciled Scots as foreigners, to deprive them of the legal basis for successful commercial activity in England, and in effect to ban the main sectors of Anglo-Scottish trade in cattle, coal, and flax. England was using a big stick to beat its small neighbour. It was the fury unleashed in Scotland by the Aliens Act which pushed the Edinburgh magistrates into demanding the death sentence for Captain Green in place of their earlier demands for simply seizing his cargo.

At this point, a historical controversy of extraordinary virulence broke out. The contestants were two lawyers — William Atwood (d. 1705), an English barrister, and James Anderson (1662–1728), an Edinburgh attorney turned antiquary. Atwood can only be described as a chauvinist and a cuss. His publications — *Jus Anglorum ab Antiquo* (1681), *The Fundamental Constitution of the English Government* (1690), and *The History and Reasons of Dependancy of Ireland* (1698) — were all designed to prove that England possessed a historical right to dominate its neighbours. His legal career reached its height in 1701, when he was appointed Chief Justice of New York. Yet within a couple of years he was back in London, having been expelled by the colony's governor for quarrelling with all and sundry. For such a character, England's problem with Scotland was a godsend. Unemployed, he sat down to write *The Superiority and Direct Dominion of the Kingdom of England over the*

Crown and Kingdom of Scotland (1704). He followed it up with an inflammatory pamphlet called *The Scotch patriot Unmask'd* (1705). He made the mistake of appealing to Anderson for confirmation of the authenticity of the historical charters from which he had liberally quoted.

Anderson was already engaged on his lifelong task of collecting and publishing Scotland's medieval archives. He immediately saw that Atwood had uncritically adopted the claims prepared for Edward I in the 1290s (see above) and that many of the so-called charters presenting Scotland as an English fief were well-known fakes. So he promptly put together *An Historical Essay showing that the Crown and Kingdom of Scotland is Imperial and Independent* (1705). When Scottish readers saw what was at stake, they were outraged. The Scottish Parliament ordered all of Atwood's work to be burned by the public hangman. In its final session of 1707, the same Parliament was to vote Anderson the handsome sum of 1,000 guineas – the money to be collected, of course, from the British Parliament in London. He never collected a penny.[27]

In a strange way, the rampant antipathies which surged through the English and the Scottish populace at this time can only have helped the cause of union. Popular opinion played no direct part in eighteenth-century decision-making. All it could do was to influence the climate in which decisions were taken by a small political elite. And the political climate both in London and Edinburgh had turned to one of severe apprehension. If a settlement to Anglo-Scottish discontent were not found swiftly, the political elite might be overwhelmed by the mob. The royal court, in particular, which was the only focus of mediation between the Queen's English and Scottish Parliaments, came under increasing strain to find a solution as soon as possible. Failure might mean war.

The Queen faced complications in each of her disgruntled kingdoms. In England, the Queen's Tory ministers showed little serious interest in union proposals. Her Whig ministers, who gained the upper hand in 1705 and pushed through the Aliens Act, were strongly in favour of union, but only on their own bullish terms. In Scotland, the pro-union Court party, led by the Dukes of Queensberry and Argyll, was opposed by a disaffected Country party, headed by the Duke of Hamilton, and by the 'New Party' of the Marquis of Tweeddale, which held the balance between them. Court and Parliament aside, the only other institution to count was the Church of Scotland, whose dour Presbyterian leaders had much in common with the English Whigs. Ninety per cent of Scotland's population would have no direct say.

The Scottish debate of 1705 centred on three issues — the principle of sovereignty, the nature of the union, and the appointment of commissioners.

On the fundamental question of sovereignty, Fletcher of Saltoun had published a text summarizing all the contending points of view. His *Account of a Conversation* . . . (1704) takes the form of an imaginary discussion between himself, the mild but pro-unionist George Mackenzie, Earl of Cromarty, and the notoriously Scotto-sceptic English MP Sir Edward Seymour.[28] Fletcher makes the case for Scotland remaining 'an independent nation' and for securing 'the honour and sovereignty of our crown and kingdom'. The Earl argues in favour of union on the grounds that 'the prince's power is . . . the very essence of monarchical government' and that the monarchy has been greatly weakened by the existence of separate kingdoms. Sir Edward splutters in protest against Fletcher's reasoned opinions:

> Here is a fair cant indeed, independent nation! honour of our crown, and what not? Do you consider what proportion you bear to England? . . . On my conscience, he has contrived the whole scheme to no other end than to set his own country on an equal foot with England and the rest of the world . . .[29]

Fletcher was clearly in favour of an equitable balance between England, Scotland, and Ireland. He did not believe that an equitable solution could be found in a centralized state inevitably dominated by the strongest of the three partners. 'That London should draw the riches and government of the three kingdoms to the south-east corner of this island', he wrote, 'is in some degree as unnatural as for one city to possess the riches and government of the world.'[30]

The exact nature of the union, therefore, carried prime importance. In the early eighteenth century, the word 'union' had no precise meaning. It bore overtones of 'harmony', 'co-operation', and 'alliance'. Most of those

Scots who spoke in favour of union in 1705–6 wanted nothing more than a treaty of cooperation with England. Those, like the Court party, who were pressing for an arrangement in which Scotland would lose its constitutional independence, had to use terms such as 'an incorporating union' or 'an entire union'.

The pacification of the Presbyterian Kirk was essential to the proceedings. The General Assembly remained in session throughout the debates on the Union. It had forbidden the Government to discuss its position with the English. But it was able to insist in advance on an 'Act for securing . . . Presbyterian Church Government' in Scotland. This was sufficient to keep the leaders of the Kirk apart from active opposition.

The naming of commissioners was also crucial. If Scotland were to appoint commissioners representing all the main shades of opinion, negotiations might be very protracted or reach no meaningful result. The matter was settled by the Duke of Hamilton, who stood up in Parliament in September 1705 and to everyone's surprise moved 'that the nomination of the commission should be left to the Queen herself'.[31] The motion was carried by four votes – a godsend to the Court party. From then on, the opponents of 'an incorporating union' had no means of giving effect to their opposition. The game had been lost and won. Henceforth, the key decisions lay beyond the Scottish Parliament's control. Hamilton had been bribed. He continued to encourage the anti-union noises coming from the ranks of the Country party in the sure knowledge that he would soon be rewarded. Within a couple of years, Hamilton's price for 'his spectacular double-cross' became manifest. He received an English dukedom (of Brandon), membership of the prestigious Orders of the Thistle and the Garter, and the plum post of the first British Ambassador to Paris.

Thanks to Hamilton's duplicity, all the commissioners belonged to their respective court circles – Godolphin's men from England and Queensberry's men from Scotland. They were chosen for opinions that would predetermine the product. When they met, they sat in separate rooms, maintaining the pretence that serious negotiations were afoot. In the event, they produced a working draft of the Treaty in ten days. All the Twenty-five Articles of Union were ready in its final form within three months on 22 July 1706. (See Appendix 35.)

Of the twenty-five articles, no less than fifteen concerned commercial or economic issues. This fact has led some historians to conclude that Scotland's acceptance of the union was driven by economic motives. To put this view crudely, the United Kingdom came into being in order to solve the economic crisis in Scotland that had been brought to a head by the Darién disaster. Such conclusions are not warranted. Analysis of the debate, and of the voting in the Scottish Parliament, shows that sovereignty was the key issue. Once sovereignty was conceded, however, the Scots were determined to drive the hardest economic bargain they could. For their part, once resistance concerning Scottish sovereignty was overcome, the English were ready to pay handsomely for their victory. They paid by conceding the principle of free trade as in Stuart's Amendment; they paid through 'the Equivalent' — the sum of compensation to be paid to Scotland in recognition of its future share of the British National Debt; and they paid in gold to bribe the Scottish parliamentarians. This last item amounted to less than £20,000 — which by the standards of the day has been described as 'modest'.[32]

The passage of the Treaty of Union through the Scottish Parliament started on 3 October 1706. Debate on Article I lasted for one month. The principle of 'the incorporating union' was finally accepted on 4 November by a vote of 116 to 83. No other clause raised so much trouble. The Church of Scotland was satisfied by an open-ended guarantee of the Presbyterian establishment. The New Party was bought off by a promise (not honoured) to give it the attractive task of overseeing the distribution of the Equivalent. Ratification was finally assured on 16 January 1707 with a comfortable majority of 45 votes.

Throughout those twelve weeks, the Scottish ministers were deluged with petitions. Not a single one expressed support for the Union. A Petition from the Convention of Royal Burghs, for example, expressed their 'Great Concern':

> The Humble Address of the Commissioners to the General Convention of the Royal Burrows of this Ancient Kingdom Convened the Twenty-Ninth of October 1706, at Edinburgh, Upon the Great Concern of the Union Prosposed Betwixt Scotland and England, . . .

Humbly Sheweth, That . . . it is our indispensible duty to signify to your grace, that, as we are not against an honourable and safe union with England, . . . far less can we expect to have the condition of the people of Scotland, with relation to these great concerns, made better and improved without a Scots Parliament. And seeing by the articles of union now under the consideration of the Honourable Estates it is agreed that Scotland and England shall be united into one kingdom, and the united kingdom be represented by one and the same Parliament, by which our monarchy is suppressed . . . And considering that the most considerable branches of our trade are differing from those of England . . . we therefore supplicate your grace and Honourable Estate of Parliament, and do assuredly expect, that you will not conclude such an incorporating union as is contained in the articles proposed, but that you will support and maintain the true reformed Protestant religion . . . as by law established, the soveraignty and independency of this crown and kingdom and the rights and privileges of Parliament . . .[33]

Protest meetings attracted large audiences. Mobs rioted. One of the commissioners, Sir John Clerk, would later admit that the Articles of Union had been 'contrary to the inclinations of at least three-fourths of the Kingdom'. In his history of union, he would estimate that less than 1 per cent of Scotland's population thoroughly approved.[34]

Before the Treaty was sent back to England for its final stages (see below), three important items remained. The first concerned the method of selecting the forty-five Scottish members who would sit in the opening session of the British Parliament. When the announcement was made that the members would not be specially elected but would be nominated by the ruling Ministry, it caused peals of outrage. But to no avail. The second item concerned the calculation of the Equivalent. The figure calculated was £398,085 10s. Of this, £232,884 5s was to be made available at 5 per cent interest to the shareholders who ten years before had subscribed to the Company of Scotland. The chief calculator, once the Chief Projector, was, very appropriately, Paterson. The third step was to amend the proposed Act of Union by a clause insisted on by the Archbishop of Canterbury. The Church of England was to be formally secured in a manner which matched the Act of Security for Presbyterian Church government in Scotland.

From then on, everything proceeded as planned. At the end of March, the Duke of Queensberry wound up the business of the Scottish Parliament for the last time. In the first weeks of April, carrying the Union documents with him, he made a triumphant progress through England reminiscent of that undertaken by James VI 103 years before:

> Southwards from Berwick, he was received with acclamations by the people, and feasted by the magistrates of every city on the road to London, while the gentlemen of each shire rode in to do him honour. 'At Barnet he was met by the Ministry of England and most of the Nobility then attending the two Houses of Parliament. Their retinue consisted of forty-six coaches and over a thousand horsemen.' Thus royal accompanied, the last Queen's Commissioner for the Scottish Parliament made entry into London through the shouting streets. The Scots in England for once found themselves popular . . .[35]

Duly signed and sealed, Scotland's assent to the Union was handed over. The Bill passed through the English Parliament without demur. The 1st of May was declared a holiday. 'The Queen, accompanied by four hundred coaches, went to yet another ceremony at St. Paul's to give thanks for the greatest of all the victories with which God had blessed her reign.'[36]

At every stage on the tortuous road which led to the formation of the United Kingdom, Scotland was England's junior, weaker, and more reluctant partner. Scotland, after all, had more to lose. Yet the smallest cogs have always had the capacity to cause the greatest trouble in even the largest machines. For this reason, Scotland's path to union is every bit as important as England's. Even a cursory examination of the Scottish story reveals much that was essential not only to the process of unification but also to the nature of the end product.

In retrospect, one sees that the window of opportunity which opened in 1705–7 was extremely narrow and to some extent fortuitous. For those two short years, the ruling circles of the two kingdoms found the psychological space and the political will to negotiate. Prior to 1705, the proposals for union were not even on the table. After 1707, when the confidence generated by Marlborough's victories ebbed away, it is doubtful whether Queen Anne's ministers would have wanted to devote time and energy to constitutional matters. Indeed, strong resentments against the union soon surfaced. In 1713, despite the presence of the sixteen Scottish peers, the House of Lords defeated a motion to abandon the union by a single vote. In this light, it is not too fanciful to conclude that the union could not have come about if the English Whigs had not adopted an aggressive strategy or if the Scots had resorted to delaying tactics. In later times, the volte-face of the Duke of Hamilton, which ensured the speedy conduct of the negotiations, was reviled in Scotland as 'the commencement of our ruin'.[37] For all who value the United Kingdom above all else, it should be celebrated as an act of consummate foresight and timing.

The financial chaos which surrounded the Company of Scotland in the period preceding the Union was by no means unique in that era of toddler capitalism. It certainly did not reflect a special brand of Scots incompetence. The Darién disaster of the 1690s did nothing to deter the English investors who inflated the South Sea Bubble scheme only sixteen years later. William Paterson's overall record is not to be slighted. The failure of the Company of Scotland was more than offset by the success both of the Bank of England and of Walpole's sinking fund, of which Paterson was also the chief author.

The road to union was not accompanied by any sense of enthusiasm or elation. The English were largely indifferent. The Scots were over-whelmingly hostile. The politicians pressed on because they felt that failure to do so would have dire consequences. To invoke a matrimonial metaphor, this was no love match. England and Scotland entered into constitutional matrimony only because they feared the worst without it. Daniel Defoe, who watched from close quarters, reflected afterwards that 'a firmer union of policy with less union of affection has hardly been known in the whole world'.[38] A historian comments: 'The Union of 1707 was conceived by *raison d'état* . . .; fittingly it would produce a union of state rather than a meeting of minds.'[39]

Nevertheless, the Scots drove a hard bargain. They were a poor, but not a defeated nation; and they extracted far more concessions from England than had been granted to the Welsh much earlier or would be granted to the Irish later. The continued existence of Scottish law and of the Scottish national Church provided a residue of separateness that would persist through all those times when the Scottish establishment in Edinburgh relied heavily on English support to overcome Scotland's own deep ethnic and social divisions. The continued existence of a Scottish Privy Council, which was envisaged by the Treaty of Union but which was arbitrarily abolished by royal decree in 1708, would have added an extra administrative dimension to that separateness.

Throughout the negotiations, the various constitutional proposals were invariably associated with the expectation of shared economic benefits. Stuart's amendment to the Act of Security may have been formally rejected; but its ghost stalked all subsequent discussions. If the Scots were to lose their sovereignty, they were always going to insist on the 'Free Trade' and the 'Liberty of the Plantations' which Stuart had raised. The one thing which had to go was the state of affairs where the English authorities could wreck the legal activities of the Company of Scotland and where an English colonial governor could issue orders to starve Scottish colonists to death.

From the start, therefore, union went hand in hand with empire. The concept of the United Kingdom was inseparable from the concept of a joint British Empire. And both concepts were turned into practical reality at a most auspicious moment. The union preceded the Treaty of Utrecht by six short years. It enabled Scotland to participate alongside England in the most lavish imperial opportunity in history. The Scots would be prevented from participating on equal terms for some time yet: but they were well qualified to do so. Proportionately they had always emigrated in greater numbers than the English, and they could now divert their migration from various traditional European destinations to the overseas empire. Thanks to the Schools Act of 1695, which was passed by the same Parliament as the act for the Company of Scotland, they were well able to compete:

To whatever land the Scotchman might wander, to whatever calling
he might betake himself, in America or India, in trade or in war, the
advantage which he derived from his early training raised him above
his competitors. If he was taken into a warehouse as a porter, he
soon became a foreman. If he enlisted in the army, he soon became
a serjeant . . .[40]

Having failed to found a separate Scottish empire, they were destined to
make a distinguished and disproportionate contribution both to the
government of the United Kingdom and to the administration of the
British Empire.

Yet the Anglo-Scottish partnership in union and empire had been
achieved through political necessity. It was not underpinned by history,
by culture, or by popular enthusiasm. An imperial British state had been
brought into being. The more formidable challenge was to forge a
community of people inspired by a strong sense of common identity and
purpose – in other words, to create not just a British state, but a British
nation. Perhaps the key factor in the long process of nation-building lay
in the fact that it was directed at a population living in new political
circumstances. For, as from 1707, the Isles were both British and imperial.

HISTORY IS WOUND FROM many strands. The shortest and simplest of them are individual human lives, which on close examination turn out to be rather complicated. The larger skeins, which are made up from the activities of whole social groups, institutions, nations, and states, are like huge cables, wound from separate strands yet twisted inseparably together. The sum of the past, therefore, can only be likened to a forest of those giant tropical lianas which coil upwards out of the earth and twist their way through the jungle cover towards the light. The history even of a single country is far too large to be examined whole. Historians must somehow reduce the tangle to manageable and comprehensible proportions. To do that, they can either pick out separate strands for detailed analysis or else they can make a series of cross-sections to expose the changing patterns within the whole. Ideally, they should try to do both.

The question then arises: where shall the cuts be made? Every cut makes an arbitrary division across a connected organism; but it has to be done. All sorts of incision points are chosen: the reigns of kings, the fall of regimes, the passing of centuries. All are unsatisfactory. Wars suit the purpose of historical dividing lines no better and no worse than the others do.

The united Kingdom of Great Britain was born in 1707 amidst the strains and stresses of the War of the Spanish Succession, a colossal conflict once described as the 'first world war'. Its formation was completed in 1801 during the struggles of the next round of all-European conflict, which goes by the name of the French Revolutionary and Napoleonic Wars, 1792–1815. It reached its peak during a third round of global conflict, this time the Great War of 1914–18.

THE FORMATION OF THE UNITED KINGDOM, 1707–1922

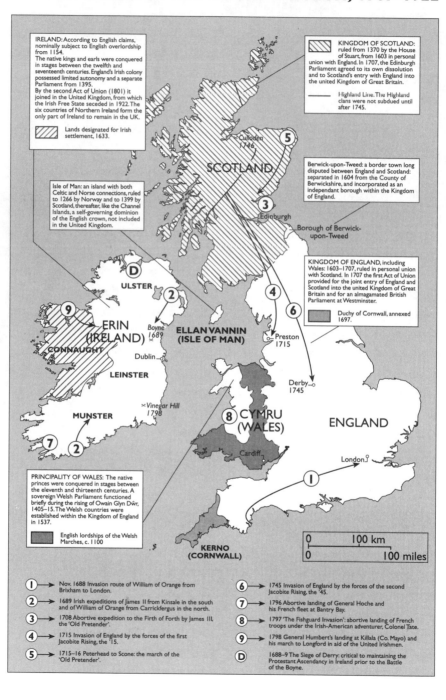

IRELAND: According to English claims, nominally subject to English overlordship from 1154.
The native kings and earls were conquered in stages between the twelfth and seventeenth centuries. England's Irish colony possessed limited autonomy and a separate Parliament from 1395.
By the second Act of Union (1801) it joined in the United Kingdom, from which the Irish Free State seceded in 1922. The six countries of Northern Ireland form the only part of Ireland to remain in the UK.

Lands designated for Irish settlement, 1633.

KINGDOM OF SCOTLAND: ruled from 1370 by the House of Stuart, from 1603 in personal union with England. In 1707, the Edinburgh Parliament agreed to its own dissolution and to Scotland's entry with England into the united Kingdom of Great Britain.

Highland Line. The Highland clans were not subdued until after 1745.

Isle of Man: an island with both Celtic and Norse connections, ruled to 1266 by Norway and to 1399 by Scotland, thereafter, like the Channel Islands, a self-governing dominion of the English crown, not included in the United Kingdom.

Berwick-upon-Tweed: a border town long disputed between England and Scotland: separated in 1604 from the County of Berwickshire, and incorporated as an independant borough within the Kingdom of England.

Borough of Berwick-upon-Tweed

KINGDOM OF ENGLAND, including Wales: 1603–1707, ruled in personal union with Scotland. In 1707 the first Act of Union provided for the joint entry of England and Scotland into the united Kingdom of Great Britain and for an amalgamated British Parliament at Westminster.

Duchy of Cornwall, annexed 1697.

SCOTLAND

Culloden 1746

Edinburgh

ULSTER

ERIN (IRELAND)

Boyne 1689

ELLAN VANNIN (ISLE OF MAN)

Preston 1715

CONNAUGHT

Dublin

LEINSTER

Derby 1745

×Vinegar Hill 1798

MUNSTER

CYMRU (WALES)

ENGLAND

Cardiff

London

PRINCIPALITY OF WALES: The native princes were conquered in stages between the eleventh and thirteenth centuries. A sovereign Welsh Parliament functioned briefly during the rising of Owain Glyn Dŵr, 1405–15. The Welsh countries were established within the Kingdom of England in 1537.

English lordships of the Welsh Marches, c. 1100

KERNO (CORNWALL)

| 0 | 100 km |
| 0 | 100 miles |

① Nov. 1688 Invasion route of William of Orange from Brixham to London.

② 1689 Irish expeditions of James II from Kinsale in the south and of William of Orange from Carrickfergus in the north.

③ 1708 Abortive expedition to the Firth of Forth by James III, the 'Old Pretender'.

④ 1715 Invasion of England by the forces of the first Jacobite Rising, the '15.

⑤ 1715–16 Peterhead to Scone: the march of the 'Old Pretender'.

⑥ 1745 Invasion of England by the forces of the second Jacobite Rising, the '45.

⑦ 1796 Abortive landing of General Hoche and his French fleet at Bantry Bay.

⑧ 1797 'The Fishguard Invasion': abortive landing of French troops under the Irish-American adventurer, Colonel Tate.

⑨ 1798 General Humbert's landing at Killala (Co. Mayo) and his march to Longford in aid of the United Irishmen.

Ⓓ 1688–9 The Siege of Derry: critical to maintaining the Protestant Ascendancy in Ireland prior to the Battle of the Boyne.

Other wars of greater or lesser consequence occurred between the major rounds. In the eighteenth century, the War of the Austrian Succession, 1740–48, the Seven Years War, 1756–63, and the War of American Independence, 1776–83, all made a deep impact on British affairs. Apart from the Crimean War, 1854–6, the nineteenth century after 1815 was relatively free of major wars that affected Britain. All in all, therefore, a summary of British history that aims to cover the ground from its beginning to the margins of living memory can reasonably be accommodated between the Treaty of Utrecht and the Treaty of Versailles – or in regnal terms, between the reign of George I and the reign of George V.

(I) The Senior Service: 'Britannia Rules the Waves'

The Navy Royal, which had become the Royal Navy by the reign of Charles I, never changed its name thereafter except during the Commonwealth. It was the principal instrument of England's, the United Kingdom's, and the British Empire's greatness. It came into being as a permanent standing fleet in England early in Henry VIII's reign. It had many antecedents, of course, in the temporary collections of converted merchantmen used by medieval kings. And it had a little-known predecessor in the late medieval Scottish fleet, which was briefly more powerful than anything possessed by England at the time. From these humble beginnings, it grew and grew until it became the equal of any fleet in Europe. In the nineteenth century, it was the absolute master of all the world's oceans.[41]

Water, it should be emphasized, is a facilitator of communication. Seas do not form a barrier. On the contary, they offer an easy means of access. Islands, therefore, can only be defended by ships, and by particular types of ship designed for warfare. The key development apparently occurred with the invention of the hinged gunport. The gunport first let ships carry heavy guns at the stern and then gave them a continuous gundeck, which allowed the firing of broadsides. Warship design was consequently transformed from that of floating castles to that of floating platforms for heavy cannon. Henry VIII's *Henry Grâce à Dieu* of 1514 was built with two stern ports, and the *Mary Rose* of 1510 was rebuilt in 1536 as an early example of the new breed of vessel with a complete line of gunports.[42]

The prime requirement for a fleet was to maintain superiority over all other ships sailing in the same waters. In England's case, the initial task was to establish an edge over those elements of the Spanish and French fleets which regularly plied the Channel. In Henry VIII's time, for instance, a new threat had been posed by French Mediterranean galleys which compelled the English fleet off Brest to retire in disorder to Plymouth in April 1513.[43] The Spanish fleet was far larger and far more varied than the fledgeling Navy Royal. At no time under the Tudors could England have sent an armada to attack France or Spain. But if it could repel a French or a Spanish attack on the English coasts, it would repay the investment.

Beyond that, the fleet served five main functions. Firstly, it was required to provide armed escort and deliver supplies for military expeditions. This capacity played a major role in England's medieval conquest of Wales and the Elizabethan conquest of Ireland. Secondly, it was required to protect merchant shipping from rivals and pirates. Thirdly, it was to serve as the link with overseas colonies, and to secure their defence. This was a task for the Stuart, but not for the Tudor navy. Fourthly, it had to project its masters' naval presence into new seas, in order to seek new colonies and new sources of trade. Drake's circumnavigation of the globe and Raleigh's ill-starred expeditions to El Dorado were motivated by these considerations.

Lastly, and most importantly, though only intermittently, the navy had to face the foe in battle. In the Tudor period,

> Having got into the wind of the enemy [got between the wind and the enemy], one bore up, 'gave him the prow' [fired the bow chasers], hauled on to a parallel course to windward to fire the lee broadside guns, luffed up to bring the stern chasers

to bear, then paid off onto the other tack to fire the other broadside. One then withdrew to a safe distance to reload before returning to 'give the charge' again. . . . In this way the English could keep the enemy under more or less continuous bombardment by a succession of ships, each of which came into action perhaps once an hour.[44]

The Navy Royal's earliest major encounter of this classic type was probably in 1588, and the tactics remained in place until supplanted by the more familiar line of battle in the 1650s. As defined in the *Fighting Instructions* of 1653,

At sight of the said fleet the vice admiral, or he that commands in chief in the second place and his squadron, as also the rear admiral, or he that commandeth in chief in the third place and his squadron are to make what sail they can to come up with the admiral on each wing, the vice admiral on the right wing, and the rear admiral on the left wing, leaving a competent distance for the admiral's squadron if the wind will permit and there be searoom enough.

As soon as they shall see the general engage, or make a signal by shooting off two guns and putting a red flag over the fore topmast-head, then each squadron shall take the best advantage they can to engage with the enemy next unto them; and in order thereunto all the ships of every squadron shall endeavor to keep in a line with the chief unless the chief be maimed or otherwise disabled (which God forbid!), whereby the said ship that wears the flag should not come in to do the service which is requisite. Then every ship of the said squadron shall endeavor to keep in a line with the admiral, or he that commands in chief next unto him, and nearest the enemy.[45]

The line of battle remained the dominant battle formation until the age of steam, although after the Battle of the Saintes (1782), the century's largest, the navy allowed admirals to cut through the enemy's line in order to break it up. This tactic was employed with great success at Trafalgar (1805) against the Franco-Spanish fleet, which anticipated Nelson's move but could not prevent it.

The maintenance of a fleet made demands on the state that were very different from those of a standing army. For one thing, it called for the permanent establishment of docks, shipyards, foundries, and storehouses, and for long-term commitments in the timber trade and the iron industry. For another, it called for a constant programme of research and development into navigational science and military technology. The royal dockyards at Deptford and Woolwich on the Thames, at Chatham on the Medway, at Portsmouth, and later at Devonport possessed the most advanced industrial workshops in the land. The magnificent stands of oak that were cut from the New Forest for Henry VIII's navy had been growing for two to three hundred years. Their loss immediately raised the question of their replacement. The earliest centres of iron forging developed in that same era in the Weald of Kent.

Naval operations, being continuous and open-ended, were inordinately expensive. Time and again, the Navy Board (which built, equipped, and maintained the ships) relaxed its efforts in peacetime, only to find major shortcomings on the outbreak of war. With time, the admirals learned that high-powered, sophisticated, long-term financing was essential to the navy's welfare. The first step was taken in 1557 with the establishment of a standing naval budget, the Ordinary. Yet a policy was being launched with fundamental consequences for the development not just of the navy but of the country as a whole. Naval finances overstretched the financial resources of the crown from the start. In the 1540s Henry VIII had an annual income of about £250,000, and from 1542–7 he spent £265,000 on the navy.[46] This was the single most important item that drove the crown into permanent partnership with Parliament. In the 1620s, the Ordinary was about £20,000; escorting Queen Henrietta Maria across the Channel in 1625 cost £35,986.[47] Most significantly, perhaps, the enormous sums earmarked for the navy in advance of war meant that relatively little was left for spending on the land forces. Once a small country like England set her sights on becoming a first-rate naval power, she automatically condemned herself to being a second-class, or even a third-class land power. This pattern never changed.

In the sixteenth century, the ships of the Navy Royal rarely ventured beyond home waters except as lone raiders. They played a vital role in securing England's supremacy in the Isles, and in assisting the Revolt of the Netherlands against Spain. But their capacity was severely reduced by the loss of Calais in 1558. Not until the defeat of the Spanish Armada thirty years later was Europe given notice of things to come.

In the seventeenth century, England's military problems were greatly simplified by the personal union with Scotland. Money that had been lavished for centuries on the English garrisons at Carlisle and Berwick could be transferred to the navy. As Chief Justice Coke once boasted, 'If Ireland is secured, [and] the Navy furnished, we will not care for pope, Turk, Spain nor all the devils in hell.'[48] Yet few serious plans were laid until provoked by England's mediocre performance in the Anglo-French and Anglo-Spanish wars, notably by the humiliating expedition to Cadiz (1625). James I's favourite, and Charles I's chief minister, the Duke of Buckingham (1592–1628), was stabbed to death by a disgruntled veteran of the Cadiz expedition; and Barbary pirates were able more than once to descend on the West Country and to carry off captives to slavery. Charles I's insistence on tunnage and poundage and his obsession with ship-money derived from his determination to built a decent fleet. In this he succeeded. In 1637 England's first ever First Rate warship, the *Sovereign of the Seas*, with 102 bronze cannon on three decks, was launched at Portsmouth at a cost of £65,586 16s 9½d.[49] The irony was that the new navy deserted the King in the 1640s and greatly assisted the victories of Cromwell's parliamentary army.

Three Dutch Wars, 1652–4, 1665–7, and 1672–4, saw the Royal Navy struggling to withstand the premier naval power of the day. The English admirals stuck to their arrogant demand that all foreign ships dip their colours and topsails in salute in the 'British Seas' (which were not defined), and they introduced the practice, soon to become standard, of random searches of foreign vessels. Nonetheless, in 1666–7 the Dutch twice blockaded the Thames, and De Ruyter captured two warships in the Medway and burned five more. The Commissioner at Chatham Dockyard, Peter Pett, was fired. But Samuel Pepys (1633–1703), the lecherous diarist, survived to make an exemplary career as Secretary to the Admiralty. Pepys's plan presented to James II in 1686 'For the Recovery of the Navy' brought startling results. By the time that King James hurriedly left England in a ketch, he was commander of 173 warships, with 6,930 guns, including 59 ships-of-the-line, and a permanent Channel squadron. Pepys, alas, is better remembered for his descriptions of the Fire of London (1666) and for his catchphrase 'And so to bed'.

In many ways, King William's War, 1689–97, must be seen as the decisive turning-point in the Royal Navy's fortunes. Louis XIV had assembled a fleet that was larger than the English and the Dutch fleets combined. And in 1690 at Beachy Head he contrived to beat them both in a grand sea battle. But whereas the French subsequently invested mainly in their land forces, and the Dutch dropped out of the reckoning, England succeeded in putting her naval finances onto a permanent footing. As a result, she finally emerged as a naval power second to none.

In the eighteenth century, the Royal Navy developed a global reach. In this, it was greatly assisted by the terms of the Treaty of Utrecht (1713), which among other things transferred Spain's monopoly slave trade contract, the *asiento des negros*, from France to the united Kingdom. The British thereby took over the intercontinental commercial networks developed by Spain in the previous two hundred years, and built a worldwide chain of naval bases, starting with Gibraltar and Bermuda. Their conquests of India and Canada (see below) can largely be explained in terms of superior naval support. Britain's pre-eminence in science was confirmed by the three remarkable voyages of the *Endeavour* under Captain James Cook (1728–79), who sailed to the South Seas on behalf of the Royal Society and made unprecedented astronomical, botanical, and geographical discoveries. It is also well illustrated by the Admiralty's

long-standing competition for a solution to the troublesome problem
of finding the longitude at sea and the production of an efficient sea-
going chronometer.[50] By the end of the century, the Royal Navy
saw no difficulty in establishing a new colony, initially for unwanted
convicts, at Botany Bay in Australia (1798), twelve thousand miles
from home. Her admirals – Anson, Byng, Collingwood, Duncan,
Hawke, Hood, Howe, Jervis, Rodney, and Vernon – had carried all
before them in a series of wars, turning distant spots like Quiberon
Bay (1759), Cape St Vincent (1797) or Aboukir (1798) into household
names. The supreme triumph came during the Napoleonic Wars off
Cape Trafalgar (21 October 1805), where Vice-Admiral Horatio
Nelson (1758–1805) crowned a scintillating career of skill and daring
with the defeat of the combined fleets of France and Spain. After
that, the world knew for certain that the Royal Navy was in a class
of its own.

In the nineteenth century, the United Kingdom's naval supremacy was rarely tested. Indeed, when sail gave way to steam, Britain's
industrial precocity (see below) only reinforced her lead. Gun-
boats were sent out to all points from Algiers (1816) to Zanzibar
(1893) to bolster British diplomacy; but the great ships-of-the-line
were never challenged. Great consternation was sown in the
1890s by Germany's naval ambitions, and by the ensuing arms race.
The *Dreadnought* (1906), which was constructed in fourteen months,
was a steel battleship of 17,900 tons that headed a force with
unheard-of firepower. But it was never involved in a fight to the
finish. At the battle of Jutland (31 May 1916), the only major naval
confrontation of the First World War, the British Grand Fleet
took some punishment, but persuaded the Germans to retire to
safety. Germany placed more hopes in its submarines than in its
battleships.

Two hundred years of unbroken mastery at sea left deep traces
on the British psyche. The British came to believe what the English
had suspected earlier, that they were invulnerable. HMS *Victory*
became the supreme symbol of British pride; and the Senior Service
was the guarantee of every Briton's liberty:

> Rule, Britannia! Britannia, rule the waves.
> Britons never, never, never shall be slaves!

And 'Sea Fever' entered into every schoolchild's mind, not excluding the millions for whom a heaving deck was a totally unknown experience:

> I must down to the sea again, to the lonely sea and the sky,
> And all I ask is a tall ship, and a star to steer her by:
> And the wheel's kick and the wind's song, and the white sail's
> shaking
> And a grey mist on the sea's face, and a grey dawn breaking.[51]

(2) THE BRITISH ARMY: 'CONTEMPTIBLY SMALL'

Standing state armies came into being in many parts of Europe during the seventeenth century. Thanks to the 'Military Revolution', they were already in evidence during the Thirty Years War, where the professional armies of France, Spain, and particularly Sweden made an international impression. In the Isles, all three kingdoms put professional state armies into the field in the 1640s – Scotland's Army of the Covenant, Ireland's Catholic Army, and the victorious New Model Army of England. These three armies were all disbanded, however, and it was left to the crown forces of Charles II to form the nucleus of the future British army. He assembled the not inconsiderable establishment of twenty thousand men. The oldest surviving regiment, now the Royal Scots, was formed in 1625 in the service of the French king and taken into the establishment in 1670. The Corps of Royal Marines had its foundation in 1664 at Portsmouth as the Duke of York and Albany's Maritime Regiment of Foot, to provide the navy with seaborne troops. The oldest regiment of the modern Household Cavalry, the Lord General's Lifeguard of Horse, was founded in 1660 and placed on the establishment in 1661. The Royal Hospital was founded at Chelsea for needy military veterans, the 'Chelsea Pensioners', in 1682. From these modest beginnings in Restoration England, the army was destined to become a branch of the permanent Establishment. It always occupied a secondary place in strategic planning; but it would play a cardinal role in the nurture of 'Britishness'.

Ever since the ship-money case (1638), when Chief Justice Finch made the famous statement that 'For us islanders, it is most necessary to defend ourselves at sea', military thinking always left the army in a subordinate role. As a result, the army quickly assumed three lasting characteristics. Firstly, by Continental standards, it was extremely small. It maintained a core of professional cadres in peacetime, in order to expand them in wartime. Secondly, since it could never compete with the major Continental armies on its own, it developed the tradition of fighting in composite allied formations. Thirdly, it constantly sought to compensate for its deficiency in size by its operational and technological efficiency. The Royal Artillery, for example, which could share the expertise and industrial base of the navy's gunners, maintained very high standards. The basic situation had still not changed by 1914. The German Kaiser dismissed the British Expeditionary Force as 'a contemptible little Army', thereby inspiring their nickname 'The Old Contemptibles'. (It was approximately one fiftieth of the size of the German army deployed in Europe at the time.) But when the Kaiser's Army encountered the BEF in October at the First Battle of Ypres, the intense and rapid rifle fire of its professionals convinced the Germans that every man had a machine-gun, and the BEF inflicted the *Kindermord* or 'Massacre of Innocents', the first great slaughter of the War.

From its origins as a royal guard essentially for internal defence – its opening engagement under Major John Churchill was against Monmouth's rebels in 1685 – the army passed under parliamentary control in 1690 and grew over a long period in two complementary directions. On the one hand, it gradually acquired a full range of specialist formations, each devoted to particular arms or functions. In addition to the four basic branches of infantry, cavalry, artillery, and marines, it assigned its technical tasks to units such as the Corps

of Engineers (1717) or in later times to such outfits as the Royal
Corps of Signals (1920), the Royal Flying Corps (1912), or the
Parachute Regiment (1940–42). The cavalry were mechanized as the
Royal Armoured Corps (1939). On the other hand, it established and
expanded its territorial base. This latter development transformed
what was essentially the army of the English crown into a truly
British army.

The first stage, which lasted for a century after 1707, saw the
gradual merger of the English nucleus with units from other parts
of the United Kingdom. The newcomers consisted in the first
instance of Lowland Scots, at a later date of Highland Scots, and,
after the second Act of Union, of a huge contingent of Irishmen.
The outcome is well reflected in the composition of the historic
Guards Division, made up of the Grenadier Guards (1656, Lord
Wentworth's Regiment), the Coldstream Guards, the Scots Guards
(1661, Scots Regiment of Foot Guards), the Irish Guards (1900), and
the Welsh Guards (1915):

> Some talk of Alexander,
> And some of Hercules,
> Of Hector and Lysander,
> And such great names as these,
> But of all the world's great heroes
> There's none that can compare
> With the tow row row, row row row row
> With the British gre-ena-adiers.[52]

Within the whole, the Highland regiments played a very particular role. Drawn from the Gaelic clans who had twice taken up arms
against the Union, they had a reputation for ferocity on the
battlefield and for fierce loyalty among themselves. Dressed in the
kilts and tartans, which all other Scots were banned from wearing
for eighty years, they were the proud remnant of a defeated race
and the government's ultimate weapon for dividing and ruling. The
Black Watch (Royal Highland Regiment), whose origins go back to

1739, the Highland Light Infantry, 1777 and 1787, the Gordon High-landers, 1787 and 1794, the Queen's Own Cameron Highlanders, 1793–4, and the Argyll and Sutherland Highlanders (Princess Louise's), 1794 and 1799, were given to insubordination and mutiny. They were men whose loyalty had been abused by clan chiefs in the government's pay. And they could be used to tame anyone in the empire who like their ancestors might dare to rebel.[53]

By the time of the Napoleonic Wars, therefore, the army had ceased to be predominantly English. At Waterloo, the Duke of Wellington commanded an army, two-thirds of which, in accordance with the principle of allied campaigning, consisted of Germans and Netherlanders. Of his own troops, over a third were Irishmen; and it was the Highland squares which finally carried the day against the charges of Napoleon's Imperial Guard (who, in large part, were Poles). Wellington (1769–1852), who himself was an Irishman, born in Dublin, once said that his army 'is composed of the scum of the earth'. Before Waterloo, he remarked, 'I don't know what effect these men will have on the enemy, but by God they terrify me!'

The second stage of the army's expansion resulted from 'localization' and (from 1881) 'territorialization' – the strategy of basing infantry regiments in the principal counties and cities of the Isles. In this way, they were linked to the militia and volunteers, serving each location with a single recruiting depot, then converting the militia and volunteer battalions into battalions of the county regiments. Men remained attached to their local regiments throughout their careers, even when they were transferred for ERE (extra-regimental experience). With time, the backbone of the army was built round regiments like the King's Own Scottish Borderers (so designated 1887), the South Wales Borderers (1881), the Royal Irish Rifles (1881), the Northumberland Fusiliers (1881), or the Gloucesters (1881), the Dorsets (1881), and the 'Ox and Bucks' (1908), who combined a strong local patriotism with the oath of allegiance to the British crown. Millions of men who passed through the ranks, especially in the age of conscription and National Service (1916–19,

1939–61), mingled with millions of other men in the same predicament. These were the cohorts, in the jumble of 'Jocks', 'Paddies', and 'Taffies', who learned to think of everyone as 'British'.

As the home base of the army expanded, however, so too did its overseas connections. In the eighteenth century, since the King of Great Britain was equally the Elector of Hanover, British troops customarily fought alongside Hanoverians. Such, for example, is the American memory of 'the redcoats' in the American War of Independence. In the nineteenth century, since the British army was given a partner in the British-staffed Indian Army (in crown control after the Mutiny of 1857), the rich variety of Britishers was joined by a still richer variety of Sikhs, Gurkhas, and Bengalis. Long after the fall of the empire, military parades led by units dressed up in Highland kit could still be watched in points round the globe from Pakistan and Uganda to Hong Kong and Fiji. In the world wars of the twentieth century, the British army called for support from the armies of all the overseas dominions. British soldiers became comrades-in-arms of Canadians, Australians, South Africans, and New Zealanders. Army service showed them that 'Britishness' was both a victorious and a worldwide phenomenon. The high point of this phenomenon, with its multitude of colourful uniforms, faces, languages, and accents, came with the Victory Parade of 1945. It was last seen, when memories of the Second World War were still fresh, at the Coronation Parade of 1953.

Like any long-standing military force, the British army lived off its legends and its heroes. These heroes, who performed exactly the same sort of feats of daring and sacrifice as their counterparts in France, Germany, Poland, or Russia, were cultivated by the soldiers and disseminated among the public at large. They once formed part of the essential knowledge of every British schoolchild. Apart from 'the Iron Duke', the popular favourites came to include General Wolfe, who died on the Heights of Abraham at Quebec (1759), General Gordon, who died surrounded by dervishes at Khartoum (1885), and Major Baden-Powell, founder of the Boy Scouts, who with the assistance of black African volunteers organized the ingenious defence of Mafeking (1900). They also included two British nurses, Florence Nightingale (1820–1910), the 'Lady with the Lamp', whose compassion lifted the darkness of the military hospital at Scutari (1854–6), and Edith Cavell (1865–1915), who was shot by a German firing-squad in Belgium for helping her prisoner-patients to escape. Her dying words were: 'I must not have hatred or bitterness to anyone' and 'patriotism is not enough'. This was refreshing. For the military view of history tends to see humanity in terms of 'Us' and 'Them'.

British army life, though a powerful motor of British identity, did not encourage social cohesion. On the contrary, its unusually rigid distinction between 'officers' and 'men' strengthened the divisions of the British class system. The British Military College (1802; Royal Military College Sandhurst from 1812) was one of the earliest in Europe. Its officer-graduates were trained in the gentleman's code of honour, duty, and sacrifice. They included many fine specimens who were not found wanting when their supreme test came in the trenches of the Great War. Their mortality rate was colossal, and generally speaking, their devotion to their men, exemplary. But they ate apart, slept apart, were decorated apart, and were buried apart. Not a few, if they survived, were given to radical politics. At the highest level, the General Staff gained an early reputation of 'Donkeys leading Lions'.[54]

As for the enlisted men of the British army, they cultivated a stoical ethos which differed markedly from the contrived bravado of the French or the studied arrogance of the Germans. Whether in the isolated outposts of empire or on the desolate beaches of Dunkirk, they knew that they lacked the safety of numbers and, though they usually ended up on the winning side, that they had never won a major war single-handed. Unlike the sailors of the Royal Navy, they could not hope to blow the enemy out of the water. So they took to irony and to self-deprecation:

> We are Fred Carno's Army, the ragtime infantry
> We cannot fight, we cannot shoot,

No bleedin' use are we.
And when we get to Berlin, the Kaiser he will say
Hoch, hoch, mein Gott, what a bloody awful lot
Are the British infantry![55]

The song was sung to the lugubrious tune of 'Greenland's Icy Mountains'. The singers would have known, and have fully shared, the grumbling humour of Kipling's perishing private on the North West Frontier:

I've a head like a concertina; I've a tongue like a button-stick.
I've a mouth like an old potato, and I'm more than a little sick.
But I've had my fun of the Corp'ral's Guard; I've made the
                                         cinders fly.
And I'm here in the Clink for a thundering drink, and for
                                         blacking the Corporal's eye!

For it's Tommy this, an' Tommy that, an' 'Chuck 'im out, the
                                         brute',
But it's 'Saviour of 'is country' when the guns begin to shoot;
An' it's Tommy this, an' Tommy that, an' anything else you
                                         please;
An' Tommy ain't a blooming fool – you bet that Tommy sees.

So:

Ship me east of Suez, where the best is like the worst,
Where there aren't no Ten Commandments, an' a man can
                                         raise a thirst:
For the temple bells are callin', an' it's there that I would be
By the old Moulmein Pagoda, looking lazy on the sea:

On the road to Mandalay
Where the old Flotilla lay
With our sick beneath the awnings
When we went to Mandalay.
Oh, the road to Mandalay,
Where the flyin' fishes play

And the dawn comes up like thunder
Outer China 'crost the bay![56]

(3) IMPERIUM: THE INNER AND THE OUTER EMPIRES

To build an overseas empire is not a simple matter. It requires more than men, money, and ships. It requires expertise, enterprise, and experience, an established tradition. The earliest European power, Spain, had all of these things. The conquistadores went straight from their triumphs in Iberia to the conquest of the Americas. The English, in contrast, initially possessed only part of the requirements. Though some historians talk of the origins of 'English imperialism' in medieval times, thinking especially of the subjugation of Ireland and Wales, the English went through a long phase when their ambitions were turned more to France than to the world's oceans. Only gradually, in the sixteenth and seventeenth centuries, did they develop the necessary imperial infrastructure. The Elizabethan conquest of Ireland was a key moment (see above). So, too, was the union with Scotland. Together they provided the politicians, the money-men, and the merchants in London with an 'inner empire' in the Isles that could serve as a springboard for the 'outer empire' overseas. The first successful English colony, in Virginia, came directly from English experience in Ireland, where Captain John Smith had served. The second conquest of Ireland by Cromwell added an extra incentive to the Navigation Acts of 1651 and 1660, which put all trade with territories ruled by England into a closed economic system. The union with Scotland followed directly Scotland's own failed experiment with colonial development (see pages 660–94, above), and closely preceded the greatly increased opportunities deriving from the Treaty of Utrecht. England was coming to maturity as an imperial power at the very time that the imperial capacity of Spain, Portugal, and the Netherlands was on the wane. France would remain as the principal rival. But the way was now open for the United Kingdom to build on England's first empire and to amass the greatest collection of colonies, dependencies, dominions, and protectorates that the world has ever seen.

The 'English Empire', as assembled in the seventeenth century, was confined almost exclusively to the Atlantic seaboard. It came about in a haphazard fashion from a variety of initiatives. Virginia (1609) was the product of a state-sponsored scheme. The colony soon sent pioneers to nearby Bermuda, and Bermuda to the Bahamas. Massachusetts, incorporated in 1629, resulted from the private enterprise of Puritan exiles. So, too, did Connecticut (1636). Rhode Island was founded by refugees from the intolerance of Massachusetts, also reinforcing England's early outposts in the West Indies, at St Kitts and Nevis (1623 and 1628). Maryland (1632) started life as a refuge for Catholic exiles under George Calvert, Baron Baltimore, who had served as clerk to the Council in Dublin. Barbados was taken over by a group of settlers under the Earl of Carlisle during Charles I's war with Spain (1625). The first English footholds in the future Canada were purely commercial. The Newfoundland Company (1605) was set up to exploit the rich coastal fishing grounds. The Hudson's Bay Company originated in explorations promoted in the 1640s by Prince Rupert, who sought to take over France's lucrative northern fur trade, and it was incorporated by Charles II in 1670. Its first governor, Charles Bayley, was a querulous Quaker imprisoned under the Test Act, who took up his post on release from the Tower of London. The first English footholds in West Africa – at James Island in the Gambia (1661), at Sierra Leone, and on the Gold Coast – originated in trading posts consolidated in 1676 under the control of the Royal African Company. Jamaica (1655) was the prize of Cromwell's war with Spain. New York (1665) and neighbouring New Jersey, which was handed by Charles II to a Jerseyman, George Carteret, were carved out of the Dutch New Netherlands, captured during the Second Dutch War. Pennsylvania (1681) arose from Charles II's debt to one of his admirals. It was given as freehold to the admiral's son, William Penn (1644–1718), who had been brought up by his Dutch mother on the family estates near Cork in southern Ireland. Himself imprisoned for

Nonconformity, Penn secured the release of twelve hundred jailed Quakers, who supplied the infant colony's initial settlers.

The 'first British Empire' – whose most valuable possessions were lost through carelessness – expanded the collection of English colonies acquired before the union. Indeed, for many decades after the union, the English were not eager to involve the Scots in their colonial ventures, and the Scots were reluctant to join in. The existing colonies in North America and the West Indies were consolidated. Georgia, which was incorporated in 1727, filled the gap separating British territory from the Spanish colony in Florida, whilst the conquest of French Canada in 1759 formed a vast block of territory stretching from Georgia to the Arctic. Further British gains from France and Spain during the Seven Years War added Dominica, St Vincent, Grenada, and Trinidad to the collection. By the 1760s, a permanent British transatlantic empire appeared to have been secured.

The British, however, had overplayed their hand. The fighting with the French in Canada had dragged the American colonists into an unwelcome conflict that greatly disturbed their relations both with the French and with the native tribes all along the open 'Frontier'. What is more, Britain's attempt to tax the colonists was grossly mishandled. Objectively speaking, it was not unreasonable or oppressive for the British crown to expect its American subjects to make a small contribution to the costs of an empire from which they, in terms of trade and commercial development, would have been among the principal beneficiaries. Americans would have had no real difficulty paying their share of Grenville's stamp duties or the derisory duty on tea. Yet the manner in which these duties were imposed caused an uproar that couldn't be quelled. The fact that the case concerning the crown's jurisdiction was put forward in a pompous and unilateral Declaratory Act (1766), exactly as in Ireland in 1720, invited the public discussion of constitutional issues that might never have been raised. Flushed with their recent victories, the British ministers did not know how to proceed with tact and restraint, and they provoked a needless disaster. In the War of

American Independence, they found out by hard experience what they should have known from the start, namely that Britain's military capacity was extremely limited. Though the Royal Navy could put a military force ashore at any point on the globe, the tiny British army did not possess the resources to master an enormous territory that was many times the size of the British Isles. As a result, a handful of redcoats were sent out to suppress a handful of colonials in the wide-open American backwoods; and they failed miserably. Even if Generals Howe and Burgoyne had eliminated George Washington's Continental Army – which was entirely possible – they could never have raised an adequate garrison to hold the colonies down for long by force. From start to finish, the birth of the USA was the product of incompetence and culpable stupidity. It need never have happened. But it did.

The 'Second British Empire', whose centre of gravity lay far to the east in the Indian and Pacific Oceans, was already in the making before the American colonies were lost. In the miraculous years of 1757–9, Robert Clive (1725–74) was putting the East India Company into a dominant position in India at the self-same time that Wolfe was capturing Canada. This time round the British learned their lesson. In India, they did not attempt to impose their will by unilateral coercion. Instead they worked with and through selected local potentates to divide and rule and to establish a highly cost-efficient hegemony. At the time when the Moghul Empire was still intact, and the French still held the lion's share of trading concessions in India, Clive showed in Bengal how a minuscule group of determined Britishers could reduce the ruling princes to puppets and then extend their own power and jurisdiction under the aegis of a nominal authority. Henceforth, as the Moghul Empire fragmented into scores of petty successor states, the British were presented with an ideal opportunity to play off one client maharajah against another, to expel the French, and to gain near total control. The Board of Control of the East India Company, established by the India Act (1784), became in effect, the central coordinating authority of a British-run confederation. The role of the British army was limited to manning a central reserve, to securing key posts on the frontier, and to training the armies of loyal clients. This system lasted for eighty years until the Indian Mutiny. But even after The Government of India Act (1858) disbanded the EIC and ushered in a regular administration under a Secretary of State and a Viceroy, the British hand on India continued to be held very lightly. In 1911, when the capital moved to Delhi, there were fewer British officials running a subcontinent of over two hundred million souls than there were Austrian officials in Prague. The Royal Navy guaranteed the imperial life-line round the Cape of Good Hope, or from 1869 via the Suez Canal. One of the grandest of the Viceroys, Lord Curzon (1859–1925), a great traveller in Asia and a great admirer of Indian civilization, foresaw the day of Indian self-government. The British, he said, were 'trustees of India's past and tutors to her future'.

India may have been 'the jewel in the crown'; but there were any number of other precious stones in the Empire's treasure-chest. From 1783 to 1920, the British Empire amassed a worldwide catalogue of some two hundred colonies, and lost none. (The Ionian Islands were given to Greece in 1864, and the rock of Heligoland was voluntarily ceded to the German Empire in 1890; all territories surrendered at the Peace of Amiens (1802) had been recovered by 1815.)

Seven or eight stages in this astonishing story may be observed. Firstly, in 1788, the unchallenged reach of the Royal Navy permitted Britain to lay claim to Australia, and to begin its colonization by Europeans at a juncture when no other power in the world was capable of doing so. The British presence in New Zealand from the 1830s was a natural corollary. Next, at the Peace of Paris (1814) after the Napoleonic Wars, the United Kingdom acquired or confirmed her occupation of a rich haul of former French, Spanish, and Dutch possessions. At the same time, through the reduction of French competition, she was able to assume control of key locations adjacent to existing possessions – hence British Guiana (1816), Singapore (1819), the Straits Settlements (1824), and others. In mid-century, the enormous prize of a decaying China came into view. As in India a century before, British policy limited itself to the acquisition of trading posts in the hope of greater gains at a later time. It was concerned not to push rival European powers into unbridled competition. Interest centred on the international port of Shanghai, and on the island of Hong Kong whose adjacent territory was secured on a hundred-and-fifty-year lease in 1847. Somewhat later, when 'the Eastern Question' came to a head through the decay of the Ottoman Empire, British policy showed restraint once again. This time the fear was to manage the ill-concealed ambitions of Russia with regards to both the Straits and the Holy Land. Even so, the British established a protectorate over Cyprus in 1878; and in 1882, by quelling a revolt, established de facto rule over Egypt as well. In the international 'Scramble for Africa', with which the century closed, no holds were barred. Full-blown, unapologetic imperialists like Joseph Chamberlain (1836–1914), or Cecil Rhodes (1853–1902), who had gone out from England to open up the diamond mines of the Rand, talked of painting the map red 'from Cairo to the Cape'. They almost succeeded; the one independent African country to block the British route was Abyssinia. Finally, as part of the settlement at the end of the First World War, the British Empire collected yet another large bag of trophies including the former German colonies, the Palestine Mandate, and part of the Near East. By that time, George V ruled over 11,400,000 square miles and 410 million subjects. (Virginia, where it all started, counted 40,000 square miles.) Here, quite literally, was an Empire 'where the sun never set'. King George's official last words were 'How is the Empire?' Unofficially, since his doctor had advised a seaside rest, they were 'Bugger Bognor'.[57]

Throughout this long process, the only people to offer sustained resistance and to force the British into two hard-fought wars were the Afrikaner 'Boers' of Transvaal. In 1881, they defeated a British force at Majuba Hill, and drove them out. In 1899–1902, having survived an attempt to overthrow their republics by the Jameson Raid, they conducted a series of brilliant campaigns against the combined might of the imperial armies. In the end, the Transvaal and the Orange Free State were added to the Cape Colony and Natal under British rule. The Union of South Africa (1910) joined Newfoundland (1855), Canada (1867), Australia (1900), and New Zealand (1907) as one of the Empire's self-governing Dominions.

No standard formula was ever devised to administer these far-flung lands. Ascension Island remained officially a naval man-of-war administered by the Admiralty. Most colonies were run by the Colonial Office, though the India Office was a separate department. Non-British Territories administered by Britain, like Egypt, came within the purview of the Foreign Office. The Channel Islands and the Isle of Man, as dependencies within the British Isles but outside the United Kingdom, answered to the Home Office. From 1865, all colonies were permitted in principle to pass their own legislation, subject only to 'the rule of repugnancy'. This meant that no colonial law should contradict the acts of the Westminster Parliament.

British imperialism, like all imperialisms, has since lost its glitter. It is widely considered today to be one of the great undiluted evils of history, involving the subjugation of the weak by the strong, the exploitation of the poor by the rich, the destruction of native cultures, and the humiliation by 'whites' of 'non-whites'. It is blamed for all sorts of current ills from poverty and political chaos in the Third World to racism and Eurocentrism. Certainly, the Empire's goals of political, economic, and cultural integration were ruthlessly pursued without too much concern for the consequences. Seen in retrospect, they belonged to a condemned system containing the seeds of its own destruction; and the reaction was bound to come.

And yet, in the eyes of its most devoted servants, there can be no doubt that British imperialism was seen as an effective force for good. Though paternalistic, it was less coercive than its counterparts run from Russia, France, or even Belgium; and it was the vehicle for improvement, bringing health, education, and increased prosperity to most of the colonial peoples. Most importantly, in the values of the day, it was the bearer of spiritual liberation and religious truth. Joseph Chamberlain, who had served as the reforming Mayor of Birmingham before serving from 1895 to 1903 as Colonial Secretary, thought of imperialism as the global equivalent of cleaning up the city slums. When he told his cheering audiences to 'Think imperially', or 'The day of empires has come', his assumption was that British imperial rule was beneficial for all, in particular for the godforsaken 'slum-dwellers' and 'heathen' of less fortunate countries than his own.[58] There was a strong sense of communal service in the Empire, and a strong streak of Protestant evangelical self-denial. All the finest imperialists, like Rudyard Kipling, born in Bombay, professed on the one hand a deep love of native cultures and, on the other, a profound moral unease at the implications of unbounded power. Kipling's moving poem 'Recessional' (1897) voices a warning against worldly arrogance: 'Lest we forget', 'Lest we forget'. The British missionaries, both Protestant and Catholic, who went out into the Empire were teaching their charges a higher message than mere political obedience. Anyone who has listened to a church choir singing in present-day Soweto or Papua New Guinea will have food for thought:

> So be it, Lord; Thy throne shall never
> Like earth's proud empires pass away
> Thy kingdom stands and grows for ever
> till all thy creatures own Thy sway.[59]

(4) THE CONTINUING PROTESTANT ASCENDANCY

Religious discrimination was the norm in early modern Europe. England was no exception. Indeed, it was less tolerant than both Scotland, where a solid Catholic block was (reluctantly) tolerated in the Highlands, and Ireland, where a tradition of multi-faith coexistence had developed early. Ever since the German princes of the 1530s, with Henry VIII's full approval, had pronounced the doctrine of *cuius regio, eius religio* (the principle that the established religion should be determined by the prince in each state) the English and later the British establishment took it to be axiomatic that its own Protestant proclivities should be formally promoted by law. So it is odd that most British historians still talk as if 'the Protestant Ascendancy' only operated in Ireland.

Yet Protestantism in the Isles was anything but uniform. Anglicans had been at odds with various brands of Nonconformists since Queen Elizabeth's day. The Church of England was at odds with the Presbyterian Church of Scotland. The only common denominator among them lay in their fear and hatred of Catholics. The essential quality of British Protestantism was a negative one: 'anti-Papism'.

In the eighteenth century, Europe as a whole grew sick of the religious conflicts that had plagued it since the Reformation, and the Age of Faith slowly gave way to 'the Age of Science and Reason'. English scientists, writers, and philosophers took a lead part in the intellectual ferment. The Royal Society for the Promotion of Natural Knowledge (1662) was Europe's premier scientific society. The Cambridge mathematician Isaac Newton (1642–1727) devised a system of natural laws which governed mankind's understanding of the universe for two hundred years. The Oxford philosopher John Locke (1632–1704), whose writings could only be published after the events of 1688–9, produced seminal works in the fields of religious practice, constitutional politics, and psychology. His *Letters* (1689–92) advocating toleration, his *Two Treatises on Government* (1690) arguing for the limitation of arbitrary rule, and especially his *Essay on Human Understanding* (1690) are regarded as classics of the age. 'All men', he wrote famously, 'are liable to error'. The poet and essayist Alexander Pope (1688–1714), who was both a Catholic and a physically disabled person, gained an international reputation with his Horatian *Essay On Criticism* (1711) and, in particular, with his wonderful *Essay on Man* (1733–4):

> Know thyself, presume not God to scan
> The proper study of mankind is Man.

Voltaire, the chief *philosophe* of the Enlightenment, took refuge in England in the 1730s and was pleasantly surprised by the relative degree of religious, political, and intellectual freedoms which he found there. The hierarchy of the Church of England was taken over by Latitudinarians, who believed in broad-mindedness and doctrinal flexibility. Deism sprang up in the religious undergrowth. Science and rationalism often went hand in hand with religious Nonconformity. The experimental physicist and chemist Joseph Priestley (1733–1804), wrote widely on all sorts of issues from liberty and electricity to freedom for the American colonies.

How far this high-minded intellectual elite was representative of the populace at large is another matter. An attempt by Parliament in 1780 to repeal the harshest provisions of anti-Catholic legislation – a century after the Test Acts – sparked off the worst riots in London's history. Led by Lord George Gordon (1751–93) and his Protestant Association, the mob attacked Catholics and their supposed supporters and ransacked their property for ten days. Twelve thousand troops restored order by summary justice. Seven hundred people were left dead; twenty-five were executed; the Lord Mayor of London was fined the vast sum of £1,000 for criminal negligence; and Gordon converted to Judaism. Eleven years later, in July 1791, another mob of similar ilk took to the streets in Birmingham. This time their target was Joseph Priestley, who had dared to hold a dinner celebrating the anniversary of the fall of the Bastille. They demolished his house and laboratory, the property of other prominent dissenters, and several Nonconformist chapels. They clearly linked religious dissent with political revolution. For that numerous part of the English population, continuing discrimination against dissenters and papists was absolutely proper.

The ideals of the Enlightenment probably made a wider appeal in Scotland. As from the 1750s, the Scottish universities produced a dazzling array of pioneering thinkers which their English counterparts could in no way emulate. (In 1753, England's greatest ever historian, Edward Gibbon, was expelled from Magdalen College, Oxford for converting to Catholicism.) The milieu in Edinburgh and

Glasgow, in contrast, encouraged speculation and free-thinking in many fields. The atheist philosopher David Hume (1711–66) wrote a highly unusual *History of England* (1762) (see below), as well as his famous follow-up to Locke in his *Enquiry concerning Human Understanding* (1746). Adam Ferguson (1723–1816), who held chairs in both mathematics and moral philosophy, wrote one of the pioneering works of sociology, his *Essay on the History of Civil Society* (1766). Adam Smith (1723–90), another professor of moral philosophy, author of *The Wealth of Nations* (1776), is seen as the father of modern economics. (See below.)

In terms of popular appeal, however, the new religious fervour of Methodism was far more influential than rational philosophy. The Revd John Wesley (1703–91), an Oxford tutor who took to open-air preaching, grew disillusioned with the stultifying conformism of the Church of England, and launched a country-wide crusade for its re-inspiration. In a long lifetime of incessant travel and proselytism, he visited the common people of virtually every parish in the land, establishing a network of preaching circuits and devotional societies, which after his death would break with the official Church for good. Wesley's Methodism stressed the inner conviction of individual believers, and the joy of redemption by God's grace. Aided by his brother Charles (1707–88), one of the greatest hymn-writers of all time, he put the soul back into English Protestantism, in a simple spirit of Christian faith that saw no one as its enemy. After Wesley, the Nonconformist camp was stronger than ever, especially in the growing industrial suburbs; and it had most of the best tunes.

Methodism made an extraordinary impact on Wales. Whether through its egalitarianism, its predilection for singing, or its rejection of the official hierarchy, it spread like wildfire through the valleys, turning Wales for two centuries into one of the great fortresses of Nonconformity. What is more, its chapels and schools provided a forum for the practice and propagation of the Welsh language. Welsh hymns married to Methodist music became one of the great art forms of British civilization; and the choirs that sang them acted

for generations as the greatest single repository of Welsh culture.
(See Appendix 55.)

> Guide me, O Thou great Jehovah
> Pilgrim through this barren land
> I am weak but Thou art mighty
> Hold me with Thy powerful hand.
> Bread of heaven, bread of heaven
> Feed me till I want no more
> Feed me till I want no more.[60]

It would be wrong, of course, to attribute the Welsh National
Revival entirely to Methodism. The revival was underway before
Wesley arrived; the great pioneer of Welsh language education,
Griffith Jones (1683–1771), experienced a religious conversion within
the Anglican context quite independent of Wesley's influence, and
his circulating Welsh schools were already making their dramatic
impact on Welsh literacy rates in the 1750s, at least one generation
ahead of the Methodist influx. Nonetheless, the conjunction of the
Welsh Revival with revivalist Methodism forged the happiest of
bonds which was to dominate Welsh life for the duration. 'The
jubilant singing of hymns with their occasional erotic images was a
sensuous experience, and the leaping characteristic of the more
exultant of the saved was even more sensuous.'[61] Cornwall, too,
was especially receptive to Methodism, developing the same blend
as Wales of religious fervour and cultural separateness.

In the nineteenth century, religious life in the Isles was dominated
by two great issues. One was 'Emancipation' – a term taken from the
campaign against slavery. The other was 'Disestablishment'.

After the Gordon Riots, a group of leading English Catholics
sought a way forward through impressing the public with their
loyalty to the state. Their Protestation (1788) formally denied the
temporal authority of the Pope. It led to the removal of the legal
ban on Catholic worship, which had been in force since 1558, but
not to an end to civil disabilities. The Union with Ireland was
pushed through on a promise of full Catholic Emancipation, but the

promise was not honoured. In consequence, Daniel O'Connor (1775–1845), a Dublin barrister, founded his Catholic Association, whose mass meetings not just in Ireland but throughout the United Kingdom turned into the most effective political lobby of the day. The threat of violence, and of another Irish Rising, was eventually sufficient to force the government to relent. The Test Acts were repealed in 1828. The Catholic Emancipation (Relief) Act (1829) rendered Catholics eligible for all offices of state except those of lord-lieutenant, lord chancellor, regent, and monarch. Catholic schools and churches proliferated. The huge influx of Irish immigrants into the new industrial cities of England and Scotland created a solid Catholic sector in the working class. British Roman Catholicism soon turned into a loyal and thriving denomination.

The repeal of the Test Acts equally removed the civil disabilities on Nonconformists. Many petty barriers remained in particular institutions like the universities, and full equality was not achieved until the 1880s. But henceforth Nonconformity flourished, and threw its weight behind the burgeoning movement for political liberalism. By the end of the century, attendance at the so called Free Churches, whether those of Old Dissent such as the Baptists, Congregational Independents, and Quakers, or those of New Dissent in the various strands of Methodism, was outstripping attendance in the Church of England.

Within Anglicanism, the double threat from liberated Catholics and Nonconformists heightened the tensions between the 'High Church' and 'Low Church'. Some parishes adopted forms of worship that were barely distinguishable from those of the dissenting chapels. Others, starting with the University parish of St Mary the Virgin in Oxford, began to imitate the liturgy and practices of Roman Catholicism. Followers of the Oxford Movement – or 'Tractarians' as they were called, from their tracts circulated in the 1840s – secured a permanent position in Anglican ranks. But their leading light, John Henry Newman (1801–90), steadily moved on until received by Rome. Founder of the Oratories in Kensington and Birmingham and first Rector of the Catholic University of Dublin, he died a cardinal.[62]

In Scotland, the elders of the Kirk took a dogged stand against the inroads both of Catholicism and of Nonconformity. With the major exceptions of the Highlands and of Glasgow, where Irish Catholics were given to battling it out on the streets with Free Presbyterians from Ulster, the general picture was more uniform until the major schism of 1843. The breakaway of the evangelical Free Church of Scotland was the culmination of tensions going back to the old struggle between episcopals and non-episcopals. The further fraction which occurred in 1900 with the defection from the Free Church of fundamentalist 'Wee Frees' rendered the final religious panorama almost as complicated as elsewhere. Religious uniformity was a chimera of the past.

The struggles over 'Disestablishment' were a natural corollary to the campaign for religious emancipation. In Ireland, for example, the liberated Catholics were no longer willing to pay tithes to the official Church; and the formal link between the Church and an unpopular state gravely undermined the Church's spiritual standing. Parallel problems arose at a later date in Methodist Wales. A solution was found in Ireland in 1871, when Gladstone's Liberal ministry cut the Gordian knot and set up the disestablished Church of Ireland. The disestablished Anglican Church in Wales did not emerge until 1930. Unreconciled opponents to this process, which is still to be applied to the Church of England, coined the longest word in the English language, namely *anti-disestablishmentarianism*.[63]

None of which cured the old disease of anti-Catholicism. On the contrary, after taking a breather in mid-century, the traditional prejudices revived in many sections of British opinion. They were fuelled by the rise of Irish nationalism, which was wrongly diagnosed as a new form of the old Popish Plot; by the remarkable resurgence of English Catholicism, which was falsely denounced as 'unpatriotic'; by the growth of solidly Catholic suburbs in all the major cities, from Belfast to Birmingham; and, after 1870, by the Vatican's pronouncement of the dogma of infallibility. Attitudes did not automatically shift in line with the liberalization of the laws. For obvious reasons, resistance to change was most entrenched in Ulster. But the Ulsterman's cry of 'No Surrender' and of 'One Faith, One Crown', still evoked huge sympathy both in England and Scotland. For the great majority of British people in the early twentieth century, God still remained a Protestant English gentleman.

(5) WESTMINSTER: 'MOTHER OF PARLIAMENTS'

There have been Parliaments in the Isles for the best part of eight hundred years. For five of those eight centuries, there were usually three Parliaments – either in London, Edinburgh, and Dublin, or, from the 1920s to the 1970s, in London, Dublin, and Belfast. During the eighteenth century, there were two Parliaments: the British or Anglo-Scottish Parliament at Westminster and the Irish Parliament in Dublin. Only in the nineteenth century, or more exactly in the years 1801–1921, was there one sole, sovereign Parliament legislating for all parts of the Isles. When popular reference works say things like 'The UK Parliament is generally considered to have started life in 1265',[64] they are repeating what most people generally consider to be the case.

Of course, the Westminster Parliament has enjoyed a remarkable run of continuity. At each step of its long story, it kept itself in being whilst new Welsh members in 1540, new Scots members in 1707, or new Irish members in 1801 were co-opted in virtually seamless mergers. In this way, the English core was able not only to keep the political initiative but also to pretend that nothing had really changed.

In reality, many important things were changing. Arguably the most fundamental element in any Parliament's make-up, the territory and population which it represents, has undergone several key shifts. The Westminster Parliament of 1999 does not serve the same country and peoples that it served in 1899, 1799, 1699, 1599, or 1499: the critical balance between English and non-English MPs has always worked strongly in England's favour; but it has varied considerably. In 1499, a House of Commons of 296 members was exclusively English.

A century later, in the late last years of Elizabeth, the 462 MPs were still exclusively English except for a handful of Welshmen. In 1659, during the Protectorate, the first all-British Parliament brought in 549 members. But the separate parliaments in Edinburgh and Dublin were restored immediately afterwards. In the eighteenth century, after the first Union of 1707, the block of English MPs constituted almost nine-tenths of the Commons, though this fell after the second Union of 1801 to about 55 per cent. In 1900, when 456 English MPs faced 101 from Ireland, 70 from Scotland, and 34 from Wales, the absolute English majority was still wafer thin. On divisive issues such as Irish Home Rule, a critical margin could be controlled by the MPs representing the universities, whose numbers varied from 12 to 20.

By general consent, the crucial moment in the growth of the standing of the Westminster Parliament occurred during the 'Revolution' of 1688–9. After a century of conflict between English Parliament and English King, Parliament came out definitively on top. In 1649, a victorious Parliament had executed the defeated King only to find that the resultant void could not be easily filled. In 1689, thanks to the exile of the King and the presence of an eager usurper, the victorious Parliament was to make less drastic arrangements, and to cement Parliament's temporary advantage into a permanent system. The system was put into place at a time when Westminster's primary competence extended only to England and Wales. But it was not successfully challenged in later times; and an English Revolution provided the guiding principles for the later 'British Constitution'.

However, since no comprehensive constitutional text was ever formulated beyond certain clauses in the Acts of Union, the very concept of a British constitution is extremely slippery. It is rooted not just in the various enactments of 1689 such as the Declaration of Rights, but equally in subsequent interpretations and in long-standing parliamentary practice which would set the precedents, refine the disputed issues, and pass the additional legislation to which all judgements had to refer. In the last resort, there was no independent constitutional court beyond Parliament that could settle disputes. 'Parliament itself decides.' Here lies the heart of what some analysts have tellingly called 'the English Ideology'. Its guiding principles, which exist implicitly in law but not explicitly in any one document, have to be summarized by every commentator as best as commentators can. But they centre on three contentions. Firstly, since Parliament determines the succession, either by naming the heirs to the throne or by legally limiting the qualified candidates, the monarchy is subservient to Parliament. What Parliament has provided, Parliament can take away. Secondly, through its financial monopoly, Parliament can insist on such control or supervision of all other governmental organs as it thinks fit. Thirdly, the entire sphere of arbitrary prerogative, once exercised by English Kings in their own right, has been transferred *in toto* to the British Parliament. Parliament is free either to exercise those prerogative powers itself, directly, or to delegate them under licence to other bodies, including the monarchy. In practice, once the electors have completed the electoral process, they surrender all their constituency rights to the elected MPs and all their collective rights to the will of Parliament. In between elections, which Parliament can if necessary postpone, they live under a legal parliamentary despotism.

Given the informality of this system, it took a little time before the full extent of Parliament's victory was realized. In the key matter of forming an executive government, for example, three or four decades passed before the realization that the government should normally and naturally be formed by the party commanding a majority in the House of Commons. William and Mary worked very closely with Parliament, relying heavily on their alliance with the Whig oligarchy that had masterminded the Settlement. But the Whig oligarchs sat in the House of Lords, manipulating the Commons through patronage and influence. Similarly, under Queen Anne, successive chief ministers – Sidney, Lord Godolphin

(1645–1712), who had made a long career in the Treasury, or the Tory Robert Harley, Earl of Oxford (1661–1724) – were chosen as much for their favour at court as for their command of the Commons. A queen who owed her throne to the parliamentary exclusion of her nephew was never going to challenge Parliament's ultimate authority. But in the absence of any newly established practice, no one stopped her from working on the assumption that her ministers were her own. The real change came during the reign of George I, when Sir Robert Walpole (1676–1745) refused the usual elevation of a chief minister to the House of Lords. By combining his twenty-year tenure of the first-lordship of the Treasury with his hold over the House of Commons, Walpole became, in effect if not in name, the united Kingdom's first Prime Minister. Even so, it was not until the middle of the nineteenth century that the cabinet of ministers automatically resigned after a general election in order to be reconstituted in accordance with the electoral results.

In those early decades, the unlimited extent of parliamentary authority may best be seen in the draconian statutes passed in the sphere of law and order. The Riot Act (1715), which dated from the time of the first Jacobite Rising, put the summary power of life and death in the hands of local magistrates. Once the magistrates had 'read the Riot Act' aloud to any unauthorized assembly of twelve or more persons, and had given them the statutory sixty minutes to disperse, they were fully empowered, by Parliament, to kill all lingerers on the spot. The Black Waltham Act (1739), which was directed against highwaymen, was still more terrifying. By the Habeas Corpus Act (1679), all prisoners had a theoretical right to be charged or released. By the Mutiny Act (1689), all soldiers were subject to military discipline in time of peace as well as in war, with a right to a court martial. But all alleged rioters, who may just have been slow to leave, and all alleged highwaymen, who may conceivably have been on their way to a masked ball, were likely to be dead without trial and with no questions asked.

The first period of British parliamentarism, however, unfolded between 1707 and 1800 in the unreformed world of patronage, clients, 'rotten boroughs', and 'pocket boroughs'. All the great aristocrats arranged for clients, usually lesser gentry from their counties, to manage their interests in the Commons. The crown could create peers from among its loyal servants in order to steer the Lords, while it kept a solid block of some two hundred 'placemen' or office-holders in the Commons to manage business there. The most famous examples of the rotten boroughs were Dunwich (Suffolk), which still returned an MP despite being washed into the sea, and Old Sarum near Salisbury, where the agent of the Duke of Newcastle would set up his electoral tent in the green pastures of a village already devoid of inhabitants. The 'pocket boroughs' were constituencies thought to be entirely in the gift of a patron. Two of them, Weymouth and Melcombe Regis in Dorset, returned a total of four MPs, the same as the City of London. When one adds to this the fact that the government of the day would spend liberal sums of secret service money to bribe electors and to reward both MPs and peers with 'annuities', it is not hard to see why the eighteenth-century Commons was entirely dependent on its social 'betters'. The historian of Parliament and prosopographist who best expounded the workings of this system, Lewis Namier, was familiar enough with aristocratic patronage from the history of his native Poland. But his findings came as a shock to his many British readers, who had imagined that the Westminster Parliament was based on high ideals. Summing up the activities of two Prime Ministers, Newcastle and Bute, of their 'squadrons' and 'electoral machines', Namier wrote somewhat cynically: 'History is made up of juggernauts, revolting to human feeling in their blindness, supremely humorous in their stupidity.'[65]

The 'English interest' was one of several parliamentary juggernauts which Namier described. Though the British Parliament in Hanoverian times was an Anglo-Scottish body, 86 per cent of the seats in the Lords and 88 per cent in the Commons were reserved for English members. No fewer than 293 MPs out of 558 sat for constituencies south of the Thames, compared with 196 from the Midlands and North, 24 from Wales, and 45 for Scotland. As time wore on, and the centre of gravity of England's population moved steadily northwards, the north of England grew to be almost as disadvantaged as Scotland was all along. Simple mathematics determined that the Scots MPs could never win a vote on their own. British democracy operated from the start on the understanding that a handful of southern English counties decided everything. Non-English members were free to participate on the basis of their freedoms being unequal to those of the English.

One of the new interests, much feared at the time, was that of 'the nabobs' – the British administrators from India, who came home with vast fortunes. Men like Robert Clive simply bought their way into Parliament without reference either to the crown or to aristocratic patrons. The so-called 'Bengal Squad' was one of the truly independent factions in Parliament, and, as such caused mortal offence to the *status possidendi*. The circles of old corruption took serious offence at the conduct of the centres of new corruption. Clive, whose finances were subject to a parliamentary inquiry, was driven to suicide. One of his successors, Warren Hastings (1732–1818), sometime Governor-General of India, was put through the ordeal of a seven-year trial that all but ruined him.

Into this maelstrom of jobbery, corruption, and chauvinism walked the rakish and libertarian figure of John Wilkes (1727–97). Elected MP for Aylesbury but not rewarded with a hoped-for posting, Wilkes turned with a vengeance against the King and the Scottish Prime Minister, the Earl of Bute (1713–92). Founding a weekly paper, *The North Briton*, he mercilessly lampooned the King and his ministers, and the official paper *The Briton*, to the point where he was charged in court with libel, and then with obscene libel. Released from the Tower because of his parliamentary immunity, he then embarked on three decades of radical protest. In and out of prison, and in and out of Parliament, he campaigned for electoral reform, for freedom of the press, and for American independence. In 1768 when Scottish troops fired on Wilkeite rioters during the Massacre of St George's Fields in London, scores of people were killed or injured. In England and the USA he is championed as a friend of liberty. In Scotland he is remembered for some of the most Scottophobic ranting on record:

> The River Tweed is the line of demarcation between all that is noble and all that is base. South of the river all is honour, virtue and patriotism. North of it is nothing but lying, malice, meanness and slavery. Scotland is a treeless, flowerless land, formed out of the refuse of the universe and inhabited by the very bastards of creation.[66]

It was apparently with Wilkes in mind that Dr Johnson made his famous quip about 'patriotism' being 'the last resort of the scoundrel'.[67]

The second period of British parliamentarism unfolded between 1801 and 1922 in the context of all-Union representation. The Irish, who commanded over 100 seats in the Commons from the start, were far stronger than the Scots and the Welsh put together; and they formed the largest single minority block. But they were still far short of the necessary votes. Apart from Catholic Emancipation (see above, page 723), the great issue of the early decades was Parliamentary Reform. Only later, after the Reform Act (1832) and the Irish famine, did the Irish question emerge as the unsolved conundrum of the age.

Oddly enough, the penultimate phase of the unreformed Parliament produced some of the most sparkling episodes of British parliamentary history. The reason, of course, lay with the onset of the French Revolution, which raised the spectre of real democracy in Europe and forced the complacent British to rake over their ideological coals. The long-running debate threw off a shower of sparks in a series of principled arguments that have defined British attitudes to radicalism and conservatism ever since. The principal contestants in the parliamentary bear-pit were Charles James Fox, MP (1749–1806), the radical; Edmund Burke, MP (1729–97), the

'Father of Conservatism'; bnand William Pitt the Younger (1759–1806), the youngest ever Prime Minister in British history and the dominant figure in government during the greater part of the French Revolutionary Wars.

Fox, a notorious roué, welcomed the French Revolution, just as he had welcomed the American Rebellion; and he stuck to his beliefs. On the Fall of the Bastille, he wrote to a friend, 'How much the greatest event it is that ever happened in the world!' Despite the excesses which followed, he held that the struggle for civil liberties posed less danger to the welfare of the people than the unending machinations of an entrenched establishment. Though never in favour of radical violence, he never ceased to raise his voice in favour of Catholic emancipation, the abolition of slavery, and parliamentary reform. Burke, too, an Irish orator of great eloquence, welcomed the French Revolution effusively. He praised the new French constitution, as he had praised Europe's first written constitution in Poland a few months earlier. But when the Revolution took to violence he held that it had disgraced itself irreparably. Burke's conservatism was not reactionary. It stood for change, but for orderly, evolutionary change. 'Good Order', he declared, 'is the foundation of all things:' but also 'a state without the means of some change is without the means of its conservation', and 'Liberty, too, must be limited in order to be possessed'. Given the revolutionaries and counter-revolutionaries on either hand, the gap between Fox and Burke was not that wide. Pitt saw virtues in them both. He concentrated on running the country. 'England has saved herself by her exertions', he declared in his last public speech, 'and will, as I trust, save Europe by her example.' The United Kingdom for Pitt was still, inexcusably, 'England'.

One says 'inexcusably', however, with a certain reservation. For the people at that period who might have been expected to insist on 'British' where 'British' was due were the very ones who willingly acquiesced. After all, it was a Scottish MP, David Scott, the member for Perthshire, who rose in the Commons in the year of Trafalgar to excuse the point:

> We commonly when speaking of British subjects call them English, be they English, Scots or Irish; he will never be offended, therefore, . . . with the word English being applied in future to express any of His Majesty's subjects, or suppose it can be meant as an allusion to any part of the United Kingdom.[68]

In this climate, Nelson had no hesitation in calling on 'every man' to 'do his duty' in the name of 'England'.

The tale of parliamentary reform is an extremely long one. Nearly two hundred years passed between the proposal for manhood suffrage from the Duke of Richmond in 1780 and the achievement of full adult suffrage for all over eighteen in 1969. Various liberal associations battled against entrenched privilege in the name of the excluded 'People'. But their democratic goals were easily smeared by association with the foreign French Revolution; and they were only ever addressed in dribs and drabs. Their greatest champion, Lord John Russell (1792–1878), was known as 'Finality Jack', because he wanted to settle it all at a stroke. But he never had his way. The working-class Chartist Movement, active 1836–58, was particularly ineffective.

The Reform Act (1832), therefore, was necessarily the first of several. It redistributed seats in the Commons, abolishing 56 rotten boroughs and giving proper representation to the growing industrial towns of northern England. And it gave the vote to large numbers of propertied males (principally £10 householders in the boroughs and 40s freeholders in the counties), raising the total electorate from 435,000 to 632,000. But it did little for the non-English constituencies and nothing for women or the working class; and it left the aristocratic interest intact in the counties. It launched the era of party-based politics but on the basis of a franchise that was far from democratic. The second Reform Act (1867) and the third Reform Act (1884) made up for some of the deficiencies by further redistribution of seats and further extensions of the male franchise. Yet all the way to 1918 a meagre 20 per cent of the United Kingdom's adult population participated in the parliamentary process. Thanks to these reforms, the relative strength of Scottish, Welsh, and Irish representation in Parliament actually decreased: at every stage, the lion's share of redistributed seats went to English constituencies.

Like parliamentary reform, the Irish question passed through many stages. Most activities took place outside Parliament. A Young Ireland group was founded in imitation of Mazzini's Young Italy in 1847; and the long active struggle for control of the land began in earnest after the Famine. In the 1860s, the Irish Republican Brotherhood, the Fenians, launched a campaign of terror-bombings and murders, provoking waves of police repression, evictions, and Coercion Acts. In 1868, the beleaguered Irish found a sympathetic English supporter in the first Liberal Government of W. E. Gladstone. But Gladstone, though he disestablished the Church in Ireland, could not stop the land war. As from 1880 the Irish Land League fought for 'the Three F's' – fair rents, free sale, and fixity of tenure. They made an example of a land agent in County Mayo, Captain Charles Boycott (1832–97), who was seen as a notorious evictor. Boycott's estates were besieged. His crops had to be harvested by an imported brigade of Ulstermen guarded by a thousand soldiers. And his name passed into the English language.

From 1877 to 1914, however, an Irish Home Rule Party pursued their demands by political action inside the British Parliament. Founded by Charles Stewart Parnell (1846–91), a Protestant landowner with an American mother, it sought leverage by the tactics of obstruction and by seeking to hold the balance between the rival 'Liberals' and 'Tories'. Parnell's great chance arose after the general election in 1885, when he did indeed hold the balance. But Gladstone's first Home Rule Bill, proposing domestic autonomy for Ireland and the restoration of a Parliament in Dublin, was voted down. The Tories under Lord Randolph Churchill (1849–95) mobilized the northern Irish Protestants, vowing 'Ulster will fight, and Ulster will be right'. Gladstone's Liberal Party fell apart; and Parnell was destroyed by a minor private scandal. The Irish MPs did not get another chance until 1910 during the Liberal government of Herbert

Asquith. Under John Redmond (1858–1918), they again held the balance in Parliament, and saw to it that a second Home Rule Bill was introduced. By that time, the Irish question had been mired with several other burning constitutional issues of the day.

Throughout its nineteenth-century heyday, the British Parliament was presented as a shining light to all peoples round the world aspiring to constitutional democracy. In 1865, the Lancashire radical John Bright (1811–89) called it 'the Mother of Parliaments'. The epithet was hardly suitable for the British Empire as a whole, where most colonies were not permitted Parliaments. But it was appropriate enough for the global 'English-speaking world' that had come into being. The US Congress, though far more democratic than Westminster, nonetheless traced its roots to the English and the British parliamentary tradition. Infant Parliaments in Ottawa, in the Canadian provincial capitals from Vancouver to Halifax, in the Australian state capitals from Perth to Brisbane, in Wellington (1907), Pretoria (1910), and Canberra (1911), all parliamentarians saw themselves as Westminster's children.

Ever since the English Parliament was transformed into the British Parliament in 1707, the House of Lords had somehow avoided reform. The citadel of the Whig oligarchy retained its hold over parliamentary procedures long after the Whigs had passed into oblivion. In particular, as the second or higher chamber of Parliament, it retained the right to veto all legislation prepared in the Commons. Despite all the cycles of parliamentary reform, the house of aristocratic privilege was still top spaniel at the start of the twentieth century. Matters came to a head in 1909–10. When Tory peers prepared to block both the 'People's Budget' and the second Home Rule Bill, Westminster's ambiguous reputation as a forum of democracy was put to the test. The passage of the People's Budget would test the British Parliament's commitment to the social and economic aspects of democracy. The fate of the Home Rule Bill would demonstrate whether the British Parliament could accommodate all the legitimate aspirations of all the peoples of the Isles.

(6) The British Aristocracy: Peerage and Baronetage

Most European countries possessed feudal aristocracies which survived into modern times. The French nobility, for example, which had been subordinated to the state by Richelieu, survived intact until 1789 and was partly restored after 1815. The Russian nobility, after a long reign as the well-heeled slaves of the Tsar, was cruelly eliminated in 1917. The *szlachta* of Poland-Lithuania, which had been the most numerous nobility in Europe and unique in having no titles, kept its privileges until the partitions of the country in the late eighteenth century. The Spanish nobility, which had once been almost as numerous as its Polish counterpart, was hobbled by the French Revolution and by the repeated republican experiments of the nineteenth century. The German aristocracy, which enjoyed a new lease of life under the Hohenzollern Empire, lost its special standing under the Weimar Republic and the Third Reich. Yet the aristocracies of England, Scotland, and Ireland were still going strong in the twentieth century. Unusual in their two-layered composition of 'peerage' and 'gentry', they had been successively merged to form a consciously British aristocracy that has long been one of the pillars of British state and society.

Reading *Burke's Peerage*, the handbook of the British aristocracy first published in 1826, one can learn more about the social aspects of British political history than from a shelf full of works of sociological analysis. It shows how this dominant caste stood at the pinnacle of a highly hierarchical social order, how it is closely bound to the monarchy, and how it was a true fusion drawn from all corners of the Isles.

The five degrees of noble peers – dukes, marquesses, earls, viscounts, and barons – and the more numerous ranks of non-noble baronets form an extraordinarily cohesive group. They are defined against the rest of society by their ancient hereditary privileges, and amongst themselves by an elaborate code of precedence. By using the criteria of seniority by rank, seniority of title by date of grant, and seniority of male and female heirs within families, *Burke's* was able to publish an annual list giving a precise place and number to every single individual. In the 93rd Edition (1953), for example, the Archbishop of Canterbury was nr. 991, HH Sultan Sir Mahomed Shah, Aga Kha nr. 18,161, and Mrs G. H. Shakerly-Ackers nr. 160,628.[69] Everyone on the list was a member of so-called 'Society'. Anyone without a number, i.e., 98.5 per cent of the population, simply did not count.

The sense of caste solidarity was reinforced not simply by centuries of interbreeding and common activities, but also by sophisticated rituals and ceremonies, by detailed dress codes and heraldry. Every degree had its specific robes for official occasions and its own form of address: and every family had a coat-of-arms designed by and registered with one of the two heraldic colleges.

The symbiosis of aristocracy and monarchy was manifest by attendance at the royal court and in the mass of court offices which the monarch dispensed. To be elevated to 'Groom of the Stool', for instance, requiring the most intimate attendance on the royal person, was not just an honour. It gave cherished access to the sovereign that any politician would lose an arm for. Noble titles had been personally bestowed by monarchs, and carried the weight of ages. The senior baron by writ, Lord De Ros, looked back to 1264. The senior English baronet, Bacon, looked back to 1611. Furthermore, the power to create new peers and baronets gave the monarch a lasting hold over the establishment. The aristocracy needed the monarchy, no less than the monarchy needed the aristocracy.

Given their feudal origins, aristocratic titles were usually linked to a particular territorial honour. All senior peers would be known and addressed by their honour rather than by their surname. Robert Devereux, Earl of Essex was known simply as 'Essex' not 'Devereux'. John Churchill, Duke of Marlborough, was known as 'Marlborough' not 'Churchill'. Bishops, too, as Lords Spiritual, were known by the name of their sees rather than by their personal names. All peers below the rank of earl possessed a territorial honour in their patent, and were known by their title, either surname, as Lord Byron, or their place, as Viscount Wellington. The practice has been carried into the age of the life peers: they are usually created with their surname as their title, unless the surname is already in use, thus 'Baroness Thatcher, of Kesteven' and 'Baroness Jay of Paddington', and are all known by the surname part of the title only. Baronets, and knights who are not peers, however, have always been known and addressed by their given name, not by their surname alone. Hence Sir Francis Drake was always addressed as 'Sir Francis', and never, as many foreigners would prefer, 'Sir Drake'.

One of the interesting things clearly visible in *Burke*'s is the long process whereby the separate peerages of the three kingdoms were gradually merged into a united British peerage with territorial honours scattered throughout the United Kingdom. In this, the distinctions deriving from the date of grant were carefully maintained. The senior non-royal duke, the Duke of Norfolk, for example, held an English peerage dating from 1483, together with the hereditary English office of Earl Marshal. The Duke of Hamilton held a Scottish peerage dating from 1643; the Duke of Leinster held an Irish peerage dating from 1766, and a viscountcy of Great Britain dating from 1747. The Duke of Portland, whose title in 1716 postdated the Union of England and Scotland, held a peerage of Great Britain. The Duke of Wellington, whose title was granted in 1814, received the first dukedom 'of the United Kingdom'. In a sense, the most 'British' of the peers were those who held titles from more than one of the constituent kingdoms. The Scottish Duke of Buccleuch and Queensberry, for example, was also the English Earl of Doncaster. The second Duke of Wellington inherited his cousin's Irish earldom of Mornington.

In the eighteenth and nineteenth centuries, the 'Britishness' of the aristocracy in general and of the peers in particular was greatly enhanced by their inimitable lifestyle. All the noble families divided their time between two residences, one in London and the other 'in the country'. In London their life centred on the court, on Parliament, and on the government offices which many held. In the country – whether at Chatsworth, Inverary, or Carton – they were the leaders of local society, patronizing the balls, the hunts, and the races: cultivating their clients, high and low: organizing the political followings which ran the parliamentary elections and the local boroughs. Their vast estates supplied them with huge independent wealth. Yet it is the common features which stand out. They sent their sons to the same schools, usually Eton or one of the 'public schools' founded for their benefit in the mid-nineteenth century, and then to Oxford and Cambridge, not to study seriously but just to be there. They 'took the waters' at Bath or wintered at the same foreign resorts, strolling along La Promenade des Anglais at Nice or the seafront at Biarritz. They fixed their calendars by the immutable dates of 'the Season' at Ascot and the 'Glorious 12th', when shooting began. They tried to marry their daughters to their social equals, or if possible to a higher rank. They followed a strict code of dress made possible by a crowd of lackeys, valets, and domestic servants, who managed the carefully calibrated wardrobe of 'morning dress', 'evening dress', 'town dress', and 'country dress'. Above all, whether their seats were in England, Ireland, Scotland, or Wales, they all spoke with the same inimitable affected southern English accent, which set them apart from the common herd and which has been accurately described as 'the voice of authority'.

Thanks to the laws of primogeniture, the practice of marriage among Anglican clergy, and the unusual tradition of commercial involvement, British aristocratic families followed varieties of activity that were almost unknown elsewhere in Europe. The eldest male heirs took the entire estate, often in entail. Second sons often took the cloth to become deans and bishops and the fathers of well-educated broods of their own. Third sons typically sought royal commissions in the navy or the army. Younger sons had none of the French aristocratic inhibitions about soiling their hands in trade and industry. Their task was to promote the family's business interests. The precocious onset of the Industrial Revolution (see below, pages 754–64) threw up opportunities which most of the great British aristocrats were eager to exploit. The Duke of Newcastle, Prime Minister, landowner, and political patron par excellence, was also the leading promoter of the Midlands coal industry. His partner and successor, the Earl of Bute, though a Scot, became heavily engaged in coal, transport, and shipping in South Wales. His neighbours, the Dukes of Argyll, took a lead in the agro-industry of the Highlands, participating in the terrible clearances of the early nineteenth century. Both the Dukes of Bedford, whose country seat was at Woburn Abbey in Bedfordshire, and the Duke of Westminster, who was based at Grosvenor House, took a lead in London property development. Old landed wealth invested heavily in the new urban and industrial wealth.

Nor was membership of the British aristocracy either closed or static. It constantly revived its ranks, and reinvigorated its blood with fresh ennoblements. In the eighteenth century, a long line of crown servants were elevated to the peerage. William Pitt the Elder (1708–78), for example, grandson of an East India merchant, started his life as MP for Old Sarum, the lowly client of a duke. Having served as Prime Minister during the triumphs of the Seven Years War, he was rewarded in 1766 with the Earldom of Chatham. In the nineteenth century, the net was cast wider. Both Benjamin Disraeli (1804–81), novelist and Conservative leader, created Earl of Beaconsfield in 1876, and Lord Rothschild, the banker (created baron in 1885), were of Jewish origin or faith. George Canning (1770–1827), son of a barrister, Sir Robert Peel (1788–1850), son of a Lancashire cotton magnate who died prematurely in a riding accident, and Mr Gladstone, who declined on principle, were the only Prime Ministers of the century who were not peers either by birth or by creation, although both Peel and Gladstone were the sons of baronets. Robert Jenkinson, Lord Liverpool (1770–1828) was the son of a royal servant elevated by George III; the formidable Henry Temple, Viscount Palmerston (1784–1865) held an Irish title; Charles, Earl Grey (1764–1845) was a peer of the United Kingdom and Robert Cecil, Marquess of Salisbury (1830–1903) was a peer of Great Britain.

The reasons for the durability of the British peerage are clearly connected with the remarkable continuity of British institutions as a whole. Unlike most Continental countries, the United Kingdom was never subject either to successful foreign invasion or to domestic social revolution. British society avoided the involuntary jolts and shocks which has made for progress elsewhere. Yet that cannot be the whole answer. British society has also avoided the sorts of democratization that were adopted in other countries uninvaded since 1815, like Sweden or Switzerland. The tenacity of the British aristocracy in maintaining its position at the top of a class-based social system had something to do on the one hand with its unparalleled penetration of all institutions, including commercial firms and businesses, and on the other hand with its masterly command of the psychology of social emulation. The aristocrats stayed on the top of the social and political ladder because so many other groups loved to co-opt or to ape them. As the English saying goes, unimaginable in France or America, 'Everyone loves a lord.' This means that when the hereditary peers eventually lose their privileges – as they undoubtedly will – the fall-out is likely to be much wider than many suspect.

The pros and cons of aristocracy have long been debated. Already in Victorian times, public opinion was turning against the concentration of vast wealth in a single heir within the family and in a few families within the state. The historian William Lecky called it 'an outrage on morality'.[70] At the same time, some people would argue that the wealth and independence of the aristocracy was a force for stability and a bulwark against despotism. The preservation of aristocracy, they would argue, was as necessary to protect the nation from the encroachments of the modern state as it formerly was to stop the pretensions of absolutist kings. For by the early twentieth century, many of the British peers had sat securely on their estates and their privileges for two, three, four, five, six, or even seven hundred years.

To take just one famous name – Byron. In 1900, George Anson, the ninth Baron Byron (1855–1917), was forty-five years old. He was the latest in fifteen generations of Byrons, who traced their roots to a fifteenth-century knight, Sir Richard Byron of Clayton and Byron in Lancashire. In the sixteenth century, the family took control of the lands and house of Newstead Abbey in Nottinghamshire which for a time was their principal seat. In 1642, Sir John Byron was present when King Charles I raised his standard at Nottingham, and was created Baron Byron for distinguished service at the Battle of Edgehill. The fifth Baron Byron (b. 1722) was tried and released by the House of Lords for killing a man in a duel. His great-nephew, George Gordon, the sixth Baron (1788–1824), was the poet. After Lord Byron's childless death at Missolonghi, the title devolved to his cousins. This had happened before and would happen again. The ninth Baron's only heir was his brother, a resident of Western Australia.

Nonetheless, the greatest shock to the standing of the aristocracy to date was administered by the Liberal ministry of 1908–15. After two decades of Conservative, imperialist rule by Lord Salisbury and Arthur Balfour, and two years of progressive Liberal reform under Henry Campbell-Bannerman (1836–1908), power fell to a cabinet headed by two men completely off 'the social map'. Both the Prime Minister, Herbert Asquith (1852–1928), a Scots orphan, and the Chancellor of the Exchequer, David Lloyd George (1864–1945), the 'Welsh wizard', had made their way to the upper reaches of British public life via the legal profession. Neither of them had any time for aristocrats and they had been angered by the obstacles placed by the Lords in the way of much of Campbell-Bannerman's legislation. So when in 1909 the House of Lords threatened to block Lloyd George's 'People's Budget' and the Irish Home Rule Bill, they countered with a Parliament Bill that threatened to abolish the House of Lords. Lloyd George appealed for popular support. 'A fully equipped duke costs as much to keep as two Dreadnoughts,' he railed; 'and dukes . . . last longer.'[71]

The sticking-point in this trial of strength was to be found in a rather technical issue, namely in Lloyd George's proposal to tax the unearned increment in land values payable on the transfer of property. Since all British citizens had been liable to pay tax on their earned income since 1851, it might have seemed eminently reasonable that landowners should have made some contribution to taxation from the soaring value of their vast estates. But transfers of property could not be avoided on the death of an owner, and 'death duty', introduced in 1894, was thought by the Lords to be the devil's own scheme. For Lloyd George, the extension of the tax was an essential buttress for his popular measures of old age pensions (1908) and national insurance (1911). For his opponents, it was an intolerable intrusion into the ancient rights of private property.

A compromise solution was eventually found in the Parliament Act (1911). The House of Lords was to remain in being, but its powers of veto over parliamentary legislation were to be drastically curtailed. To be exact, the Lords were permitted to delay the passage of financial bills for a maximum of one month and the passage of non-financial bills for a maximum of two years.

The compromise was to have momentous consequences. It ensured that the 'People's Budget' was passed after a nominal protest and a short delay. But it also ensured that the Irish Home Rule Bill, which was voted through by the Commons in January 1913, could not be enacted for two years. A further attempt to push the bill through was made in May 1914, and in July the King called a conference which failed to reconcile the Lords. When the Great War broke out the Home Rule Bill completed its passage through Parliament in September without opposition, but in the company of another bill which suspended its implementation until after the war. The Lords had saved their own skins. In the process, they had ruined the government's plan to save the integrity of the United Kingdom.

(7) The Monarchy: Alien but Inspiring

Prior to 1689, the monarchy had held its kingdoms as it were by freehold. The Stuarts had assumed that they ruled by right and by divine sanction. Any steps they took to facilitate their rule, like the calling of Parliaments, were merely seen as practical arrangements that could be graciously conceded or arbitrarily withdrawn at will.

After 1689, however, the monarchs held their kingdoms as it were by leasehold. They had come to their thrones not by right but by agreement. The terms of the contract were ill-defined and the lease was open-ended. But it was a contract all the same. The agent for the contract was Parliament, which wrote itself a permanent role into future arrangements. But the two contracting parties were on the one hand the monarchy, and on the other hand 'the people'. In late seventeenth-century political language, the people meant the narrow circle of aristocratic oligarchs who pulled all the strings. 'The people' in the later sense of the population at large did not come into it.

James II's departure from England greatly eased matters. His abdication was a legal fiction. But the lack of clear defiance at the critical moment when William of Orange was tramping across English soil gave his supporters the pretext to desert him. As one historian put it admirably, 'The Revolution was accomplished by William invading, by the Whigs rebelling, and by the Tories deserting.'[72] For a short interval during James's absence there was a vacuum – what Locke would have called the *tabula rasa*. And the vacuum permitted a completely new beginning.

Both William and Mary accepted the throne reluctantly. Mary believed that she had committed a sin against her father, but that the sin was necessary for the sake of religion. Anne shared the view, but also believed that her constant miscarriages were a sign of God's wrath. William took the throne for the sake of his grand strategy against Louis XIV. He did so with some misgivings, partly because he disliked the makeshift constitutional dispositions but also because he feared a long debilitating war in Ireland and Scotland. William was a man of action; and he knew that kings had to rule, and not just reign.

Despite later theorizing about 'limited monarchy', the settlement of 1689 did not redefine the sovereign's powers or curb them unduly. On the contrary, it was universally accepted that the monarch should exercise undivided executive power. The commanding position of Parliament in the legislative and financial sphere, and in determining the legal framework within which the monarchy was to operate, was presaged by the acts and declarations of 1689. But it only came to fruition during the twenty-five years that followed. One could say that the paper settlement of 1689 was less important than the practical settlement worked out in detail during the difficult decades of war under William and Anne.

Jacobite opposition stayed alive and active for almost exactly a century – often underground, but always smouldering. The Jacobites lay low during William's War when a single word could be interpreted as treason. Since they had to work *sub rosa*, in secret, they took to wearing white roses; and when William died after his horse stumbled over a molehill, they drank toasts 'to the little gentleman in black velvet'. But their King had heirs, which William and Anne did not. They consistently supported the claims of 'James VIII and III', the Old Pretender, who died in 1766, and of 'Charles III', the Young Pretender, who lived on until 1788, the centenary of the landing at Torbay. Throughout those decades they treated the Hanoverian Succession as a straightforward usurpation. They organized two abortive risings, in 1715 and in 1745, and they constantly dreamed of massive French backing that never materialized. They commanded considerable if unquantifiable and dwindling popular sympathy. Popular sympathy, however, decided nothing.

The Rising of '15 was confined to Scotland. After George I's accession, a disaffected Tory minister, the Earl of Mar (1675–1732), raised the Jacobite standard at Braemar on 8 September. Mar, who had served as one of the Scots commissioners during the union negotiations, had come to regard the union as a terrible mistake. So his protest was directed as much against the united Kingdom as against the Hanoverians. Yet, once again, the Lowland Scots were not prepared to see the Highlanders succeed. The Duke of Argyll with 35,000 government troops faced Mar and his clansmen at Sheriffmuir near Stirling on 13 November 1715. Though the 'Highland

Charge' appeared to carry the day, the Hanoverian professionals kept order and gained the upper hand during the ensuing chaos. The Highlanders were driven back into the mountains. By February, the Rising was quelled. Mar sailed with the Old Pretender for France, never to return.

The 'Forty-five' was a rather more serious affair. This time, in the middle of the War of the Austrian Succession, the initiative came from Versailles. A French ship put Bonnie Prince Charlie ashore at Arisaig on the west coast of Scotland on 23 July 1745 to see what would happen. The French did not want a repeat of the two earlier and disastrous expeditions to Scotland; and they had already lost seven ships in a storm off Dunkirk. They would only risk another major campaign if their Stuart client could prove his worth. The Stuart standard was raised at Glenfinnan near Fort William on 19 August. It brought out the aggrieved Macdonalds, but not the expected parade of Catholic clans. A meagre Jacobite army defeated a still more meagre Hanoverian defence force at Prestonpans on 21 September. The city of Edinburgh raised a total of four hundred men to fight for King George, though only forty-two turned out for the battle, among them the young David Hume. But it showed little more enthusiasm for 'King Charles'. The decision to march into England with a minimal army of only 5,500 men, mostly Highlanders, was carried in the Jacobite war council by only one vote. After nearly a month on the road through Cumbria and Lancashire, the wavering Jacobites were told by a Hanoverian agent at Derby, only a hundred and twenty-seven miles from the capital, that Hanoverian London would not welcome them. So the fateful decision was taken to turn back.

The story of the tragic Jacobite retreat from Derby to the day of nemesis on Culloden Moor (16 April 1746) is clouded with romantic nostalgia. Its progress filled all the newspapers throughout 1746. Despair explains all, not military dispositions. The facts are: the tiny Hanoverian force under the King's brother, the Duke of Cumberland (1721–65), did not have the means to defeat the Jacobites, had open battle been avoided; Bonnie Prince Charlie had no pressing need, other than his own mental state, to fight his pursuers on the unfavourable ground at Culloden; and he had still less reason to issue the general order of *sauve qui peut* when the battle was lost. As it was, the clansmen were ordered to charge uphill against a set position defended by massed cannon. They recited their clan genealogies in Gaelic, shouted their war cries, then moved off into a biting wind across deep heather. They faced an army of professionals that contained more Scots than their own. The Highland Charge rushed on into a shattering wall of heavy metal and fixed bayonets. It would never charge again. The survivors took to the hills. The Jacobite forces, who never even reached the battle, disbanded. The pursuing redcoats started the long job of destroying a civilization. 'Bonnie Prince Charlie' reached the Isle of Skye, dressed in petticoats and posing as Flora Macdonald's servant-girl. The court of Versailles was not sufficiently impressed to take further action:

> Speed, bonnie boat, like a bird on the wing
> Onward, the sailors cry:
> Carry the lad that's born to be king
> Over the sea to Skye.
> Loud the winds howl, loud the seas roar,
> Thunderclaps rend the air:
> Baffled our foes stand on the shore,
> Follow they will not dare.[73]

Once the Jacobite threat had died, the Hanoverian monarchy settled down to rule the united Kingdom if not with distinction at least with a modicum of undistinguished competence. It was greatly assisted by a political, economic, and intellectual climate conducive to letting the old arguments drop. The royal court provided a welcome focus for the ambitions of the all-powerful aristocracy. The informal 'King's Party' in Parliament was still more important than the formal party divisions between Whigs and Tories. All the King's most critical decisions were taken in conjunction with royal ministers who bestrode the factions in court, government, and Parliament. Divine right faded into the past. Trade flourished. The Empire expanded. Industry advanced. General prosperity increased. The Scots and the Irish had largely accepted their lot.

The Hanoverians knew their place. George I (r. 1714–27) spent half the year in Hanover, where he died. His British cabinet discussed business with him in French. George II (r. 1727–60), a cavalry officer by training, took the field in person at Dettingen in 1743, the first and last British monarch to do so. He pursued the same sort of feud with his son and heir that his father had pursued with him, thereby weakening the unity of the monarchy as a whole. But he was no cipher, least of all in foreign affairs. George III (r. 1760–1820) reigned for six whole decades. He was an active sovereign, making and breaking ministers, managing Parliament, holding strong opinions on the issues of the day. Yet he too had a stormy relationship with his dissolute son, the Prince Regent, who repeatedly took over during the periods of royal insanity. (He was probably suffering from an undiagnosed affliction by the kidney disease of porphyria.) At all events, he posed no threat to the ruling establishment of Parliament and ministers who during the Napoleonic Wars (1803–15) took an irreversible grip on policy. The first Hanoverian to be British-born and die in Britain, he benefited from loyalist sentiment during the wars, and despite losing the American colonies basked in the glow of the grandest period of imperial expansion.

In the nineteenth century, the active role of the monarchy was reduced still further. Constitutional practice was changing faster than constitutional law. Government ministers took an increasingly assertive position, looking to the monarch not for a lead but for consent and acquiescence. As the suffrage expanded, Parliament had to respond to the opinion of an ever wider political public, thereby gaining a greater sense of its own importance. Hence the relative weight of the monarch within the system as a whole was shrinking. Apart from that, the throne was successively occupied by persons of no great consequence. George IV (r. 1820–30), the former Prince Regent, was tarnished by his long-standing liaison with a Catholic woman, Mrs Fitzherbert, and later by his scandalous attempt to exclude his divorced queen from the coronation. His brother, William IV (r. 1830–37), a former admiral, succeeded to the throne at the age of sixty-five. His erratic conduct caused constitutional turmoil on more than one occasion. In 1831 he temporarily succumbed to his ministers' plan for fifty new peers to force through the Reform Bill, and in 1834 he appointed Lord Melbourne (1779–1848) Prime Minister against the wishes of the Commons. No British monarch would ever take this risk again.

The sixty-four-year reign of Queen Victoria (r. 1837–1901) stands as the centrepiece of British imperial history. It saw the United Kingdom at the peak of its international power and prestige. Victoria started off as a slip of a girl closely guided by her mentor, Lord Melbourne. She learned that she had scope for intervention in high politics, as well as for periods of calculated passivity. For twenty years, she enjoyed a blissful partnership with her consort, Prince Albert, with whom she found the touch and style for a constitutional monarchy that was still grand but largely ceremonial and not overbearing. After Albert's death, she virtually retired, but was gradually coaxed by Disraeli from her decade of mourning and emerged as the matriarch of Europe's royal families, the Empress of India, and the embodiment of British self esteem. There had been moments when the slow progress of social reform, coupled with her own withdrawal, made her unpopular. Republican attacks on her were not unknown. But by the time of her Golden Jubilee (1887), her reputation and that of the monarchy were beyond criticism. The price was paid by her son, Edward VII (r. 1841–1910), who was totally excluded from all royal business until nearly sixty years of age. Victoria saw out eleven Prime Ministers. The only one she really detested was Gladstone. 'He speaks to me', she said, 'as if I were a public meeting.'

Surprisingly perhaps, after two hundred years of the United Kingdom, the monarchy was 'British' in name only. The Hanoverians had put down roots in England alone. None of the first three Georges ever visited Scotland, Ireland, or Wales. They resided by preference at Windsor, where the Great Park was laid out for their amusement; and in 1761 they bought a second-rate palace from the Duke of Buckingham for their London home. George IV made a famous visit to Edinburgh in 1822 (see page 836, below); and Queen Victoria made a solitary and forlorn visit to Dublin on 4 August 1849, as a gesture to post-famine Ireland. Victoria and Albert bought a Scottish home at Balmoral on Teesside, and invented a tartan to go with it. Victoria even said that she 'might have been a Jacobite'. But that, like her friendship with her gillie, John Brown (1826–83), was all part of the fashion for Romantic 'Caledonianism'. It implied no solid interest in Scottish affairs.

Nonetheless, from George I to Victoria's grandson, George V (r. 1910–35), the Houses of Hanover and Sachsen-Coburg und Gotha had clearly satisfied the purposes for which they had been imported. They had provided an unbroken line of eight monarchs with no succession crises. They had not strayed from the Protestant path. They had presided over a kingdom which had grown from strength to strength until it controlled the greatest empire on earth.

Yet they had studiously preserved their Germanity. Victoria, who was obliged to surrender Hanover to an uncle, was nonetheless conceived in Germany, married to a German, and completely surrounded by German relatives. Though educated in England, she spoke German by preference, especially with Albert and their children – they called Lord Palmerston 'Pilgerstein' – and sometimes, to the annoyance of her ministers, in cabinet. She was mother to an Empress of Germany, to a Grand Duchess of Hesse, and to a Countess Battenberg; she was grandmother to a Tsarina, to a Kaiser, to a Queen of Spain, and to a Queen of Greece. It is a testament to the dedication of the Hanoverians to their German roots that every single British monarch without exception between 1714 and 1901 was married to a German spouse, thereby ensuring that every single British king had a German-born mother and a German-speaking father (see Appendix 53).

In the old days, the monarchy's German connections carried no slur. On the contrary, they linked the United Kingdom with a prominent and rising nation. But in the age of nationalism, and especially after the outbreak of war with Germany, they started to be a hindrance. On 29 October 1914 the King's German cousin, Prince Louis von Battenberg, was forced to retire as the United Kingdom's First Sea Lord, and in 1917 to change the family name to Mountbatten. George V followed suit, changing the royal family's name from Sachsen-Coburg und Gotha (Saxe-Goburg-Gotha) to Windsor. His cousin, the Kaiser, on hearing the news, cracked a rare joke about going to the theatre to see a performance of *The Merry Wives of Saxe-Coburg und Gotha*. The writer H. G. Wells remarked that the royal court was 'alien and uninspiring'; the King reacted: 'I may be uninspiring, but I'll be damned if I'm an alien.' He had his priorities wrong. In the age of modern, populist monarchies, he should have said, 'I may be an alien, but I'll be damned if I'm uninspiring.'[74]

(8) FROM CIVIL LIST TO CIVIL SERVICE

The modern distinction between executive government and the independent corps of public administrators that puts government policy into effect was unknown in early modern Europe. Public administrators were servants of the crown who paid them and who received in return their oaths of personal allegiance. They were selected either by the monarch directly or by whatever ministers happened to be in favour at the time. Their loyalty tended to be directed to their patron; and they tended to lose their employment whenever the patron lost favour. At the higher level, all the offices of state were farmed out by the crown as if on lease, and office-holders were free to appoint whatever underlings they wished on whatever conditions suited. So long as the necessary results were obtained, the government was unlikely to take any interest in questions of pay, tenure, or qualifications. Hence secretaries of state and collectors of taxes, like captains in the navy or colonels of regiments, hired and fired as they saw fit. In order to accept supplicants to their service, they routinely expected, and routinely received, a monetary inducement – that is, a bribe.

There was no concept of a 'civil service' in the United Kingdom prior to the nineteenth century. But three separate developments gradually persuaded liberal opinion that the old system could not go on for ever. One of these was the sudden growth of the crown bureaucracy during the Napoleonic Wars. The second was the drastic reduction of the so-called 'Civil List'. The third was a crisis in the government of India.

All wars require officials to run them; and the most protracted wars in British history, between 1793 and 1815, caused the largest ever expansion of British officialdom. The increase occurred not just in the departments of military and naval procurement and in the Treasury but in a wide range of offices, such as the Census or the Hydrographic Office, which had never existed before. So long as the country was at war, the government borrowed money and footed the bill. But after 1815, Parliament took a serious interest in bureaucratic retrenchment. The politicians found, however, that the new army of clerks and overseers could not be easily pruned, since as crown servants they were all paid through the Civil List – that is, the annual global grant paid to the crown for non-military purposes. No unreformed Parliament, packed with royal placemen, was going to reduce the trough from which, they, too, took their fill.

The reform of the Civil List, therefore, had to await the reform of Parliament. It took place in 1837, five years after the Great Reform Act, and immediately after the death of William IV. Parliament took direct responsibility for the maintenance of all crown officials not engaged as personal aides to the monarch, thereby introducing the crucial distinction between 'courtiers' and 'public servants'. At a stroke, the Civil List was decimated: public employees became employees of the anonymous 'state'; and the monarchy lost one of the most important of its residual powers.

The crisis in India resulted from the vigorous activities of Sir James Brown, Marquess of Dalhousie, Governor-General from 1847. At the time, the subcontinent was still administered by the East India Company, which under its latest charter of 1833 had lost its commercial monopoly but had retained its functions as a private administrative authority. Curiously enough, the company had developed far more efficient and enlightened administrative structures than the government in London. It was in Calcutta that the term 'Civil Service' had been invented after the company hived off a separate corps of highly trained administrative officials from their military counterparts. The Indian Civil Service took pride in its own strict rules, its training colleges, and its esprit de corps. Dalhousie's contribution was to engage in a series of wars and annexations, notably of the Punjab (1849), which he put under direct British control and turned into a model, modern state. Yet the wider effect was to raise the huge head of resentment in India, which in a short time caused the Mutiny and the termination of company rule. Ironically, the politicians in London, whilst contemplating the Indian crisis, could not help noticing that in the administrative sphere at least, Britain could learn much from India.

Contemplation changed to action in 1853, when W. E. Gladstone, then a junior minister in Lord Aberdeen's coalition government, called for a report on administrative reform. Prepared by Charles Trevelyan and Clifford Northcote, the report condemned recruitment of officials by patronage, advocating competitive entrance examinations, promotion by merit, and the separation of administration from executive policy-making. (There is good evidence to suggest that not only the Indian, but also the Chinese model inspired these conclusions.)

The Civil Service Commission (1855) was created to put the recommendations into effect. But nothing much happened for fifteen years, since entry to the entrance exams continued to be confined to the nominees of the ruling patrons. Only when Gladstone became Prime Minister could he finally clear away the obstacles. An Order in Council in 1870 opened the way to the emergence of a unified corps of independent administrators, observing the same rules, serving all government departments, both foreign and domestic, and offering prestigious careers to all (male) applicants of talent. In this way, the Civil Service, one of the most lasting achievements of Gladstonian liberalism, was born. Shortly afterwards, the Local

Government Board Act (1871), which transferred the duties of the Poor Law to a new department of state, took the first step in the long-running reform of local government. Within fifty years, a fully fledged state bureaucracy, fiercely jealous of its independence from politicians, was employing over two hundred thousand highly educated, and, generally speaking, highly competent 'civil servants'.

The success of the Civil Service affected many realms of British life, not least the universities, which in the 1870s were shamed into adopting their own independently assessed and written examinations for entrance and graduation. But its greatest impact was probably as an instrument of national unification. By the turn of the twentieth century, the United Kingdom employed more civil servants than military officers: and they were drawn from the brightest and best from all ends of the Isles. Though the Civil Service included a large contingent from the new English 'public schools', who were now catering for the sons of the ambitious middle classes, it also took in droves of applicants from Scotland, Wales, Ireland, and northern England, often from families with no previous administrative experience. Indeed, thanks to the special prowess of Scottish education, it took in a disproportionate number of Scots, whose prominence in the corridors of Whitehall came to mirror their ubiquitous presence in the outposts of Empire. In short, though it was firmly centralized in London, it was all-British in composition, and all-British in the scope of its activities. It was one of the main propagators of the new British ethos.[75]

(9) Workshop of the World

One of the immediate and most important effects of the Act of Union in 1707 was the creation of a united free trade area managed by the common government and legislature in London. A unified British economy took the place of the separate English and Scottish economies of the previous era. When industrialization began a few decades later, it gave rise to British industry; and when a working class came into being to work the industry, it was a British working class. When Ireland joined the Union in 1801, Irish economic operations were merged with the larger British whole. So, too, were the far-flung operations of the Empire. The consequent rise of the world's first industrial and urbanized society was connected in one way or another with all the great transformations of the era.

Anyone born in Bolton will recognize the Boltonian theory of modern history. Basically, God had blessed Bolton with the purest water for washing cloth, and the blackest coal to fire the steam engines. And in 1779 he chose Samuel Crompton of Hall i'th' Wood to invent a wonderful machine, the spinning mule, which not only produced a fine, strong cotton thread, but also proved suitable for mechanization. Soon, Bolton's magnificent cotton mills gave a chance to the struggling port of Liverpool, where the cotton bales arrived from America, to the downtrodden city of Manchester, where people could now grow rich on the Cotton Exchange, and to a number of lesser towns in the locality such as Preston, Blackburn, and Burnley, where the thread could be woven into lovely vests and shirts. Soon, Lancashire's cotton trade was putting Yorkshire woollens into the shade. It clothed millions round the world, requiring the building of the world's biggest merchant fleet to carry it and the world's strongest navy to protect it. Bolton Town Hall (1873) had the most elegant clock tower and civic centre in the land; Bolton Trinity Street was the best kept station on the L & Y; and Bolton Wanderers naturally won the first imperial cup final in the Empire Stadium at Wembley. Perhaps since the world is a wicked place, Samuel Crompton was allowed to die a pauper, and the premier borough of the United Kingdom was allowed to decline until it sank into the outer suburbs of Greater Manchester.

Not all economic historians subscribe to every detail of the Boltonian theory, but they would recognize its most essential characteristic: the interconnectedness of numerous related processes. Nowadays, there are as many theories as there are theorists; and many of the modern sociological models are as wacky as the old Boltonian one. Generally speaking, however, the semi-miraculous role once awarded to 'inventions' is discounted. So, too, is the antiquated Marxist hierarchy of the 'socio-economic base' and the political and cultural 'superstructure'. The so-called superstructure is just as likely to drive the base as vice versa. Yet two contentions would attract widespread support. One relates to the dynamic nature of economic change, of modest beginnings accelerating through several gears to the critical moment of 'take-off', of cumulative quantitative change suddenly being superseded by radical qualitative change. The other qualifies the position of industry within the wider complex of change. At one time, 'the Industrial Revolution' was taken to be the motor of everything else. It is now seen to have been the product of earlier prerequisites and transformations, and to have remained but one element in a much wider modernizing web. For today's historians, any attempt to list all the processes of modernization immediately runs into scores of headings. (See Appendix 50.)

The pre-industrial phase of the British economy, which occupied much of the eighteenth century, laid the foundations of the United Kingdom's remarkable precocity in the early nineteenth. England, and to a lesser extent Scotland, had already developed a worldwide commercial system. London had already replaced Amsterdam as the world's leading financial centre. All the prerequisites for further development – banks, venture capital, joint-stock companies, and insurance – were already in place. From the 1760s, a rapidly expanding labour market, free of the serfdom and feudal restrictions still current elsewhere in Europe, was hungry for new employment. A small, compact, and wealthy home base was waiting to service the new Empire.

In this context, the long catalogue of British discoveries and inventions appears in a rather different light. Science and technology formed part of a much broader network of action and reaction. Like thousands of others, Samuel Crompton did not act in isolation. He was responding to a demand born of the shortcomings of the spinning jenny and spinning frame, and of cotton manufactories already in production. Similarly, eighty years later, Prince Albert, as chief patron of the highly successful Great Exhibition of 1851, was very well aware of the interconnections of science, technology, industry, education, culture, social progress, and political power. Under his patronage the vast proceeds of the Exhibition were devoted not only to the foundation of the Imperial College of Science and Technology, the Science Museum, and the Natural History Museum, but also to the Royal Albert Hall, the Victoria and Albert Museum (dedicated to arts, crafts, and design), and to the Royal College of Music. London's South Kensington was transformed into the focus of an integrated all-British sphere of all-purpose endeavour.

The first name on any schoolchild's list of modern inventors always used to be that of the unforgettable Jethro Tull (1674–1741) who around 1701 experimented with a mechanical, horse-drawn seed drill on his farm in Berkshire. He was usually followed by Newcomen, T., steam engine (1705). Nowadays, Tull is not much in fashion. But he serves to underline the important fact that the ongoing Agricultural Revolution was the necessary precursor and partner of the better known Industrial Revolution. By general consent, the most influential figure was Thomas Coke, MP (1752–1842), who raised the rental income of his model estate at Holkham Hall, Norfolk from £2,000 to £20,000 p.a. and who, after fifty-six years in the Commons, became 'Father of the House'. Interestingly enough, among the numerous societies promoting scientific agriculture, the Scottish Society of Improvers (1723–) and the Irish Dublin Society (1731–) both predated the ill-named English Society of Arts (1756–).

The enclosure of communally held open land had long been the occasion both for agricultural progress and for social distress. Farmers gained control of large closed fields suitable for the production of cash crops and surpluses, whilst local peasants and humble tenants lost their means of subsistence. In England, the tempo accelerated rapidly in the decades 1755–1815, when over four thousand private Acts of Parliament resulted in the enclosure of over five million acres. General Enclosure Acts in 1801, 1836, and 1845 facilitated the process. In Scotland, the old runrig system of infield–outfield farming had been undermined in earlier, seventeenth-century legislation; private enclosure acts were rare; and the most pitiless phase of the Highland Clearances, where people were physically removed for the comfort of sheep, did not set in before 1800.

The Highland Clearances may be seen as either the culminating chapter of the disaster sparked by Culloden or as the inevitable consequence of economic progress. The vicious harrying by Cumberland's men of the Gaelic clans, who were already politically defeated and culturally condemned, was followed by the economic collapse of a society long since deprived of its immunity systems. Serious overpopulation in the marginal economy of the glens caused voluntary drift to the ports and the cities in the first instance, and determined action by the landowners in the subsequent stage. The clan chiefs, long since isolated from their clansmen's welfare, colluded. Whole communities were rounded up at an hour's notice; the crofts were set on fire to make way for sheep-walks; and the people were driven to the 'white sail'd ships' bound for Canada. Time and again, the tragedies were re-enacted. One of the most brutal actions occurred in 1819 on the estates of the Marchioness of Staffordshire in Sutherland. Another in Easter Ross in March 1854 led to a lethal attack by constables on a mass of resisting women. By that time, there were few left to be cleared. 'The Lowlander has inherited the hills, and the tartan is a shroud.'[76]

In the first flush of investigative journalism, the *Times* sent the same correspondent to the Highlands it had earlier sent to Ireland to investigate the Famine. In 1846, he found a million people in Ireland dying from starvation. The potato blight, which in England had caused minor inconvenience, was causing mass mortality in the Irish countryside. In the next five years, another million Irish would emigrate from dire necessity, many to Britain but the majority to America. Ireland's population was reduced by 20 per cent, and would not start to recover until the 1920s. Some of the lushest counties in the richest state in the world were decimated. Little relief was forthcoming. The Prime Minister, Peel, bowed to the pressures of the Anti-Corn Law League, and finally repealed the protectionist Corn Laws. This helped the cause of free trade in England, but did little to help the starving Irish. Memories of the Famine years steadily sapped the hopes that Ireland could benefit from the United Kingdom:

> A million a decade! Calmly and cold
> The units are read by our statesman sage
> Little they think of a Nation old,
> Fading away from History's page:
> Outcast weeds by a desolate sea
> Fallen leaves of Humanity![77]

The location of heavy industry was largely determined by the presence of coal. After the perfection of the steam engine in 1769 by James Watt (1736–1819), a Scot working in Birmingham, coal-fired, steam-driven machinery became the standard power source for the first wave of industrialization. Coal was not to be found either in south-east England or in Ireland; but there were plentiful supplies of it in central Scotland, on Tyneside and Teesside, in Lancashire and Yorkshire, in the west and north Midlands, and above all, in South Wales. As a result, regions which were previously underdeveloped and underpopulated suddenly sprouted mines, factories, and dirty bustling industrial towns. Within a few decades of 1760, both the economic and the demographic centres of gravity moved dramatically away from London. Glasgow, Birmingham, and Cardiff all grew with unprecedented speed. But the epitome of the age was Manchester. In 1785 Manchester was a mere village. Fifty years later it was the third city of England. Victorian Manchester was 'built on cotton bales'. It was the capital of Free Trade Liberalism and pride of the North. In 1894 it was linked to the sea by a ship canal, which made it a major port as well as a major industrial, financial, and political centre. Manchester was also the focus of a revolution in transport and communications. The Bridgwater Canal (1761), which took coal-carrying barges over an aqueduct into Manchester, improved on Liverpool's nearby Sankey Brook Navigation (1757–) by showing that water transport need not be dependent on rivers.

Within a few decades, four thousand miles of canals crisscrossed all the industrial areas. The Rainhill Trials (1830), won by George Stephenson's Rocket, launched the Railway Age by initiating the world's first public railway between Manchester and Liverpool. The enthusiasm for railways apparently saved British capitalism from financial depression in the 1840s, and gave the British economy its second wind.[78]

After the coalfields, the ports were the next great scene of industrial development, particularly of shipbuilding. London, the largest port in Europe, soon became a premier manufacturing centre. Glasgow, which served a region uniting the Midlothian coalfield, Paisley textiles, and the Clydeside docks, grew into the United Kingdom's second city. In 1800, Great Britain had been an importer of ships. By 1900, a handful of enormous dockyards – John Brown on Clydeside, Cammell-Laird's at Birkenhead, Vickers at Barrow-in-Furness, Harland and Wolff at Belfast, and Swan Hunter on Tyneside – were building half the world's ships. Both the Royal Navy and the merchant navy were the largest in the world, and almost entirely British-built. (HMS *Melita*, launched in Malta in 1888, was the only foreign-built new vessel.)

Disraeli had coined the phrase 'Workshop of the World' in 1838 in an early speech to the House of Commons. But he had done so whilst warning his compatriots against foreign competition. 'The Continent', he forecast, 'will not suffer England to be the workshop of the world.' For the time being, the United Kingdom held a lead. But front-runners are usually overtaken.

The industrial geography of Great Britain was peculiarly conducive to the growth of railways. A network of dynamic regional centres rarely more than fifty or a hundred miles apart encouraged the building first of a dense maze of local lines, and then of numerous through lines. Within twenty-five years of the Rainhill Trials, seven thousand miles of track had been laid, all the major cities were interconnected, and London was directly linked to Cornwall, to North and South Wales, to the Irish ferries at Fishguard and Holyhead, and by two main lines to Scotland. Economic historians debate questions such as the relative contribution of railways to overall economic growth. But the really important impact of railways lay in their role as a unifying force of unparalleled scope in social and national affairs. The Great Exhibition of 1851 was seen by over six million people, many of whom had never in their lives travelled beyond their native town or district. For the very first time in history, every single city in the British Isles was brought within a single day's travel of London. The citizens of the United Kingdom received their greatest stimulus to feeling 'British'.

In this brave new world of steam and smoke, the name of Isambard Kingdom Brunel (1806–59) stands supreme. Engineer of the Great Western Railway, built from Paddington to Bristol in 1835–41, he also designed and built the first transatlantic liner, the *Great Western* (1838), as a natural extension of the line. His *Great Britain* (1843) was the first ocean-going screw-driven steamship. His suspension bridges at Clifton and at the Menai Straits are monuments to Victorian confidence. His rival, Robert Stephenson (1803–59), George's son, builder of the Britannia Tubular Bridge at Menai, pushed him close. The bridges at Menai formed the most vital link in the whole system. Situated in the heart of Welsh-speaking Wales, they commanded the route from London to Dublin.

Many of the processes of modernization tended to divide rather than to unite. In another of his striking phrases, Disraeli had written of 'two nations', who barely knew each other. He meant the new rich and the new poor. It is no accident that the very idea of a social system based on class was discovered by two German exiles in early Victorian England, one working as a comfortable capitalist in the family firm in Manchester, the other reading and writing throughout his life at the same desk in the new library of the British Museum. The first joint work by Friedrich Engels (1820–95) and Karl Marx (1818–83) expounded *The Condition of the Working Class in England* (1845). It was the opening salvo in their lifelong campaign to propagate so-called 'scientific socialism'. But it was also a passionate contribution to the most burning social issue of the day, namely the division of the population into antagonistic social groups now called 'classes'. The Marxist view of class gained a keener audience abroad than in the United Kingdom, where more pragmatic and more individualistic social philosophers such as Herbert Spencer (1820–93) predominated. But the problem stood in front of everyone's eyes. Whereas the old social divisions of lord and peasant or rural farmer and urban artisan had implied considerable measure of traditional interdependence, the rise of the new upper, middle, and lower classes involved much more than a new social hierarchy. It gave a vulgar premium to mere wealth, and a stigma to poverty; and it encouraged people to follow their collective interest against others. It underlay the tense struggle over parliamentary suffrage, and the division of political allegiances between conservatives, liberals, and the long excluded labour movement. There is no more fitting place to contemplate these matters than Highgate Cemetery in North London, where 'Marx' and 'Spencer' are buried side by side.

It would be quite wrong, of course, to suggest that nineteenth-century politics can be fully explained in terms of socio-economic interests. It was far more subtle than that. Burkean Conservatism, for example, which found its greatest exponent in Disraeli, was as much a matter of temperament as of privilege. It attracted many voters fearful of radical change, who might otherwise have seen the logic of more rapid progress. Gladstonian Liberalism, too, had one foot in laissez-faire and the economic arguments of the free trade movement, and the other foot in civil liberties and the moral arguments for various forms of religious, social, and political emancipation. The centre ground of the central phase of Victorian politics, fought over by the alternating ministries of Disraeli and Gladstone, was clearly located in the broad sphere of public opinion where Disraeli's Conservatives and Gladstone's Liberals agreed.

Even so, in a setting of continuing industrialization and urbanization, the determination of the upper and the middle classes to exclude the expanding working class from political life generated strains and lasting bitterness. Ever since the vicious Combination Acts of 1799–1800, all attempts to form trade unions had been treated as revolutionary, and mild pragmatic socialists like Robert Owen

(1771–1858) were widely condemned as dangerous radicals. Rural labourers who tried to form a self-protective union, like the 'Tolpuddle Martyrs' from Dorset, were still being transported to Australia in the 1830s alongside common criminals. The first Trade Union Congress did not assemble until 1868; the tiny group of trade unionists to be elected to Parliament could only operated as 'Lib-Labs' under the aegis of the Liberal Party; and the Taff Vale Decision of 1901 laid trade unions open to crippling damages for the conse quences of strikes.

Keir Hardie (1856–1915) was the commanding figure in labour history who bridged the gap between the disillusionments of the nineteenth century and the triumphs of the twentieth. Christian, pacifist, and a passionate advocate of both temperance and women's rights, he edited the *Labour Leader* (1889–), founded the ILP in 1893, and in 1900 organized the federated Labour Representation Committee that presaged success at the polls six years later. A fatherless child miner from Midlothian, Hardie suffered years of victimization in his native Scotland before steering British socialism away from Marxism and eggheaded Fabianism. As a Scot representing the working-class London suburb of West Ham South and, from 1900–13, the Welsh mining constituency of Merthyr Tydfyl, he embodied the fact that the working class and the labour movements, like the economy itself, were all-British affairs.[79]

During the latter half of the nineteenth century, worldwide industry moved into the higher realms of steel, chemicals, and electricity. In this 'Second Industrial Revolution', though the UK's performance continued to advance in absolute terms, its relative position began to slip. In 1893, the GDP per capita of the USA surpassed that of the UK for the first time, and never looked back. What is more, the newly united German Empire was recording levels of production in key sectors such as steel, and aggregated rates of economic growth, that the British economy simply could not match. The centralized British Empire was still the largest single economic unit on the world map, holding astronomic potential for further growth and development. Whether or not that potential would ever be realized depended partly on wise management, and partly on the avoidance of major conflict. The title of a prophetic book published in 1911 said it all. The notion that the pursuit of British interests could be made to pay through war was *The Great Illusion*.[80] The economic imperative was unambiguous – it was to avoid war at almost any cost.

(10) THE STERLING AREA: LEGENDARY STABILITY

There seems to be no scholarly consensus on the origin of 'sterling', although silver coins of that name were minted in various parts of the Anglo-Saxon Heptarchy in the late eighth century. The earliest example is dated to 775. In this case, the oldest Old English coins were older than the Kingdom of England itself. 240 sterlings were coined from one pound of silver – hence the later term of 'pounds sterling'. The basic English system of 1 pound = 20 shillings = 240 pence was regularized after the Norman Conquest. It took its name of £.s.d. from the Latin terms of *libra*, *solidus*, and *denarius*.

At various points during medieval and early modern times, Welsh, Irish, and Scots coinages existed in parallel to their English equivalents. Welsh coins were only recorded in the reign of Hywel Dda (tenth century). The Kingdom of Ireland continued to mint its own coins until 1822. The Kingdom of Scotland has kept its own money to the present day, although the Scottish pound has been fixed at par with its English counterpart since the Union of 1707. Prior to the Union, the old Scottish pound had seriously depreciated in value. In the fourteenth century, it stood at 1:1, in 1430 at 2:1, in 1480 at 4:1, and after 1621 at 12:1.

The Bank of England came into being thirteen years before the United Kingdom. But as from 1707 it was the only possible candidate acting as the central bank of the British state and currency. It delegated the manufacture of coins to the mints, who in turn farmed out their operations to contractors. Sir Isaac Newton, who obtained the post of Master of the Mint in 1718, thereby amassed a tidy fortune. The last coins were being struck in Edinburgh in 1709. The headquarters of the Royal Mint moved to a site at Tower Hill in London in 1810. Copper coins were manufactured at various provincial locations – at Wolverhampton from 1700 to 1722, for example, for Ireland and America, and at the Soho Works in Birmingham from 1788 to 1875.

After numerous experiments, the British currency settled down in the eighteenth century to a standard set of coins and values. The *guinea* or 'gold crown' was worth one pound and one shilling, i.e., 21 shillings. The *shilling*, the *crown* (worth 5 shillings) and the *pound sterling* (worth 20 shillings) were all coined in silver. The *penny*, valued at twelve to one shilling, the *half-penny*, and the *farthing* or quarter-penny were coined in bronze. The issue of the old English *groat* or 4d piece was discontinued in 1662, but a British version was briefly revived in bronze form, 1836–56. The Bank of England issued a temporary £1 paper banknote in 1797.

Since the entire British Empire was treated as a single monetary union, all the countries of the Empire governed by the Bank of England came to be known as the sterling area. This state of affairs did not prevent the emergence of separate colonial coinage systems, and at a later stage, separate currencies. Gibraltar was allowed to issue its own coins in 1852, Australia in 1855, Canada in 1858, and Hong Kong in 1862. Canada was given its own dollar currency in 1871. The Indian Empire had its rupee. But the Bank of England held all the reserves in London, controlled all the exchange rates, and supervised all capital borrowing. What is more, after some delay, the City of London established a leading position in European finance. Paris had held the lead until the Franco-Prussian War, but lost it thereafter for good.

Great importance was attached to maintaining the stability of sterling, which in 1862 was the first world currency to be officially tied to the value of gold. The gold standard was held at a fixed price of £3.89 per ounce all the way to 1914. As it was gradually adopted by all other leading currencies, it encouraged a worldwide system of equally stable exchange rates. It also facilitated the regular issue of banknotes in both England and Scotland. The outbreak of the Great War forced the Bank to abandon the gold standard for eleven years. The exchange rate of the pound against the dollar fell to a low point of £1 = $3.661 in 1920. But it fared much better than the French franc; and it completely escaped the hyperinflation which destroyed the German Reichsmark. The reinstatement of the gold standard in 1925 restored sterling's robust, pre-war rate against the dollar at £1 = $4.829.

Britain had kept aloof from the various attempts to create monetary union on mainland Europe. The first of these came into being in 1834 within the framework of the German Zollverein, with nearly forty states participating. An overriding super-currency, the Vereinsmunze, was established; member states were required to adhere to one of two monetary standards, the thaler or the gulden, and the Bank of Prussia exercised overall control. The Zollverein zone merged into the German Empire in 1871. It has been seen by its admirers as the model whereby an economic grouping can be transformed into a political grouping. The Latin Monetary Union, in contrast, was created by France in 1865, and comprised eighteen countries including Belgium, Switzerland, and Italy. It had no common currency and no central bank; but its constituent currencies were tied to the French gold franc. It survived theoretically until 1926, but had started to founder at the turn of the century. The Scandinavian Monetary Union, made up of Sweden, Denmark, and Norway, lasted from 1873 to 1924. It was based on a common kronor, and held firm at least until the First World War. But the Bank of England was not interested in any of this. As Walter Bagehot, editor of the *Economist*, had said in 1877, 'Before long, all Europe, save England, will have one money.'[81]

Taking the century 1815–1914, the movement of the exchange rates of the major currencies rested somewhere between the minimal and the negligible. In all that time, the only noticeable turbulence occurred during the American Civil War, when the US dollar fell from $5.19 = £1 (1861) to $11.11 = £1 (1864) and $8.54 = £1 (1865). But it soon rose in value. Even during the First World War, the

Table 7. The exchange rates of four major currencies, 1815–1913

	UK £	France FF	Germany*	US $
1815	I	21.53	31.68 HS	
1825	I	25.21	36.92	
1835	I	25.60	13.88 m	
1845	I	25.92	13.86	
1855	I	25.47	13.52	
1860	I	25.45	13.39	5.31
1865	I	25.48	13.63	8.54
1875	I	25.49	20.71	4.856
1885	I	25.44	20.60	4.842
1895	I	25.34	20.59	4.876
1905	I	25.31	20.62	4.866
1913	I	25.56	20.78	4.868

* Germany: HS = Hamburg Schilling, m = mark

Table 8. Exchange rates, 1914–20

	£	FF	US $
1914	I	25.16	4.876
1915	I	26.51	4.748
1916	I	28.04	4.766
1917	I	27.47	4.764
1918	I	26.72	4.402
1919	I	31.75	4.429
1920	I	52.47	3.661

Allied currencies held steady, until the pressure of war debts placed sterling midway between a rising dollar and a falling franc. (See Table 7, above.)

The reason for this immobility was simple. The common currency of the world was not the pound or the dollar, but gold.[82]

Seen in retrospect, the grand era of sterling had achieved remarkable monetary soundness over a remarkably wide area and for a remarkably long time. The stability of sterling was legendary.

British people were brought up to expect it. As the saying went, it was 'as safe as the Bank of England'.

(11) British Demography: a Spate of Superlatives

Demography, the study of population, is one of the most crucial subjects for understanding the modern world. It is especially relevant to modern British history. In the period after 1750, the United Kingdom was the scene of some of the most dynamic and dramatic demographic developments. It was also the home of the most influential demographers. The Revd Thomas Malthus (1766–1834), for instance, though not the founder of the subject, published its most celebrated treatise. He was a curate in Surrey, and a teacher at the East India Company's college at Haileybury, but his *Essay on Population* (1798) caused global shock waves. He predicted that population numbers would multiply geometrically, whilst the food supply would increase only arithmetically. As he himself admitted, the outlook was rather 'melancholy'. He was predicting mass death and starvation. His arguments were typical of the anxieties of the day. But they proved to be completely false. The fact that the nineteenth century witnessed not merely an amazing increase in population but also a sensational rise in living standards gave the British a huge boost of confidence.

Once it started around 1750, the increase in the United Kingdom's population continued decade after decade with very few setbacks. By the turn of the twentieth century, the Isles were supporting between four and five times as many people as a hundred and fifty years earlier:

$$
\begin{array}{ll}
1750 & \text{c. 10.5 million} \\
1801 & \text{15.5 million} \\
1851 & \text{23.8 million}
\end{array}
$$

1901   41.5 m
1911   47.3 m[83]

The first general census was taken in 1801. Fuller statistics were collected from 1841. But the overall totals were not in doubt.

The United Kingdom's demographic ranking in Europe jumped sensationally. In 1801, at the second Act of Union, its population, though rising fast, stood at barely two-thirds of France's, and was similar to that of Spain and Portugal. In 1891, at 37.9 million, it was almost equal to France's. But by 1911, three years before the First World War, it had taken a clear lead of some 14 per cent over France, and was nearly double that of Spain and Portugal. Indeed, after the Russian Empire at c. 165 million and the German Empire at 64.9 million, it had moved up into the third position. In an age of conscription, when gross population was closely related to military strength, this was no mean consideration. Britain's performance had only been outstripped by that of the USA, which from a mere 5.3 million in 1800 had soared to 75.9 million in 1900.[84] Yet the British were not overimpressed even by the USA. The population of the United Kingdom was less important for the British than were the teeming peoples of the Empire as a whole. On this score, they put all their competitors into the shade. By 1921, when the Empire's territory had reached its maximum, its population was almost twice that of Russia, Germany, and the USA put together. (See Table 9, page 772.)

'Taking the population of the world as 1,769 millions,' a contemporary encyclopedia concluded, 'the British Empire . . . accounts for rather more than one-fourth of the whole.'[85]

The United Kingdom was the first state in the world to generate a predominantly urban society. Despite the fact that large tracts of country, even in southern England, maintained their rural character, and despite the depopulation of many upland areas, especially in Scotland, the phenomenal growth of industrial cities overshadowed all other developments. At 7.476 million (1921) and still rising, Greater London was easily Europe's largest city, containing c. 16 per

Table 9. Population of the British Empire, 1921

United Kingdom	47,300,000
Self-governing Dominions	
Canada and Newfoundland	9,000,000
Australia	5,500,000
New Zealand	1,300,000
South Africa (Union of)	5,700,000
	21,500,000
Other parts of the Empire:	
Indian Empire	319,100,000
Ceylon	4,500,000
Egypt	13,000,000
Other possessions	40,000,000
	376,600,000
Grand total	445,400,000[86]

cent of the entire British population. It was markedly larger than New York, more than twice the size of Paris, and three times bigger than Berlin. Next in size came Glasgow at 1.034 million (1921), Birmingham at 919,438, Liverpool at 803,118, Manchester at 730,551, Sheffield at 490,724, Leeds at 458,320, and Edinburgh at 420,281. At 386,947 (1911), Belfast was regularly publicized as 'Ireland's largest city', although Greater Dublin was running it very close. At 182,280 (1911), Cardiff had still not exceeded the status of a county borough. But thanks to the Merthyr Canal and the Taff Vale Railway, it was the focus of a much more extensive conurbation. Such conurbations, where strings of industrial towns merged imperceptibly with each other, were more typical of the age than planned, discrete cities of the classic type. Generally speaking, the rural sector experienced an absolute decrease after 1850, whilst the urban sector continued to grow at breakneck speed. (See Table 10, right.) The progress of urbanization was several times greater in England, Wales, and Scotland than in Ireland. (See Table 11, right.)

Table 10. The rise of urban society in the United Kingdom, 1851–1900

Decade	Urban (%)	Rural (%)
1851–1861	+21.9	+1.88
1861–1871	+28.1	–5.86
1871–1881	+25.6	–3.84
1881–1891	+18.5	–2.76
1891–1900	+15.22	+2.94[87]

Table 11. The percentage of the population of the Isles living in towns
of 10,000 or over, 1800 91

	1800–1	1850–1	1890–1
England and Wales	21.3	39.5	61.7
Scotland	17.0	32.2	50.0
Ireland	7.8	10.1	18.0[88]

From the late eighteenth to the early twentieth century, the huge movement of people from the rural areas to the cities, including that from Ireland to Great Britain, was matched by an unrelenting flood of emigration overseas. The causes varied from rural poverty, to urban overcrowding, and compulsory deportation. The leading destination was always North America, although Australia, New Zealand, and South Africa grew in prominence. Sufficient emigrants left Ulster in the late eighteenth century to make the so-called 'Scots Irish' dialect the most important single ingredient of American English accents. Such large numbers of Gaels were expelled from Scotland during the Highland Clearances (see page 758, above) that several districts of Nova Scotia and Newfoundland have remained Gaelic-speaking. The 'First Fleet' of emigrants to Australia sailed for Botany Bay in 1787 because London's prisons and convict hulks were filled to overflowing. Yet within a few decades, Australia was transformed from a convict colony into the most desirable of destinations. The state of South Australia, for instance, was laid out in 1836 round the elegant city of Adelaide as a brand-new colony for regulated settlement. Throughout the nineteenth century, the emigrant ships constantly took their human cargoes

Table 12. Emigration from Great Britain and Ireland, 1815–1905

Date	to British North America	to the USA	to Australia	to other destinations	Total
1815–52* (37 years)	1,036,714	2,064,581	313,455	51,461	3,466,211
1853–60** (8 years)	123,408	805,596	365,307	18,372	1,312,683
1861–70** (10 years)	130,310	1,132,626	267,358	41,535	1,571,829
1871–80**	177,976	1,087,372	303,367	110,204	1,678,919
1881–90**	301,922	1,713,953	372,744	169,916	2,558,535
1891–1900**	176,336	1,090,685	119,018	258,942	1,644,981
1901–05** (5 years)	181,504	290,679	27,120	85,607	584,910
Total, 1853–1905 (53 years)	1,091,456	6,120,911	1,454,914	684,576	9,351,857[89]

* All Emigrants ** British and Irish Emigrants

Table 13. Immigration to the USA by country of origin, 1871–95

		Percentage of Total Immigration
England and Wales	1,334,817	12.9
Scotland	286,807	2.8
Ireland	1,334,635	12.9
British Subjects (total)	2,956,259	28.6[90]

from all the ports of the Isles, sailing west, south, and east to the furthest corners of the globe. (See Table 12, above.)

Year in, year out, the United Kingdom was creating a worldwide network of settlements founded by 'kith and kin' such as no other country in the world possessed. Apart from an exceptional period in the middle of the century, the outflow of English emigrants was not inferior to that of Scots, Welsh, or Irish. In the years 1871–95, for example, the number of English emigrants to the USA was running at almost exactly the same level as that of the Irish. (See Table 13, above.)

Nonetheless, for all sorts of reasons, Ireland represented a very special case. Firstly, the demographic spurt in Ireland in the late eighteenth and early nineteenth century had no parallel. Secondly, industrial development in Ireland outside Ulster was modest, and failed to supply an adequate source of employment. Thirdly, the Potato Famine of 1846–9 inflicted a catastrophe on a scale unknown elsewhere in Europe. As a result, the proportion of the Irish population forced to emigrate, whether overseas or to Great Britain, was unusually high. The rate of natural increase could not keep pace with the plague of deaths and departures. Consequently and exceptionally in modern Europe, the population of Ireland fell drastically by almost a half. By 1845, on the eve of the Famine, the Irish population had passed the eight million mark. But in the succeeding years one million deaths from unnatural causes were recorded. One million emigrants left Ireland in the 1840s, a further million left in the 1850s, and 850,000 departed in the 1860s. In the last decades of the century, the rate of emigration from Ireland to the USA alone ran at 50–60,000 per annum. In the years before the First World War, the Irish population was stabilizing at about 4.4 million, the figure for 1791.[91] By then, the USA possessed three times as many citizens of Irish origin than the United Kingdom possessed Irish subjects. The phenomenon is worthy of reflection. If the Irish population had continued to multiply uninterruptedly throughout the nineteenth century at the pace of 1801–45, Ireland would have been approaching Home Rule with at least fifteen million inhabitants. At the end of the twentieth century, an Irish President could claim without any great exaggeration that there were seventy million people of Irish descent scattered around the world. The great majority of their ancestors left Ireland in the period between the Famine and the Great War.

Ireland differed from England, Scotland, and Wales in another important respect. Irish women emigrated in almost exactly the same numbers as Irish men.[92] Emigrants from the rest of the United Kingdom contained a significantly higher ratio of males to females. By 1914, Great Britain suffered from a marked surplus of spinsters. Ireland suffered from an even greater surplus of bachelors. Inexorably, for all these reasons, the balance of the nationalities within the United Kingdom was moving decisively in favour of the English. (See Table 14, overleaf.)

Table 14. The population of the Isles, 1750–1911 (millions)

	1750	1801	1851	1901	1911
England	(5.7)	} 9.1	} 18.0	32.6	34.0
Wales	(0.6)				2.0
Scotland	(1.2)	1.6	2.9	4.5	4.8
Ireland	(3.0)	5.2	6.5	4.4	4.4
UK – Total	(10.5)	15.9	27.4	41.5	45.2[93]

One must take care with these statistics, of course. The population of England was not exclusively English. By 1900, it contained large contingents of Welsh, Scots, and especially Irish migrants. Intermarriage between the different groups was widely practised in the burgeoning cities. The Irish, being Catholics, were perhaps less inclined to intermarry than the others. But young Irish lads on the loose in Great Britain must often have faced the prospect either of marrying a local girl or of staying single. So a great deal of mixing took place, and families of mixed origin undoubtedly adopted a more nuanced approach to nationality questions. Even so, the stark facts could not be denied. In 1801, roughly half of the British population lived in England. A hundred years later, roughly three-quarters of the population lived in England. One can't easily measure the effect on national consciousness. But the old tendency to confuse 'Britishness' with 'Englishness' can only have been strengthened.

A significant shift had also taken place among the United Kingdom's non-English citizens. Throughout the long Victorian Era, the Irish had always formed the second largest national group after the English. In 1901, the year of Victoria's death, they were overtaken for the very first time by the Scots. Scottish attitudes both to the United Kingdom and to the British Empire differed markedly from those of the Irish.

The most interesting feature of these figures, however, must surely lie in the way that they were commonly presented. In later times, demographic statistics would be perceived as rather dry, if not decidedly dull. But in the early twentieth century, they were viewed as a source of immense pride. A popular encyclopedia would deliver the statistics not merely in diagrams and tables but in startling graphics. (See Appendix 43.) The relative populations of 'the world's chief countries' were presented as a series of black bars, in which Britain's European rivals appeared in a corner as small chunky strips. The United Kingdom did not need to be mentioned in such company, whilst the British Empire stretched out across the page on a bar eight or nine times longer, dwarfing even China. In a representation of the world's religions, the spire of the Christian Church soared twice as high as the roofs of the 'Confucian' temple and 'Mahomedan' Mosque. The 'white race' was equal in size to the 'yellow'. The growth of population in the UK was portrayed as a line of John Bulls wearing farmer's hat, breeches, knee-boots, and a Union Jack waistcoat. In 1821 John Bull was a midget; by 1921 he had grown into a towering giant.[94] The average British reader can only have reacted with a spate of superlatives.

(12) THE RISE OF IMPERIAL ENGLISH

The genesis of the first Act of Union in 1707 lay in a political alliance between the English government of England and Wales and the English-speaking Lowland lords of Scotland. Neither the Welsh nor the Scottish Gaels were given any say. Similarly, in 1801, when the Union was extended to pre-Emancipation Ireland, it was the English-speaking Protestant Irish who fitted most easily into the new order. In such a configuration, it was absolutely natural that English language and English culture would be adopted unquestioningly as the sole medium of official communication in the United Kingdom.

Nonetheless, at the time of the Union, the reach of standard English was relatively limited. Indeed, it is open to question whether standard English itself had yet come into being. Several non-English and many non-standard, regional, or sectional cultures were functioning. It was only though a very long programme of assimilation, sometimes voluntary and sometimes involuntary, that much higher levels of standardization were achieved. Whether the developments were judged as 'good' or 'bad' depended very much on the ear of the listener.

Place-names, for example, were not systematically Englished in all parts of the Isles until the nineteenth century, although piecemeal advances were made in earlier times. Much depended on the date when particular districts received an English-speaking administration or when they were officially surveyed. In Wales, many English or Anglicized names were fixed in the reign of Henry VIII when the country was shired. So Brecheiníog became Brecknock, and Ceredigion became Cardigan. In Ireland, English names made a big step forward through the preparation of 'plantation maps' of the seventeenth century, which were drawn up by English officials in conjunction with Anglo-Irish landowners. At that time, many standard Anglicizations were adopted, such as Bally for the Gaelic *Baile*, 'city' or 'settlement', and Kill for the Irish *Cill* or 'church'. In the Gaeltaecht of Scotland, in contrast, nothing much changed until 1725, when the British military under the Irish General George Wade moved in to start the long task of building forts, roads, and bridges. It was General Wade's map-makers who made the first general assault on Gaelic nomenclature. A second assault began after the '45 Rising. Walking through the Highlands in the 1770s, Dr Johnson noted how the roadside milestones, marking the distances in English miles between places with new English names, had often been overturned by angry locals.

The decisive campaign, however, was launched with the founding of the Ordnance Survey in 1791. A general trigonometrical survey had been started in Scotland a few years earlier, but the prospect of the Revolutionary Wars led to the extension of the scheme to the whole of the United Kingdom. After 1801, Ireland was included as well. Henceforth, every single hill, stream, pass, islet, wood, farm, and hamlet, from the Shetlands to the Scillies, from Galway to Lowestoft, was given an official name; and the names were recorded on the OS maps of 1:63,000 or 1 inch to 1 mile, which from 1830 onwards were offered for sale to the public. The task was tricky enough in England. But in non-English areas it called for a large number of arbitrary decisions. In the Gaeltaecht, for example, three categories of name were used. English names were given preference wherever they existed, as at Fort Augustus (aptly named in 1721 on the birth of the Duke of Cumberland, the future victor of Culloden). More often, Gaelic names were given a simplified, Anglicized orthography. Frequently and quite attractively, hybrid names were invented or adopted, producing well-known landmarks such as Kyle of Lochalsh, the Ross of Mull, or the Spittal of Glenshee. In this way, Gaelic words such as 'glen', 'ben', 'strath', and 'loch' passed in their own right into the standard English vocabulary.

Nor was the cultural standardization of the Ordnance Survey confined to language alone. One of its many conventions was to mark Anglican parish churches in England and Ireland, and parishes of the state Kirk in Scotland, with a bold, simple cross. Roman Catholic and Nonconformist churches were marked with a less prominent symbol and called 'chapels'. Discriminatory, pre-Emancipation categories were perpetuated.

It would have been strange if some of the men performing these tasks did not become seriously interested in the intricacies of their work. Indeed, during the surveying of Ireland in the 1820s, the officials became so impressed by the knowledge of the local Irish antiquaries whom they met that they devised a scheme to accompany each of the maps with summary memoranda containing their informants' data. If pursued, the scheme would have done something to preserve the local language and lore and to offset the state-sponsored standardization. Time and expense proved exorbitant.

Surnames needed to be standardized to bring every individual citizen within the purview of officialdom. The English had used nuclear family surnames since medieval times, but the Celtic peoples had other practices. Hence, as the English administration advanced into Celtic areas, Anglicized surnames were imposed, often with eccentric results. In Wales, for instance, a small number of male Christian names were transformed into Anglicized surnames, and widely adopted en masse by the Welsh-speaking population. As a result, thousands upon thousands of unrelated families ended up with the same simple surname, usually Jones, Williams, Thomas, Edwards, Hughes, or Davies – sowing immense confusion. To this day, many individuals in each locality can only be certainly identified by the ubiquitous nicknames such as 'Jones the Milk' or 'Hughes the Post' or 'Davies the Limp'. In the Scottish Highlands, surnames only came in with the suppression of the clans in 1745. Traditionally the clanspeople had identified themselves by patronymics. But the order to register with the authorities led to the indiscriminate adoption of clan names as surnames. Once again, as in Wales, the outcome was a profusion of families all using a limited number of names – the Macdonalds, the Macleans, the Macphersons, the MacClennons.

In the eighteenth century, under pressure of Enlightenment ideas of progress, standardization was widely thought to be beneficial. The loss of particularisms and of non-standard 'peculiarities' was not regretted or resented, except of course by the people from whom they were taken away. Dr Johnson, for example, whose anti-Scottish prejudices were quite moderate by the English standards of his day, assumed that Scottish forms of speech, Lallans as well as Gaelic, would simply fade away. The goal was the elimination of difference:

> The conversation of the Scots grows every day less unpleasing to the English; their peculiarities wear fast away; their dialect is likely to become in half a century provincial and rustic, even to themselves. The great, the learned, the ambitious and the vain, all cultivate the English phrase and the English pronunciation. Scotch is not much heard, except now and then from an old lady.[95]

In such a climate, Scots were made to feel ashamed of their 'Scotsness', and many of them tried to lose it. Though opinion on the matter differs, it is likely that the use of the word 'Britain' as a synonym for the newly united Kingdom, and of 'British' as the relevant adjective, was first adopted by educated Scots who wanted to forget the uncomfortable distinction between England and Scot-

land. In the eighteenth century, the polite fashion was to refer to
Scotland as 'North Britain'. Few people mentioned 'the United
Kingdom' – a term that was not officially enthroned until the union
with Ireland in 1801. The English, of course, continued to call
everything 'England' as if nothing had changed.

Yet before one complains too bitterly, it is important to recognize that the drive for homogenization was directed just as much at
the regional dialects of England as at the Scots, the Welsh, or the
Irish. Indeed, the time would come when a crisp Scots brogue found
a prized place among the hierarchy of acceptable speech forms
within the British Establishment, every bit the equal of the lan-
guorous aristocratic affectations of the South. With time, English
prejudices against Scots speech declined, whilst class-based prejudices against the dialects of industrial regions increased. By the
early twentieth century, the ears of educated Britishers were most
offended by the supposedly crude and vulgar cadences of 'Brummie',
'Scouse', 'Geordie', and 'Cockney'.

For a long time, the advance of standard English culture was
less assisted by government policy than by the sheer weight, wealth,
and number of England's well-established cultural institutions. London's pre-eminence, already distinct before the Union, continued to
grow. London possessed more theatres, concert halls, bookshops,
publishers, libraries, newspapers, and journals than any other of the
cities of the kingdom combined. Edinburgh and, to a lesser extent,
Dublin also developed as off-centre cultural capitals; but they did so
by emulating London, not by opposing it. In the eighteenth century,
Edinburgh University outshone Oxford and Cambridge, but it did so
as a bright pupil that had bettered its English masters. St Andrews
and Trinity College, Dublin, both gripped by the Protestant monopoly, were little outposts of English culture outside England. Wales
had no institution of higher learning to call its own.

Nonetheless, compared to some of its Continental counterparts,
English language and culture still suffered from several disabilities.
There was no equivalent of Richelieu's Académie Française; royal
patronage of the arts and literature was meagre; and, until the

second half of the eighteenth century, there were no proper dictionaries.

Dr Johnson's *Dictionary of the English Language* (1755) ran into four editions during his lifetime. As he wrote in the Preface, he found the English language 'copious without order, energetic without rules'; and, after a decade of sustained labours, he tamed both its teeming vocabulary and its wayward grammar. He listed a total of 43,500 words in two huge volumes and over four thousand pages; and he supported his definitions and distinctions by 118,000 quotations from literary sources, notably from Milton. Phrasal verbs, which are highly characteristic of English morphology, but which had traditionally been shunned by classically educated analysts, were finally brought to order. The verb 'to take' was alone given twenty-one different shades of meaning in the transitive form and eleven in the intransitive. The body of the work was prefaced by a scintillating essay on the problems of lexicography; by a History of the English Language, which supplies lengthy extracts in the original from King Alfred to Alexander Pope; and by a condensed outline of English grammar. Many of the definitions, spiced with irony, became famous:

> LEXICOGRAPHER: A writer of dictionaries, a harmless drudge.
> OATS: A grain which in England is given to horses, but in Scotland supports the people.
> PATRON: Commonly a wretch who supports with insolence, and is paid with flattery.

To OATS he appended a quotation from Shakespeare: 'The oats have eaten the horses': and to HISTORIAN, 'a writer of facts and events', he added: 'Our country, which has produced writers of first figure in every other kind of work, has been very barren in good historians. – Addison'. The word ENGLISH, 'Belonging to England', is there, but not Irish, Scottish, Welsh, or British.[96]

Samuel Johnson is remembered as one of the great figures of English culture not only because of his extraordinary erudition and personality, but also because in James Boswell (1740–93) he teamed up with one of the finest of all biographers and diarists. Boswell followed Johnson round the salons of the day, recording all the aphorisms and intellectual fireworks, and in 1773 took him on a tour of the Highlands and Islands of his native Scotland. The magical combination of the canny Scot and the bullish Englishman was a wonderful epitome of British intellectual life during the Anglo-Scottish Union. When Boswell was first introduced to Johnson in 1762, he said: 'Mr Johnson, I do indeed come from Scotland, but I cannot help it.'[97]

Johnson's *Dictionary* has had numerous imitators and continuators, but two in particular deserve special mention. One of these is John Jamieson's multivolume *Etymological Dictionary of the Scottish Language* (1808), which set out to prove that Scots is not 'merely a corrupt dialect of the English'. The other, which grew from a project first mooted in the 1840s, was the Rolls Royce of all lexicons, the *Oxford English Dictionary*. The *OED*'s founding editor, James Murray, a Scot, saw the first instalment roll off the presses in 1884; the final one appeared in 1933. (See above.)

In the nineteenth century, education expanded rapidly at every level; and at every level and in all parts of the Isles English was universally mobilized as the sole medium of instruction. The new or reformed 'public schools', all of which were in reality private boarding institutions, catered from the 1830s and 40s for the sons of wealthier families. Their guru was Thomas Arnold (1795–1842), headmaster of Rugby School from 1828, who set out the model for an upbringing based on 'muscular Christianity', patriotism, discipline with responsibility, and social service. Since all the boys were boarders, they were insulated from the local population; and they were inculcated with the same ideals and the same southern English irrespective of their geographical location. Pupils of Fettes College or the Edinburgh Academy, which were located in Scotland, were virtually indistinguishable from the products of Rugby, Malvern, or Rossall, which were in the depths of the English countryside. The appearance of Roman Catholic public schools such as Stonyhurst,

Downside, or Ampleforth did something to heal the age-old religious schism in British education, whilst imparting the same ethos and the same class-based linguistic culture as that of their Protestant counterparts.

During the long mid-century debate on mass education, no educationalist was more aware of the problems and pitfalls than Thomas Arnold's son, Matthew (1822–88). Matthew Arnold is usually remembered with Tennyson and Browning as a leading Victorian poet, and as a literary, religious, and social critic. Yet he had two unusual and sometimes forgotten qualifications. For thirty-five years, he worked as the Government's Chief Inspector of Schools, gaining immense experience of education both at home and abroad, especially in France, Switzerland, Italy, and Germany; and he was one of the few prominent Victorians to possess an expert knowledge of Celtic literature. At different times in his career, he was Professor at Oxford both of Poetry and of Celtic Studies. Seen in retrospect, perhaps the most obstinate contradiction with which he wrestled rose from his love of the Celtic languages and from his desire to initiate the masses into a uniform system of effective education. In the end, having visited Berlin, where his Prussian colleagues were advocating the compulsory teaching of German to Polish children in Prussia's eastern provinces, he decided that English-language instruction should be universal in British schools. The United Kingdom's leading Celtic specialist convinced himself that Scots, Welsh, and Irish children should not be allowed to be taught in their own language.

Linguistic discrimination was simply not seen in the same light as political or religious discrimination. For Arnold was a man with a fierce liberal conscience. He was outraged, for instance, at the failure to provide the Irish Catholics with a university of their own:

> At Trinity College, Dublin, the Irish Protestants have a university instruction of the type that the Irish Catholics want. Trinity College is endowed with confiscated Catholic lands and occupies the site of a suppressed monastery. [Yet] the Catholic

majority in Ireland is neither allowed the use of the old endowments as in England and Scotland . . . nor is it allowed the aid of state grants. There is nothing like it, I repeat, in Europe.[98]

After much delay, Gladstone's first Liberal ministry launched the era of state-paid elementary education for all British children through the Education Act (1870). In 1880, attendance at school was made compulsory; and in 1882, Whitehall transferred responsibility for the provision of state-funded schooling onto the counties and country boroughs. In 1906, Asquith's Liberal government introduced free milk and cheap school meals, and from 1918 all children were obliged to stay at school until age fourteen. Scotland retained its own separate educational system, which many considered the best. But the entire United Kingdom was moving into the era of universal (English) literacy.

Few people in the centre paused to reflect on the consequences for the non-English cultures of the Isles. After all, at the height of empire, British educators were exporting English-based schooling to every continent of the globe. From London's perspective, there was no more cause for the imperial Establishment to worry about Welsh or Gaelic than about Tamil or Kikuyu. Indeed, the tidal wave of state-sponsored English teaching met with only minimal resistance. There was no repetition in the United Kingdom of the mass school strikes which broke out in Prussian Poland over the imposition there of German. Irish and Scottish Gaelic had already been reduced to the margins in Ireland and Scotland; and Scots Lallans had little visible support.

Only in the Welsh-speaking counties of Wales did extensive friction occur. There, British educators came face to face with old-established local school networks, and with people who as often as not were fully literate in Welsh. On official instructions, schoolteachers resorted to a practice that was humiliating for the children and degrading for the school. The 'Welsh Not' was a board bearing the word 'NOT' that was hung round the neck of any child caught speaking Welsh. What it stood for was 'the Saxon Commandment': 'Thou shalt not speak thy native language'.

The English language, however, was due to be handed yet more instruments of power. Like the rest of the world, the United Kingdom stood on the verge of the mass media explosion. Both cinema and radio would operate almost exclusively through the medium of English, not least because cheap, popular, and intelligible imports from the USA were readily available. The Marconi Company's patent on radio transmission was registered in 1896. The first purpose-built British cinema opened its doors in Colne, Lancashire, in 1907. The British Broadcasting Company, later Corporation, transmitted its opening programmes in 1922. Ten years later, the British government gave the BBC funds to start sending its 'Imperial Service' round the world.

The arrival of 'BBC English' in the 1920s marked the high point in the steady advance of a standardized English language. Prior to radio, written English had achieved a high degree of standardization; but spoken English had necessarily retained wide variations. Only a small sector of the population had ever been able to listen to those narrow circles of the British elite who mouthed the plummy tones of 'the King's English' or of 'Oxford English' or the much vaunted patois of London's gentlemen's clubs. Received pronunciation, as well as received spelling, style, and grammar, was now opened to all. The founder of the BBC, John Reith (1889–1971), a dour, high-handed, actively Presbyterian Scot from Kincardineshire, did not himself speak in the same prim, clipped southern accent that his employees were expected to emulate, though primness and clipping were certainly features of his own speaking style. But he set the parameters of the reigning ethos of the BBC's glory days. As Reith himself put it:

> The Broadcasters are mostly young men . . . They are rather shadowy personalities to the average man; they are aloof and mysterious. You will probably not find them at garden parties or social functions . . . [Yet] they are personages of much

importance in the land . . . It matters little to them whether it be recognised or not. In may ways, I believe, it is desirable that they should continue in their comparative obscurity . . . A place in the stars is more important than a place in the sun.[99]

'The influence of the BBC both on education and the pronunciation of "standard English"', remarked the Corporation's chief historian, 'has been noted by almost all the people who have described its work.'[100] An Advisory Committee on Spoken English was formed in 1926. It included the poet Robert Bridges, George Bernard Shaw, and later Rudyard Kipling. The Secretary was A. Lloyd James, Professor of Phonetics at London University. But it was given little to do. The Corporation led by example, not by decree. When the Committee met it discussed 'debatable words'. One of these was the name of the BBC's chief transmission station. Should it be 'Daintry', its historical pronunciation, or 'Daventry', its phonetic pronunciation? Lloyd James gave a firm ruling. 'The BBC, I think,' he said, 'has sufficient authority to decide which pronunciation it will adopt. Let it be *Daventry*.'[101]

(13) THE BRITISH: 'THE FIRST RACE IN THE WORLD'

In all probability, the first encounter between Britons and people of colour occurred in the days of Roman Britannia, when units from Africa were occasionally posted to the garrison on Hadrian's Wall. But the Romans who fostered a multiracial empire were largely indifferent to racial issues, and in any case the contacts were marginal. In subsequent centuries, such intercommunal tensions that surfaced in the Isles were centred on ethnic, cultural, or religious, rather than racial, differences. King Knútr, for instance, was concerned about conflicts between his Anglo-Saxon and his Danish subjects in England, just as Henry VIII expressed his displeasure over the perpetual animosities between English and Welsh. Regular contact with the non-European races only began in the sixteenth century, when ships from the Isles sailed to every continent of the globe and when occasional overseas visitors were brought back on board. Such early visitors were often treated as ethnographic exhibits. The most famous of them, the Algonquin princess Pocahontas (1595–1617), reached England from Virginia in 1616, and was presented at court to King James and his family. She is buried at Gravesend. Yet her fascinating story has some disgraceful aspects. Having saved the life of a Virginian colonist, Pocahontas was kidnapped and taken hostage against the good behaviour of her tribe. The circumstances of her conversion to Christianity and her marriage to an English Virginian would appear to contain an element of compulsion. The elaborate reception that was given to her in London was hardly representative of English attitudes towards native Americans in Virginia.[102]

Slavery, of course, had held a prominent position in both Anglo-Saxon and early Celtic societies. 10 per cent of England's population as recorded in Domesday Book were slaves; and slaving remained a well-established trade until the twelfth century. Yet the slaves were almost entirely of local or European origin, most frequently being drawn from prisoners-of-war. Slavery and slave trading did not assume a racial component until the rise much later of the 'Great Triangle' between Europe, Africa, and America. Sir John Hawkins of Armada fame was probably England's first slave trader. From then on, the trade increased by leaps and bounds. In the sixteenth century, it was counted in tens of thousands; in the eighteenth, when Britain established a dominant hold, in millions. Merchants from Bristol, Liverpool, Glasgow, and London led the field, and flourished.

Traditional attitudes to slavery were marked more by religious than by visual considerations. In the early modern period, European traders showed few scruples in exploiting, maltreating, and selling heathens. But they usually drew the line at keeping Christian slaves. There was also a marked contrast between the appalling treatment of blacks in the overseas colonies and their status in the home countries. The presence of black servants became increasingly common in the eighteenth century; and their legal position, though lowly, was no different from that of other exploited domestics. In the landmark case of Somerset v. Stewart (1772), the Lord Chief Justice of England, Lord Mansfield, ruled that a former slave could no longer be treated as such once he had landed on English soil. Though the issue is debatable, he is widely credited with abolishing slavery in the United Kingdom. The parallel case in Scotland of Knight v. Wedderburn (1778) established a clearer precedent whereby the Scottish courts would not uphold a slave-master's claim in pursuit of a fugitive. Evidence that blacks could be treated equally can be seen in the career of Dr Johnson's black servant, Francis Barber (1745–1803). Having no children of his own, Dr Johnson adopted Francis as his heir, gave him a gentleman's education and bequeathed him his entire fortune.[103]

However, the persistence of the slave trade and of legal slavery in the overseas empire clearly contradicted ancient English notions of liberty, not to mention the basic principles of Christianity. The horrendous hypocrisy involved can be sensed between the lines of one of the most beautiful of English hymns when one knows they were written by a former slave-trader:

> How sweet the name of Jesus sounds
> In a believer's ear
> It soothes his heart and calms his soul
> And drives away his fear.
>
> It makes the wounded spirit whole,
> And calms the troubled breasts;
> 'Tis manna to the hungry soul,
> And to the weary, rest.
>
> O Jesus! Shepherd, Guardian, Friend,
> O Prophet, Priest and King,
> My Lord, my Life, my Way, my End,
> Accept the praise I bring.[104]

The hymn's author, John Newton (1725–1807), had gone to sea as a lad, had been flogged by the navy for desertion, and had lived as a white slave in Africa. Escaping, he worked for six years as commander of a slave-ship, before experiencing conversion, studying in Liverpool, and eventually taking holy orders. Having composed many hymns, including the ever-popular 'Amazing Grace', he composed the epitaph which once hung in his church of St Mary Woolnoth, Lombard Street:

> JOHN NEWTON, Clerk
> Once an infidel and libertine
> A servant of slaves in Africa,
> Was, by the rich mercy of our Lord and Saviour
> JESUS CHRIST,
> restored, pardoned, and appointed to preach
> the Gospel which he had long laboured to destroy.
> He ministered,
> Near sixteen years in Olney, in Bucks,
> And twenty-eight years in this Church.[105]

The movement for the abolition of slavery was driven by the principled dedication of the Quakers, though its most prominent activist, Granville Sharp (1734–1813), was the Anglican grandson of an Archbishop of York. Sharp's treatise on *The Injustice of Tolerating Slavery* (1769) strongly influenced discussions surrounding the Somerset case, which in turn swelled the rising tide of protest. Sharp also took a lead in founding a colony for liberated slaves in Sierra Leone (1787). Yet the following two decades of protest coincided with a boom in slave trading. In the years 1781 to 1807, British ships carried over a million African slaves to the Americas. In the end, it was the Assembly of revolutionary France which took the lead in banning the trade. The British Parliament followed suit in 1807, but only after fears were expressed that the slave rebellion in Saint-Dominique (now Haiti) might spread to the British colonies. As for Granville Sharp, he worked tirelessly for every emancipatory movement but one. Apart from the Society for the Abolition of the Slave

Trade, he headed the African Institution, the campaign for Irish legislative independence, the British supporters of American independence, the British and Foreign Bible Society, and the Society for the Conversion of the Jews (1808). At the same time, incongruously, he served as the founding chairman of the Protestant Union (1804), dedicated to blocking Catholic Emancipation. Here were the limits to Protestant views on civil rights. African slaves, oppressed Irish, Americans, and unconverted Jews were all to be set free but not Catholics.

In Granville Sharp's later years, the baton of liberation was taken over by the evangelical philanthropist, Yorkshire MP, and former Governor of Sierra Leone, William Wilberforce (1759–1833). Wilberforce attracted a close-knit group of devoted followers known as the Clapham Sect. His allies in the House of Commons attracted the sobriquet of 'the Saints'. Once the slave trade was outlawed, their energies were directed against the institution of slavery within the Empire. Much prejudice and inertia stood in their way through two decades of Conservative government. The Act for the Abolition for Slavery was not passed until 1833, the year of Wilberforce's death, and in the tide of enthusiasm for parliamentary reform. In a very real sense, however, the crowning success of the anti-slavery movement, which had been launched when the American colonies belonged to the British Empire, did not arrive until the victory of the Unionists in the American Civil War in 1865, and the final abolition of slavery in the USA.[106]

As the (second) British Empire expanded, race relations grew more complicated. The number of British subjects from the colonies who settled in the United Kingdom was limited to a handful of isolated communities in the port cities, such as Tiger Bay in Cardiff or Bootle in Liverpool. But in the late Victorian and Edwardian era, tens of thousands of British administrators worked overseas, whilst the new dominions attracted far greater numbers of emigrants. As a result, the British public, which had long been familiar with West Africans and with Native Americans, now became familiar with Egyptians, Indians, Chinese, Polynesians, Maoris, Zulus, Bushmen, and, by reputation at least, with Australian Aborigines. The British Empire at its height took enormous pride in the multiracial make-up of its subjects.

Nevertheless, imperial pride fell far short of racial equality. Like all European imperialists of the era, the British accepted the 'White Man's Burden' as part of the divine order. They were taught, and they believed, that they were best fitted to rule over 'the lesser breeds'. Such attitudes can only be classed as racist. Yet they were not born of the fouler forms of hate-laden racism that emerged under the totalitarian regimes of a later generation. They were paternalistic and hierarchical, based on the acceptance of superior and inferior races, and hence of the duty of the favoured to lead the less fortunate. There could be no doubt who was top dog. 'We are the first race in the world,' wrote Cecil Rhodes, 'and the more of the world we inhabit, the better it is for the human race.'[107]

(14) THE BRITISH SPORTING TRADITION: 'PLAY THE GAME!'

If one goes back far enough, the concept of 'Fair Play' was reputedly invented by the Celts.[108] But there can be no doubt that organized sport and the accompanying sporting ethos was largely a product of the United Kingdom in the eighteenth and nineteenth centuries. Indeed, when all of Britain's other achievements have passed into oblivion, the world may possibly remember that the global sporting heritage first took root among the sportsmen of the Isles.

In earlier times, recreation in the modern sense was virtually unknown. The physical demands of everyday life were so great that no one thought of extra physical exercise as a desirable activity. People who worked in the fields from dawn till dusk, who spent hours every day in the saddle, or who walked for miles to church every Sunday had no spare energy for mere amusements. Games were not unknown, but they were a sporadic feature of childhood or of feast days; and they possessed no universal rules. Physical contests, too, were organized regularly. But they were either,

like boxing or wrestling, a branch of entertainment at the fair, or like
archery, a branch of officially sponsored military training. Even the
leisured classes did not understand 'sport' in the way it is understood
today. Aristocrats and landed gentlemen engaged in tournaments
well into the sixteenth century in order to refine their knightly
accomplishments. They and their hangers-on continued to engage
in hunting, shooting, and fishing not simply from sheer enjoyment,
but as a function of their social status. Oscar Wilde's magnificent
description of fox-hunting in the 1880s as 'the unspeakable in pursuit
of the inedible' precisely pinpoints the anachronism involved in the
preservation of ancient outdated attitudes to 'gentlemen's sport' in
an age of sport for everyone. Indeed, the language itself had to
change. In former times, if the word 'sport' did not refer to love-
making, it referred to hunting: 'the sport of kings'.

The aims of modern sport are radically at odds with those of
sport in earlier times. One of them, summed up in the catchphrase
of *mens sana in corpore sano*, centres on personal development
especially in young people of school age. It sets out to establish a
healthy and complementary balance between a person's physical
and intellectual development, and, by confronting the individual
with the alternating experiences of winning and losing, to inculcate
emotional stability. A second aim centres on the social benefits to
be expected from individuals who have learned to compete energetically within a framework of mutually accepted rules, to respect
the opponents whom they are trying to defeat, and to accept the
result gracefully. The third aim centres on the sphere of intercommunal, and at the highest level international conflict, where rivalries
and resentments can be effectively sublimated by transferring them
from the battlefield to the sportsfield. None of these aims could
have been envisaged in a rural, pre-modern society. It is not
surprising, therefore, that they emerged in Britain, the world's first
urban and modernized country. They were worked out in the
evolution of games which have assumed global importance – golf,
cricket, tennis, and, above all, in the various codes of football.

Scotland's major contribution lay with golf. Though the Dutch may possibly possess a prior claim, the Scots were already playing a form of golf in the fifteenth century. Numerous parliamentary edicts against 'golfe, or uther sik unprofitabill sportis' were issued from 1457 onwards because the *wapinshawingis* or 'tournaments' were interfering with archery practice. The earliest mention of the 'Royal and Ancient' course at St Andrews occurs in 1557. Both James IV and James V were keen golfers; and one of the many charges against Mary, Queen of Scots was that she had been seen playing golf shortly after the murder of her husband, Darnley. The oldest club in England, the Royal Blackheath, was founded in 1608, undoubtedly to cater for the numerous Scots who had flocked to London with James VI and I. Charles I was playing golf when news of the Irish Rebellion was brought to him in 1642. Unlike Drake, who reputedly finished his game of bowls on Plymouth Ho before tackling the Spanish Armada, King Charles broke off his round, and headed for defeat. His son, James II, was also a devotee. In 1682, partnered by an Edinburgh shoemaker called Paterson, he won a challenge match and a hefty wager. From their winnings, Paterson built a house at 79 Canongate that still stands. In the eighteenth century, the most exclusive clubs were said to be the Honourable Company of Edinburgh Golfers (1744) and the Calcutta Golf Club. The Open Championship was started in 1860 at Prestwick in Ayrshire, the original champion being Willie Park snr. of Musselburgh. It soon became an annual event, moving to England for the first time in 1897 when it was held at Hoylake, near Liverpool. The Ladies' Championship began in 1893 at St Anne's, the winner being M. Scott. Originally, golf balls were made of leather stuffed with feathers. A court decision in London in 1905, which ruled that the modern American-invented golf ball was not subject to a patent, opened the way for the game to become popular and affordable.[109]

Cricket, in contrast, was always an archetypal English game. Recorded in the fourteenth century as one of several illegal pastimes, it was originally known as 'handyn and handout'. It was condemned by a statute of 1470 which laid down the ferocious penalty of three years' imprisonment for allowing one's premises to be used for the game. The word 'cricket' appeared in 1550 in conjunction with a playing-field enclosed by one John Parish, innkeeper of Guildford in Surrey. The Elizabethan authorities closed down the Guildford ground in 1593. But in the seventeenth century, the game continued to spread. The antiquarian Dugdale substantiated his accusation about the 'dissolute and disorderly' childhood of Oliver Cromwell by the information that the future Lord Protector had been 'famous for football, cricket, wrestling and cudgelling'. Some form of cricket was being played at Winchester College during the Commonwealth. The Restoration saw the foundation of England's oldest cricket club at St Alban's in 1661. The standard eleven-man team emerged in 1697. An early rulebook was drawn up by the London Club in 1744 for a match between Kent and All-England; but the authoritative set of rules was only codified by the newly founded Marylebone Cricket Club (MCC) in 1787–8. Cricket had remained an illegal activity, however, until a decision of the Court of King's Bench in 1748 stated that it was 'a manly game, not bad in itself, but only in the ill use made by betting more than ten pounds on it'. Three years later, Frederick, Prince of Wales died from injuries sustained from a cricket ball. The length of the cricket pitch – one chain or twenty-two yards – appears to have been constant since 1700. The use of a straight willow bat was normal as from 1750. The weight of the hard, cork-filled ball was fixed at 5½ 5¾ ounces in 1774. But the eight-inch wicket with three stumps and two bails, though recorded in an oil-painting named *The Village Match* (1768), did not establish itself permanently until 1827. By that time, the MCC and its ground at Lord's in St John's Wood were universally recognized as the headquarters of the game. Thomas Lord (1757–1832) was the son of a fugitive Scottish Jacobite family. His speciality was the import of fine Scottish sea turf for the preparation of a perfectly flat and smooth grass surface. Many details, however, remained to be settled. Overarm bowling, for example, was banned in 1827 after an England side was beaten by the overarm bowlers of Sussex; and it was not legally reinstated until 1868.[110]

In the course of Queen Victoria's reign, cricket was installed as the official summer game of all the English public schools, of the English universities, and of many parts of the Empire. The game of Gentlemen versus Players, first played in 1806, became an annual event of great prestige. The Varsity Match, of Oxford versus Cambridge, took on a similar status from 1827. The competition of the so-called 'First-class Counties' started up in 1872. The first Test match, between England and Australia, was played in 1878. Cricket grew so popular in India that in due course it would be declared 'an Indian game, accidentally discovered by the English'.[111] Although Dr W. G. Grace (1848–1915) of Gloucestershire is widely acclaimed as the greatest of all cricketers, Grace's batting average of 39.1 runs per innings was easily exceeded by the 56.3 achieved by his younger contemporary, the Indian batsman Prince K. S. Ranjitsinhji, (1872–1933), who also played for England.

The geographical and organizational limitations of cricket, however, are interesting. Though the English took cricket to almost every continent on earth, they never succeeded in exporting it to Scotland, to Ireland, or to Welsh Wales. It never became the national game of the United Kingdom. What is more, the MCC, which is a private club, has retained control of the game in England to the present day.

One of cricket's most striking characteristics lies in the extreme complexity of the rules, and hence in the unparalleled arcana of cricketing jargon. Terms such as *googlie*, *lbw*, or *silly mid-off* are difficult enough to define in standard English. They are totally untranslatable into a foreign language:

RULES OF CRICKET

You have two sides, one out in the field and one in. Each man that's in the side that's in goes out and when he's out he comes in and the next man goes in until he's out. When they are all out the side that's out comes in and the side that's been in goes out and tries to get those coming in out. Sometimes you get men still in and not out. When both sides have been in and

out, including the not outs, that's the end of the game.
HOWZAT![112]

People who understand cricket form a worldwide magic circle, whose links join them, not with the United Kingdom as a whole, but with England. For this reason, a Tory ex-minister recently proposed a 'Cricket Test' to weed out would-be immigrants.[113]

Tennis had a longer history than cricket. 'Royal' or 'real' tennis was said to have its roots in the Byzantine Empire, and was a favourite pastime at the medieval French court. Once played in English monasteries, it was revived by Henry VII. The famous tennis court at Hampton Court was built by Henry VIII. The idea of playing a similar game on grass and in the open air, however, did not catch on until the 1870s. In 1877, after various trial runs, it was adopted as a secondary activity by the All-England Croquet Club at Wimbledon. It soon became a primary activity, especially after the instigation of national championships. A governing body, the Lawn Tennis Association, commenced its career in 1888. An open amateur competition operated from 1889 at the Queen's Club, West Kensington. It was won on five occasions by Sir Edward Grey, the future Foreign Minister. The Davis Cup between England and the USA, first contested in 1900, opened the era of international tennis.[114] Other tennis-like sports evolved at Badminton House, Eton and Rugby (the homes of Fives), and at Harrow (the home of racquets).

Football is probably the oldest game of all. It was known in ancient Rome. But it has always existed in numerous forms; and no attempt to reduce it to a disciplined sport was made before the mid-nineteenth century, when several rival codes were established. It came in two main variants, one where players concentrate on kicking the ball with their feet (i.e., 'football' proper), and the other where they are allowed to catch the ball with their hands and run with it. All footballers claim that their own version of the game is called 'football', whilst other people's versions are something else.

The former variant was first regulated by the Football Association at a meeting at the Freemasons' Tavern in London in 1863.

(Because of the Association's rules, it was dubbed by its enemies 'soccer'.) The latter, by tradition, traces its origins to the day in 1823 when a pupil of Rugby School, William Webb Ellis, picked up the ball and ran with it. It is the ancestor of several related games, such as American football and Rugby League, which developed somewhat later. The Rugby Football Union was founded in 1871, the year in which the FA's Challenge Cup competition was also launched. The first Football Cup Final was played at the Kennington Oval – the ground of the Surrey Cricket Club – on 16 March 1872. The finalists were the Royal Engineers and the Wanderers.

The development of football in the United Kingdom moved in two directions. After two decades of resistance, the FA lifted its opposition to professional clubs and paid players. This opened the way to the formation of the English Football League (1888), with twelve member clubs. The oldest surviving professional club, Notts County, had been launched in 1864 on an amateur basis. The first clubs to establish a permanent professional competition had originated in the industrial towns of Lancashire – notably Blackburn Rovers, Bolton Wanderers, and Preston North End. At the same time, the FA's role in England was replicated by the formation of the Scottish FA (1873), the FA of Wales (1876), and the FA of Ireland (1880). The very first international match was played between England and Scotland in Glasgow in 1872.[115]

Professionalism proved a very divisive issue. In the football world, it raised a barrier between the larger clubs and the more numerous members of the proliferating amateur leagues. Famous amateur clubs such as the Corinthian Casuals or Northern Nomads, who played an illustrious role in the early decades of the game, gradually disappeared from view. In the rugby world, professionalism caused a permanent rift between the Rugby Union, which regarded amateur status as the mark of a gentleman, and the Rugby League, which mainly catered for the working-class towns of the northern coalfields, and which could not possibly have survived without compensating its players for lost wages. The Rugby Union's long-lasting ban against anyone who had ever accepted payment for playing represented one of the clearest and ugliest manifestations of the English class system.

As with cricket, the rules of the various football codes took many years to solidify. The FA insisted on fixing a rigid crossbar to goalposts in 1883, and introduced penalty kicks in 1891. The Rugby Union kept to fifteen-player teams, whilst the Rugby League opted for thirteen-man teams. In consequence, each of the codes acted as the focus for fierce group identities and, in some instances for social friction. It was a prophet of genius who worked out that 'Rugger is a game for savages played by gentlemen, whilst soccer is a game for gentlemen played by savages.' Nonetheless, in the last resort, football was the only game to attract support from all classes and from all parts of the British Isles. Football is the nearest thing there ever was to Britain's national game.

In this formative era, British sport was almost exclusively reserved for male participants. (Women were reported playing football in Mid-Lothian as early as 1795. But their exertions gained no official recognition.) Because of this, the new sporting ethos infiltrated all the older spheres of male-dominated activity, particularly warfare and government. It was implicit in the Duke of Wellington's remark that 'Waterloo was won on the playing-fields of Eton.' And it increasingly inspired the ranks on all the far-flung battlefields of the British Empire:

> There's a breathless hush in the Close to-night
>   Ten to make and the match to win –
> A bumping pitch and a blinding light,
>   An hour to play and the last man in.
> And it's not for the sake of a ribboned coat,
>   Or the selfish hope of a season's fame,
> But his Captain's hand on his shoulder smote
>   'Play up! play up! and play the game!'
>
> The sand of the desert is sodden red, –
>   Red with the wreck of a square that broke, –
> The Gatling's jammed and the colonel dead,

And the regiment blind with dust and smoke.
The river of death has brimmed his banks,
    And England's far, and Honour a name,
But the voice of a schoolboy rallies the ranks,
    'Play up! play up! and play the game!'

This is the word that year by year
    While in her place the School is set
Every one of her sons must hear,
    And none that hears it dare forget.
This they all with a joyful mind
    Bear through life like a torch in flame,
And falling fling to the host behind –
    'Play up! play up! and play the game!'[116]

(15) BRITISH LAW: A PLANET UNTO ITSELF

Law provides one of the great normative forces of social conduct.
By laying down the rules of what is acceptable and what is
punishable, laws give expression to the shared values which all
people subject to a particular jurisdiction must either follow or defy.
In dictatorships, law reflects the principles of the dictators. But in
democratic societies, where the lawmakers are elected as popular
representatives, the correlation between law and communal values
is much closer. The laws of different democracies inevitably reflect
the differing customs and traditions of different communities. English law, for example, did not promote the same social norms as
French law, or German law. The concept of British law, however,
is especially complex; and its role in the creation of a sense of
'Britishness' is open to question.

In this sphere, a touch of lawyer's precision never comes amiss.
'The United Kingdom,' states the *Oxford Companion to Law*, 'a state

commonly but incorrectly referred to as "Great Britain", "Britain", the "British Isles" or even "England", is not truly a unitary state.'[117] Nor, one might add, has it ever been. 'There is, accordingly,' the *Companion* continues,

> no such thing as United Kingdom or British Law, though there are some rules common to all parts of the UK . . . In [those] respects in which the law varies between England, Scotland and Northern Ireland . . . the terms 'United Kingdom Law' or 'British Law' are meaningless.[118]

To explain such a statement, one needs to examine the long story of the evolution of law in the Isles. One has to look at Welsh law, at Irish law, at English law, at Scots law, and also at canon law (the law of the Roman Catholic Church, as laid down in decrees of the pope and statutes of councils) and ecclesiastical law (the law, derived from canon and civil law, but administered independently by the established Protestant Churches). After that, if one turns to the statutory law laid down by the Westminster Parliament after the Union of 1707, one may possibly conclude that 'British Law' could in some limited respects be a meaningful concept.

The customary law of Wales (see Chapter Six) was suppressed in 1284 after the English conquest. But the introduction of English law into all parts of Wales did not occur until Henry VIII's Laws in Wales Act (1535) which accompanied the formal union of the two countries. The judicial system, however, remained separate for centuries. The arbitrary courts of the Tudors' Council in Wales remained in place from 1542 to 1688. The Henrician system of King's 'great sessions' was not replaced by English-style judicial circuits until 1830. Thereafter, there was one circuit for North Wales, and another for South Wales.

Irish law as promulgated by the medieval Parliament in Dublin, but always subject to an English veto, can best be classed as a branch of English law. Yet it required a separate legal profession trained at the King's Inns; and it did not adopt all English statutes automatically. Much may be read into the fact that the English Act of Habeas Corpus (1679) did not apply in Ireland until 1781. After the Union of 1801, English law was held to prevail in Ireland whenever a conflict loomed. This state of affairs persisted right up to 1920.

English law resembles nothing else in the world except, of course, for those legal systems such as the American or the Australian, which are descended from it. It has always defied codification and systematization, and hence to the outsider appears both chaotic and obscurantist. It has developed organically over a long time, dating the central role of its royal courts to the twelfth century, the emergence of its characteristic juries to the thirteenth, and the institution of Justices of the Peace or lay magistrates to the fourteenth. Among its 'Books of Authority' it numbers Glanvill's *De Legibus* . . . (1189), Henri de Bracton's treatise of the same name (c. 1250), Littleton's *Tenures* (1481), Coke's *Institutes* (1628–44), Hale's *Pleas* (1678), and Blackstone's *Commentaries* (1765–69). Yet hardest to grasp is England's reliance on three different sources of law – common law, equity, and statute – each of which has given rise to its own distinct legal corpus.

English common law can perhaps be best described as a dense accumulation of legal cases, where more recent layers have been constructed on the decisions and opinions of the earlier layers. The guiding principle is that of precedent. Common lawyers form their view of a case by referring to decisions taken in previous cases of a similar nature. Great weight is placed on positions struck by judges, often in remote times, and in particular on the *ratio decidendi* or 'legal opinion' in which judges summarize the reasons for their decisions. These precedents can be either 'binding', as between a higher court and a lower court, or merely 'persuasive'. Both civil and criminal causes are covered. The bibles of the trade are the Year Books of cases, which are complete from the thirteenth century, and the printed Law Reports, whose runs start in the sixteenth. The principal courts have long been those of the King's Bench, the Common Pleas, and the Exchequer.

Equity, literally 'fairness', is a branch of English law that grew up in contradistinction to the inflexible and pedantic technicalities of the common law. As from the fifteenth century, petitioners began to address the King's Council directly in search of judgements based not on precedent, but on common sense and morality. The point was ceded, and a separate body of law developed using principles owing much in its early days to the canon law of the Church. The court of Chancery provided the forum.

Statutory law passed by Parliament long occupied a minor position in the overall scheme. But its importance grew with the increasingly pressing need to clarify or to summarize the state of the law on particular subjects. By the era of the Union with Scotland, parliamentary statutes were becoming the most usual method of lawmaking in England, whilst the courts of common law and equity concentrated on the application of law.

English court practice, and the resultant structure of the legal profession, is based on an ancient and rigid division between barristers and solicitors. The former, who are trained at one of the four Inns of Court in London – Gray's Inn, Lincoln's Inn, the Middle Temple, and the Inner Temple – are received at the Bar when qualified. They are then given the exclusive right of audience before a judge in the higher courts. Their senior members take the ranks of King's (or Queen's) Counsel. Solicitors, in contrast, follow a separate training from the Law Society. Until very recently they could only appear on behalf of their clients in the lower courts. Most of their work was devoted to general legal advice, to routine matters of commercial and property law, and to the preparation of briefs for barristers.

Scots law has followed a different path in almost every field of legal activity. It is the product of an older jurisdiction than England's, tracing its roots to the ninth as opposed to the tenth century. Like English law, its initial customary phase was overtaken by feudalism. But feudal particularisms lasted longer. The pre-eminence of royal justice was asserted much later. But when a decree of 1426 established that all the King's subjects were to answer to the King's laws, the theory and practice of Scots law were already developing along very specific lines. Thanks to Scotland's long alliance with France, where the influence of Roman law was strong; the top Scots lawyers were often trained in Paris or at Leyden. Stong, too, was the Romano-canonical tradition of codified laws and of centralized courts. Precedent counted for nothing. No record of cases was kept, apart from lawyers' notebooks, which became the basis of the later literature of 'practicks'. Scots lawyers follow the French method of first finding the general principles to be applied to a case, and of then reasoning one's way to a conclusion based on the specific details. The central Court of Session for civil justice dated from 1532; the Commissionary Court for ecclesiastical affairs from 1563; and the High Court of Justiciary for criminal justice from 1672. Cromwell overturned Scotland's judicial system during the English invasion of 1651. But it returned at the Restoration. During that last period of Scotland's independence, the whole of Scots law was summarized and systematized in the remarkable *Decisions of the Lords of Council & Session* and *Institutions of the Law of Scotland* (1681, 1693), the life-work of James Dalrymple, Viscount Stair (1618–95), sometime President of the Court of Session. The authoritative summary of Scots criminal law had to await the posthumous publication of David Hume's *Commentaries on the Law of Scotland respecting crimes* (1797).

Since all parts of the Isles had belonged to Catholic Christendom for a thousand years, the influence of the canon law of the Roman Church exercised a greater influence than later Protestant commentators were willing to admit. Its canons, or 'norms', which were based on Scripture and religious doctrine, injected an ethical element into all other branches of legal thought. Henry VIII banned the study of canon law; and for at least two centuries any form of contact with Roman jurists could be treated in England as treasonable. Even so, Roman norms remained the unspoken historical source of Anglican ecclesiastical law. They were more radically rejected by the Presbyterian Church of Scotland, which could look to Geneva for guidance.

≈

The Act of Union of 1707 specifically safeguarded the continued existence and separation of the English and the Scottish legal systems. In general terms, this stipulation has been honoured to the present day. On the other hand, it is impossible to deny that Scots law was put at a distinct disadvantage. By closing the Edinburgh Parliament, which alone was well versed in Scottish practice, Scots law became something of a headless chicken. The legal operations of the British Parliament were dominated by English lawyers who knew nothing of the law outside England. The chief British legal officer, the Lord Chancellor, would frequently impose English practices on Scotland out of ignorance. And the House of Lords, which now became the supreme court of appeal in Scottish cases, tended to act in the same arbitrary manner. In several respects the Act of Union was flagrantly breached. A Court of Exchequer was established in Edinburgh, for example, using English forms. After each of the Jacobite Risings, the draconian English law of treason was improperly introduced into Scotland, and prisoners illegally removed to England for trial. Bit by bit, Scottish lawyers were compelled to make recourse to precedent. Their most effective response was to move to London and, by infiltrating the legal profession of the capital, to influence English law from the inside.

It is often said that Britain has no written constitution. This is true in the sense that there is one document called 'the British Constitution'. But there are things which are particularly relevant. The Act of Union (1707), which created the united Kingdom, summarizes the constitutional framework within which the British state is supposed to function. It also defined the arrangements that accommodate English law, Scottish law, and common British statute law, as well as economic relations within the UK. This Act, as amended by subsequent statutes including the Act of Union with Ireland (1800), the Irish Home Rule Act (1914), the Government of Ireland Act (1920), the Anglo-Irish Treaty (1922), and so on, deserve more attention.

The legal scene in eighteenth-century Great Britain was dominated

by the last of the giants among English and Scottish jurists. Blackstone and Hume have been mentioned. One equally needs to
mention two others. William Murray, Lord Mansfield (1705–93), the
long-term Chief Justice of the King's Bench, incorporated and
perfected commercial law, thereby preparing the legal groundwork
for the 'Industrial Revolution'. Philip Yorke, Earl of Hardwick
(1690–1764), Chancellor from 1737 to 1756, completed the theoretical
description and the practical organization of equity. Together, they
established the guiding principles on which lawyers have drawn ever
since.

In the nineteenth century, legal reform, like parliamentary
reform, was long postponed. The delay gave Charles Dickens and
other satirists a field day. Dickens' parody of a trial in the Court of
Common Pleas in *The Pickwick Papers* became justly famous. The
action unfolds in 1827–8.

Mr Pickwick is being sued for breach of promise of marriage by
Messrs Dodson and Fogg on behalf of their client, Mrs Bardwell.
The only evidence that Pickwick had ever engaged the affections of
his former landlady, Mrs Bardwell, was contained in two brief
letters. One of them read: 'Dear Mrs. B. – Chops and Tomata sauce,
Yours, Pickwick.' The other read: 'Dear Mrs. B. I shall not be home
till to-morrow. Slow coach. Don't trouble yourself about the warm-
ing-pan.' –

> 'I wonder what the foreman of the jury . . . has got for
> breakfast,' said Mr. Snodgrass, by way of keeping up a conver-
> sation on the eventful morning of the fourteenth of February.
>
> 'Ah!' said Perker, 'I hope he's got a good one.'
>
> 'Why so?' inquired Mr. Pickwick.
>
> 'Highly important; very important, my dear sir.' Replied
> Perker. 'A good, contented, well-breakfasted juryman, is a
> capital thing to get hold of. Discontented or hungry jurymen,
> my dear sir, always find for the plaintiff.'
>
> 'Bless my heart.' Said Mr. Pickwick, looking very blank;
> 'what do they do that for?'[119]

Pickwick, of course, does not stand a chance against the conniving lawyers and the imbecile judge:

> An anxious quarter of an hour elapsed; the jury came back; the judge was fetched in. Mr. Pickwick put on his spectacles, and gazed at the foreman with an agitated countenance and a quickly beating heart.
>
> 'Gentlemen,' said the individual in black, 'are you all agreed upon your verdict?'
>
> 'We are,' replied the foreman.
>
> 'Do you find for the plaintiff, gentlemen, or for the defendant?'
>
> 'For the plaintiff.'
>
> 'With what damages, gentlemen?'
>
> 'Seven hundred and fifty pound.'
>
> Mr. Pickwick took off his spectacles, carefully wiped the glasses, folded them in their case, and put them in his pocket; then having drawn on his gloves with great nicety, and stared at the foreman all the while, he mechanically followed Mr. Perker and the blue bag out of court.
>
> They stopped in a side room while Perker paid the court fees; and here, Mr. Pickwick was joined by his friends. Here, too, he encountered Messrs. Dodson and Fogg, rubbing their hands with every token of outward satisfaction.
>
> 'Well, gentlemen,' said Mr. Pickwick.
>
> 'Well, sir,' said Dodson; for self and partner.
>
> 'You imagine you'll get your costs, don't you, gentlemen?' said Mr. Pickwick.
>
> Fogg said they thought it rather probable. Dodson smiled, and said they'd try.
>
> 'You may try, and try, and try again, Messrs. Dodson and Fogg,' said Mr. Pickwick vehemently. 'But not one farthing of costs or damages do you ever get from me, if I spend the rest of my existence in a debtor's prison.'
>
> 'Ha, ha!' laughed Dodson. 'You'll think better of that, before next term, Mr. Pickwick.'

'He, he, he! We'll soon see about that, Mr. Pickwick,' grinned Fogg.

Speechless with indignation, Mr. Pickwick allowed himself to be led by his solicitor and friends to the door, and there assisted into a hackney-coach, which had been fetched for the purpose, by the ever watchful Sam Weller.

Sam had put up the steps, and was preparing to jump upon the box, when he felt himself gently touched on the shoulder; and looking round, his father stood before him. The old gentleman's countenance wore a mournful expression, as he shook his head gravely, and said, in warning accents:

'I know'd what 'ud come o' this here mode o' doin' bisness. Oh Sammy, Sammy, vy worn't there a alleybi!'[120]

When legal reform finally came, it was far-reaching. In 1846, the modern system of county courts was created. In 1857, a Court of Probate assumed the duties of the ecclesiastical courts in probate matters, and the Matrimonial Causes Act made provision for civil divorce. A series of common law Procedure Acts in 1852, 1854, and 1860 attempted to simplify the age-old complications, whilst the Supreme Court of Judicature Act (1873) completely reorganized the central courts. Henceforth there would be a Court of Appeal and a High Court consisting of five (later three) divisions – the Queen's Bench, Chancery, Probate, Divorce, and Admiralty. The legal functions of the House of Lords were given a permanent staff; and the Law Lords heard appeals according to the original jurisdiction of the cases under consideration. In 1907, a separate Court of Criminal Appeal was set up. Masses of statutory legislation were passed in the unrelenting struggle to keep abreast of the expansion of new law, especially in the commercial, financial, and administrative fields.

After two hundred years of the Union, the question could fairly be asked just how 'British' the laws and judicial systems of the United Kingdom had become. The answer has to be that the level of homogeneity, certainly by Continental standards, was very low. Despite English intrusions, the separation of English and Scots law continued, as did the parallel structures within the English legal system. Nonetheless, it is not true to say that the label of 'British-ness' could only be attached to the characteristic diversity and muddle. It could also be observed in at least three areas – in the common body of statute law accumulated since 1707, in the super-vision exercised by British institutions over the legal affairs of India, the Dominions, and the Colonies, and in the apparently incurable habit among the dominant establishment of seeing English law and British law as identical.

Not least, one must record the extraordinary degree of isolation of British law in that period. It had very few links with the Continent. Outside the Empire, its only soul-mate could be found in the American legal system, which since 1776 had been evolving along independent tracks. It was not limited by membership of outside bodies. It was a planet unto itself.

(16) THE IMPERIAL UNIVERSE: HUNDREDWEIGHTS, RODS, AND BUSHELS

Weights and measures form a part of everyone's ingrained mental make-up. It is impossible to function efficiently in everyday life without some internalized system of measurement which enables one to judge size, volume, weight, duration, and value. Children learn one or more such systems in their early years, and adults incorporate them into their subconscious processes for the rest of their lives.

As in the rest of Europe, a plethora of weights and measures flourished during the Middle Ages in every town, locality, and kingdom of the Isles. In the former Britannia, the standardized system of Roman measures had given way to local diversity.

Standardization of weights and measures presupposes a political authority to enforce it. It was slow in coming. The old Roman mile, for example, had stood at 5,000 feet. Yet when the English mile was fixed in 1593 at 8 furlongs of 660 feet, i.e., 5,280 feet, it still left the Scottish mile of 5,952 feet and the Irish mile of 6,720 feet untouched.

Although English systems gained widespread acceptance in the eighteenth century both in the colonies and in many parts of the Isles, the United Kingdom did not attempt to introduce general uniformity until the Weights and Measures Acts of 1824, 1878, and 1897. The first of the three acts established the main categories of the British imperial system relating to length, area, liquid volume, dry measure, weight, and money. (See Appendix 45).

Complicated though it looks to modern eyes, the introduction of the imperial scheme was only a start. Particular commodities continued to be measured in units of widely differing dimensions. A bushel of English wheat was taken to be equivalent to 60 lb weight, a bushel of foreign wheat to 62 lb. A bale of American cotton was reckoned to weigh 400–500 lb, an Indian bale at 500–600 lb, an Egyptian bale at 700–740 lb. Apothecaries, jewellers, tailors, fishmongers, printers, and others kept to their own, often exotic measures. The use of non-British standards, however, such as metric measures, was declared illegal.

The Act of 1878, whilst making a number of simplifications, provided precise definitions of the basic units. The yard, for example, which had once been fixed in every reign by the King's girth, was now defined by the Standards Office of the Board of Trade as the distance between two gold plugs on a bar of iridio-platinum kept at a constant temperature of 62 °F. Copies of the bar were held at the House of Commons, the Royal Observatory, and at government offices in Edinburgh and Dublin. The standard pound of 7,000 grains was linked to the standard yard by equating one cubic foot of distilled water at 62 °F and 30 inches of barometric pressure with 62.321 lb avoirdupois. The standard imperial gallon was fixed at 277.274 cubic inches of distilled water under identical conditions. All other units of length, weight, and volume were multiples or fractions of these three basic standards.

The fact that the 1878 Act based some of its standards on metric calculations betrayed the fact that the metric system was already in use. First proposed by a French priest, Gabriel Mouton (1618–94), in the reign of Louis XIV, the metric system had been adopted by France in 1801 together with decimalization, and it was based on natural phenomena. The metre was equivalent to one 10,000,000th part of a quadrant of a great circle of the earth (i.e., of a circle whose centre is the centre of the earth, here running through the poles and Paris), or 39.37008 inches. A litre was equivalent to the volume of a cube with 10 cm sides. A gramme was equal to one cubic centimetre of water at its maximum density. These units were recommended from 1854 by the British Decimal Association and were officially approved in 1864 for limited medical and scientific purposes. The Weights and Measures (Metric System) Act (1897) abolished the penalties for possessing metric measures, thereby initiating the period when the imperial and metric systems legally existed in parallel. But it did nothing to promote metrics either in trade or in education. Indeed, the Imperial System was still being honed and refined. Under the Cran Measures Act (1908), fresh herrings were required to be sold in accordance with the ruling that 1 cran = 37½ gallons. This contrasted with the measure for smoked herrings, where 1 barrel = 26⅔ gallons. In November 1914, metric and imperial subdivisions of the inch were standardized according to the Birmingham gauge. Modern engineering and clock-making techniques were regularly demanding an accuracy of 1/2000th or 0.0005 of an inch, whilst research on micrometer screws was working to measurements of 0.00001 inch.

Despite the advances of the law, the report of a select committee in 1892 informed Parliament that local and customary denominations for weights and measures were still in widespread illegal use. To combat these deficiencies, the Educational Code of Regulations (1900) prescribed what children should be taught in English schools. Children in the third class and above should be familiar with:

  - (Weight) – ton, hundredweight, stone, pound, ounce, and dram.

- (Length) – mile, furlong, rod or pole, chain, yard, foot, inch.
- (Capacity) – quarter, bushel, peck, gallon, quart, pint.

Children in the fifth class and above should be taught:

- (Area) – square mile, acre, rood, square pole, square yd, square ft, square inch.
- (Volume) – cubic yard, cubic foot, cubic inch.

In addition, pupils from the third class upwards needed to be instructed in decimal fractions, so that by Class VII they could understand the principles of the metric system as a whole.[121]

From 1897, the imperial and the metric systems were legalized throughout the British Empire, though preference was given wherever possible to imperial units. As a result, two or three generations grew up after 1900 in a peculiar British world which was measured among other things in hundredweights, rods, and bushels. To be British involved thinking of one's body in feet and inches, and in stones and pounds. Although educated people learned how to convert from imperial to metric and vice versa, the average British subjects simply could not imagine territory that was not measured in square miles, or land that was not measured in acres, or mountains that were not measured in feet. The highest mountain in the world, Mount Everest, was, of course, British. But to reduce its stature from a soaring 29,003 feet to a paltry 8,840 metres was, to put it mildly, unthinkable.

(17) 'SPLENDID RESPONSIBILITY': THE IMPERIAL ETHOS

The history of *mentalités* is one of the many branches of history pioneered by the Annales School in Paris. It demands the analysis and description of a very elusive phenomenon, namely the 'mental furniture' which members of all communities carry in their heads, often without reflection. It is especially tricky to summarize in an objective manner; and it constantly involves questionable generali-

zations. There are always groups within groups who do not necessarily share the prevailing attitudes of the whole; there are convinced
leaders and wavering followers; and there are always individuals
who kick against the 'dominant paradigm'. And there are continuous
shifts and changes taking place. Even so, 'corporate mentalities' do
exist, and have existed in the past. And it is part of the task of
historians to draw their readers' attention to them.

In the case of the United Kingdom, and of the imperial establishment which ruled it, prevailing attitudes on several key matters
changed fundamentally in the two centuries separating the first Act
of Union from the height of Empire. To chronicle the whole story
would require more strength, skill, and space than are here present.
All that may be attempted is the briefest of subjective sketches of
four or five of the dominant traits that most frequently marked the
imperial generation coming to maturity on the eve of the First
World War. The headings are: Loyalty, Patriotism, Self-restraint,
Duty, and the Will to Rule. Each of them needs to be finessed.

British loyalty was directed to the crown – the symbol of the
political community to which all British subjects belonged. Although
the concept of the crown was focused on the person of the monarch,
to whom all office-holders swore an oath of allegiance, it was in no
way dependent on, or limited by, the particular occupant of the
throne. The personality and conduct of the monarch was like
the British weather – it was constantly in flux: good, bad, and
indifferent. But loyalty to the crown reached to a higher plane: it
was constant.

This type of loyalty might be labelled dynastic. It was typical for
the older sort of composite European states, where a collection of
countries and nations had been brought together under the common
sway of one ruling House. The British crown around 1900 found
itself in the same category as the Habsburgs of Austria-Hungary or
the Romanov Tsars of all the Russias or the Hohenzollerns of pre-
imperial Prussia. Despite what has been often said, it was *not* in the
same category as the new nation states such as Germany or Italy,
where one cohesive national community had given birth to the

state, and not vice versa. Neither the United Kingdom of Great Britain and Ireland, nor the British Empire of some hundred and fifty colonies, was a nation state. For this reason 'the loyal toast' was the focus of all public meetings:

> Here's a health unto his Majesty,
> With a fal la la la la la-a la,
> Confusion to his enemies,
> With a fal la la la la la-a la.
> And he that will not drink his health,
> We wish him neither wit nor wealth,
> Nor but a rope to hang himself.
> With a fal la la la la la la la la la,
> With a fal la la la la la la-a la.[122]

This song, composed in the seventeenth century, was still completely relevant in 1914. What was commonly called 'The National Anthem' was in reality a Hanoverian royal anthem:

> God save our gracious King,
> Long live our noble King,
> God save the King!
> Send him victorious,
> Happy and Glorious,
> Long to reign over us;
> God save the King![123]

British patriotism, therefore, was bound to be rather complicated. There was no one *patria* to be celebrated. As a result, the fashion was to be intensely patriotic, but not to define too exactly the object of one's patriotic urges. A large number of multiple identities had to be catered for. British patriotism, like the British state, was a composite construct. It was much easier to sing with gusto about the 'Land of Hope and Glory' without ever saying what the land was actually called. (See above.)

However, if one cares to analyse British patriotism of the imperial era, one soon uncovers at least three separate layers. In the first place, it was essential to pay tribute to England, the senior country in the composite realm, the founder of the inner and the outer empires, and the source of the empire's dominant traditions and institutions. England was undoubtedly Number One. But secondly, it was important to make gestures to all the lesser nations within the family, and in particular to the Welsh, the Scots, and the Irish. In the era before mass entertainment, many families would entertain themselves singing patriotic songs round the piano. And there is no School or Community Song Book of the imperial vintage which did not include a garland of popular songs from Ireland, Scotland, and Wales as well as from England. Hence 'Hearts of Oak', 'John Peel', and 'The Lass of Richmond Hill' were invariably mixed in with 'Cockles and Mussels', with 'Loch Lomond', and with that universal favourite of favourites, 'Men of Harlech'. Thirdly, it was taken to be axiomotic that a British patriot would unswervingly support all the institutions of the Kingdom and Empire – not just the Monarchy, but the Parliament, the Union, and the established Protestant Churches. For this reason, it was not always easy to be a republican, a non-English nationalist, or a Catholic without one's patriotism being questioned.

By 1900, the layer of consciousness which historians now call 'Britishness', but was rarely so called at the time, was approaching its apogee. It had been strengthened by the euphoria of Empire, by the greatly increased mobility of people within the Isles, and by all the processes of 'modernization'. It was to receive its final reinforcements by the experiences of two world wars. Although oligarchic and elitist in origin, it had won over most of the middle classes, and was seeping down into the newly literate and even the underprivileged sections of society. It was the lowest common denominator of all the other identities that had been submerged into the imperial mix; and it was open to anyone who shared their allegiance to the crown. Yet it possessed several peculiarities that have since been largely forgotten. One peculiarity was that it applied as much to the far-flung peoples of the Empire as to the peoples of the home islands. Australians, Canadians, New Zealanders, and others were taught to be ferverently 'British' to a degree that didn't always apply at home. Another peculiarity was that the great majority of English people never learned to distinguish 'Britishness' from 'Englishness'. So the common shorthand term for the multifarious British realms round the world continued to be 'England'. In common parlance at least, later terms such as 'Britain' or 'the UK' were simply not used. And when people came to write the history of this ill-defined creature, they invariably called their works 'The History of England'. Since this term was more than a little vague for everyone who intended to study the thing seriously, the Examination Decrees of Oxford University spelled it out:

> The History of England (including the histories of Scotland, Ireland, and Wales, and of British India and of British Colonies and Dependencies as far as they are connected with the History of England).[124]

Self-restraint was undoubtedly a prime characteristic of the English culture that was disseminated throughout the British realms in the Victorian era. It set the British apart from many of their Continental neighbours, especially the Latins, who showed few inhibitions about extravagant gesticulation, excitable conversation, or public displays of private emotion. It took many forms in many spheres – in the accepted code of polite manners, for example, where the British abandoned the handshake; in the disciplined conduct of public business, where 'unparliamentary language' was ruled out of order; and in the preferred modes of social behaviour, where strict hierarchical deference was observed, children were 'seen but not heard', ladies followed the rules of decorum, gentlemen affected the 'stiff upper lip', and people instinctively formed queues at bus stops. The unwritten assumption seemed to be that solid British citizens should display at all times and in every walk of life the unruffled *sang froid* and disciplined demeanour which in reality was only appropriate in extraordinary situations – on the battlefield, at the wheel of a storm-tossed ship, or in the African bush surrounded by a tumult of spear-waving natives. In literary style, self-restraint encouraged a preference for irony rather then for blunt logic. In the arts, it encouraged conservative tastes with a preference for landscapes and rural nostalgia rather than modernist experimentation, and a penchant for the colours of a subdued palette, as with Victorian stained glass. In conversational style, it fed the delightful skills of wit, ordered repartee and understatement. In the eyes of its practitioners, it was the only decent way to behave. In the eyes of foreign observers, it made the British look sometimes admirable, sometimes hypocritical, and always odd.

Where it all came from is hard to say. The subject is difficult enough to describe, let alone to explain. For a start one would have to mention the mores of Protestantism, the habits of a class-ridden society where aspirant members of the lower orders imitated their 'betters', and the ethos of a community that was told time and again of its destiny to rule over others. Yet one thing is certain. The 'imperial ethos' of the late Victorian times was very specific to the period. Though some elements of it were present earlier, and others would linger on later, it was a product of the age. It differed radically from the modes both of Elizabethan England, where Englishmen did not blush to greet each other with a kiss, and of the Georgian era, when many of the constraints of the preceding Puritan time were cast aside. And it was not destined to last indefinitely.

A sense of duty could be applied to one's family, to the local community, to society at large, to the nation, or to the whole of humanity. It is one of the key qualities in the varying relationships of state and individual. In later Victorian times, it was given great emphasis. People were repeatedly taught, in school and from the pulpit, that the constituent features of a dutiful life – self-denial, dedication, and hard work – were all Christian virtues to be admired and practised. Different individuals would react in different ways to the message. But when the Empire's premier poet sat down in 1911 to explain it to the Empire's rising generation, he had no doubt what to say. He chose the very English metaphor of gardening. (See page 867, below.)

Confidence is instilled partly by instruction and partly by experience. By the early twentieth century, four or five generations of men in the British establishment had been consciously instructed in the skills of leadership in the public schools, in the armed forces, and in the Civil Service. One large section of them was specifically prepared for careers in the distant outposts of empire. Whole dynasties of public servants had lived and worked in India or Africa for longer then anyone could remember. In all the British universities, but especially at Oxford and Cambridge, as in the ranks of the numerous missionary societies or in the officers' messes of the British army, young men would meet others for whom extended tours of service in all the continents of the world were routine. The talk was a stirring mix of adventure, of wielding authority over every race under the sun, and of unbounded success. Ever since the loss of the American colonies more than a century before, the sons of the British Empire had never encountered a setback that had not been overcome. General Gordon might have been killed at Khartoum by the Mahdi's revolt in 1885, but the Sudan, Africa's largest country, was recovered by Kitchener a decade later at the Battle of Omdurman (see below). In China, the Boxer 'Rebellion' of 1900 might have driven the representatives of the European powers from Peking, but a British-led reprisal force had retaken and looted the Forbidden City to show the Chinese who was master. In the Transvaal, the Boers might have put up a plucky show, and some of them had fought 'to the bitter end'. But the bitter end had always looked inevitable; and the Boer Republics were duly reincorporated into imperial territory. To anyone alive in those dizzy days, it can only have seemed that the trajectory of the British Empire was permanently soaring upwards. The servants of that Empire did not have to be told that they were born to rule.

In November 1900, the year of Mafeking and the Boxer Rising, a young British official celebrated both his fortieth birthday and his appointment to one of the highest posts in the Empire – First Lord of the Admiralty. A few months earlier he had hosted a private dinner party in London attended both by the Viceroy of India, who was a personal friend, and by a small group of colleagues, all of whom were to receive promotion. The Viceroy now wrote to send his congratulations:

> The Viceroy's Camp, India
> 9 November 1900
>
> Dear old boy,
>   It was grand. . . . [to hear your good news.] Well, there you all are now, ruling the Empire. Do it strenuously and nobly and with courage. Do not let that cursed Treasury sit upon you. You and St. John have got to save this country from disaster and to ensure its victory in our next big war. It is a splendid responsibility, a glorious task. All luck to you in it, old boy, from beginning to end.
>   Yours
>   affectionately,
>   Curzon[125]

There was no 'big war' in the offing at the time. But the possibility of it was clearly exercising the minds of the Empire's highest officials. When the possibility became a prospect, it would stretch their self-restraint to the full.

The late imperial British, as they would themselves have said, were 'a God-fearing race'. Overwhelmingly, they believed in God, attended church regularly, and linked their faith with patriotism. With the advent of religious toleration, however, the old Anglican monopoly faded away; and public religious practice became increasingly heterogeneous. Catholics and Nonconformists were admitted to the mainstream in the second quarter of the century, Jews in the fourth. As a result, the common religious denominator in the collective culture lay not in the ecclesiastical sphere but in the shared religious mode which informed so many of their activities. Hymn singing was one of those activities. The British sang hymns in the family circle, in their schools, and on all public occasions. They sang hymns not just in the churches, but in the town halls, in the battlefields, on the decks of their warships, under the distant 'palms and pines' of Empire, and even at the start of football matches.

The core repertoire of well-known and well-beloved hymns, therefore, supplied an essential element of British identity. It appealed both to the devout, who loved the words, and to the mass of ordinary men and women who loved the tunes. When the 'big war' finally came, the repertoire was inevitably enlarged. The most celebrated addition was the work of a lifelong British diplomat, Cecil Spring-Rice (1874–1918), who had served the Empire all over the world – in Berlin, in Teheran, and in Washington. Spring-Rice was HM Ambassador to the USA from 1913 to the end of the war. He penned his famous lines only a few days before his sudden death. They were set to music from a newly composed orchestral suite, 'The Planets', by Gustav Holst:

> I vow to thee, my country, all earthly things above,
> entire and whole and perfect, the service of my love:
> the love that asks no question, the love that stands the test,
> that lays upon the altar the dearest and the best;
> the love that never falters, the love that pays the price,
> the love that makes undaunted the final sacrifice.
>
> And there's another country, I've heard of long ago,
> most dear to them that love her, most great to them that
> know;
> we may not count her armies, we may not see her King;
> her fortress is a faithful heart, her pride is suffering;
> and soul by soul and silently her shining bounds increase,
> and her ways are ways of gentleness and all her paths are
> peace.[126]

Here was yet another candidate for a truly national anthem.

(18) Europe: the Posture of Semi-detachment

Throughout its modern existence, the United Kingdom's relationship with Continental Europe was characterized by lofty detachment and, wherever possible, by non-engagement. This posture was not due to any inherent hostility, but simply to the basic facts of the British predicament. The Empire's defence was secured by the Royal Navy, which swallowed the lion's share of defence expenditure. What is more, Britain's military potential in Continental warfare was constrained not only by the priority given to the navy, but also by the relative size of the UK's population. In the age of conscript armies, which began with the French call to arms in 1793, the British could never hope to compete on equal terms with the top-rated Continental formations. So, they wisely never tried. In 1801, at the Second Act of Union, the UK's population was barely half that of France; the British troops at Wellington's disposal numbered perhaps one twentieth of Napoleon's. In the course of the following century, the UK's population overtook that of a declining France, but was massively outstripped both by a united Germany and by a rapidly expanding Russia. Apart from that, the exponential growth of overseas Empire precluded any major involvement in Continental affairs. Not just British politics, but British trade and British culture looked in the main to more distant horizons. Despite the great improvement in communications, which brought the capitals of Europe much closer in terms of travelling time, the state of semi-detachment that had opened up at the Reformation was never remedied. The British felt no compulsion to close the gap.

Once the Napoleonic conflict was ended, the United Kingdom stood sternly aside from Continental entanglements. The British government, as one of the five major European powers, was very active in diplomacy; and HM ambassadors were among the grandest on the circuit. British naval power and British money gave the Foreign Office inordinate clout, whilst the size and splendour of the Empire created an illusion of unlimited resources. The trick, of course, was never to put those resources to the test – to threaten and cajole, to act by proxy, and to issue ringing condemnations of the other countries' despicable conduct, but not, if it all possible, to go to war. As a result, in the ninety-nine years between the Battle of Waterloo (18 June 1815) and the Battle of Mons (23 August 1914), British troops only fired shots in anger on the European mainland on one solitary occasion. Even then, in Crimea, British involvement in the fighting was inspired no less by fears for the lines of communication to India than by concern for European developments *per se*.

The Crimean War, 1854–56, confirmed earlier suspicions dating from the Afghan War of 1838–42 (when twenty thousand British soldiers had died in the retreat from Kabul), that military engagements on distant fields of glory were a recipe for disaster. After Russia invaded the Ottoman provinces of Moldavia and Wallachia, thereby posing a threat to the Straits, British troops were sent to Crimea in support of the main force of French and Turks, but their performance was hardly the cause for rejoicing. Three times as many soldiers perished from disease and ill-treated wounds than were killed in battle. The most celebrated action, the Charge of the Light Brigade, ended in unmitigated fiasco. And, after twelve months of campaigning, the combined forces of the coalition had only succeeded in capturing the one solitary Russian fortress of Sevastopol. Peace was snatched from the jaws of a prolonged impasse by the threat of British naval action in the Baltic. The Tsar sued for peace rather than leave his base at Kronstadt open to bombardment from a Royal Navy flotilla of three hundred and fifty gunships. Enough face was saved to claim a limited victory.

Yet the realities could hardly be hidden. The British public had seen the first ever front-line photographs. War correspondents, notably W. H. Russell of *The Times*, had exposed the incompetence of the military staff. And the self-publicizing talent of Florence Nightingale (1820–1910), a wealthy young woman put in charge of the base hospital at Scutari, revealed the appalling and largely unnecessary suffering of the common soldiers. In the process, the government of Lord Aberdeen had been forced to resign. The most pugnacious of all British Prime Ministers, Lord Palmerston, whose earlier advice for more extensive involvement had been ignored, came to office in the midst of a mess, where the only possible thrust of policy was to withdraw; and he never had the chance to put his more aggressive designs into effect. Palmerston's motto 'There is really nothing to be done', which had been provoked by his refusal to pursue liberal reforms, might well have been applied to British policy on the Continent. When the next crisis in the unresolved Eastern Question blew up in the following decade, and the Russians made their next bid to take the Straits, Gladstone waxed eloquent and moralistic about the 'Bulgarian Horrors'; and Palmerstonian 'jingoism' swept the music-halls:

> We don't want to fight
> But by jingo if we do
> We've got the men, we've got the ships
> We've got the money, too![127]

But the Prime Minister of the day, Disraeli, wisely declined to be drawn. In the aftermath of the recent Franco-Prussian War, he recognized that the real power in Europe now lay with Germany. So he cut a fine figure alongside Bismarck at the Congress of Berlin, collected Cyprus for his pains, and did nothing.

In the late Victorian times, the British royal family, which still fought shy of English and Catholic connections, presided over their royal and imperial relatives in the Protestant and Orthodox courts around Europe. Queen Victoria's progeny were sent off to marry in Berlin, St Petersburg, Copenhagen, the Hague, and Athens – but not, of course, Vienna, Rome, Brussels, or Madrid. Christmas at Windsor and Cowes Week in June were crowded with Hohenzollerns, Romanovs, Hesses, and Sonderburg-Glücksburgs (but not with Habsburgs, Wittelsbachs, or Bourbons). British aristocrats, who tended to prefer big American money to grand Continental partners, nonetheless took their yachts down to Biarritz or round to Cannes. The more prosperous British middle classes were acquiring a taste for outings to the Swiss Alps, for a flutter at Deauville, or for a stay in the 'Hotels Bristol' that were springing up everywhere from Warsaw to Viareggio. Railway travel and Channel ferries had put Paris within a day's travel of London.

Yet the British masses knew nothing of this. There were no European sporting links, no package holidays, no town-twinnings. As yet, the horizons of the working class were bounded by a wakes week at Blackpool or a day out on the pier at Southend. For them, 'Europe' was still a foreign country.

When the fourth or fifth round of the Eastern Question loomed, therefore, with the assassination of an Austrian archduke in Sarajevo, the British Empire was widely expected to watch from the sidelines. There had been serious fears of German naval and colonial expansion, but no expectations whatsoever of a direct German military attack on the Isles. There was an 'Entente' or friendly understanding with France, and with France's ally, Russia; but there was no binding military commitment or formal diplomatic alliance with either. Like the USA, whose military potential had never been put to the test in Europe, the United Kingdom was free to go in or to stay out as it pleased. Berlin, in particular, was acting on the assumption that London would stay neutral. No one in the United Kingdom could take pleasure from the tidal wave of anxiety emanating from Continental rivalries. Yet the military forecast was for a short, sharp conflict; and it was a reasonable calculation to make, even if mainland Europe was consumed by a more general war, that the Isles and the Empire would come through intact.

IN THE SPACE OF one generation between 1688 and 1715, the Isles experienced three momentous events which determined the principal lines of their subsequent development. The not-so-Bloodless Revolution of 1688–9 secured the Protestant Ascendancy and the Whig version of constitutional government. The Act of Union of 1707 created the united Kingdom of Great Britain, the unified British monarchy, and the growing prospect of ultimate integration with Ireland. The Treaty of Utrecht (1713) opened the way for British naval supremacy, and with it, the commercial, financial, and colonial power that would form a precondition for both imperialism and the Industrial Revolution. Each of these three great topics – Constitution, Union, and Empire – generated a literature and a body of historical writing which would promote lasting convictions about Britain's premier position in the world.

In the early eighteenth century, history was in its infancy. With the exception of Clarendon (see below), none of the 'greats' of the historical profession had yet entered the scene; and none of the rules of evidence, impartiality, and precision had yet been established. The man who probably did most to raise the standards of history-writing, both as an art and as a science, was David Hume (1711–76), a philosopher and star of the Scottish Enlightenment. When he first turned his hand to history in the 1750s, he did so because no one, in his estimation, had yet done the job properly. As he confessed to a friend:

> The more I advance in my undertaking, the more I am convinced that the History of England has never yet been written, not only for style, which is notorious to all the world, but also

for matter; such is the ignorance and partiality of all our historians.[128]

With regard to poor style, Hume was probably thinking of Bishop Burnet. On the question of partiality he was thinking not just of Burnet but of the endless stream of Protestant apologists who had already taken a dominant grip on the subject. Hume was not free of prejudices of his own. But as a principled atheist, he could hardly be charged with the reigning Protestant bias.

Prior to the appearance of Hume's *History*, the only comprehensive survey to be published was the work of a Frenchman. Paul Rapin de Thoyras (1661–1725) was a Huguenot lawyer who took refuge in the Netherlands after the Revocation of the Edict of Nantes. He joined a Huguenot unit in the army of William of Orange, landed with William at Brixham, and saw active service in Ireland. He fought at the Boyne before receiving at the Siege of Limerick a wound which ended his military career. As secretary to the Earl of Portland, and tutor to his son, he visited Versailles with the English diplomatic mission, and was able to observe the government of the Whig oligarchy from the inside. On receipt of a pension from William he retired to the Hague, and then to Wesel in Germany, where he devoted himself to writing. A political booklet, *Des Deux Partis de Whigs et des Torys* (1717), established his reputation as a commentator on British affairs; and his ten-volume *Histoire de l'Angleterre* began to appear in 1723. Rapin's *History of England*, translated by Nicholas Tindale, first appeared in a fifteen-volume edition (1726–31), and attracted numerous abridgements and continuations. It was the standard, indeed the sole work on the subject for twenty-five years.

By comparison with later works, Rapin's approach to English history was extremely simplistic – but all the more influential for that. It presented a narrative from Julius Caesar to William and Mary, and frequently supplemented the narrative with original historical documents. The essence of the argument lay in the contention that all the early Germanic peoples of Europe had enjoyed traditions of liberty and constitutional government, but that England

alone had preserved them. The pure, primeval laws which everywhere else had been overturned by absolutist monarchs had been
preserved in England by the virtuous Anglo-Saxons, by the principled
baronial authors of Magna Carta, by the constitutional instincts of
Lancastrians and Tudors, and by the wise Whig Junta of 1689. All
the English Kings from Edward II to James II who had defied this
tradition had been justly overthrown. Any reader who swallowed the
story would draw three conclusions. Firstly, the English system of
government was the product of unique continuity. Secondly, its
basic principles were eternal and unchanging; and thirdly, it was the
only subject worth discussing in the history of the Isles.

Here was 'the Whig Interpretation' in a nutshell. Montesquieu,
visiting England in 1729, was entranced, particularly by the idea of a
prehistoric political system preserved in aspic – *ce beau système . . .
trouvé dans les bois.* Voltaire was more critical, although he thought
Rapin's work to be the 'only non-partisan book worth quoting'. David
Hume was to rate Rapin as 'totally worthless'. But whilst condemning him with some reason, he missed the main point: Rapin's
primitive analysis confirmed many of the well-entrenched assumptions of his English readers. Rapin, the Huguenot, was not merely
'Our First Whig Historian'; he was one of the prime propagators of
patriotic, Anglocentric prejudice. This paradox was all the more
delicious because, with time, Rapin's own name and contribution
were completely forgotten. The irony has been savoured by one of
the most senior historians of the present day:

> It is agreeable to think that the classic and most extreme version
> of that patriotic thesis was expressed not for Englishmen or by
> an Englishman, but for foreigners by an author who had no
> great love for the English: by a French Huguenot who served
> Dutch William in Ireland [and] afterwards retired to Germany
> and wrote in French, for publication in Holland, the first
> complete history of England.[129]

In the decades of his greatest popularity, many of the people
who grasped the further implications of Rapin's work had great

difficulty in making their criticisms felt. Some of them, like the High Tory Jacobite Samuel Jebb (? 1694–1772) were every bit as simplistic. (Jebb thought that the continuous thread of English government should be traced not to the Anglo-Saxons but to the Druids.) But several others, being accomplished scholars but nonjurors, were barred from divulging their opinions openly. The nonjurors, who had refused to take the oath of allegiance to William and Mary, were a lonely company. They had broken with the Church of England, but they had not joined the Church of Rome. Yet they were widely regarded as dangerous pro-papist fellow travellers and were seriously harassed because of it. Thomas Hearne (1678–1735), for example, was forced to resign his post at the Bodleian Library in Oxford; and the contents of the commentaries in his editions of Roper's *Life of More* (1626) and of Camden's *Life of Elizabeth* (1717) inspired inquisitorial investigations by the university authorities. Another nonjuror, the Revd Jeremy Collier (1650–1726), outlawed in 1696, managed to publish his *Ecclesiastical History* (1714). He did so by burying his most risky views in the middle of long stretches of harmless, conventional narrative. Henry Wharton (1664–95), though not classed technically as a nonjuror, undoubtedly shared their outlook, and paid the price. Sometime chaplain to the Primate, he never gained further preferment after publicly exposing the errors of Bishop Burnet. Yet in some estimations his *Anglia Sacra* (1691) has won him the laurels of 'founder-member of English medieval studies'.[130] Thomas Baker (1656–1740), who refused the oath to the Hanoverians, lost his fellowship at Cambridge, and eked out a living as a penniless private scholar with no publications to his name. Like several others in his position, he spent his career working quietly on unexplored historical records, preparing the materials which could one day be used to challenge the official version.

The *History of England* (1754–61) by David Hume raised historical scholarship to heights previously unattempted; and, after a feeble start, it enjoyed enormous success. (The first volume sold just forty-five copies in one year.) Hume was a philosopher and a sceptic, whose treatises on *Human Nature* (1739), *Human Understanding*

(1748), *Natural Religion* (1750), and *The Principles of Morals* (1751) had given him a solid reputation. The six volumes of his *History*, which were not written in chronological order, covered the same span as Rapin's, from Julius Caesar to 1689. Their value lay less in the academic research, for which Hume had limited patience, than in the persuasive style, in the rich sprinkling of moral reflections, and in the entirely fresh exploration of social and economic themes. Hume had no time for the Puritans and Presbyterians who had held the limelight so long in his native Scotland, and still less for the nationalistic 'barbarians on the Thames'. He was neither Whig nor Tory, therefore, and his sceptical stance to past disputes was well matched to the demands for reconciliation after the last of the Jacobite Risings. At the same time, he viewed history as a complex process of dynamic change in which the growing sophistication of social manners reflected the steady improvement of material conditions. In short, he was the historian of progress; and the concept of progress had legions of adherents in an age when Britain's economic power was visibly rising.

Nonetheless, despite his secular stance, Hume confirmed many of the historical assumptions of his Protestant contemporaries. He denigrated the Middle Ages; he welcomed the Reformation as a step in the right direction; and he abhorred the apparent 'threat to Liberty' posed by the Stuart alliance between Kings and bishops. Yet his historical writing was remarkable for the wide range of ethical and philosophical issues which it raised. Indeed, in his *Enquiry Concerning Human Understanding* (1748) he had advertised his view that historians existed in order to service philosophy:

> [History's] chief use is only to discover the constant and universal principles of human nature, by showing men in all varieties of circumstances and situations, and furnishing us with materials from which ... we become acquainted with the regular springs of human action and behaviour.[131]

This view of history as the servant of higher realms gave his work a timeless quality. Historical events had to be described and ana-

lysed. But they were less important than the wider discussions which
they inspired. In his treatment of Cromwell's Commonwealth, for
instance, Hume devotes a long passage to the theoretical question
of whether or not the English people had a right to judge and to
execute their king. But he then moves on to a still longer passage
devoted to the permanent achievements of the period. The opening
sentences of his paragraphs convey the message admirably:

> At this era, it may be proper to stop a moment and take a
> general survey of the age, so far as regards manners, finances,
> arms, commerce, arts and sciences. The chief use of history is,
> that it affords materials for disquisitions of this nature; and it
> seems the duty of an historian to point out the proper inferences
> and conclusions . . .

> The commerce and industry of England increased extremely
> during the peaceable period of Charles's reign: the Trade to the
> East-Indies and to Guinea became considerable. The English
> possessed almost the sole trade with Spain. Twenty thousand
> cloths were annually sent to Turkey. Commerce met with
> interruption, no doubt from the civil wars and convulsions
> which afterwards prevailed; though it soon recovered after the
> establishment of the commonwealth. The war with the Dutch,
> by distressing the commerce of so formidable a rival, served to
> encourage trade in England: . . . Interest in 1650 was reduced
> to six per cent.

> The customs in England, before the civil wars, are said to
> have amounted to 500,000 pounds a year: A sum six times
> greater than during the best period in queen Elizabeth's reign:
> But there is probably some exaggeration in this matter.

> The post-house in 1653 was farmed at 10,000 pounds a-year,
> which was deemed a considerable sum for the three kingdoms.
> Letters paid only about half their present postage.

> From 1619 to 1638, there had been coined 6,900,042 pounds.
> From 1638 to 1657, the coinage amounted to 7,733,521 pounds.
> Dr. Davenant has told us from the registers of the mint, that

between 1558 and 1659, there had been coined 19,832,476 pounds in gold and silver.

The first mention of tea, coffee, and chocolate, is about 1660. Asparagus, artichoaks, cauliflower, and a variety of sallads, were about the same time introduced into England.

The colony of New England increased by means of the Puritans, who fled thither. For a like reason, the Catholics, afterwards, went over to America in great numbers, and settled the colony of Maryland.

Before the civil wars, learning and the fine arts were favoured at court, and a good taste began to prevail in the nation. The king loved pictures, sometimes handled the pencil himself, and was a good judge of art. The pieces of foreign masters were bought up at a vast price; and the value of pictures doubled in Europe by the emulation between Charles and Philip IV of Spain.

Cromwell, though himself a barbarian, was not insensible to literary merit. Marvel and Milton were in his service. Waller, who was his relation always said, that the protector himself was not so wholly illiterate as was commonly imagined. He gave a hundred pounds a-year to the divinity professor at Oxford. He intended to have erected a college at Durham for the benefit of the northern counties.

Civil wars, especially when founded on principles of liberty, are not commonly unfavourable to the arts of eloquence and composition. The speeches of the parliamentary orators during this period are of a strain much superior to what any former age had produced in England. It must, however, be confessed, that the wretched fanaticism which so much infected the parliamentary party, was no less destructive of taste and science, than of all law and order. Gaiety and wit were proscribed: freedom of inquiry detested: cant and hypocrisy alone encouraged . . .[132]

Hume then launched himself into a detailed survey of the lives and works of Milton, Hobbes, Harrington, Harvey, and Clarendon. He was writing almost exactly a hundred years after the events and people described. But he constantly relates them to his own day. He was telling his readers how much they themselves had benefited from the advancements of a period which he otherwise thought 'barbaric'.

Unlike Rapin, Hume had no narrowly political axe to grind. He was not much moved by the rights and wrongs of the Union. He was actively opposed to 'national history', and even more to history written with sectarian bias. As a son of the Enlightenment, he believed, like his friend and colleague Adam Smith, that such petty concerns were beneath him. Yet here one meets a yawning gap between the personal motivation of his writings and their public effect. The fact that Hume delivered a highly optimistic and very popular history, at a time when the Union and the Protestant Ascendancy had just passed their test of fire, could not fail to have its consequences. The concept of progress is unavoidably teleological. So, whatever his intentions, Hume's overall impact was to add a massive vote of confidence to the status quo. Hume was no political partisan and he was not a practising Protestant. But his history gave a huge impetus to the 'Whig Interpretation'. Whilst sinking Rapin without trace, it confirmed the same political message: Protestantism, the Union, and the Empire were all moving serenely in the right general direction.

It is important, however, to identify Hume's intellectual constituency. Genius, in the nature of things, is a rarity. And Hume was in no sense representative of his day. His atheism, though tolerable to the educated elite, was highly eccentric for the population at large. In the 'Age of Enlightenment' the enlightened were still a tiny, embattled minority. The majority were deeply attached to the established forms of religion. Nothing is more eloquent than the fact that in the popular market Foxe's *Book of Martyrs*, two hundred years after it was placed in every church chest, was easily outpacing the two hundred runs of Hume's *History*. Indeed, it was in the course of the eighteenth century that Foxe's monument to Protestant prejudice rose to the status of an all-time standard. As from 1732, it was regularly reprinted in the form of cheap, short and readily accessible instalments. The editions of 1761, 1776, 1784, and 1795 were not just sold by all booksellers, but were hawked round the country in all manner of popular outlets. In due course, alongside the Holy Bible and possibly Bunyan's *Pilgrim's Progress*, it became one of the few books that could be found even in working-class households. The Age of Enlightenment was also the age of John Wesley, the Methodist Movement, and religious revivalism. The Protestant Patriot was a much commoner figure than the sceptical philosopher.

In this climate, in the decades when the political Union of England and Scotland was putting down roots, two or three accompanying cultural processes also took hold. The older English apocalyptic tradition of Elizabethan vintage, which had seen England as a latter-day Israel, a 'Chosen People' battling for survival against the surrounding Philistines, was projected onto the British as a whole; the 'Protestant world-view' became the touchstone of 'Britishness'; and the maturing British nation, as it sailed into the era of imperial wealth and power, was left with an enduring conviction of its own superiority. On this subject, one can do no better than to quote the historian who has made it her own:

> the conviction that Great Britain was peculiarly blessed was not confined to the prosperous. Nor was it confined to the inhabitants of England. Nor, emphatically, was it confined to Whigs. Like all sustaining national myths, the idea that Britain was a chosen land and therefore fruitful, did not depend for its effectiveness upon its being true. Poor or not, large numbers of Protestant Britons believed – believed precisely because they *were* Protestants, and because it was comforting to believe it, – that they were richer in every sense than other peoples, particularly Catholic peoples, and particularly the French.[133]

Or again:

> Protestantism meant much more in this society than just bombast, intolerance and chauvinism. It gave the majority of men and women a sense of their place in history and a sense

of worth . . . It gave them identity . . . And as long as a sense of
mission and providential destiny could be kept alive, by means
of maintaining prosperity at home, by means of recurrent wars
with the Catholic states of Europe, and by means of a frenetic
and for a long time highly successful pursuit of empire, the
Union flourished, sustained not just by convenience and profit
but by belief as well. Protestantism was the foundation that
made the invention of Great Britain possible.[134]

A still more powerful formulation of the same sentiments was
penned by that strange mystic William Blake, in 1804–8. Set to
music after much delay by the Irish composer Sir Charles Stanford,
Blake's 'Jerusalem' opened with an oblique reference to the legend
that Jesus Christ may once have visited the Isles: 'And did those feet
in ancient time . . . ?' But it ends with an inspiring evocation of
national destiny:

> . . .
> Bring me my bow of burning gold!
>   Bring me my arrows of desire!
> Bring me my spear! O clouds, unfold!
>   Bring me my chariot of fire!
>
> I will not cease from mental fight,
>   Nor shall my sword sleep in my hand,
> Till we have built Jerusalem
>   In England's green and pleasant land.[135]

As was long the fashion, Blake said 'England'. Whether or not
Jerusalem was to be built in Ireland, Scotland, and Wales as well is
open to debate.

Just as the Act of Union does not feature very prominently in the
history books, the general issue of England's 'marriage' with Scotland
did not raise many ripples in literary circles. For those who cared
deeply, mainly in Scotland, it was, for a long time, too painful to

mention. For those who were indifferent, mainly in England, it aroused little interest.

The one literary figure of stature who was eminently qualified to turn Anglo-Scottish relations into a major focus of controversy or even protest, Sir Walter Scott, was decidedly reluctant to do so. The author of the Waverley Novels held strong views on the Act of Union; he was a writer of worldwide fame; and, as 'the father of the historical novel', he was well aware how history could be mobilized for contemporary purposes. Yet by the early nineteenth century, even fervent Scots patriots were viewing independence as a lost cause. The fiasco of two abortive Jacobite risings had knocked the stuffing out of all active resistance to the Union. So Scott's priorities did not include active opposition. He wanted to preserve Scots culture; he wanted to raise awareness of Scotland's fast evaporating history; and he wanted the English to treat Scotland better. But he was never going to raise the standard of revolt.

Walter Scott's low opinion of the Act of Union was not dissimilar to that of Robbie Burns (see Chapter Eight). The nation had been bypassed, and, in 'a Total Surrender of Independence', the Commissioners had been bought:

> The distribution of . . . money constituted the charm by which refractory Scottish members were reconciled to the Union. I have already mentioned the sum of thirty thousand pounds, which was peculiarly apportioned to the commissioners . . . I may add there was another sum of twenty thousand pounds, employed to secure . . . the party called the Squadróne Volánte . . . It may be doubted whether the descendants of the noble lords and honourable gentlemen who accepted this gratification would be more shocked at the general fact of their ancestors being corrupted, or scandalised at the paltry amount of the bribe. One noble lord accepted of so low a sum as eleven guineas; and the bargain was the more hard, as he threw his religion into the bargain, and from Catholic turned Protestant to make his vote a good one.
>
> . . . The treasure for making good the equivalent was sent

down in waggons from England, to be deposited in the castle of Edinburgh ... The dragoons who guarded the wains were loaded with execrations, and the carters, nay, even their poor horses, were nearly pelted to death, for being accessary in bringing to Edinburgh the price of the independence of the kingdom.

The public indignation was the more just, that this large sum of money in fact belonged to the Scottish nation, being the compensation to be paid for them for undertaking to pledge their revenue for a part of the English national debt ... Scotland herself was made to pay the price given to her legislators for the sacrifice of her independence.

The statesmen who accepted of these gratuities, under whatever name disguised, were marked by the hatred of the country, and did not escape reproach even in the bosom of their own families ...

Men, of whom a majority had thus been bought and sold, forfeited every right to interfere in the terms which England insisted upon ... Despised by the English, and detested by their own country; fettered, as Lord Belhaven expressed it, by the golden chain of equivalents, the Unionists had no alternative left save that of fulfilling the unworthy bargain they had made.[136]

In his novels, however, Scott was less concerned with the Union and the Jacobite Risings than with the state of Scottish society after the Jacobite cause was lost. The flagship novel, *Waverley* (1814), which gave its name to the whole series, starts symbolically in 1745 with 'the young hero setting off to join the British dragoons'. It lays out the complex relations during the Rising of a Border family, one part of which is Unionist and the other Jacobite. In the Introduction, Scott states that his interest is in 'men not manners'; and the central preoccupation of his characters is how to overcome their political differences. Edward Waverley falls in love with Flora, the sister of a Gaelic rebel, Fergus MacIvor. After meeting Bonnie Prince Charlie, he becomes embroiled in the Battle of Prestonpans on the rebel side; but he is eventually pardoned for having saved the life of a British officer. Fergus dies bravely on the gallows; Flora enters her convent; and Waverley is free to wed Rose, daughter of the Jacobite Baron of Bradwardine:

> A tear mingled with the wine which the Baron filled as he proposed a cup of gratitude to . . . 'The Prosperity of the united Houses of Waverley-Honour and Bradwardine!'[137]

The fighting was finished, Scotland had to be grateful that its two warring parties were united.

Scott's *Redgauntlet* (1824) takes the theme of insurrection one step further. This time the date is 1765; and plans are being laid for a third (and quite unhistorical) Jacobite Rising. In his zeal, the fanatical young rebel Herries of Birrenswork kidnaps his nephew to get the movement started. All ends in fiasco. It is an occasion for Scott both to parody the staid world of Edinburgh lawyers and to ridicule the very idea of rebellion.

As Scott well knew, however, the most intransigent conflict in post-Union Scotland was not the political one between Hanoverian and Jacobite, but the cultural one between Gaelic Highlander and Lallans Lowlander. For two or three generations after the '45, all hope of ending the conflict, except by the total eradication of Highland culture, appeared to be vain. Following the Act of 1746, Highland dress and the Gaelic language could only be kept alive by the British army and by the Highland Society in London. But after Waterloo, where the kilted Highland regiments distinguished themselves on the battlefield before parading to great effect in Paris, attitudes mellowed. At long last, an opportunity presented itself for reconciling Scotland's two cultural halves.

Walter Scott seized that opportunity, giving the critical impetus to a process that has radically transformed modern Scottish identity. In 1819, the Prince Regent expressed a wish to visit Scotland; and three years later, he duly appeared in Edinburgh as King George IV – the first British monarch ever to do so. Walter Scott was appointed Master of Ceremonies for the royal visit; and he chose as his deputy

David Stewart of Garth, Colonel of the Black Watch and founder of the Celtic Society in Edinburgh. Together, they took the romantic decision to 'tartanize' their country for the occasion. Colonel Stewart published his *Sketches of the Character, Manners and Present State of the Highlanders of Scotland* (1822), which contained a fine illustrated guide to which tartans should be worn by which families and by the representatives from particular districts. In due course, wearing a kilt of Royal Stewart, George IV arrived, participated in the Celtic pageant, and raised a toast to 'the chieftains and clans of Scotland'. He was warmly greeted by an array of his Scottish subjects, all sporting similar garb and joining in the fun. This was one of the great publicity stunts of British history. At a stroke, it invented a 'national tradition' in which everyone could participate, and most importantly where the dominant Lowlanders could take the Highlanders to their hearts. It issued the signal that the Highland and the Lowland traditions could be fused into one. Henceforth, when Scots started celebrating 'Burns Night' as their national day on 25 January, they saw no contradiction in people reciting verses 'To the immortal memory' in broad Lallans whilst wearing kilts, eating haggis, and downing Highland malt. When Albert of Saxe-Coburg und Gotha arrived at Balmoral with his bride two decades later, he too, thought it entirely appropriate to invent a tartan for his own family's use. And he was a *real Sassenach*.

The fact that Scotland's modern 'Highland Tradition' is entirely spurious is beside the point. It did not matter that the philibeg kilt adopted in 1822 had been created by an English industrialist for the use of his Scottish workers. It did not matter that tartans had never previously been limited to particular clans. What mattered was that the Scots had found an amusing game which was helping them to sink their differences. Only a few people objected. One of them was Walter Scott's own son-in-law, J. G. Lockart, who wrote about 'collective hallucination'. Another was Lord Macaulay, whose family had genuine Highland connections, and who was sorely offended. This absurd modern fashion, he wrote in 1850, has reached a point beyond which it was not easy to proceed. The last British king who held a court in Holyrood thought that he could not give a more striking proof of his respect for the usages which had prevailed in Scotland before the Union, than by disguising himself in what, before the Union, was considered by nine Scotchmen out of ten as the dress of a thief.[138]

Protests were in vain. The fusion of Gael and Lallander was becoming a reality. It was a historic change, nicely observed by the writer Robert Louis Stevenson (1850–94):

A century and a half ago the Highlander wore a different costume, spoke a different language, worshipped in another church, held different morals, and obeyed a different social constitution from his fellow-countrymen either of the south or north. Even the English, it is recorded, did not loathe the Highlander and the Highland costume as they were loathed by the remainder of the Scots. Yet the Highlander felt himself a Scot . . . When the Black Watch, after years of foreign service, returned to Scotland, veterans leaped out and kissed the earth at Port Patrick. They had been in Ireland, stationed among men of their own race and language, . . . but it was the soil of Galloway that they kissed at the extreme end of the hostile lowlands, among a people who did not understand their speech, and who had hated, harried, and hanged them since the dawn of history.

But now:

in spite of the difference of blood and language, the Lowlander feels himself the sentimental countryman of the Highlander. When they meet abroad, they fall upon each other's neck in spirit; even at home there is a kind of clannish intimacy in their talk. But from his [English] compatriot in the south the Low-lander stands consciously apart. He has had a different training; he obeys different laws; he makes his will in other terms, is otherwise divorced and married; his eyes are not at home in an

English landscape or with English houses; his ear continues to remark the English speech; and even though his tongue acquire the Southern knack, he will still have a strong Scots accent of the mind.[139]

R. L. Stevenson also wrote the work of fiction which best illustrates the reconciliation of Lowlander and Highlander. *Kidnapped* (1886) is one of the most thrilling and evocative adventure stories ever written. At one level, it is a tale of two wanted men hunted through the hills and the heather by the redcoats. But a large part of its charm is generated by the growing trust and friendship of a Lowlander and a Highlander thrown together by fate. The date is 1751. David Balfour is an Edinburgh lad placed on a ship bound for America by callous relatives. Alan Breck Stewart is a Jacobite fugitive and outlaw, whose Gaelic speech and devil-may-care philosophy seem completely alien. After the ship is wrecked on the coast of Mull, however, the two men stumble onto the scene of a notorious (and historical) murder – the killing of Colin Campbell, 'the Red Fox', by tenants threatened by eviction. To save their lives from the pursuing soldiery, they cross the whole of Scotland from West to East until they walk into the cobbled streets of Edinburgh. Their parting, which sends Alan Breck into exile and Davie Balfour to the bank to collect his fortune, brings tears of relief and sorrow. It is the truest of metaphors for the destiny of Scotland's two main ethnic communities. Yet a hundred years had passed before such a book could be safely written.[140]

Whilst pseudo-history and sentimental history thrived, however, the academic study of Scotland's real history was falling into abeyance. Hume and others had started a trend in Scotland which consciously adopted English history as a substitute for cultivating the past of their own country. Modern commentators say that they were forging an 'Anglo-British identity', that is, an Anglo-Scottish partnership in which the Scottish part was putting itself into voluntary liquidation. To this end, they often abandoned the name of 'Scotland' altogether, preferring to think of themselves as inhabitants of 'North Britain'. (The English never reciprocated by renaming their country as 'South Britain'.) Significantly, the last major history of Scotland before the twentieth century was published by William Robertson (1721–93) at the very time that Hume's own volumes were starting to appear. To some extent, Robertson acted as a counterweight to Hume, who rarely mentioned Scotland except to belittle it. As a young man, he had tried in 1745 to join the Jacobite army; and in his narrative of the sixteenth century he was criticized for penning 'a vindication of Mary, Queen of Scots'. Yet Robertson embodied many contradictions. A long-term member of the General Assembly of the Kirk, he served for thirty years as Principal of Edinburgh University, overseeing the decades when Scotland's foremost seat of learning became the fortress not only of the Scottish Enlightenment but also of the 'Anglo-British' tendency. He was a close friend and correspondent of Hume and Gibbon, whose approach to history he did not share. And he wrote, said Gibbon, in 'the purest English', whilst speaking a braw Scots brogue that no one in London could even faintly understand. He is best remembered for his *History of America* (1777) and particularly for his *History of Charles the Fifth* (1769), whose massive introduction is sometimes regarded as the first attempt to write a survey of medieval European history.

As a historian of Scotland, however, Robertson – whose survey appeared in 1759 – had no successors, and a dwindling readership. When his university introduced modern history as an academic discipline during the next century, it would opt to teach English, not Scottish history. St Andrews, Aberdeen, and Glasgow would follow suit, and they would persist in their Anglocentric activities until the late twentieth century. 'Scotland', in the mental sense, was going underground. 'Scottish patriotic historiography had burnt itself out,' writes a recent commentator. 'Nineteenth century Scotland was the white dwarf of Europe.'[141]

One explanation for the dissolving of Scottishness into the wider British identity must undoubtedly be sought in the extraordinary economic boom which occurred on either side of 1800. That same generation which witnessed 'the Strange Death of Scottish History' also witnessed the sudden growth of Clydeside as an imperial port, the dramatic expansion of the Scottish coalfield to supply the Clydeside steelworks, and the violent stampede of migrant workers to man the new industrial towns. What the Highlands lost, the working class of Red Clydeside gained.

Economics, in fact, was often used to explain away the whole of modern Scottish history. In the conventional view, independent Scotland had been poor and backward. So Scotland had begged to unite with England in order to grow rich. And Scotland (or parts of Scotland) *did* grow rich:

> When Scotland asked to be allowed a share in the trade with our colonies, the English Parliament answered with a contemptuous 'no'; and the result was that Scotland growled and growled . . . throughout the reign of William. But in the next reign, after long and fierce debates, the old Scottish Parliament was induced to vote for a union with the English (1708); and henceforward there was one united Parliament of Great Britain, and trade was perfectly free between the two nations. Then began the great commercial prosperity of Modern Scotland. Within fifty years Glasgow had got an enormous share of the trade with the British colonies and India, and one of the most interesting tales of town history is the story of how the grave merchants of Glasgow . . . set to work to deepen the river Clyde so as to make it easy to carry the trade which they knew would come. The first Glasgow ship for tobacco sailed to America ten years after the union, and began what is still one of Glasgow's greatest industries.[142]

Quod erat demonstrandum. It was no accident perhaps that the Oxford don who wrote those remarks in 1911 did not actually know when the Union of England and Scotland took place.

The same arguments could not be used for Ireland. Ireland was poor before the Union of 1801; and, with the exception of Ulster, it remained poor thereafter. English commentators were not slow to point out that Protestant Belfast was developing much faster than Ireland's Catholic cities. But, generally speaking, the tragedy of the Famine and the subsequent depopulation of Ireland debarred all talk of progress and prosperity. Ireland, on the other hand, had been given a direct share in the burgeoning blessings of British democracy. Indeed, in some people's estimation the Irish had been given a disproportionate share. So, if the Irish complained, they were being unreasonable. If they dared to use Britain's democratic institutions to oppose British rule, they were, in the eyes of the unreconstructed English, being disgracefully insolent:

> With the exception of those from Ulster, the Irish members of the House of Commons since the Union of 1800 have never been loyal to our system of government, but have continually cried out for a separate Parliament in Dublin. The first great agitator for this purpose was the orator Daniel O'Connell . . . He has been followed by many others, notably by Mr. Parnell, and the agitation is still continuing. In order to hush this cry, British statesmen have allowed Ireland to have many more members of the House of Commons than the population of that island warrants. More than one statesman . . . has thought of conciliating the Irish, by granting them . . . 'Home Rule' . . . But most people fear that a separate Irish Parliament would be followed by a complete separation between Ireland and Great Britain, by the establishment of an Irish Republic, and by the oppression of the well-to-do and intelligent classes of Irishmen, who are certainly loyal to the British crown. All British politicians, on both sides, have, during the last seventy years, made haste to remove every real, and, indeed, every imaginary grievance of the Irish people, though they have earned no gratitude by doing so.[143]

Put in that way, such opinions were good fertilizer for the Irish separatists. But though common enough at English tea-parties, they were becoming ever less typical of the British establishment as a whole. Sixty and seventy years on from Disraeli's denunciation of the state of Ireland and forty years after the first Home Rule Bill, most people with experience in the governance of Ireland had been won over to Gladstonian thinking; and the Home Rule Act, though in suspension during the Great War, was on the statute book. Liberal-minded 'Home Rulers' throughout the United Kingdom were looking to future opportunities, not to past mistakes:

> We hold the Ireland in the heart
> More than the land our eyes have seen,
> And love the goal for which we start
> More than the tale of what has been.[144]

Even after the Easter Rising of 1916 (see below), the hardiest Home Rulers did not despair. 'Ireland has not rebelled,' one of them argued; but 'there has been a rebellion in Ireland.'[145] They believed that all would work out at the end of war. Given her autonomy, Ireland would take her place alongside the other self-governing dominions in what they were already calling not the Empire, but the Commonwealth:

> There *is* room for *Sinn Fein* in the Commonwealth, if *Sinn Fein* will only look around with open eyes. 'Ourselves, not alone' but in a living union with other free communities, a union that leaves us still ourselves . . . This is the true motto of Ireland, as it is the true motto of all our Commonwealth.[146]

The literature of Empire took many forms. For convenience it may be classified under the headings of travel and exploration, poetry, fiction, religion, ethnology, memoirs, and history. But whatever system of classification is used, its influence on the meaning of 'Britishness' was vast.

Imperial travel and exploration was undertaken for a purpose. It was not mere wanderlust. Its priorities and directions were dictated by the state of the Empire at any particular time. Expeditions were often commissioned and financed by the British government; and their reports were frequently official documents. In the course of the eighteenth and nineteenth centuries the emphasis changed. In the time of Captain Cook's three voyages – 1768, 1772, 1776 – the main interest still lay with the oceans, and hence with the Empire's lines of communication and defence. It later moved to the interior of the great land-masses – first to the Near East and Central Asia, where 'the Great Game' against Russia was played, then to Africa and Australia. South America was the one continent in which British imperial interest was marginal.

Sir Richard Burton (1821–90), sometime officer of the Indian Army, was the archetypical Victorian traveller-explorer. In forty years of ceaseless roving, this eccentric and flamboyant character criss-crossed the remotest regions of the globe from Persia to Brazil, and wrote forty volumes of travelogues. His most famous exploit was to reach the forbidden and holy city Mecca in disguise, as related in his *Personal Narrative of a Pilgrim to El-Medinah and Meccah* (1855–6); but in geographical terms, his most important contribution, after visiting Central Africa, was to set the puzzle which fascinated a whole generation of his successors.

Burton's report on *The Lake Regions of Central Africa* (1860) alerted the world to the fact that in the age of railways and steamboats, the basic layout of Africa's rivers and watersheds still remained a mystery. The steps whereby the puzzle was gradually and belatedly solved can be followed in the pages of Sir John Speke's *Discovery of the Source of the Nile* (1863), the Revd David Livingstone's *Expedition to the Zambesi* (1865), and the work of the big-game hunter Sir Samuel White Baker on *The Nile Tributaries of Abyssynia* (1867). The man who most successfully popularized these explorations was a Welshman, John Rowlands (1841–1904), who had emigrated to America. Sent out to Africa by the *New York Herald* under his adopted name of Henry Morton Stanley, he gained huge recognition when in 1871 he succeeded in finding and rescuing David Livingstone. The evocative titles of his books, *Through the Dark Continent* (1878) and *In Darkest Africa* (1890), helped create the negative image of Africa as an evil as well as a dangerous place.

The part played by women in exploration and travel-writing was largely ignored until recently. But several fearless Victorian 'ladies' set off like the best of them to discover remote countries and to report back. The prototype was a niece of the younger Pitt, Lady Hester Stanhope (1776–1839), whose home in a ruined monastery in Lebanon acted as a staging-post for British travellers heading for the desert. But the most accomplished of them may well have been Mary Kingsley – sister of the novelist Charles Kingsley – whose *Travels in West Africa* (1897) were written with panache and with unusual sympathy for local cultures. At one point, she described a side-trip to meet another feminine stalwart, the missionary Mary Slessor:

> I made a point on this visit to Calabar of going up river to see Miss Slessor at Okÿon district . . . This very wonderful lady had been eighteen years in Calabar . . . ruling as a veritable white chief over the entire Okÿon district. Her great abilities, both physical and intellectual, have given her among the savage tribe an unique position, and won her . . . a profound esteem. Her knowledge of the native, his language, his way of thought, his diseases, his difficulties . . . is extraordinary, and the amount of good she has done, no man can fully estimate. Okÿon, when she went there alone . . . was a district regarded with fear by the Duke and Creek Town natives, and practically unknown to Europeans. It was given to killing at funerals, ordeal by poison, and perpetual internecine wars. Many of these evil customs she has stamped out, and Okÿon rarely gives trouble to its nominal rulers, the Consults in Old Calabar, and trade passes through it down to the sea-ports . . . This instance of what one white can do would give many important lessons in West Coast adminis-tration and development. Only the sort of man Miss Slessor represents is rare.[147]

(Calabar is a city in present-day Nigeria.)

One of numerous side-lined women writers was Mary Seacole (1805–81). This fascinating and intrepid woman does not rate an entry in *The Oxford Companion to English Literature* (New Edition) even though her book, *The Wonderful Adventures of Mrs Seacole in Many Lands* (1857), is a most revealing document of the times. Described as 'a coloured Creole' from Jamaica, whose soldier-father had 'good Scottish blood', she would have been placed by her contemporaries somewhere in the middle of the Empire's racial ladder – one step above the blacks, and one step below the 'white creoles'. She was the pioneer of what might be called 'reverse exploration', setting out from Jamaica to discover England, and then, as a volunteer nurse, to see the Crimean War for herself. She was deeply, even pathetically convinced of her own 'Englishness'.[148] She fills an early slot in the history of non-English literature in English. (See below.)

By 1900, few parts of the globe remained unexplored. But two remote destinations still beckoned. Both Antarctica and the Himalayas were strategically important. The former, in the hands of hostile powers, could conceivably pose a threat to the freedom of the seas. The latter was 'the Great Wall of India'. So, while the Royal Navy supported Antarctic exploration, the Government of India gave its blessing to a series of Himalayan expeditions that led inexorably to the idea of scaling Mount Everest.

British exploration of the Antarctic was accelerated by the news in 1909 that a US naval officer, Commander Robert E. Peary, had reached the North Pole. The second expedition of Captain Robert Falcon Scott RN (1868–1912) ended in failure and tragedy. Beaten in the race to the South Pole by Roald E. G. Amundsen (1872–1928), a much better trained and equipped Norwegian, the British party retraced their icy steps ever more slowly until they died of exhaustion and starvation within eleven miles of the nearest food-dump. Scott's Journal (*Scott's Last Expedition*, 1923) became a best-seller. Ending with the sentence, 'We shall stick it out to the end, but we are getting weaker, of course, and the end cannot be far', it established their heroic reputation. The self-sacrifice of Captain Laurence Oates RN, who had walked out alone into the blizzard so as not to impede the progress of his companions, was particularly admired. His was the finest example, quite literally, of 'the stiff upper lip'; and his last words – 'I am just going outside and may be some time' – became proverbial. Yet the fate of these noble individuals troubled anyone who worried about some of the arrogant assumptions underlying their exertions. It was strangely reminiscent of the death of two other British explorers, Robert Burke and William Wills, who had perished fifty years before at the opposite end of the temperature scale in the heart of the Australian outback. It never struck Scott to learn from the methods of people who lived permanently in polar conditions, just as it never struck Burke and Wills to enlist the help of Aborigines who lived without difficulty in the territory that killed them.[149]

Mount Everest was named after Sir George Everest (1790–1866), a native of Brecon, who rose to be the chief military engineer of the East India Company and Director of the Indian Trigonometrical Survey. Once mountaineering was established in late Victorian times as an imperial pastime, the highest peak of the Empire (and the world) was automatically set as the ultimate goal. Alpinists edged ever closer in the early twentieth century. George Mallory (1886–1924), whose frozen remains in their tweed suiting were not recovered till 1999, may possibly have made the summit before falling to his death. Yet it is one of the great ironies of the Everest saga that the final triumph in 1953 by the New Zealander Edmund Hillary and the Sherpa Tenzing Norgay occurred six years after the British Empire was officially dissolved. Hillary's *Ascent of Everest* (1953) represents the swansong of imperial exploration. It is equally ironic that the definitive account of life in the closed kingdom forming the northern boundary of British India, including Everest, came not from a Britisher, but from an Austrian who had escaped from detention in a British POW camp. Heinrich Harrer's *Seven Years in Tibet* (1953) marked not only a wonderful personal achievement, but a win for an alpinist from the Alps.[150]

A particularly fruitful branch of imperial exploration was devoted entirely to government-sponsored science. In the eighteenth and nineteenth centuries, botanists, zoologists, ornithologists, palaeontologists, and geologists fanned out to the farthest parts of the globe to make observations, to collect specimens, and to accumulate materials for later analysis. Botany Bay, which became the site of the first British colony in Australia, is a lasting memorial to Captain Cook's chief scientific officer, Joseph Banks (1743–1820). The voyage of HMS *Beagle*, 1831–6, which took Charles Darwin to the Galapagos Islands and was the direct stimulus to his theory of evolution and his *Origin of Species* (1859), was just one of thousands of similar but lesser known ventures.[151]

One of the most endearing of all imperial travellers was Edward Lear (1812–88), painter and poet. Unlike many, he was not a government agent. Earning a living as a commercial artist, he identified a market for drawings of tropical plants and animals and also for paintings of exotic imperial locations. To this end, he made a tour of India, returning not only with a magnificent portfolio of paintings, but also with an interesting collection of poems:

THE AKOND OF SWAT

Who, or why, or which, or *what*, Is the Akond of SWAT?

Is he tall or short, or dark or fair?
Does he sit on a stool or a sofa or chair,   or SQUAT,
                              The Akond of Swat?

. . .

Does he sing or whistle, jabber or talk,
And when riding abroad does he gallop or walk,   or TROT,
                              The Akond of Swat?
Does he wear a turban, a fez, or a hat?
Does he sleep on a mattress, a bed, or a mat,   or a COT,
                              The Akond of Swat?

. . .

Do his people like him extremely well?
Or do they, whenever they can, rebel,   or PLOT,
                              At the Akond of Swat?

If he catches them then, either old or young,
Does he have them chopped in pieces or hung,   *or shot*,
                                    The Akond of Swat?

. . .

Does he study the wants of his own dominion?
Or doesn't he care for public opinion   a JOT,
                                    The Akond of Swat?

. . .

Does he live on turnips, tea, or tripe?
Does he like his shawl to be marked with a stripe,   or a DOT,
                                    The Akond of Swat?

. . .

Is he quiet, or always making a fuss?
Is his steward a Swiss or a Swede or Russ,   or a SCOT,
                                    The Akond of Swat?

Does he like to sit by the calm blue wave?
Or to sleep and snore in a dark green cave,   or a *grott*,
                                    The Akond of Swat?

. . .

Does he beat his wife with a gold-topped pipe,
When she lets the gooseberries grow too ripe,   or ROT,
                                    The Akond of Swat?

. . .

Does he teach his subjects to roast and bake?
Does he sail about on an inland lake,   in a YACHT,
                                    The Akond of Swat?

Some one, or nobody, knows I wot
Who or which or why or what
                              Is the Akond of Swat![152]

From the author of 'The Jumblies' and 'The Dong with the Luminous Nose', one might easily dismiss the good old Akond as pure nonsense. The joke in this case is increased by the fact that Swat was a real district of the North-West Frontier, and its *akond* a genuine Indian potentate.

Imperial poetry should be clearly distinguished from any other poetry that happened to be composed during the imperial era. The former addresses imperial themes, vibrates to the rhythms of martial-imperial pride and power, and invariably leaves an imperial message. The latter need have nothing to do with Empire whatsoever. Rudyard Kipling, born in India, is the prime candidate for the Empire's poet laureate, indeed for the laurels of the Empire's writer par excellence. Kipling's poetry, though redolent of the imperial mission, was nonetheless deeply moral and reflective, and strangely prophetic. 'Recessional' (1897) evokes human vanity, foreshadowing the fall of all empires:

> Far-called, our navies melt away;
> On dune and headland sinks the fire:
> Lo, all our pomp of yesterday
> Is one with Nineveh and Tyre!
> Judge of the Nations, spare us yet,
> Lest we forget – lest we forget![153]

Two years later, on learning of the Spanish-American War and the American occupation of the Philippines, Kipling foresaw that the imperial mantle would soon be falling on other shoulders:

> Take up the White Man's burden –
> Send forth the best ye breed –
> Go bind your sons to exile
> To serve your captives' need;
> To wait in heavy harness
> On fluttered folk and wild –
> Your new-caught, sullen peoples,
> Half devil and half child.
>
> Take up the White Man's burden –
> The savage wars of peace –
> Fill full the mouth of Famine
> And bid the sickness cease;
> And when your goal is nearest
> The end for others sought,

> Watch Sloth and heathen Folly
> Bring all your hope to nought.
> . . .[154]

Many ringing phrases from Kipling's arsenal have attracted the opprobrium of later generations. It is no longer polite to mention 'lesser breeds without the law' or 'the blame of those you better'. But the critics often disregard not only Kipling's fierce love of foreign cultures, but also his essential humility and his conviction that everything in this world is temporary. It can be no accident that a hundred years after Kipling's heyday, every poll in the United Kingdom for the most popular poem in the English language always comes up with the same winner:

IF –

> If you can keep your head when all about you
> Are losing theirs and blaming it on you,
> If you can trust yourself when all men doubt you,
> But make allowance for their doubting too;
> If you can wait and not be tired by waiting,
> Or being lied about, don't deal in lies,
> Or being hated, don't give way to hating,
> And yet don't look too good, nor talk too wise:
> . . . . .
> If you can talk with crowds and keep your virtue,
> Or walk with Kings – nor lose the common touch,
> If neither foes nor loving friends can hurt you,
> If all men count with you, but none too much;
> If you can fill the unforgiving minute
> With sixty seconds' worth of distance run,
> Yours is the Earth and everything that's in it,
> And – which is more – you'll be a Man, my son![155]

If this is cliché, then cliché is a blessing.

Imperial fiction is not the same as fiction of the imperial era. One way or another, the Empire has to figure in its subject matter.

Many of its exponents, like Captain Frederick Marryat (1792–1848), G. A. Henty (1832–1902), or H. Rider Haggard (1856–1925), confined themselves to adventure stories or to juvenile books, often to considerable popular acclaim. Haggard's African stories, such as *King Solomon's Mines* (1886) or *She* (1887), which appeared at the very moment when 'the Scramble for Africa' was becoming the major international issue of the day, are filled with wonderment at Africa's wildlife, tribal society, and mysterious past. John Buchan, first Baron Tweedsmuir (1875–1940), sometime Governor-General of Canada and a prime example of a Scot who made good in Empire, enjoyed still greater fame as a novelist. A spy thriller like *Thirty-Nine Steps* (1915) is saturated through and through with the imperial spirit.

The Royal Navy maintained a constant presence in the story of Empire, and its exploits inspired a particular genre of maritime fiction. Captain Marryat, who had been a professional naval officer, pioneered the genre with *Mr. Midshipman Easy* (1836). But no writer could match the popularity of C. S. Forester (Cecil Lewis Troughton Smith, 1899–1966), who came to the fore in the mid-twentieth century, when the most glorious days of the navy were long past. Born in Egypt, educated in London, and domiciled for much of his life in the USA, Forester graduated from history books on the Napoleonic Wars to historical novels. The first of the long series of stories recounting the fictional career of Horatio Hornblower RN, *The Happy Return* (1937), seems to have had a didactic and patriotic purpose suggested by the growing international crisis of the 1930s. The later volumes which follow the rise of Hornblower from lowly midshipman to admiral and peer of the realm were essentially an exercise in imperial nostalgia.[156] Yet, once again, the best of Kipling keeps company with the very best. His *Jungle Book* (1894) and *Just So Stories* (1902) are numbered among the universal favourites of world literature, whilst *Kim* (1901) is a masterpiece with very unusual credentials.

'Kim' is the nickname of the eponymous hero of the novel, Kimball O'Hara, a ragged, orphaned urchin, who is introduced on page 1, as he sits astride a cannon beside the fort of Lahore:

Though he was burned black as any native; though he spoke the vernacular by preference; and his mother-tongue in a clipped uncertain sing-song; though he consorted on terms of perfect equality with the small boys of the bazar; Kim was white – a poor white of the very poorest. The half-caste woman who looked after him (she smoked opium, and pretended to keep a second-hand furniture shop by the square where the cheap cabs wait) told the missionaries that she was Kim's mother's sister; but his mother had been nursemaid in a colonel's family and had married Kimball O'Hara, a young colour-sergeant of the Mavericks, an Irish regiment . . . The wife died of cholera in Ferozepore, and O'Hara fell to drink . . . till he came across the woman who took opium and learned the taste from her, and died as poor whites die in India.[157]

From that point on, the readers follow Kim on his travels round northern India, learning about India as he does from the colourful people whom he meets on the road. They learn to see a rich and foreign civilization through the eyes of a bright and innocent child who in one sense is European, but who in the experience of a short lifetime has been entirely absorbed by his Indian surroundings. They listen to the teaching of Kim's chief companion, the saffron-robed lama Teshoo; and they are taught to distinguish between Buddhists, Muslims, and Hindus: between Brahmins and outcasts, between Punjabis, Pathans, and Nepalis. They are taught to reflect on the ancient wisdom of India and the dubious assumptions of assorted Christian missionaries and British officials. Above all, they are coaxed to love what they learn.

It is a great mistake to imagine that *Kim* belongs to juvenile literature simply because its hero is a growing boy. Rather, it seeks out the child in all its readers, and urges them to share in the childlike capacity to expand one's mental and moral horizons. And it does so by being filled with thrilling action as well as with rich cultural fare. Having journeyed along the Grand Trunk Road to the north, Kim becomes entangled with Russian spies and the high politics of the Great Game, and with more than one risky moment.

In the view of the novel's most distinguished editor, Kipling combined 'three wholly different sorts of fiction':

> . . . an adventure story with a spy plot of suspense and sudden action; a picaresque novel depicting the teeming human life of India present both in the brilliant, chattering, bustling crowd scenes, and in the loving, delicately humorous studies of Indian types and 'characters'; and, seemingly an impossible ingredient to mix with the other two, a delicate study of man's search . . . to find spiritual transcendence.[158]

It is a rewarding diet indeed; and it explains why 'the Little Friend of the World' has become a worldwide favourite. It should be no surprise that this fictional 'imperial waif' has long outlived the Empire from which he is undetachable.

The episodic nature of the narrative makes condensation all but pointless. *Kim* makes its impact through the constant stream of thought-provoking episodes. It is a key moment, however, when Kim meets Teshoo the lama for the very first time:

> He stopped; for there shuffled round the corner, from the roaring Motee Bazar, such a man as Kim, who thought he knew all castes, had never seen. He was nearly six feet high, dressed in fold upon fold of dingy stuff like horse-blanketing, and not one fold could Kim refer to any known trade or profession. At his belt hung a long open-work iron pencase and wooden rosary such as holy men wear. On his head was a gigantic sort of tam'-shanter. His face was yellow and wrinkled, like that of Fook Shing, the Chinese bootmaker in the bazar. His eyes turned up at the corners and looked like little slits of onyx.
>
> 'Who is that?' said Kim to his companions . . .
>
> 'A priest, perhaps,' said Chota Lal, spying the rosary. 'See! He goes into the Wonder House!'
>
> 'Nay, nay,' said the policeman, shaking his head. 'I do not understand your talk.' The constable spoke Punjabi. 'O friend of all the World, what does he say?'
>
> 'Send him hither,' said Kim, dropping from Zam-Zammah,

flourishing his bare heels. 'He is a foreigner, and thou art a buffalo.'

The man turned helplessly and drifted towards the boys. He was old, and his woollen gaberdine still reeked of the stinking artemisia of the mountain passes.

'O Children, what is that big house?' he said in very fair Urdu.

'The Ajaib-Gher, the Wonder House! Can any enter?'

. . .

'Alas! I am an old man. I did not know.'

Then, fingering his rosary, he half turned to the Museum.

'What is your caste? Where is your house? Have you come far?' Kim asked.

'I came by Kulu – from beyond the Kailas – but what know you? From the hills where' – he sighed – 'the air and water are fresh and cool.'

'Aha! Khitai [a Chinaman],' said Abdullah proudly. Fook Shing had once chased him out of his shop for spitting at the joss above the boots.

'Pahari [a hillman] from hills thou'lt never see. Didst hear of Bhotiyal [Tibetan], since you must know – a lama – or, say, a *guru* in your tongue.'

'A *guru* from Tibet,' said Kim. 'I have not seen such a man. They be Hindus in Tibet, then?'

'We be followers of the Middle Way, living in peace in our lamasseries, and I go to see the Four Holy places before I die' . . .

He fumbled in his bosom and drew forth a worn wooden begging-bowl. The boys nodded. All priests of their acquaintance begged.

'I do not wish to eat yet.' He turned his head like an old tortoise in the sunlight. 'Is it true that there are many images in the Wonder House of Lahore?' . . .

Kim clicked round the self-registering turn-stile; the old man followed and halted amazed. In the entrance-hall stood the larger figures of the Greco-Buddhist sculptures done, savants

know how long since, by forgotten workmen whose hands were
feeling, and not unskilfully, for the mysteriously transmitted
Grecian touch . . . In open-mouthed wonder the lama turned to
this and that, and finally checked in rapt attention before a
large alto-relief representing a coronation or apotheosis of the
Lord Buddha. The master was represented seated on a lotus the
petals of which were so deeply under-cut as to show almost
detached. Round Him was an adoring hierarchy of kings, elders,
and old-time Buddhas. Below were lotus-covered waters with
fishes and water-birds. Two butterfly-whinged *dewas* held a
wreath over His head; above them another pair supported an
umbrella surmounted by the jewelled headdress of the Bodhisat.

'The Lord! The Lord! It is Sakya Muni himself,' the lama
half sobbed; and under his breath began the wonderful Bud-
dhist invocation: –

'To Him the Way, the Law, apart,
Whom Maya held beneath her heart,
Ananda's Lord, the Bodhisat.'

'And He is here! The Most Excellent Law here also. My
pilgrimage is well begun. And what work! What work!'[159]

A second candidate for the title of master of imperial fiction was
the unlikeliest candidate of all. In his origins, Józef Teodor Konrad
Korzeniowski (1857–1924) was a total foreigner, a Pole from what is
now Ukraine. He was familiar with a rather nastier form of imperialism than anything in the British record; but that, in itself, was no
great qualification. He was sent away as a teenager to escape the
Tsarist oppressions of his country; and he did not return for nineteen
years. He fled first to Marseilles, and then, having gained a taste for
seafaring, spent two or three decades working his way round the
world in French and then British ships. For anyone familiar with the
travails of language-learning, it is a marvel that a half-educated lad
could ever have acquired an accurate knowledge of advanced English, not by studying on the Banbury Road, but by conversing with
fellow deckhands, by stopping in the docks of foreign ports, or even
by devouring books in his cabin. But it is no less than a miracle that,

whilst always speaking English in the stuttering guttural of his native Polish, he trained himself to write perfect English in magnificent rolling cadences and with the most idiomatic dialogue. But he did.[160]

Many of Joseph Conrad's novels are 'tales of the sea'; but many, too, are tales of distant corners of the Empire; and all are tales of the imperial era. *Heart of Darkness* (1902), for instance, is a novella about central Africa and the horrors of the Belgian colonial enterprise. It starts with the good yawl *Nellie* waiting for the tide in the estuary of the Thames before sailing for the mouth of the Congo. Conrad's evocation of 'the great spirit of the past' at the heart of the Empire acts as a foil to the contrasting passages from the heart of Africa:

> Forthwith a change came over the waters, and the serenity became less brilliant but more profound. The old river in its broad reach rested unruffled at the decline of day, after ages of good service done to the race that peopled its banks, spread out in the tranquil dignity of a waterway leading to the uttermost ends of the earth . . .
>
> Nothing is easier for a man who has, as the phrase goes, 'followed the sea' with reverence and affection, than to evoke the great spirit of the past upon the lower reaches of the Thames. The tidal current runs to and fro in its increasing service, crowded with memories of men and ships it had borne to the rest of home or to the battles of the sea. It had known and served all the men of whom the nation is proud, from Sir Francis Drake to Sir John Franklin, knights all, titled and untitled – the great knights-errant of the sea. It had borne all the ships whose names are like jewels flashing in the night of time, from the *Golden Hind* returning with her round flanks full of treasure, to be visited by the Queen's Highness and thus pass out of the gigantic tale, to the *Erebus* and *Terror*, bound on other conquests – and that never returned. It had known the ships and the men. They had sailed from Deptford, from Greenwich, from Erith – the adventurers and the settlers; king's ships and the ships of men on 'Change; captains, admirals, the

dark 'interlopers' of the Eastern trade, and the commissioned 'generals' of East India fleets. Hunters for gold or pursuers of fame, they all had gone out on that stream, bearing the sword, and often the torch, messengers of the might within the land, bearers of a spark from the sacred fire. What greatness had not floated on the ebb of that river into the mystery of an unknown earth! . . . The dreams of men, the seed of commonwealths, the germs of empires.[161]

An important subcategory of imperial literature might fairly be labelled as 'incidentally imperial'. Many English writers followed unconventional personal lives, travelled the world incessantly, and used their travels as a backdrop to their observations of human nature. Somerset Maugham (1874–1965), for instance, wrote a successful play *East of Suez* (1922), a novel, *The Moon and Sixpence* (1919), set in the Pacific Islands, and another, *The Razor's Edge* (1944), set in India. E. M. Forster (1879–1970) lived and worked in India on two occasions. His delectable *Passage to India* (1924) takes the opposite tack to Kipling's *Kim*, by viewing the subcontinent through the eyes of an English woman who moves exclusively among the taboo-ridden ghetto-dwellers of the governing British caste. Two writers of the next generation, Lawrence Durrell (1912–90) and Graham Greene (1904–91), used foreign, though not always imperial locations as a necessary stage for their work. Durrell made his reputation through fiction like *The Alexandria Quartet*, exploiting the exotics of Egypt, Lebanon, and Cyprus, Greene through a rich brew of espionage, low living, and moral adversity. As more than one critic has pointed out, 'Greeneland' is an imaginary country which may be physically located anywhere from West Africa to Cuba or Mexico, but always provides a hostile environment of stifling heat, rats, cockroaches, gamblers, hard drinkers, and crooks with which the contending parties have to struggle in their despairing attempts to preserve a modicum of faith and decency. From the British point of view, one might be tempted to say that such was the essence of the imperial challenge.

The religious impulse in the imperial enterprise should never be underestimated. The quantity of paper and print that it generated was beyond counting. All the competing missionary societies and the Bible societies produced mountains of tracts, part of which were destined for the colonials, and part for their supporters at home. Anglicans, Scots Presbyterians, Nonconformists, and Catholics all strove to construct mirror-images of themselves throughout the Empire; and all sought to convince the imperial authorities of the rightness of their cause. Their difficulties arose not from the universal gospel of Christianity, but from all the other undifferentiated cultural norms that zealous missionaries often tried to impose. One of their definite successes lay in teaching everyone missionary hymns:

> From Greenland's icy mountains,
> From India's coral strand;
> Where Africa's sunny fountains
> Roll down their golden sand:
> From many an ancient river,
> From many a palmy plain,
> They call us to deliver
> Their land from error's chain.[162]

Ethnology was understood as the study of the relationship between the culture of ethnic communities and their environment. (It is one of the precursors of modern anthropology.) It requires painstaking local research informed by language, folklore, customs, literature, history, geography, and practically everything else. For colonial administrators, it was a vital subject because it suggested how newly absorbed territories could best be governed and developed. As a result, British universities and the British Colonial Service combined to train the finest body of Arabists, Orientalists, Sinologists, Indianists, and Africanists that had ever existed. Their work turned out to be popular as well as useful. One of the prototypes was *Eothen* (1844), a record of studies on location in the Ottoman Empire undertaken by A. W. Kinglake (1809–91), a scholar who later became the official historian of the Crimean War.

In later years, the discipline was greatly refined. George Curzon, for example, the future Viceroy of India and Foreign Secretary, spent the seven years between 1887 and 1894 journeying relentlessly. He circled the world twice, but made his most determined forays into the lands of the sensitive zone between Russia and India. In 1888–9 he travelled from St Petersburg to Bokhara, Samarkand, and Tashkent. He passed 1889–90 in Persia; and in 1894 he headed for Afghanistan, crossing the mighty Pamirs and tracing the valley of the Oxus. Walking 'Through the Jade Gate' to Central Asia, he started a fashion for romantic travel in these parts, exemplified by the late Peter Fleming (1907–71) and his *News from Tartary* (1936). Curzon had put his exertions to good use. Over those same years he published three volumes of high-class scholarship – *Russia in Central Asia* (1889), *Persia and the Persian Question* (1892), and *Problems of the Far East* (1894). Those works must be counted as the foundation for all further international studies of the region.

C. M. Doughty (1843–1926), in contrast, started life as a natural history student and a glaciologist working in Norway. But his gaze was soon deflected to the Holy Land, and thence to Arabia, where he tried to emulate Burton's methods. He learned Arabic living in Damascus, then set off with the Bedouin in search of ancient ruins. His *Travels in Arabia Deserta* (1888) was written in a strange experimental English which owed much to his other interests as poet and medievalist. Its academic value was soon recognized, but its wider appeal stayed on hold until a rewritten abridgement was published as *Wanderings in Arabia* (1908). Doughty was the inspirer of an Arabist school which led directly to T. E. Lawrence and *The Seven Pillars of Wisdom* (1935). Similar pioneers worked on Indian religion and civilization such as L. D. Barnett's *The Antiquities of India* (1913).

Richard Burton's most signal contribution to oriental studies centred on so-called erotology – a subject which was long off public limits. By publishing English translations of the *Arabian Nights* (1885–8), the *Kama Sutra* (1883), and the *Perfumed Garden* (1886), even in plain-covered private editions, he ran serious risk of prosecution under the Obscene Publications Act. All his outstanding papers were burned by his widow.

Huge numbers of imperial servants wrote their memoirs. The majority of British people never went overseas in person, so there was an immense curiosity to read every detail of how the Empire was won and governed. The range of memoirs was enormous, and their value very mixed. None was more exciting than the early life of a man who hit the headlines as a journalist in the Boer War, but who had earlier charged with the lancers at Omdurman:

> The whole of the Khalifa's army, nearly 60,000 strong, advanced in battle order . . . topped the swell of ground which hid the two armies from one another, and then rolled down the gently-sloping amphitheater in the arena of which, backed upon the Nile, Kitchener's 20,000 troops were drawn up shoulder to shoulder to receive them. Ancient and modern confronted one another. The weapons, the methods and the fanaticism of the Middle Ages were brought by an extraordinary anachronism into dire collision with the organization and inventions of the nineteenth century . . .
>
> I propose to describe exactly what happened to me: what I saw and what I felt . . . The troop I commanded was, when we wheeled into line, the second from the right of the regiment. I was riding a handy, sure-footed, grey Arab polo pony. Before we wheeled and began to gallop, the officers had been marching with drawn swords. On account of my shoulder I had always decided that if were involved in hand-to-hand fighting, I must use a pistol and not a sword . . . One really had not time to be frightened or to think . . .
>
> The collision was now very near. I saw immediately before me, not ten yards away, the two blue men who lay in my path . . . I rode at the interval between them. They both fired. I passed through the smoke conscious that I was unhurt. The trooper immediately behind me was killed . . . I checked my pony as the ground began to fall away beneath his feet . . .

In one respect a cavalry charge is very like ordinary life. So long as you are all right, firmly in your saddle . . . and well armed, lots of enemies will give you a wide berth. But as soon as you have lost a stirrup, . . . or your horse is wounded, then is the moment when from all quarters enemies rush upon you. Such was the fate of not a few of my comrades . . . on my left. Brought to an actual standstill in the enemy's mass, . . . stabbed at and hacked at by spear and sword, they were dragged from their horses and cut to pieces by the infuriated foe.

I looked round . . . Once again I was on the hard, crisp desert, my horse at a trot. I had the impression of scattered dervishes running to and fro in all direction. Straight before me a man threw himself on the ground . . . My first idea . . . was that the man was terrified. But simultaneously I saw the gleam of his curved sword as he drew it back for a ham-string cut. I had room and time enough to turn my pony out of his reach, and leaning over on the off side I fired two shots into him at about three yards. As I straightened myself in the saddle, I saw before me another figure with uplifted sword. I raised my pistol and fired. So close were we that the pistol itself actually struck him. Man and sword disappeared below and behind me. On my left, ten yards away, was an Arab horseman in a bright-coloured tunic and steel helmet, with chain-mail hangings. I fired at him. He turned aside. I pulled my horse into a walk and looked around again . . .

Where was my troop? . . . There was a mass of Dervishes about forty or fifty yards away on my left. They were huddling and . . . rallying for mutual protection. They seemed wild with excitement, dancing about on their feet, shaking their spears up and down . . . I have an impression . . . of brown-clad Lancers mixed up here and there with this surging mob . . . Within a hundred yards of me I could not see a single officer or man. I looked back at the Dervish mass. I saw two or three riflemen crouching and aiming their rifles at me . . . Then for the first time that morning I experienced a sudden sensation of fear. I felt myself absolutely alone . . . What a fool I was to loiter like this in the midst of the enemy! I crouched over the saddle, spurred my horse into a gallop and drew clear of the *mêlée*.

The other three troops of the squadron were re-forming close by. Suddenly in the midst of the troop up sprung a Dervish . . . He must have leaped out of some scrub or hole. All the troopers turned upon him thrusting with their lances: but he darted to and fro causing for a moment a frantic commotion. Wounded several times, he staggered towards me raising his spear. I shot him at less than a yard. He fell on the sand, and lay there dead. How easy to kill a man!

I asked my second sergeant if he had enjoyed himself. His answer was 'Well, I don't exactly say I enjoyed it, Sir; but I think I'll get more used to it next time.' At this the whole troop laughed.

A white gunboat . . . had hurried up the river in the hopes of being of assistance. From the crow's nest, its commander . . . watched the whole event with breathless interest. Many years passed before I met this officer or knew that he witnessed our gallop. When we met, I was First Lord of Admiralty and he the youngest Admiral in the Royal Navy. 'What did it look like?' I asked him . . . 'It looked,' said Admiral Beatty, 'like plum duff: brown currants scattered about in a great deal of suet.'[163]

It is hard to believe that the same young cavalryman, Winston Churchill, who had fought the Dervishes on horseback with sabre and pistol, lived to be the Prime Minister of a nuclear power.

The histories of individual colonies or dominions were usually written soon after their formation. But it was not until the later nineteenth century that historians thought to construct a synthesis of imperial development as a whole. A lead was given by Sir Charles Dilke, Bt. (1843–1911), a promising Liberal politician whose career was blighted by the scandal of a divorce case. Dilke's two-volume *Greater Britain* (1866–7) articulated an idea, already nascent in Froude, that the British Empire was the natural, organic outgrowth of English history. The Empire was not a collection of overseas possessions or acquisitions; it was an integral part of the very sinews of the nation.

The critical exposé, however, awaited the presentation and publication of the lectures of Sir John Seeley (1834–95), Professor of Latin and later of History at Cambridge. Seeley's *Expansion of England* (1883) was vastly influential. It arrived shortly after the proclamation of Victoria as the Empress of India (1 January 1877), and shortly before 'the Scramble for Africa' brought the size and variety of the Empire's processions towards their peak. Popular enthusiasm about the growth of Empire, and official anxieties about its management, created enormous interest. Seeley answered the need by linking his analysis of the past to his predictions for the future.

Seeley's philosophy, like that of the Gladstonian 'Home Rulers' with whom he had much in common, was one of principled liberalism. He had no time either for imperialist domination or for ideas of British superiority: 'It is essentially barbaric', he wrote, 'that one community should be treated as the property of another and the fruits of its industry confiscated, not in return for benefits conferred, but by some absolute right, whether of conquest or otherwise.'[164] Or again, in relation to India: 'It is a mistake to suppose that the Empire itself is standing proof of some vast superiority in the English race over the races of India.'[165] The logical corollary insisted that the Empire must be ruled in large measure by consent.

Seeley was very conscious of past errors, particularly in America. The source of trouble in the American colonies, he judged, had lain with contradictory policies:

> The old system was an irrational jumble of two opposite conceptions. It claimed to rule the colonists because they were Englishmen and brothers, and yet it ruled them as if they were conquered Indians. And again, while it treated them as a conquered people, it gave them so much liberty that they could easily rebel.[166]

Similar confusion must not happen again. At the time of Seeley's lectures Canada and New Zealand were a self-governing dominion and colony respectively. Australia and South Africa had not been formed. But he clearly intended that all 'Englishmen and brothers' should enjoy dominion status.

Seeley saw developments in the long term. In his opening lecture, he asked the question 'What is the general drift . . . of English History?'; and he came up with an answer about the creation of internal and external empires. The internal empire he called 'the internal union of the three kingdoms' as completed by Queen Anne. The external empire was called 'a still larger Britain comprehending vast possessions beyond the sea'.[167] Here was a welcome and radical rejection of the historians' old obsession about the governance of just one kingdom – i.e., England.

Seeley was acutely aware of demographic trends. He saw the huge imbalance in the overseas Empire between the ten million people 'mainly of English blood' and the two hundred and sixty millions in India of 'a completely foreign race'. But he knew that the situation was not static. He observed the sixteenfold increase of population that had occurred in the USA between 1780 and 1880, and he projected a similar rate of increase among the British overseas: 'In not much more than half a century, the Englishmen beyond the sea – supposing the Empire to hold together – will be equal in number to the Englishmen at home, and the total will be much more than a hundred millions . . .'[168]

Fifty years from the day of utterance shows that he was thinking of 1933. This trend, he declared, 'is evidently the great fact of modern English History'. (See below.)

Criticism of Seeley's thesis inevitably homes in on his 'Anglo-centric' perspective. And it is perfectly true: his main concern was for those 'Englishmen beyond the sea'. On the other hand, he was writing at a time before the main 'Scramble for Africa', and he had many interesting comments and predictions about India. He recognized the probability of an Indian 'nationality-movement'; and he correctly foresaw the rivalry between Hindu and Muslim parties.

In the last analysis, Seeley's optimism derived from his convictions about the British Empire's benign character. It was infused, he believed, with that same spirit of freedom which had supposedly infused the whole of English history: 'Greater Britain is not in the ordinary sense an empire at all . . .; we see a natural growth, a mere normal extension of the English race into other lands . . . that our settlers took possession of . . . without conquest.' And further, 'it is not an empire attached to England in the same way as the Roman Empire was attached to Rome . . . It is self-supporting . . . It will not drag us down.'[169]

Quoting Wordsworth, he fervently believed that the river of British freedom, now flowing strongly across the globe, would never run into the sands:

> It is not to be thought of that the flood
> Of British freedom, which to the open sea
> Of the world's praise, from dark antiquity
> Hath flowed 'with pomp of waters unwithstood,'
> Roused though it be full often to a mood
> Which spurns the check of salutary bands,
> That this most famous stream in bogs and sands
> Should perish, and to evil and to good
> Be lost for ever—[170]

In those days, confidence about the Empire's future also ran high in more popular quarters. Thirty years after Seeley's lectures, C. R. L. Fletcher's textbook for the youth of the Empire made a number of fatuous comments about the peoples of the empire being eternally grateful for the blessings of British rule. Rudyard Kipling, when asked by Fletcher for a concluding poem, was more circumspect. But he produced a marvellous metaphor of perpetual regeneration:

> Our England is a garden that is full of stately views
> Of borders, beds and shrubberies and lawns and avenues,
> With statues on the terraces and peacocks strutting by;
> But the Glory of the Garden lies in more than meets the eye.
> For where the old thick laurels grow, along the thin red wall,
> You'll find the tool- and potting-sheds which are the heart of all,

The cold-frames and the hot-houses, the dungpits and the tanks,
The rollers, carts and drain-pipes, with the barrows and the planks,
. . .
Oh, Adam was a gardener, and God who made him sees
That half a proper gardener's work is done upon his knees,
So when your work is finished, you can wash your hands and pray,
For the Glory of the Garden that it may not pass away!
And the Glory of the Garden it shall never pass away![171]

In the two centuries since the Union, the public sense of 'Britishness' had grown much stronger. But it was also transformed. It was no longer confined to the population of the Isles. In the judgement of some people, like Kipling, it was open to anyone who helped to cultivate the imperial garden. In the judgement of others, it could not go beyond the Britishers' 'kith and kin'. But in everyone's judgement, it stretched right round the world.

Nonetheless, despite the essential seriousness of Britain's imperial mission, the most redeeming feature of the British imperialists undoubtedly lay in their ability to laugh at themselves. Many of them recognized the ridiculous side of their predicament. The most glorious lines on this theme and the most accurately observed were composed by a young English dramatist and lyricist as he drove along the jungle roads of Indo-China in February 1930:

> . . . . . .
> Mad dogs and Englishmen
> Go out in the midday sun,
> The Japanese don't care to.
> The Chinese wouldn't dare to,
> Hindoos and Argentines sleep firmly from twelve to one.
> But Englishmen detest a siesta.
> In the Philippines
> There are lovely screens
> To protect you from the glare.
> In the Malay States
> There are hats like plates

Which the Britishers won't wear.
At twelve noon
The natives swoon
And no further work is done.
But mad dogs and Englishmen
Go out in the midday sun.

It's such a surprise for the Eastern eyes to see
That though the English are effete,
They're quite impervious to heat,
When the white man rides every native hides in glee,
Because the simple creatures hope he
Will impale his solar topee on a tree.

Bolyboly bolyboly bolyboly baa,
Bolyboly bolyboly bolyboly baa,
Habaninny habanniny habaninny haa,
Habaninny habaninny habaninny haa.

It seems such a shame
When the English claim
The earth
That they give rise to such hilarity and mirth.
Mad dogs and Englishmen
Go out in the midday sun.
The toughest Burmese bandit
Can never understand it.
In Rangoon the heat of noon
Is just what the natives shun
They put their Scotch or Rye down
And lie down.
In a jungle town
Where the sun beats down
To the rage of man and beast
The English garb
Of the English sahib
Merely gets a bit more creased.

In Bangkok
At twelve o'clock
They foam at the mouth and run,
But mad dogs and Englishmen
Go out in the midday sun.

Mad dogs and Englishmen
Go out in the midday sun.
The smallest Malay rabbit
Deplores this stupid habit
In Hongkong
They strike a gong
And fire off a noonday gun
To reprimand each inmate
Who's in late.
In the mangrove swamps
Where the python romps
There is peace from twelve till two.
Even caribous
Lie around and snooze,
For there's nothing else to do.
In Bengal
To move at all
Is seldom, if ever done,
But mad dogs and Englishmen
Go out in the midday sun.[172]

56. Catholic martyr, 1535: St Thomas More and family.

57. The Protestant Establishment, 1547: Henry VIII
dying, Edward VI ascending, Pope Paul III agonizing.

58. 'Charles Stuart, that Man of Blood' (1649) – 'a subject and a sovereign are clean different thin

59. The Siege of Drogheda (1649) – a symbol of a cumulative calamity.

60. Willem van Oranje lands at Brixham (1688) – 'a successful invasion swiftly accomplished'.

61. Queen Anne (r. 1702–14) – from 1707 'the first British monarch both in style and substance'.

62. John Wilkes MP (1727–97), 'Friend of Liberty': 'Scotland is a treeless, flowerless land formed out of the refuse of the universe.'

63. 'Bonnie Prince Charlie', the Young Pretender, Charles III (1720–88): disguised as Flora Macdonald's servant girl.

64. Wolfe Tone (1763–98): Protestant radical, Irish separatist, founder of the United Irishmen.

65. Revd John Lingard (1771–1851), historian – 'never found his way into the company of the recognised "greats"'.

66. Rudyard Kipling (1865–1936). Imperialist, poet, inventor of the 'Little Friend of all the World'.

67. David Lloyd George (1863–1945), 'The Goat': 'a fully equipped duke costs as much as two Dreadnoughts'.

68. K. S. Ranjitsinhji (1872–1933), cricketer: leader of the batting averages.

69. HRH The Princess of Wales (1961–97): the first Englishwoman to marry a King of Britain or his heir apparent.

70. *Opposite, top:* Victoria
and Albert and offspring,
(1846) – a family of
solidly German descent.

71. *Opposite, bottom:* The
Delhi *Durbar* (1911) – the
British imitating the
Moghuls.

72. *Right:* Dublin, Easter
1916 – the first crack in
the unity of the United
Kingdom.

73. *Below:* The Western
Front, 1917. 'Lions led
by Donkeys.'

74. 'Their Finest Hour', the Battle of Britain (1940) – an RAF Spitfire of 303 (Polish) Squadron.

75. Hong Kong, 30 June 1997 – handing over the remnants of Empire.

76. TASCIOVANUS

Bronze coin of Tasciovanus, King of the Catuvellauni (late first century BC – early first century AD): probably minted at Verulamium: one of the first coins of the Isles to bear a bust.

77. CUNOBELINUS

Coin of Cunobelinus (early first-century AD), ruler of the unified Kingdom of the Catuvellauni and Trinovantes, probably minted at Camulodunum.

78. ROMAN BRITANNIA

Bronze sestertius of Emperor Antoninus Pius (AD 138–61), builder of the Antonine Wall: on the reverse, the seated figure of Britannia.

79. AETHELSTAN

King Aethelstan of East Anglia (r. c. 825–40): possibly the earliest coin to bear the legend REX ANG – King of the English.

80. ATHELSTAN

Athelstan, King of the English
(r. 924–39): the legend REX TO
BRI indicates the King's claim to
be 'King of all Britain'.

81. HYWEL DDA

Hywel Dda, 'Hywell the Good',
King of Dyfed, Seisyllwg, and
Gwynedd (r. 942–49): the only
native Welsh coinage.

82. ERIC BLOOD-AXE

Coin from the second reign of the
Viking King of Jorvik, Eric Blood-Axe
(r. 952–4), bearing the legend ERIC REX.

83. SIHTRIC SILKBEARD

Coin of the Viking King of Dublin,
Sihtric III Silkbeard (r. 989–1029):
the first native Irish issue.

84. GUILLAUME I

85. DAVID I

Silver penny from the English reign of 'The Conqueror' (1066–87) bearing the runic form of 'W', thus reading PILLELM REX: evidence for the Normans' Viking heritage.

Penny of King David I of Scotland (r. 1124–53), the first Scottish coinage: minted at Berwick, Carlisle, Roxburgh, and Edinburgh.

86. EDOUARD I

'Groat', introduced in 1279, equivalent to four silver pennies. The legend outlined the King's titles: King of England, Lord of Ireland, and Duke of Aquitaine. This was the first English coin to bear the legend DI GRA (Dei Gratia – By the Grace of God).

87. EDOUARD III

'Ship noble' of Edouard III, introduced in 1351, probably minted in Calais and valued at 6 shillings and 8 pence. The obverse, showing the King in a ship, may allude to the victory at Sluys (1340).

88. HENRY VII

12 shilling piece, or 'testoon', from the later years of the reign of Henry VII: the first English coin to bear a realistic portrait of the monarch.

89. MARY AND PHILIP

A shilling of the period of the marriage between Mary Tudor and Philip of Spain (1554–58). The busts and titles of both monarchs were displayed.

90. JAMES I

The 20 shilling 'unite' (1604) of James VI & I reflecting the new monarch's political ambitions. The reverse bore the King's new title of REX MA BRI (King of Great Britain) and the legend FACIEM EOS IN GENTEM UNAM ('I will make them one people').

91. CHARLES I

On the reverse of this gold triple unite (1644) Charles I swore to defend the Protestant religion, the laws of England, and the liberties of Parliament (RELIG PROT. LEG ANG. LIBER PAR).

92. JAMES II

Brass crown (1690) minted from melted-down cannon. Two years after James II had been deposed in England, such 'gun money' was used to pay Jacobite soldiers in Ireland.

93. ENGLISH COMMONWEALTH

Silver 5 shilling piece of 1651, the first English coin to bear an inscription
in English. Latin was apparently considered too close to Catholicism.

94. DARIÉN PISTOLE

Pistole (1701) minted using gold panned from the Scottish colony at Darién in
Central America: the obverse bore the colony's symbol of the rising sun.

95. GEORGE I

Half-penny (1723), reverse, showing the figure of Hibernia. The coin was struck for Irish use, but was withdrawn in 1724 amid allegations of corruption and was then circulated in America.

96. GEORGE II

Half-penny of George II from 1754, reverse, bearing the figure of Britannia. Restored in 1673, the figure was modelled on that used by Antoninus Pius 1,600 years before.

97. GEORGE II

Shilling of George II (1758), reverse, bearing the Hanoverians' British and German titles – 'King of Great Britain, France, and Ireland, Defender of the Faith, Duke of Brunswick and Lüneburg, High Treasurer and Elector of the Holy Roman Empire'.

98. WILLIAM IV

1837 Hanoverian Thaler, reverse, showing the combined Hanoverian and British arms of William IV: the last joint British–Hanoverian issue.

99. VICTORIA

Silver Indian rupee of 1877, the year of Victoria's coronation as Empress of India.

100. IRISH FREE STATE

Half-crown of the Irish Free State (1928), bearing the traditional Irish harp symbol. This coin was designed by an Englishman and produced at the Royal Mint in London.

101. THE EURO

The 'multinational' reverse of the 1 euro coin to be introduced into the Eurozone including Ireland on 1 January 2002 (the obverse is due to carry 'national' designs).

CHAPTER TEN

THE POST-IMPERIAL
ISLES

Since c. 1900

THE GROWTH OF THE EUROPEAN UNION, 1958–1999

Iceland

Norway

Finland
1995

Sweden
1995

Russia

Estonia

Latvia

Denmark
1973

Lithuania

Ireland
1973

United
Kingdom
1973

Russia

Belarus

Netherlands

Germany

Poland

Belgium

Luxembourg Czech Rep.

Ukraine

Slovakia

France

Switzerland

Austria
1995

Hungary

Moldova

Portugal
1986

Slovenia

Croatia

Bosnia-
Herzegovina

Yugoslavia

Romania

Italy

Spain
1986

Albania

Macedonia

Bulgaria

Turkey

Greece
1981

Morocco

Algeria

Tunisia

Libya

Egypt

Founder members 1958

Former GDR incorporated following
German reunification 1990

Member country with date joined

Next candidates for EU membership

0		300 miles
0		500 km

LONDON, FRIDAY 23 JUNE 1911. Ten years after Queen Victoria's death, the morning after her grandson's coronation, *The Times* positively throbbed with pride and excitement:

THE CORONATION

King George V. and Queen Mary were crowned yesterday in Westminster Abbey, with all the solemn rites rendered sacred by the traditions of nearly a thousand years, and in presence of an assemblage including almost all that are highest . . . in the Empire, as well . . . representatives of nearly every civilized State in the world.

The morning broke grey and gloomy, and during some hours there were occasional showers, while there was a cloudy sky all day, through which only once or twice the sun broke for a few minutes; but on the whole the weather was not unkindly . . . The great day has come and gone, the day which has filled the thoughts of the nation for months past, and has governed the plans and the movements of thousands upon thousands of men . in every region of the globe. In the venerable and beautiful Abbey of which every stone is instinct with the memories and traditions of our national life, George V. has been crowned King with all the solemnity that belongs to a ritual much of which is almost coeval with Christianity, and all the pomp and circumstance that befit the consecration of a ruler whose beneficent sway is acknowledged to the uttermost bounds of civilization . . .[1]

The meteorological bulletin formed a vital part of the psychological weather.

On the eve of the coronation, *The Times of India* had published its own estimate of the occasion:

> Today the eyes of the whole world will be turned toward the ancient shrine at Westminster where His Most Excellent Majesty George the Fifth will be crowned King of the United Kingdom of Great Britain and Ireland, and of the British Dominions Beyond the Seas, Emperor of India [sic]. The occasion is one which makes even the most thoughtless amongst us pause for a moment to consider what this great ceremony means to the British people at home and abroad and to those other peoples whose lot has become intimately intertwined with the British Empire. And the moment we reflect we are impressed, almost awed, by the antiquity of this rite. For the ceremony at Westminster carries us back to the year 785 when Ecgfrith, Prince of Mercia was 'hallowed to be king' by Offa, his father. The Coronation then, symbolises the growth of the British Nation and the British Empire through twelve centuries.[2]

George V's family consisted of the two royal parents and their six children. The King, forty-six, born as George Frederick Ernest Albert of Saxe-Coburg und Gotha, was the second son of Edward VII and Alexandra von Sonderburg-Glücksburg, sometime Princess of Denmark. Bearded, subdued, and (unofficially) 'very dull', he had spent most of his life in the Navy, and had only become his father's heir in 1892 on the death of his elder brother, succeeding in May 1910. The Queen, forty-four, formerly the Princess Victoria Marie von Teck-Württemberg, had been born in the same room in Kensington Palace as Queen Victoria; and had been briefly engaged to her husband's late brother. She took the title of Queen Mary. Prim and reserved to the point of Teutonic stiffness, and a stickler for etiquette – qualities highly prized at the time – she was said to be the dominant partner in the marriage. The heir to the throne, Edward, Prince of Wales, was celebrating his seventeenth birthday that very day. His four brothers – Princes Albert, Henry, George and John – were aged respectively fifteen, eleven, nine, and six. His sister, Princess Victoria, was just fourteen. The King's closest relatives included, on the paternal side: his uncle, Field-Marshal the Duke of Connaught; his aunts, the Duchess of Argyll, the Princesses of Hesse, and of Schleswig-Holstein, HRH the Princess Royal: the Dowager Duchesses of Albany, of Saxe-Coburg, and of Edinburgh; and his cousin, Kaiser Wilhelm II, represented at the Coronation by the Crown Prince of Germany. On the maternal side, they included a host of Sonderburg-Glücksburgs, among them the King of Denmark, the King of the Hellenes, and the Tsarina of Russia, all represented by Princes, Royal Highnesses, or Dukes.

The Queen's closest relative, her nephew, Brevet Lieutenant Colonel His Serene Highness Adolph, Duke of Teck, rode immediately behind the royal carriage in the company of the two Connaughts (father and son), Vice-Admiral Prince Louis of Battenberg, and General His Royal Highness Prince Christian of Schleswig-Holstein.

One of the most detailed contemporary accounts can be found in the pages of the *Annual Register*. The Festivities began with the Royal Procession to Westminster Abbey:

> The first procession, that of the Royal and other guests and representatives of foreign States, left Buckingham Palace (unfortunately in closed carriages) at 9.30 am. It was loudly cheered, the most cordial reception being given to the representatives of Germany, the United States, and France. Next came the procession of the Royal Family, chiefly consisting of the Princesses and their suites; the Royal children in the last carriage were received with enthusiasm all along the route. Then, leaving the Palace at 10.30, the King's procession came, headed by a military escort, on which followed carriages with officials of the household, military and naval *aides-de-camp*, high officers of the Army, the War Office Staff and Army Council, the King's Equerries and Honorary Indian *aides-de-camp* (three Indian Princes) and escorts of Colonial, Indian and British Cavalry preceding the State coach drawn by eight of the famous cream-coloured horses, and escorted by Viscount Kitchener of Khartoum, Field-Marshal commanding the troops. Throughout the route – by the Mall through the new Processional Arch and down Whitehall – the procession was received with the utmost popular enthusiasm.[3]

The ceremonies in the Abbey culminated with the act of coronation.

> Their Majesties went to the Chairs of State on the south side of
> the high altar, and the King then came forward in full view of the
> congregation to be 'presented' by the Archbishop of Canterbury for
> the Recognition, a feature dating back to the earliest days of
> European monarchy. He was acclaimed with a shout of 'God save
> King George' as the Archbishop repeated the formula of presentation
> at each of the four sides of the dais. Now followed the religious
> ceremony; the Litany, shortened and sung by two Bishops and the
> choir to Tallis's music; the ante-Communion Service, also abridged,
> preceded by Purcell's Introit and with its special collect and its
> seven-minute sermon, preached by the Archbishop of York . . . After
> this followed the Coronation Oath in its new form, taken by the
> King kneeling at the altar. Then came the Annointing, regarded as
> the central act of the religious ceremony, with the *Veni Creator*, and,
> after the special prayer, the anthem more especially associated with
> this rite, Handel's 'Zadok the priest and Nathan the prophet anointed
> Solomon King.' Hereupon the King, divested of his robes of State,
> took his seat on the Chair of King Edward, containing the Coronation
> Stone; the great Lords of the Court gathered round him; the Pall was
> held over his head by four Knights of the Garter in their robes – the
> Earls of Crewe, Rosebery, Cadogan, and Minto; and the Primate
> solemnly anointed his head, breast and hands. Next he was invested
> with the insignia of Royalty in its double capacity, ecclesiastical and
> civil; clothed with quasi-ecclesiastical robes, the *colobium sindonis*
> and the *supertunica*; presented with the golden spurs, brought from
> the altar by the Dean to the Lord Chamberlain, who lightly touched
> the King's heels with them and returned them to the altar. Then Earl
> Beauchamp, who had been bearing the Sword of State, exchanged it
> for the Sword of Offering which he delivered to the Archbishop, who
> laid it on the altar, praying that the King might use it as the minister
> of God for the punishment of evildoers and the protection and
> encouragement of those that do well. He then delivered it to the
> King, enjoining him as to its proper use; it was then returned to
> the altar and formally 'redeemed', a bag containing 100 shillings

being laid on the altar. Next the King was invested with the Armill and the Pallium or Royal robe (a gorgeous robe of cloth of gold worn by George IV, at his Coronation); and presented with the Orb by the Archbishop, with the admonition to remember 'when you see the Orb set under the Cross, that the whole world is subject to the Power and Empire of Christ our Redeemer.' Next he received the Ring and the two Sceptres, 'the ensign of Kingly power and justice' surmounted with a cross, the 'rod of equity and mercy' with a dove. Finally the Primate crowned the King, praying that God would crown him with a crown of glory and righteousness and that he might obtain the crown of an everlasting Kingdom. Hereupon the drums and the trumpets sounded, and the Abbey echoed with a shout of 'God save the King,' while the guns at the Tower announced the event to the multitude. Then, after the Benediction, the King was enthroned and received the homage of the Primate, the Prince of Wales, the Royal Princess and the Peers of the Realm.[4]

The return of the King-Emperor to Buckingham Palace was attended by a huge military parade.

Of the 60,000 troops who lined the route some 36,000 were Regulars, 17,000 Territorials, and the balance was composed of bluejackets, marines, the Special Reserve, contingents from the Channel Islands, the Dominions, some Crown Colonies, and the Federated Malay States, and a contingent fully representative of the diverse races combined in the Indian Army. The Indian troops were camped at Hampton Court, many of the others in the London Parks. There were also detachments of the Officers' Training Corps (from the Universities and Public Schools) and cadets from the naval and military colleges. The Indian and Dominion troops were posted near the Queen Victoria memorial, as was a small body of Boy Scouts.[5]

(The Boy Scouts Association was just three years old.)

In the days before TV, the *London Illustrated News* provided the main supply of pictorial images. As a guide to its pictures, it published a list of the imperial troops in the parade:

Gurkhas
Bombay Infantry
Indian Light Horse
Punjab Infantry and Cavalry
Malta Infantry and Royal Artillery
1st & 5th Bombay Cavalry
New South Wales Lancers
New Zealand Mounted Rifles
Victoria Mounted Rifles
Bengal Lancers
British Guiana Volunteers and
   Artillery
Trinidad Volunteers
21st, 22nd & 29th Saskatchewan
   Horse
19th Alberta Dragoons
23rd Alberta Rangers
7th Quebec Hussars

Transvaal Highlanders and
   Mounted Rifles and Field
   Artillery
Queensland Mounted Rifles
Natal Mounted Rifles and Field
   Artillery
Barbados Volunteers
Bermuda Volunteers
Canadian Highlanders and Cavalry
Cape Mounted Rifles
Transvaal Scottish Volunteers
Leeward Islands Volunteers
Windward Islands Volunteers
South African Police
Transvaal Cycle and Motor Corps
Kaffrarian Rifles
Transvaal Horse Artillery
Natal Carabineers[6]

Later in the parade, the crowds watched as the foreign contingents passed by. These included: from Austria, the K.U.K. Feldhaubitz-Regiment nr. 12: from Germany, the Garde-Dragoner-Regiment Königin Viktoria von Grossbritannien und Irland, the Kürassier Regiment Graf Gessler (Rheinisches) nr. 8, and the Husaren-Regiment Fürst Blücher von Wahlstatt (Pommersches) nr. 5: and from Spain, the Royal Zamora Infantry Regt, nr. 8. (Within three years, all those units except one would be enemies.)

Anyone with an eye for heraldry would have noticed important changes since the last coronation. After the Princes and Princesses of the Blood Royal, and in the middle of a group representing the orders of chivalry, parity in the parade of standards was given to the imperial dominions. In the front ranks marched the standard-bearers of South Africa, New Zealand, Australia, and Canada: in the centre, the standard-bearer of India; in the rear, the standards of Wales, Ireland, Scotland, and England preceded those of the Union and of the Monarch. For the first time, the overseas dominions were being given the same prominence as the four home countries; and India was in the heart of things.

The procession and parade were repeated on the afternoon of the second day, after which their Majesties dined with the Foreign Minister, Sir Edward Grey. On the Saturday a spectacular naval review was held:

> Next day [their Majesties] reviewed at Spithead the most formidable fleet ever assembled. It was formed in seven columns, each nearly five miles in length. The British warships present were 165 – eight Dreadnoughts, twenty-four earlier battleships, four Dreadnought cruisers, twenty-one 'armoured' and nine 'protected' cruisers, sixty-seven destroyers, twelve destroyers' depôt ships, twelve torpedo boats, and eight submarines. There were also eighteen foreign warships representing all the European Navies except that of Portugal as well as those of China, Japan, Argentina, the United States, and Chile; and in spite of the seamen's strike there were some twenty large British and foreign ocean liners and a multitude of other vessels crowded with official guests and spectators, as well as many yachts and small craft. The King and Queen, with the three elder children and the Royal guests, travelled by special train to Portsmouth and embarked in the Royal yacht *Victoria and Albert*, which steamed along the lines. As she entered the Fleet a Royal salute was fired; the King stood on her bridge, and the crew of each ship as she passed it manned the deck and cheered, His Majesty saluting in reply. After the inspection he held a reception of the British Admirals and the commanders of the foreign warships, and the yacht then left for Portsmouth, amid another Royal salute. His Majesty expressed his marked satisfaction with the Review.[7]

Outside London, every local community in the land organized some sort of celebration:

> In the country the celebrations usually began with religious services, Churchmen and Nonconformists in many cases uniting in them at the parish churches; in the afternoon there were processions and pageants, memorial trees were planted, concerts and sports were held and the elementary school children were feasted. The afternoon

unfortunately was chilly and showery in many places, though the Coronation procession in London was untouched by rain. In the evening, London was transformed by superb illuminations; all vehicular traffic was stopped, and the streets were thronged till past midnight. In other towns, too, illuminations and fireworks were very general, and the hills of the United Kingdom were adorned with some three thousand bonfires. The signal for lighting was given at 10 p.m. from the Crystal Palace.[8]

The royal pair were kept busy for the rest of the following week. The crowded programme included an opera at Covent Garden, a garden party for 6,000 guests at Buckingham Palace, a gala performance at His Majesty's Theatre, a visit to the Royal Agricultural show at Norwich, a City luncheon at the Guildhall, a children's fête for a hundred thousand at the Crystal Palace, dinner with the Prime Minister, Mr Asquith, at Downing Street, and, finally, the presentation of medals to five hundred Indian and fifteen hundred colonial soldiers. They then left for a tour to Dublin, to Caernarvon (where the Prince of Wales was invested), and to Edinburgh.

As for the wider significance of the proceedings, an extended commentary in *The Times* offered a number of exalted suggestions. It started with a eulogy of 'the Imperial idea'.

Once more we have to extend our horizon and to regard this ancient Monarchy as the mother of nations and the centre of a worldwide Empire, held together by no bonds of conquest and no assertive central authority, but by some force which none of us can properly name or define, impalpable and intangible as gravitation, yet, like that mysterious force, maintaining the system intact while allowing for all the perturbations due to the minor interactions of the several parts ... It is no mean tribute to the informing genius of our institutions that through their ancient forms the great Dominions of the CROWN can join us not only in the symbolical pageant of the Coronation, but in the processional march of the ages. Gradually, but surely and naturally, they fall into step without compulsion and almost without conscious volition, because they are of the same blood and the same fibre, only superficially affected by external conditions, and the old music to which we have been marching for eight hundred years thrills along their nerves and impels them to consentaneous motion. In that lie the greatness and the permanence of the Imperial idea, and the secret of its hold among men living in the most various conditions and drifting further with each generation from close personal connexion with the Mother Country. We should do well to consider closely what this attractive and cohesive force depends upon in the last analysis. Whether it appears to belong to consanguinity, or whether we have regard to its unquestionable power over men of other races by virtue of the appeal to universal human appreciation of the liberty and equality before the law which are fundamental principles of our polity, we must equally recognize that an Empire founded in a special and unique manner upon consent is an Empire founded upon character. Not the exploits of soldiers, not the intrepidity of seamen, not the fumbling of statesmen . . . has built up the British Empire . . . It is the product of the inner character of millions upon millions of undistinguished people who . . . have been content to do inconspicuously the duty that lay nearest them. It can be maintained only by conserving the fundamental integrity and earnestness of purpose which went to its building.[9]

It continued with a tribute to the 'Old Europe', from Portugal to Russia, where Britain was seen to have its roots:

It would be an invidious task on an occasion like this . . . to see the apportion between the nations of old Europe; the shares they have had in creating her greatness, or to appraise the good influences which they have had upon us . . . To France, to Germany, and to Italy our debt is immense, as is their debt to us. No small part of our language, as of our laws, our manners, our social habits, and our culture . . . comes to us from each of them. What would our history have been without the Norman Conquest and the French wars, without the old German Empire and the German Reformation, without the long influence of medieval Rome, and without the Italian Renaissance? No race has profited so greatly as ours by the achievements of Spain and Portugal in opening up three continents,

and it was on their soil and with their stubborn aid that WELLING-
TON struck his first deadly blows in our latest struggle against a
domination fatal to European rights. In that cause the HOUSE OF
HABSBURG was to fight by our side, as we had stood by France to
curb the overweening power of CHARLES V. and of PHILIP II.
Denmark, Sweden, and the Netherlands have all written their names
deep and large in the life of England and of Europe, and, if our
relations with our great European neighbour in Asia have not always
been cordial, we rejoice to remember that they began, in friendship,
and that never were they so friendly as they are to-day.[10]

'Our latest struggle' against domination in Europe had been waged a
hundred years earlier. 'Our great European neighbour in Asia' was Russia.
And it proceeded to a reminder of the British Empire's global reach:

But it is no longer with the old European States and peoples alone
that this world-Empire has to do. As the Dominions of the KING
have expanded, and the iron roads, which Englishmen taught the
world to build, have spread over the earth, the ancient kingdoms of
the East are more familiar to us than were wide tracts of their own
continent to our forefathers. With the remotest of them all we stand
in close alliance, and one of the most distinguished of the Princes of
Japan, with the victor of Tsushima, ADMIRAL TOGO, . . . has come
amongst us to see the descendant of KING ALFRED crowned in the
Temple of the Plantagenets. The Grand Turk, the Sophy, and Prester
John were the embodiments of half-mythical splendour to the greatest
of our poets, and yesterday the SULTAN, the SHAH, and the
EMPEROR of ABYSSINIA witnessed through their representatives the
rite by which ELIZABETH and JAMES I. were crowned. So, too, will
States and nations unborn, for generations after the last of the
Tudors was laid to rest. First of them all is that great people who
are joint heirs with us of our history from its dim beginning to the
days of FOX and of EDMUND BURKE, who speak the same mother-
tongue, whose Bible is our English Bible, given us three hundred
years ago, whose polity and laws bear the stamp of Westminster,
whose ideals of public right, of ordered liberty, and of equal justice
are our own, who are our kin in mind and feeling as they are in

blood. The choice of their representative is a sign of how fast history is made in our times. MR. HAYS HAMMOND was sentenced to death under PRESIDENT KRUGER. Yesterday he joined GENERAL LOUIS BOTHA, the Dutch-born Prime Minister of the Dominion of South Africa, in prayer for the long and happy reign of KING GEORGE V.[11]

Several newspapers commented on the abnormality of Coronation week. They noticed how political life had been suspended for the duration of the festivities. No sense of the acute tensions of the time is conveyed by the glowing passages about imperial pride and unity. In fact, the Parliament Bill, which had threatened to disrupt the working of the state completely, had only been passed before the Coronation with a few days to spare. A merchant seamen's strike, which had been paralysing the ports, held firm throughout coronation week; and troops had been used against striking coal miners at Tonypandy in South Wales. The Ulster Unionists were desperately campaigning to obstruct the progress of the Bill for Irish Home Rule. Most interestingly, only a month beforehand, the Suffragettes had laid on a show in London that rivalled the coronation parade:

It was four miles long; it contained some 40,000 women, with a comparatively small contingent, drawn largely from the Universities, of men; while massing for the march, it occupied the whole length of the Thames Embankment from Westminster to Blackfriars, together with Whitehall Gardens and Whitehall Place. It was headed by Mrs. Drummond, on horseback, with a standard bearer selected because she had endured weeks of forcible feeding in prison, and another lady personating Joan of Arc. Then came nearly a thousand 'martyrs of the cause'; a historical pageant representing women throughout English history, from Abbess Hilda of Whitby to the conspicuous figures of the nineteenth century and the voteless women after the Reform Bill; representatives of Scotland, Ireland, Wales, the Dominions, and every country in Europe, the nationality being indicated by costume or otherwise; contingents of representatives of working women, from actresses and university graduates to North country mill girls, whose attendance involved two nights in the train, of the Anglican, Roman, and Free Churches, and of all the suffrage societies, the Constitutionalists being unexpectedly strong. At the Albert Hall meeting 103,000l. was raised for the cause. The procession testified alike to the enthusiasm of the suffragists and to their artistic and organising ability; the only adverse criticism possible on it was that it was pageantry rather than politics.[12]

It is also significant, as the *Annual Register* noted, that attendance at the coronation festivities of 1911 was not as high as expected:

The frequent extra trains from the suburbs were far from full; it was unexpectedly easy to get away after the processions had passed; and holiday excursions were run from London to various seaside resorts, which acted as a further relief.[13]

Not a few Londoners preferred a day trip to Brighton to watching their King-Emperor crowned.

For monarchy and suffragettes alike, however, pageantry was a vital element of politics. What is more, British royal pageantry was evolving rapidly. Contrary to the talk about 'ancient rituals' and the unchanging practices of 'a thousand years', much of the pomp and ceremony seen in 1911 was the product of very recent decades. Exactly fifty years earlier, having watched Queen Victoria's opening of Parliament, a future Prime Minister was moved to print an anonymous article deploring Britain's lack of talent for pageantry:

Some nations have a gift for ceremonial. No poverty of means or absence of splendour inhibits them from making any pageant in which they take part both real and impressive. Everybody falls naturally into his proper place, throws himself without effort into the spirit of the little drama he is enacting, and instinctively represses all appearance of constraint or distracted attention.

But . . .

This attitude is generally confined to the people of a southern climate and of non-Teutonic parentage. In England the case is exactly the reverse. We can afford to be more splendid than most nations; but some malignant spell broods over all our most solemn ceremonials, and inserts into them some feature which makes them all ridiculous ... Something always breaks down, somebody contrives to escape doing his part, or some bye-motive is suffered to interfere and ruin it all.[14]

The first step towards a modern but ancient-looking tradition had been taken during Queen Victoria's coronation as Empress of India in 1876. The 'Imperial Assemblage' of 1877 in Delhi, which the Queen-Empress did not attend, laid the foundations for a more consciously imperial dimension to royal pageantry. Designed by Rudyard Kipling's father, it took the form of a festival which was organized, symbolically, on the site of the victory over the Indian Mutiny, and which saw seventy native princes pay their fealty to the Viceroy and his throne. As the Viceroy himself remarked: 'The further east you go, the greater becomes the importance of a bit of bunting.'[15]

Further progress was made during Queen Victoria's Diamond Jubilee of June 1897. This was the occasion when colonial troops, including the Borneo Dyak Police and the Bikanir Camel Corps, were first brought to London, and when a 'pageant of Imperialism' was consciously added to local spectacle. On the one hand, it inspired Kipling to write his 'White Man's Burden' (see above), and, on the other, it moved *The Illustrated London News* to comment on the presence of 'dusky warriors ... at the sight of whom ... the colour distinction was forgotten, even by a London crowd.'[16] The word 'even' is worth noting. The Diamond Jubilee equally moved A. C. Benson to compose the verse which was to move to the heart of the patriotic repertoire:

> Land of Hope and Glory,
> Mother of the Free,
> How can we adore Thee
> Who are born of Thee.
> Wider still and wider
> May thy bounds be set.

God, who made Thee mighty,
Make Thee mightier yet.[17]

The word 'land' is worth noting. It is entirely non-specific.

Following close on the funeral of Queen Victoria, the coronation of
Edward VII in 1902 did not make many innovations. But, by all accounts,
a decision was made in 1911 to increase the imperial component still
further. Quite apart from the festivities in London, the King-Emperor and
Queen-Empress were to travel to India and to receive the obeisance of
their three hundred million Indian subjects in person.

The Delhi *Durbar* was much more than a re-run of the 'Imperial
Assemblage' of 1877. Though staged in December 1911 on the same
site, it called for a greater degree of native participation, and it deliberately exploited the artistic and historic echoes of the Mogul Emperors
three hundred years earlier. *Durbar* was the traditional Persian word
for the Mogul court ceremony where the act of *nuzzur* or 'exchange
of gifts' symbolized the mutual rights and responsibilities of ruler and
ruled.

In 1911, therefore, the durbar took the form of a series of individual
presentations lasting five days. The Emperor and Empress sat on a raised
and covered dais, dressed in their British coronation robes but wearing
specially designed Imperial state crowns. Lines of princes and their
retinues, with their elephants and leashed tigers, moved forward. One by
one, each of the Maharajahs, Rajahiras, and Thakore Sahibs shuffled
forward under their awnings, kneeling, paying homage, and handing
over their gifts, before slowly walking backwards off the dais and
returning to their camp. At the end, the Kaiser-i-Hind addressed his
subjects, announcing the transfer of the capital of India from Calcutta to
Delhi and the eligibility of soldiers of the Indian Army for the Victoria
Cross. The usual 101-gun salute was given a miss: at the Imperial
Assemblage forty years earlier, the opening salvo of the salute had
caused a stampede of elephants that trampled numerous people. The
firework show at the Emperor's Garden Party was also cancelled, since
a spectacular fire had spectacularly destroyed the fireworks. Yet no
mishap was more shocking than the conduct of the Gaekwar of Baroda,

who in a fit of forgetfulness turned his back on the Emperor and left the dais walking forwards.

The imperial couple departed. Their empty thrones were left where they stood. But their loyal subjects still came for weeks afterwards. As reported in London on 6 January, 'tens of thousands of Indians . . . made obeisance after the King and Queen had left – many kneeling, touching the railings, and prostrating themselves in the dust'.[18]

As for the significance of the proceedings, the *Times of India* stated the obvious by a process of question and answer:

> What was signified by the presence here of His Imperial Majesty the King, Emperor of India, monarch of the mightiest empire the world has ever seen, an Empire won by the sword, may be, but held by the steady unfaltering pursuit of peace, tolerance and progress? In the ancient Abbey of Westminster the king received the homage of his own people and the Daughter Nations beyond the Sea: today, in the splendid capital of the Moghuls, Houses which never owned the Moghul allegiance gladly acknowledged his overlordship . . .
>
> What lay behind this splendid pageantry, what force was symbolised in the quiet, dignified figure receiving the acclaim of his Indian subjects? Surely none other than this – the bond of the Empire is the Crown! . . . To India . . . the Crown is the oriflamme of unity . . . to India the crown is the guarantee of stability, of fixity of purpose and continuity of policy . . . to India the crown is the pledge of tolerance and liberality . . . The unity of Empire centres in the Crown: the unity of India is enwrapped in the Crown.[19]

The Delhi Durbar was undoubtedly organized in the expectation of it being the opening event of a permanent series. Yet for reasons beyond the organizers' control, it proved to be both the first and the last. The eldest son of the King-Emperor, Prince Edward, who succeeded as Edward VIII in 1936, abdicated the throne before he could sail to India. The second son, Prince Albert, who succeeded in 1936 as George VI, was caught up almost immediately in the crisis preceding the Second

World War. By the time that George V's granddaughter succeeded to the throne only forty-two years after the Durbar, India was a sovereign republic; and the imperial memories, like those empty thrones on the plain outside Delhi, were gathering the desert dust. The Isles had ceased to be entirely British; and their Empire had ceased to exist. They were, in fact, the 'Post-imperial Isles'.

MANY HISTORIANS HAVE COMMENTED on the barbaric quality of the twentieth century. Two world wars, and the two political plagues of Communism and Fascism, brought more death and destruction to more European countries than at any time in the past. 'There are shades of barbarism in twentieth-century Europe that would once have amazed the most barbarous of barbarians.'[20]

The Isles, however, were one of the few parts of Europe to escape the brunt of those barbarities. Unlike most Continental countries, they were never subject to foreign occupation and its attendant horrors. Unlike most Continental countries, they never had to bear the imposition of either Fascism or Communism, not to mention the double dose of totalitarianism that afflicted the whole of Central Europe for decades. In the First World War, 1914–18, when all the Isles were within the United Kingdom, the British state was a major combatant power, and shed a record sacrifice of blood. Yet the blood was shed in foreign fields. The fighting never crossed onto British soil. In the Second World War, 1939–45, the Republic of Ireland was numbered, like Sweden or Portugal, among the neutrals. The United Kingdom, much reduced since 1922, came under sustained attack first from the air and then from German submarines. But once again, it pulled through intact. In the Cold War, 1948–89, when half of Europe was held in the vice of the Soviet Bloc, both Britain and Ireland contrived to avoid any physical confrontation. Both countries joined the European Economic Community in 1973, thereby propelling themselves into a new phase of their common history in which the old quarrels were in large measure defused.

The twentieth century in the Isles, therefore, has to be periodized in a slightly different way than the rest of Europe. The long

THE DEVOLUTION OF THE UNITED KINGDOM, 1922–1999

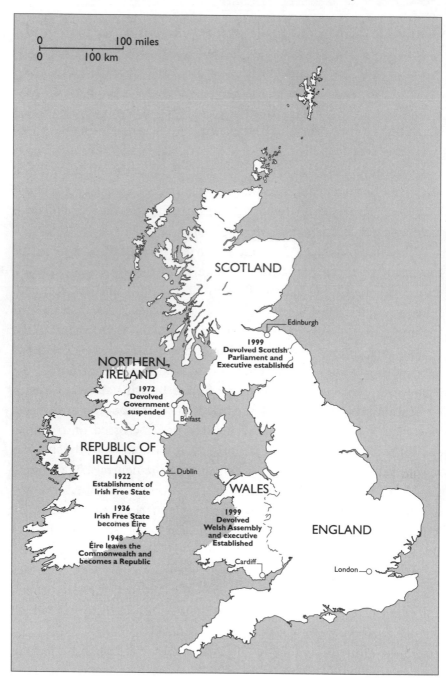

0 — 100 miles
0 — 100 km

SCOTLAND

Edinburgh

1999
Devolved Scottish
Parliament and
Executive established

NORTHERN
IRELAND

1972
Devolved
Government
suspended

Belfast

REPUBLIC OF
IRELAND

1922
Establishment of
Irish Free State

1936
Irish Free State
becomes Éire

1948
Éire leaves the
Commonwealth and
becomes a Republic

Dublin

WALES

1999
Devolved
Welsh Assembly
and executive
Established

ENGLAND

Cardiff

London

Victorian peace ran on, and left the Isles undisturbed right up to 1914. The Great War of 1914–18 saw the first act of the two-part European drama that was to be interrupted by the twenty-year interval. During the Great War, the strains between the British Government and Ireland surfaced in the Easter Rising (1916). At the start of the inter-war period, they led to the Partition that has never been healed. During the Second World War, Ireland's experience as a neutral contrasted starkly with that of a combatant Britain. The contrast continued during the first post-war generation, when Britain, though an active member of NATO and close ally of the USA, was obliged to shed her colonies, whilst Ireland, having departed the Commonwealth, entered the most isolated phase of her existence. From 1973 onwards, however, the paths of the Irish Republic and of the UK began to converge within the European framework. Among much else, they shared a common desire to see an end to the running conflict in Northern Ireland. As the pace of European integration accelerated, they were both faced with the decisions of how far to participate. In 1991, they both signed the Maastricht Treaty for closer union. In 1999, Ireland entered the euro-zone. The UK stayed out, undecided as ever whether to participate in the European movement fully or whether to remain semi-detached. As the end of the millennium approached, Britain was still refraining from casting her die. She still cultivated the special relationship with the USA, whilst continuing as a member of the EU. So long as she could ride the two horses in tandem, she was not ready to choose between them.

(1) NAVAL POWER: A SECONDARY ARM

Less than two years before the Delhi Durbar, on 25 July 1909, Louis Blériot (1872–1936) flew a 25 h.p. monoplane from Les Boraques near Calais to a meadow behind Dover Castle. He was one of three aviators competing for the £1,000 prize offered by the *Daily Mail* for the first aerial crossing of the Channel. At the time, no aeroplane had stayed aloft for more than an hour; and none had flown over the sea. Six days earlier, the British competitor, Hubert Latham, had been forced to ditch in mid-Channel through engine failure. But Blériot made the crossing at dawn in a flight of thirty-seven minutes, landing at 5.19 a.m. with the help of a colleague waving a large tricolour. 'I alighted more heavily than anticipated,' he told *The Times*, 'and the monoplane was damaged.' *The Times* commiserated with Hubert Latham, reflecting on the huge progress still to be made 'before aviation was a viable method of transportation'. *The Illustrated London News* was nearer the mark, writing of 'the inauguration of a new era in the history of the world'.[21]

If Blériot's flight had been observed from the deck of a Royal Navy warship, the sailors would undoubtedly have thought it a jolly good prank. But blessed with foresight, the observers might have realized that Blériot had done something that Vice-Admiral Villeneuve had failed to do at Trafalgar. He had demonstrated that the power of the Royal Navy could be bypassed, and that the British Empire could not be defended indefinitely by its ships. It took less than forty years for these changes to become self-evident.

For the time being, the Royal Navy was still unmatched, but not for long. During the First World War, the most important strategic development did not lie in the Royal Navy's successful maintenance of its supremacy against the German fleet. It lay in the little noticed fact that both the USA and Japan had managed to build more warships than Britain. By the end of the war, therefore, US–Japanese rivalry in the Pacific emerged as the key issue of naval strategy. What is more, at the Washington Conference on Naval Limitation, American negotiators were able to insist that the US Navy hold parity with the Royal Navy. In the Washington Treaty (1922), the world's leading naval establishments were fixed on the ratio of 5 for the US and the UK, 3 for Japan, and 1.67 for France and Italy. The Admiralty's goal as set by the Naval Defence Act (1889), of building a navy equal to the combined strength of the next two largest navies, and had been achieved by 1914. It had now vanished. Yet even parity with the US soon proved to be based on a false assessment. In 1936 the Washington Treaty expired. In September 1940, in order to defend herself against German submarines, Britain was forced through the 'Destroyers-for-Bases Deal' to acquire fifty obsolete American First World War destroyers in return for ninety-nine-year leases to the US Navy on six colonial naval bases in the British West Indies. From that point on, it was crystal clear that British naval supremacy had been lost for ever.

Developments in military technology were pointing in the same direction. Britain launched the world's first purpose-built aircraft carrier, HMS *Argus*, in 1917 but thereafter she was rapidly outstripped by the USA in the production both of aircraft and of carriers. In 1940, the RAF managed to defend Britain against the Luftwaffe by the skin of its teeth; but in the subsequent Strategic Bombing Offensive, the vastly superior capacity of the USAAF inevitably gave it a commanding role. In the key development of nuclear weapons and of intercontinental missiles, Britain played the part of a loyal but junior partner. But the general trend confirmed a state of affairs which a British Prime Minister had already realized in the early 1930s when he forecast that 'the bomber will always get through':

> The only defence is in offence, which means that you have to kill more women and children more quickly than the enemy if you want to save yourselves.[22]

Stanley Baldwin also realized that the advent of airpower had overturned the significance of traditional geographical boundaries:

> Since the day of the air, the old frontiers are gone. When you think of the defence of England, you no longer think of the chalk cliffs of Dover; you think of the Rhine. That is where our frontier lies.[23]

Thirty years after Baldwin, another Prime Minister, Harold Wilson, was saying 'Our frontier is on the Himalayas'. In the era of ICBMs, navies had been reduced to a secondary arm. The real lines of defence had moved into air and space.

Throughout the Cold War Era, the Royal Navy held its place as the number three fleet in the world, having been overtaken by the Soviet navy. But it was only able to do so by abandoning a global presence. Already in the 1940s, after the spectacular sinking of HMS *Prince of Wales* and *Repulse* by the Japanese and the disastrous fall of Singapore, Britain had silently abandoned the defence of Australasia to its own fleets. After the Suez Crisis of 1956, she could no longer mount regular patrols in the Indian or Pacific Oceans. After 1949, the great part of Britain's armed forces, including the navy, were designated to NATO. As a member of NATO, she had to subordinate all her major military policies to the decisions of an international alliance. She was forced to abandon the very idea of sovereign, independent defences.

Within this overall framework, the British Admiralty had no choice but to adapt to NATO-based structures and to accept a much reduced role. In 1961, by the Nassau Agreement, it learned that its leading weaponry was to be based on submarine-based ballistic missiles supplied by the USA. In 1964, it lost its separate standing to become one of three equal departments in a unified Ministry of Defence. In the late 1960s, when the UK's main strategic nuclear-delivery system was transferred from the RAF to the navy's *Trident*-class submarines, it could be argued that a measure of naval pride had been regained. Both the warheads and the submarines were British-built. But the victory was largely symbolic. In the sixty years since Blériot's flight, the Royal Navy had been quite literally decimated. So, too, had the merchant fleet. Britain's once mighty shipyards were fast disappearing. Expenditure on the naval sector of the defence budget had dropped from 'the lion's share' of 54 per cent in 1906 to 28 per cent in 1965.[24] Since 1945, expenditure on the army and the RAF has always exceeded that on the navy, both separately and jointly. And maintenance of the Trident system was entirely dependent on the supply of American missiles, American technology, and American good-will. The navy was almost reduced to a ferry company for the other services. In 1998 it possessed three aircraft carriers and one helicopter carrier, two assault ships, fifteen submarines, thirty-five destroyers and frigates, nineteen mine hunters, and thirty-five other vessels.[25]

In the last three decades, therefore, the United Kingdom has remained a solid, second-class power. But its freedom of manoeuvre in the military sphere is very constricted. By 1999, the idea that 'Britannia rules the waves' had become as remote as the idea that anyone but the USA ruled land, sea, air, or space.

Britain's position as a world power had been built on naval supremacy. In the second quarter of the twentieth century, Britain's naval supremacy was permanently overturned first by the rise of air power and then by the rise of the United States. Britain's position in the world inexorably declined.

(2) THE BRITISH ARMY: MEMORIES OF GLORY

Britain's military establishment has been subject to ceaseless change throughout the twentieth century. In the First World War, the army was obliged to transform itself in 1916 into a mass conscript force. For the first and only time in its history, it assumed proportions of a similar magnitude to those of its Continental counterparts. As a result, it suffered casualties on an unprecedented and unrepeated scale. As Churchill once mentioned in *My Early Life*, British soldiers during his time in the army in the 1890s had expected to survive a battle; in the trenches of the Western Front, they expected to die. Rupert Brooke (1887–1915), probably the most popular of the War Poets despite some dubious traits, was dripping with nostalgia for England when he stayed in Berlin in 1912:

> Stands the Church clock at ten to three?
> And is there honey still for tea?[26]

But when he reached the front two years later, he was consciously preparing himself for almost certain death:

If I should die, think only this of me:
> That there's some corner of a foreign field
That is for ever England. There shall be
> In that rich earth a richer dust concealed;
A dust whom England bore, shaped, made aware,
> Gave, once, her flowers to love, her ways to roam,
A body of England's, breathing England's air,
> Washed by the rivers, blest by the suns of home.[27]

The Battle of the Somme, 1 July to 18 November 1916, was a defining moment. On the first day, the British lost 57,470 casualties, mostly young volunteers. Over fourteen weeks in that one sector, they lost 419,654. Combined Allied losses reached perhaps 150 per cent of German losses. This was the catastrophe that raised the slogan 'Never Again'. It convinced the British Prime Minister, Lloyd George, of his generals' incompetence.

In the Second World War, conscript armies were raised again, but they were used with much greater caution. Thanks to the air war, the civilian population was almost as vulnerable as the military. After the disaster of 1940, when the German Blitzkrieg rapidly broke the combined French and British armies, British soldiers were never put into a major Continental campaign until they could do so in the company of American forces twice their size. The campaigns in North Africa, 1941–3, and Italy, 1943–5, were important diversions, but essentially peripheral. The D-Day Landings in Normandy in June 1944 did not take place until the Wehrmacht was already beating its long retreat in the East before a victorious Soviet Army, which inflicted 75 per cent of total German losses.

There is a curious correlation between relative military weakness and the exploitation of intelligence. Countries that can't hope to defeat the enemy through firepower will try to undermine the enemy through brainpower. Britain's Polish allies, for example, were very good at codebreaking. In 1920, they had intercepted the Red Army codes; and in the 1930s they succeeded not only in penetrating German military ciphers but also in building a model of the

Germans' secret Enigma encrypting machine. In 1939, they were able to pass on their knowledge to both the British and the French.[28] By that time German cryptology had moved on, but the British were given a head start in breaking Germany's unbreakable codes. In supplying the Allied leadership with daily doses of invaluable information from the Ultra secret, British codebreakers at Bletchley Park compensated for other shortcomings and achieved one of most priceless contributions to the war effort.[29] In the process, by constructing the Colossus machine (1943) they introduced the world to the era of computers.

In the post-war world, the bulk of British forces were assigned to NATO (1949–); National Service, i.e., conscription, was abandoned in 1961; and policy was directed to building an ever smaller but ever more efficient and technically modernized force. The statistics of British military manpower speaks worlds:

1918: 8,500,000   1944: 5,067,000   1975: 338,000   1999: 119,000.[30]

The policy of 'Appeasement', which surfaced in the 1930s, was not born from cowardice, but from the sober calculation that Britain's military resources were insufficient to meet the Empire's commitments. That calculation proved accurate. In 1940–45, Britain was only able to keep fighting by drawing on the selfless and often unappreciated sacrifice of the Dominions and the Indian Army; by deploying the substantial units of allied Poles, Czechs, and Free French; by relying on the decisive support of the United States; and, to cover the deficiencies until American might could be brought to bear, by entering an alliance with Stalin's Soviet Union. Winston Churchill, whose heroic leadership of the war effort made survival possible, had few illusions about the moral contamination that the alliance with Stalin involved. He had a sound anti-communist record. He well knew that Stalin's commitment to democracy and freedom was no greater than Hitler's. 'If Hitler invaded hell,' he once declared, 'I would make at least a favourable reference to the devil in the House of Commons.'[31] He was as good as his word.

After Hitler invaded the Soviet Union in 1941, Churchill made many favourable references to 'Uncle Joe'. And the British Government turned a blind eye to Stalin's mass crimes.

After 1945, Britain's former worldwide military commitments were bound to shrink. All engagement in India was avoided; and Britain resigned the mandate in Palestine rather than police the Arab–Israeli conflict after 1948. In the 1950s and 60s, the British army was still able to combine its standing contribution to NATO with a series of local actions provoked by decolonization in Malaya (1948–56), Kenya (1952–9), and Aden (1959–63). But after 1969, when 20 per cent of action-ready units had to be earmarked for service in Northern Ireland, and when deep financial cuts were constantly imposed, there was very little chance of involvement either outside Europe or beyond assignments paid for by others. In 1945, being counted among the victors, the United Kingdom obtained a seat on the UN Security Council. But like France she had long since ceased to play in the same military league as the USA, the USSR, or China.

Britain fought her last independent war in 1982 for the recovery of the remote Falkland or Malvinas Islands.[32] Little attention was paid to the Spanish/Argentine territorial claim, which dated from the Treaty of Tordesillas (1494) and long predated the unilateral colonization of the islands by a handful of British settlers; and diplomatic negotiations failed. The British case was greatly helped by the fact that the Argentine force was sent by a dictator hostile to US interests in South America. The British Prime Minister, Margaret Thatcher, confident of covert US political and intelligence support, launched a multi-arm task force which sailed from Portsmouth on 5 April. A Marine band on the deck of HMS *Invincible* played 'Don't Cry for Me, Argentina'. The capture of South Georgia, the sinking of the Argentine cruiser *General Belgrano* outside the war zone, and the hotly contested landing at San Carlos all prepared the way for the British advance on Stanley and the final Argentine surrender (14 June). British and Argentine dead combined did not exceed 1,000 men. By earlier standards it was a skirmish, not a war. A solution of the dispute over the sovereignty of the Falklands/Malvinas was never agreed. The ability of the British armed forces to mount another similar operation independently remained open to serious question.

Nearly twenty years later, the British military establishment had contracted still further. After the latest Strategic Defence Review (July 1998),[33] the strength of the Army's core infantry units stood at a mere forty battalions. Two of the three battle-ready divisions plus one air mobile brigade were designated for NATO's ARRC – Allied Rapid Reaction Corps. A British contingent served briefly in the Gulf War, and others were sent under UN auspices to Cyprus (1993), to Bosnia (1995), and to Kosovo (1999). The RAF possessed 798 fixed-wing aeroplanes and 116 helicopters. But the long imperial withdrawal had virtually reached its term. British troops left Gibraltar, Belize, Berlin (1994), and, most symbolically, Hong Kong (1997). Total defence expenditure has fallen in absolute terms from £24,562 billion in 1991–2 to £21,122 billion in 1997–98.[34] One single company, the Falklands Resident Infantry Company (Royal Anglian Regiment), of 120 men, stood guard on the Falklands (with a guard ship, a patrol ship, and a support tanker permanently on station) at the largest of the fourteen remaining imperial outposts beyond Europe. As a historian, it is hard not to think of the last Roman centurion and his men who once mounted the last lonely guard on Hadrian's Wall.

Nonetheless, despite realities, memories of military glory still stayed unusually strong in the United Kingdom. Unlike every other European power, the United Kingdom had the good fortune never to suffer foreign occupation or permanent defeat. In this, the British experience was much closer to that of the Americans for whom (Pearl Harbor excepted), twentieth-century war has always been a distant, foreign adventure. As a result, British myths, like the English myths before them, lived on unchallenged; and an institutionalized 'cenotaph culture' perpetuated a simplistic and moralistic view of the past. One such myth, which holds that war crimes were only committed by our enemies and never by our allies, was given legal form in the recent War Crimes Act (1991). According to the official

British definition, war crimes and crimes against humanity could only have been committed by German agents or in German-occupied territory. (The mass murder of about 27,000 Allied officers, who were all shot in the neck in 1940 on territory not yet occupied by the Wehrmacht, did not, in British law, count as a crime.)[35]

But a generational phenomenon was also in evidence. The generation who grew to maturity in 1914–18 and who lost an unequalled legion of dead and mutilated brothers, husbands, fiancés, and fathers, had still been the dominant British opinion-formers after 1945. Many of the men and women who fought the good fight in 1939–45 in conditions of unequalled social and patriotic solidarity would live to see the turn of the millennium. Their unquestioning, and occasionally nationalistic, perceptions of Britishness, as formed in the twilight era of the Empire, were still in circulation. The intense scrutiny of pre-war attitudes, which had occurred in both post-Fascist and in post-Communist countries, had never taken place on the British side of the Channel. One had to be very young indeed never to have heard a relative talking of D-Day or the Somme, or to have heard an uncle whistling 'The Road to Mandalay'.

Yet the exceptional British stance toward the World Wars was obviously as finite as the life expectancy of the generation which persisted in cultivating their memory. Soon after the turn of the millennium, British attitudes would inevitably be dominated by younger people for whome the 'war against Hitler' would be as remote as those against Napoleon or the Spanish Armada.

(3) The British Empire: All in the Past

That empires rise and fall is one of history's truisms. It is less obvious that they can be rising and falling at one and the same time. Yet such was the fate of the British Empire at the end of the First World War. A substantial piece of 'the inner empire' – Ireland – began to break away at a time when substantial items were still being added to the 'outer empire'. This was a rather more satisfactory state of affairs than elsewhere in Europe, where in 1917–18 the Russian, Austro-Hungarian, and German empires collapsed completely.

At the time, few people realized that the downward slide had started. The demand for 'Irish Home Rule' was not seen as fragmentation, but rather was explained away as a change to dominion status. In May 1917, the South African General Smuts made an optimistic overall assessment: 'The British Empire is much more than a state,' he declared. 'We are a system of states, and not a stationary system, but a dynamic and evolving system, always going forward to new destinies . . .'[36] A modern historian found a similar formula for the same idea. 'The British Empire was in reality a *cluster* of empires', he wrote, 'a congeries of different parts moving at different speeds.'[37] What is more, no deep hostility towards the Empire ever developed within British home opinion. As George Orwell noted during his visit to working-class Lancashire in the 1930s:

> at the bottom of his heart no Englishman . . . does want it [the Empire] to disintegrate. For, apart from any other consideration, the high standard of life we enjoy in England depends upon our keeping a tight hold on the Empire, particularly the tropical portions of it such as India and Africa . . . The alternative is to throw the Empire overboard and reduce England to a cold and unimportant little island where we should all have to work very hard and live mainly on herrings and potatoes.[38]

Subsequent analysis of the Empire's decline has taken two opposite directions. The more extreme of them has been described as 'downhill all the way':

> . . . the real significance of the empire for Britain was that it had cushioned her fall in the world. From 1870 to 1970 the history of Britain was one of steady and almost unbroken decline, economically, militarily and politically, relative to other nations, from the peak of prosperity and power which her industrial revolution had achieved for her in the middle of the

nineteenth century. The empire, which she had accumulated towards the end of that century, and then lost, was an incident in the course of that decline. It was acquired originally as a result of that decline, to stave it off. It was retained largely in spite of that decline. And it was eventually surrendered as a final confirmation of that decline.[39]

The opposite line of argument chose to stress the skill with which the Empire's decline was supposedly managed, and the remarkable transition from authoritarian Empire to consensual Commonwealth. It inevitably led to the interesting question, 'Why did the British Empire last so long?'[40]

By the late nineteenth century, Irish people were playing an active part not only in the United Kingdom but in the Empire at large. In 1893 John Redmond MP drew attention to their positive contributions:

In the creation of the empire, in the government of the empire, in the councils of the empire, in the exercise of those virtues and talents, which are necessary for the practice of the arts of government, I say that Irishmen have proved themselves equal to the best of Englishmen or Scotchmen or Welshmen.[41]

The Irish were widely accepted as members of the imperial family of peoples. The only trouble, as Redmond reminded Parliament, was that 'the one spot' where the Irish could not fully practise their virtues and talents was 'the land of their birth and affection'.[42] In a period of growing national sentiment, therefore (see below), the postponement in 1914 of the Home Rule Act had serious and unforeseen consequences. It led in the first instance to an armed Rising by a small group of separatists, and then, on the violent suppression of the Rising, to a rapid shift in Irish opinion. Within four years, the predominant Irish demands changed from Home Rule to independence. Ireland was to set a precedent that would reverberate throughout the Empire.

The Easter Rising of 1916 was the work of a small, and at the

time unrepresentative, group of Irish revolutionaries headed by
Patrick Pearse (1879–1916). It was the natural culmination of a
movement started three years earlier to form an armed force of
Irish Volunteers, the Oglaigh na hEireann, to oppose the Ulster
Volunteers and their attempts to obstruct Home Rule. Pearse's
group occupied the General Post Office and other strongpoints in
Dublin on 24 April, proclaimed the Irish Republic from the Post
Office steps, and held out for five days against heavy gunfire before
surrendering. From their point of view, they were seizing a moment
of British weakness during the Great War to make a dramatic
gesture for Irish freedom. From the government's point of view,
they were a senseless group of traitors, who had betrayed the
hundred and thirty thousand Irish soldiers who were loyally serving
and dying in the British army on the Western Front. Pearse and
fourteen of his companions were summarily tried and shot in
Kilmainham Jail.

On the Christmas before his death at Easter, Patrick Pearse had
made a strange pronouncement. 'The ghosts of a nation', he said,
'sometimes ask very big things, and they must be appeased, whatever the costs.'[43] Committed Irish republicans have been appeasing
those ghosts ever since. Their credo lies in the words of Pearse's
Proclamation:

> Irishmen and Irishwomen! In the name of God and of these
> dead generations from which she receives the tradition of
> nationhood, Ireland, through us, summons her children to the
> flag . . . We declare the right of the people of Ireland to the
> ownership of Ireland and to the unfettered control of Irish
> destinies, to be sovereign and indefeasible. The long usurpation
> of that right by a foreign people and government has not
> extinguished the right, nor can it ever be extinguished except
> by the destruction of the Irish people. In every generation the
> Irish people have asserted it in arms. Standing on that funda-
> mental right and again asserting it in arms in the face of the
> world, we hereby proclaim the Irish Republic as a Sovereign

Independent State, and we pledge our lives and the lives of our comrades-in-arms to the cause of its freedom, and its welfare and its exaltation among the nations.

The Irish Republic is entitled to, and hereby claims the allegiance of every Irishman and Irishwoman. The Republic guarantees religious and civil liberty, equal rights and equal opportunities to all its citizens, and declares its resolve to pursue the happiness and prosperity of the whole nation and of all its parts, cherishing all the children of the nation equally, and oblivious of the differences, carefully fostered by an alien government, which have divided a minority from the majority in the past. We place the cause of the Irish Republic under the protection of the Highest God ... In this supreme hour, the Irish nation ... must, by the readiness of its children to sacrifice themselves for the common good, prove itself worthy of the august destiny to which it is called.[44]

At the time, it was a despairing, defiant gesture.

Nonetheless, the Rising provoked the intended effect. The mood changed both in Ireland and abroad. Within six months of the Rising's suppression, W. B. Yeats was penning the lines that would make it famous:

> I write it out in verse –
> MacDonagh and MacBride
> And Connolly and Pearse
> Now and in time to be,
> Wherever the green is worn,
> Are changed, changed utterly:
> A terrible beauty is born.[45]

In 1917–18, educated British opinion found it increasingly difficult to explain why independence should be recommended for assorted Czechs, Poles, and Arabs, but not for the Irish. Irish Catholic opinion swung dramatically beyond Home Rule to favour a republic. After the General Election of December 1918, seventy-eight Sinn Féin MPs refused to take their seats at Westminster, preferring to create their own Dáil or republican Parliament in Dublin.

The British–Irish War of 1919–21 is known in Ireland as the War of Independence. It saw state terror perpetrated by units of the paramilitary 'Black and Tans' answered by a terrorist campaign of assassinations and bombings organized by 'the Big Fellow', Michael Collins (1890–1922), a survivor of the Easter Rising. Perhaps the most damaging incident occurred at Croke Park, Dublin, where, in a reprisal raid, a British armoured car drove onto the pitch of a Gaelic football match and opened fire on the players. A footballer was shot dead; dozens were killed in the stampede; and the infuriated crowd lynched some men thought to be auxiliaries. Within a year, all the institutions of British government, including the burned-out tax offices, were paralysed in all parts of Ireland except eastern Ulster. Lloyd George's policy of Irish Home Rule could not be implemented except in Northern Ireland (see below). For many months preceding the truce of 11 July 1921, the authorities of the British crown and those of the rebel Republic operated in parallel.

The Anglo-Irish Treaty, negotiated in 1921 and ratified in 1922, was the fruit of mutual concessions. Lloyd George abandoned Home Rule under Westminster. Michael Collins abandoned the claim to a fully independent sovereign republic. Both in practice abandoned a united Ireland and reluctantly accepted the fait accompli of Partition. Six counties of Ulster were to remain within the United Kingdom as the self-governing province of Northern Ireland. The remaining twenty-six counties were to form an Irish Free State with dominion status similar to that of Canada or Australia; and all Free State officials were to swear allegiance to the British crown. In the United Kingdom, the Treaty caused unresolved turmoil that continued to the end of the century. In the Free State, it provoked a vicious civil war. The 'pro-treaty' party was defeated; Michael Collins was assassinated. The hard-line anti-treaty faction of another survivor of the Easter Rising, Eamon de Valera (1882–1975), triumphed. It was only a matter of time before de Valera's government would denounce the Treaty and overthrow the Free State.[46] Few people in the British Isles noticed that the United Kingdom had lost a larger percentage of its territory than Germany had.

Throughout the twentieth century, a secret society of Irish republican fundamentalists continued to wage war and terror for their unrealized ideals. They traced their roots to the Irish volunteers of 1913, but took their name of the Irish Republican Army (IRA) during their struggle against the 'Free Staters' in 1922–3. They gave rise to the Fianna Fáil Party of de Valera; but then turned against his accommodation with the Commonwealth. In the post-war decades, they concentrated on the struggle for what they saw as 'the liberation' of Northern Ireland. Outlawed both in the Republic and in the Kingdom, they were increasingly driven into criminal activities of all sorts. After incessant splits and feuds, a new Sinn Féin emerged as the political wing of the (Provisional) IRA. Only at the end of the century did one branch of the movement show signs of wanting to pursue their goals by political as distinct from violent means.

The two inter-war decades saw some parts of the British Empire flourish, whilst others floundered. At the end of the First World War, the United Kingdom claimed three prizes. It took the entire German High Seas fleet, the most modern units of which, eleven battleships, five battle-cruisers, eight light cruisers, and fifty destroyers, were interned under the terms of the Armistice only to be scuttled by their commander. It received a game-bag of ex-German colonies including Tanganyika, South-West Africa, and New Guinea. And it obtained League of Nations mandates to govern the ex-Ottoman territories of Palestine, Transjordan, and Iraq. The ex-German colonies completed the dream of Cecil Rhodes for a continuous British domain 'from the Cape to Cairo', whilst constituting a fund for colonial sub-lets administered by the dominions.

The League of Nations mandates caused nothing but trouble. In Palestine, the Arab population became outraged not only by the influx of Jewish settlers but also by the Zionist interpretations of

the Balfour Declaration (1917) which took British support for a Jewish 'national home' to mean British support for an exclusive
Jewish state.[47] In Jordan and Iraq, armed force was used to suppress opposition before independent monarchical states could be
established.

In 1931, by the Statute of Westminster, the British Commonwealth of Nations came into existence as a distinct grouping of
states within the Empire. In the first instance, it consisted of the six
self-governing 'white' dominions – Canada, Newfoundland, Australia, New Zealand, South Africa, and the Irish Free State – though it
was consciously intended as a model for future developments. Yet
the overcaution of British policy was demonstrated by events in
India. The forum of local politics, the Indian National Congress, had
been operating since 1885. But in successive Government of India
Acts, 1919 and 1935, Indian leaders were granted no more than a
subordinate role, and all central powers remained with the Viceroy.
During riots in 1930 provoked by a salt tax, Mohandas Gandhi
(1869–1948), 'the Mahatma', launched a mass campaign of non-
violent civil disobedience, which, with time, became unstoppable.

The causes of the Empire's decline are easy to recognize in
retrospect. 'Imperial Overstretch', which was apparent before the
Second World War and which became acute thereafter, obviously
stands high on the list. So, too, do the export of European-style
nationalism to every continent of the globe, and the growing climate
of 'anti-colonialism' which gathered pace after the founding of the
United Nations. Yet, in the British case, special factors were at work.
One of these was the 'Economic Dunkirk' which stared Britain in
the face after 1945. Another from 1941 onwards was Britain's growing
dependence on the USA, a dominant ally which used anti-imperial
rhetoric whilst itself pursuing an informal variant of imperialism
exercised largely by economic means. The intricacies of the Anglo-
American Alliance, both during and after the war, ensured that
decolonization would take place, but also that it would not be given
absolute priority over the exigencies of the Cold War.

Strategic factors, not fully formulated at the time, also played a crucial part. In 1939, the United Kingdom faced a terrible dilemma – either to re-enter the European arena, as in 1914, and to put the Empire at risk, or, by giving priority to the preservation of the Empire, to leave Europe to the tender mercies of Hitler and Stalin. Unwilling though he was, the Prime Minister, Neville Chamberlain, eventually chose to intervene in Europe. By so doing, he accelerated the processes by which Britain would lose its empire.

By 1945, the Labour government of Clement Attlee realized that Britain was fast losing the means to hold down its Empire by force. The British army was being demobilized. The Indian Army could no longer be relied on. Communist forces had swallowed Eastern Europe whole, and were threatening Greece. Palestine was the scene of Zionist terrorism: India of mass civil disobedience. A wartime round-up of Congress Party activists in India, including Jawaharlal Nehru (1889–1964), had only increased unrest, and Field Marshall Wavell, Viceroy since 1943, was advocating retreat. 'The really fatal thing for us', he advised, 'would be to hang on to responsibility when we had lost the power to exercise it.'[48] Ernest Bevin, the Foreign Secretary, considered Wavell a defeatist. In the end, Attlee opted for a middle course of orderly retreat dressed up as a deliberate, forward-thinking, liberal policy. The vital decisions were taken amidst the power cuts and food shortages of Christmas 1947. The defence of Greece was to be left to the Americans; and Palestine was to be handed to the UN. India was already being granted full self-government within the Commonwealth.

The transfer of power in India was put into the hands of Admiral Louis Mountbatten (1900–79), created Earl Mountbatten of Burma in 1947 and the last Viceroy. He was given a tight schedule, and told that British troops must not be used to keep the peace. As a result, he could not prevent the partition of India, the emergence of the Muslim Republic of Pakistan, and the separation of both Burma and Ceylon. Five hundred thousand people lost their lives in communal violence. But Mountbatten and his consort, Lady Edwina, pulled out in style; and no British soldiers were killed. Churchill, now leader of HM Opposition, was horrified:

The British Empire seems to be running off almost as fast as the American Loan. The steady and remorseless process of divesting ourselves of what has been gained by so many generations of toil, administration and sacrifice continues. In the case of Burma . . . this haste is appalling. 'Scuttle' is the only word that can be applied.[49]

Independent Burma left the Commonwealth. Ceylon became a dominion.

The Conservative Governments of Churchill (1951–5) and Anthony Eden (1955–7) conducted themselves with considerably less *sagesse*; and were virtually stampeded by events. Churchill in his old age had no heart for decolonization. His Foreign Secretary, Eden, proved to be a complacent gradualist. Only Harold Macmillan, Minister of Defence, seemed to have some sort of vision of moving towards 'a third British Empire'. In 1951, they were taken by surprise by the nationalization of Persian oil, and in 1952 by the revolution in Egypt. The Suez Crisis of 1956 brought British fortunes to their nadir. At least rhetorically, Eden considered President Nasser a new Hitler; and he treated the nationalization of the Suez Canal Company as a more immediate threat to British interests than Hitler's invasion of Poland. Worst of all, having plotted with the French and the Israelis, he failed to tell Washington about his plans for military intervention. The outcome was a fiasco. The Franco-British expeditionary force was obliged to withdraw from Egypt under American pressure. Nasser triumphed. One of Eden's critics called it 'Britain's Waterloo'. The psychological trauma, as observed by a colonial governor, looked irreparable:

[O]ne of the worst things that has happened to us . . . particularly since Suez, is that in the Middle East we have lost confidence in our ability to deal with situations. The loss of confidence is a very odd thing – it is something, which has happened inside us and bears no particular relation to the facts as observed in the field. Our Suez fiasco seems, in effect, to have left a far deeper mark on ourselves than on the Arabs.[50]

It is all to the credit of the ensuing government of Harold Macmillan, therefore, that the torrent of ensuing colonial crises was handled with skill and aplomb. Special credit is usually awarded in this to Iain Macleod, who was Colonial Secretary for only two of Macmillan's six years in office, but who left his stamp on the overall strategy. Macmillan set out to ride the tide, not to stop it. At every turn, whether by establishing sovereign bases in Cyprus or a long lease on the Valetta dockyard in Malta, he sought to grant independence on terms that were favourable to Britain. He was keen on regional federations, as in the West Indies or in Central Africa. They didn't often work; but they acted as a useful transitional stage towards full independence. Above all, he sought to find moderate leaders in the nationalist movements, who would act as partners and buffers against extremism.

In Africa, the charismatic figure of Kwame Nkrumah, from his base in the Gold Coast (Ghana), was advocating a Pan-African revolution. Foreign Office advice was unequivocal:

> Nkrumah is our enemy, he is determined to complete our expulsion from an Africa which he aspires to dominate absolutely . . . We, being white, cannot hope to fight him openly in Africa. Ergo: we must find blacks who can; and although it would be counter-productive to damn them with our old colonial kiss, yet surely it is not beyond our ingenuity to find effective ways of affording them discreet and legitimate support?[51]

Here were the circumstances in which Macleod came into his own. He stood behind Macmillan's famous 1960 speech about 'A wind of change blowing through Africa' which was delivered first in Accra (Ghana) and then in Cape Town (South Africa), actively encouraging demands for decolonization. He accelerated the timetable of independence in several colonies, on average by ten years; and he recruited former opponents, like Jomo Kenyatta, the convicted leader of the Mau Mau in Kenya, as partners. By 1964 the process of decolonization was essentially complete. Rhodesia alone remained intractable. But, by and large, the British had avoided the blood and chaos surrounding the imperial retreat of France and Belgium. Power had gone; influence remained.

The Empire had evaporated with amazing speed. The historic name was dropped in 1958 when 'Empire Day' was changed to 'Commonwealth Day'. But the Commonwealth declined almost as speedily. From being a tightly knit association of ex-Imperial nations, it soon became a marginalized talking-shop with very limited political clout. In 1949, the 'British' label was dropped even there. South Africa, which left in 1961, was readmitted in 1994. Ireland, which had left in 1949, did not apply to rejoin. The Commonwealth's newest member was Cameroon, which joined in 1995.

The impact of the Empire on perceptions of Britishness, however, was enormous. Some historians have argued that the growth of empire overseas had been even more critical in the crystallization of British consciousness than were the home-grown factors of naval power, monarchy, Protestantism, and English culture.[52] What is certain is that Empire engendered no simple or universal view of Britishness. In some people, it encouraged feelings of xenophobia and superiority, strengthening the older English traditions of domination and exclusivity:

> There cannot be the slightest doubt that empire was a major
> component in British people's sense of their own identity, that
> it helped to integrate the United Kingdom, and to distinguish it
> in the eyes of its own citizens from other European countries.
> Empire reinforced a hierarchical view of the world, in which
> the British occupied a pre-eminent place among the colonial
> powers, while those subjected to colonial rule were ranged
> below them in varying degrees of supposed inferiority.[53]

In other people, empire was mainly associated with pride in liberal values, with the spread of freedom and self-government over five governments and the worldwide struggle for decency and civilization. In the minds of just a few, it provoked feelings of shame. Whatever it did, whether as a nightmare or the dream of a lost golden age, it was all in the past.

On 30 June 1997, the British withdrew in style from their last major colony – Hong Kong. Elgar's *Nimrod* was played. Royal Marine buglers sounded the Last Post. The dignitaries stood to attention. The guard of Gurkhas saluted. The flags were lowered in the teeming, tropical rain. The last Governor wept. The hand of the incoming Chief Executive, representing People's China, was shaken. The official party departed aboard the Royal Yacht *Britannia* on her last voyage before the scrapyard. They were treated to a grand naval review by the largest fleet of British ships to sail the China Seas since the fall of Singapore. They were then put ashore in order to be flown home. The next day, the last Governor was carrying his own cases at Heathrow and looking for a taxi.[54]

(4) PROTESTANT SUPREMACY: 'AN EXPRESSION OF CULTURE'

Shortly after the Napoleonic Wars, when the old Kingdom of Prussia was reconstructed to absorb both the Catholic Rhineland and other new territories with a predominantly non-Lutheran tradition, the Prussian authorities felt impelled to create a united Protestant state Church. Without such an organization, it was felt, the Protestants of Prussia could not speak with one voice and could not exercise their customary ascendancy. No such step was ever taken in the United Kingdom. Despite its Erastian origins, the Church of England never caught up with the successive modifications in the state and the monarchy. It has not been a true state Church since 1707. It saw no reason to change its ways when the state became British instead of English, nor when the state took on a large contingent of Irish Catholics in 1801. As a result it has had to watch as its former standing eroded. Barred by the Act of Union from touching the

Church of Scotland, it lost its privileged position in Ireland and in Wales; and it survived with the trappings of establishment but with the substance of a regional sect. It was entirely dependent on the British state. Its bishops were appointed by the Crown on the advice of Prime Ministers who did not need to be either English or Christians, let alone Anglicans. The legislation of its General Synod was still subject to Parliament, even though the majority of parliamentarians became non-believers. Yet the Anglican hierarchy had no special authority in the kingdom as a whole. The Church of England was *not* the established Church of the United Kingdom. The Archbishop of Canterbury was *not* the British Primate. He had no right to speak on behalf of British Protestants, let alone of all British Christians. On the eve of the twenty-first century, the British state had never addressed an issue which Prussia resolved at the start of the nineteenth. The status quo persist through sheer inertia. After all that time, it had no chance whatsoever to be solved on the Prussian model.

In essence, the Church of England could have chosen to do one of two things. It could have stayed as it was, the plaything of 'godless political machinery'. Or, as some of its thoughtful clergy now said openly, it could have accepted realities and begged for its freedom.[55] If it had done the latter and accepted disestablishment, it would have finally lost 'the chains' that were forged by Henry VIII. But it would also have driven the final nail into the coffin of the Protestant Establishment. That might have been no retrograde step. For in the United Kingdom as a whole, the Protestant Establishment, and the accompanying political ideology of the Protestant Ascendancy, had been dead as dodos for decades past.

In the 1990s, the religious scene in the United Kingdom had been largely determined by a series of fundamental shifts that made themselves manifest in the course of the twentieth century.

Almost all the religious denominations in the United Kingdom, for example, formed part of worldwide communities that had long since outdistanced any national boundaries. The Church of England stood at the centre of a global episcopalian communion, whose practicants elsewhere in the English-speaking world outnumbered those in England itself. The Church of Scotland was the mother of an international Presbyterian family that was widely represented in the old dominions. All the Nonconformist Churches had a strong presence overseas. The three Roman Catholic provinces in the United Kingdom answered to the Vatican in Rome, as did all other provinces of the world's largest Christian Church. Religion could no longer be seen in purely national or religious terms.

After many tribulations, the Roman Catholic Church had finally won parity of esteem. Having shaken off its historic shackles, it now commanded a larger body of churchgoers than any other denomination. The almost universal chorus of acclaim which attended the death of Cardinal Basil Hume (1923–99), a model Englishman, a Benedictine monk, and for twenty-three years the Archbishop of Westminster, could only partly be explained by his personal virtues. So, too, could his award of the Order of Merit. It also marked a change in public attitudes. His funeral was attended among others by the Prime Minister and the Prince of Wales. Until recently, such things had not happened. In 1943 when a predecessor, Cardinal Heenan, died, King George VI was advised not to permit any official representation at the funeral.

Over the same decades, the non-Christian faiths had established a firm presence. The large influx of East European Jews in the 1880s and 1890s brought all the varieties of Reformed, Orthodox, and Chassidic Judaism to all British cities. More recently, Muslim mosques and Hindu temples became an accepted feature of the landscape. England and Wales were home to as many Muslims as Methodists. Immigration from the West Indies brought previously unseen groups like the Rastafarians onto British streets. The contemporary approach to pick 'n' mix religions had encouraged the growth of every conceivable tradition, faith, sect, and society from Scientologists and Satanists to Pagans and Buddhists.

Most striking of all was the post-war collapse in religious belief itself. In 1945, the great majority of the British people were practising Christians. Almost everyone was baptized, married, and buried in some sort of a religious ceremony. Not just the middle classes, but the greater part of the British working classes were still attached in varying degrees to their churches and chapels. The Education Act of 1944 made religious education a compulsory subject in all schools. Fifty years later, the traditions of centuries had all but vanished. An absolute majority of British citizens never set foot in a place of worship. Many couples neither bothered with a church wedding, nor even a marriage, nor baptized their children. The Christian sabbath, once a universal day of rest, had been turned into just another day for trading. Consumerism ruled. A government driven by populist considerations was building a Millennium Dome in which the religious core of the millennium – the two thousandth anniversary of Christ's birth – was struggling to find a corner. One wondered how many visitors to the Dome would have been able to talk for even one minute about the basic principles of Christianity, let alone to profess any brand of faith whatsoever. Official statistics confirmed these impressions. Non-belief was predominant. The denominational balance among believers had changed out of all recognition. In 1994, published figures for the UK put the self-professed non-religious at 24 per cent, Roman Catholics at 9 per cent, practising Anglicans at 4 per cent, Presbyterians at 3 per cent, Muslims and Methodists at 2 per cent each, Hindus at 1 per cent, and the residue of other Christian denominations at 4 per cent.[56] (As always, people with no religious faith to declare were recorded as 'non-practising Anglicans'.) This meant that the number of active Roman Catholics had overtaken the number of active Anglicans, to become the largest single denomination. The proportion of principled non-religious people was higher than in any other European state except the Netherlands. Neither England nor the United Kingdom as a whole could reasonably claim to be a Protestant country.

Since becoming a beleaguered minority, British Christians were slowly learning to forget their differences. Where once the great divide had stood between Protestants and Catholics, it now set Christians apart from non-Christians. After centuries of sectarian conflicts, Ecumenism was finally finding fertile ground. In its initial form, the ecumenical movement in Britain strove to unite the Protestants. The British Council of Churches attracted support from both Anglicans and Nonconformists in work both at home and abroad. Among the Nonconformists, the English Congregationalists joined with the English Presbyterians to form a United Reformed Church. Methodists and Anglicans began to discuss an end or at least a truce, to their two-hundred-year-old schism.

More recently, the Roman Catholic Church entered ecumenical circles. In 1982, Pope John Paul II was welcomed to Canterbury Cathedral – an event previously unimaginable. Anglican–Roman contacts remained sensitive not only through the historical legacies of Cranmer and Newman but also through contemporary issues such as that of women priests. But they kept going. Slowly, surely, ecclesiastical Christianity in the United Kingdom was growing more charitable, more recognizably Christian. In June 1999, the Polish-born ex-Jewish Cardinal-Archbishop of Paris, Jean-Marie Lustiger, preached the annual John the Baptist's Day Sermon at Magdalen College, Oxford, once a High Church fortress whose fellows had been expelled by James II. His text was taken from Isaiah xl, 'A voice crying in the wilderness'. In July 1999, St Paul's Cathedral in London hosted an inter-faith memorial service for King Hussein of Jordan. The reading was taken from the Koran. The Muslims present, recognizing the prophetic status of Christ, were invited to join in the recital of 'Our Father'. The times were definitely changing.

Granted such a background, it came as a shock to find that there were still enclaves in the Isles where the old religious bigotry reigned undisturbed. One such enclave was Glasgow Rangers Football Club, which employed no Catholic players until the mid-1990s and which in 1999 was obliged to fire its chairman for celebrating a cup-win with an evening of rabidly anti-Catholic songs –

> We're up to our knees in Fenian blood,
> Surrender or you'll die!

The Edinburgh Festival of 1999 was due to open with a lecture called 'Scotland's Shame' by the composer James MacMillan, who contended that anti-Catholic bigotry was still endemic. In the Republic of Ireland, the Roman Catholic Church had aspired for most of the century to a brand of clerical authoritarianism that would have been unthinkable among Catholics in England. Nothing, however, compared to the sectarian hatreds which were still thriving in the retarded time capsule of Protestant Ulster.

The British Province of Northern Ireland, which was set up by the Government of Ireland Act (1920) and confirmed by the Anglo-Irish Treaty (1922), was designed from the start as a Protestant reservation. Its roots went back, of course, to the Ulster Plantation of 1608 (see above); but its modern origins can be traced to the movement against Irish Home Rule stirred up in the 1880s by Lord Randolph Churchill. In 1912, the Unionist MP Edward Carson (1854–1935) organized the Ulster Volunteers to fight against Home Rule. Their revival of the old slogan 'Ulster will fight, and Ulster will be right' revealed their aims. Since the British General Staff of the era contained an unusually high proportion of Ulstermen who would probably have refused to confront their own, the government's scope for action was limited. In 1914, British soldiers stationed at the Curragh were told:

> In view of the possibility of active operations in Ulster, officers whose homes are actually in the province of Ulster who wish to do so may apply for permission to be absent from duty during the period of operations [i.e., suppressing the Ulster Volunteers if they attempted to capture army equipment], and will be allowed to "disappear" from Ireland. Such officers will subsequently be reinstated and will suffer no loss in their careers. Any other officer who from conscientious or other motives is not prepared to carry out his duty as ordered, should say so at once. Such officers will at once be dismissed from the Service.[57]

Most of the officers in 3rd Cavalry Brigade opted for dismissal, but were persuaded to stay in service on the assurance that the government would not use the army 'to crush political opposition to the policy or principles of the Home Rule Bill'.[58] In the event, they were not put to test because Home Rule was postponed by the outbreak of war and the Ulster Volunteers were sent off to die in the mud of the Somme. The blood sacrifice only strengthened Ulster's resolve. In 1918 the electoral victory of Sinn Féin in all the southern counties of Ireland made partition virtually inevitable. Belfast was preparing 'to go it alone', long before London or Dublin resigned themselves to the arrangements.

The nature of Northern Ireland's 'democracy' therefore was inseparable from the sectarian culture which gave it birth. It was secured firstly by the findings of a Boundary Commission, which deliberately excluded three of Ulster's ancient nine counties for having too many Catholics, and secondly by a provincial Parliament at Stormont, which accordingly enjoyed an in-built Protestant majority. From then on, legal means could be used to enforce a manifestly oppressive regime. Protestant politicians could boast of their democratic credentials whilst voting for undemocratic measures, upholding a judiciary and a militarized police force recruited exclusively from Protestants, justifying social and economic politics which deliberately marginalized Catholics, and turning a blind eye to the activities of openly sectarian associations and gangs. Ulster Protestantism was not homogeneous. In religious matters it was divided between the disestablished Episcopalians of the Church of Ireland and the more fundamentalist Free Presbyterians. In political matters, it was divided between the mainstream Ulster Unionists (UUP), who were represented in Westminster as well as running Stormont, and their more extreme and more recent opponents, notably the Democratic Unionist Party (DUP) of the Revd Ian Paisley (1926–). Many members of these groups shared the ancient visceral hatred of Catholicism, and a deep fear of the neighbouring Irish Republic, whose constitution from 1937 to 1998 laid claim to the whole of Ireland. They called themselves 'loyalists', being loyal not to the United Kingdom as it really was, but rather to an antiquated perception of the United Kingdom as an unalterably Protestant country. They persisted in their beliefs, even when they found themselves ever further out of step with British public opinion and with the British government.

The reaction against the Ulster system was slow in coming; but a broad-based Civil Rights Association, with a membership drawn from liberals, trade unionists, and students as well as from Catholics and Nationalists, broke into the open in the late 1960s. Peaceful protests proved pointless. Civil rights marches were set on by Protestant mobs. Sympathetic politicians were denounced as traitors. The marches turned into riots. The riots boiled over into intercommunal warfare. The Royal Ulster Constabulary and its notorious 'B-Specials' lost control. The British army was called in. On 'Bloody Sunday', 30 January 1972, a banned march was fired on by British paratroopers in Derry, and thirteen unarmed civilians were shot dead. The descent into terror and counter-terror had begun.

For thirty years thereafter, Northern Ireland was virtually ungovernable. Forced to suspend the discredited Stormont regime, the British government introduced direct rule from London. Yet every attempt to restore self-government on the basis of Protestant–Catholic partnership was frustrated by loyalist strikes. Generous schemes to re-house slum dwellers on a non-sectarian basis were defeated. On the streets, the IRA re-emerged from the shadows of its earlier existence in the Republic to recruit support in the Catholic ghettos, to challenge the British army, to defy the precepts of the Catholic Church, and to indulge in a protracted campaign of indiscriminate bombings. It was accompanied by similar republican groups as the 'Continuity IRA', the 'Real IRA', and the Irish Nationalist Liberation Army. It was opposed by similar Protestant terror-groups – the Ulster Defence Association or Ulster Freedom Fighters, the Loyalist Volunteer Force, and the Ulster Volunteer Force. Terrorists from both sides fought each other, whilst ruling by gunlaw over their respective communities. When the regular courts were suspended, they were interned in the purpose-built Maze

Prison at Long Kesh with its separate Loyalist and Republican wings. But a mixture of intimidation and hunger strikes rendered internment unworkable. On the political front, the extreme Republicans and the extreme Loyalists thrived on each other's barbarities. By 1992, the death toll passed three thousand. Catholics mourned Catholic victims. Protestants mourned Protestants. A depoliticized, but still overwhelmingly Protestant, RUC struggled manfully to hold the ring, suffering hundreds of casualties of its own. The stalemate seemed total, not least because the Unionists held disproportionate influence over Conservative governments in London. The utter barbarity of the violence could not be overestimated. Catholic families were routinely burned out of Protestant streets and Protestants driven from Catholic districts. Tit-for-tat sectarian killings were a regular occurrence. 'Knee-capping' and 'tar-and-feathering' were meted out to anyone who crossd the thugs. People were 'disappeared' – i.e., killed and secretly buried, often for trivial offences. One Catholic woman was 'disappeared' for giving comfort to a dying British soldier. The bombers struck without mercy – in town centres, at public gatherings, in crowded streets. In Omagh in 1998 a recalcitrant republican faction planted a bomb that killed over thirty people *after* a ceasefire was called. Far more civilians were killed than soldiers. And, despite the IRA being regarded in Britain as the chief terrorist group, more Catholics died than Protestants.

Progress towards a settlement was agonizingly slow. It was only made possible by three landmark events. One of these was the gradual rise since 1970 of the SDLP, a brave, moderate anti-terrorist and non-sectarian party. It gradually won the confidence of the majority of Catholic voters and offered the only plausible partnership for moderate unionists. The second was the Anglo-Irish Agreement of 1985, which ensured close cooperation between London and Dublin. The third was the appearance of the New Labour Government of Tony Blair, who, owing nothing to Unionist support, could not be pressured like its predecessors by 'the Orange Card'.

The two years between the summer of 1997 and that of 1999 were warmed by rising hopes. Comprehensive negotiations sponsored by the British and Irish Governments mobilized all parties including Sinn Féin to sign a Good Friday Agreement (1998) setting out the pathway towards power-sharing in a restored Northern Ireland Assembly and Provincial Executive. The Nationalists were persuaded to sign by clauses providing for cross-border cooperation and for the involvement of the Irish Government. The Unionists were persuaded by a categoric assurance that the Province would remain within the UK so long as a democratic majority so wished. Yet the provision for regular referenda on this point promised constant instability. A ceasefire was instituted. The Agreement was approved by a massive 71 per cent vote in a popular referendum. For their pains, the two leading politicians of the province, David Trimble of the Ulster Unionists and John Hume of the SDLP, were awarded the Nobel Peace Prize.

The award was premature. The Agreement had provided for the 'elimination of all paramilitary weapons by May 2000'. But Unionist and Loyalist opinion immediately raised fresh demands, including the advance disarmament of the IRA. Stalemate set in. The ceasefire held. But other forms of violence persisted. In July 1999 the Unionists failed to meet the deadline for forming the planned Executive. Yet again, hopes for peace and partnership had been dashed. If the Unionists were not allowed to play the political game according to their own rules, they would not play at all. A commission for the even-handed reform of the RUC was bound to sow dissension.

Meanwhile the old Loyalist rituals continued. Man and boy, Ulster Protestant males drilled throughout the winter to prepare for their summer parades. Year in, year out, members of the Orange Order insisted on holding their marches. In the 'marching season' of July, hundreds of 'lodges' sent tens of thousands of men to don their 1920-style outfits – dark suit, bowler hat, furled umbrella, and orange sash – and to fall in behind the drums and pipes. They sang incongruous hymns like 'What a Friend We Have in Jesus' and a more fitting repertoire of rousing songs such as 'The Sash my Father Wore' (see Appendix 33) or 'The Billy Boys'. They insisted on walking the routes laid down some two hundred years before, irrespective of offence caused. They regarded all complaints as a challenge to their 'rights'; and they rejected all comments about 'Protestant triumphalism' . Whenever anyone tried to stop them, they vowed to have their way.

Since 1996, Portadown in County Armagh became a flashpoint of the marching season. In that year, the Orange march was re-routed after protests from Catholic residents. The police ruled that the Orangemen could parade as usual to the annual service at the Church of the Ascension in the village of Drumcree, but that they were not to return to Portadown through the Catholic housing estate beside the Garvaghy Road. A Loyalist mob then assaulted and pelted the police cordon for several days until the Orangemen surged through. In 1997, 1998, and 1999 the security line at Drumcree held firm. But the Orangemen solemnly swore each year that they would be back.

The symbolic details of this scene were worth noting. Thirty years before, one of the best known citizens of Portadown was the rose-grower Sam McCredy. It was in his nursery on the slopes leading to Drumcree that he bred the world-famous Gold Medal rose, to which he gave the patriotic British name of 'Elizabeth of Glamis'. In the 1970s, unsettled by the Troubles, he emigrated to New Zealand. The site of his nursery on the Garvaghy Road was sold to provide land for the housing estate. Catholic residents took over from Protestant roses. The rituals of the Orange 'marching season' are clearly a case for anthropologists specializing in tribalism. A well-respected leader of the Catholic community had no doubts about their purpose: 'People [in Northern Ireland] don't march as an alternative to jogging', he said, 'They do it to assert their supremacy. It is pure tribalism, the cause of troubles all over the world.'[59] But the Orangemen disagreed. Marching wherever and whenever they wished was 'an expression of their culture'.

(5) Parliaments and Assemblies: a Grand Gamble

British Parliamentary democracy reached its zenith in December 1918. At the time of the first general election after the Great War, amidst delicate slogans such as 'Hang the Kaiser', the Imperial Parliament at Westminster exercised a legislative monopoly throughout the British Isles and colonies and a supervisory role over the parliaments of the self-governing dominions. The monopoly lasted for less than twelve months, the supervisory role for twelve years.

The parliamentary franchise, however, was still expanding. In 1918, the Representation of the People Act gave the vote to men over twenty-one and to women over thirty. This was seen both as a victory for the suffragettes and a recognition of women's contribution to the war effort. In reality, it was rather faint-hearted. In 1928 the vote had to be extended to all women over twenty-one and in 1969 to men and women over eighteen.

The breach in Westminster's monopoly was engineered by seventy-three Irish MPs who following the election of 1918 refused to take their seats in Westminster, setting up the Dáil Éireann in Dublin instead. Among them was Constance Gore-Booth, Countess Markiewicz (1868–1927), a radical English aristocrat who had been sentenced to death after the Easter Rising. Though never installed in the Commons, she was Britain's first woman MP. Thereafter, the Dáil settled down as the sovereign, bicameral assembly of the Irish Free State and Republic. It took the place of the subordinate assembly which the Home Rule Act had foreseen for Dublin but which never met.

The provincial Parliament of Northern Ireland first assembled at Stormont Castle near Belfast in 1921. It was completely dominated by Protestant Unionists, who also ran the provincial executive until the imposition of direct rule from London in 1972 (see above). Nonetheless, Stormont set the precedent for the institutions of 'devolved' government, which were granted to Scotland and Wales over ninety years later. It was due to be restored in accordance with the Good Friday Agreement of 1998.

As part of the scheme, which formally established the British Commonwealth in 1931, Westminster resigned all its residual powers relating to the parliaments of the dominions. It was retracting in the direction of becoming a purely UK institution. Henceforth, the dominions had no institutional link with the British state, except with the crown and, in matters of legal appeal, with the Privy Council.

The concept of devolution – that is, the partial transfer of powers from central government to legislative and executive organs in the regions – had underlain the whole sad story of Irish Home Rule. It had not worked in Ireland, having first provoked Partition and then, in Northern Ireland, a provincial system that had to be suspended. Yet it resurfaced in the United Kingdom at the very time when the troubles in Northern Ireland were starting to rage. The Kilbrandon Report (1973) recommended the formation of legislative assemblies in Scotland and Wales and the calling of a referendum to obtain democratic consent. Public opinion, however, proved hostile. A Referendum Act set 40 per cent of the popular vote as the threshold for acceptance. In the referenda of 1979, pro-Devolution voters polled only 33 per cent in Scotland, and a derisory 12 per cent in Wales. The project was shelved.

In that same decade, the United Kingdom joined the European Economic Community at the third attempt. Membership began on 1 January 1973. After the fall of the Conservative Government of Edward Heath, who had negotiated British entry, the decision was challenged by certain elements of the in-coming Labour Government. The new Prime Minister, Harold Wilson, had no choice but to put it to a referendum. A decisive vote of 67 per cent in favour during the Referendum of 5 June 1975 settled the matter once and for all. No option was left open for renegotiations.

It has to be said, however, that the issues surrounding membership of the EEC (later the European Union) were imperfectly expounded in public debate. The opponents of membership presented an extreme and extremely emotional case, predicting chaos and national ruin. The advocates of membership confined their arguments largely to the prospect of economic benefits. The British public were given the distinct impression that they were joining nothing more than 'the Common Market'. For whatever reason, they did not fully understand that by signing up to the Treaty of Rome the United Kingdom was committed to a movement aiming at ever closer integration. Equally, many people did not seem to realize that membership of the European Community automatically reduced (though did not totally overturn) the sovereign powers of the British Parliament. As from 1973, the parliamentarians at Westminster were no longer the undivided masters of their own house.

In the nature of things, the impact of the European Union on the British Parliament has been incremental. Westminster did not lose its basic right to approve the actions of the British representatives, who, as members of the Council of Ministers, participated in the highest decision-making body of the Union. But once the collective decisions were made, Westminster was treaty-bound to implement them. All relevant directives of the European Commission had to be incorporated into British law. At the same time, Westminster had to cooperate in the development of a parallel, Union-wide European Parliament based in Strasbourg. This body was carefully designed so as not to infringe the rights of the existing legislatures of member states. Certainly in the early days, MEPs were a lower form of life than MPs were. They only possessed powers of review and advice. Even so, in 1999, through a determined review of financial accounts, they forced the resignation of the entire European Commission. Surprisingly enough, the British public were not impressed. In the subsequent European election, less than a quarter of British citizens bothered to exercise their vote.

The rise of the European Union was undoubtedly a factor in a growing feeling that the British Parliament was losing its former vigour and status. But other factors were at work as well. One of these related to the poor calibre of the latest generation of MPs, many of whom possessed no experience beyond a career in the apparatus of their political party. Another was linked to the tendency for governments to bypass Parliament, and to discuss political issues directly with the electorate through manipulation of the press and television. In the late 1990s, political 'spinning' in the media seemed to attract greater attention than traditional debate in the Commons. The Cabinet Office, answerable solely to the Prime Minister, was the fastest growing body in sight. In between elections, the Prime Minister acted as if he possessed unprecedented extra-parliamentary powers.

A further source of discontent lay with the system of parliamentary elections in which the candidate 'first past the post' was judged the sole winner. The system favoured the two main parties, Conservative and Labour, but ill served the smaller parties. In the 1980s and 90s, for instance, the third largest party, the Liberal Democrats, obtained up to a quarter of the popular votes cast, but never won more than 1 or 2 per cent of the parliamentary seats. Many analysts thought that a system of proportional representation (PR) would be much fairer. In 1997, however, having won an absolute victory under the old system, 'New Labour' had no need of PR or of Lib-Dem support. So an independent commission was asked to examine it under Lord Jenkins.

The Jenkins Commission had been handed a brief for which bodies such as the Electoral Reform Society had been pressing since 1884. The electoral system of 'First Past the Post' had made many enemies, not only in the UK but equally in Canada, India, and the USA. In the British Election of 1997, it had caused 14.7 million voters to cast ineffective votes. Unfortunately, since 'Proportional Representation' came in many different forms, none of the numerous alternative systems could command decisive support. In the end, when it reported in October 1998, the commission rejected the well-backed Single Transferable Vote (STV) system, and opted instead for an obscure system called Alternative Vote Top-up (AV+). For the time being, the government did nothing.[60]

'New Labour', however, had also re-embraced Devolution. Eighteen years of Conservative government had witnessed an unparalleled mania for centralization. Margaret Thatcher weakened local government, abolished the Greater London Council, and favoured the south-east of England. Scotland and Wales in particular felt an acute sense of neglect. The fortunes of the Scottish Nationalist Party (SNP) and Plaid Cymru revived. As a result, the modernization of the opposition Labour Party was undertaken under the Welsh Socialist Neil Kinnock (1942–) and the Scots Socialist John Smith (1938–1994) with a strong commitment to de-centralizing policies and regional development. 'New Labour' was dominated by politicians from Scotland, Wales, and the North of England; and their election manifesto inevitably contained a promise to reintroduce 'Devolution'. In 1997, all the Conservative MPs in Scotland and Wales lost their seats, thereby reducing their party to an exclusively English base. This time, in the 1998 Referendums, Government-backed proposals for restoring a Scottish Parliament and a Scottish executive to Edinburgh were passed by a resounding 71 per cent vote. Similar proposals for a Welsh Assembly and Executive in Cardiff scraped through by a whisker. Even so, the change of mood since 1979 was striking. Proposals for the Northern Ireland Assembly were agreed in principle, but not implemented.

The inauguration of the Scottish Parliament and the Welsh Assembly in the summer of 1999 ushered in a new era. For the first time in its history, the British Parliament had willingly agreed to share power with a comprehensive system of subordinate legislatures. The declared aim was to restore a better balance between the aspirations of England and those of Scotland, Wales, and Northern Ireland, and thereby to preserve the Union. The policy was equally well matched to the EU's strategy of 'subsidiarity' and its promotion of 'a Europe of the Regions'. To anyone who remembered and admired the Imperial Parliament of 1918 it was anathema.

Seen in the historical perspective, the British government was applying similar measures to the 'inner empire' to those which were once applied to the dominions of the 'outer empire'. The eventual result could well have been the same. Devolution could easily have proved to be the stepping-stone to disintegration. It destroyed Westminster's monopoly, but it did not initiate a coherent federal or confederal system. It had not been well prepared; and it left England in a state of limbo. It could have diffused the strains of the Union for a season; but in the long term, it could also have encouraged the destabilizing and centrifugal forces of imbalance, nationalism, and separatism. One could say without equivocation that Britain had taken a grand gamble.

(6) The Hereditary Peers: an Endangered Species

Ever since the crisis of 1910–11 (see below), the British peerage had clung to its wealth and privileges with remarkable tenacity. Reform had been constantly mooted, and repeatedly postponed. The hereditary peers held on to their private judicial system – the right to be judged only by each other – until 1948. They kept their powers to delay parliamentary bills until 1949 and their monopoly in the House of Lords until 1958. Generally speaking, they also kept hold of their wealth. In 1999, of Britain's ten richest people, one was the monarch; another was heir to the throne; and the Duke of Westminster was number four.

The passage of the Life Peerage Act (1958) cut into the hereditary monopoly for the first time. It created a body of both men and (importantly) women, who had obtained their titles through achievement and who could be expected to be more active in the everyday work of Parliament. In forty years, the steady flow of life peers had brought a wealth of experience to the Lords from all fields of life, and had reduced the in-built Conservative bias of their hereditary fellows. In 1999, one could count among the more prominent names Lord Callaghan and Lady Thatcher, both former prime ministers; Lord Jenkins and Lord Dahrendorf, both former European commissioners; Lord Howe and Lord Healey, the sheep and the sheep-beater; Lord Dacre and Lord Bragg, a historian and a novelist.

For the last ninety years, the House of Lords had survived by making itself useful and by avoiding major confrontations with government or Commons. After 1945, faced by a crushing Labour Party victory in the General Election, the Peers voluntarily adopted the so-called Salisbury Convention. According to this doctrine, it was judged improper to reject or delay measures that had received 'the clear endorsement' of the democratic electorate.[61]

Supporters of the Lords stressed its expertise as a revising chamber and the absence of a suitable alternative. Neither point was relevant to the running sore of continuing hereditary privilege. But Conservative governments were unlikely to undermine an undemocratic institution that bolstered their parliamentary advantage.

Reform, therefore, had to await a non Conservative government. It was promised by the General Election Manifesto (1997) of 'New Labour', which contained a firm commitment to the abolition of hereditary peerage. The promise was adopted as government policy; and in accordance with the Salisbury Convention should presumably have been accepted by the Lords without demur. But the hereditary peers still had a say in the manner and timing of their demise. The absence of a clear plan for the profile of a reformed second chamber caused protracted delay.

One aspect of House of Lords reform received less airing than was desirable. The reform was initiated at the same time that Westminster was preparing to devolve important powers to the restored Parliament to the new assemblies in Wales and Northern Ireland. Since none of the devolved assemblies were expected to be bicameral, the reformed House of Lords was likely to remain the sole second chamber in the whole of the United Kingdom; and the exact relationship between the Lords of Westminster and the legislators in Edinburgh, Cardiff, and Stormont was a matter of utmost importance. It was every bit as crucial as their position vis-à-vis the Commons. Ever since the incorporation of representatives of Scottish and Irish peers in 1707 and 1801, the Lords had been a bastion of Britishness. And so they had remained. Lord Longford, a Labour peer, held an Irish title. The late Viscount Tonypandy, needless to say, was a Welshman. The Duke of Hamilton, whose hereditary duty was to carry the Scottish regalia into the reopening of Scotland's Parliament, had not yet lost his seat at Westminster. This British dimension would be ignored by parliamentarians at their peril. Pro-unionists needed to pay it careful attention. Anti-unionists needed to keep quiet.

In the meantime, as House of Lords reform pended, the hereditary peerage continued to expand. The latest recruit in 1999 was the Earl of Wessex, who added an earldom to his titles by virtue of nothing more than his mother's whim. No new, non-royal peerages had been created since the government of Mrs Thatcher. But lordly sons continued to inherit their lordly titles from their lordly fathers. One of the very last elevations was that of the former Prime Minister, Harold Macmillan, to be the Earl of Stockton. It says much of present circumstances that Macmillan's grandson Alexander, the second Earl (1943–), apart from being a scion of London's most eminent publishing house, chose to seek election to the European Parliament. The hereditary peers knew perfectly well that they were an endangered species.

In Scotland, the practices of large absentee aristocratic landowners had long been under siege. Crofters' associations struggled dourly to establish elementary land rights. The sale of huge estates to foreigners or to commercial concerns interested only in exploiting the hunting or the fishing was widely criticized.[62] 'New Labour' threatened punitive taxes. (See Appendix 61.)

In England, the landed fortunes of the aristocracy had long looked more of a burden than an asset. Some five hundred country houses were demolished after 1945. Twice as many were sold off as hospitals, schools, or hotels. The Dukes of Bedford, Northumberland, and Devonshire were crippled by death duties. The government actually refused to accept the gift of Chatsworth in lieu of taxes. Hereditary fortunes were being squeezed dry. Then Margaret Thatcher rode to the rescue. Rising land prices, a prolonged stock market boom, reduced taxation, and the encouragement of entrepreneurial ventures turned desperation to delight in a decade. Over a hundred hereditary peers returned to the country's 'rich list'. Their titles may have been in danger; but their bank accounts were not.[63]

(7) THE HOUSE OF WINDSOR – A WAY FORWARD

After three hundred years, there could have been little surprise that the unreformed British monarchy was riddled with problems and anomalies. What was surprising was how little discussion was directed to the long-term issues, as opposed to the trivial misde meanours of individual royals. The prospects were graver than the tabloids imagined. Indeed, the tittle-tattle of royal scandal helped to keep more serious matters off the agenda.

Despite a large body of modern legislation that outlawed racial and religious discrimination, the British monarchy remained legally tied to the old concept of a Protestant Establishment in its crudest anti-Catholic form. Here the relevant documents are not just the Act of Settlement (1701), which only applied to England and Wales, but the joint Act of Union (1707), which incorporated and adapted clauses from the earlier English Act. The Act of Union states that 'all Papists and persons marrying papists' shall for ever be excluded from 'the Imperial Crown of Great Britain and the Dominions thereunto belonging'.[64] Interpretations can differ. But what this seems to mean is that a future monarch could belong to the Revd Ian Paisley's Free Presbyterian Church or arguably to the Mormons, but not to the Church which had the strongest support and the longest connections. Whether he or she would be debarred through dabbling in Orthodoxy, Judaism, Islam, Druidism, or multi-faith practices, was unclear.

The British monarch remained Supreme Governor of the Church of England, a body which was itself in serious decline. The monarch held no special position in the Church of Scotland or in any other denomination. The scope for confusion was limitless. It was uncertain whether the Supreme Governor must also be a regular communicant. Yet no barrier seemed to exist to the monarch or the heir to the throne breaking the ecclesiastical rules of the Church. The remarriage of the monarch, though not possible at that time in Westminster Abbey (or Westminster Cathedral), might have been perfectly feasible in a Nonconformist chapel or perhaps in Crathay Church. The British monarchy was also inextricably entangled with the peerage and hence with the outdated principles of hereditary privilege and hierarchical castes. All the princes of the royal blood, from the Prince of Wales to the Earl of Wessex, were automatically members of the House of Lords. For the British government to abolish the hereditary peerage as proposed, but without damaging the monarchy, was well-nigh impossible.

British monarchs entered the twentieth century as emperors and empresses. When the Empire disappeared, Elizabeth II set great store on her duties as Head of the Commonwealth. But now that the Commonwealth was no longer British, the point of her headship was unsure. Her inherited position as Queen of Canada, Australia, and New Zealand was also under fire. If in the prospective referendum of 1999 her Australian subjects were to vote for 'a resident President', the general prestige of the monarchy would sink yet another step lower. And after Australia, some other nation would want its say. The general trend was downwards.

The British monarchy had never dealt properly with the basic problem of its origins and identity. In the eighteenth century, it had no call to conceal its Germanity. But in the nineteenth century it consciously adopted the aura and ideology of Englishness. The court assumed the affectations of aristocratic southern English speech. In all official publications the line of succession was presented as a simple continuation of the English monarchs. Elizabeth II was so designated because she was counted a successor to Elizabeth I of England, despite being the first queen of that name to reign over the UK. Royal genealogies publicized 'the Firm's' descent from Alfred, Eadgar, or Ecgfrith, not from Robert the Bruce, Owen Tudor, Geoffroi Plantagenêt, or Hrolf the Walker.[65] Scottishness and Welshness were permitted in small doses; Irishness was avoided;

and the the German connections were denied even if one wrote direct to the Duke of Edinburgh to ask for his family name.[66] The Queen Mother, a Scot, who was the first non-German to marry into the top echelon of British royals, habitually referred to Germans in Captain Mainwaring fashion as 'the Huns'. 'When Philip's princely relatives came to Balmoral . . . she told members of her staff: "You certainly don't curtsey to Germans." '[67] If similar instructions had been given a generation or two earlier, curtseying would have completely died out. Diana, Princess of Wales (1961–97), 'England's Rose', was the first person of English descent ever to approach the British throne. Her Englishness was one of the few attributes that was never held against her.

Like all their British subjects, all members of the British royal family have recently become citizens of the European Union. As a family of almost unblemished German descent, they were no doubt well qualified. But the change had potential legal implications. British courts were never likely to consider a case directed against the crown in whose name they exercise their jurisdiction. European courts could conceivably adopt a different stance.

For much of the twentieth century, British monarchs benefited from the aura of deference with which they and their relatives were surrounded. Their high public standing was greatly enhanced by the cultivation since late Victorian times of royal pomp and ceremony, by the patriotic social climate of two world wars, and by the mystery which distanced the royal circle from the lives of ordinary people. Prior to the televised Coronation of 1953, which persuaded many British families to buy their first television set, most British people had never seen their monarch as a living, moving, speaking person. Since then, the deferential instincts of British society were much diminished. American-style familiarity was spreading. The most powerful man in the land, the Prime Minister, signed letters to unknown constituents as 'Tony'. The titling, the curtseying, the bowing and scraping of royal etiquette looked increasingly out of line not only with public sentiment but also with the chosen poses of monarchical marketing. Rightly or wrongly, a monarchy which was neither completely remote nor truly familiar sent out confused signals that invited misinterpretation.

Diminishing deference, however, brought increasing demands for accountability. In the 1950s, the monarch faced no questions when she dropped Queen Victoria's custom of paying income tax like all her subjects. In the 1990s, when questions began to be asked, she was allowed to pay income tax on a voluntary basis and at an undisclosed rate. In an era when financial auditing was becoming universal, such exceptional arrangements were not likely to be tolerated for long.

In the post-war era, the British monarchy was sucked into a strategy where the ubiquitous techniques of PR and advertising were used to promote the ideal 'Royal Family'. Such operations were unthinkable in former times. The private lives of royals could be scandalously licentious because they were carefully screened from the public gaze. But once they were opened to media scrutiny, new expectations were set; and the expectations could not be realized. The trend began under George VI, apparently at the initiative of the present Queen Mother, who at the age of ninety-nine was probably set to be the last beneficiary. It continued in the 50s, 60s, and 70s under Elizabeth II and her apparently exemplary brood. It began to disintegrate in the 1980s amidst the personal tribulations of the Queen's sister and daughter; and it reached an all-time low amidst a torrent of lurid and embarrassing revelations about the youngest generation of royals. The monarch's own family was shown to be as dysfunctional as any in the world of soap opera or the underclass. The royal mystique, once judged essential to the survival of the monarchy, was dispelled for ever.

The tragedy of Diana, Princess of Wales brought the wider catastrophe to a head. A vulnerable untrained girl, with a personality deeply scarred by her own family traumas, was snatched from her job as a kindergarten teacher by an heir to the throne under orders to find a bride. She was thrust without warning into a luxurious but psychologically hostile circle where newcomers were simply expected to cope and to conform. Her husband, as it turned out, was another complex psychological invalid, who had never really parted with the only love of his life. Their mismatch was played out in the full glare of cruel media attention. The fairy-tale wedding dissolved into psychiatric disorders. Both royal partners used the media for their own ends. The court, the public, and the media were split into pro-Charles and pro-Diana factions. But Charles could compete neither with Diana's glamour, nor with her touching devotion to offbeat charities, nor with her ultimate weapon – a spectacular death in the company of an Arab playboy in a speeding black Mercedes in a Paris underpass at midnight.

The spontaneous outpouring of public grief at Diana's death surpassed anything that Britain had hitherto known. Indeed, in the sour eyes of the critics, the mountains of flowers, the seas of candles, and the miles of roadside shrines and icons were thought to have a suspect, and distinctly un-British flavour. But they were produced by a greater head of affection and emotion than was ever generated by royal pomp. Princess Diana won the hearts of everyone who has ever had to struggle with their own weaknesses. A woman who once appeared to have won the ultimate prize in life's lottery ended as the heroine of the underprivileged, the disabled, the outcast, the neglected. At the funeral, her brother – another flawed aristocrat playing the populist – drew ripples of applause in the Abbey, and the sympathy of the watching millions, by openly criticizing the Royal Family, who had meanly deprived Diana of the title of HRH. 'She needed no royal title', Earl Spencer said, 'to continue to generate her particular brand of magic.'[68] The monarchy was the chief casualty. The damage, which was all beneath the surface, could yet prove irreparable.

A few months earlier, Princess Diana had comforted the pop singer Elton John during the funeral of Gianni Versace, the designer. He repaid the complement at Diana's funeral, by singing a rewritten version of a maudlin song first composed for Marilyn Monroe:

> Goodbye England's rose;
> May you ever grow in our hearts

You were the grace that placed itself
where lives were torn apart.
You called out to our country,
and you whispered to those in pain.
Now you belong to heaven,
and the stars spell out your name.
And it seems to me you lived your life
Like a candle in the wind
Never fading with the sunset
When the rain set in.
And your footsteps will always fall here
Along England's greenest hills;
Your candle's burned out long before
Your legend ever will.[69]

Princess Diana's death gave the Royal Family a transient respite. Yet the stream of attacks, slights and self-inflicted injuries continued unabated. The government slashed the Queen's proposed pay rise by two-thirds because of 'overgenerous' payments in the past.[70] The official set of forty-eight stamps marking Britain's achievements during the millennium made no single reference to the monarchy.[71] In a survey of Britain's 'Powerful and Influential People', the monarch was placed 100th out of 100. (See below.) Senior royals broke their age-old silence and began to express public opinions. The Queen publicly defended the Foreign Secretary after a chaotic tour of India.[72] The Prince of Wales, a doughty environmentalist, sounded off on everything from ugly buildings to genetically modified foods. The Duke of Edinburgh added to the catalogue of his allegedly racist remarks. A serious rift opened up between the Prince and his mother over his continuing adulterous relationship with the woman whom Diana had once described as one of the 'three in the marriage'. The Prince had to deny a rumour of begging his mother to abdicate.[73] The Queen Mother alone (1900–) seemed to be above the fray. She was the one person holding 'the Firm' together. Yet a gushing biography for her ninety-ninth birthday contained some hidden barbs. A noted spendthrift herself, she was reported as seeing the Queen's decision to pay tax as a betrayal. She felt 'Diana was a very silly girl with a poor sense of . . . *devoir*'. She indulged Prince Charles 'as the son she never had'. 'Granny is the mother he feels he never had.' Her horizons were parochial. Her beloved Bertie once let slip that 'Abroad is bloody.'[74] New constitutional roles loomed, particularly in Scotland, where the procedure of appointing a chief executive would be different from that in London. And new assaults loomed in the Commonwealth, notably in Australia.

The survival of the British monarchy had no parallel among the grander dynasties of Europe. It lived on, in a state of animated suspension, in a country that had never been tested by defeat. So it was difficult to guess whence the fatal blow would fall. Popular opinion was unlikely to be decisive. Opinion polls taken on the streets of Paris in 1789, or of Vienna in 1918, would have given resounding support to the Bourbons or the Habsburgs. Even the Romanovs had their equivalent of the 'Way Forward Group'. Dynastic crises of the killer type develop suddenly, like heart attacks. One cannot prepare for them except by keeping in all-round robust health. Yet the British monarchy, as an institution, did not enjoy such vigour. Almost all the constituents of the ancient body politick on which it was formerly built had withered or wilted. In which case, though out of sight, the end could hardly be far away. Sooner rather than later, the *soi-disant* Windsors were bound to join their relatives, the Hohenzollerns and the Romanovs, on one of the various ex-royal circuits.

The scene had been described in fiction long since. Jack Barker's People's Republican Party won the 1993 election, and the Royals had to be told that they would be moving into new accommodation:

> The Queen winced as Jack Barker ground his cigarette out on the silk rug . . . Prince Charles bent down and picked up the cigarette stub [and] slipped it into his pocket.
> Princess Margaret said, 'Lilibet, I've *got* to have a fag. Please!'

'May we open the windows, Mr. Barker?' asked the Queen. Her accent cut into Jack like a crystal . . .

'No chance,' he replied.

'Am I to have a house of my own, Mr. Barker, or must I share with my daughter and son-in-law?' The Queen Mother gave Jack her famous smile . . .

'You'll get a pensioner's bungalow. It's your entitlement as an ordinary citizen of this country.'

'A bungalow, good. I couldn't manage stairs. Will my staff be living in or out?

'You don't seem to understand. There'll be no staff, no dressers, no cooks, secretaries, cleaners, chauffeurs.'

Turning to the Queen he said, 'You'll have to nip in now and then to help your mum out. But she'll probably be entitled to Meals on Wheels.'

'Under the People's Republican Party's rule, nobody in Britain will starve,' said Jack.

Prince Charles cleared his throat and said, 'Er, may one, er enquire as to where . . .? That is, the location . . .?'

'If you're asking me where you're all going, I'm not telling you.'

Inside the Centre Room the Queen waved Margaret's cigarette smoke away and asked, 'How long have we got?'

'Forty-eight hours,' said Jack.

The Queen said, 'That is very short notice, Mr. Barker.'

Jack said, 'You should have known your time was up years ago . . . You'll be notified of your removal dates.'

To Charles he said, 'Relieved, eh?'[75]

(8) THE CIVIL SERVICE: CONTINUITIES AND DISCONTINUITIES

Eugène Ionesco wrote 'Civil Servants don't make jokes'.[76] The observation, around 1958, was not entirely true. But one can hardly claim that their history was uproarious. In the twentieth century,

British civil servants were multiplied, retrained, dispersed, unionized, and, in part, privatized and Europeanized. If the typical civil servant in 1918 was a pinstriped mandarin strolling down Whitehall with bowler hat and rolled umbrella, the representative figure at the end of the century could easily have been a nuclear scientist at Harwell or a Welsh-speaking woman administrator in Cardiff or even a British bureaucrat on secondment in Brussels.

The exponential growth in Civil Service numbers must largely be attributed to the long list of new tasks undertaken by government, especially in education and social services, and post-1945 to the growth of the welfare state. The figures speak for themselves:

1815	25,000
1851	39,000
1871	54,000
1891	79,000
1939	87,000
1979	730,000[77]

The numerical increase was particularly great in the lower grades, creating a clear divide between the top-level staff of policy advisers and the army of clerks and bottle washers. The Haldane Report (1918) complained that senior civil servants had no time to think.

By the late 1950s, alarms were sounded about the negative effects of the sheer size of the service. The vast amorphous horde was thought to be losing its sense of direction. The Plowden Report (1961) revealed that HM Treasury lacked any proper means of forecasting or controlling income and expenditure. Forecasting and control agencies soon became ubiquitous.

The Fulton Report (1968) deplored the cult of the gentleman amateur and called for the employment of specialist experts and for an emphasis on training. One result was the creation in 1970 – a century after the service's foundation – of the Civil Service College at Sunningdale Park in Berkshire.

The concentration of civil servants in London was also criticized. With the growth of modern communications, there was no need for government institutions to be located in one place; and there was much to be said for redeployment to regional centres. As from the 1970s, therefore, the precedent set fifty years earlier by the move of the Welsh Health Board to Cardiff was repeated many times over. The Royal Mint moved to Llantrisant; the Patent Office to Newport; the Inland Revenue to a number of new locations. In the late 1990s, the process of dispersal was given a further boost by the introduction of devolved government for Scotland and Wales. The Scottish Office was largely demobilized and transferred to Edinburgh as the secretariat of the new Scottish Executive. Only a small caretaker staff and minister were left in Whitehall. The staff of the Welsh Office largely decamped to Cardiff to serve the executive of the Welsh National Assembly. From the political point of view, the leading question was whether British civil servants would retain their former metropolitan outlook or whether they would begin to identify with the cities and regions where they now worked.

The welfare state carried enormous ideological implications. Though much of the groundwork had been laid earlier, the practical measures were introduced by Attlee's post-war Socialist government. The scheme was the brainchild of the Keynesian economist William Beveridge (1879–1963), who set out to banish the plague of social misery and unemployment manifested during the pre-war Depression. By promising state support to all citizens 'from the cradle to the grave', it quickly became a source of great pride, distinguishing Britain, as was thought, from many less fortunate countries. Yet in the course of forty years, it began to absorb 40 per cent of the state budget, and was increasingly seen by its critics to be creating 'a dependency culture', a half-educated underclass of 'drop-outs' living on 'hand-outs'. The Thatcherite government of the 1980s was particularly hostile to what was now called 'the Nanny State'. Huge sectors of government activity, such as the utilities (gas, water, and electricity), were turned into private companies and sold off on the stock market. Hundreds of operations once run directly by government departments were handed over to the so-called Quangos – Quasi-Autonomous Non-Governmental Organizations. And the number of civil servants was slashed. By the 1990s, the Civil Service had been slimmed down by about a third. In 1998, the number employed stood at 463,270.

Battles over the welfare state were mirrored in battles over the trade unions. In its early days, the Civil Service had nothing to do with the unions. But in the 1970s large sectors were unionized. NALGO, NUPE, and COHSE figured among the most active and numerous unions. Top civil servants organized their own 'professional body' – the First Division Association. In the 1980s, the Thatcher government resisted a determined attempt to unionize the Government Communications HQ at Cheltenham.

The Civil Service still set great store on its high standards of conduct. As amended in May 1999, the Civil Service Code laid out its objectives for all to see:

> The constitutional and practical role of the Civil Service is, with integrity, honesty, impartiality and objectivity, to assist the duly constituted Government of the United Kingdom, the Scottish Executive or the National Assembly for Wales . . . whatever their political complexion, in formulating their policies, carrying out decisions, and in administering the services for which they are responsible.[78]

Point 2 stated 'Civil servants are servants of the Crown'. This could be seen to underline the crucial role of the monarchy within the British system. In reality, the abstract concept of 'the Crown' could continue without a monarch. As indicated in Footnote 1, 'we use the [American] term Administration to mean Her Majesty's Government of the United Kingdom, the Scottish Executive or the National Assembly for Wales.'[79] The important issue here was to avoid the impression that Scotland or Wales had their own 'governments'.

How far the code matched reality was a matter of opinion. One view held that 'the grovel factor' ensured that forceful politicians could always get their way with obsequious administrators. Another more popular view, brilliantly portrayed in the BBC TV series *Yes, Minister*, held that unscrupulous mandarins, whilst feigning subservience, could manipulate their political masters at will. The truth did not necessarily lie in the middle. As shown by the very first encounter between Jim Hacker MP and Sir Humphrey Appleby, the ideal of Open Government lay tantalizingly out of reach:

> JIM HACKER: Opposition is about asking awkward questions.
> SIR HUMPHREY: And government is about not answering them.
> JIM HACKER: Well, you answered mine anyway.
> SIR HUMPHREY: I'm glad you thought so, Minister.[80]

That programme was aired in 1980. The Major government published its own white paper on Open Government in 1994.

In the post-war era, growing public concern was expressed about the Civil Service's habitual addiction to secrecy. Unlike some other countries, such as the USA, which had a long tradition of governmental transparency, the British political establishment had a long tradition of keeping information to itself. For decades, there had been no discussion at all. But in the 1970s, when the Franks Report (1972) recommended reform of the Official Secrets Act and when a Liberal MP, Clement Freud, made the first vain attempt to force through a Freedom of Information Bill, public awareness of the problem grew. It turned out that Section 2 of the Official Secrets Act (1911), to which all higher-grade civil servants had to subscribe, had made it a criminal offence to disclose without prior authorization *any* information on *any* subject whatsoever. The Act had originally been passed to deal with naval espionage. But it had been used for sixty years to keep a lid on literally everything. It could only be likened to the famous directive of the Soviet censorship – making it illegal to admit to the existence of a directive denying the existence of the Soviet censorship. If one thought about it, it was an offence in Britain to make any authorized disclosure about the nature of the Official Secrets Act. Anything more contrary to the spirit of democracy it would be hard to imagine.

Throughout the 1980s and 90s, seven or eight further attempts to introduce Freedom of Information bills were defeated in Parliament. A number of piecemeal measures, however, were passed. The

Data Protection Act (1984) gave individuals the right to see data stored on government computers. The Local Government (Access to Information) Act (1985) gave the public limited access to papers and reports used in council meetings. The Access to Personal Files Act (1987) and the Access to Health Records Act (1990) increased the public's rights. In 1989, the Thatcher government replaced the old Official Secrets Act with a new one, which still guarded information about wide areas of 'security', defence, international relations, and policing, and which still permitted convictions without proof of harm.

The on-going debate was fuelled by the actions of civil servants who rebelled against the restrictions. In 1984, a young Foreign Office clerk was jailed for releasing information about the deployment of cruise missiles. In 1984, an official in the Minister of Defence was charged in court for revealing that Ministers had misled Parliament over the facts of the sinking of the cruiser *Belgrano* during the Falklands War. He was acquitted by a jury, which believed that he had told the truth. A great fuss surrounded the autobiography of a rogue intelligence officer, Peter Wright, whose book *Spycatcher* (1987), published in Australia, became a worldwide best seller.[81]

Wright's revelations centred on the continuing attempts to root out the ramifications of a high-powered Soviet spy ring that had operated inside the highest levels of the British Civil Service since the 1930s. Guy Burgess (1911–63) and Donald Maclean (1913–83), both Foreign Office officials, defected to Moscow in 1951. Kim Philby (1912–88), variously head of British counterespionage against Stalin's USSR, MI6's chief liaison officer with the CIA and FBI, and a major general of the KGB, followed them twelve years later. Sir Anthony Blunt (1907–83), sometime Surveyor of the Queen's Pictures, was uncovered in 1964, and publicly exposed in 1979. John Cairncross (1913–95), who was thought to be the last of the Soviet moles, had penetrated Churchill's wartime cabinet. But sure enough, in 1999 yet another Soviet spy was unmasked in the person of Melita Norwood (1912–), who was alive and well in unruffled suburban retirement. Codenamed 'Hola' by the Soviets, Norwood had worked for decades

at the British Non-Ferrous Metals Research Association. She systematically purloined information that greatly accelerated Stalin's programme for exploding an atomic bomb in 1949. Britain's cult of
secrecy had provided cover for the biggest gang of traitors in
Britain's history.[82] The official admission that the British intelligence
services really did exist in a real building on the banks of the Thames
did not occur until after the end of the Cold War. It revealed a
world apart from the political culture of the USA, where the US
Secret Service could be contacted through a telephone number in
every directory. Not surprisingly, the Blair Government's Freedom
of Information Bill as presented in May 1999 failed to meet cam-
paigners' expectations. It threatened to confirm the famous obituary:

> Here lies a civil servant. He was civil
> To everyone, and servant to the devil.[83]

Talk of falling standards was unavoidable. Ten thousand men
and women working at Bletchley Park in wartime did not spill a
bean at the time or for thirty years afterwards. And now former
British intelligence officers were routinely circulating their complaints on the Internet.[84] Greed accompanied indiscretion. The
media imported the term 'fat cat' from America to describe the
unscrupulous directors of privatized companies, very often ex-civil
servants from the government departments which once ran them.
They were not quite in the same bracket as the highest fliers in the
City. But then they were not entrepreneurs or risk-takers. Their
apparent betrayal of the ideal of service seemed all the greater.[85]

Over those same decades, however, the international framework
within reach the British Civil Service worked, had been radically
transformed. In the 1960s, there was still a large contingent who
had once served in India or the Colonies. In the 1990s, a similar
contingent was gaining its experience in the highest institutions of
the EU. 'Europe' loomed ever larger. The CSC at Sunningdale was
running courses on 'Demystifying Brussels' or 'Westminster Scrutiny
of European Law' or even 'Working in French'. For anyone familiar

with bygone traditions, this last development could only be treated as that rare commodity in the Civil Service – a joke.

(9) THE BRITISH ECONOMY: NOT THE ONLY ROAD TO SUCCESS

Throughout the twentieth century, the British economy followed a steady path of growth and progress. The troughs caused by the strains of two world wars, and by the Depression of the 1930s, were all been followed by new peaks; and the overall trend was upward. The collective wealth of the United Kingdom was much greater in 1999 than it was in 1899. The average income of its citizens had risen many times over. Their standard of living in terms of material wealth, and their quality of life as reflected in working conditions, social services, housing, recreation, health, environment, and longevity, had vastly improved. Whatever problems remained, anyone thinking of raising the theme of decline had to keep the overall, historic picture in mind. British people, whose grandparents lived predominantly in a world of slums, soot, insecurity, and back-breaking toil, now saw their grandchildren entering a far gentler world of motor cars, the welfare state, domestic appliances, regular holidays, and universal education.

Much of what people felt to be economic decline was really a part of industrial modernization. The old heavy industries on which 'the Workshop of the World' had been built wasted away to the point of near extinction. Coal mining, iron and steel, textiles, machinery, and shipbuilding held their own until 1945. But they began to slide, by coincidence, at the same time as the British Empire; and they suffered the same fate. In three or four decades, the towns that had been the powerhouses of the Industrial Revolution, had quite literally run out of steam. By the 1990s there were no coalmines left in Merthyr Tydfil. There were virtually no steelworks in Sheffield, no working cotton mills in Bolton, no major shipyards on Clydeside or Tyneside. Most symbolically, British Railways transferred in the 1970s from native coal to foreign diesel.

Yet importantly, new industries and new services appeared to replace the old. Britain gained a respectable share in high-tech industries – in aerospace, electronics, biotechnology, telecommunications, materials science, and defence systems. Thriving light industry sprang up, often in new locations, whilst the industrial districts of the older ports and cities emptied and rusted. The City of London kept its position as the leading provider of financial services in the world. The net product was better than it had been.

Britain's industrial transformation, however, did not take place without serious consequences for the future. One such worrying development lay in the acute reduction of the manufacturing sector. Britain lost its former reputation for 'making things'. Another source of worry lay in the fact that Britain's performance did not keep pace with the competitors. A third factor was connected with the dramatic geographical redistribution of economic activity.

The reasons why the British economy performed well, but less well than most other advanced industrial countries, was the subject of considerable controversy. Historians would stress historical factors – such as the burden of antiquated plant, ancient infrastructure, and unreformed practices in the world's oldest industrial society. They would also point out that Britain escaped the physical destruction and the psychological trauma which her wartime enemies encountered. For, as the experience of Germany and Japan well illustrates, wartime defeat can prove briefly devastating, but in the long-term extremely stimulating. Anthropologists would point to an industrial culture where confrontations between management and unions blighted industrial relations from the 1940s to the 80s; and to a class culture where the distance between employer and employee was rigorously maintained. Sociologists would stress the damaging effects of a failing state educational system, where standards of literacy and numeracy were often poor to middling, and of the growth of a large underclass, which was permanently unemployed, vulnerable to crime, and subject to despair.

Table 15. Industrial production, 1994–98

Total industry (excluding construction) 1995 = 100

	1994	1995	1996	1997	1997 Sep	1998 Sep
EU-15	96.8	100.1	100.8	104.1	105.2	108.3
EUR-11	96.7	100.0	100.1	104.2	105.3	108.9
B	93.6	100.0	100.8	105.6	106.2	108.4
DK	96.0	100.0	101.1	105.6	108.5	107.5
D	96.9	100.0	100.4	103.9	105.3	109.4
F	98.0	100.0	99.9	103.9	105.2	108.5
IRL	84.1	100.0	108.0	124.5	130.6	150.5
I	94.2	100.0	97.2	99.8	100.9	101.2
NL	97.2	100.0	102.7	104.7	104.5	105.7
S	88.8	100.0	103.1	111.2	115.0	116.1
UK	98.7	100.6	101.2	102.4	101.5	102.4
US	95.3	100.0	103.5	108.6	112.2	115.1
JP	96.7	100.0	102.0	105.7	107.2	99.6[86]

The British car industry was one of several sectors that failed the test. In 1950, it was producing a full range of best-selling products from the luxury Rolls Royces to the popular Austins and Morrises. By 1995, though the car market had quintupled, British-owned car makers had disappeared. British drivers preferred Japanese and Continental makes. Rolls Royce and Rover were both subsidiaries of German firms. Ford and Vauxhall belonged to American conglomerates. The United Kingdom had no equivalent of the German VW, the Italian Fiat, or the French Renault and Peugeot.

Explanations are one thing. Facts are another. Whatever index one cares to take, Britain's economic performance was not so good as that of many rivals, to whom fifty years ago she could show a clean pair of heels. The statistics of industrial production, for instance, shows the UK advancing, but advancing at a lower rate than its competitors. (See Table 15, above.)

The statistics for Gross Domestic Product (GDP) reveal a similar pattern (see Table 16, overleaf).

Table 16. GDP per capita (in PPS), 1995–98

	1995	1996	1997	1998
I Economic Areas				
EUR-11	17,539	18,303	19,171	20,012
EU-15	17,253	18,095	19,010	19,819
G7	21,559	22,797	23,938	24,732
II Main Economic Partners				
USA	25,687	27,142	28,784	30,173
JPN	20,370	21,905	22,482	22,023
CAN	20,631	21,564	22,690	23,005
AUS	18,766	19,895	20,936	
III EU-Member States				
B	19,646	20,411	21,439	22,531
DK	19,990	21,269	22,349	22,922
D	18,971	19,923	20,759	21,677
EL	11,485	12,243	13,051	13,572
E	13,222	14,010	14,844	15,660
F	18,504	19,032	19,886	20,746
IRL	16,329	17,090	19,147	20,576
I	17,621	18,376	19,096	19,679
L	29,545	30,505	32,615	34,674
NL	18,509	19,050	20,211	21,097
A	19,113	20,336	21,229	22,168
P	12,138	12,670	13,450	14,281
FIN	16,657	17,281	18,749	19,941
S	17,427	18,027	18,623	19,321
UK	16,592	17,840	19,032	19,776
IV EFTA				
CH	23,153	22,923	23,822	24,693[87]

Wherever one looked in the 1990s, the same conclusions are self-evident. Britain's relative economic decline was remarkable. The country which had always thought of itself as number one could not usually be found in the top ten. Methods of calculation may vary. But from 1992 the UK was number four in Europe with regards to the total size of its GDP, following Germany, France, and Italy. But in terms of GDP per capita (PPS), it was number eleven: in terms of GDP growth it was number thirteen; and in terms of the growth of industrial output, number sixteen.[88] Even in car owner-ship (1994) it only came in at number ten. These figures, though not disgraceful, were bound to generate a feeling of malaise.

Nonetheless, aggregated all-statistics cover only one part of the story. The redistribution of economic activity, and the relative wealth of the constituent regions within states, are every bit as important. In the United Kingdom, dramatic changes took place. In the early days of Union and Empire, British heavy industry devel-oped most strongly on the geographical periphery, especially in the North and the West. Apart from the Midlands, the great coalfields were located in South Wales, Lancashire, and Yorkshire, Durham and Tyneside, and central Scotland. The great shipbuilders were located in Belfast, Clydeside, and Tyneside. Apart from London and Birmingham, the great conurbations grew up round Cardiff, Man-chester and Liverpool, Leeds, Bradford and Sheffield, Newcastle and Middlesbrough, and Glasgow. Their industries kept the periphery chained to the capital in London. Thus, Scotland, Northern Ireland, and Wales were intimately and organically linked with England.

The disappearance of heavy industry was one of several factors that created entirely new patterns of distribution. In England, a new divide opened up between a prosperous, high-tech South-east and the old struggling rust-belts of the North. The age-old imbalance between England and Ireland had been largely rectified. The indus-trial area round Dublin was acting as a regional magnet for busi-nesses and workers on both sides of the Irish Sea. The economic links between the old industrial centres and London were signifi-cantly weakened. In South Wales, for instance, the disappearance of the mining industry did far more than blight the local communities of the valleys. It started to heal the rift which once existed between rich industrial English-speaking Wales and the poor, rural, Welsh-

Table 17. Direction of United Kingdom exports, 1935–1973 (per cent)[89]

	1935–8	1950–4	1955–9	1960–4	1965–9	1970–3
Western Europe	27	26	27	35	39	43
USA	5	6	8	9	12	10
Old Dominions	29	30	26	22	20	17
Eastern Europe, USSR, and Japan	5	1	2	4	5	5
Former Colonies	19	23	23	17	12	10
Latin America, Middle East, and rest of world	15	14	14	13	12	15

speaking Wales; and it blew away the assumption that Wales's prosperity was indefinitely bound to a centralized British economy run from England. In all parts of the Isles, the rapid growth of direct economic links with industrial and commercial partners in Western Europe was destroying the traditional insular framework of the British economy.

The economic effects of decolonization turned out to be far less drastic than was anticipated. Since almost everyone from Lenin upwards had assumed that the wealth of imperial powers derived from the exploitation of colonies, it followed that the loss of colonies would trigger a marked decline in the wealth of ex-imperial powers. Exactly the opposite happened. In the years 1951–73, when decolonization was at its height, the real GDP of the United Kingdom was increasing. The annual average growth rate of 3 per cent outstripped that of any period since early Victorian times. The only possible conclusion is that economically 'the Empire was more burden than benefit'.[90]

Still more surprisingly, as trade with the dominions and colonies declined, trade with other regions of the world either held steady or improved. British exports increased with the USA but more dramatically with the countries of Western Europe. (See Table 17, above.)

The conclusion here was fairly obvious: if, after the loss of

Empire, the UK did not want to be tied to the economic coat-tails of the USA, her best course of action was to join the European Common Market. In the 1960s and 1970s, the economies of Common Market members showed unparalled dynamism.[91]

Since the 1970s, the European factor became a permanent and prominent element of the economic equation. Ireland was a prime example of a small country that benefited mightily from membership of the EEC and EC. It performed much better outside the United Kingdom than it ever did inside it. By the same token, the Regional Development Policies of the EEC, which have greatly assisted Wales, Scotland, and parts of Northern England, pointed to alternative paths of economic development. Even in Belfast, the realization must have dawned that belonging to Britain was not the only road to economic success.

Ireland's economic revival undoubtedly raised the hopes of the Scottish nationalists. The SNP claimed that a future independent Scotland would surge ahead within the EU. Their opponents claimed that independence would cost £10 billion: a rise of income tax to 38p, an exodus of 92,000 jobs, and a 50 per cent hike on business tax.[92] Wishful thinking grappled with scaremongering. Both sides needed to reflect on the truth that important issues like independence were never settled by economic calculations alone.

(10) FROM STERLING TO EURO: AN UNFINISHED TALE

In modern economies, the stability of money provides one of the most potent motors of public confidence. Individuals need to know what the fruits of their labour will buy both today and tomorrow. Businesses can plan ahead. Monetary instability produces the opposite effects – anxiety, lethargy, despair.

By the second quarter of the twentieth century, the British people treated the stability of sterling as part of their favoured birthright. No one could remember a time when the pound was not 'as good as gold'. Monetary crisis in Britain, therefore, stood to have a disproportionate psychological effect. It was not surprising that a defeated Germany had suffered monetary collapse. But that victorious imperial Britain might be threatened with something similar was bewildering. Yet for the rest of the century Britain was to experience a whole series of monetary crises. In the end, the pound sterling survived. But it had absorbed a number of body blows that had considerably weakened its former position. By 1999, the British government was seriously considering what even fifty years before had been unimaginable – to join the latest variant of monetary union.

The first blow descended in 1931. Thanks to the Wall Street crash two years before, and the onset of worldwide Depression, the Bank of England decided that the pound would have to be slightly devalued and the gold standard abandoned. The practical effects of the decision were modest. The pound did not slump in the exchange rates. But the shock to British prestige was tremendous. Several countries, including Canada, were to leave the Sterling Area, which in its diminished form was renamed the Sterling Bloc. The US dollar, which did *not* leave the gold standard, gained in reputation if not – for the time being – in market value. The dollar, like the pound, endured a brief dip in 1933–4 before recovering. By 1939, at £1 = $4.460, the exchange rate was back to where it had been in 1918.

During the Second World War, Britain's finances were all but bankrupted. Colossal borrowing from the USA piled up unrepayable debts. The fact that the pound–dollar rate was fixed at £1 = $4.03 from 1940 to 1945 concealed the underlying problems. Seeing that the advent of peace could bring financial chaos, President Roosevelt convened an international conference at Bretton Woods, New Hampshire in July 1944 to establish a global system of financial management. The outcome was the creation of three portentous organizations – the International Monetary Fund (IMF) for stabilizing currencies, the International Bank for Reconstruction and Development (World Bank) for channelling investments, and the General Agreement on Tariffs and Trade (GATT) for settling problems of international commerce. By joining these organizations,

Britain, like all the other members, was accepting limitations on her previously untrammelled financial sovereignty. Bretton Woods also established a new system of international exchange rates based on the US dollar. The pound sterling was publicly knocked off its perch as the world's leading currency.

The British economist John Maynard Keynes (1883–1946) played a prominent role at Bretton Woods, whose decisions were largely determined by his economic philosophy. A strong believer in international interdependence, he had resigned as British delegate to the Paris Peace Conference in 1919, protesting against the punitive reparations imposed on Germany. An advocate of limited state management of the financial and labour markets, as expressed in his *General Theory of Employment, Interest and Money* (1936), he discredited the contention of the classical economists that optimum economic efficiency could be obtained without government intervention. He also expounded the links between economic progress and education and culture. 'Keynesianism' was to become the economic orthodoxy of post-war Britain. Its practitioners might well have taken heed of their guru's warnings: 'Practical men,' Keynes wrote, 'who believe themselves to be exempt from any intellectual influences, are usually the slaves of some defunct economist. Madmen in authority . . . are distilling their frenzy from some academic scribbler of a few years back.'[93]

Keynes harboured no regrets about the Second World War. 'We threw good housekeeping to the winds,' he philosophized, 'but we saved ourselves, and we helped save the world.'[94] Nonetheless the bill for the bad housekeeping was still waiting to be paid. The imminent collapse of sterling was repeatedly warded off by drastic cuts in government expenditure, especially on the defence of the Empire, and by massive injections of Marshall Aid. By 1949, however, the moment of truth arrived. The Attlee Government took a deep breath and devalued the pound by 33 per cent, from $4.03 to $2.80. In the prevailing opinion of the day, the largest devaluation in British history was a humiliating defeat.

In the following decades, the British public learned that there *was* life after devaluation. Foreign travel for pleasure was rendered virtually impossible by export controls which recorded the minute sums of permitted currency in the back of every would-be tourist's passport. But industrialists welcomed the competitiveness of the low pound, and foreign commerce revived rapidly. The most galling spectacle lay in the fact that the economy and currency of the supposedly defeated Germany were advancing much better than Britain's. It provided the most persuasive argument for joining 'the Six'. In 1967, the Wilson government was pushed into a further but smaller devaluation of the pound from $2.80 to $2.40. This occurred in the middle of a phase when the value of the Deutschmark against the pound almost doubled in six years – from 10.971 DM = £1 in (1967) to 6.540 DM = £1 (1973).

Anticipating membership of the EEC, the Wilson government announced in 1965 its intention of introducing a decimalized currency. Six years later, on 15 February 1971, the pound sterling was effectively divided into 100 'new pence', designated as 'p'. New coins went into circulation in denominations of 50p, 20p, 10p, 5p, 2p, 1p, and ½p. The old coins were withdrawn. The half-crown, the florin, the 'bob', the 'tanner', and the 'thre'pny bit' passed into history. A new generation grew up for whom calculation in £. s. d. was an arcane and an archaic mystery. (For those who believe that nothing is new under the sun, the florin coin, worth 2s or ¹⁄₁₀ of a pound, had been introduced in 1849 in anticipation of a decimalization policy that only materialized a hundred and twenty-one years later.)

Britain's entry into the EEC triggered several important monetary changes. For one thing, it rendered the upkeep of the Sterling Bloc pointless. By 1980, the Sterling Bloc, once the pride of the British Empire, had ceased to exist except for a handful of tiny dependencies such as Tristan da Cunha and the Falkland Islands. For another, it occurred on the eve of the worldwide oil crisis that finally knocked the almighty dollar off the gold standard and ushered in the era of floating exchange rates. Once again, however, it was the pound that fared badly, despite a short spell inside the so-called 'snake'. By 1978, the pound had fallen to $1.92 and to DM 3.85. In that same year, the European Commission introduced a voluntary monetary system, the EMS, possessing a mechanism to regulate exchange rates (ERM) and a common unit of account, the ecu. Britain did not join.

From 1979 to 1990, all aspects of British policy were dominated by the most forceful of prime ministers of modern times, Margaret Thatcher (1925–). An eager disciple of 'monetarism', a theory associated with the American economist Milton Friedman, she believed fervently in the freedom of markets and of unrestrained competition in all fields – that is, not just in the social and economic spheres but in the arts, in education, and in science. In this, she overturned not only the prevailing wisdom of Keynesian economics but also the hard-won moderation of 'One-Nation Toryism' as practised by her Conservative predecessors, Macmillan and Heath. Her philosophy led her into a principled stand against Communism, for which the peoples of Eastern Europe will be eternally grateful, and into a natural bond of mutual sympathy and affection with the right-wing American President Ronald Reagan. But it also led her into a merciless assault on the trade unions and into a deeply suspicious stance vis-à-vis the EEC, where a very different 'social market' philosophy was in vogue. Oddly enough, by hacking her way through the lower levels of bureaucracy and the institutions of local government, which she held to be unwanted obstacles to her beloved market forces, Mrs Thatcher unwittingly ended up as the greatest centralizer in British history. She believed, in theory, in minimizing government intervention. In practice, she cleared the way for government interventionism on an unprecedented scale. She was also a passionate English nationalist of the cruder ilk. She consistently confused 'Britain' with 'England', posed during the Falklands War like Henry V before Agincourt, and so offended the Scots and the Welsh that, again unwittingly, she brought back devolution from the dead. Finding all markets irresistible, she was persuaded against her better judgement to accept the Single European Act. But there was no question of joining the ERM.[95]

The Major government's dalliance with the ERM, from 1990 to

1992, started in ebullience and ended in tears. Britain's participation was intended to protect the pound from the dollar and the Deutschmark. But the bullish pronouncements of Britain's Chancellor of the Exchequer, that the pound would be defended to the last, were so unconvincing that an American speculator decided to take him on. Borrowing an astronomic sum on the money market for only a couple of days, George Soros single-handedly forced the Bank of England to devalue, drove the UK out of the ERM, and having cashed his borrowings at the new rate, walked away with a cool profit of billions. How the mighty had fallen! The Bank of England, which began with £1.2 million and a head start of three hundred years, had been thrashed by a Hungarian emigrant who began without a cent in his pocket.[96] In theory, Mrs Thatcher should have cheered.

The disaster of 1992 inevitably blighted all British attempts to approach the next round of European integration with equanimity. The introduction of a single currency by participating member states within the EU had been planned since Maastricht. The policy required a strict timetable which foresaw the fixing of conversion rates for the euro in May 1998, the adoption of the euro as the common currency of transaction on 31 December 1998, and the adoption of euro notes and coins on 1 January 2002.

In the event, only eleven of the fifteen member states joined 'Euroland'. The Republic of Ireland was one of the eleven participants. The UK was one of the four abstainers. Britain's abstention came as no surprise. The Major government had been hamstrung by a Conservative Party deeply split on European issues. British public opinion was unprepared and disorientated. The media was predominantly hostile. 'New Labour', though generally well disposed, feared another disaster. The Prime Minister, Tony Blair, having promised a future referendum, warily kept his options open.

The establishment of the euro was fiercely criticized by those who felt that the EU should have had other priorities. It had been given preference over other matters, such as the reform of the Common Agricultural Policy and expansion to the east, which many thought more urgent and more important. In this regard it was

Table 18. The Isles: total population, 1901–99

1901	1911	(1922)	1930	1940	1950	1960	1970	1980	1991	1999
44.5	45.2	47.4	48.8	51.2	53.5	55.2	58.6	59.7	61.8	63.9*[97]

* Estimated

likened to the Franco-German circle installing computerized air-conditioning in the western wing of the European house while the inhabitants of the eastern wing still struggled to mend the roof and fix the water supply. It certainly divided the EU into high-speed and low-speed zones.

Yet the significance of the Eurozone in world money markets was not confined to Europe. It was larger than the dollar zone, and a potential challenger for global leadership. If the euro were to falter, the whole European adventure would be at risk. But if the dollar faltered and the euro flourished, perhaps through the extraordinarily high level of US debt, the euro could conceivably assume the mantle of the world's premier reserve currency. In that case, Britain would definitely want to join. The euro would merely be taking over where sterling had once left off.

(II) DEMOGRAPHY: TROUGHS AND PEAKS

During the twentieth century, the population of the Isles continued to increase, but at a much reduced rate. (See Table 18, below.)

An outstanding change came with the secession of the Irish Free State from the United Kingdom. From 1921, Irish and British statistics were recorded separately. (See Table 19, overleaf.)

Urbanization reached its peak in the larger conurbations in the 1950s and 60s. Improved communications meant that people could still work in the cities while residing in the new satellite towns or in the countryside. Greater London peaked at 8.348 million in 1951, south-east Lancashire 2.428 million in 1961, the West Midlands at 2.372 millions in 1971. Some of the old industrial towns like Belfast or Halifax fell into absolute decline. But others, like Bolton or

Table 19. The population of the individual countries, 1922–99

	1922	1930	1940	1950	1960	1970	1980	1991	1999
England & Wales	38,205	39,801	41,862	44,020	45,775	48,891	49,603	48,968	53,319[*]
Scotland	4,898	4,828	5,065	5,168	5,177	5,214	5,153	4,957	5,142[*]
Northern Ireland	1,269	1,237	1,299	1,377	1,420	1,527	1,547	1,583	1,695[*]
UK total	44,370	45,866	48,226	50,565	52,372	55,632	56,303	55,508	60,156[*]
Rep. of Ireland	3,022	2,927	2,958	2,969	2,832	2,944	3,428	3,621	3,756[*,98]

[*] Estimated

Swansea, managed to survive the post-war recession and to re-expand. Many of the smaller and middle-sized cities have witnessed unbroken growth.

Table 20. Population growth of smaller and middle-sized cities, 1901–81

	1901	1931	1961	1981
Aberdeen	154,000	167,000	185,000	204,000
Bolton	168,000	177,000	161,000	261,000
Bournemouth	47,000	117,000	154,000	146,000
Cambridge	38,000	67,000	96,000	91,000
Halifax	105,000	98,000	96,000	87,000
Luton	36,000	69,000	140,000	165,000
Oxford	49,000	81,000	106,000	99,000
Swansea	95,000	165,000	167,000	187,000
Worcester	47,000	51,000	66,000	75,000[99]

In Ireland, an important reversal of fortunes took place, with symbolic as well as purely economic consequence. As Belfast waned, Dublin waxed strong. From the time it became the capital of the Republic, Dublin never looked back. Indeed, it was entering the new millennium on the jaws and claws of the self-proclaimed 'Tiger Economy'. (See Table 21, right.)

Birth rates, which had risen steadily through the early nineteenth century to a peak of around 36 per 1,000 in the 1870s, have been gradually falling ever since. As one would expect, sudden 'baby booms' occurred after each of the world wars – a jump from 18.5 to

Table 21. Population growth of Ireland's chief cities, 1901–81

	1901	1931	1961	1981
Belfast	349,000	438,000	416,000	306,000
Dublin	291,000	473,000*	537,000	526,000[100]

* 1936

25.5 per 1,000 in 1919–20, and another from 15.9 to 20.5 per 1,000 in 1945–47 – but the general trend moved downwards to around 13 per 1,000 in 1980. Contrary to widespread belief, the birth rate in Ireland was consistently lower than in Great Britain throughout the nineteenth century, although it has stayed extraordinarily constant throughout the history of the Republic, starting at 19.5 per 1,000 in 1922 and reaching 21.9 per 1,000 in 1980.[101]

Death rates have fallen slowly but steadily. In England and Wales, they reached 25 per 1,000 in 1849, and stood at 11.2 per 1,000 in 1980. The key index of infant mortality, which started at 151 per 1,000 live births in 1839, did not fall below 100 per 1,000 until the First World War, and not below 20 per 1,000 until 1965.[102]

Emigration has also continued, although the numbers involved have tailed off considerably since the 1960s. In the period after the Second World War, emigration persisted at a high rate alongside the unprecedented wave of Commonwealth immigration. Emigration to the USA, for instance, has kept going with surprising regularity. Apart from one or two exceptional years, the absolute number of emigrants leaving Ireland for the USA exceeded those from Great Britain until 1904. Since then, British emigrants have exceeded Irish emigrants.

Table 22. Emigrants to the USA from Great Britain and Ireland, 1900–79

	1900	1910	1920	1930	1940	1950	1960	1970	1979
Great Britain	13,000	69,000	38,000	31,000	6,200	13,000	20,000	14,000	16,000
Ireland	36,000	30,000	9,600	23,000	800	5,800	6,900	1,200	800[103]

The aggregated total of emigrants from the Isles cannot be precisely calculated. But a hundred years after Seeley's prediction, there could be no question: his estimate of a hundred million Britishers at home and abroad had been surpassed. The President of Ireland, Mary Robinson, once reputedly boasted that the world contained seventy million people of Irish origin alone.

The socio-economic status of the emigrants changed as well. Until the Second World War, poverty was the driving force. After 1945, it was skilled and educated people who predominated, until 'the brain drain' became a recognized phenomenon. Similar patterns were observable in outward flows to Canada, Australia, New Zealand, and South Africa. In the case of South Africa, which left the Commonwealth in 1961, political obstacles acted as a brake.

The net result of two hundred years of emigration was an enormous worldwide community of communities who in one way or another had maintained ties with their original homelands in the Isles. In the twentieth century, almost all these overseas emigrants organized institutional links with their 'Mother Country'. Most of their organizations were cultural, though some were overtly political. Many hovered midway between the cultural and the political.

The English-Speaking Union (ESU), for example, was founded in 1918 by Sir Evelyn Wrench (1882–1966) and Dr Walter Hines Page, the US Ambassador in London. The second chairman, 1921–6, was Winston Churchill. On the surface, the ESU looked more like a cultural society, promoting exchanges, conferences, scholarships, and international use of the English language. Yet despite its self-definition as a 'non-political association', it has a manifest political purpose. Its founding document talks of maintaining 'the unity in purpose of the English-speaking democracies' and 'a good understanding between the peoples of the USA and the British Commonwealth'. Its two main headquarters were in London and New York, though it had branches round the world.[104] Whether intentionally or not, it served as a major prop to the Anglo-American alliance.

The Cambrian Societies accentuated the cultural less ambiguously. Their prime concern had always been associated with the Welsh heritage of language, song, and literature. The National Welsh–American Foundation, based in Pennsylvania, had counterparts in Canada, Australia, New Zealand, even in Oslo.[105] An eisteddfod or a Cymanfa Ganu, a 'Festival of Song', was something to be seen and heard. They were part of a worldwide Celtic Revival (see above).

The overseas Irish organizations were probably the most numerous of all. They varied from the Ancient Order of Hibernians, which was an old-established society for lay Catholics,[106] to bodies which existed to fund and publicize the IRA. The political muscle of this 'Irish Lobby' had been steadily growing throughout the twentieth century. Several American presidents, from Kennedy to Nixon, Reagan and Clinton, traced their roots to the Irish emigrant ships; and their role as arbiters in the British–Irish conflict has inevitably grown.

As for demographic patterns within the Isles themselves, two contemporary features stood out at the approach of the millennium. One of these was the further crushing preponderance of England, which by 1999 had risen to 78 per cent of the total population from 58 per cent in 1800. Within the UK, it was still higher, at 83 per cent. This preponderance undoubtedly inflamed resentments against 'the Centre' and encouraged the revival of 'Devolution'.

The other feature related to a marked imbalance within England itself. Whereas the second half of the nineteenth century saw a centrifugal movement of population to the North and West, the second half of the twentieth has seen the opposite – a centripetal concentration of both numbers and wealth back to the South-east. One has only to look at the relative growth of the counties. (See Table 23, overleaf.) At 7.678 million (1981), Greater London, though slightly reduced from its former peak, was still larger than all the other major conurbations put together. Overall, the South-east contained no less than 32 per cent of England's, and 29 per cent of the UK's, citizens.

Quite apart from the horrors of congestion, pollution, and vehicular gridlock, the sheer size of the South-East was sure to have political consequences. It would make London government look increasingly like a regime for the benefit of the Home Counties. It could possibly bring the English regions closer to Wales and Scotland

Table 23. Population of the counties and new regions, 1891–1981 (thousands)[107]

	1891	1981	*Growth per cent*
Orkney	30	19	−36.7
Western Isles	45	32	−28.9
Cumbria and Borders	130	100	−23.1
Powys	117	111	−5.2
Highland	201	200	−0.5
Cumbria	432	487	+12.7
West Yorkshire	1,598	2,037	+127
Lancashire	890	1,377	+155
Kent	710	1,468	+207
Cambridgeshire	277	579	+209
Oxfordshire	232	519	+224
Bedfordshire	163	507	+311
Berkshire	211	681	+328
Buckinghamshire	167	568	+340
West Sussex	177	662	+374
Essex	367	1,474	+402
Hertfordshire	214	957	+447
Surrey	217	1,004	+463

in a common cause against London. And it would strengthen the tendency of less favoured areas to look beyond London to Brussels for help against the spreading tentacles of the south-eastern monster.

Over the century, Britain's international demographic ranking had dropped several places. Gone were the days when it could turn to the Empire and claim to be the world's number one. In 1999, it was number three in Europe after Russia and Germany. It was number two out of fifteen in the European Union. Vis-à-vis the USA, the UK had almost dropped out of sight. With roughly half of the USA's population in 1900, it could now only reach just over a quarter. The British had to reconcile themselves to the fact that they now belonged to a middle-sized nation.

On this score, the Republic of Ireland had more to rejoice about. Demographically, Ireland was tiny. It could be likened in size to

Israel, to Iceland, Cambodia, New Guinea, or to South-east Lanca-shire. Among EU members, it was half the size of Austria, a third of the size of Belgium, a quarter of the size of the Netherlands. Luxembourg alone was smaller. But Ireland had prospered more than its British neighbours had; and it had a voice at all the top tables. Within the communal framework, it was living proof not just that 'small is beautiful' but that 'small is effective'.

On the brink of the twenty-first century, globalization was everywhere persuading sovereign states to join larger political and economic groupings. Both Britain and Ireland were members of the European Union, a grouping with a population of 375 million that dwarfed both of them. Safety was thought to lie with the big numbers. And for those who took pride in the size of things, the European Union was about to expand further. By the time it had absorbed the next wave of prospective entrants, including 40 million Poles, 10 million Czechs, 10 million Hungarians and 2 million Slovenians, it would contain almost exactly the same number of people as the late British Empire at its height. If only they could see it, the British were moving from the psychological point of view, out of a trough and back towards a peak.

(12) LANGUAGE AND CULTURE: CENTRIFUGAL TENDENCIES

Despite what many English people believe, British culture is extremely complex. Quite apart from English culture, which comes in a dozen major regional variations, a vibrant group of non-English counter-cultures developed in the nineteenth and early twentieth centuries. In origin, each of the counter-cultures was based on a Celtic language. Hence there was a strong revival of Welsh literature written in Welsh, there was a determined campaign by Irish nationalists to rescue Erse, and in the Highlands and Islands of Scotland there was a parallel movement to preserve Gaelic. Yet each of these Celtic movements was accompanied by an important shadow – by a movement which used the English language as a medium for promoting non- or even anti-English purposes. Thus there was a distinct Welsh literary community writing in English, and similar Irish and Scottish communities doing the same. In Scotland, yet another variation arose, namely a movement to revive Lallans as an alternative both to Gaelic and to English. All in all, if the count is correct, the realm of standard English was challenged from at least seven directions at once. And all that happened before the influx of a still richer mix of non-British Englishes from all over the world (see below).

Throughout the modern period, standard English passed almost without comment as the accepted vehicle of state-backed power. 'It hath ever been the use of the conqueror,' Edmund Spenser had written, 'to despise the language of the conquered.' Ever since England's union with Wales, it was assumed that 'diversity of language must ultimately be eradicated.'[108]

All minority languages, literatures, and regional cultures which existed were tolerated because they were thought to lack political ambition. They had no significance beyond some peripheral locality or small eccentric grouping. All the leading non-English writers and thinkers of the age from Edmund Burke and David Hume to Bernard Shaw and Oscar Wilde were drawn into the mainstream of the English-speaking British literary establishment.

However, from the early nineteenth century onwards, language has assumed a repertoire of new roles in modern society that was at the best latent in former times. On the one hand, philology, linguistics, and hermeneutics have developed as major scholarly disciplines. They have come to exercise a profound influence on the study of the humanities in general and on history-writing in particular.[109] Hermeneutics, for instance, which is concerned with the interpretative principles used in textual analysis, is the key subject for understanding both 'postmodernist' literary theory and the postmodernist assault on the established historiographical canon.[110] On the more practical level, language has become a vehicle for new forms of national consciousness, in particular for contemporary nationalist movements. In their ineffable imperial confidence, British

scholars often assumed that language-based nationalisms only operated on the Continent. Yet they have been present all along in the
Isles; and they have been growing in prominence.

In Wales, or at least in the northern and western districts of
Wales, the Welsh language had sturdily held its own against the
English advance. It was the bedrock of religious life in the chapels,
and it commanded a healthy secular sector, which grew increasingly
critical of chapel-inspired puritanical ways. The 'neo-druidism' that
accompanied the revival of the annual sessions of the National
Eisteddfod from the 1860s must be recognized as entirely bogus. But
the really interesting feature of that revival is that it possessed no
nationalist, let alone anti British overtones. A picture of the National
Eisteddfod at Aberystwyth in 1865, as published in the *Illustrated
London News*, shows a hall bedecked with Union Jacks and a banner
in English to Queen Victoria's son: 'God Bless the Prince of Wales'.
The mix of religion and romanticism that is evident in the work of
Victorian Welsh writers was well matched to the romantic English
vogue for Welshness as launched by the highly popular travelogue
of the Revd George Borrow, *Wild Wales* (1862).

The resurgence of Welsh literature with clear political ambitions
was delayed until the early twentieth century, and it followed a
plethora of mutually incompatible paths.[111] The Welsh language
sector, which had old-established traditions of its own, did not
always take kindly to Anglo-Welsh literature written in English.
Two men helped to bridge the gap – Emrys ap Iwan (Robert
Ambrose Jones, 1848 1906), sometimes dubbed 'the father of Welsh
Nationalism', and John Morris-Jones (1864–1929), the first Professor
of Welsh language at University College, Bangor. The latter provided modern Welsh with two indispensable aids – his *Welsh
Grammar* (1913) and his *Cerdd Dafod* (1925) on Welsh poetics.

Ideological discordance was no less divisive than the language
issue. Nationalist literature in Welsh usually cultivated the rural idyll
of the North, while Anglo-Welsh writers from the South were more
often absorbed by Socialist politics and by urban-industrial issues. It
is not without significance that the pioneer of modern Welsh lyric

poetry, John Ceiriog Hughes (1832–87), lived and worked as a railway official in Manchester. His successors included T. Gwynn Jones (1871–1949), Robert Williams Parry (1884–1956), and T. H. Parry-Williams (1887–1975).

The literature of the 'Valleys' was not written exclusively in English. J. Kitchener Davies's successful play *Cwm Glo*, 'Coal Valley' (1935), was first presented in Welsh. An influential writer, Caradoc Evans (1878–1945), emerged with a searing novel, *My People* (1915), which attacked both the hypocrisy of chapel society and the high-minded myth of the *gwerin*, the noble common folk. The novel by Richard Llewellyn (1906–83), *How Green was My Valley* (1939), broke out of the Welsh compound and became a worldwide best seller.

As a political figure, however, no contemporary Welshman could compare with J. Saunders Lewis (1893–1985). Born in Liverpool of Welsh-speaking parents, he was a convert to Catholicism, and in 1925 a founding member of the Welsh National Party, Plaid Cymru. His literary work was mainly as a dramatist, but his reputation was made as a political activist. He combined passionate Welsh patriotism with a strong belief in a Pan-European civilization based on the heritage of Christianity. In this respect, he has been likened to T. S. Eliot. Lewis first hit the headlines in 1936 after an arson attack on the RAF bombing range at Penyberth. He and his companions were found guilty, but only after the trial had been transferred from Caernarvon to the Old Bailey. Nearly thirty years later, his BBC Radio Lecture 'Tyged yr Iaith' ('The Fate of Language', 1962) brought disputes over Welsh language rights to a head. Threats of hunger-strikes, campaigns against English road signs, and more violent attacks on English-owned holiday homes surrounded the government's decision to pursue a bilingual policy throughout Wales – in schools, in the media, in the courts and administration. The Cymdeithas yr Iaith Gymraeg (the Welsh Language Society) was founded that same year. Since then, the social constituency of the Welsh Language has been steadily expanding. 'Civilisation must be more than an abstraction,' Saunders Lewis wrote, 'it must have a local habitation and a name. Here, its name is Wales.'[112] After the death of Saunders Lewis, one of the upcoming Welsh poets, Alan Llywd (1948–) wrote 'Tranc y Cof' ('The Passing of Memory'):

> Mae ein Cof fel ogof laith, – ond di-swn
>> Yw'r atseinio hirfaith
> O'i mewn, lle clywem unwaith
> Lenwi'r hollt gan lanw'r iaith
>
> *(Our Memory is like a damp cave, but soundless*
>> *Is the long echoing*
> *Inside it, where once we heard*
> *The gap filled by the tide of language)*[113]

Dylan Thomas (1914–53) achieved for Welsh literature in English what Saunders Lewis achieved for the Welsh language. Habitually playing up to his chosen role as a drunk and a social pest, he died early, but not before putting the cadences and the inimitable articulation of English as spoken in Wales into the ears of people around the world. He did it, a month before his death, through his radio 'play for voices', *Under Milk Wood*:

[*Silence*]

FIRST VOICE (*Very softly*)
To begin at the beginning:
It is spring, moonless night in the small town, starless and bible-black, the cobble streets silent and the hunched, courters'-and-rabbits' wood limping invisible down to the sloeblack, slow, black, crowblack, fishingboat-bobbing sea. The houses are blind as moles (though moles see fine to-night in the snouting, velvet dingles) or blind as Captain Cat there in the muffled middle by the pump and the town clock, the shops in mourning, the Welfare Hall in widows' weeds. And all the people of the lulled and dumbfound town are sleeping now.[114]

The action takes place in the imaginary village of Llareggub, which, as someone worked out, when read backwards turns into 'Bugger

All'. In the initial broadcast on 25 January 1954, the First Voice was read by Richard Burton.

Post-war Welsh literature undoubtedly possessed a desperate streak. Welsh nationalists regarded both the pseudo-investiture of the Prince of Wales in 1969 and the defeat of the Devolution Referendum in 1979 as unmitigated disasters. For a time, they felt they were fighting the last battle of a dying nation:

> Where can I go, then, from the smell
> Of decay, from the putrefying of a dead
> Nation? I have walked the shore
> For an hour and seen the English
> Scavenging among the remains
> Of our culture . . ., of elbowing our language
> Into the grave that we have dug for it.[115]

R. S. Thomas (1913–) was among the generation that had learned Welsh as an adult. Angharad Tomos (1958–) was one of Wales's female bards. Her novel *Yma O Hyd*, 'Still Here' (1985) was written as an ironic account of national failure. Its title was borrowed for a popular song, and transformed into a defiant anthem of optimism. It was composed at the time when the Thatcher government was destroying the South Wales coal industry – an event which promised to do more to reunite the Welsh people than anything else in living memory.

The cultural scene in late Victorian Ireland bore little resemblance to that in Wales. The Irish language was almost defunct, whilst the politicization of the people was far advanced. The Irish Revival, therefore, followed its own priorities.

The *spiritus movens* was Douglas Hyde (1860–1949), the first Professor of Irish at Dublin's National University. The son of a Protestant clergyman, Hyde wrote a pioneering *History of Irish Literature* (1892); and he set high hopes on so reviving Gaelic that it would become the national language of the future republic. (His ambitions can only be likened to those of the Jews of Eastern Europe who at the very same time were setting out to revive Hebrew as the language of the future, as yet non-existent Israel.) The Gaelic League was founded in 1893 at Hyde's instigation, and the Abbey Theatre staged some of his Gaelic plays. Hyde was duly rewarded, being elevated to the presidency of the Irish Republic, 1938–45.[116]

The Gaelic League addressed a population which by then was 90 per cent English-speaking. It provided materials for self-teaching – used, for instance by Eamonn de Valera, the future premier – and laid the groundwork for schooling in Gaelic. In the long run it could only press for limited aims: to preserve the native language in the shrinking western Gaeltacht, and to introduce a degree of bilingualism in the rest of Ireland.

Not everyone in the Irish Revival, however, shared Hyde's enthusiasm for teaching Gaelic. Many thought that the most urgent priority was to collect traditional folklore and to publish it in an accessible form in England. This task was undertaken by Samuel Ferguson (1810–86), sometime keeper of the Records in Dublin. Ferguson's *Songs of the Western Gael* (1865) and his epic poem *Congal* (1872), which celebrated the last stand of the Irish pagans against Christianity, were immensely suggestive. His posthumous collection *Ogham Inscriptions in Ireland, Wales and Scotland* (1894) provided materials for later scholars. Others thought that the establishment of a sound framework for Irish history should have precedence. This task was taken on by one Standish James O'Grady (1846–1929). 'Like the fool he was', one critic comments, O'Grady 'rushed in where the angels of scholarship feared to tread.'[117] The product was the excruciatingly awful *History of Ireland: the Heroic Period* (1880). It had chapter after chapter on the Ice Ages and on racial fantasies, and never proceeded beyond the era of legends. It was, as the author unfortunately explained, 'the kind of history which a nation deserves to possess'.[118] For two decades, it was the only history which the nation could get. Still others believed that top priority should be given to the creation of a national theatre. This was done in 1899 by W. B. Yeats and Lady Gregory, whose Irish Literary Theatre joined forces with the Abbey Theatre five years later.

William Butler Yeats (1865–1939) came onto the scene quite early. The son of a highly sophisticated painter, he was educated partly in London, and won over to Irish nationalism by a family friend, an ex-Fenian. He saturated himself for years in folklore, and was a great admirer of O'Grady. 'He made the old Irish heroes alive again,' he recalled, 'and that was all that mattered.'[119] Yeats, however, rejected Hyde's ideal of 'De-anglicising Ireland'. He did not accept Hyde's assertion that the Irish language was 'the best claim we have upon the world's recognition of us as a separate nationality'. Instead, he set out to create a special brand of English, which had 'an indefinable Irish quality of rhythm and style'. The rest, one is tempted to say, was just language – searing, super-charged, magnificent language:

> What wounds, what bloody press
> Dragged into being
> This loveliness.[120]

Yeats was able to achieve his new synthesis of Irish English because he had mastered the English classics no less than Irish folklore. In the early years when he published *The Wanderings of Oisin* (1889), *Fairy and Folk Tales of the Irish Peasantry* (1892), and *The Celtic Twilight* (1893) he was also editing the works of William Blake and the poems of Edmund Spenser. He was awarded the Nobel Prize for Literature in 1923.[121]

Ireland's literary giants followed thick and fast. J. M. Synge (1871–1909) was viciously denounced both by Yeats and Patrick Pearse for his drama *The Playboy of the Western World* (1907). The plays of Sean O'Casey (1880–1964), such as *The Plough and the Stars* (1926), aroused such uproar in Dublin that he moved permanently to England. Samuel Beckett (1906–89), author of *En attendant Godot* (1952; *Waiting for Godot*, 1954) and another Nobel laureate, settled permanently in Paris. Seamus Heaney (1939–), a third Irish Nobel Prize winner, was born in Northern Ireland, so was technically

British. But such details were of secondary importance. Their Irishness shone through everything.

There was a powerful, unmistakeable Irish flavour, too, in the genial writings of James Joyce (1882–1941), who was criticized in some quarters for 'turning his back on Ireland'. Pan-European in outlook, and a peripatetic polyglot, Joyce had little interest in everyday Irish politics, and spent most of his life abroad – in Trieste, in Zurich, and in Paris. Yet his masterpiece, *Ulysses* (1922), is a magnificent distillation of turn-of-the-century Dublin. In one of its teeming, chaotic episodes, the young Stephen Daedalus is learning simultaneously about the English, about money and about history during a hilarious meeting with his eccentric headmaster, Mr Deasy:

> —Because you don't save, Mr Deasy said, pointing his finger. You don't know yet what money is. Money is power, when you have lived as long as I have. I know, I know. If youth but knew. But what does Shakespeare say? *Put but money in thy purse.*
>
> —Iago, Stephen murmured.
>
> He lifted his gaze from the idle shells to the old man's stare.
>
> —He knew what money was, Mr Deasy said. He made money. A poet but an Englishman too. Do you know what is the pride of the English? Do you know what is the proudest word you will ever hear from an Englishman's mouth?
>
> The seas' ruler. His seacold eyes looked on the empty bay: history is to blame: on me and on my words, unhating.
>
> —That on his empire, Stephen said, the sun never sets.
>
> —Ba! Mr Deasy cried. That's not English. A French Celt said that. He tapped his savingsbox against his thumbnail.
>
> —I will tell you, he said solemnly, what is his proudest boast. *I paid my way.*
>
> Good man, good man.
>
> . . .
>
> —Mark my words, Mr Dedalus, he said. England is in the hands of the jews. In all the highest places: her finance, her

press. And they are the signs of a nation's decay. Wherever they gather they eat up the nation's vital strength. I have seen it coming these years. As sure as we are standing here the jew merchants are already at their work of destruction. Old England is dying.

He stepped swiftly off, his eyes coming to blue life as they passed a broad sunbeam. He faced about and back again.

—Dying, he said, if not dead by now.

> The harlot's cry from street to street
> Shall weave old England's winding sheet.

His eyes open wide in vision stared sternly across the sunbeam in which he halted.

. . .

—History, Stephen said, is in a nightmare from which I am trying to awake.

From the playfield the boys raised a shout. A whirring whistle: goal. What if that nightmare gave you a back kick?

—The ways of the Creator are not our ways, Mr Deasy said. All history moves towards one great goal, the manifestation of God.

Stephen jerked his thumb towards the window, saying:

—That is God.

. . .

Mr Deasy halted, breathing hard and swallowing his breath.

—I just wanted to say, he said. Ireland, they say, has the honour of being the only country which never persecuted the jews. Do you know that? No. And do you know why?

He frowned sternly on the bright air.

—Why, sir? Stephen asked, beginning to smile.

—Because she never let them in, Mr Deasy said solemnly.[122]

From the national point of view, Scotland was in the most miserable condition at the turn of the century. The few lonely voices, such as

those of Keir Hardie and James Mackinnon, who were calling for
Home Rule, were crying in the wilderness. They did not have the
local backing that the Irish did. Nothing was done, even when John
Buchan, by then a famous novelist and MP for the Scottish Universities, addressed the House of Commons in 1932:

> . . . I believe that every Scotsman should be a Scottish nation-
> alist. If it could be proved that a separate Scottish Parliament
> were desirable . . . Scotsmen would support it . . . The main
> force is clearly . . . the cultural force, the desire that Scotland
> shall not lose her historic personality . . .
>
> May I be allowed to say a word to my friends who regard
> this whole question as trivial . . . compared to the great
> economic problems with which we are faced? . . . Believe me,
> this question is not trivial. It goes to the very root . . . of Britain
> and the Empire. Britain cannot afford . . . a denationalised
> Scotland. In Sir Walter Scott's famous words,
> 'If you un-Scotch us, you will make us damn mischievous
> Englishmen.'
>
> We do not want to be like the Greeks, powerful and
> prosperous wherever we settle, but with a dead Greece behind
> us. We do not want to be like the Jews of the Dispersion – a
> potent force everywhere on the globe, but with no Jerusalem.[123]

This was a manifesto.

Buchan stressed 'the cultural force'. The fact of the matter
was that Scotland's cultural forces were desperately enfeebled. The
independent literary tradition had almost died out. The man
who revived it, in the first instance almost single-handedly, was
Christopher Murray Grieve (1892–1978), a native of Langholm
in the Borders, who survived the trenches of the Western Front
with a burning conviction about the urgency of both social and
cultural revolution. A founder member of the Scottish National
Party (SNP) in 1928, he was expelled five years later when he
joined the Communist Party, from which he was also expelled,
and then rejoined. He is numbered among the many inglorious

poets who once wrote a *Hymn to Lenin*. Forty years later he explained:

> I must be a Bolshevik
> Before the Revolution, but I'll cease to be one quick
> When Communism comes to rule the roost,
> For real literature can exist only when it's produced
> By madmen, hermits, heretics,
> Dreamers, rebels, sceptics –
> And such a door of utterance has been given to me.[124]

In the 1920s, Grieve took the pen name of Hugh MacDiarmid. His life's work was dedicated thereafter to 'the encouragement of Scots and Gaelic, the necessity of Scottish independence, and the recognition that . . . a deep-seated Radicalism . . . is a prime require-ment of Scottish conditions today.'[125] He left the Gaelic to others; but he reinvented a synthetic Scots or Lallans for contemporary use. His masterpiece is, by general acclaim, 'A Drunk Man Looks at the Thistle' (1926):

> Whatever Scotland is to me
> Be it aye pairt o' a' men see
> O' Earth and O' Eternity
> Wha winna hide their heids in't till
> It seems the haill o' space to fill,
> As 'twere an unsurmounted hill.
>
> He canna Scotland see what yet
> canna see the Infinite,
> And Scotland in true scale to it.[126]

MacDiarmid's legacy includes the SNP, which by the 1990s was competing for power in Scotland: the Lallans Society, which was pressing for the replacement of standard English in schools, and above all, the continuing 'deep-seated radical tradition'. One writer in this tradition, Tom Nairn (1932–), author of *The Break-up of Britain* (1977), saw the root of Scotland's distress in her 'cultural self-emasculation':

the relationship between civil society and state in Scotland precluded a fully national culture . . . Instead, what it led to was a strange sort of . . . stunted, caricatural . . . 'cultural sub-nationalism.' It was cultural of course because it could not be political; on the other hand this culture could not be straight-forwardly nationalist either . . .[127]

By the late twentieth century, normal Scottish nationalism had finally surfaced.

Within the hierarchy of Scottish woes, the distress of the Gaelic-speaking community was by far the most acute. The Highlands and Islands had supplied the largest cohorts of emigrants. Until 1918, there was no provision whatsoever for Gaelic education. The punitive 'hanging stick' – the equivalent of the Welsh 'not' – was still in use until the 1960s. The Post Office refused to deliver letters addressed with Gaelic names. Effective secondary education in Gaelic had never been provided. Numbers fell alarmingly. The census of 1881 showed 245,415 Gaelic-speakers or 6.84 per cent of Scotland's population. By the 1990s, the total had fallen below 90,000, or 1.8 per cent. Ever since its foundation in 1899, the An Comunn Gaidhealach, or 'Gaelic Society', had been fighting a rearguard action.[128]

The Gaelic Revival of the 1970s, therefore, came at 'five to midnight'. Gaelic radio, a Gaelic TV channel, bilingual road signs, a Gaelic College, the Sabhal Mor Ostaig on Skye, a Gaelic arts agency, and annual Gaelic song festivals have been among the first fruits. And those melancholy Gaelic laments were still being written:

> 'S chan aithne dhomh ceart d' fhiamh no do dhòigh
> an dèidh còig bliadhna shiantan
> tìme dortadh eadar mise 's tù.[129]
>
> (I do not right know your appearance or your manner
> after five years of showers
> of time pouring between me and you.)

≈

European connections featured prominently in all these 'non-metro-politan perspectives'. Many of the Welsh writers were strong Euro-peanists. Saunders Lewis saw Catholic Europe as his main inspiration. Most of the Irish pantheon, too, despised insularity. James Joyce could write to Ibsen in Norwegian. Beckett preferred to write in French. MacDiarmid saw himself as an internationalist first, and a nationalist second. They all valued their languages because they valued the wider heritage embodied in them.

Nonetheless, as Ireland demonstrated, the loss of language does not by any means equate with the death of identity. The last native Cornish speaker died in 1799. Yet, two hundred years later, Cornish Societies were among the most energetic on the worldwide Celtic circuit. (One could even contact Los Hijos de Kernow in Albuquer-que, NM.) The Cowethas Kelto-Kernuak, or 'Celto-Cornish Society', had been thriving since 1901. The Gorsedh Kernow held annual bardic rallies on the model of the Welsh eisteddfodau from 1940s onwards. The lost language was reconstituted by scholars such as Henry Jenner and Morton Nance (1873–1959). And Cornish poets broke once more into song:

> My a gews hep let, my a gan a goll . . .
>
> *(I talk without hindrance, I sing of a loss.)*[130]

The Manx language expired on 27 December 1974 with the death at Glen Chiass, Port St Mary, of the last native speaker, Ned Maddrell, aged ninety-seven. 'At the funeral, not a word of his native language was spoken or sung.' But his passing did not go unnoticed. It was noticed, among others, by the Regius Professor of History at Oxford, himself a Celtic speaker.[131] But funerals are not the end. Celtic scholars were hard at work.[132] As Cornish had demonstrated, there was a real hope that dead voices could sing.

Oddly enough, at the very moment when the standard-bearers of standard English might have been thought to have conquered the world, they faltered in their step. Standard English fell out of fashion. The all-conquering hero, which had an unassailable position in the Isles and which was now, in conjunction with its American cousin, the *lingua franca* of world science, global communications, and international affairs, suffered a minor stroke at home, a loss of confidence. To what extent the crisis was caused by the end of Empire is open to question. It may have been coincidental. But the historic drive to have everyone in the United Kingdom using a similar pronunciation and following the same rules of grammar and punctuation simply ground to a halt. In the mid-1960s, regional accents came back into vogue. BBC presenters no longer tried to be speak-alikes. The Prime Minister, Harold Wilson, who was schooled in Lancashire, took pride in his northern accent. Suddenly, the Scouse of the Beatles was as good as cut-glass Cheltenham or educated Edinburgh. Regional diversity was back in fashion for the first time since early Victoria. Small boys who passed their scholarship exam to grammar school were no longer sent for 'helocution' lessons. Indeed, there were no more grammar schools to send them to. In the parallel mode for child-centred education, schools stopped inflicting grammar on children altogether. University students could obtain a degree without ever learning the difference between *its* and *it's*. Sloppy speech habits were not to be corrected. Under the influence of transatlantic imports, anyone could feel free to speak 'on-line', 'in-house', or 'off-beat' as fancy dictated. Within a generation, encouraged by complacent broadcasters, the 'slurping and grunting' of Estuary English had become the prevalent mode of speech of millions (see below). Standard English was in no less need of protection than Gaelic was. So, too, were genuine Cockney, Geordie, and Scouse.[133]

The academic study of English literature lost its way during the same years. Contrary to popular impressions, Faculties of English were a relatively recent addition to England's universities. They had been pioneered in Scotland in the eighteenth century, and had spread to the USA, Australia, and New Zealand in the nineteenth.[134] But they only reached England in the twentieth. (Oxford's Faculty of English dates from 1921.) The English people apparently did not feel the need to propagate their literature like the colonials once did, as a form of cultural cement. As a result, barely fifty years separated the establishment of English literature as a recognized discipline and the onset of deconstructionist literary theory, which blighted the subject thereafter. Literary appreciation was left to the uninitiated.

On the international front, a new language called 'World English' emerged. It was the LCD of all the other Englishes. But it was in universal use – on the Internet, by air traffic control, and, as a second language, by hundreds of millions the world over. In 1999, it was even given its own dedicated dictionary by the efforts of Microsoft Corp.[135] In the enlarged European Union of 'Fifteen', it was suddenly the means whereby Finns could converse with Greeks, or Danes with Portuguese.

The language crisis in the European Union had been long foreseen and long neglected. When the British stayed out in the 1950s, the Francophone *énarques* of the European movement established French as their working language; German was often used from the Messina Conference onwards, but only unofficially. All the languages of all member states received equal status in all formal sessions and documents. But it was English, not German, that was added as an official working language in 1973 after the entry of Ireland and the UK. A quarter of a century later, the policy was splitting at the seams. The costs of translation and simultaneous interpretation were astronomic. In July 1999, when Finland accepted the EU's rotating presidency, it was announced that translation services for all informal meetings in Finland would be confined to English, French, and Finnish. The German government announced a boycott.[136] After all, 90 million of the EU's 370 million spoke German as their native tongue.

Europe remained a Tower of Babel. But bluffs and boycotts could solve nothing. Misunderstandings were rife enough as it was. One foreign minister, who had used a metaphor about 'shooting rapids', was thought by his colleagues to have pronounced on 'shooting rabbits' and inadvertently started a debate about pest control. In practice, neither French, nor German, nor Standard

English nor World English was the Union's lingua franca. It was English pidgin that ruled the roost. With the imminent advent of these paragons of simplicity Polish, Czech, Hungarian, and Slovenian, the cacophonous cooing and crowing was set to deteriorate still further.

Sooner or later, one common lead language would have to be adopted for the whole of the Union, in precedence over all other bilingual or trilingual strategies; and it would have to be systematically taught to all. The Father of the European Parliament, Dr von Habsburg, once tried out a speech in Latin. But he was three hundred years too late. For the purposes of the twenty-first century, there was only one possible candidate. If only Britain's Europhobes could see it, this fact could turn them into Europhiles overnight.

(13) Multiracial Britain: 'A New Way of Being British'

Views on 'Race' have undergone enormous changes in the course of the twentieth century. A hundred years ago, genetic science was incapable of explaining human differentiation sensibly. In Britain, as elsewhere, pseudo-science flourished, and eugenics was a popular and respectable subject. The British, who were familiar with horse-breeding, tended to think of 'human breeds' in the same terms. They certainly confused 'race' with 'nation', assuming that the 'English Race' and the 'Scottish Race' were biologically distinct. They were also acutely aware of 'colour', although they had no better guide than the crude 'Five Race Scheme' of black, brown, red, white, and yellow that had been current throughout the nineteenth century. They went along with the dubious equation of 'white' with 'European', variously misdescribed as 'Aryan' or 'Caucasian'. The primitive and unacceptable state of prevailing 'race theory' was not properly exposed and discredited until 1945, when the full horrors of the German Nazis' pseudo-science became apparent. The discovery of DNA by two British scientists in 1953 placed informed discussion onto a completely new plane. Henceforth, no one could seriously contest the fact that all human beings share a hugely similar genetic make-up.

The first major modern influx of foreign immigrants was that of East European Jews in the period 1885–1905. Fleeing the poverty of the Jewish Pale of Settlement in the Russian Empire, as well as the fear of persecution, Yiddish-speaking Jewish immigrants arrived in a sudden, uncontrolled flood, quickly transforming the East End of London and similar districts in other major cities into predominantly Jewish districts. They were far from uniform. Some were highly educated and assimilated into Russian or Polish culture. Most, however, belonged to Orthodox or Chassidic religious groups, who followed strict practices of dress, diet, and hygiene, and separate residence. Their arrival was greatly assisted by existing institutions such as the Chief Rabbinate (1758) and the Board of Deputies of British Jews (1760), and, at the political level, by the Anglo-Jewish Association (AJA). Their numbers – about a hundred thousand in total – caused the British government to pass the Aliens Act (1906); and the incidence of anti-Semitism increased, especially during the short-lived appearance of the British Union of Fascists in the 1930s. Nonetheless, the dispersion, integration, and in large measure the assimilation of Jewish immigrants was essentially complete by 1939. One last wave arrived immediately before the Second World War from the highly modernized Jewish communities of Germany and Austria. Since then, their contribution to British life has been outstanding.

In Victorian and Edwardian times, of course, Jews were seen as a racial group, not just as a religious one. This view was strengthened by the tenets of Orthodox Judaism, which forbade intermarriage and which automatically regarded all children of Jewish mothers as Jews. Assimilation, therefore, was not a simple matter. It was helped by the rise of Reform Judaism, which relaxed many of the 613 religious rules. But its demands forced many Jews to abandon their community, to adopt radical social or political philosophies, and very often to Anglicize their names.

One solution for ambitious youngsters was to conceal their Jewishness. As is now well documented, this was the life strategy of Leopold Amery (1873–1955), the son of an immigrant mother from Hungary, who made a brilliant career as an ultra-patriotic British Conservative. Born in India, where his father had worked as a minor official, Amery cruised through Harrow, Balliol, and All Souls into the British Cabinet, where he served both as Colonial Secretary and, under Churchill, as Secretary of State for India. Even in his autobiography he provided false information to conceal his origins. Since Amery was the author of the Balfour Declaration, the founder of the Jewish legion, a close friend of Jabotinsky, a vehement opponent of controlled immigration to Palestine, and the man who in 1939 brought down Neville Chamberlain, quoting Cromwell's words in the Commons – 'In the name of God, go!' – his conduct is not exactly irrelevant. But it becomes tragic, when one learns that his elder son, John Amery (1912–45), became a principled Fascist and anti-Semite, a determined collaborator with Franco, with Vichy, and with the Nazis. The younger son, Julian Amery (1919–97), followed his father into a high flying political career. John Amery was hanged for treason in December 1945.[137] The roots of the tragedy had to be sought in the strains of immigration.

In the First World War, the British Empire made use of huge numbers of Indian Army troops on the Western Front. A Prime Minister, Lord Salisbury, had callously pointed to this prospect earlier, referring to India as 'an English barracks in the oriental seas from which we can draw any number of troops without paying for them'.[138] In the Second World War, a politicized Indian Army could no longer be exploited so easily in this way. It was used in the Asian theatre, of course, but only sparingly in North Africa and Italy.

During and after the Second World War, the United Kingdom received the first large group of foreigners to be officially resettled as an act of government policy. One Polish Army, based in Scotland 1940–45, landed and fought in Normandy; another, which had been evacuated from Russia, fought alongside the Allies all the way from Tobruk to Monte Cassino. At the end of the war, the Poles in

Britain, who numbered about five hundred thousand, were urged to
go home by a British government that didn't seem to notice that
the greater part of Poland had been annexed by the USSR. So about
half of them stayed. The Polish Resettlement Corps, 1947–9, eased
the transition from military to civilian life for the ex-soldiers and
their numerous dependants.[139]

As the Poles settled in, still larger cohorts of economic migrants
began to arrive, largely from the West Indies and from the Indian
subcontinent. The first ship, the *Empire Windrush*, landed 492 Jamai-
cans at Tilbury on 22 June 1948. Given the post-war shortage of
labour, the government followed an open-door policy throughout
the 1950s. Major organizations such as London Transport or the
National Health Service were able to recruit directly. But the
population of immigrants without work rose steadily; and from 1962
the Commonwealth Immigration Act limited the influx to persons
with a work voucher from the Ministry of Labour, to their dependants, and to students. In the forty years since then, the number of
foreign-born residents in the British population has risen to 7 per
cent – a rather lower percentage than in several other European
countries such as France or Germany. Their achievements were
manifold. The 'corner shop', for instance, one of the mainstays of
British urban life, was saved by immigrant shopkeepers. Chinese and
Indian restaurants added much-needed variety to the British diet.
One quarter of British doctors and nurses were foreign-born.

Nonetheless, the opposition to Commonwealth immigration
grew more and more vocal. One reason was purely economic.
British workers and trade unions feared for their jobs, whilst
government agencies watched anxiously at the strain placed on the
social services. Another reason was cultural. British society was still
extraordinarily traditional in outlook. The sound of steel bands, or
the sight of a mosque in Regent's Park, were unfamiliar, and often
thought inappropriate. Yet another reason was educational. A recent
study has shown that through all the pre-war and most of the post-
war periods, some British history textbooks were still preaching a
message of moral and cultural superiority.

In this connection, the concept of 'moral racism' has been coined. It refers to a well-documented tendency to attribute the success of Western nations to their supposedly innate abilities and capacity for freedom. The Victorian imperialist Charles Dilke (see above) had written in the 1860s of 'a moral dictatorship of the globe' justified by 'Saxon institutions and the English tongue'. He had also praised the USA as 'an amplifier for England's voice'. A hundred years later there were academic voices still analysing the Cold War in similar terms, praising the 'neo-moralism' of US foreign policy and presumably of 'the special relationship'. The key to the development of Third World countries lay in the small number of men who had attended Western universities: 'Sitting in cafés and lecture rooms in London and elsewhere these people had discussed free choice and democratic government. They contrasted such European principles with the attitude of the colonial governments they knew.'[140] At the bottom of it, one suspects there lay a substantial element of sheer racial prejudice.

In 1968, a prominent British Conservative politician, Enoch Powell MP (1912–98), chose to speak out against Commonwealth immigration in the most ominous tones. Powell was no crude demagogue. He was a highly sophisticated intellectual, a sometime Professor of Classics, who spoke with precision and authority. These qualities made his views all the more inflammatory. His speech at Birmingham on 20 April 1968 was littered with classical references: 'Those whom the gods wish to destroy,' he announced,

> they first make mad. We must be mad, literally mad, as a nation to be permitting the annual inflow of some fifty thousand dependants, who are for the most part the material of the future growth of the immigrant descended population. It is like a nation busily engaged in heaping up its own funeral pyre . . . As I look ahead I am filled with foreboding. Like the Roman, I seem to see 'the River Tiber foaming with much blood.'[141]

Powell's worst predictions were not realized. Race riots, though evident enough at Notting Hill (1968) or at Toxteth (1981), did not become a prominent feature of the British scene. The post-war British National Party (BNP), which openly campaigned on racist lines, loitered, like the pre-war British Union of Fascists, on the extra-parliamentary fringe. Powell's influence collapsed. He ended his career in the ranks of the Ulster Unionists.

The Race Relations Act (1976) and the resultant Commission for Racial Equality (CRE) came into being in part through fears of Powellite rhetoric, but largely through the growing confidence of the immigrant communities and their friends. The act rendered all forms of racial discrimination unlawful, and made provision for the compensation of victims of harassment and prejudice.

By 1999, the CRE was one of the more active of government propaganda agencies. It aimed to promote a positive image of multiracial Britain, among other things by popularizing a particular view of British history. 'Britain has always been a mixed society', it teaches, 'ever since the Bronze Age.' Or again, 'most people in Britain today are either immigrants or the descendants of immigrants'.[142] At a time when historians are stressing the relatively small genetic impact of successive invasions, this had to be a particularly contentious opinion. It is only true if one refers back to the main repopulation of the Isles after the Ice Age. (See Chapter One.)

More seriously, one must question some of the assumptions which surround many of the well-meaning activities of the anti-racist lobby. Terms such as 'the Black and Asian community' do less than justice to the fact that there are numerous different black communities and still more numerous ethnic and religious communities from Asia. By stressing colour, there is a definite danger of forgetting the primacy of culture. Black evangelical Protestants who march with the Orange Parades in Liverpool may have more in common with other British Protestants than with Rastafarians from Jamaica or African immigrants from Nigeria or Ghana. Pakistani Muslims, Punjabi Sikhs, and Indian Hindus do not necessarily have much in common beyond skin colour, whilst other Asians, like the Chinese, belong to a totally different world from that of the Subcontinent.

Anti-racist politics have equally been complicated by the old confusion over 'race' and 'nation'. In recent years, an increasing number of complaints to the CRE have involved accusations of 'white' against 'white'. In 1998, a Danish van driver in Sheffield won a landmark case against his employers. 'The fact of Mr. Svensborg being white', the CRE commented, 'made no difference so far as allegations of racism are concerned.'[143] As national consciousness rose in Scotland, so, too, did the incidence of English people invoking the law against alleged discrimination by Scots. It could well be that the CRE will have to work its way towards the wider position of its EU counterpart, the Commission against Racism and Intolerance.

Even so, nothing in the 1990s matched the well-deserved outcry surrounding the *Report of the Stephen Lawrence Inquiry* (1999). Five years after the gratuitous murder of a black teenager on a London street, the independent report not only found that police investigations had been pathetically inadequate, but also that the British police force was suffering from 'institutionalised racism'.[144] Here was a clarion call to signal how far contemporary Britain stood from the ideal of a country free from 'discrimination on grounds of colour, nationality, citizenship, ethnic or national origin'.[145]

One of the most positive products of post-war immigration was found in the rise of a new branch of English literature: or rather, the further expansion of a genre first pioneered by Joseph Conrad. Immigrant writers' use of the medium of English to sublimate their often painful encounters with post-imperial Britain was once described as 'The Empire Writes Back with a Vengeance'. It is a delicious thought:

> Wat a joyful news, Miss Mattie,
> I feel like me heart gwine burs'
> Jamaica people colinizin
> Englan' in reverse.[146]

The variety of authors was as wide as the former Empire. V. S. Naipaul (1932–), Samuel Selvon (1923–), and George Lamming (1927–) were born in the West Indies: Salman Rushdie (1947–) in India: Timothy Mo (1950–) in Hong Kong: Abdulrazak Gurnah (1948–) in Zanzibar. The titles of their novels needed no explanation: *The Lonely Londoners*, *In the Castle of My Skin*, *Pilgrim's Way*. There was, it emerged, a Muslim Britain, a Caribbean Britain, an Irish Britain, a Jewish Britain, an Antipodean Britain. The central theme, inevitably, was that of displaced identity. Hanif Kureishi, for instance, started a novel with a manifestatory sentence.

'My name is Karim Amir, and I am an Englishman born and bred, almost.' But then there is the obligatory exhortation:

> It is the British, the white British, who have to learn that being British isn't what it was … There must be a fresh way of seeing Britain: and a new way of being British … The failure to grasp this opportunity … will be more insularity, schism, bitterness and catastrophe.[147]

(14) BRITISH SPORT: A HISTORIC RELAPSE

One of the most attractive elements of the old British sporting tradition was found in the conviction that winning is not the be-all and end-all. Sportsmen played to win, but not to win at any cost. Sport was seen as part of a way of life that was governed in its entirety by spiritual values and by moral purpose. To win by cheating, for instance, was not just unspeakable. It was pointless. Sport was also perceived as an aesthetic activity. The rhythms and patterns and varied emotions of a game were considered equivalent to those in a work of art or a piece of music.

No one better embodied these attitudes than the critic and writer Neville Cardus (1889–1975). Born in the backstreets of Victorian Manchester, Cardus taught himself to write. In time, he became the *Manchester Guardian*'s cricket correspondent in the summer, the paper's leading music critic in the winter, and a national celebrity. For him, cricket and music were two sides of the same coin:

> One day I sat at a table outside the little café at Lord's, talking to the cricket correspondent of *The Times* . . .
>
> 'Has it occurred to you that we are paid to do this?' . . .
>
> I was also being paid to go after a day at Lord's to Covent Garden and hear Lehman in *Rosenkavalier*.
>
> 'Yes', said *The Times* correspondent, '. . . And it's too good to be true, isn't it?'
>
> 'Yes', I replied, 'it can't last.'[148]

It was the summer of 1938.

H. D. 'Donnie' Davies (1895–1958) belonged to the same school. Under the pen name of 'Old International', he was the *Manchester Guardian*'s football correspondent. Of a penalty kick, he could write that the ball struck the crossbar 'like a tuning fork striking the rostrum, in the perfect pitch of A'. He would die in the Munich air disaster.[149]

Post-war sport was subject to pressures that killed off these high-minded attitudes. Rampant commercialization had much to answer for. Sport became big business, closely dependent on the media and advertising. Professional teams were paid by results. Amateur sport shrank as would-be players were drained off to become spectators or couch potatoes.

In football, for example, a handful of rich clubs came to dominate the game. Leeds, Liverpool, Newcastle, Manchester United, Arsenal, Chelsea, and others outgrew their competitors not only on the field of play but equally in the huge market for team merchandise. Attitudes changed. Buying star players was more important than training youngsters. Losing was a disaster. Tribalism among rival supporters threatened to slide into violent hooliganism. 'Some people think football is a matter of life and death,' declared one doughty manager; 'I can assure them it is much more serious than that.'[150]

British sport kept up its high reputation throughout the first half of the century. In cricket, England were still the side to beat, though Australia were pushing them hard. In 1931, a diplomatic crisis loomed when the Australians officially objected to England's unfair tactics of 'bodyline bowling'. In 1936 the Men's Singles at Wimbledon was won by Fred Perry. As late as 1953, the English football team still had the confidence to take on a side from 'The Rest of the World'.

Sport, being intimately tied up with national pride, contains a stronger political dimension than most participants realize. It can easily be turned into an instrument of state policy. Everyone now knows how the Communist states of Eastern Europe used international sport in general, and the Olympic movement in particular, to bolster their power and prestige. But power politics has not been entirely divorced from sport even in the Isles. The history of Gaelic Football is a case in point. As from 1884, when the Gaelic Athletic Association was founded in Ireland, Irish youngsters played the game because it was their own. It provides a glorious spectacle, full of graceful leaping and powerful running in a vast arena. (It is the direct ancestor of 'Aussie Rules' football as played with such enthusiasm in Australia.) The British authorities regarded it as a source of sedition. During the reign of terror of the 'Black and Tans', its clubs were targeted. Yet decades after it ceased to be a political issue, British commentators could not always bring themselves to write about it objectively. The relevant entry in a recent edition of the *Encyclopædia Britannica* began as follows – Gaelic football, 'sometimes described as "unmitigated mayhem" ... still resembles a free-for-all, but...'[151] Irish sportsmen, in consequence, remain under greater pressure on national matters than their British counterparts. When the Jordan Formula One team won a Grand Prix event in 1999, their leader was immediately asked whether he really knew the words of 'Amhrán na BhFiann'. 'Do you really have any idea', he exploded, 'how many times we used to sing it as kids in Synge Street?'[152] No one bothers to ask British sportsmen if they know the words of 'God Save the Queen'.

Britain's fall from grace in the rankings of world sport proceeded unchecked throughout recent decades. Apart from one solitary win in 1966 on home turf, England's football team has shown little sparkle in World Cup tournaments. In 1999, the country that invented football was placed eleventh in the FIFA rankings. English cricket fared no better. Isolated victories over stronger teams from South Africa, Australia, or the West Indies had to be greeted as epoch-making triumphs. In the unofficial Wisden World Test-match Rankings for 1999, England occupied the ninth of nine designated places. In the cricket World Cup '99, England, the home of cricket, was knocked out in the first round together with the likes of Bangladesh, Kenya, and (wait for it) Scotland. In lawn tennis, no British male player had won a singles title at Wimbledon since Fred Perry, no British woman since Virginia Wade in 1977. In rugby, another British invention, as in Association Football, England stood lower than France. In golf, the highest ranked British player, the Scot Colin Montgomerie, was at number five. In the last Olympic Games of the millennium (1996), Britain obtained no gold medals compared with forty-four for the US, fifteen for France, and seven for Poland. National rankings obviously move up and down in all sports. But it is very hard to avoid the conclusion that in the last quarter of the twentieth century British sport had suffered a historic relapse.

Analysis of the phenomenon uncovered a wide spectrum of causes. One vital factor undoubtedly lay with the uncharacteristic neglect of sport in British state schools. Given the former traditions, the sale of playing fields by cash-strapped educational authorities could only be likened to a sale by a bishop of half his parish churches. Sport cannot be nurtured without sports grounds.

Yet at the so-called national level British sport has suffered from a deficiency that points to a deeper malaise. For all the misplaced rhetoric about a nation state, the United Kingdom had never developed a system of national sports teams. Even more to the point, a large proportion of the supporters were blissfully unaware of the fact that an English team was not the same as a British team. In 1966, when England won the World Cup, Wembley was awash with Union Jacks. Hardly anyone at the scene seemed to notice that the Union Jack was not, and never had been, the flag of England. Only through a sustained campaign by the Scottish authorities did English supporters begin to wave the appropriate flag of St George. But they still did not have an English anthem to sing. In 1999, the so-called 'Barmy Army', which follows the England cricket team abroad, was there in Australia without a proper flag in sight. Their one moment of constitutional nicety came with their stalwart singing at the MCG, of 'God Save *Your* Gracious Queen'. The English RFU thought in desperation to adopt an American spiritual, 'Swing Low', for its song.

National identity is no trivial matter. It is the psychological cement which binds communities together. The Scots knew who they are. So, too, did the Welsh and the Irish. But a large part of the English were manifestly bewildered. The widespread failure to create teams representing the entire United Kingdom must be seen as a symptom of the wider failure to complete the construction of a British nation. One of the few major multinational teams, the British and Irish Lions, drew rugby players not just from the UK but from the Isles as a whole.

As the hotchpotch of sporting teams from different parts of the United Kingdom continued to perform poorly, the prominence of European competitions steadily increased. The standing of football's European Cup, for instance, rose to new heights; and individual clubs from Britain rose to meet the challenge. Liverpool FC won the European Cup on four occasions, Manchester United on two. In 1998, Chelsea FC – a London club with an Italian manager and few English players – won the European Cup Winners' Cup. In 1999, Manchester United – an English club with a Scots manager – won three cups in a row. Their late winning goal against Bayern Munich was scored by a Norwegian. It was a sign of the times. If current trends continued, few all-British teams would ever be organized. But sports people from the UK could win respect by preserving the old traditions in new ways. Atheletics supplied an excellent example of the potential of multicultural Britain.

HM Government could not fail to be aware of the crisis in British sport. In 1995, a policy paper called 'Raising the Game' sounded the alarm, and it resulted in the reorganization of all the UK's top sports bodies. As in many other spheres, the chosen solution was devolutionary. In 1997, the GB Sports Council, which had a remit for the whole United Kingdom, was abolished. It was replaced by four separate Sports Councils – one each for England, Scotland, Wales, and Northern Ireland. A residual body called UK Sport assumed responsibility for matters requiring coordination, including a proposed UK Sports Institute. The largest of the new organizations, Sport England, was to answer to the English Department of Culture, Media and Sport in London. The other councils were to be controlled by the newly devolved executive bodies in Edinburgh, Cardiff, and Belfast.[153] They were embarking on an experiment that was being repeated many times over in very many aspects of British life. The experiment was designed to raise the standards of sporting activities. But whether it could address the specifically British dimension to sporting deficiencies was more than doubtful.

(15) BRITISH SOVEREIGNTY: A DIVISIBLE QUANTITY

Towards the end of the nineteenth century, the world of British laws and lawyers was as sovereign as sovereign could be. No outsiders could tell them what to do. Reform could only come from internal sources. With time, however, the external framework altered to such an extent that by the end of the following century, external pressures had become the main motor of change. Indeed, the question was posed how far the United Kingdom was a truly sovereign country in the legal field.

It would be invidious to try to summarize in a few sentences the vast transformations to the law which have taken place since 1914. But one can at least summarize the categories of change. For convenience, these categories may be listed as substantive change, organizational change, and philosophical change.

The substance of the law has probably been transformed more by accretion than by modification. Huge bodies of new legislation came into being in the fields of administration, social welfare, taxation, and road traffic, which simply did not exist a hundred years previously. The revision of existing law also proceeded apace. In 1925–6, for example, the laws of property and succession were radically revised to sweep away essentially feudal practices.

Organizational reforms saw, among other things, the growth of delegated legislation, of administrative tribunals, and of the quasi-judicial powers of administrators. The judiciary was subjected to successive reconstructions. The partition of Ireland in 1920–22, for example, required the establishment of a completely new and separate judicial system in Northern Ireland, which inherited the only corpus of Irish law to survive within the United Kingdom. The outbreak of terrorism resulted in the establishment from 1973 of a Belfast Recorder's Court trying criminal offences without a jury. In England and Wales, a joint Court of Appeal with civil and criminal divisions was created in 1966. The Crown Court for criminal cases replaced the old Assizes and Quarter Sessions in 1971. A Crown Prosecution Service (CPS) was established as late as 1986.

The resultant judicial structure, though simplified, was still complicated and fragmented. Only two courts in the United Kingdom possessed undivided competence throughout the territory of the state. One of them was the Courts-Martial Appeal Court for the armed services; the other, from 1966, was the Restrictive Practices Court.[154]

The philosophy underlying the making and the application of law evolved extensively during the twentieth century. Three or four shifts may fairly be mentioned. Much greater weight was paid to the rights and treatment of defendants and convicts. As a result, a series of acts on the law of evidence was passed in 1938, 1968, and 1972. Separate Juvenile Courts have existed since 1908. The Criminal Justice Act (1956) greatly diminished the grounds for capital punishment, and the death penalty had not been used since 1965. The immunity of the crown has been greatly diminished. From 1947, crown agents have been subject to the same liability in contract and property law as any other company or individual. Finally, the fiction concerning an ancient unchanging law, whose judgements had to be recovered and applied to every new situation, was increasingly overtaken by the concept of an evolving corpus of law requiring constant revision by statute. The Law Revision Committee (1934) and, since 1965, the permanent Law Commission, embodied the more modern attitudes. Much of the contemporary emphasis on a humane and ethical approach to law can be traced to Jeremy Bentham's groundbreaking *Introduction to the Principles of Morals and Legislation* (1789). But 210 years have not sufficed to realize the one thing which Bentham thought most essential – namely, the introduction of a systematic legal code.

Notwithstanding the internal reforms, it is arguable that external factors delivered a still greater impact. The United Kingdom's membership of international organizations, the independence of Ireland, the loss of Empire, and the entry to the European Community have all combined to redesign the overall framework within which 'British law' operated.

Prior to the end of the nineteenth century, international law had little institutional standing. Ever since Grotius, principles had evolved whereby sovereign states, if so inclined, could settle their disputes. Yet Great Powers, like Britain, were often more inclined to argue their case with a gunboat than with a team of lawyers. What is more, both England and Scotland had been completely isolated since the Reformation from the *corpus iuris* of the Catholic

Church, which had maintained the tradition of supra-national legal norms in many Continental countries.

The UK's first modern contact with a supra-national legal authority occurred in 1899, when the International Court of Arbitration at the Hague, otherwise the 'Hague Tribunal', was recognized. The Tribunal was the fruit of an international conference on peace convened by the Tsar of Russia, and the British government immediately saw its advantages. The second case ever brought before the Tribunal involved a claim by Britain, Germany, and Italy against Venezuela. The three powers had mounted an abortive naval blockade of Caracas in order to extract payment from residents of Venezuela whom they regarded as debtors. By submitting their claim to the Tribunal, they agreed to honour the arbitration award of the Tribunal's judges. The three judges were duly appointed. They were a lawyer from St Petersburg, a professor from Vienna, and the Tsar's Minister of Justice, M. Muraviev. The award in 1903 was made in favour of the blockading powers. HMG felt encouraged to submit more claims.

In that pre-1914 era, the Powers were not accustomed to submit to arbitration without making a formal reservation of their sovereign rights. (The earliest instance was at the so-called Jay Treaty (1794) between the United Kingdom and the USA.) But, bit by bit, they were weaned to the idea that international justice could best be administered by supra-national institutions and by collective action. The slaughter of the First World War underlined the cost of unrestrained sovereignty, and the League of Nations was specifically designed as a forum for settling international disputes by peaceful collective means. By joining the League, Britain explicitly undertook to respect its rules, and to this extent accepted a measure of restraint on British sovereignty. Similarly, by recognizing the World Court, which was administered by the League as a continuation of the Hague Tribunal, she implicitly accepted a valid sphere of law beyond British jurisdiction.

The bloodletting of the Second World War once again brought home the consequences of unbridled sovereignty. By the time that the International Court of Justice was re-established at The Hague in 1946 under the aegis of the United Nations, the old assumptions about unqualified national rights were fading. The United Kingdom was a founder member of UNO, and a permanent member of the Security Council. Henceforth, Britain would be bound by the collective decisions and the norms of the organization.

Less confidence could be placed in the international tribunals set up after 1945 in Nuremberg and Tokyo to try the crimes of the defeated Axis Powers. The political decision to take such action was justified on moral grounds. The crimes of the Nazi Reich and of Imperial Japan were thought, probably correctly, to be too abhorrent to go unpunished. Yet the desirable action was achieved by the undesirable manoeuvre of keeping silent about mass crimes perpetrated on a massive scale by one of the prosecuting powers, the Soviet Union. International legal action only becomes fully legitimate when it is administered by authorities who are neutral and who themselves admit to the principle of the rule of law.[155]

The secession of the Irish Free State from the United Kingdom in 1922 followed a precedent set up by the USA, whilst setting an example that would be repeated many times over throughout the Empire. Henceforth, a legal tradition that was largely English in origin would be subject to an independent national legislature and would develop in its own independent orbit. Irish law would gradually become genuinely Irish, Indian law genuinely Indian, Israeli law genuinely Israeli.

The loss of Ireland might well have alerted the British authorities to the implications of Britain's declining imperial status. But it didn't. No effective thought appears to have been given, for example, to the shrinking constituency within which legal definitions of British nationality and citizenship could operate. To anyone who has looked closely at the issue, the legal nature of 'Britishness' was 'fuzzy', 'vague', and 'malleable'. In British practice, the concepts of nationality and citizenship were consistently confused. The only coherent concept was that of 'subjecthood', which applied to all subjects of the crown across the Empire. No legal distinction was made between British subjects born and resident in the United Kingdom, and those born and resident outside it. The movement of those subjects round the Empire was only regulated by immigration controls that were frequently arbitrary. From the Aliens Act (1905) onward, great efforts were directed to the negative definition of persons who were not so-called British 'nationals', rather than to a precise definition of the various categories of people who could be accepted as British subjects. For decades, the old practical distinction was maintained between British residents of the 'United Kingdom and Dominions' as opposed to those of the Colonies. Yet only in 1977 did a Government Green Paper openly admit that 'Britain is no longer an imperial power' and that 'the all-embracing concept of nationality' needed urgent revision. The result was the British Nationality Act (1981), which for the first time put British citizenship onto the statute book.[156]

Even so, the definition of citizenship was unusually narrow. A British citizen was simply a person with the right of entry to the UK. And there were many anomalies. Irish citizens also possessed right of entry, as from 1991 did the citizens of other EU countries. It was 1998 before the British government extended the full rights of citizenship to residents of the UK's remaining Overseas Territories – which no longer included Hong Kong. For seventeen years, this particular group of people had lingered in the extraordinary limbo of BSWC – British Subjects Without Citizenship.[157]

Britain's entry into the European Community in 1973 initiated a long and accelerating process of legal change that showed no signs of slowing down after a quarter of a century. On the one hand, within the sphere of Community affairs, it subjected the British government to the superior authority of the Community's courts – the European Court of Justice and the European Court of First Instance. On the other hand, it required the British government to give community directives the force of law by incorporating them into British legislation. Here was a delicious paradox. Prior to 1973, the concept of purely 'British law' was limited by the fragmented nature of the United Kingdom's various legal systems. After 1973, the scope of British law began to grow rapidly by the incorporation of directives which most British people were accustomed to think of as 'European law'. The fact was: this new body of law was both 'European' *and* 'British'.

In November 1998, the latest momentous step in merging European and British law was taken by the Human Rights Act, which incorporated the European Convention on Human Rights (ECHR) into domestic British law. As a founding member of the Council of Europe, Britain had played an active part in formulating the ECHR and had ratified it in 1952. But British subjects had only been able to avail themselves of the Convention by applying to the Council's European Court in Strasbourg, and with little hope of seeing a decision enforced. Now they could apply directly to the British courts, and target their claims not only against individuals but also against any 'public authority'. Such far-reaching rights had never before existed in the United Kingdom. What is more, the Human Rights Act stood fair to force change in further areas of legislation. English judges were given powers to declare existing laws 'incompatible' with the Convention, and to demand harmonization. Scottish judges were to be given the extraordinary power to declare statutes 'invalid'. Exceptionally, appeals were to be made not to the House of Lords, but to a judicial committee of the Privy Council. The standing of judges looked to be enormously increased. The possibility of conflicting opinions between English and Scottish judges loomed. Once again British law was being expanded, not diminished, by European law.

Having once lived within the unbounded realms of empire, British people had been brought up to think of sovereignty, like virginity, as an absolute item. It was either intact or it was not. Yet the experience of the twentieth century showed that absolute sovereignty was a myth, or, if not a myth, an impossible ideal. In a world where all states and nations belonged to some form of international or supranational groupings, it was inevitable that individual rights be balanced against collective responsibilities. Sovereignty was better seen as a divisible quantity – to be pooled in some quarters and to be retained in others. By sharing a part, one did not lose the whole. One could belong to the family and still be a completely unique individual.

(16) Metrication: a Slowly Changing Mental World

For most of the twentieth century, though the imperial and the metric systems of weights and measures enjoyed legal parity in the United Kingdom, they were not treated equally. The imperial system was regarded as native, and was in everyday use. The metric system was thought foreign, and was little used outside scientific work. The First World War, which took millions of Britons to France, probably did something to improve popular knowledge of metrics. But the Second World War, which brought millions of Americans to Britain, can only have strengthened the imperials. For the Americans used a set of weights and measures which was based on the old, unreformed, pre-1824 English system, and which was an older variant of the imperial.

After 1945, the Imperials held their own for two more decades. They were encouraged by Britain's membership of American-led NATO, by joint UK–US scientific ventures, and by the British government's habit of keeping its distance from the European movement. At the same time, several factors began to work in favour of metrics. One was the marked growth of trade with 'the Six'. The other was the related decision in 1961 to apply for membership of the Common Market. The socialist government of Harold Wilson, which was strongly influenced by scientific advice, went ahead in 1965 with the policy of giving preference to the teaching of metrics in British schools.

For the first twenty years after Britain's entry to the European Community, the dual system, which had existed in theory since 1897, at last became the practical reality. Metric measures took their place alongside their imperial equivalents. The dual labelling of goods spread far and wide. Speed clocks in cars, for example, were marked in kilometres as well as in miles. Petrol pumps were marked in both litres and gallons. A compromise phenomenon called 'soft imperial' made its appearance, especially in the building trade. The standard imperial 9 inch brick and the 6 foot 6 inch wooden door continued to be used. Only now they were called the 225mm brick and the 1981mm door. Neither the imperialists nor the metricists could claim outright victory.

The Maastricht Treaty of 1991, however, contained undertakings for further harmonization throughout the 'Single European Market'. So a new Weights and Measures Act (1995) put the emphasis decisively in favour of metrics. Henceforth the metric system was established in the UK as the sole legal standard. A limited number of imperial measures were to be retained for a temporary period ending 31 December 1999, and a very small residue for an indefinite period after that. As from 2000, the use of non-approved imperials was liable to be treated as an illegal deed.

Among the imperials granted temporary reprieve in 1995 were pints for the sale of specified drinks in returnable containers, therms for gas supply, and fathoms for marine navigation. Imperial weights could still be used for wholesale goods when sold in bulk, but not for the same items when sold retail. One was permitted to buy two tons of apples from the farmer, but not two pounds of apples from the corner shop.

The list of imperial items that were approved for indefinite use included pints for draught beers and ciders, acres for land registration, troy ounces for precious metals, and measures of speed and distance for the purposes of road traffic management, such as miles per hour.

In practice, innumerable exceptions and anomalies remained. Since all British machinery, from carpet looms to wood lathes, had been calibrated in imperials ever since the Industrial Revolution, it was idle to assume that the entire plant of the country could be rejigged or replaced in the space of five or ten years. There was no chance that carpet retailers, for instance, could abandon the dual system by the end of the century.

What is more, all realms of life not classified as trade or business were free to persist with traditional measures. Horse-racing showed no intention of abandoning hands (for the height of horses), furlongs (for the length of races), or guineas (for the calculation of prize money). Golf courses were still to be measured in yards.

Opposition to metrication aroused passionate feelings in a number of disparate quarters. One group represented by the British Weights and Measures Association (BWMA) believed that the compulsory metrication constituted an attack on British culture and a breach of civil rights. A second group headed by the Dozenal Society based its opposition on the belief that base 12 provides a better foundation for mathematical calculations than the decimal base 10 does. A third group was connected to the New Age lobby, which saw metrication as part of the dehumanizing drive of modern civilization. All groups tended to look to the USA as the one major country in the world that had stoutly defended the principles both of cultural continuity and of freedom of choice. The British anti-metricators were inevitably joined by an Irish Anti-metric League.

The publications of the BWMA in particular were well worth reading, not simply for the arcane metrological arguments but also for an insight into the workings of the Europhobic mind-set. One recurrent assumption was that nothing in Britain – usually called England – has ever changed in hundreds if not thousands of years. An article on 'The 10,000-year-old Inch' said it all.[158] Another assumption was that metrication and decimalization were the work of cunning conspirators, always unnamed but always located somewhere 'in Europe' or among the faceless 'technocrats and bureaucrats' 'in Brussels'. (Not in the NATO district of Brussels, you understand.) Most persistently, one encountered the assumption that metrication was the result of an 'undemocratic', 'impractical', or downright 'wanton' assault on a timeless heritage: '. . . traditional units are a part of our language. They are built into our historic buildings and live in our literature. If we abandon them, we lose a valuable heritage, handed down over centuries. [We] should oppose cultural vandalism . . .'[159]

Read in isolation, some of the arguments could be persuasive. But rarely did they convey the slightest inkling either that a nation's heritage is never static, or that the late twentieth-century drive for metrication was the concluding phase of a trend started well over a hundred years previously.

Nonetheless, the state of play in the 1990s was ironic, to say the least. The United Kingdom found itself in the final phase of adopting a system invented in Revolutionary France. The British Imperial System, as regularized in 1824, had been reduced to a marginal residue. It had only remained as the standard in places such as the Bahamas, Myanmar, or Micronesia. Yet the Old English or Colonial System, now discreetly called 'Customary', was alive and well in the world's largest economy. Indeed, through US leadership of the North American Free Trade Area, it was starting to spread into Central and Latin America. Through American domination of the worldwide computer industry, where printers are measured by the ten-thousand-year-old inch, not by millimetres, it stood a good chance of expanding its reach still further.

In essence, therefore, the controversy over metrication was a case study in miniature of Britain's basic dilemma, whether to side with 'Europe' or to side with the USA. In this case, the crucial shifts had occurred long since. Yet hope sprang eternal that the trends of decades could yet be reversed. Just as the Astronomer Royal wrote to *The Times* in 1869 to object to the adoption of metrics for scientific purposes, so letter-writers to the *Daily Telegraph* were still pleading for the preservation of 'our' 'convenient' 'superior' and 'functional' units:

> Three-quarters of people in Britain prefer customary units, as do a majority even of those aged 15–24, despite years of one-sided education and propaganda. Yet the sale of apples or potatoes priced by the pound is due to become a criminal offence in less than six months' time. Wake up, democracy![160]

One thing is certain: the mental worlds in people's heads change rather more slowly than official policies do. Many of the older

English units abolished in 1824 were still going strong in the 1890s (see below). At that rate, many of the imperial units outlawed in 1995 would still be going strong in 2065, the centenary of preferential metrical education.

(17) THE POST-IMPERIAL ETHOS: THE *ESPRIT COMMUNAUTAIRE*

As people grow older, they have a natural tendency to look back with fond nostalgia to the 'good old days'. The present is always seen to be deteriorating. The 'Golden Age' is invariably perceived in the past.

For the British, who lost their enviable status of top dog, the temptations of nostalgia were particularly acute. Older people remembered the purposeful, high-minded approach to life which characterized their youth. They remembered the social solidarity of the war years, and the unwavering patriotism. They remembered the good manners, the codes of dress, deportment, and etiquette which lubricated everyday life, and the strict sexual mores. They took pride in the hard physical work which they had to perform in every daily task. And they let the younger generation know. 'There was no going down to the Social Security to collect your cheque in those days.' 'We had to scrape and save every penny to make ends meet.' 'Your grandfather and grandmother walked to church twice every Sunday – three miles there and three miles back.' 'And I had to walk to school, rain or shine. No one ever heard of a school run.' 'Your mother used to look after the war widow next door, you know.' 'We used to stand to attention to listen to the King's Christmas message on the wireless.' 'Once upon a time, boys raised their caps to grown-ups in the street, if you can imagine it; and girls were not allowed to wear trousers for anything.' 'Gentlemen opened doors for ladies, and gave up their seats in buses.' 'And everyone knew what to do.' 'If you weren't back in the house by ten o'clock, you'd get a clout across the ear.' 'When our unmarried cousin Ethel announced she was having a baby, her father showed her the door.

It was terrible.' 'When your Uncle Ken was called up to fly the bombers, he told us he'd get killed. But he had to go. No one thought of refusing.' 'There weren't any easy-iron shirts, you know. Your grandfather had to have a fresh-starched dicky and a stiff collar every morning.' 'And who do you think polished his boots?'

The litany of complaints about the younger generation was endless. 'Have you not thought of getting yourself a proper job?' 'They spend more on a night out at the pub than we would spend in a month.' 'They didn't even know that the Queen's message was on.' 'Have you seen how they all put their feet on the seats in the trains?' 'And it's the young women who smoke the most.' 'Nobody bothers if young lads nick things from the shops.' 'He brought his girlfriend to stay the night without even asking and she helped herself from the fridge.' 'They drop litter everywhere.' 'She calls herself an eco-warrior, whatever that is.' 'They all got drunk at the office party, you know, and no one batted an eyelid.'

For the historian, the problem is to sort subjective reactions from objective changes. There is no doubt that social attitudes changed almost beyond recognition in the last three or four decades of the twentieth century. But it is very difficult to separate the decline of specifically British values from the rise of all pervasive pop culture, consumerism, and general Western decadence. Nor is it possible to accept that everything in the old-style society was good, and that everything in contemporary lifestyles is bad. Social discipline had suffered a serious decline. Juvenile crime and loutish behaviour were in evidence on all sides. On the other hand, the old starched-front propriety concealed much hidden cruelty, secret abuse, thoughtless exploitation, and despicable hypocrisy.

Traditional loyalty to the crown had not disappeared completely. Indeed, opinion polls in the 1990s still showed a majority in favour of retaining the monarchy. Most British people could not imagine a suitable alternative. But the old deferential mode had evaporated. In the early twentieth century members of the royal family could commit any form of indiscretion in the sure knowledge that it would not be reported. From the 1980s, the British media showed no scruple in publishing the most embarrassingly intimate details of the Prince of Wales's phone call to his mistress or of Princess Diana's 'Squidgy tapes'.[161] Respect for the institution of monarchy had plummeted in line with the exposés of individuals.

By 1999, when the Queen Mother reached her ninety-ninth birthday, the tide of disrespect was seeping into the innermost sanctum of the Royal Family. The Queen Mother was as old as the century, and was widely regarded to have been the real power behind the throne since the late 1930s. She still attracted the affections of many. But her critics showed no pity. One senior commentator concluded that the 'Queen Mum', like Lenin's mummy in Red Square, was something 'to be disposed of'.[162] Anything less deferential could not be imagined.

Patriotism of the old sort had equally passed out of fashion. Two generations of British citizens had grown up without ever being been ordered to lay down their lives for their country. The military form of national service was terminated in 1961, but not replaced by a civil form of national service. So the idea of 'serving one's country' as a universal stage in public education, at least for males, was allowed to lapse. Young people still had loyalties. But they were much less focused on their country than previously. Though not in the same proportions as young people in the Continental countries, an increasing minority thought of themselves as 'Europeans'.

Even so, patriotic sentiments still tugged strongly at many hearts. In 1953, the popular BBC Promenade Concerts in the Royal Albert Hall devised a patriotic programme for the closing night of the season. The programme started with Elgar's rendering of 'Land of Hope and Glory', raced through medleys of popular songs and sea shanties, and finished with rousing choruses of 'Rule, Britannia!' and Parry's 'Jerusalem'. Forty-six years later, the formula was still evoking immense enthusiasm. One suspects that the 'Last Night of the Proms' could still be going strong long after the last promenaders of 1953 vintage had passed on.

The characterization of patriotism had also changed, though it was in a state of considerable confusion. Perhaps under American influence, many people now accepted themselves to be 'Brits' who lived in the UK, especially when faced with the issue abroad. They retained much affection for Canadians, Australians, and New Zealanders, but they now viewed the inhabitants of the former dominions as members of separate nations. Most obviously, the secession of Ireland, and the reassertion of Scots and Welsh identity, put increasing strains on the traditional equation of 'British' and 'English'. In the late 1990s, one of the topics of public concern centred on the prospect of an 'English backlash'.[163] It was becoming entirely possible that the mood of the English would turn ugly, and that the English would begin to demand their own separate rights and institutions. Under Devolution, the Welsh might wonder why they had been granted fewer powers than the Scots, whilst the Scots might resent continuing control from London. The people of Northern Ireland, having voted overwhelmingly for the Good Friday Agreement, were left simmering in despair that the agreement was not being implemented. In the summer of 1999, the latest obstacle lay with the proposed reforms of the RUC. The Unionists respected a force that had bravely borne the brunt of the Troubles. The Nationalists only saw a force that was still 92 per cent Protestant and that they wanted to be disbanded. Most tellingly, the former British minister who chaired the commission on police reform concluded that the RUC could only be retained if it dropped the British crown from its insignia, changed its name to the Northern Ireland Police Force, and stopped flying the Union Jack. The British establishment was growing indifferent to traditional 'Britishness'.[164]

Old-fashioned mores of self-restraint had gone through the window. The causes were manifold. Religious upbringing had ceased to exist for the majority. The hierarchy of class was dissolving. The familiarity of travel introduced the young to the 'American hug' and the French custom of cheek kissing. 'Doing one's own thing' was acceptable. British ways were not necessarily the best. Above all, the sexual revolution of the 1960s undermined the most deep-seated of social taboos. Young people no longer knew what was wrong with 'living in sin'. Teenage sex became so rife that Britain topped the European league for schoolgirl motherhood. Mothers who remained single by choice bore no stigma. Indeed they received special support from the social services of the state. Child poverty rose to shameful levels. Personal preferences performed in private were no longer an issue. Homosexuality was legalized, and in some quarters celebrated. Divorce rates rocketed. The concept of duty sank, as the preoccupation with individual rights rose.

A fine example of the older generation's distress was contained in a *cri de cœur* from a distinguished senior writer: Peregrine Worsthorne (1923–), a champion of traditional British conservatism, went into print with the confession 'I have fallen out of love with England.' He recited the standards of his youth. He was 'King George V's loyal subject . . . for right or wrong, in sickness and in health, for ever and ever, amen.' 'Patriotism . . . was in the very air one breathed.' 'Love of country went hand in hand with . . . veneration of country.' But now, fifty years on, 'such strength of emotion about England strikes me . . . as absurd.' The reasons given were not just the obvious ones – globalization and the loss of empire – but the degradation both of the physical environment and of English culture:

> Then there are the truly appalling new Britons . . ., not so much aliens as enemies. Even the grunting and slurping language they speak . . . jars unbearably. Most shameful of all, M. Santer, president of the European Commission, speaks the Queen's English rather better than our . . . own . . . politicians, who go in for mid-Atlantic English.[165]

The article was accompanied by a cartoon showing one wasp asking another: 'Has it occurred to you that the Queen is a single mother?'

Attitudes that had been specifically fostered by the imperial experience could not be salvaged. The confidence of a ruling elite that knew it was born to rule was inevitably sapped. The best that the British elite could do was, like Harold Macmillan, to strike the pose of a defeated Greek left to teach the arts of civilization to the all-powerful transatlantic Romans, or like a later Foreign Secretary, Douglas Hurd, to talk optimistically about 'punching above our weight'.[166] In a strange way, racial tolerance also diminished. Formerly, the habits of the white sahib, who may have kept himself and his family apart from the natives, nonetheless contained a strong streak of respect. For one thing, he was living in their country; he encountered their culture on a daily basis; and he belonged to a vulnerable foreign minority. For another, Indians and Africans posed no threat whatsoever to his job or status. Yet the white sahib's grandchildren, who had never seen Asia or Africa, could not share his outlook. Unaccustomed to black faces, ignorant of foreign cultures, and living in a majority community threatened by widespread unemployment, the post-war Briton was far less likely to think of Commonwealth immigrants with equanimity. The fiction of the great happy family of the Imperial peoples no longer carried any weight. The reality of a British underclass competing for jobs and housing on their own ground placed serious obstacles in the path of a compassionate multiculturalism.[167]

Above all, Britons in the late twentieth century no longer possessed the strength to think of either 'dominating' or 'helping' the world in a major way on their own. They could obtain a frisson of the old superiority complex by cultivating the supposed 'special' relationship with the USA. The Americans, after all, had inherited a considerable dose of English 'moralistics' and they were the only people left to put it into practice. In 1999, an American President and British Prime Minister felt entirely justified in joining forces to break international law and to bomb a sovereign state in the name of their own interpretation of morality. One could praise or condemn their action. But one could not deny that NATO's campaign against Serbia was a good example of the old way of doing things.[168] It was a very particular interpretation of the Foreign Office's stated intention of pursuing 'an ethical foreign policy'.

By the late 1990s, politicians were reaching a consensus in their conviction that the moral rot had somehow to be stopped. But they had few practical ideas about where to start. The Conservative Prime Minister, John Major, had tried to launch a campaign of 'Back to (unspecified) Basics', and ran into a barrage of derision. His 'New Labour' successor, Tony Blair, was soon calling for 'a new sense of moral purpose', and risked the same reaction. Britain was entering a phase of agonized soul-searching. Yet there appeared to be very little willingness to discern the different sources of different sorts of dysfunction. Reactionary critics tended to assume that all was part of a package, that the 'old culture' which had once made Britain great had been replaced by an irresponsible, libertarian 'new culture' that was dragging Britain down.

In a searing attack called *The Abolition of Britain*, a forthright journalist analysed the long list of self-inflicted injuries that had supposedly damaged the 'old culture' almost beyond repair. Much of the argument was rigorously consequential. Britain's loss of confidence went back to the wartime 'American Occupation'. Churchill's funeral in 1965 marked the last occasion when the old values still held sway. The unseemly proceedings at Princess Diana's funeral in 1997 exposed the silent revolution that had been accomplished in the intervening years. Britain's sense of history had been wrecked by a historical profession uninterested in the nation's heritage. Britain's schoolchildren had been led astray by teachers indifferent to educational standards. The Church of England had been reduced to anarchy by bishops who no longer upheld the Faith. 'Dumbed-down' television and the insatiable appetite for entertainment had undermined cultural pursuits. Patriotism and respect for British institutions had been mocked by the prevalence of satire. The satirical show *Beyond the Fringe* (1962–3) and in particular, the playwright Alan Bennett (1934–) had apparently much to answer for. The National Council for One-Parent Families, whilst championing a feckless minority, ruined the matrimonial harmony of millions. The National Association for Teaching English raised a generation that was all but ignorant of the English literary canon. The unsuccessful prosecution in 1960 of the publisher of *Lady Chatterley's Lover* had opened the floodgates for pornography and ever more offensive breaches of the obscenity laws. The culture of the Pill and the condom separated sexuality from its proper context of love, partnership and marriage. The long reign of Margaret Thatcher, who worshipped the market but cared nothing for culture or morality, carried no less blame than that of her socialist opponents . . .[169]

Here was the honest voice of unashamed reaction, which longed to reverse the changes of the post-war era and to return to a mythical age of innocence. 'Britain', wrote Peter Hitchens, 'is the only virgin in a Continent of rape victims.'[170] This was possibly an apt metaphor for 1945, but hardly for 1999. In the terms of Hitchens's own polemic, the one-time British virgin had spent the last forty years demeaning herself. What is more, every single aspect of her ruin was attributed to internal failures and to domestic traducers. Not one of the catalogue of disasters could be pinned on European influences. Britain's soaring teenage pregnancy rate could hardly be blamed on Brussels. In which case, it was entirely illogical to pour quite so much venom on the European union, and on the prospect of joining the Eurozone. If one were to believe such conclusions, one might think that to lose the pound sterling was the ultimate disgrace, the final downfall of British maidenhood in a European gang-rape. What a lovely non-sequitur! If poor old Britannia were really in the sick and sorry state that Mr Hitchens so cogently described, then she was in urgent need of care and company. For her to live on her own, and to fend for herself, would be the worse possible remedy. Far better to join the European Club of Victims

Anonymous, and to convalesce in a comforting community of fellow-sufferers.

All the while, within the everyday work of the European Union, both British and Irish were having to learn new ways of governing. Not everything about the *esprit communautaire* was attractive. Brussels was a Tower of Babel not only of foreign languages but also of competing political cultures. Yet no one nation dominated. All decisions had to be made by seeking a consensus. A spirit of cooperation and dedication to the cause of peace and prosperity were essential. Compromise and comradeship were de rigueur. In 1900, a grand British Viceroy could set out his colleague's ministerial aims as ensuring the country's victory 'in our next big war'. (See above.) His counterpart in 1999 would probably find such a thought as disgraceful as it was impractical. He could still tell his colleague to resist 'that cursed Treasury'. But, as the minister left on Eurostar for a top table at Brussels, the talk would have been about 'taking the lead', 'trading this for that', and 'not letting the bureaucrats grind you down'.

(18) BRITAIN AND EUROPE: A CHOICE FOR THE MAKING

In the course of the twentieth century the Isles were pulled by stages into a position of ever increasing intimacy with the European mainland. In part, the shift could be explained through far-reaching changes in the patterns of communication and trade. In part, and especially in the second half of the century, it could be attributed to the effects of globalization and the ever-diminishing significance of the old sovereign states. But it must also be seen as the cumulative consequence of three key political decisions – in 1914, in 1939, and in 1972. The end result was not in doubt. In the 1890s the United Kingdom of Great Britain and Ireland was still holding on to its traditional 'semi-detached' stance with regards to the Continent (see below). In the 1990s, both the United Kingdom and the Republic of

Ireland were permanently and institutionally engaged in the European Union.

The revolution in communications was there for all to see. If mid-Victorian travellers were thrilled to get from London to Paris in a single day, their mid-century counterparts a hundred years later were accustomed to make the journey in less than an hour. Regular air services round Europe began in the 1920s. Initially, they were very uncomfortable, very expensive, and very exclusive. But from the 1960s commercial jets put air travel within almost everyone's reach. Package holidays boomed. For the first time in history, ordinary British working-class families could take their holidays in Greece, in Italy, or in Spain. On the Mediterranean beaches, and in the *tavernas*, they met millions of other Europeans enjoying themselves in exactly the same way. Their ability to mingle, especially linguistically, was not perfect. But they came back home with the fruits of a learning experience such as no previous generation had been given. They developed a taste for wine; they took a liking to *moussaka, pizza,* and *paella*; and they learned the inestimable lesson that the British way of doing things was not necessarily the best. Indeed, if one needed to bag a deckchair and a beach umbrella, the German habit of rising at six o'clock proved rather more effective than the British habit of rising at eight or nine. By the 1990s, a family trip to Corfu or to the Costa del Sol was just as routine as their grandparents' outings to Blackpool or Brighton. What is more, the *tavernas* of Brighton were matched by the chip shops on Corfu.

Every other form of communication developed at the same dizzy pace. Roll-on, roll-off car ferries replaced cargo ships that had winched tourists' vehicles onto the open deck with a crane. Hovercraft overtook the ferries. Motorways on either side of the Channel put Brussels as close to London as Manchester had been. High-speed rail links – speedier in some countries than others – whisked travellers to and fro with famous despatch. Money-changing, which was once done clumsily with travellers' cheques and suspicious bank clerks, could now be effected instantly at Continental ATMs that

accepted British bank cards. Satellite TV brought Continental programmes into British living rooms. The ultimate step was taken in
1994, when the Channel Tunnel was opened. One could travel from
Folkestone to Boulogne by land. Great Britain had ceased to be an
island for the first time in about seven thousand years.

Globalization drove similar changes into the organizational
sphere. All manner of operations once conducted by local or national
organizations were now taken over by international bodies that
bestrode frontiers and oceans. The phenomenon was by no means
limited to Europe. Indeed, its motive force could often be traced to
the USA. But it was particularly relevant to a European continent
that had hitherto been fragmented by dozens of sovereign states.
Indeed, it promised to give Europe the same economic, transporta-
tional, and commercial benefit that a huge country like the USA
enjoyed. Early steps were taken by international organizations in the
postal and transportation spheres. Large multinational firms, like
Royal Dutch Shell (1907), were already in existence before the First
World War. By the end of the century, there was no important
activity in Europe that was not run, regulated, or coordinated by
some sort of transitional authority. Britain was locked into the lives
of its neighbours as never before.

Changing British trade patterns revealed a growing concentration on export and import with Europe. The trend was in
progress several decades before the demise of the British Empire
(see above); but it provided a ready-made alternative when 'imperial
preference' came to an end in the 1960s. Thanks to the contiguity of
the Continent, it developed further and faster than Britain's second
line of commercial expansion with the USA. The Confederation of
British Industry (CBI) inevitably grew into a fundamental supporter
of 'pro-European' sentiment.

Twice in the first half of the twentieth century, British governments faced a decision of absolutely capital importance – whether
to intervene in a general European war, or, in the interests of the
overseas Empire, to stay out. On both occasions, the decision was
taken to put Britain's interests in Europe first; and a long series of

consequences ensued. In August 1914, the British government had no obligation to enter the European war. Whereas France and Russia were bound together by the terms of a formal alliance, Britain was only linked to France and Russia by an informal entente. The British could have steered clear. They could have solved the problem with Belgium by accepting German assurances that Belgian independence was only temporarily interrupted. The German command fully expected them to do so. But they chose to go in. And by going in, they committed the United Kingdom to a chain of unending European involvements. Whatever the damage that would be done to the Empire, priority was given to dealing with a perceived threat from Germany to the security of the Isles in Europe.

In 1939, the same dilemma reappeared in a slightly different form. But the same decision was taken. As in 1914, the British government was not prepared to let the danger of German hegemony over mainland Europe pass unchallenged. This time round, Britain did possess an obligation to intervene, in the shape of the British Guarantee to Poland and the subsequent British–Polish Alliance (25 August 1939). But that obligation, though providing the *casus belli*, can hardly be considered as the main justification of the decision. Britain in 1939 had no means of giving direct military assistance to Poland. The Guarantee had been no more than an act of bluff in the much wider game of trying to deter Hitler. (It was not invoked as a *casus belli* against the Soviet Union, when Stalin's troops joined Hitler's in Poland.) It was one small link in the long chain of events leading back to the fateful summer of 1914. To have stood back in 1939, and to have let German expansion continue unchecked, would have betrayed the 700,000 or more British soldiers who had died in the unfinished war against Germany only twenty years before.[171] But it would also have run much greater risks. The Nazi regime was a far more hostile beast than the Kaiser had ever been. And Göring's Luftwaffe presented a much sharper threat to the Isles than the Kaiser's fleet had done. So the pressure to intervene on Chamberlain and Halifax was much more acute than that on Asquith and Grey. The latter, who had never known a European war in the whole of their careers, almost strolled into the conflict, oblivious of the outcome. The former, both of whom had the tragedy of 1914–18 before their eyes and both of whom understood the implications for the Empire – Halifax had been Viceroy of India – re-entered the conflict with well-justified forebodings. The results are in the record. The United Kingdom emerged from the war on the winning, Allied side. It achieved its prime objectives in Europe, by seeing an end to the prospect of German hegemony. But it paid for that success by losing its grip on the Empire, by accepting a position of political, economic, and military dependence on the USA, and by colluding in the rise of the USSR.

In the second half of the twentieth century, therefore, an entirely new European challenge emerged. As the Soviet army occupied the eastern half of Europe, as Britain's dependence on the USA was prolonged, and as the remnants of the Empire sank from view, British politicians watched as the European movement in Western Europe went from strength to strength. The question was: to join or not to join. In the late 1940s, the Attlee government showed no inclination. In the 1950s the Conservative governments of Churchill and Eden stayed aloof. But by the early 1960s the Macmillan government reached the point of applying for membership. In 1963 and in 1967, General de Gaulle stopped the application dead. Together with the Suez catastrophe in 1956, the French vetoes brought the British people face to face with reality. Britain's absolute sovereignty was an illusion. Britain could only act on the world scene as a client state of the USA. Yet even in European affairs she carried no more clout than her neighbours so recently regarded as second-raters. It was a sobering thought.

With such a prelude, the decision to enter the European Community after General de Gaulle's death took place in much chastened circumstances. Negotiated by the Heath government in 1970–72, it took effect in January 1973, and committed the United Kingdom to all the clauses of the Treaty of Rome. In particular, despite the scepticism of many British politicians, it included a commitment to the objective of 'an ever closer union'.

From then on, the British were treaty-bound to participate in all the complex activities of the EEC. They were also required to take a position on each of the community's strides towards further integration. The Single European Act (1986) was adopted by the Thatcher government. The Exchange Rate Mechanism (ERM), a transitional stage on the road to full monetary union, was embraced by Britain in 1990 then abandoned, humiliatingly, in 1992. The Treaty of Maastricht (1991), which set out a far-reaching programme of integrationist measures, was signed by John Major with a couple of opt-outs. In 1999, the introduction of a common European currency, the euro, evoked a stance of wait-and-see from the Blair government. At every stage, the benefits of membership had to be weighed against the limitations placed on every member's freedom of manoeuvre. For the first time in its history the United Kingdom had to adjust to the unfamiliar condition of acting collectively with its partners in the club.

The Republic of Ireland joined the EEC at the same time as the United Kingdom. The former rebel was transformed overnight into an equal partner. The configuration of the key relationship within the Isles was put onto a healthy footing for the first time in fifty years. British–Irish cooperation improved by leaps and bounds.

The principal inhibitor to Britain's membership of the EEC (from 1991, the European Union) lay not in the memories of Empire, but in the habit of clinging to America's apron strings. From 1973 onwards, Britain was standing astride two galloping horses, which could not be guaranteed to run in step indefinitely. In the early post-war decades, American leaders encouraged Britain's involvement in 'Europe', since the US needed prosperous trading partners, and the UK could act as a useful bridge for an American-led NATO. From the 1950s to the early 1990s the EEC and NATO, which possessed a long list of common members, interacted in a mutually complementary fashion. The one took care of the economic development: the other of strategic security.

As the end of the twentieth century approached, however, strains began to appear on all sides; and Britain's balancing act became increasingly precarious. The collapse of the Soviet Bloc made NATO's former role redundant, whilst opening up the prospect of eastward expansion by the EU. From the American standpoint, the much enlarged EU, now with a population of 320 million and a common currency, started to look less like an economic partner and more like a potential rival. As it strove for greater integration and for greater harmony of purpose, its strivings inevitably threatened to complicate its good relations with Washington. At the same time, NATO was left searching for gainful employment. The implosion of the Soviet Union removed at a stroke the original purpose for America's dominant European presence. For the time being, conflicts in the former Yugoslavia provided a field for common endeavour. But they fed the Americans a sense of frustration at having to do tasks that the Europeans could well do for themselves. And they gave the Europeans a strong and unpalatable taste of their political and military impotence.

In Britain, the future of 'Europe' caused more dissension than any other political issue. The Conservative government of 1992–97 was paralysed by the in-fighting of its 'Europhile' and 'Eurosceptic' wings. Public opinion as a whole appeared to be increasingly polarized. The strong pro-American lobby, led by Conservatives like Lady Thatcher, considered support for NATO and opposition to further integration of the EU as two sides of the same coin. The pro-Europeans, in contrast, who were pressing for British entry to the Eurozone, were standing to offend the Atlanticists. On the verge of the new millennium, Britain still possessed strong connections with both 'America' and 'Europe'. But the balancing act could not go on for ever. Sooner or later, she would have to choose. Nothing was yet decided. One could only guess from the precedents. But if Britain were to take the first capital decision of the twenty-first century in line with the three capital decisions of the twentieth century, the decision would go with 'Europe'. After all, the Atlantic was a hundred times wider the Channel; and all the political, economic, and cultural barriers, which had kept the Isles apart from the Continent, were falling fast.

1999. MORE THAN A HUNDRED and fifty years ago, one of Britain's most prominent historians, Lord Macaulay, mused about the future of his country. Conscious of the frailty of all human institutions, he imagined a time when England would no longer exist. Influenced no doubt by the famous account of Edward Gibbon, who had sat among the ruins of the Colosseum and reflected on the passing of ancient Rome, Macaulay had imagined the passing of London. He described the day when 'some traveller from New Zealand shall . . . take his stand on a broken arch of London Bridge to sketch the ruins of St Paul's'.[172] In some respects, the picture has already been proved false. The German bombs which fell through the roof of St Paul's in 1940 failed to explode, and the London Bridge which Macaulay knew has been transported brick by brick to Arizona. But in general terms, the contention is undeniable. In the long term, London 'will be one with Nineveh and Tyre'. The only question is: When?

Early in 1999, a senior British politician hinted at an answer to the question by publishing a party polemic called *The Death of Britain?*.[173] The title was rather more memorable than the content, which suggested that Britain's death, if it occurred, could be solely attributed to eighteen months of New Labour's misrule. Nonetheless, it was a sign of the times. At no other point in the twentieth century would any British politician have reflected, even by way of hyperbole, on the possible demise of the state. The author was exercised by what he saw as a constitutional crisis. But many people, for several years, had been worrying and writing about 'a crisis of identity'.

≈

The things which the British people were told about their history clearly had bearing both on their view of themselves and on their assessment of current problems. In the twentieth century, however, they were not well served. For whatever reason, historians did not keep pace with the demands of a rapidly changing world. After several decades of holding to the old ways, they eventually retreated either into social history or into the ultra-specialization which divorced them from the general public.

For much of the twentieth century, there was no dearth of general Histories of England written by distinguished scholars. One has to mention Pollard (1912), the American, Lunt (1928), Chrimes (1948), Feiling (1950), and Clark (1971).[174] Yet they all wrote very much to a pattern. They usually started with Roman Britain and ploughed on to the First World War. Since all of them, with one exception, were late medievalists or early modernists, they placed special stress on the Tudors and Stuarts. They all gave special prominence to the evolution of Parliament. And they all wrote almost exclusively about England. None of them paid more than passing attention to the creation of the United Kingdom. Chrimes, who 241 years after the Act of Union was still calling his work *English* Constitutional History, did not even mention it. Sir George Clark, writing at the very time when the UK was negotiating to join the EEC, summed up the common outlook:

> The purpose of this book is to show how the English people came to form a community . . . There are communities within England, such as villages, towns and counties. Around it . . . are such neighbouring communities as Wales, Scotland, Ireland and France, and many others further away. There are international communities, like the churches, and the many political or other associations in which England has shared. I have not shared the histories of any of these communities except in as far as they explain the growth and action of England. By that I mean England in the strict sense, not Great Britain or the British Isles.[175]

It is perfectly evident that England was still regarded as a discrete community, frozen in time and free as a bird. If any of Clark's readers had tried to relate this picture to contemporary events, they could have been forgiven for thinking that Edward Heath was Prime Minister of England.

Arnold Toynbee (1889–1975), though a British historian, was not especially concerned with British history. He was a historical theoretician; and his twelve-volume synthetic *Study of History* (1939) has been variously described either as 'the most ambitious historical work . . . since Gibbon' or as 'hopelessly schematic'. Nonetheless, Toynbee had his strong views on Britain's place in the past; and in the early pages of his *Study*, where he is searching for 'an intelligable field of study', he tests out the British case:

> Great Britain seems to be as good a choice as any. She is not merely a national state but a Great Power. Her principal constituent, England, who incorporated herself into Great Britain two centuries ago without any breach of continuity or change of identity is . . . on the whole as important a figure [as France], though she has performed quite a different historical function. Her particular merit . . . is that, to any exceptional degree, she has been kept in isolation – first by her physical geography and secondly by a certain policy on the part of her statesmen in the age during which she has been most creative and most powerful.[176]

After examining the main features of Britain's past from 'The Industrial Revolution' to 'the Conversion of the English', Toynbee reached a conclusion that was either far ahead of or, at the very least, completely out of step with his generation. He concluded that neither Great Britain nor any other nation-state was worthy of his attention in itself:

> Thus British national history is not, never has been, and almost certainly never will be an 'intelligible field of study' in isolation: and if that is true of Great Britain, it must surely be true *a fortiori* of any other national state.[177]

In 1931, such statements were close to heresy.

Two history books of that era, however, stand out from the crowd. One was written by a Frenchman, the other by a man who carried the grandest name in British historiography.

Élie Halévy (1870–1937) was a typical left-wing French intellectual, author of histories of philosophic radicalism and of European Socialism. He was not the most obvious candidate to teach the British people about their past. What is more, his six-volume *Histoire du Peuple Anglais* (1913) was confined to nineteenth-century affairs. Yet when the English translation volumes began to appear from 1924 onwards, they won instant acclaim. The range of topics was astonishingly comprehensive. The style was clarity itself. And the tone was unmistakably sympathetic. Halévy apologized in the preface for having 'to learn with great difficulty . . . a multitude of things which even an uneducated Englishman knows, so to speak, by instinct.'[178] But he then proceeded to demonstrate his mastery of everything from Methodism in volume I to 'the Irish Revolt' in volume 6. He was the perfect example of an outsider who becomes the insiders' favourite. 'England is a free country,' he concluded on the last page of volume 1, 'this means at bottom that England is a country of voluntary obedience, of an organization freely initiated and freely accepted.'[179] If a Frenchman said such things about the English, they had to be true. French editions of Halévy's work were still being produced in the 1960s.

The Whig tradition, which Halévy had learned with such difficulty, had surrounded George Macaulay Trevelyan (1876–1962) since birth. The nephew of Lord Macaulay, he was born with the proverbial silver spoon and progressed effortlessly to be Regius Professor of Modern History at Cambridge and Master of Trinity. His studies of *Garibaldi and the Making of Italy* (1911) and *The Life of John Bright* (1913) were infused with classic British Liberalism. His one-volume *History of England* (1926), therefore, carried an unusual weight of authority. Edition followed edition both before and after the Second World War. Together with his *English Social History* (1942), they made him the most popular historian of his generation.

Yet Trevelyan's opinions were strangely antiquated. If one were unkind, one would have to say that he was pandering to his readers' prejudices. The first part, up to 1066, which was published by popular demand as a separate volume, was called, like some Victorian pseudo-scientific study, *The Mingling of the Races*. Exceptionally among his contemporaries, he wrote in the later chapters about 'Britain', not just 'England', and he paid tribute to 'the joyful pride' and 'mutual advantage' of the Anglo-Scottish 'partnership'.[180] Yet he was constantly going on about Britain's 'greatness' and 'uniqueness' without any qualifications of time. Once Britain had established itself as 'a leader in the world's affairs', the distinct impression was conveyed that this felicitous condition was immutable:

> In the sphere of pure politics, Britain is famous as the mother of Parliaments. In answer to the instincts and temperament of her people, she evolved in the course of centuries a system which reconciled three things that other nations have often found incompatible – executive efficiency, popular control, and personal freedom.[181]

This sort of comment was no preparation for a Britain that in Trevelyan's own lifetime was actively committed to joining those 'other nations' in permanent partnership.

Churchill apart, no historian of stature Trevelyan and Clark attempted to write a compact synthesis of national history. The historical profession was rapidly becoming more specialized. Authors were unwilling to write outside their own particular patch or period. Publishers were advised to commission either collaborative works by numerous contributors or, more frequently, massive, multi-volume series on the model of the prestigious Oxford History of England. Both strategies raised the academic standard of works available to the general reader. At the same time, they served to fragment historical knowledge, and all too often to destroy the public's appetite for it. Collaborative works were notoriously lacking in zest and good style; whilst the sheer scale of the multi-volume series deterred all but the most tireless devotees.

National history in any case was slipping out of fashion. So, too, was the readiness to appreciate a broad-based historical vision. Indeed, from the 1970s, History itself was under attack. The academic market place was filling up with any number of new stalls – economics, sociology, political science, gender studies, race studies, and many others, all of which preferred contemporary analysis. History came under pressure to contract, and increasingly to limit its horizons to the twentieth century. Academics with different priorities could resist for a while. But they were undermined by the advent of student-centred syllabuses and by course selection *à la carte*. In the 1980s, when academic life was handed over to the book-keepers and auditors, administrators would question the value of 'minority courses' that packed fewer bodies into classrooms, and would shamelessly axe them. As universities trained graduates lacking in comprehensive knowledge, so teachers trained pupils with the same deficiencies. Step by step, the day approached when Oxbridge admissions tutors would complain that candidates with the highest grades in A-level history had no knowledge or interest beyond Hitler and Stalin.[182]

Trends in school history-teaching had much to answer for. Early in the century, when history was established as a school discipline, patriotic and moral objectives predominated. 'The formation of an ethos for the English race', announced a History Association pamphlet for 1909, 'was central to the mission of history as a lesson.'[183] Teaching was robotic. The rote-learning of the names and dates of monarchs was commonplace. More surprisingly, history textbooks prepared before the First World War often continued in widespread use until well after the Second. A warhorse text such as *The Groundwork of British History*, by G. T. Warner and C. H. K. Marten, which was first published in 1912, was still being reprinted (as *The New Groundwork*, by Warner, Marten, and Muir) in 1964. A breakdown of its contents reveals all the old stereotypes: 'the mingling of races', England's sterling national character, the benefits of the Reformation, the absence of revolution, the pursuit of liberty, the 'savagery' of Ireland, and the beneficent effects of empire:

> Britain believed that her rule was beneficial . . . She used her capital to develop backward lands, and she tried to give justice to all citizens – and all this was summed up in what was called 'the civilizing mission of the Anglo-Saxon race'.[184]

After 1945, however, new winds began to blow through history lessons. UNESCO promoted an effective campaign of 'History for World Citizenship'. Internationalism was to replace nationalism. The Council of Europe promoted a parallel 'History for European Citizenship'. National histories were to give ground to the common heritage of Western Europe. Most significantly, a number of educationalists exposed the dangers of bias in history. A study by E. H. Dance, *History the Betrayer* (1960), was well received by the teaching profession.[185] Demands then surfaced, firstly for an emphasis on the teaching of historical skills, secondly for the study of selected periods in greater depth, and thirdly for the replacement of political by social history. At the same time, teachers concerned for the less able pressed for more varied pedagogical approaches including 'the lines of development' technique and exercises in empathy. In themselves, each of these proposals carried conspicuous merit. But their collective impact was undoubtedly to sow disarray. In an era when the state sector of British education was being turned upside down by the introduction of comprehensive schooling, and when the syllabus was being stretched by the entry of numerous new subjects, history-teaching was one of the losers. In 1943, the Norwood Report had called confidently for a 'British-centred History Curriculum' – British meaning both home and overseas. Thirty and forty years later, no end of committees could succeed in bringing order to the reigning chaos.

One of many organizational problems derived from the absence of any all-British consensus. The so-called National Curriculum only applied to England and Wales, and even Wales enjoyed special provisions. Schools in Scotland and Northern Ireland ran their own

curricula. So if the long-running committee, which had been following a brief to reintroduce a balance between British and general
history, had actually pushed its recommendations into reality, they
would have only applied to part of the country. Yet in 1999 the battle
for a coherent approach to history in education appeared to be lost.
Regional examination boards, which also enjoyed autonomy, were
trying to drop medieval history completely. Students at the leading
universities like Oxford were following 'pick 'n' mix' courses which
allowed them to graduate in complete ignorance of whole swaths of
British history.[186] And if press reports were correct, the government
was introducing yet another scheme for English schoolchildren
between five and fourteen where there was no prescribed content
whatsoever and no requirement to teach history in chronological
sequence. 'If these proposals are adopted,' commented the director of
a professional association that was critical of the trend, 'they will
destroy history as a subject that has traditionally given schoolchildren
a sense of national identity. History-teaching will become a total free-
for-all.'[187] He was echoing the opinion of a senior government adviser
who had earlier warned that Britain's national identity was being
undermined. 'A society that failed to pass on "the great tradition"'
from one generation to the next 'was nearing its terminal stage'.[188]

Extraordinary though it may seem, one of the main reasons for the
confusion in schools and university must be attributed to the fact
that most British historians could not actually say with any certainty
what British history was. The old Anglocentric tradition, as defined
most recently by Clark (see above), was fading fast. But it had not
been replaced by any coherent British scheme before the ultra-
specialists, the pick 'n' mixers, the advocates of contemporary history, and all the other vultures moved in. It took a clear-thinking
New Zealander to tell the British what their history consisted of.

Professor John Pocock (1924–) was a historian of political thought,
who had published on Locke, and Harrington and seventeenth-
century feudal law. But he looked at British history from what he

called a 'South Pacific perspective' – yet another example of the far-sighted outsider. He seems to have been worried in the early 1970s that Britain's entry into the EEC would swing the pendulum of historical interest too far in the direction of European subjects. But he was obviously most concerned that none of his colleagues in the United Kingdom possessed any clear idea of what they should be defending against the expected European onslaught. Hence, only one year after Clark's publication of yet another depressing 'History of England', he set out his plea in a local New Zealand journal. It was entitled 'British History: a plea for a new subject'. He had set a really sharp-clawed and sharp-eyed cat among the slow-footed academic pigeons.

Pocock's article was reprinted in the USA, re-presented in conference, re-formulated in a paper for the Centre for the Study of Public Policy, and republished in revised form. It was obligatory reading for anyone who wanted to understand how peculiar the dominant tradition of history-writing in Britain had become and how difficult it was to escape from it. Its chief target, of course, was the apparently nonsensical construct which equated 'Britain' with 'England' and 'England' with 'Britain'. But it took a much sharper turn by arguing that the construct was not just a harmless myth or a simple piece of misunderstanding. It was the product of a political strategy to uphold the domination of the English over all the other peoples of the Isles. A few random quotations and telling phrases must convey the drift of twenty closely-argued pages:

— 'British History [is] too serious to be left to the English.'
— 'the need to write it as the history of the interaction and expansion of a number of cultures originating in an archipelago off the north-west coast of Europe.'
— 'Because Britain is an effect of English domination over adjacent cultures, it has no history other than English History . . .'
— 'The English have little belief in "Britain" . . . unless assured that the word is a synonym for themselves.'

— The United Kingdom arose from 'a Whig experiment in empire' coinciding with 'the golden age of aristocratic parliamentarianism.' 'It is not clear that the two can survive one another.'

— 'When George III declared that he "gloried in being a Briton" he meant to say that he was not a Hanoverian, but he was accused of saying that he was a Scot.'

— In the Scottish Enlightenment 'the Scots' took to 'writing the History of England better than the English could do for themselves.'

— 'The English are not conducting the affairs of the United Kingdom as if it were a state, so much as a series of appendages to themselves. Only British Marxists talk of the British state, and that as a prelude to predicting its overthrow.'

— 'England is not a self-contained whole, as its myths suggest, but a creation of history.'

— 'The myths and symbols of an English *patria* remain heavily southern and agrarian.'

— 'the recurrent need to choose between *kleinenglisch* and *grossbritannisch* solutions.'

— 'It seems evident that British history must be constructed as that of many peoples, interacting, destroying and creating one another.'

— 'The Whig gravitational pull.'[189]

Seeing that British history and British historiography had been in the making for over two and a half centuries, one can only say that Pocock's strictures were slightly overdue. They provoked the predictable outbursts. One of the most offensive came from one of Pocock's original interlocutors, A. J. P. Taylor, who callously asked: 'But what have the Scots ever contributed to History?'[190] At the time, Taylor the 'tele-don' was the most listened-to historian in the land. What could a mere colonial hope to achieve against the likes of him?

≈

People's personal memories are a powerful factor in contemporary historical consciousness. The various shifts in Britain's position in the world were spread out at intervals throughout the century. So people of different ages had different memories. The secession of Ireland, for instance, took place in the 1920s. The full independence of the dominions was granted in the 1930s. The disintegration of the overseas Empire began in the 1940s and continued until the late 1960s. The entry into the European Community occurred in the 1970s. And constitutional devolution within the UK began in the 1990s. Every decade with the exception of the 1980s witnessed a sizeable reconfiguration. These facts have no small impact on the debate which was getting under way at the end of the century. Presuming that political awareness does not develop until one's teens, one needed to be a nonagenarian in 1999 to remember either the Great War or the days when the United Kingdom included the whole of the British Isles. Only octogenarians could remember the days of untrammelled Empire; and only OAPs in their seventies could clearly recall the Second World War and the loss of India. Sixty-year-olds, born about 1939, might have some slight awareness of the wartime 'blackout' or post-war rationing. But their fuller understanding of political events could not have begun much before Suez. Fifty-year-olds and over could remember the Beatles in their prime and the terrible shock of de Gaulle's veto. Forty-year-olds might just remember Britain and Ireland joining 'the Common Market' and the European Referendum of 1975. But every single man and woman under thirty years of age had lived the whole of their lives as members of the European Community. For them, if not for their parents and grandparents, the gradual almost imperceptible movement towards closer European Union was part of their everyday existence. And time was on their side. The United Kingdom in 1999 had a Prime Minister aged forty-six who could not possibly have remembered Churchill, except perhaps his funeral; who could not have had any clear recollections of the Empire; and who entered university in the year that Britain entered the European Community. His mental picture of the world, and that of the generation which he led, was formed by very different experiences from those of all his predecessors.

The state of play at the turn of the millennium can only be described as unresolved. The sources of consternation were manifold. Quite apart from the problem of British history, one would have to outline the effects of devolution, the changing patterns of power and influence, and the ubiquitous feeling of national decline.

The confusion over British history was by no means confined to the academic and the educational sectors. It was greatly magnified by government support for the concept of 'Heritage', and for the methods by which the concept was applied. Anyone concerned to foster a sense of British identity was bound to consider the concept deficient and the methods crass. History is all about change and conflict. It is not a comfortable subject. 'Heritage', in contrast, was developed as an idea for preserving the memories and monuments of the past in a prim, static mode which would appeal to the casual tourist but not to anyone seriously interested in past realities. It had distinct commercial overtones, being a product of the 1980s when markets ruled all and the chief concern was for the output of the turnstiles. It summoned up the noun 'theme park' and the adjective 'twee'. It aimed to dress up the past for the entertainment of its consumers. Worst of all, it bore no relation to the common history of the United Kingdom. When the scheme was launched in 1984, the principal body was named English Heritage with a remit confined exclusively to England. Parallel bodies were set up for Scotland, Wales, and Northern Ireland, each of which was now presented as possessing its own 'heritage'. The idea of *British Heritage* did not come into it, except as the title of a magazine to encourage foreign visitors to tour the United Kingdom.

The literature distributed by English Heritage, by far the largest of the four organizations, was well worth examining. It described EH as 'the national body created by Parliament [and] charged with the protection of the historic environment'. It did not specify which nation was referred to, nor whose Parliament was responsible. If one read the Welcome Message from the Chairman, it was peppered with phrases such as 'our historic environment', 'our understanding of the past', and 'the protection of our heritage'. The only thing he did not clarify was who 'we' were.[191] The prize exhibit, of course, was Stonehenge. (See above.) As an exercise in strengthening British identity, the creation of English Heritage was a disaster. It played into the hands of all separatists.

Museums were in a similar state of disarray, at least on this central question of fostering national identity. Britain in the 1990s possessed a plethora of museums. In addition to all the traditional historical, local, military, and maritime museums there were museums of everything from Agriculture to Dance and Toys, even Fishing. Museum-going was popular. Yet the sheer mass of museological exhibitions was causing disorientation. No museum-goer could obtain a coherent view of the past. The British Museum had a huge international collection. Alone, the new Museum of Scotland, opened in 1998, projected a national mission – and the mission was not British.[192]

In all but name, therefore, the policy of devolution had been accepted by the Thatcher government in the cultural and educational sphere many years before it was adopted in the constitutional sphere by 'New Labour'. The cumulative effects were bound to be far-reaching. The Scots and the Welsh, and to some extent the Northern Irish, were given a strong injection not only of self-esteem but also of separation. The English were left feeling bewildered. Of all the British peoples, the English were by far the most disconcerted about who they really were. In the late 1990s, the issue began to be debated with some vigour.

In a sense, the contemporary debate about 'Englishness' went all the way back to George Orwell (1903–50) and to his wartime book, *The Lion and the Unicorn* (1941). Orwell, an ex-Etonian socialist, possessed one of the great minds of the century. His *Animal Farm* (1945) and *Nineteen Eighty-four* (1949) exposed the lies of totalitarianism like nothing else in literature. Yet, having banged the drum of internationalism between the wars, he was at pains under the Blitz to prove his patriotism. The result was a book whose first part, called 'England your England', was devoted to an attempt to define the qualities which made 'Englishness' admirable. It contains some wonderfully critical comments. 'England is the most class-ridden society under the sun', he wrote, '- a land of snobbery and privilege run largely by the old and the silly.' Or again: 'What was it', he asked of the 1930s, 'that made every British statesman do the wrong thing with such unnerving instinct?' At the same time, he was very proud of his compatriots, especially the common people. He hated ladies in Rolls-Royces, who, he raged, were 'more damaging to morale than a fleet of Goering's bombing-planes'. Yet he had great faith in the steadfastness of ordinary folk, and their ability to pull through. In the end, he concluded, touchingly, that the most marked characteristic of 'English civilisation' was its 'gentleness'. In a famous passage, later to be quoted by a Prime Minister, John Major, he conjured up some of the gentle images which he took to be 'characteristic of the English scene':

> The clatter of clogs in the Lancashire mill towns, the to-and-fro of the lorries on the Great North Road, the queues outside the Labour Exchanges, the rattle of pin tables in the Soho pubs, the old maids biking to Holy Communion through the mists of the autumn morning—[193]

'I believe in England,' he finished, 'and I believe that we shall go forward.'[194]

These words were often quoted when the topic came back onto the agenda fifty years later. But Orwell had been writing when 'England' was not generally distinguished from the United Kingdom as a whole; and as the son of a colonial family, born in Bengal, he was using 'England' and 'English' in the old imperial sense. So his remarks were not strictly relevant to the anxieties of post-imperial generations.

From the mass of articles on the subject, which were falling thick and fast after 1997, three may be selected for approaching the issue from three separate vantage points. Professor Jeremy Black, writing in *History Today*, took the long historical view. A 'sense of Englishness' has been built on since the tenth century, layer on layer. But for three hundred years since the creation of the Union and the Empire, it became so entangled in overlapping concepts of Britishness and imperial loyalty that its previous clarity became hopelessly blurred. The pre-imperial benchmarks of English no longer applied. The post-imperial version would have to be rediscovered.[195]

Antonia Byatt (1936–), a perspicacious novelist in her own right and a Yorkshirewoman, was commissioned in the mid-1990s to edit *The Oxford Book of English Short Stories*. She hesitated to accept, partly because English literature seemed to be sinking beneath something called British Cultural Studies and partly because her publishers had already dealt with Scots, Irish, Welsh, Canadian, and Australian stories. (Typical, one might think, that English was the last category to come to mind.) Anyhow, she did accept and made her first rule 'to be strict about Englishness'. The experience turned out to be extremely pleasurable. Thirty-seven authors from Anthony Trollope and William Gilbert, father of W.S.G., to P. G. Wodehouse and Evelyn Waugh. And it was even possible to make some generalizations. There was nothing unexpected in Byatt's conclusion that English writing was extremely 'mongrel rich', varying from grim realism to irony, farce, and 'the wildly surreal'. But her willingness to commit herself to two recurrent English characteristics was unexpected, especially as there turned out to be three of them. The first generalization was 'The English like solidity.' The second was their 'preoccupation with wickedness'. The third was 'the shiftingness, the twisting, [which] I have come to think of as English'.[196] Political students of *Albion perfide* would certainly agree with the last one.

Jeremy Paxman (1950–) was known as the country's most provocative television interviewer. He sought answers to his quest for Englishness over several years 'by travelling, talking and reading'. He came up with a highly intelligent panorama that was as fascinating in its detailed observations as it was lacking in firm conclusions. In answer to the question 'What are the English supposed to be celebrating?' Paxman comes up, off the top of his head, with:

> 'I know my rights', village cricket and Elgar, Do-it-Yourself, punk, street fashion, irony, vigorous politics, brass bands, Shakespeare, Cumberland sausages, double-decker buses, Vaughan Williams, Donne and Dickens, twitching net curtains, breast-obsession, quizzes and crosswords, country churches, dry-stone walls, gardening, Christopher Wren and Monty Python, easy-going Church of England vicars, the Beatles, bad hotels and good beer, church bells, Constable and Piper, finding foreigners funny, David Hare and William Cobbett, drinking to excess, Women's Institutes, fish and chips, curry, Christmas Eve at King's College, Cambridge, indifference to food, civility and crude language, fell-running, ugly caravan sites on beautiful clifftops, crumpets, Bentleys and Reliant Robins, and so on.[197]

Where, one wonders, was John Betjeman? But Betjeman was there all right: and Betjeman's own list was not so very different:

> For me, England stands for the Church of England, eccentric incumbents, oil-lit churches, Women's Institutes, modest village inns, arguments about cow parsley on the altar, the noise of mowing machines on Saturday afternoons, local newspapers, local auctions, the poetry of Tennyson, Crabbe, Hardy, and Matthew Arnold, local talent, local concerts, a visit to the cinema, branch-line trains, light railways, leaning on gates, and looking across fields.[198]

Betjeman (1906–84), after all, was nearly half a century in front of Paxman:

> Phone for the fish knives, Norman
> As Cook is a little unnerved;
> You kiddies have crumpled the serviettes
> And I must have things daintily served.[199]

Paxman's survey was not without its ascerbities. He was particularly good on the romantic rural myths of an overwhelmingly urban society. He noted the racism of football hooligans, and the occasional anti-Semitism – though he thought that these contemporary phenomena could be more attached to 'Britain' than to 'England'. He likened England's imperial legacy to 'being chained to a corpse'. In place of a conclusion, he remarked that there was 'something positive about the fact that [the English] have not devoted a lot of energy to discussing who they are':

> The English have not spent a great deal of time defining themselves, because they haven't needed to. It is a mark of self-confidence. Is it necessary to do so now? I can only answer that it seems something that the English can no longer avoid.[200]

The distribution of power and influence is of prime importance for any assessment of a country's condition. A study of the United Kingdom undertaken in 1998 produced some telling results. Dr Terry Kellard, a political psychologist, used eleven different criteria to measure the relative power and influence of two hundred key figures and of the interest groups to which they belonged. The rank, fame, and office of prominent personalities were put into the balance alongside other factors such as the size of the constituency influenced or the scope of the person's position. (See Appendix 57.) It came as no surprise that the Prime Minister, Tony Blair, occupied the number one position. But many of the other placings within the top hundred were not easily predictable. Among the politicians, for example, members of the executive held a crushing advantage over parliamentarians as a whole. Only two non-government MPs, the Speaker of the Commons at nr.54 and the Leader of HM Opposition at nr.68, reached the list. Among the leading ministers of the (New Labour) government, the Scots were neck and neck with the English at 5:5, probably for the first time in British history. Two politicians from Northern Ireland, one Unionist and one Republican, also held high places. Among the non-political categories, several 'global' foreigners made a strong showing. They included Bill Gates, nr.2; Conrad Black, the Canadian media tycoon, nr.4; George Soros, the Hungarian-American financier, nr.7; Rupert Murdoch, of News International, nr.13; and the Pope, nr.44. The average standing of key figures in the media and advertising, at 40, was significantly higher than that of people in business and finance, at 53. But both categories easily surpassed all others except for politicians and administrators. In religion, both the Pope and the leader of Britain's Muslims were well ahead of the Archbishop of Canterbury. Neither wealth nor royalty proved to carry special weight. Queen Elizabeth II, who was both the Head of State and the country's wealthiest person, only just crept onto the list at 100th equal. Her richest subject, Lord Sainsbury, came in at nr. 88. The survey can hardly have been welcome in Buckingham Palace. No doubt others with other criteria would produce a different pecking order. But if the prime symbol of Britishness, to whom all British subjects owed allegiance, could only come 100th out of 100, the prospect for 'Britishness' was bleak indeed.[201]

As the pundits pondered, and the analysts analysed, the pollsters went out to ask the people. A National Opinion Poll survey conducted in May 1998, and supposedly left unpublished by the government, produced strong support for the notion that Britain was a 'once great country in decline':

QUESTION: Is Britain
– a once great country in decline?   44 per cent
– a once great country on the way back?   30 per cent
– always one of the leading countries?   25 per cent
(Don't know)   1 per cent

On European issues, the survey found 'Euroscepticism' in a minority, but alive and kicking:

QUESTION: Should Britain leave the European Union
and become independent once more?

Disagree	58 per cent
Agree	40 per cent
Don't know	2 per cent

No less than 59 per cent of the people asked thought that a United States of Europe would have come into existence within twenty years, i.e. by 2018. The pollsters did not give their respondents the chance of stating that 'the return to independence' was impossible, even if Britain left the Union.

In the year that the European single currency was about to be launched, British opinion was shown to be evenly divided. Whilst 73 per cent of respondents thought it right to leave the decision open, the numbers for and against eventual membership were running neck and neck:

QUESTION: Should Britain eventually become a
member of the single currency?

In favour	48 per cent
Not in favour	46 per cent
Don't know	6 per cent

Colleagues in the EU were urging the British government to commit itself to joining, but the dilemma was plain to see.[202]

On the EU question, as on so many others, 'New Labour' had turned the tables completely round. In 1980, the Labour Party in opposition passed a Party motion 'to disengage Britain from the EEC institutions'. The vote was five million to two million. But bit by bit as the Thatcherite Conservatives grew more anti-European, the moderate Labourites grew into pro-Europeans, on good terms with their Social Democratic partners in France and Germany. Tony Blair, whose earliest political act had been to vote 'Yes' in the European Referendum of 1975, came to power in 1997 with a huge parliamentary majority, and promptly declared himself in favour of a 'people's Europe'. In March 1998, he travelled to Paris, and delivered a speech in passable French to the Assemblée Nationale.[203] This brave gesture did not make him appear any less British. Yet two months later, in May 1998, as current President of the EU, he chaired the meeting where eleven of fifteen member states, but not Britain, pledged themselves to complete economic and monetary union. Once again, Britain's uncertainties about herself and her future condemned her to stand on the sidelines.

Official reactions to the multiplying crises of confidence took several forms. The British government, for example, took the extraordinary step of rebranding itself in the manner of a failing business company that has changed its publicity manager. On 1 April 1998 (April Fool's Day), the Foreign Secretary solemnly announced that henceforth the United Kingdom would be known as 'Cool Britannia'. The gesture changed nothing. But it convinced many observers in the growing belief that New Labour's real forte lay in marketing and manipulation of the media.

In rebranding Britain, the government was only following the lead of commercial companies. In 1995, the greetings-card retailer Clinton's produced its first ever card to celebrate St George's Day on 23 April (Shakespeare's birthday.) Within two years, it was selling fifty thousand. English football fans followed suit. In 1996, at the European Cup, thousands painted their faces with the red cross of St George instead of the traditional Union Jack. British Airways took a similar tack. In 1997, it announced that the Union Jacks painted on the tailfins of its aircraft were to be replaced at a cost of £60 million by a multifarious collection of 'ethnic designs'. Two years later it announced that the experiment had been a marketing disaster with its British passengers, and that an artistic variation on the Union Jack theme would gradually be reintroduced. Virgin Airways promptly introduced a new livery emblazoned with regulation Union Jacks.[204] The net result could only be described as mystification.

In the BBC, top executives decided to bring up the corporation's vocabulary up to date. In March 1999, a new guide to style and language was issued under the title of *The Changing UK*. It was prompted by the imminent opening of the Scottish Parliament and the Welsh Assembly and by the need to report accurately on the complex division of powers between Westminster, Edinburgh, and

Cardiff. Much of the glossary was devoted to differentiating between correct usage in England and Scotland:

England	Scotland
the defendant	the accused
barrister	advocate
alimony	ailment
arbitrator	arbiter
reserved judgement	avizandum
bailiff	sheriff officer
NSPCC	Children First
FA Premiership	Scottish Premier League
injunction	interdict
manslaughter	culpable homicide
plaintiff/claimant	pursuer
arson	wilful fire-raising

In the general section of the guide, many points were unobjectionable. 'The words "British" and "English"' for example, 'are *not* interchangeable.' But in one of the Key Points, an instruction appeared in bold print: **"Don't talk about "the nation" when you mean "the UK"'**. An explanation elaborated: 'We broadcast to an audience in the nations of England, Scotland and Wales . . . It is better that programmes which are broadcast throughout the United Kingdom talk about things happening "across the United Kingdom" or "UK-wide"'.[205] Parts of the press were outraged. The *Sunday Times* ran a front-page headline: 'Revealed: the nation that dare not speak its name.' The British Broadcasting Corporation, one of the most prestigious UK-wide institutions, had worked for nearly seventy years under the motto: NATION SHALL SPEAK PEACE UNTO NATION. But it was now denying the status of 'nation' to the British peoples for whose service it existed. Better proof could not be found that, at least in the eyes of some very influential officials, 'the British nation' was an unacceptable fiction. *O tempora! O mores!*

≈

Historians have no special powers of prophecy. But they are trained to take the longer view. And the longer view gives them the chance not only of exploring the roots of the present but also, and more practically, of assessing the progress of long-running trends. On this score, five general propositions concerning the present condition of the Isles may be ventured. They relate to the nature of the British and Irish states; to the existence, or non-existence of a British nation; to the growth of multiple identities; to the decay of traditional 'Britishness'; and to the strategic choices that loom ahead.

(1) *The United Kingdom is not, and never has been, a nation-state*

In this, it must be contrasted with the Republic of Ireland, which is a nation-state and which approximates much more closely to the nation-states of the Continent such as France or Italy or Germany. By the terms of its inception in 1707, the United Kingdom has been prevented from developing either the federal or the unitary structures which have elsewhere fostered homogeneity. The Federal Republic of Germany, for instance, may be regarded as a German nation-state since each of the constituent *Länder* of the federation were established on an equal basis and none were designed to dominate the others. The Republic of France, which until recently possessed a highly centralized, unitary character, was the prime example of a nation-state where a political nation grew up in very close coincidence with the state territory. But the UK is neither the one nor the other. It is essentially a dynastic conglomerate, which could never equalize the functions of its four constituent parts and which, as a result, could never fully harmonize the identities of the national communities within its borders. The UK, for example, has no one established Church. (It has two of them.) It has no unified legal system, no centralized educational system, no common cultural policy, no common history – none of the institutional foundations, in other words, on which nation-states are built.

Many misunderstandings surround these elementary truths. One derives from the fact that England, prior to its incorporation into the UK, *was* a nation-state or well on the way to being so. Founded in the tenth century (see above), it enjoyed six centuries of consolidation before it annexed Wales, and swallowed the first of several meals that could not be completely digested. Even so, the Tudor Kingdom of England and Wales, under one powerful monarchy, one authoritarian Anglican Church, and one representative Parliament, did create a strong national community. The trouble begins when historians present the rest of modern history as a simple continuation of the Tudor-built nation-state from Elizabeth I to Elizabeth II. What really happened, of course, is that England tied itself to another nation-state, Scotland, and then to Ireland. At each of these stages, the nation-building process had to start anew in complicated circumstances which permitted, at the most, only partial success.

A second misunderstanding derives from terminology. Like all ruling elites who wanted their citizens to form a coherent national community and to identify themselves with the interests of the state, the British establishment deliberately confused the concepts of citizenship and nationality. Indeed, in British usage, citizenship actually came to be called 'nationality', whilst citizens – or rather subjects – were called 'nationals'. This linguistic manoeuvre did much to create the false impression that everyone who carried a British passport was automatically identified with the same national group.

(2) *The British nation, therefore, is not coterminous with 'all the citizens of the United Kingdom'; and it is a body with a fluid membership*

Unlike citizenship, which is granted by the state, nationhood depends on individual people's readiness to be identified with a national community. From the individual's standpoint, one's citizenship is an external, legal matter: one's nationality is the result of an internalized psychological process. In the British case, the historic task of the United Kingdom was to foster a common sense of national belonging among people who had previously identified themselves exclusively with England, Wales, Scotland, or Ireland. The task was undertaken by all the long list of instruments outlined in Chapter Nine – among them, the monarchy, to which all were required to own allegiance, the anti-Catholic ideology of the Protestant Ascendancy, which set Britain apart from its neighbours, and the Empire, in whose benefits all could participate. The important thing to remember, however, is that the invisible bonds which bind a national community together are not static. They fluctuate. They strengthen and weaken in different periods of time and among different constituent groups.

In the eighteenth century, for example, the British nation attracted one group of Scots, the 'North Britons', whilst failing to win over many Highlanders or Jacobites. It also failed to enlist a substantial body of obdurate English, like John Wilkes, who thought the union with Scotland an unmitigated disaster. In the nineteenth century, thanks to rising prosperity and the success of Empire, the British national community probably recruited the majority of UK citizens, although it always faced an uphill struggle in Ireland. If 'Home Rule' had been effectively introduced in the decades when many Irish Catholics were sitting on the psychological fence, it could conceivably have taken them in as well. But it didn't. In the twentieth century, having offloaded the southern Irish, who by then were thoroughly disaffected, it rose to new heights of fervency during the common struggle of the Second World War. This uplifting sense of national solidarity, at the peak of British patriotism in 1939–45, was an experience to which the older generation now looks back with such admiration and nostalgia.

At this point, a touch of political theory may come in handy. Scholars are generally agreed that there are two main types of national community. One of them, generated 'from above' by governmental policy, relies either on brute force or on sentiments usually labelled as 'civic nationalism'. The other, generated from below by grass-roots action, is directed against government policy and relies on 'ethnic' or 'popular' nationalism. The former is an enterprise of the state. The latter is an enterprise of the common people, or of particular groups within the population. According to their varying numbers or aspirations, popular nationalists may limit themselves to cultural goals. In other circumstances, they may press for political objectives ranging from provincial autonomy and regional self-government to unconditional independence. In any composite state or dynastic empire, the two types of national community exist side by side and compete with each other. As the state establishment and its supporters endeavour to persuade their fellow citizens to join their state-backed national community, the popular nationalists are working against them in their efforts to create their own sort of breakaway nation.

The old Tsarist Empire, for instance, contained a huge variety of peoples, each with its own history, its own language, and its own religious affiliations. Over the centuries, the Tsars and their ministers set out quite consciously firstly to enforce the loyalty of this kaleidoscope of subjects, and then, through education, to Russify them and to turn them all into a homogeneous Russian nation. The leaders of the Soviet Union, who stepped into the shoes of the Tsars, followed similar policies, except in their case they aimed to create an entirely new species called 'Soviet Man'. At the selfsame time, all the peoples who had been taken into the Tsarist Empire or the Soviet Union strove for generations to resist government policy, to preserve their own culture, to raise their own separate national consciousness, and in the later stages to break free completely. The final result of this competition is now known. The Tsarist Empire and the Soviet Union both enjoyed a period of temporary success. But they both fell apart under the strain. In their place, a swath of triumphant nation-states has been established across the map of Europe. One of them, Finland, which broke away in 1917–18, is already a member of the European Union. The others find themselves in varying stages of rehabilitation or invalidity. The Russian nation, deprived of its empire, has been left in a state of total bewilderment, not knowing what to believe about its past or its present or its future.

People in the United Kingdom would be well advised to take stock of the Russian/Soviet example – but for one purpose only. In most important respects, the UK of today is as different from the late USSR as chalk from cheese. It is small; it is democratic; and as Orwell stated, by international standards it is gentle. In terms of complexity, political culture, social relations, and historical traditions, it is light-years apart from Russia. Yet in one respect, and one respect only, the parallel appears relevant. Many indications suggest that in composite states of imperial origin, the competition between the state-backed imperial nation and the overlapping popular nations may be an essential feature of political life. In those states where a strong imperial nation has much to offer, the popular nations will sink back into the status of regional curiosities. In those states where the imperial nation loses the citizens' trust, the popular nations will revive, turn militant, and restore their sovereign status. In those states, where neither the imperial nation nor the popular sub-nations can establish a clear advantage, they can coexist in equilibrium almost indefinitely.

On these topics, intelligent historians are always looking for comparisons. Pocock, for example, was drawn to the example of Austria and Germany, and hence to his discussion of the *kleinenglisch* and *grossbritannisch* models – 'Little England' versus 'Great Britain'. One could equally try out the example of Austria-Hungary, where the multinational *Kaisertreu* establishment in Vienna would take the part of the British, the Magyars would take the part of the Scots, and the Czechs, Slovaks, and Croats would become the Irish, the Scottish Gaels, and the Welsh. Unfortunately, all such games can never quite fit.

In the last resort, the most vital requirement for nations is that their constituent supporters believe in them. National communities are held together by belief. If the belief evaporates, the community disintegrates. Most academics would now agree that 'the British nation' was an invention, and an invention 'not much older than the United States'.[206] It has been buttressed by all sorts of myths and fictions, not least about its history. But so long as the system of invented belief was intact it could inspire men and women to work and to die for it. When the flag waved, hearts fluttered.

In this light, the most ominous sign for the health of the United Kingdom would lie in the fading of belief in the British nation. Its advocates do exist, and in all walks of life. But they grow ever older and fewer. If the BBC's guide is correct, Broadcasting House still believes in the four 'popular nations' of the Isles, but not in a British nation (see page 1035, above). Senior academics agreed. 'Though there *was* a British state,' wrote one of them, as recently as 1997, 'there was never a British nation.' Even the state was put into the past tense.[207]

(3) *Multiple identities are a natural feature of the human condition*

Everyone feels a sense of belonging to a complex network of communities; and there is no necessary tension or conflict between them. Everyone belongs to a family, and beyond the immediate family to wider kinship groups. Every single person on earth has a maternal kin and paternal kin. Most people have a spouse or a partner, with another set of relatives or in-laws to cope with. Most identify with their place of birth or the town of their youth or the county of their residence. They also identify to a greater or a lesser degree with their fellow workers in the institutions which they serve, with their fellow worshippers in the churches which they attend, with their fellow players and supporters in the sports which they follow. Reconciling these multiple attachments and ordering them psychologically into some sort of bearable hierarchy is an exercise which everyone performs. Failure to do so results in the well-known pathology of *alienation*.

For some reason, this universal human mechanism was not applied until recently to the issue of national identity. In the age of nationalism, it was somehow thought unnatural for someone to be French and English at one and the same time. One was either one or the other. Yet there is no insuperable reason why an individual born to an English father and a French mother should not feel equally attached to England and to France. As society becomes more and more mobile, the incidence of mixed nationality grows ever more commonplace. Indeed, if only the truth be known, every human being is a mongrel. What is also true, however, is that all individuals, when ordering their personal hierarchy of identities, will choose to emphasize or to overlook different elements in their overall make-up and will produce different solutions to suit different situations. Siblings born of the same parents are perfectly capable of choosing opposite identities according to their individual inclinations. George III told a British audience that he was a true 'Briton'. In Hanover, he could have said with absolute truth and conviction that he was a German through and through.

If one looks at the British nation, from the point of view of its constituent individuals, therefore, one finds a very complex picture. After three hundred years of coexistence, the intermingling of the English, Irish, Welsh, and Scots is pretty far advanced. And after fifty years of Commonwealth immigration, the admixture of Caribbean and Asian elements is spreading. The permutations are almost infinite. The crucial matter is how those individuals see themselves.

On this score, three points must be made. Firstly, in accordance with the law of multiple identity, most people will find no difficulty in thinking of themselves as 'British and Scots' or 'British and Pakistani' or 'part English and part Welsh', or 'Liverpool Irish' or whatever. Secondly, those same people will describe themselves differently in different contexts. When faced with a gang of Manchester United supporters, a group of Arsenal fans will forget their internal differences as Cockney, black, or Jewish and will think of themselves as Londoners. When faced with a crowd of Germans on the beach at Marbella, those same lads could all become British or English at a stroke. Thirdly – and most interestingly for the historian – people can change their dominant identity in the course of their lives. One sees this quite clearly in Scotland. Twenty or thirty years ago, when Scottish nationalism was still weak, most Glaswegians or Aberdonians would say that they were 'British'. (They would *never* say they were English.) Nowadays, a considerable proportion would say that they were primarily Scots – 'British citizens, yes, but Scots at heart.' Every community to which individuals belong has its own gravitational pull. As the pulls wax and wane, the identity of individuals gravitates with them.

This particular problem of historical change in identity is particularly relevant in Southern Ireland. Anyone born in Dublin before 1948 was automatically a British subject. Many of the men fought in the British army and swore an oath of loyalty to the British crown. Then, suddenly, when Éire left the British Commonwealth, those same Dubliners could not remain 'British and Irish', even if they wanted to.

Or think for a moment about Eamonn de Valera, long-term Prime Minister of the Irish Republic. Born in New York in 1882 of a Spanish father and an Irish mother, he was an American citizen. In other circumstances, he might easily have stressed the American part of his identity. If he had followed his father to Cuba, he had all the credentials to be a Spaniard or a Cuban. But he chose to follow his mother's connections, and came to Dublin at a time when Ireland was still British. Yet he had no intention of accepting the official view of his nationality. On the contrary, he put himself at the head of the popular Irish national movement against British rule, led Ireland to independence, and made himself unambiguously Irish. The story may sound complicated. But it reflects a complicated reality.

In the last quarter of the twentieth century, yet another factor was thrown into the mix. As from 1973, every resident of the United Kingdom and the Republic of Ireland was equally living in the EEC, and from 1995 in the EU. In the 1990s, European Union passports, which also named the holder's British or Irish citizenship, were phased in. So yet another layer was added to the existing collection of multiple identities. Every inhabitant of the Isles was officially a 'European'. But it should have caused no problem. No Englishman need feel less English for also being British; and no Britisher need feel any less British for also being a European.

(4) *All the foundations of historic 'Britishness' were in an advanced state of decay*

The pillars of the state as formerly constituted were crumbling. Some of them had already crumbled. Seapower, Empire, the Protestant Ascendancy, and 'the Imperial Universe' had all passed on. The 'Mother of Parliaments', the monarchy, the sporting tradition and the Imperial ethos were all falling from grace. The British economy and British law were almost inextricably entangled in Europe-wide institutions. The pound sterling was one stop from extinction. In the course of the twentieth century, the United Kingdom had lost one quarter of its territory. In one of the UK's remaining provinces civil war had raged for nearly thirty years. A settlement to the conflict in Northern Ireland was agreed in 1998; but by the middle of 1999 it had not been put into effect. After two attempts at devolution, the British government belatedly granted differing measures of self-government to Scotland and Wales. In 1999, the Queen duly opened the Scottish Parliament and the Welsh Assembly. Only two years previously, a Conservative Prime Minister was saying that any such measures would spell the end of the Union. Britain's military power was largely committed to the NATO alliance. British independence as understood at any time prior to the Second World War had ceased to exist. Britain's performance in a wide range of economic, educational, and social fields lagged behind its competitors. Such was the scenario which inspired books with titles like *The Death of Britain?* or *The Abolition of Britain*.

The sudden death of states was a very familiar theme in the 1990s. For forty-five years after the last war, British people were told, and quite correctly, that they were threatened by an aggressive superpower armed with an arsenal of nuclear weapons of unimaginably lethal potency. Whilst the British Empire declined and disappeared, the Soviet Union was thought to be terribly strong. It held half of Europe in thrall, and was telling all its captive peoples that the 'end of capitalism' was nigh. It even attracted the admiration of a none too tiny coterie of Western intellectuals. Its last leader was widely acclaimed as a great reformer and a fine statesman. And then it died on its feet. It expired like a dinosaur that had suffered a heart attack. Not a shot was fired. Not a single leading Sovietologist predicted its fate. For a time, the collapse of the Soviet Bloc seemed to confirm the unquestioned validity of Western democracy. It inspired an American political scientist to proclaim 'the End of History'. But to anyone interested in the life and death of states it could only have sent one message. Surface appearances meant nothing. Diseased organisms could conceal their terminal maladies until the very last moment. Statesmen should look to the internal health of their charges.

Yugoslavia was another composite state that fell apart, and just at the time when the 'British' debate was starting. Serbia was the 'England' of Yugoslavia, and in the hands of an ex-Communist nationalist wreaked havoc in Croatia, Bosnia, and Kosovo. Yet the political climate in Yugoslavia could not have been more distant from that in Britain. Ethnic hatreds were murderous. Wholesale slaughter and 'cleansing' were the order of the day. No one thought that the Balkans could throw much light on Britain's problems.

Historians struggled for precedents. Most former states in the twentieth century had been destroyed by war. Prior to 1989, there were few examples of natural demise. Even the Byzantine Empire, which had slowly shrunk over several centuries to the bounds of its capital city, had to be finished off by a fierce Ottoman assault. Even the French Revolution did not involve the dismemberment of France. On the contrary, though it swept away the monarchy and the *ancien régime* in a sea of terror, it propelled a reinvigorated France into a phase of unparalleled vigour and aggrandizement. In any case, people who were closest to the death throes of a state or a regime were invariably unable to read the symptoms. In 1789, the prospects for the French patient looked much better than in 1788. Remedial action was being taken. Yet, as Gorbachev learned, remedies could kill. One is reminded of the apocryphal conversation between a German and an Austrian general on the crumbling front in October 1918. The German general says: 'The situation is serious, but not hopeless.' The Austrian replies: 'No, the situation is hopeless, but not serious.'

There, surely, was the most crucial point of all. Many of Britain's traditional institutions appeared to be on their last legs. Many aspects of life in the United Kingdom were being transformed out of all recognition. But did it really matter? No one was facing pestilence, war, or starvation. Interest rates were low. Incomes, by historic standards, were high. Music was still being played. The public were still buying history books. For those who believed, God was still in His heaven.

(5) *Discussions about alternative visions of the future suddenly came into vogue*

As the debate about 'Britishness' persisted, and the gloom deepened, it was noticeable that leading commentators began to make explicit choices, about future action. One of these choices concerned the future role of England within the changed UK. The other addressed the wider national scene. With whom did Britain's destiny lie?

Once Scotland and Wales were granted their assemblies, only the dimmest of wits could continue to pretend that 'Britain' and 'England' were one and the same thing. The great English myth was finally shattered. One English journalist shouted, 'Let's stand up for Englishness.'[208] Another appealed, 'England, don't arise!'[209] At the more practical level, voices were raised to call for the creation of a purely English Parliament to match the new legislatures in Edinburgh and Cardiff and the prospective Assembly in Belfast.[210] In that case, the United Kingdom would begin to assume the guise of a federation. Other calls were made for parliaments to be set up in each of the English regions. A step in that direction was taken when 'New Labour' announced the restoration of local self-government in London with mayoral elections to be held in May 2000. As in 1979, constitutionalists were exercised once again by the so-called Midlothian Question, i.e., the anomaly that Scottish MPs could vote on English matters at Westminster, whilst English MPs could not vote on Scottish matters at Edinburgh. Conservatives were exercised by the fact that in 1997 they had lost all their parliamentary seats outside England. For the first time in their history, they had been reduced to their English base. They would be sorely tempted to play to the gallery of English nationalism, which everyone now saw as a distinct phenomenon. Certain essential matters were being clarified. If the Irish, the Welsh, and the Scots could have their nationalisms, the English must have theirs as well.

On the international front, a gulf opened up between those who felt that Britain's future lay with the Atlantic Alliance and the USA, and those who saw it with the European Union. The Atlanticists were the more aggressive. They were not satisfied just to praise Britain's links with the USA and Canada. They were actively hostile to the European Union and all who supported it. Some of them, like Conrad Black, the media tycoon, had argued for some time that the UK should withdraw from the EU and join NAFTA.[211] Others argued that Britain's culture was more compatible with that of Canada and America than with the chaotic diversity of the Continent.[212] The Baroness, who led the fray, poured contempt on those, like the mandarins of the Foreign Office, who supposedly wanted 'to dissolve our national independence in the European Union'. She then stated her convictions in the most straightforward language:

> We have much more in common with the United States than with Europe as has been shown time and again in war and in peace.
>
> The transatlantic relationship with the United States must remain at the heart of our foreign policy.
> – Margaret Thatcher, House of Lords[213]

The pro-Europeans were led by a cross-party lobby group, 'Britain in Europe'. Compared to their opponents, they were strangely subdued, partly because they wished to avoid the charge of anti-Americanism, partly because their ardour had been doused by the advent of the euro. An articulate group of opinion-makers who had backed the EU throughout the 1990s felt that the euro was a step

too far, that it was inhibiting the more urgent tasks of EU reform
and expansion to the East. Others, notably among the Liberal
Democrats, bravely called for the acceptance both of the euro
in particular and of European integration in general. Nonetheless,
the campaign had to proceed, if only to counter the accusations
of the Atlanticists. It had several strands. The CBI based its support
on the simple fact that nearly 60 per cent of Britain's trade was with
the EU. Former Conservative heavyweights defied their party by
holding that early entry into Euroland was not impossible. A prominent group of diplomats was convinced that more influence in
international relations could be wielded by a joint European chorus
than by Britain's lone voice. A group of Christians, mainly Catholics,
took up the Pope's appeal for a Europe united by its ancient
Christian heritage. To begin with, the Prime Minister held back. He
wanted to keep his options open. But in the summer of 1999 he was
forced to lend his weight to the campaign, but still with no clear
indications of his immediate plans. The battle lines were drawn. But
as yet no cannonballs had been fired. The senior journalist who had
published a lengthy history of Britain's sorry post-war relations with
the European movement concluded with the sentence: 'There now
was a Prime Minister . . . untroubled by the demons of the past,
[and] prepared to align the island with its natural hinterland'.[214]
(This seemed to indicate that Northern Ireland did not belong to the
deal.)

It was twenty-two years since the radical Scots writer Tom
Nairn had first floated the shocking idea of 'The Break-up of Britain'. But no one had dared to imagine how the breakup would look
or when and in what circumstances it might happen. Could there
be a replay in Edinburgh of that moving ceremony in Hong Kong?
When elections for the Scottish Parliament took place, however,
the pro-Union Labour Party fought off the challenge of the SNP;
and it was Donald Dewar of 'New Labour' who emerged as Scotland's First Minister and welcomed the Queen to the opening of
the Edinburgh Parliament. In Wales, too, 'New Labour' held off
Plaid Cymru and took charge of the Welsh executive. In Northern

Ireland, there was stalemate, not least because the Unionists claimed that the ceasefire was being violated. The Good Friday Agreement had not been implemented. But for the time being, the rot had been stemmed. So a planned and orderly retreat was not on the immediate cards. And the much advertised 'English Backlash' had not yet materialized.

No one seemed prepared to hazard a guess about what was going to happen. Most British people, preoccupied with their daily lives, never gave it a thought. There were few outwards signs of present danger. All the world's trouble spots seemed to be abroad. Many probably thought that nothing much would change, that Britain could continue its balancing between 'Europe' and the USA indefinitely. Most assumed that the UK would survive in its current form. That was possible, though its defenders were doing little to cure the population of their age-old complacency. A tiny minority thought that they were standing on the edge of an explosion. They saw that the foundations of 'Britishness' had long been losing their substance; and they refused to close their eyes to the basic facts. They suspected they were entering the lull before the storm. Scots nationalists were talking openly of an independent Scotland within a decade. Some Irish nationalists felt that a United Ireland was finally within their grasp.

Yet explosions, typhoons, and volcanic eruptions were hardly the right metaphors. Britain was not Yugoslavia, or a Soviet Union. There was no head of political steam, except in Norther Ireland, no great well of suppressed anger. Inertia, not fanaticism, was the enemy. The better metaphors were probably those of a quietly gathering avalanche that could strike out of the blue in the best of weather, or possibly a minor landslip. With no way of measuring the extent of the hidden damage, no one could exactly predict what might be swept away. And no one could imagine what trifling incident could set it off.

≈

At the end of a long narration, historians can feel the urge to cast their narrator's mask aside and to speak personally and plainly. I don't see what's wrong with that.

I happen to belong to a minority who hold that the breakup of the United Kingdom may be imminent. I could be wrong. But the sense of foreboding has grown steadily over the last decades as I sat at my desk thinking and writing about long-term history. In this connection, there is nothing to match the experience of writing a survey of European history from beginning to end. One receives the overwhelming impression that all states and empires are ephemeral; that all of them pass away; and that something is always found to take their place. The death of a state may have overtones of sadness; but it is not necessarily an unmitigated tragedy.

Five or six years ago, when drawing up a table of European states and their respective ages, I noticed that the United Kingdom was one of the oldest.[215] I even expressed a doubt whether the UK would live to see its three hundredth birthday in 2007.[216] I have not changed my mind, though I now think that the belated introduction of devolution may prolong the UK's life for an extra season or two. At bottom, I belong to the group of historical colleagues who hold that the United Kingdom was established to serve the interests of Empire, and that the loss of Empire has destroyed its *raison d'être*. I myself remember the old imperial world-view of history from my student days. It has evaporated in the space of a lifetime.

It is not inconceivable, of course, that the British Establishment may yet wake up to its predicament. It may even set in motion a plan to create the structures of a British nation-state and to recover pro-British sentiment. If so, it would be running against the contemporary tide. In my estimation, it would deliver too little, and too late.

The resurgence of pride and consciousness among the 'popular nations' of the Isles causes me little unease. Patriotism is a healthy quality; and patriotism is one of the sentiments which has been seeping away from the state-backed 'British nation'. England is a great country with enormous resources of fine people, high culture,

economic wealth, and worldwide support. It would probably do better
on its own than at the head of unwilling satellites. If the Republic of
Ireland can flourish independently, then so too can Scotland. Wales
is set to gain a greater degree of unity than at any point in modern
times (see above). Northern Ireland was an artificial creature from
the start. Its leaders must surely see that the benefits of being tied to
a fading Britain are sinking fast. It pays a heavy fine every day for
keeping its distance from a prospering Republic. In the long run, its
destiny can only lie in a united Ireland, perhaps as an autonomous
province. But to reach that point, the men of violence on all sides
have to throw their guns aside; the courage of the Unionists has to be
matched by the magnanimity of the Nationalists; and someone has to
remind them all that when Protestant England practised a sectarian
monopoly, the glory of Irish patriots, from Wolfe Tone to Patrick
Pearse, lay in their preaching of religious tolerance.

Perhaps the main source of optimism lies in the existence of the
European Union. Unfortunately, the most positive aspect of the EU
is rarely noticed. It is obscured by the misplaced obsession with
purely economic considerations. But it is this: it gives a place in the
sun to Europe's smaller and middle-sized nations. Economics were
never at the top of the agenda of the fathers of the European
movement. It was always a means to a higher end. It was the means
of forging a prosperous community in which all member states, both
large and small, could live in peace. For this reason, the European
ideal is despised by those who wish to hang on to the vestiges of a
superior status and of national domination. In the old European
jungle of sovereign states, an independent Scotland, or an independent Wales, or even an independent England would have been
vulnerable creatures living precariously among larger predators. But
the jungle has been banished. Under the umbrella of the European
Union, a 'Scotland-in-Europe', a 'Wales-in-Europe' and an 'England-
in-Europe' have every chance of doing as well as an 'Ireland-in-
Europe'. No one seems to notice that the richest and most satisfied
country in Europe is Luxembourg.

It is a great pity that the British people, having won the Second

World War (as they think), have largely forgotten what caused it. In the 1930s, Europe was a continent of the independent sovereign states which today's Eurosceptics so strangely admire. And it was a bear garden. When Mussolini marched into Abyssinia in 1934, nobody tried to stop him. When Hitler's Wehrmacht marched into Austria in 1938, no one stopped him. When Hitler threatened to march into Czechoslovakia in 1938, the great and the good tried to stop him by conceding his outrageous demands. So he marched in all the same. In 1939, when Hitler and Stalin marched their armies into Poland, the United Kingdom and France decided to cry 'enough' and declared war on one of the aggressors. The result was a titanic conflict that did more to damage the standing of Britain and France than anything else in their modern history.

Sixty years later, Italy, Austria, Germany, France, and Britain all belong to the same supra-national organization, together with ten other members. The Czech Republic, Poland, Hungary, and Slovenia are standing on the threshold, and there is a long line of applicants behind them. The European Union has many grave faults. The list of necessary reforms is as long as the Channel Tunnel. The decision to launch the euro was probably mistimed. But if one has to state the obvious, the new game of fighting with words in the council rooms of Brussels over the best way to reform and to strengthen the Union is infinitely preferable to the old game of fighting with tanks over the remaking of Europe's frontiers.

In this context, the gloom which surrounds 'the decline of Britain' is surely misplaced. Even if Britain were to break up, all that is really valuable would remain. There could be a sovereign Scotland. There could be an English Republic. It could be better than the last one. There might even be a consolidated Wales, and an Ireland at peace with itself. But one would still be able to listen to Elgar's cello concerto. One could happily sing 'Land of Hope and Glory' whilst dreaming of the land of one's preference. One could still watch Bolton Wanderers. The Royal Shakespeare Company would stay in business. And one would follow the performance of *Much Ado About Nothing* with new insight.

I am not unduly impressed by the armchair doom-mongers, who live comfortably in rather agreeable surroundings. This may well be due to my own experiences. When I was a student in Oxford, my tutor, A. J. P. Taylor, who was a leading light in the Campaign for Nuclear Disarmament (CND), used to scare us with stories of impending Armageddon. Taylor was convinced that the superpowers were about to blow the world to pieces. But they did not. A little later I found myself living, almost by accident, in Central Europe, in a country whose people had suffered more than most British and Americans could begin to imagine. And the country's ordeal did not end with the war. My father-in-law had spent most of the time between 1939 and 1945 in the Nazi concentration camps of Dachau and Mauthausen, simply because of what he was. He was then tortured and flung into a Soviet prison, simply because he had survived Dachau and Mauthausen. One of my senior colleagues in the History Faculty where I studied was a hero of the wartime Resistance. He had had spent many years under sentence of death in a Communist jail, simply because Communists could not stand the idea of non-Communist heroes. A medievalist whom I knew had lost an arm fighting the Nazis. Another older friend had lost his legs, and then became a pioneer and a champion of legless ski-ing. A fifth of the population had been killed in the war. Every family had lost relatives and friends and neighbours in the acts of genocide and ethnic clearances which the Nazi and Soviet invaders had perpetrated. All these people had loved the independent country, which they had lost through no fault of their own. Having no free voice of their own, they had to listen in silence as others reviled it. Yet they had to find ways of living their lives without it. At the time, there was no hope of restoring it. So they found the means of coping, and sometimes of coping cheerfully. Shortly before he died, my ex-Resistance colleague gave his verdict on the Communist regime. 'We will outlive them,' he said.

In my honest view, therefore, the most pertinent contributions to the present debate about Britain were the ones which betrayed the least anxiety. We live in a fortunate, and relatively gentle part of the Continent. I particularly welcomed the comments of my fellow historian, Felipe Fernández-Armesto, a colleague who is both insider and outsider rolled into one:

> The English have a remarkably uniform set of assumptions about themselves – almost all of which are false. They think they love animals, but they impose quarantine. They proclaim fair play but inhabit perfidious Albion. They say they are reserved when they are repressed; they claim they are uncomplaining when they are uncommunicative. Before the world they affect sang-froid but at home they honour *Men Behaving Badly*. They call indiscipline individualism and bloody-mindedness common sense. They espouse a mythic past and mistake it for a progressive story of peaceful change and democratic climacteric. They name themselves the Bulldog Breed but their bark is worse than their bite. They inhabit clouded hills and think they are in Jerusalem. Good for them. I love their magnificent irrationality. There has never been nationhood without falsehood. But now, . . . the English have an opportunity to discard myths and face a reality which could be so much better. Otherwise, the vaunted 're-awakening of England' will be only a prolongation of dreams – or a stirring of nightmares.

And finally, there were those wonderful notes of an American, who sometimes forgot his politest vocabulary, but who spoke, as one should, from the heart. He had been living in Yorkshire, somewhere in the vicinity of *Wuthering Heights*:

> It looked so peaceful and wonderful that I could almost have cried, and yet it was only a tiny part of this small, enchanted island. Suddenly, in the space of a moment, I realized . . . that I loved . . . all of it. Every last bit of it, good and bad – Marmite, village fêtes, country lanes, people saying 'mustn't grumble' and 'I'm terribly sorry but', people apologizing to *me* when I conk them with a careless elbow, milk in bottles, beans on toast, haymaking in June, stinging nettles, seaside piers, Ordnance Survey maps, crumpets, hot-water bottles as a necessity, drizzly Sundays – every bit of it.

What a wondrous place this was – crazy as fuck, of course, but adorable to the tiniest degree. What other country, after all, could possibly have come up with place names like Tooting Bec and Farleigh Wallop, or a game like cricket that goes on for three days and never seems to start? Who else would think it not the least odd to make their judges wear little mops on their heads, compel the Lord Chancellor to sit on something called the Woolsack, or take pride in a naval hero whose dying wish was to be kissed by a fellow called Hardy? ('Please, Hardy, full on the lips, with just a bit of tongue.') What other nation in the world could have given us William Shakespeare, pork pies, Christopher Wren, Windsor Great Park, the Open University, *Gardeners' Question Time*, and the chocolate digestive biscuit? None, of course.

How easily we lose sight of all this. What an enigma Britain will seem to historians when they look back on the second half of the twentieth century. Here is a country that fought and won a noble war, dismantled a mighty empire in a generally benign and enlightened way, created a far-seeing welfare state – in short, did nearly everything right – and then spent the rest of the century looking on itself as a chronic failure. The fact is that this is still the best place in the world for most things – to post a letter, go for a walk, watch television, buy a book, venture out for a drink, go to a museum, use the bank, get lost, seek help, or stand on a hillside and take in a view.

All of this came to me in the space of a lingering moment. I've said it before and I'll say it again. I like it here. I like it more than I can tell you.[217]

How generous of an American to say that we won the war.

Bryson visited London like most other places in Britain. 'I can never understand', he wrote, 'why Londoners fail to see that they live in the most wonderful city in the world.'[218] St Paul's was still standing. A third London Bridge spanned the River Thames. And, despite Lord Macaulay's fears, there were no ruins in sight.

NOTES

Introduction

1. D. Cannadine, G. M. Trevelyan: a life in History (London, 1992), p. xii. **2.** A. J. P. Taylor, *English History 1914–1945* (The Oxford History of England), vol. 15 (Oxford, 1965), Preface, p. v. **3.** Simon Schama, *The Embarrassment of Riches: an interpretation of Dutch Culture in the Golden Age* (London, 1988), and *Citizens: a chronicle of the French Revolution* (New York, 1989); F. Fernández-Armesto, *Millennium* (London, 1996); O. Figes, *A People's Tragedy: the Russian Revolution, 1891–1924* (London, 1997). **4.** James Shapiro, 'Yes, a big seller can have footnotes', *The New York Times Book Review*, 15 February, 1997. **5.** L. Brockliss, D. Eastwood, eds, *A Union of Multiple Identities: the British Isles, c. 1750–c. 1850* (Manchester, 1997). **6.** 'Churchill may fall victim to history shake-up', *The Advertiser* (Adelaide), 30 March 1999, quoting the *Daily Mail*. See P. Hitchens, 'Born Yesterday', in *Abolition of Britain* (London, 1999), pp. 33–55. **7.** R. Strong, *The Story of Britain* (London, 1998); Kenneth O. Morgan, ed., *The Oxford History of Britain* (Oxford, 1999); and Antonia Fraser, *The Lives of the Kings and Queens of England* (London, 1997). **8.** Stong, op. cit., p. 1. **9.** A. L. Rowse, *The Story of Britain* (London, 1979, revised 1993), p. 7. **10.** Ibid., p. 178. **11.** *The Oxford English Dictionary* (Oxford, 1994), p. 561. **12.** Ibid., pp. 562–3. **13.** *The Shorter Oxford English Dictionary*, p. 223. **14.** OED, op. cit., p. 561. **15.** Ibid. **16.** SOED, op. cit., p. 611. **17.** Morgan, op. cit., p. v. **18.** Ibid., p. vi. **19.** John Guy, 'The Tudor Age', ibid., p. 257. **20.** John Morrill, 'The Stuarts', ibid., p. 327. **21.** Ibid., p. x. **22.** Fraser, op. cit., p. 9. **23.** Christopher Lee, *This Sceptred Isle* (London, 1997). **24.** Paul Johnson, *The Offshore Islanders: a History of the English People* (London, 1995). **25.** OLIS – Oxford University libraries' online catalogue, as at May 1999. **26.** *Library of Congress Catalogue* (Washington D.C., 1990), p. 1777. **27.** Ibid. **28.** Ibid. **29.** A. M. Pankratova, *A History of the USSR* (Moscow, 1947–8), 3 vols. **30.** Cannadine, op. cit., p. 213.

One: The Midnight Isles

1. Nigel Hawkes, 'History Teacher Bones Up on an Ancestor', *The Times*, 8 March 1997. On Cheddar Man, see T. C. Darvill, *Prehistoric Britain from the Air* (Cambridge, 1996), pp. 23–5; also L. B. Thornycroft, *The Story of Cheddar* (London, 1949).

2. T. C. Darvill, *Prehistoric Britain* (London, 1987), p. 43 puts the date at 6000 BC. See also: R. J. O. Hamblin, *The Geology of the English Channel* (London, 1992); J. A. Williamson, *The English Channel: a History* (London, 1959); J. A. Steers, *Introduction to Coastline Development* (London, 1971).   **3.** E. G. Bowen, *Britain and the Western Seaways* (London, 1972).   **4.** *Albion.* The name derives from the Celtic root of *alp*, meaning 'peak' or 'height'. It is akin to the better known etymology of Alps and Apennines. When encountered by the Romans, however, it was wrongly thought to derive from the Latin *albus*, 'white', which nicely matched the appearance of the cliffs equally well. The enthusiasm of classical scholars has enshrined the Romans' mistake in popular wisdom.   **5.** See Darvill, op. cit., Chapter III 'Harvest for the Year: early agriculturalists 3500–2500;' also R. Bradley, J. Gardiner, eds, *Neolithic Studies: a Review of some Current Research* (Oxford, 1984), and Julian Thomas, *Rethinking the Neolithic* (Cambridge, 1991).   **6.** M. Richards, H. Corte-Real, et al., 'Paleolithic and Neolithic Lineages in the European Mitochondrial Gene Pool', *American Journal of Human Genetics*, vol. 59 (1996), pp. 185–203. **7.** 'Samphire' in Norman Davies, *Europe: a History* (Oxford, 1996), p. 82, quoting Jane Renfrew, *Food and Cooking in Prehistoric Britain: History and Recipes* (London, 1985).   **8.** R. Hippisley Cox, *The Green Roads of England* (London, 1914).   **9.** See J. C. Richards, *English Heritage Book of Stonehenge* (London, 1991), also G. S. Hawkins, *Stonehenge Decoded* (London, 1966), and D. Souden, *Stonehenge Revealed* (New York, 1997).   **10.** Alexander Thom, *Megalithic Sites in Britain* (Oxford, 1967), 'The sixteen-month calendar', pp. 109–17.   **11.** See A. H. Grundy, *Britain's Prehistoric Achievements* (Lewes, 1964); for an opposite view, A. Burl, *Prehistoric Astronomy and Ritual* (Princes Risborough, 1983).   **12.** The ley-line craze was started by one Alfred Watkins, author of *Early British Trackways* (1922) and *The Old Straight Track* (1925). It has since been adopted by New Age occultists who see the lines as magical sources of power and energy.   **13.** R. Mercer ed., *Beakers in Britain and Europe: Four Studies* (Oxford, 1977), also R. J. Harrison, *The Beaker Folk: Copper Age Archaeology in Western Europe* (London, 1980).   **14.** Wessex Culture.   **15.** Harrison, op. cit., pp. 123–4.   **16.** Ibid., p. 102.   **17.** Plumpton, East Sussex.   **18.** Heathery Burn, Durham.   **19.** Jarlshof, Shetland.   **20.** Llyn Fawr, Glamorgan. J. and C. Hawkes, op. cit., p. 123–4.   **21.** See Barry Cunliffe, *Danebury: anatomy of an Iron Age Hill Fort* (London, 1983).   **22.** B. Cunliffe, D. Miles, eds, *Aspects of the Iron Age in Central Southern Britain* (Oxford, 1984).   **23.** J. and C. Hawkes, *Prehistoric Britain* (Harmondsworth, 1942), p. 138: Chysauster (Cornwall).   **24.** Ibid., pp. 140–44. Glastonbury (Somerset).   **25.** See Neal Ascherson, *Black Sea* (London, 1995), pp. 210–28.   **26.** J. and C. Hawkes, op. cit., p. 30.   **27.** Ann MacSween, *Prehistoric Scotland* (London, 1989).   **28.** Great Orme's Head, Llandudno.   **29.** Mount Sandel, Co. Derry.   **30.** The Great Clare Hoard, from Mooghaun North, Co. Clare. **31.** MacSween, op. cit.   **32.** Fort Navan, Co. Armagh.   **33.** Peter Harbison, *Pre-Christian Ireland: from the First Settlers to the Early Celts* (London, 1988), p. 191. **34.** Cessair's Tale: see P. B. Ellis, *A Dictionary of Irish Mythology* (London, 1987), also his *Dictionary of Celtic Mythology* (London, 1992); M. Dames, 'Original

Landings', *Mythic Ireland* (London, 1992), pp. 145–49. **35.** E. Hull, 'The Hawk of Achill', in C. and J. Matthews, eds, *The Encyclopaedia of Celtic Wisdom* (Shaftesbury, 1994), p. 75. **36.** Robert Graves, *The White Goddess: a Historical Grammar of Poetic Myth* (1948), G. Lindop, ed. (Manchester, 1997), p. 9. Graves pointedly wrote that 'English poetic education should really begin not with *The Canterbury Tales* . . . but with *The Song of Amergin*', ibid. **37.** Jacquetta Hawkes, *A Guide to the Prehistoric and Roman monuments in England and Wales* (London, 1951), pp. 288–9. **38.** Ibid., *passim*. **39.** *The Times*, 1 March 1997, regarding Aubrey Burl, author of *A Guide to the Stone Circles of Britain, Ireland and Brittany* (New Haven, 1995), and his more recent hypothesis in the current issue of the *Wiltshire Archaeological Journal*. **40.** *Independent*, 1 March 1997. **41.** *Archaeology*, vol. 50, no. 4 July/August 1997. **42.** Patrick Ashmore, *Calanais: the Standing Stones* (Urras nan Tursachan, 1995). Foreword by Magnus Magnusson. **43.** *British Archaeology*, no. 17, Sept 1996.

Two: The Painted Isles

1. John Davies, *Hanes Cymru* (London, 1990), p. 22. **2.** John Davies, *A History of Wales* (London, 1993), p. 22. **3.** Hazel Mary Martell, *Na Ceiltigh* (Baile Átha Cliad, 1995), p. 4. **4.** Hazel Mary Martell, *The Celts* (London, 1995), p. 4. **5.** Ibid., pp. 42–3. **6.** Ibid., pp. 44–5. **7.** The spelling of Gaelic names varies widely according to dialect and period. See E. Dwelly, *The Illustrated Gaelic–English Dictionary* (Edinburgh, 1993); D. S. Thompson, ed., *The Companion to Gaelic Scotland* (Oxford, 1983). **8.** D. Norton-Taylor et al., *The Celts* (New York, 1974); G. Herm, *The Celts: the People who Came out of the Darkness* (London, 1976). See also P. B. Ellis, *The Celtic Empire: the First Millennium of Celtic History* (London, 1990). **9.** T. G. E. Powell, *The Celts* (London, 1980). **10.** 'Celtic Tomb Found in Poland', *The Times*, 29 August 1997, describes the burial of a man 6 feet 3 inches tall and a sword of 3 feet 3 inches in length. See Zenon Wozniak, *Osadnictivo celtyckie w Polsce* (Wrocław, 1970); J. Rosen-Przeworska, *Spadek po Celtach* (Kraków, 1979). **11.** This is the thesis of the most recent overview by Barry Cunliffe, *The Ancient Celts* (Oxford, 1997). See also Frank Delaney, *The Celts* (London, 1986); Miranda J. Green, ed., *The Celtic World* (London, 1995). **12.** *Encyclopædia Britannica* CD (1998), 'Celtic Languages'. **13.** 'Dlaczego wyspy Brytyjskie a nie Krutyjskie?' ('Why "British Isles" and not "Cruttish Isles"?'), W. Liponski, *Narodziny Cywilizacji Wysp Brytyjskich* (Poznań, 1995), pp. 91–5. **14.** *Encyclopædia Britannica*, XIth Edition, vol. XIV, p. 758, 'Ireland – Early History'. **15.** Jacquetta and Christopher Hawkes, *Prehistoric Britain* (London, 1947), pp. 129–31. **16.** F. J. Byrne, *Irish Kings and High-kings* (London, 1973); T. F. O'Rahilly, *Early Irish History and Mythology* (Dublin, 1946). See also P. B. Ellis, *A Dictionary of Celtic Mythology* (London, 1992). **17.** Hugh Kearney, *The British Isles: a History of Four Nations* (Cambridge, 1989), p. 20. **18.** Now Stanwick Hill, Yorkshire. **19.** Now Danebury, Hampshire.

20. H. Ramm, *The Parisi* (London, 1978).   **21.** Barry Cunliffe, *Hengistbury Head* (London, 1978), p. 9.   **22.** Ibid.   **23.** *Dictionary of National Biography* (*DNB*), vol. XIX, pp. 127–9.   **24.** Generally thought to be near the modern Wheathampstead. **25.** *DNB*, vol. III, pp. 1179–80.   **26.** W. G. Boswell-Stone, *Shakspere's Holinshed: the Chronicle and the Historical Plays Compared* (London, 1896), p. 7.   **27.** Cloten: *Cymbeline*, III, i.   **28.** Boswell-Stone, op. cit., p. 14.   **29.** D. F. Allen, *An Introduction to Celtic Coins* (London, 1978). See also J. P. C. Kent, 'The Origins of Coinage in Britain', in B. Cunliffe, ed., *Coinage and society in Britain and Gaul*, Council for British Archaeology, Research Report No. 38, pp. 40–42.   **30.** D. F. Allen, *Sylloge of Coins of the British Isles: the Coins of the Coritani* (London, 1963), p. 38.   **31.** On Celtic religion, see Miranda Green, 'The Gods and the Supernatural', in *The Celtic World*, op. cit., no. 26; ibid., 'Celtic goddesses, warriors, virgins and mothers'; and G. A. Wait, *Ritual and Religion in Iron Age Britain* (Oxford, 1985).   **32.** At Lydney, Gloucestershire.   **33.** On Celtic Art, see I. Finlay, *Celtic Art: An introduction* (London, 1973); M. R. Megaw, *Celtic Art: from its Beginnings to the Book of Kells* (New York, 1991); and M. Jope, 'The Social Implications of Celtic Art, 600 BC – AD 600', in Green, op. cit., no. 22.   **34.** See P. B. Ellis, *Celt and Roman: the Celts in Italy* (London, 1998).   **35.** See N. Pennick, *Runestaves and Oghams* (Cambridge, 1997).   **36.** On Old Irish Literature, see P. MacCana, 'Mythology and the Oral Tradition' in Green, op. cit., no. 39; also R. Thurneysen, *An Old Irish Reader* (Dublin, 1949); and P. Mallony in B. Scott etc., *Studies in Early Ireland* (Belfast, 1981).   **37.** From 'The Plot to Steal the Bull', in I. Zaczek, *Chronicles of the Celts* (London, 1996), pp. 32–3.   **38.** Ibid., pp. 37–8.   **39.** Lipoński, op. cit., p. 68. **40.** The first volume of the *Oxford History of England*, R. G. Collingwood and J. N. L. Myres, *Roman Britain and the English Settlements* (Oxford, 1936), was replaced by two separate volumes – P. Salway, *Roman Britain* (Oxford, 1981), and J. N. L. Myres, *The English Settlements* (Oxford, 1986). But no volume on the pre-Roman period was ever announced.   **41.** E. H. Carter, R. A. F. Mears, *A History of Britain* (Oxford, 1937), 4 vols: I, p. 7.   **42.** c.v. Barry Cunliffe, 'The Insular Tradition of Vernacular Literature' in *The Ancient Celts*, op. cit., and K. Jackson, *The Oldest Irish Tradition* (Cambridge, 1964).   **43.** Dr Simon James of Durham University as quoted in the *Guardian*, 13 March 1998.   **44.** Ibid. A similar line is followed by a contributor on 'The Celts' to *The Oxford Companion to British History* (Oxford, 1997) who states (p. 182): 'the supposed "expansion" of the Celts is largely a product of the misinterpretation of the archaeological record' and, 'if we accept there were never any Celts in antiquity in Britain,' . . . 'the description of the Welsh, Irish and Scots as "Celts" [is] without any historical foundations'. This is a fine example of an old trick whereby an *a priori* definition is set up in order that it can be denied.   **45.** On the Celtic debate, see J. V. S. and M. R. Megaw, 'Ancient Celts and Modern Ethnicity', *Antiquity* 70, no. 267 (1996), pp. 175–81; and, in response, S. James, 'Celts, Politics and Motivation in archaeology', ibid., 72, nr. 275 (1998), pp. 200–209.   **46.** Myles Dillon, *The Celtic Realms* (1972), quoted by Colin Renfrew, *Archaeology and Language* (London, 1987), p. 244.   **47.** Geoffrey of

Monmouth, *History of the Kings of Britain*, trans S. Evans (London, 1963), pp. 4, 25–6. **48.** Ibid., pp. 27, 63. **49.** J. Davies, *History of Wales*, op. cit., p. 303. **50.** John Toland, *Hypatia* (1753): also *A Critical History of the Celtic Religion and Learning* (London, 1815). **51.** *DNB*, vol. XIX, pp. 127–9. Stukeley's publications include *Itinerium Curiosum* (1724); *Palæographi Sacra* (1736), which attempts to reconcile British prehistory with the Old Testament; *Stonehenge, a Temple restor'd to the British Druids* (1740); *Palæographia Britannica* (1743–52); and *The Coins of the Ancient British Kings* (n.d.). **52.** Revd D. McNicol, *Remarks on Dr. Samuel Johnson's Journey to the Hebrides* (London, 1779), p. 68. **53.** William Blake, 'The Voice of the Ancient Bard,' Songs of Innocence, *Complete Writings* (Oxford, 1972), p. 126. **54.** Malcolm Chapman, *The Celts: the Construction of Myth* (London, 1992). **55.** E. M. Quiggin, 'The Celts', *Encyclopædia Britannica*, XIth Edition, 1911. **56.** Susan Bassnett, *Comparative Literature: a Critical Introduction* (Oxford, 1993), p. 48. **57.** Seamus Heaney, *An Open Letter* (Derry, 1983). **58.** P. Beresford Ellis, *The Creed of the Celtic Revolution* (London, 1969). **59.** Ian Howie-Willis, 'The Celts in Cyberspace: the Electronic Celtic Revival', speaking notes for Beechworth Celtic Festival, Australia, 14 November 1998. **60.** See T. O. Clancy, G. Markus, *Iona: the Earliest Poetry of a Celtic Monastery* (Edinburgh, 1995). For the Iona Community: <http://www.iona.org.uk>. **61.** From A. Duncan, *A Little Book of Celtic Prayer* (London, 1996), quoting B. O'Malley, *Cydymaith y Pererin* ('The Pilgrim's Companion') (Llandysul, 1989). **62.** See P. Cherici, *Celtic Sexuality: Power, Paradigms and Passion* (London, 1994), W. Y. Wentz, *The Fairy Faith* (Gerards Cross, 1977); L. Spence, *The Magic Arts in Celtic Britain* (New York, 1992). **63.** Celtica, Y Plas, Machynlleth, Mid-Wales, SY20 8ER. (Tel: 01654 702702, <http://multiweb. ruralwales.net/~celtica/>.

Three: The Frontier Isles

1. AUC: *ab urbe condita*, from the building of the city (in 755 BC). **2.** *Corpus Inscriptionum Latinarum* (Berlin, 1876), vol. VI, no. 920, p. 165. The inscription was seen in the ruins of the Claudian Arch in the sixteenth century, but miscopied. Only a fragment from the left-hand side of the original text has survived. The rest has been reconstructed by scholars. See A. A. Barrett, 'Claudius' British Victory Arch in Rome', *Britannia*, vol. 22 (1991), pp. 1–19; also D. R. Dudley, *Urbs Roma* (London, 1967), p. 185. **3.** *Suétone: vie des douze Césars*, H. Ailloud, ed. (Paris, 1932), vol. II, pp. xvi–xvii. **4.** *Ad Quintum Fratrem* 21 (III, 1) 10, in D. R. Shackelton Bailey, ed., *Cicero: Epistulae ad Quintum Fratrem et M. Brutum* (Cambridge, 1980), p. 80. **5.** Leonard Cottrell, *The Great Invasion* (London, 1958), p. 84. **6.** Benjamin Isaac, *The Limits of Empire: the Roman Army in the East* (Oxford, 1992), especially Chapter IX, 'Grand Strategy', pp. 388 ff. **7.** F. Bucheler, A. Risée, eds, *Anthologia Latina* (1894), no. 419, quoted and translated by D. Braund, *Augustus to Nero: a Source Book on Roman History, 31 BC – AD 68* (London, 1985), p. 87. **8.** Bucheler, op.

cit., no. 423; Braund, ibid., p. 87. **9.** Tacitus, *Agricola*, in Cornelius Tacitus, *Opera Minora*, M. Winterbottom, R. M. Ogilvie, eds (Oxford, 1975), p. 21. **10.** Cottrell, op. cit., p. 144. **11.** Tacitus, *Agricola*, op. cit, 40, 5. **12.** Gibbon, *The Decline and Fall of the Roman Empire* (Everyman, London, 1910), vol. I, pp. 3–4. **13.** See [HERMAN] in Norman Davies, *Europe: a History* (Oxford, 1996), p. 827. **14.** See P. Filtzinger, *Limesmuseum Aalen*, Württembergischer Landesmuseum (Stuttgart, 1991); also Margot Klee, *Der Limes zwischen Rhein und Main* (Stuttgart, 1989). **15.** After T. Cornell, J. Matthews, *Atlas of the Roman World* (Oxford 1982). **16.** Edith Hall, *Inventing the Barbarian: Greek self-definition through tragedy* (Oxford, 1989). **17.** Neal Ascherson, *The Black Sea* (London, 1995), p. 49. **18.** Aelii Spartiani, *De Vita Hadriana* 5, 1–2 in *A Commentary on the Vita Hadriani in the Historia Augusta*, H. W. Benario, ed. (Chico, CA, 1980), p. 21. **19.** Ibid., II, 2 (p. 27). **20.** (R.I.C. II, p. 447; no. 845). **21.** *Roman Inscriptions of Britain*, R. G. Collingwood and R. P. Wright, eds, vol. I, *Inscriptions in Stone*, no. 1051, pp. 349–51. About seven lines of the full inscription are missing from the surviving fragments between COSIII and DIFFVSIS. **22.** After 'Finn and the Salmon' in Iain Zaczek, *Chronicles of the Celts* (London, 1996), p. 84. **23.** From *Fragments of Ancient Poetry collected in the Highlands of Scotland and Translated from the Galic or Erse language* (1760), in J. Macpherson, *The Poems of Ossian* (Edinburgh, 1805, reprinted 1971), II, p. 385. **24.** After C. J. Marstrander et al., eds, *Dictionary of the Irish Language* (Dublin, 1913–76), 4 vols. **25.** B. R. Hartley, R. L. Fitts, *The Brigantes* (London, 1988). **26.** See A. D. Divine, *The North-West Frontier of Rome: a Military Study of Hadrian's Wall* (London, 1969); also S. Johnson, *English Heritage Book of Hadrian's Wall* (London, 1989). **27.** See A. K. Bowmen, J. D. Thomas, *The Vindolanda Writing Tablets* (Newcastle, 1974); also R. Birley, *Vindolanda* (Greenhead, 1991). **28.** Peter Salway, *The Frontier People of Roman Britain* (London, 1965), Appendix. 'Inscriptions and Sculptures', No. 61, pp. 235–6. **29.** Ibid., No. 27, p. 221. **30.** Ibid., No. 13, pp. 213–14. **31.** Ibid., No. 14, p. 214. **32.** A. S. Robertson, *The Antonine Wall: a Handbook to the Surviving Remains* (Glasgow, 1990). **33.** J. Hawkes, *A Guide to the Prehistoric and Roman Monuments in England and Wales* (London, 1973), p. 213. **34.** See Isabel Henderson, *The Picts* (London, 1967); see also F. T. Wainwright, ed., *The Problem of the Picts* (Westport, Conn., 1970). **35.** Ian Adamson, *Cruthin: the Ancient Kindred* (Newtownards, Co. Down, 1974). See also M. Hall, *Ulster: the Hidden History* (Belfast, 1986), and ibid., *The Cruthin Controversy* (Newtownabbey, 1994). The implication here is that the resettlement of the Ulster plantation by Scots in the seventeenth century saw 'the Ancient Kindred returning home'. One is not supposed to ask whether the hypothesis has been influenced by contemporary politics. **36.** Lloyd and Jenny Lang, *The Picts and the Scots* (Dover, NH, 1993), pp. 100–61. **37.** Peter Salway, *Roman Britain* (Oxford, 1981), pp. 18–19. **38.** See A. Birley, *The People of Roman Britain* (London, 1979), Chapter IX, 'British Soldiers in the Roman Army'; also P. Holder, *The Roman Army in Britain* (London, 1982). **39.** R. W. Bagshawe, *Roman Roads* (Aylesbury, 1979). **40.** G. Milne, *Book of Roman London* (London, 1995); J. P. Alcock, *Londinium: a Practical Guide to the Visible*

Remains (London, 1977).   **41.** Barry Cunliffe, foreword to K. Branigan, *Roman Britain* (London, 1980), p. 6.   **42.** See J. M. C. Toynbee, *Christianity in Roman Britain* (1953)   **43.** *The Poetical Works of Thomas Moore* (Edinburgh, n.d. *c.* 1865), p. 431.   **44.** Rudyard Kipling, 'The Roman Centurion's Song', in *Complete Verse* (London, 1990), p. 586.   **45.** Paul Anderson, *With the Eagles* (London and New York, 1929), p. 8.   **45.** C. R. L. Fletcher, *A History of England* (London, 1911), pp. 19–21.   **46.** Ibid.

Four: The Germanico-Celtic Isles

1. G. Jack, *Beowulf: a student edition* (Oxford, 1994), 'The Fight at Finnsburgh', lines 37–40, pp. 215–16.   **2.** 'Beowulf', lines 1106–27, ibid., pp. 93–4.   **3.** 'Beowulf', lines 1157–9, ibid., p. 98.   **4.** D. Wright, *Beowulf: a prose translation* (London, 1957), p. 52; also M. Alexander, *Beowulf: a verse translation* (Penguin, London, 1973).   **5.** See Norman Davies, *Europe: a History* (Oxford, 1996), p. 215ff.   **6.** Quoted by N. Davies, *God's Playground: a history of Poland* (Oxford, 1981). I, p. 46.   **7.** St Ursula: D. Attwater, ed., *The Penguin Dictionary of Saints* (Harmondsworth, 1965), pp. 333–4.   **8.** Gordon Ward, *Hengest: an Historical Study of his Danish Origins and of his Campaigns in Frisia and South-east England* (London, 1949), p. 25.   **9.** John Morris, *The Age of Arthur: a History of the British Isles from 350 to 650* (London, 1939), p. 39.   **10.** Ibid., *passim.*   **11.** Notably J. N. L. Myres, *The English Settlements* (Oxford, 1986).   **12.** St Germanus: Attwater, op. cit., p. 152.   **13.** E.g. by P. B. Ellis, *Celt and Saxon* (London, 1993), p. 31ff.   **14.** Quoted by Morris, op. cit., p. 14.   **15.** Ibid., pp. 57–8.   **16.** Bede, *History of the English Church and People*, I, 15 (Penguin translation), (London, 1955).   **17.** *The Anglo-Saxon Chronicle* (Everyman edn., London 1953).   **18.** Morris, op. cit., p. 66.   **19.** Barbara Yorke, 'Fact or Fiction? The Written Evidence for the Fifth and Sixth Centuries AD', *Anglo-Saxon Studies in Archaeology and History*, vol. 6 (1993), pp. 45–50.   **20.** See J. R. R. Tolkien, *Finn and Hengest: the Fragment and the Episode*, A. Bliss, ed. (London, 1982).   **21.** Ward, op. cit., ch. XII.   **22.** Sir Frank Stenton, *Anglo-Saxon England* (Oxford, 1998).   **23.** See J. B. Johnston, *The Place-names of Scotland* (London, 1934).   **24.** Morris, op. cit., p. 72.   **25.** Ibid., p. 76.   **26.** *The Anglo-Saxon Chronicle*, 473. This is the English version. Generally speaking, *The Anglo-Saxon Chronicle* only takes notice of Anglo-Saxon victories and Anglo-Saxon advances. Celtic sources tend to be similarly tendentious. The essential task is to consider all sources, which usually turn out to be mutually complementary.   **27.** *The Anglo-Saxon Chronicle*, 477.   **28.** St Patrick, 'Letter to Coroticus', in R. P. C. Hanson, *The Life and Writings of the Historical Saint Patrick* (New York, 1983), pp. 58–73. See also: E. A. Thompson, *Who was Saint Patrick?* (Woodbridge, 1985), pp. 125–43; L. Bieler, *Studies on the Life and Legend of St. Patrick* (London, 1986); D. N. Dumville et al., eds, *Saint Patrick, AD 493–1993* (Woodbridge, 1993).   **29.** See J. Ryan, *Irish Monasticism* (Dublin, 1931).   **30.** T. Cahill, *How the Irish saved Civilisation* (London, 1995).   **31.** See D. Ó Corráin, in R. Foster, ed., *The*

Oxford Illustrated History of Ireland (Oxford, 1989): also F. J. Byrne, *Irish Kings and High Kings* (London, 1973). **32.** S. J. Connolly, 'Brehon law', 'Law – Early Irelanad', *The Oxford Companion to Irish History* (Oxford, 1998), pp. 57, 305–6. **33.** Quoted by Ó Corráin, op. cit., pp. 6–7. **34.** Quoted by Morris, op. cit., p. 232. **35.** J. Morris, ibid. **36.** From Aneirin, *Y Gododdin: Britain's Oldest Poem*, ed. A. O. H. Jarman, (Llandysul, 1988), pp. 7–9. **37.** From the cross in the kirk of Ruthwell, Dumfries and Galloway, quoted by B. Kay, *Scots: the Mither Tongue* (Edinburgh, 1986), p. 32. **38.** See A. B. Scott, *The Pictish Nation: its People and its Church* (Edinburgh, 1918): also E. Sutherland, *In Search of the Picts* (London, 1994). **39.** Morris, op. cit. **40.** J. Davies, *A History of Wales* (London, 1993), p. 63. **41.** See Chapter I, note 6. **42.** Bede II, 2, pp. 100–101. **43.** Ibid., I, 27, p. 76; I, 30, pp. 86–7. **44.** Morris, op. cit., p. 395. **45.** 'Sutton Hoo', *Oxford Companion to British History* (Oxford, 1997) p. 904. **46.** Ibid., p. 704. **47.** Kearney, op. cit., pp. 40–2. **48.** *The Anglo-Saxon Chronicle*, ed. M. J. Swanton (London, 1997), pp. 54–5. **49.** Bede V, 23, p. 325. **50.** J. Davies, op. cit., p. 63. **51.** Susan Pearce, *The Kingdom of Dumnonia* (Padstow, 1978); also A. K. H. Jenkins, *Cornwall and its people* (London, 1970). **52.** Norman Davies, op. cit., pp. 223–4. **53.** 'The Tywyn Inscribed Stone' in Ifor Williams, *The Beginnings of Welsh Poetry: Studies* (Cardiff, 1972). *The Beginnings of Welsh Poetry*, Rachel Bromwich, ed., pp. 25–40. **54.** J. Davies, op. cit., p. 45. **55.** Edward Gibbon, *The Decline and Fall of the Roman Empire* (Everyman, London, 1910), vol. I, p. 5. **56.** David Hume, *A History of England from the Invasion of Julius Caesar to the Revolution of 1688* (London, 1807) vol. I, p. 26. **57.** Ibid., I, p. 473. **58.** Ibid., I, p. 21. **59.** V. G. Wexler, *David Hume and the History of England* (Philadelphia, 1979), p. 8 **60.** Charles Dickens, *A Child's History of England* (1852) in *The New Illustrated Dickens* (Oxford, 1958), vol. XII, pp. 139–40. **61.** J. R. Green, *A Short History of the English People* (London, 1874). **62.** John Carey, *The Irish National Origin-Legend: Synthetic Pseudo-history* (Quiggin Pamphlets, Cambridge, 1994), p. 24. **63.** *The Sunday Times*, 21 June 1998, 'Oxford dons try to slay Beowulf'. **64.** *Beowulf*, Encyclopædia Britannica, CD (1998). **65.** J. R. R. Tolkien, *The Lord of the Rings* (London, 1954), p. 5. **66.** Sir Thomas Malory, *The Tale of the Death of King Arthur*, E. Vinaver, ed. (Oxford, 1955), p. 80. **67.** J. F. Palmer, 'The Saxon Invasion and Its Influence on our Character as a Race', *TRHS* (New Series), vol. II (1885), pp. 173–96. **68.** See S. Scammell, *Mary of Nazareth, Joseph of Arimathea and the early Celtic Church* (Crosby Ravensworth, 1995). **69.** W. D. Simpson, *St. Ninian and the Origins of the Christian Church in Scotland*, (Edinburgh, 1940): also *The Penguin Dictionary of Saints* op. cit., p. 255. **70.** See Ellen Murray, *Peace and Adventure: the Story of Iona* (Glasgow, 1987); also T. O. Clancy, G. Marcus, *Iona: the Earliest Poetry of a Celtic Monastery* (Edinburgh, 1995). **71.** Deidre O'Sullivan, Robert Young, *English Heritage Book of Lindisfarne, Holy Island* (London, 1995); G.W. Dunleavy, *Colum's Other Island: the Irish at Lindisfarne* (Madison, Wisconsin, 1960); P. Hunter Blair, *Northumbria in the Days of Bede* (London, 1976). **72.** See D. du Maurier, *Vanishing Cornwall: the spirit and history of Cornwall* (Harmondsworth, 1972). **73.** D. Delap, A. Lockhart, eds, *Celtic Saints* (London, 1955), p. 5. **74.** See

the Introduction to the Quiggin Pamphlets Series, Carey, op. cit., p. viii.
75. Melvyn Bragg, *Credo* (London, 1996), p. 431.

Five: The Islands in the West

1. R. I. Page, *Chronicles of the Vikings: Records, Memorials and Myths* (London, 1995), pp. 46–8. 2. *Egils Saga Skalla-Grímssonar*, S. Nordal, ed. (Reykjavík, 1933), p. 185. 3. Ibid., p. 172. 4. Page, op. cit., pp. 134–5. 5. Snorri Sturluson, *Heimskringla*, B. Aðalbjarnarson, ed. (Reykavík, 1941–51), vol. I, pp. 188, 194. 6. *Landnámabók*, the 'Book of Settlements', in Page, op. cit., pp. 64–5. 7. *Islendinga bók Landnámabók*, J. Benediktsson, ed. (Reykjavík, 1968), p. 102. 8. *Hávamál*, D. A. H. Evans, ed. (London, 1986), p. 54. 9. Page, op. cit. 10. See N. Pennick, *Runestaves and Oghams* (Cambridge, 1997) 11. See Peter Sawyer, *The Age of the Vikings* (London, 1962), the first historical account to stress the economic aspect of Viking expansion and to rationalize the causes of Viking savagery. 12. 'Ships, Shipwrights and Seamen', J. Graham-Campbell, *The Viking World* (London, 1989), pp. 37–63. 13. J. Wallace-Hadrill, Simon Keynes, 'Vikings' in Michael Lapidge, ed., *The Blackwell Encyclopaedia of Anglo-Saxon England* (Oxford, 1999), p. 99. 14. R. Southern, *The Normans' Self-Image*. 15. *Anglo-Saxon Chronicle*, 793, Swanton, op. cit., pp 55–6 16. Annals of Lindisfarne. 17. *Orkneyinga Saga*, F. Guðmundsson, ed. (Reykjavík, 1965), p. 15. 18. After *Cogadh Gaedhel re Gallaibh*, trans. J. H. Todd (London, 1867), p. 79. Quoted by T. W. Moody and F. X. Martin *The Course of Irish History* (Cork, 1994), p. 104. On Clontarf, see D. O'Corráin, *Ireland before the Normans* (Dublin, 1972). 19. *Brennu-Njal's Saga*. E. O. Sveinsson, ed. (Reykjavík, 1954), pp. 459–60. 20. *Anglo-Saxon Chronicle*, 936: quoted by P. B Ellis, *Celt and Saxon*, op cit., p. 211–12. 21. See D. Dunville, 'Brittany and Armes Prydain Vawr', *Études Celtiques*, 20 (1983), pp. 145–83. 22. *Anglo-Saxon Chronicle*, 832, Swanton, op. cit., p. 62. 23. See A. J. Frantzen, *King Alfred* (Boston, 1986): also A. P. Smythe, *King Alfred the Great* (Oxford, 1995). 24. J. Davies, *A History of Wales* (London, 1993), pp. 100–101. 25. See Gwn Jones, *The Mabinogion* (Everyman, London, 1950). 26. *Macbeth*, III, v, 135–7. 27. Ibid., V, v, 22–7. 28. See J. D. Mackie, *A History of Scotland* (London, 1964), chapter 5, 'The House of Canmore'. 29. See F. M. Stenton, *Types of manorial structure in the northern Danelaw* (Oxford, 1910). 30. From the *Nóregs Konunga tal*, after Page, op. cit., pp. 32–3. 31. A lavish British Museum exhibition in 1991 entitled 'The Making of England' confined itself to the period 597–890. See Patrick Wormald, 'The Making of England' in 'On Second Thoughts . . .', *History Today*, February 1995, pp. 26–32. 32. J. Davies, op. cit., p. 97. 33. R. R. Davies, 'The Peoples of Britain and Ireland, 1100–1400', *T.R.H.S.* (Sixth Series) IV, (1994), p. 6. 34. Wormald, op. cit., p. 32. 35. See N. F. Blake, ed., *The Saga of the Jomsvikings* (London and New York, 1962); also H. Loyn, *The Vikings in Wales*, The Dorothy Coke Memorial Lecture (London, 1976), p. 11 ff. 36. Dimitri Obolensky, *The Byzantine Commonwealth: Eastern Europe, 500–1453* (Lon-

don, 1971), p. 307.   **37.** See M. K. Lawson, *Cnut: the Danes in England* (London, 1993).   **38.** See E-G. Léonard, *Histoire de Normandie* (Paris, 1948).   **39.** Snorri Sturluson, *King Harald's Saga* (Penguin, London, 1966), p. 62.   **40.** See A. C. Reeves, *The Marcher Lords, 1063–1536* (Llandybie, 1983).   **41.** A. Jones, ed., *The History of Gruffydd ap Cynan* (Manchester, 1910), pp. 146–7.   **42.** See D. A. Kibbee, *For to speke Frenche trewely: The French language in England, 1000–1600* (Amsterdam, 1997); also D. Gray, ed., *Middle English Studies presented to Norman Davis*, (Oxford, 1983).   **43.** H. Loyn, op. cit., p. 21.   **44.** W. Bell Scott, *Scenes from Northumbrian History: the mural paintings at Wallington Hall, Northumberland* (Newcastle, 1972).   **45.** For example, A. Bourcher, *The Land Seekers* (London, 1964) and *The Sword and the Raven* (London, 1969): Nathaniel Benchley, *Beyond the Mists* (New York, 1975).   **46.** For example, Henry Treece, *The Last of the Vikings* (Leicester, 1964) about Harald Hardrada, and *Man with a Sword* (London, 1962) about Hereward: T. Jones, *The Saga of Eric the Viking* (London, 1983).   **47.** For example, Henry Treece, *The Road to Miklagard* (London, 1957): Rosemary Sutcliff, *Blood Feud* (New York, 1977): and G. Finkel, *The Long Pilgrimage* (Sydney, 1967).   **48.** Other titles include Theodora du Bois, *The High King's Daughter* (London, 1966) about the Viking Age in Ireland: Henry Treece, *Viking Sunset* (London, 1969): R. Klein, *Berk the Berserker* (Adelaide, 1987): and Rosemary Sutcliff, *Sword Song* (London, 1997).   **49.** Charles Dickens, *A Child's History of England* (London, 1852), p. 202.   **50.** Clare A. Simmons, *Reversing the Conquest: History and Myth in Nineteenth Century British Literature* (New Brunswick, 1990), Chapter I: 'Early Conceptions of Saxons and Normans'.   **51.** W. P. James, *King Alfred Surveying the University of Oxford at the Present Time, A Prize Poem Recited in the Theatre, Oxford, June 4th 1856* (Oxford, 1856), p. 6.   **52.** Ibid., p. 7.   **53.** Alfred Austin, 1897. Quoted by Simmons, op. cit. p. 175.   **54.** Ibid., p. 188.   **55.** Ibid., p. 187.   **56.** Ibid., p. 188.   **57.** E. A. Freeman, *Poems Legendary and Historical* (London, 1850), quoted by Simmons, op. cit., p. 141.   **58.** E. A. Freeman, *The Norman Conquest: its Causes and its Results* (London, 1875–9), vol. III, p. 503.   **59.** Bulwer-Lytton (1848), quoted by Simmons, op. cit., p. 156.   **60.** Charles Kingsley, 'Swan-Neck', in *The Poems of Charles Kingsley* (London, 1927).   **61.** Charles Kingsley, *Hereward the Wake, 'Last of the English'* (London, 1902), pp. 3–4.   **62.** Ibid., p. 4.   **63.** Ibid., p. 367.   **64.** Ibid., p. 369.   **65.** Ibid., p. 370.   **66.** Sir James Henry Ramsay, *The Foundations of England* (London, 1898): T. Hodgkin, *The History of England from the Earliest Times to the Norman Conquest* (London, 1906): and Sir Charles Oman, *England before the Norman Conquest* (London, 1910).   **67.** F. M. Stenton, *William the Conqueror and the Rule of the Normans* (New York, 1908): *Anglo-Saxon England* (Oxford, 1943).   **68.** Simon Keynes, 'Anglo-Saxon History after *Anglo-Saxon England*', in D. Matthews, ed., *Stenton's Anglo-Saxon England Fifty Years On* (Reading, 1994), p. 83 ff.   **69.** W. C. Sellars, J. B. Yeatman, *1066 and All That* (London, 1935).   **70.** Lewis Carroll, *Alice's Adventures in Wonderland* (1865), (Penguin, London, 1998), p. 25.   **71.** J. R. Strayer, *On the Medieval Origins of the Modern State* (Princeton, 1970).   **72.** See R. Chatterton Newman, *Brian Boru: King of Ireland*, (Dublin, 1996).   **73.** Quoted by P. B. Ellis,

Macbeth, High King of Scotland, 1040–57 AD (London, 1980), p. 117. **74.** Quoted by Ellis, ibid., p. 123.

Six: The Isles of *Outremer*

1. Steven Runciman, *A History of the Crusades*, vol. II, *The Kingdom of Jerusalem* (Cambridge, 1952), Chapter III, 'Fiasco'. **2.** Henry, Archdeacon of Huntingdon, *Historia Anglorum – The History of the English People*, D. Greenway, ed. (Oxford, 1996), pp. 752ff. **3.** G. M. Trevelyan, *English Social History* (London, 1942), p. 1. **4.** *Historia Anglorum*, op. cit., pp. 752–3. **5.** *De Expugnatione Lyxbonensi: The Conquest of Lisbon*, C. W. David, ed. (New York, 1936, 1976), pp. 132–3. **6.** Ibid., pp. 184–5. **7.** Amin Maalouf, *The Crusades through Arab Eyes* (London, 1984), p. 148. **8.** William of Tyre, *A History of Deeds done beyond the Sea*, trans. E. Babcock, A. C. Krey (New York, 1943), p. 190. **9.** Maalouf, op. cit., pp. 149–50. **10.** William of Tyre, op. cit., p. 195. **11.** Runciman, op. cit., II, p. 288. **12.** Henry of Huntingdon, op. cit., p. 700. **13.** Ibid., pp. 702–5. **14.** Ibid., pp. 710–11. **15.** Ibid., pp. 738–41. **16.** Ibid., p. 788. **17.** Ibid., pp. 794–7. **18.** See François Dornic, *Histoire de l'Anjou* (Paris, 1961). **19.** 'Fri et Tremble', in Jean-Claude Marol, *L'Amour libéré(e): ou l'érotique initiale des troubadours* (Paris, 1998), pp. 148–51. **20.** On Aliénor and her background, see Margaret Trouncer, *Eleanor: Two Marriages of a Queen* (London, 1967): W. W. Kibler, ed., *Eleanor of Aquitaine, Patron and Politician* (symposia in the Arts and Sciences, nr. 3), University of Texas (Austin, Texas, 1976): C. Higounet, *Histoire de l'Aquitaine* (Toulouse, 1971): M. Meade, *Eleanor of Aquitaine: a biography* (New York, 1977). **21.** See F. Vaux de Foletier, *Piotou* (Guide Bleu), (Paris, 1960). **22.** Henry of Huntingdon, in *The Plantagenet Chronicles*, ed. E. Hallam (London, 1986), pp. 82–4. **23.** Ibid., p. 84. **24.** Ibid., pp. 84–5. **25.** Ibid., p. 85. **26.** Henry of Huntingdon, op. cit., pp. 776–7. **27.** *The Anglo-Saxon Chronicle*, trans. Michael Swanton (London, 1997), pp. 268–9. **28.** K. O. Morgan, *Oxford History of Britain* (Oxford, 1993), p. 123. **29.** Compiled from R. W. Eyton, *Court, Household and Itinerary of King Henry II* (London, 1878), pp. 133–53. **30.** T. Percy, *Reliques of Ancient English Poetry* (London, n.d.), quoted by D. D. R. Owen, *Eleanor of Aquitaine: Queen and Legend* (Oxford, 1993), I, pp. 121–24. **31.** T. W. Moody and F. X. Martin, *The Course of Irish History* (Cork, 1994), p. 130. **32.** *The Song of Dermot and Earl Richard Fitzgilbert*, Denis Conlon, ed. (Frankfurt, 1992), p. 32, line 461 ff. **33.** Ibid., lines 777 ff. **34.** Ibid., p. 218, lines 3436 ff. **35.** R. R. Davies, 'The Peoples of Britain and Ireland, 1100–140: II Names, Boundaries and Regal Solidarities', *Transactions of the Royal Historical Society* (1995), p. 18. **36.** John Davies, *A History of Wales* (London, 1993), p. 1. **37.** See R. Williams, *The Lords of the Isles* (London, 1984). **38.** John Gillingham, 'The Beginnings of English Imperialism', *Journal of Historical Sociology*, vol. 5 (1992), pp. 392–409. **39.** W. J. Warren, 'What was Wrong with King John?', *History Today* (1957), pp. 806–12. **40.** See N. Denholm-Young, *Richard of Cornwall* (London, 1947). **41.** F. W. Maitland, 'A Song on the Death of Simon de Montfort', *English Historical Review* (1896), p. 317, verse 28. **42.** R. F. Treharne, 'The Personal Role of Simon de Montfort . . .', Raleigh Lecture 1954, *Proceedings of the British Academy* (1954), pp. 75–102. **43.** A. Wachtel, 'Die sizilische Thronkandidature des Prinzen Edmund von England', *Deutsches Archiv für Geschichte des Mittelalters*, IV (1944), (London, 1983). **44.** *The Song of Lewes*, C. L. Kingsford, ed. (London, 1890), lines 9–10. **45.** 'Song on the Death of Simon de Montfort', op. cit., p. 318, verse 41. **46.** Susan Reynolds, 'How Different was England?', *Thirteenth Century England VII. Proceedings of the Durham Conference*, 1997 (Woodbridge, 1999), p. 15. **47.** Moody and Martin, op. cit., p. 136. **48.** J. Davies, op. cit., pp. 143–53. **49.** See R. Williams, *The Lords of the Isles* (London, 1984). **50.** F. M. Powicke, *King Henry III and the Lord Edward*, (Oxford, 1947), 'Epilogue'. **51.** *Dictionary of National Biography*, VI, p. 433. **52.** Harding, op. cit., p. 323. **53.** J. E. Morris, 'Two Documents Relating to the Conquest of Wales', *English Historical Review*, 1899, p. 507. **54.** J. Davies, op. cit., p. 161. **55.** Michael Lynch, *Scotland: a New History* (London, 1992), p. 113. **56.** Ibid., p. 118. **57.** Dante Alighieri, *Paradiso* xix, 121–3; Dante equally blames the Scots. **58.** *Braveheart*, Paramount Pictures, 1995, starring Mel Gibson as William Wallace. **59.** Tom Scott, ed., *Penguin Book of Scottish Verse* (Harmondsworth, 1970), p. 59. **60.** G. M. Trevelyan, *A History of England* (London, 1937), p. 218. **61.** *DNB*, vol. III, p. 121. **62.** J. Fergusson, ed., *The Declaration of Arbroath* (Edinburgh, 1970), quoted by P. H. Scott, *Scotland: An Unknown Cause* (Edinburgh, 1997), p. 5. **63.** Ibid., p. 6. **64.** *DNB*, vol. III, p. 127. **65.** R. R. Davies, op. cit., I, pp. 18–30. **66.** From T. F. Tout, *Chapters in the Administrative History of Mediaeval England*, 6 vols. (Manchester, 1920–33). **67.** Paul Studer, 'An Anglo-Norman Poem by Edward II', *Modern Languages Review* (1921), p. 40, lines 1ff, 17ff. **68.** Alan Harding, *England in the Thirteenth Century* (Cambridge, 1993), 'Introduction', pp. 1–67, which provides a comprehensive survey of the historiography. **69.** Shakespeare, *King John*, V, vii, 112–14. **70.** Harding, op. cit., p. 30. **71.** Hume quoted by Harding, ibid., p. 32. **72.** Quoted by Harding, p. 43. **73.** T. F. Tout: see Harding, passim. **74.** Edwin Jones, 'John Lingard and Modern Historiography', in *The English Nation: the Great Myth* (Stroud, 1998), pp. 168–217. **75.** H. G. Richardson and G. O. Sayles, *The Governance of Mediaeval England* (Edinburgh, 1963), see Harding, op. cit., passim. **76.** G. O. Sayles, *The Functions of the Medieval Parliament* (London, 1988), see Harding, op. cit., passim. **77.** Quoted by Stephen Knight, *Robin Hood: a Complete Study of the English Outlaw* (Oxford, 1994), 'The Theatre of the Fifteen-nineties', pp. 98ff. See also J. C. Holt, *Robin Hood* (London, 1982). **78.** Knight, op. cit., passim. **79.** Andrew of Wyntoun, quoted by Knight, op. cit., p. 32. **80.** Joseph Ritson, ed., *Robin Hood: a Collection of All the Ancient Poems, Song, and Ballads* (London, 1832). **81.** J. Walker Mc-Spadden, *Stories of Robin Hood and his Merry Outlaws, Retold from the Old Ballads* (London, 1905), with numerous reprintings. **82.** Walter Scott, *Ivanhoe*, ed. G. Tulloch (Edinburgh, 1998), p. 16. **83.** Ibid., p. 375. **84.** See J. B. Gillingham, *Richard the Lionheart* (London, 1989). **85.** David Hume, quoted by Dr S. D. Lloyd,

The Oxford Companion to British History (Oxford, 1997), p. 266. **86.** Runciman, op. cit., III, p. 480. **87.** Dom David Knowles, *The Religious Orders in England*, vol. III (Cambridge, 1959), p. 468. **88.** Edwin Jones, op. cit., p. 143: especially his Chapter IV, 'The Mediaeval Background to Reformation Historiography', pp. 115–48. **89.** Geoffrey Chaucer, *The Canterbury Tales*, General Prologue, lines 118–62. **90.** John Barbour, from 'The Bruce'. John MacQueen, Tom Scott, eds, *The Oxford Book of Scottish Verse* (Oxford, 1966), p. 10. **91.** Robert Burns, 'Scots, Wha Hae', ibid., p. 413.

Seven: The Englished Isles

1. *English Historical Documents*, vol. IV, ed. A. R. Myers (London, 1969), nr. 4, pp. 52–3. **2.** As reported by Froissart. Quoted by J. F. C. Fuller, *The Decisive Battles of the Western World*, vol. I (London, 1954), p. 447. **3.** Geoffrey le Baker, *Chronicon Galfridi le Baker de Swynebroke*, ed. E. M. Thompson (Oxford, 1889), [1328], quoted by E. Hallam, ed., *Chronicles of the Age of Chivalry* (Godalming, 1995), p. 232. **4.** After 'William de la Pole Account for wool exported to Dordrecht in 1337, (Latin)', A. R. Myers, ed., *English Historical Documents* (London, 1969), vol. IV, nr 581, pp. 1017–18. **5.** Ibid., IV, nr 12. **6.** Ibid., IV., nr. 18, pp. 66–7. **7.** Ibid., IV, nr. 21 (ii), p. 70. **8.** N. A. M. Rodger, *The Safeguard of the Sea. A Naval History of Britain, Volume One 660–1649* (London, 1997), pp. 97–8. **9.** Ibid., pp. 97–8. **10.** 1 mark = 13s 4d. After T. F. Tout, D. M. Broome, 'A National Balance Sheet for 1362–3', *English Historical Review*, vol XXXIX (1924), pp. 404–19. **11.** J. F. C. Fuller, *The Decisive Battles of the Western World*, vol. I (London, 1954), 'The Battles of Sluys and Crecy', pp. 444–68. **12.** Ieuan Gethin, quoted by P. Ziegler, *The Black Death* (London, 1970), p. 197. **13.** 'Oh for the good times', *English Historical Documents* vol. IV, nr. 694, p. 1,182. **14.** Chaucer, 'Book of the Duchesse', in A. C. Baugh, ed., *Chaucer's Major Poetry* (London, 1963). **15.** T. A. Knott and D. C. Fowler, eds, *Piers the Plowman: a Critical Edition of the A-version* (Baltimore, 1952), lines 1–6, p. 67; *Visions from Piers Plowman*, trans. N. Coghill (London, 1949), p. 15. **16.** Basil Cottle, *The Triumph of English, 1350–1400* (London, 1969), p. 15. **17.** *English Historical Documents*, op. cit., nr. 251, pp. 483–4. **18.** Cottle, op. cit., p. 16. **19.** Ibid., pp. 16–17. **20.** D. Crystal, ed., *Cambridge Encyclopaedia of the English Language* (Cambridge, 1995), p. 31. **21.** 'Sumer is icumen in', *Oxford Book of English Verse* (Oxford, 1953), nr. 1, p. 2. **22.** Cottle, op. cit., p. 19. **23.** Ibid., p. 20. **24.** Ibid., p. 22. **25.** See: Philippe Contamine, *La Guerre de Cent Ans* (Paris, 1968). **26.** R. R. Davies, *The Revolt of Owain Glyn Dŵr* (Oxford, 1995), p. 158. **27.** Ibid., p. 415. **28.** François Villon, from 'Ballade des dames du temps jadis', St John Lucas, ed., *The Oxford Book of French Verse* (Oxford, 1957), p. 37. **29.** R. A. Griffiths, R. S. Thomas, *The Making of the Tudor Dynasty* (New York, 1993). **30.** G. R. Elton, *The Tudor Revolution in Government* (Cambridge, 1953). **31.** G. Bray, ed., *Documents of the English Reformation* (Cambridge, 1994), p. 78; quoted by Edwin Jones, *The*

English Nation: the Great Myth (Stroud, 1998), p. 34. **32.** Bray, op. cit., pp. 113–14: Jones, op. cit., p. 34. **33.** Bray, op. cit., p. 79: Jones, op. cit., p. 36. **34.** Jones, op. cit., p. 37. **35.** T. W. Moody and F. X. Martin, *The Course of Irish History* (Cork, 1994), p. 180. **36.** W. C. Dickinson, ed., *A Source Book of Scottish History*, vol. III (Edinburgh, 1961), pp. 176–7. **37.** *First Book of Discipline*, ibid., pp. 176–7. **38.** Andrew Melville, 1596. Quoted by Michael Lynch, *Scotland: a New History* (London, 1992), p. 228. **39.** Dickinson, op. cit., vol. III, pp. 22–5. **40.** See F. Fernández-Armesto, *The Spanish Armada* (Oxford, 1988); also J. A. Froude, *The Spanish Story of the Armada*, reprint (Stroud, 1988); G. Mattingly, *The Defeat of the Spanish Armada* (2nd edition), (London, 1983). **41.** H. Kearney, *The British Isles: a History of Four Nations* op. cit., p. 155. **42.** Ibid., p. 139. **43.** Especially J. Gillingham, 'The Beginnings of English Imperialism'. See Chapter Five, note 38. **44.** William Dunbar, 'Ane Ballat to Our Lady', J. MacQueen and T. Scott, eds, *The Oxford Book of Scottish Verse* (Oxford, 1966), nr. 30, pp. 109–11. **45.** G. Chaucer, 'General Prologue to the Canterbury Tales', lines 1–4, 12–18, The Riverside Chaucer (Oxford, 1987), p. 23. **46.** Quoted by Jones, op. cit., p. 35. **47.** A. L. Rowse, *Tudor Cornwall: Portrait of a Society* (London, 1941), pp. 282–6. **48.** Edmund Spenser, 'A Ditty in praise of Eliza: Queen of the Shephards', *The Oxford Book of English Verse* (Oxford, 1939), nr. 89, p. 111. **49.** *The Booke of the Common Prayer and Administracion of the Sacramentes, and other Rites and Ceremonies of the Churche: after the vse of the Churche of England*, Londini in officina Edouardi Whitchurche . . . Anno do 1549, Mense Martii. **50.** *The First and Second Prayer-Books of Edward VI*, Everyman's Library no. 448 (London, 1910), p. 348. **51.** Ibid., p. 394. **52.** Ibid., p. 410. **53.** Ibid., p. 424. **54.** See Edwin Jones, 'England's Past in the Seventeenth Century', *The English Nation*, op. cit., pp. 61ff. **55.** Burnet, 1679. Quoted by Jones, op. cit., p. 71. **56.** Ibid. **57.** Jones, op. cit., pp. 76–8. **58.** V. H. Galbraith, 'A New Life of Richard II', *History* (1942). **59.** Shakespeare, *King Richard the Second*, III, ii, 54–62. **60.** Shakespeare, *King Henry the Fifth*, Prologue, 11–14. **61.** Shakespeare, *Richard II*, II, i, 40–50. **62.** Ibid., lines 63–6. **63.** *King Henry the Fifth*, III, i, 1–34. **64.** Ibid., III, ii, 1, 20. **65.** See Catherine Belsey, 'Making History', in G. Holderness, ed., *Shakespeare's History Plays: Richard II to Henry V* (Basingstoke, 1992), pp. 103 ff. **66.** K. B. McFarlane, 'The Lancastrian Kings', in *The Cambridge Medieval History*, vol. VIII. **67.** Shakespeare, *King Henry the Eighth*, V, iv, 17–20. **68.** Ibid., III, ii, 455–8. **69.** *A Man for All Seasons* (1966), directed by Fred Zinnemann. **70.** 'More, Thomas', in Margaret Drabble, ed.,*The Oxford Companion to English Literature*, (Oxford, 1985), p. 668. **71.** S. T. Bindoff, *Tudor England*, (Harmondsworth, 1950). **72.** John Lingard, *A History of England*, 8 vols. (London, 1819–30): abridged and continued by James Burke (London, 1855): abridged and continued by Dom Henry Birt (London, 1903). **73.** *Lingard's History*, Birt's Abridgement, p. 261. **74.** Ibid., pp. 304–5. **75.** Ibid., p. 351. **76.** *Elizabeth*, directed by Shekhar Kapur, starring Cate Blanchett (Gramercy Pictures, 1998). **77.** *Lingard's History*, Birt's Abridgement, op. cit., p. 322 **78.** Ibid., p. 392. **79.** Ibid. p. 392. **80.** Ibid., p. 329. **81.** Ibid., p. 415. **82.** Ibid., p. 418 **83.** *Lingard's History*, Burk's

Abridgement, op. cit., p. 459. **84.** Charles Dickens, *A Child's History of England* (1851–3), New Oxford Illustrated Dickens (Oxford, 1958), p. 369. **85.** William Cobbett, from the *History of the Protestant 'Reformation'* (London, 1824). **86.** Evelyn Waugh, *Edmund Campion* 3rd edition,(London, 1961): also H. C. Gardner, *Edmund Campion, hero of God's underground* (London, 1957). **87.** Prefatory notes by 'Vindicator' in *A True Account of the Gunpowder Plot etc* (London, 1851), p. xi. **88.** Quoted by E. Jones, *The English Myth*, op. cit., passim. **89.** J. A. Froude, *History of England from the fall of Wolsey to the defeat of the Spanish Armada*, new edition (London, 1893); A. F. Pollard, *History of England, 1547–1603* (London, 1910), J. E. Neal, *Queen Elizabeth I* (London, 1952). **90.** C. R. L. Fletcher, *A History of England* (London, 1911), pp. 121–2. **91.** Ibid., p. 137. **92.** Rudyard Kipling, 'Together', p. 138. **93.** G. G. Coulton, *Ten Mediaeval Studies* (Cambridge, 1930). **94.** E. B. Wernham, 'The Tudor Revolution in Government', *English Historical Review*, 1956. **95.** G. R. Elton, *The Practice of History* (Sydney, 1967): *Return to Essentials* (Cambridge, 1991). See K. Jenkins, 'On Geoffrey Elton', *On 'What is History?'* (London, 1995). **96.** G. R. Elton, *The Future of the Past; an Inaugural Lecture* (London, 1968), p. 4. **97.** Ibid., pp. 9–10. **98.** G. R. Elton, *The English* (Oxford, 1992). **99.** His publications on Tudor England include *Christopher Marlowe* (1964), *The Elizabethan Renaissance* (1971–2), *The England of Elizabeth* (1950), *The Expansion of Elizabethan England* (1955), *Eminent Elizabethans* (1983), and *The Poems of Shakespeare's Dark Lady* (1978); on Cornwall, *Tudor Cornwall: Portrait of a Society* (1941), *A Cornish Childhood* (1942), *A. L. Rowse's Cornwall, a Journey Through Cornwall's Past and Present* (1988), *The Cornish in America* (1969), etc., see also *All Souls and Appeasement* (1961). **100.** John Guy, Chapter 5, 'The Tudor Age', in K. O. Morgan, ed., *The Oxford History of Britain*, Updated Edition (Oxford, 1993), pp. 257–326. **101.** Colin Kidd, *Subverting Scotland's Past: Scottish Whig historians and the creation of an Anglo British identity, 1689–c. 1830* (Cambridge, 1993), p. 211. **102.** *Schiller's Maria Stuart*, freely translated by Stephen Spender (London, 1959), p. 63. **103.** J. Słowacki, *Dzieła Wszystkie* (Wrocław, 1952), vol. I, p. 191. **104.** Alexander Montgomerie, 'To His Maistress', J. MacQueen, T. Scott, eds, *The Oxford Book of Scottish Verse* (Oxford, 1966), no. 73, pp. 236–7. **105.** Henry Stewart, Lord Darnley, 'To the Queen', ibid., no. 69, pp. 232–3.

Eight: Two Isles: Three Kingdoms

1. 'Proclamation of his Majesties titill to the croune of England', *The Register of the Privy Council of Scotland*, D. Masson, ed. (Edinburgh, 1884), vol. VI, pp. 552–3. **2.** J. E. Neale, *Queen Elizabeth I* (London, 1934), p. 390. **3.** G. P. V. Akrigg, ed., *Letters of King James VI and I* (Berkeley, 1985), No. 92, pp. 206–7. **4.** Charles Williams, *James I* (London, 1934), pp. 172–4. **5.** Akrigg, op. cit., Introduction, p. 3. **6.** Francis Watt, *The Book of Edinburgh Anecdotes* (Edinburgh, 1913), p. 115. **7.** See E. Cheetham, *The Prophecies of Nostradamus* (London, 1973), quoted by Norman

Davies, *Europe: a history* (Oxford, 1996), pp. 546–7. **8.** Ibid., *Prophecies* x.39. **9.** From 'The Essayes of a Prentice in the Divine Art of Poesie' in G. G. Smith, ed., *Specimens of Middle Scots* (Edinburgh, 1902), pp. 227–30. **10.** Most of James VI/I's works exist in modern reprints or facsimile editions. See *Basilikon Doron* (Cardiff, 1931): *The True Law of Monarchies* (Toronto, 1996): *Daemonologie, The essays of a prentise . . ., A counter-blast* (Amsterdam, 1969): *The Poems of James VI of Scotland* (Edinburgh, 1955–8): *Minor prose works: including a Declaration of Sports* (Edinburgh, 1982): *Political Works* (Cambridge, Mass., 1918). **11.** G. P. V. Akrigg, op. cit., 'Introduction', p. 3. **12.** *Letters*, nr. 91, op. cit., pp. 204–5. **13.** The full text is in Caroline Binghem, *James VI of Scotland* (London, 1979), Appendix, p. 175. **14.** James VI and I, 'To his son, Prince Henry' (April 1603). The text has been Anglicized and modernized. In G. F. Maine, ed., *A Book of Scotland* (London and Glasgow, 1950), pp. 189–90. **15.** Williams, op. cit., p. 171. **16.** Ibid., p. 176. **17.** B. Galloway, *The Union of England and Scotland 1603–8* (Edinburgh, 1986), p. 8. **18.** *Register of the Council*, op. cit., V, p. 596. **19.** J. P. Sommerville, ed., *King James VI and I: Political Writings* (Cambridge, 1994), p. 135. **20.** Ibid., pp. 136–7. **21.** Ibid., p. 136. **22.** *The Holy Bible Containing the Old and New Testaments translated out of the original tongues, and with the former translations diligently compared and revised by His Majesty's special command . . .* (1611), p. 5. **23.** Antonia Fraser, *The Gunpowder Plot: terror and faith in 1605* (London, 1996) p. 295. **24.** Quoted P. B. Ellis, *Macbeth* (London, 1980). **25.** Quoted in *Encyclopædia Britannica*, XIth Edition, vol. x, p. 458 under 'Flags'. **26.** See Theodore K. Rabb, *Jacobean Gentleman: Sir Edwin Sandys, 1561–1629* (Princeton, 1998). **27.** Quoted by B. Coward, *The Stuart Age* (London, 1994), p. 137. **28.** See M. Merriman, 'James Henrisoun and great Britain: British Union and the Scotish Commonwealth', in R. Mason, ed., *Scotland and England, 1286–1815* (Edinburgh, 1986). **29.** *Political Writings*, op. cit., 31 March 1607, p. 160. **30.** Ibid., p. 161. **31.** Ibid., p. 161. **32.** Ibid. p. 162. **33.** Ibid., p. 178. **34.** D. H. Willson, *King James VI and I* (London, 1956), p. 251. **35.** Galloway, op. cit., p. 175. **36.** For recent studies on early seventeenth-century religious history, see P. O. G. White, *Predestination, policy and polemic* (Cambridge, 1992): L.A. Ferrell, *Government by polemic: the king's preachers and the rhetoric of conformity* (Stanford, 1998): Julian Davies, *The Caroline Captivity of the Church . . . 1625–41* (Oxford, 1992): H. Trevor-Roper, *Archbishop Laud* (Basingstoke, 1988). **37.** See N. Carlin, *The Causes of the English Civil War* (Oxford, 1999): A. Hughes, *The Causes of the English Civil War* (Basingstoke, 1998). **38.** From J. R. Green, *A Short History of the English People* (London, 1892–4). **39.** See C. B. Falls, *The Birth of Ulster* (London, 1936): Lord Hamilton, *The Irish Rebellion of 1641 . . .* (London, 1920): Eamon Phoenix, *Two Acres of Irish History* (Belfast, 1988). **40.** See L. Brockliss, D. Eastwood, *A Union of Multiple Identities, c 1750–c 1850* (Manchester, 1997), especially 'Introduction', pp. 1–8. **41.** See Conrad Russell, *The Origins of the English Civil War* (Basingstoke, 1973); *The Causes of the English Civil War* (Oxford, 1988): 'The British Problem and the English Civil War' in R. Cust, A. Hughes, eds, *The English Civil War* (London, 1997). **42.** Conrad Russell, 'The Emergence of Adversary Politics in the Long Parliament',

in Cust, Hughes, op. cit.   **43.** S. R. Gardiner, *History of the Great Civil War, 1642–49*
(London, 1886–9), vol. I, p. 168.   **44.** Oliver Cromwell, after the Battle of Marston
Moor, 1644, quoted by John Buchan, *Oliver Cromwell* (London, 1934).   **45.** John
Davies, *A History of Wales* (London, 1934), pp. 277–80.   **46.** Charles I, 30 January
1649: Pauline Gregg, *King Charles I*, (London, 1981), p. 444.   **47.** See Tom Reilly,
Cromwell: an Honourable Enemy (Brandon, 1999).   **48.** Ronald Hutton, *The British
Republic, 1649–60* (London, 1990), p. 49.   **49.** 'To the Lord Cromwell, May 1652',
Milton's Sonnets, E. A. J. Honigman, ed., (London, 1966), p. 19. *maw* = stomach,
appetite.   **50.** See 'England', in *Encyclopaedia Judaica* (Jerusalem, 1970); also Victoria
and Albert Museum, *Catalogue of the tercentenary exhibition of Anglo-Jewish Art and
History* (London, 1956).   **51.** Quoted by J. G. Simms, in T. W. Moody, F. X. Martin,
eds, *The Course of Irish History* (Dublin, 1967, 1994).   **52.** J. Swift *Works* (1910), IV,
94, quoted by Simms, op. cit., pp. 205–6.   **53.** John Milton, 'The History of Britain,
that part now call'd England . . .' in *Works* (New York, 1932), vol. xx, pp. 1–325.
54. Michael Lynch, *Scotland: a new History* (London, 1992), pp. 295–6.   **55.** Godden
v. Hales (1686), *English Constitutional Documents, 1558–1783*, C. 256.   **56.** John Morrill,
'The Stuarts', *Oxford History of Britain* (Oxford, 1999), p. 384.   **57.** *House of Lords
Journal* (for 1707), vol. XVIII, p. 272.   **58.** Ibid., XVIII, p. 272.   **59.** Ibid., XVIII,
p. 272.   **60.** Ibid. Bills 2–3   **61.** Ibid. Bills 5–8   **62.** P. H. Stanhope, *A History of
England comprising the Reign of Queen Anne until the Peace of Utrecht, 1701–13* (London,
1870), pp. 279–80.   **63.** *The Journals of the House of Commons, 1705–1708*, vol. XV,
p. 326.   **64.** The document may be examined in the House of Lords Record
Office.   **65.** Queen's Proclamation. *Commons Journal*, op. cit., p. 392.   **66.** Quoted
by Moody and Martin, op. cit., p. 219.   **67.** A. Young, *A Tour of Ireland* (1780), II,
pt 2, pp. 35–6, quoted by Moody and Martin, op. cit., p. 221.   **68.** From 'Holyhead,
Sept. 25, 1727', in T. Kinsella, ed., *The New Oxford Book of Irish Verse* (Oxford, 1986),
pp. 186–7.   **69.** *Danta Diadha Uladh*, E. O'Muirgheasa, eds (Dublin, 1930),
pp. 281–3, quoted by Moody and Martin, op. cit., p. 224.   **70.** NB. The Kingdom
of Great Britain, 1707–1800, though created from the union of England and
Scotland, had not formally adopted the title of 'United Kingdom'.   **71.** T. Carlyle
from *Heroes and Hero-worship* (1838), quoted by Margaret Drabble, ed., *Oxford
Companion to English Literature* (Oxford, 1985), p. 242.   **72.** Antonia Fraser, *Cromwell:
Our Chief of Men* (London, 1973), p. 700.   **73.** Ibid., p. 706.   **74.** From the Earl of
Clarendon, *The History of the Rebellion and Civil Wars in England* (1702–4), vol IV;
quoted in J. R. Hale, *The Evolution of British Historiography* (Cleveland, Ohio, 1964),
pp 140–1   **75.** Prefatory remarks by 'Vindicator' to *A True Account of the Gunpowder
Plot etc* (London, 1851), p. viii.   **76.** Garry Wills, *Witches and Jesuits* (New York,
1995).   **77.** Fraser, op. cit., *passim*.   **78.** Herbert Butterfield, *The Whig Interpretation
of History* (London, 1931), p. 11.   **79.** John Derry, 'Herbert Butterfield', in J. Cannon,
ed., *The Historian at Work* (London, 1980), p. 174.   **80.** J. H. Hexter, 'Storm over
the Gentry', *Re-appraisals in History* (Chicago, 1979), pp. 117–62.   **81.** Edward
Burroughs, quoted by Christopher Hill, *The World Turned Upside Down: Radical
Ideas during the English Revolution* (London, 1972), p. 386. See also C. Hill,

Economic Problems of the Church from Archbishop Whitgift to the Long Parliament (London, 1956): *Society and Puritanism in Pre-Revolutionary England* (London, 1964): and *Intellectual Origins of the English Revolution* (Oxford, 1965). **82.** Thackeray, quoted by W. Speck, 'Thomas Babington Macaulay', in J. Cannon, ed., *The Historian at Work* (London, 1980), pp. 55–69. **83.** T. B. Macaulay, *The History of England* (Everyman, (London, 1911), vol. II, pp. 488–9. **84.** See A. Maurois, *The Three Musketeers: a study of the Dumas Family* (London, 1957); D. Welsh, *Sienkiewicz's Trilogy: a study in novelistic technique* (Rome, 1971). **85.** W. Harrison Ainsworth, *The Lancashire Witches* (London, 1849); R. Neill, *Mist over Pendle* (London, 1951). See also E. Peel, *The Trials of the Lancashire Witches* (Hendon, 1985). **86.** Sir Walter Scott, 'Rokeby', *Poetical Works* (London, 1878), p. 224. **87.** Sir Walter Scott, *A Legend of Montrose* (London, 1901), pp. 1–3. **88.** Ibid., pp. 248–52. **89.** R. D. Blackmore, *Lorna Doone*, Everyman Edition (London, 1911), p. 484ff. **90.** Ibid., p. 464ff. **91.** R. S. Hawker, from *Cornish Ballads* (1869), in W. Henley, ed., *Lyra Heroica* (London, 1920), pp. 169–70. **92.** Walter Scott, 'Bonny Dundee'; his *Poetical Works* (London, 1878) do not include this item, although it figures on a list drawn up by the Scottish Arts Council for a new national anthem for Scotland. <http://www.scot.demon.co.uk/scotfaq/4_2.html> **93.** Macaulay, op. cit., vol. IV, pp. 538–42. **94.** J. R. Green, (1874) quoted by Mackie, op. cit., p. 262. **95.** Robbie Burns, 'A Parcel of Rogues', J. Kinsley, ed., *Poems and Songs* (London, 1969), pp. 511–2. **96.** OLIS (Oxford University libraries' online catalogue, using subject headings from the Library of Congress, Washington, D.C.)

Nine: The Imperial Isles

1. John Keats, 'On First Looking into Chapman's Homer', A. Quiller-Couch, ed., *Oxford Book of English Verse* (Oxford, 1939), nr. 641, p. 759. **2.** W. Marston Acres, *The Bank of England from within, 1694–1900* (London, 1931), p. 9. **3.** W. D. Bowman, *The Story of the Bank of England* (London, 1937), p. 11. **4.** Ibid., p. 35. **5.** Lord Macaulay, *The History of England* (1848), Everyman edn. (London, 1906), vol. IV, p. 466. **6.** Ibid., vol. IV, pp. 469–71. **7.** J. S. Barbour, *A History of William Paterson and the Darien Company* (Edinburgh, 1907), Appendix A, pp. 201ff. **8.** Michael Lynch, *Scotland: a New History* (revised edition: London, 1992), p. 308. **9.** Barbour, op. cit., pp. 253–84. **10.** Macaulay, op. cit., vol. IV, p. 481. **11.** John Prebble, *The Darien Disaster* (London, 1968), p. 196. **12.** Ibid., p. 197. **13.** Ibid., p. 205. **14.** Ibid. **15.** Ibid., p. 206–7. **16.** Ibid., p. 197. **17.** Macaulay, op. cit., p. 489. **18.** *Observator's Trip to Scotland* (1708), quoted by G. M. Trevelyan, *England under Queen Anne*, vol. II, *Ramillies and the Union with Scotland* (London, 1932), pp. 175 . **19.** David Daiches, ed., *Andrew Fletcher of Saltoun: Selected Political Writings and Speeches* (Edinburgh, 1979), pp. 70–72: quoted in P. H. Scott, *Scotland, an unwon cause: an Anthology with a Commentary* (Edinburgh, 1997), pp. 38–40. **20.** Daiches, op. cit., pp. 74–5; Scott, op. cit., pp. 41–2. **21.** P. H. Scott, *Andrew Fletcher and the Treaty of Union*

(Edinburgh, 1992), pp. 230–31. **22.** Stuart's Amendment, ibid., p. 232. **23.** Daniel Defoe, quoted by P. H. Scott, op. cit., p. 44. **24.** Prebble, op. cit., p. 8. **25.** Ibid., p. 9. **26.** Ibid., pp. 9–10. **27.** William Ferguson, *The Identity of the Scottish Nation: an Historic Quest* (Edinburgh, 1998), 'The Dawn of Enlightenment', pp. 173–95. **28.** Andrew Fletcher, *An Account of a Conversation Concerning a Right Regulation of Government for the Common Good of Mankind* (Edinburgh, 1704), in P. H. Scott, *Scotland*, op. cit., pp. 44–51. **29.** Ibid., pp. 45, 51. **30.** Ibid., p. 49. **31.** Lynch, op. cit., p. 312. **32.** Ibid. **33.** Address from the Convention of Royal Birghs (1706), in P. H. Scott, op. cit., pp. 56–7. **34.** 'Sir John Clerk's observations on the present circumstances in Scotland' (1730), quoted by Lynch, op. cit., p 312. **35.** Trevelyan, op. cit., vol. II, p. 285. **36.** Ibid. **37.** Sir George Carnwarth, *Memoirs* (1830), quoted by Lynch, op. cit., p. 312. **38.** Daniel Defoe, *Union and no Union* (1713). Lynch, ibid. **39.** Lynch, ibid. **40.** Macaulay, op. cit., vol. IV, p. 302. **41.** See J. R. Hill ed., *The Oxford Illustrated History of the Royal Navy* (Oxford, 1995), p. 697. **42.** N. A. M. Rodger, *The Safeguard of the Sea. Volume One, 660–1649* (London, 1997), pp. 209–10. **43.** N. A. M. Rodger, 'The Development of Broadside Gunnery, 1450–1650', *Mariner's Mirror*, Vol. 82, No. 3, August 1996, p. 303. **44.** Ibid., pp. 307, 309. **45.** J. S. Corbett, ed., *Fighting Instructions 1530–1816* (London, 1903), pp. 99–104. **46.** Rodger, *The Safeguard of the Sea*, op. cit., p 237. **47.** Ibid., p. 370. **48.** Norman Longmate, *Island Fortress: The Defence of Great Britain, 1603–1945* (London, 1991), p. 11. **49.** Rodger, *The Safeguard of the Sea*, op. cit., p. 388. **50.** See Dava Sobel, *Longitude* (London, 1996). **51.** 'Rule, Britannia!', James Thompson, 1740: John Masefield, 'Sea Fever' from 'Salt-water Ballads', *Collected Poems* (London, 1927), pp. 27–8. **52.** 'The British Grenadiers', from *The Oxford Song Book*. **53.** J. Prebble, *Mutiny: Highland Regiments in Revolt, 1743–1804* (London, 1975). **54.** Alan Clark, *The Donkeys (1961)* (London, 1961). **55.** From Theatre Workshop, *Oh! What a lovely war* (London, 1976). **56.** Rudyard Kipling, from 'Cells', 'Tommy' and 'Mandalay' in *Barrack-room Ballads and Other Verses* (1892), in C. Carrington, ed., *The Complete Barrack-room Ballads of Rudyard Kipling* (London, 1973), 37, 31–33, 64–66. **57.** J. M. & M. J. Cohen, *The Penguin Dictionary of Quotations*, p. 175. **58.** See Denis Judd, *Radical Joe: a Life of Joseph Chamberlain*, (Cardiff, 1993): also J. Enoch Powell, *Joseph Chamberlain*, (London, 1977). **59.** Revd R. J. Ellerton, *Hymns Ancient and Modern* (London, 1940), no. 477, p. 410. **60.** William J. Williams, *The Church Hymnary* (London, 1898), no. 295, p. 382. **61.** J. Davies, op. cit., p. 39. **62.** See I. T. Kerr, *John Henry Newman: a biography* (Oxford, 1990). **63.** P. M. H. Bell, *Disestablishment in Ireland and Wales* (London, 1963). **64.** *Hutchinson Multimedia Encyclopedia*, V. EB Micropedia IX. **65.** Sir Lewis Namier, *England in the Age of the American Revolution* (London, 1930), Chapter II. See also his *The Structure of Politics at the Accession of George III* (London, 1929). **66.** On Wilkes's Scottophobia, see Linda Colley, *Britons: Forging the Nation, 1707–1837* (New Haven, 1992), pp. 113–17, 120–21. **67.** Ibid., p. 110. **68.** Ibid., p. 162. **69.** B. and A. P. Burke, 'Key to Relative Precedence', in E. M. Swinhoe, ed., *A Genealogical and Heraldic History of the Peerage . . .* 93rd Edition (London, 1935), pp. xxi–xci. **70.** W. Lecky, *A History of*

England (London, 1878), vol. I, p. 182.   **71.** Speech at Newcastle, 9 October 1909.
72. J. R. Western, *Monarchy and Revolution: The English State in the 1680s* (London,
1972), p. 283.   **73.** 'The Skye Boat Song', *Oxford Song Book*, op. cit.   **74.** *Oxford
Dictionary of Twentieth Century Quotations* (Oxford, 1998), p. 126.   **75.** See W.
Griffith, *The British Civil Service, 1854–1954* (London, 1954).   **76.** John Prebble, *The
Highland Clearances* (London, 1963), p. 304.   **77.** From Lady Wilde, 'The Exodus',
in C. Morash, ed., *The Hungry Voice: the Poetry of the Irish Famine* (Dublin, 1989),
p. 219.   **78.** See E. Hobsbawm, *The Age of Capital, 1848–75* (London, 1997).   **79.** K.
O. Morgan, *Keir Hardie: radical and socialist* (London, 1975).   **80.** Norman Angell,
*The Great Illusion: a Study of the Relation of Military Power in Nations to their
Economic and Social Advantage* (London, 1910): see also his *Fruits of Victory* (1921)
and *The Defence of the Empire* (1937).   **81.** Sam Vaknin, 'A History of Previous
European Currency Unions', <http://www.geocities.com/Athens/Forum/6297/
nm032.html>.   **82.** B. R. Mitchell, ed., *British Historical Statistics* (Cambridge,
1988), pp. 702–3.   **83.** J. Gardiner, N. Wenborn, eds, *The History Today Companion
to British History* (London, 1995), 'Population', pp. 610–11.   **84.** A. Hammerton, ed.,
Harmsworth's Universal Encyclopaedia (n.d. c. 1930), 'Population and the Census',
p. 6526ff.   **85.** *Encyclopædia Britannica* (XIth edition), 'United States of America'.
86. Ibid., p. 6257.   **87.** *Enclyclopædia Britannica* (XIth Edition), vol. XVIII, p. 432.
88. Ibid.   **89.** Ibid.   **90.** Ibid.   **91.** S. J. Connolly, ed., *Oxford Companion to Irish
History* (Oxford, 1998), p. 170.   **92.** Connolly, ibid., p. 170.   **93.** Various sources,
esp. B. R. Mitchell, op. cit., pp. 11–13.   **94.** Harmsworth's *Universal Encyclopedia*,
op. cit.   **95.** S. Johnson, *A Journey to the Western Islands of Scotland* (1775), reprinted
(New Haven, 1971).   **96.** See A. H. Reddick, *The Making of Johnson's Dictionary
1746–1773* (Cambridge, 1990).   **97.** See G. Clingham, *New Light on Boswell: critical
and historical essays* (Cambridge, 1991).   **98.** Matthew Arnold, 'The Irish University
Question' (1879), in *English Literature and Irish Politics* (Ann Arbor, 1973), pp. 56–60.
99. J. C. W. Reith, *Broadcast Over Britain* (London, 1924). pp. 51–2.   **100.** Asa
Briggs, *The History of Broadcasting in the United Kingdom. Volume 1. The Birth of
Broadcasting, 1896–1927* (Oxford, 1995), p. 222.   **101.** Ibid., p. 222.   **102.** G. S.
Woodward, *Pocahontas* (Normal, Oklahoma, 1969).   **103.** Rajeev Syal, 'Dr John-
son's black servant "proved to be my ancestor"', *Sunday Times*, 1999; see also
'Revealed: the Queen's black ancestors', ibid., 6 June 1999.   **104.** 'How Sweet
the Name', *Church Hymnary*, op. cit., nr. 201.   **105.** See <http://www.tch.
simplenet.com.bio/n/jnewton.htm>.   **106.** See E. Lascelles, *Granville Sharpe
and the freedom of slaves in England* (Oxford, 1928).   **107.** See T. O. Ranger, *Rhodes,
Oxford and the study of Race Relations* (Oxford, 1987).   **108.** See G. Jarvie, *Sport
in the Making of Celtic Cultures* (London, 199).   **109.** See G. Cousins, *Golf in
Britain: a social history* (London, 1973).   **110.** See T. Bailey, *A History of Cricket*
(London, 1979): P. Wynne-Thomas, *The History of Cricket* (Norwich, 1989).
111. From Mark Whittaker, 'Game of Empire', BBC Radio 4, 20 May, 1999.
112. By acknowlegement of the Marylebone Cricket Club.   **113.** Attributed to Lord
Tebbit.   **114.** See E. B. Noel, *A History of Tennis* (London, 1991).   **115.** See J.

Walvin, *The People's Game: the history of football revisited* (Edinburgh, 1994). **116.** Sir Henry Newbolt, 'Vitai Lampada (They Pass on the Torch of Life)'. **117.** D. M. Walker ed., *The Oxford Companion to Law* (Oxford, 1980), p. 1250. **118.** Ibid., p. 251. **119.** Charles Dickens, *Pickwick Papers*, Oxford Illustrated Dickens (Oxford, 1948), p. 464. **120.** Ibid., pp. 487–8. **121.** *Encyclopædia Britannica* (XIth edition), 'Education'. **122.** 'Here's a health' *Oxford Song Book*, op. cit. **123.** 'God Save Our Gracious King' (c. 1745). The original version contained a stanza, since dropped: 'God grant that Marshal Wade / May by thy mighty aid, / Victory bring; / May he sedition hush / And like a torrent rush / Rebellious Scots to crush. / God Save the' King!' **124.** *University of Oxford Examination Decrees and Regulations*: Faculty of Modern History (Oxford, 1958). **125.** Lord Curzon to the Earl of Selborne, 9 IX 1900, D. G. Boyce, ed., *The Crisis of British Power . . . 1895–1910* (London, 1990), nr. 60. **126.** See D. H. Burton, *Cecil Spring Rice: a diplomat's life* (London, 1990). **127.** Music hall song by G. W. Hunt (1878): *Concise Oxford Dictionary of Quotations* (Oxford, 1964), p. 112. **128.** J. Y. T. Greig, ed., *The Letters of David Hume* (Oxford, 1932), quoted by Hugh Trevor-Roper, *From Counter-Reformation to Glorious Revolution* (London, 1992), p. 265. **129.** Hugh Trevor-Roper, 'Our First Whig Historian', ibid., pp. 249–65. **130.** Edwin Jones, *The English Nation: the Great Myth* (Stroud, 1998), p. 88. **131.** Quoted by Edwin Jones, ibid., p. 152. **132.** Hume, *History of England*, op. cit. **133.** Colley, *Britons*, op. cit., 'Jerusalem the Golden', p. 30ff. **134.** Ibid., pp. 53–4. **135.** William Blake, 'Jerusalem', quoted ibid., p. 50. **136.** Walter Scott, 'A Total Surrender of Independence', from *Tales of a Grandfather*, quoted by P. H. Scott, op. cit., pp. 62–4. **137.** Walter Scott, *Waverley* (n.d.), p. 552. **138.** Lord Macaulay, quoted by H. Trevor-Roper in T. Ranger, E. Hobsbawm, eds, *The Invention of Tradition*, (London, 1983). **139.** R. L. Stevenson, from 'The Foreigner at Home' (1887), quoted by P. H. Scott, op. cit., p. 74–5. **140.** R. L. Stevenson, *Kidnapped* (1886). **141.** Colin Kidd, op. cit., p. 280. **142.** C. R. L. Fletcher, op. cit., p. 181. **143.** Ibid., pp. 226–7. **144.** Quoted by Ernest Barker, *Ireland in the Last Fifty Years (1866–1916)* (Oxford, 1917). (Sir Ernest Barker (1874–1960) was later the first Professor of Political Science at Cambridge.) **145.** Ibid., p. 97. **146.** Ibid., p. 108. **147.** Mary Kingsley, 1897: quoted by Simon Gikandi, *Maps of Englishness: Writing Identity in the Culture of Colonialism* (New York, 1996), p. 143. **148.** Ibid., pp. 125–43. **149.** See Apsley Cherry-Garrard, *The Worst Journey in the World* (London, 1994): A. Moorehead, *Cooper's Creek* (London, 1961). **150.** J. Hunt, *The Ascent of Everest* (London, 1953): H. Harrer, *Seven Years in Tibet* (London, 1953). **151.** C. Darwin, *The Voyage of the Beagle* (Penguin, London, 1989). **152.** Edward Lear, 'The Akond of Swat', *Nonsense Songs and Stories* (London, 1894), pp. 84–6. **153.** Kipling, 'Recessional', in *Definitive Verse* (London, 1940): published in *The Times*, 17 July 1897. **154.** Kipling, ibid.: published in *The Times*, 4 February, 1899. **155.** 'If—', ibid., published in *The Times*, 4 February 1899. **156.** See C. S. Forester, *The Hornblower Companion* (London, 1964). **157.** R. Kipling, *Kim*, Centenary Edition (London, 1981), p. 1. **158.** Angus Wilson, 'Introduction' to *Kim*, ibid., p. v. **159.** Ibid., pp. 6–8. **160.** J. Baines, *Joseph Conrad: a critical* *biography* (London, 1960): Z. Najder, *Conrad: a chronicle* (London, 1983). **161.** From 'Heart of Darkness' (1908) in J. Conrad, *Youth, Heart of Darkness, The End of the Tether* (London, 1974), pp. 46–7. **162.** 'From Greenland's Icy Mountains', *The Church Hymnary*, op. cit., nr. 441. **163.** Winston Churchill, *My Early Life: a Roving Commission* (London, 1930), pp. 200ff. **164.** Sir J. R. Seeley, *The Expansion of England* (London, 1914), p. 78. **165.** Ibid., p. 272. **166.** Ibid., p. 81. **167.** Ibid., p. 11. **168.** Ibid., p. 14–15. **170.** Ibid., pp. 343–44, 354. **170.** William Wordsworth, quoted by Seeley, ibid. **171.** Rudyard Kipling, 'The Glory of the Garden', *Definitive Verse*, op. cit. **172.** Noël Coward, *The Lyrics* (London, 1983), pp. 122–3.

Ten: The Post-Imperial Isles

1. *The Times*, 23 June 1911. **2.** *The Times of India*, 22 June 1911. **3.** *The Annual Register for 1911* (London, 1912), pp. 145–6. **4.** Ibid., pp. 146–7. **5.** Ibid., pp. 148. **6.** *Illustrated London News*, 24 June 1911. **7.** *Annual Register*, op. cit., p. 149. **8.** Ibid., p. 148. **9.** *The Times*, 23 June 1911. **10.** Ibid. **11.** Ibid. **12.** Annual Register, op. cit., p. 144. **13.** Ibid., p. 145. **14.** Lord Salisbury, quoted by David Cannadine, in E. Hobsbawm, T. Ranger, eds, *The Invention of Tradition* (Cambridge, 1983). **15.** Lord Lytton, ibid. **16.** *Illustrated London News*, 26 June 1987. **17.** A. C. Benson, 'Land of Hope and Glory'. **18.** *Illustrated London News*, 6 January 1912. **19.** *Times of India*, December 1911. **20.** Norman Davies, *Europe: a history* (Oxford, 1996), p. 897. **21.** *Illustrated London News*, 31 July 1909. **22.** Speech to House of Commons, 10 November 1932. **23.** Speech to House of Commons, 30 July 1934. **24.** 'British Defence Spending', B. R. Mitchell, ed., *British Historical Statistics* (Cambridge, 1998). **25.** 'Defence' in *Britain 1999*, Office for National Statistics (London, 1998), pp. 96–104. **26.** Rupert Brooke, from 'The Old Vicarage, Grantchester', *The Collected Poems with a Memoir* (London, 1942), p. 97. **27.** From 'The Soldier', ibid., p. 150. **28.** See J. Garliński, *Intercept: the Enigma War* (London, 1979). **29.** See F. H. Hinsley, *Codebreaker: the inside story of Bletchley Park* (Oxford, 1993). **30.** I. C. B. Dear, M. R. D. Foot, eds, *The Oxford Companion to the Second World War* (Oxford, 1995): also HMSO, *Britain 1999* (Oxford, 1998). **31.** *Oxford Dictionary of Twentieth Century Quotations*, op. cit., p. 68. **32.** See Max Hastings, Simon Jenkins, *The Battle for the Falklands* (London, 1997). **33.** At <http://www.mod.uk/policy/sdr/index.htm>. **34.** 'Defence' in *Britain 1999*, op. cit. **35.** J. K. Zawodny, *Death in the Forest: the story of Katyn Forest Massacre* (London, 1971). The Soviet President Mikhail Gorbachev admitted in 1990 to Soviet guilt for the crime. On the War Crimes Act (1991) see 'An Act to confer jurisdiction ... in respect of ... violations of the laws ... of war committed in German-held territory ...', at <http://www.hmso.gov.uk/acts/summary/01991013.htm>. **36.** Jan Smuts, May 1917, quoted by Paul Kennedy, *Strategy and Diplomacy* (London, 1983), p. 209. **37.** Paul Kennedy, ibid., p. 207. **38.** George Orwell, 'The Road to Wigan Pier', in *The Penguin Complete Longer Non-fiction of George Orwell* (London,

1983), pp. 139–40. **39.** B. Porter, *The Lion's Share* (London, 1975), pp. 353–4, quoted by Kennedy, op. cit. **40.** P. Kennedy, 'Why did the Empire last so long?', ibid., pp. 199–219. **41.** Quoted by P. J. Marshall, 'Imperial Britain,' *JICH*, vol. XXII (1994), nr. 3, p. 385. **42.** Ibid. **43.** *Oxford Book of Twentieth Century Quotations*, op. cit., p. 246: and quoted by Conor Cruise O'Brien in *Ancestral Voices* (Dublin, 1994). **44.** Gerry Adams, *Before the Dawn: an Autobiography* (London, 1996), p. 74. **45.** W. B. Yeats, 'Easter 1916' (1921). **46.** See R. E. Foster, 'The De Valera Dispensation', *Modern Ireland, 1600–1972* (London, 1988), pp. 536–68. **47.** See J. Reinharz, *Chaim Weizman: the making of a statesman* (Oxford, 1993). **48.** Wavell, quoted by Wm Roger Louis, 'The Dissolution of Empire', *The Oxford History of the British Empire* (Oxford, 1999), vol. IV, *The Twentieth Century*, p. 5. **49.** Churchill, ibid., p. 11. **50.** Sir Charles Johnston, Governor of Aden, ibid., p. 17. **51.** John Russell, H.M. Ambassador in Addis Ababa, ibid., p. 23. **52.** E.g. Edward Said, *Culture and Imperialism* (London, 1993). **53.** P. J. Marshall, op. cit., p. 384. **54.** Chris Patten, speech in Oxford, 1 July 1999. **55.** See C. O. Ogilvie, *Cut the connection: disestablishment and the Church of England* (London, 1994). **56.** Clive Carpenter, ed., *The Guinness European Data Book* (London, 1994), p. 81. **57.** Field Marshal Lord Carver, *Britain's Army in the Twentieth Century* (London: 1998), p. 22. **58.** War Office memorandum, 23 March 1914, quoted in ibid., p. 24. **59.** Lord Fitt (Gerry Fitt), former leader of the SDLP, in *The Times*, 4 August 1994. **60.** At <http://www.represent.org.uk/democ/report.html>. **61.** Donald Shell, *The House of Lords* (London, 1992), p. 10–13. **62.** Auslan Cramb, *Who owns Scotland now? The use and abuse of private land* (Edinburgh, 1966). **63.** Dominic Hobson, *The National Wealth* (to be published: extracted as 'Dynasty: How the Aristocracy is making a fortune', *Sunday Times*, 1 August 1999). **64.** The Treaty of Union (1707), clause II, P. H. Scott, op. cit., p. 202. **65.** See Alison Weir, *Britain's Royal Families: the complete genealogy* (London, 1996). **66.** Private correspondence. **67.** Graham Turner, 'The Real Queen Mother', *Daily Telegraph*, 7 July, 1999. **68.** *Guardian*, 8 September 1997. **69.** Elton John, 'Candle in the Wind', revised version, 1997, original version, 'Goodbye, Norma Jean . . .' (1973). **70.** 'Brown Slashes Queen's Pay Rise', *Sunday Times*, 6 September 1998. **71.** 'A History of Britain in 48 stamps: Monarchy is ignored . . .', *The Times*, 13 November 1998. **72.** Peter Hitchens, 'The Queen of Cool', *Spectator*, 2 May 1998. **73.** 'Prince Denies Plea to Abdicate', *The Times*, 9 November 1998. **74.** Turner, op. cit. **75.** Sue Townsend, *The Queen and I* (London, 1992), pp. 18–25. **76.** Eugène Ionescu, *The Killer* (London, 1958). **77.** *British Historical Statistics*, op. cit., Chapter II, passim. **78.** The Civil Service Code (1999), issued by the Cabinet Office, Central Secretariat, Horse Guards Parade, London SWIP 3AL. **79.** Ibid., Footnote 1. **80.** BBC, 'Minutes of Yes Minister Season 1 Episodes': <http://www.yesminister.demon.nl/ymseas1.htm>. **81.** Peter Wright, *Spycatcher: the candid autobiography of a British intelligence officer* (Sydney, 1987). **82.** Christopher Andrew, 'The KGB's most valuable female spy', *The Times*, 11 September 1999: see his *KGB: The inside story of its foreign operations from Lenin to Gorbachev* (New York, 1991). **83.** From C.

H. Sisson, *The London Zoo* (London, 1961).   **84.** Notably, the 'Shaylergate' website of ex-MI5 agent, David Shayler.   **85.** See Dominic Hobson, 'Loot: Why are the British so greedy?', *Sunday Times*, 25 July 1999: extracts from *The National Wealth* (London, 1999).   **86.** Industrial Production: Total industry (excluding construction, 1995 = 100; Eurostat Press Office, May 1999.   **87.** GDP per capita in PPS GDP per capita in ECU. Ibid.   **88.** Ibid.   **89.** After Charles Feinstein, 'The End of Empire and the Golden Age,' in P. Clarke, C. Trebilcock, eds, *Understanding Decline: perceptions and realities of British economic performance. Essays presented to Barry Supple* (Cambridge, 1997), p. 229.   **90.** Ibid., p. 215.   **91.** See Norman Davies, *Europe*, op. cit., pp. 1080–82.   **92.** '£10 billion: the true cost of Independence', *Scotland on Sunday*, 25 April 1999.   **93.** J. M. Keynes, *General Theory* (1947 edition): see also R. J. A. Skidelsky, *John Maynard Keynes: a biography* (London, 1983–92), 2 vols.   **94.** Quoted by A. J. P. Taylor, *English History, 1914–45* (Oxford, 1965).   **95.** See Hugo Young, *The Iron Lady: a biography of Margaret Thatcher* (London, 1989).   **96.** See George Soros: *Soros on Soros: staying ahead of the curve* (New York, 1995).   **97.** *British Historical Statistics*, op. cit., p. 9ff: *Britain 1999*, op. cit.: *History Today Companion to British History*, op. cit., under 'Population'.   **98.** Ibid.: for Ireland, see <http://aoife.indigo.ie/'cronews/census>.   **99.** *B.H.S.*, op. cit.   **100.** *B.H.S.*, op. cit.   **101.** *B.H.S.*, op. cit., p. 40ff.   **102.** Ibid., p. 52ff.   **103.** Ibid., p. 81ff.   **104.** English Speaking Union, Dartmouth House, London WiX 8AB. Information Service.   **104.** Gydliad Cenedlaethol Cymru-America (National Welsh-American Foundation), <http://www.wales-usa.org/>.   **106.** M. McCormack, 'The Ancient Order of Hibernians,' <http://www.aoh.com/history/main.htm>.   **107.** *B.H.S.*, op. cit., pp. 38–9.   **108.** R. R. Davies, 'Language and Historical Mythology', *TRHS* (Sixth Series), vol. VII (1997), p. 15.   **109.** R. J. W. Evans, *The Language of History and the History of Language: an Inaugural Lecture . . . 11 May 1998* (Oxford, 1998).   **110.** See Richard J. Evans, *In Defence of History* (London, 1997).   **111.** Dafydd Johnston, *The Literature of Wales* (Cardiff, 1994): see also M. Wynn Thomas, *Corresponding Cultures: the two literatures of Wales* (Cardiff, 1999).   **112.** Johnson, op. cit., p. 137.   **113.** Ibid., p. 130.   **114.** Dylan Thomas, *Under Milk Wood: a play for voices* (London, 1954), p. 1.   **115.** From R. S. Thomas, 'Reservoirs', Johnston, op. cit., p. 124: see also Tony Conran, 'The new frontier: R. S. Thomas', in Tony Conran, *Frontiers in Anglo-Welsh Poetry* (Cardiff, 1997).   **116.** J. E. and G. W. Dunleavy, *Douglas Hyde: a maker of Modern Ireland* (Oxford, 1991).   **117.** Vivien Mercier, *Modern Irish Literature: Sources and Founders* (Oxford, 1994), p. 95.   **118.** Ibid., p. 96.   **119.** Ibid., pp. 98–9.   **120.** Quoted by V. Mercier, 'W. B. Yeats: Master Craftsman', op. cit., pp. 158.   **121.** See Roy Foster, *W. B. Yeats: a life*, vol. I (Oxford, 1997).   **122.** James Joyce, *Ulysses*, First Unlimited Edition (London, 1937), pp. 27–33.   **123.** John Buchan, *Hansard*, vol. 272, 24 November 1932, quoted by P. H. Scott, *Scotland: an unwon cause* (Edinburgh, 1997), pp. 131–4.   **124.** From 'Talking to Five Thousand People in Edinburgh' (1972), *Oxford Dictionary of Twentieth Century Quotations*, op. cit., p. 198.   **125.** H. MacDiarmid, *Letters*, ed. A. Bold (London, 1984), p. 873.   **126.** H. MacDiarmid, *A Drunk Man Looks at the Thistle*

(1926) (Edinburgh, 1987), quoted by P. H. Scott, op. cit., pp. 136–7. **127.** Tom Nairn, *The Break-up of Britain* (London, 1977), pp. 152–7. **128.** *Scottish Gaelic – a Brief History*, <http://www.dalriada.co.uk/scotland.htm>, (unsigned). **129.** Iain Crichton Smith, quoted by Derick S. Thomson, 'Poetry in Scottish Gaelic, 1945–92', *Poetry in the British Isles: Non-metropolitan perspectives*, H.-W. Ludwig, L. Fietz, eds. (Cardiff, 1995), p. 162. **130.** Edin Chirgwin (1892–1960), quoted by D. Annear, 'The Modern Revival' (1998), Cornish Language Centre, <http://home-pages.newnet.co.uk/lindamarriott/kernewek/revival.html>. **131.** R. J. W. Evans, op. cit., p. 22. **132.** The Manx Gaelic Society, Yn Cheshaght Ghailckagh, founded in 1899, was at hand. **133.** S. Laville, 'Scouse accent sinking into the estuary, says academic', *Daily Telegraph*, 1 June 1999. **134.** R. Crawford, ed., *The Scottish Invention of English Literature* (Cambridge, 1998). **135.** *Encarta World English Dictionary* (1999): <http://www.worldenglishdictionary.com/>. **136.** 'Language "snub" infuriates Berlin', *Guardian*, 2 July 1999; Roger Boyes, 'Germans fight attempt to finish EU label', *Times*, 27 July 1999. **137.** William Rubinstein, 'The Secret of Leopold Amery', *History Today* (February 1999), pp. 17–23. **138.** Quoted on the official website of the Commission for Racial Equality (1999), <http://www.cre.gov.uk>. **139.** See K. Sword, J. Ciechanowski, N. Davies, *The Formation of the Polish Community in Great Britain, 1939–49* (London, 1985). **140.** L. E. Snellgrove, *The Modern World Since 1870* (London, 1968), and C. F. Strong, *The Story of the Twentieth Century* (London, 1966), quoted by Dr Athena Syriatou, 'Treacherous and unreliable: Race and ethnicity in British history books in the twentieth century', paper presented to the 68th Anglo-American Conference of Historians, Institute of Historical Research, London, 1 July 1999. **141.** Enoch Powell, in *Oxford Dictionary of Twentieth Century Quotations*, op. cit., p. 255. **142.** CRE Web site, op. cit. **143.** Ibid. **144.** W. Macpherson, *The Stephen Lawrence Report*, HMSO (London, 1999). **145.** CRE Web site, op. cit. **146.** Louise Bennett, in *Jamaica Labrish* (1966), quoted by Susheila Nasta in A. Robert Lee, *Other Britain, Other British* (London, 1995), p. 48. **147.** Hanif Kureishi, quoted by A. Robert Lee, ibid., p. 77. **148.** Neville Cardus, *Autobiography* (London, 1947), p. 201. **149.** Jack Cox: *Don Davies, 'Old International'* (London, 1962). **150.** Bill Shankly, of Liverpool FC, in *Sunday Times*, 4 October 1981. **151.** *Encyclopædia Britannica* (XVth Edition), Micropaedia (1998). **152.** Eddie Jordan, *Irish Times*, 5 July 1999. **153.** Sport England Website: <http://www.english.sports.gov.uk>. **154.** See D. M. Walker, ed., *The Oxford Companion to Law* (Oxford 1980), under 'United Kingdom'. **155.** Norman Davies, *Europe: a history*, op. cit. pp. 1048–55. **156.** Rieko Karataini, *Defining British Citizenship, 1980–81*, D.Phil. thesis in International Relations, Oxford University 1999, unpublished. **157.** 'Outposts of Empire regain Citizenship', *The Times*, 10 September 1998. **158.** Nigel Corrigan, 'The 10,000-year-old inch,' *The Dozenal Journal*, nr. 8: published on the Internet at <http://www.shaunf.dircon.co.uk/shaun/metrology/inch.html> (1999). **159.** British Weights and Measures Association, 'Statement of Views and aims', <http://users.aol.com/footrule/index.html> (1999). **160.** R. Carnahan, *Daily Telegraph* letters, 7 July 1999; Sir John

Herschel, letter to *The Times* 30 April 1869: <http://www.users.zetnet.co.uk/estatopia/inch3.htm>. **161.** See A. Morton; *Diana: her true story* (London, 1992); J. Dimbleby, *The Prince of Wales: a biography* (London, 1994); Anna Pasternak, *Princes in Love* (London, 1996). **162.** Will Self, 'Bigoted, snobbish, profligate'; Profile: The Queen Mother, *Independent on Sunday*, 8 August 1999. **163.** G. Wheatcroft, 'As Britain Breaks Up, let's stand up for Englishness', *Sunday Telegraph*, 18 April 1999: 'Top Tories call for English Parliament,' *Sunday Times*, 4 October 1998. **164.** Patten Report on Policing in Northern Ireland, September 1999. **165.** Peregrine Worsthorne, 'Land of Concrete and Wapping Lies, I Love You No More,' *Spectator*, 20 February 1999, p. 34. **166.** See Alistair Horne, *Macmillan* (London, 1988–9), 2 vols.; Douglas Hurd, *The Search for Peace* (London, 1997). **167.** See J. Rex, *The Ghetto and the Underclass* (Aldershot, 1988). **168.** See N. Malcolm, *Kosovo: a short history* (London, 1998): Amnesty International, *Kosovo: after tragedy, justice?* (London, 1999). **169.** Peter Hitchens, *The Abolition of Britain from Lady Chatterley to Tony Blair* (London, 1999). **170.** Ibid., p. 297. **171.** Field Marshal Lord Carver, op. cit., p. 130. **172.** T. B. Macaulay, *Critical and Historical Essays* (London, 1862), vol. III, p. 101. **173.** John Redwood, *The Death of Britain?* (London, 1999). **174.** A. F. Pollard, *The History of England: its political evolution* (Oxford, 1912); W. E. Lunt, *History of England* (New York, 1928); S. Chrimes, *A Constitutional History of England* (Oxford, 1948); Keigh Feiling, *A History of England* (London, 1950); Arthur Bryant, *The Story of England* (London, 1961); Sir G. Clark, *English History: a survey* (Oxford, 1971). **175.** Clark, op. cit., p. v. **176.** Arnold Toynbee, *A Study of History*, Vol. I (London, 1931), p. 17. **177.** Ibid., p. 21. **178.** Élie Halévy, *A History of England in the Nineteenth Century*, vol. I (London, 1961), p. xii. **179.** Ibid., p. 591. **180.** G. M. Trevelyan, *History of England* (London, 1952), p. 482. **181.** Ibid., p. xix. **182.** Dr Alexander Murray, Letter to *The Times*, July 1999. **183.** Quoted by Dr Athena Syriatou, *Educational Policy and Educational Content: the Teaching of European History in Secondary Schools in England and Wales, 1945–75*, Ph.D. Thesis, University College (London, 1997). **184.** Ibid., p. 201. **185.** E. H. Dance, *History the Betrayer: a study in bias* (London, 1960). **186.** 'Oxford graduates have degree of ignorance about history', *Sunday Telegraph*, 27 October 1998. **187.** 'Kings, Dates, Battles – they are all history in the new curriculum', *Daily Telegraph*, 3 August 1999. **188.** Nick Tate (Qualifications and Curriculum Authority, ibid. **189.** J. G. A. Pocock, 'The Limits and Division of British History', Centre for the Study of Public Policy, Paper nr. 31 (Strathclyde, 1979): other versions in *New Zealand Journal of History* 8 (1) 1972; *Journal of Modern History*, 47 (4), 1975: *American History Review*, 87, 1982. **190.** Ibid. (1972), passim. **191.** English Heritage (1999): <http://www.english-heritage.org.uk/>. **192.** Museum of Scotland, <http://www.nms.ac.uk>. **193.** George Orwell, *The Lion and the Unicorn: Socialism and the English Genius* (London, 1941), passim. **194.** Ibid., p. 126. **195.** Jeremy Black, *History Today* (March 1998). **196.** A. S. Byatt, *Oxford Book of English Short Stories* (Oxford, 1998): also 'What it means to be English', *The Times*, 6 April 1998. **197.** Jeremy Paxman, *The English* (London, 1998): also 'The English', extracts *Sunday Times*, 27 September

1998.   **198.** Quoted by Paxman, 'The Land of Lost Content', *Sunday Times*, 4 October 1998.   **199.** J. Betjeman, from 'How to get on in society' (1954). **200.** Paxman, 'What it means to be English', op. cit.   **201.** Dominic Hobson, *The National Wealth*, op. cit.: extracts in *The Sunday Times*, 1 August 1999.   **202.** ' "Cool" Britain still feels it is in decline', *Sunday Times*, 17 May 1998.   **203.** Hugo Young, *This Blessed Plot: Britain and Europe from Churchill to Blair* (London, 1998), p. 491. **204.** 'BA to fly the flag again and ditch ethnic tailfins', *Sunday Times*, 23 May 1999. **205.** *The Changing UK*, BBC, March 1999.   **206.** P. Scott, *Knowledge and Nation* (Edinburgh, 1990), p. 169.   **207.** John Cannon, ed., *Oxford Companion to British History* (Oxford, 1997), preface p. vii.   **208.** See note 163.   **209.** Peregrine Worsthorne, 'England, don't arise', 19 September 1998.   **210.** 'Top Tories Call for English Parliament', *Sunday Times*, 4 October 1998.   **211.** Conrad Black, *Britain's Final Choice: Europe or America* (London, 1998).   **212.** William Rees-Mogg, 'How the West is One', 'The Atlantic option is better suited to British interests and character', *The Times*, 26 July 1999.   **213.** Margaret Thatcher, *Sunday Telegraph*, 11 July 1999.   **214.** Hugo Young, op. cit., p. 515.   **215.** Norman Davies, *Europe: a history* op. cit., p. 1268.   **216.** Ibid., p. 1075.   **217.** Bill Bryson, *Notes From a Small Island* (London, 1995), pp. 351–2.   **218.** Ibid., p. 46.

Notes to Illustrations

Section One   **1.** The Isles; satellite image of Great Britain and Ireland. *Photo: PLI/ Science Photo Library, London.*   **2–17:** *Artwork for flags copyright Raymond Turvey* **2.** St Andrew, an early Christian martyr, was first linked to Scotland when a relic of his was brought to Mucross (now St Andrews) in the ninth century. He was depicted in art as an old man holding a Gospel and leaning on the transverse cross on which he was martyred. The white saltire on a blue field is traditionally said to have been adopted by the Kings of the Scots after their victory over the Anglo-Saxon army of King Athelstan.   **3.** In widespread use since the thirteenth century, the English flag of a red cross on a white field predates the adoption of St George as England's patron saint under Edouard III.   **4.** The red saltire of St Patrick, which resembles the blue saltire of St Andrew, had no general currency in Ireland prior to its incorporation into the Union Flag of 1801. The traditional Irish flag bore a Celtic harp and was adopted by Henry VIII as King of Ireland. **5.** St Piran or Pirin, who lived in the sixth century, became the patron saint of Cornish tin miners. The flag of a white cross on a black field has medieval origins. It is recognized by the Cornish national movement but not by the British authorities.   **6.** The Red Dragon (Y Ddraig Goch) was reported to be the emblem of Macsen (d. 388) in the late fourth century. In its present form, the Welsh flag of a red dragon on a green and white field dates from Henry Tudor, who included it amongst his banners at Bosworth Field in 1485.   **7.** The *Trinacria* or 'Legs of Man' has been in evidence as the Manx emblem for at least three hundred years.

As redesigned in 1968 it was adopted as the official flag of the Isle of Man, which though a crown dependency does not form part of the United Kingdom. **8.** The Channel Islands are the only residue of the Duchy of Normandy to remain after 1214 as a dependency of the English crown. Guernsey used the flag of St George until 1985, when the yellow cross of 'the Conqueror' was added as a reminder of the island's Norman origins. **9.** There seems no logical reason why Jersey should have adopted a red saltire like that of St Patrick in the nineteenth century. The three Plantagenet lions were added in 1981 as a reminder of the link with England since the reign of King John. **10.** The 'Great Union' flag, as designed by the heralds of King James VI & I in 1606, was chosen from several alternative designs. It combined the saltire of St Andrew with the cross of St George, and marked the King's determination to declare himself King of Great Britain despite the rejection of his scheme for an Anglo-Scottish constitutional union. **11.** In 1649, when Scotland declared for Charles II, the Free State and Commonwealth set up by the English parliamentary regicides consisted only of England and Ireland. Hence the Commonwealth's flag portrayed a St George's cross vertically alongside the Irish harp. **12.** Following Cromwell's suppression of the monarchy in Scotland, the Protectorate controlled all the British Isles. Hence the Protectorate's jack showed an Irish harp superimposed on the 'Great Union' flag. **13.** The triple combination of the crosses of St George, St Andrew, and St Patrick derived from the creation of the United Kingdom of Great Britain and Ireland in 1801. It is worth noting that the Union Jack was not appropriately modified when the Irish Free State left the United Kingdom in 1922 – thereby promoting the myth of continuity. **14.** The Irish tricolour, Green representing the nationalist tradition, Orange the Protestant tradition, and White the peace and reconciliation between them, was used by the illegal Republican movement from 1916 onwards. It became the official flag of the Irish Free State from 1922. **15.** The flag of Northern Ireland as created in 1920 shows the Red Hand of Ulster superimposed on the cross of St George, thereby emphasizing the Province's historic link with England. It functioned as the official flag of the Province until the imposition of direct rule in 1972, since when the Union Jack has been reintroduced. The Red Hand remains the emblem of the Loyalist community. **16.** The Orcadian flag, which has no official standing, places the red and yellow of the Scottish royal standard in the form of a Scandinavian cross. It is a twentieth-century invention. **17.** The flag of Shetland portrays a Scandinavian cross in the blue and white colours of Scotland. Like its counterpart in Orkney, it marks an unofficial move to stress the islands' historic connections both with Scotland and with Norway. *18–29: Artwork for standards copyright Raymond Turvey.* **18.** The Confessor's standard predates the systematization of English heraldic practices. Its cross and five doves resemble standards borne by his tenth-century predecessors, Edgar and Æthelred. It continued in use until St Edward was overtaken as England's patron saint by St George. **19.** Duke Rollo sported a lion on his banner, and the two lions passant gardant had become the traditional arms of Normandy by the early eleventh century. Brought to England by the Conqueror, they remained as the basis for the English royal standard until 1189. (Henri II Plantagenêt claimed the English throne through his Norman mother, Mathilda.) **20.** Guillaume le Lion, King of Scots, took the lion as his emblem from the arms of his father, Henry, Earl of Huntingdon. The lion rampant was adopted henceforth as the prime symbol of Scotland. The surrounding tessure of a double line of fleurs-de-lys, added by Alexander II (r. 1214–49), is traditionally said to recall the 'Auld Alliance' with France. **21.** The single lion passant was the traditional emblem of Aquitaine, and was used to augment the two lions of Normandy by Richard Cœur de Lion, Duke of Aquitaine and, from 1189, King of England. From then onwards, the three lions became the usual arms of the Plantagenet dynasty. **22.** From 1340, when Edouard III claimed the thrones both of France and of England, the Plantagenet lions were quartered on the royal standard with the lilies of France. Henry IV later reduced the number of lilies from six to three. The royal standard of England remained unchanged throughout the fifteenth and sixteenth centuries. **23.** In 1603, James VI of Scotland ascended the thrones of England and Ireland. As a result, the arms of England were quartered on the royal standard with the lion of Scotland and the harp of Ireland. This design was employed by the House of Stuart throughout the seventeenth century. **24.** The personal arms of the Lord Protector Cromwell showed the lion of Huntingdon superimposed on a standard quartered with the cross of St George, the cross of St Andrew, and the Irish harp. **25.** After the death of Mary in 1694, William III & II adopted a standard where the arms of the House of Orange-Nassau were superimposed as an 'escutcheon of pretence' on the earlier standard of the Stuarts. **26.** As the mark of her elevation to the throne of a united Kingdom of Great Britain, Queen Anne's standard was altered in 1707 to include two joint Anglo-Scottish quarters (England impaling Scotland), a single quarter for the Irish harp, and a quarter for the lilies of France. **27.** From 1714, the royal standard of the House of Hanover saw one of the Anglo-Scottish quarters replaced by the arms of Hanover. The claim to the French throne, and hence the French lilies, remained in place until 1801. **28.** From 1801, the Hanoverians were Kings of the United Kingdom and from 1814, Kings, as opposed to Electors, of Hanover. The royal standard of George III, therefore, was radically altered to show the crowned arms of Hanover superimposed as an 'escutcheon of pretence' over the double quarters of England and the single quarters of Scotland and Ireland. **29.** In 1837, Queen Victoria was debarred by the Salic law from the Kingdom of Hanover. As a result, the royal standard only reflected her position as Queen of the United Kingdom of Great Britain and Ireland. It is interesting to note that from Victoria's reign the ancient practice of modifying the royal standard in line with each monarch's particular titles and claims has been dropped. The only minor change since 1837 occurred in 1901 when Edward VII agreed to a modification in the design of the Irish harp. Apart from that, the royal standard has been frozen in time, with no attempt being made to reflect the changing circumstances either of the reigning dynasty or of the United Kingdom in the nineteenth and twentieth centuries. The public image of an ancient and unchanging tradition is a modern invention. **30.** Celtic Bard – bearer of the older tradition; *The Bard* by Thomas Jones. *Photo: National Museum and Gallery, Cardiff.* **31.** The last invasion of the Northmen (1066); *The Body of Harold brought before William the Conqueror*, 1844–61, Ford Madox Brown (1821–93). *Photo: Bridgeman Art Library/Manchester Art Gallery.* **32.** Dispersal of the Spanish Armada (1588); *The Armada* by Nicholas Hilliard (1547–1619). *Photo: Bridgeman Art Library/Society of Apothecaries, London.* **33.** George IV enters Holyrood (1822). Tradition invented. *The Entrance of George IV at Holyrood House* by David Wilkie (1785–1841). *Photo: Royal Collection,* © *HM Queen Elizabeth II.* **34.** 'King Billy Rides Again', Belfast, 1970. Belfast wall paintings. Taken by H. Sykes, 1970. *Photo: Camera Press, London.* **35.** Mrs McCarron and guest, Glasgow, 1999. The Queen joined Mrs Susan McCarron for tea in her home in the Castlemilk area of Glasgow, July, 1999. *Photo: PA Photos, London.*

Section Two **36.** Roman Centurion at Hadrian's Wall (c. AD 122). *The Building of the Roman Wall* by William Scott Bell (1856), Wallington House, Northumberland. *Photo: National Trust Photographic Library.* **37.** Vortigern makes a treaty with the Saxon leaders Hengest and Horsa (AD 428 or 449). From Cassell's *History of England. Photo: Mary Evans Picture Library, London.* **38.** King Arthur, as a champion of medieval chivalry; *King Arthur and the Thirty Kingdoms* from the *Chronicle* of Peter of Langtoft. *Photo: Bridgeman Art Library/British Library, London.* (Roy 20 A II f. 4r) **39.** Sveyn Forkbeard lands on Humberside (AD 1013); *The Arrival of King Svevyn and Danish Troops in England* (vellum). *Photo: Bridgeman Art Library/British Library, London.* (Harl 2278 f. 98v) **40.** Magna Carta (1215): England a papal fief. *Magna Carta and the Charter of the Forests signed by King John, 15 June 1215*, engraved by A. W. Warren. *Photo: Bridgeman Art Library.* (Private collection) **41.** Robin Hood: fact or folk legend? Friar Tuck and Robin Hood. Illustration by Saloman van Abbe (1883–1955) from *Robin Hood, the Prince of Outlaws* by Carola Oman, published by J. M. Dent & Sons Ltd., 1939. *Photo: Bridgeman Art Library, London.* (Private collection) **42.** The reconstructed head of the Cheddar Man (c. 7000 BC), a Continental, produced by the University of Manchester. *Photo: Natural History Museum, London.* **43.** Patricius (b. c. AD 372). British bishop, Irish saint; St Patrick by an unnamed artist. *Photo: Mary Evans Picture Library, London.* **44.** Alfred, King of Wessex (d. 899), 'hero of our race'. Statue of King Alfred the Great from Winchester, Hampshire. *Photo: Mary Evans Picture Library, London.* **45.** Macbeth of Moray, King of Scots (r. 1040–57); an engraving by J. Hall. *Photo: Mary Evans Picture Library, London.* **46.** Owain Glyn Dŵr (c. 1359–1416), last Prince of Wales; an engraving by Forrest, from the seal engraved in the 'Archaelogica'. **47.** Margaret Tudor, Queen of Scotland (r. 1503–15); an engraving by J. Cochran. *Photo: Mary Evans Picture Library, London.* **48.** Thomas Cromwell, first Earl of Essex, executed 1540: English ideologue. After Hans Holbein. *Photo: National Portrait Gallery, London* (1497/8–1543). **49.** Hugh O'Neill, Earl of Tyrone, (1540–1616) by an unnamed artist. *Photo: Ulster Museum, Belfast.* **50.** The Plantagenêt tombs at Fontevrault: Henri II (1133–89), Aliénor of Aquitaine (c. 1122–1204), Richard I (1157–99), and Isabella of Angoulême (d. 1246). *Photo: Bridgeman Art Library, London.* (Private collection) **51.** Edouard I in Parliament by Wriothesley. *Photo: Royal Collection © HM Queen Elizabeth II.* **52.** Braveheart (1305). William Wallace in chains on trial before Edouard I at Westminster. From a painting by Daniel Maclise, RA. *Photo: Mary Evans Picture Library, London.* **53.** Edouard I Plantagenêt pays homage to Philip I of France for Gascony (1272). *Photo: Royal Collection © HM Queen Elizabeth II.* **54.** The Battle of Sluys (1340), a strategic victory. From Froissart's *Chronicle. Photo: Bridgeman Art Library/Bibliothèque Nationale, Paris, France.* **55.** Henry V at Harfleur (1415): 'this Blessed Plot'. *Photo: Mary Evans Picture Library, London.*

Section Three **56.** St Thomas More, Catholic martyr (1535); his father, his household and his descendants (1593). By Rowland Lockey (fl. 1593–1616). *Photo: National Portrait Gallery, London.* **57.** The Protestant Establishment (1547); Edward VI and the Pope (1570). Artist unknown. *Photo: National Portrait Gallery, London.* **58.** 'Charles Stuart, that Man of Blood' (1649); an eyewitness representation of the execution of King Charles I of England (1600–49), (oil on canvas). By Weesop (fl. 1641–9). *Photo: Bridgeman Art Library, London.* (Private collection) **59.** Oliver Cromwell besieges Drogheda (1649–50); English School (eighteenth century). *Photo: Bridgeman Art Library, London.* (Private collection) **60.** Willem van Oranje lands at Brixham (1688); Dutch School (seventeenth century). *Photo: Royal Collection © HM Queen Elizabeth II.* **61.** Anne (r. 1702–14), Queen of Great Britain (1703); by Edmund Lilly (fl. 1702–16). *Photo: Bridgeman Art Library/Blenheim Palace, Oxfordshire.* **62.** John Wilkes MP (1727–97), Scottophobe; by an unnamed artist. *Photo: Mary Evans Picture Library, London.* **63.** Bonnie Prince Charlie (1720–88); Charles Edward Stuart, the Young Pretender, in disguise (1746), by an unnamed artist. *Photo: Mary Evans Picture Library, London.* **64.** Theobold Wolfe Tone (1763–98), Irish patriot; engraving by F. Scriven. *Photo: Mary Evans Picture Library, London.* **65.** Revd John Lingard (1771–1851), historian. *Photo: Ushaw College, Durham, (with thanks to Sutton Publishing).* **66.** Rudyard Kipling (1865–1936), imperial poet; woodcut by Sir William Newzam Prior Nicholson (1872–1949). *Photo: Bridgeman Art Library, London.* (Private collection) **67.** David Lloyd George (1863–1945), People's Chancellor; by an unnamed artist. *Photo: Mary Evans Picture Library, London.* **68.** Prince K. S. Ranjitsinhji (1872–1933). *Photo: Hulton Getty.* **69.** HRH The Princess of Wales (1961–97). *Photo: Snowdon/Camera Press.* **70.** The Royal family in 1946 by Franz Xaver Winterhalter (1805–73). *Photo: Royal Collection © HM Queen Elizabeth II.* **71.** The first and last Durbar, Delhi, 1911. *Photo: Illustrated London News Picture Library, London.* **72.** Dublin, Easter 1916: 'a terrible beauty'; British troops behind a barricade of barrels during the Easter Rising. *Photo: Hulton Getty.* **73.** The Western Front, 1917: 'a foreign field'; *The Harvest of Battle* by C. R. W. Nevinson (1921). *Photo: Imperial War Museum, London.*

74. 'Their Finest Hour', (1940); a Spitfire of the 303 (Polish) Squadron.   75. Hong Kong, End of Empire, 30 June 1997; an aide-de-camp presents the outgoing Hong Kong Governor Chris Patten with a Union Flag. *Photo: David Gray/ Popperfoto.*

Section Four   *76–101: Coin photos courtesy of the trustees of the British Museum except 87, 95, 100 – Spink & Son; 101 – The Royal Mint.*   76. Tasciovanus. 77. Cunobelinus.   78. Roman Britannia.   79. Aethelstan.   80. Athelstan. 81. Hywel Dda.   82. Eric Blood-Axe.   83. Sihtric Silkbeard.   84. Guillaume I. 85. David I.   86. Edouard I.   87. Edouard III.   88. Henry VII.   89. Mary and Philip.   90. James I.   91. Charles I.   92. James II.   93. English Commonwealth. 94. Darién Pistole.   95. George I.   96. George II.   97. George II.   98. William IV. 99. Victoria.   100. Irish Free State.   101. The Euro.

APPENDICES

Appendix 1

The Isles

'... this royal throne of kings ... this sceptr'd isle ... this earth, this realm, this England'
– William Shakespeare

'Britain is an island' – Roy Strong (1996)

'Great Britain, two partitioned, poly-cultural islands' – *Oxford History of Britain* (1999)

'In Britain everything is different ... when people say "England", they sometimes mean
"Great Britain", sometimes "the United Kingdom", sometimes the "British Isles"
– but never just England.' – George Mikes (1946)

The Polyglot Isles

Countries

English	England	Wales	Ireland	Scotland	Cornwall
Welsh	Lloegr	Cymru	Iwerddon	Yr Alban	Cernyw
Irish	Sasana	An Bhreatain Bheag	Éire	Albain	Corn na Breataine
Scots	Sasann	a' Chuimrigh	Eirinn	Alba	a' Chorn
Cornish	Pow Saws	Kembra	Ywerdhon	Alban	Kernow
French	L'Angleterre	Le Pays de Galles	L'Irelande	L'Écosse	Cornouaille
Latin	Britannia	Cambria	Hibernia	Caledonia	Cornubia
Old Norse	England	Vair	Irland	Skotland	
Old English	Englalond	Wealon	Yra land	Scotland	Kern-Wealhas

Seas

English	North Sea	Irish Sea	Channel
Welsh	Môr Y Gogledd	Môr Iwerddon	Môr Udd
Irish	An Mhuir Thuaidh	Muir Meann	Muir nIocht
Scots	An Cuan Tuah	Curan Eirinn	An Caolas Sasannach
Cornish	An Mor Cleth	Mor Ywerdhon	An Chanel
French	La Mer du Nord	La Mer d'Irlonde	La Manche

Isles

English	Shetland	Orkneys	Man	Anglesey
Welsh	Ynysoedd Shetland	Ynysoedd Erch	Ynys Manaw	Ynys Môn
Irish	Sealtainn	Inse Orc	Oileán Mhanainn	Inis Môn
Scots	Sealtainn	Arcaibh	Eilean Mhannainn	
Cornish			Enys Man	
French	Shetland	Les Isles d'Orcades	Île de Man	Anglesey
Old Norse	Hjaltland	Orkneyjar		
Manx			Ellen Vannin	

Appendix 3

Place Names in the Isles

The Midnight Isles

Afternoon Country – *Wales*
Cliff Country – *England*
Corner Land – *Kent*
Dark Water Valley – *Thames valley*
Eight Sisters – *Seven Sisters*
Furthest Isles – *Shetland Islands*
Great Isle – *Britain*
Green Isle – *Ireland*
Headlands – *Cornwall*
Middle Sea – *Irish Sea*
Midnight Isles – *Inner Hebrides*
Midway Island – *Isle of Man*
Misty Country – *Scotland*

Noonday Riviera – *South Coast*
North Strait – *Little Minch*
Outer Isles – *Outer Hebrides*
Penultimate Isles – *Orkney Islands*
Sacred Island – *Anglesey*
Southern Straits – *Straits of Dover*
Sunrise Coast – *East Coast*
Sunrise Sea – *North Sea*
The Sleeve – *The Channel*
Valley of Kings – *Boyne valley*
Western Wetlands – *Somerset Levels*
Eastern Wetlands – *Fens*

The Painted Isles

Tailltin – *Teltown, Co. Westmeath*
the Plain of Adoration – *Now in Co.
    Cavan*
Ulaidh – *Ulster*
Cruchain – *Connaught*
Laighin – *Leinster*

Mumha – *Munster*
Mide – *Meath*
Mai Din – *Maiden Castle, Dorset*
Din Albion – *Hengistbury, Dorset*
Lughdun – *London*
Mon – *Anglesey*

The Frontier Isles and Roman Europe

Aballava – *Burgh-by-Sands*
Anderida – *Pevensey*
Aquae Sulis – *Bath*
Arbeia – *South Shields*
Arconium – *Ercing*
Argentoratum – *Strasbourg*
Augusta Treverorum – *Trier*
Batavia – *The Netherlands*
Branodunum – *Brancaster*
Bremenium – *High Rochester*
Brigantium – *Bregenz*
Cambria – *Wales*

Calleva Atrebatum – *Silchester*
Camboglanna – *Caltlesteads*
Camulodunum – *Colchester*
Cantium – *Kent*
Cataractonium – *Catterick*
Cilurnum – *Chesters*
Cimbrian Peninsula – *Jutland*
Coriosopitum – *Corbridge*
Deva – *Chester*
Dolaucothi – *Gold mines on the River
    Cothi in the Cambrian Mountains,
    Wales*

Dubris – *Dover*
Durovernum – *Canterbury*
Eboracum – *York*
Forum Julii – *Fréjus*
Gallia Narbonensis – *Provence*
Gaul – *France*
Glevum – *Gloucester*
Hibernia – *Ireland*
Isca, Isca Dumnoniorum – *Exeter*
Isca Silurum – *Caerleon*
Isurium – *Aldborough, North Yorkshire*
Lindum Colonia – *Lincoln*
Londinium – *London*
Lugdunum – *Lyons*
Lugovallium – *Carlisle*
Magnis – *Carvoran*
Mare Germanicum – *North Sea*
Massilia – *Marseilles*
Moesia – *A province between the Danube and the Black Sea*
Mogontiacum – *Mainz*

Novaesium – *Neuss*
Noviomagus Regnensium – *Chichester*
Ostia – *Ostia*
Pannonia – *Western Hungary and eastern Austria*
Pons Aelius – *Newcastle*
Portus Adurni – *Portchester*
Ripuarium – *Richborough*
Rutupiae – *Rochester*
Sequana – *Seine*
Tamesis – *Thames*
Vectis – *Isle of Wight*
Venta Icenorum – *Caistor St Edmund*
Vercovicium – *Housesteads*
Viroconium Cornoviorum – *Wroxeter*
Verteris – *Brough-under-Stainmore, Cumbria*
Verulamium – *St Albans*
Vindolanda – *Chesterholm*
Vindovala – *Rochester*

The Germano-Celtic Isles

Caerel   *Carlisle*
Catraeth – *Catterick*
Dinbych-y-Pysgod – *Tenby*
Isca – *Exeter*

Ynys Glannauc – *Puffin Island, River Wye*
Ynys Medgawdd – *Lindisfarne*

The Isles in the West

Aclea – *Oakley (Hampshire)*
Cernemude – *Charmouth (Dorset)*
Hengestoune – *Hingston Down (Cornwall)*

Jorvik – *York*
Swanawic – *Swanage*

Late Bronze Age and early Iron Age settlements in the Isles

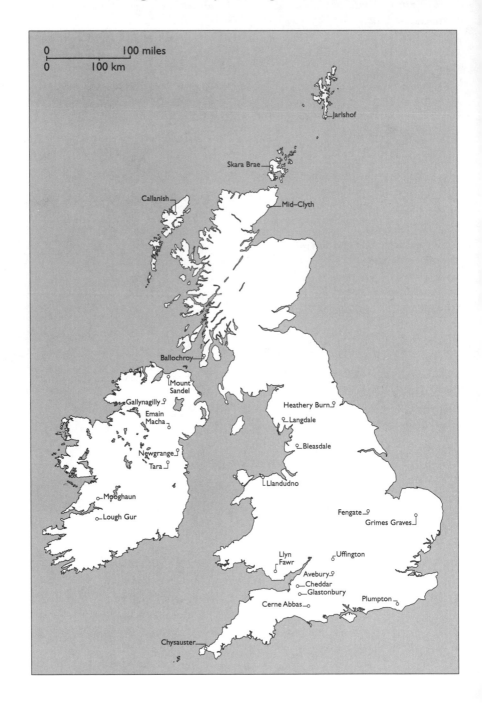

The Middle Sea

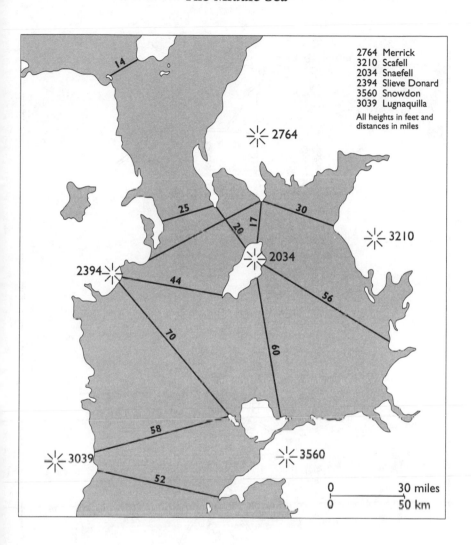

2764 Merrick
3210 Scafell
2034 Snaefell
2394 Slieve Donard
3560 Snowdon
3039 Lugnaquilla

All heights in feet and
distances in miles

Hadrian's Wall in the Second Century

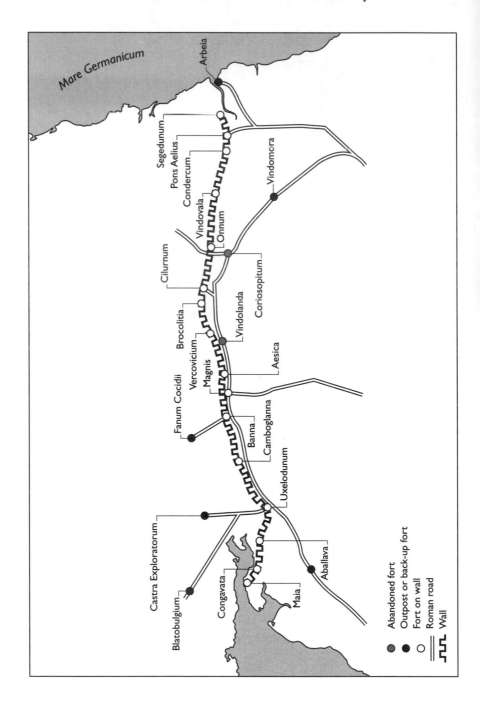

Roman London in the Third Century

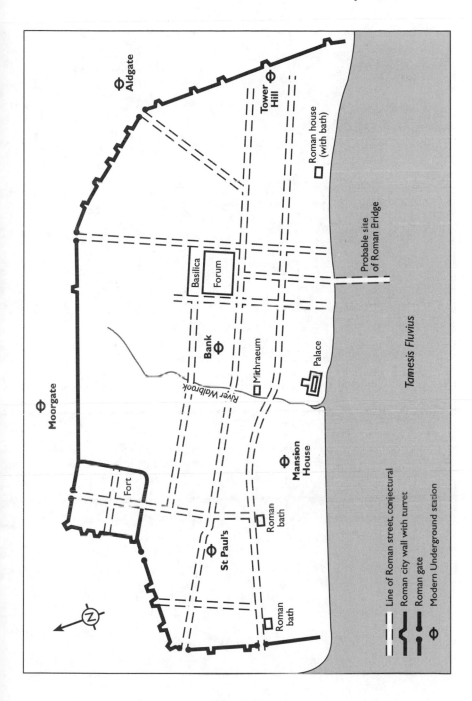

The Spread of Christianity in the Fifth to the Ninth Centuries

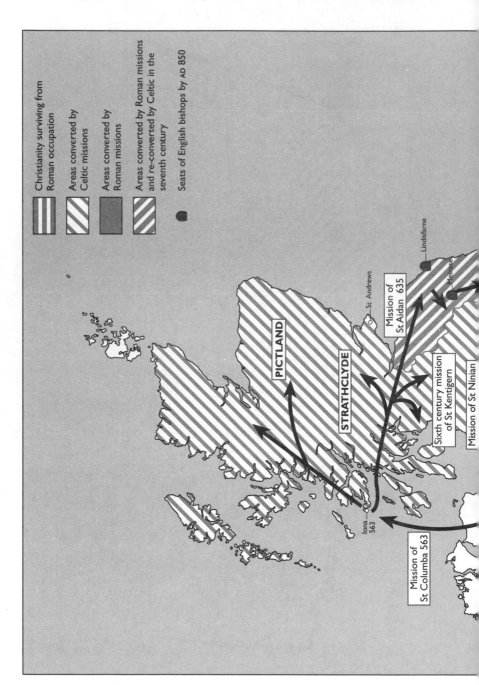

Christianity surviving from Roman occupation

Areas converted by Celtic missions

Areas converted by Roman missions

Areas converted by Roman missions and re-converted by Celtic in the seventh century

● Seats of English bishops by AD 850

PICTLAND

STRATHCLYDE

St Andrews

Lindisfarne

Melrose

Mission of St Aidan 635

Sixth century mission of St Kentigern

Mission of St Ninian

Iona 563

Mission of St Columba 563

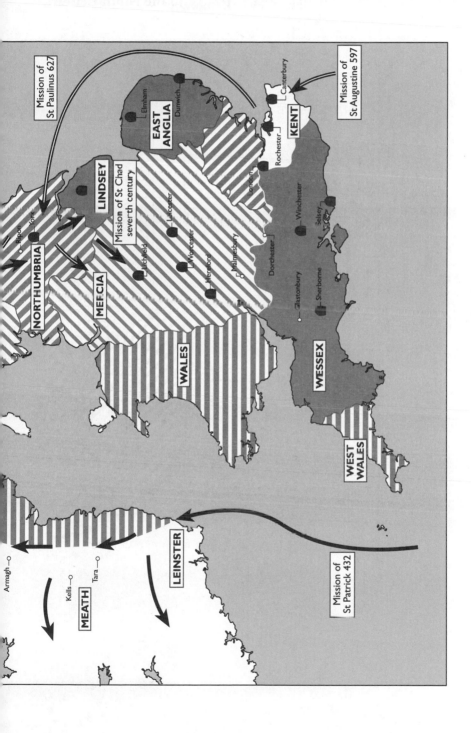

The Celtic Languages

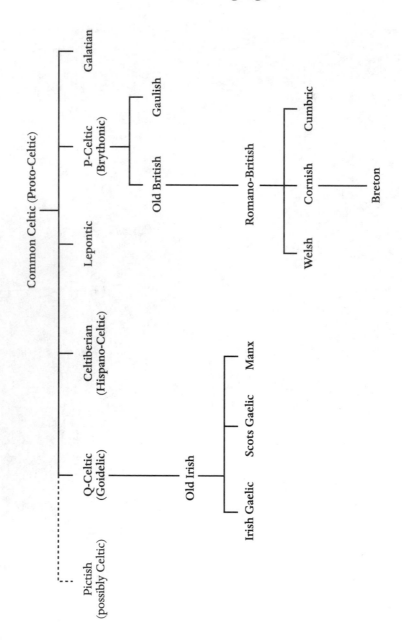

The Provinces and Territories of Early Scotland,
c. the Eighth Century

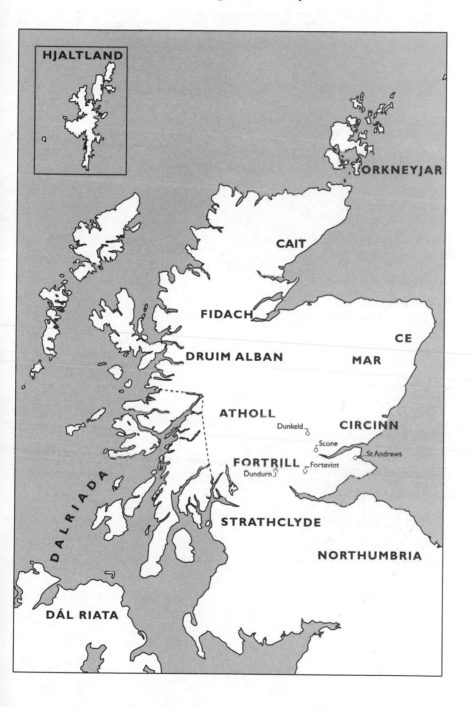

Wales – the Early Kingdoms in the Eighth and Ninth Centuries

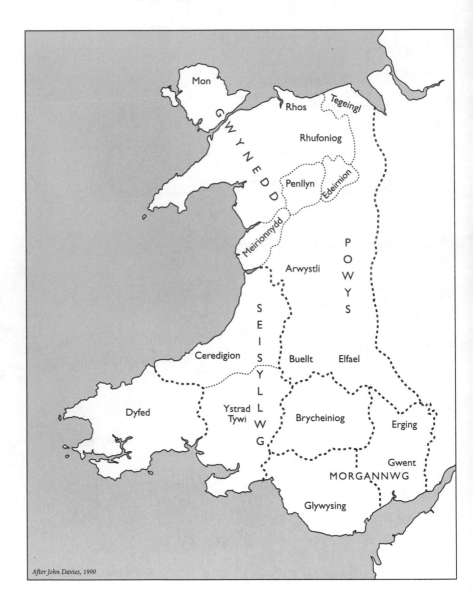

Mon

GWYNEDD

Rhos

Tegeingl

Rhufoniog

Penllyn

Edeirnion

Meirionnydd

Arwystli

POWYS

SEISYLLWG

Ceredigion

Buellt

Elfael

Ystrad
Tywi

Brycheiniog

Erging

Dyfed

Gwent

MORGANNWG

Glywysing

After John Davies, 1990

The Viking Seaways in the Tenth Century

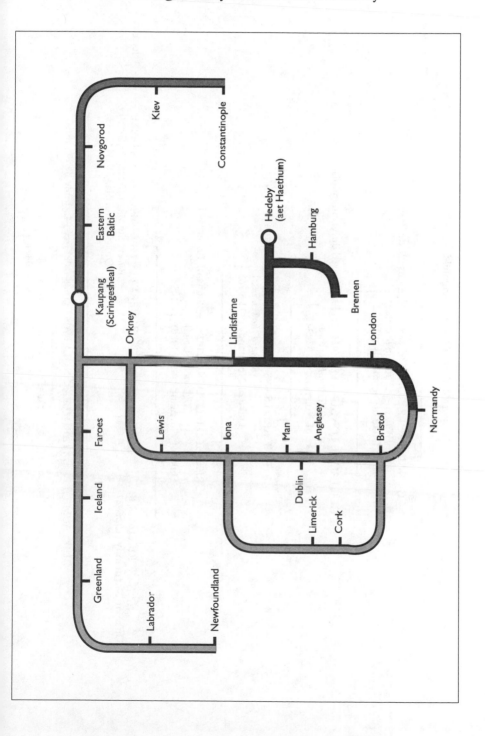

The Descendants of Göngu Hrolf

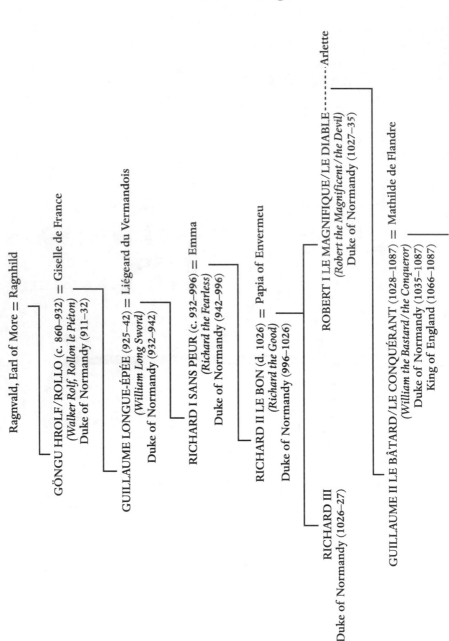

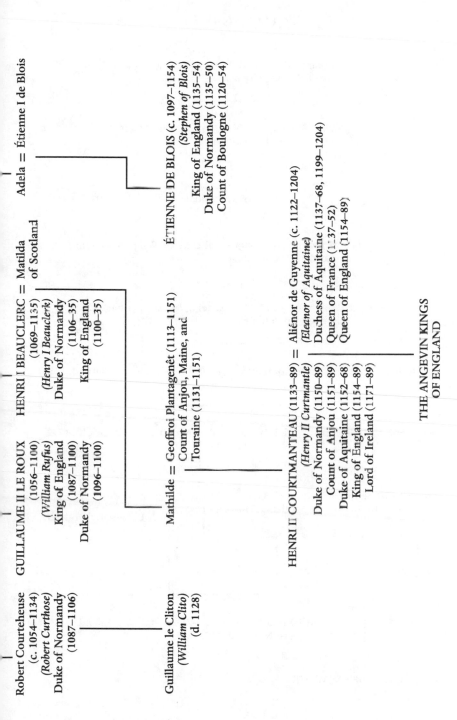

Robert Courteheuse
(c. 1054–1134)
(*Robert Curthose*)
Duke of Normandy
(1087–1106)

GUILLAUME II LE ROUX
(1056–1100)
(*William Rufus*)
King of England
(1087–1100)
Duke of Normandy
(1096–1100)

HENRI I BEAUCLERC = Matilda
(1069–1135)   of Scotland
(*Henry I Beauclerc*)
Duke of Normandy
(1106–35)
King of England
(1100–35)

Adela = Étienne I de Blois

Guillaume le Cliton
(*William Clito*)
(d. 1128)

Mathilde = Geoffroi Plantagenêt (1113–1151)
              Count of Anjou, Maine, and
              Touraine (1131–1151)

ÉTIENNE DE BLOIS (c. 1097–1154)
(*Stephen of Blois*)
King of England (1135–54)
Duke of Normandy (1135–50)
Count of Boulogne (1120–54)

HENRI II COURTMANTEAU (1133–89) = Aliénor de Guyenne (c. 1122–1204)
(*Henry II Curtmantle*)   (*Eleanor of Aquitaine*)
Duke of Normandy (1150–89)   Duchess of Aquitaine (1137–68, 1199–1204)
Count of Anjou (1151–89)   Queen of France (1137–52)
Duke of Aquitaine (1152–68)   Queen of England (1154–89)
King of England (1154–89)
Lord of Ireland (1171–89)

THE ANGEVIN KINGS
OF ENGLAND

The De Brus Dynasty

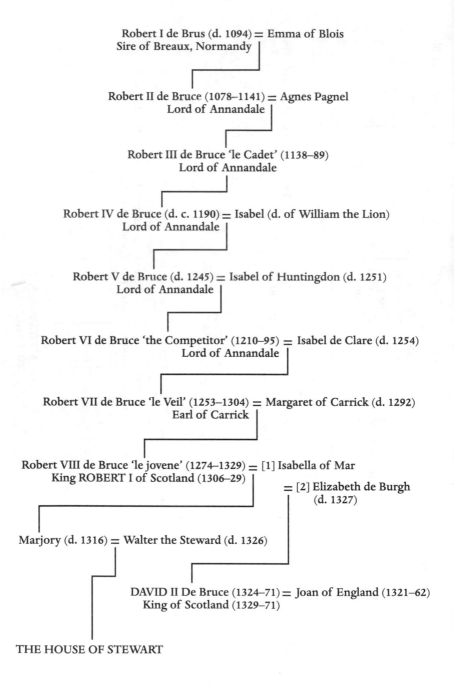

Robert I de Brus (d. 1094) = Emma of Blois
Sire of Breaux, Normandy

Robert II de Bruce (1078–1141) = Agnes Pagnel
Lord of Annandale

Robert III de Bruce 'le Cadet' (1138–89)
Lord of Annandale

Robert IV de Bruce (d. c. 1190) = Isabel (d. of William the Lion)
Lord of Annandale

Robert V de Bruce (d. 1245) = Isabel of Huntingdon (d. 1251)
Lord of Annandale

Robert VI de Bruce 'the Competitor' (1210–95) = Isabel de Clare (d. 1254)
Lord of Annandale

Robert VII de Bruce 'le Veil' (1253–1304) = Margaret of Carrick (d. 1292)
Earl of Carrick

Robert VIII de Bruce 'le jovene' (1274–1329) = [1] Isabella of Mar
King ROBERT I of Scotland (1306–29)
= [2] Elizabeth de Burgh
(d. 1327)

Marjory (d. 1316) = Walter the Steward (d. 1326)

DAVID II De Bruce (1324–71) = Joan of England (1321–62)
King of Scotland (1329–71)

THE HOUSE OF STEWART

Normandy in the Eleventh Century

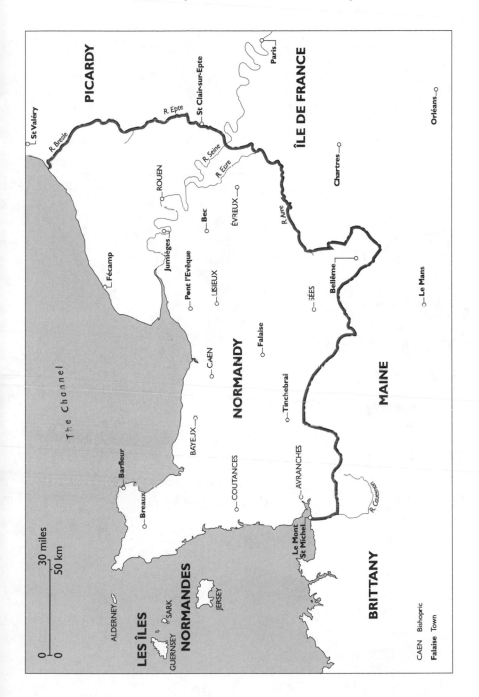

The Norman Conquest, 1066

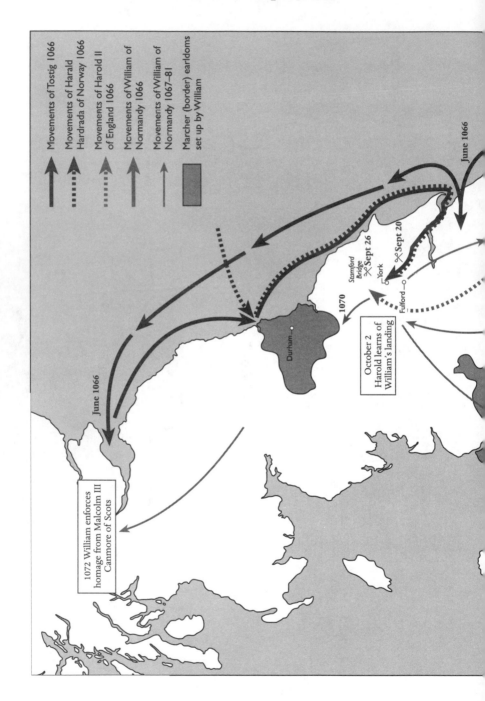

Movements of Tostig 1066

Movements of Harald Hardrada of Norway 1066

Movements of Harold II of England 1066

Movements of William of Normandy 1066

Movements of William of Normandy 1067–81

Marcher (border) earldoms set up by William

June 1066

June 1066

Stamford Bridge ✕ Sept 26

York

Sept 20

Fulford

1070

Durham

October 2
Harold learns of
William's landing

1072 William enforces
homage from Malcolm III
Canmore of Scots

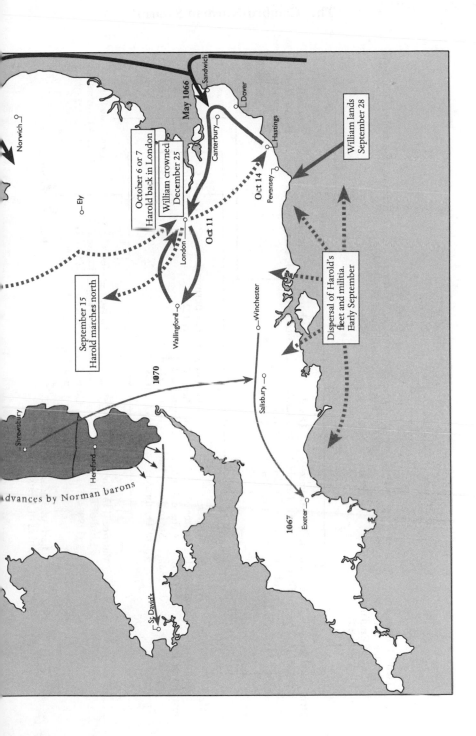

Norwich

Sandwich

May 1066

Dover

Canterbury

Hastings

October 6 or 7
Harold back in London

William crowned
December 25

Fevensey

Ely

Oct 14

William lands
September 28

Oct 11

London

September 15
Harold marches north

Dispersal of Harold's
fleet and militia.
Early September

Wallingford

Winchester

1070

Salisbury

Shrewsbury

Hereford

advances by Norman barons

1067   Exeter

St David's

The 'Cambro-Norman Swarm'

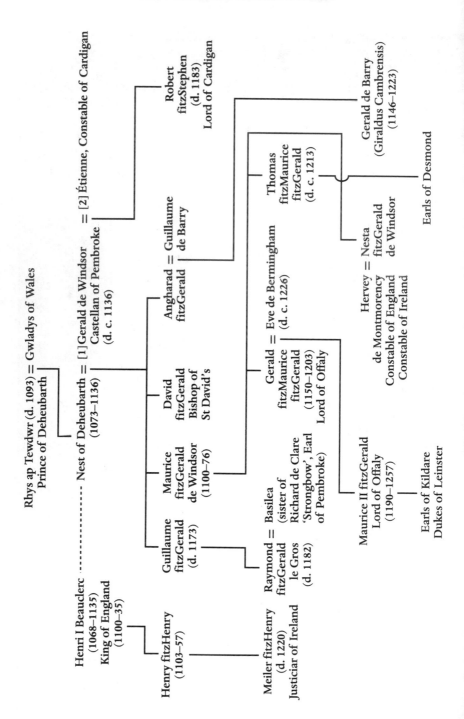

Henri III's Family Connections

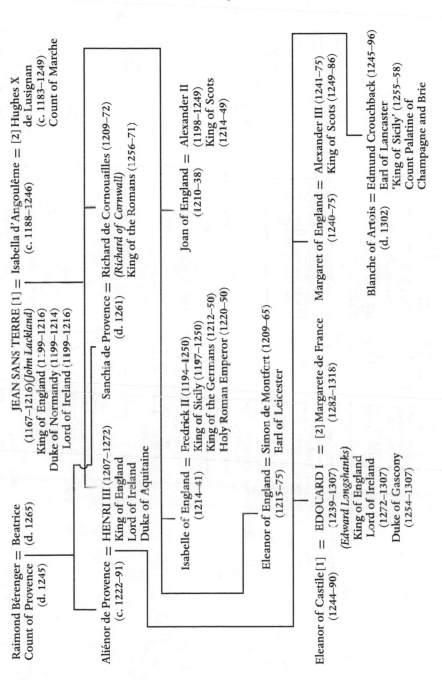

The Plantagenêt Dynasty

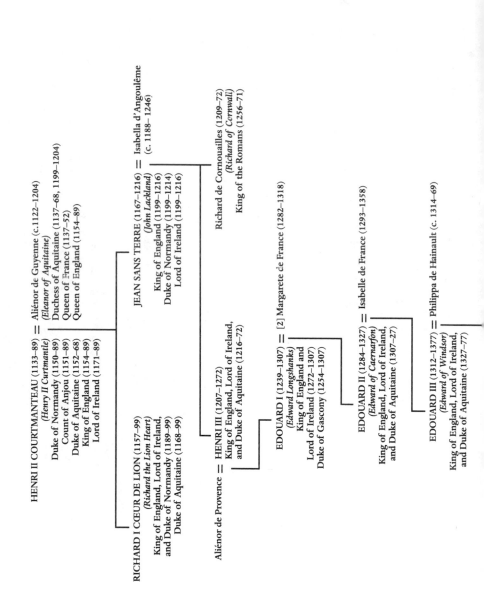

HENRI II COURTMANTEAU (1133–89) = Aliénor de Guyenne (c.1122–1204)
(*Henry II Curtmantle*)   (*Eleanor of Aquitaine*)
Duke of Normandy (1150–89)   Duchess of Aquitaine (1137–68, 1199–1204)
Count of Anjou (1151–89)   Queen of France (1137–52)
Duke of Aquitaine (1152–68)   Queen of England (1154–89)
King of England (1154–89)
Lord of Ireland (1171–89)

JEAN SANS TERRE (1167–1216) = Isabella d'Angoulême
(*John Lackland*)   (c. 1188–1246)
King of England (1199–1216)
Duke of Normandy (1199–1214)
Lord of Ireland (1199–1216)

Richard de Cornouailles (1209–72)
(*Richard of Cornwall*)
King of the Romans (1256–71)

RICHARD I CŒUR DE LION (1157–99)
(*Richard the Lion Heart*)
King of England, Lord of Ireland,
and Duke of Normandy (1189–99)
Duke of Aquitaine (1168–99)

Aliénor de Provence = HENRI III (1207–1272)
King of England, Lord of Ireland,
and Duke of Aquitaine (1216–72)

EDOUARD I (1239–1307) = [2] Margarete de France (1282–1318)
(*Edward Longshanks*)
King of England and
Lord of Ireland (1272–1307)
Duke of Gascony (1254–1307)

EDOUARD II (1284–1327) = Isabelle de France (1293–1358)
(*Edward of Caernarfon*)
King of England, Lord of Ireland,
and Duke of Aquitaine (1307–27)

EDOUARD III (1312–1377) = Philippa de Hainault (c. 1314–69)
(*Edward of Windsor*)
King of England, Lord of Ireland,
and Duke of Aquitaine (1327–77)

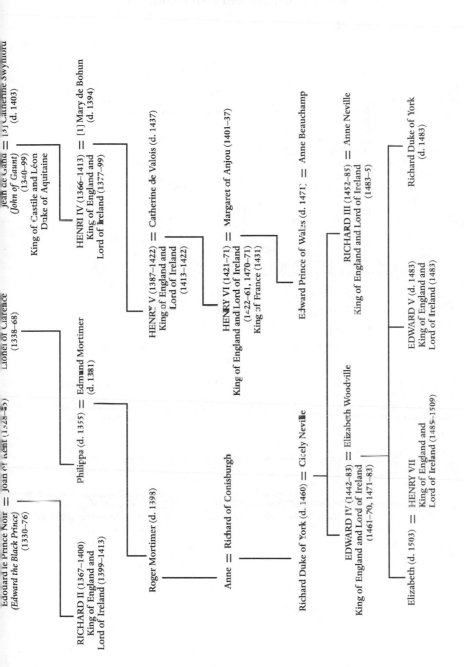

The Genealogy of France *Outremer*

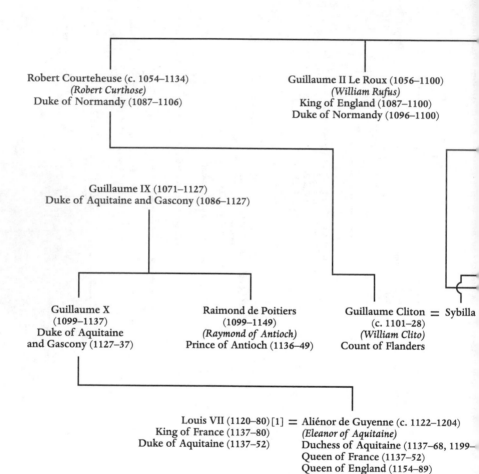

Robert Courteheuse (c. 1054–1134)
(Robert Curthose)
Duke of Normandy (1087–1106)

Guillaume II Le Roux (1056–1100)
(William Rufus)
King of England (1087–1100)
Duke of Normandy (1096–1100)

Guillaume IX (1071–1127)
Duke of Aquitaine and Gascony (1086–1127)

Guillaume X
(1099–1137)
Duke of Aquitaine
and Gascony (1127–37)

Raimond de Poitiers
(1099–1149)
(Raymond of Antioch)
Prince of Antioch (1136–49)

Guillaume Cliton = Sybilla
(c. 1101–28)
(William Clito)
Count of Flanders

Louis VII (1120–80) [1] = Aliénor de Guyenne (c. 1122–1204)
King of France (1137–80)   *(Eleanor of Aquitaine)*
Duke of Aquitaine (1137–52)   Duchess of Aquitaine (1137–68, 1199–
                                   Queen of France (1137–52)
                                   Queen of England (1154–89)

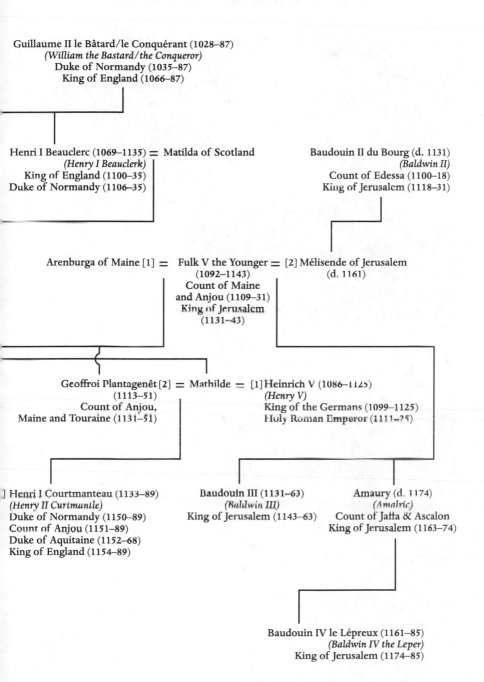

Angevin Possessions in France, c. 1190

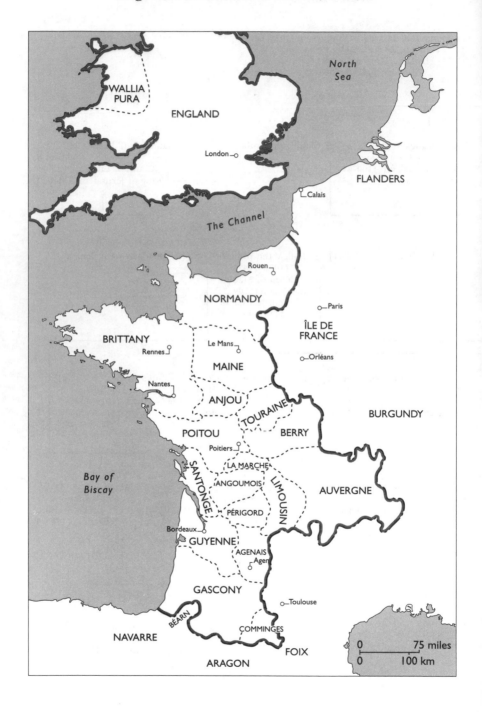

Wales in 1300 – the Marcher Lordships

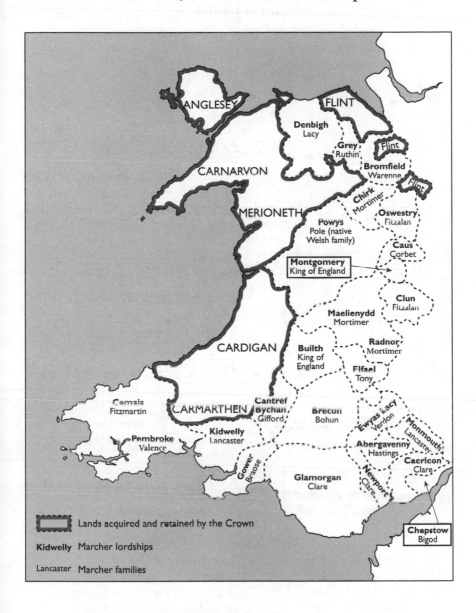

Appendix 23

'Rhyfelgyrch gwyr Harlech'
'Men of Harlech'

English words: A. P. Graves   Composer: unknown

1.

We le goelcerth wen yn fflamio,
A thafodau tân yn bloeddio,
Ar i'r dewrion ddod I daro,
    Unwaith eto'n un.
gan fanllefau tywysogion
Llais gelynion, trwst arfogion,
A charlamiad y marchogion,
    Craig ar graig a grýn!

Arfon byth ni orfydd,
Cenir yn dragywydd;
    Cymru fydd fel Cymru fu,
Yn glodus yn mysg gwledydd.
Yng ngwyn oleuni'r goelcerth acw,
Tros wefusau Cymro'n marw,
Annibyniaeth sydd yn galw,
    Am ei dewraf dyn.

1.

Fierce the beacon light is flaming,
With its tongues of fire proclaiming,
'Chieftains, sundered to your shaming
    Strongly now unite!'
At the call all Arfon rallies,
War cries rend her hills and valleys,
Troop on troop, with headlong sallies,
    Hurtle to the fight,

2.

Ni chaiff gelyn ladd ac ymlid-
Harlech! Harlech! cwyd iw herlid;
Y mae Rhoddwr mawr cin Rhyddid,
    Yn rhoi nerth i ni.
Wele Cymru a'i byddinoedd,
Yn ymdywallt o'r mynyddoedd!
Rhuthrant fel rhaeadrau dyfroedd,
    Llamant fel y lli!
Llwyddiant i'n lluyddion!
Rwystro bâr yr estron!
    Gwybod yn ei galon gaiff,
Fel bratha cleddyf Brython;
Y clêdd yn erbyn clêdd a chwery,
Dûr yn erbyn dûr a dery,
Wele faner Gwalia'I fyny,
    Rhyddid aiff a hi!

Chiefs lie dead and wounded,
Yet, where first 'twas grounded,
    Freedom's flag still holds the crag,
Her trumpet still is sounded,
O there we'll keep her banner flying,
While the pale lips of the dying,
Echo to our shout defying,
    'Harlech for the right!'

2.

Shall the Saxon army shake you,
Smite, pursue and overtake you?
Men of Harlech, God shall make you
    Victors, blow for blow!
As the rivers of Eryri
Sweep the vale with flooded fury,
Gwalia from her mountain eyrie,
    Thunders on the foe!
Now avenging Briton,
Smite as he has smitten!
    Let your rage on history's page,
In Saxon blood be written!
His lance is long but yours in longer,
Strong his sword, but yours is stronger!
Onc stroke morel and then your wronger
    At your feet lies low!

The Kings of France: Capetian and Valois, 1270–1483

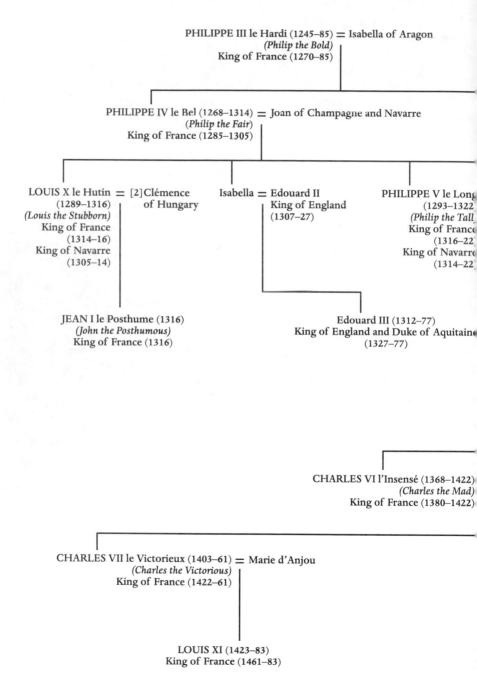

PHILIPPE III le Hardi (1245–85) = Isabella of Aragon
(Philip the Bold)
King of France (1270–85)

PHILIPPE IV le Bel (1268–1314) = Joan of Champagne and Navarre
(Philip the Fair)
King of France (1285–1305)

LOUIS X le Hutin = [2] Clémence
(1289–1316)   of Hungary
(Louis the Stubborn)
King of France
(1314–16)
King of Navarre
(1305–14)

Isabella = Edouard II
King of England
(1307–27)

PHILIPPE V le Long
(1293–1322)
(Philip the Tall)
King of France
(1316–22)
King of Navarre
(1314–22)

JEAN I le Posthume (1316)
(John the Posthumous)
King of France (1316)

Edouard III (1312–77)
King of England and Duke of Aquitaine
(1327–77)

CHARLES VI l'Insensé (1368–1422)
(Charles the Mad)
King of France (1380–1422)

CHARLES VII le Victorieux (1403–61) = Marie d'Anjou
(Charles the Victorious)
King of France (1422–61)

LOUIS XI (1423–83)
King of France (1461–83)

Charles (d. 1325) Comte de Valois,
Alençon, Chartres, and Le Perche

an de
urgundy

CHARLES IV le Bel = [3] Joan
(1294–1328) d'Évreux
(Charles the Fair)
King of France
(1322–28)
King of Navarre
(1322–28)

PHILIPPE V de Valois = [1] Joan de
(1293–1350) Burgundy
(Philip of Valois)
King of France
(1328–50)

JEAN II le Bon (1319–64) = Bonne de Luxembourg
(John the Good)
King of France (1350–64)

ARLES V le Sage (1338–80) = Joan de Bourbon
(Charles the Wise)
King of France (1364–80)

sabella von Bayern

Catherine de Valois (d. 1437) = Henry V (1387–1422)
King of England (1413–22)

Henry VI (1421–71)
King of England (1422–61, 1470–71)
Titular King of France

Chronology of the Hundred Years War

The Sluys Period

1337 Edouard III claims the throne of France.

1340 Battle of Sluys – an English naval victory over the French.

The Crécy Period

1346 Battle of Crécy – an English victory.

1347 Calais falls to the English.

The Poitiers Period

1350 Philippe VI of France succeeded by Jean II.

1356 Battle of Poitiers – English victory with capture of King Jean.

1360 Peace of Brétigny – Aquitaine surrendered to England and Edouard III renounces claim to Normandy.

French Recovery

1364 Jean II of France succeeded by Charles V.

1369 Charles V retakes Aquitaine – hostilities recommence.

1370 English massacre at Limoges.

1372 Battle of La Rochelle – French naval victory.

1373 Jean de Gand (John of Gaunt) leads his *chevauchée* from Calais to Bordeaux.

1376 Death of the Black Prince.

1377 Death of Edouard III of England – succession of Richard II.

1380 Death of Charles V of France – succession of Charles VI.

1386 French planned invasion of England abandoned.

1389 Truce of Leulinghen between French and English.

The Uneasy Truce

1396 Peace of Paris – England retained only Calais and part of Gascony.

1399 Richard II deposed and succeeded by Henry IV.

1402 French support to Scottish invasion of England.

1403 French raids on the English coast.

1405 French support to Owain Glyn Dŵr.

1406 French attacks on English possessions in France.

1407   Assassination of Duke of Orléans – results in war between Burgundy and Orléans.

1411   Burgundy and Orléans appeal to England.

1412   Duke of Clarence leads a *chevauchée* from Normandy to Bordeaux.

1413   Death of Henry IV and succession of Henry V.

England Ascendant

1415   Henry V invades France. Capture of Harfleur. English victory at Agincourt.

1419   Fall of Rouen to English.

1420   Treaty of Troyes – Henry V recognised as heir to Charles VI. English occupy Paris.

1421   Battle of Baugé – French victory and death of Duke of Clarence.

1422   Death of Henry V. Death of Charles VI. Henry VI King of France north of the Loire – Charles VII King of France south of the Loire.

1423   Battle of Cravant – English victory.

1424   Battle of Verneuil – English victory.

1428   Siege of Orléans begun.

French Revival

1429   Joan of Arc relieves Orléans. Charles VII crowned at Rheims.

1430   Joan of Arc captured by English.

1431   Execution of Joan of Arc. Henry VI crowned in Paris

1435   Treaty of Arras – ends Burgundian–Armagnac war.

1436   French recapture of Paris.

1444   Treaty of Tours – five-year truce.

France Triumphs

1448   English surrender Maine to French.

1450   Battle of Formigny – French victory. French reconquer Normandy.

1451   French reconquer Guyenne.

1453   Battle of Castillon – French victory. Fall of Bordeaux. England retains only Calais.

The Tudor Dynasty

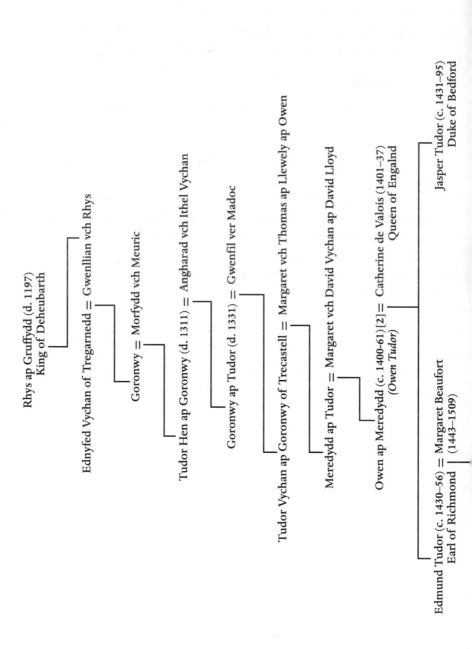

Rhys ap Gruffydd (d. 1197)
King of Deheubarth

Ednyfed Vychan of Tregarnedd = Gwenllian vch Rhys

Goronwy = Morfydd vch Meuric

Tudor Hen ap Goronwy (d. 1311) = Angharad vch Ithel Vychan

Goronwy ap Tudor (d. 1331) = Gwenfil ver Madoc

Tudor Vychan ap Goronwy of Trecastell = Margaret vch Thomas ap Llewely ap Owen

Meredydd ap Tudor = Margaret vch David Vychan ap David Lloyd

Owen ap Meredydd (c. 1400-61) [2] = Catherine de Valois (1401–37)
(Owen Tudor)   Queen of Engalnd

Jasper Tudor (c. 1431–95)
Duke of Bedford

Edmund Tudor (c. 1430–56) = Margaret Beaufort
Earl of Richmond   (1443–1509)

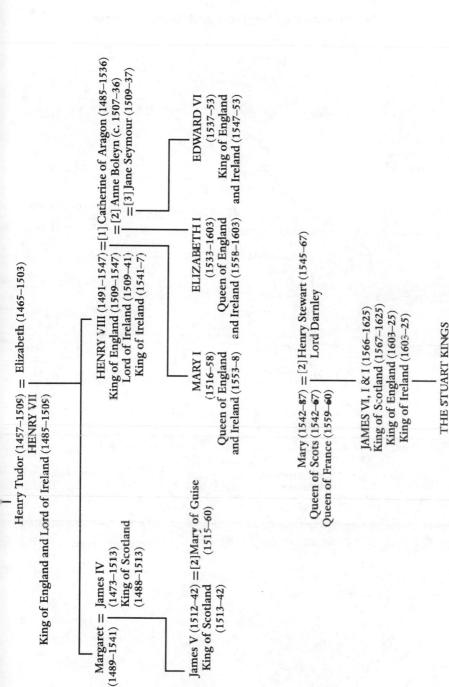

Henry Tudor (1457–1509) = Elizabeth (1465–1503)
HENRY VII
King of England and Lord of Ireland (1485–1505)

Margaret = James IV
(1489–1541) (1473–1513)
King of Scotland
(1488–1513)

James V (1512–42) = [2]Mary of Guise
King of Scotland (1515–60)
(1513–42)

HENRY VIII (1491–1547) = [1] Catherine of Aragon (1485–1536)
King of England (1509–1547) = [2] Anne Boleyn (c. 1507–36)
Lord of Ireland (1509–41) = [3]Jane Seymour (1509–37)
King of Ireland (1541–7)

MARY I
(1516–58)
Queen of England
and Ireland (1553–8)

ELIZABETH I
(1533–1603)
Queen of England
and Ireland (1558–1603)

EDWARD VI
(1537–53)
King of England
and Ireland (1547–53)

Mary (1542–87) = [2] Henry Stewart (1545–67)
Queen of Scots (1542–67) Lord Darnley
Queen of France (1559–60)

JAMES VI, I & I (1566–1625)
King of Scotland (1567–1625)
King of England (1603–25)
King of Ireland (1603–25)

THE STUART KINGS

The Counties of England and Wales, c. 1536

The Dissolved Monasteries – A Selection

'Song of the Western Men'

Words: Revd R. S. Hawker (1803–75)   Music: Cornish Traditional

1.

A good sword and a trusty hand
A merry heart and true!
King James' men shall understand
What Cornish lads can do
And have they fixed the where and when?
And shall Trelawny die?
Here's twenty thousand Cornishmen
Will know the reason why!

     A good sword and a trusty hand
     A merry heart and true!
     King James' men shall understand
     What Cornish lads can do

2.

Out spake their captain brave and bold,
A merry wight was he:
'If London Tow'r were Michael's Hold,

We'll set Trelawny free!
We'll cross the Tamar, land to land,
The Severn is no stay,
With "One and All" and hand in hand,
And who shall bid us nay?'
      Out spake a captain brave and bold,
      a merry wight was he:
      'If London Tow'r were Michael's Hold,
      We'll set Trelawny free!'

3.
And when we come to London Wall,
A pleasant sight to view,
Come forth! come forth! ye cowards all,
Here's men as good as you!
Trelawny he's in keep and hold,
Trelawny he may die,
But twenty thousand Cornish bold,
Will know the reason why!
      And when we come to London Wall,
      A pleasant sight to view,
      'Come forth! Come forth! Ye cowards all,
      Here's men as good as you!'

The Stuart Dynasty

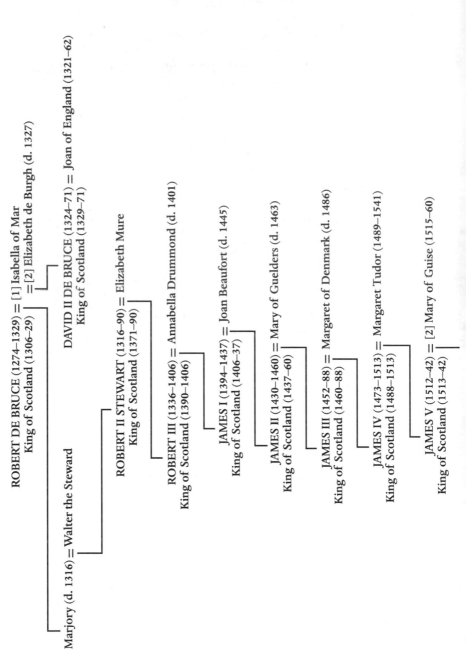

ROBERT DE BRUCE (1274–1329) = [1] Isabella of Mar
King of Scotland (1306–29)
= [2] Elizabeth de Burgh (d. 1327)

DAVID II DE BRUCE (1324–71) = Joan of England (1321–62)
King of Scotland (1329–71)

Marjory (d. 1316) = Walter the Steward

ROBERT II STEWART (1316–90) = Elizabeth Mure
King of Scotland (1371–90)

ROBERT III (1336–1406) = Annabella Drummond (d. 1401)
King of Scotland (1390–1406)

JAMES I (1394–1437) = Joan Beaufort (d. 1445)
King of Scotland (1406–37)

JAMES II (1430–1460) = Mary of Guelders (d. 1463)
King of Scotland (1437–60)

JAMES III (1452–88) = Margaret of Denmark (d. 1486)
King of Scotland (1460–88)

JAMES IV (1473–1513) = Margaret Tudor (1489–1541)
King of Scotland (1488–1513)

JAMES V (1512–42) = [2] Mary of Guise (1515–60)
King of Scotland (1513–42)

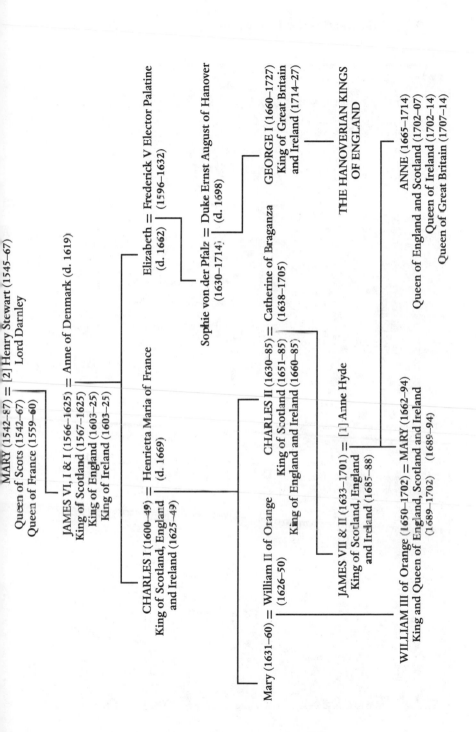

MARY (1542–87) = [2] Henry Stewart (1545–67)
Queen of Scots (1542–67)　　　Lord Darnley
Queen of France (1559–60)

JAMES VI, I & I (1566–1625) = Anne of Denmark (d. 1619)
King of Scotland (1567–1625)
King of England (1603–25)
King of Ireland (1603–25)

Elizabeth = Frederick V Elector Palatine
(d. 1662)　　　(1596–1632)

Sophie von der Pfalz = Duke Ernst August of Hanover
(1630–1714)　　　(d. 1698)

GEORGE I (1660–1727)
King of Great Britain
and Ireland (1714–27)

THE HANOVERIAN KINGS
OF ENGLAND

ANNE (1665–1714)
Queen of England and Scotland (1702–07)
Queen of Ireland (1702–14)
Queen of Great Britain (1707–14)

CHARLES I (1600–49) = Henrietta Maria of France
King of Scotland, England　　　(d. 1669)
and Ireland (1625–49)

CHARLES II (1630–85) = Catherine of Braganza
King of Scotland (1651–85)　　　(1638–1705)
King of England and Ireland (1660–85)

JAMES VII & II (1633–1701) = [1] Anne Hyde
King of Scotland, England
and Ireland (1685–88)

Mary (1631–60) = William II of Orange
(1626–50)

WILLIAM III of Orange (1650–1702) = MARY (1662–94)
King and Queen of England, Scotland and Ireland
(1689–1702)　　　(1689–94)

The Colonization of Ireland in the Seventeenth Century

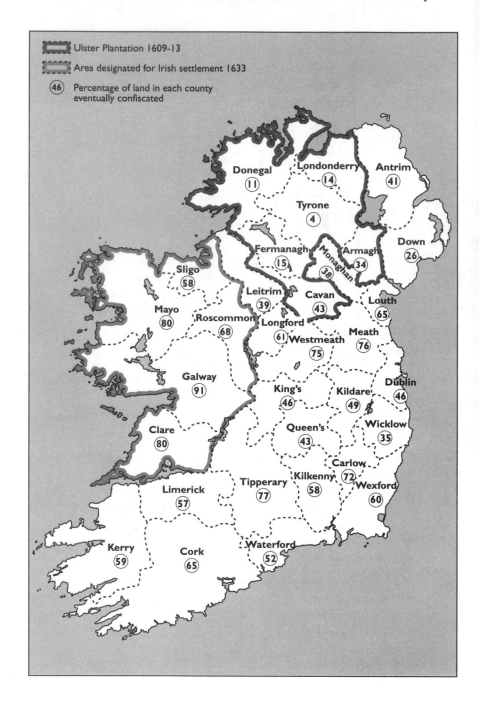

Ulster Plantation 1609-13

Area designated for Irish settlement 1633

(46) Percentage of land in each county eventually confiscated

Donegal (11)
Londonderry (14)
Antrim (41)
Tyrone (4)
Fermanagh (15)
Monaghan (38)
Armagh (34)
Down (26)
Sligo (58)
Leitrim (39)
Cavan (43)
Louth (65)
Mayo (80)
Roscommon (68)
Longford (61)
Westmeath (75)
Meath (76)
Galway (91)
King's (46)
Kildare (49)
Dublin (46)
Clare (80)
Queen's (43)
Wicklow (35)
Carlow (72)
Limerick (57)
Tipperary (77)
Kilkenny (58)
Wexford (60)
Kerry (59)
Cork (65)
Waterford (52)

'Lilliburlero'

Music attr. Henry Purcell (1659–1695)

1.

Ho! bruder Teague, dost hear de decree?
 Lilli burlero, bullen a-la,
Dat we shall have a new deputie,
 Lilli burlero, bullen a-la,
  Lero, lero, lilli burlero, lilli burlero, bullen a-la,
  Lero, lero, lilli burlero, lilli burlero, bullen a-la.

2.
Ho! by shaint Tyburn, it is de Talbote:
 Lilli burlero, bullen a-la,
And he will cut the Englishmens'
  troate.
 Lilli burlero, bullen a-la,
  Lero, lero, etc.

3.
But if dispence do come from de pope,
 Lilli burlero, bullen a-la,
We'll hang Magna Charta and dem in
  a rope.
 Lilli burlero, bullen a-la,
  Lero, lero, etc.

4.
For de good Talbot is made a lord,
    Lilli burlero, bullen a-la,
And with brave lads is coming abroad.
    Lilli burlero, bullen a-la,
        Lero, lero, etc.

6.
Arrah! But why does he stay behind?
    Lilli burlero, bullen a-la,
Ho! by my shoul 'tis a Protestant
        wind.
    Lilli burlero, bullen a-la,
        Lero, lero, etc.

8.
And he dat will not go to de mass,
    Lilli burlero, bullen a-la,
Shall be turn out, and look like an ass.
    Lilli burlero, bullen a la,
        Lero, lero, etc.

5.
Who all in France have taken a sware,
    Lilli burlero, bullen a-la,
Dat they will have no Protestant heir.
    Lilli burlero, bullen a-la,
        Lero, lero, etc.

7.
But see Tyrconnel is now come
        ashore,
    Lilli burlero, bullen a-la,
And we shall have commissions galore.
    Lilli burlero, bullen a-la,
        Lero, lero, etc.

9.
Now, now de hereticks all go down,
    Lilli burlero, bullen a-la,
By Chrish and Shaint Patrick, de
        nation's our own.
    Lilli burlero, bullen a-la,
        Lero, lero, etc.

'The Sash My Father Wore'

D. Timothy and A. Darnell

1.

It is old but it is beautiful, and its colours they are fine,
It was worn at Derry, Aughrim, Enniskillen and the Boyne:
My father wore it when a youth in the by-gone days of yore:
So on the 12th I always wear the Sash my father wore.

2.

Here am I a loyal Orangeman just come across the sea;
For singin' and for dancin' I hope that I please thee;
I can sing and dance like any man as they did in days of yore;
And on the 12th I always wear the Sash my father wore.

3.

It is now I'm going to leave you all, so good luck to you I'll say;
And when I'm on the ocean, for me I hope you'll pray,
I am going to my native land, to a place they call Dromore:
Where on the 12th I love to wear the Sash my father wore.

4.

And whenever I come back again my brethren here to see,
I hope in fine old Orange style, they will always welcome me;
My favourite tune Boyne Water will please me more and more;
And make my Orange heart feel glad in the Sash my father wore.

The Darién Settlement, 1698–1700

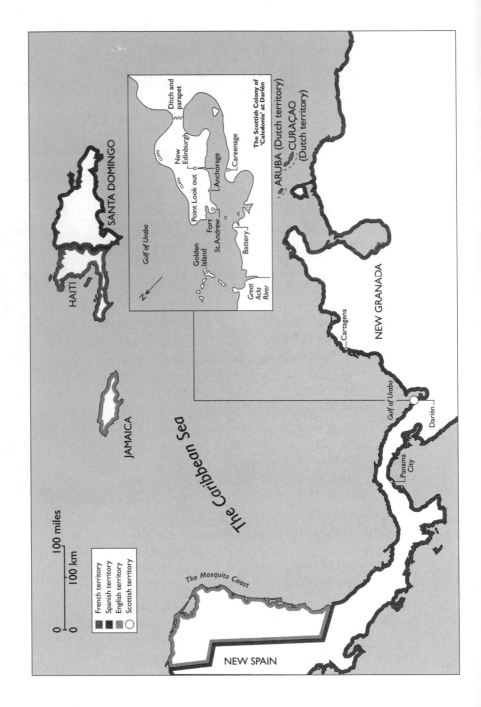

The Articles of the Act of Union, 1707

I   That the two kingdoms of England and Scotland shall for ever after be united into one kingdom by the name of Great Britain.

II   That the succession to the monarchy of the united kingdom of Great Britain be to the most excellent Princess Sophia of Hanover, and their heirs of her body being Protestants.

III   The the united kingdom of Great Britain be represented by one Parliament.

IV   That all the subjects of the united kingdom of Great Britain shall have full freedom of trade within the said united kingdom.

V   That all ships belonging to her Majesty's subjects of Scotland be deemed as ships of Great Britain.

VI   That all parts of the united kingdom shall have the same allowances and be under the same prohibitions and regulations of trade and liable to the same Customs and duties on import and export.

VII   That all parts of the united kingdom be liable to the same Excise upon all excisable liquors.

VII   That all foreign salt imported into Scotland shall be charged the same duties as [in] England. But Scotland shall, for seven years, be exempted from playing [the duty] in Scotland for salt made there.

IX   That Scotland shall not be charged the sum of forty-eight thousand pounds as the quota of Scotland to a land tax.

X   That Scotland shall not be charged with the same duties on stamped paper, vellum and parchment in force in England.

XI   That Scotland shall not be charged with the duties payable in England on windows and lights.

XII   That Scotland shall not be charged with the duties payable in England on coals, culm and cinders consumed there, but shall be charged for all coals, clum and cinders not consumed in Scotland.

XIII   That Scotland shall not be charged with the duty payable in England upon malt.

XIV   That Scotland be not charged with any other duties except these consented to in this treaty.

XV   It is agreed that Scotland shall have an equivalent for what [her] subjects shall be charged towards payment of the debts of England . . . the sum of three hundred ninety-eight thousand and eighty-five pounds ten shillings.

XVI   That the coin shall be of the same standard and value throughout the united kingdom.

XVII   That the same weights and measures shall be used throughout the united kingdom.

XVIII That the laws concerning regulation of trade, Customs and Excises be the same in Scotland as in England.

XIX   That the Court of Session shall remain within Scotland as it is now constituted by the laws of that kingdom.

XX   That all heritable offices be reserved to the owners thereof in the same manner as they are now enjoyed by the laws of Scotland.

XXI   That the rights and privileges of the royal burghs in Scotland remain entire after the union.

XXII   That of the peers of Scotland sixteen shall be the number to sit and vote in the House of Lords, and forty-five the number of the representatives of Scotland in the House of Commons of the Parliament of Great Britain.

XXIII That the sixteen peers of Scotland shall have all privileges which the peers of England now have.

XXIV   That after the union there be one great seal for the united kingdom of Great Britain, which shall be different from the great seal now used in either kingdom.

XXV   That all laws in either kingdom contrary to or inconsistent with the terms of these articles shall cease and become void.

The 57 Stuart *Rejetés*

1   Charles Edward Stuart – the Young Pretender (1720–88)
2   Anne Marie, Duchess of Savoy
     3   Philip, Prince of Piedmont
     4   Charles, Duke of Aoust
5   Louis, Dauphin of France (d. 1765)
6   Louis, Prince of Austria
7   Don Philip, infant (brother of above)
8   Don Ferdinand, infant (brother of above)
9   Elisabeth Charlotte, Duchess of Orléans
  10   Philip, Duke of Orléans (1674–1723)
    11   Louis, Duke of Chartres
    12   Duchess of Berry
    13   Mlle. of Orléans
    14   Mlle. of Valois
    15   Mlle. of Montpensier
    16   Mlle. (b. 1714)
  17   Elisabeth, Duchess of Lorraine
    18   Leopold, Prince of Lorraine
    19   Francis, Prince of Lorraine
    20   Charles, Prince of Lorraine
    21   Elisabeth Therese, Princess of Lorraine
    22   Anne Charlotte, Princess of Lorraine
23   Louis Otto, Prince of Salmes
  24   Dorothea Françoise
  25   Elizabeth Alexandrina
  26   Christina Anne
27   Adelaide (sister of 23)
28   Eleonora Christina (sister of 23)
29   Anne Henrietta, Princess of Conti
  30   Louis, Duke of Bourbon (1692–1740)
  31   Charles of Charleois
  32   Count of Clermont
  33   Mary Anne of Bourbon
  34   Louisa, Princess of Conti
  35   Mlle. of Charolais
  36   Mlle. of Clermont
  37   Mlle. of Vermandy
  38   Mlle. of Sens
  39   Mary, Princess of Conti
    40   Louis, Prince of Conti
    41   Mary, Duchess of Bourbon
    42   Mlle. of Conti
  43   Louisa, Duchess of Main
    44   Louis Augustus, Prince of Dombes
    45   Louis Charles
    46   Mlle. of Main
  47   Mary, Duchess of Vendôme
48   Benedicte Henriette, Duchess of Hanover (sister of 29)
  49   Charlotte, Duchess of Modena
    50   Françoise Marie, Princess of Modena
    51   Jean Frederica, Princess of Modena
    52   Benedictine Erneste, Princess of Modena
    53   Amelia Josepha, Princess of Modena
    54   Henrietta, Princess of Modena
  55   Wilhelmina Amelia, Archduchess of Austria
    56   Mary Josepha
    57   Mary Amelia
58   George, Elector of Hanover (1660–1727)

'Scots Wha Hae'

Words: Robert Burns (1759–1796)   Music: Scottish Traditional

1.
Scots, wha hae wi' Wallace bled,
Scots, wham Bruce has aften led,
Welcome to your gory bed,
Or to victorie!

2.
Now's the day, and now's the hour;
See the front o' battle lour!
See approach proud Edward's power –
Chains and slaverie!

3.
Wha will be a traitor knave?
Wha can fill a coward's grave?
Wha sae base as be a slave?
Let him turn and flee!

4.
Wha for Scotland's King and law
Freedom's sword will strongly draw,
Freeman stand, or freeman fa'?
Let him follow me!

5.
By oppression's woes and pains!
By your sons in servile chains!
We will drain our dearest veins,
But they shall be free!

6.
Lay the proud usurpers low!
Tyrants fall in every foe!
Liberty's fall in every foe!
Let us do or die!

Appendix 38

'Flower of Scotland'

Words and Music: Roy Williamson (1936–1990)

1.

O flower of Scotland
When will we see
Your like again,
That fought and died for
Your wee bit hill and glen
    And stood against him
    Proud Edward's army
    And sent him homeward
    Tae think again.

2.

The hills are bare now
And autumn leaves lie
Thick and still
O'er land that is lost now
Which those so dearly held
    Chorus

3.

Those days are passed now
And in the past
They must remain
But we can still rise now
And be the nation again
    Chorus

'God Save the Queen'

Words and Music: attr. Henry Carey (1687–1743)

I.

God save our gracious Queen;
Long live our noble Queen;
    God save the Queen!
Send her victorious,
Happy and glorious,
Long to reign over us
    God save the Queen!

2.

O Lord our God arise,
Scatter her enemies,
    And make them fall:
Confound their politics,
Frustrate their knavish tricks,
On Thee our hopes we fix;
    God save us all!

3.

Thy choicest gifts in store
On her be pleased to pour;
    Long may she reign:
May she defend our laws,
And ever give us cause
To sing with heart and voice,
    God save the Queen!

(4.

God grant that Marshall Wade,
May by thy might aid,
    Victory bring,
May he sedition hush,
And like a torrent rush,
Rebellious Scots to crush
    God save the King!)

'Recessional'

Rudyard Kipling

God of our fathers, known of old—
      Lord of our far-flung battle-line—
Beneath whose awful Hand we hold
      Dominion over palm and pine—
Lord God of Hosts, be with us yet,
      Lest we forget, lest we forget!

The tumult and the shouting dies—
      The captains and the kings depart—
Still stands Thine ancient sacrifice,
      An humble and a contrite heart.
Lord God of Hosts, be with us yet,
      Lest we forget, lest we forget!

Far-call'd our navies melt away—
      On dune and headland sinks the fire—
Lo, all our pomp of yesterday
      Is one with Nineveh and Tyre!
Judge of the Nations, spare us yet,
      Lest we forget, lest we forget!

If, drunk with sight of power, we loose
      Wild tongues that have not Thee in awe—
Such boasting as the Gentiles use
      Or lesser breeds without the Law—
Lord God of Hosts, be with us yet,
      Lest we forget, lest we forget!

For heathen heart that puts her trust
      In reeking tube and iron shard—
All valiant dust that builds on dust,
      And guarding calls not Thee to guard—
For frantic boast and foolish word,
      Thy Mercy on Thy People, Lord!

'Rule, Britannia!'

Words: James Thomson (1700–1748)   Music: Dr Thomas Arne (1710–1778)

1.
When Britain first, at Heaven's command,
Arose from out the azure main,
This was the charter of the land,
And guardian angels sang this strain –
> 'Rule, Britannia! Britannia, rule the waves;
> Britons never, never, never will be slaves.'

2.
The nations, not so blest as thee,
Must in their turns to tyrants fall,
Whilst thou shalt flourish great and free,
The dread and envy of them all.
> Rule, Britannia! etc.

3.
Still more majestic shalt thou rise,
More dreadful from each foreign stroke,
As the loud blast that tears the skies,
Serves but to root thy native oak.
          Rule, Britannia! etc.

4.
Thee haughty tyrants ne'er shall tame,
All their attempts to bend thee down,
Will but arouse thy generous flame,
And work their woe and thy renown.
          Rule, Britannia! etc.

5.
To thee belongs the rural reign,
Thy cities shall with commerce shine,
And thine shall be the subject main,
And every shore it circles thine.
          Rule, Britannia! etc.

6.
The Muses, still with freedom found,
Shall to thy happy coast repair,
Blest isle with matchless beauty crowned,
And manly hearts to guard the fair.
          Rule, Britannia! etc.

'The Wearing of the Green'

Words: Author unknown   Music: Irish Street Ballad (1798)

1.

Oh, Paddy dear, and did you hear the news that's going round?
The shamrock is forbid by law to grow on Irish ground;
Saint Patrick's Day no more we'll keep, his colours can't be seen,
For there's a cruel law against the wearing of the green.
I met with Napper Tandy, and he took me by the hand,
And he said "How's poor old Ireland, and how does she stand?"
She's the distressful country that ever yet was seen;
They're hanging men and women there for wearing of the green.

2.

Then since the colour we must wear is England's cruel red,
Sure Ireland's sons will ne'er forget the blood that they have shed;
You may take the shamrock from your hat, and cast it in the sod,
But 'twill take root and flourish there, tho' underfoot 'tis trod.
When law can stop the blades of grass from growing as they grow,
And when the leaves in summertime their verdure dare not show,
Then I will change the colour that I wear in my caubeen;
But till that day, please God, I'll stick to wearing of the green.

3.

But if at last our colour should be torn from Ireland's heart,
Her sons, with shame and sorrow, from the dear old isle will part;
I've heard whisper of a country that lies beyond the sea,
Where rich and poor stand equal in the light of freedom's day.
Oh, Erin! Must we leave you, driven by a tyrant's hand?
Must we ask a mother's blessing from a stange and distant land?
Where the cruel cross of England shall never more be seen,
And where, please God, we'll live and die still wearing of the green.

Nineteenth-Century Demography

From *Harmsworth's Universal Encyclopaedia*

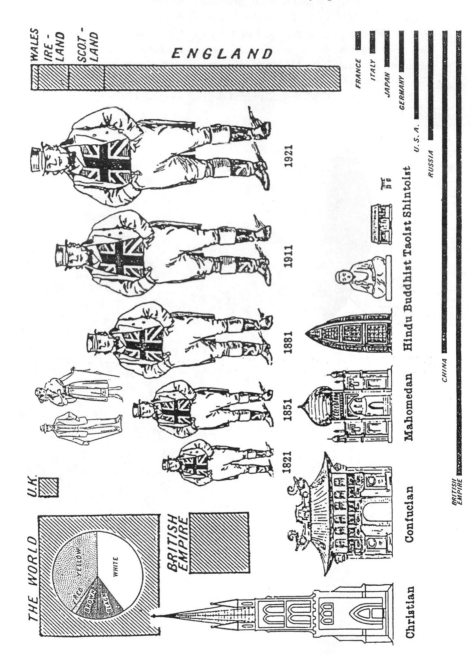

Demographic Change in the United Kingdom: percentage share of each nation in their combined population totals, 1803 and 1999–2000

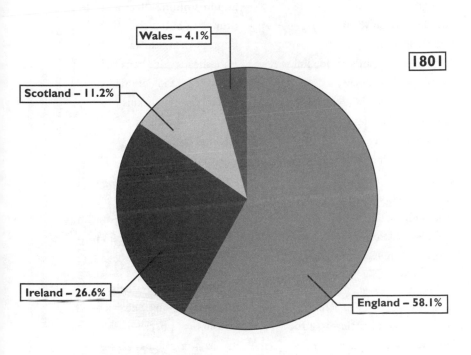

Wales – 4.1%

Scotland – 11.2%

Ireland – 26.6%

England – 58.1%

1801

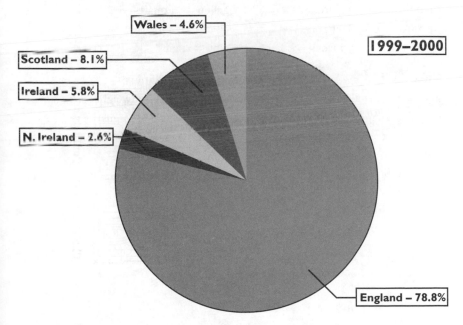

Wales – 4.6%

Scotland – 8.1%

Ireland – 5.8%

N. Ireland – 2.6%

England – 78.8%

1999–2000

Imperial Weights and Measures
(from 1824)

Length

1 mile = 1,760 yards

1 furlong = 220 yards

1 chain = 22 yards = 100 links

1 rod, pole or perch = 5½ yards

1 yard = 3 feet = 36 inches

1 foot = 12 inches

1 span = 9 inches*

1 hand = 4 inches*

1 nail = 2¼ inches (for cloth)*

1 inch = 1/36 yard

1 fathom = 6 feet

1 cable = 600 feet

1 nautical mile = 6,080 feet

Area

1 square mile = 640 acres

1 acre = 10 sq. chains = 4 roods

1 rood = 40 sq. poles

1 sq. pole = 30¼ sq. yards

1 sq. yard = 9 sq. feet

1 sq. foot = 144 sq. inches

Money

1 guinea = 21 shillings

1 pound sterling = 20 shillings

1 crown = 5 shillings

1 shilling = 12 pence

1 penny = 4 farthings

Liquid Volume (Beer and Ale)

1 tun = 2 butts

1 butt = 2 hogsheads

1 hogshead = 1½ barrels

1 barrell = 2 kilderkins

1 kilderkin = 2 firkins

1 firkin = 9 gallons

1 gallon = 4 quarts

1 quart = 2 pints

1 pint = 4 gills

1 gill = 5 fluid ounces

1 fluid ounce = 8 fluid drachms

1 fluid drachm = 60 minims

Dry measure

1 chaldron = 36 bushels

1 quarter = 8 bushels

1 bushel = 4 pecks

1 peck = 2 gallons

1 gallon = 4 quarts

1 quart = 2 pints

1 pint = 4 gills

Weight Avoirdupois

1 ton = 20 hundredweight (cwt)

1 hundredweight = 4 quarters

1 quarter = 2 stones

1 stone = 14 pounds (lb)

1 pound = 16 ounces (oz) = 7,000 grains

1 ounce = 16 drams = 437½ grains

1 dram = 27.34 grains

---

* Not statutory. There was considerable non-statutory local variation. Some of these units (e.g. the nautical mile) have changed their value since 1824.

'Land of Hope and Glory'

Words: Arthur C. Benson (1862–1925)   Music: Edward Elgar (1857–1934)

Dear Land of Hope, thy hope is crowned.
God make thee mightier yet!
On Sov'ran brows, beloved, renowned,
Once more thy crown is set.
Thine equal laws, by Freedom gained,
Have ruled thee well and long;
By Freedom gained, by Truth maintained,
Thine Empire shall be strong.

Chorus   Land of Hope and Glory,
Mother of the Free,
How shall we extol thee,
Who are born of thee?
Wider still and wider
Shall thy bounds be set;
God, who made thee mighty,
Make thee mightier yet.

Thy fame is ancient as the days,
As Ocean large and wide:
A pride that dares and heeds not praise,
A stern and silent pride:
Not that false joy that dreams content
With what our sires have won;
The blood a hero sire hath spent
Still nerves a hero son.

Chorus

'Amhrán na bhFiann'

'The Soldier's Song'

Words: Peadar Kearney (1883–1942)   Music: Patrick Heeney (1881–1911)

Sinne Fianna Fáil,
A tá faoi gheall ag Éirinn,
Buíon dár slua
Thar toinn do ráinig chugainn,
Faoi mhóid bheith saor,
Sean tir ár sinsear feasta
Ni fhágfar faoin tiorán ná faoin tráill
Anocht a théam sa bhearna baoil,
Le gean ar Ghaeil chun báis nó saoil,
Le gunna scréach faoi lámhach na bpiléar,
Seo libh canaig amhrán na bhFiann.

Soldiers are we,
Whose lives are pledged to Ireland,
Some have come
From a Land beyond the wave.
Sworn to be free,
No more our ancient sire land
Shall shelter the despot or the slave.
Tonight we man the gap of danger
In Erin's cause, come woe or weal
'Mid cannons' roar and rifles peal,
We'll chant a soldier's song.

Appendix 48

'Yma O Hyd'
'We're Still Here'

Dafydd Iwan

'Dwyt ti'm yn cofio Macsen	*You don't remember Macsen*
'Does neb yn ei 'nabod o	*Nobody ever knew him*
Mae mil chwe chant o flynyddoedd	*One thousand and six hundred years*
Yn amser rhy hir i'r co'	*Is too long ago to recall*
Ond daeth Magnus Maximus o Gymru	*But Magnus Maximus left Wales*
Yn y flwyddyn tri chant wyth tri	*In the year three hundred and eighty three*
A'n gadael yn genedl gyfan	*And left the nation as one*
A heddiw, deled hi!	*And today, look at her!*
Cytgan	Chorus
R'yn ni yma o hyd	*We're still here (We're still standing)*
R'yn ni yma o hyd	*We're still here*
Er gwaetha pawb a phopeth	*Despite everybody and everything*
Er gwaetha pawb a phopeth	*Despite everybody and everything*
Er gwaetha pawb a phopeth	*Despite everybody and everything*
R'yn ni yma o hyd	*We're still here*
R'yn ni yma o hyd	*We're still here*
Er gwaetha pawb a phopeth	*Despite everybody and everything*
Er gwaetha pawb a phopeth	*Despite everybody and everything*
Er gwaetha pawb a phopeth	*Despite everybody and everything*
R'yn ni yma o hyd	*We're still here*
Chwythed y gwynt o'r dwyrain	*Winds will blow from the east*
Rhued y storm o'r môr	*Storms will rage from the sea*
Hollted y mellt yr wybren	*Lightning will rip through the skies*
A gwaedded y daran yn un côr	*The thunder will roar as one*
Llifed dagrau'r gwangalon	*Tears flow from the faint-hearted*
A llyfed y taeog y llawr	*And the villein/churl still suffers*
Er dued y fagddu o'n cwmpas	*When the darkest clouds loom –*
R'yn ni'n barod am doriad y wawr	*We're ready for the dawn*
Cytgan	Chorus
Cofiwn i Facsen Wledig	*We remember that Macsen Wledig*
Aduel ein gwlad yn un darn	*Left our country as one*
A bloeddiwn gerbron y gwledydd	*And we'll call out to all nations*
Byddwn yma hyd Ddydd y Farn	*'We'll be here until Judgement Day'*
Er gwaetha pob Dic Siôn Dafydd	*Despite every Dic Siôn Dafydd*
Er gwaetha 'rhen Fagi a'i chriw	*Despite Maggie and her crew*
Byddwn yma hyd ddiwedd amser	*We'll be here until the end of time*
Bydd yr iaith Gymraeg yn fyw	*The Welsh Language will live!*
Cytgan	Chorus

The Counties of Ireland

Galway English name

Gaillimh Gaelic name

—·— Border of Northern Ireland

(8) Approximate meaning of
Gaelic name

(1)

Donegal
Dún na Ngall

(London)Derry
Doire

Antrim
Aontroim

(2)

Tyrone
Tír Eoghain

(3)

(4)

Down
Dún

Fermanagh
Fir Manach

(7)

Armagh
Ard Macha

(5)

Monaghan
Muineacháin

(6)

Sligo
Sligeagh

Leitrim
Liatroim

Cavan
Cabhán

Louth
Lú

Mayo
Maigh Eo

(8)

Roscommon
Ros Comán

Longford
Longfort

Meath
Mí

(9)

Westmeath
Iarmrmhí

Galway
Gaillimh

Offaly
Ua Fáilghe

Kildare
Cill Dara

Dublin
Baile Átha Cliath

(10)

Clare
Clár

Laois
Laois

Wicklow
Cill Mhantáin

(15)

Tipperary
Tiobraid Árainn

(14)

Carlow
Ceatharlach

Limerick
Luimneach

(12)

Kilkenny
Cill Chainnigh

Wexford
Loch Garman

(11)

(13)

Kerry
Ciarraí

Cork
Corcaigh

Waterford
Port Lairge

(16)

1	Fortress of the foreigners	9	St Coman's Wood
2	Oakwood	10	Church of Oak
3	Land of Eoghan	11	Barren land
4	Macha's Hill	12	The Well of Ara
5	The men of Manach	13	Church of St Canice
6	Fortress	14	Four Lakes
7	A place of little hills	15	St Mantan's Church
8	The plain of yews	16	Marsh

Modernization – the Component Processes

(The Industrial Revolution)

1. Scientific and mechanized agriculture
2. Mobility of Labour: enclosures, emancipation of the serfs
3. New sources of power: coal, steam, gas, oil, electricity
4. Power-driven machinery
5. Heavy industry: mining and metallurgy
6. Factories and factory towns
7. Improved transport: canals, roads, railways, flight
8. Communications: post, telegraph, telephone, radio
9. Capital investment: joint-stock companies, trusts, cartels
10. Expanding domestic markets: new industries, internal trade
11. Foreign trade: import and export, colonies
12. Government policy
13. Demography: rapid population growth and its consequences

14. The money economy: wages, prices, taxes, paper money
15. Marketing skills: advertising, stores, sales distribution
16. Science and technology: research and development
17. Financial services: credit, savings banks, insurance
18. Standardization of weights, measures, and currencies

19. Urbanization: town planning, public services
20. New social classes: middle classes, domestics, 'workers'
21. Transformation of family structures: 'the nuclear family'
22. Women: dependency and subordination
23. Migration: local, regional, international
24. Public health: epidemics, hygiene, medical services
25. Poverty: unemployment, vagrancy, workhouses, slums
26. Exploitation: child labour, female labour, sweatshops
27. Organized crime: police, detectives, criminal underclass
28. Private charities

29. Education: primary, technical, scientific, executive, female
30. Literacy and mass culture

31. Leisure: organized recreation and sport
32. Youth movements
33. Religious trends: fundamentalism, temperance, worker priests
34. Social sciences: economics, anthropology, ethnography, etc.

35. Collectivism: industrial and urban psychology
36. Consumerism
37. Class consciousness
38. National consciousness
39. Political consciousness

40. Extension of the electorate: universal suffrage, suffragettes
41. Political parties with mass constituencies
42. State-run welfare: pensions, social insurance, benefits
43. Elaborate social legislation
44. Expansion of the civil service: state bureaucracy
45. Reorganization of local government
46. Political associations and pressure groups: trade unions
47. Imperialism
48. Total war: conscript armies, mechanized warfare, home front

'Hen Wlad fy Nhadau'
'Land of my Fathers'

Welsh words: Evan James   English words: A. P. Graves   Music: James James

1.
Mae hen wlad fy nhadau yn anwyl i mi,
Gwlad beirdd a chantorion, enwogion o fri;
Ei gwrol rhyfelwyr, gwlad garwyr tra mâd,
Tros ryddid collasant eu gwaed.

> Gwlad, Gwlad, pleidiol wyf i'm gwlad,
> Tra môr yn fur,
> I'r bur hoff bau,
> O bydded i'r heniaith barhau.

1.
O land of my fathers, O land of my love,
Dear mother of minstrels who kindle and move,
And hero on hero, who at honour's proud call,
For freedom their lifeblood let fall.

> *Wales! Wales! O but my heart is with you!*
> *As long as the sea*
> *Your bulwark shall be,*
> *To Cymru my heart shall be true.*

2.

Hên Gymru fynyddig, paradwys y bardd,
Pob dyffryn, pob clogwyn, i'm golwg sydd hardd;
Trwy deimlad gwladgarol, mor swynol yw si
Ei nentydd, afonydd, i mi.
         Gwlad, gwlad etc.

2.

O land of the mountains, the bard's paradise,
Whose precipice proud, valleys lone as the skies,
Green murmuring forest, far echoing flood,
Fire the fancy and quicken the blood.
         Wales! Wales! etc.

3.

Os treisiodd y gelyn fy ngwlad dan ei droed,
Mae hen iaith y Cymry mor fyw ag erioed;
Ni luddiwyd yr awen gan erchyll law brad,
Na thelyn burseiniol fy ngwlad.
         Gwlad, gwlad etc.

3.

For tho' the fierce foeman has ravaged your realm,
The old speech of Cymru he cannot o'erwhelm,
Our passionate poets to silence command,
Or banish the harp from your strand.
         Wales! Wales! etc.

The wives and husbands of the Kings and Queens of Great Britain and the United Kingdom, George I to George VI

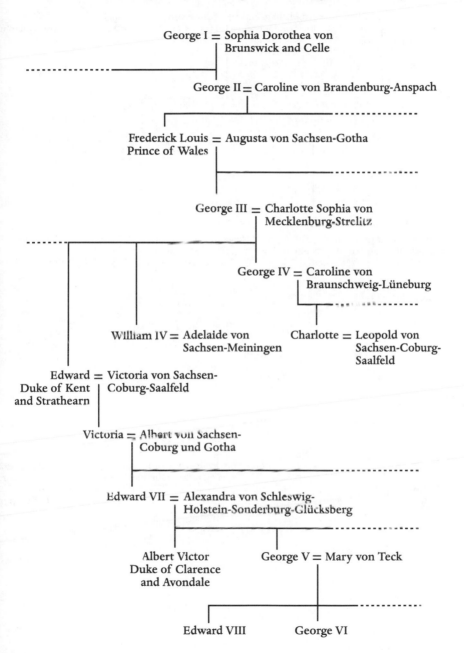

The House of Windsor and its Predecessors

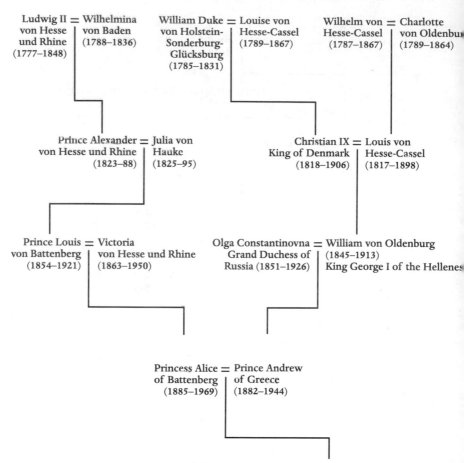

Ludwig II = Wilhelmina
von Hesse | von Baden
und Rhine | (1788–1836)
(1777–1848)

William Duke = Louise von
von Holstein- | Hesse-Cassel
Sonderburg- | (1789–1867)
Glücksburg
(1785–1831)

Wilhelm von = Charlotte
Hesse-Cassel | von Oldenbur
(1787–1867) | (1789–1864)

Prince Alexander = Julia von
von Hesse und Rhine | Hauke
(1823–88) | (1825–95)

Christian IX = Louis von
King of Denmark | Hesse-Cassel
(1818–1906) | (1817–1898)

Prince Louis = Victoria
von Battenberg | von Hesse und Rhine
(1854–1921) | (1863–1950)

Olga Constantinovna = William von Oldenburg
Grand Duchess of | (1845–1913)
Russia (1851–1926) | King George I of the Hellenes

Princess Alice = Prince Andrew
of Battenberg | of Greece
(1885–1969) | (1882–1944)

Philip von Schleswig-Holstein-Sonderburg-Glücksburg (1921
(Philip Mountbatten) Prince of Greece and Denma
Duke of Edinbur
Earl of Merione

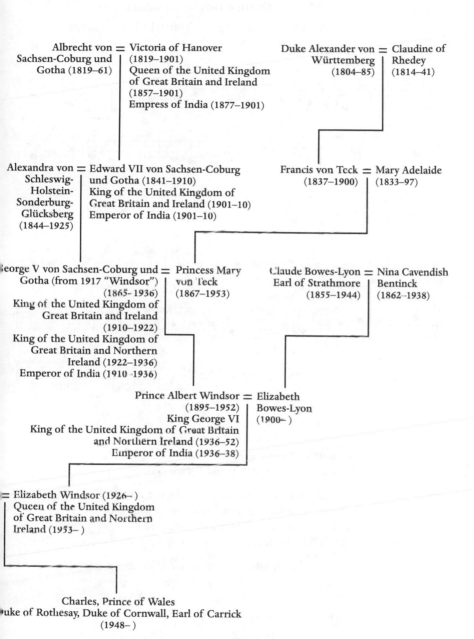

Albrecht von = Victoria of Hanover
Sachsen-Coburg und | (1819–1901)
Gotha (1819–61) | Queen of the United Kingdom
of Great Britain and Ireland
(1857–1901)
Empress of India (1877–1901)

Duke Alexander von = Claudine of
Württemberg | Rhedey
(1804–85) | (1814–41)

Alexandra von = Edward VII von Sachsen-Coburg
Schleswig- | und Gotha (1841–1910)
Holstein- | King of the United Kingdom of
Sonderburg- | Great Britain and Ireland (1901–10)
Glücksberg | Emperor of India (1901–10)
(1844–1925)

Francis von Teck = Mary Adelaide
(1837–1900) | (1833–97)

George V von Sachsen-Coburg und = Princess Mary
Gotha (from 1917 "Windsor") | von Teck
(1865–1936) | (1867–1953)
King of the United Kingdom of
Great Britain and Ireland
(1910–1922)
King of the United Kingdom of
Great Britain and Northern
Ireland (1922–1936)
Emperor of India (1910–1936)

Claude Bowes-Lyon = Nina Cavendish
Earl of Strathmore | Bentinck
(1855–1944) | (1862–1938)

Prince Albert Windsor = Elizabeth
(1895–1952) | Bowes-Lyon
King George VI | (1900–)
King of the United Kingdom of Great Britain
and Northern Ireland (1936–52)
Emperor of India (1936–38)

= Elizabeth Windsor (1926–)
Queen of the United Kingdom
of Great Britain and Northern
Ireland (1953–)

Charles, Prince of Wales
Duke of Rothesay, Duke of Cornwall, Earl of Carrick
(1948–)

Appendix 54

'Danny Boy'

Words: F. E. Weatherly (1848–1929)   Music: Irish Traditional

Oh Danny boy, the pipes, the pipes are calling
From glen to glen, and down the mountain side
The summer's gone, and all the flowers are dying
"Tis you, 'tis you must go and I must bide.

But come ye back when summer's in the meadow
Or when the valley's hushed and white with snow
'Tis I'll be there in sunshine or in shadow
Oh Danny boy, oh Danny boy, I love you so.

And if you come, when all the flowers are dying
And I am dead, as dead I well may be
You'll come and find the place where I am lying
And kneel and say an 'Ave' there for me.

And I shall hear, tho' soft you tread above me
And all my dreams will warm and sweeter be
If you'll not fail to tell me that you love me
I'll simply sleep in peace until you come to me.

The British Empire and Imperial Territories at their Zenith

This list shows all the major territories under direct and indirect control of the United Kingdom in 1922.

Date	Name in 1922	Date	Name in 1922
1583	Newfoundland	c. 1788	Alberta
1605	St Lucia	1788	New South Wales
1609	Bermudas	1794	Seychelles
c. 1618	Gambia	1795	Cape of Good Hope (Cape Colony)
1623	Nova Scotia		
1623	St Christopher (St Kitts)	1795	Ceylon
1628	Nevis	1796	Demerara, Berbice, Essequibo
1605–25	Barbados		
1632	Antigua	1797	Trinidad
1632	Montserrat	1800	Malta
1638	British Honduras	1803	Tasmania
c. 1650	Gold Coast Colony	1810	Mauritius
1655	Jamaica	1811	Manitoba
1666	Bahamas	1819	Singapore
1670	Cayman Is.	1821	British Columbia
1670	Rupert's Land and North-West Territory	1821	Vancouver I
		1824	Natal
1608–85	Bombay	1824	Queensland
1704	Gibraltar	1826	Western Australia
1713	New Brunswick	1834	Victoria
1666–72	Virgin Islands	1836	South Australia
1758	Prince Edward I.	1839	Aden
1758	Cape Breton I.	1840	New Zealand
1761	Dominica	1841	Hong-Kong
1762	Grenada	1759–90	Ontario
1762	St Vincent	1849	Punjab
1763	Tobago	1759–90	Quebec
1765	Falkland Is.	1825–26	Eastern Bengal and Assam
1766	Saskatchewan	1861	Lagos
1787	Sierra Leone	1864	Bhutan

Date	Name in 1922	Date	Name in 1922
1868	Basutoland	1919	Palestine
1870	Manitoba	1919	South West Africa
1824–52	Burma	1919	Tanganyika Territory
1878	Cyprus	1919	Togoland
1881	British North Borneo	1920	Iraq
1882	*Egypt*	1920	Transjordan
1887	Zululand	1877–81	Transvaal
1888	Brunei	1874–95	Federated Malay States
1888	Kenya Colony	1884–86	British Somaliland
1888	Sarawak	1884–86	Nigeria
1890	Swaziland	1885–91	Bechuanaland Protectorate
1890	Zanzibar Protectorate	1888–93	Rhodesia
1891	Nyasaland Protectorate	1890–96	Uganda
1899	*Anglo-Egyptian Sudan*	1639–1748	Madras
1848–54	Orange River Colony	1633–1765	Bengal
1919	Cameroon	1786–1824	Straits Settlements

Twentieth-Century Demographics:
The Domination of South-east England

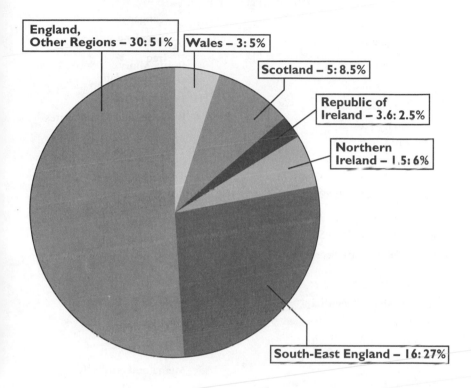

England,
Other Regions – 30: 51%   Wales – 3: 5%

Scotland – 5: 8.5%

Republic of
Ireland – 3.6: 2.5%

Northern
Ireland – 1.5: 6%

South-East England – 16: 27%

Region name – Population in millions, 1991: Percentage of total population

Power and Influence in the United Kingdom (1998): The Top Hundred

Individual People ranked 1–100

Politicians

In Government

1 Tony Blair

= 4 Defence Secretary

= 9 Deputy PM
Lord Chancellor
Foreign Secretary
Education Secretary

= 18 Chancellor of Exchequer

= 24 Home Secretary

= 46 Northern Ireland Secretary

= 68 Social Security Secretary

In Opposition

= 41 Tory Party Chairman

= 68 William Hague

= 21 David Trimble, UUP

= 31 Gerry Adams, Sinn Fein

= 54 Speaker of the Commons

Appointed Administrators

3 Lord Chief Justice

= 6 Head of MI6

8 Chief of the Defence Staff

= 13 Head of MI5

16 Deputy Chief of Defence Staff

= 18 Governor of the Bank of England

39 Chief Inspector of Schools

Appointed Administrators

92 Prime Minister's Spokesman

97 Leader of GMB, trade unionist

Business and Finance

2 Bill Gates, Microsoft

7 George Soros

= 46 Richard Branson, Virgin

= 46 CEO of BT

= 54 CEO, Ispat Steal

= 56 CEO, GEC

= 58 CEO, Mercury Assets

= 75 Sir Terence Conran

= 84 Mohammed Al Fayed

= 88 Lord Sainsbury, the UK's richest person

Media and Advertising

= 4 Conrad Black

= 13 Rupert Murdoch

= 13 Editor of *The Sun*

= 21 David D. Frost, presenter

= 24 Head of ITV

= 29 Director-General, BBC

= 29 CEO, Channel 4

51 Chris Evans, DJ

58 Lord Saatchi

60 Editor, *Daily Mirror*

After Dr. Terry Kallard – *Sunday Times*, 18 October 1998

Media and Advertising

79 Editor, *Hello*

93 Chairman, Granada

Science, Academia, Professions

28 Director, LSE

36 Helena Kennedy, QC

37 Head of Roslin Inst

41 Harry Kroto

50 Cherie Booth, QC

= 56 Jonathan Porritt

= 60 Steve Hawking

Religion

= 44 The Pope

= 44 Zaki Badawi, Muslim leader

= 68 Archbishop of Canterbury

72 Cardinal Hume

Music and the Arts

33 Paul McCartney

= 65 Andrew Lloyd Webber

77 Lord Rogers, architect

= 79 Germaine Greer

= 79 Jeffrey Archer

= 84 Oasis

Sport

= 84 Alan Shearer, England
      Football Captain

= 97 Glen Hoddle, England
      Manager

Royalty

= 100 HM The Queen

= 100 Prince Charles

= 100 Prince William

EU Institutions

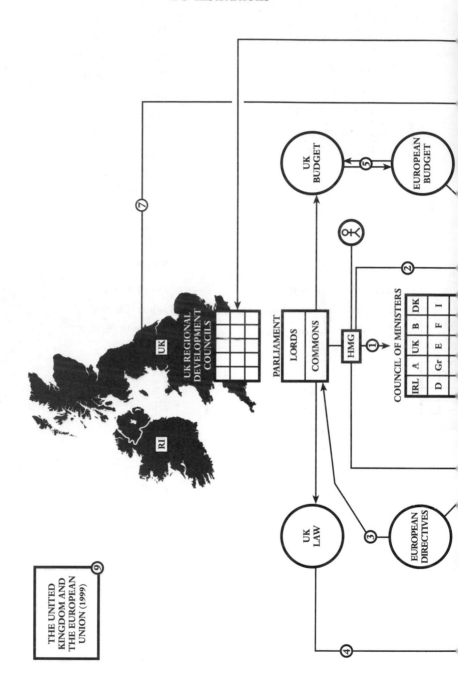

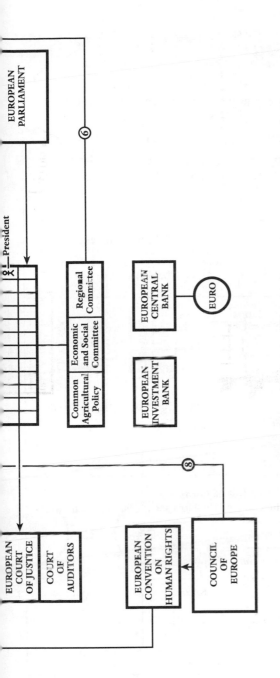

① The British Government has a permanent seat on the Council of Ministers, the EU's supreme Executive.

② HMG appoints two of the twenty-four commissioners who administer EU policy.

③ European directives only become law after being scrutinised and passed by national legislatures.

④ The European Convention on Human Rights was incorporated into a British Human Rights Act (1998).

⑤ The UK both contributes to, and receives a rebate from the European Budget.

⑥ EU Regional Funds are distributed to member states, in the UK through Regional Development Councils.

⑦ M.E.Ps from the UK are directly elected to the European Parliament, which has advisory and auditory powers.

⑧ The UK is a founder-member of the Council of Europe – a separate organization with cultural and legal functions.

⑨ The UK is a member of the EU by virtue of signing the Treaty of Rome as amended by the Single European Act (1993).

Appendix 59

Judicial Structures in the United Kingdom, 1999

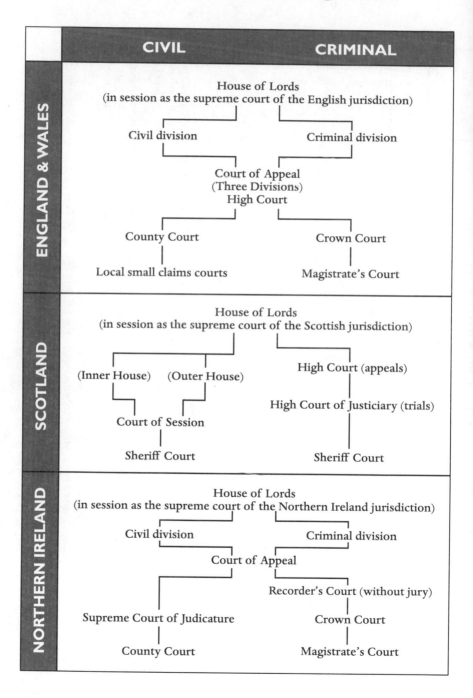

The Top Twenty Landowners in Scotland?

Most private estates are held in trust, which means that the Duke of Atholl, for example, only 'owns' a few thousand acres himself. The list, however, identifies the main beneficiaries and families behind the key estates. The acreages were, in most cases, supplied by the owners, and may not accord with detailed map-based calculations.

	Acres	
1	1,600,000	Forestry Commission
2	270,000	Duke of Buccleuch/Lord Dalkeith *Four estates in the Borders*
3	260,000	Scottish Office Agriculture Department *Ninety per cent crofting land*
4	190,000	National Trust For Scotland *Includes 75,000 acre Mar Lodge*
5	135,000	Alcan Highland Estates *Land used for electricity generation*
6	130,000	Duke of Atholl, Sarah Troughton *Estates around Dunkeld/Blair Atholl*
7	125,000	Capt. Alwyn Farquharson *Invercauld on Deeside/Smaller estate, Argyll*
8	120,000	Duchess of Westminster, Lady Mary Grosvenor *Grosvenor Sporting Estates, Sutherland*
9	105,000	Earl of Seafield *Seafield estates, Speyside*
10	100,000	Crown Estate Commission *Three main estates, including Glenlivet*
11	100,000	Edmund Vestey and four sons *Assynt, mountain property*
12	92,000	South Uist Estate Co. (syndicate) *Sporting estate with 900 crofts*
13	90,000	Sir Donald Cameron of Lochiel, and family *Sporting/forestry centred on Achnacarry Castle*
14	90,000	Countess of Sutherland, Lord Strahnaver *Sporting estates in Sutherland*
15	87,400	Royal Society for the Protection of Birds *Fifty-two seperate reserves*
16	87,000	Paul Van Vlissingen *Letterewe 'wilderness', Wester Ross*
17	84,400	Scottish Natural Heritage *Nature reserves*
18	80,000	Robin Fleming and family *Blackmount/Glen Etive*

From Auslan Cramb, *Who Owns Scotland Now? The Use and Abuse of Private Land*, Mainstream Publishing (Edinburgh, 1996).

| 19 | 77,000 | Hon. Chas. Pearson *Dunecht* |
| 20 | 73,000 | Lord Margadale *Islay* |

Major Foreign Landowners (not already listed)

	Acres	
1	70,000	Unknown Malaysian businessman (Andras company) *Glenavon, Cairngorms (40,000) also Braulen, Inverness-shire (30,000)*
2	63,000	Mohammed bin Raschid al Maktoum, Arab billionaire *Glomach, West Benula, Inverinate, Wester Ross*
3	50,000	Kjeld Kirk-Christiansen, head of Lego, Denmark *Strathconon, Mid Ross*
4	48,000	Profs Joseph and Lisbet Koerner, Swedish Tetra Pak heiress *Corrour, Lochaber*
5	30,000	Stanton Avery, US billlionaire *Dunbeath, Caithness*
6	30,000	Mohammed Fayed, owner of Harrods *Balnagowan, Ross and Cromarty*
7	26,000	Urs Schwarzenberg, Swiss businessman *Ben Alder, Inverness-shire*
8	20,000	Count Knuth, Danish aristocrat *Ben Loyal, Sutherland*
9	20,000	His Excellency Mahdi Mohammed Al Tajir, United Arab Emirates *Blackford, Perthshire*
10	17,200	Prof. Ian Roderick Macneil of Barra, American clan chief *Barra and islands*
11	16,000	Eric Delwart, Belgian *Kilchoan, Knoydart*
12	10,000	Lucan Ardenberg, Dane *Pitmain, Inverness-shire*
13	7,400	Marlin Maruma, German spiritual artist *Island of Eigg*
14	4,000	Fred Olsen, Norwegian shipping magnate *Forest Estate, Galloway*
15	4,000	Dr Sybrand and Feya Heerma van Voss, Dutch *Blar a' Chaoruinn, Fort William*
16	4,000	Hans Depre, Belgian businessman *Clova, near Lumsden, Aberdeenshire*

The Counties of Scotland before 1975

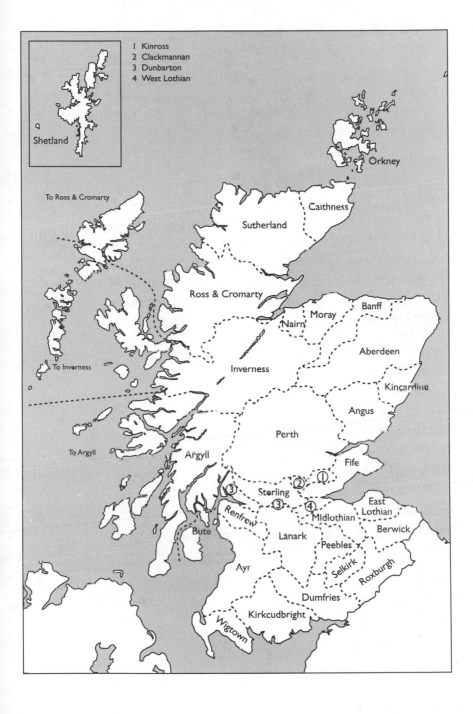

1 Kinross
2 Clackmannan
3 Dunbarton
4 West Lothian

Shetland

To Ross & Cromarty

To Inverness

To Argyll

Orkney

Caithness

Sutherland

Ross & Cromarty

Banff

Moray

Nairn

Aberdeen

Inverness

Kincardine

Angus

Perth

Fife

Argyll

Sterling

East Lothian

Midlothian

Renfrew

Berwick

Bute

Lanark

Peebles

Ayr

Selkirk

Roxburgh

Dumfries

Kirkcudbright

Wigtown

Appendix 62

Shadow of Empire

Current British Dependencies

Anguilla

Ascension Island

Bermuda

British Virgin Islands

Cayman Islands

Channel Islands

Falklands Islands

Gibraltar

Isle of Man

Montserrat

Pitcairn Island

Turks and Caicos Islands

St Helena

Commonwealth

Antigua and Barbuda* (1981)

Australia* (1931)

The Bahamas* (1973)

Bangladesh (1972)

Barbados* (1966)

Belize* (1981)

Botswana (1966)

Brunei (1984)

Cameroon (1995)

Canada* (1931)

Cyprus (1961)

Dominica (1978)

Fiji (1970, 1997)

The Gambia (1965)

Ghana (1957)

Grenada* (1974)

Guyana (1966)

India (1947)

Jamaica* (1962)

Kenya (1963)

Kiribati (1979)

Lesotho (1966)

Malawi (1964)

Malaysia (1957)

The Maldives (1982)

Malta (1964)

Mauritius (1968)

Mozambique (1995)

Namibia (1990)

Nauru (1968)

New Zealand* (1931)

Nigeria (1960)

Pakistan (1947)

Papua New Guinea* (1975)

St Christopher and Nevis* (1983)

St Lucia* (1979)

St Vincent and the Grenadines* (1979)

Seychelles (1976)

Sierra Leone (1961)

Singapore (1965)

Solomon Islands* (1978)

South Africa (1931)

Sri Lanka (1948)

Swaziland (1968)

Tanzania (1961)

Tonga (1970)

Trinidad and Tobago (1962)

Tuvalu* (1978)

Uganda (1962)

United Kingdom*

Vanuatu (1980)

Western Samoa (1970)

Zambia (1964)

Zimbabwe (1980)

Countries that have left the Commonwealth

Fiji (1987, rejoined 1997)

Republic of Ireland (1949)

Pakistan (1972, rejoined 1989)

South Africa (1961, rejoined 1994)

---

* Have the Queen as Head of State.

Aristocratic Incomes (1999)

Creation	Acreage c. 1880	Income c. 1880 (£ est)	Present acreage	Present wealth (£m est)	
1874	19,749	325,000	148,300	1,700	Duke of Westminster
1800	—	—	7,300	500	Earl Cadogan
1694	198,572	180,990	70,000	390	Duke of Devonshire
1873	33,001	100,000	3,100	260	Viscount Portman
1597	—	—	3,110	250	Lord Howard de Walden and Seaford
1766	186,379	176,000	90,200	250	Duke of Northumberland
1694	86,335	225,000	13,000	175	Marquess of Tavistock
1812	23,501	23,870	30,000	150	Marquess of Northampton
1833	1,358,545	141,679	16,500	150	Duke of Sutherland
1796	116,668	153,000	53,990	130	Marquess of Bute
1682	51,085	56,266	52,000	120	Duke of Beaufort
1789	20,202	60,000	13,000	120	Marquess of Salisbury
1815	33,991	41,288	12,000	100	Marquess of Cholmondeley
1837	44,090	59,578	26,000	100	Earl of Leicester
1838	6,834	7,037	15,000	100	Marquess of Normanby
1742	12,944	24,528	—	100	Viscount of Petersham
1703	70,137	98,000	18,000	100	Duke of Rutland
1929	43,586	141,224	10,150	95	Sir Anstruther-Gough-Calthorpe
—	183,199	107,920	17,000	85	Lady Anne Bentinck
1551	44,806	77,720	14,000	80	Earl of Pembroke
1765	27,185	46,764	13,500	80	Earl Spencer
1765	24,870	42,900	10,000	75	Earl of Radnor
1707	60,418	50,917	65,600	75	Duke of Roxburghe
1837	56,893	84,649	27,000	75	Earl of Yarborough
1703	—	—	22,400	72	Earl of Rosebery
1611	3,377	5,358	13,000	60	Sir Nicholas Bacon
1697	19,389	34,599	9,000	60	Earl of Jersey

Incomes: after Dominic Hobson, *The National Wealth* (London, 1999); extracted in *The Sunday Times*, 1 August 1999. Tourist draws source: British Tourist Authority, 1996.

1944	—	—	18,000	55	Earl of Halifax
1776	49,074	42,968	33,800	55	Earl of Mansfield
1783	34,010	35,870	12,000	55	Sir Tatton Sykes
1313	132,220	74,006	75,700	55	Baroness Willoughby de Eresby
1698	104,194	97,398	53,000	50	Baron Barnard
1789	55,574	68,015	10,000	50	Marquess of Bath
1963	109,935	88,112	14,000	50	Baron Egremont
1663	460,108	232,000	275,000	45	Duke of Buccleuch
—	115,743	138,800	—	45	Lady Juliet de Chair
1485	68,942	163,273	27,000	45	Earl of Derby
1743	—	—	3,000	45	Earl of Portsmouth
1299	34,776	32,613	26,000	40	Baron Clinton
1812	29,620	38,118	—	40	Earl of Harewood
1701	—	—	18,000	40	Marquess of Lothian
1639	69,875	28,592	37,300	35	Earl of Airlie
1772	13,663	21,168	15,000	30	Earl Bathurst
1675	25,773	39,284	10,500	30	Duke of Grafton
1702	23,511	36,557	11,500	30	Duke of Marlborough
1815	—	—	2,500	30	Earl of Verulam
1892	—	—	14,000	30	Marquess of Zetland
1711	99,576	54,014	14,000	28	Baron Middleton

Top Draws in the Tourist Kingdom

Property	Owner	Visitors	Admission charge (£)	Income (£m)
Beaulieu Abbey	Lord Montagu	506,352	8/2.80	3.40
Blenheim Palace	Duke of Marlborough	419,902	7.50	3.10
Chatsworth House	Duke of Devonshire	404,721	5.75	2.30
Harewood House	Earl of Harewood	254,000	6.00	1.50
Castle Howard	Simon Howard	200,000	6.50	1.30
Weston Park	Earl of Bradford	164,256	5.00	0.82
Bowood House	Earl of Shelburne	154,804	4.80	0.74

INDEX